A Review of the Events of 1974

The 1975 World Book Year Book

The Annual Supplement to The World Book Encyclopedia

Field Enterprises Educational Corporation

Chicago   Frankfurt   London   Paris   Rome   Sydney   Tokyo   Toronto

Staff

Editorial Director
William H. Nault

Editorial Staff

Executive Editor
Wayne Wille

Managing Editor
Paul C. Tullier

Chief Copy Editor
Joseph P. Spohn

Senior Editors
Robert K. Johnson,
Edward G. Nash,
Kathryn Sederberg,
Darlene R. Stille,
Foster P. Stockwell

Senior Index Editor
Pamela Williams

Editorial Assistants
Deborah Ellis, Cynthia Hillman

Executive Editor,
The World Book Encyclopedia
A. Richard Harmet

Art Staff

Executive Art Director
William Dobias

Art Director
for Year Book
Alfred de Simone

Senior Artist
Gumé Nuñez

Artists
Roberta Dimmer,
Wilma Stevens

Photography Director
Fred C. Eckhardt, Jr.

Photo Editing Director
Ann Eriksen

Senior Photo Editors
Blanche Cohen, Marilyn Gartman,
John S. Marshall, Mary Tonon

Assistant Photo Editor
Karen Christoffersen

Art Production Director
Barbara J. McDonald

Art Quality Control
Alfred J. Mozdzen

Research and Services

Director of Educational Services
John Sternig

Director of Editorial Services
Carl A. Tamminen

Head, Editorial Research
Jo Ann McDonald

Head, Cartographic Services
J. J. Stack

Cartographer
H. George Stoll

Cartographic Designer
Paul Yatabe

Manufacturing Staff

Executive Director
Philip B. Hall

Production Manager
Jerry R. Higdon

Manager, Research
and Development
Henry Koval

Manager, Pre-Press
John Babrick

Assistant Manager, Pre-Press
Marguerite DuMais

Year Book Board of Editors

Harrison Brown, Alistair Cooke, Lawrence A. Cremin, John Holmes, James Murray, Sylvia Porter, James Reston

World Book Advisory Board

Phillip Bacon, Professor and Chairman, Department of Geography and Anthropology, University of Houston; Jean Sutherland Boggs, Director, The National Gallery of Canada; George B. Brain, Dean, College of Education, Washington State University; Alonzo A. Crim, Superintendent, Atlanta Public Schools; John H. Glenn, Adviser to the National Aeronautics and Space Administration; William E. McManus, Director of Catholic Education, Archdiocese of Chicago; Robert K. Merton, University Professor, Columbia University; A. Harry Passow, Jacob H. Schiff Professor of Education and Chairman, Department of Curriculum and Teaching, Teachers College, Columbia University; John Rowell, Director, School Libraries Programs, School of Library Science, Case Western Reserve University; William M. Smith, Professor of Psychology and Director, Office of Instructional Services and Educational Research, Dartmouth College.

Copyright © 1975 by Field Enterprises Educational Corporation, Chicago, Illinois 60654. Portions of the material contained in this volume are taken from The World Book Encyclopedia, Copyright © 1975 by Field Enterprises Educational Corporation, and from The World Book Dictionary, Copyright © 1974 by Doubleday & Company, Inc. All rights reserved. This volume may not be reproduced in whole or in part in any form without written permission from the publishers.

Printed in the United States of America
ISBN 0-7166-0475-2
Library of Congress Catalog Card Number: 62-4818

Preface

Two new pieces of equipment were much in evidence in YEAR BOOK offices while this edition was being prepared. One was an electronic calculator; the other was a long list of conversion factors for changing customary measurements—feet, pounds, acres, gallons, and so forth—into metric. It was all part of a new service to our millions of readers, and another demonstration of WORLD BOOK's innovative leadership. With its 1975 edition, WORLD BOOK becomes the first major encyclo-

One Gram
About the weight of two paper clips

One Kilogram
About the weight of the U-V volume of WORLD BOOK

A switch to metrics calls for a switch in the way we think about familiar objects. These pictures are from "Metric System" article on page 568.

pedia to provide its users with both customary measurements and their metric equivalents throughout the set. And the YEAR BOOK is doing the same, beginning with this edition. In the "Geology" article in the Year on File section, for example, you will read that, "In some cases, the vessels went far below the depths ordinary submarines could reach—more than 9,000 feet (2,700 meters)." In addition, we have reprinted the new "Metric System" article from the 1975 WORLD BOOK; it begins on page 568. And on page 110, you will find a Special Report, "The Move to Metric."

The United States, of course, has not yet adopted metrics as its official measurement system, but few doubt that this will occur within the next several years. In 1974, one branch of the U.S. government officially encouraged the use of metrics. This was done in an amendment to the Elementary and Secondary Education Act, in which Congress said, "It is the policy of the United States to encourage educational agencies and institutions to prepare students to use the metric system of measurement with ease and facility. . . ." That is our policy, too.   WAYNE WILLE

Contents

A chronology of some of the most important events of 1974 appears on
pages 8 through 14. A preview of 1975 is given on pages 613 and 614.

Contributors

Abrams, Edward, Ph.D.; Director of Technical Development, Chemetron Corporation. [CHEMICAL INDUSTRY]

Alexiou, Arthur G., M.S., E.E.; Associate Director, Office of Sea Grant Programs, National Science Foundation. [OCEAN]

Anderson, Joseph P., M.S., LL.D.; Director, Social Legislation Information Service, Inc. [POVERTY; Social Organizations]

Araujo, Paul E., Ph.D.; Assistant Professor, Food Science Department, University of Florida. [NUTRITION]

Banovetz, James M., Ph.D.; Chairman, Department of Political Science, Northern Illinois University. [CITY; City Articles; HOUSING]

Barabba, Vincent P., B.S., M.B.A.; Director, United States Bureau of the Census. [CENSUS, U.S.]

Barber, Peggy, B.A., M.L.S.; Director, Public Information Office, American Library Association. [AMERICAN LIBRARY ASSOCIATION]

Bautz, Laura P., Ph.D.; Associate Professor of Astronomy, Northwestern University. [ASTRONOMY]

Bazell, Robert J., B.A., C. Phil.; News Writer, *New York Post.* [SCIENCE AND RESEARCH]

Beaumont, Lynn ; Travel and Public Relations Consultant. [FAIRS AND EXPOSITIONS; TRAVEL]

Beckwith, David C., J.D.; Correspondent, *Time* Magazine. [COURTS AND LAWS; CRIME; PRISON; SUPREME COURT]

Benson, Barbara N., A.B., M.S.; Instructor, Biology, Cedar Crest College. [BOTANY; ZOOLOGY]

Berkwitt, George J., B.S.J.; Chief Editor, *Industrial Distribution Magazine.* [MANUFACTURING]

Bornstein, Leon, B.A., M.A.; Labor Economist, U.S. Dept. of Labor. [LABOR]

Boyum, Joy Gould, Ph.D.; Professor of English, New York University. [MOTION PICTURES]

Bradley, Van Allen, B.J.; former Literary Editor,*Chicago Daily News.* [LITERATURE]

Bradsher, Henry S., A.B., B.J.; Correspondent, *Washington Star-News.* [Asian Country Articles]

Brown, Kenneth, Editor, *United Kingdom Press Gazette.* [EUROPE; Western Europe Country Articles]

Brown, Madison B., M.D.; Senior Vice-President, American Hospital Association. [HOSPITAL]

Cain, Charles C., III, B.A.; Automotive Writer, Associated Press. [AUTOMOBILE]

Carroll, Paul, M.A.; Professor of English, University of Illinois at Chicago Circle. [POETRY]

Constantine, Gus, A.B.; Editor, National and Foreign News, *Washington Star-News.* [Special Report: TO INCREASE KNOWLEDGE AMONG MEN]

Cook, Robert C., former President, Population Reference Bureau. [POPULATION, WORLD]

Cromie. William J., B.S.; Director of Research and Development, Field Enterprises Educational Corporation. [Special Report: LEARNING FOR LIVING IN A SILENT WORLD; SPACE EXPLORATION]

Csida, June Bundy, former Radio-TV Editor, *Billboard* Magazine. [RADIO; TELEVISION]

Cuscaden, Rob, Editor, *Building Design & Construction* Magazine. [ARCHITECTURE; ARCHITECTURE (Close-Up)]

Cviic, Chris, B.A., B.Sc.; Editorial Staff, *The Economist.* [Eastern Europe Country Articles]

Dale, Edwin L., Jr., B.A.; Reporter, *The New York Times,* Washington Bureau. [INTERNATIONAL TRADE AND FINANCE]

Davies, Richard P., B.S.; Medical Writer. [HEALTH AND DISEASE; MEDICINE; MENTAL HEALTH]

DeFrank, Thomas M., B.A., M.A.; Correspondent, *Newsweek.* [NATIONAL DEFENSE]

Delaune, Lynn de Grummond, M.A.; Assistant Professor, College of William and Mary; Author. [LITERATURE FOR CHILDREN]

Derickson, Ralph Wayne, Public Information Associate, Council of State Governments. [STATE GOVERNMENT]

De Simone, Daniel V., LL.B., J.D.; Deputy Director, Office of Technology Assessment, U.S. Congress. [Special Report: THE MOVE TO METRIC; WORLD BOOK SUPPLEMENT: METRIC SYSTEM]

Dewald, William G., Ph.D.; Professor of Economics, Ohio State University. [Finance Articles]

Dixon, Gloria Ricks, B.A.; Director of Public Relations, Magazine Publishers Association. [MAGAZINE]

Douglas, William O., LL.B., M.A., LL.D.; Associate Justice, Supreme Court of the United States. [SUPREME COURT (Close-Up)]

Eaton, William J., B.S.J., M.S.J.; Washington Correspondent, *Chicago Daily News.* [U.S. Political Articles; WATERGATE]

Edsforth, Ronald W., Research Aide, Washington Center for Metropolitan Studies. [WORLD BOOK SUPPLEMENT: WASHINGTON, D.C.]

Evans, Earl A., Jr., Ph.D.; Professor of Biochemistry, University of Chicago. [BIOCHEMISTRY; BIOLOGY]

Farr, David M. L., D. Phil.; Professor of History, Carleton University, Ottawa. [CANADA; LÉGER, JULES; TRUDEAU, PIERRE ELLIOTT]

Feather, Leonard, Professor of Jazz History, University of California at Riverside; Author, *The Encyclopedia of Jazz in the Sixties*. [MUSIC, POPULAR; RECORDINGS]

Flynn, Betty, B.A.; former United Nations Correspondent, *Chicago Daily News.* [UNITED NATIONS]

French, Charles E., Ph.D.; Head, Agricultural Economics Department, Purdue University. [AGRICULTURE]

Gayn, Mark, B.S.; Asia Bureau Chief, *The Toronto Star;* Author. [ASIA and Asian Country Articles]

Goldner, Nancy, B.A.; Critic, *Dance News, The Nation,* and *Christian Science Monitor.* [DANCING]

Goldstein, Jane, B.A.; U.S. Representative, International Racing Bureau. [HORSE RACING]

Goy, Robert W., Ph.D.; Director, Wisconsin Regional Primate Research Center; Professor of Psychology, University of Wisconsin. [PSYCHOLOGY]

Grasso, Thomas X., M.A.; Associate Professor and Chairman, Department of Geosciences, Monroe Community College. [GEOLOGY]

Graubart, Judah L., B.A.; Columnist, *Jewish Post and Opinion* (Chicago). [JEWS]

Grier, Eunice S., B.S.; Research Aide, Washington Center for Metropolitan Studies. [WORLD BOOK SUPPLEMENT: WASHINGTON, D.C.]

Griffin, Alice, Ph.D.; Professor of English, Lehman College, City University of New York. [THEATER]

Gwynne, Peter, M.A.; Science Editor, *Newsweek.* [Special Report: PSYCHIC POWERS: FACT OR FRAUD?]

Havighurst, Robert J., Ph.D.; Professor of Education and Human Development, University of Chicago. [OLD AGE]

Healey, Gerald B., Midwest Editor, *Editor & Publisher* Magazine. [NEWSPAPERS]

Hechinger, Fred M., B.A.; member, Editorial Board, *The New York Times.* [EDUCATION]

Henahan, John F., B.S.; Free Lance Science Writer. [Special Report: DOOM FOR THE GIANTS OF THE SEA?]

Hsieh, Chiao-min, Ph.D.; Professor of Geography, University of Pittsburgh. [Special Report: THE NEW FACE OF CHINA]

Jacobi, Peter P., B.S.J., M.S.J.; Professor and Associate Dean, Medill School of Journalism, Northwestern University. [MUSIC, CLASSICAL]

Jessup, Mary, E., B.A.; former News Editor, *Civil Engineering* Magazine. [DRUGS; Engineering Articles; PETROLEUM AND GAS]

Joseph, Lou, B.A.; Manager, Media Relations, Bureau of Public Information, American Dental Association. [DENTISTRY]

Kind, Joshua B., Ph.D.; Associate Professor of Art History, Northern Illinois University; Author, *Rouault;* Midwest Correspondent, *Art News.* [VISUAL ARTS]

Kingman, Merle, B.A.; Senior Editor, *Advertising Age.* [ADVERTISING]

Kisor, Henry, B.A., M.S.J.; Book Editor, *Chicago Daily News.* [LITERATURE (Close-Up)]

Klie, Robert H., B.E.E.; Head, Transmission Methods Department, Bell Telephone Laboratories, Inc. [COMMUNICATIONS]

Klie, John R., M.S.; Director of Publications, Institute of Food Technologists. [FOOD]

Koenig, Louis W., Ph.D., L.H.D.; Professor of Government, New York University; Author: *Bryan; A Political Biography of William Jennings Bryan.* [CIVIL RIGHTS]

Levy, Emanuel, B.A.; Editor, *Insurance Advocate.* [INSURANCE]

Lewis, Ralph H., M.A.; Collaborator, Division of Museum Services, Museum Operations, National Park Service. [MUSEUMS]

Lisagor, Peter, A.B.; Washington Bureau Chief, *Chicago Daily News.* [Special Report: FROM TRIUMPH TO TRAGEDY]

Litsky, Frank, B.S.; Assistant Sports Editor, *The New York Times.* [Sports Articles]

Livingston, Kathryn Zahony, B.A.; Senior Editor, Special Projects, *Town and Country.* [FASHION]

Maki, John M., Ph.D.; Professor of Political Science Dept., University of Massachusetts. [JAPAN]

Marty, Martin E., Ph.D.; Professor, University of Chicago. [PROTESTANT; RELIGION]

Mattson, Howard W., B.S.; Director of Public Information, Institute of Food Technologists. [FOOD]

Miller, J. D. B., M.Ec.; Professor of International Relations, Research School of Pacific Studies, Australian National University. [AUSTRALIA; NEW ZEALAND; PACIFIC ISLANDS; WHITLAM, EDWARD GOUGH]

Morton, Elizabeth H., LL.D.; former Editor in Chief, Canadian Library Association. [CANADIAN LIBRARY ASSOCIATION; CANADIAN LITERATURE]

Moss, Robert, M.A.; Special Correspondent, *The Economist.* [LATIN AMERICA and Latin American Country Articles]

Mullen, Frances A., Ph.D.; President, International Council of Psychologists, Inc. [CHILD WELFARE]

Neil, Andrew, M.A.; Political Correspondent, *The Economist.* [GREAT BRITAIN; IRELAND; NORTHERN IRELAND]

Nelson, Larry L., Ph.D.; Executive Vice-President, Snyder Associates, Inc. [AGRICULTURE]

Newman, Andrew L., M.A.; Information Officer, U.S. Department of the Interior. [CONSERVATION; ENVIRONMENT; FISHING; FOREST AND FOREST PRODUCTS; HUNTING; INDIAN, AMERICAN]

O'Connor, James J., E.E.; Editor in Chief, *Power* Magazine. [ENERGY]

Offenheiser, Marilyn J., B.S.; Editor, *Electronics Magazine.* [ELECTRONICS]

O'Leary, Theodore M., B.A.; Special Correspondent, *Sports Illustrated* Magazine. [BRIDGE, CONTRACT; CHESS; COIN COLLECTING; GAMES, MODELS, AND TOYS; HOBBIES; PET; STAMP COLLECTING]

Pearl, Edward; Supervisory Meteorologist, University of Chicago. [WEATHER]

Peterson, J. L., M.S.E.; Supervisor, Acoustic and Environmental Studies, Bell Telephone Laboratory. [TELEPHONE]

Plog, Fred, Ph.D.; Associate Professor of Anthropology, State University of New York, Binghamton. [ANTHROPOLOGY; ARCHAEOLOGY]

Poli, Ken, ; Editor, *Popular Photography.* [PHOTOGRAPHY]

Rabb, George B., Ph.D.; Deputy Director, Chicago Zoological Park. [ZOOS AND AQUARIUMS]

Reichler, Joseph L.; Special Assistant to the Commissioner of Professional Baseball. [WORLD BOOK SUPPLEMENT: BASEBALL]

Roberts, John Storm, M.A.; former Editor in Chief, *Africa Report.* [AFRICA and African Country Articles]

Rogers, Morris E., B.S.; former Chicago Area Editor, *Drovers Journal.* [INTERNATIONAL LIVE STOCK EXPOSITION]

Rowen, Joseph R., A.B.; Vice-President, National Retail Merchants Association. [RETAILING]

Rowse, Arthur E., I.A., M.B.A.; President, Consumer News, Inc. [CONSUMER AFFAIRS]

Schaefle, Kenneth E., M.B.A.; former President, The Communication Center, Inc. [AVIATION; RAILROAD; SHIP AND SHIPPING; TRANSIT; TRANSPORTATION; TRUCK AND TRUCKING]

Schmemann, The Reverend Alexander, S.T.D., D.D., LL.D., Th.D.; Dean, St. Vladimir's Orthodox Theological Seminary, New York. [EASTERN ORTHODOX CHURCHES]

Schubert, Helen C., B.S.; Home Furnishings Writer. [INTERIOR DESIGN]

Shaw, Robert J., B.S.B.A.; former Editor, *Library Technology Reports,* American Library Association [LIBRARY]

Shearer, Warren W., Ph.D.; former Chairman, Department of Economics, Wabash College. [ECONOMICS]

Sheerin, John B., C.S.P., A.B., M.A., LL.D., J.D.; Editor Emeritus, *New Catholic World.* [ROMAN CATHOLIC CHURCH]

Shidler, Atlee E., President, Washington Center for Metropolitan Studies. [WORLD BOOK SUPPLEMENT: WASHINGTON, D.C.]

Spencer, William, Ph.D., Professor of History, Florida State University; Author, *Land and People of Algeria.* [MIDDLE EAST and Middle Eastern Country Articles; North Africa Country Articles]

Steffek, Edwin F., B.S.; Editor, *Horticulture* Magazine. [GARDENING]

terHorst, Jerald F., B.A.; Columnist, *The Detroit News-Universal Press Syndicate;* Author, *Gerald Ford and the Future of the Presidency.* [WORLD BOOK SUPPLEMENT: FORD, GERALD RUDOLPH]

Thompson, Carol L., M.A.; Editor, *Current History* Magazine. [U.S. Government Articles]

Tofany, Vincent L., B.L.; President, National Safety Council. [SAFETY]

von Smolinski, Alfred W., Ph.D.; Assistant Professor of Chemistry, University of Illinois at the Medical Center. [CHEMISTRY]

Warner, John W., LL.B.; Administrator, American Revolution Bicentennial Administration. [BICENTENNIAL CELEBRATION]

White, Thomas O., Ph.D.; Physicist, Department of Nuclear Physics, Oxford University, Oxford, England. [PHYSICS]

Contributors not listed on these pages are members of the WORLD BOOK YEAR BOOK editorial staff.

Chronology 1974

January

Sun	Mon	Tue	Wed	Thu	Fri	Sat
		1	2	3	4	5
6	7	8	9	10	11	12
13	14	15	16	17	18	19
20	21	22	23	24	25	26
27	28	29	30	31		

1   **Greek President** Phaidon Gizikis abolishes a court that was to prepare for new elections.

2   **Carlos Arias Navarro** is sworn in as the first civilian president of Spain; he replaces 11 of 19 Cabinet ministers.

8   **Sweden rations gasoline and heating oil,** the first West European country to do so.

11-18   **U.S. Secretary of State** Henry A. Kissinger negotiates a troop disengagement accord between Egypt and Israel.

12   **Chile's military rulers** begin prepublication censorship of all newspapers and magazines.

13   **The Miami Dolphins** football team wins its second straight Super Bowl, beating the Minnesota Vikings, 24 to 7.

Jan. 11-18   Feb. 8

Feb. 13

14-18   **The International Monetary Fund** meets in Rome to discuss world currency system reform and effects of higher Middle East oil prices.

15   **Brazil elects generals** Ernesto Geisel and Adalberto Pereira dos Santos president and vice-president, respectively.
Conference on Security and Cooperation in Europe reconvenes in Geneva, Switzerland.

19   **France allows** its currency to float freely in the international monetary exchange markets.

19-20   **Chinese jets and troops** take the Paracel Islands in the South China Sea from a small South Vietnamese force.

21   **The 93rd U.S. Congress** opens its second session.

22-23   **Heads of the 10 Canadian provinces** discuss oil policy in Ottawa.

23   **Alaskan pipeline construction** permit is issued by the U.S. Department of Interior. Project had been blocked by environmental lawsuits since 1970.

26   **The Turkish Cabinet** re-forms with Bülent Ecevit as the new prime minister.

30   **President Nixon** delivers his State of the Union message to Congress, saying "One year of Watergate is enough. . . ."

February

Sun	Mon	Tue	Wed	Thu	Fri	Sat
					1	2
3	4	5	6	7	8	9
10	11	12	13	14	15	16
17	18	19	20	21	22	23
24	25	26	27	28		

3   **Chairman Mao Tse-tung** launches a new cultural revolution in China.

4   **President Richard M. Nixon** submits a $304.4-billion budget to Congress for fiscal 1975, the first federal budget to exceed $300 billion.
Patricia Hearst, granddaughter of the late newspaper publisher William Randolph Hearst, is kidnaped in Berkeley, Calif., by a group called the Symbionese Liberation Army. The group demands food for the poor as ransom.

7   **Prime Minister Edward Heath** calls a general election for February 28 following a threat to strike by British coal miners.
Grenada, one of six Caribbean islands in the West Indies Associated States, gains full independence, ending 200 years of British rule.

8   **Final *Skylab* mission ends.** Three astronauts land safely after a record-breaking 84 days aboard the orbiting space laboratory.

11   **Independent truckdrivers** in the United States end their 12-day strike over increased diesel fuel costs, widespread fuel shortages, and lower speed limits.

13   **Major oil-consuming nations** propose international cooperation in dealing with the worldwide energy crisis and economic instability resulting from Arab oil embargoes.
Russia deports Alexander I. Solzhenitsyn to West Germany and strips him of his citizenship for his book *Gulag Archipelago, 1918-1956*, a critical study of the Soviet penal system.

19   **Randolph Hearst** announces details of a $2-million food giveaway to gain release of his daughter Patricia.

20   **J. Reginald Murphy,** editor of the *Atlanta Constitution*, is kidnaped by a group calling itself the American Revolutionary Army; he is released unharmed three days later.

25   **Herbert W. Kalmbach,** President Nixon's personal lawyer, pleads guilty to two charges of illegal campaign financing.

March

Sun	Mon	Tue	Wed	Thu	Fri	Sat
					1	2
3	4	5	6	7	8	9
10	11	12	13	14	15	16
17	18	19	20	21	22	23
24	25	26	27	28	29	30
31						

1 **Watergate grand jury** indicts seven presidential aides, a former attorney general, and two Nixon campaign aides on charges of conspiracy, obstruction of justice, and perjury; reportedly, a sealed report names President Nixon as an unindicted co-conspirator.

2 **Italy's 35th government** since World War II collapses. Prime Minister Mariano Rumor resigns, then agrees to try to form a new government.
President U Ne Win of Burma returns political power to the People's Assembly after 12 years of dictatorial rule.

4 **British Prime Minister** Edward Heath resigns after failing to form a coalition government. Labour Party leader Harold Wilson succeeds him. No party won a majority of seats in February elections.

7 **Presidential aides** John D. Ehrlichman, Charles W. Colson, and four others are indicted in connection with the burglary of the office of psychiatrist Lewis J. Fielding, who treated Pentagon Papers defendant Daniel Ellsberg.

9 **Turkey lifts** its two-year ban on the farming of the opium poppy. The United States had urged the ban to help control illegal drug traffic.

12 **Carlos Andrés Pérez** becomes president of Venezuela, vows to nationalize the foreign-owned oil industry.

18 **Seven Arab countries** agree to lift their oil embargo on the United States, in effect since October, 1973.

20 **Attempt to kidnap** Princess Anne fails in London; attacker wounds chauffeur, bodyguard, and a policeman before he is captured.

21 **Sweden and the United States** name new ambassadors, ending 15-month rift that followed Swedish criticism of U.S. bombing of North Vietnam.

29 *Mariner 10* space probe passes within 466 miles (750 kilometers) of the planet Mercury; 800 close-up photos reveal a surface similar to that on the moon. Earlier, the craft flew by Venus.

April

Sun	Mon	Tue	Wed	Thu	Fri	Sat
	1	2	3	4	5	6
7	8	9	10	11	12	13
14	15	16	17	18	19	20
21	22	23	24	25	26	27
28	29	30				

1 **U.S. Supreme Court** upholds the 1970 Bank Secrecy Act that allows federal government access to the records of individual bank customers.

2 **President Georges Pompidou**, 62, dies of cancer in France. Alain Poher, president of the Senate, becomes acting president.
Oscar awards go to *The Sting*, as best picture; Glenda Jackson, best actress; and Jack Lemmon, best actor, at 46th annual Academy of Motion Picture Arts and Sciences presentation.

Mar. 4

Mar. 12

Apr. 10

3 **Patty Hearst** says in taperecorded statement that she has decided "to stay and fight" with the Symbionese Liberation Army.
U.S. Lutheran and Roman Catholic theologians declare accord on the issue of papal primacy, which was a factor in the division of the two church groups in the 1500s.

4 **The North Atlantic Treaty Organization** (NATO) observes its 25th anniversary in Brussels, Belgium.

5 **Laotian King Savang Vatthana** decrees a coalition government that includes representatives of the pro-Communist Pathet Lao Party.

8 **President Nixon** signs a bill that will boost the minimum wage in stages from $1.60 to $2.30 per hour by Jan. 1, 1976.
Outfielder Hank Aaron hits his 715th career home run in Atlanta stadium, breaking the record set by Babe Ruth.

10 **Israel's Prime Minister Golda Meir** resigns, bringing down her month-old coalition government.

14 **Gary Player wins** his second Masters golf tournament in Augusta, Ga.

15 **Niger's president** is ousted by the army.
Federal Bureau of Investigation links Patty Hearst to a San Francisco bank robbery.

16 **U.S. Secretary of Army** Howard H. Callaway halves the sentence of former Army Lieutenant William L. Calley, Jr.

18 **The U.S. Department of Commerce** announces a 5.8 per cent drop in the gross national product for the first quarter of 1974, the largest quarterly drop since 1958.

May 8   May 9

May 17

succeed the retiring Michael Ramsey as head of the Church of England.

6   **Willy Brandt resigns** as chancellor of West Germany after a top member of his staff is unmasked as an East German spy.

7   **The Federal Energy Administration** is created by a bill signed into law by President Nixon.

8   "**No confidence" vote** in Canada's House of Commons topples Prime Minister Pierre Elliott Trudeau's minority Liberal Party government.
Daniel Oduber Quirós is inaugurated as president of Costa Rica.

9   **Iceland's Prime Minister** Olafur Johannesson dismisses parliament and schedules new elections for June 30.
Impeachment hearings of the U.S. House Judiciary Committee begin.

10   **White House denies** rumors that President Nixon will resign.

15   **General António de Spínola** becomes provisional president of Portugal; he vows restoration of democracy and self-determination for African colonies.
Twenty-six Israelis die in attack on village of Maalot by three Palestinian commandos.

15-16   **West Germany** elects Walter Scheel president, Helmut Schmidt, chancellor.

16   **Former Attorney General** Richard G. Kleindienst pleads guilty to charge that he refused to testify "accurately and fully" before a Senate committee.

17   **Six die in Los Angeles** gun battle and fire; victims are identified as members of the Symbionese Liberation Army.

18   **India explodes** a nuclear bomb, and becomes the sixth nation to make and test such a weapon.

19   **France elects** a new president, former Finance Minister Valery Giscard d'Estaing.

22   **Patty Hearst** is formally charged in Los Angeles County with 19 crimes.

27   **Jacques Chirac** is named premier of France.

28   **Northern Ireland** returns to British rule following a general strike by militant Protestants that toppled the coalition government of Brian Faulkner.

29   **Australia's Labor Party** claims victory in the close May 18 general elections.

30   **President Tito** is named head of Yugoslavia's Communist Party for life at the 10th party congress.

20   **Japan and China** begin mutual airline service.

21   **Alfonso Lopez Michelsen** is elected president of Colombia in the first free elections in 20 years.

25   **Portuguese army coup d'état** ends 40 years of civilian dictatorship.

28   **Former Nixon Cabinet members** John N. Mitchell and Maurice H. Stans are acquitted of federal charges relating to secret campaign contributions by financier Robert L. Vesco.

29   **President Nixon** announces in a television address that he is releasing edited transcripts of 31 taped Watergate-related conversations. He declares he "had nothing to hide."

May

Sun	Mon	Tue	Wed	Thu	Fri	Sat
			1	2	3	4
5	6	7	8	9	10	11
12	13	14	15	16	17	18
19	20	21	22	23	24	25
26	27	28	29	30	31	

2   **Maryland court** bars former Vice-President Spiro T. Agnew from practicing law.

4   **New Archbishop of Canterbury,** F. Donald Coggan, 64, is named by Queen Elizabeth II to

June

Sun	Mon	Tue	Wed	Thu	Fri	Sat
						1
2	3	4	5	6	7	8
9	10	11	12	13	14	15
16	17	18	19	20	21	22
23	24	25	26	27	28	29
30						

1   **Israel and Syria** begin exchanging prisoners of war as part of a troop disengagement accord.

3   **Israeli Knesset** approves a three-party coalition government with Yitzhak Rabin as prime minister.
Charles W. Colson, a former Nixon aide, pleads guilty to a charge of obstruction of justice in connection with the 1971 trial of Pentagon Papers defendant Daniel Ellsberg.

6   **White House admits** that Watergate grand jury voted in February to name President Nixon as an unindicted co-conspirator in the Watergate case.

9   **Russia and Portugal** re-establish diplomatic ties that were ended with the Russian Revolution in 1917.

10   **Prime Minister Rumor's** Cabinet, 36th in Italy since World War II, resigns.

11-12   **U.S. Congress approves** the Energy Supply and Environmental Coordination Act of 1974, a bill that relaxes environmental standards in view of energy shortages.

12   **France raises taxes** and plans to reduce energy consumption in an effort to slow inflation and improve balance of payments.

14   **Presidents Nixon and Sadat** sign accord in Cairo by which the United States agrees to supply nuclear technology to Egypt for peaceful purposes.

17   **France and China** explode nuclear devices in the atmosphere.

23   **Rudolph Kirchschlaeger** is elected president of Austria; he succeeds Franz Jonas, who died in April after nine years in office.

25   **Russia launches** an earth-orbiting research station called *Salyut 7*.

26   **North Atlantic Treaty Organization** state leaders sign a pact affirming their "common destiny" at a meeting in Brussels, Belgium.
West German bank, Bankhaus I. D. Hersttat in Cologne, collapses following heavy losses in the trade of foreign currencies.
Army General Augusto Pinochet Ugarte assumes full executive powers of Chile's military government.

27   **President Nixon** arrives in Moscow for his third summit meeting with Communist Party Secretary Leonid I. Brezhnev.

July

Sun	Mon	Tue	Wed	Thu	Fri	Sat
	1	2	3	4	5	6
7	8	9	10	11	12	13
14	15	16	17	18	19	20
21	22	23	24	25	26	27
28	29	30	31			

1   **President Juan Perón,** 78, of Argentina dies. His wife, Vice-President María Estela (Isabel) Martínez de Perón, becomes first female chief of state in the Americas.

8   **Canadian** Prime Minister Pierre Elliott Trudeau's Liberal Party wins a majority of seats in the House of Commons.

10   **Arab oil** countries lift their embargo against the Netherlands.

12   **John D. Ehrlichman,** former Nixon aide, is convicted of charges stemming from the 1971 burglary of Daniel Ellsberg's psychiatrist's office.

13   **Portugal's president,** António de Spínola, names army leaders to Cabinet posts. Colonel Vasco dos Santos Gonçalves becomes prime minister.
The Senate Watergate Committee releases its final 2,250-page report on the Watergate burglary and other crimes during the 1972 presidential campaign; it recommends 35 election-campaign reforms, but makes no formal accusations.

14   **Inflation** replaces the energy crisis as the most important issue facing Americans, according to a Gallup Poll.

15   **Cypriot National Guard,** led by Greek officers, overthrows President Archbishop Makarios III; Makarios flees to London.

20   **Turkey invades Cyprus.** Greece mobilizes its armed forces.

22   **Greece and Turkey** accept a United Nations cease-fire for Cyprus.

23   **Greece's military junta** resigns because of its failures in the Cyprus war. Civilian government is restored as Constantin Karamanlis returns from exile to be prime minister.

24   **The U.S. Supreme Court** rules 8-0 that President Nixon must produce subpoenaed tape recordings and documents as evidence in the trial of six former aides.

27-30   **House Judiciary Committee** approves three articles of impeachment charging President Nixon with obstructing justice, abusing the powers of the presidency, and defying legitimate congressional subpoenas for evidence. Two proposed articles are rejected.

29   **John B. Connally, Jr.,** former U.S. treasury secretary, is indicted in connection with the campaign contributions of milk producers.

August

Sun	Mon	Tue	Wed	Thu	Fri	Sat
				1	2	3
4	5	6	7	8	9	10
11	12	13	14	15	16	17
18	19	20	21	22	23	24
25	26	27	28	29	30	31

5   **President Nixon** releases a statement and transcripts of tape recordings implicating him in the Watergate cover-up.

8   **Nixon goes on television,** admits "some" wrong judgments, and says he will resign.

9   **President Nixon resigns.** Vice-President Gerald R. Ford succeeds him.

July 23

Aug. 8

General Motors Corporation announces a hike of nearly 10 per cent in its automobile prices, the largest single auto price increase ever.

14 **President Ford** signs a bill that ends a 40-year ban on private ownership of gold.

14-15 **Turkey resumes fighting** in Cyprus; Greece decides to withdraw its troops from the North Atlantic Treaty Organization.

The Episcopal Church's governing clerical body rules invalid the July 29 ordination of 11 women to the priesthood.

15 **The wife** of South Korean President Chung Hee Park is murdered by a gunman attempting to assassinate Park.

17 **Fakhruddin Ali Ahmed** is elected president of India by its parliament and state assemblies.

19 **United Nations** conference on world population opens in Bucharest, Romania; 130 nations are represented.

Greek Cypriots kill Ambassador Rodger P. Davies during a demonstration at the U.S. embassy in Nicosia.

19-23 **United Mine Workers** observe "memorial week" for those miners killed or maimed in mines, and their action shuts down the nation's coal mines.

20 **President Ford nominates** Nelson A. Rockefeller to be Vice-President.

Atomic Energy Commission study says the chance that a nuclear power plant accident would kill more than 1,000 people is one in a million.

27 **Emperor Haile Selassie** is ordered by the ruling Armed Forces Committee in Ethiopia not to leave the capital.

Aug. 20

Sept. 18-19

Sept. 12

Iceland's President Kristján Eldjárn asks Independent party leader Geir Hallgrimsson to form a coalition Cabinet; Olafur Johannesson is named justice and commerce minister.

29 **UN Conference** on the Law of the Sea adjourns in Caracas, Venezuela, after representatives of 148 nations fail to reach any formal agreements.

31 **West Germany** agrees to loan Italy $2 billion.

September

Sun	Mon	Tue	Wed	Thu	Fri	Sat
1	2	3	4	5	6	7
8	9	10	11	12	13	14
15	16	17	18	19	20	21
22	23	24	25	26	27	28
29	30					

2 **General Francisco Franco** resumes power as Spain's chief of state after recovering from phlebitis; Prince Juan Carlos had served as chief of state since July 19.

Pension reform bill is signed into law by President Ford; measure sets standards for eligibility, vesting, and funding of benefits.

8 **President Ford grants** a "full, free, and absolute" pardon to former President Nixon for all crimes he may have committed while President.

9-10 **Finance ministers** from 10 major industrial nations in the International Monetary Fund meet in Basel, Switzerland, to discuss problems following several bank failures in various countries.

10 **Portugal ends colonial rule** in Guinea-Bissau; Portugal's provisional President António de Spínola formally recognizes independence of African state.

12 **Emperor Haile Selassie,** 82, of Ethiopia is deposed by military leaders.

Boston busing plan stirs some violence and boycotts at public schools as classes begin.

Wholesale prices rose at an annual rate of 46.8 per cent during August, the U.S. Department of Labor reports.

16 **Wounded Knee trial ends** in dismissal of charges against American Indian leaders Dennis Banks and Russell Means; judge cites government misconduct.

Earned amnesty plan is announced by President Ford for Vietnam War draft evaders and deserters.

General Alexander M. Haig, Jr., former White House chief of staff, is nominated supreme commander of the North Atlantic Treaty Organization.

17 **The UN General Assembly** convenes in New York City for its 29th annual session.

18-19 **Hurricane Fifi** ravages Honduras, leaving some 5,000 dead and 60,000 homeless, and causing millions of dollars in damage, officials estimate.

24 **The U.S. Department of Agriculture** lowers its estimates of grain crops as early fall frosts damage corn, soybean, and wheat crops.

25 **Judge overturns conviction** of former Lieutenant William Calley for murdering civilians in South Vietnam; prejudicial pretrial publicity is given as the main reason for reversal.

27-28 **President Ford** holds an economic summit meeting and asks all Americans to "become inflation fighters and energy savers;" he names a new Economic Policy Board to coordinate and implement economic policy.

30 **António de Spínola,** Portugal's provisional president, quits, saying "a general climate of anarchy" exists in Portugal; General Francisco da Costa Gomes, 59, replaces Spínola, while Prime Minister Vasco dos Santos Gonçalves retains power.

Canadian Parliament opens in Ottawa; government pledges to attack inflation by cutting spending and expanding production.

October

Sun	Mon	Tue	Wed	Thu	Fri	Sat
		1	2	3	4	5
6	7	8	9	10	11	12
13	14	15	16	17	18	19
20	21	22	23	24	25	26
27	28	29	30	31		

1   **Chinese Communists** celebrate 25 years of rule, but ailing Chairman Mao Tse-tung, 80, and Premier Chou En-lai, 76, miss ceremonies.

1-4   **International Monetary Fund** governors and World Bank officials discuss global imbalances in payments caused by high oil prices at annual meeting in Washington, D.C.

3   **Rumor Cabinet resigns** again in Italy because of economic policy dispute.

8   **Franklin National Bank** of New York City becomes the largest U.S. bank ever to fail. European-American Bank and Trust Company buys its assets.
   President Ford, to halt inflation and avoid further recession, calls for voluntary energy conservation and a 5 per cent surtax on corporate profits and personal incomes.

9-15   **Secretary of State Kissinger** visits seven Middle East capitals to promote peace talks.

10   **British Labour Party** wins a three-seat majority in the House of Commons in British elections.

12   **Leon Jaworski** resigns as Watergate special prosecutor, effective October 25.

14   **Watergate cover-up prosecution** of five former aides to President Nixon begins in Washington, D.C. Prosecutor says the scandal involved "the most powerful men in the U.S. government . . . even the President himself."

15   **Federal election** campaign-funding reform bill is signed into law. Sets spending limits for presidential, House, and Senate races; provides public financing for presidential elections.

16   **Congress overrides** Ford veto for first time, gives $7 billion to the Railroad Retirement System.

17   **President Ford testifies** voluntarily before a House judiciary subcommittee about his pardon of former President Nixon; says Nixon brought "shame and disgrace" on the office.
   Congress adjourns for elections.
   A's win the World Series for the third straight year. Oakland beats the Los Angeles Dodgers 3-2, winning the series 4 games to 1.

20   **Swiss voters reject 2 to 1** a proposal that would have deported about 500,000 foreign workers.

21   **Mexican President** Luis Echeverría Alvarez holds talks with President Ford.

24   **Greece exiles** former dictator George Papadopoulos and four generals who helped him seize power in 1967.

26   **Secretary of State Kissinger** concludes 3½ days of arms-limitation negotiations with Russian leaders in Moscow.

27   **Chancellor Helmut Schmidt's** ruling Social Democratic Party loses elections in Bavaria and Hesse, West Germany.

28   **Arab chiefs recognize** guerrilla Palestine Liberation Organization as "the sole legitimate representative of the Palestinian people"; approve $3.5 billion in military assistance for Arab states.

29   **U.S. Department of Commerce** reports its economic indicators dropped more in September than in any other month in 23 years.

30   **Former President Nixon** goes into shock following blood-clot surgery.
   West German Chancellor Schmidt ends talks in Moscow with Communist Party chief Brezhnev.
   Muhammad Ali wins back the heavyweight boxing title by knocking out champion George

Oct. 28   Nov. 5

Oct. 30

Foreman in the eighth round of their fight in Kinshasa, Zaire. The bout began at 4 A.M. in Zaire (10 P.M. E.S.T.).
South Vietnamese President Thieu fires three top military corps commanders amid growing unrest and charges of corruption.

November

Sun	Mon	Tue	Wed	Thu	Fri	Sat
					1	2
3	4	5	6	7	8	9
10	11	12	13	14	15	16
17	18	19	20	21	22	23
24	25	26	27	28	29	30

3   **Expo '74 World's Fair** closes in Spokane, Wash., after 184 days and more than 5.2 million visitors.

5   **Democrats sweep off-year elections.** Watergate, the Nixon pardon, recession, and inflation are cited as reasons for the large Republican losses.
   UN World Food Conference opens in Rome to discuss ways to avoid widespread starvation.

Nov. 12

Dec. 7

Nov. 23-24

Irish President Erskine H. Childers dies at 68 after a heart attack.

19 United States automakers announce widespread layoffs as car sales plummet.
U.S. consumer confidence in October hits a seven-year low, a private research group reports.

20 European Community countries support the continued existence of Israel in the UN "Question of Palestine" debate.
The U.S. Department of Justice files an anti-trust suit against American Telephone and Telegraph Company, the world's largest privately owned company.

23-24 Russia and the United States agree to limit, but not reduce, offensive nuclear weapons at Ford-Brezhnev Vladivostok meeting.

24 New Ethiopian Military Council executes General Aman Andom and 59 others.

26 President Ford signs an $11.8-million mass-transit aid bill that will subsidize operating expenses for the first time.
Japanese Prime Minister Kakuei Tanaka resigns over an alleged financial scandal.

December

Sun	Mon	Tue	Wed	Thu	Fri	Sat
1	2	3	4	5	6	7
8	9	10	11	12	13	14
15	16	17	18	19	20	21
22	23	24	25	26	27	28
29	30	31				

6 Argentina's President Isabel Perón suspends civil rights to help police end political terrorism that has claimed more than 135 lives since July.

8 Eight Ohio National Guard men are acquitted of charges in connection with the 1970 Kent State shootings that killed four students.

9 Secretary of State Kissinger ends an 18-day, 27,000-mile (43,500-kilometer) trip that took him to 17 countries. The Middle East situation dominated his talks.
Israeli Finance Minister Yehoshua Rabinowitz announces a stiff austerity package that includes a devaluation of the pound, higher food prices, and increased taxes.
Reverend Alison Cheek becomes first woman to celebrate communion in an Episcopal Church in the United States.

12 South Africa is suspended from the 1974-1975 UN General Assembly for its racial policy.
United Mine Workers strike, idling 70 per cent of U.S. coal production.

13 "The Question of Palestine" goes before the UN General Assembly. Yasir Arafat, leader of the Palestine Liberation Organization, calls for "one democratic state" to replace Israel. Yosef Tekoah, chief Israeli delegate, denounces Arafat's speech in rebuttal.

14 Former President Nixon goes home from the hospital after a three-week stay.

17 President Ford flies to Japan for talks with Prime Minister Kakuei Tanaka.
Greek voters elect Prime Minister Constantin Karamanlis in first free elections in 10 years.

4 Prime Minister Trudeau meets President Ford in Washington, D.C., to discuss Canada's plans for reduced oil exports to the United States.

5 Nationwide coal strike ends officially after 24 days as officers of the United Mine Workers sign a three-year contract.
Danish Prime Minister Poul Hartling dissolves parliament over economic policy dispute.
West German Chancellor Schmidt confers with President Ford in Washington, D.C.
Russian-French summit meeting begins in Paris on issues of oil, security, and the Mideast.

7 Archbishop Makarios returns to Cyprus; vows to resist the partition of the island into Greek and Turkish sectors.
Italy's new Prime Minister Aldo Moro gains a vote of confidence on anti-inflation bill.

8 Greece votes 2 to 1 to become a republic; abolishes the monarchy that dates from 1832.
Soyuz 16 manned spacecraft lands safely after a six-day flight rehearsal for the planned 1975 Russian-U.S. space mission.

9 Takeo Miki formally becomes Japan's prime minister and names a new Cabinet.

9-10 Common Market heads of state meet in Paris to discuss energy, regional differences.

16 Presidents Ford and Giscard d'Estaing of France end talks in Martinique by agreeing to coordinate their energy policies.

18 Michael Stassinopoulos becomes the Greek provisional president by vote of Parliament.

19 Nelson A. Rockefeller is sworn in as the 41st Vice-President of the United States.
Cearbhall O Dalaigh becomes the fifth president of the Irish Republic.

20 The 93rd Congress adjourns after passing a trade bill that allows removal of tariffs on Russian goods.

30 Watergate jury begins deliberations that end on Jan. 1, 1975, with guilty verdicts for four of the five former Nixon aides.

Section One

The Year In Focus

THE YEAR BOOK Board of Editors analyzes some significant developments of 1974 and considers their impact on contemporary affairs. The Related Articles list following each report directs the reader to THE YEAR BOOK's additional coverage of related subjects.

Focus on The World

John Holmes

**The remarkable fact about 1974 may have been
not the extent of disagreement, but rather the
effort made on so many fronts to seek agreement**

It was like a recurrent earthquake. The international structure, fashioned through long years of struggle and experience, seemed about to fly apart. Democratic government, it was widely said, might not survive inflation and shortages. The banking system was said to be at the mercy of the Arabs. The oil shortage, which had set off the panic, did ease temporarily, but the prospects were not at all reassuring. The poor countries suffered most, but the Western countries saw their comfortable world disintegrating. Resentful but somewhat conscience-stricken, they had to adjust to the intransigent assertions of the third world of nonaligned, developing countries. There was less bloodshed than in many recent years, but there was an alarming amount of the purposeful killing that is harder to contain than open warfare.

Statesmen, continuing their desperate effort to settle man-made disputes of long standing, were overwhelmed by the need to cope with the consequences of natural disasters. There were floods in South Asia and bad monsoons, inexorable famine in Africa, poor crops in North America and Europe.

But, although there were few solutions as yet, governments were responding to calamity with unprecedented efforts to cope through international action. Fear that the effort could be wrecked at any moment by passion and impatience, that time was running out for the internationalist approach, was forcing governments—even great powers—away from entrenched positions and to the bargaining table.

The effort to hold things together had to be maintained at two levels —that of the world's immediate problems and that of planetary survival. Issues of planetary survival crowded on us sooner than expected. Although they dwarfed in significance continuing attempts to liquidate the bitter heritage of the Cold War and imperial dismemberment, failure in the latter threatened progress in the former. The situation in Southeast Asia was still turbulent, though it seemed, by tacit acquiescence of the great powers, to have been decoupled from détente. When the fragile structure of peace collapsed in Cyprus in July, the major powers, while still conscious of rivalry, did recognize their greater interest in keeping the lid on. The crisis, in fact, provoked a political change in Greece that promised more stability in the eastern Mediterranean. Farther east, however, the Arab-Israeli conflict remained a major obstacle to East-West détente and a coherent attack on the planetary issues. The linkage was clear. The Middle Eastern oil producers in 1973 had used their power for political as well as economic purposes, and this had induced the industrial countries to face more soberly in 1974 the meaning of global interdependence in supplies and resources. It had created a financial crisis that threatened the most sacred structures. But the Arabs had lined up the developing

John Holmes

17

world behind their struggle over Palestine, and they were not likely to act "reasonably" in international institutions until there was a settlement in the Middle East.

So U.S. Secretary of State Henry A. Kissinger continued his indefatigable negotiations. In the first half of the year, remarkable progress was made in separating Arab and Israeli soldiers, with United Nations (UN) peacekeeping forces installed on both the Egyptian and Syrian fronts. There was almost universal, if sometimes grudging, support for Kissinger's efforts. The principal worry abroad over the upheavals in Washington, D.C., called "Watergate" was that he might be sacrificed. One result of the crisis of American government was to induce a better appreciation by both friendly and unfriendly powers of how essential a strong United States committed to outward-looking policies is to the international system. The Russians, of course, could not be expected to like Kissinger's central role in the Arab-Israeli negotiations, and they tried to get them back to the multilateral forum in Geneva, Switzerland. They supported the Arabs, but they didn't upset the delicate balance. They could not have enjoyed the American rapprochement with the Arabs, climaxed by President Richard M. Nixon's triumphant visits to Egypt and Syria in June. Later in the year, the Egyptians restored their maneuvering position by mending relations with Moscow. But by then, the issue had passed from the heady stage of setting the tables for negotiation to swallowing the hard terms that would be required, and the atmosphere inevitably deteriorated. Threats and alarms are to be expected whenever bargaining reaches this stage, as there is unlikely to be compromise without them. Nevertheless, the violence of language and of terrorist action in the autumn were ominous reminders of what could happen if the momentum toward peace could not be maintained.

In spite of these alarms and some resistance in the U.S. Congress, Kissinger doggedly sought to keep the planet on an even keel, to maintain equilibrium by workable if not necessarily affectionate relations with friends and adversaries. But unlike during the old balance-of-power game, he had to resist playing off one power against the other. The considerable attention devoted to United States-Soviet détente aroused the suspicions of China, which aligned itself with the lesser powers in protest against "the double hegemony" of the two dominant powers. So, to reassure the Chinese, Kissinger went to Peking following the meeting of President Gerald R. Ford and Communist Party General Secretary Leonid I. Brezhnev in Vladivostok, Russia, in November. It was all part of the supreme effort to hold the framework together.

Few countries opposed this policy of rapprochement, but older friends of the United States had been feeling neglected. A presidential visit was therefore arranged for Japan and South Korea. The secretary of state was able to devote a little more time to Latin America, where his pragmatic approach to a volatile relationship seemed welcome. Another exercise in defusing hostility was Kissinger's visit to India in

Threats and alarms are to be expected at this stage of bargaining

Kissinger holds a press conference

October. By concentrating on the practical aspects of issues of mutual interest, he helped considerably to repair a relationship that had gone very sour.

The question of India's willingness to continue in the paths of constructive internationalism was raised by its explosion of a nuclear device on May 18. That event forced one of the older planetary problems, nuclear proliferation, back on the priority agenda. It was very discouraging. The Indians said their exercise was for peaceful purposes only, but this was regarded elsewhere as a meaningless distinction. The danger was that all controls would be rejected as futile. It was compounded by the greatly increased sale and construction of nuclear reactors to meet the threatening shortage of energy. And China, India, Brazil, and other countries that have refused to sign the Nuclear Non-Proliferation Treaty complained that the superpowers had not kept their part of the bargain, which was to begin dismantling their terrifying capacity for overkill.

The traditional alignments were shifting under the pressure of economic issues

They had a point. There was little solid achievement in the continuing Strategic Arms Limitation Talks between the Russians and the Americans. When Kissinger went to Moscow in June, he was unable to get the "conceptual breakthrough" for which he hoped, but at Vladivostok in November, Ford and Brezhnev reached an agreement in general terms that, if it can be translated into specific action, would be the most encouraging step yet toward assured détente. Other East-West exercises in limiting competition—the conference on reduction of forces in Central Europe and the Conference on Security and Cooperation in Europe—were also at the holding stage in 1974. It seemed as if the discussions might go on forever, that they might turn into permanent institutions, struggling not so much for elusive "solutions" as to maintain whatever kind of stability was possible in changing circumstances.

Traditional alignments were shifting under the pressure of economic issues that conflicted with strategic interests. Allies were being shrill with each other. Sometimes it seemed as if the most dependable partnership was the curious lock step in which the Russians and Americans were involved.

The Atlantic community was restless. Western cohesion was recognized as inadequate alone to cope with either the immediate or the planetary problems. However, North Atlantic Treaty Organization (NATO) unity was one pillar of a détente based on the strength and confidence of each side, and the NATO powers had to stick together for this strategic purpose at least. With the exception of the French, they joined in the American-sponsored agency for the pooling of energy resources in time of crisis. The framework for this body was not NATO, however, but the Organization for Economic Cooperation and Development, which includes other industrial states such as Japan and the European neutrals. It could be regarded, therefore, as directed not against the Eastern bloc but against the oil states or the clamoring have-not countries. It did represent a greater disposition to firmness

Ford and Brezhnev meet in Vladivostok

and collective bargaining in Washington's attitude to the third world, especially the newly rich. But the intention of the new agency was to promote "cooperative relations with oil-producing countries and with other consuming countries." Simple confrontation was to be avoided. So was appeasement.

In spite of the impressive vote totals it could ring up at the UN, the so-called third world itself appeared less monolithic in the crisis, as the gaps between those rich in oil, those with other resources, and those poor in everything became more apparent. There was talk of the third, fourth, and fifth worlds. And the "industrial rich" were insisting that the "oil rich" play their part in helping the poor before they committed themselves to sharing. The latter, particularly Iran, gave some indications of their new responsibility, but they did not like being pressured by those whom they accused of raising the price of other commodities. Even the Russians and to a lesser extent the Chinese were being put on the spot. It was their large purchases of grain for their own consumption that had diminished the resources from which certain capitalist countries had been sustaining starving peoples in previous famines.

The need to face together the problems of survival may have brought the needed element of sobriety into the policies of the superpowers toward each other. Although the militancy of the developing countries presented constant temptations to Cold Warriors to play off one side against the other, the militants seemed more interested in action than in blandishments. The UN General Assembly majority showed its power by suspending South Africa from attendance and by providing Yasir Arafat of the Palestine Liberation Organization with a legitimate platform. The developing countries were making strong demands for a more equitable sharing of the world's resources, but their dependence on the world economy and their own conflicting interests forced them also to recognize interdependence as a fact of life. "If it is a dialogue that is wanted," said President Houari Boumediene of Algeria to the General Assembly at the special session in the spring, "we are in favor of dialogue."

The most basic dialogue took place in November at the World Food Conference in Rome, which set up a World Food Council and adopted certain specific programs to deal with present famine and perpetual starvation. It seemed very little, and no one was satisfied, but both givers and receivers made clear they wanted to break out of the old pattern of emergency handouts. It was agreed that poor countries would have to be helped to feed themselves. The fact that Western countries could not feed countries with uncontrolled populations was better understood than at the World Population Conference in Bucharest, Romania, in August. The groundwork was laid in Rome for still more haggling in new councils—for the scoring of ideological points and no action, or for a transformation of man's concept of international institutions.

The same might be said of the UN Conference on the Law of the

Arafat at the UN

Sea in Caracas, Venezuela, in the summer. It was a notable effort by the international community to organize a regime of self-discipline to cover 70 per cent of the earth's surface. Earlier conferences in Geneva had sought to codify customary law, which favored the large maritime powers, but at Caracas, they were framing regulations based on equity for all—or the nearest thing obtainable by rough consensus. Because genuine contradictions of interest had to be worked out and a grand package compromise put together, no specific agreements were reached at Caracas. Few were expected at this stage. There had, after all, never been anything quite like this before—the entire world involved in an effort to create international law. A significant factor at Caracas was that, though the posture of confrontation between rich and poor persisted, the issues themselves (exploiting the resources of the sea, controlling pollution, regulating fishing and navigation) cut across conventional alignments. Coastal states, landlocked states, states with long coastlines, and those that practice long-range fishing formed temporary blocs regardless of race and ideology. It sounded confusing, but it was perhaps a healthier mix for the international community than the polarization of blocs.

The UN system provided the means to act internationally

In the long perspective, the remarkable fact about 1974 may be not the extent of disagreement, but the effort on so many fronts to seek agreement. We were into the crunch stage when the answers are exceedingly hard to find. On the level of negotiation, this meant not just agreeing to talk, but actually accepting borders or guarantees or talking with people long considered unacceptable. The failure to agree is not necessarily evidence of a lack of will to do so. The issues are baffling, and the risks are high. It is a time when brinkmanship is to be expected. At the end of 1974, there was no verdict in the struggle between the forces of integration and of disintegration. The struggle is permanent. The next conference on food or resources or the law of the sea could break up in disorder—or never take place. The next Middle East war could at any moment shatter the whole fabric of détente. Still, it was something for the framework of international negotiation to have held in such a climactic year. Although decisions taken or not taken in the Security Council or the General Assembly were as usual praised and denounced, it was the United Nations system that provided the means and also the compulsion to act internationally. The habits developed since its founding in 1945 were perhaps deeply rooted enough to resist the threatening anarchy.

Related Articles

For further information on international relations in 1974, see the articles on the various nations in Section Four, and also the following:

Africa	International Trade	Middle East
Asia	and Finance	Pacific Islands
Europe	Latin America	United Nations

Law of the Sea meeting

Focus on The Nation

James Reston

It may be that, in the perspective of history, 1974 was not a bad year, but an instructive one that proved the strength of our institutions

In general, it is probably wrong to try to measure history by years. This is a form of calendar worship. The life of nations and the human family usually moves much more slowly, by drifts and tendencies over decades and even generations. But occasionally there is a year that is very special in the life of a country, that sets it apart from all others, and therefore can fairly be called "historic." The year 1974 was such a one in the United States.

For the first time in the long story of the republic, a President of the United States, Richard M. Nixon, resigned from the highest office in the land. And by the end of the year, the United States had a new President and a new Vice-President, Gerald R. Ford of Michigan and Nelson A. Rockefeller of New York, neither of whom had been elected by the votes of the American people.

These extraordinary political events took place during the most serious American economic recession in more than a generation—with the highest unemployment rate and the lowest stock market level in a dozen years— and in the midst of a worldwide crisis over the fourfold increase in the price of industrial fuel. The psychological effect of these events was profound.

During the Vietnam War, it had been demonstrated that money and machines, two commodities on which America had placed great trust, were not necessarily the answer to limited wars far from home. Now it was demonstrated in 1974 that the nation's assumption of unlimited supplies of cheap fuel and food was not valid, and even that the integrity of the presidency could not be taken for granted.

This confused and even startled the nation. It had a political crisis, a fuel crisis, rising inflation and unemployment for most of the year, a new President, a new Vice-President, and a new balance of political power in Congress—all at the same time.

There was even talk that the United States was headed in the 1970s for the sort of economic depression it had endured in the 1930s. The capitalist countries were all in trouble in 1974: over 20 per cent inflation in Great Britain and Japan, virtual bankruptcy in Italy, political turmoil in Greece and Turkey, rising economic difficulties in France and West Germany, and the threat of a fifth Arab-Israeli war and another oil embargo in the Middle East.

Yet it may be that, in the perspective of history, 1974 was not a bad year but an instructive year that brought the nation back to the hard realities of political and economic life and actually proved, not the weakness, but the strength of its political and economic institutions.

In the first place, the gloomy comparisons of 1974 with 1932 were historically inaccurate. There was a temporary depression of the

James Reston

American spirit in 1974 but not of the American economy in terms of the 1930s. Unemployment rose at the end of 1974 to about 6.5 million — some 7.1 per cent of the total work force and much higher for blacks and auto workers. Car sales were way down, food prices and interest rates were way up. Old people and others living on fixed incomes and young people trying to buy houses at annual interest rates of over 10 per cent were in trouble.

The burden of debt in America in 1974 was staggering. Even *Business Week* magazine, which concerns itself primarily with the business interests of the country, seemed worried about the rising debt of America.

"The United States is the Debt Economy without peer," it reported in its Oct. 12, 1974, issue. "It has the biggest lenders, the biggest borrowers, the most sophisticated financial system. The numbers are so vast that they simply numb the mind: $1 trillion in corporate debt; $600 billion in mortgage debt; $500 billion in U.S. government debt; $200 billion in state and local government debt; $200 billion in consumer debt."

In short, to deal with nearly 30 years of economic boom at home and export it abroad, the United States had borrowed an average net of $200 million a day, every day, since the end of World War II in 1945.

This was not only an economic and financial question, but also a philosophic question for America in 1974. This would, *Business Week* said, "be an awesome burden of debt even if the world's economic climate were perfect. It is an ominously heavy burden with the world as it is today—ravaged by inflation, threatened with economic depression, torn apart by the massive redistribution of wealth that has accompanied the soaring price of oil."

Yet comparisons of 1974 in the United States with the depression year of 1932 were highly misleading. In 1932, there were between 15-million and 17 million persons unemployed in the United States. Average wages that year for Americans lucky enough to have jobs were a little over $16 a week. In 1974, over 80 million Americans were working at the highest wages of any nation in the world. And, unlike 1932, the nation had a social security system, an unemployment benefits system, a health insurance system, and a public-works program, all backed by the federal government, to ease the pressures on the unemployed and relieve the anxieties of the old and the sick. Thus, 1974 was a time of trouble and reappraisal, with spectacular losses in the investments of the rich and the middle class, but it was not a disaster for the poor, as in 1932.

All historical judgments are relative. Going into 1975 meant going into the last quarter of the 20th century. In the first quarter, there was a savage world war—actually a civil war among the Western nations. The second quarter of the century was marked by the world economic depression, the second world war, and the emergence of the United States and Russia as the predominant military powers in the world. But it also was marked by the revival of Europe and Japan.

Comparisons of 1974 with the depression year of 1932 are very misleading

The old team

The third quarter of the century, from 1950 to 1975, saw the rise of new power centers not only in Japan and Europe, but also in China and particularly in the oil-producing states of the Middle East. Finally, in 1974, it became clear in the United States that power and nations beyond its control could change the life of America—force the American people to line up in the morning to pay double for gasoline and change many other aspects of their lives. All this taxed not only the American pocketbook, but also the American mind.

In this third quarter, the United States had gone through two savage limited wars in Korea and Vietnam. But unlike the first and second quarters, it had avoided world war, and coming into the last quarter of the century, it was dealing with more subtle and ambiguous problems.

Mainly, 1974 was a time of testing and challenge for the American system of constitutional government. It began with dramatic charges of illegal corruption against the President and members of his White House staff and Cabinet, which were denied. It ended with the resignation of President Nixon and a spectacular trial of his principal political aides. Only a presidential pardon and illness kept Nixon himself out of the criminal courts.

At the beginning of the year, in his nationally televised State of the Union message, President Nixon tried to interfere with the responsibilities of Congress and the courts to look into the charges of corruption in his Administration and see that the laws were "faithfully executed." He presented a 10-point program to Congress, accompanied by a 22,000-word program on how to check inflation; lessen the energy crisis; institute domestic reforms in the fields of health, welfare, and transportation; and promote world peace.

His appeal was clear. Maybe mistakes and even misjudgments had been made in the past, but the great issues of peace abroad and economic security at home were more important. He would, he said, cooperate with Congress and the courts to look into charges of espionage, sabotage, burglary, perjury, and obstruction of justice in his Administration, but he tried to turn the investigations off. "One year of Watergate," he said, "is enough."

Three historic decisions in 1974 rejected Nixon's appeal and insisted on abiding by the laws and the Constitution. On February 6, the House of Representatives voted, 410 to 4, to grant broad constitutional power to its Judiciary Committee to gather all the facts bearing on the possible impeachment of the President.

On July 24, the Supreme Court of the United States voted 8 to 0 that Nixon had to produce "forthwith" all relevant tape recordings and documents relating to 64 conversations he held with his aides in the White House. The tapes had been subpoenaed by Watergate special prosecutor Leon Jaworski for use in the pending cover-up trial of six of Nixon's former assistants.

In late July, after almost six months of investigation, the Judiciary Committee of the House of Representatives voted in nationally tele-

Mainly, 1974 was a time of testing for the American system of government

The new team

25

vised hearings to recommend three articles of impeachment. The first, voted on July 27, charged that President Nixon had personally engaged in a "course of conduct" designed to lead to obstruction of justice in the Watergate scandal. Six Republicans joined all 21 Democrats on the committee in the 27 to 11 vote.

The second, voted 28 to 10 on July 29, charged that he had "repeatedly" failed to carry out his constitutional duties in a series of alleged abuses of presidential power. The third, on July 30 in a 21 to 17 vote, accused him of unconstitutional defiance of Congress and its subpoenas.

Even then, Nixon insisted that he would not resign, but on August 5, when the transcripts of three of his conversations on June 23, 1972 – only six days after the Watergate break-in – were made public, it was disclosed that he had personally been involved in obstructing justice. Further, he had concealed the evidence from his own lawyers and from his supporters who were defending him against impeachment in the House Judiciary Committee.

At that point, it was clear that the constitutional process had worked its way, and he had no choice but to resign, and save his presidential pension, or be impeached and convicted. On August 8, he announced on national television that he would resign, and the next day he left the White House with the expressed hope that his departure would start a "process of healing that is so desperately needed in America." On August 9, Gerald R. Ford was sworn in as the 38th President of the United States and declared that "our long national nightmare is over." He pledged to preside over an open and candid Administration and asked the nation to pray that Richard Nixon, "who had brought peace to millions," might "find it for himself."

For the rest of 1974, the business of the nation went on under President Ford and Vice-President Rockefeller about as before. None of the disasters predicted by followers of President Nixon took place. The new President and the new Vice-President were received in Washington, D.C., with a sense of relief and accepted abroad by the leaders of Russia, Europe, and Japan without regret or question.

Meanwhile, by the end of 1974, Congress acted to correct the mistakes of the Vietnam War and the Watergate affair. It passed a war-powers bill that prohibited a President from committing U.S. troops to war overseas for more than 60 days without the approval of the members of the House and Senate. It moved against the money-corruption of the Watergate affair by providing up to $20 million in public money for major candidates in presidential elections, and it created new safeguards against wiretapping or bugging of private citizens.

Accordingly, by the beginning of 1975, there was a new spirit and a new balance of power in American politics. The relations between the White House, Congress, and the press were much more open. The Democrats came into the 94th Congress early in January, 1975, with much larger majorities than in 1974, and President Ford was calling

By the end of 1974, Congress had acted to correct some past mistakes

Nixon resigns

for political unity to deal with the economic problems of the nation.

By early in 1975, however, with an unelected President in the White House, the political struggle to replace him in 1976 had already started. The leading candidate of the Democratic Party, Senator Edward M. Kennedy of Massachusetts, announced that, for personal reasons, he would not be a candidate, and the new President indicated that he would seek election in his own right.

Thus, the normal constitutional procedures were operating again by 1975. Congress had regained some of the authority it had handed over to the President in the previous generation. The dangers of political corruption, of improper campaign financing, and of political espionage and sabotage were all under better supervision and control; and while the nation was preoccupied with serious economic difficulties, it was ready to deal with them in 1975 in a much more orderly and trustful spirit.

By 1975, the normal U.S. constitutional procedures were operating again

Related Articles

For further information on United States affairs in 1974, see also Section One, FOCUS ON THE ECONOMY and FOCUS ON EDUCATION; Section Two, FROM TRIUMPH TO TRAGEDY; Section Five, FORD, GERALD RUDOLPH; and the following articles in Section Four:

Focus on The Economy

Sylvia Porter

The year 1974 saw the twin nightmares of a deepening business decline and a galloping inflation—but is a depression ahead? No!

Slumpflation was the name of the nightmare "game" we endured in 1974—a wretched combination of deepening business decline side by side with relentlessly galloping inflation. The absolute worst of the alternates with which I closed my report on 1973's joyless boom came through with a force no one could have anticipated without foreknowledge of how the Watergate affair would paralyze all government economic policymaking for most of the year. In fact, until the very end of the year, the United States new leaders also appeared to be impotent to deal with the dilemma of exploding energy and food costs in a period of spreading economic decay.

The cost of living continued to soar at an intolerably rapid rate. The rise in the consumer price index was at a murderous rate of more than 12 per cent, the biggest one-year jump since 1947. In the first half of 1974 alone, electricity rates of the nation's 50 largest utilities rose an average of 55.4 per cent. At year's end, it cost more than $1.55 to buy the market basket of goods and services that $1 bought as recently as 1967. At 1974's rate of increase, the price level in the United States would double in merely five to six years—making any sort of sound advance planning an impossibility. Despite pay hikes, the average worker's "real" earnings—pay after deductions for Social Security taxes and federal income taxes and adjusted for inflation—went down substantially from 1973. The longer the squeeze lasted, the harder it became to take. As a result, consumers bought fewer luxuries and tried to cut their own budgets as much as they could on their own.

And the business retreat went far beyond "stagnation" or other terms the politicians preferred to use. The "feel" as well as the fact of recession was all around us. The decline became much worse than the slowdown that began in 1973 as an inevitable backing away from the unsustainable boom artificially created in 1972 to help ensure the re-election of President Richard M. Nixon.

In duration, this business decline seemed destined to be the longest of the entire post-World War II generation. Assuming its beginning is dated in November, 1973, the recession was 13 months old as 1975 began, already longer than the postwar average of 11 months. If a real recovery doesn't start until mid-1975—the earliest recovery date expected by many authorities—the recession will have lasted twice as long as most of the setbacks of the 1950s and the 1960s.

In depth, this decline appeared likely to be among the most severe of the past 28 years as well. Unemployment rose sharply above its low of 4.2 per cent in autumn, 1973, and the rate was clearly heading toward well over 7 per cent in early 1975. The number of unemployed approximated 6.5 million, the highest total since the Department of Labor began computing these figures in 1948.

Sylvia Porter

The government's key barometer of leading business indicators— yardsticks that usually telegraph in advance that a business decline is on the way—was plunging at the steepest rate in more than 23 years as 1974 closed.

After a 45-month boom, machine tool orders slipped, and while business continued to spend huge amounts for new plants and equipment, these outlays were becoming increasingly vulnerable to cutbacks.

On the surface, profits seemed to be the best ever, with a few exceptions. But the gains were mostly phony, reflecting windfalls on inventories bought earlier at much lower prices. With inventory profits eliminated, before-tax earnings generally were not up, but actually *down*. Some industries were outright disasters—housing, autos, new appliances. And the business decline had the usual multiplier effect as it spread out and fed on itself. (For instance, a house that isn't built doesn't use lumber or glass or need bathtubs or appliances or furniture, drapes, and so forth.) The total output of goods and services declined throughout the year, qualifying 1974 for a "recession" label by any acceptable definition.

As for Wall Street, that was a debacle. While there was havoc in the housing industry, there was nothing short of a catastrophe in the securities industry. The number of member firms of the New York Stock Exchange, the world's greatest securities market place, fell to the lowest level since the late 1800s—down from 622 to 515 in the past five years alone. Other exchanges shriveled even more as brokerage firms went out of business, merged, were forced into consolidations, or were quietly taken over.

In many ways, 1974 saw the worst stock market decline since the cataclysmic crash of 1929-1932—almost half a century ago. Hundreds of solid stocks had lost 80 to 90 per cent of their value since the start of the decade. For less than $10, you could have bought a share of stock in more than one-third of the companies listed on the New York Stock Exchange—or 620 out of the 1,543 stocks representing the top of American industry and business.

The bitter irony of all this is that at the same time, the securities markets are being called upon to supply additional trillions of dollars to help finance an imperative expansion of industry's efficiency (productivity) and capacity to produce. Yet, with stock prices at 1974's levels, raising the funds through the issuance of new stocks is next to impossible. In the first half of 1974, only $2.3 billion of new stocks was issued against $9.3 billion in 1973 and $15.3 billion in 1972. It wasn't merely too expensive for companies to raise money by issuance of new shares at last year's low prices. Equally as depressing, after years of losing money, many investors didn't want to buy the stocks.

Why so horrible a stock market record since the mid-1960s? Unquestionably, the prime factor has been the virulence of this era's inflation, sending interest rates skyrocketing, making fixed-income securities (short-term money market issues and long-term bonds) ex-

In many ways, Wall Street had its worst drop since 1929-1932

How the Bear Markets Compare

Bear Market	Drop in Dow (%)	Duration (Months)
1929-32	89	34
1937-38	49	13
1938-42	41	42
1946	23	4
1953	13	8
1956-7	13	10
1957	19	3
1960	17	10
1961-62	27	6
1965	11	1½
1966	25	8
1967-68	13	6
1968-70	36	18
1973-74	40	24

tremely attractive in comparison with stocks, and threatening the very survival of our economic system.

But why the virulence of inflation? "If I had to populate an asylum with people certified insane, I'd just pick 'em from all those who claim to understand inflation." A smart-alecky crack from one of today's smart-alecky university economists? No. It was Will Rogers, America's beloved humorist, who, in a much simpler age long ago, came up with that almost incredibly up-to-the-minute observation. And I suppose that with Rogers' warning ringing in my ears, I should now subside. But I'm too serious a commentator on economics to default on even an attempt at explanations for this wretched era. So herewith—first with the "simple" answers and then with the truly fundamental causes of today's nightmare of slumpflation.

For decades we spent recklessly, and now we see the end result

Bad weather, droughts, and crop disasters the world over have clearly played an enormous part in sending food prices soaring in recent years. Shortages of other crucial raw materials also have developed. The Arab oil boycott, the quadrupling of oil prices in one year, and the resulting spiral in prices for all forms of energy are obvious forces. The successive devaluations of the U.S. dollar to a point where it sank in 1973 to among the world's most undervalued currencies expanded our exports, but the devaluations also greatly boosted the costs of our imports. And since the exports included huge amounts of agricultural products and the imports raised prices of many goods essential to us, the devaluations hardly helped the U.S. consumer.

At the same time, while crops and other raw materials have been restricted and prices of energy have been skyrocketing, demands for foodstuffs and all types of goods and services have ballooned throughout the world. As our economic expansions in the post-World War II period were fed by massive U.S. government spending and easy credit, so expansions elsewhere were fed by similar spending and credit policies. By extraordinary coincidence, the upturns ran into each other and into the limits of world resources in 1973. It was beyond the capacity of individual nations to produce enough to satisfy billions of new customers clamoring for the first time in history to move up the scale of living standards toward the lofty levels set by the United States.

Indisputably, all these have been great factors. But most fundamental is the fact that we are finally reaping the economic whirlwind of decades of reckless spending, straining even the United States magnificent resources and technology. The excesses began with World War II and reached a first peril point in the creation of the Marshall Plan— an unprecedented gesture of generosity and enlightened self-interest by which the United States poured billions of dollars into the economic streams of our war-devastated allies (and enemies). That spending alone turned our war-swollen balance-of-payments surpluses into an annual chain of balance-of-payments deficits.

The excesses reached a second peril point in the mid-1960s, when President Lyndon B. Johnson would not admit that Vietnam was a

Drought

war and thus refused to insist on raising revenues sufficient to finance it. Our balance of payments plunged into an ocean of red ink.

They reached a third peril point when President Nixon failed to stick to any solid anti-inflation programs and instead went on a wild inflation-creating spree in 1972 to assure his re-election. And our excesses reached a fourth peril point when Watergate overwhelmed the White House and crippled U.S. economic policy for the prolonged and critical period from 1973 to mid-1974.

The things that went right were tragedies that did not happen

There can be no quick and easy answers—not with this background. Economies as complex as ours cannot be turned on a dime, and in defense of President Ford, he inherited a terrible economic legacy when he took over from Nixon in late summer.

To remind you: In August, the inflation rate already was at 12 per cent, double the rate when Nixon came in; the prime rate that banks charge to their top borrowing customers also was at 12 per cent, against 7 per cent in 1969; the federal budget was at $305 billion, nearly two-thirds larger than spending in the year ending June 30, 1969. And we were well into the second recession since 1969.

Didn't anything go right on the economic front in 1974? Sure, many things of great importance, but they primarily fall into the category of tragic events that could have happened but did not:

▪ The major oil-consuming nations *did not* turn inward and become bitter competitors for any oil the producers agree to supply. On the contrary, the countries of the Western world that import 80 per cent of the world's oil formed a counter-cartel to "secure oil supplies on reasonable and equitable terms." This recognition that we are now all parts of a world economy and that the trading nations will go up or down together is in itself good news of potentially enormous meaning.

▪ The international banking system *did not* break down, despite failure of a major bank in West Germany and of lesser institutions in Italy, Great Britain, and elsewhere, plus the two largest bank failures in U.S. history. The central bankers actually publicly stated they would assist banks that get into trouble and threaten to set off a dominolike series of financial catastrophes.

▪ Even the weakest among our European allies *did not* collapse. Italy was rescued again, Great Britain—through some genius of its own—was still muddling through at year-end, and the European Community (Common Market) was very much alive and indulging in its usual cranky squabbling.

▪ A predicted mass flight from the U.S. dollar into "things" *did not* occur—even through the months that our economic policies were non-policies. United States consumers instead raised their rate of savings to almost 8 cents out of every $1 of disposable income, in face of the fact that real incomes were down from a year ago. While this reflected a deep sense of insecurity, it also indicated a continued faith in the U.S. dollar as a medium of value.

▪ The dire forecasts of fundamental and prolonged scarcities of vital products and raw materials *did not* hold up. Shortages eased in areas

Gasoline shortage

ranging from nails to newsprint, from copper to cotton, from utility poles to electric wire and cable. Shortages were expected to ease for many more products in 1975, including such essentials as fertilizer and chemical fibers.

■ We *did not* suffer a devastating credit crunch. Credit was excruciatingly tight for most of 1974, with mortgage money all but unavailable in some regions, and loans were horribly expensive. But the eerie credit squeezes of 1966 and 1970—when money just seemed to disappear—were not repeated. Federal Reserve Board Chairman Arthur F. Burns promised to keep credit flowing—and it flowed slowly until mid-1974, then became perceptibly easier and cheaper to get as the Federal Reserve acknowledged the accelerating recession.

■ The United States *did not* retreat in foreign trade. In fact, when the perversions caused by our expensive oil imports and huge agricultural exports are eliminated, we showed impressive competitive gains in trade with our major commercial rivals and trading partners. The red ink in our balance of payments resulting from oil imports was far different from the destructive deficits resulting in the early 1970s from the fact that our dollar was dreadfully overvalued. The U.S. dollar today is more fairly priced than in many years, and it has more than held its own as an international medium of exchange during a period when all currency rates have been "floating" in value against each other. Floating also has not become a synonym for "drowning," and the world is accepting an evolution of our monetary system.

■ Finally, the world *did not* crash into the calamitous depression (of the 1929-1932 variety) feared by more than half of all Americans, according to a Gallup Poll late in the year.

And now? Now the probability is growing that inflation will moderate and that with restimulative economic policies, the recession will end before 1976. The debate centers not on whether or when the downturn will end but, rather, on whether it will end in a V-shape or a saucer-shape—a sharp down and a brisk up or a slow down, a long bumping along bottom, and a sluggish swing up. The answer will depend on policies still to be adopted by the White House and Congress, on events in the Middle East, oil diplomacy, and other developments that simply cannot be glimpsed at this point. But depression? Despite the doomsayers, *no*.

The probability is growing that the recession will end in 1975

Related Articles

For further information on economics in 1974, see Section Four, Agriculture; Banks and Banking; Economics; International Trade and Finance; Labor; Manufacturing; Stocks and Bonds.

Arthur F. Burns

Focus on Science

Harrison Brown

For perhaps the first time, scientists showed a willingness to accept restrictions on their freedom to do research of their own choosing

In July of 1974, a group of 11 molecular biologists who had been brought together by the U.S. National Academy of Sciences called for a temporary ban on certain kinds of experiments that involve the genetic manipulation of living cells and viruses. For many decades, biologists have accepted severe restrictions on experimentation on humans. Aside from that, this may be the first time that scientists have indicated a willingness to accept restrictions upon their freedom to undertake research of their own choosing.

Shortly after the discovery of nuclear fission in 1939, American nuclear physicists accepted, upon the urging of the late Leo Szilard and Enrico Fermi, a self-imposed ban on publishing certain of their research results. Recognizing that the development of an atomic bomb might be possible, there was no desire on the part of the American scientific community to help the Germans under Adolf Hitler develop such a weapon. But, although there was a self-imposed moratorium on publication of their findings, the research on nuclear fission went full speed ahead. In the case of the group of 11, headed by Professor Paul Berg, chairman of the Biochemistry Department of Stanford University, an outright ban on certain experiments on bacteria and viruses, as distinct from human beings, has been proposed.

The motivation for the proposal stems from the development of a new technique that makes use of a newly discovered class of enzyme that operates on deoxyribonucleic acid (DNA) molecules. These spiral molecules are inside the nucleus of every cell and are the basic self-replicating units of life, producing fragments that are able to recombine. The recombined fragments give rise to new forms of DNA molecules that can, under the right circumstances, infect bacteria and reproduce themselves within the cells. These new DNA molecules are called "recombinant" DNA.

Professor Stanley Cohen and his co-workers at Stanford University have linked DNA from two separate microorganisms, and the recombined DNA has been shown to replicate well in *Escherichia coli* (*E. coli*, in shorthand) a species of bacteria in common laboratory use that thrives abundantly—but for the most part harmlessly—in the human intestine. Similarly, segments of DNA from the chromosomes of fruit flies have been recombined with bacterial DNA to yield hybrid molecules that can also replicate satisfactorily in *E. coli*. And, frog genes have been introduced into bacteria.

The most obvious concern of the group of 11 scientists is that new types of bacteria and viruses, to which human beings have not been exposed, can now be created. The potential danger is that these new viruses and bacteria might infect the human population.

The group specifically proposes a moratorium on two related types

Harrison Brown

of experiments, at least until the scientists—working with their governments—have had the opportunity to consider the dangers, as well as the opportunities, in depth. In the absence of such a moratorium, this particular research field might well grow too rapidly and become too large to be controllable.

According to the group, the first type of experiment to be avoided is one that inserts into bacteria genes that enable them to resist antibiotics or to form dangerous bacterial toxins. The thought of a new form of bacterium that is injurious to humans, yet resistant to our more clinically useful antibiotics, is indeed a disturbing one.

The second type of experiment to be avoided is one that links segments of DNA's from likely cancer-producing viruses, or other animal viruses, with elements of DNA's that are capable of reproducing themselves in bacterial populations that live in humans and other animals. Such recombinant DNA molecules might possibly increase the incidence of cancer or other diseases.

Finally, the group cautions that the arrangement of the amino acids in many types of animal cell DNA's is similar to that in certain tumor viruses. Under the circumstances, the group recommends caution in any experiment involving the joining of any foreign DNA to a DNA replication system that creates new recombinant DNA molecules with unpredictable biological properties.

The group stresses that its concern is based more upon judgments of potential danger than upon demonstrated risk. Nevertheless, it urges the director of the National Institutes of Health to consider establishing an advisory committee to evaluate the potential hazards of recombinant DNA molecules and develop procedures and guidelines to minimize the dangers.

The concern expressed about this problem has by no means been uniquely American. Nobel laureate Sir John Kendrew, in his presidential address before the British Association for the Advancement of Science, stressed the need for a permanent international body that would make a continuing assessment of the benefits and dangers of such genetic experiments. In Great Britain, the Medical Research Council issued a moratorium call similar to that of the group of 11 in the United States. As a result, the Advisory Board for the Research Councils has set up a scientific committee "to make an authoritative assessment of the potential benefits and potential hazards of techniques which allow experimental manipulation of the genetic composition of microorganisms." Because of such concerns, an international meeting of scientists who work in the field was scheduled to be held in the United States in early 1975 to review scientific progress in this area and to discuss ways of dealing with the potential hazards.

Thus far, the concept of a moratorium has been well received by scientists working in the field. The need for caution is obvious, and even those who might oppose the moratorium will be under considerable moral pressure to refrain from undertaking such experiments until such time as the situation has been fully evaluated. Nevertheless,

The concern is based more upon judgments of potential danger than proven risk

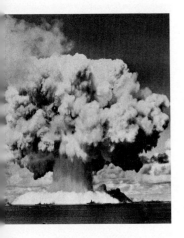
Atomic bomb blast

most scientists take a positive attitude and stress that "safe" techniques can be devised for manipulating altered DNA's and bacteria. Over the years, for example, chemists and biologists have learned how to handle dangerous quantities of radioactive substances by remote control in such a way that humans are not harmed.

Most scientists agree, however, that it would be unfortunate if it became necessary to maintain a moratorium for a prolonged period of time. The ultimate medical benefits of such research could be substantial. Furthermore, there are enormous insights to be gained concerning the genetics of living organisms.

Clearly, the development of this new technique is the most spectacular achievement in genetics since 1969, when Jonathan Beckwith and his collaborators at Harvard Medical School succeeded in isolating a pure gene from a living organism. At the time, the Harvard group warned that genetic manipulation can be fraught with danger. The ability to develop new DNA's brings us one step closer to the time when genetic engineering in man, with its promise and with its dangers, becomes a reality.

It would be unfortunate if the moratorium lasted for a long period

Now that genetic engineering in bacteria is a reality, public concern over the potential benefits and hazards of genetic engineering in man will almost certainly increase. For the foreseeable future, however, genetic manipulations on human beings will almost certainly be confined to single gene traits where the success of molecular genetics has thus far been confined. Such traits include, however, a significant number of genetic defects. We must keep in mind the fact that 5 out of every 100 children born have genetic defects that are immediately apparent or that will affect them later in life. There are substantial technical obstacles yet to be overcome before such single-gene defects can be corrected, but it seems likely that we are not far removed from the time when such corrections can be made.

In contrast with traits that are determined by single genes, many human traits depend upon the sum of the contributions of many genes interacting with the environment. These contributions and their interactions are so complex that it will be a long time, if ever, before such polygenic traits as intelligence, temperament, size, and shape can be altered predictably by gene manipulation. Thus, fears that a tyrant might specify the precise genetic composition of his subjects are unwarranted, at least for the time being.

Another major category of genetic manipulation is *cloning*, the production of an exact gene copy of an individual. This is done by removing the nucleus from any female's egg and replacing it with a nucleus obtained from a body cell of any individual. This has already been accomplished with frogs, and it may become feasible in mammals in the future. Certainly the incentive to create exact genetic duplicates of prize cattle will be strong. Indeed, the creation of an exact genetic duplicate of oneself would represent a major step toward the achievement of immortality. Once cloning becomes truly feasible on a substantial scale, the moral and ethical issues will be formidable.

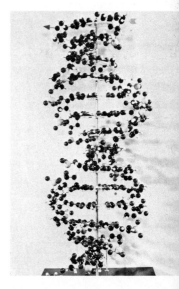

DNA model

**One form of
human genetic
engineering
is now in use**

In one sense, human genetic engineering—in the form of genetic diagnosis—is already being used on a substantial and increasing scale. In 1969, a group at the University of Wisconsin reported that it had obtained and cultivated cells from the amniotic fluid of a 22-week fetus (this is the fluid in the sac in which the fetus floats). After chemical analysis, the group diagnosed the fetus as a mutant male suffering from the Lesch-Nylan syndrome, which is a genetic error of metabolism that results in severe neurological and developmental disorders.

In five short years, this new technique, known as *amniocentesis*, has been refined and applied to several thousand pregnant American women. Using the refined techniques, a quantity of amniotic fluid is extracted at about the 12th to 16th week of pregnancy, and fetal cells are cultured and analyzed. In this manner, genetic defects associated with 40 or more diseases can be detected. In the event of the discovery that the fetus is afflicted with a genetically caused illness, it can be aborted if the parents so desire. The parents can, if they wish, follow up with another pregnancy, and the new fetus can be tested. The procedure can be repeated until a child free of inherited disease is conceived.

Of all genetic diseases, Mongolism is perhaps the most widely known and feared. This is a combination of physical and mental abnormalities caused by the presence of an extra chromosome, a rod-shaped body in the nucleus of a cell that carries the genes that control the development of the organism. Mongoloid children can have intelligence quotients as low as 20; seldom are they higher than 70. They are prone to repeated infections and generally have a greatly shortened life span. They do not become independent members of society. At present, somewhere between 6,000 and 8,000 Mongoloid babies are born each year in the United States, and care of the children is estimated to cost about $2 billion annually.

Prior to the development of amniocentesis, prospective parents could, through genetic counseling, obtain an estimate of the probability of their conceiving a Mongoloid child—or, for that matter, a child handicapped by any one of a variety of genetic defects. Yet every woman who wanted a child had to take her chances. She might use the probability estimate as a guide, but as gamblers know, statistical estimates tell us nothing about the outcome of individual events.

Now amniocentesis makes it possible for a woman to learn definitely whether the fetus she is carrying is Mongoloid or whether it suffers from any of a variety of genetic diseases. Even in the extreme case of the identification of a Mongoloid fetus, the finding presents serious ethical, moral, and emotional problems to the parents. A young couple who do not wish to bear the emotional and financial burden of the deformed child might well decide upon an abortion. A middle-aged couple who want a child badly might decide to have the child rather than risk not being able to conceive again. But at least parents are able to make decisions based upon certain knowledge as distinct from estimates of probabilities.

Paul Berg

Now that prenatal genetic diagnosis is an established medical technique, we can expect increasing numbers of parents, as well as society, to be confronted by perplexing social and ethical dilemmas. The decision to abort a fetus is seldom an easy one. At one extreme, if amniocentesis shows that the fetus suffers from Tay-Sachs disease, where the child is born normal but quickly develops mental and physical abnormalities that lead inevitably to death by the age of 4, the decision might be a relatively easy one. But what about the decision to abort a fetus because of its sex? Suppose the parents already have several boys and want a girl? Amniocentesis tells them the sex of the fetus. Do the parents have the right to abort the fetus simply to satisfy their desires as to the sex of the child?

During the past decade, research in medical genetics has progressed with unprecedented rapidity. The social consequences both for good and for bad are enormous. It is clear that an informed public should play a major role in formulating the necessary decisions. But in order to play this role, the public must be well informed concerning both the available techniques and the consequences of their use. Unfortunately, the mass media and the schools have tended to avoid the subject or have focused mainly upon the medical advances rather than on the social, ethical, and political dilemmas.

The public should play a major role in formulating needed decisions

Related Articles

For further information on science and technology in 1974, see the articles on the various sciences in Section Four.

Focus on Education

Lawrence A. Cremin

**Events in the United States in 1974 raised anew
the old dilemma of maintaining a common, public
school system in a diverse, pluralistic society**

Conflicts over values crackled across the American educational scene in 1974. As if in a changing weather system of opinion and belief, the schools found themselves caught amid the lightning and thunder of intense ideological controversy.

In January, a federal district judge in New York City ruled that the Mark Twain High School had been illegally segregated according to race and ordered city authorities to come up not only with an integration plan for the school, but also with an integration plan for the surrounding public housing. In April, several speakers before a convention of the National School Boards Association in Houston deplored the erosion of local school board authority in matters such as Bible reading, recital of the pledge of allegiance, and the use of standardized tests, and criticized the growing power of the courts and of teacher organizations in the development of public school policies.

In July, the Supreme Court of the United States struck down an arrangement between the city of Detroit and some of its suburban school districts under which inner-city black children would be bused each morning to predominantly white suburban schools. In September, tempers flared so violently in Boston, where new school desegregation measures had been introduced under federal court order, that school buses were stoned, thousands of children were kept home by their parents, and the governor of Massachusetts eventually had to call out the National Guard. And in Kanawha County, West Virginia, that same month, disagreements over textbooks that had been introduced in connection with a new language arts program became so heated that several men were shot or beaten and a number of school buildings were actually fire-bombed or dynamited.

There were various ways of perceiving what was happening. In one sense, the controversies merely testified to the fact that any program of education invariably incorporates some view of the good life, that citizens in a democracy will inevitably disagree on what the good life really is, and that therefore those same citizens will inevitably disagree in matters of education.

In another sense, however, the controversies of 1974 had a different cast about them. For they frequently went beyond the usual differences among ordinary citizens as to what constitutes good education to involve two additional sorts of conflict. They often pitted one level of government against another—the federal courts, for example, insisting that a local school district take a particular action and the local school district resisting; and they often pitted lay people against professionals, especially the professionals who operated the schools.

Two controversies during the year were particularly illustrative of these phenomena: the controversy over school busing in Boston and

Lawrence A. Cremin

**Integration, some
Bostonians said,
was being forced
on them by others**

the controversy over school textbooks in Kanawha County. Like many controversies over racial integration during the 20 years since the Supreme Court handed down its celebrated *Brown v. Board of Education of Topeka* decision of 1954, the one in Boston began with a federal court order instructing local school authorities to come up with a plan to achieve better "racial balance" in the schools. As was often the case in Northern cities, the distribution of housing in Boston was such that if all children attended neighborhood schools, some schools ended up mostly black and other schools ended up mostly white. Therefore, if a different racial balance was to be achieved, substantial numbers of children would have to be transferred to schools in different parts of the city. The Boston school board—with little enthusiasm, one might add—proceeded to draw up a plan whereby some 20,000 of the city's 94,000 public school pupils would be transported each day to schools outside their neighborhoods. And the plan was put into effect on September 12, the first day of the fall term.

What followed included shoving bouts in the affected schools, beatings, boycotts on both sides, protest marches, attacks on school buses, and the deployment of large numbers of local and state policemen and then of National Guard men. Resistance came primarily from the so-called South Side of the city, a neighborhood inhabited mostly by white people of Irish background. Their views were well expressed by Thomas O'Connell, an organizer of a rally held on September 9, at which feeling ran so high that Senator Edward M. Kennedy (D., Mass.), long a favorite in the area, was actually prevented from speaking. Integration, O'Connell contended, was something that was being forced upon the city's ethnic and working-class neighborhoods by outside liberals who resided in the wealthier suburbs and who therefore did not have to live with its effects. Mayor Kevin H. White responded that integration was the law of the land and that Boston would have to comply with it. "No man, not even a President, stands above the law," Mayor White maintained. "And no city, or group within it, can stand in defiance of the law." The violence peaked during the latter days of September and then subsided, only to flare up again in December with a stabbing and a near riot at South Boston High School.

In Kanawha County, which includes the city of Charleston (West Virginia has county boards of education but no separate administrative arrangements for cities within the counties), both the issues and the political situation were fundamentally different. There, the school authorities had come under attack from members of the local board of education as well as from a number of fundamentalist Christian ministers and their supporters in the community. The controversy began in the spring of 1974, when Superintendent of Schools Kenneth V. Underwood asked the board to adopt several series of textbooks for a language arts program that was to be inaugurated in September. In all, some 96,000 books were involved, under 325 titles, at a cost of $400,000. The titles had been chosen by a committee of professional

Buses in Boston

educators associated with the Kanawha County schools, from an approved state list that had been compiled in accordance with a new state requirement that textbooks for the public schools be "multi-ethnic." That is, the books had to draw their material from a variety of ethnic, racial, and cultural traditions, and they had to portray blacks and whites in situations where they do things together. In response to the superintendent's request, the board voted tentative adoption.

One member of the board, however, Alice Moore, the wife of a local Baptist minister, argued that the board should assume a more active role in such decisions and asked for an opportunity to read some of the books. Once she had done so, she charged that they were absolutely unfit for school use, claiming that they undermined the Christian religion, employed "filthy language," featured the writings of convicted criminals, subverted traditional morality, and advanced unpatriotic ideas. Despite her charges, the board voted in June, by a majority of 3 to 2, to adopt the books.

Mrs. Moore and her supporters were outraged and set out to get the decision reversed. By the time the schools opened on September 3, a boycott had been organized and the county was in turmoil. Shootings, fire-bombings, and dynamiting occurred, and for a time the schools were actually shut down, not by the boycotters but by Superintendent Underwood, who feared for the safety of the children. Meanwhile, the board temporarily removed the disputed books and created a committee of 18 citizens to review them and bring back recommendations. After several weeks of tumultuous meetings, the committee advised that the texts be returned to the schools. The board, taking a conciliatory line, accepted the committee's recommendation but added a proviso that no child whose parents objected to the books would be forced to read them. In the end, the violence slowly abated, but the ugliness remained, leaving Kanawha County a fearful and divided community.

What had so exercised Mrs. Moore and her fellow critics? Essentially, they claimed, it was the substance of the books and the assumptions of their authors concerning what was appropriate for schoolchildren to be reading and thinking about. They objected, for example, to the presence of certain words and phrases in some of the stories and poems—words such as "damn" or "hell" or "bastard" or "whore"—that the authors deemed realistic but that the critics deemed obscene. They objected to the inclusion of certain protest poems raising questions about the fairness of the military draft or the wisdom of the United States involvement in Vietnam, as utterly unpatriotic and subversive of legitimate authority.

They objected to the presence of Lawrence Ferlinghetti's poem "Christ Climbed Down," which Ferlinghetti wrote as an attack on the commercialism of Christmas but which they saw as crassly sacrilegious. And they objected to the recounting of "Jack and the Beanstalk" followed by questions as to whether it might ever be right for

Some people in Kanawha County opposed use of "unfit books"

Books in Kanawha County

43

people to steal, charging that the questions themselves made ethics seem "relative." They found these and dozens of other items offensive to their own deepest beliefs and utterly intolerable when put forward as part of an organized instructional program for their children supported by public funds. And the fact that the books were prepared by experts, or that many of the disputed passages were written by world-famous authors, or that many members of the community, including clergymen, defended the books (one Episcopalian minister referred to them as "delightful, delectable, delicious . . . the best reading I have done in years"), or even that a majority of the school board had found the books acceptable, carried very little weight with them.

The question was how to define the "public interest" in such conflicts

The issues raised in Boston and Kanawha County went to the heart of some of America's most cherished educational values. At one level, they posed the simple question of the right to dissent from legal public decisions. What were the rights, if any, of the Irish parents of Boston's South Side neighborhood not to have their children bused to other parts of the city (or to refuse to have children bused from other parts of the city to "their" neighborhood schools)? What were the rights, if any, of the fundamentalist Christian parents in Kanawha County not to have their children taught from books they deemed offensive and sacrilegious?

In another sense, the two controversies posed the equally fundamental question of the rights of local or neighborhood communities to dissent from the decisions of larger communities, be they counties or cities or states or nations. In an era of much talk about "community control" of schools, the several levels of community were frequently at odds and the question became one of *which* community would control.

But there was yet another question, especially in the Kanawha County controversy, that may have been the most difficult of all. It concerned the definition of "the public interest" in conflicts between parents and school authorities. The issue in one form or another went all the way back to the conflict in ancient Athens that led to the trial and condemnation of Socrates. The distinguished American journalist Walter Lippmann discussed it almost half a century ago in some reflections on the Scopes trial published under the title *American Inquisitors*. The Scopes trial had taken place in 1925 and had attracted worldwide attention. The state of Tennessee had passed a law that year prohibiting the teaching of the theory of evolution in the state's public schools because it conflicted with the story of the Creation as told in the Bible. John Scopes, a high school science teacher in Dayton, Tenn., had deliberately taught the theory of evolution in his biology classes as a means of testing the legality of the statute. He had been arrested, tried, convicted, and fined $100. Later, the case had been appealed to the Tennessee Supreme Court, which had sustained the constitutionality of the statute but remitted Scopes's fine.

In Lippmann's view, two deeply held American principles had collided head-on. Scopes, as a teacher, had seen his responsibility as one

Walter Lippmann

44

of conveying the truth, and the truth as he and scientists around the world understood it included the theory of evolution. William Jennings Bryan, who represented the parents of Dayton (most of whom were fundamentalist Christians), had insisted that public control of public education meant that parents had the right to have their children taught by teachers who did not subvert their most fundamental beliefs about the world. In Dayton, the result had been a stand-off: Both sides had claimed victory but neither had really won. Elsewhere, the conflict seemed unending. "If I read the signs rightly," Lippmann observed in 1928, "we are at the beginning of a period of intense struggle for the control of public education." He saw too little likemindedness in many communities between teachers and the mass of their fellow citizens for the schools to carry on their work with ease and openness, and he saw the situation compounded by the incessant strife among political groups for the allegiance of those fellow citizens. In the end, he thought, the results would be beneficial, since open conflicts between reason and political authority would themselves constitute victories for reason. And for Lippmann that was all to the good. But he was by no means certain as to what the short-run cost would be, in the flight and surrender of able and dedicated schoolteachers or in some more general decline of the quality of public education.

A struggle over the control of public education seemed certain

Now, Lippmann, with his lifelong preference for reason, was precisely the sort of liberal "intellectual" the South Side parents and the Kanawha County critics saw as the main source of their difficulties. And there was no denying, too, that the battle over evolution during the 1920s was somewhat different—though not entirely so—from the battle over standards of taste and value during the 1970s. Yet Lippmann's analysis of 1928 seemed strangely pertinent to the situation of 1974. A period of intense struggle for the control of public education seemed to loom on the horizon, and it promised to raise anew all the time-honored dilemmas of maintaining a common, public school system in a diverse, pluralistic society. And no one could foretell what the outcomes would be or whether those outcomes would be beneficial—to truth, or to American parents and their children, or to all three.

Related Articles

For further information on education in 1974, see Section Two, LEARNING FOR LIVING IN A SILENT WORLD; and Section Four, EDUCATION.

William Jennings Bryan

Focus on The Arts

Alistair Cooke

**Television is the liveliest of the popular arts,
but under what conditions do its artists—writer,
producer, director, film crew—do their best work?**

It shows how fettered we all are to an old-fashioned, almost an Edwardian, view of the arts that in a dozen years or more of this Focus report, television has been paid only the passing tribute of a bow. "The arts" are conventionally assumed to include painting, sculpture, music, ballet, theater, literature, and—only within living memory—the motion picture. Yet, television is far and away the liveliest of all the popular arts, and—as a decade of assassinations, military coups, sky-jackings, kidnapings, Asian wars, religious wars, and Watergates has amply demonstrated—it is universally the most potent of the news media. Scholars, historians, sociologists, and newspaper reporters have an obvious stake in the printed word, and they persistently think of themselves as the most "serious" documentarians of the life of nations. But news is nothing less than history on the wing, and no medium yet discovered travels so fast or observes more intently than the fly on the wall that is television. The view of the world and its woes held by many of the $3\frac{1}{2}$ billion humans alive today is overwhelmingly impressed on them by TV—or, in the poorer countries, by the transistor radio.

I begin with television "news," at a point seemingly furthest removed from the arts, to make the point that everything televised is a form of art: The shortest and the longest newsclips are conscious or unconscious dramatizations of a part of life, since *somebody* has to decide in the first place what "shots" to take and in the last place (the film-editing room) how to combine them to inform or alarm or reassure or otherwise move the viewer. Of course, the parade of images we see in our living rooms will never be more memorable than the combined insights of the cameraman, the director, and the film editor. And much of the time in the United States, especially in the televising of official events and even more often in the dramatizing of history, banality is conditioned by the stereotypes already implanted in the minds of the writer, the director, and the camera crew. The shooting script of a White House press conference, the arrival of a head of state, or an inauguration can be guessed at before the event takes place. An episode in the life of one of the Founding Fathers is predetermined by the writer's reverential view of all Founding Fathers, by the need to employ actors (who are rarely acquainted with either the public or private life of statesmen), and by the determination of the art director to dress everybody up in the most exotic exhibits from the costume wing of the nearest museum.

Occasionally, history—both past and present—is made to come alive by the accident of an actor who forgets his historic role and starts to behave instead of to act. A contemporary news event is suddenly unforgettable, because the camera catches one onlooker who is more worried about his sneezing neighbor than about the soaring rhetoric of

Alistair Cooke

47

the President. In the three-hour television drama *The Missiles of October*, based on the Cuban missile crisis, William Devane's easy and precise mimicry of the voice and accent of John F. Kennedy was enough to bring to life the ordeal of the presidency and to cut through the surrounding pomp and self-conscious "statesmanship" like a knife through butter. And all the Sunday-go-to-meeting cordiality of Vice-President Nelson A. Rockefeller's inauguration a day later, on December 19, was unforgettably blasted by one bleary-eyed senator who clapped mechanically through an interminable yawn.

The artistic claims of television plays, operas, and social documentaries are more obvious, since it is assumed that the writer and director start from scratch to create a story or an argument out of a welter of human experience. But in all television—from the most fanciful fairy tale to the most humdrum photography of fact—the best that appears on the screen is due to the freedom of the director and his crew (the writer included) to express themselves in their chosen medium with no outside interference.

And that, in American television, is the rub. Because a commercial network is only incidentally an artistic medium. It is primarily a showcase for mass-market products. And, in the system that has developed in the United States in the past 50 years, the sponsor and his field commander, the advertising man, are directly interested in the artistic role of the writer and the director. Their preoccupation is with attracting the largest possible audience. Consequently, they come to take the most unflagging interest in any show they have bought that seems to them to drag or is oversubtle or disturbing or too low-key in its dramatic line. In other words, the prime concern is to keep a mass audience attentive enough to be on hand when the sponsor presents his commercials.

It is always difficult for an artist to do his best work when his own aims are prescribed from the outside. There are portrait painters who refuse to work to commission, because invariably the client has a view of a face that is different from the view of the painter commissioned to re-create it. ("A good likeness, but there's something wrong with the mouth" is the bane of a portrait painter's life.) A novelist who was required to satisfy the publisher's prejudice about divorce or physical suffering would plainly be a huckster. And even the brassiest Broadway audience would howl in revolt if, after a Hamlet soliloquy, a pause was called for to expound the virtues of a "whiter than white" detergent or the latest in nutritious cat foods. Yet, three generations of Americans have been bred on the broadcasting-sponsorship system, and while they may find it wearisome, they do not think it odd.

It is instructive, if sad, to recall the different ways in which the Americans and the British developed their separate systems. It is all the more ironical to reflect that they started with opposite aims and eventually exchanged them. For the first British broadcasting organization, formed in 1922, was something called the British Broadcasting *Company*; that is to say, a commercial association of radio-set manufac-

John Maynard Keynes

A commercial TV network is only incidentally an artistic medium

turers. After several years during which it became plain that the manufacturers would be bound to dictate the programs, there was a Royal Commission (a sort of amalgam of a presidential commission and a Senate investigation). It began to cast around to discover the ideal broadcasting institution. Much under the influence of economist John Maynard Keynes, who proposed that the commanding body should be neither a commercial company nor a government agency, it was decided—initially on the analogy of the Port of London Authority —to replace it on Jan. 1, 1927, with a public corporation, to be known as the British Broadcasting *Corporation* (BBC). It is unfortunate for an American's elementary understanding of the setup that the word corporation was chosen precisely to convey that it was not a commercial enterprise, whereas a corporation in the United States is exactly that, what the British call "a limited liability company." At any rate, the BBC—which even *The New York Times*, in nodding moments, calls the British Broadcasting Company—was set up *by* the government to be independent both *of* the government and of commercial sponsorship. Its revenues came, and come, from a license fee imposed on the owners of all sets and paid into the Post Office. A few years ago, Parliament weakened the BBC's always dangerous power as a monopoly by introducing another independent broadcasting authority to manage an alternative commercial outlet. But even here—after a careful scrutiny of the American system—it was decided to prohibit outright sponsorship of programs. The programs are made by separate production companies, and shown on the independent network. Advertising time is sold by the network to all comers; but they buy time, not programs, as newspaper advertisers buy space and not the editorial slant.

The American broadcasting experience began, as one might have guessed from the mere fact that the United States spans a continent, with a cluster of local stations producing their own programs mostly with local talent. Pretty soon, commercial firms saw the advantage to them of sponsoring orchestras and vaudeville talent. But they were almost fearfully aware of radio as a public resource, and their commercials were no more than a bald sentence inserted at the beginning or end of a program. A few stations began to allow a flattering substantive clause to be attached to the mere identification of the sponsor. In 1922, Herbert Hoover, then secretary of commerce, called the first "Radio Conference," which consisted entirely of representatives of the radio industry. He pronounced the following remarkable warning: "It is inconceivable that we should allow so great a possibility for service . . . to be drowned in advertising chatter." Since almost everybody present held the then-universal view that broadcasting was a public resource, like a library or an opera house, the conference passed a resolution that "direct advertising . . . be absolutely prohibited and that indirect advertising be limited to the announcement of the call letters of the station and the name of the concern responsible for the matter broadcasted."

The BBC is free of government and of commercial sponsorship

TV commercial

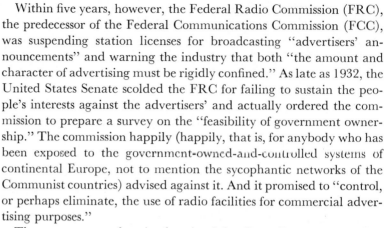

Within five years, however, the Federal Radio Commission (FRC), the predecessor of the Federal Communications Commission (FCC), was suspending station licenses for broadcasting "advertisers' announcements" and warning the industry that both "the amount and character of advertising must be rigidly confined." As late as 1932, the United States Senate scolded the FRC for failing to sustain the people's interests against the advertisers' and actually ordered the commission to prepare a survey on the "feasibility of government ownership." The commission happily (happily, that is, for anybody who has been exposed to the government-owned-and-controlled systems of continental Europe, not to mention the sycophantic networks of the Communist countries) advised against it. And it promised to "control, or perhaps eliminate, the use of radio facilities for commercial advertising purposes."

Then came the deluge—the billion-dollar big business of radio and TV

The country was then in the pit of the Great Depression, and it would have seemed heartless, and highly impractical, to deny business —big or little—the stimulus of exposure over the radio. Direct sponsorship supplemented and supplanted mere "advertising announcements," and after that came the deluge—the billion-dollar institution of television and radio commercial entertainment that Herbert Hoover had thought "inconceivable."

Throughout the decade when the advertising issue was joined, the government, the radio-station managers, and the advertisers alike constantly stressed their common understanding that broadcasting was primarily a "public service." Yet, only in the past dozen years or so have we in the United States come to develop the alternative of an American public television network—the Public Broadcasting Service (PBS). In the past year, popular appreciation of the PBS has been greatly stimulated by its presentations of British dramas of enviable style and character. In earlier years, many of these classical plays— adapted from the works of Henry James, Fyodor Dostoevsky, Thomas Hardy, James Fenimore Cooper, and Dorothy L. Sayers—were produced by the BBC and sold as a package to the PBS. But the series that had 20 million Americans canceling Sunday-night invitations to supper in 1974 was the story of an upper-crust Edwardian London household that offered the viewer an "Upstairs, Downstairs" view of life. Such is the transatlantic reputation of the BBC for superior television, and such is the American awareness of the BBC's freedom from all advertising, that the BBC finds itself regularly praised in the United States for "Upstairs, Downstairs" and "A Family at War," when they are, in fact, the products of two independent British producing companies—London Weekend and Granada respectively—and are shown on the British commercial network.

Herbert Hoover

The excellence of many U.S.-produced programs shown over the PBS—social documentaries and children's shows in particular—and the feast of imported drama really began to offer this country an alternative, noncommercial network, until a new financing setup in effect almost destroyed the PBS as a network. For the public system gets its money partly from the federal government, partly from grants given by industrial and other corporations, and partly from voluntary subscriptions by the viewers. The essential modicum of federal funding used to go to the PBS as a central programming authority–buying and creating and commissioning programs it then broadcast over its 246-station network. But the new setup scatters the federal money among the individual stations and leaves them free to devise and produce their own shows. It sounds eminently democratic. Its first effect, however, has been to deprive the small nucleus of stations that came up with truly creative programs–Boston's WGBH, New York City's WNET, and San Francisco's KQED are distinguished examples–of the extra money they need to set a superior example for the entire network. At the same time, it has given more money, and independent programming authority, to scores of stations that have never shown a spark of originality and that will now be encouraged more than ever to bow to the local commercial or Establishment view of what is entertaining, safe, and "noncontroversial."

This sudden withdrawal of funds has forced the few creative stations to rely more and more on the business corporations "who made possible the preceding program" by a grant of money. This expedient is no blow to the corporations, especially to the oil industry. On the contrary, in a time of alarming inflation, they manage to get the best of both the commercial and the public-service worlds by seeming to promote splendid shows on their own initiative, and actually doing so by spending on every hour of television only about one-tenth or less of what it would cost them to sponsor anything on a commercial network. The tempting danger ahead is for industries to retreat to public broadcasting stations and step up the newspaper and magazine advertising of the programs they have helped to underwrite by suggesting that they inspired or created and produced the programs that they bought, in fact, as a cheap import. The day may come when authentic sponsors, not to mention the FCC, may begin to put the question to the PBS: When is a public network a commercial vehicle?

I hope this survey, which is surely long overdue, has answered the question that was implicitly posed at the beginning of this article: Under what conditions can the artists–writer, producer, director, film crew–do their best work? Or, in the rhetorical version gasped out by naïve but delighted viewers: "Why are these British plays so much better than most of ours?" The answer is: the total freedom from outside interference that has been achieved in Britain by both the BBC and the commercial network. When the advertiser's power is reduced to that of an honest tradesman buying time but not programs, the air is free for the independent exercise of the best that is in the people who write and produce the shows.

Why are these British plays so much better than most of ours?

"Upstairs, Downstairs"

Related Articles

For further information on the arts in 1974, see Section Two, To Increase Knowledge Among Men.

Focus on Sports

Jim Murray

He never really wanted to be known as a home-run hitter, but Henry Aaron of the Atlanta Braves broke baseball's most cherished record in 1974

"Sneaking a fast ball past Henry Aaron is like sneaking a sunrise past a rooster." —From the collected sayings of Don Drysdale, a right-handed pitcher.

The most famous apocryphal story about Henry Aaron (they will multiply over the years) concerns the time, early in his career, when he came to bat with Yogi Berra behind the plate. "Hey, kid," Yogi said, pointing to the bat. "You're holding that all wrong. You're supposed to have the label up." Aaron barely paused. "Mr. Berra," he said, "I didn't come up here to read."

Berra grinned. But the point is, if Aaron had added, "I came up here to break Babe Ruth's record," there would have been a coast-to-coast guffaw and people would have come from miles around to point at him and fall down laughing.

The Henry Aaron of the time was a slim, graceful, graduate short-stop of medium height and build, late of the Mobile, Ala., sandlots and the Indianapolis Clowns' infield. He became a slick outfielder, but he was a singles hitter, a line-drive batter, as self-effacing as a monk, as silent as an iceberg. Everyone knew what an all-time home-run hitter looked like. A bawdy old character with a face like a custard pie, a belly like a department-store Santa Claus, sausages for fingers, wagon tongues for wrists, and a terrible memory for names.

There is a story in baseball of a famous old slugger who once watched a gung-ho rookie skittering around the bases on a home run in about 9 seconds flat. The old timer, who never completed *his* home runs in under a minute, drawled, "Hey, kid. Leave those home runs to those of us who can act them out."

Babe Ruth might have said the same thing to Henry Louis Aaron. Not holding the label up was the least of Hank Aaron's faults. He hit off the wrong foot. He batted cross-handed as a kid and looked as if he came up to the plate for a nap. He hit 13 home runs his first full year with the Milwaukee Braves. Babe Ruth hit more than that when he was still a pitcher. But Aaron ended the 1974 season with a career total of 733 home runs, 19 more than Ruth's old record.

Henry was the unlikeliest "Sultan of Swat," "Maharajah of Mace," and the other alliterations of the Ruthian saga the game ever saw. He didn't have this big, leg-twisting, hat-falling-off, 360-degree swing the art demanded. He didn't jump on a pitch like a puma pouncing on a pigeon. He just sort of flicked at the ball at the last second as the ball was disappearing into the catcher's glove. He was more surprised than anyone when it went over instead of against a fence.

He didn't bludgeon his way to the record. He crept up on it, like a commando with lampblack on his face, under radio silence, squeezing under barbed wire. Nobody heard him coming. Babe Ruth came into

Jim Murray

the home-run record like a guy jumping through a skylight with a blazing pistol. He set a new record every day for 15 years and no rockets went off, no national television was on hand, no calls came from the White House.

Babe Ruth *grew* into his legend. Henry's came down on him like Halley's Comet. Nobody was looking. Two years before he broke the record, all eyes were on Willie Mays. The years before *that*, they were on Mickey Mantle, Harmon Killebrew, Ernie Banks—*anybody*, even his own *teammate*, Eddie Mathews.

Henry Aaron's very *presence*, to say nothing of prowess, was a secret to all but a few National League pitchers. *They* knew Henry, all right. Sandy Koufax, no less, dubbed him "Bad Henry." The pitchers knew appearances were deceptive. Henry Aaron came to the plate with his bat on his shoulder like a kid approaching a creek with a fishing pole. Once there, he lashed at anything hittable. Don Drysdale once pitched him carefully to 3-and-2 and then came in with a pitch Aaron parked out in the street. "What'd he hit?" the press wanted to know later. "Ball four," said Drysdale laconically.

The word spread gradually around the infields and the outfields of the league—but it was slow getting to "The Ed Sullivan Show" or *Sports Illustrated* (which had Eddie Mathews on its first-ever cover). Part of the problem was who he was. Part of it was where he was. Milwaukee is 1,000 miles (1,600 kilometers) from the Great White Way as the crow flies—and light-years away as the TV industry flies. Besides, in New York City, Willie Mays's hat was falling off, his legs were coming out from under him as he made spectacular catches, he was being covered by 10 reporters if he only played stickball in the streets, he was "Say, Hey!," and he was doing it all in New York.

Full many a homer was born to blush unseen in Wisconsin air, 398 of them, in fact. Henry was handicapped in another particular. He made it look so *easy*. His hat never flew off. He appeared to be *meeting* pitches, not mugging them. In the outfield, he'd *glide*. He played the game as if he were on tracks, battery-operated. He was as emotional as a clock. As far as Broadway was concerned, it was an out-of-town try-out. The critics ignored it.

In his 13th year with Milwaukee, Hank Aaron got an extraordinary break. They didn't take the act to Broadway, but the front office took it to Atlanta. He could still go on "What's My Line?" unmasked and in full uniform and stump the panel, but what made Atlanta felicitous was its altitude. There are three things a home-run hitter needs: a good swing, durability—and a friendly park. When they moved Babe Ruth into the Yankee Stadium in 1923 with its 296-foot (90-meter) right-field fence, the poets of the press box called it "The House that Ruth Built." "The House that Was Built for Ruth" was more like it.

Atlanta wasn't built for Henry Aaron, but it is the highest in altitude of any big league city. For some reason, maybe *that* one, balls seemed to jump out there like popcorn.

Aaron hit 398 home runs in his 12 years at Milwaukee and 335 in

Babe Ruth hits one

One handicap to fame was that Aaron made it all look so easy

his nine years at Atlanta. But he was 32 years old by the time he got to Atlanta and, in his last two years at Milwaukee, he had dwindled down from highs of 44 and 45 to lows of 24 and 32. In Atlanta, Hank promptly hit 44 again, never dipped lower than 29, and hit his career high of 47 at age 37.

But while Henry may have liked the climate meteorologically, he cared less for it sociologically as he neared Ruth's record. This was Henry's "Dear Nigger" period. The shock of bigotry directed against a man who had never been heard to raise his voice, who had showed up for work every day for 21 years, who really had had no designs on Babe Ruth's records but just looked up one day and there it was, dismayed a sport that thought it had put all that behind it with the signing of Jackie Robinson.

The ironic thing about Henry Aaron is, he never really wanted to be known as a home-run hitter in the first place. He didn't want to be a freak, he wanted to be a mechanic. Temperamentally, he was as far from the flamboyant Ruth as a stagehand from a star.

He didn't hit his home runs in clusters, as Ruth did. Most of Aaron's early homers were accidents. Aaron never "called his shot" because, if the pitch was out and away from him, he just tried to hit it somewhere. Ruth struck out more than 100 times (and once 170) in 13 different seasons. Aaron never did.

Even when he neared the record, Aaron preferred to decline the honor. "I don't want people to think of me as a home-run hitter," he told a reporter quietly one night as he prepared to step into a batting cage. "I want to be remembered as a *hitter*, not a slugger." He got his 3,000th base hit as early as 1970. Babe Ruth never got his.

The simple recital of 733 home runs doesn't begin to grasp the enormousness of the feat. If Aaron were to top out at 800 home runs (not likely but possible), it has to be considered that this is the equivalent of hitting 40 home runs a year for 20 years. Even to hit 750— which Aaron surely will—means hitting 37 home runs a year for 20 years. A leaf through any record book will show you that most major leaguers don't get 733 *hits* lifetime.

One unforeseen happening is that Aaron destroyed not only the Ruth record, but also the Ruth legend. For the Babe, it was a claying feat. You may remember when we last saw the Babe heading for That-Big-Clubhouse-in-the-Sky, he was the idol of every red-blooded American, the guy-who-never-let-the-kids-down. The Aaron fortune unearthed a rash of biographies of the Babe that looked beyond the Hall of Fame and blurred that image. They revealed The Big Guy as a human being whose private life was more of a morass than a myth. But they could not dim his genius. Or his orphan asylum childhood that inspired a genuine lifelong love of kids.

The record Aaron broke was set on a rainy day in Pittsburgh in 1935, with Babe Ruth in an alien uniform, far from "The House that Ruth Built" to say nothing of "The People that Ruth Built It For." Paunchy, a sideshow attraction and not really a player, the Babe, like

In temperament, Hank Aaron was no match at all for Babe Ruth

Aaron gets number 715

Samson in Gaza, called once more on the strength he had once known, one last shakedown of thunder from the sky. He crashed three home runs, one of them so mighty it soared clear out of Forbes Field over the high, distant right-field fence, the first ball ever hit that far and out of that park. There were only a few thousand people at the park that day and most of them hooted. No one bronzed the ball, no "I Was There" buttons were passed out. The Babe had broken a record every time he hit a home run for more than a decade, but this was the last record he would break.

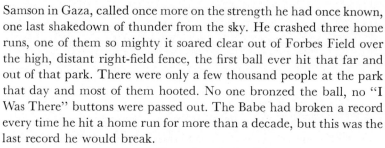

With a bat in his hands, Aaron is one of sports' greatest heroes

Forty years from now, will readers find a Henry Aaron different from the public image? Hardly. With a bat in his hands and a number on his back, Henry Aaron is a hero, one of sports' greatest. With a briefcase in his hands and a sincere tie on, Henry is just another decent citizen who showed up for work every day for 22 years, did what he was told, and made no waves. The fact that what he did had never been done before impressed a lot of people more than it impressed Henry Aaron.

The whole world looked on when Henry Aaron broke the record. It was as carefully orchestrated as Madison Avenue could make it. It was more like an inauguration than a ball game. Politicians ran for office on it, hustlers made their move with pennants and "I Was There" certificates, television manufacturers and television networks got in on the act. To some extent they cheapened it. But they could never cheapen the man. Henry Aaron walked with quiet dignity through every one of those 733 home runs—and all the time in-between.

Baseball fans are jealous of their game's records. They are resistant to change, prone to ancestor worship. They are impatient with sporadic brilliance. "Streak hitters!" they contemptuously refer to its displayers. Still, there is a great contentment when a record is broken by someone they deem worthy. In other sports, spurts of brilliance may be tolerated. An unknown can win the U.S. Open. A substitute can run wild in the Rose Bowl. A much-defeated old warhorse can land a lucky punch and win the heavyweight title. Hats never flew in the air when Roger Maris broke Ruth's one-season record. One season does not a career make.

But Henry Aaron had a 22-year streak. He was the most *known* player left in the lists. The game's most cherished record now belongs to one of its most cherished players.

Aaron addresses Congress on Flag Day

Related Articles

For further information on sports in 1974, see SPORTS and the articles on individual sports in Section Four.

Section Two

Special Reports

Seven articles give special treatment to subjects
of current importance and lasting interest.

From Triumph To Tragedy

By Peter Lisagor

Just 21 months after his landslide re-election, Richard Milhous Nixon—in a drama unparalleled in U.S. history—was forced to resign as President

On Aug. 9, 1974, Richard Milhous Nixon resigned as the 37th President of the United States, climaxing a political and constitutional drama without parallel in American history. He departed unceremoniously from the White House a tormented figure, his 30-year career in politics and government dissolved in scandal and ignominy. The nation was relieved that power was transferred to his successor, Gerald R. Ford of Michigan, with a minimum of rancor and recrimination. But though the saga of Nixon the President was over, Nixon the man had made too much history, touched too many passions, and left too vivid an imprint on his generation to be dismissed and forgotten. The transgressions against the law that brought him down, the corruption and abuses of power popularly known as "Watergate," had cut too deeply into the public consciousness to be easily wiped out.

Richard Nixon entered history with the perverse distinction of being the first President forced from office. During the last hours of his presidency, he revealed facets of character that make him one of the most intriguing and perplexing politicians of his time. On the night of August 8, in a 16-minute televised speech from the Oval Office of the White House, he notified the American people that he was abandoning a two-year struggle to survive the Watergate scandal. He was

As helicopter whisks Richard Nixon away from the White House, soldiers roll up red carpet down which he walked for the last time as President.

neither vengeful nor contrite, admitting no guilt and making no apologies for the actions that forced him to quit.

Instead, he explained that he no longer had "a strong enough political base in the Congress" to justify further efforts to vindicate himself. "I have never been a quitter," he said. "To leave office before my term is completed is opposed to every instinct in my body. But as President I must put the interests of America first. America needs a full-time President and a full-time Congress, particularly at this time with problems we face at home and abroad. To continue to fight through the months ahead for my personal vindication would almost totally absorb the time and attention of both the President and the Congress in a period when our entire focus should be on the great issues of peace abroad and prosperity without inflation at home. Therefore, I shall resign the presidency effective at noon tomorrow."

The absence of any hint of complicity or guilt outraged his detractors and critics; the absence of self-pity and sanctimony pleased his supporters. His appeal "to begin healing the wounds of this nation" and "to put the bitterness and divisions of the recent past behind us and to rediscover those shared ideals that lie at the heart of our strength and unity as a great and as a free people," won him substantial praise. Many had feared that this enigmatic man of controversy and crisis would bow out in a spasm of recriminations.

The next morning, in a final scene in the White House East Room, he did yield to the bitterness that seethed just below the thin façade of his disciplined dignity. With live television cameras present, he met with members of his Cabinet and his staff and indulged in a tensely emotional, stream-of-consciousness flashback of his life and career. He rambled on for nearly 20 minutes about his saintly mother and his humble father, about sadness and disappointments, about the valleys and peaks of public life, and about his political idol Theodore Roosevelt. In a curious passage tinged with irony, he said that no one in his Administration "ever profited at the public expense or the public till." He had chosen to forget or ignore the fact that his first Vice-President, Spiro T. Agnew, had been forced to resign in October, 1973, for evading income taxes and allegedly accepting bribes and that he himself had been charged with improving his properties in San Clemente, Calif., and Key Biscayne, Fla., at government expense.

To anti-Nixon observers, this was vintage Nixon, a man haunted by self-pity, suspicion, and distrust. But to his loyal staff, many in tears, he was seen as a heroic victim of implacable enemies, misguided associates, and wayward circumstances. To his family standing behind him on the platform—wife Pat, daughters Tricia and Julie and their husbands—he was being unjustly driven from office and demeaned by malignant forces.

At the end of his talk, he and his family made their way down the marble staircase to the South Lawn, where the presidential helicopter, *Army One*, awaited them. There he was met by Vice-President Ford,

The author:
Peter Lisagor is chief of the *Chicago Daily News* Washington bureau. His colleagues rate him the "all-around best correspondent" in the nation's capital, *Time* magazine said in 1970.

Events in the summer of 1972 set the scene for President Nixon's eventual downfall. In Miami, he is nominated for a second term. In Washington, D.C., a security guard, Frank Wills, discovers the break-in at Democratic Party Headquarters in the Watergate complex.

who at high noon, 90 minutes later, would be sworn in to succeed him as the 38th President.

The party moved stiffly down a red carpet to the copter's ramp, and said a brisk farewell, without ruffles or flourishes. The last to climb up the short ramp, Nixon paused at the top to look around for the last time at a scene of many triumphs and one irrevocable tragedy during his 2,027 days in the White House. As he had done countless times before, he lifted his arms in the air and spread his fingers in the V-for-victory sign, a tight smile on his face, determinedly rejecting the reality of his fall from grace. However, when Ford later offered him a full and free pardon for any crimes he committed or may have committed, Nixon accepted.

Never before in its 198 years had the nation witnessed the forced resignation of a chief executive. But the resignation was neither sudden nor surprising, in retrospect. For more than two years, the Watergate scandal had gnawed away at the heart of the Nixon presidency. His closest White House and political associates—chief of staff H. R. (Bob) Haldeman; domestic adviser John D. Ehrlichman; counsel John W. Dean III; former Attorney General John N. Mitchell; and aides Charles W. Colson, Egil Krogh, Jr., Jeb Stuart Magruder, and Herbert W. Kalmbach, to name only a few of the more prominent—had marched into federal courtrooms as indicted or confessed accomplices in a sprawling conspiracy that ironically was calculated to keep the President in power.

The nature of the illegal acts they committed was most graphically described by Senator Sam J. Ervin, Jr., the North Carolina Democrat who was chairman of the Senate Select Committee on Presidential Campaign Activities, familiarly known as the Watergate Committee:

After a landslide win in the November, 1972, election, a triumphant President Nixon arrives for his second-term inauguration ceremony.

"...the presidential aides who perpetrated Watergate were not seduced by the love of money, which is sometimes thought to be the root of all evil. On the contrary, they were instigated by a lust for political power, which is at least as corrupting as political power itself."

They placed President Nixon's re-election to a second term in 1972 beyond all other considerations. Their lust for power, in Ervin's view, "blinded them to ethical considerations and legal requirements; to [Greek philosopher] Aristotle's aphorism that the good of man must be the end of politics; and to [President] Grover Cleveland's conviction that a public office is a public trust." Ervin, a constitutional scholar, rebelled at the notion that any President can put himself above the Constitution or can suspend its provisions to promote "his own political interests or the welfare of the nation."

Ervin's committee uncovered the evidence that ultimately destroyed Nixon. Almost accidentally, committee investigators discovered while questioning former presidential assistant Alexander P. Butterfield that Nixon had installed a tape-recording system in the White House, ostensibly to compile a historical record of his presidency. According to later testimony, this voice-actuated system was put in early in 1971, at the seemingly casual suggestion of Haldeman.

Once the existence of the tapes became known, it set in motion a series of legal subpoenas by the Watergate Committee, by the successive special Watergate prosecutors, and later by the House Judiciary Committee after it began an impeachment inquiry. Nixon fought each set of subpoenas in court, but each time the courts forced him to yield the tapes or risk being held in contempt.

On April 30, 1974, the White House released a thick volume of the edited transcripts of tapes already in the hands of the House Judiciary Committee and the special prosecutor. Its contents created waves of shock, dismay, and disgust in Congress and among the people. The transcripts cast the President in a pitiless light, revealing his vulgar contempt for Congress, his disregard for the sensitivity of such institutions as the Federal Bureau of Investigation (FBI), the Central Intelligence Agency (CIA), and the Internal Revenue Service (IRS). The transcripts also revealed a basic mistrust of the people and a flawed moral vision of the character of a free society. Senate Republican leader Hugh D. Scott, Jr., of Pennsylvania, who had staunchly defended the President up to that point, called the transcripts "disgusting, shabby, immoral."

From April 30 on, the White House was like a wartime bunker, with the President and his dwindled cast of associates fighting a defensive battle against a steady drumfire of charges and allegations. The bunker collapsed on August 5, when the transcript of a single day's taped conversations between Nixon and Haldeman was released.

Federal Judge John J. Sirica, *left,* who tries the Watergate burglars in January, 1973, is convinced the case is more than the third-rate burglary the White House claims it is. In March, James W. McCord, Jr., *above,* tells Sirica that the Watergate defendants were pressured to keep silent.

The fateful conversations had occurred on June 23, 1972, six days after the burglary and bugging of the Democratic National Committee Headquarters in the Watergate Office Building in the section of Washington, D.C., known as "Foggy Bottom." The transcript provided indisputable evidence linking the President directly to the Watergate cover-up. This amounted to an obstruction of justice—an impeachable offense—and condemned Nixon to an irreversible process that culminated in his resignation four days later.

Watergate had been spread on a canvas of revelations and rebuttals, of deceit, confusion, anger, and fear. It had been a spectacle of steady and inexorable White House retreat. As the unrelenting tides of scandal engulfed high officials of his Administration, the President scrambled to find higher ground for himself. Many Americans were unwilling to believe that the President would associate himself with men involved in burglaries, bribes, illegal campaign contributions, perjury, obstruction of justice, and other abuses and violations of the public trust. They found it even harder to accept that he could be personally involved in an illegal cover-up and could have practiced a massive deception on the people for more than two years.

John Dean testifies at the Senate Watergate Committee hearings in June, 1973, that Nixon knew about the cover-up, *facing page.* Then, on July 16, Alexander P. Butterfield tells the senators about the secret White House tape recordings, *above.*

Nixon's decline and fall were cruelly ironic. Historians are almost sure to conclude that the abuses of Watergate were politically unnecessary. Nixon needed no committee to re-elect him, no extralegal investigative group to plug the news leaks he feared for political reasons, no campaign to harass his real or imagined enemies with income tax audits and illegal surveillance. As the 1972 re-election campaign approached, he had written a record that virtually assured him a second term.

He had carried out a televised and dramatically staged journey to Communist China in February, 1972, clinking glasses with Premier Chou En-lai, standing on the Great Wall of China, strolling through the snow-covered Imperial Gardens of the Forbidden City in Peking. The 800-million Chinese, depicted by Nixon earlier in his career as fire-breathing expansionists, were now being lured back into the community of civilized nations. A few months later, in May, Nixon was exchanging vodka toasts with Russian leader Leonid I. Brezhnev in Moscow. Televised in full color again, Nixon and Brezhnev signed a treaty to limit nuclear weapons and to brake the deadly spiral of arms that jeopardized mankind. A policy of relaxing tensions, described as détente, was replacing the Cold War that had dominated Soviet-American relations for 25 years. And Nixon brought an end to U.S. combat involvement in the long, costly, and divisive Vietnam War, blunting the chief campaign argument of his Democratic presidential opponent, Senator George S. McGovern of South Dakota.

With a rare sense of timing and his noted manipulative skills, Nixon transformed his foreign-policy maneuvers into an insurmountable obstacle for any opponent. He was re-elected in November by a landslide. He sat astride a world of power far beyond a small-town Califor-

Some of Nixon's closest associates get caught in the Watergate web. They include, *left to right,* Attorney General Richard G. Kleindienst, former Attorney General John N. Mitchell, top White House aides John D. Ehrlichman and H. R. Haldeman, former CRP director Jeb Stuart Magruder, and acting FBI director L. Patrick Gray.

nia boy's dreams. But instead of opening him up and mellowing him, success seemed to sharpen the edges of his personality, to turn him even more inward. Nixon had reached the pinnacle of a career distinguished by crisis and bitterness, survival and revival. But he seemed unable to overcome qualities of mind and character that contrived in the end to destroy him—a suspicious nature that turned political foes and critics into enemies; a secretive bent that led him to exclude those who might have turned him away from the excesses of Watergate; a mistrust of intellectuals, journalists, or anyone else he felt had scorned or derided him; deep and abiding insecurities; and a belief that victory was worth any cost.

The actual burglary of Democratic Party Headquarters in the Watergate complex on June 17, 1972, was merely the focal point of a scandalous mosaic that involved illegal invasions of privacy, attempted misuse of the IRS to harass political opponents, and efforts to abuse the functions of the FBI and the CIA. The Watergate break-in was neither the beginning nor the end of the wrongdoing and corruption of which Nixon and his associates finally stood accused.

Much of it might never have surfaced were it not for such determined people and institutions as John J. Sirica, then chief judge of the U.S. District Court, Washington, D.C., who was skeptical of the tale told by the arrested burglars; the diligent *Washington Post* reporters Bob Woodward and Carl Bernstein and other newspapers and magazines; special Watergate prosecutors Archibald Cox and Leon Jaworski; the Senate Watergate Committee; the House Judiciary Committee; and the Supreme Court of the United States.

And in a saga laced with ironies, President Nixon was himself a source of fatally damaging evidence. In a statement issued on May 22, 1973, Nixon revealed that as early as the spring of 1969, the White House had tapped the telephones of a number of Henry A. Kissinger's National Security Council staff members and the phones of some jour-

nalists. The President claimed he was trying to find out who leaked information about sensitive national security operations to the press.

In his May 22 statement, Nixon also claimed that, during the spring and summer of 1970, he was disturbed by bomb threats and campus demonstrations that reached "critical proportions" and by deteriorating relations between the FBI and other intelligence agencies in the federal government. To rectify the situation and strengthen the government's intelligence operations, he approved a secret plan for covert activity in July, 1970. This plan authorized surreptitious entry—breaking and entering, in effect—in certain special situations related to national security. FBI Director J. Edgar Hoover adamantly opposed it, however, and Nixon said he felt obliged to rescind it within five days.

His preoccupation with national security leaks led President Nixon to set up an investigative unit in the White House itself—"the plumbers." The principal purpose of the plumbers, Nixon said, was to "stop security leaks and to investigate other sensitive security matters." This unit was spawned by the publication of the so-called Pentagon Papers, which began appearing in *The New York Times* on June 13, 1971. These voluminous documents, prepared by the Department of Defense as a detailed post-mortem on U.S. involvement in the Vietnam War, were leaked to the press by Daniel Ellsberg, one of the authors of the report.

A week after the first installment appeared in print, Nixon approved the creation of the plumbers under Ehrlichman's general supervision. Ehrlichman's chief assistant, Egil Krogh, was put in direct charge of the secret unit. Among its operatives were G. Gordon Liddy and E. Howard Hunt, later arrested in the Watergate burglary.

According to the President's own version of events, he instructed the plumbers unit to find out "all it could about Mr. Ellsberg's associates and his motives. Because of the extreme gravity of the situation, and not then knowing what additional national secrets Mr. Ellsberg might

President Nixon orders the special prosecutor, Archibald Cox, *above,* fired in October, 1973, in a dispute over the tapes. Attorney General Elliot L. Richardson, *right,* resigns rather than discharge Cox. But the firing is carried out.

disclose, I did impress upon Mr. Krogh the vital importance to the national security of his assignment. I did not authorize and had no knowledge of any illegal means to be used to achieve this goal."

But the unit did resort to illegal means. On Sept. 3, 1971, a group of plumbers led by Hunt and Liddy broke into the Los Angeles office of Lewis Fielding, Ellsberg's psychiatrist, seeking information to discredit Ellsberg. Ehrlichman, Krogh, Liddy, and another member of the plumbers unit, David R. Young, Jr., were ultimately indicted by a federal grand jury in connection with the break-in of Fielding's office. Ehrlichman and Krogh were convicted of violating the psychiatrist's civil rights. White House assistant Charles Colson, also implicated in the Fielding affair, went to jail after pleading guilty to a charge of obstructing justice.

Then, in April, 1973, while Ellsberg was on trial in a Los Angeles federal court for alleged mishandling of confidential government documents, Ehrlichman held two secret meetings with the trial judge, W. Matthew Byrne, Jr. They discussed the possibility of Byrne becoming FBI director. Nixon and Ehrlichman later denied that they were trying to influence Byrne's conduct of the trial. Because the government had withheld evidence of the break-in of Fielding's office, the case against Ellsberg was dismissed by Judge Byrne on May 11, 1973.

In addition to the questionable wiretaps and the creation of the plumbers, the White House had also compiled an "enemies list" of political foes and private citizens–journalists, intellectuals, even movie stars–deemed unfriendly to the Nixon Administration. There were hints of scandal involving the International Telephone and Telegraph Company and campaign contributions from milk producers. But these and other transgressions, improprieties, and abuses remained a secret to the public until the Watergate burglary occurred.

Watergate itself was a bizarre operation whose purpose remains in dispute. Theories abound, but the most reasonable conjecture is that the Committee to Re-Elect the President (CRP) was hoping to obtain information that might prove embarrassing or damaging to the Democrats in the 1972 election campaign. For months, CRP had planned a campaign of surveillance and information gathering. On Jan. 27, 1972, Mitchell, then U.S. attorney general, was visited in his Justice Department office by acting CRP director Jeb Stuart Magruder, Liddy, and Dean. Liddy, who had then surfaced as the committee's general counsel, outlined for the group an intelligence scheme against the Democrats calling for an outlay of $1 million and including, according to what Mitchell later said, "mugging squads, kidnaping teams, prostitutes...and electronic surveillance."

Magruder later testified before the Watergate Committee that Mitchell told Liddy to go back and devise a "more realistic" plan. The revelation that illegal actions were freely discussed in the office of the Administration's chief law enforcement official shocked members of the Watergate Committee.

In March, 1972, after Mitchell had resigned his Justice Department post to assume command of CRP, Magruder discussed the revised intelligence plan, scaled down to cost only $250,000. In testimony later, Magruder said Mitchell approved the plan, while Mitchell contended that he never specifically approved the Watergate crime. But clearly someone had authorized it, as well as the spending of committee funds to finance it. For as events unfolded, money laundered

Rose Mary Woods, the President's personal secretary, shows how she may have caused part of an 18½-minute tape erasure by pressing the wrong button on the recorder and holding the foot pedal down while she answered a phone.

After the Cox firing and the tape erasures, Nixon's popularity plunges, and calls for his removal increase.

through a Mexican bank to conceal its original source was found in the Miami bank account of Bernard Barker, one of the Watergate burglars. It was later determined that the money was part of $89,000 in illegal campaign contributions.

The actual Watergate break-in was incredibly botched. It was staged by five men—former CIA agent and CRP security coordinator James W. McCord, Jr., and four Cuban refugees—Barker, Eugenio R. Martinez, Virgilio R. Gonzalez, and Frank A. Sturgis. Hunt and Liddy were in a motel room across the street from the Watergate complex, masterminding the operation through walkie-talkie radios.

Just after midnight on June 17, 1972, private security guard Frank Wills noticed that a door lock in the Watergate had been taped. He removed the tape. But a short time later, he again found it taped and called the police. McCord, Barker, Gonzalez, Martinez, and Sturgis were arrested in the Democratic Headquarters, with their telephone-bugging equipment in hand.

The police also found thirty-two $100 bills numbered in sequence on Barker's person, and established that the money had come from Barker's account in a Miami bank. Hunt and Liddy were traced by FBI agents through information gleaned from address books of Barker and Martinez. Thus an investigation was triggered that would, two years later, force an American President out of office.

From the beginning, the White House tried to dismiss the affair. Presidential press secretary Ronald L. Ziegler called it a "third-rate burglary attempt" and charged that "certain elements" might try to blow it all out of proportion. But the conspiracy to cover up the Watergate affair began almost immediately. Three days after the burglary, Dean examined the contents of a safe in Hunt's office in the Executive Office Building. The contents of the safe provided evidence that the tentacles of Watergate would reach far afield. Dean discovered documents dealing with the Pentagon Papers case and a forged diplomatic cable that appeared to implicate the late President John F. Kennedy in the 1963 assassination of South Vietnamese President Ngo Dinh Diem. A year later, Dean testified before the Watergate Committee that Ehrlichman had instructed him to shred the documents and to drop a briefcase containing surveillance items belonging to Hunt into the Potomac River. Dean said, however, that he did not do so. Instead, he gave some of the documents to FBI Acting Director L. Patrick Gray III, warning him they were "political dynamite."

Despite a steady stream of White House denials that greeted stories dug up by Woodward and Bernstein and published in the *Washington Post*, the Nixon tapes, when they were finally released, disclosed that as early as June 23, 1972, less than a week after the Watergate burglary, President Nixon became a participant in the cover-up. He ordered Haldeman to enlist the CIA in an effort to thwart an FBI inquiry into the source of the funds found on Barker.

Haldeman and Ehrlichman called in CIA Director Richard M.

The President greets a crowd of well-wishers in Michigan in April, 1974, as part of his strategy of taking his case to the people. He emerges from seclusion in an effort to shore up his slipping support.

Helms and Deputy Director Vernon A. Walters. Although Helms ruled out the possibility that any covert CIA operations in Mexico would be compromised by an FBI investigation, Haldeman had Walters ask Gray to forego any FBI probe of the Mexican connection. As the tape transcripts later revealed, Nixon and his aides hoped that the role of the White House and CRP could be concealed by aborting the FBI inquiry. Simultaneous with the cover-up moves, plans were approved to have Nixon's personal attorney, Herbert W. Kalmbach, distribute CRP funds to the Watergate defendants and their lawyers.

While the backstage cover-up progressed, the President and his spokesmen steadfastly maintained in public that the White House was not involved. At a news conference on Aug. 29, 1972, Nixon said that Dean had conducted a thorough investigation of the episode. The President stated "categorically" that "no one in this Administration, presently employed, was involved in this very bizarre incident."

In his testimony before the Watergate Committee in June, 1973, Dean denied that he ever made any investigation, a denial that was supported by tape transcripts that later became public. For example, in a Sept. 15, 1972, conversation with Dean recorded in the Oval Office, President Nixon told Dean in a congratulatory tone, "The way you, you've handled it, it seems to me, has been very skillful, because you–putting your fingers in the dikes every time that leaks have sprung here and sprung there."

But in the fall of 1972, the public was unaware of any of these behind-the-scenes maneuvers. The voters paid scant attention to the *Washington Post* disclosures, and on November 7, Nixon and Agnew were re-elected by one of the greatest landslides in U.S. history.

In January, 1973, Hunt and the four Cuban Americans pleaded guilty on all counts before Judge Sirica. But Sirica stated that, despite claims "no higher-ups" were involved, the whole story had not been told. Investigative reporters continued to publish stories about political saboteurs hired to disrupt the Democratic campaign, and the White House continued to condemn them as the work of political enemies. Nevertheless, the accounts prodded the Senate to vote 70 to 0 on February 7 to set up the Watergate Committee of four Democrats and three Republicans.

The unraveling process began on the last day of February, when the Senate Judiciary Committee opened hearings on Gray's nomination as FBI director. To the deep dismay of the White House, Gray revealed that he had passed FBI reports on Watergate to Dean and linked the President's appointments secretary, Dwight L. Chapin, and his personal lawyer, Kalmbach, to Republican espionage and sabotage activities against the Democrats. Kalmbach was eventually convicted of collecting illegal campaign contributions. On April 26, a Watergate Committee member told the press that Gray had destroyed evidence taken from Hunt's safe, and the following day Gray resigned as FBI acting director.

Transcripts of taped conversations released later told of deepening White House efforts at that time to cover up. The President was informed that Gordon C. Strachan, a Haldeman aide acting as liaison with CRP, had lied to federal investigators. One of the most damaging disclosures in the tape transcripts occurred on March 21, 1973, when Nixon was discussing Hunt's demands for hush money. The President exclaimed, "For Christ's sake, get it!"

Meanwhile, on March 19, 1973, McCord, one of the original Watergate burglars, wrote a letter to Judge Sirica, asserting that the defendants had committed perjury in the Watergate trial because they were under pressure to plead guilty and remain silent. When Sirica released the letter in open court four days later, it fell like a bombshell on the White House and sparked the attention of the public. But the White House continued its "stone wall" policy. Ehrlichman informed Attorney General Richard G. Kleindienst that no one in the White House had prior knowledge of the burglary, and Ziegler told the press that "no one in the White House had any involvement or prior knowledge of the Watergate event."

In April, the stone wall began to show signs of crumbling. Magruder informed the U.S. attorneys that he had perjured himself as a witness in the Watergate trial. He also implicated Dean and Mitchell in the Watergate affair. Dean advised Nixon on April 15 that he had begun to cooperate with the prosecutors. And Kleindienst told the President the prosecutors had evidence that top aides—Haldeman, Ehrlichman, and Dean—and lesser White House officials were involved in the cover-up.

The clerk of the House Judiciary Committee tallies the vote on an impeachment article. After months of investigation, the committee votes three impeachment articles, on July 27, 29, and 30, 1974.

The second Watergate special prosecutor, Leon Jaworski, wins release of 64 White House tapes when the Supreme Court denies Nixon's claim of executive privilege on July 24, 1974.

On April 30, Nixon announced the resignations of Haldeman and Ehrlichman, yet he praised them as "two of the finest public servants it has been my privilege to know." He also announced that Dean was forced to resign, and Kleindienst quit, saying close friends of his were involved in the scandal. Defense Secretary Elliot L. Richardson was nominated to be attorney general with authority to appoint a special Watergate prosecutor. On May 18, Richardson selected Archibald Cox, a Harvard University law professor who had served as solicitor general in the John F. Kennedy Administration, as the special prosecutor.

The Senate Watergate Committee opened its televised hearings on May 17, and the White House began to take on the appearance of a decimated command post under siege. The President was forced to admit that a cover-up effort existed in the White House, but he grimly denied any personal involvement in it. However, his denial ran squarely into the face of the dramatic testimony before the Watergate Committee of John Dean, who, in five days before the television cameras from June 25 to 29, drew a devastating picture of official life in the White House. In a soft but menacing monotone, the youthful (34 years old) White House counsel opened with this charge:

"To one who was in the White House and became somewhat familiar with its inner workings, the Watergate matter was an inevitable outgrowth of a climate of excessive concern over the political impact of demonstrators, excessive concern over leaks, an insatiable appetite for political intelligence, all coupled with a do-it-yourself White House staff, regardless of the law." Dean also charged that the President knew about the cover-up as early as Sept. 15, 1972.

The White House immediately struck back, charging that Dean himself had masterminded the cover-up. Ehrlichman and Haldeman, when they appeared before the Senate committee, maintained that Dean was its chief architect and that they and Nixon were innocent.

But even the Dean testimony was overshadowed on July 16, when Alexander Butterfield reported the existence of a secret tape-recording system. Historians will debate for years why the President did not at that point order the tapes destroyed, claiming it was a national security measure. Equally mystifying was why he had permitted his own involvement in the cover-up to be taperecorded.

Cox and Ervin immediately requested the relevant tapes. But on July 23, the President turned down their requests on the grounds of executive privilege. Ervin and Cox then issued subpoenas—and the tapes issue went into the courts. Nixon continued to insist he knew nothing of the cover-up, declaring on August 15, "Not only was I unaware of any cover-up, I was unaware there was anything to cover up." On August 29, Judge Sirica ordered Nixon to yield the tapes of nine White House conversations subpoenaed by Cox. Nixon appealed the decision.

In October, while waiting for the appellate court verdict, the Administration was further rocked and undermined by the forced resignation of Vice-President Agnew, charged with income tax evasion and other alleged criminal acts. On October 12, the same day that the President nominated House Minority Leader Gerald R. Ford as the new Vice-President, the U.S. Circuit Court of Appeals sustained Sirica's ruling that Nixon turn over the tapes.

The President tried to compromise on the tapes, offering to produce a summary of them that would be checked for accuracy by the respected Senator John C. Stennis (D., Miss.). But Cox refused the compromise. On Saturday, October 20, the President ordered Rich-

Three Republican leaders, Senators Hugh D. Scott and Barry Goldwater and Congressman John Rhodes, meet with reporters on Aug. 7, 1974. They say they have just told the President he has lost most of his support in Congress because of tapes that disclose his part in the cover-up.

ardson to fire Cox. Richardson resigned as attorney general rather than violate his agreement that he would support Cox's efforts–even if they led to the Oval Office. Deputy Attorney General William D. Ruckelshaus also quit over the issue. That same day, Nixon made Solicitor General Robert H. Bork the acting attorney general, and Bork then fired Cox.

This "Saturday Night Massacre" shook the Nixon Administration to its foundations. Major U.S. newspapers demanded Nixon's resignation, congressional offices were swamped with telegrams of indignation, and the White House switchboard was backed up for hours with outraged calls.

Following this wrathful backlash, the House Democratic leaders began an inquiry into the possible impeachment of the President. Peter W. Rodino, Jr. (D., N.J.), chairman of the House Judiciary Committee, began the long and laborious planning for a process that had been set in motion only once before in U.S. history–in 1868, when President Andrew Johnson was impeached (but acquitted by one vote in the Senate).

Meanwhile, on October 23, the President agreed to surrender the

Crowd listens outside the White House on the night of August 8, 1974, as President Nixon announces to the nation that he will resign from office the following day.

subpoenaed tapes, and on November 1, he appointed Texas lawyer Leon Jaworski to pick up where Cox left off. Nixon promised the new special prosecutor total cooperation from the executive branch.

Throughout this period, other disclosures kept the scandals at fever pitch. Entire tapes were reported missing, and a critical discussion between Haldeman and Nixon on June 20, 1972, was obliterated in an unexplained 18½-minute gap. Nixon's personal secretary, Rose Mary Woods, claimed to have caused part of the gap by accidentally erasing the tape when she was typing the transcript.

As 1974 began, the President had little reason to believe he could regain the equilibrium and confidence needed to govern effectively. On March 1, 1974, the Watergate grand jury in Washington, D.C., indicted seven former Nixon associates in the conspiracy to cover up and obstruct justice—Mitchell, Haldeman, Ehrlichman, Strachan, Colson, CRP deputy manager Robert C. Mardian, and a CRP attorney, Kenneth W. Parkinson. In a secret report to Judge Sirica, the grand jury also named the President as an unindicted co-conspirator. It acted on the principle that a President cannot be indicted until impeached and removed from office.

On April 30, the White House released tape transcripts that further tarnished the image of the President and his Administration. These tapes, already in the hands of special prosecutor Jaworski and the House Judiciary Committee, went far toward corroborating many of the allegations leveled at the White House and the President by his chief accuser, Dean.

The House Judiciary Committee, composed of 21 Democrats and 19 Republicans, began formal impeachment hearings on May 9. It began its televised public debate on July 24. The committee's chief counsel, John M. Doar, and its minority counsel, Albert E. Jenner, Jr., constructed a powerfully persuasive case against President Nixon.

The President was further staggered on July 24 when the Supreme Court ruled 8 to 0 (Associate Justice William H. Rehnquist, who had served in the Justice Department under Nixon, disqualified himself) that he had to turn over 64 tapes subpoenaed by special prosecutor Jaworski. Although Nixon had indicated through his defense counsel, James D. St. Clair, that he might defy the Supreme Court, he knew that even his staunchest supporters on the House judiciary panel would consider such defiance an impeachable offense. He agreed to obey the court order and turn over the tapes.

On July 27, in full televised view of the American people, the House Judiciary Committee, by a 27 to 11 vote, passed its first article of impeachment, recommending to the full House that the President be impeached because his actions amounted to a "course of conduct or plan" to obstruct justice through the cover-up. On July 29, it passed, 28 to 10, a second article, alleging abuses of power in the use of the IRS, the FBI, and other government agencies to violate the constitutional rights of U.S. citizens. On July 30, it adopted, by a 21 to 17

After submitting his letter of resignation, a shattered Nixon bids farewell to his staff and Cabinet members the morning of Aug. 9, 1974.

vote, a third article recommending impeachment for unconstitutional defiance of congressional subpoenas. Nevertheless, White House officials clung to the belief that while the House might vote to impeach the President, he still had a chance of escaping conviction and removal in the Senate, where a two-thirds vote was required.

Meanwhile, the President continued his campaign to prove that Watergate was merely an aberration and could be overcome by displays of competence and skill in the conduct of foreign policy. In mid-June, he traveled to the Middle East, despite a risky case of phlebitis in his left leg. (The phlebitis would force him to enter the hospital – seriously ill – twice in 1974 after leaving office.) He was received enthusiastically in Egypt. Multitudes lined the streets of Cairo and Alexandria, hailing his overtures to the Arab countries, his effort to strike a balance between the Arabs and Israelis. He also visited Israel, Saudi Arabia, Jordan, and Syria. At the end of June, after returning to Washington for a brief rest, he flew off to Russia for another summit meeting with Brezhnev. But the world travels failed to stay the inexorable course of Watergate and its attendant scandals. In August, events moved swiftly toward their conclusion.

The final, fatal blow was inflicted by the President himself on August 5. He was compelled to admit that on June 23, 1972, he knew of the involvement of his re-election committee and his White House aides in the Watergate cover-up, and that he, in effect, was part of it. In a public statement, he said that portions of the June 23 tape "are at variance with certain of my previous statements." Reportedly, his attorney, St. Clair, and his new chief of staff, Alexander M. Haig, Jr., had urged him to make a statement revealing the contents of the tape, because it was already in the hands of the special prosecutor and would, in any case, eventually become known.

Nixon's admission destroyed more than two years of denials and confirmed the deceptions practiced by the President and his associates upon the American people. Still, Nixon seemed torn by the course he would take. On August 6, amid a clamor that he resign, he told his Cabinet that he would not resign and thought that the constitutional process of impeachment should be allowed to run its course. On August 7, he met for half an hour in the late afternoon with Senate Republican leader Hugh Scott, House Republican leader John J. Rhodes of Arizona, and Senator Barry Goldwater of Arizona. They told him that he had a meager 10 votes against impeachment in the House and probably only 15 votes against conviction in the Senate. He was then apparently persuaded he could not "tough it out," and on August 8, he made his final address to the nation announcing he would resign the next day.

The presidential jet flying the Nixons to seclusion at San Clemente was somewhere over Missouri at noon on August 9, when Richard Milhous Nixon ceased officially to be President of the United States, 895 days short of completing his second term.

His presidency near an end, Richard Nixon walks to a waiting helicopter
with his wife, Pat, and soon-to-be-President Gerald Ford and his wife, Betty.

Psychic Powers: Fact or Fraud?

By Peter Gwynne

While some still scoff, other scientists are stepping up their research into parapsychological phenomena, trying to prove that they exist and learn how they work

In the spacious living room of a London town house, a small but eager audience watches Uri Geller, a young professional magician from Israel who claims that his feats result from psychic—mental—powers rather than more conventional magician's skills. Geller's dark eyebrows draw together in concentration as he gently strokes a key he has borrowed from one of the spectators. "I'm not sure this will work," he mutters. Then, as the watchers crane forward, the key apparently starts to bend. Geller continues stroking it, and the bend becomes more obvious. By the time he gives it back to the astonished owner, it is distorted at a 30-degree angle—useless for opening locks, but a potent demonstration of what Geller claims are his psychic powers.

Across the Atlantic Ocean, in a laboratory in New York City's Maimonides Medical Center, scientists undertake a more rigorous psychic study with volunteer students who claim no unusual powers. One volunteer, wired to brain-monitoring equipment by electrodes taped to her scalp, settles down to sleep in a soundproof room. When the monitors in another room indicate that she is dreaming, another volunteer concentrates on a picture of Rodin's sculpture *The Thinker*, trying to send its details to the dreamer by telepathy. After a short "transmission," the scientists wake the sleeper and ask what she remembers of her dreams. She tells of a man sitting in front of her—hardly an exact description, but close enough to suggest that something might have been transmitted to her while she dreamed.

Psychic success seems to occur more readily in certain altered states of consciousness, such as those found in deep meditation or under hypnosis.

Clairvoyance enables
the psychic to see
what is hidden —
such as the face of
a turned-down card.

At the Psychical Research Foundation in Durham, N.C., volunteers sit before four lights, colored red, yellow, green, and blue. They press buttons in front of the lights to indicate which color they think will light up next. The order in which the lights flash on is determined by the radioactive decay of strontium-90 atoms, one of the most unpredictable processes known. Yet, physicist Helmut Schmidt, who directs the experiments, finds that a few volunteers predict the lighting order with an accuracy that defies all statistics.

These are just three examples of the growing interest—both popular and scientific—in events for which there are no obvious scientific explanations. For centuries, folklore has held that certain persons possessed mysterious powers not held by the rest of humankind—powers to see the future and to transmit messages across space and time. For centuries, doubters have scoffed at such claims.

But in recent years, the general public, college and university students and professors, and even some adventurous scientists have jumped onto the fast-moving parapsychological bandwagon. Parapsychology, popularly known as extrasensory perception (ESP), comes from the Greek word *para*, meaning *beside* or *beyond*, and is concerned with phenomena that lie outside the realm of orthodox psychology. Researchers are investigating subjects that range from forecasting the future and identifying the contents of sealed envelopes to studying *poltergeists* (unexplained noises and movements) and haunted houses.

Some scientists argue that today's psychic phenomena are the prelude to tomorrow's physics. One proponent is William Tiller, chairman of the Department of Materials Science at Stanford University in California, who argues: "Parapsychology is a new realm of physics more relevant than anything that has been discovered since the days of the Greeks. My goal is to do the kind of work that convinces serious scientists that there is something important here."

Parapsychology has always attracted some attention, but the current surge of interest seems more widespread than normal. In 1969, the Parapsychological Association gained a certain scientific respectability when the American Association for the Advancement of Science elected it to membership. The move was prompted by the passionate advocacy of anthropologist Margaret Mead, who argued, "The whole history of scientific advance is full of scientists investigating phenomena that the establishment did not believe were there. I submit that we vote in favor of this association's work."

The author:
Peter Gwynne is
science editor for
Newsweek magazine.
His articles on various
aspects of science
have appeared in
many magazines.

Parapsychology is also gaining more importance among the general public because of its relationship to various aspects of the youth culture, such as drugs, transcendental meditation, and Oriental religions. The packed houses that greeted the movies *Rosemary's Baby* and *The Exorcist* indicate the strong public interest in the occult. Parapsychologists deplore any connection with the supernatural, but some of this interest in the mystic nevertheless has spilled over into the psychic arena. Students at more than 100 colleges and universities in the

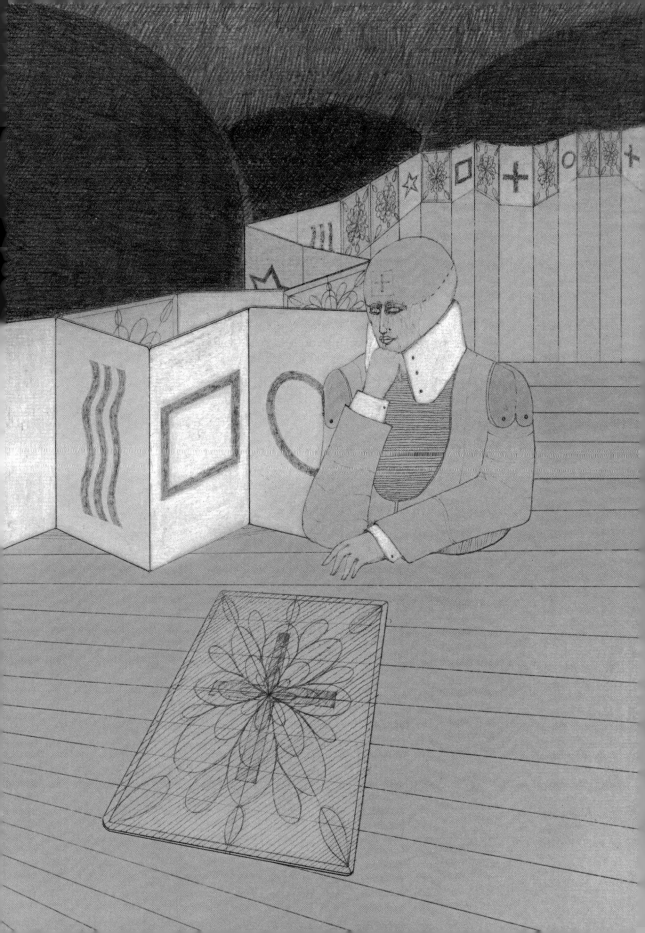

United States are signing up for courses ranging from somewhat dubious attempts to teach students to "develop their own ESP" to in-depth investigations of current psychic research.

Much of the current interest seems to be centered in the United States, where 19 of the 23 full-time academic parapsychologists in the world are at work and more than 200 researchers from other disciplines are active in the field. But the paranormal phenomenon is international. In Great Britain, for example, the scientific weekly *New Scientist*, whose worldwide readership consists largely of level-headed scientists and laymen with more than a passing knowledge of science, received more than 1,700 replies to a questionnaire it published in 1973 on parapsychology. Editors were amazed to find that two-thirds of those answering believed that paranormal powers were worth investigating scientifically.

Outside the United States, Russia seems to be the most active in psychic investigation. The most striking difference between the two countries is in their approach to research. United States efforts are devoted largely to proving the existence of ESP and understanding how it operates. Russian scientists, on the other hand, seem to have few doubts about the existence of psychic powers, and are seeking practical applications of these phenomena. The Russian activity is one reason the U.S. government is keeping a close eye on the progress of parapsychological research.

In the present intellectual climate, parapsychology is receiving more notice than it has since the 1880s, when the German philosopher-psychologist Max Dossier coined the word. Dossier was one of many philosophers and psychologists of his day who were interested in reports of strange effects that seemed to defy the Victorian picture of the world as a perfectly functioning piece of clockwork. Earlier scientists had probed the surface of psychic phenomena, but serious intellectual investigation did not really begin until 1882, when the Society for Psychical Research was founded in England. The society's main aim was to collect anecdotal information on such events as hauntings and poltergeists. But, even though the group included many eminent scientists of the day, including Nobel Prizewinning physicist Baron Rayleigh, most of the intellectual community frowned on its efforts.

"We were told somewhat roughly," wrote classicist Henry Sidgwick of Trinity College, Cambridge, the society's first president, "that being just like all other fools who collected old women's stories and solemnly recorded the tricks of imposters, we only made ourselves the more ridiculous by assuming the aims of a scientific society and varnishing this wretched nonsense with technical jargon."

In the early 1900s, parapsychological studies became more organized. Instead of simply recording paranormal happenings, scientists in both Britain and the United States (including U.S. philosopher-psychologist William James) began to try deliberately to induce such phenomena. In a typical experiment, one person would draw a geometric figure, and then try to send the figure mentally to someone in another room, who would attempt to reproduce the drawing.

But it was left to an extraordinary pioneer at Duke University in Durham, to approach the subject in a truly quantitative manner. J. B. Rhine, who at 80 remains an active researcher, became interested after reading and hearing lectures about psychic effects. In 1932, he decided to test these phenomena, using a statistical approach that demands hundreds and thousands of trials to repeat a single effect. He designed a special pack of 25 cards, called Zener cards, including five each with a circle, a square, a cross, a star, and a set of wavy lines. He then enlisted volunteers to try to transmit the symbols to other volunteers in other rooms or buildings, and he measured the rate of correct guesses against the number expected on the basis of pure chance. Rhine found that some subjects obtained consistently high scores with odds of millions, and even billions, to one against them.

Current investigations are moving away from Rhine's approach of trying to prove simply that paranormal phenomena exist. Instead, researchers are using chemical, physical, and medical equipment and techniques to determine exactly what physical and physiological changes occur when psychics perform their paranormal feats.

This new approach reflects the growing interest in what are known as altered states of consciousness. Brain experts have become convinced in recent years that they cannot get a total picture of how man's mind operates simply by studying him in his normal state of wakeful consciousness. They also need to observe the brain in a variety of conditions, or states of consciousness, such as those experienced during dreaming, and even under the influence of drugs.

An obvious indicator of such an altered state is the person's behavior. But more reliably measured are such factors as blood chemistry, obtained by conventional chemical analysis, and brain waves, charted by electroencephalographs. During intense meditation, for example, the brain-wave pattern is dominated by alpha waves, at a rate of 8 to 14 cycles a second. Theta brain waves, at 4 to 7 cycles a second, predominate in the drowsy period just before one falls asleep. Other altered states of consciousness, such as those induced by drugs or hypnosis, have their own characteristic patterns. If psychics are genuine, one secret of their success might be their ability to slip at will into altered states of consciousness, dominated by alpha or theta brain waves. Charles Tart, psychologist at the University of California at Davis, explains: "In certain altered states of consciousness, parapsychological events seem to be quite natural; they don't appear as great mysteries that have to be explained, but are relatively common." If this is so, it may be possible to foster paranormal skills in normal people by nudging them into an altered alpha-wave state—through hypnosis, for example.

There are five basic paranormal skills. *Clairvoyance* is the ability to receive information from inanimate objects, such as the hidden face of

a playing card, or a drawing inside a sealed envelope. *Telepathy* is the ability to transmit thoughts and read the minds of other persons. *Precognition* is the ability to foretell future events. *Psychokinesis* is the power to influence inanimate objects–bending them, for example, or altering their temperatures–by willpower alone. And *psychic healing* is the art of reducing disease symptoms by the laying on of hands.

Clairvoyance, telepathy, and precognition all involve a certain amount of statistics. The chance that one will name correctly a face-down card is a matter of simple mathematics. If, for example, you are asked to name each card in a pack of 52 as the cards are laid facedown in front of you, you can guarantee that you will score one correct by naming the same card every time; sooner or later that card will turn up. The statistical chance of correctly naming one card is 1 in 52.

Some persons, however, seem to beat these odds consistently. At the Foundation for Research on the Nature of Man, in Durham, former Yale law school student William Delmore over and over names 4 or 5 cards correctly in a pack of 52. Occasionally, he feels especially certain about a particular card and makes what he terms a "confidence call." More than 70 per cent of those calls are right.

Delmore has not been wired up to brain-monitoring equipment during his card feats, but, at the nearby Psychical Research Foundation, psychic Sean Lalsingh of Trinidad has. The measurements show that when Lalsingh scores high in the clairvoyance tests, his brain is producing large amounts of alpha waves–the brain waves associated with deep meditation.

Charles Honorton, parapsychologist at the Maimonides Medical Center, uses hypnosis to elicit clairvoyance. His subjects, most of them students, are all volunteers who have no known psychic skill. Honorton first asks them to guess the colors and shapes of prints sealed inside envelopes in front of them. Then he hypnotizes the volunteers and repeats the test. He has found that his hypnotized subjects do appreciably better at guessing the colors and shapes than they do normally.

Precognition, the ability to predict the future, is tested by forecasting events so unpredictable that no one has any idea what might happen next.

One of the best-known telepathic experiments of recent years was that in which U.S. astronaut Edgar D. Mitchell tried to send information to Chicago psychic Olof Johnsson during Mitchell's *Apollo 14* moon flight in 1971. At set times during the flight, Mitchell attempted to send Zener card pictures to Johnsson. Johnsson correctly identified 51 out of 200 "transmissions," against 40 expected by chance.

Beyond that, however, Mitchell experienced a strange state of euphoria on the trip. He refuses to term it a mystical experience, but says: "You cannot go into space and look at this planet without experiencing a deep sense of the insignificance of man and this planet, as compared with the universe. It opens one's mind to consider new and unusual phenomena, which lie outside present physical theory, as definite possibilities."

The experience led Mitchell to devote full time to promoting parapsychology. When he joined the astronaut corps, he was an engineer

Telepathy enables thoughts to be sent directly from one mind to another. It may be a remnant of a primitive communication system.

with only slight interest in the mystical. But after his *Apollo* flight, he says, "I grew dissatisfied with the idea that science was ignoring a phenomenon that was happening to thousands of people every day." He resigned his astronaut duties and founded the San Francisco-based Institute of Noetic Sciences (sciences dealing with the mind) to coordinate support for ESP research. As president, he is now a major spokesman and fund-raiser for psychic studies.

Meanwhile, telepathic experiments have overtaken the rather limited technology of Mitchell's space-based efforts. At the Newark (N.J.) College of Engineering, researcher E. Douglas Dean uses an instrument called a plethysmograph to study the unconscious reception of telepathic messages by volunteers. The instrument, which fits over a fingertip, measures the contraction in blood volume, a response that generally accompanies stress. During experiments, a volunteer tries to send lists of names by telepathy to a person wearing the plethysmograph. Measurements suggest that the receiver's blood vessels constrict when names emotionally significant to him are transmitted, even though he may not be aware of receiving any telepathic message.

It is in precognition, the ability to foretell the future, that objective scientific measurements offer the best opportunity to overcome previous limitations. The object of precognitive experiments is to choose events so random that neither the experimenter nor his subjects can have any inkling of what will happen next. Thus, Helmut Schmidt uses the radioactive decay of strontium-90 atoms to control the flashing lights in his project at Durham's Psychical Research Foundation.

Of all the parapsychological arts, psychic healing is the one that has the greatest impact on the lives of the general public. All too often, patients regarded as incurable by physicians are persuaded to submit, for a hefty fee, to the ministrations of so-called psychic healers. In some of the most irresponsible instances, healers with no medical skills and no knowledge of sterilization procedures claim, with a great flourish, to remove "tumors" from terminal cancer patients. In several cases, analysis of the tumors has shown that they were not human at all, but tissue from some small animal.

Yet, a small percentage of psychic healing incidents seem to have some credibility, resulting in the disappearance of all symptoms previously observed. Lawrence LeShan, a New York City psychologist who has pioneered in the study of psychic healing, says that about 10 per cent of the cases he has studied can be classified as "unquestionably valid and unattributable to other causes." But even in valid cases, he adds, "We do not have to accept the healer's explanation of how he did it." LeShan believes that most psychic healing is actually accomplished by the patient's own self-healing mechanisms, which are somehow mobilized telepathically by the healer.

Some scientists are trying to discover exactly what, if any, mental and physical changes take place during encounters between healers and their patients. One technique used in studying psychic healers is a

Psychokinesis is the
ability to influence
inanimate objects.
Keys bend, watch dials
spin, and books rise—
through willpower alone.

form of photography known as the Kirlian effect, named after Semyon and Valentina Kirlian, the Russian husband-and-wife team who invented it in 1939. It is, in effect, a sophisticated fingerprinting technique. After the subject places a fingertip against the emulsion of an ordinary photographic film in a darkened room, an electric spark is sent across the fingertip and the film. When the film is developed, it reveals a colored corona surrounding the fingertip that varies with the individual's emotional and physical state. Some researchers believe this corona may be the "psychic aura" that has been reputed to surround wizards, sensitives, and psychics since the Middle Ages. But physicists can easily explain the colors and shapes of the coronas in terms of the normal chemicals found on the skin.

What is interesting about the photographs, however, is that a psychic healer's Kirlian signature seems to change during the healing process. Pictures taken during and after an encounter show that the healer's corona appears to shrink while the patient's corona grows stronger. This does not prove that any healing takes place, but some parapsychologists believe that it may indicate a flow of some sort of energy between healer and patient.

Undoubtedly the most controversial parapsychological experiments of recent years have been those dealing with the clairvoyant, telepathic, and psychokinetic abilities of Uri Geller. Since Geller first visited the United States in 1972, he has become a violently controversial figure in both laboratories and theaters. That he sometimes resorts to magic tricks during his performances is hardly open to dispute; even the best psychic has off days, and, when he is a magician, the show must go on. But Geller's supporters argue that he really does use psychic abilities at times.

Physicists Russell Targ and Harold Puthoff, financed by Mitchell's Institute of Noetic Sciences, set out in early 1973 to test Geller's claims at the Stanford Research Institute. In their experiments, they did their best to prevent fraud by removing all the normal props on which traditional magicians rely. They then observed Geller as he identified the contents of sealed envelopes, picked out the single film canister in 10 that was filled with water, and caused the needle on a sealed laboratory balance to move, apparently by sheer willpower. The first two experiments were performed in "double blind" fashion; that is, neither the experimenters nor Geller knew what shapes were in the envelopes, or which canister was filled with water.

When Stanford issued its Geller report in the spring of 1973, the two scientists did not actually admit a belief in Geller's psychic claims, but they said: "We observed certain phenomena for which we have no scientific explanation." Critics greeted the report with scorn. George Lawrence of the U.S. Defense Department's Advanced Research Projects Agency, who watched Geller in person and also saw films of the Stanford experiments, called Geller "nothing more than a magician." And Ray Hyman of the University of Oregon said the Stanford tests

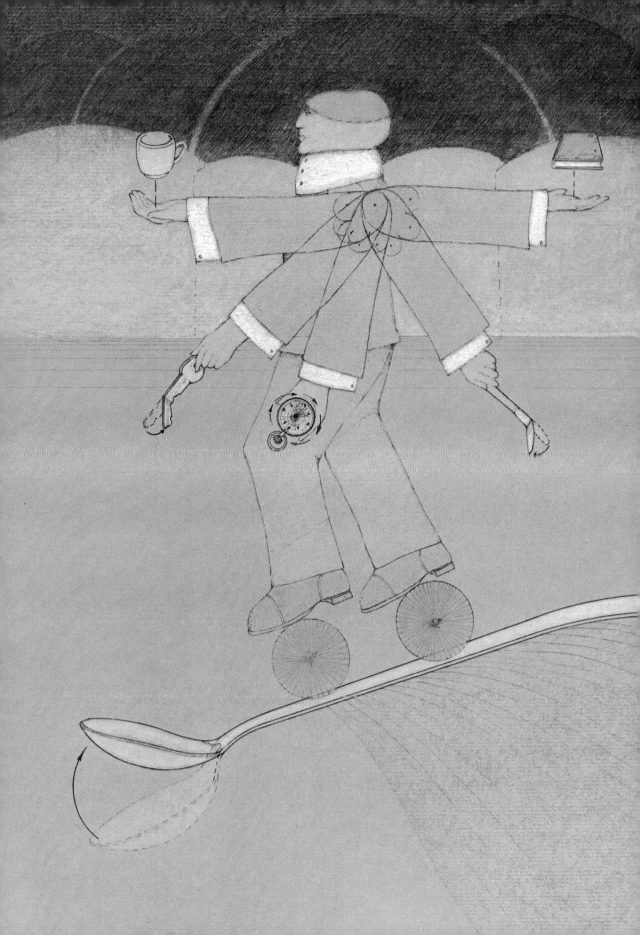

were conducted with "incredible sloppiness." Nevertheless, the experiments gained a certain scientific respectability when they were published in the conservative British journal *Nature*. Publication did not, of course, represent a scientific seal of approval for the research. "What we are saying to scientists," commented *Nature* editor David Davies, "is, 'Here is what is being done in the name of science. Here are the accusations. Now go back and have another look.'"

Other institutions are bidding to conduct further studies with Geller, but the young Israeli seems reluctant to undergo any more testing. "I can't dance at two weddings or three weddings," he says with some petulance. "I'm not that eager to give myself to science so much. I enjoy girls and speedboats—I like living. I don't want to be locked up and studied all the time, no matter how important people think it is."

Meanwhile, Targ and Puthoff are continuing to conduct similar experiments with others who claim psychic powers. At the same time they were studying Geller, they also were investigating the abilities of New York artist Ingo Swann, who claims to be able to influence the temperature of objects shielded from him. Currently, they are studying a retired California police commissioner named Pat Price. After meeting a person who then travels to a new location several miles away, Price seems able to describe that person's new surroundings with uncanny accuracy.

The most convincing critics of Geller and of others who claim psychic powers are magicians. James Randi, a New Jersey magician who performs as the Amazing Randi, can duplicate virtually all of Geller's demonstrations using stage magic. The key-bending trick, for example, is done by applying pressure with the help of another hard surface, such as a tabletop, while the audience's attention is misdirected. "Geller is a very good magician," Randi says. "He can take advantage of any situation. And people want to believe in him."

Randi also recalls one of Geller's more painful failures, on television's "Tonight Show." On that occasion, Randi and host Johnny Carson, himself a former stage magician, had rigged the props so as to prevent the normal magician's tricks—and Geller could not perform a single psychic act. Geller, not knowing of Carson's magician background, claimed his failure was due to Carson's hostility.

Milbourne Christopher, head of the Occult Investigative Committee of the Society of American Magicians, has harsh words for people who claim extrasensory powers they do not have. "One of the troubles of modern life is the will to believe in the marvelous," says Christopher. "Uri Geller goes on television and says that he bends metal with his mind. Any magician immediately recognizes how the fellow does it, but the audience cannot. The gullible public should know that charlatans are deluding them."

But surely, one might argue, hard-nosed scientists would not be fooled by magic tricks. On the contrary, say the critics. "Physicists often go on the assumption that there is no fraud," declares Martin

Gardner, a writer for *Scientific American* and an expert amateur magician. "Their acute attention to detail often makes them the easiest to fool with magicians' tricks."

Of course, not even the most skeptical critics believe that the scores of volunteers involved in parapsychological experiments are all deliberately deceiving the scientific establishment. But they do contend that parapsychologists are not as rigorous in their experiments as they would be if they were undertaking an investigation in, say, physics or biology. "They are looking so strongly for positive results that they are bound to find them," Gardner says. And many parapsychologists agree that many experiments are carried out and interpreted in a somewhat sloppy fashion. But they counter that the critics demand more precise controls for parapsychological experiments than normal scientific studies require.

A more serious problem is that of outright fraud. Parapsychologists were shocked to learn in August, 1974, that some of the most promising precognition experiments being conducted in Durham had been tampered with by the chief investigator. At the Foundation for Research on the Nature of Man, Walter Levy, Jr., had wired animal cages in such a way that half of each cage was electrified by the impact of cosmic rays bombarding the earth from outer space. It was supposedly impossible to know which half of the cage would be electrified at any moment, but mice, gerbils, and other small rodents appeared to beat the statistical odds by jumping from one half of the cage to the other just before a jolt arrived. The results had offered some of the strongest and most objective support for psychic phenomena, and it was considered a serious setback to psychic research when it was revealed that Levy had been falsifying data from a follow-up series of experiments for which he hoped to receive foundation funding. Although Levy's original experimentation was not implicated in the fraud, his action clearly tarnished all his research.

Another thorny question for parapsychologists is whether their experiments can be repeated. One of the foundations of modern science is the belief that no experimental result can be regarded as definitely established until it has been obtained by more than one group of researchers, working under the same set of circumstances. Yet this repeatability has been noticeably lacking in psychic investigations. Trying to explain the inconsistent results, ex-astronaut Mitchell says, "We are dealing with subtle interior states. You can't treat a subject like a black box." The introduction of electronic and physical equipment in parapsychological laboratories may help researchers in devising experiments that can be duplicated by others.

Also hindering the progress of parapsychology is the carnival atmosphere that surrounds such performers as Geller. Some researchers believe that unquestioning enthusiasm may hurt the future of psychic investigation as much as stubborn skepticism. California's Targ worries: "We may be replacing irrational opposition to the idea of the

paranormal with irrational acceptance of every claim for it. The fact that we know scientifically that inexplicable things happen sometimes is no reason to believe every bit of nonsense that comes along."

One question, almost entirely ignored at present, involves the reason for psychic effects. The Russians have a theory involving *bioplasma*, a term they coined to describe a fourth state of matter that constantly interacts with other states, just as water becomes steam or ice. The flow of bioplasmic energy is responsible for such effects as psychokinesis and the Kirlian corona, according to this theory. Other investigators believe that eventually some rational explanation will emerge that fits in with current laws of physics. Among the possibilities is a new type of force so weak that it has not yet been detected. To those who scorn this idea, parapsychologists point out that the two forces that hold atomic nuclei together—the strong nuclear force and the weak nuclear force—were not discovered until this century. Indeed, for some physicists, parapsychology represents a challenge as deep, in many ways, as elementary particle physics.

One measure of the impending arrival of parapsychology as a valid area of scientific endeavor is the increasing involvement of many official organizations in psychic research. The National Institute of Mental Health, for example, has given two grants to the Maimonides Medical Center to finance its investigations of thought transmission. Institute experts hope that such work may eventually allow psychiatrists to use ESP to improve their empathy with patients.

The Florida Department of Health and Rehabilitative Services is studying the use of parapsychology in caring for the handicapped. The National Aeronautics and Space Administration has financed a program at the Stanford Research Institute to teach agency personnel how to use ESP, with the thought that telepathy may someday prove useful as an alternative form of long-range communication. The Central Intelligence Agency has asked at least two parapsychology professors whether psychics can jam computers and radar screens. And the Defense Department's Advanced Research Projects Agency, while denying that it conducts psychic research, is monitoring developments closely, partly because of the intense interest shown by the Russians. On the business scene, several large drug companies, among them Hoffmann-LaRoche, are exploring means of training the mind to control stress. And at least one management consultant, John Mihalasky of the Newark College of Engineering, suggests that intuition plays an important part in business success and advises that potential executives be tested for ESP ability.

Plainly, parapsychology is now at the crossroads. Increasing numbers of scientists are undertaking experiments designed not only to show that psychic powers exist, but also to prove that, in suitable situations, each one of us can use them. But the critics remain unconvinced, and undoubtedly will continue so until the caliber of parapsychology research is proved to be as high as that in other sciences.

Psychic healers claim to cure by the laying on of hands. Some persons believe the process may occasionally activate a patient's self-healing mechanism.

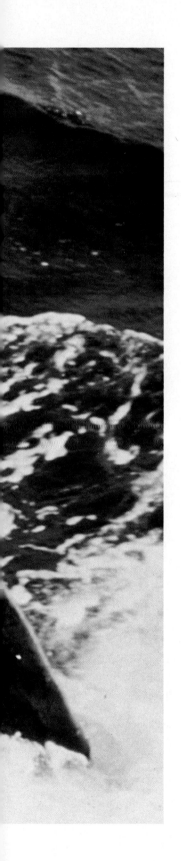

Doom for The Giants Of the Sea?

By John F. Henahan

**Many conservationists fear the continuing slaughter
of whales is pushing these animals toward extinction**

Wispy white geysers spout up against the background of blue sea and sky. Now and then, a great barnacle-encrusted back bursts through the surface, and with a loud huff, a whale spouts air and water through its blowhole. It cruises along on the surface for a few minutes, and then, with a powerful thrust of its tail, dives, leaving behind a patch of calm water on the otherwise rippled sea. The gray whales are on the move again.

Every winter, from November to February, the California gray whales travel some 6,000 miles (9,600 kilometers) from their summer homes in the Bering Sea to their winter breeding grounds in the warm lagoons of Baja California. In March and April, they head back north again. Some 11,000 gray whales make the annual trips up and down the west coast of North America. This is a remarkable number, considering that twice they were almost completely wiped out by the whaler's harpoon—once in the late 1800s and again in the 1930s. Now, most biologists agree, these gray whales will survive and prosper if they are left alone.

But other whales have not been so fortunate, and some conservationists fear that many whale species are headed for extinction. Once, a mighty herd of gray whales migrated along the coast of South Korea. Since none of these whales has been sighted since the late 1960s,

A woodcut details the dangers whalers faced in the 1800s, when they attacked their quarry from small wooden boats with hand-held harpoons.

The author:
John F. Henahan is a science writer and former editor of *Chemical and Engineering News*.

they probably are gone forever. The blue whales, largest animals that have ever lived on land or in the sea, also face a bleak future. Some are more than 100 feet (30 meters) long, twice as large as the prehistoric dinosaurs, and weigh at least 250,000 pounds (113,000 kilograms). These whales appear doomed to the same fate as the dinosaurs—extinction. In similarly dire straits are the humpback whales. Only a few remain to sing their weirdly melodic songs as they travel across the world's oceans. Their numbers probably have dwindled past the biological point of no return. And the list of whales that may succumb to the relentless harpoon goes on: the finback, sei, and maybe even the huge sperm whales, cousins of the legendary Moby Dick.

In 1974, about 37,500 whales were killed. This was the quota prescribed by the 15-nation International Whaling Commission (IWC), the organization that supposedly regulates world whaling activities. About 85 per cent of those whales were destroyed by Japan and Russia, with Australia, Brazil, Canada, Chile, Denmark, Iceland, Norway, Peru, Portugal, South Africa, and Spain making smaller contributions to the whale's demise.

If many whale species are doomed to extinction, the trend was set in motion when large-scale whaling began about 700 years ago. During the 1200s, Basque fishermen began using sailing ships, which carried small catcher boats, to hunt for whales in the Bay of Biscay. They mainly went after the slow-moving right whale, so named because it was rich in oil, moved slowly, floated after it was killed, and was therefore the "right" whale to hunt. When a whale was sighted, the men would row the smaller boats close to the whale so that they could plunge their harpoons deep into the animal's side. The whale would then dive or swim until it was exhausted, and then the whalers would move in for the kill.

Whales had at least half a chance against the hand-held harpoons of these early whalers. But since then, the odds against the whale have increased enormously as one technological advance was piled on another, each aimed at finding and killing whales easier, faster, and more cheaply. In the mid-1800s, after a cannon-propelled harpoon with a deadly exploding tip was invented and steam-powered vessels replaced sailing ships, bigger, faster whales came within easy reach.

Modern factory ships, with their fleets of diesel-powered catcher boats, appeared in 1925. These huge, seagoing processing plants can convert a whale into oil, meat, and bone in less than an hour. Today, with sonar, radar, aerial surveillance, and even bigger and faster ships adapted to the whaling industry, there is no hiding place left for any whale, large or small, fast or slow.

With each step forward in whaling technology, the whales took at least two steps back. By 1920, the right-whale population had dropped to about 4,000. Previously it had been found in large but uncounted numbers in the Atlantic Ocean off the coast of Greenland, in the North Pacific Ocean, and throughout the Southern Hemisphere. Finally, in 1935, a worldwide ban on hunting the right whale was put into effect by international agreement.

Although the U.S. government declared the California gray whale officially off-limits to American whalers in 1937, the Russians and Japanese continued large-scale killing of grays until 1947. In fact, the Russians still kill about 150 gray whales a year and sell the meat to Eskimos living in the northernmost reaches of the Soviet Union. But the gray whale had its darkest days in the late 1800s, when U.S. whalers discovered their breeding grounds in Baja California. The blue lagoons were stained blood-red as whalers indiscriminately killed adult males, pregnant females, and even young grays.

A Japanese whaler on a modern diesel-powered catcher boat aims his bomb-tipped harpoon at a minke whale surfacing in the Pacific Ocean.

After 30 years of limited protection, many scientists believe the gray-whale population is at least stabilizing. "I don't think their population will get much bigger," says Raymond M. Gilmore, a research associate in marine mammals at the San Diego Museum of Natural History and one of the best-informed scientists on the comings and goings of the gray whale. "They are protected from the whaling industry, but now they are being harassed by all the fishing boats and excursion vessels that go down to Baja. This limits the amount of space they can occupy in the lagoons and certainly must have some effect on their breeding patterns."

Scientists and the whaling industry estimate the original population of blue whales in the Antarctic at around 150,000, but there may now be as few as 2,000. Ironically, the fading of the blue whale was due in large part to a poorly conceived conservation scheme concocted in 1946 by the International Convention for the Regulation of Whaling, the predecessor of the IWC.

The convention attempted to limit the total whale kill by declaring that the Antarctic season would begin on January 7 and end when the equivalent of 16,000 blue whales had been taken. They devised a rating system by which 1 blue whale equaled, for example, 2 1/2 humpbacks or 6 of the small sei whales. As a result, whalers found themselves under heavy pressure to bring in as big a catch as they

Men at a processing plant in the Faeroe Islands *flense* (strip the skin and blubber from) a sperm whale. Some whaling fleets process the catch on special factory ships

could in the shortest possible time. This period in the late 1940s came to be known as the "whale olympics." The blue whales, being the biggest, were the best whales to hunt. And so, this quota system served to cut deeper and deeper into the Antarctic blue-whale population.

By 1966, it was no longer profitable to hunt the few blue whales that remained, so they were given protection throughout the world by international agreement. But many marine scientists are extremely pessimistic about the blue whale's prospects for survival. The sea is so large and there are so few blues that it becomes increasingly difficult for a male to find a female and mate to sustain the species. The hump-back whales, which also received complete protection in 1966, are in even greater danger for the same reason.

What is now left to the whalers are the smaller brydes, minke, and sei whales and the large sperm and finback whales. The finbacks have already been reduced to about one-fifth of their original population, but there are apparently still large numbers of sperm whales left, even though they have been hunted fairly heavily for several centuries. However, there is no doubt that their population will fall off rapidly if

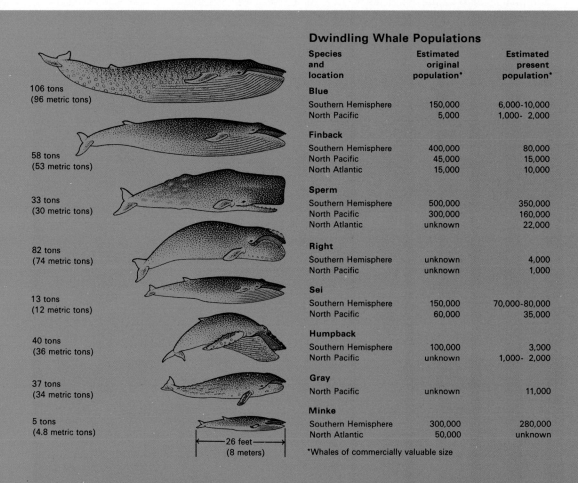

Weight	Species and location	Estimated original population*	Estimated present population*
106 tons (96 metric tons)	**Blue**		
	Southern Hemisphere	150,000	6,000-10,000
	North Pacific	5,000	1,000- 2,000
58 tons (53 metric tons)	**Finback**		
	Southern Hemisphere	400,000	80,000
	North Pacific	45,000	15,000
	North Atlantic	15,000	10,000
33 tons (30 metric tons)	**Sperm**		
	Southern Hemisphere	500,000	350,000
	North Pacific	300,000	160,000
	North Atlantic	unknown	22,000
82 tons (74 metric tons)	**Right**		
	Southern Hemisphere	unknown	4,000
	North Pacific	unknown	1,000
13 tons (12 metric tons)	**Sei**		
	Southern Hemisphere	150,000	70,000-80,000
	North Pacific	60,000	35,000
40 tons (36 metric tons)	**Humpback**		
	Southern Hemisphere	100,000	3,000
	North Pacific	unknown	1,000- 2,000
37 tons (34 metric tons)	**Gray**		
	North Pacific	unknown	11,000
5 tons (4.8 metric tons)	**Minke**		
	Southern Hemisphere	300,000	280,000
	North Atlantic	50,000	unknown

Dwindling Whale Populations

*Whales of commercially valuable size

26 feet (8 meters)

Whale meat is cut into slabs and sold cheaply in Japanese food markets. Japan claims it is an important protein source.

the current IWC quota, allowing 23,000 sperm whales to be killed each year, is maintained for very long.

Why were whales hunted on such a large scale in the past, and why does the practice continue? Because whales provide industry with commercially valuable products. Every part of the whale's body seems to be good for something. Whalemeat is a high-protein food that can be eaten by human beings and animals. Whalebone was used in the past for such items as corset stays, buggy whips, and umbrellas. Ambergris, an intestinal secretion of sperm whales, is used to enhance the fragrance of expensive perfumes. But whale oil has traditionally been the most sought-after product. The prized blue whale yielded an average of about 11 to 14 tons (10 to 12.7 metric tons) of oil. Oil is found predominantly in the whale's blubber (fatty overlayer), bones, meat, and blood. Once the oil is removed, the residue can be used for fertilizer or as a high-protein animal feed.

Whale oil was burned in lamps until the mid-1800s, when it was replaced by less costly petroleum products, such as kerosene. The oil is still used in the manufacture of soap, cosmetics, shoe polish, paint, car wax, oilcloth, linoleum, and some margarine. It is also used in wool processing and leather tanning. Conservationists point out that only the low price of whale oil has kept these uses alive, and that in each case, whale oil can be replaced by other materials, just as plastics have replaced whalebone. For example, most of the world's margarine supply is now made from fish or vegetable oil. Sperm-whale oil, although inedible, is used as a lubricant for fine machinery. Again, conservationists point out there are alternative materials for such lubricants.

If there are substitutes for all whale products, why not stop hunting whales? The Japanese insist that their major reasons for keeping the whaling industry alive are that it provides work for about 50,000

A mural on the side of a semitrailer, owned by an ecology-minded trucking firm in Chicago, carries the antiwhaling message along the highways, *top*. A demonstrator on Wall Street in New York City protests against Japan's whaling industry, *above*.

persons and that whalemeat supplies Japan with a much-needed source of protein. In 1973, the Japanese consumed about 122,000 tons (110,000 metric tons) of whalemeat.

On the first count, some conservationists argue that, if the Japanese are really interested in keeping those people working, killing off all the whales is not the way to go about it. Once the whales are gone, everyone in Japan's whaling industry will be unemployed. As for providing protein, conservationists maintain that the Japanese get only 1 per cent of their total meat protein from whales; giving up that small amount in the name of preserving a species is not asking too much. The Japanese argue that they need all the protein they can get. They point out that American conservationists, who can afford to eat beef, tell the Japanese not to eat cheaper whalemeat when a pound (0.45 kilogram) of beef in Japan costs about $7.

The Japanese also complain that Americans, who have not depended on whales in any major way since the U.S. Civil War, are being overemotional in asking that whales be saved for the saving's sake. This stings conservationists to reply that the whales belong to everybody and the decision to destroy them should not go wholly to the Japanese—or the Russians.

While Japan is vocal in defending its whaling interests, Russia has been silent on the subject. Many observers believe the main reason for Russia's whaling activity is to obtain oil for ball bearings and delicate machinery, particularly military equipment.

During the last few years, agitation for saving whales has increased among conservationist groups throughout the world. One of the most active antiwhaling groups is Project Jonah, a volunteer U.S. organization of concerned citizens formed in 1971 and based in Bolinas, Calif.

To dramatize the need to halt whaling activity, Project Jonah sent three children from Canada, Sweden, and the United States to Japan in June, 1974, to deliver 7,500 antiwhaling letters and children's drawings to the office of Japanese Prime Minister Kakuei Tanaka.

"Many people consider that our asking protection for whales just because they deserve to live is radical and oversentimentalized," says Gail Madonia, Project Jonah's treasurer. "I don't agree. Scientists are now learning that whales have their own methods of communication, their own culture and societies. There is every reason why we should protect them in advance, before their numbers get so low that they're doomed to biological extinction."

Taking a more direct hit-them-in-the-pocketbook approach, the Animal Welfare Institute (AWI), based in Washington, D.C., has been urging a boycott on Japanese and Russian goods. It is difficult to determine how the campaign will affect Russian attitudes, but there is evidence that Japanese businessmen are feeling the weight of world opinion. According to AWI President Christine Stephens, U.S. representatives of Nissan Motor Corporation, producer of the Datsun automobile, have informed the Japanese government that they "received hundreds of letters from concerned people who are saying that they will not purchase Datsuns or any other Japanese products until the excessive killing of whales is stopped."

Japan and Russia are also feeling a delicate political pressure from the U.S. government, which has quietly informed them that the United States might embargo all of their fishery products if they do not cooperate with international whale-conservation measures. This would be a severe blow to Japan, which exports about $200 million worth of fish and seafood to the United States every year.

The IWC is charged with regulating its member nations' whaling activities, but conservationists claim that its efforts have been aimed mainly at making sure there are enough whales left to keep the industry alive, rather than at saving the whales. "The IWC has been a publicity sop, an honorary gathering set up to benefit the whaling industry," says Madonia.

There is some evidence that she may be right. The IWC has made it very easy for its members to flout commission directives. For example, a majority at the 1973 meeting of the IWC voted to end finback-whale hunting by 1976, set regional quotas for sperm whales, and set an annual worldwide minke-whale quota of 5,000. But Russia said it would ignore the quotas and suggested it would simply leave the IWC if such attitudes persisted. Also, since 1972, Japan and Russia have successfully blocked a U.S. call for a 10-year moratorium on the killing of all whales. The moratorium would allow scientists to determine just how many whales of each species remain and would also allow some of the most hard-pressed species to rebuild their populations.

Frustrated by the IWC's shortcomings, some countries have taken steps to limit their own whaling operations and whale imports. In

Sea World scientists
study the respiratory
system of Gigi, a captive
gray whale, to determine
how long she can hold
her breath and what gases
are in her blood when she
dives to great depths.

1971, Great Britain, Norway, and the Netherlands stopped their whaling activities in the Antarctic. Great Britain also limited its whale imports to products of the still-plentiful sperm whale. In 1970, following extremely strong conservationist pressure on Congress, the United States placed eight whale species on the endangered animal list and banned the import of all whale products. Those actions effectively killed the U.S. whaling industry, and in 1971, the last whaling vessel sailed back into port in Richmond, Calif.

Robert Casebeer, one of the last of the Richmond whalers, now works for a fish market. He believes that U.S. whaling operations, carried out by small whaling vessels with four or five crewmen, had little effect on the whale population. He thinks U.S. whalers were forced out of business because of the sins of the Russian and Japanese whalers, with their huge factory ships. Nevertheless, Casebeer favors a moratorium on whaling.

"I'm in favor of stopping all whaling right now," he says. "I don't believe the whales will ever build their populations back to where they once were. But I don't think we should deplete them completely. I guess you can ask what good they are, but you can ask that about a coyote or a mountain lion. They're there, and they must have been put there for a purpose."

Biologists and conservationists say that a full moratorium would give them time not only to count the surviving whale populations, but also to learn more about whale behavior than has ever been possible in the past. Previously, scientists obtained most of their biological data from dead whales. And whale counting was left to the whaling industry, hardly an unbiased institution. It would be in the industry's interest to exaggerate the number of existing whales to justify increased annual whaling quotas. And conservationists suspect that the Japanese are doing just that.

"Any way you look at it, keeping track of whales is an expensive, time-consuming process," says Kenneth Norris, professor of natural history at the University of California at Santa Cruz and one of the foremost authorities on marine mammals. "Whales spend about 90 per cent of their time underwater, which means that scientists usually spend 95 per cent of their time looking for whales and 5 per cent of their time gathering data. We think that entirely new approaches to studying and counting whales are needed."

And Norris is trying out new approaches to answer some questions about whale behavior. He and his colleagues have been working with the gray whales that swim along the California coast. In 1973, the group lassoed seven baby grays in Baja California's Magdalena Bay. They outfitted the captured whales with sensor-equipped harnesses that record such data as heart rate, stomach temperature, and diving and navigation behavior.

So far, they have carried out the experiment only for short periods of time and close to the lagoons. But the next step is to try the system

out in the open water as the whales make their way back north to the Bering Sea. They plan to outfit whales with radio transmitters that can beam data about their behavior to ships, aircraft, and eventually, satellites. The team is also trying to develop improved photo-reconnaissance techniques so that large-scale, long-term movements of whales can be photographed from aircraft. To monitor the movements of individual whales from aircraft, ships, and satellites, Norris and his colleagues plan to "brand" an identifying mark on the skins of whales with a harmless beam of laser light.

Other researchers are making underwater recordings of the sounds that different whales make to determine where, when, and how they migrate, how deep they dive, and other unresolved aspects of whale behavior. For example, biologist Roger S. Payne of Rockefeller University in New York City found that different families of humpback whales have sound patterns and dialects as distinctive as birdsongs. The humpback "songs" range from long sepulchral groans to ghost-like screams. William C. Cummings of the Naval Underseas Research Center in San Diego recorded sounds made by all kinds of whales, from the high-pitched whistle of porpoises and killer whales to the powerful low-frequency bellow of blue whales.

One of the most detailed studies of a whale's physiology was carried out by scientists at Sea World in San Diego between March, 1971, and March, 1972. They raised a gray whale named Gigi in captivity, watching her grow from a 4,300-pound (1,950-kilogram) baby to an adolescent weighing 14,000 pounds (6,350 kilograms). During Gigi's stay, the San Diego scientists developed volumes of valuable data about whale behavior and biology. But by the end of a year, Gigi had grown so large and had become so costly to feed that they were forced to return her to the Pacific Ocean.

Before setting Gigi free in the Pacific Ocean, scientists fitted her with a radio transmitter to check migration patterns. For six months, the device sent a signal each time Gigi came to the surface.

Most conservationist concern has been centered on the great whales. But one of the smallest whales, the porpoise, is also running into trouble. According to Norris, from 200,000 to 400,000 porpoises are killed every year because they swim with schools of tuna and get tangled in fish nets. American tuna fishermen are under heavy federal pressure to end porpoise killing by 1976, or they will no longer be able to bring their catch into the United States.

There are sound scientific reasons for ensuring that whales survive. Ecologists know little about the web of life in the oceans. If the whales completely disappear, this could throw the food chain out of balance. For example, the largest whales consume up to 1.5 tons (1.36 metric tons) of food each day. Some whales eat *plankton* (small plants and animals that float on the surface of the water), others devour fish and squid. No one knows what the effect would be on ocean life if there were no whales to eat the excess fish, plankton, and squid.

Another ecological mystery is the question of what happens when a community of whales becomes unbalanced because of overkilling. The great whales' only natural enemy is the killer whale, a large porpoise. No one knows how many killer whales populate the oceans or how they will be affected if other whales are wiped out.

The 1974 IWC meeting in London produced the first indications that the save-the-whale movement may have made some headway. Once more, the U.S. proposal for a 10-year blanket moratorium on the killing of all whales was rejected, but the Australian delegation made an alternative proposal—a selective moratorium on any population of whales that drops below a number considered dangerous to its survival. Most experts agree that a moratorium on the rapidly dwindling finback whale will be suggested at the 1975 meeting.

Under present IWC rules, Japan and Russia are free to turn thumbs down on the Australian proposal, but some experts believe they may not. "There's been a big change in the attitude of most of the countries represented at this year's IWC meeting," says U.S. delegate Prudence Fox, a National Oceanic and Atmospheric Administration official. "In the past, many countries haven't been very aggressive about suggesting reduced quotas because they were afraid that the Japanese and Russians wouldn't go along. This year they've been willing to propose things whether those countries are willing to go along or not. The present feeling is that once Japan and Russia see that every other country is bound and determined to get real conservation, they will have to take note of it and react to it. For that reason, I'm quite optimistic that they will go along with it."

Even with a blanket moratorium on whaling, there may be little hope that the blue whale and other dwindling species can reproduce themselves back to biological survival. But without a moratorium, we may never have an opportunity to find out. So the problem comes down to two questions: Can we afford to let the whales live? Or, can we afford to live without them?

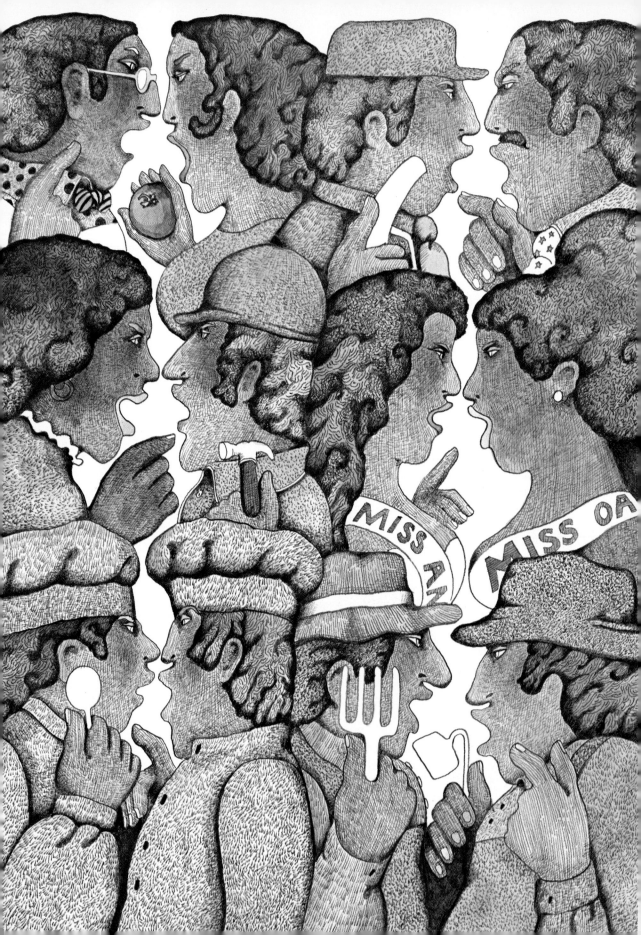

The Move
To Metric

By Daniel V. De Simone

The measurement debate has lasted nearly 200 years, but slowly the United States is moving toward joining the rest of the world in a common system

What does the United States have in common with Barbados, Burma, Gambia, Ghana, Jamaica, Liberia, Nauru, Oman, Sierra Leone, Tonga, Trinidad, and Yemen (Aden)? Answer: They are the only countries not yet committed to the metric system.

Since 1945, more than 1 billion people throughout the world have started using a new language when they speak of the speed of an automobile, the weight of a bag of flour, the height of a ceiling, the distance to the moon, and other measurements. They have joined more than 2 billion others who were already talking this language: the metric system of measurement.

The United States is an island in a metric sea. It is the only major nation that clings to the "customary" system of measurement— pounds, inches, gallons, acres, and a host of other units so numerous that no one fully comprehends them all.

When it comes to the language of measurement, the United States is a Tower of Babel. Men and women in every walk of life speak their own special dialects. The two "pure" tongues, customary and metric, are often intermingled with such special-purpose "slang" units as barn, furlong, board-foot, pica, face-cord, therm, and electron volt.

In general, people who must communicate regularly with one another can do so with minimum confusion. But the proliferation of measurement terms has caused some difficulties. In certain highly technical industries, for example, research scientists use only metric terms, while production engineers work with customary units. Before engineers can turn a researcher's idea into a product, someone must translate the measurements.

Clearly, there would be less chance of confusion if everyone agreed to use the same language of measurement. But which of the two major measurement languages should be the standard?

No other measurement system that has actually been used matches the simplicity of the *Système International d'Unités,* the modernized metric system. It was designed deliberately to fill the needs of scientists and engineers. Laymen need know and use only a few simple parts of it: those concerned with length (meter), mass or weight (kilogram), time (second), temperature (degree Celsius), and electricity (ampere). Other units of measurement are derived from these basic units. For example, area is measured in square meters, speed in meters per second, and density in kilograms per cubic meter.

Another advantage is that the metric system is based on the decimal system. Units of different sizes are always related by powers of 10. There are 10 millimeters in 1 centimeter; 100 centimeters in 1 meter; and 1,000 meters in 1 kilometer. This greatly simplifies converting larger to smaller units. For example, in order to calculate the number of centimeters in 3.794 kilometers, multiply by 1,000 and then by 100 (move the decimal point five places to the right) and the answer is 379,400. By comparison, in order to find the number of inches in 3.794 miles, it is necessary to multiply 3.794 by 5,280 and then by 12.

The customary system seems to lack any logical patterns. But it does have its own practical merits. Many customary units are closely related to everyday experience and human anatomy, from which they were derived centuries ago. A foot is roughly the length of a human foot; a yard is approximately the distance between a man's nose and his outstretched fingertips; a mile is about 2,000 paces.

The great abundance of units is often a convenience for those who use them. Most people find it easiest to comprehend numbers that are between 1 and 1,000 – preferably between 1 and 10. By picking from the wide assortment of customary units, it is usually possible to work with a convenient number. Some householders buy a few tons of coal for the winter. The farmer delivers a few hundredweight of fruit or vegetables to the market. The grocer sells potatoes by the pound. Some pipe tobacco is sold by the ounce, and diamonds by the carat.

Many of the multiples used in the customary system are based on powers of 2 and 12, which have practical virtues in doing arithmetic.

The author:
Daniel V. De Simone is deputy director of the U.S. Office of Technology Assessment. He was director of the group that prepared the U.S. Metric Study for Congress in 1971.

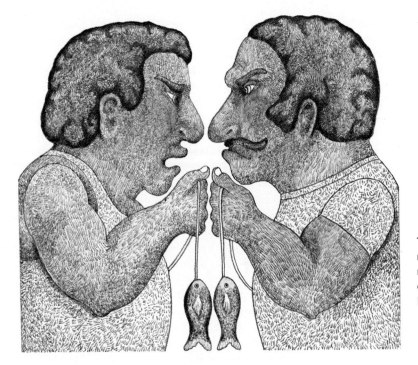

The proliferation of measurement terms makes comparing things difficult unless they can be viewed side by side.

Even the French, fathers of the metric system, recognize the handiness of 12. A few years ago, a British building contractor, specializing in partially prefabricated construction, decided to convert his plans to modular units of 40 inches on the theory that this length was close enough to 1 meter (39.37 inches) so that he could bid on school buildings in France. He was surprised to learn later that French schools were being designed to modular units of 1.2 meters, because these could be divided into 200-, 300-, 400-, and 600-millimeter subunits.

In addition to the customary and metric measurements, there are a host of miscellaneous units that certain groups use almost as private languages. Printers still talk of picas and points. Horse-racing fans are committed to the furlong. Every commodity seems to be measured in a different way; there are such oddities as cords and board-feet of wood. Even scientists and engineers speak special measurement dialects. There are, for instance, more than a dozen units of energy, including ergs, electron volts, horsepower-hours, joules, kilowatt-hours, watt-seconds, British thermal units, metric tons of TNT, and calories.

Whether in customary or metric, a few things are still measured crudely. One can make sure a shoe fits only by trying it on. A "mile down the road" may be as much as 3 miles; a "kilometer down the road" may be just as vague. And cooks add a "pinch" of this or a "dash" of that, whether they use metric or customary recipes.

The customary system of measurement in the United States is part of the cultural heritage from the British. It started as a hodgepodge of Anglo-Saxon, Roman, and Norman-French weights and measures.

Since medieval times, commissions appointed by various English monarchs have tried to reduce the chaos by setting specific standards for some of the most important units. Early records, for instance, indicate that an inch was defined as the length of "three barleycorns, round and dry" when laid together; a pennyweight, $\frac{1}{20}$ of a Tower ounce, was equal to 32 wheatcorns from the "midst of the ear." The U.S. gallon is the British wine gallon, standardized about 1700 (and about 20 per cent smaller than the imperial gallon that the British adopted in 1824). In short, the United States inherited a makeshift system based largely on folkways.

In his first presidential message in 1790, George Washington suggested to Congress that it was time for the United States to set its own standards of weights and measures. The matter was referred to Secretary of State Thomas Jefferson, who proposed the adoption of a standard of length based on a simple pendulum: a cylindrical iron rod of such length that a swing from one end of its arc to the other and back again would take two seconds. He also recommended that the U.S. system of weights and measures be based on decimal ratios, which the United States had adopted for its coins. He suggested retaining some of the old names for frequently used units, and he also urged that the new units should be as close as possible in size to the old ones. His new "foot," based on the pendulum, would be nearly as long as an old foot, but it would be divided into 10 new "inches." Jefferson's report was accepted by Congress, but no further action was taken.

Converting recipes to metric terms may create some confusion in the kitchen. But cooks will probably continue to use a "pinch" of this or a "dash" of that in creating many dishes.

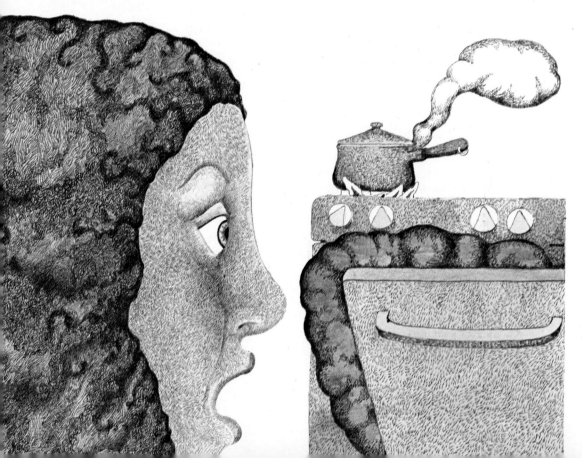

Meanwhile, a new measurement system had been born in the intellectual ferment of the French Revolution. In 1790, the Paris Academy of Sciences constructed a radically different system that was wholly rational, quite simple, and internally consistent. Its keystone was the meter, a unit of length defined as a specific fraction of the earth's circumference. For a while during the Revolution, Frenchmen even lived on a 10-day week.

But the metric system was not an unqualified success, even in France. In 1812, Napoleon Bonaparte partially reinstated the old system while retaining metric standards. Only after a lapse of 25 years was the metric system officially restored in France when an 1837 law made it compulsory after Jan. 1, 1840. After that, the system rapidly spread to other countries. By 1850, the Netherlands, Greece, Spain, and parts of Italy had adopted it. By 1880, 17 other nations—including Germany, Austria-Hungary, Norway, and most of South America— were using the metric system. And 18 more were added by 1900.

The United States showed little interest in standardizing measurements until President James Madison reminded Congress in 1816 of the need for uniform weights and measures. The result was John Quincy Adams' *Report Upon Weights and Measures*, submitted in 1821. Adams recommended, first, standardization of the familiar English units, followed by negotiations to establish a uniform international system. Congress took no action on the Adams report, and the question again languished.

In 1866, Congress legalized the use of metric weights and measures, but did not make the system compulsory. Another small step came in 1875, when the United States joined 16 other nations in signing the Treaty of the Meter, endorsing the metric system as the preferred system of weights and measures. But the nation made no effort to use the system it had approved. A number of attempts to convert the nation to the metric system were made between 1896 and 1907, but opponents raised such an outcry that further legislative proposals were bottled up in committee.

The controversy then moved to the pages of newspapers and magazines. Only two congressional hearings were held, though 40 bills were introduced. Then, with the onset of the Great Depression of the 1930s, the metric question was shoved aside and remained dormant for almost three decades.

Then came Russia's first *Sputnik* satellite in 1957, an event that suddenly focused U.S. attention on science and technology. The U.S. government again turned serious attention to adopting the metric system, the predominant measurement system of science. The metric momentum intensified as other major uncommitted nations began to convert; by 1965, even Great Britain announced it would forsake inches and pounds. Finally, in 1968, Congress commissioned a major assessment of the metric issue. Metric legislation passed the U.S. Senate in 1972, but the House of Representatives failed to follow suit and,

One mile is

1 yard

1 inch

A yard is one sash length

Fathom is Viking's arm spread

One acre is amount plowed in one day

1 foot

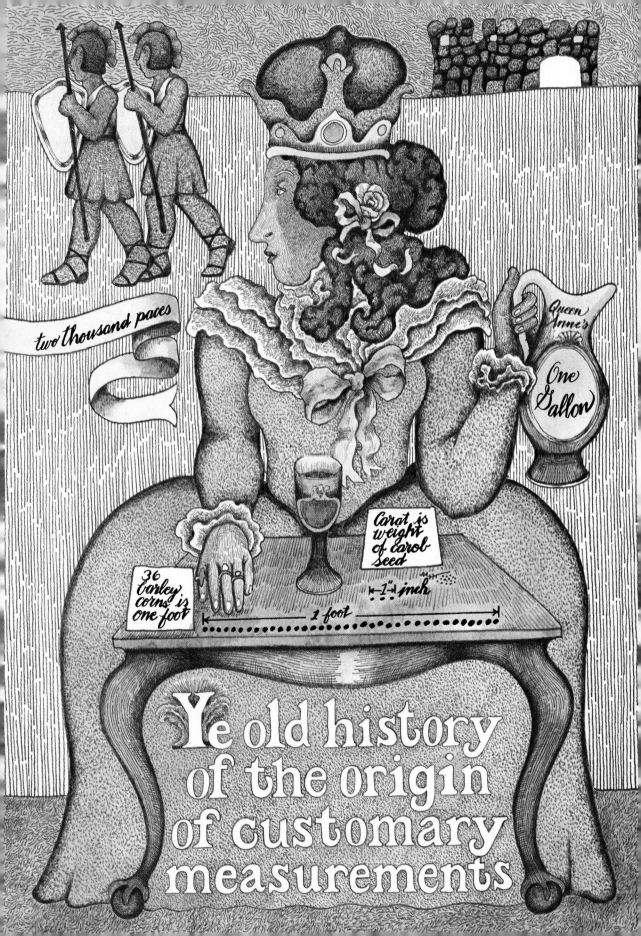

Ye old history of the origin of customary measurements

at the end of 1974, Congress was still struggling with the issue. However, the U.S. government made its encouragement of metric conversion a matter of policy in August, 1974, by enacting an amendment to an education bill that authorized $50 million to be spent through 1978 to prepare students to use the metric system.

Strongest opposition to the metric conversion bill comes from a small group of labor representatives who want federal subsidies to pay for all costs of converting tools and equipment. Supporters of the bill refuse to go along with such an amendment, arguing that subsidies would encourage wastefulness and the American taxpayer would have to pay. They point out that the bill does not exclude technical and other assistance for small businesses and self-employed craftsmen. Nor does it exclude some help in the form of accelerated depreciation of tools and equipment and investment tax credits. Even under present tax laws, metric conversion costs would be tax deductible.

The bill is expected to be reintroduced in 1975. But even without official commitment, the metric system is advancing in the United States, though its progress is sporadic and piecemeal. With few exceptions, the language and tools of U.S. science are entirely metric. Many schools teach the metric system, even to very young children. Soldiers speak casually of "advancing 3 kilometers to Hill 803," an unnamed hill that is 803 meters high; their ammunition is measured in millimeters. The National Aeronautics and Space Administration and the National Bureau of Standards use metric terms in their documents.

Automobile mechanics have added metric tools to their tool boxes to repair foreign vehicles built to metric specifications. Even some automobiles made in the United States are being assembled with such engines, transmissions, and other parts. Leading corporations, such as General Motors, Ford, and Honeywell, are taking steps to assure a smooth and economical changeover to metric standards. Many swimming pools are built to metric dimensions so that U.S. swimmers can practice for international events measured in meters. American skis, once made to standard feet and inch lengths, are now sold in centimeter sizes. The width of photographic film is expressed in millimeters, even though sprocket holes are spaced six to an inch. Standards for automobile emissions of hydrocarbons, carbon monoxide, and nitrogen oxides read in "grams per mile"–another metric infiltration.

The main reason "going metric" has been so controversial is that it was never clear what the debate was really all about. Some people assumed that at some future date, the inch and the pound would suddenly be outlawed. Others foresaw a painless and casual drift toward the use of more metric measurements.

But the United States will not go metric in either of these ways. An abrupt and mandatory changeover would be so disruptive, it would be intolerable. On the other hand, if the changeover is left to chance, without coordination, the United States would probably still be painfully straddling two measurement systems at the end of this century.

Mere legalization is hardly enough. The experience of other industrial nations shows that success in going metric depends on planning, coordination, and scheduling. To minimize costs and maximize benefits, suppliers of standard parts and materials need to know what buyers will need. Buyers need to know when suppliers will be ready. Workers and consumers need to acquaint themselves with new units of length, mass, volume, and temperature. And educators and publishers need to anticipate changes.

The United States can learn a number of things from the experience of such other countries as Japan and Britain. Japan began its metric program years before it emerged as an industrial power. In 1921, Japan had three officially recognized measurement systems: metric, customary, and a traditional system based on the *shaku* (11.930 inches) and the *kan* (8.267 pounds). In that year, the metric system was introduced into primary schools and plans were made for public utilities, government agencies, and a few industries to convert to metric over a 10-year period. Other sectors of the economy were allowed 20 years to make the change. But conversion, interrupted first by the Great Depression and then by World War II, progressed slowly and the deadlines were extended. In 1939, a new law restored the shaku-kan system to equal footing with metric and also postponed final conversion to metric until 1958. The changeover was essentially completed in the early 1960s.

There are two lessons in the Japanese changeover. First, the educational efforts begun in the schools more than a generation earlier greatly facilitated the final changeover. Second, Japan's zigzag route to metric conversion was largely due to the lack of strong promotion in the beginning; educating only the children was not enough.

Many mathematical calculations can be greatly simplified by metric measurements.

The British took much longer to make up their minds, but once they decided to go metric, they moved steadily forward. A study showed that the manufacturing industry could make the change efficiently and economically only if the economy as a whole proceeded on a similar time scale, that a Metrication Board should be established to coordinate the planning, and that any legal barrier to the use of the metric system—such as regulations written in customary measurements—should be removed. In 1965, the government set 1975 as the target date for conversion, with the possibility that some sectors of the economy might convert earlier or later.

British metrication got off to an auspicious start in January, 1970, when construction, one of the most complicated industries to change, led the way. Its activities are closely interlocked with those of a host of manufacturing industries—including steel, glass, plastics, and timber. It employs a wide variety of skilled and professional people, including architects, civil engineers, electricians, steam fitters, and experts in heating, ventilation, and building maintenance. All the major materials manufacturers have now arranged their own metrication programs to mesh with that of construction.

The British solved a number of minor but bothersome technical problems with interesting ingenuity. The gasoline industry, for example, realized it faced a two-pronged problem: Service stations were going to have to dispense gasoline by the liter—and price it in the new decimal currency, which was adopted in February, 1971. They designed a price-computing pump with a convertible head that could be easily adjusted for changes in both money and measurement. All gasoline pumps installed since October, 1968, have been of this kind.

In the drug industry, there was some worry about medicine taken in liquid doses. Most consumers had only the vaguest notion of the size of a milliliter. To avoid possibly disastrous confusion, drug manufacturers supplied pharmacists with cheap plastic spoons that held exactly 5 milliliters. One spoon was given away with each bottle of medicine.

Not all the knotty little problems of metrication have yet been solved. The dairy industry, for instance, is still worried about the size of the metric milk bottle. The British householder is accustomed to buying milk in one-pint bottles, and if milk is sold in the comparable metric size—500 milliliters—he is not likely to change the number of bottles he orders. Unfortunately, 500 milliliters is about 10 per cent less than a British pint. British milk companies have reason to fear consumption would slump, as happened in Kenya when the 500-milliliter bottle was adopted. A similar fear need not trouble the United States, however, because the U.S. quart is about 5 per cent smaller than 1 liter. If the same psychology were to apply, milk consumption would rise by roughly 5 per cent when Americans begin buying their milk in liters.

Virtually all the British Commonwealth countries are in the process of converting to the metric system—notably Canada, Australia, and

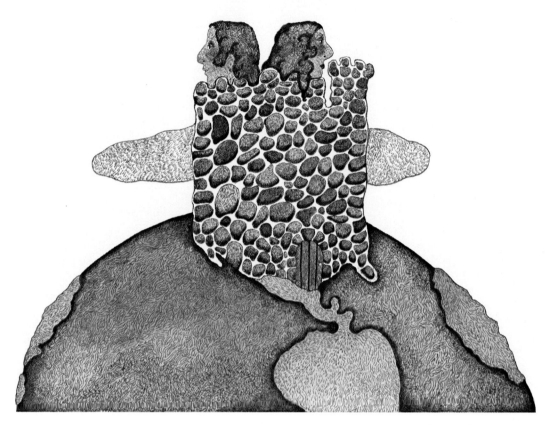

The United States stands virtually alone in a metric world. It is the only major nation not committed to the metric system.

New Zealand. Australia's timetable calls for conversion to be completed by 1976, but by early 1974, the country was already more than halfway there. Australians had been buying sugar by the kilogram for more than a year, and gas pumps were converted to liters in 1974. The government is spending the equivalent of $450,000 to educate motorists to metric road signs, which went up on July 1, 1974.

Canada is moving more slowly, hampered because its chief trading partner, the United States, has not yet decided to go metric. In spite of that, a number of metric advances are being made. Projections are that Canada will be totally metric by 1980. Weather reports will be given in degrees Celsius beginning in April, 1975, and the government has also set 1975 as the target date for total use of metric teaching in the primary grades. A packaging act passed in 1974 requires that all products state weights and measures in metric units.

In going metric, countries must consider two kinds of changes, "soft" and "hardware." A soft change is simply a trade of one measurement language for another; the weather announcer who reports the temperature in Celsius instead of Fahrenheit degrees is making a soft change. Hardware changes involve altering the sizes, weights, and other dimensions of physical objects. For example, if the dairy industry starts selling milk by the liter (1.05 quarts), the milk distributor has to modify his machinery to fill a slightly larger container.

A hardware change is almost always preceded by a soft change. Suppose that new cookbooks are written with recipes in metric language–for example, milliliters. If a recipe calls for 250 milliliters of oil, the housewife looks at a conversion table that translates milliliters to liquid ounces, then measures out slightly more than 8 ounces (1 cup) of oil. So far she has made only a soft change. If she breaks her measuring cup and buys a new one marked off in milliliters, this is a hardware change–at no extra cost, because she had to buy a new cup anyway. But if the conversion table confuses her and she throws away her ounce-marked cup in frustration, the price of the new metric measure is an extra hardware cost of conversion.

Many industries would make metric changeovers much as the housewife did when she broke her measuring cup. A pump in a chemical factory, for example, might last 10 years before it had to be replaced. But if a critical part failed after, say, five years, the user might decide to buy a new pump built to metric standards.

Some measurements would never need to be changed. It would be preposterous for the United States to tear up all its railroad tracks just to relate them to some round-number metric gauge. Nor would Americans be likely to translate into metric such sayings as "a miss is as good as a mile" or to rewrite the words to the song "I Love You a Bushel and a Peck."

Nor is going metric likely to present much of a problem in sports. Internationally, soccer is the most popular game; however, there is no standard size for a soccer field. Most of the nations in the old British Empire will presumably cling to the traditional imperial dimensions of the cricket pitch. Similarly, it would be unnecessary to change the length of U.S. football fields. And no announcer who wants to keep his audience would ever seriously say: "The Miami Dolphins have the ball; first down and 9.144 meters to go."

Some nonmetric units may continue to be used wherever they make communications and calculations clear and easy. Meteorologists in metric countries still speak of bars, one bar being roughly normal atmospheric pressure on earth. Astronomers talk of distance in light-years, instead of many trillions of kilometers.

Each time the U.S. Congress considered adopting the metric system in the past, action was postponed, often because the United States major trading partners were not then metric. Now, every other major nation has converted to the metric system or plans to do so, and this obstacle has been removed.

Among other advantages, the metric system would aid the United States in its international relations. Many present U.S. engineering standards–based on the inch and other customary units–are incompatible with standards used elsewhere. A potential customer in another country may prefer a certain U.S. machine, but he is less likely to import it if standard parts for repair and maintenance are not readily available in his country. As the rest of the English-speaking world completes its change to metric, this will become even more of a handicap for U.S. manufacturers.

Along with Canada, Mexico is among those nations most anxious for the United States to speed its metric changeover. Mexico, long a metric nation, must maintain a manufacturing capability in both the metric and customary systems in order to trade with the United States. Mexico is forced to bear the cost of maintaining this dual capability as long as the United States uses the customary system.

A U.S. decision to go metric would be welcomed also by its military allies. The compatibility and interchangeability of equipment between the United States and its allies would expedite repairs, make possible mutual military support in areas where such support is now nonexistent, and simplify procurement across national boundaries.

In outer space, too, international standards are needed, especially now that the United States and Russia are cooperating in such programs as the *Apollo-Soyuz* rendezvous in 1975. Uniform hatches and docking equipment are a must if the two nations are to operate space vehicles jointly.

The question is no longer whether or not the United States should switch to metric measurements. The question is how and when America will make the change. It is primarily a question of timing and preparation. Will the nation convert according to a specific plan over a comparatively brief period of 10 to 15 years? Or will it continue to drift aimlessly toward metric usage?

Legislation now before Congress calls for a coordinated and flexible program that would encourage the various sectors of society to deal with their particular problems voluntarily. Within this framework, each sector could work out its own timetable and program, dovetailing them with those of other sectors. Formal education in metric usage would be buttressed by encounters with the metric system in everyday life—hearing weather reports in degrees Celsius, buying cloth by the meter, potatoes by the kilogram, and milk by the liter.

There will be costs and difficulties in the change, even if it is carefully coordinated, but these can be minimized by using common sense. In even a concerted program for going metric, some things would be changed fairly soon, some slowly, and some never. Almost all machinery could continue in use until it wears out or becomes obsolete. Many machine tools can produce metric parts with only minor modifications. Schoolbooks are usually out of date in a few years; when updated, metric conversions can easily be inserted. As the British have found, retraining workers is unexpectedly easy—they learn on the job what they need to do their work. These examples illustrate what would be involved in a reasonable approach to conversion.

In any case, one thing is certain—eventually the United States will join the rest of the world in using the metric system as the common language of measurement.

See also Section Five, METRIC SYSTEM.

To Increase Knowledge Among Men

By Gus Constantine

**James Smithson's little gift to a new nation
has grown into a multifaceted cultural complex**

Near the center of Washington, D.C.'s famed Mall, a bronze fountain spouts 12 jets of water high into the air, and carefully positioned floodlights illuminate the dancing spray. The fountain stands directly south of a reflecting pool sunk in a garden of buff colored gravel, which serves as the focal point for the exhibit of some of the finest pieces of sculpture produced in the 1800s and 1900s. This is the face of the Joseph H. Hirshhorn Museum and Sculpture Garden, the newest addition to the Smithsonian Institution.

The Smithsonian includes what is perhaps the world's greatest complex of museum buildings, but it is far more than a museum. It is a vast government assembly of scholars, performing artists, research facilities, exploration stations, scientific objects, works of art, and memorabilia. So extensive are its activities that 150 pages were required to describe them during a 1970 congressional hearing. And the complex is continually growing. More than 18 million visitors flock to the Mall every year to stare in fascination at the institution's diverse, colorful, and artfully displayed exhibits. Officials envision a crush of 30 million tourists during the 1976 U.S. bicentennial celebration.

The Hirshhorn Museum was officially opened to the public on Oct. 4, 1974. But on the three preceding nights, members of Congress, the Cabinet, the Supreme Court of the United States, the diplomatic corps, and scholars, art patrons, and dues-paying members of the Smithsonian paraded through the four floors of the circular concrete structure and its plaza for a preview of Washington's most contempo-

The entryway to the doughnut-shaped Hirshhorn Museum is a brilliant arc of concrete and glass at night. The Capitol dome glows in the background.

George Segal's sculpture *Bus Riders* dominates one gallery in the new Hirshhorn Museum.

The author:
Gus Constantine is an editor of national and foreign news for the *Washington Star-News*.

rary art museum. The widely publicized preview was much in keeping with the style of the Smithsonian–a mixture of serious scholarship and extravaganza designed to catch the public's fancy.

The Joseph H. Hirshhorn Museum came into being in 1966, when Hirshhorn, a Latvian-born American businessman and avid collector of contemporary art, deeded to the federal government his collection of some 6,000 pieces, 2,000 of them sculptures. The collection, worth an estimated $40 million to $50 million, has statues by Auguste Rodin, Henry Moore, and Alberto Giacometti, and paintings by Pablo Picasso, Andrew Wyeth, and Ben Shahn. In return, the government spent $16 million to fulfill Hirshhorn's wish for a building on the Mall housing his collection and bearing his name–middle initial included.

Hirshhorn came to America at the age of 6. He worked his way up from a $12-a-week office boy to Wall Street broker, then invested in Canadian uranium mines and became a multimillionaire. He began buying art in 1917, covering the walls of his homes and offices in both the United States and Canada. When he announced that he was giving his collection to the public, many museums expressed interest. He finally decided to give it to his adopted country, and President Lyndon B. Johnson accepted it on behalf of the Smithsonian.

An intramural Smithsonian fight followed between advocates of the need for another Smithsonian modern art museum and those who thought that the Smithsonian already had the nucleus of such a museum – the National Collection of Fine Arts – and should build on that. But, with the Smithsonian's well-established tradition of acquiring objects and finding homes for them, it really wasn't a contest.

With the opening of the Hirshhorn, the Smithsonian now has seven art museums on or near the Mall. The others are the National Gallery of Art, the Freer Gallery of Art, the National Collection of Fine Arts, the National Portrait Gallery, the Renwick Gallery, and the Hillwood Museum, which has not yet officially opened.

There are also three science museums: the National Museum of Natural History, the National Museum of History and Technology, and the National Air and Space Museum. The latter, now in temporary quarters on the Mall, will make its public debut in still another museum building on the Mall in 1976, in conjunction with the United States bicentennial celebration.

Such is the character of the Smithsonian that it defies definitive classification, even in terms of something as physically conspicuous as a museum. For example, consider the Smithsonian's Anacostia Neighborhood Museum, set up in a converted movie theater across the Anacostia River in a largely black community of Washington. Some people question whether it is really a museum. The Smithsonian calls it a public service. It was created in the late 1960s at the height of the civil rights movement as an "innovative experiment in public education," and it is operated in close cooperation with the local community. Museum director John Kinard captured the flavor of the times, and provoked some hostility at the opening, by staging an exhibit on rats in order to dramatize how poor blacks suffer in run-down ghetto housing projects.

Outside the museum field, the Smithsonian has drawn into its administrative bosom the stately Kennedy Center for the Performing Arts and the National Zoological Park, which houses more than 3,000 animals. These include two pandas that were presented to the United States by Chairman Mao Tse-tung during the 1972 visit to the People's Republic of China by President Richard M. Nixon.

However, the hydra-headed nature of the Smithsonian becomes most evident in the diversity of projects it has undertaken away from Washington, D.C. It operates the Smithsonian Astrophysical Laboratory at Cambridge, Mass., where scientists study the mysteries of the universe. There, also, is the Center for Short-Lived Phenomena, which has focused its attention on such things as a falling meteor, a fleeting migration of squirrels in the Appalachians, and an oil spill in a Hungarian river. There is a Tropical Research Center in Panama, an Oceanographic Sorting Center in Tunisia, and other specialized study centers in various parts of the world.

It is estimated – nobody knows for sure – that the Smithsonian provides a home for about 70 million objects, both animate and inanimate, and that its collection is growing at the rate of a million objects a

Diffused ceiling light
and spacious circular
galleries help display
the Hirshhorn's modern
paintings and sculptures
to their best advantage.

year. It owns the prototype of the Boeing 707 airplane, and about 20 million insects. It keeps more than 20,000 skeletal remains, about 2,000 of which are skulls neatly tucked away in drawers in the basement of the Museum of Natural History. Those who favor such voracious hoarding of dissimilar things regard the Smithsonian as the nation's mantelpiece. Others sometimes call it a cluttered attic.

To keep it operating, the Smithsonian in 1973 received $62.7 million from Congress. In 1974, the institution asked Congress to increase this to $76 million. It has a staff of 3,100, including more than 300 scholars and scientists.

As if the phenomenal growth of the Smithsonian were not impressive enough, its plans for the 1976 bicentennial call for still more

has ever produced. The show will be called "A Nation of Nations," and its theme will be the peopling of America by immigrants from all over the world. "Never have so many people moved to one place in such a short period of time," Smithsonian officials point out. "As a result of their decision, a new nation and a new people came into being." Officials promise they will not ignore the difficulties faced by the new immigrants, difficulties of adjustment, joblessness, and discrimination that have made many question whether America is indeed the melting pot that we would like it to be.

In the National Museum of Natural History, the institution will erect four habitats re-creating views of life during the epoch before man, the era of colonization, the time of national independence, and

The World Book Map of Washington, D.C.

This exclusive WORLD BOOK map illustrates west-central Washington, the site of most of the city's main points of interest. Buildings and monuments are shown in blue and marked with a number on the map. To identify a blue-colored structure, look up its number on the map index. For example, the building marked number 66 is the Smithsonian Building. To learn the location of a particular place, begin with the map index, which is arranged in alphabetical order. For example, to locate the White House, find "White House" in the index. The index entry indicates that the building is number 78 and that it can be found at D 4 using the map's grid system.

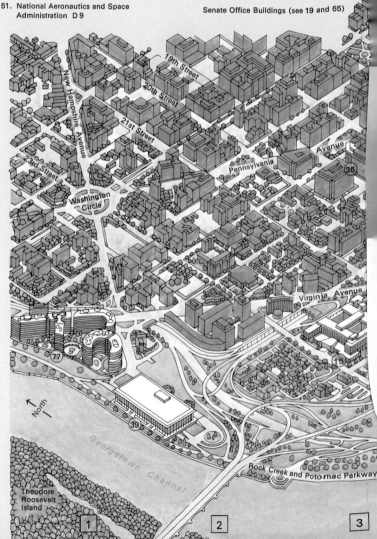

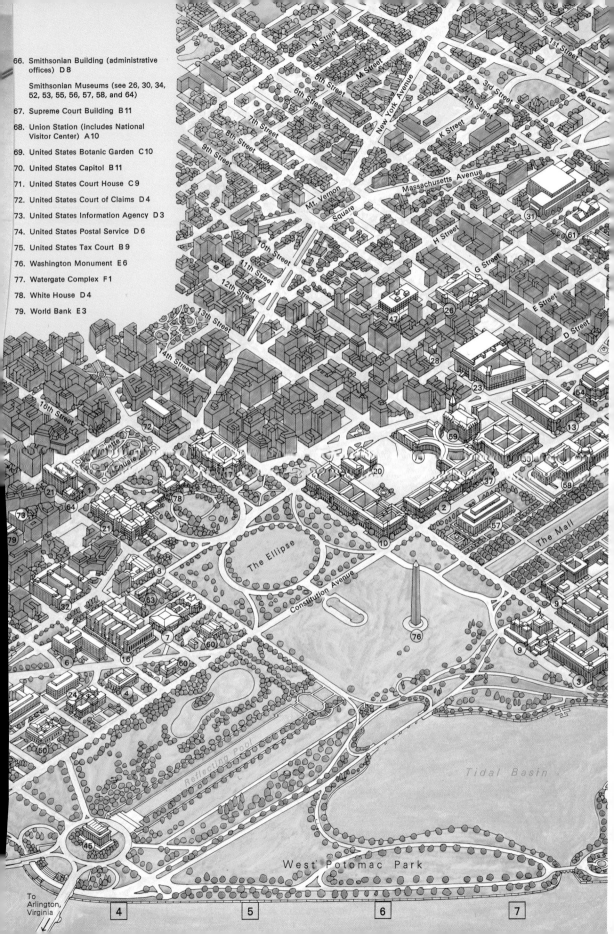

building and even greater displays. The National Air and Space Museum, now under construction on the south side of the Mall, will be three city blocks long. The Smithsonian has always wanted a home for the airplanes and space capsules it owns, but the nation, faced with the staggering cost of the Vietnam War, kept deferring this expenditure. Now, the new museum will provide a home for the Wright brothers' *Flyer*, Charles A. Lindbergh's *Spirit of St. Louis*, the Apollo 11 command module and lunar landing module used by astronaut Neil A. Armstrong in 1969 for man's first landing on the moon, and the first Air Force intercontinental ballistic missile.

At the west side of the Mall, adjacent to the Museum of History and Technology, the Smithsonian plans to have the largest exhibition it

Fold out page 130

North Capitol

68

33

Street

New Jersey Avenue

Louisiana Avenue

Delaware Avenue

6th Street

5th Street

3rd Street

2nd Street

East Capitol Street

A

49

27

43

B

19

65

1st Street

67

42

5

75

Constitution Avenue

70

44

40

46

C

48

71

62

South Capitol Street

14

56

69

Canal Street

Pennsylvania Avenue

25

The Mall

Independence Avenue

11

55

53

17

11

34

D

66

52

11

Interstate 95

22

G Street

18

29

30

6th Street

E

12

I Street

41

7th Street

M Street

3

Maine Avenue

F

Washington Channel

38

East Potomac Park

This map was drawn by George Suyeoka.
Reference material was provided by Sanborn Map Co. and Air Photographics, Inc.
The map was critically reviewed by the National Capital Planning Commission.
Copyright © 1975, U.S.A. by Field Enterprises Educational Corporation

G

Potomac River

8   9   10   11   12

The painting *Arcturus II*
by Victor Vasarely
is a colorful part of the
Hirshhorn collection.

the present. These are intended to show the ecological impact man has made on his environment.

The Arts and Industries Building will house a "Victorian extravaganza" that will hopefully capture the spirit of the United States 100 years ago, when it celebrated its centennial. There will also be a show on urban design, replete with street lights, bus stops, and trash cans, and an exhibition of about 150 paintings to portray how the artist's vision has changed under the crush of urbanization.

Almost all the Smithsonian family members have been assigned some part in commemorating the bicentennial. There will be a showing of crafts and decorative arts of the Western Hemisphere; a gallery of portraits and accompanying biographical material to tell the story of the American Revolution; scale models of the city of Washington, D.C., at significant stages in its development; and an exhibition on the arts of Asia in the 1700s. It may surprise some that 18th-century Asian art has a part to play in celebrating the American Revolution, but the Freer Gallery—the Smithsonian's Asian art museum and part of the official family—is entitled to celebrate.

It would astonish the man responsible for calling the Smithsonian Institution into existence to view this complex, ever-growing storehouse of art and science today. James Smithson, its originator, was an English scientist, the illegitimate son of the Duke of Northumberland, Hugh Smithson. He never visited America and never met an American. But he admired both the American and French revolutions and saw the United States as an emerging giant with a significant scientific contribution to make to mankind. Smithson was an eccentric figure who yearned to be a famous chemist rivaling Antoine L. Lavoisier or Joseph Priestley. But he never achieved much scientific recognition, and today is remembered chiefly as the discoverer of a zinc-containing mineral called *smithsonite*.

As the years passed, Smithson's health began to fade and, with it, his hopes. He drew up a will providing that if his nephew and heir died without offspring, his estate would pass to the United States to create "an Establishment for the increase and diffusion of knowledge among men." Smithson died in 1829, his nephew in 1835. There were no offspring, and the United States inherited a special-purpose fund worth precisely $508,318.46.

Today, it is difficult to imagine how a half-million-dollar gift could spark a controversy and be viewed as a constitutional challenge. However, that is what happened in the case of Smithson's bequest, largely because some Americans felt that the United States should not be beholden to an alien who owed his allegiance to a monarchy. Finally, the government did what almost any inheritor would do—it kept the money, deposited it in the U.S. Treasury, and began drawing interest on it. To govern the institution, Congress set up a Board of Regents in August, 1846, that would be answerable to the "Establishment" that Smithson referred to in his will. That Establishment—it is even called

that today—consists of the President of the United States, the Vice-President, the chief justice, and the heads of executive departments.

But the Smithsonian has never projected an image that is an extension of the Establishment. Its character, its interests, its specializations have all been expressions of the personalities of the eight scholars who have served as secretary of the Smithsonian Institution, the institution's executive head.

For example, the first was Joseph Henry, a noted physicist who made several discoveries in the field of electromagnetism. He nudged the Smithsonian into an extensive program of publishing scientific findings. The second, Spencer Fullerton Baird, was a naturalist who promoted many exploratory expeditions to gather materials for the development of museums.

Its current secretary, S. Dillon Ripley, is a bird specialist and a man with a flair for the spectacular. He has pushed the institution in the direction of a series of large, eye-catching projects. And this explains the acquisition and lavish promotion of the Hirshhorn collection.

This also explains another Smithsonian venture, the launching of the *Smithsonian* magazine in April, 1970, over the objections of several regents who felt it would be a misuse of federal funds. When it began, advertisers were promised a circulation of 175,000, and the Smithsonian delivered. The magazine offered a brilliant array of color photography in the style of *Life* magazine, hiring as its editor Edward K.

King and Queen, one of the many works by sculptor Henry Moore owned by the Hirshhorn, is in the museum's sculpture garden.

Thompson, a former *Life* editor. The circulation has since soared to over 500,000. When the magazine was unveiled, it appeared with a giant elephant on its cover. And politically conscious Washington did not miss the point that the chosen portrayal of natural history was also the symbol of the Republican Administration then in power.

Leading Smithsonian officials like to bill themselves as a community of scholars engaged in the "increase and diffusion of knowledge" that Smithson mandated in his will. And few would doubt that the Smithsonian does conduct a vast amount of significant research. Yet, the tenacity with which this image of scholarship is fostered, coupled with the showmanship and polish of its museum displays, tempts one to look for contradictions. Why, some ask, with its vast resources, has the Smithsonian been unable to produce a single Nobel medalist, something that institutions less richly endowed have accomplished? Is it too big or too specialized? Is it too diverse in its interests to concentrate its resources in an area of activity that might produce a major scientific breakthrough? Or is it just a matter of unfortunate coincidence?

But whatever one may say of the Smithsonian's merits as a center of scholarship, its unquestionable ability to put on a cultural show makes it unique in American life. A visitor arriving in Washington during the first week in July catches the Smithsonian dressed at its best. This is the time of the American Folklife Festival, started by the Smithsonian in 1967 as an annual display of the diverse life styles of this country.

Gaily colored tents dot the Mall area from the Washington Monument to the science and art museums. Eskimos are flown in from Alaska to demonstrate whalebone carving, and Indians come from all over the United States to teach their age-old crafts. Appalachian hill-folk impart their skills in quilt-making and pewter work, and immigrants of every ethnic group sing, dance, cook outdoors, and sell their wares. The folk festival is part state fair and part learning experience that enables visitors to understand the complex mix of cultural and ethnic groups that form the United States of America.

Touring the bewildering array of exhibits that is the Smithsonian can be a unique educational experience. Its unusual development mirrors, in a way, the surprising growth of a mighty world power from 13 humble, struggling colonies.

"The Smithsonian's facilities have grown with the passage of time along with the national collections, the range of responsibilities and programs, the size of the staff, and, indeed, with the city of Washington and the nation itself," says one of the institution's official publications. It is one of its few understatements.

The growth is hardly the natural process of ordered expansion that the Smithsonian portrays. Instead, it is the result of a frenetic determination by the institution's leaders to make it the world's largest storehouse of art and science, as well as the greatest show on earth. Given this drive, one might ask: Where will hydra grow its next head?

The New Face of China

A scholar takes a close look at the sweeping changes in China since Communists seized power 25 years ago

The platform stage is draped in red and gold banners, and there are massive bouquets of paper flowers at each end. A group of 5-year-old boys and girls with scrubbed faces and dressed in bright colors dance onto the stage to the strains of accordion music. At a signal from their teacher, they begin to sing and act out a popular song: "It is ridiculous to have two Chinas; we are determined to liberate Taiwan!" They raise their fists in revolutionary determination and make fierce expressions with their faces. The song ends: "The poor people of the world must win victories."

The occasion is International Children's Day. And the scene takes place in the People's Park near Peking's Tien An Men Square in the People's Republic of China. For several hours on this June 1, thousands of children and adults have marched there from all over the city. They are dressed in brightly colored clothing, and some carry wreaths and large paper flowers. Almost every child wears a red neckerchief, signifying membership in the national children's organization, the Little Red Soldiers. They also wear badges praising Communist Party

Children in today's China climb on the statues in Peking's Forbidden City. Their grandparents could not even enter the area in the old days, but the fabled Imperial Palace and grounds are now a public museum.

A boy demonstrates t'ai chi chu'an, an ancient martial arts exercise, during the International Children's Day festival, held on June 1 in the People's Park in Peking.

The author:
Chiao-min Hsieh is professor of geography at the University of Pittsburgh and author of *China: Ageless Land and Countless People* and *Atlas of China*.

Chairman and leader of the country Mao Tse-tung. The children's day is filled with demonstrations of acrobatics, skits, dances, and puppet shows. Almost all of these include some political message, but a few are just for fun.

Twenty-five years ago this park was a private one, owned by a single rich family for its personal enjoyment. There were none of the festive celebrations that now mark national and international holidays. Groups of beggars, both adults and children, huddled on every street corner in Peking, and rickshaw pullers formed long lines to wait for possible customers. World War II had ended, but the cessation of the long conflict with Japan brought no peace. Instead, China became embroiled in civil war between the Nationalists and the Communists and battles between local warlords. Hordes of starving peasants roamed the countryside, while smallpox, plague, cholera, and malaria reached epidemic proportions. Few schools existed, and the nation had one of the highest rates of illiteracy in the world. Roads were poor and badly in need of repair. Railroads lay unused because the Japanese had removed many sections of iron track for use in making armaments. Japan also left the country with little heavy industry. What Japan neglected to dismantle in Manchuria, the Russians later removed as war reparations due them for having defeated the Japanese in Manchuria. Then, high inflation rocked the government.

Today, however, 25 years after Mao's army seized control of the country, China, once the most conservative and underdeveloped nation in the world, is the most radical and rapidly developing one. Since 1949, new railroads and highways have been built, and new irrigation and water-control projects have been completed. Agriculture has been expanded, new industrial regions have appeared, and new urban centers have developed. The Communists have created a new system of government, controlled inflation, nationalized businesses, enforced economic planning, indoctrinated the minds of people, and mobilized the poor. They also have created the foundations of modern industry, science, and technology.

The most dramatic change in the 25 years of Communist rule has come in agriculture—not in terms of how farming is done, but in terms of how it is organized. Farming occupies the energies of about 8 out of every 10 Chinese, and it is still essentially unmechanized. Farmers do not have much chemical fertilizer, and most of them use water buffaloes, horses, donkeys, and mules instead of tractors. Most of the country lies between the same latitudes as the continental United States. The north has cold Siberian winters, the south has lush tropical

China's 25 Years of Growth: Cities and Railroads

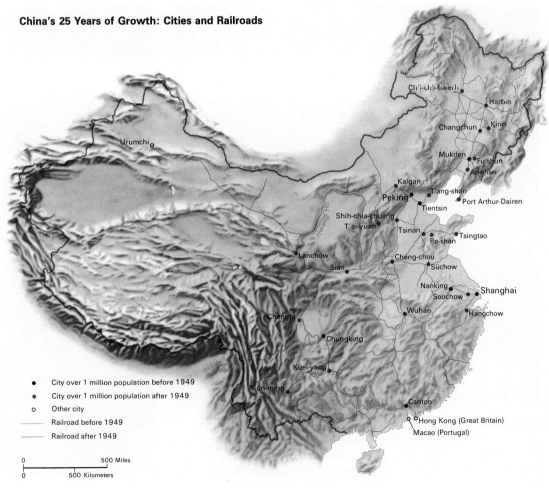

● City over 1 million population before 1949
● City over 1 million population after 1949
○ Other city
——— Railroad before 1949
——— Railroad after 1949

0   500 Miles
0   500 Kilometers

growth, and the southwest has the mighty Tibetan plateau, "the roof of the world." But the 830 million mainland Chinese are almost four times as numerous as Americans and constitute more than one-fifth of the world's population. Yet, 96 per cent of the Chinese live in the eastern half of the country, many of them along the valleys and plains of three great rivers, the Hwang Ho (Yellow River), Yangtze, and Si Kiang. As a result, cultivation in these valleys is probably more intensive than anywhere else in the world.

The sweeping organizational changes in agriculture began in 1949 with a nationwide land-reform campaign, which was completed in only four years. The program was necessary if the new government was to institute effective political control of the vast rural areas and also secure the popular support of the poor peasants. Under the program, the government broke up large, privately owned estates and distributed the land and other properties, such as draft animals, farm implements, and horses, among the more than 300 million peasants who owned no land.

Water buffaloes still pull most of the plows in China's rice fields, though tractors and other mechanical equipment are used on some of the communes. Workers have built new stone-walled terraces on the hillsides of many communes, so crops can be cultivated in these areas.

The government next turned its attention to merging the millions of small, individually owned farms into larger, cooperative units. In 6 years, the Chinese Communists completed what it took Russia 17 years to accomplish. By 1957, the individual farms that had dominated Chinese agriculture for thousands of years had virtually disappeared, and 97 per cent of the peasant households were consolidated and organized into agricultural cooperatives.

In 1958, under the slogan of agriculture as the "foundation of the economy" and industry as the "leading factor," the cooperatives were reorganized into still larger units, or communes. By the end of the year, there were 26,578 communes, with more than 90 per cent of the farm households participating. Most of the communes covered an entire township, with several thousand families in each. Mergers later cut the number of communes briefly to 24,000, and still later subdivisions in some provinces tripled that total. But the commune remains today the form that merges all the cooperative farming in the country, and to which practically all the peasants belong.

The commune's scope of activities is far broader than that of the cooperatives. It is a social, economic, and administrative unit engaged in both agricultural and nonagricultural activities, including trade, education, and military training, whereas the cooperative was almost entirely an agricultural organization. Furthermore, because the communes are big farms, they can be cultivated with modern tractors and combines when more of these machines become available. This was never possible on the tiny, inefficient, individual farms of 25 years ago that were the size of family garden plots by American standards.

The organization of China's millions into communes has the additional benefit of forming large labor forces for such tasks as building irrigation projects and planting forests. Not since the construction of China's Great Wall, begun sometime before 220 B.C., have so many people been gathered together to erect dams, cut roads through mountains, and turn the course of rivers. Even units of the army have been enlisted in these programs to convert acres or hectares of unusable land into commune farmland.

What strikes most visitors to China and its communes are the old and the new existing side by side, vivid reminders that, while great progress has been made, it is at best uneven. Less than 2 miles (3.2 kilometers) from Tien An Men Square and the ultramodern buildings that surround it, one can watch water buffaloes pulling wooden plows on a commune. Industrial exhibits display hydraulic dump trucks, mechanical rice planters, and other agricultural machinery, yet the communes have few of these mechanical tools. Brigades that work from dawn to dusk do all the plowing and harvesting. Boeing 707s and fast Ilyushin jets (assembled in China from parts imported from Russia) flash across the sky, but most farm goods are transported in caravans of horse-drawn carts and two-wheeled vehicles pulled by men.

The changes brought by the creation of communes have been paralleled by a revolution in family relations. The ideals enunciated at the start of the Communist regime in 1949 have remained constant—that the traditional family structure should be retained and its strengths used. However, the primary commitment of each individual is expected to be to the state or to the commune, rather than to the elders of the family. Abhorrent feudal customs were quickly broken, such as the parents' stranglehold over the lives of their children. Children now are allowed to marry without parental interference, and the buying and selling of child brides is forbidden.

Women, for the first time, have individual rights under the law, and are no longer considered the property of a husband and his mother. Big, ostentatious, and wasteful wedding feasts have also been prohibited. Commune women, just as men, are expected to work in the fields, as women always have in rural China, but now child care is provided. In the cities, nurseries have been established so that the women can easily join in productive work. Many women have entered higher educational institutions and become government officials.

中国共产党万岁

国家大文立

毛主席万岁

毛主席万岁

伟大的

伟大的

无产阶级文化大

China's urban population has doubled in the past 25 years. And pictures of Mao are ever present in the rapidly growing and crowded cities.

At sporadic intervals, children and young people have been urged to take the lead in showing their parents how to rid themselves of old feudal ideas. This, too, represents a change in family relationships. Children in the old China were expected to obey their parents in all things. Youths were particularly extolled in 1966 for taking a lead in the Cultural Revolution. This was a massive political campaign to recapture the idealism of the early days of the Chinese Communist movement, to eradicate and change the remnants of feudal thinking, and a campaign that sometimes led to senseless destruction and sloganeering. Today, youths play an active political role. This is important, because half of the country's population is under 21 years of age.

In China, education has traditionally been the channel through which the young succeeded their elders and achieved power, wealth,

Primary school students work at their productive labor project, placing seals in bottle caps. All schoolchildren do such work, and primary students spend about 10 days each semester working and visiting factories and communes.

and prestige. The Cultural Revolution, in one sense, was a massive campaign to alter this traditional practice. Schools were closed for many months. Entrance examinations were abolished and, when the schools reopened, political commitment became the primary requirement for admission to higher educational institutions. Examinations have since been reinstated, but they are no longer the sole qualification for entry. All secondary school students must go to work in the fields or factories after graduation. Then the most conscientious and politically dedicated are selected by their fellow workers and team members to study in the universities.

But the Cultural Revolution could not weaken education's importance in China. Even before the Communist take-over in 1949, the Chinese regarded education as the most basic way of indoctrinating the young. They have never considered education a market place where ideas are exchanged. They believe that the values established by education determine the kind of leadership the nation will get in the future. Therefore, the present educational program demands no less than the establishment of a new society, and calls for new customs, new habits, and new patterns of thought and behavior. From nursery school to university, the school system is the most important instrument for this reshaping of the culture and consciousness that is the primary goal of the Chinese revolution. Textbooks, songs, and even children's ballets are fashioned to expound the importance of Mao Tse-tung's thought.

During the 1950s, the country's elementary school enrollment tripled, secondary school enrollment increased ninefold, and higher education, six. When the Cultural Revolution started, the country had 100 million students in school—more than the United States and Russia combined. It was turning out 70,000 engineers each year, the third highest total in the world after Russia and the United States.

Education was also the method by which the new Chinese government confronted the age-old problem of disease. It began a crash program to train many new health workers and a mass propaganda program to improve public sanitation and health. By 1965, this had produced more than 100,000 new physicians and some 170,000 assistant doctors (medical personnel with three rather than five years of training). But even this supply of new doctors could not satisfy the needs of such a large population, so the government began training paramedical workers called *barefoot doctors*. (The term is used to designate closeness to a peasant's life, and does not indicate a lack of shoes.) The barefoot doctors generally receive from three to six months' initial training, followed by continuing on-the-job medical education. They work part of the time as farmers or factory laborers and part of the time in the commune health stations. They are trained to identify and treat easily diagnosed medical problems, and to refer patients they cannot treat to more advanced medical centers.

The Chinese have combined Western medicine with their traditional techniques, such as acupuncture, herbal remedies, and exercise. Students in China's Western-style medical schools are also taught traditional medicine, and those who study traditional medicine also learn Western practices.

In assessing Chinese science and technology, it should not be forgotten that the Chinese have been contributing to the sum of human knowledge for nearly 3,000 years. Chinese made the first magnetic compass, paper, and gunpowder, as well as the first wheelbarrow, crossbow, and kite. They were the first to cast iron, to make iron suspension bridges and canal lock gates, and to develop a technique for deep-well drilling.

Yet, such inventiveness came to an end after 1600. The Chinese emperors decided to avoid war by disbanding their contacts with the rest of the world. They destroyed their own navy and ships, and the country became isolated and economically backward. After 1949, the Communists began training large numbers of scientists and engineers in the hope of catching up with the West. The synthesis of insulin in 1958 by a group at the Biochemical Institute in Shanghai was an achievement hailed by biochemists and other scientists throughout the world. By 1964, China had exploded an atomic bomb, and by 1970 it had launched its first space satellite. A team of British scientists reported after touring the country in 1962 that the Chinese were "surprisingly advanced" in electronics and solid state physics.

The scientific advances are a reflection of the many gains that the Chinese have made in industrial production. They began their development from a very low level of per-capita production, and the level is still low. But they have overcome decades of war and public anarchy.

The arts are designed to indoctrinate as well as entertain. One popular opera-ballet is *The Red Detachment of Women,* which depicts the life of a woman soldier during the bloody civil war between the Communist and Nationalist Chinese.

China today is a nation at the beginning of industrialization, but one that has the potential to be the largest self-sufficient industrial nation on earth. It is also a testing ground for new methods of flood control, irrigation, and other technologies associated with agriculture, which will have relevance for other food-producing countries.

Before 1949, China imported all its big machinery from Japan, Europe, and the United States. Now it produces its own high-grade steel, and makes its own automobiles, ships, and railroad equipment. It is difficult to determine the extent of Chinese production, because the government publishes no figures. But the visitor sees the new products, new industrial plants, and new housing in all the cities and throughout the countryside. Visitors also point out that there seems to be no shortage of clothing, food, and other consumer necessities.

China has made work, and the resulting product, identical with the highest national purpose. The people work hard, six days a week and without vacations, and they are paid in accordance with the work performed and the number of hours they work. In this, the Chinese rely heavily on organization. They describe their economic system as a great battalion in which some lead and many march. The workers are called on to duplicate the soldiers' sense of purpose. The campaign has involved unremitting exhortation to work hard to build the nation, to advance the revolution, to ensure Chinese independence, and, of course, to please Chairman Mao.

Intensive geological exploration has located vast new oil fields and coal deposits. The Chinese claim overall coal resources of 10.6 trillion tons (9.6 trillion metric tons). While this amount might be exaggerated, China's coal reserve is definitely one of the world's largest, along with those of the United States and Russia. Newly discovered oil fields in Manchuria and in the ocean off the east coast are said to be larger than existing U.S. fields.

The key to economic development in China has been the creation of an effective transportation system. Throughout China's history, distribution was always the fundamental economic problem. The country's huge size—slightly larger than the United States—and mountainous landscape made road-building difficult. Recognizing this, the Communist government made the development of modern transportation facilities one of the most important parts of its successive five-year plans. China now has more than 23,000 miles (38,000 kilometers) of railroads, an increase of 6,800 miles (10,900 kilometers) since World War II. Today, only six countries have more railroad mileage than China.

The growth of industry and new transportation systems have brought many people to the cities, and the urban population has doubled during the past 25 years. China has 31 cities of 1 million or more people—more than any other country. Industrial concentration has also shifted from the coastal cities, where all the heavy industry once was, to newly industrialized cities situated close to the inland areas where raw materials are found. Strategic considerations probably played a part in this shift, too. Industrial concentrations along the eastern coast are far more vulnerable to attack than those scattered among inland cities.

The Communists are also apparently determined to end the traditional distinction between the cultured city and the backward countryside. Every large city factory has a garden plot where industrial workers gain experience in agriculture. And every agricultural commune has workshops—actually medium-sized factories—that not only make the traditional farm tools, but also can repair all mechanized equipment. Many of these produce bricks and other construction materials, but some produce their own electric motors and pumps, some make electric light bulbs, some produce medicines, and a few even build threshing machines. By linking the agricultural and industrial resources of several adjacent communes, provincial authorities have literally moved mountains (or tunneled through them) without getting subsidies or materials from the central government.

Administrative groups called three-in-one committees do all the economic and social planning in China. These are composed of young activists who rose to prominence during the Cultural Revolution, older leaders who had been managers and administrators prior to the Cultural Revolution, and soldiers from the People's Liberation Army. This is to ensure the participation of all three age categories.

The three-in-one committee structure began in 1967, during the last stages of the Cultural Revolution, in an effort to rebuild the administrative apparatus that was disrupted by Red Guard attacks during the initial stages of the Cultural Revolution. According to Mao, the "three-in-one combination" was to "exercise unified leadership, eliminate redundant or overlapping administrative structures, and organize a revolutionary leading group that keeps in contact with the masses." It appears to be an effective system of administration and a way of developing continuing leadership.

The men and women who work in this T'ai-yuan iron and steel plant built the factory themselves. Their story is typical of this industrial city. The workers elect their managers, and they insist that all plant officials must work on the production line at regular intervals.

Of course, the top leadership in the country rests with Chairman Mao. Everywhere in China—in every home and on every billboard—there are pictures of Mao with one or more quotations from his writings. This adulation of a living personality is somewhat offensive to many Westerners, but the cult built around Mao is nothing new in China. For thousands of years there were emperors and emperor worship. Mao, though he undoubtedly has tremendous power, tends to operate through groups rather than by dictatorial fiat. Many of the decisions he is credited with making are probably those of administrative committees, and Mao's role has been one of summing up and presenting the group consensus as if it were his own thought.

Mao has the support of one of the largest armies in the world—almost 2½ million men—though visitors report that an armed man is rarely seen in China. A few armed soldiers guard the foreign embassies and legations in Peking, but the city police carry no weapons. The People's Liberation Army, which undoubtedly contains tough military units, combines many duties in its daily activities that would be carried out in the United States by county agricultural agents, public health authorities, 4-H club members, amateur drama groups, and Army engineers. Each army division produces its own grain and meat, runs its own hospital, maintains tailoring and shoe-repair facilities, and has its own theatrical troupe. Officers and enlisted men wear identical uniforms, with no distinguishing insignia, except that officers' jackets have four pockets instead of two.

A vast civilian militia of perhaps 30 million persons supplements the army. It includes men, women, and children in every factory, school, urban district, and commune village. Militia members know their own territory, tree by tree and rock by rock. They dig their own shelters and caves for possible guerrilla activity, and would probably be a crucial factor in any war fought on the Chinese mainland.

Napoleon Bonaparte warned 150 years ago against meddling with this country. China, he argued, was a sleeping dragon that had best be left to slumber lest it destroy those who awaken it. But empire seekers who came after Napoleon disregarded his advice. Great Britain declared war on China in 1839—the so-called Opium War—to win profitable trading rights. Soon after this, France, Russia, and other nations demanded similar treaties and forced concessions from the decaying Manchu dynasty. Shanghai, for example, was divided into sections, with one belonging to the French and one to the British.

As a result of this, the Chinese react whenever they believe their borders are threatened. They fought United Nations troops in Korea when they believed these forces might cross the Yalu River and enter China. They battled with India over their Himalayan border, and they periodically come into armed conflict with Russia over the ill-defined border along the Amur River. During the Vietnam War, China gave armaments, food, and other supplies to the North Vietnamese, fellow Communists whose territory borders China.

The chief point of conflict between the People's Republic of China and the United States concerns the Nationalist government on Taiwan, which the U.S. government continues to support while trying to cultivate friendly relations with the People's Republic. There is, of course, no realistic way at present for the People's Republic to "liberate" Taiwan, and Nationalist China has little hope of retaking the mainland. Meanwhile, the communiqué released by President Richard M. Nixon and Premier Chou En-lai in February, 1972, acknowledged that all Chinese agree that Taiwan is a part of China. The key to the eventual improvement of relations between the mainland and Taiwan may rest simply in the passage of time.

In trade, China has had to balance its imports with its exports, because it receives little foreign aid and investment. The government looks upon foreign trade as a means of acquiring goods and capital for

Huge poster in Soochow urges people in the developing countries to fight imperialists. Such propaganda posters replace the advertising signs that are found in most other countries.

industrialization. It has not allowed ideological differences to stand in the way of trade. As a result, China now does business with 120 nations, including Australia, Canada, England, Japan, West Germany, and the United States. The two-way trade with the United States in 1974 totaled $1.25 billion. Most of the manufactured goods that China exports are produced by light industries, which require little technology and can utilize the country's low production costs. These include cotton and silk fabrics, brooms and brushes, and tin products. In return, China imports such goods as wheat, fertilizers, industrial chemicals, and passenger aircraft.

China's image of the contemporary world is basic in forming her foreign policy. In Peking's eyes, as its representative told the United Nations on April 10, 1974, the international political scene is composed of three distinct elements—the two superpowers, the other economically developed countries, and the third world. The two superpowers are Russia and the United States. The third world is composed of the underdeveloped countries of Asia, Africa, and Latin America. China has associated itself with this group of countries, most of which are now deeply involved in establishing their own nations and in developing their own independent economies.

The Chinese "model" apparently offers several attractions to some third world countries, such as the example of self-reliance and rapid nation-building from a backward technological base, and "no-strings-attached" foreign aid. Such Asian countries as Pakistan, the Khmer Republic, Burma, and Indonesia regard China as much more dynamic and attractive than India. China has acted as a helpful friend to such African countries as Guinea and Mali, and has challenged Arab leadership on the black continent. The Chinese provided the interest-free loans and technical help needed by Tanzania to build a major rail line. However, China's foreign aid appears insignificant compared to Russia's and the United States. It is true that Peking has offered more aid to several nations—such as Zaire, Tanzania, Zambia, Burma, the Khmer Republic, Sri Lanka, and Nepal—than Russia. But the sizable Russian aid to Algeria, Indonesia, Egypt, and other nations overshadows the Chinese effort. American aid is even more impressive.

Any country's international relations are closely tied to its domestic affairs. Thus, the great convulsions of the Cultural Revolution disrupted diplomatic relations with many nations for a time. So far, however, this has not happened with the new wave of turmoil that began in China late in 1973 after the death of Marshal Lin Piao, commander of the army and alleged leader of a plot to overthrow the government. There has been a major military shakeup resulting in the transfer to new commands of many long-time regional military commanders. Because Lin was an admirer of Confucius, attacks on the writings of this ancient sage have been renewed. Confucius is accused of having advocated slavery and of opposing change. Western music, specifically that of Beethoven and Respighi, has also been denounced as decadent and bourgeois, and there has been an attempt to tie admiration for Confucius with admiration for Western culture.

Although much of this internal conflict and criticism seems obscure to Westerners, the future of China is at issue: Who will lead in the post-Mao era? And what direction will they take? One group in China seeks a centralized state apparatus and an active role in international affairs. Another believes that international involvement will corrupt the Chinese people and make it difficult for them to achieve ideological unanimity in the face of the Western challenge. So far, despite the sporadic turmoil, there has been little of the disruption that characterized the events of 1966, when every institution was enmeshed in debate and youthful Red Guards marched throughout the country.

In this light, China's ability to start a war, which frequently concerns observers in the West, is diminished. Its armed forces—mostly a land-based army and civilian guerrillas—seem ill prepared for warfare far outside China's borders. There may continue to be border skirmishes, which have occurred periodically with India and Russia, until all sides agree to well-defined boundaries. Of the countries that have a common frontier with China, only Russia is capable of invading and fighting on Chinese territory. Yet, Russia would hardly risk nuclear war, even though the Chinese claim there is a million-man Russian army poised on the Sino-Russian border prepared to take such action.

As to exactly who will lead China after Mao, no one can say. It will be a major change, of course, but probably not as radical a change as most people in the West assume. After all, the government of China is run more by committee than by Mao's whim. In December, 1974, he turned 81 years old, but was still active and apparently in good health. Also, the three-in-one committee structure seems to assure a leadership blend of youth and experience at all levels of administration. For example, the recently elevated Wang Hung-wen, now one of the three or four top national leaders, is in his late 30s. Wang, a Shanghai factory worker, made his meteoric rise to national power in 1973 largely on the basis of his role in the Cultural Revolution.

Some concern was evidenced in the spring and summer of 1974 when Premier Chou En-lai, who then was 76, was hospitalized and had to turn over his duties to subordinates. Chou was back on his feet, however, for the October 1 celebration of the founding of the People's Republic. He made a speech at a public reception in Peking, lauding the nation's 25 years of progress. During his illness, there were signs that Mao and the other top officials were hunting for ways to prevent a leadership struggle should Chou have to resign because of ill health. One of these signs was the stress on unity in the editorials of official journals and newspapers in September.

The real test of cohesion, however, will come only after Mao and Chou die. When that happens, it is anyone's guess whether their survivors can muster sufficient self-discipline and farsightedness to ensure a completely peaceful transition to new leadership.

Learning for Living in a Silent World

By William J. Cromie

**Students and faculty at a unique school
try new methods of teaching deaf children
how to learn better and live more fully**

The walls of the one-story high school are splashed with color, and the main room, with its library and surrounding study areas, vibrates with dissonant sounds. In the snack bar, two teen-agers dance to blaring radio music, while a third beats time with drumsticks on a counter top. A small group practices conversational Spanish in the language skills area, and nearby, a 15-year-old boy rehearses the song "Born Free."

The students—in fact, all 131 students in that unusual building on the Gallaudet College campus in northeast Washington, D.C.—are deaf. Not knowing this, a visitor might think they were a normal group of high school students with a lot of freedom. And that is exactly how the faculty and administration of this unique school for the deaf intend it to be.

"Deaf kids want to be like everyone else. The deaf are not, as many people believe, mute and retarded," says faculty member Bill Grant, who sports a large "Deaf and Bright" button.

"The deaf are plagued with the 'I can't' syndrome," growls another faculty member, Don Pettingill. "Parents say, 'My child can't hear, so he can't do this and he can't do that.' Kids come to me and say, 'I can't do this because I'm deaf.' I answer, 'So what? So am I.' I tell them that deafness is a nuisance, not a handicap."

This is the basic attitude at the Model Secondary School for the Deaf (MSSD), the first such federally funded school in the United States. Since it began operating in 1969, the school's purpose has been to update methods of educating the deaf and make these methods available to other schools for the deaf throughout the country. MSSD students come from a five-state area around Washington, D.C. Kendall elementary school, which became a federally funded demonstration school in 1970 and serves deaf children in the Washington area, is also on the Gallaudet campus. Both of these model schools serve as training grounds for deaf college students who are majoring in education, counseling, and audiology (the science of hearing) at Gallaudet College. Gallaudet is the world's only accredited liberal arts college and graduate school for the deaf.

Of the estimated 330,000 young Americans (under 25) with hearing difficulties, about 55,000 are enrolled in special school programs for the deaf. However, deaf education generally has not kept pace with such modern advances as open classrooms, team teaching, and visual aids. Also, according to a government study, less than 10 per cent of deaf high school graduates continue their education, compared to about 50 per cent of hearing graduates. The goal of MSSD is to help close these gaps between the hearing and the deaf.

It was no accident that Gallaudet was chosen as the site for these model schools. Gallaudet, founded as the Columbia Institution for the Deaf and Dumb by a wealthy businessman, Amos Kendall, in 1857, has a long tradition of service to the deaf. From 1857 until 1910, the institution was headed by Edward Miner Gallaudet, son of the pioneering deaf educator, Thomas Hopkins Gallaudet. In 1864, Congress gave the school authority to grant degrees, and the name was changed to Gallaudet College in 1954. In addition to the elementary and secondary schools, its 92-acre (37-hectare) campus houses a preschool; centers for research, adult education, and medical testing; public-information services about hearing impairment; psychological and career counseling; and social services for the deaf and their families. A sprawling $15-million facility is being built to house the expanding MSSD. It is scheduled to be completed by early 1976, and school officials expect the student body to reach its maximum of 600 deaf children by 1980.

In its first four years of operation, MSSD has made no startling breakthroughs. However, the school is experimenting with several

The author:
William J. Cromie is
Director of Research
and Development
for Field Enterprises
Educational Corporation
and a free-lance writer.

Parents of deaf children meet with a counselor, *above,* to work out problems they have in understanding and communicating with their children. Kendall preschoolers, *right,* learn about shapes and colors and explore their small world while a teacher explains that world to them by total communication, using many forms of expression, including sign language.

A teacher tests a toddler's hearing, *left,* by pounding a drum. An older child, *above,* moves a bead each time she hears a sound.

promising innovations, including more efficient methods for the deaf to communicate and computer programs and instructional packages that allow each child to learn at his or her own pace. The instructional packages contain learning goals or objectives, activities—such as reading, watching films, or writing papers—and tests to determine if the objectives have been achieved. A total of 108 instructional packages were under development in 1974, ranging from a short course in basic movements on the trampoline to a one-semester course in biology called "The Human Body." Eventually, these will be passed on to other schools for the deaf.

Open classrooms for the deaf—learning areas without real walls— were pioneered at Kendall and MSSD. "Physical openness provides

A speech therapist teaches a child using a powerful hearing aid how to make vowel sounds, *below.* In the Kendall school's open classroom, *right,* two students and a teacher practice spelling, while the group beyond a room divider tackles math.

Kendall students play a total-communication word game and show they know the word on the blackboard by pointing to their ears, using sign language, or trying to pronounce it, *above.* A Gallaudet College student teacher watches, *right,* as two Kendall students take a test.

visual stimulation for deaf kids, the way sound provides an awareness of surroundings for hearing kids," a school official points out. "We arrange room dividers and furniture in various ways to determine which provides the best learning situation."

It is extremely difficult for persons who can hear to comprehend the isolation experienced by persons who are deaf. "Consider that our students never have heard their fathers or mothers talk about their work, or about money problems," says Pettingill. "Most of the kids don't even understand what their parents do for a living, much less what *they* can expect when they go to work."

Because people who are deaf from birth have never heard words being spoken, they have problems with language. So they are sometimes mistakenly thought of as retarded. "Deaf children do learn more slowly," explains Edward C. Merrill, Jr., president of Gallaudet. "This is because hearing loss presents surprisingly difficult learning problems that center around language development. I don't mean just speech, but vocabulary, style–in short, understanding."

Degrees of deafness in children accepted at MSSD vary from those who are able to hear speech as an indistinguishable murmur to those who live in the silent world of the profoundly deaf. How then, does someone who is totally deaf–who does not even understand what sound is–learn to make the sounds of spoken language?

"Most don't," says Pettingill. "The speech of a deaf person is usually very difficult to understand."

Pettingill, an outspoken advocate of deaf rights, served as president of the National Association of the Deaf from 1972 to 1974. Pettingill considers himself to be an exception among the deaf because he speaks well enough to be understood by hearing people. But Pettingill was not deaf from birth. He could hear and speak normally until he was 5 years old, when his hearing organs were damaged by disease. Therefore, he knew how words should sound.

"When I lost my hearing," he says, "the family's reaction was: 'So you're deaf. So what?' It was a big family–my parents had nine children–so I was treated like everyone else. That's the best thing that could ever have happened to me."

Pettingill recalls psychological problems beginning when he entered a school for the deaf. "There were deep divisions between the teachers and the students. Hearing educators planned our lives for us. They tried to make hearing people out of us. They would not accept us as normal people who happen to be deaf."

They taught only speech and lip reading at the schools Pettingill attended. "We were forced to speak and we were punished if we used sign language," he says. "So those who could not learn to speak and read lips began to feel inferior and guilty. They began to withdraw."

Educators of the deaf disagree on the best way to teach those who cannot hear to communicate. Ordinary speech clearly helps a deaf person get along better in a hearing world. To hearing people, signing is literally a foreign language, because the hand signals used in sign language represent objects and ideas, not the words of English or any other spoken language. Also, many speech advocates believe that learning signs and finger spelling early in life endangers a deaf child's ability to develop speech and lip-reading skills later. Educators in favor of teaching sign language argue that denying young deaf children a clear means of communication results in emotional harm and intellectual retardation that is far more serious than the alleged interference with learning to speak and read lips.

Kendall and MSSD try to solve the oral versus sign-language dilemma by teaching their students both methods. However, some educators maintain that the two methods interfere with each other when they are taught at the same time. Teachers at MSSD and Kendall believe their experience indicates otherwise.

For example, Peggy Harrison could speak well but had never learned sign language. Her mother feared that learning a new communication method at MSSD would interfere with Peggy's speaking skill. "As it turned out," says her mother, "Peggy's vocabulary actually has grown because she gained more confidence by learning a second communication skill."

The Gallaudet schools also are experimenting with a method known as "cued speech," developed in 1966 by R. Orin Cornett, vice-president of Gallaudet College. Cues consist of 12 hand signals that, when used with lip reading, allow a deaf person to see clearly any word that is spoken. Lip movements for some speaking sounds, such as *pet, met,* and *bet,* are the same. Cued speech symbols represent sounds and tell a deaf person which of a number of possible words is being spoken. For example, the signal for the *p* sound would show that the spoken word was *pet,* rather than *bet.*

But how does a deaf child learn about concepts, such as love? "Total communication," says Pettingill. "We say it so the child can see the word on our lips; show it in sign language, in our facial expressions; and we use our bodies to hug the child, for example." Nevertheless, it is extremely difficult for a deaf child to understand more subtle meanings, such as the difference between love and compassion.

Although educators have different opinions about what is the best method of teaching the deaf, they agree completely on the importance of identifying the problem as early as possible to take advantage of any residual hearing ability. "Most deaf persons have some residual hearing, and, if possible, they should be fitted with a hearing aid before they are a year old," says MSSD audiologist Vern Larson. "An early start in identifying different sounds makes speaking and learning language much easier in the school years."

"If we get kids early enough and start them dealing with sound and language, then by the time they finish high school they will be less handicapped–maybe some won't be handicapped at all," adds science teacher Robert Wehrli, the hearing father of three deaf children.

High school students study in the circular library in
the center of the Model Secondary School for the Deaf,
top. While a literature teacher leads a discussion about
a story projected on the screen, television cameras film
the class session, *left.* Later, students can study the
tape to see how well they communicate. Students in a
drama class, *above,* improvise to act out an everyday
situation — starring mom, dad, and the family dog. The
goal is total communication, using body language
and pantomime. This skit also is filmed for analysis.

163

MSSD chemistry students use instructional packages during a class session, *top.* One watches a videotape, another does an experiment, and others consult with the teacher. A social studies class, *above,* discusses a newspaper story. Students also learn practical skills, such as how to cook, *top right,* and drive a car, *right.*

Widespread ignorance about deafness can make early identification of the problem a difficult and traumatic experience. Wehrli called in a local public-health nurse when his first deaf child, Joan, shattered the family composure with unnerving screams. The nurse concluded that the only thing the child needed was a good spanking. The Wehrlis then took their infant daughter to doctors, but none of them were able to identify the problem. Finally, when Joan was almost 2 years old, they took her to the Boston Children's Hospital. "It was like a whole new world," says Wehrli. "Those people really knew what they were doing. They fitted Joan with a hearing aid and started her in a day-school program at the hospital."

Although the Wehrlis went through that experience more than 20 years ago, several parents of preschool children currently enrolled at Kendall tell about similar incidents. "From the time my daughter Cathy was 4 months old until she was 2½, doctors kept telling me that she was too young for a hearing test," recalls the mother of a preschooler. "They told me that even if she was deaf, there was nothing I could do about it. It is very painful to look at your child and know you need help, but not be able to get it. We finally had Cathy tested at a large children's hospital, where they fitted her with a hearing aid. Now she's able to take advantage of what little hearing ability she has to distinguish different types of sounds."

Identifying a child's hearing problem is only the first step in dealing with deafness. A deaf child born of hearing parents can create serious problems within the family. Kendall's testing, counseling, and social services provide information on the capabilities of the children and help parents adjust to their children's deafness. In addition, the school sponsors meetings and discussion groups where parents of deaf children can get together to share common problems. "This really helps us to have a normal family life," observes the mother of two deaf preschoolers. "You find out everyone has the same problems you do. You realize you don't have to spend the rest of your life catering to your handicapped children. You spank them when they need it, and love them when they need it—just like any other child."

The facility also teaches parents how to help educate their child. "To understand your child's problems, and to give help, you need to be able to communicate effectively," notes Robert R. Davila, the deaf director of Kendall. So parents can learn such skills as sign language and finger spelling and how to work at home with a deaf child.

All the students, from preschool to college, concentrate heavily on learning language skills. Although MSSD accepts young people between the ages of 14 and 19, their reading levels range from 3rd to 10th grade. Because of this, curriculum is highly individualized—each student sets personal goals and learns at his or her own pace. In some English courses, teachers encourage students to talk and argue with each other. They discuss things of general interest to teen-agers—cars, sports, dates. "They want to be like normal kids," says one staff mem-

Dough

Sew

Toe

An instructor shows how to help a lip reader distinguish between similar-sounding words — dough, sew, toe — by use of cued speech. Hand signals represent the different sounds to indicate which of the words is being spoken.

ber, "but it takes 12 to 15 years of schooling to raise a deaf person to a fifth-grade language and reading level. Most teen-agers consider fifth-grade work 'baby stuff,' but it may be all they can handle."

Most of the students accepted at Gallaudet College must spend one year in a preparatory class where they receive extensive instruction in English and language development. Only then can they enter the regular four-year degree program. In that program, new words are explained in different contexts, using both speech and sign language, before each lecture begins.

MSSD is experimenting with teaching deaf students a foreign language, Spanish, by using cued speech. "You can't teach conversational Spanish by using sign language because signs for English and Spanish — for example, *house* and *casa* — are the same," explains a teacher. So the students watch the teacher or a videotape to learn the lip movements for Spanish words and cues for the different sounds. Because they never hear themselves speaking Spanish, the students measure their progress in learning Spanish by comparing videotapes of themselves talking with tapes made by instructors.

By much the same method, deaf students also learn to sing songs. The student watches a videotape of someone else singing the song. Then the student practices, makes a videotape, and compares it with that of the original performer.

With the help of earphones, amplifiers, and hearing aids, some youngsters can hear the music. Those who are totally deaf feel the vibrations of sound waves, particularly those of low frequency. A school dance at MSSD is an uproarious affair; students turn the music volume up all the way to produce enough sound so they can feel the vibrations in their ears, or through the floor.

In addition to the academic curriculum, which includes English, mathematics, science, and social studies, physical education is a required course at MSSD. Most students participate in some sport. Basketball is the favorite, and the high school has both varsity and junior varsity teams that play other high schools in the area.

The students also play football, and MSSD hopes to have a school team soon. Football is an old tradition at Gallaudet. The college team plays to the booming, low-frequency beat of a huge drum. In the huddle, players agree that the ball will be snapped to the quarterback on a certain beat of the drum, say, the third or fourth boom. "At first, the drum may confuse players on hearing teams," laughs a coach. "Someone will start to move at the first sound of the drum, and they get an offside penalty."

There are no structured classes, letter grades, or age groups at MSSD. "We bring students together on the basis of their needs and interests," comments Doin Hicks, director of MSSD. The teen-agers go to school year-round in five 9-week terms. Students are evaluated on the basis of whether they accomplished the goals set for them in various required and elective courses. Evaluation of their progress also

A deaf student uses cued speech to learn a song. She watches a videotape of someone else singing and cueing the sounds, *above.* Then she makes a videotape of her own performance, *left,* to compare with the original.

takes into account such factors as self-confidence, motivation, attitude, and ability to handle responsibility.

A round library occupies the center of MSSD's hangarlike main building, with study areas scattered outside this book-lined hub. Faculty-student relations appear to be warm and informal. In study areas, students, usually dressed in jeans, work alone or in small groups.

"The school has a minimum of rules and regulations," Hicks points out. "This increases the chances that students are going to make mistakes. But we prefer they make them while we're around to help them pick up the pieces. We try to direct them by encouragement and goals, rather than by regulation and punishment. Our objective is to make them become responsible for their own learning and behavior. This is the only way they are going to be able to handle real-life situations." The faculty at MSSD is equally concerned with their students' social development. An administrator noted that "the emotional and social levels of our kids vary from those who drive cars downtown to shop or see a movie to those who are afraid to ride a bus."

Fear of riding on a bus or of going to a store is often a sign of other, deeper problems that arise because the deaf child is unable to communicate with hearing people. "When there is a breakdown of communication, this scares people and often creates embarrassing situations," says Pettingill. "Deaf people don't want to get into embarrassing situations, so they withdraw." Deprived of ordinary experiences with everyday situations, deaf children begin to doubt their ability to cope in a hearing world.

When a new deaf student enters MSSD, the faculty members try to determine his or her main talents or interests, what areas are best for the student's self-expression. For example, when Joe Sprowl first came to MSSD, he had quite a negative attitude toward education—probably because he was afraid of failing. But Joe liked to play basketball and he liked to box. So his teacher encouraged him to practice and become skilled in these sports. Joe's success gave him greater self-confidence and self-respect, and his new attitude toward himself carried over to his schoolwork and his social life.

To help students through the transition from the sheltered surroundings of the school to holding a job and coping with the hearing world, MSSD has a Department of Off-Campus Study coordinated by Pettingill. "We try to equip deaf kids to go out and get whatever piece of the world they can handle," says Hicks.

With this goal in mind, MSSD puts all of its first-year high school students through an 18-week orientation course, a kind of consciousness-raising for the deaf. "In addition to teaching them how to get and keep a job, we want to teach them pride and self-respect and to accept their deafness," says Pettingill. In this orientation course, new students tell how they feel about their deafness. Responses range from "Hearing people make fun of me," to "I can't do anything," to "It doesn't make any difference."

They also discuss proper attitudes, good work habits, the requirements of employers, job responsibilities, and what kind of jobs are available. Then students go through a step-by-step work program, progressing from two-hour-a-week jobs on the campus to full-time, off-campus employment. "Even students planning to continue their education after graduation are encouraged to work off-campus, because jobs enrich their knowledge and experience," notes Hicks. "We want students to be familiar with real work situations, but, more important, we want them to interact with the hearing world and gain exposure to both good and bad situations."

As with academic tasks, faculty members believe that the best policy is to let students make mistakes while there are adults around to help

During a typical day on the campus, *clockwise from above,* students gather to visit before class and in the snack bar at lunchtime. After classes, the college football team practices to the low-frequency beat of a drum. A group of MSSD girls relax in a dormitory, and a student works at an off-campus pet clinic.

The MSSD drama class builds props and creates a skit on the theme of Evel Knievel's next stunt — all within an hour. An MSSD girl plays Evel, waving proudly from the launch ramp. But the vehicle catches fire and explodes, and the injured Evel is carried off atop a Volkswagen ambulance.

them correct the mistakes. Pettingill tells about one deaf student who was fired from jobs four times in four weeks: "We picked him up each time, brushed him off, explained why it happened, and got him ready to try again."

There are plenty of jobs on the Gallaudet campus—in the libraries, gyms, lunchrooms, and dormitories. When students feel they want an outside job, they are encouraged by the MSSD faculty to look for it themselves. "That's when we find out how well we've trained them," says Pettingill. "When a student locates a job, in a newspaper ad, for example, we contact the employer and help the student fill out the job application. We advise him or her on how to dress, act, and compete with hearing people for the job."

Ninety-six of the 120 high school students worked part time during the first five months of 1974, and 40 got full-time jobs during the summer. They worked for employers ranging from the computer department at a National Aeronautics and Space Administration center to restaurants and dry-cleaning shops. Ten students even worked as messengers for Watergate special prosecutor Leon Jaworski.

However, MSSD and its programs have not won unanimous acceptance among educators of the deaf. The school has been criticized for lack of structure and discipline, and for being too liberal. Administrators of other schools complain that they do not have the time, money, or staff to implement MSSD-invented techniques. Some believe that the model school's $4-million annual budget would be better spent if the funds were distributed among established schools to improve their programs and facilities.

Hicks replies that "MSSD expects to develop a kind of educational menu from which other schools can choose servings of materials and methods that best suit their educational appetite." He also tells about such students as Joe, who was 15 years old and could barely communicate in sign language when he enrolled at MSSD. But by the time Joe graduated, he had become a model of cooperation and was accepted into Philadelphia Community College. The MSSD faculty points to many other cases of students who had serious problems. "We are convinced that these kids would never have received the attention and recognition they needed in a conventional school for the deaf."

Joseph Rosenstein, director of MSSD's Office of Research and Evaluation, defends the model-school concept. "State schools often lack money for educational change and the development of materials and techniques. Also, many of these schools are characterized by a lack of desire to disturb the status quo. Our function is to do what other schools are unable, or unwilling, to do—close the gap between innovation and education."

"The significance of our school," says Hicks, "must be measured not on the basis of how well we educate a particular group of deaf kids, but on what other schools can learn from our efforts. We are a proving ground for institutions for the deaf."

A Year In Perspective

THE YEAR BOOK casts a backward glance at the furors, fancies, and follies of yesteryear. The coincidences of history so revealed offer substantial proof that, although the physical world continually changes, human nature—in all its inventiveness, amiability, and even perversity—remains fairly constant, for better or worse, throughout the years.

1874

1974

Crises, Crusades, And Courage

By Paul C. Tullier

It took persistent optimism, mixed with homespun humor, to help brighten the year's generally gloomy outlook

In 1974, no one could really say with any conviction that the world was his or her particular oyster. Nor could it be said that the year's events were everyone's cup of tea. For the haves as well as the have-nots, 1974 was pure potluck.

Global finances were at low ebb. Interest rates were sky high. Many nations were running horrendous balance-of-payments deficits. Labor was restless. Living costs spiraled ever upward. Housewives everywhere—from Singapore to Spain, from Uruguay to the United States—complained in a multilingual chorus about the high prices of food; at the same time, the farmers who produced the world's food were bitter about the low financial return for their labor. The world's collective temper, already burning on a short fuse, was further aggravated by an international fuel shortage. Admonitions that people not be "fuelishly" wasteful did nothing to dampen the fires.

The fates, too, seemed to be weaving a global pattern of political turmoil and tension. In Indochina, where a war had allegedly come to

Farmers, unhappy with low profits, insisted others were getting rich off the sweat of their brows.

The author:
Paul C. Tullier is Managing Editor of THE WORLD BOOK YEAR BOOK.

an end, deviousness was the order of the day. Peace treaties signed with avowals of sincerity were constantly being violated by the regime in Hanoi. Northward, Russia was reportedly massing troops along its border with China. And in the United States, the sun set on the scandal-riddled administration of an American President.

These were the ingredients that made life in 1974 an almost unpalatable mix. But in essence, they were no different than those that had simmered on history's back burners a hundred years earlier. For the deviousness in Indochina, the Russo-Chinese border threat, and the presidential crisis in the United States—to say nothing of the chaotic state of the world's economy, labor unrest, a fuel shortage, and soaring living costs—were much like the trials and tribulations that confronted the average world citizen in 1874.

It was evident, from the overall view, that the world was in an unsavory mess. But on closer inspection, on a less-earthshaking level, there were signs that men would rise above it. In New York City, the piers of the New York and Brooklyn Bridge were beginning to emerge from the turbulent waters of the East River. In Philadelphia, the Girard Avenue Bridge, billed as the widest bridge in the world—100 feet wide by 1,000 feet long (about 30 by 300 meters)—was formally opened on July 1, 1874. (On that same day, the Philadelphia Zoological Gardens—America's first—were opened to the public.) St. Louis, Mo., proudly unveiled its noteworthy example of bridge building three days later, on July 4. Called the Eads Bridge after its designer, James B. Eads, it was the first permanent span built across the Mississippi River that could accommodate railroad traffic.

The Old World was not to be outdone. In Scotland, work was underway on a bridge over the estuary of the River Tay. It was an innovative eye-popper, 1 mile (1.6 kilometers) long, a curved bridge that its designer maintained would make straight ones obsolete. Paris and London, meanwhile, had agreed to burrow a tunnel under the English Channel, and designs were under consideration. (The two countries were still initiating new construction plans in 1974.)

Inventiveness—and an ingenious use of materials and techniques—played a large role in these then-huge projects. But smaller ones required inventiveness, too. One man, H. S. Parmalee of New Haven, Conn., patented the sprinkler head, without which no modern-day building would be complete. In Rochester, N.Y., the Sargent & Greenleaf Company began manufacturing a newfangled time lock, and no bank worth its salt would be without one today. An adhesive-and-medicated plaster with a rubber base, a forerunner of today's Band-Aid, was put into production in East Orange, N.J. The electric streetcar, a vehicle run with electric current generated by a stationary dynamo and invented by S. D. Field of Stockbridge, Mass., was successfully tested in New York City. Its use of the "third rail" principle was both timely and fortuitous: It would satisfy a growing need for rapid municipal transportation.

Inventiveness that catered to the taste buds was displayed by one R. M. Green of Philadelphia. In 1874, he concocted and began selling ice cream sodas. Inventiveness of a different sort made its bow in *Harper's Weekly* in 1874. The widely read periodical published the first cartoon to use the elephant as the symbol of the Republican Party. Entitled "Third Term Panic," the cartoon drawn by Thomas Nast reflected Republican concern that President Ulysses S. Grant would run for a third term on *their* ticket.

Other "firsts" that would become a permanent part of the American way of life were introduced during the year. On August 16, 163 German-speaking Mennonite immigrants from the southern Russian steppes reached Kansas' Marion County, bringing with them quantities of a strain of wheat they called Turkey Red. It was so named for its color and because the seed had originally been obtained from Turkey. It was a hardy winter wheat that would flourish and eventually make Kansas the granary of the United States. Among other beneficial innovations that year, the first corset manufactured solely as a health item went into production in McGraw, N.Y. America's first hospital record system was introduced at Bellevue Training School for Nurses in New York City. Andrew T. Still of Baldwin, Kans., announced a new medical discipline—osteopathy.

These were medical breakthroughs that reflected an abiding concern for the human condition. But they were not the only ones in 1874 that brought out crusaders with a cause. Tobaccophobes were indignant about the "obnoxious fumes" from cigars and pipes that "clouded the air, assailed the delicate membranes of the nostrils and caused the eyes to smart painfully." They peppered municipal officials with demands that separate facilities be provided on public transportation for those enamored of the tobacco weed. The Pullman Company, a prime target of their wrath, eventually set aside "smoking cars" to segregate the incorrigible "public nuisances" from the pure-air enthusiasts.

Alcohol, "the brew of the devil," was another target of the reform-minded citizenry. Then, as now, they considered "booze" the root of all evil, and their efforts to eradicate it were strenuously and widely

The Eads Bridge at St. Louis was an 1874 engineering marvel. It was the first permanent structure designed to carry railroad traffic across the Mississippi.

The elephant was first used as a symbol of the Republican Party in a cartoon drawn by Thomas Nast in 1874.

supported. The entrenched establishment, however, was formidable and resistance was spirited. According to available statistics, 78,000 persons were engaged in the liquor business in Pittsburgh alone. One newspaper estimated that 7 million bushels of grain were used annually in the making of alcoholic beverages for clients in Chicago. To curtail this evil, 135 women met in Cleveland's Second Presbyterian Church in November to organize the National Woman's Christian Temperance Union.

Crime, a sometimes handmaiden of alcohol, was omnipresent. And just as statistics in 1974 showed it was most prevalent in the big cities, the same was true in 1874. In New Orleans a hundred years ago, the French Quarter was the focal point of crime. A much-favored rendezvous for assorted muggers, footpads, cutpurses, and other criminals was Pig-Trough Carrie's on Gallatin Street. In Chicago, the sin section was called The Levee. One of its most iniquitous dives, the Lone Star, was notorious for an alcoholic specialty named for its bartender-owner, Mickey Finn. A popular itinerant "singer" who cadged coins in the bars was a tall, thin young man with long black hair. His name was Tiny Tim.

Popularity of a different sort was enjoyed by a lottery craze that swept the United States and other countries in 1874. Local lotteries were conducted clandestinely by back-door solicitations. Two kinds of bets could be placed—capital (in which the gambler picked one number) or gig-and-saddle (in which the gambler picked three). Lottery was especially popular in Louisiana until an investigation by state authorities revealed that the daily drawings were crooked. This information did little to discourage the gamblers, who diverted their bets instead to the Royal Havana Lottery of Cuba. It promised, through U.S. newspaper ads, that $1.2 million in prizes would be distributed monthly but that a total of only 16,000 tickets would be sold. The Royal Saxon Government Lottery of Leipzig, Germany, offered the same tempting sum at the same odds.

These diversions, though considered shady by the more staid and proper, paled beside two others of 1874. The first involved William Marcy Tweed, political boss supreme of New York City, who was serving time for fraud involving city and state funds. His downfall could be traced to the erection of the Tweed Courthouse, which was built at a cost of about $12.5 million. According to chroniclers of the times, the actual cost was only one-third of that and the remaining two-thirds was graft—or "boodle," as it was called. (This drafty and soot-splotched monument to municipal corruption was declared a historic landmark by New York City in 1974.)

The second and most widely deplored crime of all occurred in Germantown, a wealthy suburb of Philadelphia. On July 1, a 4-year-old boy, Charley Ross, was lured into a wagon and carried away by two men who demanded $20,000 for his return. His kidnaping, which received unprecedented news coverage around the world, was the first for ransom in U.S. history.

Russian Mennonites who emigrated to Kansas in 1874 brought a new strain of wheat that would help make America the world's breadbasket.

Little Charley would become a footnote in history. But many infants born the year he was kidnaped would eventually warrant more prominent space. Included among the newcomers in 1874 were authors G. K. Chesterton, W. Somerset Maugham, Gertrude ("A Rose is a Rose is a Rose") Stein, Ellen Glasgow, and Lucy (*Anne of Green Gables*) Montgomery; poets Robert Frost, Amy Lowell, and Robert W. (*The Shooting of Dan McGrew*) Service; composers Arnold Schönberg, Charles Ives, and Gustav (*The Planets*) Holst. There were wireless inventor Guglielmo Marconi, magician Harry Houdini, and industrialist Karl Bosch. Future statesmen included Britain's Winston S. Churchill, Israel's Chaim Weizmann, and, from Canada, W. L. Mackenzie King and Arthur Meighen. All their names would be glowingly alive a hundred years later, along with that of oil tycoon John D. Rockefeller, Jr., whose son Nelson—in 1974—would be nominated for Vice-President of the United States.

But their accomplishments were all in the future, and little note was made, by the press, of their births. More immediate doings, such as spectator sports, were preferred as a daily diet by the periodicals of the day. Some notable "firsts" were reported in 1874. The first international rugby football game was played at Cambridge, Mass., on May 14, 1874, between teams representing Harvard and McGill University of Canada. Another trailblazing event was the European tour of the

Women opposed to the use of alcohol held prayer meetings outside saloons. Their efforts led to the formation of the Woman's Christian Temperance Union in 1874.

Charley Ross, 5, who was the first American kidnap victim held for ransom, vanished July 1, 1874.

William Tweed, a corrupt New York City politician once considered beyond the law's reach, spent most of 1874 in jail.

National Association's Philadelphia Athletics and the Boston team. They were the first professional U.S. baseball clubs to play abroad. They competed in 14 ball games and 7 cricket matches during a tour of England and Ireland. Earlier, in July, a baseball tournament in Watertown, N.Y., attracted 14 amateur clubs from the United States and Canada to a competition that was marred only by baseball's perennial enemy – rain.

Women were active in the sports arena. In the spring of 1874, Mary Ewing Outerbridge introduced lawn tennis to the United States. Remembering a game she had seen while visiting Bermuda, she set up a net on the grounds of the Staten Island Cricket and Baseball Club and, with a friend, played the first game of tennis in the United States. In July, Sophie Stevens won the gold opera chain offered as first prize in a "ladies' swimming contest" held at Fort Hamilton Beach, N.Y.

The music gourmets, like the sportsmen, found much to whet the appetite in 1874. Johann Strauss's *Die Fledermaus* made its U.S. debut at New York City's Thalia Theatre on November 21. In March, the first performance of Johann Sebastian Bach's *The Passion According to St. Matthew* was given its U.S. première (in part) by the Cecilia Society of Boston. Richard Wagner's *Lohengrin* was added to the repertory of the prestigious New York Academy of Music on March 23.

Other musical treats were offered the public in 1874. Bach's *Christmas Oratorio* was presented in England for the first time in Christ Church Cathedral, Oxford, as the anthem for a special service. Giuseppe Verdi's *Requiem Mass*, written to commemorate the death of the Italian author Alessandro Manzoni, was sung in Milan, Italy, on May 22. The international hit concert of the year – from a gourmand's viewpoint – was a mammoth soundfest given in Rome's Piazza del Popolo in June. About 3,500 musicians, representing all of the city's military bands, united under one baton and blared martial airs for the hordes of tourists who had invaded the city.

The literary world, at home and abroad, was agog with news of the trials and tribulations to which Russia's Alexander Solzhenitsyn, winner of a Nobel Prize for literature, was subjected by the Kremlin regime in 1974. But the literary world of 1874 was equally aroused by Ralph Waldo Emerson's criticism of Algernon Charles Swinburne's poetry. His characterization of it as "smutty" touched off a transatlantic controversy.

Controversy notwithstanding, the year produced some tasty literary morsels. Among them was Francis Parkman's *The Old Regime in Canada*, a volume in his great cycle of histories about the struggle of the English and French for the North American dominion. Edward Eggleston published *The Circuit Rider*, a major novel about a pioneer preacher whose pulpit was the saddle of his horse. Another best seller was *Professor Fowler's Great Work on Manhood, Womanhood and their mutual interrelations; Love, its Laws, Power, etc.* Intriguingly enough, it was available by mail only; the publishers sent it in a plain envelope.

The other arts flourished in 1874, notably in France, where Rosa Bonheur was decorated with the French Cross of the Legion of Honor for her celebrated canvases, including *The Horse Fair*. Other French artists fared less well, including Claude Monet, Pierre Renoir, Camille Pissarro and their friends who rented a place on the Boulevard des Italiens in Paris to exhibit their work—which no reputable gallery would show. One critic, looking at a Monet oil that represented Le Havre harbor at sunrise and that was titled *Impression*, derisively spoke of all the paintings on exhibit as "impressionism." Ironically, that word would eventually name the most popular movement in modern art history.

For those who preferred to satisfy their aesthetic appetites with drama, the theater was alive and well. In March, Lotta Crabtree opened a three-week run in Fred Marsden's *Zip* at Booth's Theatre in New York City. Joseph Jefferson, a Philadelphian, was touring in *Rip Van Winkle*. As a showplace with international flavor, a Colosseum modeled after its London namesake opened on January 10 in New York City. Inside, it presented cycloramas of London and Paris. Outside, for passers-by, the bells in the tower pealed the St. Paul and Westminster chimes. The building had a third, built-in asset: It was considered the biggest cast-iron structure in America.

European stars, sometimes known as "scenery chewers," because of their histrionic techniques, were popular on the international circuit in 1874. Among them was Sarah Bernhardt, a rising young actress who was growing restive under contract to the Comédie Française in Paris. On Aug. 6, 1874, a not yet "divine" Sarah opened in a drama by Voltaire in which she played the title role, Zaïre. One hundred years later, there would be an African country by that name.

Many people in 1874, however, took a dim view of any pursuits other than those calculated to satisfy man's spiritual needs. For them, "soul" food was the essential ingredient of life. A newly founded sect in Philadelphia was thriving under Charles Taze (Pastor) Russell who preached that the millennium (the period of the Second Advent of Christ) had begun invisibly in 1874. His followers, who were known as Russellites or Millennial Dawnists (after his book *Millennial Dawn*), helped spread his teachings through a publication entitled the *Watchtower*. Today, they are known as Jehovah's Witnesses.

Two dedicated Protestants pooled their efforts in 1874 to establish a center in the United States where Bible instruction would be readily available to Sunday school teachers. One was John Heyl Vincent, a Methodist minister who also edited the Methodist *Sunday School Journal*. The other was Lewis Miller, an Akron, Ohio, mill owner, inventor, and philanthropist. Working tirelessly, the two men eventually established a center at Fair Point, a piece of land jutting out slightly into Chautauqua Lake in western New York. Opening-day ceremonies were attended by 142 Sunday school teachers from 25 states, as well as Canada, Ireland, Scotland, and India. In the decades to come,

A spectacular performance of Richard Wagner's *Lohengrin* at the New York
Academy of Music on March 23, 1874, won plaudits from lovers of grand opera.

Professional baseball won international exposure in 1874 when the championship
Boston team joined the Philadelphia Athletics on a trailblazing tour of Europe.

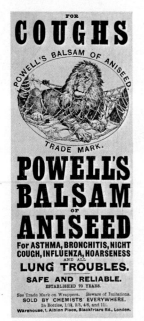

FOR

COUGHS

POWELL'S BALSAM OF ANISEED

TRADE MARK.

POWELL'S
BALSAM
OF
ANISEED

**For ASTHMA, BRONCHITIS, NIGHT
COUGH, INFLUENZA, HOARSENESS**
AND ALL
LUNG TROUBLES.
SAFE AND RELIABLE.
ESTABLISHED 70 YEARS.

See Trade Mark on Wrappers.   Beware of Imitations.
SOLD BY CHEMISTS EVERYWHERE.
In Bottles, 1/1½, 2/3, 4/6, and 11/.
Warehouse, 1, Albion Place, Blackfriars Rd., London.

Herbs were a basic
ingredient of patent
medicines. Their
cure-all claims were
as extravagant as
their trademarks.

the Chautauqua system, as well as the Tent Chautauquas, would mold the tastes of America.

Hinduism was enjoying a widespread vogue in the Western world in 1874, thanks to the teachings of one Swami Dayananda Saravasti, a forerunner of today's Maharaj Ji. In England, a group known as Cabalists were dabbling in occultism; in Italy, readers enjoyed *The Journals of the Disciples of Satan*, reportedly owned by the Mafia.

Religious beliefs may have been varied, but hearth and home, then as now, remained stable. For most homemakers, domestic considerations took precedence over all issues. Many, even as today, had domestic or personal problems; consequently, they turned to the increasingly popular advice columns that were becoming fixtures in the popular press. Today's anguished readers address their woeful pleas for guidance to Dear Abby or Ann Landers. In 1874, the expert to consult was Jenny June. Her columns of advice, which ran in *Demorest's* magazine, were wide ranging and not to be taken lightly. Female readers were told how to entertain a gentleman caller or resnare an errant husband. Youngsters were advised that pimples could be eliminated by breakfasting daily on cold oatmeal topped with cranberry sauce.

Physical pain, as opposed to mental anguish, required a different approach. No medicine chest could be considered up to date in 1974 unless it reflected the current rage for products containing herbal essences. But in 1874, herbs were already in vogue. Pennyroyal and St.-John's-wort were strong-scented, highly prized herbs admired for their medicinal properties. The well-stocked medicine chest was sure to have a bottle of *Dr. Wm. Hall's Balsam for the Lungs,* known parenthetically as "the great American consumptive remedy." As an all-around performer, the balsam-based panacea also promised "to cure coughs, colds, pneumonia, bronchitis, asthma, spitting of blood, croup, and whooping cough." Bitter-tasting tamarind seeds were a favorite cathartic; only a few critical viewers were aware of this while watching a movie titled *The Tamarind Seed* a hundred years later.

Through it all, the average man a hundred years ago retained his sense of humor as a way of coping. "Bread rises faster when leavened with the salt of wit," runs an old adage, and most people in 1874 obeyed the saying with gusto. "If a Bedouin had all his teeth pulled," went a joke much favored in vaudeville routines, "what language would he speak?" The answer: gum-Arabic. One that tickled everyone's fancy appeared in *Leslie's Illustrated Weekly Newspaper* toward the close of 1874. It was widely reprinted in the English-language periodicals of the day. "The woman who made a pound of butter from the cream of a joke," ran the gag, "and a cheese from the milk of human kindness, has now washed the close of a year and hung it out to dry on a beeline. She did it with tongue-in-chic."

This reassuring ability to smile despite a plethora of problems, including inflation, labor difficulties, and fuel shortages, gives the student of history—present or past—ample food for thought.

The Year On File, 1974

Contributors to THE WORLD BOOK YEAR BOOK report on the major developments of 1974 in their respective fields. The names of these contributors appear at the end of the articles they have written. A complete roster of contributors, giving their professional affiliations and listing the articles they have prepared, appears on pages 6 and 7.

Articles in this section are alphabetically arranged by subject matter. In most cases, titles refer directly to articles in THE WORLD BOOK ENCYCLOPEDIA. Numerous cross references (in bold type) are a part of this alphabetical listing. Their function is to guide the reader to a subject or to information that may be a part of some other article, or that may appear under an alternative title. *See* and *See also* cross references appear within and at the end of articles and similarly direct the reader to related information contained elsewhere in THE YEAR BOOK.

ADVERTISING

ADVERTISING. The U.S. advertising business, beset by inflation, had a sluggish year in 1974. Early estimates from McCann-Erickson's media department showed that spending for advertising in the United States increased 5.9 per cent to about $26.5 billion. But the increase came almost entirely from media rate boosts, not increased advertising.

The rate increases sent many advertisers scurrying to find better media buys to ease the sting. Available daytime television time for the fourth quarter was already scarce by midyear. Some sponsors appeared to have fled to daytime TV to escape big price hikes in evening prime-time rates. There were also delays in selling prime time. But the year's final figures were expected to show network television with an 8 per cent gain in dollar revenue over 1973, the biggest increase of all major media. Spot TV advertising, on the other hand, was up only about 4 per cent, primarily due to price hikes.

Inflation Fighters. The government in 1974 favored a slight moderation in consumer spending to combat inflation. One question was whether advertisers and retailers, whose function is to sell goods and services at a profit, should cut back on advertising to dampen spending. Understandably, most advertisers resolved to hold the line on advertising in the conviction that cutbacks in ad spending would not help the fight against inflation.

Antismoking warnings continue to receive top priority in public service ads from such groups as the American Heart Association.

Herbert Stein, chairman of the Council on Economic Advisers, offered an alternative in August. He urged advertisers to help the inflation fight by stressing price in their advertising. "It would be good for the economy if consumers reward sellers who offer the best values," he said. "Since consumers don't know who has the best values, this is where advertising can help."

Many advertisers took that tack. Within weeks after Stein's suggestions, Sears, Roebuck and Company announced it would conduct an aggresive national price promotion effort in the fall. Sears, which spends an estimated $470 million on advertising annually, traditionally had used its national efforts to build its image or establish brand names. Price advertising was left to the local stores. Other giant retailers also stressed price advertising.

Others pushing price in their ads included the Gillette Company, which ran TV commercials saying its White Rain shampoo cost less than other brands; General Mills, whose new ads for Hamburger Helper pointed out the price per serving was only 50 cents, including the ground beef; and Black & Decker, which ran TV spots showing that four of its products cost less today than comparable models of eight to 10 years ago.

Leading Advertisers. Compilations by *Advertising Age* showed that nine of the 10 largest national advertisers in the United States had increased their advertising expenditures as they entered 1974 (one held even), and nine of the top 10 advertising agencies had increased their billings. The U.S. government joined the top 10 national advertisers for the first time, spending about $99 million in 1973.

Oil Advertising. One category that cut back its ad spending was the oil industry. Federal Energy Administration chief John C. Sawhill warned the 20 major oil companies in mid-August that a return to "hard-sell tactics" for gasoline and other petroleum products might force his office to take "strong action to curb" such activity.

Until then, no such warning appeared necessary. The biggest oil companies all had cut ad expenditures during the previous year as their price hikes and windfall profits during the gas shortage prompted them to assume a low profile. All three oil companies on *Advertising Age*'s list of the 100 largest national advertisers – Exxon Corporation, Shell Oil Corporation, and Standard Oil Company of Indiana – reduced advertising in 1973. Three others previously on the list – Texaco, Mobil Oil Corporation, and Gulf Oil Corporation – dropped off the list entirely.

Although the oil companies reduced their gasoline advertising earlier in 1974, this policy appeared to change with October and November campaigns for lead-free gas. In the vanguard was Amoco Oil Company with multipage color inserts in newspapers and magazines and TV spots explaining the catalytic converters on new cars and the reported benefits of lead-free gas. The drive replaced a TV campaign for tires, batteries, and accessories, but Paul D. Collier, Amoco manager of merchandising, said the intent was educational, not "to promote gasoline per se."

The Federal Trade Commission (FTC) released a rash of complaints and consent settlements against gas-mileage claims made by automobile makers. The FTC accused General Motors and Chrysler Corporation of distorting gas economy test results. General Motors was accused of misrepresenting Environmental Protection Agency tests for the Cadillac Eldorado. Chrysler was said to have misstated the relative performance of Chryslers and Chevrolet Novas.

The FTC also proposed a ban on premiums in TV cereal ads directed at children. The cereal industry proposed a self-regulatory plan as an alternative, but this appeared to make little impression on consumerists and the FTC. In other action, the Federal Communications Commission urged TV stations to separate advertising and program content on children's shows.

A study by the American Association of Advertising Agencies showed that agency net profit increased for the second year in a row, to 3.87 per cent of gross income in 1973, up from 3.62 per cent in 1972. A further rise was expected in 1974. Biggest account shift of the year occurred when Uniroyal moved its $10-million tire account from Doyle Dane Bernbach to Ogilvy & Mather.   Merle Kingman

AFGHANISTAN. The government of President Mohammad Daoud marked economic gains and held broad public support in 1974, its first year in power. There was no effective organized opposition to the republican regime.

The tranquil political climate enabled Daoud to continue planned economic development and the elimination of governmental corruption. A one-year plan went into effect on July 16, the republic's first anniversary. It envisaged government investment of $99 million, 43 per cent of it drawn from foreign sources. An end to the three-year drought and a 14 per cent increase in exports were encouraging signs.

Petroleum deposits estimated at 7 million short tons (6 million metric tons) were discovered in May in Jowzjan Province as well as a new natural gas field with about 400 billion cubic feet (11.3 billion cubic meters) of reserves. Russia, major purchaser of Afghan gas, agreed in July to purchase 100 billion cubic feet (2.8 billion cubic meters) at 34 cents per 1,000 cubic feet (28 cubic meters), an increase of $14\frac{1}{2}$ cents, effective October 1. A five-year Soviet-Afghan aid agreement signed on August 30 committed Russia to expand production of Afghanistan's Jeraqduq gas field. A Russian-built thermal power plant at Mazar-i-Sharif went into operation on August 9, giving that impoverished area 36,000 kilowatts of new power.   William Spencer

See also ASIA (Facts in Brief Table).

Be your own keeper.

It would be great if we could protect you and your family from accidents, but all we can do is remind you to take time to be safe. If you want to be your brother's keeper, start with yourself.

National Safety Council

GREEN CROSS FOR SAFETY · NATIONAL SAFETY COUNCIL

If you don't like thinking about safety, think where you'd be without it.

The National Safety Council broadened its public service ad campaign in 1974 to caution against all types of accidents.

AFRICA. Black African nationalists won a monumental victory in 1974 when Portugal granted independence to its African colonies. A six-year drought in nations south of the Sahara continued to wipe out cattle and crops, forcing starving human beings to leave their homes. African plans for agricultural development were at least temporarily thwarted by the high price of oil.

Portuguese Turnabout. In February, General António de Spínola, deputy chief of the general staff and a former commander of Portuguese forces in Guinea-Bissau, published a book stating that Portugal could not defeat the black nationalist guerrillas in Angola, Guinea-Bissau, and Mozambique. He advocated making these African holdings states in a Federal Republic of Portugal.

Spínola was fired. But army officers overthrew the Portuguese government on April 25, and the new government eventually decided to grant full independence to the colonies. See PORTUGAL.

Independence Problems. On September 10, Guinea-Bissau became the first to gain independence. Because Guinea-Bissau's liberation movement was united, it was able to negotiate a settlement with Portugal. See GUINEA-BISSAU.

But Angola and Mozambique, which border on white-ruled Rhodesia and South Africa, presented thorny problems. The black liberation movement in Mozambique was united and agreed to independence in 1975. But a large class of white settlers objected to the independence agreement and began rioting in September. See MOZAMBIQUE.

Angola's liberation movement was divided into three main factions, each claiming to be the sole representative of the people. So there was no strong, united group to negotiate with Portugal. Angola also has a large white population. To complicate the matter, Cabinda, an oil-rich enclave, asked to negotiate a separate independence agreement with Portugal. See ANGOLA.

Isolated White Minorities. The fall of Portuguese colonialism radically altered the balance of power between black- and white-ruled African nations. Except for a small common border with South Africa, Rhodesia is completely surrounded by black nations. Consequently, Rhodesia's white-minority government was anxious to reach a settlement with the nation's black population. It made some progress in December, including a cease-fire with nationalist guerrillas. While South Africa's security was not seriously threatened, its white-minority government was concerned about maintaining economic ties with the new black government in Mozambique. See RHODESIA; SOUTH AFRICA.

Sahelian Drought. The drought in the nations just south of the Sahara, in a desolate zone known as

A camel caravan, sponsored by the United Nations Food and Agriculture Organization, carries food to remote drought-stricken areas of Niger.

Tanzanian Prime Minister Rashidi Kawawa leans from a train to greet
Chinese engineers who worked on the Great Uhuru Railway link with Zambia.

the Sahel, continued. It took its toll not only in starvation and malnutrition, but also in disrupted social patterns among nomadic people, who suffered immense cattle losses. The drought was most severe in Chad, Ethiopia, Mali, Mauritania, Niger, Senegal, and Upper Volta, but its effects were felt in many other African nations. Observers estimated in September that drought would destroy about 40 per cent of Zambia's maize crop. Ivory Coast's coffee crop dropped an estimated 30 per cent, and coffee production in Kenya and Tanzania also was down. In addition, Tanzania alone lost about 250,000 head of cattle to the drought.

Some scientists speculated that the drought signaled a permanent climatic change in the area. However, significant amounts of rain had fallen by June in many parts of the Sahel. Ironically, two drought-stricken nations – Mali and Niger – suffered from flooding caused by heavy summer rains.

The United Nations (UN) Food and Agricultural Organization reported in August that more than 3.5-million head of cattle died of hunger and thirst in the Sahel during 1973. Although estimates varied, more than a million persons may have died and up to 5-million may have been driven from their homelands by the drought.

According to the UN, 17 of the 39 nations south of the Sahara were affected by the drought and many of these countries were threatened with bankruptcy

and starvation. The people of 20 African nations had dangerously low average calorie intakes. Some of these people were already below the recommended daily minimum calorie intake, and others ran the risk of being forced below it by a combination of natural disaster and soaring grain, fertilizer, and oil prices.

The Oil Crisis. Africa also had to contend with oil shortages during the year, and the price of oil contributed to high inflation rates, which reached 40 per cent in some countries. High oil prices also promised future hardships, threatening to wreck African agricultural plans. These developing countries place a high priority on agricultural development and the Green Revolution of high-yield grains. But for this, they need large quantities of chemical fertilizers, which are made from petroleum products.

The Arab nations refused to sell oil to African nations at reduced prices. However, the Arabs guaranteed Africa a steady supply of oil and established a $200-million African Development Fund for making loans to purchase oil. Nevertheless, this did not promise to eliminate the African oil crisis.

The increased value of oil made oil exploration a major preoccupation on the African continent. Exxon Corporation and Texaco, Incorporated, planned a joint oil and natural gas drilling project in Mali and Mauritania. Exploratory drilling by U.S. interests was underway in Chad, and U.S. companies got permission in July to search for oil in the northeastern part of Kenya.

There were disagreements between various African governments and foreign oil companies over how to exploit oil deposits. In May, Cameroon warned foreign oil companies that the government would revoke their licenses to operate if they attempted to put Cameroon's oil resources "on reserve" instead of developing them rapidly. Dahomey nullified a 10-year-old agreement with Union Oil Company, claiming that the company had deliberately delayed bringing an oil deposit into production. Nigeria and Zaire began nationalizing their oil industries.

Arab Relations. African nations had hoped that they could win oil concessions from Arab oil-exporting nations by taking a united pro-Arab stance on the Middle East. Four nations–Botswana, Ivory Coast, Kenya, and Liberia–had cut diplomatic ties with Israel in 1973, as the oil crisis loomed.

However, the African nations became increasingly disappointed by the lack of Arab response. In June, a Kenyan government official said that Kenya had not benefited by its break with Israel. Kenya had lost Israeli foreign aid but had not gained any concessions from the Arabs on oil prices. This indicated that Kenya might reconsider its pro-Arab position. See KENYA; MIDDLE EAST.

Portugal's Dwindling Empire

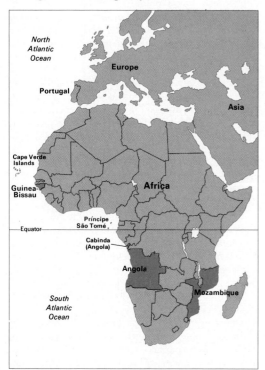

Oil politics were a major factor in tension over what many black African nations saw as increasing Arab influence in the Organization of African Unity (OAU). The issue surfaced at the OAU summit meeting held in Mogadishu, Somalia, in June. The Somali candidate for secretary-general was opposed by many African nations because Somalia had joined the Arab League in February. A long-standing territorial dispute between Ethiopia and Somalia also complicated the matter. After 18 ballots failed to break a deadlock between the Somali and Zambian candidates, a compromise nominee, William Eteki Mboumoua of Cameroon, was elected unanimously. He replaced Nzo Ekangaki, who had resigned.

Egypt and Zambia announced in March they were considering setting up a copper-manufacturing company in the Suez Canal area. Copper provides more than 90 per cent of Zambia's export earnings. Most of the copper is sent to Europe for manufacture. But it would cost less to transport the copper to Egyptian factories on the new Tanzania-Zambia railroad and through the Suez Canal, which was scheduled to reopen in 1975.

Far Eastern Relations. Japan and the People's Republic of China played increasingly important roles in African affairs. Japan, in need of raw materials for its industry, expanded its investments in the minerals and other resources of black Africa.

However, Japan's relations with black nations were complicated by expanding Japanese trade with the white-minority-ruled nations of Rhodesia and South Africa. The OAU charged that Japan was the "most notorious sanctions buster" of the UN's trade embargo against Rhodesia. As a result, the Japanese government considered reducing trade with South Africa and cutting off trade with Rhodesia.

China continued to supply aid to black African nations. Senegal received a $48-million, interest-free loan for agricultural diversification, and Tanzania got $77.5 million to develop coal and iron-ore deposits. China had already supplied Tanzania with funds and the technical aid needed to build the Tanzania-Zambia railroad. China and the Malagasy Republic signed economic cooperation agreements on January 18, and China reportedly continued secret military aid to black nationalist guerrillas during the year.

Nationalization Policies. Several African nations began taking economic control of industries away from foreigners. Togo nationalized a multinational phosphate company in January. President Gnassingbe Eyadema was almost killed in a plane crash shortly after he announced that Togo would take a 51 per cent share in the company. The Togolese government claimed the plane crash was a murder attempt by the company.

In July, Gabon took a controlling interest in a proposed iron-ore project involving the United States, and French, West German, and other Euro-

Facts in Brief on African Political Units

Country	Population	Government	Monetary Unit*	Foreign Trade (million U.S. $) Exports	Imports
Algeria	16,930,000	President Houari Boumediene	dinar (4.18 = $1)	1,802	2,338
Angola	6,111,000	Governor General Silvino Silverio Marques	escudo (24.7 = $1)	499	436
Botswana	750,000	President Sir Seretse Khama	rand (1 = $1.45)	42	75
Burundi	3,913,000	President & Prime Minister Michel Micombero	franc (78.8 = $1)	30	32
Cameroon	6,168,000	President Ahmadou Ahidjo	CFA franc (234.75 = $1)	353	335
Central African Republic	1,786,000	President of the Government Jean Bedel Bokassa; Premier Elizabeth Domitien	CFA franc (234.75 = $1)	36	39
Chad	4,022,000	President N'Garta Tombalbaye	CFA franc (234.75 = $1)	39	63
Congo	1,043,000	President Marien N'Gouabi; Prime Minister Henri Lopes	CFA franc (234.75 = $1)	47	93
Dahomey	3,048,000	President & Premier Mathieu Kerekou	CFA franc (234.75 = $1)	47	86
Egypt	37,519,000	President Anwar al-Sadat; Prime Minister Abdul Aziz Hegazi	pound (1 = $2.56)	1,119	905
Equatorial Guinea	301,000	President Francisco Macias Nguema	ekpwele (56.8 = $1)	23	9
Ethiopia	27,436,000	Military Administrative Committee Chairman Brigadier General Teferi Benti	dollar (2.07 = $1)	240	215
Gabon	531,000	President Omar Bongo	CFA franc (234.75 = $1)	241	142
Gambia	402,000	President Sir Dawda Kairaba Jawara	dalasi (1.72 = $1)	24	32
Ghana	9,904,000	National Redemption Council Chairman Ignatius Kutu Acheampong	new cedi (1.17 = $1)	393	293
Guinea	4,400,000	President Ahmed Sekou Toure; Prime Minister Lansana Beavogui	sily (20.5 = $1)	58	70
Guinea-Bissau	467,000	President Luis de Almeida Cabral	escudo (24.7 = $1)	no statistics available	
Ivory Coast	4,864,000	President Felix Houphouet-Boigny	CFA franc (234.75 = $1)	857	710
Kenya	13,421,000	President Jomo Kenyatta	shilling (7.14 = $1)	461	615
Lesotho	1,038,000	King Motlotlehi Moshoeshoe II; Prime Minister Leabua Jonathan	rand (1 = $1.45)	5	32
Liberia	1,788,000	President William R. Tolbert	dollar (1 = $1)	289	193
Libya	2,320,000	Revolutionary Command Council President Muammar Muhammad al-Qadhaafi; Prime Minister Abd al-Salam Jallud	dinar (1 = $3.38)	2,308	1,038
Malagasy	7,563,000	President Gabriel Ramanantsoa	franc (234.75 = $1)	203	203
Malawi	5,044,000	President H. Kamuzu Banda	kwacha (1 = $1.19)	96	141
Mali	5,582,000	President & Prime Minister Moussa Traore	franc (469.5 = $1)	40	92
Mauritania	1,313,000	President Moktar Ould Daddah	ouguiya (47 = $1)	100	69
Mauritius	878,000	Governor General Sir Abdul Raman Osman; Prime Minister Sir Seewoosagur Ramgoolam	rupee (5.7 = $1)	132	171
Morocco	17,047,000	King Hassan II; Prime Minister Ahmed Osman	dirham (4.2 = $1)	634	765
Mozambique	9,164,000	High Commissioner Victor Crespo; Prime Minister Joaquin Chissano	escudo (24.7 = $1)	175	327
Namibia (South West Africa)	891,000	Administrator B. J. van der Walt	rand (1 = $1.45)	no statistics available	
Niger	4,547,000	Supreme Military Council President Seyni Kountche	CFA franc (234.75 = $1)	57	68
Nigeria	62,481,000	Federal Military Government Head Yakubu Gowon	naira (1 = $1.52)	3,358	1,874
Rhodesia	6,272,000	President Clifford Dupont; Prime Minister Ian D. Smith	dollar (1 = $1.68)	499	453
Rwanda	4,299,000	President Juvenal Habyarimana	franc (92.8 = $1)	31	32
Senegal	4,424,000	President Leopold Sedar Senghor; Prime Minister Abdou Diouf	CFA franc (234.75 = $1)	194	360
Sierra Leone	2,750,000	President Siaka P. Stevens; Prime Minister Sorie Ibrahim Koroma	leone (1 = $1.17)	132	158
Somalia	3,148,000	Supreme Revolutionary Council President Mohamed Siad Barre	shilling (6.3 = $1)	39	121
South Africa, Republic of	25,268,000	President Jacobus Johannes Fouche; Prime Minister Balthazar Johannes Vorster	rand (1 = $1.45)	3,528	5,397
Sudan	17,862,000	President Sayed Gaafar Mohamed Nimeiri	pound (1 = $2.87)	434	436
Swaziland	464,000	King Sobhuza II; Prime Minister Makhosini Dlamini	rand (1 = $1.45)	70	60
Tanzania	15,094,000	President Julius K. Nyerere; Prime Minister Rashidi Kawawa	shilling (7.14 = $1)	368	425
Togo	2,257,000	President Gnassingbe Eyadema	CFA franc (234.75 = $1)	57	95
Tunisia	5,743,000	President Habib Bourguiba; Prime Minister Hedi Nouira	dinar (1 = $2.29)	386	608
Uganda	11,363,000	President Idi Amin Dada	shilling (7.14 = $1)	326	162
Upper Volta	5,971,000	President & Prime Minister Sangoule Lamizana	CFA franc (234.75 = $1)	21	62
Zaire	25,640,000	President Mobutu Sese Seko	zaire (1 = $2.00)	684	626
Zambia	4,774,000	President Kenneth David Kaunda; Prime Minister M. Mainza Chona	kwacha (1 = $1.56)	1,142	604

*Exchange rates as of Dec. 2, 1974

189

pean interests. Gabon also intended to seek funds for a railroad that would link its major iron-ore deposits with Atlantic Ocean ports.

Zaire began giving its citizens control over foreign-owned operations and nationalized several oil companies. However, foreigners were invited to stay on as managers. Nigeria and Kenya also pursued local-control programs. See NIGERIA; ZAIRE.

Military Regimes. Coups increased the number of African nations ruled by military regimes. The military in Ethiopia carried out a coup that began in February, when army units mutinied and forced the Cabinet to resign, and ended on September 12, when Emperor Haile Selassie I was deposed.

One of the major causes of the revolt was Ethiopia's feudal tenant-farmer system. The system's hardships on the peasants were aggravated by the drought. The military also accused Selassie's government of widespread corruption. See ETHIOPIA.

A military coup headed by Lieutenant Colonel Seyni Kountche toppled the civilian government of President Hamani Diori in Niger on April 15. The military said they had acted because Diori had failed to deal effectively with the suffering caused by the six-year drought. See NIGER.

Claiming that "politicians playing politics" were hampering attempts to strengthen the nation's drought-ravaged economy, President Sangoule Lamizana of Upper Volta announced an army takeover on February 8. He suspended the Constitution and dissolved Parliament. Lamizana remained as president.

Nigeria's military government had promised a return to civilian rule by 1976. However, on October 1, President Yakubu Gowon postponed the end of military rule, saying he feared a return to "the old cutthroat politics."

Mali citizens overwhelmingly voted their approval on June 2 for a new Constitution that will eventually bring back civilian rule. Mali has been ruled by a military regime headed by Moussa Traore since 1968. The Constitution provides for a single political party, a president, a national legislature, and five more years of military rule.

In January, political opponents attempted to overthrow Lesotho's Prime Minister Leabua Jonathan. The coup failed, and by March, hundreds of opposition party supporters reportedly had been killed. The Lesotho government introduced a law forbidding foreign aid to political parties in Lesotho.

There were continuing reports during 1974 of torture and murder under the Uganda military regime headed by Idi Amin Dada. One escaped prisoner charged in December that cannibalism was practiced in prison camps and that prisoners were forced to kill other prisoners.

Student unrest was widespread during 1974. There were demonstrations in Congo, Dahomey, Ethiopia, Kenya, and Nigeria.   John Storm Roberts

AGRICULTURE. Problems plagued world agriculture in 1974. The most trying ranged from unfavorable weather, overwhelming food demands, and expensive, often scarce fertilizer and other production necessities to complaints about high food prices, drastically fluctuating farm prices, and relatively lower farm incomes.

Weather problems have harassed farmers in many parts of the world for a number of growing seasons. There has been a six-year drought in Africa, plus droughts in Australia, India, and Russia–and a shift in ocean currents temporarily halted Peruvian anchovy fishing. Primary causes of the gloomy 1974 picture were dry summers and early frosts in the United States and Canada and severe floods in Bangladesh and widespread droughts in Africa and India. A drought in the Southwestern United States cut into pasture, grain sorghum, and feed production in 1974. Corn Belt farmers experienced the worst farming weather in 40 years: Heavy spring rains delayed planting; a bad drought raised havoc in midseason; and several early frosts damaged unharvested crops and further cut production estimates.

World Production stayed about the same as in 1973, based on preliminary estimates. Despite declines in the United States, Canada, Russia, and southern Asia, there were increases in other areas, especially Africa, eastern and western Asia, and Latin America.

However, food production and especially percapita food production declined. Preliminary estimates placed total world grain output at 1.24 billion short tons (1.12 billion metric tons), down 40.8 million short tons (37 million metric tons) from the record high set last year.

Livestock production was up after the sharp drop in 1973, but lower prices and higher feed costs caused by short grain supplies caused economic problems for livestock producers in most parts of the world.

Coffee production jumped by more than 25 per cent to the highest level since 1966.

World food demands on U.S. farmers were highlighted at the World Food Conference in Rome in November. The United States was sharply criticized for eating too much and not sharing enough with the world's hungry people. Already criticized for high food prices, partly because of a liberal food-export policy, U.S. farmers felt misunderstood and caught in the middle.

High Food Prices brought consumer resistance in the United States, which worried farmers, especially in the face of growing livestock supplies. "Consumers in this country and around the world are trimming back their budgets and often their diet expectations," said Assistant Secretary of Agriculture Clayton K. Yeutter on September 26. "They are spending more of their incomes for gasoline, the electric bill, and medical care, which makes it difficult to spend more for food, too."

Kansas cornfield shows the disastrous effects
of Midwest drought. Dry weather and early
frosts reduced U.S. corn and soybean crops.

Skyrocketing prices and middleman profits for some items, such as sugar, incensed both consumers and farmers. Price variations made commodity markets suspect. At least four legislative proposals were offered for revising and strengthening federal regulation of futures markets, and Congress passed, and President Gerald R. Ford signed, the Commodity Futures Trading Commission Act of 1974 in October.

Farm income, estimated at $27 billion in 1974, was down $5 billion from the 1973 record. Incomes varied greatly among farmers. Especially hard hit were crop farmers, whose harvests were reduced by drought, and cattle feeders, many of whom went bankrupt. Total sales by farmers rose in 1974, but the increased revenues were more than offset by the sharply higher fuel, fertilizer, and feed costs that farmers had to pay.

Livestock Production. Sharply reduced feed-grain supplies hit U.S. livestock producers especially hard. The feed grain supply was the lowest since 1957, yet farmers had to feed 40 per cent more cattle, 80 per cent more poultry, and 8 per cent more hogs than in that year. Only dairy cattle showed a decline, down 40 per cent from 1957.

AGRICULTURE

The high livestock prices of recent years plus early optimistic estimates of 1974 crop production resulted in expanded livestock production. Thus, the output of such major meat items as beef, pork, and chicken equaled or surpassed 1973 levels. The tight feed-grain supply that developed later, however, curtailed livestock production in several areas. Late in the year, 7 per cent fewer sows were farrowing than at the same time in 1973, and further decline was expected in 1975. Increased beef slaughter resulted largely from slaughter of range animals, which are fed little or no grain. This rising proportion of range cattle reflects the lack of profit in cattle feeding. Cattle-on-feed inventories in late 1974 were the lowest in over six years, and a number of marginal feed-lot operations ceased production altogether.

U.S. Crop Production dropped off sharply. The effect of weather was dramatically reflected in United States Department of Agriculture (USDA) forecasts of 1974 corn production as successive onslaughts of unfavorable weather steadily reduced expected output:

Predicting Bad News

Date	Crop Forecast (billion bushels)
March 15	6.7
July 1	6.4
September 1	5.0
November 1	4.6

The all-crops production index stood at 110 (1967=100), compared with an index of 120 for 1973 and 113 for 1972. The chief decline came in feed grains (corn, oats, barley, sorghum), which fell from a 1973 index of 115 to only 92.

The American crop picture was not all gloomy, however. Production of food grains (wheat, rye, rice), spurred by record wheat and rice crops, rose 5 per cent to an index of 119, up from 113 in 1973. Vegetables, fruits and nuts, and tobacco production also rose over 1973 levels.

Farm Prices showed a mixed trend. Prices received for crops, spurred by the small harvest, were generally above 1973 levels, but livestock prices were down substantially. The November 15 index of prices received by farmers was 182 (1967=100), up from 181 in 1973.

The index of prices paid by farmers, however, rose sharply from a 1973 index of 152 to 178.

U.S. Agricultural Exports, following a 60 per cent increase to $12.9 billion in 1973, rose another 65 per cent in 1974 to $21.3 billion. The unprecedented rise resulted primarily from sharply higher prices, but it also reflected an increase from 92 million short tons (83 million metric tons) in 1973 to over 100 million short tons (91 million metric tons), compared to only 55 million short tons (50 million metric tons) in 1970. Exports of crop items amounted to 43 per cent of farmers' cash receipts for crop items

in 1974. The following table shows those items for which the volume of exports was at least 40 per cent of production in 1974:

Exported Crops

Product	Per cent of Production	
	1973	1974
Rye	33	102*
Wheat	77	67
Dry edible peas	85	59
Dry whole milk	63	56
Rice (rough)	69	52
Cattle hides (whole)	52	48
Soybeans	56	47
Tallow	40	45
Almonds	40	45
Cotton	34	44
Tobacco	36	41

*Includes export of carry-over production from 1973.

The high level of exports created a record $11.3-billion agricultural trade surplus, despite a 30 per cent gain in agricultural imports to $9.5 billion, also a record.

United States farm exports totaled over $1 billion to each of four major markets—Japan, West Germany, the Netherlands, and Canada. Japan, the leading buyer of U.S. products, purchased more than $3 billion in farm products, an increase of 49 per cent.

Exports to the People's Republic of China increased fourfold to $852 million. Most of the purchases were in wheat ($317 million), corn ($189 million), cotton ($188 million), and soybeans ($142-million).

Federal Farm Policy was the same market-oriented, expanded trade policy that has kept Secretary of Agriculture Earl L. Butz in the news since 1972. As the year ended, some wavering from this trade policy was in evidence. The sharp reduction in U.S. production of feed grains, and consumer clamor, brought pressure to limit food exports. President Ford personally stopped a $500-million corn and wheat export commitment to Russia on October 3. Federal approval procedures of export sales were substantially tightened and sales were closely monitored by the White House at year's end.

Community development programs continued to be emphasized. Assistant Secretary of Agriculture Will Erwin said on August 7 that the USDA's Farmers Home Administration put $3.6 billion in loans into rural areas to "improve living conditions and enhance employment opportunities" in fiscal 1974. Under the Rural Development Act, nearly $1.8 billion went to construct, purchase, and improve more than 100,000 homes and apartments for rural residents of low and medium income. Loans were also made for the construction of water and waste-disposal systems for rural families.

Butz summed up his policy on September 22:

"Our national agricultural policy will continue to assure farmers of as little government control over production and marketing as possible. Our national policy will continue to assure competitive access to world markets for U.S. agriculture." He defended the program with pride, pointing out that he had eliminated more than 75 per cent of the $4-billion annual subsidy to farmers and had made a net contribution to the fiscal 1974 balance of payments of $11.3 billion – 25 per cent above fiscal 1973. Yeutter contended on November 25 that "food prices have gone up despite our farm policy, not because of it." Despite widespread clamor about food exports, Butz and his staff expanded exports and continued to resist export controls.

United States farm price and income policy was substantially accommodated to global food policy. Speaking in Rome on September 4, Butz reaffirmed the U.S. government's desire to increase food production in developing countries, improve consumption patterns in all countries, make world food supplies more secure, and improve world trade. He made it clear, however, that the United States was not going to do this alone. With respect to food aid, he said, "The United States is prepared to make a firm commitment . . . but we don't intend to wait for reserves to meet food aid needs. Neither do we intend that the reserve system become simply a food aid cushion discouraging production in developing nations."

Agriculture's Competitive Structure came under government scrutiny and federal agencies took a tougher antitrust line on agribusiness. A far-reaching Department of Justice consent-decree order in August to the Associated Milk Producers, Incorporated, one of the major dairy cooperatives, warned agriculture cooperatives on monopolistic and other illegal practices. Widening profit margins made food corporations suspect. In a federal court in San Francisco, the Great Atlantic & Pacific Tea Company was found guilty on July 25 of price manipulation and was instructed to remit nearly $33 million to six livestock producers.

Crop Technology helped the troubled farmer in subtle ways. Among the new developments were *herbigation*, in which herbicides are applied in irrigation water, and *spray tillage*, in which troublesome wheat grasses are sprayed with contact herbicides rather than plowed under. High-moisture grain-handling systems were used widely and cut costly grain drying time. *Double-cropping* (producing two crops instead of one) increased production on many farms. Crop breeders focused on improving protein content, particularly in crops such as soybeans. Farmers got special incentive from reports of high-yielding Brazilian soybeans that produced a crop 30 per cent greater than 1973 and double that of 1972, as that country became an important factor in the world bean trade.

Agricultural Statistics, 1974

World Crop Production
(million units)

Crop	Units	1973	1974	%U.S.
Corn	Metric tons	311.6	297.5	42.6
Wheat	Metric tons	367.4	351.8	13.8
Rice	Metric tons	307.6	NA	1.3[1]
Barley	Metric tons	155.6	157.3	4.5
Oats	Metric tons	53.7	52.3	18.0
Rye	Metric tons	28.8	29.3	1.7
Soybeans	Metric tons	57.8	NA	73.8[1]
Cotton	Bales[2]	62.4	62.4	20.5
Coffee	Bags[3]	63.2	80.1	0.2
Sugar	Metric tons	81.7	NA	6.6[1]

[1] Based on 1973 production
[2] 480 lbs. (217.7 kilograms) net
[3] 132.276 lbs. (60 kilograms)
NA Not available

Output of Major U.S. Crops
(millions of bushels)

Crop	1962-66[†]	1973	1974[*]
Corn	3,876	5,643	4,621
Sorghums	595	936	609
Oats	912	664	649
Wheat	1,229	1,711	1,781
Soybeans	769	1,567	1,244
Rice (a)	742	928	1,148
Potatoes (b)	275	299	339
Cotton (c)	140	130	121
Tobacco (d)	2,126	1,743	1,962

[†] Average; [*] Preliminary
(a) 100,000 cwt. (4.54 million kilograms)
(b) 1 million cwt. (45.4 million kilograms)
(c) 100,000 bales (50 million lbs.) (22.7 million kilograms)
(d) 1 million lbs. (454,000 kilograms)

U.S. Production of Animal Products
(millions of pounds)

	1957-59[†]	1973	1974[*]
Beef	13,704	21,277	22,940
Veal	1,240	357	425
Lamb & Mutton	711	514	465
Pork	10,957	12,751	13,780
Eggs (a)	5,475	5,545	5,483
Chicken	5,292	11,225	11,250
Turkey	1,382	2,445	2,590
Total Milk (b)	123	116	114

[†] Average; [*] Preliminary
(a) 1 million dozens
(b) 100 million lbs. (45.4 million kilograms)

Livestock Technology also moved forward. New imported beef breeds, particularly from Europe, became increasingly popular. Scientists at the USDA's Beltsville, Md., laboratories successfully used frozen boar sperm for artificial breeding. New uses were found for the annual U.S. production of 2 billion short tons (1.8 billion metric tons) of animal waste. Chicken droppings, with 11 per cent protein, have been recycled into poultry feed, cattle feed, and lamb feed. But waste disposal was still a serious problem. Environmental Protection Agency guidelines were expected to require 40 per cent of dairy farmers to install run-off water systems for the disposal of animal waste at an estimated cost of $300 million.

French farmers block roads with tractors in September to protest falling farm prices. The action spread to other European Community countries.

The U.S. Farm Labor Force numbered 4.8 million persons in September, down from 4.9 million in 1973. The average wage rate, without room and board, was $2.22 per hour on October 1, up from $1.98 per hour on Oct. 31, 1973. The Supreme Court of the United States settled a labor problem dating back to 1947 when it ruled on November 25 that Mexican field workers may legally commute to the United States for seasonal work.

U.S. Farmers' Financial Status, as of Jan. 1, 1974, was boosted by a record increase of $82.8 billion in owned equity in farm assets. The previous record increase in equity was $36.6 billion in 1972. Overall, farmers owned assets worth $478.8 billion and owed debts of $84.1 billion, leaving an equity of $394.7 billion.

Preliminary forecasts for Jan. 1, 1975, showed another big jump in farm assets, debts, and net worth. Assets were estimated at $520 billion, debts at $95 billion, and net worth at $425 billion. On March 1, 1974, U.S. farm real estate values were an astounding 25 per cent above 1973 levels. The average value of an acre of U.S. farmland rose to $310.   Charles E. French and Larry L. Nelson

AIR FORCE, U.S. See NATIONAL DEFENSE.

AIR POLLUTION. See ENVIRONMENT.

AIRPORT. See AVIATION.

ALABAMA. See STATE GOVERNMENT.

ALASKA. See STATE GOVERNMENT.

ALBANIA suddenly showed interest during 1974 in better relations with its neighbors, Greece and Yugoslavia, while maintaining implacable hostility toward Russia and its allies. In a speech on October 3, Enver Hoxha, the Albanian Communist Party first secretary, referred to Bulgaria as a Russian colony ready to allow itself to be used as a launching pad for aggression against Yugoslavia, Albania, Greece, and Turkey. He also warned Romania and Yugoslavia against taking part in the Russian-sponsored European Communist Parties Conference in 1975, lest they become "accomplices of Soviet counter-revolutionaries." Albania boycotted a preparatory meeting in Warsaw, Poland, in October.

General Beqir Balluku, a reputed advocate of a friendlier policy toward Russia, was purged in July. He had been a member of the ruling Politburo since 1948 and defense minister since 1953. But his purge meant no easing of the regime's hard stance toward the United States. United States diplomatic overtures for a resumption of relations were brusquely rejected. But relations continued to develop with Italy, Austria, Norway, and France. A new trade agreement was signed with Switzerland in October.

Albania's gross national product increased by 11 per cent in 1974, but shortages of spare parts threatened further rapid industrialization.   Chris Cviic

See also EUROPE (Facts in Brief Table).

ALBERTA. See CANADA.

ALGERIA. Foreign Minister Abdelaziz Bouteflika's election as president of the United Nations General Assembly for its 1974 session symbolized Algeria's emerging role as a leader of the developing nations and a mediator in international disputes. President Houari Boumediene was credited in large measure with the agreement between Portugal and nationalists in Guinea-Bissau on independence for the former Portuguese colony.

Boumediene was also instrumental in convening a special General Assembly session on raw materials and development in April to consider radical changes in the relationship between the industrialized and the developing nations. The Algerian government was among the first to lift the oil embargo imposed by Arab oil-producing states in October, 1973. Diplomatic relations with the United States were restored on November 12.

Domestic Affairs. The government continued gradually to restore parliamentary government. About 78 per cent of the electorate voted in elections on June 2 for the popular assemblies of Algeria's 15 *wilayas* (provinces). The elections resulted in a territorial reorganization on July 7 to ensure greater popular representation and direction of local affairs by the assemblies. Sixteen new wilayas were formed.

Relations with France continued to improve. On September 25, the government released all remaining blocked accounts – about $8 million – belonging to French citizens who left the country after Algeria gained independence. New agreements with France and West Germany in April provided guaranteed employment on four-year contracts and wage increases for Algerian workers in the two countries.

Economic Developments. A four-year plan put into effect on June 24 envisaged expenditures of $12⅓ billion to establish a 15 per cent annual growth rate. The $6-billion 1974 budget was 38 per cent greater than 1973's.

Production started on May 22 at a new gas liquefaction plant at Skikda and a paper mill at Mostaganem. The contract between Sonatrach, the state oil organization, and El Paso Natural Gas Company for long-term gas deliveries to the United States was annulled because the U.S. Federal Power Commission failed to ratify it. But Algerian oil and gas continued to find ready markets. New delivery agreements were made with Spain and Brazil, the latter with a Brazilian commitment to invest $39 million in oil prospecting. Sonatrach signed several major development contracts, including one with Great Britain for expansion of the Hassi R'mel-Skikda gas pipeline and one with an Italian firm for a new Skikda refinery. New steel plants were dedicated in August at Oran and Djidjelli. Algeria received $157.5-million in loans from the World Bank for natural gas and railway projects. William Spencer

See also AFRICA (Facts in Brief Table).

AMERICAN LEGION. See VETERANS.

AMERICAN LIBRARY ASSOCIATION (ALA) held its annual conference in New York City in July, 1974. It set a new attendance record of 14,058. Edward G. Holley, dean of the University of North Carolina School of Library Science, took office as president. Allie Beth Martin, director of the Tulsa, Okla., City/County Library, is president-elect.

One of the major programs during the conference focused on the independent learner. It featured reports on the programs of public libraries participating in projects sponsored by the Office of Library Independent Study and Guidance Projects of the College Entrance Examination Board. Through such independent study projects, library users can complete course work and receive credits without enrolling in a formal education program.

Affirmative Action and fair employment were frequent issues at the conference. For example, a women's task force held an institute before the conference and approached the membership with resolutions regarding equal opportunity for women.

A number of major 1974 association developments also focused on affirmative action. The Association of College and Research Libraries, an ALA division, received a $350,000 grant from the Andrew W. Mellon Foundation to fund an internship program for librarians in predominantly black American colleges. The ALA also received a $25,000 grant from the U.S. Office of Education to conduct an institute on the design of affirmative action plans for librarians and libraries.

A major legislative achievement for librarians was the enactment of the Education Amendment of 1974. The bill extends and amends the Elementary and Secondary Education Act of 1965, including the school library program.

The Year's Awards. Two ALA units shared the 1974 J. Morris Jones-World Book Encyclopedia-ALA Goals Award: the American Association of School Librarians (to develop a national certification model for media personnel), and the Association of College and Research Libraries (for phase two of the revision of *Standards for College Libraries*).

Paula Fox won the Newbery Medal for her novel *Slave Dancer*, the most distinguished children's book in 1973. Margot Zemach received the Caldecott Medal for illustrating *Duffy and the Devil*, the most distinguished children's picture book. The Mildred L. Batchelder Award for the most outstanding children's book originally published in a foreign language went to *Petra's War*, by Aliki Zei, translated from Greek by Edward Fenton, and published by E. P. Dutton & Company. Augusta Baker, former coordinator for children's services, New York City Public Library, received the Clarence Day Award for leadership in children's books. Peggy Barber

See also CANADIAN LIBRARY ASSOCIATION (CLA); LIBRARY.

ANDORRA. See EUROPE.

ANGOLA. The political status of this Portuguese colony changed radically in 1974, following the overthrow of Portugal's government in April. Portugal announced it planned to grant Angola independence. However, the announcement led to racial violence and a power struggle between three African nationalist groups – the Popular Movement for the Liberation of Angola (MPLA), the National Front for the Liberation of Angola (FNLA), and the National Union for the Total Independence of Angola (UNITA). See PORTUGAL.

Because of racial disturbances, the Portuguese Army on May 26 banned all political meetings. Then a strike by black workers on July 15 touched off a week of rioting that left at least 43 persons dead and more than 160 injured. About 50 persons were killed and 250 injured in August race riots in Luanda.

On July 23, a military council was set up to handle the transition to independence. It called on the three nationalist groups to join a coalition government. But each group said it was the sole representative of the independence movement. However, in January, 1975, the groups set aside their differences and negotiated a settlement, with Angola's independence scheduled for Nov. 11, 1975.   John Storm Roberts

See also AFRICA (Facts in Brief Table).

ANIMAL. See CONSERVATION; INTERNATIONAL LIVE STOCK EXPOSITION; PET; ZOOLOGY; ZOOS AND AQUARIUMS.

ANTHROPOLOGY. Members of a joint French and United States anthropological expedition in Ethiopia announced on Oct. 25, 1974, that they had found fossilized human remains from 3 million to 4 million years old. Preliminary dating indicated that the fossils were as much as 1.5 million years older than the remains found in Kenya in 1972 by Richard Leakey, and that they are by far the oldest relics of humans that have ever been found. The find includes a complete upper jaw with all the teeth in place, and half of an upper jaw and half of a lower jaw.

The expedition was led by Donald Carl Johanson of Case Western Reserve University in Cleveland and Maurice Taieb of the French Scientific Research Center in Paris. They discovered the remains near the Awash River in central Ethiopia.

Leakey, director of Kenya's National Museum, said that the discovery confirmed his belief that man and apes had developed side by side from a common ancestor much earlier than previously believed. "I expect someone will find a link between Homo [man] and Australopithecus [apelike primate] and their ancestor in Africa at 4 to 5 million years."

Man in North America. New dating techniques showed that human beings may have lived in North America more than 48,000 years ago. The results were announced on May 14 by Jeffrey L. Bada and Roy Schroeder of the Scripps Institution of Oceanography at La Jolla, Calif., and George Carter of Texas A&M University. Until now, the oldest scientifically dated human fossil in North America was a skull known as "Los Angeles man," dated by University of California, Los Angeles, scientists at 23,600 years old.

The newly dated remains include a skull found in a sea cliff near Del Mar, Calif., dated at 48,000 years old, and a 44,000-year-old skull fragment found near La Jolla, Calif. The new dating technique, called *racemization*, measures amino acids in human bones. In crystalline form, these acids rotate light waves passed through the crystals. In living bone tissue, they always rotate the light to the left. After an organism dies, the amino acids gradually change their geometry so the light is rotated to the right. The age of the fossil can be determined by measuring the amount of left-handed and right-handed amino acids in it. The dating method is considered a major breakthrough in fossil dating because the carbon-14 method is reliable only to about 40,000 years into the past.

Biology and Culture. Two 1974 studies suggest a close relationship between man's biological constitution and his culture. In one, Richard S. Spielman and James V. Neel of the University of Michigan and Ernest C. Migliazza of the University of Maryland found a relationship between biological and linguistic change among the primitive Yanomamas, a South American tribe that has been isolated until recently.

The oldest known song, written in Syria about 1400 B.C., was deciphered at the University of California and played by Richard Crocker.

Their study focused on seven Yanomama groups with different dialects, all within the Yanomama territory. The scientists defined what they call a linguistic distance between these areas by studying similarities and differences in words, grammar, and *phonology* (sounds). They compared the degree of linguistic distance with the similarities and differences in characteristics of blood proteins, separating the groups. As the Yanomama population grew and new villages were founded, the blood protein differences and linguistic differences between Yanomama groups grew at about the same rate, indicating that biological and cultural change rates correspond closely.

Solomon H. Katz, Mary Hedeger, and Linda Valleroy of the University of Pennsylvania completed another study that shows the close relationship between biology and cultural behavior. They studied American Indian groups that cook corn in water to which an alkaline substance, such as wood ash, lye, or alkali, has been added. The scientists found that cooking corn with an alkaline substance improves the quality of the corn's protein. They found in a study of 51 American tribes that most of those practicing alkali cooking depend heavily on corn as a food resource. Without this process, the corn does not have enough nutritional value to serve as the tribe's primary food source. ⸱ Fred Plog

ARAB EMIRATES, UNITED. See UNITED ARAB EMIRATES.

ARCHAEOLOGY. Two Canadian archaeologists studying an 11,000-year-old burial in Montana reported that the hunters of that time used more sophisticated spearing methods than scientists had previously believed. L. Lahren of the University of Calgary in Alberta and R. Bonnichsen of the National Museum of Man in Ottawa found a spearpoint attached to a peculiar bone object that they believe was a foreshaft. It was used by the Clovis men, primitive hunters who hunted mammoths and other large game in Canada and the western United States. A wooden lance was inserted into the other end of the bone object. The foreshaft would have increased the hunters' efficiency by reducing the possibility of breaking the lance and permitting deeper penetration of the spearpoint into the animals.

Migration. Martin H. Wobst of the University of Massachusetts used computer simulation techniques to determine the rate of early man's spread through the New World. Assuming that only 25 individuals originally crossed the Bering land bridge between Russia and Alaska and that the population grew slowly, Wobst concluded that the New World would have become populated in only 3,000 years. While this spread seems at first glance to be rapid and archaeological evidence might suggest a rapid migration, Wobst found that a slow increase in human occupation of territory, about 3 miles (5 kilometers) per year, would have resulted in the occupation of

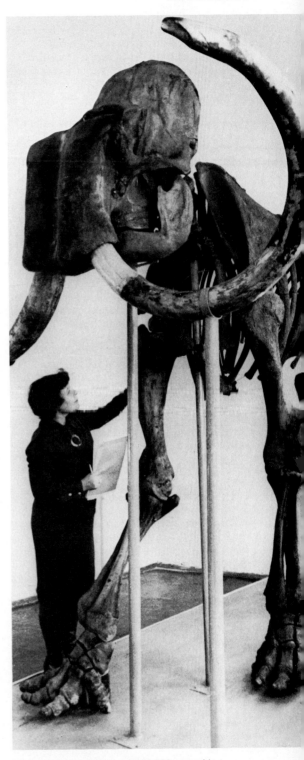

Well-preserved skeleton of a 20,000-year-old mammoth, found by Russian archaeologists in Siberia, is one of the largest ever discovered.

the entire New World. Thus, it seems that North and South America were populated by slow territorial expansion rather than a conscious migration.

Mayan Agriculture. B. L. Turner II of the University of Wisconsin studied archaeological evidence of Mayan agriculture and produced the first detailed study of such a system for the Rio Bec region of Mexico's Yucatan Peninsula. Turner discovered that there were terrace systems covering an area of 623 square miles (1,600 square kilometers) and raised fields covering more than 46 square miles (120 square kilometers). He concluded that the former served to contain water run-off and to build up topsoil, while the latter served to reclaim lowland that was flooded during some seasons of the year. Modifying the earth in this way, the Maya could have practiced intensive, near-annual cultivation between A.D. 350 and 1540 rather than the periodic slash-and-burn agriculture they were once believed to have practiced.

Turner's study also sheds light on the eventual Mayan abandonment of the area. The extent to which the Maya modified the land surface might have led to major environmental changes that would have forced them to abandon the area.

The Colossi. Robert F. Heizer and a group of researchers at the University of California, Berkeley, used a technique called neutron activation analysis to find the origin of the raw materials used by the ancient inhabitants of Thebes, Egypt, to construct the Colossi of Memnon. The Colossi are two giant statues weighing 720 short tons (653 metric tons) each. In neutron activation analysis, a rock sample is irradiated in an atomic reactor to make some of its atoms radioactive. The intensity and progressive decay of the radioactive atoms can then be precisely measured.

The chemical composition of the quartzite from which the statues were made was compared with that of quartzite from quarries in different parts of Egypt. A quarry near Cairo, 420 miles (676 kilometers) downstream from Thebes was identified as the source of the material. Transporting the statues upstream for that distance was clearly a major undertaking that must have involved many laborers.

China. Archaeologists in the city of Changsha in Southern China discovered many manuscripts in August in a Han dynasty tomb. The find included historical, philosophical, and medical treatises that were produced about 2,000 years ago on bamboo strips. There is a 4,000-word essay on how to judge horses; a treatise on the movement of the stars; a book advising rulers to combine punishment with virtue; primitive scientific texts on the elements; philosophical teachings of Lao Tzu, the legendary founder of Taoism; and a 12,000-word manuscript, *Annals of the Warring States*, more than half of which was hitherto unknown. The medical scripts were part of a lost work, *The Yellow Emperor's Classic of External Medicine.*   Fred Plog

ARCHITECTURE. The death of Louis I. Kahn in New York City on May 17, 1974, removed the last of this century's architectural form-givers. Kahn, along with Frank Lloyd Wright, Le Corbusier, and Ludwig Mies van der Rohe, had signaled the direction and shaped the form of much of this century's most significant architecture. See Close-Up.

Expo Architecture. Spokane, Wash., hosted a world's fair–Expo '74. The fair, which opened on May 4, centered around environmental themes, and was located next to the famous Spokane Falls.

It was a modest exposition, as world's fairs go. The U.S. Pavilion, designed by the architectural firm of Naramore, Bain, Brady, & Johnanson, was the largest structure, a tent 130 feet (40 meters) high. The pavilion's central exhibit was a large fountain composed of various bathroom fixtures–shower heads, sinks, bathtubs–by sculptor Harold Rosenthal.

The Washington State Pavilion was a sturdy-looking masonry and glass building by the Spokane architectural firm of Walker, McGough, Koltz, & Lyerla. It will become the city's new opera house.

Although the exposition was fairly devoid of architectural excitement, the American Forest Industry sponsored an interesting, regionally inspired pole-framed structure. It was designed by Seattle architect Miles Yanick. See Fairs and Expositions (Close-Up).

AIA Convention. The annual meeting of the prestigious American Institute of Architects (AIA) is generally a sedate, low-key affair, free of internal strife. But delegates to the 1974 convention, held in Washington, D.C., in May, were confronted by Judith Roeder, who stridently insisted that they stop being "lackeys of the establishment" and start creating "humane architecture" more responsive to people's needs. Roeder, an architect with the Department of Planning in Pittsburgh, said, "What architects have always done is to monumentalize the establishment, rather than reflect and provide for the needs of the whole society."

Notable New Buildings. The Joseph H. Hirshhorn Museum and Sculpture Garden opened on October 4 in Washington, D.C. Critics had no doubts about the art treasures inside the $16-million structure–6,000 modern paintings and sculptures from the private collection of industrialist Joseph H. Hirshhorn. But there was a good deal of doubt about whether the building itself was much of an architectural treasure.

The museum, designed by Gordon Bunshaft of Skidmore, Owings & Merrill, is a circular, reinforced concrete structure with an open inner core. The three-story building is raised 14 feet (4.3 meters) above its plaza on four massive piers. Its exterior surface is pink granite. There are no windows on this somewhat monolithic structure, only a single, narrow balcony slit, which makes it resemble the military defense bunkers of World War II. *The New York Times* architecture critic Ada Louise Huxtable called the

A Great Form-Giver

Louis I. Kahn was the last of modern architecture's form-givers, those architects who revolutionized building design in the first half of the 1900s. The least known and the least celebrated of the form-givers, Kahn died as he had worked for most of his life—alone and unrecognized.

The 73-year-old master suffered a fatal heart attack on March 17, 1974, in New York City's Pennsylvania Station. His body lay unclaimed in the city morgue while his wife called distant parts of the world, trying to locate him.

Kahn's work was not recognized as a major influence on modern architecture until late in his career. For years, he was considered out of step with the architectural trends set by the international form-givers of our age: Frank Lloyd Wright, who advocated blending the building with its natural surroundings; Le Corbusier, who elevated elegant cubes above the ground on concrete pillars; Ludwig Mies van der Rohe, whose sleek steel and glass skyscrapers dominate skylines throughout the world. In contrast, Kahn preferred simple geometric shapes and basic building materials—brick and concrete.

Kahn, born in Estonia in 1901, lived most of his life in Philadelphia, where his family had immigrated in 1905. He worked his way through the University of Pennsylvania by playing the piano and organ in silent-movie houses. After earning a degree in architecture in 1924, he rented an office in a shabby part of Philadelphia and remained there for the rest of his life. After all, he needed only a drafting table.

The shy, introspective young architect did not impress prospective clients. So he supported himself, his wife, and daughter for many years by teaching. He had only an occasional, unimportant commission to design a building. But during those decades of neglect, Kahn acquired an unmatched architectural vision. He began asking very basic questions, trying to discover "what the building wants to be."

Concerned with the nature of the material, Kahn once said, "I asked the brick what it wanted. And the brick replied, 'I want to be an arch.'"

He developed a concept of *served* and *servant* spaces. Servant space contains such functional equipment as pipes and air ducts. He regarded these as part of the building's aesthetic design and refused to hide them.

His first major commission was the Yale Art Gallery, completed in 1951. Public reaction to his design was mixed. Some people considered it raw and crude, particularly the rough concrete ceiling, which exposed the building's air and heat ducts and also the lighting equipment.

Then, suddenly, Kahn was discovered. In 1960, he startled the architectural world with his Richards Medical Research Building at the University of Pennsylvania. The tough, bold design was the first outstanding example of Kahn's served-servant space concept. He grouped the building's functional equipment—stairwells, elevators, laboratory exhaust systems—into four seven-story brick towers. He interspersed the served spaces (laboratories) among these servant towers.

At last, the commissions began to roll in libraries, museums, synagogues. His most famous buildings include the Salk Institute for Biological Studies in La Jolla, Calif.; the Kimbell Art Museum in Fort Worth, Tex.; and a complex of government buildings in Dacca, Bangladesh. At the time of his death, he was working on the Yale Center for British Art and the Institute for Management in Ahmadabad, India.

Kahn was also concerned with the way his designs interacted with light. "The sun never knew how great it was until it hit the side of a building," he was fond of saying.

Kahn's buildings of brick and concrete proclaimed their weight and strength and purpose. He provided a legitimate alternative to the modern vocabulary of steel and glass, the so-called International School's rigid dependence on skin-and-bones architecture. There is an intensity and commitment to everything he designed that proclaims him the architect's architect. Architecture "may be expressed as a world within a world," he once said. And the world Louis Kahn has left as his design legacy will not soon be forgotten.   Rob Cuscaden

Louis I. Kahn
1901-1974

Four-level Florida residence designed by William Morgan Architects of Jacksonville won an American Institute of Architects Honor Award in 1974.

on a two-story addition to the 70-story RCA Building in New York City's Rockefeller Center. The addition will be constructed on the 12th-floor setback of the famed building, erected in 1933. Designers Ford & Earl came up with a two-story glass structure, made up of lightweight, prefabricated modular units. Because of the large expanses of glass, solar energy will be used to heat and cool it.

Not quite a building per se, the Canadian National Tower in Toronto, Ont., topped out at 1,805 feet (550 meters), making it the world's largest free-standing structure. The $29.5-million communications and observation tower was designed by John Andrews and Webb, Zerafa, Menkes, Housden. It was scheduled to open early in 1975, complete with a 400-seat revolving restaurant in its seven-story "sky pod" about 1,100 feet (335 meters) aboveground.

New York City planners announced that a 4-acre (1.6-hectare) recreational park will be built in the East River, north of the Brooklyn Bridge. It will be shaped like a boat, constructed on piles, and connected to the shore by two gangplanklike bridges. Architects Venturi & Rauch included an athletics field, children's playground, senior citizens' area, and a swimming pool on a barge.

Architectural Forum, the 82-year-old trade magazine, suspended publication in March, because advertising revenues could not keep pace with soaring production costs.   Rob Cuscaden

building "the biggest doughnut in the world." See Section Two, To INCREASE KNOWLEDGE AMONG MEN.

The proposed John Fitzgerald Kennedy Library at Harvard University in Cambridge, Mass., already 10 years in the planning, continued to generate more controversy than actual construction. In 1973, I.M. Pei & Partners had presented a design for a glass pyramid structure 85 feet (30 meters) high to house the library. A smaller-scaled building for the academic facilities of Harvard's Kennedy School of Government and Politics would be wrapped around the library. Cambridge neighborhood groups vehemently opposed this original conception, objecting that it would become too prominent a tourist attraction.

I.M. Pei went back to the drafting board. Late in 1974, the architects disclosed revised plans. The new, low-scaled version completely separated the two structures and eliminated the glass pyramid. But, the same neighborhood groups repeated their objections, and the year ended without a final decision being made.

The Grand Ole Opry in Nashville, Tenn., moved to a new home on March 16. Architects Welton Beckett & Associates designed a $15-million brick and concrete auditorium with a seating capacity of 4,400 persons and what is claimed to be the world's largest radio and television broadcasting studio. Construction was scheduled to begin early in 1975

ARGENTINA.
President Juan D. Perón died on July 1, 1974. He was immediately succeeded in office by his third wife, María Estela (Isabel) Martínez de Perón. Mrs. Perón, who had been serving as vice-president, inherited a political legacy that verged on civil war. See PERÓN, MARÍA (ISABEL).

The diverse Peronista groups that had rallied around the former dictator's name were once again at each other's throats, and political terrorism took a high toll in the months that followed. Against this background, the question that most overshadowed Argentine politics became: How soon would the armed forces, which had renounced power at the start of 1973, feel compelled to intervene again?

Domestic Politics were dominated by a left wing, right wing tussle within the Peronista camp. The right, led by the astrologer-turned-social-welfare-minister, José López Rega, emerged as the victor. After Perón's death, López Rega succeeded in appointing his old political cronies to key posts; thus, in an August Cabinet reshuffle, Alberto Rocamora became minister of the interior and Alberto Sabino minister of defense. The conservative Alberto Villar had been reinstated as police chief on April 10. López Rega's hold became complete when he got rid of his chief political rival, the left-leaning economy minister, José Ber Gelbard, on October 12.

Rampant Terrorism, and the failure of the security forces to contain it, was again the key political issue.

Mourners bid farewell to Argentina's President Juan D. Perón. Isabel Perón, who succeeded her husband, stands at foot of draped coffin.

The Economy suffered less than might have been expected from the political instability and the breakdown of Perón's "social compact," a program designed to restrict wage increases to 20 per cent a year. The growth rate in the first half of 1974 was 6.2 per cent. Long-term problems were building up, however, through the heedless expansion of the monetary supply by about 70 per cent and of the budgetary deficit of about 30 per cent. The government managed to confine the rise in the cost-of-living index to about 25 per cent, but at the cost of price controls that severely tightened the profit margins for private enterprise and created a booming black market.

Cattlemen suffered from the beef glut in Europe and the resulting ban, until October, of beef imports into the European Community (Common Market). Argentina's beef sales in the first half of 1974 were down by 29 per cent in value and 47 per cent in quantity. This was one reason for the government's bitterly contested proposals for a new agrarian law based on the principle that land should belong to those who work it. Minister of Agriculture Horacio Gilberti planned by land redistribution to open up vast tracts of the pampa, the fertile plain around Buenos Aires, to more intensive cultivation; only 20 per cent is now planted in crops. The rise in world grain prices was the secret of Argentina's favorable trade balance in 1974.   Robert Moss

See also LATIN AMERICA (Facts in Brief Table).

Three main groups were responsible: the Trotskyite People's Revolutionary Army, led by Roberto Santucho; the left wing Peronist Montoneros, led by Mario Firmenich, who declared open war on the government in early September after a brief honeymoon; and the extreme right wing Argentine Anti-Communist Alliance, better known as the "Triple A."

Scores fell victim to the left wing terrorists. Among them were a number of leading political and military figures, including Arturo Mor Roig, a former minister of the interior; Colonel Jorge Crassi; Jordan Bruno, a well-known conservative intellectual; Ricardo Goya, labor relations director of IKA-Renault; and the federal police chief, Alberto Villar, who was killed by a bomb while sailing on the Paraná River on September 9. In revenge, the Triple A killed several left wing figures and threatened the lives of prominent men associated with the short-lived administration of President Hector José Cámpora in 1973. There was widespread speculation that the Triple A was in fact supported by the Peronist right.

Kidnapings for ransom continued, and a number of foreign companies, including the U.S.-owned Ford Motor Company, recalled their expatriate executives from Argentina. The most spectacular abduction was that of Jorge and Juan Born on September 19. The brothers controlled the trading conglomerate Bunge and Born, one of the country's largest financial empires.

ARIAS NAVARRO, CARLOS (1908-   ), was sworn in as Spain's president on Jan. 2, 1974 (see SPAIN). He is the first civilian head of government since General Francisco Franco began his dictatorial rule in 1939. He succeeded Admiral Luis Carrero Blanco, who was assassinated on Dec. 20, 1973.

Arias immediately named 11 new ministers, older men who are fiercely loyal to Franco. However, he promised some political reform, including election of certain officials and legalization of political parties and labor unions within the state-run unions.

Arias was born in Madrid on Dec. 11, 1908. After earning a law degree from the University of Madrid, he entered the civil service. A public prosecutor in Málaga when civil war broke out in 1936, he sided with Franco's Nationalist forces and became a vigorous military prosecutor.

From 1944 to 1957, Arias served as governor of several provinces. He built a tough, law-and-order reputation as director general of security, Spain's top police post in the interior ministry, from 1957 to 1965. He was mayor of Madrid from 1965 until June, 1973, when he succeeded Carrero Blanco as interior minister.   Robert K. Johnson

ARIZONA. See STATE GOVERNMENT.

ARKANSAS. See STATE GOVERNMENT.

ARMY, UNITED STATES. See NATIONAL DEFENSE.

ART. See ARCHITECTURE; DANCING; LITERATURE; MUSIC, CLASSICAL; POETRY; VISUAL ARTS.

ASIA

Mercifully, the big conflicts were ended. In their wake, Asia had only mini-wars in 1974 – in Vietnam, in Khmer, and in the southern islands in the Philippines. They were savage enough, but at least they were containable. In the place of armed struggle, there were economic crises that were almost as punishing. "We're obsessed," said a senior Indian official, "with the three terrible F's – food, fuel, and fertilizer. We've trimmed everything to the bone, but we still cannot find the resources to buy all we need."

In this desperate year, Asians from Japan to Pakistan were caught in a crisis they could not have anticipated. On the western edge of the continent, the sun-parched kingdoms, sheikdoms, and emirates of the Middle East gained power and wealth beyond their wildest dreams, but this was at the expense of the Asians. Some bankers thought the oil-rich states (a few smaller than a middling U.S. city) would earn $50 billion before the year's end. Much of this vast fortune was taken away from the Asians – some (Japan and Taiwan) who could afford it and some (India, Pakistan, Bangladesh, and Sri Lanka) who were brought near bankruptcy.

Economic Slump and human suffering were a major by-product of the oil squeeze in Asia. Japan

Khmer government forces use landing boats
to take fleeing civilians out of Kampot,
a provincial capital besieged by guerrillas.

Indira Gandhi said that in August, 1974, anxious leaders wondered how they could get enough drinking water to the people in the parched western states of India. It was only the providential rains in September that averted calamity. But even as some states suffered for lack of water, others in India's north, as well as in much of Bangladesh, were inundated by the monsoon rains. Thousands died in the floods, and crops were washed away.

The scale of the year's disaster could have been reduced by a vast program of public works. But there was no such program in Asia—except in China. There, the effect of the drought was greatly reduced by an immense irrigation system, and the flood damage by huge dikes. True, compulsion was used to provide the needed labor in China. But, with tens of millions of landless laborers, India and Bangladesh could have accomplished what China had. What was absent was the will of the governors.

Problems of the Green Revolution. In this troubled year, many in Asia were tempted to blame their woes on the failure of the Green Revolution. But this was the judgment of the ignorant. It was the Green Revolution that boosted the yield of wheat in India and Pakistan, and of rice in the Philippines, Taiwan, and South Korea, far beyond anything known before. But the Green Revolution had stern prerequisites. It demanded a controlled water supply, vast quantities of fertilizer, and improved seed. India and Pakistan were the prime examples of places where farmers had been allowed to slip back to their pre-Green Revolution methods of farming. When there was enough fertilizer, the peasants used less than they should have—and the state did not provide new seed varieties quickly enough.

But the Green Revolution has only been briefly slowed down. A breakthrough in rice production is certain in India, Bangladesh, and Sri Lanka. In Thailand, the farmers still produce a single rice crop where they could have two, and they employ methods used a century ago. Since this nation produces large surpluses of rice for export, no one worries much—yet. But Thailand's population is growing at 3.2 per cent a year, and all the land that can be used to grow rice has now been used. Soon this rice granary of Asia will also have to embrace the Green Revolution or go hungry. And China, with 15 million mouths added to its population each year, will also have to consider such modern methods.

Time for Change. Thailand has always been known as a land of peaceful lotus-eaters, and when the students poured out into the streets in October, 1973, to overthrow the military dictatorship, it surprised most observers. A Western diplomat listed

and Bangladesh alike sought desperately to cut down on their use of fuel. But, invariably, this meant smaller crops and industrial stagnation. In India, where half the energy comes from such fuels as firewood, charcoal, and cow dung, rather than oil, the rate of growth still sank to near zero—as it also did in Japan for a time. The poor starved, the black market grew, and India's agents scoured the world markets in search of grain on long, easy credit. There was little grain to be bought, and the credit was tight.

Drought and Floods. But oil prices, more than tripled overnight, were not the only reason for the crisis. Much of Asia still lay at the mercy of nature. Drought killed India's crops, and its herds of cattle were decimated for lack of grass. Prime Minister

this as one of his major discoveries: "The Thais, we now know, are prone to mayhem." But, in fact, the air in all of Asia was heavy with violence in 1974, born of discontent with man's unhappy fate.

The political structures of the governments in Asia range from the heavy-fisted North Korean regime of Kim Il-song – "the beloved and respected leader," as the press there calls him – to the relative democracy of Indira Gandhi in India. In between, there are dictators, some in civilian clothing and more in uniforms, some medieval in their philosophy and others spouting liberal slogans. They hold power by exploiting fears of Communism, or fears of hostile neighbors, or even of vague external threats (as in "socialist" Sri Lanka and the "guided democracy" of Burma). And there is always China, with its "dictatorship of the proletariat," which sacrifices private lives to the goals of the leaders in Peking.

Varied as these regimes are, they are all aware of the popular yearning for a change among their people. When violence breaks out in the streets, the causes often seem trivial. But a closer look shows that the underlying reason is discontent with the system and its leaders. This was the case in Djakarta, Indonesia, where students rioted in January, ostensibly in protest against a visit by Japan's Prime Minister Kakuei Tanaka. It was the case in September, when a frail Gandhian, Jayaprakash Narayan, led a campaign to unseat the Indian state government of Bihar. By the year's end, the campaign had spread to other Indian states and to Delhi, and Gandhi's own powerful Congress Party was badly shaken by Narayan's charges of ineptness and corruption.

No Opponents. Heavy-handed repression – and the absence of alternatives – helped most of these regimes to survive. The two Asian liberals, Gandhi and Singapore's Prime Minister Lee Kuan Yew, hesitated only a little longer to put their dangerous foes behind bars than did the generals who ruled South Vietnam and South Korea. Much of Asia had earlier spurned the Western notions of democracy, and it was still in pursuit of a viable and enlightened political philosophy. It was a symptom of Asia's futile search for alternatives that India had three, and possibly four, Communist parties, each worshiping its own Marxist gods and each warring fiercely against its Communist rivals.

For most leaders and rebels alike, the West was the whipping boy. The Communists attacked the West with zeal and so did the liberals, who conveniently forgot that Western aid was keeping many of them afloat.

But almost all the Asians had failed to grasp the implications of the oil crisis, which overnight changed the patterns of wealth and power. Although India and Sri Lanka inveighed against the new U.S. naval base on Diego Garcia Island in the Indian Ocean, what was threatening them both was not the U.S. Navy, but the Arab oil stranglehold. Yet, in 1974,

none in Asia went so far as to wag a reproachful finger at the oil producers.

Too Many Babies. One of Asia's tragedies remained its awesome birth rate – and the failure to control it. In five years, India had brought its birth rate down from 40 births per thousand people to 37. But it was unclear if this was the result of the nation's family-planning program or of some natural demographic phenomenon. In those five years, India's population had grown by about 65 million, to a total of about 600 million. But the grain yield had, if anything, declined.

India, of course, was not alone. Its birth rate was matched by Pakistan's. Thailand, with the highest birth rate in Asia, expected to have 40 million people by the year 2000. And China, which in 1974 admitted having "nearly" 800 million people, probably had many more and may reach 1 billion by the year 2000, according to some experts.

The problem was muddied by politics. For instance, India, the first Asian nation to launch a birth-control program, remained mute when the Chinese spokesman at the World Population Conference in Bucharest, Romania, in August, in effect denounced family planning as a capitalist conspiracy meant to subjugate the have-not countries. Many felt that what was needed, instead of such political talk, was an open and forceful appeal for birth control by the leaders of the world's two most populous states, China and India.

The U.S. Withdrawal from Vietnam in 1973 did not have the dire consequences so many Americans had feared. There was no sudden falling of Asian countries into the Communist orbit. Yet the effect has been deep and wide. For one thing, China and Russia reduced the flow of their military hardware to North Vietnam as U.S. troops pulled out of South Vietnam. One result of this was to defuse Vietnam, at least for the moment, as an international bomb.

Even more important, the United States, no longer the dominant power in Asia, intent on keeping the Communists at bay, was now free to play a far more subtle game called *triangle*. By establishing ties with Peking, the United States could now exploit the merciless struggle between the two Communist giants, China and Russia.

President Gerald R. Ford visited Japan and South Korea during an eight-day November trip to Asia and met with Russian leader Leonid I. Brezhnev in Vladivostok, Russia, while Secretary of State Henry A. Kissinger flew to Peking to see China's Premier Chou En-lai. Ford was criticized for visiting South Korea on the grounds that this symbolized U.S. support for the repressive policies of the Seoul government. However, Kissinger argued that not to go would "raise grave doubts" about the American commitment to South Korea.

United States-Chinese relations remained correct rather than warm, in 1974. When Kissinger made

Facts in Brief on the Asian Countries

Country	Population	Government	Monetary Unit*	Foreign Trade (million U.S. $) Exports	Imports
Afghanistan	19,142,000	President & Prime Minister Mohammad Daoud	afghani (55.1 = $1)	90	113
Australia	13,713,000	Governor General Sir John R. Kerr; Prime Minister Edward Gough Whitlam	dollar (1 = $1.32)	9,538	7,658
Bangladesh	81,355,000	President Mohammadullah; Prime Minister Sheik Mujibur Rahman	taka (8.1 = $1)	74	127
Bhutan	932,000	King Jigme Singhi Wangchuk	Indian rupee	no statistics available	
Burma	30,750,000	President U Ne Win; Prime Minister U Sein Win	kyat (4.9 = $1)	110	96
China	830,491,000	Communist Party Chairman Mao Tse-tung; Premier Chou En-lai	yuan (1.96 = $1)	3,055	2,775
India	601,503,000	President Fakhruddin Ali Ahmed; Prime Minister Indira Gandhi	rupee (8 = $1)	2,942	3,006
Indonesia	129,133,000	President Suharto	rupiah (415 = $1)	3,062	2,410
Iran	33,383,000	Shah Mohammed Reza Pahlavi; Prime Minister Amir Abbas Hoveyda	rial (71.4 = $1)	6,943	3,442
Japan	110,528,000	Emperor Hirohito; Prime Minister Takeo Miki	yen (300 = $1)	36,982	38,347
Khmer (Cambodia)	7,326,000	President Lon Nol; Prime Minister Long Boret	riel (375 = $1)	7	80
Korea, North	15,948,000	President Kim Il-song; Prime Minister Kim Il	won (1.1 = $1)	128	252
Korea, South	34,623,000	President Chung Hee Park; Prime Minister Kim Jong Pil	won (399 = $1)	3,200	4,219
Laos	3,253,000	King Savang Vatthana; Prime Minister Souvanna Phouma	kip (600 = $1)	3	44
Malaysia	11,770,000	Paramount Ruler Abdul Halim Muazzam; Prime Minister Abdul Razak	dollar (2.42 = $1)	2,950	2,402
Maldives	118,000	President Ibrahim Nasir; Prime Minister Ahmed Zaki	rupee (7.2 = $1)	4	3
Mongolia	1,434,000	People's Revolutionary Party First Secretary & Premier Yumjaagiyn Tsedenbal	tugrik (3.2 = $1)	75	104
Nepal	12,101,000	King Birendra Bir Bikram Shah Deva; Prime Minister Nagendra Prasad Rijal	rupee (10.6 = $1)	31	46
New Zealand	3,032,000	Governor General Sir Denis Blundell; Prime Minister Wallace E. Rowling	dollar (1 = $1.31)	2,599	2,178
Pakistan	70,474,000	President Fazal Elahi Chaudhry; Prime Minister Zulfikar Ali Bhutto	rupee (9.7 = $1)	961	981
Philippines	42,660,000	President Ferdinand E. Marcos	peso (6.9 = $1)	1,778	1,773
Russia	255,543,000	Communist Party General Secretary Leonid I. Brezhnev; Premier Aleksei N. Kosygin; Supreme Soviet Presidium Chairman Nikolai V. Podgorny	ruble (1 = $1.29)	16,510	17,290
Sikkim	231,000	Maharaja Palden Thondup Namgyal	Indian rupee	no statistics available	
Singapore	2,282,000	President Benjamin H. Sheares; Prime Minister Lee Kuan Yew	dollar (2.4 = $1)	3,605	5,063
Sri Lanka (Ceylon)	13,950,000	President William Gopallawa; Prime Minister Sirimavo Bandaranaike	rupee (6.7 = $1)	388	421
Taiwan	15,957,000	President Chiang Kai-shek; Vice-President C. K. Yen; Prime Minister Chiang Ching-kuo	new Taiwan dollar (37.5 = $1)	4,378	3,797
Thailand	39,310,000	King Phumiphon Aduldet; Prime Minister Sanya Thammasak	baht (20.5 = $1)	1,584	2,057
Vietnam, North	23,596,000	President Ton Duc Thang; Premier Pham Van Dong	dong (2.35 = $1)	114	212
Vietnam, South	20,843,000	President Nguyen Van Thieu; Vice-President Tran Van Huong; Prime Minister Tran Thien Khiem	piaster (670 = $1)	13	707

*Exchange rates as of Dec. 2, 1974

Foreign ministers of Bangladesh, India, and Pakistan happily salute
agreement they reached in April that normalized their relations.

his seventh Peking visit in November, the final communiqué could offer nothing more substantial than the word that President Ford would visit China in 1975. Still, with each of the Communist capitals worried lest the other one become too intimate with Washington, the United States retained its political leverage.

The Sino-Russian Feud continued to cast its shadow over Asia. When the Russians provided arms to India, the Chinese supplied them to Pakistan. And when Afghanistan baited China's ally Pakistan over the issue of border tribesmen, it counted on Moscow's support. In India and Indonesia, rival Communist parties reflected the views of the two big Communist powers. In Laos and Khmer, the Russians and the Chinese checked and counterchecked each other's intricate moves.

If there were victims of this feud, they were in the main the revolutionaries of various countries in Southeast Asia. After decades of battling the governing reactionaries, they suddenly found themselves forsaken. Both the Russians and the Chinese were engaged in a competitive wooing of the established Asian governments, and they were ready to abandon the rebels in the process.

The diplomatic maneuvering was rewarding for the small Asian countries that once dreaded the Communists no less than did Washington. One after another turned to thoughts of an accommodation with Moscow or Peking. In 1974, Malaysia, Singapore, the Philippines, and Thailand sent emissaries to China, and some sent missions to the semiannual trade fair in Canton. In November, Thailand annulled an old law that banned commerce with China. And Imelda Marcos, the wife of the Philippine president, managed to bewitch the leaders in Peking during her visit to China in September.

Nuclear Blasts. Not all the portents were quite as pacific. China continued to develop long-range missiles, and India exploded a nuclear device in May. India thus became the sixth member (and the second in Asia) to join the nuclear club. Japan, with its advanced industry, was debating whether to manufacture atomic weapons, and even Indonesia spoke of "going nuclear."

Sikkim's Status. After many months of conflict, India's tiny protectorate of Sikkim, which borders Tibet, became an associate state of India in September. The powers of Sikkim's ruler, Palden Thondup Namgyal, were curtailed by this action, and the move was criticized abroad, particularly by China. Sikkim's government moved to oust the ruler in November, but Gandhi reportedly counseled against any "hasty decision."   Mark Gayn

See also the various Asian country articles; Section One, Focus on The World; Section Two, The New Face of China.

ASTRONAUTS. See Space Exploration.

ASTRONOMY. A clearer picture of Jupiter's size, structure, and radiation belts emerged in 1974, as astronomers analyzed data returned by *Pioneer 10*, which passed within 81,000 miles (130,000 kilometers) of the planet in December, 1973. *Pioneer 11* returned additional data when it looped around Jupiter in December, 1974. At its equator, Jupiter's diameter is 88,733 miles (142,800 kilometers), and at its poles, 82,966 miles (133,520 kilometers). The flattening occurs because Jupiter rotates even faster than the Earth, spinning around its poles in just under 10 hours. *Pioneer 10* measured Jupiter's mass at 317.8 times that of the Earth.

Jupiter's outer, visible layers are hydrogen-rich clouds of ammonia-ice crystals. The clouds stretch around the planet, banding it with 17 colored stripes that parallel its equator. Light-colored stripes are warm-weather features that well up through the atmosphere, while reddish-brown areas are cooler features falling back to lower levels. Below the clouds, scientists believe that there is a gaseous, turbulent atmosphere where temperature and pressure rise steadily until the pressure forces hydrogen into its liquid state. Most of the interior is an immense hydrogen ocean from 25,000 to 30,000 miles (40,000 to 48,000 kilometers) deep. At the very center, Jupiter may have a small rocky core with a composition like the Earth, which is mostly iron and nickel. The center is hot, perhaps as high as 54,000° F. (30,000° C), having been heated as Jupiter slowly contracted from a larger size. The Great Red Spot is a hurricanelike storm in Jupiter's upper atmosphere.

Astronomers discovered a 13th moon of Jupiter in September on photographs taken at the Hale Observatories in California. The moon is small, perhaps only a few miles or kilometers across. It moves in a direct (counterclockwise) orbit about 7.7 million miles (12.4 million kilometers) from the parent planet. It belongs to a middle group of three other Jovian satellites. It circles Jupiter in 282 days.

Multiple Mirror Telescope. The Smithsonian Astrophysical Observatory in Cambridge, Mass., and the University of Arizona in Tucson are jointly attempting a new concept in optical telescopes – one made from six separate 72-inch (183-centimeter) mirrors mounted in a circle around a smaller guiding telescope. The telescope will be installed on Mount Hopkins near Tucson late in 1975 or in 1976. Light collected by the six mirrors will be focused on one spot, giving the arrangement the equivalent light-gathering power of a 176-inch (447-centimeter) conventional telescope. The main advantage will be the saving in cost, because the six medium-sized telescopes are much less expensive than one large telescope. Each will be of a Cassegrain configuration; that is, incoming starlight will be reflected from the primary mirror to a smaller secondary mirror before coming to a focus. A third, flat mirror in each telescope will deflect the focusing beams to a central

Astronomers got their first detailed look at the cratered surface of Mercury when *Mariner 10* swung around the planet in March, 1974.

detector, where all six signals will be simultaneously recorded for total brightness or for intensity differences according to wave length.

The design requires special care that all six mirrors of each type be identical or the images will not add together correctly, thus destroying the planned advantage. Also, the six component telescopes must be aligned to point in exactly the same direction at all times. A laser beam will continuously reflect through the system, feeding alignment information to corrector motors behind each secondary mirror. These motors will make minor adjustments to compensate for small wanderings of the component telescopes.

Compact Cluster. Observers at Lick Observatory in Mount Hamilton, Calif., have found that a group of about 24 faint objects is a cluster of galaxies rather than a cluster of stars, as thought earlier. The brighter galaxies in the group have such high surface brightness that one can barely distinguish them from stars on photographs taken with moderate magnification. This caused the earlier misconception. Their light is shifted by about 12 per cent toward redder, or longer, wave lengths than originally emitted, indicating that the objects are moving away from the Earth at about 18,450 miles (29,700 kilometers) per second. A high-magnification photograph shows clearly that the objects are galaxies. Normal galaxies receding at such a speed are estimated to be 2.3-billion light-years away.

Two features are remarkable. First, the galaxies concentrate most of their luminosity in a small area, putting them in the class called *compact* galaxies. Second, the ones measured are all moving at about the same speed, meaning there is little internal motion within the cluster. Internal motion measures the total mass of a cluster; the lack of internal motion indicates that the cluster's mass is small when compared to its brightness. It resembles a cluster of giant groupings of stars, such as a scaled-up version of the globular star clusters in the halo of the Milky Way, our Galaxy.

Extraterrestrial Communication. Radio astronomers occasionally search for signals from possible advanced civilizations on planets around other stars. The most likely candidates are the nearby, solar-type stars Tau Ceti and Epsilon Eridani. Such searches generally use wave lengths around 21 centimeters, the same frequency emitted by the neutral hydrogen atom, on the theory that a civilization desiring to make its presence known would use this frequency because other civilizations would be listening on it.

Astronomers reported in 1974 that a search of 10 stars conducted with antennas at the National Radio Astronomy Observatory in Green Bank, W. Va., failed to reveal any signs of other civilizations. This led to speculation that advanced civilizations may black out radio signals near 21 centimeters to allow clearer reception of natural radio signals from interstellar hydrogen gas clouds. Searches for other civili-

zations will continue intermittently, using large radio telescopes, especially that at Arecibo, Puerto Rico.

A View of Mercury. *Mariner 10* made two close passes to Mercury in 1974, the first on March 29 and the second on September 21. The main aim of the mission was to obtain the first clear pictures of Mercury's terrain. The first approach came within 431 miles (690 kilometers) of the surface, much closer than the second, which passed about 29,930 miles (48,170 kilometers) from Mercury for more coverage.

At close range, Mercury looks very much like the Earth's Moon. Its surface is covered with craters, ranging from large basins up to 800 miles (1,300 kilometers) across down to tiny ones barely seen on the clearest pictures. Smooth floors in some craters indicate they were flooded with volcanic material in the past. Large plains areas resembling the lunar *maria* (seas) also support the idea of volcanic flooding in Mercury's hotter early history. Sharp-rimmed craters imply that there has been no erosion and, hence, no significant atmosphere since the craters were formed, perhaps 4 billion years ago.

Brief Notes. A rough wheel of stones laid out on the ground at Medicine Mountain in Wyoming's Bighorn National Forest may be an Indian observatory dating back to 1760. The Medicine Wheel is about 80 feet (25 meters) across and has 28 stone spokes radiating from a central *cairn* (heap of stones). Six other large cairns are piled up on or near the rim. Alignment of pairs of cairns point to astronomically significant points on the horizon, such as the rising and setting points of the sun at summer solstice – the longest day of the year – and the points where the stars Aldebaran, Rigel, and Sirius rise. The site is accessible only in summer because of heavy snow the rest of the year.

A total solar eclipse occurred on June 20 over extreme southwestern Australia and the Indian Ocean. Ground observers saw the moon completely cover the sun for 5 minutes. This was extended to 7 minutes 9 seconds for some observers and newsmen who chased the moon's shadow in a jet aircraft.

Comet Kohoutek, although not as bright as predicted in advance, yielded much new information on comets. In particular, it provided the first conclusive evidence that water exists in comets. Bright yellow and red emission features were identified as being caused by ionized water vapor in the comet's tail. This discovery confirmed the popular dirty iceberg model for comets, proposed in 1950 by Fred L. Whipple of the Harvard College Observatory.

The catalog of molecules found in interstellar space acquired an especially interesting addition with the discovery of methylamine, which can combine with formic acid (already known to exist in space) to form glycine. Glycine is the simplest amino acid – a unit leading to proteins, the building blocks of life.   Laura P. Bautz

ATOMIC ENERGY. See ENERGY.

AUSTRALIA. Growing inflation, problems in the rural areas, and vigorous parliamentary opposition to the governing Labor Party's policies characterized 1974. Prime Minister Edward Gough Whitlam asked for dissolution of both houses of Parliament in April. The general election on May 18 left the Labor government in command of the House of Representatives but still with a minority in the Senate.

A series of Senate votes against government-proposed bills culminated in open defiance on April 2 when Whitlam announced that a prominent member of the Democratic Labor Party, Senator Vincent Gair, would be appointed ambassador to Ireland. The opposition rightly interpreted this move as an attempt to gain a Senate seat for the Labor Party in Gair's state of Queensland in the May elections. The government took up the challenge by obtaining from the governor general, Sir Paul Hasluck, the third double dissolution of Parliament in history. What was to have been an election for half the Senate became one for the entire Parliament.

The main issue for the Labor Party was the blockage of government legislation by the opposition-controlled Senate, which had defeated several measures passed by the House of Representatives. The election was called after the Liberal and Country parties voiced opposition to appropriations bills needed to finance the government's operation.

The Election resulted in the disappearance of the Democratic Labor Party from the 60-seat Senate and a stalemate between the government and its main opposition (the Liberal and Country parties). The balance of power rested in the hands of two independents who favored the opposition. The government's majority in the 127-seat House of Representatives was reduced from nine to five. Four constitutional referendums were defeated.

A joint meeting of both houses of Parliament, on August 6 and 7, the first in history, passed several bills that had previously been rejected by the Senate after passing the House of Representatives. The joint sitting gave Whitlam a slim three-vote majority, needed to get the legislation passed.

Economic Conditions declined markedly from 1973, though export prospects for minerals and certain other products continued to be bright, and Australia's near self-sufficiency in oil shielded it from the worst aspects of the energy crisis.

On July 31, the government announced that Australia had a balance-of-payments deficit of $1 billion for the fiscal year, compared to a surplus of $1.5-billion the previous year. The deficit was attributed to the smallest inflow of capital since 1952-1953 and to an increase of 50 per cent in imports. The import increase resulted from an upward revaluation of the Australian dollar in September, 1973, along with

Darwin, Australia, is a scene of chaotic ruin after Christmas Day cyclone killed at least 48 persons and damaged 90 per cent of the city's buildings.

Australian Aborigines look at uranium found on their land. They turned down a fortune by refusing to let mining companies develop the deposit.

cuts in tariffs and the lifting of import quotas on textiles. Australia's official reserves stood at $5.5-billion on June 30, a decline of 15 per cent from the previous year.

Subsequently, the building trade slackened considerably, while the flood of imports led to unemployment in the textile, clothing, and automobile industries. To meet balance-of-payments problems, the Australian dollar was devalued by 12 per cent on September 25 in order to make it easier to sell Australian goods overseas and to safeguard jobs threatened by imports. At the same time, the fixed link with the United States dollar was cut. Future exchange rates will be based on changes in the values of a number of foreign currencies that are significant in Australian trade.

The Budget, introduced on September 17, was not notably anti-inflationary. It included a substantial increase in government spending and a tax increase on higher incomes and capital gains. Tight credit and high interest rates were prominent most of the year, though modified in the later months because of growing unemployment. The government moved to reduce the import of cheap textiles from Asian countries. The rise in prices was estimated at around 15 per cent, but incomes generally rose more rapidly. However, some estimates indicated that the rate of inflation would reach 20 per cent by year-end.

Whitlam announced new economic measures on November 12 that would lower income taxes and reduce company taxes from 47.5 per cent to 45 per cent. Import duties on motor vehicles were increased 10 per cent. Also, $196 million was provided to banks for housing construction loans. Whitlam said the new economic measures would promote investment, restore business confidence, enhance profits, and increase employment. The government also supported the principle of wage indexation, which would ensure that wages were adjusted to cost-of-living increases. However, Whitlam asked unions to minimize their wage demands in the light of the additional take-home pay provided by the income tax cuts. Earlier economic measures were announced on November 10 to get investment money, especially foreign funds, flowing more freely.

Rural Difficulties arose from heavy flooding of large parts of the continent in January and March, and from a decline in beef exports to the three main markets–Japan, the United States, and the European Community (Common Market). Wool brought good returns early in the year, but the Australian Wool Commission had to buy much of it in later sales. A floor price for wool began operating for the first time on September 1.

Wheat and sugar continued to sell well abroad, in spite of the failure of negotiations to provide regular supplies of sugar to Great Britain. The Labor government's tax policies proved unpopular with farmers, as did its decision to remove the subsidy on phosphate fertilizer on December 31.

Mineral Resources. Mineral exports continued to improve, especially exports of coking coal, the highest grade of bituminous coal, and iron ore. The minister for minerals and energy announced on October 9 that contracts for coking coal exports in 1975 would probably bring in $1.1 billion, up from $630 million in 1974. Iron ore contracts for 1975 would also total about $1.1 billion, up from $784-million.

The government's earlier enthusiasm for total Australian control of mineral resources had been much reduced by November 3, when Whitlam announced less stringent guidelines for the use of private foreign capital in mineral exploration. He also recognized the right of mining companies to have a return on capital in line with the high risks sometimes involved in exploration and development.

Medical Teams bringing emergency food, blood plasma, and other relief supplies flew into the cyclone-devastated city of Darwin at the end of December in the largest relief operation since World War II. Cyclone Tracy leveled the northern Australian port city on Christmas Day, leaving at least 48 persons dead, hundreds injured, and half of the city's 40,000 residents homeless. Thousands of refugees were evacuated to the south.

Foreign Relations continued along the lines set in 1973. A trade mission to North Vietnam, announcement of the first trade agreement with East Germany, establishment of diplomatic relations with North Korea, and an Australian trade fair in China showed how far Australia had moved from its previous reluctance to deal with those countries.

Relations with Japan continued to be good. Throughout the year, officials worked steadily toward a treaty that would embody joint interests, to be known as the Treaty of Nara. Japan's Prime Minister Kakuei Tanaka visited Australia between October 31 and November 6.

Other state visitors included President Julius K. Nyerere of Tanzania in March, President U Ne Win of Burma in May, and the shah of Iran in September. Australia pursued its policy of cultivating relations with the third world of developing nations by unsuccessfully voting for South Africa's expulsion from the United Nations in October, and by joining the International Bauxite Association. This group was established after a meeting in Guinea in March to coordinate policy on the ore used in making aluminum. However, Australia made it clear that it would not ignore the interests of the consumer countries.

The Australian government signed a new agreement with the United States on March 21 giving

Police try to shield Prime Minister Edward Gough Whitlam, who is being pushed, punched, and pelted with rubbish at an election rally in March.

Australia greater control over the operation of the Northwest Cape Naval Communications Station in Western Australia. The station, which would be highly important in case of nuclear war, had been operated since 1963 by the United States alone. Under the new agreement, it will be a joint facility of the two countries, and the United States will retain exclusive rights to only one communications building.

The government asked both the United States and Russia to use restraint in the build-up of naval forces in the Indian Ocean. Australia also protested nuclear tests by France and China.

Immigration Declined in the face of growing economic difficulties. The government temporarily suspended the admission of immigrants on October 2 and indicated that future immigration would depend upon the availability of jobs. Even before the announcement, Australia had reduced the expected number of immigrants from 110,000 to 80,000.

More attention was paid to language training and other forms of assistance to migrants already in Australia. New visa requirements were to become effective in 1975 for visitors from Britain, Ireland, Canada, and Fiji, because the old "easy visa" system enabled migrants to enter illegally and take jobs. However, Australia continued to operate its immigration system without reference to ethnic origins.

The Aborigines. The government was committed to improving the condition of the Aborigines, but their status continued to cause concern. There were upheavals in the Department of Aboriginal Affairs, and constant argument between the federal and Queensland governments. Western Australia handed over control of its Aboriginal affairs to the federal government on July 1. The government accepted recommendations in May for increasing Aboriginal land rights in the Northern Territory. Spending on Aboriginal welfare continued to increase rapidly. However, Aborigine demonstrators jeered Prime Minister Whitlam on the steps of Parliament House on October 30.

Social Change. The Conciliation and Arbitration Commission ruled on May 2 that equal pay for men and women would be fully effective by June 30, 1975. The minimum wage was also raised. Sir John Kerr, chief justice of New South Wales and the son of a Sydney boilermaker, was named in February to succeed Sir Paul Hasluck as governor general. He took over the post in June. "Advance Australia Fair" was adopted on April 9 as the national anthem in place of "God Save the Queen."

In sports, Think Big won the Melbourne Cup, Richmond won the Victorian Football League Grand Final, and Eastern Suburbs took the Sydney Rugby League Grand Final. Victoria won the Sheffield Shield for cricket.   J. D. B. Miller

See also ASIA (Facts in Brief Table); WHITLAM, EDWARD GOUGH.

AUSTRIA. Rudolf Kirchschlaeger, the foreign minister since 1970, was elected president on June 23, 1974, maintaining the Socialist Party's unbroken hold on the presidency since World War II. He had a 4 per cent lead over the conservative People's Party candidate, Alois Lugger, mayor of Innsbruck. Kirchschlaeger, 59, took nearly 52 per cent of the votes and nearly 64 per cent in Vienna, the capital. He succeeded Franz Jonas, federal president since 1965, who died on April 23. See KIRCHSCHLAEGER, RUDOLF.

In provincial elections in Lower Austria on June 9, the ruling Socialists lost a provincial assembly seat to the People's Party. The People's Party then held 31 seats to the Socialists' 25.

The Austrian schilling was effectively revalued upward by 3 per cent on May 16 when the national currency was withdrawn from the European joint float. The central bank had been forced to buy $30-million in U.S. currency to maintain the schilling's exchange rate relative to other currencies. National bank experts said the schilling would be kept broadly in step with the main joint-float currencies, notably that of West Germany, but they were anxious to counter inflation by cutting import prices.

Critics of the revaluation claimed it would worsen Austria's unprecedented drop in tourism in 1974. Foreign currency revenue from tourism dropped by 25 per cent, while Austrians spent 5 per cent more abroad. Tourism is a major economic factor; it accounted for 23 per cent of visible export earnings in 1973. The government promised federal aid and credits for tourist enterprises hurt by the revaluation.

Inflationary Trends. Business expansion continued against a background of nearly fully utilized resources, rising prices, and labor shortages. However, the growth rate of capital investment declined to only 3 per cent from 11 per cent the previous year because of the government's credit curbs. The gross national product nearly equaled the target growth rate of $4\frac{1}{2}$ per cent, despite the oil crisis. Austria's "partnership" approach to wages and prices, under which the government, management, and trade unions negotiate centrally through a joint wage and price commission, produced lower unit labor cost rises than the European average. But prices rose about 10 per cent and threatened the partnership. At year's end, the government was considering a ceiling on the permissible number of foreign workers, currently estimated to be 10 per cent of the work force.

A European Center for Coordinating Social Welfare is to be set up in Vienna with United Nations backing. In September, Vienna Mayor Leopold Gratz promised to relocate the city's Red Cross Center that assists Jews emigrating from Russia. Residents near the center had feared possible Arab terrorist attacks.   Kenneth Brown

See also EUROPE (Facts in Brief Table).

AUTOMOBILE. For the world's automakers, 1974 began badly – and ended worse. The Middle East oil embargo, drastically higher fuel costs, and much higher price tags for new cars destroyed consumer enthusiasm. As new-car sales slumped, layoffs and plant closings increased, and corporate profits declined. Late in the year, U.S. automakers announced production cutbacks and plant closings that idled more than 200,000 workers. There were also extensive layoffs in Europe, where roughly 1 job in 10 depends on the auto industry.

By October, sales were down 33 per cent in Italy, and 25 per cent in Germany. November sales were down 35 per cent in France, and most other countries fared little better. The United States had 34 per cent fewer sales in November, 1974, than in November, 1973. It was the worst drop for any month in 1974. United States sales improved very slightly in early December, which registered 29 per cent fewer sales than in December, 1973.

Auto sales in the United States came to about 14.6 million units in 1974, down 13 per cent. That put total worldwide car sales in the area of 23.5 million cars.

U.S. Auto Production for 1974 was estimated at about 7.3 million cars, 24 per cent fewer than 1973's record 9.7 million. Sales of domestic and imported cars also dropped sharply from the record 11.4 million cars in 1973 to an estimated 8.9 million, down 22 per cent.

The sales drop hit the auto firms right in the pocket. General Motors Corporation (GM) earnings for the first nine months of 1974 were off 77 per cent, with a third-quarter drop of 94 per cent. Ford Motor Company earnings were off 60 per cent for the nine months, and Chrysler Corporation was down 88 per cent. United States carmakers sold 7,448,921 cars in 1974, down from 9,669,689 in 1973.

Import Cars had their problems in the U.S. market. They got about 16 per cent of the market – virtually the same slice they had in 1973 – but the piece came out of a much smaller overall market this time. Through the first 11 months of 1974, dealers sold 1,323,638 imported cars, compared to 1,620,811 in the same 1973 period.

Volkswagen (VW), the leading import, was among the hardest hit. Its 11-month sales totaled 316,087 cars, down from 443,969 for the same period a year earlier. Two Japanese cars, Toyota (227,094) and Datsun (178,213) ran next to VW in this period.

Market Mix. One of the industry's problems was trying to determine the customer's buying taste. Many auto men thought that the demand for compact and subcompact cars would skyrocket because of the fuel shortage and high cost of gasoline. But, after a strong first six months for the small cars, standard and luxury models sold better than expected in the second half of 1974. By mid-November, the small cars and standard-sized cars were running virtually

Gas shortages, price hikes, and recession fears brought slumping auto sales, big factory inventories, and drastic production cutbacks.

neck and neck. Small cars took 35.46 per cent of sales; standards, 34.93; and intermediates, 25.51.

Car prices jumped substantially on the U.S.-made 1975 models. However, the price picture was difficult to clarify, because automakers shuffled standard and optional equipment on their cars. The trade publication *Automotive News* said its study of 270 models available both in 1973 and 1974 showed new prices were up an average of $449.86, or 10.19 per cent. The remainder of the 307 models offered in 1975 were new, and no comparison could be made.

Automotive News figured that American Motors prices were up $382.62, or 13.02 per cent; GM $429.68, or 9.47 per cent; Chrysler $432.20, or 9.97 per cent; and Ford $540.36, or 12.26 per cent. More price shuffling went on throughout the year. Ford's Pinto price was cut $150 in late November to $2,769. Ford said this made it the lowest-priced domestic car. When the federal government decreed that the unpopular ignition-seat belt interlock system could be abolished, GM cut its prices $13. The device requires drivers and front-seat passengers to fasten their seat belts before the car's ignition can be turned on.

GM Appeal. In statements presented to a Senate subcommittee in December, GM called for a moratorium on design and engineering changes that are required to meet federal safety and emissions standards. Just meeting current federal safety standards cost $400 a car, GM said, of which $155 was for a

Fuel economy heightened consumer interest in foreign and domestic compact cars after the Middle East oil embargo cut gas supplies.

stronger bumper system. It said 1976 standards would require stronger brakes and bumper changes, while 1977 standards call for stronger seats and a passive-restraint system such as airbags. If forced to meet these standards, GM said, the price of cars would go up another $350, making the three-year total for safety items alone $750.

The GM plea for government relief also said that the cost of meeting air-emission standards for 1975 cars was $215. This figure would go up to $475 in meeting the standards proposed through 1978.

"Thus, by 1978," GM said, "consumers would have to pay $1,225 per car just for equipment to meet federal safety and emissions standards."

Fuel Conservation. The auto industry also objected to government fuel-consumption standards. Spokesmen said that about 430 pounds (195 kilograms) must be added to the car's weight in order to comply with all existing and proposed safety and emissions standards. It said that emissions standards suggested by some for 1977 would mean an additional loss of 15 to 20 per cent in fuel economy. Environmental Protection Administrator Russell E. Train pointed out that after Jan. 1, 1975, auto firms can request a one-year suspension of the proposed 1977 standards for reducing hydrocarbons and carbon monoxide emissions. He said that hearings would then consider the ability of the auto firms to meet the 1977 standards and their ability to increase gaso-

line mileage 40 per cent by 1980, as requested by President Gerald R. Ford. Train said the auto firms had told him they could not meet the fuel-economy goal unless the government agreed to a freeze on safety and emissions standards.

Experimental Engines. Automakers, faced with the fact that gasoline was likely to become scarcer and more expensive, continued to work on various experimental engines, ranging from electric to steam. No breakthroughs were reported. Chevrolet, which had announced it would probably put some cars powered by Wankel rotary engines on the road in 1974, postponed the plan because of lab problems. Declining corporate profits caused automakers to delay or cancel other research projects.

Gains and Losses. A hopeful Philadelphia entrepreneur, Malcolm Bricklin, formed the first new company to try the mass production of automobiles in North America since Preston Tucker tried to market the Tucker Torpedo in the late 1940s. More than 700 Bricklins, two-seat sports cars, were manufactured in 1974 at Bricklin's Canadian plant in St. John, New Brunswick. Bricklin hopes eventually to produce 50,000 cars a year.

Meanwhile, Aston Martin, the British maker of expensive sports cars, announced on December 30 that it was going out of business. The company blamed the economic crisis for its decision, which idled 500 company workers.   Charles C. Cain III

AUTOMOBILE RACING. Emerson Fittipaldi became a winning driver at the age of 7, when he won a soap-box derby in his native São Paulo, Brazil. In 1974, at the age of 27, he won the world drivers' championship for the second time in three years.

This title, the most coveted in the sport, was decided in 15 Grand Prix races around the world. The competition among the sleek Formula One cars was so close that three drivers entered the final race, the $300,000 United States Grand Prix on October 6 in Watkins Glen, N.Y., with a chance for the world title.

The three were Fittipaldi, driving a Team McLaren chassis with a Ford-Cosworth V-8, 3-liter engine; Clay Regazzoni of Switzerland in a Ferrari with a Ferrari engine; and Jody Scheckter of South Africa in a Tyrrell-Ford. Jackie Stewart of Scotland won the 1973 title in a similar Tyrrell-Ford, then retired.

Carlos Reutemann of Argentina won the United States Grand Prix in a Brabham-Ford. Regazzoni and Scheckter broke down. Fittipaldi finished fourth, and became world champion again.

Of the 14 Grand Prix races earlier in the year, Fittipaldi won in Brazil, Belgium, and Canada; Ronnie Peterson of Sweden (Lotus-Ford) in Monaco, France, and Italy; Reutemann in South Africa and Austria; Scheckter in Sweden and Great Britain; Niki Lauda of Austria (Ferrari) in Spain and the

Emerson Fittipaldi finishes fourth in the U.S. Grand Prix at Watkins Glen, N.Y., on October 6 to clinch his second world drivers' title.

Netherlands; Regazzoni in West Germany; and Denis Hulme of New Zealand (McLaren-Ford) in Argentina. The 12-cylinder Ferraris were the fastest cars, but they frequently broke down.

In the series for the world manufacturers' championship, in races that lasted from 6 to 24 hours, the idea was to keep the cars from breaking down. Matra-Simca of France won the title for the third year in a row, and its team of Henri Pescarolo and Gerald Larrouse won the series' (and Europe's) most celebrated race, the 24 Hours of Le Mans. Pescarolo was unhappy after Le Mans, saying, "I don't like it very much. It's bloody too long and it's very difficult, much more difficult, driving at less than the car's limit, to stay far from your own limit."

Indianapolis 500. America's premier race, the Indianapolis 500, had a new look on May 26. After almost annual accidents—some of them fatal, involving both drivers and spectators—safety walls were redesigned, emergency procedures were introduced, new and younger officials ran the race, gasoline tanks were smaller, and more pit stops were required.

In an almost accident-free race, Johnny Rutherford of Fort Worth, Tex., won in a Team McLaren-Offenhauser and split the winner's purse of $245,031 with car owner and crew. The total purse was $1,015,686, a record for the sport. Bobby Unser of Albuquerque, N. Mex., driving an Eagle-Ford, was second at Indianapolis and first in the California

500, and he won the United States Auto Club's Championship Trial for Indianapolis-type cars.

Stock Cars. The other major type of racing peculiar to the United States was the National Association for Stock Car Auto Racing (NASCAR) Grand National series for late-model sedans. Richard Petty of Randleman, N.C., won his fifth Grand National driving title, a record. Petty, driving a 1974 Dodge, and Cale Yarborough of Timmonsville, S.C., in a 1974 Chevrolet, each won 10 of the 30 races. The richest NASCAR race was the $275,000 Daytona 500 on February 17 in Daytona Beach, Fla. Petty won for a record fifth time when Donnie Allison's left front tire was shredded with less than 28 miles (45 kilometers) to go. Petty's earnings for the year were $278,175.

The Canadian-American Challenge Cup (Can-Am) series was dominated by UOP Shadows driven by Jackie Oliver of England and George Follmer of Arcadia, Calif. Oliver won four of the five races, and Follmer seethed. He resented orders from the pits to let Oliver win. The 1975 Can-Am series fell victim to inflation, however. It was canceled in November.

In the seven-race Formula 5000 series, the Lola-Chevrolets driven by Brian Redman of England and Mario Andretti of Nazareth, Pa., won three races each, and Redman won the series. These cars looked like Indianapolis cars, but their stock-block engines were much cheaper.   Frank Litsky

AVIATION

AVIATION stalled in 1974 as spiraling jet-fuel prices combined with slumping passenger and air-cargo traffic late in the year to produce growing losses on many of the world's airline routes. A poor safety record added to the airlines' woes. As a result, 1974 was the airlines' worst year ever, according to Knut Hammarskjoeld, director general of the International Air Transport Association. He said the world's air transport industry would register an operating loss of 3 per cent for 1974, before taxes and interest on capital.

Nevertheless, United States scheduled airlines had one of the most profitable years in their history, despite the uncertainty with which 1974 began and ended. Profits were $365 million, about 70 per cent higher than in 1973. Unexpectedly heavy traffic on domestic routes during the first half of the year, flight reductions made in response to the 1973 oil embargo, revenue gains from numerous fare increases, and the phasing out of old aircraft were the chief factors responsible for the U.S. industry's improved profits.

Domestic airline traffic increased 2.5 per cent, most of the gain coming during the first six months when traffic was up 6.3 per cent. Most of the gain reflected the public's confusion about the fuel situation during the first quarter. Many who normally traveled by automobile turned to air transportation rather than risk being unable to obtain the fuel they would need. Industry sources estimated that this factor may have contributed as much as three percentage points of the total traffic gain when its effect was at its peak in March. But in October, a sharp drop in domestic traffic began, and the declines in November and December were among the sharpest since World War II. As in winter, 1973, airline officials anticipated the need for reduced schedules by grounding some aircraft.

Air freight revenues reached $1.1 billion, a 10 per cent increase over 1973's revenues. Total air freight increased by about 5.3 per cent. Domestic air freight was up 2.1 per cent, while international air freight hauled by U.S. carriers rose 10.3 per cent.

International Problems. The two major U.S. international air carriers—Pan American World Airways (PanAm) and Trans World Airlines (TWA) —were deep in debt and asked the federal government for help. By midyear, PanAm, having lost $174 million over the previous six years, had just about run out of cash. TWA was in better shape but predicted a pretax loss of about $47 million on its 1974 international operations. Soaring fuel costs and a 10 per cent decline in international passenger traffic threatened the airlines' survival.

Consequently, both carriers requested emergency federal subsidies. TWA did not specify an amount,

A giant circular terminal dominates the new Charles de Gaulle Airport at Roissy, France. It dwarfs a *Concorde* supersonic transport, left.

The new Lockheed SR-71, truly faster than a speeding bullet, lands in England after crossing the Atlantic Ocean in 1 hour 55 minutes.

but on August 23, PanAm sought $10.2 million a month retroactive to April to help pay its bills. The proposal was rejected in September by the Civil Aeronautics Board (CAB), the agency responsible for approving airline subsidies. Administration officials said President Gerald R. Ford decided that it was not "fair to the nation's taxpayers" to ask them to support international airlines "with direct cash subsidy payments."

President Ford, however, did direct that a strong effort be made to improve the competitive climate in which U.S. international air carriers operate, including "corrective action" against foreign governments that discriminate against U.S. lines by charging excessive fees.

In October, the two air carriers agreed to reduce their competition by swapping or dropping certain routes, saving an estimated $50 million annually. In December, PanAm pilots reportedly accepted an 11 per cent wage cut in return for PanAm's withdrawal from an industry mutual strike-aid pact, effective Jan. 1, 1976.

PanAm and TWA were not alone in crisis. Worldwide inflation, skyrocketing fuel costs, and slumping passenger volume produced 1974 losses of about $500 million for the world's international airlines.

Alitalia, the Italian national airline, announced plans on November 29 that it hoped would reduce its 1975 operating deficit by $90 million. The plans included a 17 per cent reduction in North Atlantic service. The company reported a 1974 loss of about $100 million. Air France, the French national air carrier, expected a similar $100-million deficit, while the British and Belgian carriers placed their losses at about $40 million each. Industry observers believe that the international airlines can be profitable only if they cooperate in reducing the number of flights, eliminate unfair competition, and raise fares to cover costs.

Supersonic Transport. The future of the British-French *Concorde* looked increasingly bleak; leaders in both countries dubbed the project a financial fiasco. The plane continued to be dogged by cost overruns. Originally budgeted at $480 million, the project had used up $3 billion, and the price of each aircraft had risen from $15 million to $65 million.

As a result, the only firm orders for the *Concorde* remained captive ones from the British and French state airlines–Air France for four planes and British Airways for five. The two countries hoped to sell planes to oil-rich Iran and perhaps even China, but prospects for the vital U.S. market were dim because of the *Concorde*'s poor economics. It would cost eight times as much as a Boeing 747 for from two to three times the speed, one-third the seating capacity, and triple the fuel consumption.

Meanwhile, Russia's TU-144 was racing the trouble-plagued *Concorde* to become the world's first supersonic jet transport operating commercially. It was slated for commercial service late in 1975.

Air Safety. More than 1,200 persons were killed in air crashes throughout the world, making 1974 the worst year for aviation safety in history. The world's two worst air disasters occurred, and 1974 also produced the worst U.S. record of fatalities since 1960.

In the world's worst air crash, 346 persons died when a Turkish DC-10 jumbo jet plunged into a forest after take-off from Orly Airport outside Paris on March 3. The second worst air disaster in history occurred on December 4 when a Dutch DC-8 charter flight carrying 182 Moslem pilgrims to Mecca and a crew of nine crashed in Sri Lanka.

The year also saw the first fatal crash of a Boeing 747 jetliner. Fifty-nine persons were killed on November 20, when a Lufthansa 747 crashed shortly after take-off near Nairobi, Kenya. However, 98 others aboard the plane survived.

A total of 467 persons were killed on U.S. scheduled airline flights in nine crashes. This was more than twice the number in any of the five previous years. See DISASTERS (Aircraft Crashes).

In many cases, a mechanical defect or an error committed by a flight crew caused the crash. As a result, questions were raised about the performance of the Federal Aviation Administration (FAA), the government agency primarily responsible for protecting the flying public. After a nine-month study, a House subcommittee issued a report in December charging the FAA with "sluggishness which at times approaches an attitude of indifference to public safety."

The FAA was criticized in connection with the March DC-10 crash near Orly. It was widely suspected that a cargo door, found intact miles from the crash site, may have been improperly latched and came off in flight. The loss of the door could have caused sudden decompression of the cargo cabin, crushing the cabin floor and thereby severing vital control cables.

Such a cargo-door incident nearly caused a DC-10 to crash near Detroit in 1972. This incident prompted the FAA to prepare an "airworthiness directive" to McDonnell Douglas Corporation, maker of the DC-10, demanding cargo-door design changes. The manufacturer appealed the decision, and a less formal "general notice" was sent to each DC-10 owner instead.

In March, McDonnell Douglas officials conceded that the Turkish DC-10 had left its Long Beach, Calif., factory in December, 1972, without a vital cargo-door improvement, even though the company's records indicated a change had been made. For its part, the FAA said in April it would order safety-related design changes in the future, rather than leaving such changes to the manufacturer and the airlines to work out. Kenneth E. Schaefle

AWARDS AND PRIZES presented in 1974 included the following:

Arts Awards

American Institute of Architects. *Allied Professions Medal,* Kevin Lynch, Cambridge, Mass., for work in urban design and environmental planning. *Architecture Critics' Medal,* Walter McQuade, New York City, for architectural criticism. *Craftsmanship Medal,* Sheila Hicks, Paris. *Fine Arts Medal,* Ruth Asawa Lanier, San Francisco, *Twenty-Five-Year Award,* Johnson's Wax Company Administration Building, Racine, Wis., designed by Frank Lloyd Wright.

Brandeis University *Creative Arts Awards. Medal for Dance,* Anna Sokolow. *Medal for Poetry,* Robert Francis. *Medal for Sculpture,* Tony Smith. *Medal for Theater Arts,* Helen Hayes.

Capezio Dance Award. Robert Joffrey, founder and director of the City Center Joffrey Ballet, New York City.

National Academy of Design. *Benjamin Altman Prize for Figure Painting,* Charles Reid, for *Friends; Landscape Painting,* Reuben Tam, for *Lava Mountains.*

National Academy of Recording Arts and Sciences. *Grammy Awards: Record of the Year,* "Killing Me Softly with His Song" by Roberta Flack. *Song of the Year,* "Killing Me Softly with His Song," written by Norman Gimbel and Charles Fox. *Album of the Year, Pop,* "Innervisions" by Stevie Wonder. *Classical,* Bartok's *Concerto for Orchestra* with Pierre Boulez conducting the New York Philharmonic. *Best Classical Performance, Orchestra,* the New York Philharmonic, conducted by Pierre Boulez in Bartok's *Concerto for Orchestra; Soloist with Orchestra,* Vladimir Ashkenazy for the five Beethoven Piano Concertos, with the Chicago Symphony Orchestra, conducted by Georg Solti; *Best Solo Classical Performance,* Puccini's "Heroines" by Leontyne Price; *Best Chamber Music Performance,* Scott Joplin's "The Red Back Book" conducted by Gunther Schuller. *Best Opera Recording,* Bizet's *Carmen* with Leonard Bernstein conducting the Metropolitan Opera. *Best Jazz Performance, Big Band,* "Giant Steps" by Woody Herman; *Group,* "Supersax Plays Big Bird" by Supersax; *Solo,* "God Is in the House" by Art Tatum. *Best Country Vocal Performance, Female,* "Let Me Be There" by Olivia Newton-John; *Male,* "Behind Closed Doors" by Charlie Rich. *Best Contemporary Vocal Performance, Female,* Roberta Flack with "Killing Me Softly with His Song"; *Male,* Stevie Wonder for "You Are the Sunshine of My Life"; *Combo,* Gladys Knight and The Pips for "Neither One of Us." *Best New Artist of the Year,* Bette Midler.

National Academy of Television Arts and Sciences. *Emmy Awards: Best Actor and Actress in a Special,* Hal Holbrook in "Pueblo" and Cicely Tyson in "The Autobiography of Miss Jane Pittman." *Best Actor and Actress in a Series,* Alan Alda in "M·A·S·H," and Mary Tyler Moore in "The Mary Tyler Moore Show." *Best Supporting Actor and Actress,* Michael Moriarty and Joanna Miles in "The Glass Menagerie." *Best Dramatic Series,* "Upstairs, Downstairs," produced by Rex Firkin and John Hawkesworth. *Best Comedy Series,* "M·A·S·H," produced by Gene Reynolds and Larry Gelbart. *Best Music-Variety Series,* "The Carol Burnett Show," to Carol Burnett and producers Joe Hamilton and Ed Simmons. *Best Dramatic Special,* "The Autobiography of Miss Jane Pittman," produced by Robert Christiansen and Rick Rosenberg. *Best Comedy, Variety, or Music Special,* "Lily," to Lily Tomlin and producers Irene Pine, Herb Sargent, and Jerry McPhie. *Best Children's Special,* "Marlo Thomas and Friends in Free To Be . . . You and Me," produced by Marlo Thomas and Carole Hart. *Best Director of a Series,* Robert Butler for "The Blue Knight." *Best*

Director of a Special, Dwight Hemion for "Barbra Streisand and Other Musical Instruments."

National Institute of Arts and Letters and American Academy of Arts and Letters. *Award for Distinguished Service to the Arts,* Walker Evans. *Award of Merit for the Novel,* Nelson Algren. *Arnold W. Brunner Memorial Prize in Architecture,* Hugh Hardy, with Malcolm Holzman and Norman Pfeiffer. *E.M. Forster Award,* Paul Bailey. *Charles E. Ives Award,* the Charles E. Ives Society. *Gold Medal for Graphic Art,* Saul Steinberg. *Loines Award for Poetry,* Philip Larkin. *Richard and Hinda Rosenthal Foundation Awards,* Julie Curtis Reed and Alice Walker. *National Institute Awards. Art,* Perle Fine, Richard Fleischner, Marilynn Gelfman-Pereira, George Griffin, Nancy Grossman, Ibram Lassaw, and Charlotte Park. *Literature,* Ann Cornelison, Stanley Elkin, Elizabeth Hardwick, Josephine Johnson, Donald Justice, David Rabe, Charles Rosen, Sam Shepard, James Tate, Henry Van Dyke, Lanford Wilson. *Music.* Richard Felciano, Raoul Pleskow, Phillip Rhodes, Olly Wilson.

Journalism Awards

American Association for the Advancement of Science (AAAS). *AAAS-Westinghouse Science Reporting Award,* David Brand, staff reporter, *The Wall Street Journal,* for three articles dealing with protein research, solar energy, and artificial intelligence.

The Newspaper Guild. *Heywood Broun Award,* Donald L. Barlett and James B. Steele, the *Philadelphia Inquirer,* for a series exposing discrimination by judges and prosecutors and uneven treatment in the sentencing and jailing of accused persons, some of whom were innocent of the charges.

Columbia University. *Maria Moors Cabot Awards,* for distinguished journalistic contributions to the advancement of Inter-American understanding, Don Bohning, Latin American editor, *The Miami Herald;* William D. Montalbano, Latin American correspondent, *The Miami Herald;* Fernando Pedreira, editor-in-chief, *O Estado Do São Paulo,* Brazil.

Long Island University. *George Polk Memorial Awards: Book,* David Wise for *The Politics of Lying: Government Deception, Secrecy, and Power. Foreign Reporting,* Henry S. Bradsher, Hong Kong correspondent of the *Washington Star-News,* for articles on China. *Investigative Reporting,* Seymour Hersh, *The New York Times,* for reporting on the American air raids on Cambodia in 1969 and 1970 and the government cover-up of the raids. *Magazine Reporting,* John Osborne, for his column "The Nixon Watch" in *The New Republic. Metropolitan Reporting,* James Savage and Mike Baxter of *The Miami Herald,* for their articles about illegal political fund-raising. *National Reporting,* Andrew H. Malcolm, *The New York Times,* for articles about illegal no-knock raids by federal narcotics agents. *News Photography,* George Brich of the Associated Press for a picture of an American prisoner of war returning from North Vietnam. *Television,* the Public Broadcasting Service and the National Public Affairs Center for Television, for coverage of the Senate Watergate Committee hearings. *Special Award,* Donald L. Barlett and James B. Steele of the *Philadelphia Inquirer* for articles about the oil shortage.

National Cartoonists Society. *Reuben,* Dik Browne, for the comic strip "Hagar the Horrible."

New York Women in Communications. *Matrix Awards,* for exceptional achievement in the communications industry: *Books,* Marya Mannes, author of *Last Rights. Newspapers,* Charlotte Curtis, Associate Editor, *The New York Times. Magazines,* Shana Alexander, *Newsweek* columnist. *Broadcasting,* Rita Sands, WCBS-Newsradio.

Famous Spanish guitarist Andrés Segovia, left, receives the Sonning Music Prize from Danish composer Borge Friis in Copenhagen in June.

The Society of Professional Journalists, Sigma Delta Chi. *Newspaper Awards: General Reporting,* James R. Polk, *Washington Star-News,* for his stories revealing secret national political campaign contributions by financier Robert Vesco. *Editorial Writing,* Frank W. Corrigan, *Newsday,* for his timely and thorough discussion of the energy crisis. *Washington Correspondence,* James M. Naughton, John M. Crewdson, Ben A. Franklin, Christopher Lydon, and Agis Salpukas of *The New York Times* Washington Bureau for their coverage of Vice-President Spiro T. Agnew's "plea bargaining" to avoid prosecution and possible imprisonment. *Foreign Correspondence,* Jacques Leslie, *Los Angeles Times,* for his detailed reports on Vietnam after the cease-fire. *News Photography,* Anthony K. Roberts, free-lance photographer, for a series of photographs documenting an attempted kidnaping in Los Angeles, which ended in the assailant's death. *Editorial Cartooning,* Paul Szep, *The Boston Globe,* for his pungently humorous and timely political cartoons. *Public Service in Newspaper Journalism, Newsday,* Garden City, N.Y., for a 32-article series, "The Heroin Trail," which traced in detail the movement of heroin from the poppy fields of Turkey to the streets of Long Island. *Magazine Awards: Reporting,* Floyd Miller, *The Reader's Digest,* for a story about a 1972 train-bus crash in Congers, N.Y. *Public Service, Philadelphia* magazine, for an article by Mike Mallowe, "Willie Lee Weston Is Armed and Dangerous." The article studied the dangers of poorly trained armed security guards. *Radio Awards: Reporting,* Eric Engberg, Washington News Bureau, Group W, Westinghouse Broadcasting Company, for his live, 10-minute, spot news report on the resignation of Vice-President Spiro T. Agnew. *Public Service,* WMAL Radio, Washington, D.C., for a 27-

part series, "The Legend of Lenient Justice," on Washington's criminal-court system. *Editorializing,* WGRG Radio, Pittsfield, Mass., for a thoughtful series of editorials on Watergate. *Television Awards: Reporting,* correspondent Steve Young and producer Roger Sims, Columbia Broadcasting System News, for a three-part series, "Deprogramming: The Clash Between Religion and Civil Rights," which documented the capture of a young member of a fundamentalist sect and her subsequent "deprogramming" at the request of her parents. *Public Service,* WSOC-TV, Charlotte, N.C., for "Police File," a series of stories about unsolved crimes. *Editorializing,* KRON-TV, San Francisco, for editorials about a dangerous stretch of highway near the Golden Gate Bridge. *Research in Journalism,* Philip Meyer, Knight Newspapers, for his book, *Precision Journalism,* which deals with the use of surveys and public-opinion polls in the news media. *Distinguished Teaching in Journalism,* John Hohenberg, professor emeritus, School of Journalism, Columbia University, New York.

Literature Awards

Academy of American Poets. *Lamont Poetry Selection Award,* John Balaban, for his first book of poems, *After Our War.*

American Library Association. *Beta Phi Mu Award,* Martha Boaz, Dean, School of Library Science, University of Southern California, Los Angeles. *Caldecott Medal,* Margot Zemach, for illustrating *Duffy and the Devil. Francis Joseph Campbell Citation,* for outstanding contributions to advancing library services to blind people, to Senator Randolph Jennings (D., W. Va.). *Melvil Dewey Medal,* for creative professional achievement, to Robert B. Downs, Dean of Library Administration, University of Illinois. *Joseph W. Lippincott Award,* for distinguished service in the library profession, to Jerrold Orne, Professor, School of Library Science, University of North Carolina, Chapel Hill, N.C. *Newbery Medal,* to Paula Fox, author of *The Slave Dancer,* the most distinguished contribution to children's literature.

Copernicus Society of America. *Copernicus Award* to poet Robert Lowell. *Edgar Allen Poe Award,* to poet Mark Strand.

The Mystery Writers of America. *Edgar Allan Poe Awards. Best Mystery,* The Dance Hall of the Dead by Tony Hillerman. *Best First Mystery,* The Billion Dollar Sure Thing by Paul E. Erdman.

National Book Committee. *National Book Awards: Arts and Letters,* Pauline Kael, for *Deeper into Movies. Biography,* Douglas Day, for *Malcolm Lowry: A Biography. Children's Literature,* Eleanor Cameron, for *The Court of the Stone Children. Contemporary Affairs,* Murray Kempton, for *The Briar Patch: the People of the State of New York v. Lumumba Shakur et al. Fiction,* Thomas Pynchon, for *Gravity's Rainbow;* and Isaac Bashevis Singer, for *A Crown of Feathers and Other Stories. History,* John Clive, for *Macaulay: the Shaping of the Historian. Philosophy and Religion,* Maurice Natanson, for *Edmund Husserl: Philosopher of Infinite Tasks. Poetry,* Allen Ginsberg, for *The Fall of America: Poems of These States, 1965-1971,* and Adrienne Rich, for *Diving into the Wreck: Poems, 1971-72. Science,* S. E. Luria, for *Life: the Unfinished Experiment.*

University of Chicago. *Harriet Monroe Poetry Prize,* to Elizabeth Bishop.

Nobel Prizes. See NOBEL PRIZES.

Public Service Awards

American Institute of Public Service. *Award,* to Elliot L. Richardson, former U.S. attorney general, for the greatest public service performed by an elected or ap-

Byron B. Brenden was named the first Inventor of the Year in February for his acoustical holography work. He holds several patents.

pointed official. *Award,* to Ralph Nader, consumer advocate, for the greatest public service performed by a private citizen. *Award,* to Mayor Maynard Jackson of Atlanta, Ga., for the greatest public service performed by an American under the age of 36.

Lyndon Baines Johnson Foundation. *Award,* to Ivan Allen, Jr., former mayor of Atlanta, Ga., and Franklin A. Thomas, president of the Bedford-Stuyvesant Redevelopment Corporation, New York City.

National Association for the Advancement of Colored People. *Spingarn Medal,* to Federal Judge Damon J. Keith of Detroit.

Ramon Magsaysay Award Foundation. *Magsaysay Awards For International Understanding,* William F. Masterson, S.J., an American missionary and educator. *Journalism, Literature, and Creative Communications,* Zacarias B. Sarian, a Filipino editor. *Government Service,* Hiroshi Kuroki, a Japanese public official. *Community Leadership,* Fusaye Ichikawa, a member of the Japanese parliament. *Public Service,* Shrimati M.S. Subbulakshmi, an Indian singer.

Templeton Foundation. *Prize for Progress in Religion,* Brother Roger Shutz, prior of the ecumenical Taizé community in France, for worldwide work among the young and his efforts for "renewal and reconciliation."

Science and Technology Awards

American Chemical Society. *Arthur C. Cope Award,* Donald J. Cram, professor of chemistry, University of California, Los Angeles. *Priestley Medal,* Henry Eyring, Distinguished Professor of Chemistry and Metallurgy, University of Utah.

American Section, Society of Chemical Industry. *Perkin Medal,* Edwin H. Land, chairman, president, and research director of Polaroid Corporation.

American Institute of Aeronautics and Astronautics. *Goddard Awards,* Paul D. Castenholz, Rockwell International Corporation; Richard C. Mulready, United Aircraft Corporation; John L. Sloop, National Aeronautics and Space Administration. *Louis W. Hill Space Transportation Award,* Kurt H. Debus, director, John F. Kennedy Space Center, National Aeronautics and Space Administration.

American Institute of Physics. *Dannie Heineman Prize for Mathematical Physics,* Subrahmanyan Chandrasekhar, Morton D. Hull Distinguished Service Professor of Astronomy and Astrophysics, University of Chicago, for his theoretical work on stellar structures.

American Physical Society. *Bonner Prize in Nuclear Physics,* Denys H. Wilkinson, professor of experimental physics, Oxford University, England. *Buckley Solid State Physics Prize,* Michael Tinkham, Gordon McKay Professor of Applied Physics, Harvard University. *High-Polymer Physics Prize,* Frank A. Bovey, head, Bell Laboratories Polymer Chemistry Research Department. *Langmuir Prize,* Harry G. Drickamer, University of Illinois, Urbana. *Davisson-Germer Prize,* Norman Ramsey, Higgins Professor of Physics, Harvard University. *Leo Szilard Award,* David R. Inglis, University of Massachusetts.

Columbia University. *Louisa Gross Horwitz Prize,* for outstanding research in biology, to geneticist Boris Ephrussi, professor emeritus of biology, University of Paris, and director of the French Center for Molecular Genetics. *Vetlesen Prize,* for achievement in the earth sciences, to Chaim Leib Pekeris, professor of applied mathematics, Weizmann Institute of Science, Rehovoth, Israel.

Franklin Institute. *Franklin Medal,* to Nikolai Bogolyubov, Director, Laboratory for Theoretical Physics, Joint Institute for Nuclear Research, Dubna, Russia, for mathematical discoveries in the field of mechanics.

Geological Society of America. *Penrose Medal,* awarded posthumously to W. Maurice Ewing, founder and director, Lamont-Doherty Geological Observatory, Columbia University. *Arthur L. Day Medal,* to Alfred E. Ringwood, professor of geology, Australian National University in Canberra.

Albert and Mary Lasker Foundation Awards. *Albert Lasker Clinical Medical Research Award,* to John Charnley, professor of orthopedic surgery, and director of the Centre for Hip Surgery, Wrightington Hospital, Wigan, England, for developing surgical methods to completely replace injured or diseased hip joints. *Albert Lasker Basic Medical Research Awards,* to Ludwik Gross, chief of the Cancer Research Unit, Veterans Administration Hospital, Bronx, N.Y., for the discovery of leukemia-inducing and cancer-inducing viruses in mammals; Howard E. Skipper, president, the Southern Research Institute, Birmingham, Ala., for contributions to the chemotherapy of cancer; Sol Spiegelman, director of the Institute of Cancer Research, College of Physicians and Surgeons, Columbia University, for contributions to molecular biology, and the first synthesis of an infectious nucleic acid; and Howard M. Temin, American Cancer Research Professor at the University of Wisconsin, Madison, for contributions to the biology of RNA-containing cancer viruses.

National Academy of Engineering. *Founders Medal,* J. Erik Jonsson, former mayor of Dallas and honorary chairman of the board of Texas Instruments, Incorporated, for contributions to engineering and society. *Zworykin Award,* Ivar Giaever, physicist at the General Electric Research and Development Center, Schenectady, N.Y., for his "contributions to the fields of electronic tunneling, superconductivity, and *in situ* protein detection."

National Academy of Sciences (NAS). *Henry Draper Medal,* Lyman Spitzer, Jr., Young Professor of Astronomy and director of Princeton University Observatory, for his investigations in astronomical physics, studies of the chemical composition and interactions of interstellar matter, and research in plasma physics and controlled nuclear fusion. *Gibbs Brothers Medal,* Phillip Eisenberg, president, Hydronautics, Incorporated, Laurel, Md., for contributions to naval architecture and marine engineering, including his work on hydrofoil boat development. *NAS Award for Environmental Quality,* G. Evelyn Hutchinson, Sterling Professor of Zoology emeritus, Yale University, for "scientific contributions to limnology and ecology and especially for continuing public advocacy . . . of the desperate need for man to understand, preserve, and protect the environment in which he lives." *Selman A. Waksman Award,* Renato Dulbecco, assistant director of research, Imperial Cancer Research Fund, London, for his studies in animal cell biology, which concerned the interaction of animal cells with tumor viruses. *U.S. Steel Foundation Award in Molecular Biology,* David Baltimore, American Cancer Society Professor of Microbiology, Massachusetts Institute of Technology, for "discoveries of the reproduction and enzymology of RNA viruses, [which have] greatly advanced the science of molecular biology."

Theater and Motion Picture Awards

Academy of Motion Picture Arts and Sciences. *"Oscar" Awards:* Best Picture, *The Sting,* Universal Studios. *Best Actor,* Jack Lemmon in *Save The Tiger. Best Supporting Actor,* John Houseman in *The Paper Chase. Best Actress,* Glenda Jackson in *A Touch of Class. Best Supporting Actress,* Tatum O'Neal in *Paper Moon. Best Director,* George Roy Hill for *The Sting. Best Foreign Language Film,* François Truffaut's *Day for Night. Best Original Screenplay,* David S. Ward for *The Sting. Best Documentary, The Great American Cowboy,* produced by Keith Merrill. *Best Song,* "The Way We Were," by Marvin Hamlisch. *Special Oscar,* The Marx Brothers, accepted by Groucho Marx.

Antoinette Perry (Tony) Awards. *Drama: Best Play, The River Niger* by Joseph A. Walker. *Best Actor,* Michael Moriarty in *Find Your Way Home. Best Actress,* Colleen Dewhurst in *A Moon for the Misbegotten. Best Director,* José Quintero for *A Moon for the Misbegotten. Musical: Best Musical, Raisin. Best Actor,* Christopher Plummer in *Cyrano. Best Actress,* Virginia Capers in *Raisin. Best Choreographer,* Michael Bennett for *Seesaw. Composer of the Best Music,* Frederick Loewe, for *Gigi. Writer of the Best Lyrics,* Alan Jay Lerner, for *Gigi.*

Cannes International Film Festival. *Grand Prix International, The Conversation,* United States, written and directed by Francis Ford Coppola. *Best Actor,* Jack Nicholson, *The Last Detail. Best Actress,* Marie José Nat, *Les Violons du Bal. Best Screenplay, Sugarland Express,* written by Hal Barwood and Matthew Robbins.

New York Drama Critics' Circle Awards. *Best Play of 1973-1974, The Contractors,* by David Storey. *Best Musical, Candide,* music by Leonard Bernstein.

New York Film Critics Awards. *Best Film, Day for Night,* directed by François Truffaut. *Best Actor,* Marlon Brando in *Last Tango in Paris. Best Actress,* Joanne Woodward in *Summer Wishes, Winter Dreams. Best Director,* François Truffaut for *Day for Night. Best Screenwriting,* George Lucas, Gloria Katz, and Willard Huyck for *American Graffiti.* Edward G. Nash

See also LITERATURE, CANADIAN; JACKSON, GLENDA; LEMMON, JACK; LITERATURE FOR CHILDREN; MIDLER, BETTE; PLUMMER, CHRISTOPHER.

BAHAMAS. See WEST INDIES.

BAHRAIN. The government acquired complete control over operations of the Bahrain Petroleum Company (BAPCO) in September, 1974, mirroring the worldwide trend among oil-producing states toward nationalization of the industry. Government control extended equally to local marketing, oil exports, and natural gas production averaging 250,000 barrels daily.

Bahrain's oil production of about 66,000 barrels daily represented a slight decrease, but the nationalization enabled the state to show a healthy increase in income and a surplus of $48 million over expenditures. The revised budget, approved by Amir Isa bin Salman Al Khalifa and the National Assembly that was elected in December, 1973, put Bahrain's 1974 revenues at $227 million and expenditures at $177 million.

Work began in July on a huge industrial complex on Sitrah Island, an area of reclaimed land that will provide BAPCO with additional storage facilities and encourage chemical and other petroleum-related industries to establish plants in Bahrain. Construction contracts were awarded to United States, British, and German firms. On August 9, Bahrain sold 3,000 short tons (2,700 metric tons) of aluminum to the People's Republic of China, its first direct sale to China since the two states opened relations.   William Spencer

See also MIDDLE EAST (Facts in Brief Table).

BALLET. See DANCING.

BALTIMORE. A public employee strike in July, 1974, left Baltimore streets buried under tons of garbage and greatly reduced police protection. The trouble began on July 1, when sanitation workers staged a wildcat strike to protest a 6 per cent wage increase. About 3,000 city workers left their jobs during the dispute. Some 1,400 policemen joined the other strikers on July 11. State police were called in to help deal with outbreaks of looting and violence. The union leaders were threatened with jail terms unless the illegal walkouts ended by July 15.

The municipal employees accepted a negotiated settlement on July 15, but the striking police officers demanded a general amnesty. The matter was resolved on July 16 when the union promised to negotiate any action taken against individual strikers.

Combating Crime. A comparative study by two political scientists of the criminal justice systems of Baltimore, Chicago, and Detroit, released in September, revealed that Baltimore convicted 43.7 per cent of its accused felons in 1972 and sent 63.1 per cent to prison. The study found that Baltimore, with the harshest criminal justice system of the three cities, had the lowest rate for crimes against persons.

In August, the Baltimore Police Department started paying $50 for every handgun voluntarily surrendered to them and a bounty of $100 for information leading to the arrest of persons possessing illegal guns. The program was an immediate success.

More than 7,000 weapons were turned in during the first week. Police also claimed that gun-related crimes dropped after the program began.

The Federal Bureau of Investigation reported on October 3 that crime in Baltimore was up 10.9 per cent during the first six months of 1974 over the same period in 1973.

Baltimore County Executive N. Dale Anderson was convicted on March 20 of 28 counts of conspiracy and extortion and four counts of income tax evasion. Anderson was a close associate of former U.S. Vice-President Spiro T. Agnew and succeeded Agnew as Baltimore County's chief executive officer. His conviction stemmed from the same investigation that led to Agnew's resignation in October, 1973.

Living Costs. Baltimore's cost of living rose 13.5 per cent and food costs increased 14.3 per cent between June, 1973, and June, 1974. The average factory worker's income was $10,098 per year as of July. Yet, Department of Labor figures indicated an average family of four needed more than $13,200 to live in moderate comfort in Baltimore.

Baltimore's urban homesteading program, which allows individuals to obtain abandoned homes by promising to repair them, was attacked for failing to serve the poor. A Baltimore Department of Housing official reported that high repair costs limited the program to middle-income buyers.   James M. Banovetz

A Baltimore policeman checks some of the 7,000 handguns voluntarily turned in by citizens after the city began paying $50 for each weapon.

BANGLADESH looked forward to its best year in 1974. Then came the summer floods starting in June, the worst in two decades. The government reported that 1,300 people were drowned, and 27 million were driven from their homes. More than 1 million short tons (0.9 million metric tons) of rice, still in the fields or already harvested, were lost. Vast quantities of jute, the country's primary export money earner, were destroyed.

Widespread Hunger. By October, food supplies were short. The government said that "fewer than 5,000 had died of hunger." But soup kitchens ran out of gruel, warehouses were looted, and officials forecast disaster unless 2.3 million short tons (2.1 million metric tons) of grain could be procured abroad. In fact, only a little more than half that much had been pledged, most of it by the United States and Canada. On November 28, a cyclone swept in from the Bay of Bengal and caused heavy property damage.

Even before the summer floods, the nation was crippled economically. Oil, which ate up one-fifth of the earnings in 1973, took half of them in 1974. The price of imported grain more than doubled. Meantime, the jute crop had dropped from 6.2 million bales in 1973 to around 4 million, and possibly as much as one-fourth of it was smuggled to India.

Law and Disorder. The war of 1971 had left Bangladesh with both weapons and many men eager to use them. To keep law and order, the government formed a force of about 30,000 called Jatyo Rakkhi Bahini. Heavily armed and heavy-handed, these government units themselves became the prime element of lawlessness.

Prime Minister Sheik Mujibur Rahman continued to dominate the scene. But much of the trouble stemmed from his ineptness as an administrator. He insisted on making all decisions, even the trivial ones. Corruption spread, and some of his relatives were accused of enriching themselves. On December 28, the government declared a state of emergency in order to stamp out what it called internal subversion, lawlessness, and political killings.

Reconciliation and Discord. Relations with Pakistan remained strained. In February, Mujibur flew to the Islamic conference in Lahore, Pakistan, where he and Pakistani President Zulfikar Ali Bhutto somewhat reluctantly embraced each other. In early April, Bangladesh, Pakistan, and India agreed that the Pakistani prisoners of war held in India would be sent home. Bangladesh also agreed it would not try 195 Pakistani prisoners on war crimes charges. The omens, therefore, looked good when Bhutto returned to Dacca, the Bangladesh capital. But he and Mujibur disagreed on many issues, and Bhutto left in a huff.

Perhaps the only happy events for the country were Bangladesh's admission to the United Nations in September and the signing of contracts to drill for oil in the Bay of Bengal.   Mark Gayn

See also ASIA (Facts in Brief Table).

BANKS AND BANKING throughout the world weathered a series of disturbances in 1974. These developments led some commentators to draw parallels to the period from 1929 to 1933 and the onset of the Great Depression.

Several of the world's large banks failed, including the Franklin National Bank in New York City, the largest of several banks that failed in the United States. Bankhaus I. D. Herstatt in Cologne, West Germany, collapsed on June 26 after suffering heavy foreign exchange losses. Three smaller German banks closed shortly after. The Banca Privata Italiana of Milan, Italy, closed its doors in September, with a group of other enterprises taking over its liabilities.

An arrest warrant was issued in Italy for financier Michele Sindona, the principal stockholder in Banca Privata Italiana, Franklin National, and one of the smaller German banks. He was charged with fraud in connection with his Italian bank holdings. In New York City, the Securities and Exchange Commission filed suit against Sindona and others in October for violations of securities laws at Franklin National, particularly in hiding losses sustained in foreign exchange speculation and in overvaluing the bank's securities portfolio.

Speculation in foreign currencies led to trouble for a number of banks. Banque de Bruxelles, Belgium's second-largest commercial bank, announced on October 14 that it had lost up to $96 million from unauthorized currency speculation. Three other major European banks also had large losses in foreign exchange, though, like the Brussels bank, they continued to operate. They were the Union Bank of Switzerland, Westdeutsche Landesbank Girozentrale of West Germany, and Lloyd's Bank in London, whose losses occurred through a Swiss branch.

The Franklin National Bank failure on October 8 was the largest bank failure in U.S. history. It came less than a year after the previous record failure, that of the United States National Bank of San Diego in October, 1973. Franklin National was the 20th largest bank in the United States.

Unlike the 1930s, not a single dollar was lost by depositors, not even by those who had more than the $20,000 maximum insured by the Federal Deposit Insurance Corporation (FDIC) at the time. Other creditors did not fare as well, and stockholders were not expected to salvage anything.

The FDIC arranged for the European-American Bank and Trust Company to take over the offices of the defunct Franklin National, its remaining deposits, and selected loans and investments. The failure demonstrated that deposit insurance insures deposits, but not the bank itself. A few weeks after the failure, the maximum insured deposit was raised to $40,000.

Federal Reserve Role. The U.S. Federal Reserve System (Fed) was created in 1913, following a careful study of the bank panic of 1907. It is empowered to act as a lender of last resort to shore up failing banks and to prevent individual bank failures from threatening the entire banking system.

From May to October, 1974, the Fed loaned Franklin National the enormous sum of $1.75 billion, temporarily staving off its failure and allowing massive withdrawals by depositors whose accounts exceeded the insured maximum. Beyond this direct support, the Fed was ready to lend to other banks or to buy securities and pump money into the banking system if a run on other banks occurred. It failed to save the Franklin National, but the operation kept the disaster from spreading to other banks, unlike the situation in the 1930s when thousands of banks failed and billions in savings were lost.

Criticism of the Fed continued on two fronts in 1974. On the one hand, there was a popular outcry that the Fed was responsible for high interest rates that distorted credit-financed spending, especially for housing. Some critics argued that the Fed should have pumped more money into the economy during the year to support legitimate credit demands.

On the other hand, the monetarist economists argued that the Fed had pumped far too much money into the economy in an effort to prevent interest rates from rising very much. According to the monetarists, this policy had backfired by accelerating inflation, which in turn had increased interest rates. The monetarists held that the Fed had overemphasized its role in cushioning financial markets from disturbances such as bank failures, but had not emphasized enough its direct effects on the money supply and spending in the economy.

Restrictive Policies. Even without President Gerald R. Ford's proposed 5 per cent surtax on 1975 incomes, government fiscal policy – its use of spending and revenue-producing activities to achieve certain goals – was very restrictive in 1974. The Administration put a damper on spending increases, and incomes and prices built up by inflation raised income and sales tax collections. When the government raises taxes or lowers spending, the flow of income drops, thus reducing overall demand.

Monetary policy, the Fed's management of the money supply as measured by interest rates or by the rate of monetary growth, also became very restrictive during the third quarter. The economic situation in the first half was clouded by the oil crisis and associated cutbacks in employment and production, but in the third quarter, it was clear that restrictive policies had triggered the second recession of the Nixon-Ford Administration. As the recession deepened late in the year, the Fed began loosening its restrictive policies.

Savings Competition. Inflation and high interest rates through midyear played havoc with savings institutions as depositors withdrew funds in search of higher returns elsewhere. Savings and loan associations, facing record withdrawals in July and August,

Penny-pinching Americans caused a coin shortage in 1974. Officials estimate that U.S. hoarders have stored 30 billion pennies over the past decade.

increased their borrowings from Federal Home Loan banks by nearly $10 billion and cut back normal mortgage lending. Savings accounts were tapped by savers for funds to invest directly in securities such as 9 per cent Treasury notes and comparably priced variable interest notes issued by major banks. The latter matured in about five years, with rates of return adjusted every six months to prevailing short-term interest rates. In 1974, these issues yielded much more than the 5¼ per cent maximum interest on passbook savings and the 7½ per cent maximum yields on long-term certificates of deposit.

To protect savings institutions from such competition, a House-Senate conference committee agreed on legislation that would allow the Fed to set ceilings on issues of variable rate securities by bank holding companies. In contrast, President Richard M. Nixon had proposed in 1973 that ceilings on savings rates be eliminated and housing be subsidized by granting tax credits to lenders. The proposal was designed to prevent distortions in credit flows when market interest rates exceed ceilings on savings rates. Also being considered were proposals to tie interest rates to price level changes.

Mortgage Rates. Reflecting high building costs and interest rates, new housing starts in the United States plummeted in 1974 to less than half the 2.5-million starts of late 1972 and early 1973. Various government programs cushioned the decline. Yet mortgage rates reached all-time peaks of 9 per cent and more in September before tailing off as the money markets generally eased. The average rate for new home loans fell for the first time in 19 months when it dropped from 9.19 per cent to 9.17 per cent in October. However, the mortgage rate of loans for existing houses continued to climb, reaching a record 9.51 per cent in October. The prime rate for top-rated business loans dropped to 10.25 per cent, from a peak of 12 per cent in July. This also was expected to filter down and help ease mortgage rates.

President Ford, in his anti-inflation message on October 8, proposed that the Federal National Mortgage Association aid housing by buying up to $7.75-billion of conventional, as well as government-guaranteed, mortgages. Previously, only the Federal Home Loan Mortgage Corporation held both types of mortgages.

Private Gold Holdings. After 40 years, a ban against U.S. citizens holding monetary gold was lifted effective Jan. 1, 1975. Since 1933, gold had been held exclusively by the government for use in redeeming dollars owed to official foreign holders. The price had remained at $35 a troy ounce (31 grams) until Aug. 15, 1971, when the United States stopped selling gold. Subsequently, gold has been officially revalued, first to $38 an ounce in 1971, and then to $42.22 in 1973. Official holdings of gold, at the official price, total about $11 billion for the United States and $40 billion for the rest of the world. But the official price is largely meaningless, because the Treasury has not been willing to sell. The open market price of gold overseas rose to over $190 an ounce in November and fluctuated wildly in December in anticipation of legalized U.S. trading.

The changing status of gold served to emphasize the United States policy favoring relatively more freedom in pricing international currencies. The most widely held medium of international exchange is the U.S. dollar. By the end of July, foreign holders had accumulated $107 billion in U.S. dollars, up 15 per cent over the previous year and 264 per cent in 10 years. Due to increases in oil prices, oil-exporting nations accumulated about $35 billion in foreign currencies in the first nine months of 1974, including about $8 billion in U.S. dollars.

The dollar – like most other currencies – was floating in 1974; that is, its value in terms of other currencies depended on the supply and demand for dollars and not on government buying and selling of dollars in exchange for gold or other currencies to maintain a fixed price.

International Reform. In June, 20 nations that had been negotiating international monetary reform under auspices of the International Monetary Fund (IMF) abandoned the task of achieving permanent reform. But they published some general conclusions about what the reformed system should be like. They recommended that countries should maintain "par values" – the relation of one currency to another – within an agreed margin, but added that currencies should be permitted to float with IMF approval. Par-value changes should be encouraged in order to eliminate balance-of-payments surpluses or deficits. See INTERNATIONAL TRADE AND FINANCE.

The group disagreed about the role of gold. Also undetermined were controls on growth of worldwide primary reserves, such as gold and the U.S. dollar. The huge build-up in foreign holdings of dollars in previous years had been interpreted as a source of worldwide inflation in the 1970s.

The group also recommended that primary reserves include Special Drawing Rights (SDR) certificates, a form of international money issued by the IMF. The IMF took a major step in internationalizing reserve assets in June by basing the SDR value on a composite of 16 currencies.   William G. Dewald

BARBADOS. See WEST INDIES.

Washington Star Syndicate, Inc.

IF I COULD AFFORD TO PAY THAT KIND OF INTEREST... I WOULDN'T NEED THE LOAN –

LOANS 11%

7-3 BRICKMAN

BASEBALL

BASEBALL made history in several ways during and after the 1974 season. The key figures included Henry Aaron, who broke Babe Ruth's lifetime home-run record; Lou Brock with his base-stealing; Nolan Ryan with his fast-ball pitching; Frank Robinson, who became the major leagues' first black manager; and the rowdy, always-feuding Oakland A's, who won their third straight World Series.

Aaron was playing his 21st season for the Braves (12 in Milwaukee, 9 in Atlanta). He started the season with 713 career home runs, one short of probably the most celebrated record in all sports. The Braves opened the season against the Reds in Cincinnati, and they wanted to keep Aaron on the bench so he could tie and perhaps break the record a few days later before a home crowd in Atlanta.

But Commissioner Bowie Kuhn ordered the Braves to play Aaron in Cincinnati. Aaron played on April 4 in the opening game, and on his first swing of the season, he hit his 714th home run, tying Babe Ruth. "I thought that tying the record would mean a lot to me," he said, "but it was just another home run."

On April 8, the Braves played the Los Angeles Dodgers in Atlanta. Before a stadium crowd of 53,000 and a Monday-night national television audience of 35 million, Aaron hit his 715th home run and broke the record. He said, "When I hit it, all I could think about was that I wanted to touch all the bases . . . . It's the Cadillac of baseball records. But Babe Ruth will still be regarded as the greatest home-run hitter who ever lived."

At the age of 40, Henry Aaron seemingly had everything. He was earning $200,000 a year from the Braves, and another $200,000 a year for five years from Magnavox Company to publicize its television sets. He finished the season as the major-league all-time leader in home runs (733), games played (3,076), at bats (11,628), total bases (6,591), extra-base hits (1,429), and more. But he was not content.

Aaron had said that he was not interested in managing. But when the Braves fired Manager Eddie Mathews in July, Aaron was peeved that he was not offered the job (which went to Clyde King). Later, he changed his mind about retiring, perhaps because he was dissatisfied with the salary (he said it was $30,000) the Braves had offered him to become a public relations man. He wanted more responsibility and more money.

Aaron decided he wanted to continue playing one more year, and not for the Braves of the National League but for the Milwaukee Brewers of the American League, because he had spent so many happy years in Milwaukee. The Braves obliged and in November traded him to the Brewers, where he signed a two-year contract and became a potential designated hitter and later a front-office executive.

Final Standings in Major League Baseball

American League	W.	L.	Pct.	GB.
Eastern Division				
Baltimore	91	71	.562	
New York	89	73	.549	2
Boston	84	78	.519	7
Cleveland	77	85	.475	14
Milwaukee	76	86	.469	15
Detroit	72	90	.444	19
Western Division				
Oakland	90	72	.556	
Texas	84	76	.525	5
Minnesota	82	80	.506	8
Chicago	80	80	.500	9
Kansas City	77	85	.475	13
California	68	94	.420	22

Leading Batters
Batting Average—Rod Carew, Minnesota .364
Home Runs—Dick Allen, Chicago 32
Runs Batted In—Jeff Burroughs, Texas 118
Hits—Rod Carew, Minnesota 218

Leading Pitchers
Games Won—Jim Hunter, Oakland; Ferguson Jenkins, Texas 25
Win Average—Billy Champion, Milwaukee (11-4) (162 or more innings) .733
Earned-Run Average—Jim Hunter, Oakland (162 or more innings) 2.49
Strikeouts—Nolan Ryan, California 367

Awards
Most Valuable Player—Jeff Burroughs, Texas
Cy Young—Jim Hunter, Oakland
Rookie of the Year—Mike Hargrove, Texas
Manager of the Year—Billy Martin, Texas

National League	W.	L.	Pct.	GB.
Eastern Division				
Pittsburgh	88	74	.543	
St. Louis	86	75	.534	1½
Philadelphia	80	82	.494	8
Montreal	79	82	.491	8½
New York	71	91	.438	17
Chicago	66	96	.407	22
Western Division				
Los Angeles	102	60	.630	
Cincinnati	98	64	.605	4
Atlanta	88	74	.543	14
Houston	81	81	.500	21
San Francisco	72	90	.444	30
San Diego	60	102	.370	42

Leading Batters
Batting Average—Ralph Garr, Atlanta .353
Home Runs—Mike Schmidt, Philadelphia 36
Runs Batted In—Johnny Bench, Cincinnati 129
Hits—Ralph Garr, Atlanta 214

Leading Pitchers
Games Won—Andy Messersmith, Los Angeles; Phil Niekro, Atlanta 20
Win Average—Andy Messersmith, Los Angeles (20-6) (162 or more innings) .769
Earned-Run Average—Buzz Capra, Atlanta (162 or more innings) 2.28
Strikeouts—Steve Carleton, Philadelphia 240

Awards
Most Valuable Player—Steve Garvey, Los Angeles
Cy Young—Mike Marshall, Los Angeles
Rookie of the Year—Bake McBride, St. Louis
Manager of the Year—Walter Alston, Los Angeles

There it goes! Henry Aaron's expression tells the story as his record 715th home run soars out of the Atlanta park in April 8 night game.

(five in a row). Manager Walter Alston of the Dodgers said of the A's, "Their record speaks for itself. They play the game the way it should be played. They don't make any mistakes."

Four of the five World Series games, including the finale, were decided by 3-2 scores. The heroes of the last game, and the heroes of the series, were outfielder Joe Rudi and relief pitcher Rollie Fingers. Rudi's home run won the game, and Fingers and his Svengali mustache pitched in relief for the fourth time in the series (the A's won those four games).

Major-League Races. When the A's won the World Series in 1972 and 1973, their manager was Dick Williams. He quit after the 1973 series because of continual interference by Charles O. Finley, the club owner. Two days before training camp opened in February, Finley hired Alvin Dark as manager. Dark had managed the A's before, when they played in Kansas City. But Finley fired him in 1967.

All season, Finley telephoned instructions to Dark in the dugout, and Dark had little chance to do his own managing. Sal Bando, the A's third baseman and captain, thought that made little difference because, he said, Dark "couldn't manage a meat market."

Despite all their problems and locker-room fights, the A's won the American League West without a threat. The Baltimore Orioles beat the resurgent New York Yankees by two games in the East by winning

A Black Manager. A few blacks had managed in the minor leagues and winter leagues, but no black had managed in the major leagues. In 1974, 28 years after Jackie Robinson had become the first black player in the major leagues, Frank Robinson (no relation to Jackie) became the first black manager.

Frank Robinson was 39 years old and still playing. In 19 major-league seasons, he had 2,900 hits, 574 home runs, 1,778 runs batted in, and a .295 batting average. He had managed five years for Santurce of the Puerto Rican Winter League. Late in the 1974 season, the Cleveland Indians obtained him (and his $175,000 salary) on waivers from the California Angels, and when the season ended, the Indians gave him a one-year contract as playing manager in 1975. Ted Bonda, executive vice-president of the Indians, said frankly, "We needed somebody to wake up the city. We felt we had to generate excitement."

World Series. The Oakland A's, with their green and gold uniforms, white socks, and overstated mustaches, looked like a cross between a softball team and a summer-stock company. But they could play baseball, and when they defeated the Los Angeles Dodgers, 4 games to 1, in the World Series, they had won their fourth straight Western Division title, third straight American League pennant, and third straight World Series. The only teams to have won more consecutive World Series were the New York Yankees, starting in 1936 (four in a row) and 1949

Frank Robinson listens quietly as he is named manager of the Cleveland Indians, the first black manager in big-league baseball history.

15 of their last 17 games and 27 of their last 33. In the play-offs for the American League pennant, the A's defeated the Orioles, 3 games to 1.

In the National League, the Dodgers solidified themselves before the season with trades that brought Mike Marshall from Montreal and Jim Wynn from Houston. Marshall, a relief pitcher, set a major-league record by appearing in 106 of the 162 regular-season games. He also pitched in all five World Series games. Wynn, a center fielder, provided power.

The Dodgers led in the West from the first week of the season. The Pittsburgh Pirates, after a horrendous start, won their fourth Eastern Division title in five years but lost to the Dodgers in the play-offs.

Top Players. Lou Brock of the St. Louis Cardinals, at the age of 35, stole 118 bases, breaking Maury Wills's 1962 record of 104. Nolan Ryan of the Angels pitched the third no-hitter of his career, posted a 22-16 won-lost record, struck out 367 batters in 332 innings, struck out 19 in a nine-inning game (a major-league record), and had his fast ball timed at 100.9 miles per hour (162.4 kilometers per hour), the fastest ever recorded.

Al Kaline, a Detroit Tigers outfielder for 22 years, became the 12th man in major-league history to reach 3,000 hits. Rod Carew of the Minnesota Twins won his third straight American League batting championship. Jim (Catfish) Hunter of the A's won more than 20 games for the fourth straight year, then was declared a free agent on December 16 by an arbitrator because the A's had not lived up to the terms of his contract. After spirited bidding, Hunter agreed to a five-year contract with the New York Yankees for a reported $3.75 million on December 31.

Gaylord Perry of the Indians pitched 15 consecutive victories before losing six games in a row. Steve Busby of the Kansas City Royals pitched a no-hit game on June 19 against Milwaukee. On July 19, Dick Bosman of the Cleveland Indians pitched a no-hitter against the A's.

Arbitration. For the first time, club owners and players agreed on binding arbitration if they could not agree on salary. Under the agreement, each side would present a figure, and the arbitrator would have to choose one or the other. In all, 29 players went to arbitration and 16 won. The highest paid was Reggie Jackson, the A's outfielder. Jackson was offered $100,000 by Finley, but asked for $135,000 and got it.

Hall of Fame. For the first time, writers voted teammates (and, in this case, roommates) into the Baseball Hall of Fame together in January. They were outfielder Mickey Mantle and pitcher Whitey Ford, who starred for the Yankees in the 1950s and 1960s. The Negro Leagues committee chose James (Cool Papa) Bell, and the veterans committee selected the late Jim Bottomley, the late Sam Thompson, and umpire John (Jocko) Conlan.   Frank Litsky

See also Section One, FOCUS ON SPORTS; Section Five, BASEBALL.

BASKETBALL. North Carolina State became national collegiate basketball champion in 1974, ending the dominance of the University of California, Los Angeles (UCLA), at least temporarily. The professional champions were the Boston Celtics in the National Basketball Association (NBA) and the New York Nets in the American Basketball Association (ABA).

The Bruins of UCLA had won seven straight National Collegiate Athletic Association (NCAA) championship tournaments and nine in 10 years. They had won 88 consecutive games, a record for colleges, until a 71-70 loss on January 19 to Notre Dame. Then UCLA lost to Oregon on February 15, and to Oregon State on February 16. On February 17, it held an unprecedented Sunday practice.

In the NCAA championship semifinals on March 23 in Greensboro, N.C., North Carolina State beat UCLA, 80-77, in double overtime. North Carolina State defeated Marquette in the final, 76-64, and finished the season with a 30-1 won-lost record. The loss was to UCLA by 18 points early in the season.

Coach Norm Sloan of North Carolina State said, "People give coaching too much credit. Players win the games, not the coaches." Nevertheless, the Associated Press named the 47-year-old Sloan as Coach of the Year. United Press International picked Richard (Digger) Phelps of Notre Dame, and the

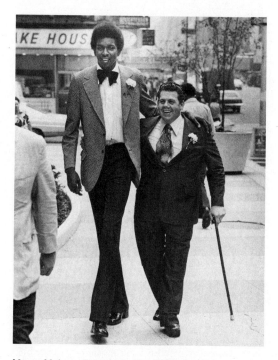

Moses Malone, Petersburg, Va., high school star, with Utah Stars owner James Collier after signing a 10-year, $3-million pro contract.

228

National Association of Basketball Coaches chose Al McGuire of Marquette.

The Player of the Year was David Thompson, a 6-foot 4-inch (193-centimeter) forward for North Carolina State. Bill Walton, UCLA's 6-foot 11-inch (211-centimeter) center, who had won that honor the two previous seasons, was hampered by chronically bad knees. Thompson and Walton were chosen for most all-America teams along with John Shumate of Notre Dame, Marvin Barnes of Providence College, and Keith Wilkes of UCLA.

In the NBA. From 1957 to 1969, the Boston Celtics won 11 NBA titles. In 1974, a balanced, fast-breaking Celtic team won again, defeating the Milwaukee Bucks in the play-off finals, 4 games to 3. John Havlicek, the 34-year-old captain, was a link to the glory days. He explained the success of the modern Celtics by saying, "This team has a lot of pride. The younger guys don't want to hear about the old Celtics anymore. They want to prove that they have championship quality themselves."

The Bucks were led by 7-foot 2-inch (218-centimeter) Kareem Abdul-Jabbar, the NBA's Most Valuable Player for the third time in four years. The Rookie of the Year was Ernie DiGregorio, a guard who led the league in assists and free-throw accuracy and led the Buffalo Braves to their first play-off berth. The Coach of the Year was Ray Scott, who, in his first full season, got the Detroit Pistons into the play-offs. Bob McAdoo of Buffalo led the league in scoring and field-goal accuracy. The all-star team consisted of Abdul-Jabbar at center, Havlicek and Rick Barry of Golden State at forward, and Walt Frazier of New York and Gail Goodrich of Los Angeles at guard.

The NBA voted a franchise to New Orleans for the 1974-1975 season for $6.15 million and one to Toronto for 1975-1976 for a higher price.

New Orleans quickly made a monumental trade to acquire Pete Maravich of Atlanta, a favorite in Louisiana from his high-scoring college days at Louisiana State University. In return for Maravich, Atlanta received New Orleans' number-one draft picks in 1974 and 1975, its number-two picks in 1975 and 1976, and the first guard and forward chosen by New Orleans in the expansion draft. Those players, hand-picked by Atlanta, were Dean Meminger of New York and Bob Kauffman of Buffalo.

In the ABA. The New York Nets, who spent their early years playing in desolate suburban arenas, became champions by winning 12 of their 14 play-off games. They defeated the Utah Stars, 4 games to 1, in the finals. The Nets were coached by Kevin Loughery, in his first ABA season. The average age of the starting five was only 23. The star of the Nets, and the ABA's Most Valuable Player and scoring champion, was Julius Erving, perhaps the most exciting pro player.

The all-star team had Erving and George McGinnis of Indiana at forward, Artis Gilmore of Ken-

Final Standings in Major League Basketball

National Basketball Association

Eastern Conference

Atlantic Division	W.	L.	Pct.
Boston	56	26	.683
New York	49	33	.598
Buffalo	42	40	.512
Philadelphia	25	57	.305

Central Division	W.	L.	Pct.
Capital	47	35	.573
Atlanta	35	47	.427
Houston	32	50	.390
Cleveland	29	53	.354

Western Conference

Midwest Division	W.	L.	Pct.
Milwaukee	59	23	.720
Chicago	54	28	.659
Detroit	52	30	.634
Kansas City-Omaha	33	49	.402

Pacific Division	W.	L.	Pct.
Los Angeles	47	35	.573
Golden State	44	38	.537
Seattle	36	46	.439
Phoenix	30	52	.366
Portland	27	55	.329

Leading Scorers	G.	FG.	FT.	Pts.	Avg.
Bob McAdoo, Buffalo	74	901	459	2,261	30.6
Pete Maravich, Atlanta	76	819	469	2,107	27.7
Kareem Abdul-Jabbar, Milw.	81	948	295	2,191	27.0
Lou Hudson, Atlanta	65	678	295	1,651	25.4
Gail Goodrich, Los Angeles	82	784	508	2,076	25.3

American Basketball Association

Eastern Division	W.	L.	Pct.
New York	55	29	.655
Kentucky	53	31	.631
Carolina	47	37	.560
Virginia	28	56	.333
Memphis	21	63	.250

Western Division	W.	L.	Pct.
Utah	51	32	.607
Indiana	46	38	.548
San Antonio	45	39	.536
San Diego	38	47	.447
Denver	37	48	.435

Leading Scorers	G.	FG.	FT.	Pts.	Avg.
Julius Erving, New York	84	897	454	2,299	27.3
George McGinnis, Indiana	80	784	488	2,071	25.8
Dan Issel, Kentucky	83	826	457	2,118	25.5
George Gervin, San Antonio	74	664	378	1,730	23.3
Willie Wise, Utah	82	712	396	1,826	22.2

College Champions

Conference	School
Atlantic Coast	North Carolina State
Big Eight	Kansas
Big Ten	Indiana-Michigan
Ivy League	Pennsylvania
Missouri Valley	Louisville
Ohio Valley	Austin Peay
Pacific-8	UCLA
Southeastern	Vanderbilt
Southwest	Texas
Western Athletic	New Mexico

tucky at center, and Jimmy Jones of Utah and Mack Calvin of Carolina at guard. The Rookie of the Year was Swen Nater of San Antonio.

Merger moves between the NBA and ABA broke down again, and the ABA sued the NBA for $300-million for alleged antitrust violations and an additional $300 million for what the ABA called breach of contract, fraud, and actual damages. The ABA club owners and the NBA players had agreed on merger terms that would have eliminated the option clauses binding players to their teams, but the NBA club owners refused to accept those terms.

The Players. Utah of the ABA signed 19-year-old Moses Malone of Petersburg, Va., the nation's outstanding high school player, in late August, a day after he was supposed to have started freshman classes at the University of Maryland. His contract had a potential value of $3 million over 10 years. Malone, 6 feet 11 inches (211 centimeters) tall, had been sought by more than 300 colleges.

Walton, courted by both pro leagues, signed with Portland of the NBA in May for an estimated $2.5-million for five years (see WALTON, BILL). Wilt Chamberlain coached San Diego of the ABA but missed as many practices as he attended and later retired. Oscar Robertson of Milwaukee became a commentator on NBA telecasts. Jerry West of Los Angeles and Willis Reed of New York – also among the game's great players – also retired.   Frank Litsky

BELGIUM. For the first time, one of the three "federalist" parties that advocate greater regional autonomy for Belgium's linguistic communities joined the government on June 10, 1974. Prime Minister Leo Tindemans added the French-speaking Walloon Union to his Social Christian – Liberal coalition three months after the March 10 general election. With the Walloons' 12 added seats, Tindemans gained a nine-seat parliamentary majority. But without the support of the other two federal groups, the Flemish-speaking People's Union and the French-speaking Democratic Front of Brussels, he still lacked the two-thirds majority necessary for constitutional reforms. The move was seen as a major step toward resolving difficulties created by the three mutually jealous districts of Brussels, Flanders, and Wallonia.

Government Crisis. The coalition government of Edmond Leburton resigned on January 19 in a crisis precipitated when Iran withdrew from a joint $200-million oil refining project near Liège, Belgium. In the March 10 elections, the Social Christians and the Socialists consolidated their positions at the expense of the federalists. The Social Christians gained five seats, giving them 72 of the 212 seats in the lower house. But talks to form a coalition of the three major parties broke down on April 19 when the Socialists refused to work with the Liberals. The situation was not resolved until the Walloons joined the Social Christians' and Liberals' coalition two months later.

Oil Crisis. Two-thirds of the automobile industry's manpower, 22,000 workers, were laid off in February because of the energy crisis and lagging parts supplies. By March 15, gasoline pumps were dry, and there was no oil for heating because oil companies refused to import oil until they were allowed to raise prices to reflect the increased cost of petroleum. The caretaker government allowed a price rise of $31 a ton on April 1, and deliveries resumed.

Inflation Continued, reaching an annual rate of 15 per cent in 1974. The government acted on August 12 to contain it at this figure by limiting mortgages to 60 per cent of the market value of property. On August 16, it cut retail prices by 2.4 per cent on beef and 5 per cent on pork. Rising unemployment and an illegal immigrant work force of 15,000 to 20,000 led the government to ban the entry of foreign workers on August 2. Belgian farmers, supporting a call by the European Farmers' Organization for an 8 per cent increase in guaranteed producer prices in the European Community, blocked roads on August 20 and September 2.

Legislation passed on August 19 will cut military service in half for 40,000 conscripts over the next five years. About 6,000 soldiers will be recruited annually to take their places.   Kenneth Brown

See also EUROPE (Facts in Brief Table).

BELIZE. See LATIN AMERICA.

BHUTAN. See ASIA.

BICENTENNIAL CELEBRATION. In 1974, the United States moved with vigor and imagination toward the celebration of its 200th birthday. Unlike the centennial celebrations of 1876, which were concentrated in Philadelphia, the 1976 bicentennial will not be confined to one city. Instead, it will involve projects in cities, towns, and hamlets of all size throughout the 50 states, the District of Columbia, Puerto Rico, and the three U.S. territories.

About 1,900 U.S. communities have been designated as official bicentennial participants and about 3,100 more are expected by 1976. In many, preparations were already underway during 1974. In South Bend, Ind., more than 400 citizens volunteered to paint all of the town's 4,800 fire plugs to resemble Revolutionary War soldiers. Yankton, S. Dak., residents were planning 19 projects that ranged from a Bicentennial Ball to a concerted drive to eradicate Dutch elm disease. In mid-June, the Smithsonian Institution opened its four-part major exhibition dramatizing the Revolution with the display "In the Minds and the Hearts of the People: Prologue to Revolution, 1760-1774" in the National Portrait Gallery in Washington, D.C.

This was only one of the many museum displays, restorations of old buildings, and dramatizations of historical events either being planned or getting started in 1974. In Louisiana, volunteers were working on 158 bicentennial projects that included the establishment of a riverfront park in Baton Rouge and a small museum in the Chitamacha Indian Reservation. Twenty counties in Florida planned a variety of festivities, including a concert featuring the works of American composer Charles Ives.

Other Activities. Books, souvenirs, coins, and plates were on sale in many cities. In midyear, first proofs of the new bicentennial dollar, half dollar, and quarter were struck at the Philadelphia Mint. The new coins carry the familiar Washington, Kennedy, and Eisenhower busts on their faces but will be double-dated 1776-1976. On the reverse side, a drummer boy will appear on the quarter, Independence Hall on the half dollar, and the Liberty Bell and the moon on the dollar.

John W. Warner was named administrator of the American Revolutionary Bicentennial Administration in April. Previously, bicentennial planning was the responsibility of a 50-member commission. Among the newly constituted administration's goals is a plan to encourage a greater involvement of foreign governments in the bicentennial celebrations. By year's end, some 40 countries, including Australia, Greece, Japan, and Venezuela, had indicated that they plan to join in the observance.   John W. Warner

Leaders from the 13 original U.S. colonies meet in Carpenters' Hall, Philadelphia, to mark the first Continental Congress, held in 1874.

BIOCHEMISTRY. Intensive research and clinical testing continued in 1974 on prostaglandins, members of a large family of chemicals that possess extraordinary physiological activity. Fourteen prostaglandins occur naturally in human tissues of the lung, liver, uterus, and gastrointestinal tract, and chemists have synthesized hundreds of similar molecules called analogues. Medical researchers have been investigating their use in treating asthma, peptic ulcers, and high blood pressure, and for inducing labor in high-risk pregnancies. One prostaglandin is now being marketed for use by physicians in selected U.S. hospitals for therapeutic abortions.

In 1930, two New York gynecologists noted that human seminal fluid causes powerful contractions of smooth uterine muscle. Three years later, Swedish physiologist Ulf von Euler isolated a component of semen that not only contracted smooth muscle, but lowered blood pressure in animals. He named it prostaglandin because he believed that an unsaturated fatty acid from the prostate was the active substance. Later findings showed that minute quantities of prostaglandins are manufactured and released by most organs of the body.

In 1957, Professor Sune Bergström and his associates at the Karolinska Institute in Stockholm, Sweden, first isolated two crystalline prostaglandins in pure form from biological sources. By 1962, researchers had used such techniques as X-ray crystallography to determine the structure of several prostaglandins, but a limited natural supply of the chemicals hampered further work. Since about 1968, however, several methods have been perfected to synthesize prostaglandins, and researchers now understand their chemical structures in great detail.

Complexities Involved. Understanding the physiological roles of the prostaglandins is more complex, because these substances seem to play different roles in each organ, possibly in each tissue and cell. Certain prostaglandins stimulate contraction of the uterine muscles, while others inhibit it. Likewise, some prostaglandins boost blood pressure by direct action on the muscle of the blood vessels, while others lower it. Certain prostaglandins act as tranquilizers, others inhibit gastric secretion, and the actions of some are inhibited by anti-inflammation drugs.

In view of this diversity of effects, biochemists have proposed several general theories on how prostaglandins act. One proposal involves the important cellular compound cyclic AMP (3′,5′-adenosine monophosphate) that is synthesized in cell membranes by an enzymatic adenyl cyclase as a result of the interaction between specific hormones and their target cells. The level of cyclic AMP determines the extent of the cell's physiological response to the hormonal stimulus. Depending upon the tissue studies, the prostaglandins affect the level of cyclic AMP either by stimulating or inhibiting its synthesis or by inhibiting its destruction by hydrolytic enzymes.

Stopping Runaway Growth. Such human abnormalities as *acromegaly* (enlargement of bones in the face, hands, and feet), gigantism, and dwarfism result from abnormal functioning of the pituitary gland. If the *anterior* (forward) portion of the gland secretes too much of the growth hormone somatotropin, excessive skeletal growth and gain in body weight result. Injury or removal of a child's pituitary gland results either in a greatly retarded growth rate or no growth.

In April, 1974, Samuel S. C. Yen and his collaborators from the University of California's San Diego School of Medicine reported on the treatment of five acromegalic patients with a substance that inhibits the release of somatotropin. The inhibiting agent, called somatostatin, was first isolated from hypothalamus extracts in 1973 by Paul Brazeau and Roger Guillemin at the Salk Institute in San Diego.

Somatostatin consists of a long peptide chain of 14 amino acids and can now be synthesized in the laboratory. Scientists believe that it inhibits the secretion of growth hormone (as well as affecting the secretion of other pituitary hormones) by acting directly on the cells of the pituitary gland.

Yen's group found a definite, though short-lived, decline in the rate of growth hormone secretion in every acromegalic patient to whom somatostatin was administered. They concluded that somatostatin's inhibitory effect is nearly complete and that its biological action is brief.

The use of somatostatin may eventually allow doctors to control oversecretion of growth hormone without surgery or X-ray treatment, but some basic questions remain unanswered. Most biologists believe that the hypothalamus portion of the brain controls the rate of release of growth hormone from the pituitary gland. However, researchers have not yet found a growth hormone releasing factor.

The Cyclic Messengers. The role of cyclic AMP has now been firmly established as a second messenger in the physiological action of many hormones. That is, many hormones either increase or decrease the amount of cyclic AMP that in turn controls numerous metabolic processes in living cells. However, in addition to those hormones that act by way of cyclic AMP – epinephrine, glucagon, and almost all the pituitary and hypothalamic hormones – there are others, such as insulin, the steroid hormones, the thyroid hormones, and various plant hormones, that apparently do not involve cyclic AMP.

Biochemical researchers attempted in 1974 to verify the suggestion first made by Nelson D. Goldberg at the University of Minnesota, that the analogous cyclic GMP (3′,5′-guanosine monophosphate) may regulate this second group of hormones. Goldberg and other researchers now believe that hormonal regulations may be based on the balance between the cellular concentration of cyclic AMP and a far lower quantity of cyclic GMP.   Earl A. Evans, Jr.

BIOLOGY. Thanks to the nine-banded armadillo, scientists announced in 1974 that they are now able to prepare useful quantities of lepromin, a substance that physicians use to screen leprosy patients. Lepromin may help eradicate the ancient skin disease. Leprosy afflicts from 10 to 20 million people living in the tropical areas of the world, despite the availability of drugs that can arrest, if not cure, it.

A biochemist reported at the third World Congress of the International Society for Tropical Dermatology, held in São Paulo, Brazil, in August, that an armadillo about the size of a football, infected with 300 trillion leprosy bacilli, would furnish about 1,600 quarts (1,500 liters) of the diagnostic serum. Eleanor E. Storrs, a biochemist with the Gulf South Research Institute in New Iberia, La., estimated that a single armadillo could supply enough lepromin to test 15-million persons. At the same meeting, Wayne Meyers of the University of Hawaii reported on tests of leprosy patients in Zaire. He found that armadillo lepromin produced the same response as lepromin prepared from the tissues of untreated lepers, except that the armadillo lepromin produced a somewhat more severe reaction.

With an abundant, reliable source of leprous armadillo tissue available for the first time, researchers hope to discover why the well-known organism that causes leprosy, *mycobacterium leprae*, does not grow in an artificial medium, despite its proliferation in lepromatous sores.

Caution for Genetic Research. The recent discovery of the restriction endonucleases, a new class of enzymes that act on genetic DNA in bacterial extracts, makes it possible to alter genes in a fashion hitherto impossible. These enzymes fragment enormously long DNA molecules into smaller pieces that are roughly the size of a single gene. Some restriction enzymes cut the double strand of the DNA helix at a point on one strand several bases lower than on the other strand to form "sticky ends."

Because a DNA fragment from a particular living species that has been cut by a specific restriction enzyme will have the same sticky ends as the fragment formed from a different DNA species cut by the same enzyme, the two fragments can fuse to form a hybrid DNA molecule. New genetic elements can be transferred into the bacterial cell if a bacterial DNA component known as a plasmid is used as one of the two components of the hybrid. The plasmid DNA enters the cell and is reproduced along with the hybrid component by the enzymes of the bacterial cell.

Using this technique, investigators have created plasmids containing genetic fragments from other bacteria that confer resistance to antibiotics. They have also created gene fragments from such other species as the toad (*Xenopus laevis*) and the fruit fly (*Drosophila*) that can infect and reproduce in the common human intestinal bacterium, *Escherichia coli* (*E. coli*).

A single nine-banded armadillo, infected with leprosy, provides physicians with enough diagnostic serum to test 15 million patients.

The possibility that some of these artificial recombinant molecules could prove biologically hazardous has led a group of 11 scientists to form a Committee on Recombinant DNA Molecules that is chaired by biochemist Paul Berg of Stanford University, Stanford, Calif.

Urge Experiment Ban. In a letter simultaneously published in July issues of *Science* and *Nature*, the Berg group asked for a temporary, self-imposed ban on experiments that involve inserting into bacteria (1) genes that confer either resistance to antibiotics or the ability to form bacterial toxins (such as the diphtheria toxin), and (2) the genes of such viruses as tumor viruses. The biologists are concerned with the remote possibility that *E. coli* bacteria carrying such antibiotic-resistant or tumor-producing genes might escape and infect the population. Experiments in which animal genes are inserted into bacteria "should not be taken lightly," according to the letter.

Reaction to this proposal is mixed, but the ban is being studied by a number of committees in the United States and Great Britain. An international meeting to discuss the problem is scheduled for February, 1975, in Washington, D.C. But it is already apparent that such experiments must be carried out with the most careful precautions. See Section One, FOCUS ON SCIENCE.   Earl A. Evans, Jr.

BIRTHS. See CENSUS, U.S.; POPULATION, WORLD.

BLINDNESS. See HANDICAPPED.

BOATING. The American defender *Courageous* routed the Australian challenger *Southern Cross* in four straight races in September, 1974, off Newport, R.I., to retain the America's Cup. It was the 22nd consecutive U.S. victory in the 123 years of yacht racing's most important competition.

The yachts were aluminum sloops of the 12-meter class, about 65 feet (20 meters) long and designed for speed, with no creature comforts. The races attracted international attention, but the real excitement came in the trials to choose a defender.

There were three candidates—*Courageous, Mariner,* and *Intrepid. Courageous* and *Mariner* were new yachts built for this competition by Eastern syndicates. They were made of aluminum, which was allowed for the first time. *Intrepid,* a wooden yacht, defended the cup successfully in 1967 and 1970. In 1973, a West Coast group bought it—hull, two masts, and 31 sails—for $95,000 and had it redesigned. The group raised $750,000 from 900 contributors for its campaign.

The radically designed *Mariner* did badly in the trials. *Courageous* and *Intrepid* were evenly matched, and in the end, *Courageous* was chosen as defender because of the excellence of its new skipper, Frederick E. (Ted) Hood, a sailmaker from Marblehead, Mass.

Southern Cross earned the right to challenge for the cup by winning four straight races from the French sloop *France,* the only other aspirant. *Southern Cross* was owned by Alan Bond, a brash, outspoken, 36-year-old land developer from Western Australia. In the trials, its unusual design seemingly had it flying when the wind was to its back. But against *Courageous,* in 24.3-mile (39.1-kilometer) races over six-sided courses, it was beaten by huge margins for such races —4 minutes 54 seconds, 1 minute 11 seconds, 5 minutes 27 seconds, and 7 minutes 19 seconds.

Other Yachting. The year's major ocean race was the 625-mile (1,006-kilometer) sail from Newport to Bermuda, starting June 21. *Scaramouche,* a 55-foot (17-meter) sloop owned by Charles E. Kirsch of Sturgis, Mich., was the handicap winner. In February and March, *Scaramouche* had finished second in the Southern Ocean Racing Conference's prestigious six-race series. The series winner was *Robin Two II,* which Ted Hood sailed, owned, designed, and built.

Powerboats. Carlo Bonomi of Italy, the 1973 world offshore champion, again dominated that series in *Dry Martini,* a 36-foot (11-meter) Cigarette hull with twin 468-cubic-inch (7,700-cubic-centimeter) Kiekhaefer Aeromarine engines. Art (Snapper) Norris, a 23-year-old vice-president of the Detroit Red Wings hockey team, won the national offshore title for inboards in *Slap Shot,* a 36-foot (11-meter) Cigarette with twin 482-cubic-inch (7,900-cubic-centimeter) MerCruiser engines. The unlimited hydroplanes champion and winner of the Gold Cup and President's Cup was the 1973 champion, *Pride of Pay 'N' Pak* of Seattle, driven by George Henley of Eatonville, Wash.   Frank Litsky

BOLIVIA. President Hugo Banzer Suarez clung to power in 1974 despite determined efforts by a young army officers' movement to oust him. On June 5, the dissidents tried to mount a coup d'état. The leaders, Colonel René López Leyton and Colonel Gary Prado Salmón, managed to rally a section of the Tarapacá armored regiment, but were quickly routed and forced to flee the country.

Reacting to the coup attempt, Banzer set up a new Cabinet that was entirely composed of right wing senior officers, in which the dominant figure was General Juan Lechín Suárez, nominally responsible for the "coordination of the presidency." This led to friction with the civilian leaders of the Nationalist Popular Front, which had previously supported Banzer.

The main political question was whether the country would be returned to constitutional rule. Banzer, who had come to power in August, 1971, by overthrowing the leftist government of Juan Jose Torres, made a series of inconclusive statements before scheduling new elections for mid-1975. On November 9, however, the Cabinet resigned after the military called for a new government, and the elections were postponed indefinitely.

Foreign Policy continued to be overshadowed by Banzer's sympathy for the regime in Brazil. He was originally carried to power by the strong Santa Cruz agro-industrialists, who have always tended to look to Brazil rather than La Paz.

On May 22, Bolivia contracted to sell natural gas to Brazil on a long-term basis in return for a pledge of $600 million in Brazilian investments. Brazil also agreed to provide Bolivia with a $60-million loan, most of it to develop the Mutún iron ore deposits.

The Brazilian connection partly explained Bolivia's new friendliness with the right wing Chilean junta. Presidents Banzer and Augusto Pinochet Ugarte of Chile met at President Ernesto Geisel's inauguration in Brasília on March 16, the first time that Bolivian and Chilean heads of state had talked face to face in 12 years. The Bolivians toned down their traditionally strident claims to the coastal territories annexed by Chile in the 1800s. As a result of the meeting, a Council of 50 was set up on April 6 to study the problem of providing landlocked Bolivia with access to the Pacific Ocean.

Continuing Inflation resulted in serious labor unrest during the year. The most dramatic flare-up occurred on January 28 when peasants in Cochabamba Province set up barricades during a demonstration against the doubling of the prices of some staple foods. The army mounted a combined land and air operation to crush the uprising. Another revolt led by dissident army officers on November 7 was also suppressed by the government.   Robert Moss

See also LATIN AMERICA (Facts in Brief Table).

BOOKS. See CANADIAN LITERATURE; LITERATURE; LITERATURE FOR CHILDREN; POETRY.

BOSTON. Long-simmering racial tensions and the school busing issue combined in 1974 to turn Boston's public school system into a battleground between black and white. A federal court ordered busing to achieve racial balance when schools opened for the fall term in September. This touched off weeks of violence that left dozens of persons injured and forced the governor to mobilize the National Guard.

United States District Court Judge W. Arthur Garrity ruled on June 21 that the Boston school system was deliberately and unconstitutionally segregated, and he ordered busing to achieve integration. The students were principally from the black Roxbury and white South Boston neighborhoods.

However, Boston voters had rejected busing as a means of achieving integration by a 13-to-1 margin in an advisory referendum on May 21. Tension mounted, and on September 9, Senator Edward M. Kennedy (D., Mass.) was booed and pelted with food as he attempted to address a protest meeting.

Busing Violence. School opened on September 12 amid protests and violence, and 35 per cent of the pupils boycotted school the first day. On September 20, a high school was closed following a racial clash between 1,500 black and white youths.

Violence reached its peak on October 7, when a white mob beat a black motorist stuck in a traffic jam and whites stoned buses carrying black students. Mobs of blacks then began attacking whites in the Roxbury area. Two days later, Massachusetts Governor Francis W. Sargent ordered 400 extra policemen into Boston to help maintain order.

Sargent mobilized the National Guard on October 15, after racial fights again broke out at a high school. He also requested federal troops, but was turned down by President Gerald R. Ford. Although the violence began to subside, absenteeism was still running at 28 per cent in late October. Violence again erupted and some schools were closed following the December 11 stabbing of a white student. On December 27, Judge Garrity held three schoolboard members in contempt of court for refusing to approve a busing plan for the entire city.

The Economy also suffered as Boston became the city with the highest cost of living in the nation. According to the U.S. Department of Labor, an average family of four needed more than $9,400 a year to maintain a minimum standard of living and more than $15,600 to live in moderate comfort. Yet, the average factory worker in the Boston area earned only $9,470 a year as of July.

Living costs in Boston rose 9.7 per cent between April, 1973, and April, 1974, while food costs went up 15 per cent in the one-year period ending in June. Blue-collar earnings, however, rose only 5.7 per cent.

Crime increased markedly. According to the Federal Bureau of Investigation, serious crimes in the Boston area increased 20.6 per cent during the first six months of 1974. *James M. Banovetz*

BOTANY. After 15 years of measurements, Wayne T. Swank and James E. Douglas of the Southeastern Forest Experimental Station at Franklin, N.C., reported in 1974 that they had discovered a 20 per cent reduction in the amount of water in the streams flowing through a forest after a stand of hardwood trees was replaced by softwood eastern white pines. They attributed the loss of water from the streams to increased *transpiration* from the trees. In transpiration, water enters the roots of a plant, moves through the cells and eventually leaves the plant by evaporation. It is essential to the tree's life because it provides the energy for moving nutrient soil materials up from the roots through the plant. Swank and Douglas concluded from their study, made in the Appalachian Mountains area, that the favored practice of planting white pines on municipal watersheds is not wise because it might substantially reduce water supplies.

Seeds and Sounds. Gaylord T. Hageseth of the University of North Carolina at Greensboro performed experiments in 1974 to determine if sound affects seed germination. He found that single-frequency sounds (pure tones) hastened the onset of germination by several hours. He experimented with frequencies of 100, 1,000, 2,000, 4,000, and 9,000 vibrations a second. The loudness or intensity in all tests was constant at 100 decibels. The frequency used was unimportant as long as the sound was a pure tone of one frequency. Broadband noise (a mixture of many frequencies) did not accelerate seed growth. Though germination was speeded up when the seeds were exposed to the pure tones, all seeds eventually achieved 98 to 99 per cent germination whether they were exposed to pure tones or broadband noise. Thus, the Hageseth finding, though it increases our knowledge about plant growth, is of little practical use because the sound speeds up germination by only a few hours.

Effects of the Moon. Quite unexpectedly, Frank A. Brown, Jr., of Northwestern University in Evanston, Ill., and Carol S. Chow of the Marine Biological Laboratory at Woods Hole, Mass., found that the water uptake of pinto beans varied according to the phase of the moon. The investigators set out to determine what effect the distance between plants had on bean water uptake. In their experiments, they placed 20 beans in screen baskets. The scientists then dipped them in water, blotted them dry, weighed them, resubmerged them for four hours, then blotted and weighed them a final time. Maximum water uptake occurred at the new moons, full moons, and quarter moons, or about every seven days. The researchers do not know exactly what physical force created by lunar periodicity the beans responded to. The magnitude of the force is very small, and more experiments are necessary before other botanists accept the results of this experiment. *Barbara N. Benson*

BOTSWANA. See AFRICA.

BOWLING. In the world of professional bowling, where many of the outstanding men wore mod clothes and long, styled hair, the star of 1974 was Earl Anthony, a self-described square with a crew haircut. Anthony, a 35-year-old left-hander from Tacoma, Wash., won two of the major competitions – the $125,000 Firestone Tournament of Champions in April in Akron, Ohio, and the $75,000 Professional Bowlers Association (PBA) championship in June in Downey, Calif. He also won in San Jose, Calif., in June; Fresno, Calif., in July; and Cleveland and Newark, Ohio, in October.

In 1971, Johnny Petraglia of Brooklyn, N.Y., set the all-time single-season earnings record of $85,065. Anthony ran his 1974 earnings to $100,155 for the year by finishing second to Petraglia in the Brunswick World Open in Chicago in November and winning the Hawaiian Invitational in December. Anthony is a quiet family man who was voted 1973 Athlete of the Year in the state of Washington.

The PBA Tour consisted of 31 tournaments from January to November. Total purses reached $2,048,500, a record for the 16th consecutive year. The first major championship was the $85,000 United States Open held in February in New York City. Larry Laub of Santa Rosa, Calif., won by rolling 246, 245, and 258 in the last three games of the sudden-death finals.

Paul Colwell of Tucson, Ariz., won the American Bowling Congress (ABC) Masters tournament in April in Indianapolis. He was too keyed up when he averaged 187 for his first four-game set. After a good night's sleep, he averaged 242 for the next four games and survived the first eliminations. Then he rolled four-game sets averaging 250, 236, 238, 230, 225, 242, and 242.

Women Bowlers. Pat Costello of Oklahoma City won two key championships with last-minute heroics. She captured the United States Open in May in Irving, Tex., by rolling two strikes in the final frame. She won the Professional Women's Bowlers Association title in August in Flint, Mich., with three strikes in the last frame. In each case, she relegated Betty Morris of Stockton, Calif., to second place. Morris had a great year, winning three tournaments, finishing second in eight, and earning a record $30,037. She averaged 210 for all of her competitive games during the year.

Judy Cook Soutar of Grandview, Mo., was the major winner at the WIBC tournament. She won the all-events title in the overall competition in May. And she won the Queens title by rolling 199, 257, 236, and 247 for her final four-game set.

Lorrie Koch of Carpentersville, Ill., captured the Brunswick World Open. Loa Boxberger of Russell, Kans., won the Red Crown Classic in January in Baltimore, a tournament that set women's records for prize money ($85,000) and first-place money ($12,500).

Frank Litsky

BOXING. Muhammad Ali won the two most important and lucrative fights of 1974. He outpointed Joe Frazier in January in New York City and then regained the world heavyweight title by knocking out champion George Foreman of Hayward, Calif., in October in Kinshasa, Zaire. Ali and Frazier earned $2.6 million each for their fight, the highest purses in boxing history until Ali and Foreman earned $5 million each for their meeting.

Ali was the champion from 1964 to 1967. Then boxing officials stripped him of the title after he refused induction into the United States Army. Frazier eventually won the title, then lost it to Foreman in 1973. Ali, at 32, remained as talkative and controversial as ever. He was also boxing's greatest box-office attraction, and the record purses were a tribute to his ability to lure customers to theaters for closed-circuit showings of his fights.

Ali's 12-round decision over Frazier and Foreman's second-round knockout of Ken Norton of San Diego in a March title fight in Caracas, Venezuela, made a Foreman-Ali match attractive. Most of the money for the fight was put up by a Panamanian company based in Switzerland, of which the African nation of Zaire owned 95 per cent. President Mobutu Sese Seko of Zaire envisioned the fight as a way to publicize his nation, gain prestige, and attract tourists.

He did not succeed entirely. Fight tours from the

World Champion Boxers			
Division	**Champion**	**Country**	**Year Won**
Heavyweight	Muhammad Ali	U.S.A.	1974
Light-heavyweight (disputed)	*Victor Galindez	Argentina	1974
	†John Conteh	England	1974
Middleweight (disputed)	*Carlos Monzon	Argentina	1970
	†Rodrigo Valdez	Colombia	1974
Junior-middleweight	Oscar Alvarado	U.S.A.	1974
Welterweight	Jose Napoles	Mexico	1971
Junior-welterweight (disputed)	*Antonio Cervantes	Colombia	1972
	†Perico Fernandez	Spain	1974
Lightweight (disputed)	*Roberto Duran	Panama	1972
	†Gattu Ishimatsu	Japan	1974
Junior-lightweight (disputed)	*Ben Villaflor	Philippines	1973
	†Kuniaka Shibata	Japan	1974
Featherweight (disputed)	*Alexis Arguello	Nicaragua	1974
	†Bobby Chacon	U.S.A.	1974
Bantamweight (disputed)	Rodolfo Martinez	Mexico	1974
	*Soo Hwan Hong	South Korea	1974
Flyweight (disputed)	*Susumu Hanagata	Japan	1974
	†Shoji Oguma	Japan	1974

*Recognized by World Boxing Association
†Recognized by World Boxing Council

Muhammad Ali watches heavyweight champ
George Foreman, the victim of a knockout,
crash to the canvas in their bout in Zaire.

United States to Zaire were overpriced, and only 35 Americans, rather than the anticipated 5,000, made the trip. Closed-circuit-television prices were high, averaging from $15 to $20 in the United States. Drive-in theaters charged $80 per car, and the Waldorf Astoria Hotel in New York City charged $80 plus the price of a room to have the room wired for the fight. The promotion lost perhaps $5 million, but artistically and dramatically, the fight was a success.

Ali, a 4-to-1 underdog, let Foreman punch himself out, then knocked him out with two seconds remaining in the eighth round. It was Foreman's first professional defeat, and Ali said, "Foreman was humiliated. I told you he was nothing, but did you listen? He punched like a sissy." Foreman said of Ali, "I think he should be respected."

Ali, who had said he would retire after the Foreman bout, seemed ready to change his mind. He reportedly had been offered a $10-million guarantee for his next title bout.

In the other weight divisions, the world champions with the longest reigns were Carlos Monzon of Argentina, middleweight champion since 1970, and Jose Napoles of Mexico, welterweight champion since 1971. In one of the year's most attractive fights, Monzon knocked out Napoles in seven rounds in February in Paris. Frank Litsky

BOY SCOUTS. See YOUTH ORGANIZATIONS.
BOYS' CLUBS. See YOUTH ORGANIZATIONS.

BRAZIL. It was an unlucky year in many ways for President Ernesto Geisel, who was sworn in on March 15, 1974. Disastrous floods struck the state of Santa Catarina in March, claiming 3,000 lives and leaving more than 250,000 people homeless. A meningitis epidemic that broke out in São Paulo and other major towns in July killed an estimated 1,000 (see HEALTH AND DISEASE). And on November 15, the government suffered a severe reversal in the congressional elections, which had previously been regarded as little more than a ritual act. See GEISEL, ERNESTO.

General Geisel began his term by making a fairly clean sweep of the ministers associated with his predecessor, General Emílio Garrastazú Médici. The new Cabinet that was sworn in on March 17 had only two carryovers: Air Force Minister Brigadier Joelmir Campos de Araripeas and João Paulo dos Reis Velloso as planning minister. In a subsequent reorganization of the administration, their powers were expanded into those of two economic "superministers." Despite early hopes that the changes might bring a more liberal policy, however, pressure from the conservatives in the high command compelled the government to maintain a tough line on press censorship, the treatment of *cassados* (those whose political rights were "temporarily" suspended after the 1964 coup), and internal security.

Voters Dissatisfied. The November elections showed the growing restlessness with a regime that seemed incapable of containing inflation or sustaining the "economic miracle" of the late 1960s and early 1970s. Well-known figures from the pro-government National Renewal Alliance, such as Nestor Jost, president of the Banco do Brasil, and Carvalho Pinto, a former finance minister and governor of São Paulo, were trounced by younger, all-but-obscure candidates from the opposition Brazilian Democratic Movement (MDB) in the Senate elections. In the elections held for the state legislatures, the MDB also won control of the country's most densely populated provinces, including São Paulo and Rio Grande do Sul. The results encouraged speculation that General Geisel might eventually be forced to resign in favor of a more hard-line soldier, or else devise a way to return the country to civilian rule in 1975.

Foreign Relations. Brazil continued its cautious relations with the East European Communist bloc by raising to ambassadorial levels its diplomatic representations with Romania, Hungary, and Bulgaria in May and by recognizing the People's Republic of China on August 15. The year presented a number of delicate diplomatic problems, particularly in relations with the new regime in Portugal (and its African territories); the Arab oil producers; and neighboring Spanish-speaking countries that had not entirely willingly slipped into the Brazilian sphere of influence.

A series of important economic agreements were concluded with neighboring Latin American countries, including one to exploit Bolivian natural gas

Brazilian housewives in Tubarão wait for rations in wake of nationwide floods in March that killed thousands and disrupted food distribution.

and a long-term agreement to buy Colombian coal. An agreement was signed with Paraguay on May 17 to develop the Itaipu hydroelectric complex on the Paraná River. An investment of at least $3 billion was involved. Brazil remained the rallying point for conservative movements in Latin America as well as the principal ally of the United States in South America, but there were signs that economic demands were leading to a more flexible foreign policy.

The Economy. Brazil, which produces only 180,000 of the 900,000 barrels of oil it consumes daily, was badly affected by the successive price rises instituted by the Organization of Petroleum Exporting Countries. These contributed both to inflation, which reached an annual rate of about 35 per cent, and to the mounting current account deficit, which, by the end of 1974, was about $7 billion. Under these conditions, Brazil's creditable export drive counted for less than it would have under normal circumstances; the value of exports rose from $6.2 billion in 1973 to over $7 billion. The total foreign debt had climbed to $18 billion by the end of the year, a gain of $5-billion. Although most foreign investors continued to regard Brazil as a safe bet, there was less non-Arab capital available. In September, the finance ministry felt compelled to lower the minimum period for foreign loans from 10 years to 5.   Robert Moss

See also LATIN AMERICA (Facts in Brief Table).

BRIDGE. See BUILDING AND CONSTRUCTION.

BRIDGE, CONTRACT. Italy successfully defended its world bridge team championship by winning the Bermuda Bowl, played in Venice in May, 1974. The Italians won by 29 international match points over the Dallas Aces in the finals. The victory was Italy's 12th Bermuda Bowl triumph and its 15th world title since the world famous Italian Blue team began playing in 1957.

Giorgio Belladonna, Benito Garozzo, and Pietro Forquet were at the heart of the Italian victory. They were supported by Benito Bianchi, Arturo Franco, and Soldano de Falso. The Aces entered the 96-deal final with a two-point advantage. However, the Italians erased that on the first deal. The North American team was led by Bob Wolff and Bob Hamman of Dallas and Eric Murray and Sam Kehela of Toronto, Canada.

A Canadian-Californian team won the Harold A. Vanderbilt knockout team championship on April 1 at the American Contract Bridge League (A.C.B.L.) spring national championships in Vancouver, B.C. It was the first major title for Joe Silver and Eric Kokish of Montreal and Bob and Dave Crossley from San Rafael, Calif.   Theodore M. O'Leary

BRITISH COLUMBIA. See CANADA.

BRITISH COMMONWEALTH OF NATIONS. See AUSTRALIA; CANADA; GREAT BRITAIN; NEW ZEALAND; and articles on other Commonwealth countries.

BUILDING AND CONSTRUCTION. Spending for construction in the United States in 1974 was $143-billion, up only 5 per cent over 1973's record $136.4-billion. The forecast for spending in 1975 is $149.5-billion – a rise of 12 per cent, but probably all due to inflation. Spending for housing in 1974 was down 15 per cent to $49.7 billion.

Declining markets caused an alarming increase in the jobless rate among construction workers in September. The unemployment rate of 12.4 per cent was the highest in four years and more than double the nation's overall jobless rate.

Labor contract negotiations ran heavier than usual. As of mid-July, there had been 97 strikes, involving 104,841 workers. The average 1974 wage increase in 388 settlements reported to the Associated General Contractors was 8.9 per cent, but cost-of-living escalator clauses were causing concern for 1975 and 1976. California plumbers and painters won the greatest escalator protection with increases of $2.07 and $3.51, respectively.

Codes and Specifications. U.S. cities strengthened their building codes in 1974 to combat fires in high rise buildings. Fire department officials agreed that people should not place too much reliance on fire departments, even those in big cities with the most sophisticated equipment and methods. Instead, they said, protection begins with the designer, the materials used, and proper building techniques. The Occupational Safety and Health Administration will study and try to improve the building codes of seven engineering and contracting organizations.

Revision of building codes on the West Coast was concerned with protection against earthquake damage. Vincent E. McKelvey, director of the U.S. Geological Survey, reported to the American Association for the Advancement of Science in February that a devastating earthquake "is inevitable in the San Francisco area" sooner or later, and that structures must be designed with that in mind.

New Building Techniques. To accommodate its additional space needs, the Chicago Board of Trade is building a new floor midway between its existing trading floor and its 75-foot (23-meter) ceiling. The new $2.5-million floor, built of steel trusses and beams and a concrete deck, will provide 20,000 square feet (1,860 square meters) of space. A major advantage is that the project permits business to go on as usual, because all work is done after trading hours and on weekends.

At the end of 1974, Russia was completing a 240-unit apartment building, school, and shopping center in Riverdale, N.Y., to serve as the headquarters for its United Nations mission. The complex was built from the top down. At the heart of the system are two concrete core pillars holding stairways and elevator shafts. A floor of steel and concrete, completely finished and equipped with all utilities, was built around the core every four or five days and then hoisted to the top. Because the work could be dovetailed, the job took only 15 months and saved $1 million.

New Buildings. New Orleans resumed work in April on the $162-million Louisiana Superdome, which will be the world's largest roofed stadium. Supporting the roof are 2,500 prestressed concrete piles. The roof has an insulation layer of polyurethane foam, which delayed the project because of fire-safety concerns. However, the material was deemed completely safe after extensive review. An elevated gutter at the roof's edge holds 350,000 gallons (1.3 million liters) of run-off water, thus avoiding further overloading New Orleans' overtaxed storm drainage system. A network of pipes drains off the water during dry periods.

A planned conference center in New York City will use solar energy to provide part of its heat. The $6-million structure, to be built by Rockefeller Center, Incorporated, and the RCA Corporation, will be constructed around an *atrium*, or court. The part containing the meeting rooms will have black, windowless walls. Solar collectors will be attached to the south wall and the roof. Other energy-conservation features include a heat-recovery system to collect and store excess energy; a computerized monitoring system to regulate all building systems to save on energy consumption; and insulating glass for the atrium.

New Bridges. Brazil opened a $232-million bridge across Rio de Janeiro's Guanabara Bay in March. The bridge is the first direct connection between Rio de Janeiro and the bayside city of Niterói, and will be a key link in Brazil's coastal highway. The project replaced a 45-minute ferry crossing.

W. J. Wilkes, chief of the U.S. Federal Highway Administration (FHWA) bridge division, reported in February that a nationwide survey indicated that 25,000 bridges and viaducts in the United States need to be replaced, at a cost of $5 billion. So far, FHWA has approved replacement of only 223 of these structures at a cost of $265 million.

Dam Building. Completion of two major dams suffered setbacks in 1974. Central Asia's showpiece, the Nurek Dam, straddling the Vakhsh River in Russia, will be the world's highest rock-fill dam when finished, and the power source for industrial and agricultural development near the Afghanistan border. However, delays in reaching its full power capacity and unexpected costs have put it behind schedule.

Similarly, completion of Pakistan's record $623-million Tarbela Dam was delayed when failure of a tunnel intake gate in August caused the reservoir behind the huge dam to drain.

Two California dams moved toward construction when the U.S. Army Corps of Engineers opened bids in March for the construction of New Melones Dam on the Stanislaus River and called for bids for first-phase construction of Warm Springs Dam on Dry Creek. New Melones, a rock-fill dam, will store water for power generation, irrigation, flood and water-

Excavators clear chalk away from the Dover cliffs in preparation for construction of an English Channel tunnel between England and France.

quality control, and recreation. It is expected to be completed in 1979. Warm Springs, an earth-fill dam, is scheduled to be completed in 1980.

New Tunnels. With $1.2 billion in construction contracts already awarded, the Metro Subway in Washington, D.C., is one of the world's biggest public works projects. It is also one of the world's major tunneling projects. Some stations on the 90-mile (145-kilometer) line extend 120 feet (37 meters) below street level. Many existing buildings are being underpinned by extending the old, shallow foundations to get below the Metro tunnel.

The Bay Area Rapid Transit system opened a tunnel under San Francisco Bay to train traffic on September 16. This connected for the first time four other segments in the 75-mile (120-kilometer) system. Actually, the tunnel was the first section of the completely automated, $1.6-billion line to be completed, but its use was delayed until a faulty electric detection system could be corrected.

After years of study, Chicago and its Metropolitan Sanitary District (MSD) may have found the answer to the waterway pollution in the area that results from overflows of combined sanitary and storm sewers. The MSD plans a $1.3-billion system of deep rock tunnels and three reservoirs. The deep tunnels will capture storm water and run-off sewage and carry it to the underground reservoirs for storage until it can be treated.   Mary E. Jessup

BULGARIA expanded its relations with the non-Communist world in 1974 but without abandoning its policy of integration with Russia. Bulgaria appointed an ambassador to West Germany in February, and West German Foreign Minister Walter Scheel visited Sofia in March. Officials signed an agreement on industrial, economic, and technical cooperation with West Germany in June. Deputy Prime Minister Ivan Popov visited the United States at the end of September to discuss business cooperation with government and business leaders.

Communist Party First Secretary Todor Zhivkov visited Iraq in April, and Egyptian President Anwar Sadat traveled to Sofia in June. On July 31, a council on foreign economic relations was set up to promote business cooperation with non-Communist countries.

Three young Communist Party Politburo members were purged on July 3. Ivan Abadzhiev, Venelin Kotsev, and Kostadin Gyaurov were given ambassadorial posts abroad. All three had allegedly been lukewarm about plans for speeding up Bulgaria's total economic integration with Russia.

Russian assistance with several prestige projects was announced on the 30th anniversary of Bulgaria's Communist regime on September 9. These projects included a new chemical complex, a natural gas pipeline linking Bulgaria and Russia, and a nuclear power station, the first in the Balkans.   Chris Cviic

See also EUROPE (Facts in Brief Table).

BURMA. Chairman U Ne Win on March 2, 1974, proclaimed the end of the "colonels' revolution" he launched 12 years earlier. Power, he said, would be "returned to the people." But the change was largely one of appearance. The Revolutionary Council of 15 military officers and Marxist ideologists was replaced with a National Congress of 450 members. But Ne Win retained power as president of Burma, and his close associate, Brigadier Sein Win, became premier of a Cabinet in which 15 of the 18 members were active or retired army men.

The face-lifting did not change the realities for this nation of 30 million people. Because they have been neglected and paid poorly for their rice, Burmese farmers funnel their grain into the black market. In midsummer of 1973, when Burma was said to be producing a bumper rice crop, rice exports had to be suspended. In 1974, this one-time rice bowl of Asia did not have enough rice to feed its own people.

Unrest and Violence. Inflation (54 per cent in two years) and the lack of rice set off riots in May. These began in the north and rolled southward. Dockers refused to load rice for export, and industrial workers seized 42 Rangoon factories. They demanded higher pay, more rice at the official price (one-third of that in the black market), and dissolution of the junta-controlled workers' councils.

On June 6, troops fired on Rangoon demonstrators, killing 22 and wounding 60. The following day, all schools were closed. To placate the public, the regime promised to import food, clothing, and spare parts for cars and industry. But it had no reserves for shopping abroad, and Burmese banknotes were worth little. Floods in August and September made things worse by destroying much of the unharvested rice crop.

Row over Corpse. U Thant, the former United Nations secretary-general, died in New York City on November 25. One of Burma's most eminent men, he had been an ally of Ne Win's bitter rival, ex-premier U Nu. U Thant's body arrived in Rangoon on December 1, but the public was barred from the airport. It lay in state at a race track for four days while the government and U Thant's family argued about the burial place.

On December 5, several thousand students and Buddhist monks seized the coffin and took it to the University of Rangoon campus for burial in a mausoleum they were going to build. Troops and police stormed the campus on December 11 and seized the body. This set off riots, and martial law was proclaimed. Some observers believed that the battle over U Thant's body was merely a symptom of the public hatred for the regime.   Mark Gayn

See also ASIA (Facts in Brief Table).

BURUNDI. See AFRICA.

BUS. See TRANSIT; TRANSPORTATION.

BUSINESS. See ECONOMICS; LABOR; MANUFACTURING; Section One, FOCUS ON THE ECONOMY.

CABINET, U.S. The same U.S. Cabinet served under two Presidents in 1974—Richard M. Nixon, who resigned on August 9, and Gerald R. Ford. Ford promised that under his Administration the Cabinet would have greater responsibilities and influence. See FORD, GERALD R.; NIXON, RICHARD M.; PRESIDENT OF THE UNITED STATES; U. S. GOVERNMENT.

When Ford took office, he asked that all Cabinet members stay on at least temporarily to ensure a smooth transition of government. All the Cabinet members agreed to do so. However, Ford began to make some changes late in the year in the Cabinet and in Cabinet-level posts.

Ford's Appointments. Attorney General William B. Saxbe announced on December 13 that he would resign to become ambassador to India. Laurence H. Silberman was in line to be acting attorney general after Saxbe's departure in early 1975. Roy L. Ash, director of the Office of Management and Budget, announced on December 17 that he would leave that post in late January or early February, 1975. Ford's choice to succeed Ash was James T. Lynn, secretary of housing and urban development.

Secretary of Transportation Claude S. Brinegar resigned on December 18, effective Feb. 1, 1975. Brinegar intended to return to private life.

One of the most powerful Cabinet-level positions in the Ford Administration was that of White House staff coordinator and senior adviser to the President. Ford appointed Donald M. Rumsfeld to that post on September 24.

There were rumors that Ford would make further Cabinet changes in 1975, but observers believed he would retain Secretary of the Interior Rogers C. B. Morton, Secretary of State Henry A. Kissinger, and Secretary of the Treasury William E. Simon. Simon, formerly head of the Federal Energy Office, had replaced George P. Shultz as treasury secretary on April 30. See SIMON, WILLIAM E.

Kissinger Crisis. The wide-ranging Watergate investigation revealed in January that the White House plumbers unit, in an attempt to stop suspected national security leaks, had tapped the telephones of 13 government officials and four newsmen. Kissinger had testified at his 1973 Senate confirmation hearings that he had only supplied the White House with the names of persons having access to secret information.

Nevertheless, there were reports that Kissinger had ordered the wiretaps. On June 11, Kissinger threatened to resign unless he was cleared of all suspicion. The Senate Foreign Relations Committee affirmed on August 6 that the new information did not conflict with Kissinger's 1973 testimony. See KISSINGER, HENRY A.   Darlene R. Stille

CALIFORNIA. See LOS ANGELES-LONG BEACH; SAN FRANCISCO-OAKLAND; STATE GOVERNMENT.

CAMBODIA. See KHMER.

CAMEROON. See AFRICA.

CAMP FIRE GIRLS. See YOUTH ORGANIZATIONS.

CANADA

Canada plumped for a strong government in 1974 to deal with problems of inflation and economic slowdown. A national election on July 8 gave Prime Minister Pierre Elliott Trudeau's Liberal government a resounding vote of confidence. The minority position the Liberals had held since 1972 was turned into a comfortable majority, while the opposition parties lost ground.

This was a remarkable result. The Canadian vote went against the trend in many other Western countries, where divided and confused electorates have withheld backing for a single leader or party. The result also upset the tradition in Canada that a leader who suffers a reverse at the polls – as Trudeau did in 1972 – rarely wins his way back into public favor. Trudeau successfully challenged both these trends in 1974. He broke the pattern of minority government established in five of the last seven Canadian elections and installed his government securely in power.

Uneasy Coalition. The election was brought on by the dramatic defeat of the Trudeau government's budget in the House of Commons on May 8 – the first budget defeat in Canadian history. The Liberals, who held only 109 Commons seats after the 1972 election, depended on the votes of 31 New Democratic Party (NDP) members to stay in office. With this support, they were able to repel the attacks of the 106 Progressive Conservative members, who were usually joined by the 15 members of the Social Credit Party. On this basis, the Liberals managed to survive from January, 1973, to May, 1974. During this period, they won 19 votes of confidence on critical issues. But the linkage with the NDP was not without danger to both parties. For the Liberals, it meant devising legislation with one eye always on NDP preferences; for the NDP, the association meant a blurred image in the public eye.

Steadily growing strains between the two parties widened into a definite breach in May when Finance Minister John N. Turner presented his third budget. Under pressure from the NDP, Turner proposed stiffer taxes on corporations, but he went only a short distance to satisfy his critics' demands in this area. He rejected as "cosmetic policies" the NDP's calls for a subsidy to be used to lower mortgage interest rates and for a two-price system by which Canadian primary products would be sold at a lower price at home than abroad. The finance minister also poured

scorn on the Conservatives' advocacy of temporary wage and price controls. Turner said such controls had not worked in the United States and Great Britain and were unsuitable for Canada, which imported so many products from other countries.

Parliament Dissolved. The contents of the budget, coupled with Turner's uncompromising defense in presenting it on May 6, immediately ranged the Conservatives and NDP against the government. Two days later, by a vote of 137 to 123, they passed a motion of lack of confidence in the financial policies of the Trudeau Administration. Faced with this defeat in the House of Commons – only the third in Canadian history – Trudeau had two options. He could go to the governor general and offer his resignation, in which case someone else would be asked to form a government. Or he could ask that Parliament be dissolved, meaning that the country would be asked to pass judgment through a general election. Trudeau chose the second alternative, and the voting was set for July 8.

The resulting campaign was long and unexciting. Trudeau emphasized that leadership was the real issue and that only his government had the capacity to deal with the complex economic questions facing Canada. The Conservative leader, Robert L. Stanfield, opposing Trudeau for the third time, failed to generate mass enthusiasm for the Tories. Stanfield's quiet and deliberate manner could not match the vitality and flair projected by Trudeau and his young wife, Margaret. Public opinion polls during the campaign usually showed Stanfield trailing Trudeau in popularity.

The Liberal Victory. In the polling, the Liberals established an early lead in the Atlantic Provinces and held it across Canada. They made heavy gains in Ontario, where they won 55 seats compared to the 36 held before, and in British Columbia, where they increased their representation from 4 to 8 seats. They did poorly in Manitoba, and Alberta again denied them a single seat. But the result was satisfying for Trudeau's Liberals. They gained 32 seats across the country, giving them 141 of the 264 seats in Parliament. They won 42.4 per cent of the popular vote, compared with 38 per cent in 1972. The election corrected a weakness in their 1972 showing – a heavy dependence on Quebec. After the May election, they had a justified claim to a national standing, with solid support in every region.

The Conservatives were bitterly disappointed in the results. From their position in October, 1972, when they had 107 seats, only 2 less than the Liberals, they had dropped in two years to a group with 46 fewer members. Their total strength in the new House of Commons stood at 95, scattered over every province except Quebec, which returned only 3 Conservatives. Their share of the popular vote remained at 34.8 per cent, but too much of this figure was drawn from western districts and not enough

Prime Minister Pierre Elliott Trudeau and his wife, Margaret, beam with delight after the Liberal Party election victory on July 8.

from the populous central Canadian cities. Stanfield made it clear that he would not lead the party in another election.

The NDP also fared badly. Their share of the popular vote fell from 17.2 to 15.1 per cent, and their strength in the House of Commons fell from 31 to 16. They lost 9 seats in British Columbia and 3 in Ontario, where their veteran leader, David Lewis, was defeated. There seemed little doubt that some of the NDP's former support had moved, or returned, to the Liberals, especially in Ontario.

The fourth party, Social Credit, held its own in its stronghold, Quebec. It won 11 Quebec seats and 4.9 per cent of the total Canadian vote, compared with 15 seats and 7.4 per cent of the vote in 1972. Réal Caouette, the party's driving force, campaigned quietly in 1974 because of illness. Nevertheless, he held off a determined Liberal drive to take Social Credit seats in Quebec.

After the Election. In retrospect, it appeared that the Conservatives had made a tactical error in stressing wage and price controls during the campaign. The average voter was suspicious, fearing that controls would be ineffective and that they might limit his ability to cope with inflation through higher wage settlements. The NDP probably suffered from the feeling that it had selfishly exploited its minority situation since 1972 for party advantage.

Thus, the Liberals may have benefited from negative attitudes toward both the Conservatives and the NDP. The Liberal strategy of emphasizing the need for majority government and claiming that it was the only party capable of winning support in every region made a powerful impact upon a worried electorate. Trudeau's role in defining the issues and giving an impression of cool capability was also a major factor in the Liberal victory.

Trudeau shuffled his Cabinet a month after the election. The most important change was the exchange of jobs between Mitchell Sharp, who had been secretary of state for external affairs since 1968, and Allan J. MacEachen, who was president of the privy council and government leader in the House of Commons. One member of the Cabinet, Jack Davis, minister of the environment and fisheries, had to be replaced after being defeated in the election. Six other ministers were transferred to different departments and six were dropped, with the number of Cabinet posts reduced from 31 to 29.

Parliament's Work in 1974 was interrupted by the May dissolution and the election. Because the legislature's life was shorter than in previous years, much legislation had to be held over. Actual legislative accomplishments were limited.

In January, Parliament passed a measure regulating election-campaign expenses and providing for

The Spectator, Hamilton, Ont.

public disclosure of donations of more than $100. It was amended 70 times as it made its way through the House of Commons. Another measure laid down regulations governing wiretapping and other forms of electronic surveillance. Parliament also approved measures for the emergency allocation of oil supplies – not required in the winter of 1973-1974 – and for an export tax on petroleum.

A number of taxation changes suggested by Finance Minister Turner in his abortive May budget were brought back before the new House in a second budget introduced on November 18. Turner hoped to keep the economy expanding in order to prevent prices from being pushed up by a shortage of goods and services. He promised cuts in personal income taxes, assistance to prospective home buyers and the elderly, concessions to small investors, and increased taxes on luxury items. He forecast a budget surplus of $250 million for the 1974-1975 fiscal year, based on revenues of $25.1 billion and expenditures of $24.8 billion.

The budget's proposed new taxes on oil and mining industries brought angry protests, especially in Alberta, which produces 85 per cent of Canada's oil. The key proposal was that provincial taxes and royalties will no longer be deductible in calculating federal income taxes.

The Canadian Economy, faced with rapid inflation, wage-cost pressures, and depressed foreign markets, showed little real growth in 1974. The gross national product reached an estimated $139 billion, representing a real growth rate of 4.2 per cent, down from 1973's rate of 7 per cent.

The economic slowdown in the United States affected Canada. During the first half of 1974, the volume of exports south of the border fell by 8 per cent. Lumber was especially hard hit, but there were also declines in metals, automotive equipment, and chemicals. The Canadian wheat crop, forecast at 522.5 million bushels, was smaller and poorer in quality because of bad weather conditions. Total exports to all markets for the first nine months of the year reached $23.1 billion. Imports for the same period were $22.6 billion.

The unemployment rate for December, adjusted to discount seasonal factors, reached 6.1 per cent, up from 5.5 per cent in November. Total employment remained steady at 9.25 million persons, but unemployment rose from 542,000 to 597,000.

Inflation continued at a high level, with the consumer price index for December at 175.8 (1961 = 100), a gain of 12.4 per cent. This was the highest yearly rise since August, 1951.

Oil and Gas. Canada weathered the energy crisis during the winter of 1973-1974 without imposing restrictions on the use of oil. Additional supplies were brought to eastern Canada, which is normally dependent on offshore oil, by vessel and tank car from the western provinces. Plans were made to extend the Interprovincial Pipe Line to Montreal; the line now links the Prairie Provinces with Chicago and southwestern Ontario.

The Canadian tax on oil exports, first collected in October, 1973, aroused sharp criticism in the United States Senate in January. The outburst was touched off by the announcement that the tax would be raised to $6.40 a barrel after February 1.

Donald S. Macdonald, Canada's minister of energy, mines, and resources, went to Washington, D.C., on January 30 to explain the higher tax to William Simon, President Richard M. Nixon's chief energy adviser. Macdonald pointed out that the proceeds from the tax would subsidize the high cost of imported oil needed in Quebec and the Maritime Provinces. American companies importing Canadian oil would pay world prices, just as Canada had done in 1972 when the United States froze domestic prices, but allowed export prices to rise.

Simon was apparently convinced by the Canadian minister's argument. In a statement after the meeting, he said that it was "inequitable" for Canada to have to buy expensive oil from abroad while selling cheaper oil to the United States. Simon agreed that Canada was entitled to remove the disparity through the export tax, though he hoped that Canada "could be a little more reasonable" about the tax level.

The Canadian export tax, tied to the price of imported non-Canadian oil at Chicago, was lowered to $4 a barrel following a meeting between Prime Minister Trudeau and the provincial premiers on March 27. The meeting established a uniform price for domestic crude oil across Canada. After June 1, the export tax rose to $5.20 a barrel. It continued at this rate for the rest of the year, though the level on exports of heavy crude oil was reduced in November as prices fell for this type of oil.

Energy Conference. Canada sent two Cabinet ministers to the energy conference held in Washington, D.C., on February 11 and 12. At the meeting, External Affairs Minister Mitchell Sharp explained that Canada's oil exports to the United States would probably decline during the remainder of the 1970s. He said Canada's proven reserves of oil were limited and it was doubtful whether the vast Alberta oil sands could be developed quickly enough to supply U.S. petroleum needs. There were formidable technological, environmental, and financial problems connected with exploiting the tar sands.

Sharp's forecast of declining exports was confirmed during the following months when Canadian oil shipments to the United States leveled off at about 900,000 barrels a day, compared to the daily average of 1.15 million barrels in 1973. The Canadian government announced in November that shipments to the United States would be cut to 800,000 barrels a day on Jan. 1, 1975, with further cuts possible. The announcement fueled the battle between the government and the Canadian oil industry. The oil indus-

The Ministry of Canada
In order of precedence

Pierre Elliott Trudeau, prime minister
Mitchell Sharp, president of the queen's privy council
Allan Joseph MacEachen, secretary of state for external affairs
Charles Mills Drury, minister of science and technology, and public works
Jean Marchand, minister of transport
John Napier Turner, minister of finance
Jean Chrétien, president of the treasury board
Donald Stovel Macdonald, minister of energy, mines, and resources
John Carr Munro, minister of labor
Gérard Pelletier, minister of communications
Stanley Ronald Basford, minister of national revenue
Donald Campbell Jamieson, minister of regional economic expansion
Robert Knight Andras, minister of manpower and immigration
James Armstrong Richardson, minister of national defense
Otto Emil Lang, minister of justice and attorney general of Canada
Jean-Pierre Goyer, minister of supply and services
Alastair William Gillespie, minister of industry, trade, and commerce
Warren Allmand, solicitor general of Canada
Hugh Faulkner, secretary of state of Canada
Marc Lalonde, minister of national health and welfare
Daniel J. MacDonald, minister of veterans affairs
André Ouellet, minister of consumer and corporate affairs
Jeanne Sauvé, minister of the environment
Eugene Whelan, minister of agriculture
Bryce Mackasey, postmaster general
Raymond Perrault, leader of the government in the senate
Barnett Danson, minister of state for urban affairs
Judd Buchanan, minister of Indian affairs and northern development
Romeo Leblanc, minister of fisheries

Premiers of Canadian Provinces

Province	Premier
Alberta	Peter Lougheed
British Columbia	David Barrett
Manitoba	Edward R. Schreyer
New Brunswick	Richard B. Hatfield
Newfoundland	Frank Moores
Nova Scotia	Gerald A. Regan
Ontario	William G. Davis
Prince Edward Island	Alexander B. Campbell
Quebec	J. Robert Bourassa
Saskatchewan	Allan Blakeney

Commissioners of Territories

Northwest Territories	Stuart M. Hodgson
Yukon Territory	James Smith

try, already angry over increased tax proposals, resented the cutback in its lucrative U.S. market. Canadian shipments account for almost 25 per cent of U.S. oil imports and 6 per cent of total U.S. consumption.

Other U.S. Negotiations. Worried about the possible connection between the growth hormone diethylstilbestrol (DES) and cancer, Canada decided in April to ban the import of cattle treated with DES. After difficult negotiations with the United States, a suitable procedure was worked out to certify that cattle imported from the United States were free of DES, and the ban was lifted in early August. But the Canadian government then announced a quota system for beef imports in order to protect the Canadian cattle industry. The United States protested and, in retaliation, introduced its own quotas on imports of Canadian beef and pork in November. United States Secretary of Agriculture Earl L. Butz said the U.S. quotas would be dropped if Canada would drop its restrictions.

The two countries were more cooperative in drawing up a new airlines agreement in May that allocated 28 new routes across the border to American operators and 18 to Canadian airlines. On June 20, the two countries signed a coastal pollution agreement setting up procedures to deal with pollution from oil carriers and offshore drilling rigs.

Foreign Affairs. Canada's warm friendship with India was strained when India exploded an underground nuclear device on May 18. There seemed little doubt that the plutonium used in the explosion had been produced in a Canadian reactor provided India in 1956 with the understanding that it would be used for nonmilitary purposes. Although the Indian government insisted that its nuclear power was being developed for peaceful purposes, Canada was concerned that India had struck a blow at the principle of the nonproliferation of nuclear powers. The Canadian Cabinet suspended further deliveries of nuclear equipment to India and stopped training Indian atomic scientists in Canada. However, the government stopped short of cutting off shipments of food and agricultural equipment.

Prime Minister Trudeau underlined the importance of stronger trade links with Europe when he paid a five-day visit to Paris and Brussels, Belgium, beginning on October 21. About 12 per cent of Canada's 1973 exports went to the countries of the European Community (Common Market), Canada's main trading partner after the United States.

The French visit symbolized the restoration of normal relations with France, which had been cool since French President Charles de Gaulle encouraged Quebec separatism in a 1967 speech in Montreal. Trudeau's state visit to France was the first by a Canadian prime minister since Lester B. Pearson visited Paris in 1964. Trudeau told President Valery Giscard d'Estaing that Canada would like France's

A Canadian technician measures ice movement to determine whether a pipeline can be built to carry natural gas south from the Arctic islands.

assistance in working out a preferential trading arrangement with the Common Market. Trudeau then went on to Brussels where Belgian Prime Minister Leo Tindemans encouraged Canada's trade objectives.

Peacekeeping Duties. In the Middle East, 1,100 Canadians served with the United Nations (UN) truce supervisory force established in the Suez Canal area in late 1973. After Israel and Syria drew their troops back from the Golan Heights in May, 150 Canadian soldiers were transferred from the Suez area to the new truce line.

When political unrest, the Turkish invasion, and civil war turned Cyprus into a battleground in July, the Canadian government doubled its 500-man UN contingent there. In the weeks that followed, Canadians were often caught in cross fire between Greeks and Turks. Two Canadian soldiers lost their lives in these incidents. Nine other Canadians died when Syrian anti-aircraft fire brought down a transport aircraft on a UN mission in Syria on August 9.

The Provinces

Alberta gained the first American Indian lieutenant governor in Canadian history when Ralph Steinhauer was appointed as queen's representative in May. A former chief of the Cree Indian Saddle Lake band, Steinhauer was a founder of the Indian Association of Alberta. In August, the Alberta government bought Pacific Western Airlines, the third largest airline in Canada. The province in December relaxed taxes and royalties on oil in an effort to spur further exploration.

British Columbia, under the NDP government of Premier David Barrett, continued to buy into privately owned companies in 1974. In January, the province purchased over 1.1 million shares of Westcoast Transmission Company, which operates a gas pipeline running 1,500 miles (2,400 kilometers) from northeastern British Columbia to Vancouver and the United States border. Shortly afterward, the government made its fourth purchase in the forest industry by buying Kootenay Forest Products of Nelson.

Manitoba added up the cost in October of an expensive venture, Churchill Forest Industries, located 450 miles (725 kilometers) north of Winnipeg. The complex was built after 1966 to develop the timber resources of the area. It went into receivership and was taken over by the government in January, 1971. A judicial inquiry reported in October that the province, after lending over $92 million to the enterprise, had wound up with a plant valued at only $7 million. The inquiry criticized the current NDP government and its Conservative predecessor for lax supervision of the project.

New Brunswick voters went to the polls in a general election on November 18. Premier Richard B. Hatfield's Conservative government, first elected in 1970, easily won re-election, taking 33 legislative seats to the Liberals' 25. The major parties shared the popular vote equally, each winning about 47 per cent. The election campaign was quiet, with no single issue dominating the public discussion.

Newfoundland. The provincial government acted on March 28 to coordinate hydroelectric power developments on the upper and lower stretches of the Churchill River in Labrador. It purchased almost 5-million shares, valued at $160 million, from Brinco, Limited, the Montreal-based owner of the Churchill Falls power scheme. Brinco, controlled by Rio Tinto Zinc Corporation of London, England, refused to sell until Premier Frank Moores threatened to nationalize the company.

Nova Scotia. Premier Gerald A. Regan's Liberal government, in power since 1970, won a sweeping

victory in a general election on April 2. The Liberals gained 6 seats, increasing their standing to 31 in the 46-seat legislature. The Conservatives gave up 6 seats, mainly on Cape Breton Island, to come out of the contest with 12 members. Three NDP members were elected, a gain of 1, but the party's share of the popular vote almost doubled.

Ontario acquired the first woman lieutenant governor in Canada's history in January when Pauline McGibbon, 63, chancellor of the University of Toronto since 1971, was named to be the 22nd holder of the provincial viceregal post. The legislature adjourned on June 28 after passing 69 bills, including a guaranteed income scheme for the elderly, blind, and disabled; a Health Disciplines Act that defined the scope and practice of five professions in the health field; and a controversial 50 per cent tax to be levied on the profits from land speculation. At year-end, the legislature was considering an amendment to lower the tax to 20 per cent.

Prince Edward Island, Canada's smallest province, gave Premier Alexander B. Campbell's Liberal administration a vote of confidence on April 29. In power since 1966, the Campbell government scored its third straight electoral victory by winning 26 seats in the 32-seat assembly. The budget, announced on April 2, featured the largest general tax reductions in the island's history, including the removal of the 8 per cent sales tax on a number of items.

Quebec. Political controversy centered on a measure that made French the official language in the province. The National Assembly passed the bill on July 30 by a vote of 92 to 10. The vote did not reflect the bitter struggle that accompanied each stage in the passage of the legislation. The English-speaking minority saw the bill as striking at the survival of their language; the immigrant viewed it as an effort to compel him to educate his children in French; and the separatist Parti Québécois regarded it as ineffectual in protecting the position of the French language. Several groups announced they would challenge its constitutionality in the courts.

Saskatchewan joined the other western provinces in imposing heavier taxes on natural resources in 1974. Oil and potash were among the minerals singled out for new forms of taxation. The province, which was an early pioneer in providing state-supported hospital care and physicians' services, announced in 1974 that it would pay for prescription drugs for all residents, with only a dispensing fee charged to the individual.

Facts in Brief: Population: 22,916,000. Government: Governor General Jules Léger; Prime Minister Pierre Elliott Trudeau. Monetary unit: Canadian dollar. Foreign Trade: exports, $26,309,000,000; imports, $24,918,000,000.   David M. L. Farr

See also CANADIAN LIBRARY ASSOCIATION (CLA); CANADIAN LITERATURE; LÉGER, JULES; TRUDEAU, PIERRE ELLIOTT.

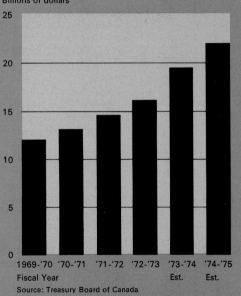

Federal Spending in Canada

Estimated Budget for Fiscal 1975*

	Millions of dollars
Health and welfare	6,855
Public debt	2,925
Economic development and support	2,672
Defense	2,365
Fiscal transfer payments to provinces	1,839
Transportation and communications	1,637
General government services	1,105
Internal overhead expenses	969
Education assistance	599
Culture and recreation	550
Foreign affairs	507
Total	22,023

*April 1, 1974, to March 31, 1975

Spending Since 1969

Billions of dollars

1969-'70 '70-'71 '71-'72 '72-'73 '73-'74 '74-'75
Fiscal Year   Est.   Est.
Source: Treasury Board of Canada

CANADIAN LIBRARY ASSOCIATION (CLA) held its 29th annual conference in Winnipeg, Man., from June 22 to 28, 1974. More than 1,200 persons attended. The central conference theme was Canadian library systems and networks – their planning and development. The participants discussed questions relating to national, provincial, and municipal library planning and development, cooperation between the public and private sectors, and the financing of library and information services.

The CLA's board of directors set a course in 1974 for the association and its management for the years ahead. The number of directors was increased from 6 to 10 to improve the work of the association and its divisions.

Medals and Awards. The Book of the Year for Children Medal was awarded to Elizabeth Cleaver, author and illustrator of *The Miraculous Hind* (English). No award was made for a French title. The Amelia Frances Howard-Gibbon Medal for illustrations was awarded to William Kurelek for *A Prairie Boy's Winter*. The Merit Award of the Canadian Library Trustees Association went to Ray Culos of the Burnaby Public Library Board in British Columbia. The sixth Howard V. Phalin-World Book Graduate Scholarship in Library Science was awarded by a CLA standing committee to Nancy Williamson, assistant professor, faculty of library science, University of Toronto. The scholarship was sponsored by World Book – Childcraft of Canada, Limited.

Publications. *The National Library of Canada* by F. Dolores Donnelly (Sister Francis Dolores) is a historical analysis of the forces that contributed to the establishment of the library. Published by the CLA, it identifies the National Library's role and responsibilities. Donnelly is associate professor of library science at the University of Toronto. *Cataloguing Standards: The Report of the Canadian Task Group on Cataloguing Standards; Recommendations to the National Librarian* was published by the National Library of Canada. Its 58 recommendations would affect every library and librarian in Canada.

Libraries. The new $3.7-million Ottawa Public Library building, opened in May, is designed to provide all types of community services. The John M. Cuelenaere Library of Prince Albert, Sask., honors a former mayor and library board member. It is a resource center for the area students, and the city's main public library. The National Science Library of Canada, Ottawa, which also serves as the Library of the National Research Council of Canada, was moved into a spacious new building early in 1974.

National Library. An Ethnic Canadiana program was established to acquire and maintain a collection of Canadian newspapers in languages other than English and French. The program has organized a center for rotating books in ethnic languages to public and regional libraries.　　Elizabeth Homer Morton

CANADIAN LITERATURE was notable in 1974 for its longer fiction, its short stories, and regional settings of works dealing with the land and its people. *Canada*, a volume with 54 color photographs and poetry in English and French that had been selected "to reflect the grandeur of the land and the life of its people," is an example of the emphasis on rural scenes and natural phenomena.

Literature. *Supplement to the Oxford Companion to Canadian History and Literature*, the work of 37 contributors edited by William Toye, covers French and English literary development from 1967 to 1972. *The Canadian Experience; a Brief Survey of English Canadian Prose*, edited by A. J. M. Smith, covers three periods of Canadian literature: pre-Confederation (before 1867); Confederation to World War I; and the 60 years after the war. It contains excerpts from diaries and novels, and some short stories.

Fiction. *The Diviners* by Margaret Lawrence is the most full-bodied of this accomplished writer's works. *The Lark in Clear Air* by Dennis T. Patrick Sears re-creates rural Ontario life in the 1930s.

Indian folklore is a popular theme in *Revenge of Annie Charlie* by Alan Fry; *The Vanishing Point* by W. O. Mitchell; *Riverrun* by Peter Such; and *We, the Wilderness* by Thomas York. *Thirty Indian Legends*, by Margaret Bemister, is illustrated by Indian artist Douglas Tait.

Outstanding short story collections by individual authors include *Something I've Been Meaning to Tell You* by Alice Munro; *Blood Flowers* by W. D. Valgardson; and *Women and Children* by Beth Harvor. Anthologies are *Stories from Atlantic Canada* by Kent Thompson and *New Canadian Stories, 73*, edited by David Helwig and Joan Harcourt.

Drama. *Dramatists in Canada*, edited by William H. New, includes a survey of Canada's dramatic heritage as well as a discussion of contemporary drama. *The Brock Bibliography of Published Canadian Stage Plays in English, 1900-72*, compiled by the Brock University Department of Drama, is indispensable for anyone interested in Canadian theater.

Poetry. *What's So Big About Green?* by Earle Birney; *Crusoe; Eli Mandel*, selections chosen by Margaret Atwood and Dennis Lee; and *Thanks for a Drowned Island*, poems by Alfred G. Bailey, are examples of the year's output. An important study is *E. J. Pratt, the Evolutionary Vision*, by Sandra Djwa.

Fine Arts. *Indian Arts in Canada* by Olive Patricia Dicason, handsomely illustrated, is, in the words of one reviewer, an "assessment of an ancient tradition and a heritage whose importance the 20th century is now beginning to evaluate properly." *Canadian Native Art* by Nancy-Lou Patterson surveys all art forms from every area. *High Realism in Canada* by Paul Duval describes and attempts to analyze the work of 13 Canadian artists, and it includes biographical notes. *Pellan* by Germain Lefebvre is notable for the brilliant fidelity of the color reproduction.

Canadian author Max Braithwaite discusses his latest novel, *A Privilege and a Pleasure,* with students at Port Colborne High School in Ontario.

History and Politics. The period of the Great Depression is portrayed in *Ten Lost Years, 1929-1939* by Barry Broadfoot, and in *Men Against the Desert* by James H. Gray. *Canada, 1896-1921; A Nation Transformed* by Robert Craig Brown and Ramsay Cook is a study of a complicated period of political, economic, and social change. *The Selection of National Party Leaders in Canada* by John C. Courtney analyzes the Liberal and Progressive Conservative party procedures. *Mike: the Memoirs of the Right Honorable Lester B. Pearson, Volume 2 (1948-1957)* covers Pearson's life from his entrance into politics to his acceptance of the Nobel Peace Prize.

Education. *Halfway up Parnassus* by Claude Bissell recounts social upheavals and other changes during his 39 years on the University of Toronto campus, from student to president.

Canada's North. *Arctic* by Fred Bruemmer includes 80 of his full-color and 150 black-and-white photographs, and the text describes the land, sea, plants, animals, people, and history as he learned it on his trips to Canada's Arctic Islands. *Tales from the Igloo,* edited and translated by Maurice Metayer, includes 22 tales collected from the Copper Eskimos of the Canadian Arctic, with colored illustrations by Agnes Nanogak, an Eskimo artist. *A History of the Original Peoples of Northern Canada* by Keith J. Crowe, a work by an Eskimo-speaking civil servant working with a team of native researchers, is the best history

of the North to date and a first move in re-educating people about the North.

Quotations. *Colombo's Canadian Quotations* and *"Quotations" from English Canadian Literature,* compiled and edited, respectively, by John Robert Colombo, Canadian poet, and David Strickland, teacher of Canadian studies at the Séminaire de Québec, present the personal choices of a poet and a teacher in pithy quotations.

Governor-General's Literary Awards for books published in 1973 went to Rudy Wiebe for *The Temptations of Big Bear* (English fiction); Miriam Mandel for *Lions at Her Face* (English poetry); Michael Bell for *Painters in a New Land* (English nonfiction); Réjean Ducharme for *L'hiver de Force* (French fiction); Albert Faucher for *Québec en Amérique au XIXe siècle* (French nonfiction); and Roland Giguère for *La main au feu* (French poetry). Giguère declined the award.

Stephen Leacock Memorial Award for humor went to Donald Jack for *That's Me in the Middle.*

Canada Council Translation Prizes recognize the increasingly important role of translation in communications, arts, and culture in Canada. Alan Brown won the award for his English translation of *L'Antiphonaire* (*The Antiphonary*) by Hubert Aquin, and Jean Paré for his translation of *The Scalpel and the Sword* (*Docteur Bethune*) by Sydney Gordon and Ted Allan.　　　　Elizabeth Homer Morton

CELEBRATIONS and anniversaries observed in 1974 included the following:

Aquinas-Bonaventure Septicentennial. On October 29, the University of Chicago began a four-week schedule of religious and cultural events commemorating the 700th anniversary of the deaths of two noted theologians: Saint Thomas Aquinas and Saint Bonaventure. A "celebration of the medieval heritage," the series was organized by the Jesuit School of Theology in Chicago and the Catholic Theological Union. It included 20 major lectures, exhibitions of art and the printed word, and musical and theatrical performances.

Anton Bruckner Memorial. The 150th anniversary of the Austrian composer's birth was celebrated by the world's major symphony orchestras. Special all-Bruckner concerts were performed by the Vienna Philharmonic and Amsterdam's Concertgebouw Orchestra.

Robert Frost Centennial. The 100th anniversary of Robert Frost's birth was commemorated in an exhibition entitled "Robert Frost 100." The exhibition, which consisted of 100 prized items, included Frost's first book, a collection of five poems he had privately printed in 1894. The exhibition, which began its tour in May, was shown at Princeton University, the University of Chicago, the University of Virginia, and other centers of learning.

Herbert C. Hoover Centennial. The 100th anniversary of the 31st President's birth was celebrated on August 10 in his birthplace, West Branch, Iowa. A highlight of the weeklong event was a wreath-laying ceremony at Hoover's grave.

Charles Ives Centennial. The 100th anniversary of the New England composer's birth was celebrated with performances of his works by major symphony orchestras, including those of San Francisco, Rochester, Minnesota, Boston, Philadelphia, and Detroit. Ives festivals were also held in Miami, New York City, and Danbury, Conn.

Guglielmo Marconi Centennial. A bronze bust was unveiled on October 14, the 100th anniversary of the birth of the inventor of wireless telegraphy at Southwellfleet, Mass. The ceremony was held near the beach where Marconi sent the first transatlantic message from the United States to England in 1903.

Pierpont Morgan Library Quinquagenary. A special eight-week exhibition of treasures called "Great Acquisitions of Fifty Years: 1924-1974" went on view February 15 in the New York City library founded by financier and art collector J. Pierpont Morgan. Among the 200 works shown were manuscript pages of Franz Schubert's *Die Winterreise* and Charles Dickens' "Our Mutual Friend" and such rarities as letters from Machiavelli, Erasmus, and Francis Bacon.

Winston Churchill, namesake of Britain's World War II leader, views a sculpture of his grandfather at a Churchill Centennial show in London.

Oxygen Discovery Bicentennial. Ceremonies in August at the Joseph Priestley house in Northumberland, Pa., celebrated the 200th anniversary of Priestley's discovery of oxygen on Aug. 1, 1774. The American Chemical Society unveiled a plaque dedicated to Priestley and to the fact that discussions at the centennial on Aug. 1, 1874, led to the founding of the American Chemical Society in 1876.

Petrarch Sexcentennial. The 600th anniversary of the death of Petrarch, the great Italian poet and scholar whose works had an unparalleled influence on world literature, was commemorated April 6 to 12 by an International Petrarch Congress in Washington, D.C. Activities included special concerts, a scholar's mass, a day at the National Gallery of Art, and a reading of excerpts from Petrarch's "Coronation Oration" on the steps of the Capitol.

Arnold Schönberg Centennial. The creator of the 12-tone system of musical composition was honored on his 100th birthday with performances of his works by symphony orchestras in Chicago; Philadelphia; Cincinnati; Boston; Los Angeles; Milwaukee, Wis.; and Tanglewood, Mass.

Yale Law School. A three-day observance from November 1 to 3 marked the 150th anniversary of the founding of the Yale Law School at New Haven, Conn. Activities included seminars, luncheons, dinners, and speeches by university officials and distinguished alumni.   Paul C. Tullier

CENSUS, U.S. The number of United States households rose to an estimated 70 million in 1974, some 6.5 million more than at the start of the present decade, according to the U.S. Bureau of the Census.

Households made up of persons living alone or with nonrelatives accounted for nearly half the increase. This is the fastest-growing type of household in the nation, showing an increase of 25 per cent during the 1970s. Contributing to this growth are older persons who live alone after their families have matured and young, single persons who have left the parental home.

Of the estimated 70 million households, 46.8-million, or 67 per cent, were husband-wife households; 8.1 million, or 12 per cent, were families in which no spouse of the family head was present. The great bulk of the latter are headed by women. The remaining 14.9 million households consist of people living alone or with nonrelatives.

There were 16 million households headed by women in 1974, compared with 13.4 million in 1970. Families headed by women increased as much during the period 1970-1973 – from 5.6 million to 6.6-million – as they did throughout the 1960s. Because of their rapidly growing numbers, women family heads have become a source of increasing concern among social scientists as well as public and private officials. Although no hard data are available on the causes of the rapid increase in women family heads,

the makeup of the group has shown considerable change over the years. Compared to previous years, for example, 1974 women family heads are younger on the average; more likely to be divorced or separated; less likely to be widowed; more often single; and more often employed.

The United States had an estimated population of 211.6 million persons on Jan. 1, 1974, according to Census Bureau officials. This included the populations of the 50 states and the District of Columbia, and the armed forces and federal employees overseas and their dependents living with them.

The net gain in population during 1973 was an estimated 1.5 million, compared with 1.6 million during 1972 and 2 million in 1971. The bureau estimates that the net gain was the result of about 3.1 million births, 2 million deaths, and 350,000 added by immigration. Although population increased, the total fertility rate remained below the *replacement rate* (the birth rate needed for the population to replace itself) for the second year in a row, declining to 1.9 children per family from 2.03 children in 1972.

As of Dec. 31, 1974, the U.S. population was estimated at 213.2 million, an increase of 1.6 million for the year.   Vincent P. Barabba

CENTRAL AFRICAN REPUBLIC. See AFRICA.

CEYLON. See SRI LANKA.

CHAD. See AFRICA.

CHEMICAL INDUSTRY continued operating at full plant capacity in the United States during 1974. Heavy demand for major chemicals, plastics, and synthetic fibers produced a third consecutive year of growth. However, most of the earnings gains resulted from higher prices, about 21 per cent above last year's levels. Demand declined at year's end, but prices and production both remained high. The monetary value of the nation's chemical inventories climbed 17 per cent.

The Arab oil embargo, which was lifted in March, intensified existing energy and raw-material shortages and sent prices skyrocketing. Hardest hit were the petrochemical industries, which use petroleum products as raw ingredients as well as fuel. Automobile owners felt the effects of petroleum shortages late in the year when antifreeze supplies vanished. Where available, prices jumped from about $1 to over $5 a gallon.

Despite inflation and high interest rates, domestic capital spending rose 36 per cent to $6.07 billion. Foreign capital investment was boosted by 68 per cent to $2.5 billion. Most of the money was spent in European Community countries and Latin America. Sales from overseas subsidiaries rose from $21.5 billion in 1973 to about $27.5 billion.

Pollution Control requirements opened at least three new large markets for lime: to remove sulfur dioxide in stack gas scrubbers; to remove phosphates

Smoke billows from ruins of the Nypro chemical plant near Scunthorpe, England, following an explosion on June 2 that killed 29 persons.

from sewage; and to control acidity in sewage plants. Capital investment for air- and water-pollution control rose to $609 million for the chemical industry.

Chemicals and Health. In July, the U.S. Food and Drug Administration (FDA) approved Aspartame, a new sweetener made by G. D. Searle & Company. Reportedly 180 times sweeter than sugar, it was approved for all uses except in cooking and bottled soft drinks. However, this authorization was delayed in August pending a study of allegations that Aspartame might cause brain damage to children who eat it with monosodium glutamate (MSG), a common food additive. In September, the FDA rejected a petition by Abbott Laboratories to return the sweeteners called cyclamates to the market. The U.S. Department of Agriculture urged a reduction in the use of nitrates and nitrites for curing and preserving meats because they are converted into cancer-producing nitrosamines in the digestive tract.

On February 11, the Occupational Safety and Health Administration (OSHA) issued rules for protection of workers from exposure to 14 cancer-causing substances. Vinyl chloride monomer was implicated in the liver-cancer deaths of a number of workers, and in April, OSHA set an emergency interim exposure limit of 50 parts per million (ppm). The ceiling was lowered to 1 ppm on October 1. The FDA and the Environmental Protection Agency (EPA) requested removal from the market of aerosol-spray products and pesticides using vinyl chloride monomer as a propellant.

Sales of flame-retardant treatments for fibers and plastics used in clothing, home furnishings, and automobile and plane interiors increased by 18 per cent. In July, the Federal Trade Commission (FTC) ordered 25 plastics companies and their trade association – the Society of the Plastics Industry – to stop advertising their foamed plastics as "nonburning." The FTC said the products do burn, and ordered the group to start a $5-million research program on ways to minimize their fire-hazard potential.

Pesticides. Increased planting acreage resulted in a record year for pesticides, up 10 per cent to $1.4-billion. Dichlorodiphenyl-trichloroethane (DDT), which was banned in 1972 by the EPA, was approved in March for a one-time use against the tussock moth in the forests of the Pacific Northwest and the pea weevil in Washington and Idaho. At about the same time, the University of Illinois in Urbana received a patent for a biodegradable relative of DDT that is less poisonous to animals.

Pennwalt Corporation gained commercial marketing approval from the EPA for Penncap-M, a microencapsulated pesticide. It will be used on alfalfa, cotton, and sweet corn. On October 1, the EPA ordered suspension of marketing of Shell Chemical Company's aldrin and dieldrin, which were found to cause liver tumors in rats.   Edward Abrams

253

CHEMISTRY. Teams of Russian and United States chemists both took credit for the 1974 discovery of a new element that has 106 protons and 157 neutrons in its nucleus. A team of scientists headed by Albert Ghiorso and Glenn T. Seaborg produced the new element (called element 106-263) in September in the super heavy-ion linear accelerator (Super HILAC) at the University of California's Lawrence Berkeley Laboratory (LBL) in Berkeley. Its chemical properties are expected to be similar to chromium, molybdenum, and tungsten. However, Seaborg predicts that element 106-263 may differ from these metals because of relativistic effects caused by the large size of its nucleus.

The LBL group bombarded californium-249 with oxygen-18 ions to create element 106-263. Within seconds, the isotope spontaneously decays to the known isotope rutherfordium-259 (LBL's name for element 104-259) and then to nobelium-255.

Researchers at Russia's Joint Institute for Nuclear Research at Dubna, near Moscow, claimed in June that they made the 106th element of the periodic table. They bombarded lead nuclei with chromium ions to form a compound nucleus. The Russians based their claims on the fission products that are formed when the compound nucleus spontaneously breaks apart. The Russian and U.S. groups clashed in the 1960s over which first discovered elements 104 and 105. The International Union of Pure and Applied Chemistry has twice avoided a decision on the issue. Until it rules, the elements will continue to be called rutherfordium and hahnium in the West, and kurchatovium and niels bohrium in the East.

Molecules in Space. Using a radio telescope 36 feet (12 meters) in diameter at the National Radio Astronomy Observatory (NRAO) at Kitt Peak, near Tucson, Ariz., an international team of scientists discovered ethanol molecules in interstellar space. They identified the molecule's emission lines in the millimeter-wave portion of the spectrum of radio frequencies from Sagittarius B2, a vast cloud of dust and gas near the center of the Milky Way.

Ethanol (C_2H_5OH) is the second nine-atom hydrocarbon molecule to be found so far. According to Patrick E. Palmer of the University of Chicago and Mark A. Gordon of NRAO, "ethanol has a very rich spectrum, and it promises to be a very useful tool to probe for conditions in space." In November, several members of the team discovered the molecule silicon monosulfide, SiS, the 32nd molecule to be identified in interstellar space.

Arthritis Cure? The free radical superoxide may have severely damaging effects in rheumatoid arthritis, according to Joe M. McCord of Duke University Medical Center in Durham, N.C. McCord believes that superoxide is responsible for the degradation of synovial fluid, a viscous liquid that lubricates normal bone joints.

Superoxide can be produced in the body by *autoxidation* of a number of compounds. Autoxidation is oxidation by direct combination with oxygen. For example, Bernard B. Babior of Tufts New England Medical Center in Massachusetts has shown that a large amount of superoxide is released when blood cells called polymorphonuclear leukocytes destroy bacteria.

Within the living cell, the enzyme superoxide dismutase converts superoxide radicals to hydrogen peroxide, which can be converted to water by such enzymes as catalase and peroxidases. Because fluids outside the cell contain only trace amounts of superoxide dismutase, they cannot convert superoxide radicals to hydrogen peroxide.

In rheumatoid arthritis, polymorphonuclear leukocytes accumulate in the synovial fluid, which often breaks down and loses its ability to lubricate. According to McCord, hyaluronic acid, a high-molecular-weight polysaccharide, determines the proper viscosity of synovial fluid, and both superoxide and hydrogen peroxide are involved in its breakdown. His studies show that by adding either superoxide dismutase or catalase to whole bovine synovial fluid, its viscosity can be preserved in the presence of superoxide. Should similar results be found in human synovial fluid without unwanted side effects, superoxide dismutase might become an effective means for treating rheumatoid arthritis. Alfred W. von Smolinski

See also BIOCHEMISTRY; NOBEL PRIZES.

CHESS. World champion Bobby Fischer did not play competitively in 1974, but he was much in the news. In April, Edmund E. Edmondson, president of the United States Chess Federation, announced that Fischer would play in the 1974 World Chess Olympics only if he could play in a building separate from the one in which the other matches were played. Fischer's request was denied. The Chess Olympics took place in Nice, France, in June. Russia won the tournament for the 11th consecutive time. Yugoslavia was second, and the United States placed third.

World Championship Preparations. On June 28, Fischer notified the International Chess Federation that he was renouncing his world championship. He would not defend it in 1975 unless the rules of the competition were changed to conform to his wishes. The federation had limited the championship series to 36 games; the first player to win 10 games would be declared champion. Fischer demanded that no limit be set on the number of games played. Reportedly, the American Olympiad team asked the federation to reconsider its rules to appease Fischer. But, on July 25, the federation said Fischer would be stripped of his title on April 1, 1975, unless he dropped his demands for rules changes.

If Fischer does play, his opponent will be Anatoly Karpov, 23, of Russia. In a series of games played in Moscow, Karpov defeated Viktor Korchnoi, also of Russia. The two had emerged from a series of world

Swimmers play chess on floating chessboards
in an outdoor swimming pool in Budapest,
Hungary, to celebrate the first day of spring.

CHICAGO. Criminal charges against some of his political associates and his own illness plagued Chicago Mayor Richard J. Daley in 1974. Alderman Thomas E. Keane, Daley's most powerful political ally and the City Council floor leader, was convicted in November on federal charges of mail fraud and conspiracy. He was sentenced to five years. Two other aldermen and Daley's former press aide also were convicted on criminal charges during the year.

Daley suffered a stroke on May 13, his first serious illness during 20 years as mayor. He underwent vascular surgery on June 2, and returned to his office on September 3. On December 9, Daley announced that he intended to run in 1975 for an unprecedented sixth term as mayor.

Regional Transit Plan. Voters on March 19 approved the formation of a Regional Transportation Authority (RTA) to coordinate all public transportation in the Chicago metropolitan area's six Illinois counties and aid the financially failing Chicago Transit Authority (CTA). However, the RTA was hindered by disputes over funding and the selection of an RTA board chairman.

Accidents as well as funding problems plagued the CTA during the year. Four separate elevated train crashes injured nearly 300 persons.

Multimillion-Dollar Robbery. Thieves stole about $4 million from the vault of an armored express

candidates matches played during 1974. If Fischer does not play, the championship match will probably be between Karpov and Korchnoi.

In one semifinal, Karpov defeated a former world champion, Russian Boris Spassky, 4 games to 1. In the other, Korchnoi defeated former world champion Tigran Petrosian, also a Russian, 3 games to 1.

Henrique Mecking, the temperamental Brazilian grandmaster who lost a quarter-final match to Korchnoi in February in Augusta, Ga., charged the Russian with "war propaganda and political warfare, not chess." He said Korchnoi disturbed him by "making grunting noises, continually clearing his throat, and laughing audibly."

Other Winners. Walter Browne, an Australian now living in New York City, won the United States Chess Championship in Chicago on August 2. The prize was $2,250. In the United States Open Chess Championship, which ended on August 23 in New York City, Vlastimil Hort of Czechoslovakia and Pal Benko of New York City tied for first place with 10 victories and 2 defeats each.

Anthony John Miles of Great Britain won the World Junior Chess Championship in Manila, the Philippines, on August 23. Three residents of Warwick, R.I., set a world record for marathon chess play on August 10 by completing 104 hours and 11 minutes of play. They were Philip Hirons, Gilbert Steinle, and Keith Kaplan.   Theodore M. O'Leary

A mounted policeman patrols the area around Chicago's Buckingham Fountain. Mounted patrols were resumed to combat crime in the parks.

company on October 20. In an attempt to conceal the robbery, they set fire bombs in the vault to destroy the remaining cash. However, the robbery was discovered when the fire broke out. Police and Federal Bureau of Investigation (FBI) agents arrested a guard employed by the company and five other men. See CRIME.

According to the FBI, serious crime increased 5 per cent in Chicago during the first six months of 1974. To cut down on crime in city parks, police began riding horses in those areas.

On February 11, Daley appointed James M. Rochford as superintendent of the police force, which had been wracked by scandals. In December, the federal government cut off the city's revenue-sharing funds until alleged discriminatory police-hiring practices could be corrected.

The Cost of Living in Chicago rose 10.8 per cent between June, 1973, and June, 1974, while the wages of the average factory worker rose only 8.4 per cent during the year ending in July. At the same time, department store sales rose 11.1 per cent, construction activity dropped 5.9 per cent, and employment went up 0.7 per cent. The federal government released $7 million to the city on October 3 to provide jobs for the hard-core unemployed.

The city lost one of its four major daily newspapers when *Chicago Today* ceased publication on September 13. James M. Banovetz

CHILD WELFARE. Child advocacy centers continued to be established on a demonstration basis across the United States in 1974 in a slowly growing federal program. Between 1970 and 1973, the government funded 11 demonstration projects at a total cost of $2.5 million. More were inaugurated in 1974. Rather than providing direct services, these centers seek to assure that each child receives the services to which he is entitled, and to arouse the conscience of the public, the agencies, and the legislatures to the gaps that need filling.

One of these, the Syracuse (N.Y.) Center for Human Policy, is staffed by attorneys, special educators, and graduate researchers and advocates. It has filed class-action suits in the courts on behalf of handicapped children. Where feasible, it negotiates with institutions, school districts, or other agencies to secure the services children need. In the courts of New York, it won the right for child advocate groups to inspect all children's institutions. Through legal workshops, publications, and specially developed memos, it also helps parents act as advocates for their own children.

Legal rights of children received increased attention through such activities as a joint project of the national Parent-Teacher Association and the National Council of Juvenile Court Judges. The judges' group also convened the first National Conference on Juvenile Justice with the National District Attorneys Association in January. The alleged deprivation of juvenile legal rights in courts, schools, and community was high on the agenda.

Child Abuse. The Child Abuse Prevention and Treatment Act became federal law in 1974. The Department of Health, Education, and Welfare subsequently established a National Center on Child Abuse and Neglect within its Children's Bureau to coordinate government policies and plans.

All states have been urged to improve their statutes on child abuse, to improve reporting procedures, to protect the victims, and to provide curative and preventive methods. The existing model law is being revised under a federal grant.

Individual cases of child abuse continued to arouse public furor and professional responses. Vincent J. Fontana, director of pediatrics at St. Vincent Hospital in New York City, reported that 200 children died of maltreatment in New York City in 1973. Rowine Brown, medical director of Cook County Hospital in Chicago, reported that hospital records indicate that 10 per cent of the abused children treated there and returned home as medically cured are brought back to the hospital dead within 90 days.

Transracial Adoptions. The adoption of black children by white families subsided in 1974. Adoptions by black families apparently have increased enough to reduce substantially the need for transracial placements. Also, many black social workers have disapproved of the transracial adoptions. However, not all black children needing homes can be placed. An article in the March, 1974, issue of *Child Welfare* magazine argues that the need continues and suggests guidelines.

Hyperactive Children. The Food and Drug Administration (FDA) continued to monitor the use of stimulants to calm hyperactive children. Amphetamines and methylphenidate are currently approved for children with hyperactivity or minimal brain disfunction, but only under FDA's most restrictive schedule for marketed drugs.

Considerable publicity has been given to the possibility that such drugs are being prescribed for nothing more than normal childhood boisterousness. Educators are sensitive to the charge, because they are sometimes a link in the chain of events that leads to the prescription. But the FDA does not believe that this occurs often enough to warrant withdrawing marketing approval.

Day Care for preschool children with working mothers received gradually expanding federal support in recent years, but this trend appears over. There are new ceilings on federal day-care funds and cutbacks or limited growth in state support. Only 10 per cent of the 6 million U.S. preschool children with working mothers are currently enrolled in any kind of licensed day-care program. Frances A. Mullen

CHILDREN'S BOOKS. See LITERATURE FOR CHILDREN.

Conflict between church and state erupts publicly in Chile in April as
Raul Cardinal Silva Henriquez, left, denounces military junta's policies.

CHILE. The new military regime faced difficulties in consolidating its position in 1974. It found itself isolated internationally; it was also in danger of losing the support of some of the civilian groups that had approved of its Sept. 11, 1973, coup d'état against the regime of Salvador Allende Gossens.

During 1974, it became clear that there would be no early return to constitutional government. The electoral registers were burned, the junta extended the state of emergency, and it governed according to Chile's stern code of military law. It also became clear, with the naming of General Augusto Pinochet Ugarte as supreme chief of state on June 26, that the army had successfully asserted its primacy over the other services.

The Domestic Economy. The junta's economic policy called for monetary restraint, a balanced budget, a return to a free market system of pricing, and fewer restraints on private enterprise. The economic legacy of the Allende regime could not, however, be shrugged off in a single year, and there was a bitter social cost involved in the junta's attempts to restore a market system. Inflation in 1974 was about 350 per cent, according to official figures. Real wages dropped as state import subsidies for food and consumer goods were cut back, and prices were allowed to rise to a world level.

The denationalization of Chilean industries proceeded apace. Chile also adopted an open-door policy toward foreign investors, but at the cost of cooling relations with its neighbors in the Latin American Free Trade Association.

Political Unrest, which had been expected to rise dramatically as a result of unpopular economic measures and the suppression of opposition parties and trade unions, did not find many outlets inside Chile. The guerrilla left failed to mount any significant operations. A conflict with the Roman Catholic Church and with the Christian Democratic Party, on the other hand, caused the junta growing concern. On April 23, in a letter signed by 28 bishops, the church hierarchy complained about the regime's arrests and summary executions. Many Christian Democrats objected to the junta's January 21 ruling that non-Marxist parties would have to confine future activities to those of an "administrative" nature; they could not, for example, hold political meetings.

The Foreign Image of the junta continued to deteriorate in the wake of hostile press reports about repression, torture, and arbitrary arrests and inquiries by such bodies as Amnesty International and the Human Rights Commission of the Organization of American States (OAS). Many observers were surprised that the junta allowed these groups to investigate; the OAS had been refused permission to study conditions in Cuba and Brazil.   Robert Moss

See also LATIN AMERICA (Facts in Brief Table).

CHINA, NATIONALIST. See TAIWAN.

CHINA, PEOPLE'S REPUBLIC OF

CHINA, PEOPLE'S REPUBLIC OF. With red banners, crashing cymbals, fireworks, and dancing in the parks, China marked the 25th anniversary of the People's Republic on Oct. 1, 1974. It was a significant date, for a revolution that survives a quarter of a century has proven its vitality. But there were other items to please the leadership in Peking. The harvest was excellent. Industry continued to make progress, and foreign trade kept expanding. While China kept a low profile in world affairs, the country stayed on cordial terms with other countries, save hated Russia, Russian allies, and India.

Strains Show. But the picture of calm and contentment was deceptive. The question of succession to Chairman Mao Tse-tung remained unresolved, and increasingly it affected domestic politics. Mao was 81 years old on Dec. 23, 1974, and he could not remain at the top much longer. Thus, the year was marked by a sharp struggle for advantage among the most powerful factions. The generals were elbowed out of the way in December, 1973, when eight of the 11 regional commanders were moved from the areas where they were dominant to new commands where their influence was limited.

This left two major groups contending for power and the right to make policy, the Old Guard and the Radicals. The Old Guard in Peking – tough but aged men – with Mao, had been the makers of this revolu-tion. Their ranks, however, were beginning to shrink as infirmity or death claimed them. Premier Chou En-lai, for example, spent much of 1974 in a hospital, all but retired from an active role. His loss was griev-ous, both to China and to the Old Guard; almost single-handedly, he kept the nation from plunging into revolutionary chaos during the Cultural Revo-lution that broke out in 1966. With Chou in virtual retirement, the task of administering this vast coun-try fell on 70-year-old Deputy Premier Teng Hsiao-ping, a veteran of party battles but lacking Chou's prestige.

The Rebels. The Old Guard wanted normality, order, and firm central controls. It wanted the revo-lutionary turmoil muted so that production could advance. And it wanted to remain in power after Mao's passing, so as to ensure China's steady military and economic growth.

But, increasingly, the Old Guard found itself challenged in 1974 by the younger, more militant Radicals, whose power base was apparently in Shanghai and whose allies included Mao's wife, Chiang Ching.

The revolution, the Radicals cried, was not yet complete. They wanted all true Maoists, and es-pecially the young, to mount the revolutionary bar-ricades, to combat all Old Guard efforts to leave things as they were, to seek out the hidden enemies,

Premier Chou En-lai meets with Imelda Marcos, wife of the Philippines' president, during her September visit to negotiate a trade agreement.

and to carry on what Mao called an "uninterrupted revolution."

Verbal Duel. In September, 1973, the initial issue of the theoretical magazine *Study and Criticism* came out in Shanghai. It was the first new journal to appear since the Cultural Revolution that ended in 1968. The new magazine expounded themes often different from those championed by the party's official *People's Daily* in Peking.

It was *Study and Criticism* that fired the opening gun in the curious campaign against the ancient sage Confucius and Mao's former heir-designate Marshal Lin Piao, who allegedly died in a plane crash in 1971 while trying to escape to Russia. The campaign was aimed at replacing Confucius' ideas of an orderly society obedient to its elders with Mao's view of a society in constant flux and with no reverence for elders. But, more significantly, it was believed to be directed against the Old Guard in Peking, who opposed change and disorder.

The *People's Daily* kept appealing for "unity," for obedience, for production, and for revolution – in that order. The Radicals employed Maoist slogans, "To rebel is justified" and "Daring to go against the tide" (defying the party command when one felt it was wrong).

Rallies, Too. But the duel was not confined to words. In the spring, many provinces saw mass rallies directed against "U.S. imperialism." Here and there, in the Southwest and West, exhibits were opened to display crude tools with which U.S. intelligence agents who worked in China during World War II allegedly tortured revolutionaries. The campaign was probably meant to embarrass Premier Chou and the Old Guard, who had toiled hard to open cordial relations with the United States.

When the Radicals denounced Western composers – including Beethoven – as a tool with which the capitalists sought to weaken revolutionary vigilance, they were perhaps trying to undermine Premier Chou, who brought leading Western orchestras to Peking in 1973. When the Radicals denounced the efforts to expand book learning in the schools and universities, they were likely aiming their cannon at the Old Guard. The Old Guard was trying to raise the levels of education, which had been lowered disastrously after the Cultural Revolution.

The fortunes of battle changed from month to month. In the spring, the Radicals held the advantage; in July, the Old Guard won its fight to give priority to production. But the long-range advantage seemed to be with the Radicals. They were younger.

The Posters. In some ways, 1974 was reminiscent of the years of turmoil during the Cultural Revolution. At first, the government set up criticism groups to carry on the anti-Confucius campaign. These soon were converted into an army of theorists, whose prime task was to keep the propaganda drive at a feverish pace.

By late spring, the walls in the cities, factories, and universities displayed a coat of posters complaining against injustice – at work, in dealings with the government, or at the hands of the police. The poster-writers then turned on national leaders. But the latter managed to keep the passions under control.

The massive movement of high school graduates to the villages continued, but to ensure better treatment by the hostile peasantry, the government now sent along cadres to see to it that the young strangers were given adequate housing and grain rations. Hong Kong authorities also estimated that some 8,230 young escapees from South China managed to slip into the British colony in the first six months of 1974. Most of these were city youths who disliked the hardships of farm life.

Population. Long reluctant to reveal the size of its population, the Chinese government finally reported on August 22 that the nation was "nearing 800 million." Some Western observers believed that the figure was closer to 830 million. At the same time, Peking spokesmen at the United Nations World Population Conference in Bucharest, Romania, joined some African states in rejecting family planning for developing nations. Poverty, China argued, was the result of imperialist exploitation rather than too many mouths to feed. Nevertheless, the government pressed its birth-control program with vigor. In 1974, the population growth rate was put at around 2 per cent, which was still lower than most other Asian countries. But this meant more than 15 million new mouths to feed each year.

Increased grain output, therefore, was of crucial importance. Chinese estimates for 1974 put the yield at around 280 million short tons (250 million metric tons), or equal to the record harvests of 1971 and 1973. In addition, China expected to import around 9 million short tons (8 million metric tons) of grain from Canada, Australia, and the United States. The last had also become China's principal supplier of raw cotton.

Industrial Growth continued. The steel output was expected to top 26 million short tons (24 million metric tons), close to that of Great Britain. But the pacesetter once again was the young oil industry, whose output was expected to pass 60 million short tons (54 metric tons). China had also begun to buy equipment for offshore exploration and drilling from the United States and other countries. These offshore areas were claimed by other Asians; and in January, China and South Vietnam battled over the disputed Paracel Islands in the South China Sea, thought by some to lie above a pool of oil.

Foreign Trade continued to expand. It topped the 1973 record of $2 billion with Japan, and was expected to reach $1.25 billion with the United States, thanks mainly to U.S. grain and cotton sales. As in the previous year, Peking continued to buy complete factories in 1974. Typical was the purchase of two

Peasants of Talin Commune in northeastern China read posters calling on them to criticize the late Lin Piao and the thinking of Confucius.

strip mills, at a cost of $382 million, from Japan and Western Germany to be added to China's steel complex in Wuhan.

China continued to forge new air links with the world. In September, Japan opened an air route to Peking – at the price of losing its profitable air route to Taiwan. A line linked China with Canada, and a Chinese airliner made a test flight to New York.

Foreign Affairs. Peking's feud with Moscow continued. The Chinese took part in international conferences, but sometimes it seemed as if their main aim was to hurt the Russians. China's envoys urged North Atlantic Treaty Organization countries to stick together against the Russian threat, and encouraged Japan to press its claim to four northern islands seized by Russia in the final moments of World War II.

The Sino-Russian border talks in Peking broke down in midsummer after yet another effort in June to revive them. They were overshadowed by a Chinese refusal to release a Russian helicopter and its three-man crew that Russia said had strayed into China's far northwest on March 14. See RUSSIA.

Diplomatic relations with the United States were correct but cool. President Gerald R. Ford appointed George Bush, former chairman of the Republican Party, to replace David K. E. Bruce as head of the U.S. mission in China.   Mark Gayn

See also ASIA (Facts in Brief Table); Section Two, THE NEW FACE OF CHINA.

CHIRAC, JACQUES (1932-   ), was appointed premier of France by President Valery Giscard d'Estaing on May 27, 1974 (see FRANCE). A career civil servant, Chirac held several Cabinet posts under Giscard d'Estaing's predecessor, Georges Pompidou. Chirac's blunt approach to solving problems, along with his towering, 6-foot 7-inch (201-centimeter) frame, prompted Pompidou to call him his "bulldozer."

Jacques Chirac was born in Paris on Nov. 29, 1932. After graduating from high school, he attended a summer session at Harvard University and toured the United States. Returning to Paris, he studied at the Institute of Political Studies, then attended the cavalry officers' training school in Saumur. Following military service in Algeria, he earned a graduate degree from the National School of Administration.

In 1962, Chirac was assigned to the staff of Georges Pompidou, who was then premier under President Charles de Gaulle. He was elected to the National Assembly in 1967 and served as secretary of state for social affairs in charge of employment. In 1968, he became deputy to Giscard d'Estaing, then minister of finance. Chirac later served as minister of parliamentary relations, minister of agriculture, and interior minister.   Robert K. Johnson

CHRONOLOGY. See Pages 8 through 14.

CHURCHES. See EASTERN ORTHODOX CHURCHES; JEWS; PROTESTANT; RELIGION; ROMAN CATHOLIC.

CITY. A survey of 47 major cities of the world released in September, 1974, by the Business International Corporation, a research firm, rated Tokyo as the city with the highest cost of living. The cost of living in Tokyo was more than 131 times that in Washington, D.C. Close behind Tokyo were Osaka-Kobe, Japan; Stockholm, Sweden; and Oslo, Norway. New York City finished in a tie with The Hague, the Netherlands, for 10th place, while Chicago was 13th. San Francisco was 16th, and Washington, D.C., was 17th. Bombay, India, was the least expensive city.

Aid for U.S. Cities. The Housing and Community Development Act of 1974, a major legislative objective of urban leaders for several years, was signed into law by President Gerald R. Ford on August 22. The new law authorized more than $11-billion for local governments.

The act consolidated 10 different urban development programs into a single block-grant program as of Jan. 1, 1975. The new block grants replaced such previous programs as Model Cities, urban renewal, open space, water and sewer, and public facility loans. The amounts allocated will be based on population, and the seriousness of problems in housing,

Outdoor murals grew in popularity in many cities in 1974. This giant mural in Cincinnati, Ohio, calls for citizens' control of their own communities.

overcrowding, and poverty. No local matching funds are required, and local officials will have great flexibility in how they use the funds.

Eighty per cent of the available funds will go to metropolitan areas; the balance is for less populated areas. The act also will make more mortgage credit available to aid the United States housing industry and to finance more public housing. See HOUSING.

White House Meetings. President Ford received a delegation of mayors at the White House on August 14, the first such White House reception in three years. The group was led by San Francisco Mayor Joseph L. Alioto, president of the U.S. Conference of Mayors, and Los Angeles Mayor Thomas Bradley, president of the National League of Cities. The mayors and the President agreed that, to aid the fight against inflation, the cities would sacrifice some programs in return for an opportunity to have some voice in formulating the federal budget.

Another delegation of mayors met with the President on October 1 to discuss mass-transit legislation. Led by Alioto, New York City Mayor Abraham D. Beame, and Chicago Mayor Richard J. Daley, the 20-member delegation came away with a promise that Ford would support an $11.8-billion mass-transit aid bill. It was finally passed by Congress on November 21 and signed November 26. See TRANSIT.

Revenue Sharing. The National League of Cities and the U.S. Conference of Mayors issued a joint pre-election statement calling upon their members to obtain commitments from 1974 congressional candidates to support extension of the revenue-sharing program beyond its 1976 expiration date. President Ford, in the August meeting with mayors, pledged to support the program.

A federal judge ruled in April that the antidiscrimination requirements of the revenue-sharing law permit the U.S. Treasury Department to withhold revenue-sharing payments from local governments judged guilty of discriminating against minorities or women. The ruling was made in a case charging that Chicago's police department discriminated in personnel practices, and in December, the government cut off Chicago's revenue-sharing funds.

Growth Limits. An increasing number of U.S. cities have been trying to limit their population growth. According to a survey by the U.S. Department of Housing and Urban Development, 226 cities have imposed moratoriums on building permits, water or sewer connections, new subdivisions, and rezoning to permit development and taken other measures designed to stop or slow the rate of population growth. Cities usually justified such action by pointing to problems with overburdened water and sewage facilities, environmental factors, or the tax increases needed to finance new schools, roads, or utilities. Some simply cited a desire to maintain small-town life styles.

The city council of St. Petersburg, Fla., in March,

passed an ordinance establishing a maximum population of 235,000 for the city. This was 25,000 fewer persons than the number already estimated to be living there. So the city required the 25,000 persons who had moved into the city since July, 1973, to apply for permanent residency. If they could not be fitted into the 235,000 limit, they would have to move within six months. However, the ordinance was reversed on April 4, because the city lacked a way to enforce it and there were also questions about its constitutionality.

On April 29, 1974, a federal judge ruled a similar ordinance in Petaluma, Calif., invalid as an unconstitutional infringement of the right to travel. Confronted with a rapidly growing population, Petaluma had passed an ordinance in August, 1972, limiting the number of new homes to 500 a year for five years. Petaluma voters approved the action by a 4-to-1 margin. However, local real estate interests challenged the ordinance in court. In his ruling, the judge stated, "Every city has to take its fair share of the population growth," and warned the city not to try limiting its growth by any other zoning regulation. The city appealed the decision.

Other lawsuits were pending as the year ended. More than a dozen suits were filed against Aspen, Colo., and surrounding Pitkin County for more than $32 million damages because the city and county enacted regulations to curtail building in the area. The growth-limitation efforts in Aspen appeared to be headed for a constitutional test in the Supreme Court of the United States.

Growth and Discrimination. Growth-limiting policies became an issue at a conference sponsored by the National Committee Against Discrimination in Housing in January. Avery Friedman, a member of Lawyers for Housing in Cleveland, questioned the nongrowth advocates' motives, particularly on race. "It is not coincidental," said Friedman, "that the nongrowth philosophy has grown during the same period that the suburbs are beginning to open up to minorities."

Earl Finkler, chief planner for Tucson, Ariz., argued that "rapid, unchecked growth is no guarantee of social justice, equal housing, or other worthy goals." He pointed to Chicago and Orange County, California, as examples of communities that have grown rapidly and yet found themselves with some of the most extreme racial segregation in the nation.

Busing Curb. On August 21, President Ford signed a new education act imposing curbs on school busing as an integration tool. The new law restricts federal courts from ordering busing of children beyond the second closest school to a child's home. However, it gives judges some leeway when needed to ensure the constitutional rights of black children. The law's supporters said that Congress wanted to make clear its opposition to busing across school district lines.

Minneapolis shoppers stroll through the glass-roofed court of a new building complex that includes a 51-story tower, the city's tallest.

The Supreme Court ruled against such a court-ordered plan in Detroit in July, and court-ordered busing brought racial violence to Boston when the schools opened in September. See BOSTON; DETROIT; EDUCATION; Section One, FOCUS ON EDUCATION.

Urban Crime. The Federal Bureau of Investigation reported in October that serious crimes in U.S. cities rose 16 per cent during the first six months of 1974. President Ford told the International Association of Chiefs of Police on September 24 that the federal government was launching a new program to work with state and local law enforcement agencies to take the "career criminal . . . out of circulation." The new program will keep better track of repeat offenders and speed prosecution of cases in which repeaters are involved.

Body armor for policemen came into more frequent use to protect officers from serious bullet wounds. Los Angeles made bullet-proof vests mandatory equipment for its policemen after an officer wearing such a vest received only a flesh wound from a bullet fired from a distance of 2 feet (61 centimeters) on May 31. San Francisco, New York City, and Detroit were reported to be considering similar equipment.

City police departments also employed more women as police officers and assigned them to patrol and other crime-fighting duties. By midyear, more than 3,000 women were serving as patrol police officers in cities such as Atlanta, Chicago, Dallas, Detroit, New York, and Washington, D.C. The first policewoman killed in the line of duty was shot in Washington, D.C., in September.

Cost of Living. United States cities were afflicted with an average increase of 11.1 per cent in living costs between June, 1973, and June, 1974. The average income of urban blue-collar workers rose only 8.6 per cent during the same period.

Inflation caused added financial woes for hard-pressed cities, particularly the sharp rise in interest rates caused by a tight money supply. Testifying before the Senate finance subcommittee in August, San Francisco Mayor Alioto urged legislation allowing commercial banks to underwrite revenue as well as general obligation bonds issued by cities.

Problem-Solving Innovations. The federal government announced on October 15 that it would offer $15 million to cities willing to experiment with banning or limiting autos in downtown areas. To limit autos, motorists would be charged fees to enter congested areas.

The nation's 26 largest cities and six of its largest urban counties joined in a major effort to increase the use of modern technology in solving operating problems. The municipal groupings, called the Urban Consortium for Technology Initiatives, was funded by the National Science Foundation and the U.S. Department of Transportation.   James M. Banovetz

CIVIL RIGHTS remained a global concern in 1974. Rebel military officers ousted Portugal's dictatorship on April 25 and pledged a democratic government. Among the beneficiaries of the bloodless revolution were the overseas territories of Angola, Mozambique, and Guinea-Bissau, to which the new government promised independence. On July 23, the military junta that had ruled Greece for seven years collapsed, and a democratic government was installed. See PORTUGAL; GREECE.

Russia criticized novelist Alexander Solzhenitsyn in January for publishing abroad *The Gulag Archipelago, 1918-1956*, an epic history of Russian labor camps. The government charged Solzhenitsyn with treason on February 13 and banished him, stripping him of citizenship. See LITERATURE (Close-Up).

School Desegregation. In the United States, angry, rock-throwing crowds tried to prevent the beginning of classes as a court-imposed busing program to integrate Boston's public schools got underway. After violence broke out, police began escorting buses carrying black students into predominantly white South Boston. See BOSTON.

President Gerald R. Ford urged the citizens of Boston to "respect the law," but added that busing for integration was "not the best solution to quality education in Boston." This was the first time since the Supreme Court of the United States decision in

Divorced fathers campaign for equal rights
to the custody of children as the issue
of "male liberation" becomes a new cause.

Brown v. Board of Education of Topeka in 1954, that a U.S. President expressed disagreement with a court desegregation order. Mayor Kevin White of Boston said Ford's statement "fanned the flames of resistance." In contrast, Denver's public schools desegregated without incident. Enrollments reached 93 per cent of their expected total.

Northern school desegregation plans fared badly in the courts in 1974. In a 5 to 4 decision on July 25, the Supreme Court ruled that busing across school district lines in Detroit was improper. It ruled that lower courts had exceeded their authority in ordering the establishment of a "super school system" involving the exchange of students between Detroit and its suburbs. School desegregation was also slowed in the South when the Supreme Court on April 22 upheld desegregation plans for Memphis that preserved all-black schools in an effort to save money and limit busing.

In Housing, the U.S. Commission on Civil Rights criticized federal agencies for their lax enforcement of fair-housing standards. The commission charged on August 12 that state and local officials freely circumvented standards, using zoning regulations, building codes, and highway construction to keep poor, minority-group families out of suburban areas or force them to relocate.

Black Political Gains. Elections proved fruitful for blacks. By April, 108 cities had elected black mayors; there were 82 at the same time in 1973. Most, however, were elected in cities with predominantly black populations, and most were in the South.

The second National Black Political Convention was held in March in Little Rock, Ark. The rhetoric was milder and there were fewer controversial issues than at the first convention in 1972. However, leading black mayors and congressmen, and heads of such organizations as the National Association for the Advancement of Colored People and the National Urban League were again conspicuously absent.

A milestone in the recognition of black members by previously all-white organizations came in August when Frederick W. Morton, Jr., a justice of the New York Supreme Court, was elected judge-advocate-general of the Veterans of Foreign Wars (VFW). It was the first time in its 75-year history that the VFW had chosen a black for a leadership post.

Personal Privacy. A U.S. Senate subcommittee reported in June that various executive agencies have over a billion pieces of personal information about Americans, most of it stored in computers. This spurred legislators to promote, unsuccessfully, a "right to privacy" bill to protect citizens from governmental collection of personal information.

A federal court of appeals ruling in July significantly enhanced protection of individual liberties. The court ruled that the Federal Bureau of Investigation must expunge a person's arrest record from

Christine Gonzales, first woman engineer on the Santa Fe System, after a year of training, begins full-fledged job in Hurley, N. Mex.

its criminal files if the arrested person was exonerated and released without charges. A Supreme Court decision on May 13 seemed certain to wipe out the convictions of over 600 drug offenders. The court ruled that a group of narcotics sellers was illegally convicted because the Department of Justice obtained evidence against them with invalid wiretapping orders.

But the courts took a more restrictive view of civil liberties in other rulings. On April 1, the Supreme Court upheld the 1970 Bank Secrecy Act, which requires banks to keep extensive records of bank accounts and depositors' identities and to report certain major transactions to the government as an aid in catching tax dodgers.

News Media had another tough year. The Columbia Broadcasting System (CBS) and American Broadcasting System television networks in April accused the Richard M. Nixon Administration of instigating an antitrust suit against them for refusal to "play ball" with the Administration. The networks charged that CBS White House correspondent Dan Rather was "quietly and privately" threatened by members of the White House staff.

Network executives called for repeal of the Federal Communications Commission's Fairness Doctrine, which requires broadcasters to provide equal time for all parties on controversial matters. In a year of repeated verbal attacks on the news media by the Nixon Administration, the doctrine was seen as a tool for potential government influence over the news.

In a landmark decision, the Supreme Court ruled on July 15 that a newspaper cannot be compelled to provide free rebuttal space to an individual who is criticized in its pages. A right of reply, the court concluded, amounted to a censorship as compelling as instructing the press on what it must not print.

For Women, it was a year of distinctive civil rights gains. On June 3, the Supreme Court upheld the Equal Employment Opportunity Act of 1972 requiring that employers pay women equal wages for equal work. A national law adopted in August dented the long-entrenched bias against credit for women. It prohibits discrimination against women on mortgage credit. In October, an amendment to the federal deposit insurance legislation contained antidiscrimination provisions applicable to all types of personal and commercial consumer credit for women.

Women's groups were critical, however, of limitations on punitive damages and enforcement procedures. On June 18, the U.S. Department of Health, Education, and Welfare published proposed regulations to end sex discrimination in education. The rules would permit athletic teams of mixed sexes and would bar the practice of restricting home economics courses to girls and shop courses to boys.   Louis W. Koenig

See also articles on individual countries; COURTS AND LAWS.

CLEVELAND. The federal district court's chief judge acquitted eight former Ohio National Guard men on Nov. 8, 1974, in the May, 1970, Kent State shootings. He ruled that the government had not proved beyond a reasonable doubt that the guardsmen had deprived students of their rights. Four Kent State students were killed and nine others wounded during shooting at a campus demonstration. The trial in Cleveland followed a ruling on April 17 by the Supreme Court of the United States that authorized the families of slain and wounded students to file civil suits seeking damages from state, school, and military officials.

Cleveland's 800 garbage truckdrivers struck on April 15, demanding a 45-cent-an-hour pay increase and a guarantee against layoffs. City officials had offered a 25-cent raise and contended that layoffs were determined by the city's financial condition. Garbage went uncollected for 17 days until the drivers accepted a 37-cent-an-hour pay hike.

Cleveland Mayor Ralph J. Perk lost in his bid for election to the U.S. Senate in the November 5 elections. Perk, who had won the Republican nomination in the May 7 Ohio primary, was defeated by former astronaut John H. Glenn.

Urban Violence. More than 100 policemen fought an hour-long gun battle with members of the Sunni Orthodox Muslim sect in East Cleveland on May 30. Seven persons, including five policemen, were wounded. The incident began when sect members apparently attempted to kidnap a suspected drug dealer. The Muslims had vowed to eliminate all drug pushers in the area.

On August 10, Mayor Perk vetoed a gun registration bill that the city council had passed on July 29 by a one-vote margin. The bill would have banned the sale of cheap handguns and required registration of existing handguns within three months.

The Federal Bureau of Investigation reported that crime in Cleveland rose 13 per cent during the first six months of 1974. However, this was less than the 16 per cent increase noted nationally during the same period.

Cost of Living. Inflation hit hard in Cleveland as the cost of living increased 10.2 per cent between May, 1973, and May, 1974. Food costs rose about 13 per cent during the year ending in June. Department of Labor figures showed that the average family of four needed an annual income of more than $13,500 to live in moderate comfort in Cleveland, while more than $8,500 was required to maintain a minimum standard of living.

Chester Commons minipark, which opened in 1973 in downtown Cleveland, was the site of numerous weddings, fashion shows, and picnics. The three-dimensional park, built by pushing the earth into sculptured mounds of abstract objects, cost $307,000 to develop.   James M. Banovetz

CLOTHING. See FASHION.

COAL mines in the United States were shut down in late 1974 by a United Mine Workers (UMW) strike. About 120,000 UMW members struck on November 12, but UMW and coal industry negotiators reached a tentative new contract two days later. It had to be changed before union members ratified it on December 4 and 5. See LABOR.

A long coal strike would have seriously hurt the slumping U.S. economy and depleted an already tight energy supply. Surprisingly, government officials who were planning the nation's long-term answers to shrinking domestic supplies of oil and natural gas in 1974 emphasized the role of coal far less than had been anticipated earlier in the year. Federal Energy Administrator John C. Sawhill outlined the nation's energy options on November 12 when he presented the results of a seven-month, $5-million study called Project Independence. The report pictured coal production rising from 1973's total of about 600 million short tons (544 million metric tons) to only 1.1-billion short tons (998 million metric tons) in 1985 unless a heavy commitment is made to boost production. Accelerated development could roughly double the 1985 production projection.

Vast Reserves. Carl Bagge, president of the National Coal Association, called the report "a flawed document that fails to recognize coal's vast potential." Indeed, the United States has an estimated 429 billion short tons (389 billion metric tons) of recoverable coal reserves. The extent to which these reserves will be tapped and electric utilities will switch from oil to coal depends largely on two pieces of federal legislation. One is the Clean Air Act of 1970, which contains a provision that prohibits "significant deterioration" of air quality. The other is a strip-mine-control bill that President Gerald R. Ford pocket-vetoed on December 30. The bill's congressional backers plan to reintroduce it in 1975 and perhaps strengthen key provisions that would require the restoration of strip-mined land, allow land owners to block strip-mining of federally owned coal under their land, and tax mined coal to help finance the reclamation of already stripped and abandoned land.

If strictly interpreted, the "significant deterioration" clause of the Clean Air Act could prevent almost all energy-related construction in the West, according to the coal industry and electric utilities. In August, the Union Electric Company of St. Louis filed a suit asking that federal sulfur dioxide (SO_2) pollution limits be set aside for its three biggest generating stations.

On April 30, the U.S. House of Representatives appropriated $2.27 billion for energy research during fiscal year 1975. About $80 million was earmarked for coal gasification, and about $87 million for coal liquefaction. On a larger scale, 10 major utilities announced plans for coal gasification projects, each costing about $500 million.   Mary E. Jessup

See also MINES AND MINING.

COGGAN, F. DONALD (1909-   ), succeeded Michael J. Ramsey as archbishop of Canterbury and head of the Church of England in December, 1974. A renowned Biblical scholar, Coggan is the first Low Church, or Evangelical, Anglican in 126 years to be the spiritual leader of the church, which includes some 3.5 million Episcopalians in the United States.

Frederick Donald Coggan was born on Oct. 9, 1909, in Highgate, a London suburb. He gained a reputation as a brilliant student of Oriental languages and theology at St. John's College, Cambridge, where he received his M.A. degree and was ordained in 1935.

He was curate at the Church of St. Mary in Islington, a working-class London district, until 1937. For the next seven years, Coggan was professor of New Testament studies at Wycliffe College in Toronto, Canada. Returning to England in 1944, he became principal of the London College of Divinity. He was consecrated as bishop of Bradford in 1956, and archbishop of York in 1961.

Archbishop Coggan is an able administrator and generally conservative in his views. However, he urged in 1968 that the priesthood be opened to women. A strong opponent of South Africa's policy of apartheid, or racial separation, Coggan plans to address the problems of underdeveloped nations.

Coggan and Jean Braithwaite Strain were married in 1935 and have two daughters.   Robert K. Johnson

COIN COLLECTING. The continuing trend toward investing in precious metals as a hedge against inflation sent coin prices soaring again in 1974 and resulted in records for both individual rare-coin prices and total value of sales at coin auctions. An all-time high price of $200,000 for a single coin was paid at a New York City auction on May 24 for a 1907 Roman-numeral, ultrahigh-relief, proof U.S. $20 gold piece. The coin, of which only from 13 to 16 are believed to exist, was designed by sculptor Augustus Saint-Gaudens at the request of President Theodore Roosevelt. At the same auction, an 1875 proof U.S. $5 gold coin brought $150,000. Sales at the auction totaled a record $2,384,547.

Both records were broken a few days later in Zurich, Switzerland, where an ancient Athenian silver decadrachm sold for $272,240. A total of 253 ancient Greek coins, with an estimated catalog value of $2,755,000, sold at that auction for a record total of $4,584,000.

A Penny Shortage and inflated penny prices afflicted the United States in 1974 as a result of widespread penny hoarding. The hoarders were anticipating the possibility that copper might reach such a high price that it would be profitable to melt down the copper pennies. Penny hoarding was also encouraged by rumors that the U.S. Mint would substitute an aluminum alloy for copper in pennies. In April, the U.S. Department of the Treasury prohibited both the melting and the export of pennies. In June, the mint issued a public appeal for citizens to return pennies to circulation.

In February, "fast buck" dealers began advertising $50 bags of San Francisco Mint 1974 pennies for $99.50. The advertised price soon rose to $900. Mary Brooks, director of the U.S. Mint, countered by announcing in June that at least 400 million 1974 pennies would be minted in San Francisco. They would be mixed with pennies minted in Denver and Philadelphia and shipped to all parts of the country. Brooks assured collectors that they would be able to buy plenty of the San Francisco pennies at face value.

The U.S. government revealed the commemorative coin designs for the U.S. bicentennial on March 7. The special designs will appear on the reverse sides of dollars, half dollars, and quarters. The Liberty Bell, superimposed on an image of the moon, will appear on the dollar. The half dollar will show an outline of Independence Hall, and the quarter will carry a colonial drummer boy. The fronts of the coins will be the same but double-dated 1776-1976.

The U.S. Mint planned to release 225 million of the dollar pieces, 400 million half dollars, and more than a billion quarters for general circulation. In addition, the mint is going to offer 45 million silver-clad proof and uncirculated specimens at premium prices.   Theodore M. O'Leary

Liberty bearing a torch decorates one side of the ultrahigh-relief U.S. 1907 $20 gold piece, which sold for $200,000 on May 24.

Supporters of presidential hopeful Alfonso Lopez Michelsen gather for a campaign rally in Medellín, Colombia. He won by a landslide in April.

COLOMBIA. Liberal Party member Alfonso Lopez Michelsen was sworn in as president on Aug. 7, 1974. He had been elected on April 21 by an overwhelming majority of more than a million votes.

The election was significant in two ways. First, more than half of the 9 million eligible voters cast ballots, thus reversing a trend of 50 per cent to 67 per cent voter absenteeism over the past decade. Second, the election, in which seats in the Congress, the state assemblies, and the municipal councils were at stake, marked the end of a 16-year arrangement by which the Liberal and Conservative parties had alternated every four years in the presidency and shared equally in legislative seats and other political posts.

President Lopez campaigned on a platform advocating a much more independent foreign policy than that of the preceding Conservative administration. He also called for trade relations with China and an end to the trade embargo imposed on Cuba by the Organization of American States. In addition, he strongly criticized United States policy toward Latin America. On domestic issues, he advocated moderate social, economic, and political reforms to solve Colombia's problems. These included runaway inflation that was rising at the rate of 17 per cent annually, unemployment that had reached 20 per cent of the labor force, and inequities in income.

Decrees Issued. On September 17, Lopez declared a state of emergency; between September 18 and October 13, a series of decrees was issued to help solve the nation's problems. To stimulate local food production, a government subsidy of wheat imports was ended. Sales taxes were increased, and other taxes, including those on income and property, were reformed to shift the tax burden from the poor to the rich. Government ministries began trimming budgets and eliminating such departments as public relations. New sales taxes were imposed on luxury items; export subsidies were reduced up to 70 per cent.

Initially, most of the measures won popular support. By early November, however, various groups began expressing dissatisfaction with the government's policies. The business community charged that the tax reforms and the discouragement of exports were stimulating a higher rate of inflation. Other groups, such as the National Federation of Merchants, accused the government of unleashing a new price spiral. However, both the Liberal and Conservative parties generally gave their support to the decrees.

Labor Unions. Legal recognition was given on August 20 to the Colombian Workers Syndical Confederation and the General Labor Confederation. It was the first time in 16 years that Communist unions had been given official recognition.   Paul C. Tullier

See also LATIN AMERICA (Facts in Brief Table).

COLORADO. See STATE GOVERNMENT.

COMMON MARKET. See EUROPE.

COMMUNICATIONS. Domestic and worldwide communications in 1974 continued the burgeoning expansion of recent years. New transmission systems went into operation, satellite communication expanded, and research progress continued.

Domestic Communications. The Bell System began service in March over a new coaxial cable transmission system between Pittsburgh and St. Louis. This new telecommunications superhighway provides 108,000 two-way telephone channels over a cable containing 22 coaxial tubes.

American Telephone and Telegraph Company (A. T. & T.) also introduced Data Under Voice (DUV), a technological development by Bell Laboratories that permits digital signals, such as computer data, to be transmitted in the unused lower end of the radio frequency spectrum transmitted by microwave radio relay systems. DUV, part of the Bell System's Dataphone Digital Service, allows 1.5 million bits of information to be transmitted per second. Dataphone Digital Service, an interstate service transmitting data-processing information, is in limited service pending a review of its rate structure by the Federal Communications Commission (FCC).

The FCC approved the use of a new communications band for mobile telephone service in May. The Bell System is developing a high-capacity land mobile telecommunications system for part of this band, which will allow a greater number of mobile telephones. Service areas would be divided into small "cells" so that many customers in a large urban area could use the same channel simultaneously without interference. Fixed antennas on building tops, linked to electronic switching centers, would maintain the continuity of a telephone call as the vehicle moved from one cell to another.

Satellite Services. RCA Global Communications and RCA Alaska Communications in January inaugurated a satellite communications service linking cities in Alaska and the contiguous 48 states.

Western Union launched its first *Westar* satellite in April, and private service began immediately. The first space mail (Mailgrams) was transmitted in September, as a joint Western Union-U.S. Postal Service venture. *Westar II* went up in October.

A. T. & T., together with the General Telephone & Electronics Corporation, started building earth stations that are to be used in domestic satellite service scheduled to begin in 1976. The Comsat General Corporation will own and operate the satellite.

Construction continued on three *Intelsat IV-A* satellites, scheduled for delivery in 1975. They will be used over the Atlantic region as part of the global communications satellite system. Each satellite will have almost 8,000 voice circuits, and will also carry television programs.

New Technology. Construction began in June on the first link of a new transmission system called millimeter waveguide. The first installation will be used to evaluate construction techniques and to test performance under field conditions. When fully developed, the new system will carry nearly 500,000 simultaneous telephone conversations.

Bell Laboratories developed a low-loss light fiber for optical communications systems. In these experimental systems, information is carried on a beam of light as it passes along a hair-thin glass fiber. A cable with 100 of these fibers would have many times the capacity of any present cable transmission system.

International Communications. A new submarine cable connecting Hawaii to the mainland began service in September. This cable, called Transpac 2, provides 845 voice circuits. It will be extended during 1975 to Guam and Okinawa, where connections can be made to Australia, Japan, and other parts of the Orient. Partly as a result of this installation, A. T. & T. was able to reduce rates between Hawaii and the mainland in May.

Another major submarine cable opened in 1974 provides 1,840 two-way voice channels across the Atlantic Ocean, more than all other existing cable systems combined. The complete system, which cost $80 million, was a joint project of the British Post Office and the Canadian Overseas Telecommunications Corporation. R. H. Klie

CONGO (BRAZZAVILLE). See AFRICA.
CONGO (KINSHASA). See ZAIRE.

Western Union's *Westar* communications satellite is launched on April 13. In September, it began transmitting Mailgrams—the first space mail.

CONGRESS OF THE UNITED STATES

CONGRESS OF THE UNITED STATES. Despite the focus of its second session on the possible impeachment of President Richard M. Nixon, the 93rd Congress made some major legislative achievements in 1974. It passed measures in the fields of housing, minimum wages, social security reform, campaign-financing reform, equal treatment for women, and regulation of private pensions and made changes in its own system of handling federal budget proposals.

The Second Session of the 93rd Congress convened on Jan. 21, 1974; recessed from October 17 to November 18 to campaign for the November 5 elections; and finally adjourned on December 20.

In the House of Representatives, there were 243 Democrats, 188 Republicans, 1 Independent, and 3 vacancies. The Senate had 57 Democrats, 41 Republicans, 1 Conservative (aligned with the Republicans), and 1 Independent (with the Democrats).

In the Senate, Mike J. Mansfield (D., Mont.) continued to serve as majority leader; Robert C. Byrd (D., W. Va.) was Democratic whip. Hugh D. Scott, Jr. (R., Pa.), was once again minority leader. Robert P. Griffin (R., Mich) was minority whip.

Carl B. Albert (D., Okla.) was re-elected speaker of the House. Thomas P. O'Neill, Jr. (D., Mass.), continued to serve as House majority leader; John J. McFall (D., Calif.) continued as majority whip. Minority leader in the House was John J. Rhodes

(R., Ariz.); Leslie C. Arends (R., Ill.) served as minority whip.

On December 10, Wilbur D. Mills (D., Ark.) gave up his chairmanship of the House Ways and Means Committee. Mills was hospitalized on December 3 for exhaustion, in the wake of criticism of his relationship with an exotic dancer. House Democrats then moved to reform the committee by increasing its membership and stripping it of the power to make committee assignments to Democratic congressmen. Also, the full House had voted in October that the committee divide into at least four subcommittees.

The Budget. On February 4, President Nixon sent Congress a record $304.4-billion budget for fiscal 1975 (July 1, 1974, to June 30, 1975). The proposed budget increased defense spending to $87.7 billion. Spending for income-security programs, such as social security, rose to more than $100-billion. Nixon estimated that the federal deficit for fiscal 1975 would total $9.4 billion. However, on November 26, Gerald R. Ford, who replaced Nixon as President on August 9, gave Congress a revised budget of $302.2 billion for fiscal 1975.

Congress passed, and on June 30 President Nixon signed, a bill raising the federal temporary debt ceiling by $19.3 billion to a record $495 billion until March 31, 1975. This was less than the Administration's request for a raise to $505 billion through June

30, 1975. The national debt in 1974 was estimated at $475 billion.

The Congressional Budget and Impoundment Control Act of 1974, designed to give Congress some control over the budget, passed the House on June 18 and the Senate on June 21, and President Nixon signed it on July 12. The law provided that budget committees be established by both houses of Congress; that either house could veto any presidential impoundment of funds by passing a resolution; and that the President could not cancel a program established by Congress without congressional consent. The law also changed the beginning of the federal fiscal year from July 1 to October 1, as of 1976. Congress also passed, and Nixon signed into law on March 2, legislation providing for Senate approval of the directors and deputy directors of the Office of Management and Budget.

The Economy. The President's power to set wage and price ceilings under the Economic Stabilization Act expired on April 30. The next day, the Senate voted 57 to 31 to deny President Nixon the power to impose price or wage controls. However, Congress complied with President Ford's request and passed legislation, which the President signed on August 24, establishing an advisory Council on Wage and Price Stability. The council will monitor prices and wages, but it does not have the power to impose controls.

The Housing and Community Development Act of 1974 was passed by the Senate on August 13 and by the House on August 15 and was signed into law on August 22. It authorized $11.1 billion over the next three years for private housing and community development, including financial assistance for home buyers and builders. The act also allowed communities more control and flexibility in planning low-income housing. See CITY; HOUSING.

The Emergency Home Purchase Assistance Act of 1974 provided further aid for the hard-pressed housing industry. The measure, which President Ford signed on October 18, authorized the Government National Mortgage Association to buy up to $3 billion worth of mortgages.

Minimum-Wage Law. For the first time since 1966, Congress on March 28 passed legislation raising the minimum wage. President Nixon signed the measure on April 8. For most workers covered by the legislation, the minimum wage was raised from $1.60 to $2 an hour as of May 1; to $2.10 an hour on Jan. 1, 1975; and to $2.30 an hour on Jan. 1, 1976. Federal minimum-wage standards were extended to domestic servants and to state and local government workers. The new law covers 55 million Americans.

Pension Protection. The Employee Retirement Income Security Act of 1974, passed by Congress on August 22, signed by Ford on September 2, provided protection for some 23 million workers against the loss of their retirement benefits because of company bankruptcies, union corruption, or the loss of their jobs. Public disclosure of information about employee benefits was required for plans affecting another 12 million persons. The act authorized a pension guarantee corporation to be established under the jurisdiction of the U.S. Department of Labor. See OLD AGE; LABOR.

Energy Legislation. On May 7, Nixon signed a bill creating the Federal Energy Administration with the power to institute emergency rationing programs. On October 11, Ford signed a bill creating the Energy Research and Development Administration to replace the Atomic Energy Commission.

The Senate completed congressional action on the Energy Supply and Environmental Coordination Act of 1974 on June 12. The act, which encouraged the use of coal instead of gas or oil in electrical plants, was signed by President Nixon on June 26.

On January 2, President Nixon signed legislation requiring the states to establish speed limits of 55 miles (89 kilometers) per hour on their highways in order to qualify for federal highway trust funds.

Year-around daylight-saving time, which had been put into effect in 1973, was revoked in 1974.

President Gerald R. Ford appears before a House
judiciary subcommittee on October 17 to
explain why he pardoned former President Nixon.

Members of the United States House

The House of Representatives of the first session of the 94th Congress consists of 291 Democrats and 144 Republicans (not including representatives from the District of Columbia, Puerto Rico, Guam, and the Virgin Islands), compared with 243 Democrats, 188 Republicans, and 1 Independent, with 3 seats vacant, for the second session of the 93rd Congress. This table shows congressional districts, legislator, and party affiliation. Asterisk (*) denotes those who served in the 93rd Congress; dagger (†) denotes "at large."

Alabama
1. Jack Edwards, R.*
2. William L. Dickinson, R.*
3. William Nichols, D.*
4. Tom Bevill, D.*
5. Robert E. Jones, D.*
6. John H. Buchanan, Jr., R.*
7. Walter Flowers, D.*

Alaska
† Don Young, R.*

Arizona
1. John J. Rhodes, R.*
2. Morris K. Udall, D.*
3. Sam Steiger, R.*
4. John B. Conlan, R.*

Arkansas
1. Bill Alexander, D.*
2. Wilbur D. Mills, D.*
3. J. P. Hammerschmidt, R.*
4. Ray Thornton, D.*

California
1. Harold T. Johnson, D.*
2. Don H. Clausen, R.*
3. John E. Moss, D.*
4. Robert L. Leggett, D.*
5. John L. Burton, D.
6. Phillip Burton, D.*
7. George Miller, D.
8. Ronald V. Dellums, D.*
9. Fortney H. Stark, D.*
10. Don Edwards, D.*
11. Leo J. Ryan, D.*
12. Paul N. McCloskey, Jr., R.*
13. Norman Y. Mineta, D.
14. John J. McFall, D.*
15. B. F. Sisk, D.*
16. Burt L. Talcott, R.*
17. John J. Krebs, D.
18. William M. Ketchum, R.*
19. Robert J. Lagomarsino, R.*
20. Barry M. Goldwater, Jr., R.*
21. James C. Corman, D.*
22. Carlos J. Moorhead, R.*
23. Thomas M. Rees, D.*
24. Henry A. Waxman, D.
25. Edward R. Roybal, D.*
26. John H. Rousselot, R.*
27. Alphonzo Bell, R.*
28. Yvonne B. Burke, D.*
29. Augustus F. Hawkins, D.*
30. George E. Danielson, D.*
31. Charles H. Wilson, D.*
32. Glenn M. Anderson, D.*
33. Del M. Clawson, R.*
34. Mark W. Hannaford, D.
35. Jim Lloyd, D.
36. George E. Brown, Jr., D.*
37. Jerry L. Pettis, R.*

38. Jerry M. Patterson, D.
39. Charles E. Wiggins, R.*
40. Andrew J. Hinshaw, R.*
41. Bob Wilson, R.*
42. Lionel Van Deerlin, D.*
43. Clair W. Burgener, R.*

Colorado
1. Patricia Schroeder, D.*
2. Timothy E. Wirth, D.
3. Frank E. Evans, D.*
4. James P. Johnson, R.*
5. William L. Armstrong, R.*

Connecticut
1. William R. Cotter, D.*
2. Christopher J. Dodd, D.
3. Robert N. Giaimo, D.*
4. Stewart B. McKinney, R.*
5. Ronald A. Sarasin, R.*
6. Anthony J. Moffett, D.

Delaware
† Pierre S. du Pont IV, R.*

Florida
1. Robert L. F. Sikes, D.*
2. Don Fuqua, D.*
3. Charles E. Bennett, D.*
4. William V. Chappell, Jr., D.*
5. Richard Kelly, R.
6. C. W. Young, R.*
7. Sam M. Gibbons, D.*
8. James A. Haley, D.*
9. Louis Frey, Jr., R.*
10. L. A. Bafalis, R.*
11. Paul G. Rogers, D.*
12. J. Herbert Burke, R.*
13. William Lehman, D.*
14. Claude D. Pepper, D.*
15. Dante B. Fascell, D.*

Georgia
1. Ronald Ginn, D.*
2. Dawson Mathis, D.*
3. Jack T. Brinkley, D.*
4. Elliott H. Levitas, D.
5. Andrew Young, D.*
6. John J. Flynt, Jr., D.*
7. Lawrence P. McDonald, D.
8. Williamson S. Stuckey, Jr., D.*
9. Phillip M. Landrum, D.*
10. Robert G. Stephens, Jr., D.*

Hawaii
1. Spark M. Matsunaga, D.*
2. Patsy T. Mink, D.*

Idaho
1. Steven D. Symms, R.*
2. George Hansen, R.

Illinois
1. Ralph H. Metcalfe, D.*
2. Morgan F. Murphy, D.*
3. Martin A. Russo, D.
4. Edward J. Derwinski, R.*
5. John C. Kluczynski, D.*
6. Henry J. Hyde, R.
7. Cardiss Collins, D.*
8. Dan Rostenkowski, D.*
9. Sidney R. Yates, D.*
10. Abner J. Mikva, D.
11. Frank Annunzio, D.*
12. Philip M. Crane, R.*
13. Robert McClory, R.*
14. John N. Erlenborn, R.*
15. Tim L. Hall, D.
16. John B. Anderson, R.*
17. George M. O'Brien, R.*
18. Robert H. Michel, R.*
19. Thomas F. Railsback, R.*
20. Paul Findley, R.*
21. Edward R. Madigan, R.*
22. George E. Shipley, D.*
23. Charles Melvin Price, D.*
24. Paul Simon, D.

Indiana
1. Ray J. Madden, D.*
2. Floyd J. Fithian, D.
3. John Brademas, D.*
4. J. Edward Roush, D.*
5. Elwood H. Hillis, R.*
6. David W. Evans, D.
7. John T. Myers, R.*
8. Philip H. Hayes, D.
9. Lee H. Hamilton, D.*
10. Philip R. Sharp, D.
11. Andrew Jacobs, Jr., D.

Iowa
1. Edward Mezvinsky, D.*
2. Michael T. Blouin, D.
3. Charles E. Grassley, R.
4. Neal Smith, D.*
5. Tom Harkin, D.
6. Berkley Bedell, D.

Kansas
1. Keith G. Sebelius, R.*
2. Martha E. Keys, D.
3. Larry Winn, Jr., R.*
4. Garner E. Shriver, R.*
5. Joe Skubitz, R.*

Kentucky
1. Carroll Hubbard, Jr., D.
2. William H. Natcher, D.*
3. Romano L. Mazzoli, D.*
4. Marion Gene Snyder, R.*
5. Tim Lee Carter, R.*
6. John B. Breckinridge, D.*
7. Carl D. Perkins, D.*

Louisiana
1. F. Edward Hébert, D.*
2. Lindy Boggs, D.*
3. David C. Treen, R.*
4. Joe D. Waggoner, Jr., D.*
5. Otto E. Passman, D.*
6. W. Henson Moore, R.
7. John B. Breaux, D.*
8. Gillis W. Long, D.*

Maine
1. David F. Emery, R.
2. William S. Cohen, R.*

Maryland
1. Robert E. Bauman, R.*
2. Clarence D. Long, D.*
3. Paul S. Sarbanes, D.*
4. Marjorie S. Holt, R.*
5. Gladys N. Spellman, D.
6. Goodloe E. Byron, D.*
7. Parren J. Mitchell, D.*
8. Gilbert Gude, R.*

Massachusetts
1. Silvio O. Conte, R.*
2. Edward P. Boland, D.
3. Joseph D. Early, D.
4. Robert F. Drinan, D.*
5. Paul E. Tsongas, D.
6. Michael J. Harrington, D.*
7. Torbert H. Macdonald, D.*
8. Thomas P. O'Neill, Jr., D.*
9. John J. Moakley, D.*
10. Margaret M. Heckler, R.*
11. James A. Burke, D.*
12. Gerry E. Studds, D.*

Michigan
1. John Conyers, Jr., D.*
2. Marvin L. Esch, R.*
3. Garry Brown, R.*
4. Edward Hutchinson, R.*
5. Richard F. Vander Veen, D.*
6. Bob Carr, D.
7. Donald W. Riegle, Jr., D.*
8. Bob Traxler, D.*
9. Guy Vander Jagt, R.*
10. Elford A. Cederberg, R.*
11. Philip E. Ruppe, R.*
12. James G. O'Hara, D.*
13. Charles C. Diggs, Jr., D.*
14. Lucien N. Nedzi, D.*
15. William D. Ford, D.*
16. John D. Dingell, D.*
17. William M. Brodhead, D.
18. James J. Blanchard, D.
19. William S. Broomfield, R.*

Minnesota
1. Albert H. Quie, R.*
2. Thomas M. Hagedorn, R.
3. Bill Frenzel, R.*
4. Joseph E. Karth, D.*
5. Donald M. Fraser, D.*
6. Richard Nolan, D.
7. Bob Bergland, D.*
8. James L. Oberstar, D.

Mississippi
1. Jamie L. Whitten, D.*
2. David R. Bowen, D.*
3. G. V. Montgomery, D.*
4. Thad Cochran, R.*
5. Trent Lott, R.*

Missouri
1. William L. Clay, D.*
2. James W. Symington, D.*
3. Leonor K. Sullivan, D.*
4. William J. Randall, D.*
5. Richard Bolling, D.*
6. Jerry Litton, D.*
7. Gene Taylor, R.*
8. Richard H. Ichord, D.*
9. William L. Hungate, D.*
10. Bill D. Burlison, D.*

Montana
1. Max S. Baucus, D.
2. John Melcher, D.*

Nebraska
1. Charles Thone, R.*
2. John Y. McCollister, R.*
3. Virginia Smith, R.

Nevada
† James Santini, D.

New Hampshire
1. Norman E. D'Amours, D.
2. James C. Cleveland, R.*

New Jersey
1. James J. Florio, D.
2. William J. Hughes, D.
3. James J. Howard, D.*
4. Frank Thompson, Jr., D.*
5. Millicent Fenwick, R.
6. Edwin B. Forsythe, R.*
7. Andrew Maguire, D.
8. Robert A. Roe, D.*
9. Henry Helstoski, D.*
10. Peter W. Rodino, Jr., D.*
11. Joseph G. Minish, D.*
12. Matthew J. Rinaldo, R.*
13. Helen Meyner, D.
14. Dominick V. Daniels, D.*
15. Edward J. Patten, D.*

New Mexico
1. Manuel Lujan, Jr., R.*
2. Harold Runnels, D.*

New York
1. Otis G. Pike, D.*
2. Thomas J. Downey, D.
3. Jerome A. Ambro, Jr., D.
4. Norman F. Lent, R.*
5. John W. Wydler, R.*
6. Lester L. Wolff, D.*
7. Joseph P. Addabbo, D.*
8. Benjamin S. Rosenthal, D.*
9. James J. Delaney, D.*
10. Mario Biaggi, D.*
11. James H. Scheuer, D.
12. Shirley Chisholm, D.*
13. Stephen J. Solarz, D.
14. Frederick W. Richmond, D.
15. Leo C. Zeferetti, D.
16. Elizabeth Holtzman, D.*
17. John M. Murphy, D.*
18. Edward I. Koch, D.*
19. Charles B. Rangel, D.*
20. Bella S. Abzug, D.*
21. Herman Badillo, D.*
22. Jonathan B. Bingham, D.*
23. Peter A. Peyser, R.*
24. Richard L. Ottinger, D.
25. Hamilton Fish, Jr., R.*
26. Benjamin A. Gilman, R.*
27. Matthew F. McHugh, D.
28. Samuel S. Stratton, D.*
29. Edward W. Pattison, D.
30. Robert C. McEwen, R.*
31. Donald J. Mitchell, R.*
32. James M. Hanley, D.*
33. William F. Walsh, R.*
34. Frank Horton, D.*
35. Barber B. Conable, Jr., R.*
36. John J. LaFalce, D.
37. Henry J. Nowak, D.
38. Jack F. Kemp, R.*
39. James F. Hastings, R.*

North Carolina
1. Walter B. Jones, D.*
2. L. H. Fountain, D.*
3. David N. Henderson, D.*
4. Ike F. Andrews, D.*
5. Stephen L. Neal, D.
6. L. Richardson Preyer, D.*
7. Charles Rose, D.*
8. W. G. Hefner, D.
9. James G. Martin, R.*
10. James T. Broyhill, R.*
11. Roy A. Taylor, D.*

North Dakota
† Mark Andrews, R.*

Ohio
1. Willis D. Gradison, Jr., R.
2. Donald D. Clancy, R.*
3. Charles W. Whalen, Jr., R.*
4. Tennyson Guyer, R.*
5. Delbert L. Latta, R.*
6. William H. Harsha, R.*
7. Clarence J. Brown, R.*
8. Thomas N. Kindness, R.
9. Thomas L. Ashley, D.*
10. Clarence E. Miller, R.*
11. J. William Stanton, R.*
12. Samuel L. Devine, R.*
13. Charles A. Mosher, R.*
14. John F. Seiberling, D.*
15. Chalmers P. Wylie, R.*
16. Ralph S. Regula, R.*
17. John M. Ashbrook, R.*
18. Wayne L. Hays, D.*
19. Charles J. Carney, D.*
20. James V. Stanton, D.*
21. Louis Stokes, D.*
22. Charles A. Vanik, D.*
23. Ronald M. Mottl, D.

Oklahoma
1. James R. Jones, D.*
2. Theodore M. Risenhoover, D.
3. Carl B. Albert, D.*
4. Tom Steed, D.*
5. John Jarman, D.*
6. Glenn English, D.

Oregon
1. Les AuCoin, D.
2. Al Ullman, D.*
3. Robert B. Duncan, D.
4. James Weaver, D.

Pennsylvania
1. William A. Barrett, D.*
2. Robert N. C. Nix, D.*
3. William J. Green, D.*
4. Joshua Eilberg, D.*
5. Richard T. Schulze, R.
6. Gus Yatron, D.*
7. Robert W. Edgar, D.
8. Edward G. Biester, Jr., R.*
9. E. G. Shuster, R.*
10. Joseph M. McDade, R.*
11. Daniel J. Flood, D.*
12. John P. Murtha, D.*
13. Lawrence Coughlin, R.*
14. William S. Moorhead, D.*
15. Fred B. Rooney, D.*
16. Edwin D. Eshleman, R.*
17. Herman T. Schneebeli, R.*
18. H. John Heinz III, R.*
19. William F. Goodling, R.
20. Joseph M. Gaydos, D.*
21. John H. Dent, D.*
22. Thomas E. Morgan, D.*
23. Albert W. Johnson, R.*
24. Joseph P. Vigorito, D.*
25. Gary A. Myers, R.

Rhode Island
1. Fernand J. St. Germain, D.*
2. Edward P. Beard, D.

South Carolina
1. Mendel J. Davis, D.*
2. Floyd D. Spence, R.*
3. Butler C. Derrick, Jr., D.
4. James R. Mann, D.*
5. Kenneth L. Holland, D.
6. John W. Jenrette, Jr., D.

South Dakota
1. Larry Pressler, R.
2. James Abdnor, R.*

Tennessee
1. James H. Quillen, R.*
2. John J. Duncan, R.*
3. Marilyn Lloyd, D.
4. Joe L. Evins, D.*
5. Richard H. Fulton, D.*
6. Robin L. Beard, Jr., R.*
7. Ed Jones, D.*
8. Harold E. Ford, D.

Texas
1. Wright Patman, D.*
2. Charles Wilson, D.*
3. James M. Collins, R.*
4. Ray Roberts, D.*
5. Alan Steelman, R.*
6. Olin E. Teague, D.*
7. Bill Archer, R.*
8. Bob Eckhardt, D.*
9. Jack Brooks, D.*
10. J. J. Pickle, D.*
11. W. R. Poage, D.*
12. James C. Wright, Jr., D.*
13. Jack Hightower, D.
14. John Young, D.*
15. Eligio de la Garza, D.*
16. Richard C. White, D.*
17. Omar Burleson, D.*
18. Barbara C. Jordan, D.*
19. George H. Mahon, D.*
20. Henry B. Gonzalez, D.*
21. Robert Krueger, D.
22. Robert R. Casey, D.*
23. Abraham Kazen, Jr., D.*
24. Dale Milford, D.*

Utah
1. K. Gunn McKay, D.*
2. Allen T. Howe, D.

Vermont
† James M. Jeffords, R.

Virginia
1. Thomas N. Downing, D.*
2. G. William Whitehurst, R.*
3. David E. Satterfield III, D.*
4. Robert W. Daniel, Jr., R.*
5. W. C. Daniel, D.*
6. M. Caldwell Butler, R.*
7. J. Kenneth Robinson, R.*
8. Herbert E. Harris, D.
9. William C. Wampler, R.*
10. Joseph L. Fisher, D.

Washington
1. Joel Pritchard, R.*
2. Lloyd Meeds, D.*
3. Don Bonker, D.
4. Mike McCormack, D.*
5. Thomas S. Foley, D.*
6. Floyd V. Hicks, D.*
7. Brock Adams, D.*

West Virginia
1. Robert H. Mollohan, D.*
2. Harley O. Staggers, D.*
3. John M. Slack, D.*
4. Ken Hechler, D.*

Wisconsin
1. Les Aspin, D.*
2. Robert W. Kastenmeier, D.*
3. Alvin J. Baldus, D.
4. Clement J. Zablocki, D.*
5. Henry S. Reuss, D.*
6. William A. Steiger, R.*
7. David R. Obey, D.*
8. Robert J. Cornell, D.
9. Robert W. Kasten, Jr., R.

Wyoming
† Teno Roncalio, D.*

Nonvoting Representatives
District of Columbia
Walter E. Fauntroy, D.*

Guam
Antonio Won Pat, D.*

Puerto Rico
Jaime Benitez, D.*

Virgin Islands
Ron de Lugo, D.*

Members of the United States Senate

The Senate of the first session of the 94th Congress consists of 60 Democrats, 37 Republicans, 1 Independent, and 1 Conservative, with 1 seat contested, compared with 57 Democrats, 41 Republicans, 1 Independent, and 1 Conservative for the second session of the 93rd Congress. Senators shown starting their term in 1975 were elected for the first time in the Nov. 5, 1974, elections. Those shown ending their current terms in 1981 were re-elected to the Senate in the same balloting. The second date in each listing shows when the term of a previously elected senator expires. For organizational purposes, the one Independent will line up with Democrats, the one Conservative with Republicans.

State	Term	State	Term	State	Term
Alabama		**Louisiana**		**Ohio**	
John J. Sparkman, D.	1946—1979	Russell B. Long, D.	1948—1981	Robert Taft, Jr., R.	1971—1977
James B. Allen, D.	1969—1981	J. Bennett Johnston, Jr., D.	1972—1979	John H. Glenn, D.	1975—1981
Alaska		**Maine**		**Oklahoma**	
Theodore F. Stevens, R.	1968—1979	Edmund S. Muskie, D.	1959—1977	Henry L. Bellmon, R.	1969—1981
Mike Gravel, D.	1969—1981	William D. Hathaway, D.	1973—1979	Dewey F. Bartlett, R.	1973—1979
Arizona		**Maryland**		**Oregon**	
Paul J. Fannin, R.	1965—1977	Charles McC. Mathias, Jr., R.	1969—1981	Mark O. Hatfield, R.	1967—1979
Barry Goldwater, R.	1969—1981	J. Glenn Beall, Jr., R.	1971—1977	Robert W. Packwood, R.	1969—1981
Arkansas		**Massachusetts**		**Pennsylvania**	
John L. McClellan, D.	1943—1979	Edward M. Kennedy, D.	1962—1977	Hugh Scott, R.	1959—1977
Dale Bumpers, D.	1975—1981	Edward W. Brooke, R.	1967—1979	Richard S. Schweiker, R.	1969—1981
California		**Michigan**		**Rhode Island**	
Alan Cranston, D.	1969—1981	Philip A. Hart, D.	1959—1977	John O. Pastore, D.	1950—1977
John V. Tunney, D.	1971—1977	Robert P. Griffin, R.	1966—1979	Claiborne Pell, D.	1961—1979
Colorado		**Minnesota**		**South Carolina**	
Floyd K. Haskell, D.	1973—1979	Walter F. Mondale, D.	1964—1979	Strom Thurmond, R.	1956—1979
Gary Hart, D.	1975—1981	Hubert H. Humphrey, D.	1971—1977	Ernest F. Hollings, D.	1966—1981
Connecticut		**Mississippi**		**South Dakota**	
Abraham A. Ribicoff, D.	1963—1981	James O. Eastland, D.	1943—1979	George S. McGovern, D.	1963—1981
Lowell P. Weicker, Jr., R.	1971—1977	John C. Stennis, D.	1947—1977	James G. Abourezk, D.	1973—1979
Delaware		**Missouri**		**Tennessee**	
William V. Roth, Jr., R.	1971—1977	Stuart Symington, D.	1953—1977	Howard H. Baker, Jr., R.	1967—1979
Joseph R. Biden, Jr., D.	1973—1979	Thomas F. Eagleton, D.	1968—1981	William E. Brock III, R.	1971—1977
Florida		**Montana**		**Texas**	
Lawton Chiles, D.	1971—1977	Mike Mansfield, D.	1953—1977	John G. Tower, R.	1961—1979
Richard B. Stone, D.	1975—1981	Lee Metcalf, D.	1961—1979	Lloyd M. Bentsen, D.	1971—1977
Georgia		**Nebraska**		**Utah**	
Herman E. Talmadge, D.	1957—1981	Roman Lee Hruska, R.	1954—1977	Frank E. Moss, D.	1959—1977
Sam Nunn, D.	1972—1979	Carl T. Curtis, R.	1955—1979	Edwin Jacob Garn, R.	1975—1981
Hawaii		**Nevada**		**Vermont**	
Hiram L. Fong, R.	1959—1977	Howard W. Cannon, D.	1959—1977	Robert T. Stafford, R.	1971—1977
Daniel K. Inouye, D.	1963—1981	Paul Laxalt, R.	1975—1981	Patrick J. Leahy, D.	1975—1981
Idaho		**New Hampshire**		**Virginia**	
Frank Church, D.	1957—1981	Thomas J. McIntyre, D.	1962—1979	Harry F. Byrd, Jr., Ind.	1965—1977
James A. McClure, R.	1973—1979	Contested		William L. Scott, R.	1973—1979
Illinois		**New Jersey**		**Washington**	
Charles H. Percy, R.	1967—1979	Clifford P. Case, R.	1955—1979	Warren G. Magnuson, D.	1944—1981
Adlai E. Stevenson III, D.	1970—1981	Harrison A. Williams, Jr., D.	1959—1977	Henry M. Jackson, D.	1953—1977
Indiana		**New Mexico**		**West Virginia**	
Vance Hartke, D.	1959—1977	Joseph M. Montoya, D.	1964—1977	Jennings Randolph, D.	1958—1979
Birch Bayh, D.	1963—1981	Pete V. Domenici, R.	1973—1979	Robert C. Byrd, D.	1959—1977
Iowa		**New York**		**Wisconsin**	
Richard C. Clark, D.	1973—1979	Jacob K. Javits, R.	1957—1981	William Proxmire, D.	1957—1977
John C. Culver, D.	1975—1981	James L. Buckley, Cons.	1971—1977	Gaylord Nelson, D.	1963—1981
Kansas		**North Carolina**		**Wyoming**	
James B. Pearson, R.	1962—1979	Jesse A. Helms, R.	1973—1979	Gale W. McGee, D.	1959—1977
Robert J. Dole, R.	1969—1981	Robert Morgan, D.	1975—1981	Clifford P. Hansen, R.	1967—1979
Kentucky		**North Dakota**			
Walter Huddleston, D.	1973—1979	Milton R. Young, R.	1945—1981		
Wendell H. Ford, D.	1975—1981	Quentin N. Burdick, D.	1960—1977		

Senator Jacob Javits (R., N.Y.), left, listens as Nelson Rockefeller testifies at Senate hearing considering his nomination as Vice-President.

Congress passed a bill in September returning the nation to standard time from the last Sunday in October to the last Sunday in February. President Ford signed the bill on October 5.

Civil Rights Measures. After months of debate, Congress passed a compromise education bill authorizing $29 billion for federal education programs over the next four years. The act limited, but did not ban, the busing of schoolchildren to achieve racial balance. President Ford signed the bill on August 21. See EDUCATION.

In August, President Ford signed legislation forbidding discrimination against women applying for mortgage credit. The Federal Reserve Board must work out regulations to enforce the law within a year.

On October 9, the House passed the Depository Institutions Amendments Act of 1974, forbidding any kind of credit discrimination based on sex or marital status. The Senate approved the bill the next day, and President Ford signed it on October 29.

Foreign Policy. Congress often clashed with the weakened executive branch in 1974, particularly in foreign affairs. On April 4, the House refused to approve additional aid to Vietnam. The Senate voted its refusal on May 1.

Congress wanted to cut off aid to Turkey because the Turks had used U.S. equipment in their invasion of Cyprus. But on October 18, Congress voted to continue aid to Turkey until December 10 and, in December, extended aid to Feb. 5, 1975 (see CYPRUS; TURKEY). In December, Congress also voted to cut off military aid to Chile after learning of Central Intelligence Agency involvement in Chile's internal affairs.

In December, Congress passed a trade bill attempting to force Russia to allow Jews to emigrate in return for liberalized U.S.-Soviet trade.

Other Measures passed by the second session included:

- Establishing a $60-million national center to deal with problems of child abuse and child neglect.
- Authorization of $566.9 million in benefits for disabled veterans.
- Establishment of a federal program of legal aid for the poor.
- Legislation allowing Americans to buy and sell gold after Dec. 31, 1974.
- An $11.8-billion mass transit program.
- A one-year program providing $2 billion in guaranteed loans for livestock producers.
- Changes in the Freedom of Information Act of 1966 to make government information more accessible to private citizens, passed over President Ford's veto.
- A total of $851 million for vocational rehabilitation of the handicapped.
- A program to provide jobs and to increase unemployment compensation.

Senator Henry M. Jackson (D., Wash.) administers oath to oil executives
called to testify at a Senate hearing investigating industry profits.

- Stringent penalties for antitrust violations.
- Federal standards for pure drinking water.

Vetoes and Overrides. On January 4, Nixon
pocket-vetoed a bill that would have allowed cities
to use some federal-aid funds to purchase buses. On
March 6, he vetoed an emergency energy bill because it contained a provision for rolling back oil
prices. On August 8, hours before he resigned, Nixon
vetoed a bill appropriating $13.5 billion for the
Department of Agriculture and consumer affairs
and environmental agencies.

President Ford vetoed more than 20 measures.
However, the Congress overrode four of those vetoes,
including a railroad retirement bill; a bill increasing veterans' benefits; an $851-million appro-
priation for rehabilitating the handicapped; and
an amendment to the Freedom of Information Act
of 1966.

Congress and Watergate. On June 30, the Senate Select Committee on Presidential Campaign
Activities concluded its 20-month investigation of
the Watergate affair and its related scandals, stemming largely from President Nixon's re-election
effort. The committee released its final report, including suggestions for campaign reform, on July 13.

The Campaign Financing Reform Act of 1974,
passed by Congress and signed by President Ford on
October 15, marked a major advance in the effort to
end corruption in campaign financing. The act provided public financing of presidential primaries and
national election campaigns. It also created an independent Federal Elections Commission to administer the law. Criminal violations are to be
handled by the Department of Justice.

On February 6, the House of Representatives
voted 410 to 4 to give its Judiciary Committee broad
power – including subpoena power – to investigate
possible grounds for the impeachment of President
Nixon. After long investigation and a televised debate, the House committee in late July approved
three articles of impeachment. After Nixon resigned,
the House formally ended its inquiry without debate
on August 20.

Later in the year, a House Judiciary Committee
subcommittee undertook an inquiry into President
Ford's pardon of former President Nixon. Ford appeared personally before the subcommittee on
October 17 to answer their questions.

After four months of hearings, mainly into his
finances, Congress on December 19 finally approved
the nomination of Nelson A. Rockefeller as the new
Vice-President.   Carol L. Thompson

See also FORD, GERALD RUDOLPH; NIXON,
RICHARD MILHOUS; PRESIDENT OF THE UNITED
STATES; ROCKEFELLER, NELSON ALDRICH; WATER-
GATE; Section One, FOCUS ON THE NATION; Section
Two, FROM TRIUMPH TO TRAGEDY.

CONNECTICUT. See STATE GOVERNMENT.

CONSERVATION. International action on environmental issues produced mixed results in 1974. Russell Peterson, chairman of the U.S. Council on Environmental Quality, said on April 23 that ending pollution and the depletion of resources depends on solving the population crisis. Such a solution was rejected at the United Nations (UN) World Population Conference. Representatives of 135 nations attended that meeting in Bucharest, Romania, in August. Supported by Russia, the developing nations defeated U.S. efforts for a goal of reducing the number of births to an average of two children per family by the year 2000.

United States representatives to the 1974 annual meeting of the International Whaling Commission in London demanded a 10-year moratorium on commercial whaling. Conservationists applauded the request as the only way to prevent the whale's extinction, but Japan and Russia, who harvest about 85 per cent of the world's catch each year, opposed the move. On June 19, a week before the meeting started, seven wildlife and conservation groups stepped up their joint campaign for a boycott of Japanese and Russian products. See FISHING INDUSTRY; Section Two, DOOM FOR THE GIANTS OF THE SEA?

The UN Law of the Sea Conference in Caracas, Venezuela, in August ended without agreement.

FAMED AS AVIATOR, ECOLOGIST

LINDBERGH DIES

"He was a good friend."

The conference will convene again in Geneva, Switzerland, in March, 1975. See OCEAN.

In the United States, balancing energy needs and environmental goals dominated conservation activities in 1974. At the Natural Resources, Recreation, and Environmental Conference on Inflation in Dallas on September 16, for instance, discussion centered almost entirely on energy problems. For the most part, U.S. conservation organizations successfully protected basic environmental legislation from being weakened by hasty action inspired by the energy crisis. An increasing number of conservation activists served as constructive consultants on environmental issues rather than as obstructionists.

National Parks and Recreation. Ronald H. Walker, director of the National Park Service since late 1972, resigned on September 11 but was asked to remain in the post until the end of 1974. Walker resigned during Senate hearings in which he was charged with awarding a contract to a personal friend. A former Walker associate headed the Park Reservation Service, Incorporated, which was awarded a contract to operate a computerized telephone system to handle campsite reservations at 21 parks in the National Park System. Walker denied favoritism in awarding the contract. The reservation system, which went into operation on July 1, was terminated on August 29 after complaints of overloaded telephone circuits that left an estimated 38,000 phone calls unanswered.

Camping fees were reinstated in federal campgrounds in June. Congress had restricted the charges to campgrounds with highly developed facilities in 1973. Most conservation groups favored the congressional reversal because an estimated loss of $7-million in fees had limited improvements in the national recreation areas.

Gasoline shortages early in the year significantly reduced travel to park and other recreational areas. At the peak of the summer vacation season, the credit crunch, caused by inflation and high interest rates, kept tourists away. The National Park Service noted a new trend in travel habits in which Americans visited fewer parks and stayed longer in each park. Vacationers also visited parks close to home.

After four years of controversy and litigation, a giant, 307-foot (94-meter) tower on the edge of the National Gettysburg Battlefield Historical Park in Pennsylvania opened on August 17. Historians and conservationists had challenged construction of the tower by Thomas R. Ottenstein, a millionaire businessman, as a "crass intrusion" on America's most famous Civil War battlefield. Suits to halt construction were defeated in state courts.

A fire, which started when lightning struck on June 17, was left to burn out on its own in Wyoming's Grand Teton National Park. Under a national policy, park officials had designated about 124,000 acres (50,000 hectares) in which fires started by natural causes would be allowed to burn out naturally. Residents of Jackson, Wyo., originally approved the plan in early June, but, as smoke hung over more than 3,500 blackened acres (1,400 hectares) beside Lake Jackson three months later, residents and tourists began pressuring the Department of the Interior for a reversal of its new policy.

The Wilderness Act, landmark legislation designed to preserve the U.S. natural heritage of unspoiled wilderness areas, was 10 years old in September. Under its provisions, Congress has expanded the National Wilderness Preservation System to 11 million acres (4.5 million hectares) of park, national forest, and wildlife refuge land. Over 100 additional wilderness proposals were before Congress in 1974. The Land and Water Conservation Fund Act also marked its first 10 years in September.

Wildlife Protection. The U.S. Fish and Wildlife Service stepped up enforcement of the Endangered Species Act of 1973. The new legislation ensures greater protection for more than 400 species of wildlife that are in danger of extinction. The new law creates a new list of threatened species for animals likely to become endangered. It also prohibits the unauthorized import or interstate sale of endangered species. The service assigned 220 agents to crack down on illegal traffic in furs, shells, and feathers from endangered species.

Under pressure from Western senators and woolgrowers, the Interior Department on May 30 authorized the use of cyanide guns for killing coyotes. Sheep ranchers had charged that the ban in March, 1972, on the use of poisoned bait in predator animal control had resulted in the annual destruction of 800,000 sheep by coyotes.

The Interior Department asked Congress in July for new legislation to assist in managing wild horse herds. The department wanted to use surface vehicles and aircraft in gathering herds for culling.

The National Park Service issued an environmental impact statement on October 13 defending its grizzly bear management program in Yellowstone National Park. The agency estimated that its program, which has been attacked by some conservation groups, was perpetuating a "wild, free-ranging grizzly bear population" of about 300 in the park. In 1970, the service closed access to garbage dumps to encourage the bears to seek food in the natural environment and to reduce opportunities for human contact with the grizzly bears.

In March, the Environmental Protection Agency lifted its 1972 ban against dichlorodiphenyl-trichloroethane (DDT) for use against the tussock moth and pea weevil in the Pacific Northwest. Later, hunters were warned that DDT levels were above the safety limits in certain game.   Andrew L. Newman

See also ENVIRONMENT.

CONSTITUTION, UNITED STATES. See UNITED STATES CONSTITUTION.

CONSUMER AFFAIRS. American consumers endured a year of increased turmoil in 1974. The chief irritant was the continuing upward spiral of living costs. By November, the U.S. Department of Agriculture reported food prices had risen 15 per cent during the year.

Some increases bordered on the spectacular. Pork prices were up 26 per cent; fresh milk, 30 per cent; and white flour, 68 per cent. Sugar prices rocketed up 300 per cent and dried beans, 400 per cent. Nonfood prices also rose substantially. The Consumer Price Index, prepared by the U.S. Bureau of Labor Statistics, showed prices up 66 per cent for fuel oil and coal, and 38 per cent for gasoline and motor oil. The prices of 1975 cars rose from $500 to $1,000 per vehicle. High interest rates and a shortage of loanable funds at banks and lending institutions—largely because savers chose to shift their funds into high-yield bonds—made it virtually impossible for buyers to obtain home mortgages. See BANKS AND BANKING; HOUSING.

President Gerald R. Ford declared inflation "public enemy number one," when he assumed office in August, and set up a series of economic "summit conferences" to get public views on what should be done. After the conferences, he presented a broad program calling for voluntary fuel and food conservation. He also proposed a grass-roots citizen

The Consumer Product Safety Commission, with power to set standards and ban products, uses a toll-free telephone number for complaints.

campaign featuring distribution of WIN (Whip Inflation Now) buttons. In his speeches, Ford offered
homespun advice reminiscent of World War II days,
urging people to plant WIN gardens and save fuel
wherever possible.

However, Ford's advice and the program aroused
considerable criticism and derision among consumer
and business leaders. They contended that most
people in the United States were already doing all
they could to help. General Motors Corporation
took out full-page newspaper ads in the fall urging
people to buy new cars rather than save their money,
as the President had requested. And a Gallup Poll
reported in November that 62 per cent of those in-
terviewed preferred price and wage controls as the
way to beat the inflation.

Legislative Changes. Consumer gains in Congress
increased slightly. Important new laws dealt with
housing, pensions, and credit. A new housing law
approved by Congress on August 15 and signed by
Ford on August 22 increased the amount of government guarantees on Federal Housing Administration (FHA) and Veterans Administration (VA)
mortgages and lowered the proportion of down payment required. Pension legislation passed on August
22 and signed on September 2 set up a large new
government program to protect those in private pension funds from precarious financing and other abuses
that have left many people without the retirement
payments they thought they had earned. Amendments to credit laws raised the maximum insurance
on bank deposits from $20,000 to $40,000, banned
discrimination against women in the granting of
credit, established new rights for persons victimized
by billing errors, and provided new rights for credit-
card holders who withhold regular payments when
merchandise proves to be defective.

But a House-passed bill that would set up a long-
sought federal consumer agency to monitor other
agencies was killed in September by a Senate fili-
buster. An unprecedented fourth attempt to shut off
debate and bring the bill to a vote failed by two votes
to get the necessary two-thirds margin. Consumer
advocates vowed to submit a stronger bill in the next
Congress.

At the state level, the most popular consumer
issues were no-fault auto insurance, licensing of auto
repair establishments, and creation of public advocacy offices. There were also increasing efforts to
require adequate representation of consumers before regulatory boards, particularly public-utility
commissions. Several states overturned bans on advertising prescription drugs as a result of citizen
lobbying efforts.

Law Enforcement. The Federal Trade Commission (FTC) began to require restitutions and arbitration for the first time. One consent order, announced on March 26, may bring millions of dollars
back to buyers of land from GAC Corporation, a

major land developer based in Miami, Fla. Another
required arbitration for the first time at no expense
to customers of Josephs Furniture Company, a New
York City retailer. The store was also required to
grant customers an unprecedented 10 days to cancel
a sale and get their money back.

The FTC even went after the nation's largest
retailer – Sears, Roebuck and Company – in July,
charging the firm with using "bait-and-switch" tactics in the selling of certain household appliances. It
charged the company lured customers to its stores
by advertising a relatively inexpensive item, then
tried to get them to buy more expensive models.
Sears denied the charges.

The FTC also jumped into the controversial field
of nutritional claims for food with proposed regulations to require minimum quantities of nutrients before certain comparative claims could be made. The
rules were similar to ones proposed earlier by the
Food and Drug Administration for food labels. The
FTC also proposed to ban television commercials
using premium offers to sell items to children.

Whether the FTC was doing enough to protect the
public, however, became a hotly argued topic. A
subcommittee of the House Committee on Interstate and Foreign Commerce released a critical staff
report in March noting that the number of complaints issued by the FTC had dropped from 210 in
1971, 105 in 1972, and 99 in 1973 to only 6 in the
first nine months of fiscal 1974. The subcommittee
said that the 1974 cases were "not sufficiently significant to explain the large reduction in output."

Business Initiatives. Business interests continued
to create new programs to meet consumer demands
and counteract complaints about product quality
and deceptive selling practices, as well as soaring
prices. The U.S. Chamber of Commerce announced
its support of "a nationwide system of voluntary and
judicial procedures designed to guarantee consumer
justice in all consumer-business transactions." The
program, outlined in a 24-page booklet, called for
greater use of arbitration and small claims courts,
though the chamber acknowledged that, "by and
large, the nation's legal system has failed to provide
accessible and effective consumer justice."

The National Association of Homebuilders created
a 10-year warranty for new houses, and the International Franchise Association adopted voluntary
standards that require members to disclose all pertinent information to prospective franchise owners.
The National Institute for Automotive Service Excellence published the first national directory of
automobile mechanics who have passed written tests
to measure competence. Manufacturers voluntarily
labeled air conditioner "Energy Efficiency Ratios"
to make comparison shopping easier, and many food
chains put nutritional values on their labels.

Consumer Organizations. Private citizens continued to form voluntary groups to fight against

consumer abuses in almost every area of economic activity. But this consumer representation was divided, and results were limited.

Voluntary groups scored the most success where their organization was best. One of the more effective was the Virginia Citizens Consumer Council, which won campaigns to overturn a state ban against advertising prescription drug prices and to require open dating of baby formulas and prohibit the sale of outdated ones.

One of the more significant developments was the first national conference of state and local consumer officials, held in Washington, D.C., in June. It was organized and financed by the Office of Consumer Affairs in the U.S. Department of Health, Education, and Welfare. Participants set up their own organization to foster the exchange of information about consumer abuses and to explore ways to improve federal-state consumer programs.

Perhaps the most significant development, however, was the noticeable increase in citizen awareness of their rights and problems as consumers, in the face of historic price increases and other market place aggravations. More and more Americans reversed old patterns—conserving high-priced fuel, foregoing expensive meat cuts, buying used cars instead of new ones, and generally trying to save more and spend less.   Arthur E. Rowse

COSTA RICA. See LATIN AMERICA.

COURTS AND LAWS. Repercussions from the Watergate scandal buffeted the United States legal, judicial, and criminal justice systems in 1974. The most controversial act was the pardon awarded former President Richard M. Nixon by President Gerald R. Ford on September 8, a move that touched off a storm of criticism. The American Bar Association (ABA) board of governors formally deplored the timing of the pardon, prior to filing of charges and full assignment of blame for the Watergate affair. Harry Kalven, Jr., a distinguished congressional law professor at the University of Chicago, summarized the criticism: "Ford fatally prejudiced the legal system ... the trial of Nixon represented the last real institutional chance to allocate blame properly, to get the matter finally resolved. The public's nose is rubbed in the inconsistency between the treatment of Nixon and treatment of other people presumed involved in the same offense." See PRESIDENT.

Bar Discipline. An unprecedented number of former public officials were suspended or disbarred during the year. Nixon's letter of resignation from the California bar, dated September 11, was finally accepted. Nixon's first Vice-President, Spiro T. Agnew, was disbarred by the Maryland Court of Appeals on May 2, as a result of his no-contest plea in October, 1973, to felony tax evasion charges. Five former presidential advisers were relieved of their law licenses as a result of Watergate-related convictions.

Former Army Lieutenant William L. Calley, Jr., top, is paroled in November after serving three years for his part in My Lai massacre.

They are Charles W. Colson, John W. Dean III, John D. Ehrlichman, Herbert W. Kalmbach, and Egil Krogh, Jr. But a federal court in Washington, D.C., ruled on August 16 that the disbarment of former Attorney General Richard Kleindienst would be "unwarranted."

The ABA endorsed ethics education as a prerequisite for a law school diploma, a move prompted in part by the overwhelming percentage of accused Watergate figures who were attorneys. The members called for "equal justice under law" for all.

Revision and Reform. At year's end, Congress passed and sent to the President a total revision of the federal criminal code and rules of evidence. Ford signed it on Jan. 4, 1975. The new law requires freeing defendants who are not brought to trial within 100 days of their arrest.

Attempts to reintroduce the death penalty, last imposed in the United States in 1967 and formally banned by the Supreme Court of the United States in 1972, continued. In October, the Supreme Court agreed to review the matter in 1975 on an appeal from North Carolina, one of 28 states that has approved new death penalty laws attempting to remove the "arbitrary and capricious" incidence of death imposition found unconstitutional by the High Court. David C. Beckwith

See also CIVIL RIGHTS; CONSUMER AFFAIRS; SUPREME COURT OF THE UNITED STATES.

Investigators view $1.45 million found buried in a cellar. It was part of $4.3 million stolen from Purolator Security vaults in Chicago.

CRIME. Kidnapings, bombings, and murders for alleged political reasons became almost commonplace throughout the world in 1974. Meanwhile, property crimes and white-collar crimes (among businessmen and government officials) jumped dramatically. Charges of misconduct in top government office led to the downfall of West German Chancellor Willy Brandt in May, President Richard M. Nixon in August, and Japan's Prime Minister Kakuei Tanaka in November.

Crime in the United States, which had appeared to be leveling off in recent years, resumed its sharp upward trend. Statistics compiled by the Federal Bureau of Investigation (FBI) revealed that the incidence of major crime rose 16 per cent during the first six months of 1974, the largest increase in six years.

The FBI statistics reflected a moderate increase in four violent crimes—8 per cent in forcible rape, 7 per cent in aggravated assault, 5 per cent in robbery, and 5 per cent in murder. But the three property crimes listed, which comprise the bulk of reported offenses, showed startling increases, including a 20 per cent jump in larceny-theft, a 16 per cent increase in burglary, and a 4 per cent boost in auto theft. As in recent years, crime in suburban areas (up 21 per cent) and rural areas (up 19 per cent) showed the greatest increase. Urban crime rose 13 per cent for the period.

Law enforcement officials, including Attorney General William B. Saxbe, called for a severe crackdown on violators, particularly high-level white-collar criminals and repeat offenders, in hopes of reversing the new trend.

A spectacular spree by a California group, the Symbionese Liberation Army, highlighted the year's crime news. On February 4, Patricia Hearst, 19, granddaughter of newspaper publisher William Randolph Hearst, was abducted from her Berkeley apartment. See Close-Up.

Discothèque Fire. The year's most deadly crime occurred at a crowded nightclub in Port Chester, N.Y., on June 30, when smoke from a fire that had been set deliberately trapped and killed 24 patrons. Police charged an unemployed Greenwich, Conn., man with arson, alleging that he had started the blaze to cover traces of a burglary he had committed at a bowling alley next door.

Four Black Muslims were indicted by a California grand jury on May 16 on murder and conspiracy charges. San Francisco police said the arrests solved at least 12 "zebra" killings in the city over two years in which white victims were murdered at random.

Mrs. Martin Luther King, Sr., 69, mother of slain civil rights leader Martin Luther King, Jr., was killed in Atlanta, Ga., on June 30 by a young black gunman. The shooting took place during church services being conducted by Mrs. King's pastor-husband. Other worshipers at the Ebenezer Baptist

Terrorism: A Political Plague

Political terrorism continued at a frightening pace throughout the world in 1974. And in the United States, it adopted a startling new form.

The terrorism of the late 1960s and the 1970s was not greatly different from that of the 1800s, when revolutionaries tried to destroy governments with random bombings and murders. Groups or individuals still murder and maim to dramatize causes that range from simple greed to what they regard as high ideals of patriotism or humanitarianism. Skyjackers hold innocent passengers hostage, demanding huge sums of money. The smoke of terrorist bombings hangs over England and Northern Ireland, and bloody Arab and Israeli attacks and reprisal raids constantly wrack the Middle East.

In Latin America, both right wing and left wing guerrillas kidnap foreign diplomats and businessmen. In August, terrorists even kidnaped the 83-year-old father-in-law of Mexico's President Luis Echeverría Alvarez. Late in 1974, political assassinations in Argentina rose to a reported average of one a day.

Vicious terrorists of the Japanese Red Army, who massacred 26 persons in Tel Aviv's Lod Airport in 1972, seized the French Embassy in The Hague, the Netherlands, in September, 1974. In several U.S. cities, there were terrorist bombings and shootings in 1974.

But on February 4, one of the strangest terrorist bands surfaced in the United States. This small group, calling itself the Symbionese Liberation Army (SLA), kidnaped Patricia Hearst, 19-year-old daughter of San Francisco newspaper magnate Randolph A. Hearst. For more than three months, the SLA held U.S. radio, television, and newspaper audiences spellbound, awaiting each installment in the kidnaping-terrorist-adventure tale.

Unlike Palestinian refugees or Irish patriots, the SLA members formed an unlikely cast for this bizarre version of guerrilla theater. They included escaped convict Donald D. DeFreeze, who called himself General Field Marshal Cinque; Nancy Ling Perry,

daughter of a California businessman; Patricia Soltysik, active in radical feminist activities; Emily Harris, a former junior high-school teacher; and Camilla Hall, daughter of a Lutheran minister.

Patty Hearst's captors sent taped messages and letters to radio stations to air their demands. They said they had declared war on the "fascist capitalist class" and had kidnaped Patty Hearst as its symbol.

The SLA guerrillas styled themselves as saviors of the poor. They demanded that Hearst show good faith in negotiating for his daughter's release by providing free food for all the poor in California, which would have cost more than $230 million. Hearst compromised by setting up a $2-million food-giveaway program.

But the drama took an unexpected twist on April 3, when Patty Hearst announced she chose to remain with the terrorists. She took the name Tania, and allegedly made her first public appearance on April 15 as a bank robber. Although bank security cameras photographed her holding a gun, police at first had doubts that she took part voluntarily.

Patty allegedly was involved in a shooting at a suburban Los Angeles sporting goods store on May 16. Law officers picked up the SLA trail there, and the next day, most of the SLA was wiped out in a spectacular shoot-out. Six SLA members died in a burning, bullet-riddled building. Patty and two remaining members disappeared. Two others were in prison for the November, 1973, murder of an Oakland, Calif., school official.

The SLA apparently inspired the kidnaping of J. Reginald Murphy, editor of the *Atlanta Constitution*, on February 20. His abductors claimed to be members of a right wing American Revolutionary Army. But it proved to be only a husband and wife after $700,000 ransom.

Guns, bombs, and even the mass media have made terrorism grimly effective. But the specter of an even greater horror has begun to haunt the world. Could terrorists steal enough nuclear material to hold an entire city hostage under the threat of atomic destruction?   Darlene R. Stille

Patricia Hearst

Church subdued Marcus W. Chenault, 23, of Dayton, Ohio, but not before he had also killed Deacon Edward Boykin and wounded a third churchgoer. On September 12, Chenault was sentenced to die in the electric chair.

Six persons, including four customers, were slain on October 19 during the holdup of a New Britain, Conn., bakery. Police charged two men in the slayings. A Pasadena, Tex., man was accused of fatally poisoning his own son on Halloween night with strychnine-laced candy. He had earlier insured the boy's life for $61,000.

First Policewoman Slain. A 24-year-old Washington, D.C., policewoman, Gail A. Cobb, was shot and killed on September 20 by a robbery suspect she had chased into a garage. According to the FBI, she was the first female police officer slain in the line of duty in the United States.

The largest cash theft in U.S. history resulted in the arrest of six Chicago-area men, charged with the $4.3-million burglary of a Chicago security firm on October 20. A portion of the haul was later found buried under a cement floor in a Chicago cellar. The rest may have been deposited in secret bank accounts in the Bahamas.   David C. Beckwith

See also CHICAGO; COURTS AND LAWS; HOUSTON; SAN FRANCISCO; SUPREME COURT OF THE UNITED STATES.

CUBA. A resolution to lift diplomatic and economic sanctions imposed against Cuba in 1964 by the Organization of American States was defeated on Nov. 12, 1974, at a meeting of the group in Quito, Ecuador. Supporters of the resolution maintained that sanctions against the regime of Prime Minister Fidel Castro were "anachronistic, uneffective, and inconvenient." Twelve Latin American countries favored the resolution, but three voted against it, and six – including the United States – abstained. The resolution thus lacked the required two-thirds majority.

In September, U.S. Senators Claiborne Pell (D., R.I.) and Jacob K. Javits (R., N.Y.) of the Senate Foreign Relations Committee visited Cuba to review possibilities of improving ties between the two countries. Although they recommended resuming diplomatic relations, the committee tabled their suggestion for future consideration.

Provincial Election. The first election held in Cuba since 1958 took place in Matanzas Province on June 30. It was part of efforts to establish a stable political structure through which Cubans would run local affairs. Voting was secret, direct, and on a voluntary basis; the voting age was set at 16.

Voters elected municipal government administrators; eventually, an executive committee will run the province. Matanzas was chosen as a test province because of its small size and population.

Fidel Castro welcomes Cuban athletes home from the XII Central American and Caribbean Games, which were held in February in Dominican Republic.

The Economy showed signs of vigor during the year, and the annual growth rate of 8 per cent was expected to continue through 1975. The average gain in per capita output in goods and services was also 8 per cent. Much of the economic upswing was attributable to the world price of sugar – Cuba's principal crop – which sold at an export price of 53 cents a pound (0.45 kilogram). Higher export prices on other goods, including nickel, citrus fruits, tobacco, and seafood also boosted the economy.

Rents were being held to 10 per cent of monthly wages. Health care, education, and sports events were free. Tourism appeared to be reviving; an estimated 15,000 visitors toured the island during the year compared to a mere 5,000 in 1973. Despite these gains, food, clothing, soap, toothpaste, and most other consumer goods, such as household appliances, were rationed.

Foreign Relations. On February 16, the Canadian International Development Agency announced Canada had signed a three-year, $9-million, technical assistance agreement with Cuba that will expand agricultural and foodstuffs industries. Later in the month, about 200 Argentine businessmen visited Havana to consolidate purchasing agreements under a $1.2-billion credit granted by Argentina. Trade missions from East Germany, North Vietnam, and Algeria also visited Havana.   Paul C. Tullier

See also LATIN AMERICA (Facts in Brief Table).

British Prime Minister Harold Wilson, right, greets Archbishop Makarios III in London after the deposed president's escape from Cyprus.

CYPRUS. The Cypriot National Guard, led by Greek officers, ousted President Archbishop Makarios III on July 15, 1974. Only a week earlier, Makarios had accused the Greek government of conspiring to seize control of Cyprus. The rebels said Makarios was dead, but he escaped and made a clandestine radio broadcast. He announced dramatically, "I am alive," and urged Cypriots to resist the rebels, then went to Great Britain. The rebels named Nikos Sampson, a newspaper publisher, president.

Fighting continued between rebels and Makarios supporters for five days on the island, a republic in which 4 out of 5 citizens are Greek Cypriots and most of the rest are Turkish Cypriots. The situation worsened as Great Britain, Greece, and Turkey, bound by a treaty to guarantee the Constitution of Cyprus, sought solutions. The United States tried to prevent Turkish military intervention, while the North Atlantic Treaty Organization backed a British move for peace talks in London.

Turkey Attacks. But on July 20, Turkish forces invaded Cyprus by sea and air. Vacationers and non-Cypriots sought shelter at British bases on the island as civilian and military casualties mounted. The United Nations (UN) negotiated a cease-fire on July 22, ending the heavy fighting around Nicosia. Having failed in its attempt to control Cyprus, the military government of Greece resigned on July 23. With the return of civilian rule in Greece, Glafcos Clerides,

president of the Cypriot House of Representatives, replaced Sampson as president of Cyprus.

A preliminary peace agreement that left Turkey's invasion forces strongly entrenched on the island was signed on July 30. Greece threatened to boycott further peace talks in Geneva, Switzerland, unless Turkey withdrew from areas it had occupied after the July 30 agreement. A UN buffer zone failed to halt Turkish advances. The peace talks resumed in Geneva on August 8 but broke down on August 14.

Two hours after the talks collapsed, Turkey launched massive air, artillery, and tank attacks. When the Turks announced a cease-fire on August 16, the northeastern third of Cyprus, the richest part of the island, was in their hands. By August 18, almost half the Greek Cypriots in the region had fled their homes.

U.S. Ambassador Rodger Paul Davies was shot dead on August 19 while a mob of Greek Cypriots was attacking the U.S. Embassy in Nicosia during an anti-American demonstration.

Makarios Returns. On December 7, Makarios returned to the island amid jubilation by thousands of Greek Cypriots. He rejected the Turkish peace plan that would partition the island into Greek Cypriot and Turkish Cypriot sectors and transfer the population accordingly.   Kenneth Brown

See also GREECE; MIDDLE EAST (Facts in Brief Table); TURKEY.

CZECHOSLOVAKIA expanded its political and economic relations with the West in 1974, but maintained strict vigilance against Western influences at home. In July, West Germany and Czechoslovakia ratified a treaty that normalized relations. Czechoslovak Foreign Minister Bohuslav Chnoupek visited Bonn later that month. Relations with Austria improved so much that Czechoslovakia ceded a small strip of territory on the Austrian frontier in June.

U.S. Relations. On April 25, Prague ratified a consular treaty that had been signed in 1973 with the United States. The United States and Czechoslovakia reached a preliminary agreement on July 5 settling mutual post-World War II financial claims. Under the agreement, Czechoslovakia will pay some compensation for about $80 million worth of American property that was nationalized by the Communists in 1948. In return, the U.S. government will release about 20.5 short tons (18.4 metric tons) of Czechoslovak gold held by the United States, France, and Great Britain in their Tripartite Gold Commission.

Talks with the Vatican continued despite the sudden death of Stepan Cardinal Trochta, 68, on April 6. He died of a heart attack following a long interview with a government official. The government denied reports he had been bullied and abused.

April marked the fifth anniversary of the removal of former liberal leader Alexander Dubček. The Communist Party restated its hard line in several party newspapers and magazines. However, no action was taken against Dubček, who had allowed a letter criticizing the regime's oppressive policies to be published in an Italian Communist magazine in March. Two leading critics of the regime, Jiri Hochmann and Ota Filip, were allowed to emigrate to West Germany in July, but two politically inspired trials were held outside Prague.

The Economy. On June 25, Finance Minister Jaroslav Tlapak reported an increase of 15.1 per cent in national income and 14.4 per cent in consumption over the first three years of the current five-year plan. Czechoslovakia had a record grain harvest in 1974, and industrial output increased by 6.2 per cent in the first six months compared with the same period in 1973. About 90 per cent of that increase was achieved through higher productivity.

Industry was hard hit by the increase in oil and other commodity prices on world markets. About $480 million was earmarked for subsidies to cushion industry from the effects of higher world prices. Imports from the West increased by 55 per cent in the first six months of the year. Acute labor shortages continued to threaten economic growth. Czechoslovakia was talking with Yugoslavia and other exporters of labor at year's end. Chris Cviic

See also EUROPE (Facts in Brief Table).

DAHOMEY. See AFRICA.
DAIRYING. See AGRICULTURE.

DALLAS-FORT WORTH. Voters in Dallas on Sept. 10, 1974, rejected a proposed 1 per cent payroll tax on persons working within the city. The earnings tax, on salary in excess of $5,000, was designed to affect only suburban commuters, because Dallas homeowners would have received a credit against their property taxes for any earnings taxes paid.

Problem Airport. The $700-million Dallas-Fort Worth Regional Airport, which opened in 1973, ran into difficulties during its first year of operation. Airtrans, the computerized transit system designed to move passengers within the terminal area, frequently malfunctioned, causing passengers stranded along the route to miss planes. The baggage-handling system damaged luggage, and passengers complained about the costs of airport services and about its remote location.

All eight major airlines serving the area moved their operations to the new airport when it opened, leaving only Southwest Airlines operating out of Dallas' Love Field. Southwest's profits immediately jumped 100 per cent, and other airlines wanted to return to the old facility, located closer to downtown Dallas. The Dallas and Fort Worth city councils tried in mid-April to stop the airlines from leaving the new airport by passing ordinances banning commercial airline flights from all other municipal fields. Implementation of the order, however, was stayed pending the outcome of several lawsuits.

Significant Crime Increase. The Federal Bureau of Investigation (FBI) reported on October 3 that the crime rate increased 23 per cent in Dallas and 20 per cent in Fort Worth during the first six months of 1974. However, a Law Enforcement Assistance Administration (LEAA) study, released on January 27, indicated that FBI statistics did not give an accurate view of the crime situation. The LEAA study showed that for every crime reported in Dallas, 2.6 went unreported.

Economic Conditions in the Dallas-Fort Worth area were relatively good. The number of jobs increased 1.9 per cent, construction activity was up 0.8 per cent, and department store sales rose 10.1 per cent during the one-year period ending in July. The cost of living rose 9.7 per cent between May, 1973, and May, 1974, but the wages of factory workers nearly kept pace, increasing 7.7 per cent to an annual average of $7,808 by midyear. However, according to the U.S. Department of Labor, this amount failed to meet the estimated $8,018 needed to maintain a minimum standard of living for a family of four.

In early 1974, the city and a private investment group joined forces to develop a 53-acre (21-hectare) tract of land at the edge of the Dallas business district. Development plans include a hotel, transportation center, shopping complex, and a tower topped by a revolving restaurant. James M. Banovetz

DAM. See BUILDING AND CONSTRUCTION.

DANCING

Viewed from the short range, dance appeared to flourish in 1974. The dance capital of the world, New York City, had its busiest season yet. Many other large cities across the United States were visited by at least half a dozen major dance troupes. An increasing number of small and medium-sized modern-dance groups were able to keep their dancers on the payroll for longer periods of time by touring college campuses. And a national poll showed that dance attendance at universities for the first time was on a par with rock concerts.

But the long-range picture was gloomy. Government subsidies clearly could not keep abreast of rising costs. Private patrons disappeared, and foundation support dwindled or depended on matching grants from other sources, as in the case of the Ford Foundation's $6.3-million grant to the New York City Ballet and New York City Opera.

The most ominous event was the June 12 announcement that the National Ballet of Washington, D.C., was disbanding immediately. Its board of directors said that it was impossible to raise the $300,000 needed to balance the budget, or a similar amount needed to open the fall season. The National Ballet was founded in 1963 with the aid of a 10-year Ford Foundation grant and gained a reputation with productions of full-length classics. Some critics accused the company of sinking too much money into glamour productions and failing to cultivate home-grown choreographers and a distinctive dance style of its own. However justified the criticisms, the quick extinction of the National Ballet made the dance world nervous.

The National Ballet was not alone in its troubles. The San Francisco Ballet began a last-ditch fund-raising appeal in September. The Harkness Ballet, which opened the new $1-million Harkness Theater in New York City with great fanfare on April 9, announced on October 9 that it would disband in April, 1975, unless it could raise $1 million from sources other than its sole patron, Rebekah Harkness. The New York City Ballet announced an increased deficit, and American Ballet Theatre said its future was imperiled if it did not obtain funds.

The Eliot Feld Ballet, a new company, was the one bright spot. With almost 20 ballets to his credit, Feld is considered the most able choreographer of the younger generation in the United States. The Eliot Feld Ballet was aided by a Rockefeller Foundation subsidy and rent-free use of the Newman Theater in Joseph Papp's Public Theater complex in New York City. In its première season, May 30 to June 16, the company presented two new Feld ballets, *Sephardic Song* and *Tzaddik*, the Hebrew word for *sage*. The critics marveled at how cohesively and beautifully the new company performed.

In the fall, the Feld group became a resident of the Public Theater complex and danced there during December. Aware of the financial situation affecting the dance world, the company has kept its operation modest. There is no live orchestra and only a small repertory and roster. Also, there are only 300 seats to fill at the Newman Theater.

New Productions. *Coppelia*, restaged by George Balanchine and Alexandra Danilova, was the most heralded new production. The New York City Ballet brought the work to New York City in November. For *Coppelia*'s third act, Balanchine choreographed a brilliant new set of pure-dance variations. Danilova, fondly remembered for her witty interpretation of the ballet's heroine in the 1940s, staged the first two acts based on her memory of the original Petipa choreography. As the leads, Patricia McBride and Helgi Tomasson confirmed the opinion that they are two of America's most splendid dancers.

McBride and Tomasson were also the leads in Jerome Robbins' *Dybbuk*, first seen May 16 during the City Ballet's spring season in New York City. Their dramatic performances, plus the attention accorded the score by Leonard Bernstein, who conducted at the première, caused *Dybbuk* to be much talked about but not universally acclaimed.

Visitors from Abroad. Just as talked about, and also praised to the skies, were the first American performances of Mikhail Baryshnikov. The Latvian-born Baryshnikov, an extraordinary dancer in the classic tradition, was a leading member of Leningrad's Kirov Ballet in Russia. He defected in Toronto, Canada, on June 29 while touring with a group of Russian dancers. American Ballet Theatre (ABT) quickly recruited him as guest artist for several appearances during its engagement at the State Theater in New York City from July 2 to August 10. By coincidence, ABT was presenting a new production of *La Bayadère*, a staple for a male Russian virtuoso. Baryshnikov was able to step into this famous role right away, as well as that of Albrecht in *Giselle*. After guesting with two Canadian companies, Baryshnikov again danced with ABT in Washington, D.C., from October 22 to November 3.

The Kirov Ballet's highly anticipated summer visit was canceled because of the controversy surrounding ex-Kirov star Valery Panov and his dancer-wife, Galina. After a two-year struggle to obtain Russian exit visas, the Panovs were finally allowed to emigrate to Israel on June 15.

The Royal Ballet of Britain was at the Metropolitan Opera House in New York City from May 7 to

Helgi Tomasson and Patricia McBride dance in Jerome Robbins' *Dybbuk*, a poetic story of a wandering spirit who enters his lover's body.

The Alvin Ailey dance company fuses jazz and blues with Latin American and African techniques in such works as José Limón's *Missa Brevis*.

26, and at the Kennedy Center in Washington, D.C., for the next two weeks. They offered only one new work, and not a very good one—Kenneth Mac-Millan's *Manon*. But the general level of dancing was so high that the visit was a success.

The National Ballet of Canada also did well on a transcontinental tour in March and April. But it probably owed its success to just one dancer, Rudolf Nureyev. By virtue of phenomenal stamina, he appeared in just about every performance.

Old and New. The Martha Graham Dance Company, continuing its comeback, appeared on Broadway from April 15 to May 4. The season was marked by two new works, *Holy Jungle* and *Chronique*, and by revivals of several important ballets that had been feared lost when Graham retired from dancing. However, she invented a new stage role as the hostess of lecture-demonstration programs.

The Alvin Ailey company brought new life to what Ailey terms America's "black tradition" by reviving works of black choreographers Janet Collins and Pearl Primus in May at the New York City Center.

Modern-dance choreographer Paul Taylor may have started a new trend in dance crossovers by inviting Nureyev to join his company for a guest appearance in *Aureole* in New York City on October 14. Also on the program during the one-week engagement was Taylor's *Sports and Follies*, which premièred August 7 at Lake Placid, N.Y. Nancy Goldner

Russian dancer Mikhail Baryshnikov, right, who defected in Toronto in June, won warm praise when he made his U.S. debut in *Giselle* in July.

DEATHS OF NOTABLE PERSONS in 1974 included those listed below. An asterisk (*) indicates the person is the subject of a biography in THE WORLD BOOK ENCYCLOPEDIA. Those listed were Americans unless otherwise indicated.

Abrams, General Creighton W. (1914-Sept. 4), U.S. Army chief of staff. He was commander of U.S. forces in South Vietnam from 1968 until 1973.

Allan, Andrew (1907-Jan. 15), pioneer of Canadian radio and television.

Alsop, Stewart (1914-May 26), author, columnist, and political analyst. He had suffered from leukemia and wrote a book about his impending death called *Stay of Execution: A Sort of Memoir.*

Anderson, Edward (1900-April 26), retired football coach at Holy Cross College and the University of Iowa, and member of the football Hall of Fame.

Antoniutti, Ildebrando Cardinal (1898-Aug. 1), former Italian papal diplomat who was prefect of the Sacred Congregation for Religious and Secular Institutions from 1963 until he retired in 1973.

Arquette, Cliff (1905-Sept. 23), actor who created the homespun Charlie Weaver character on television.

*** Asturias, Miguel Angel** (1899-June 9), Guatemalan novelist, poet, and diplomat who won the 1967 Nobel Prize for Literature.

*** Ayub Khan, Field Marshal Mohammad** (1907-April 19), president of Pakistan from 1958 to 1969.

Bates, H. E. (Herbert Ernest) (1905-Jan. 29), English author whose novels included *Fair Stood the Wind for France* (1944) and *The Purple Plain* (1947).

Bates, Marston (1906-April 3), cultural biologist and professor emeritus of zoology at the University of Michigan. One of the United States ranking naturalists, he was known for his ability to turn scientific findings into readable prose for the general public.

*** Benny, Jack** (1894-Dec. 26), one of America's top comedians, whose career spanned some 60 years. He carried his role as a violin-playing tightwad from vaudeville to the golden days of radio to television. A master of comic timing, he could get big laughs with a simple "hmmm-m-m-m."

Bickel, Alexander M. (1924-Nov. 7), Sterling Professor of Law at Yale University and one of the top authorities on the U.S. Constitution.

*** Bohlen, Charles E. (Chip)** (1904-Jan. 2), U.S. diplomat and one of the leading experts on Russia. He was said to have spent more time with Joseph Stalin than any other American.

Braddock, James J. (1905-Nov. 29), who won the heavyweight boxing title in a stunning upset of Max Baer in 1935 and lost it to Joe Louis in 1937.

Brennan, Walter (1894-Sept. 21), veteran actor who won three Academy Awards for "best supporting actor." He also starred in the television series "The Real McCoys."

Brogan, Sir Denis W. (1900-Jan. 5), Scottish historian, author, and lecturer who was professor of political science at Cambridge University, England, from 1939 to 1968, then emeritus professor.

*** Bush, Vannevar** (1890-June 28), electrical engineer and president of the Carnegie Institution of Washington from 1939 to 1955. He marshaled U.S. technology for World War II as director of the Office of Scientific Research and Development.

*** Chadwick, Sir James** (1891-July 24), British winner of the Nobel Prize for Physics in 1935 for his discovery of the neutron.

Childers, Erskine (1905-Nov. 17), president of Ireland since June 25, 1973. Through his mother, he was descended from John Adams and John Quincy Adams.

Alan F. Guttmacher, leader in the family-planning movement.

Vannevar Bush, an electrical engineer.

Georges Pompidou had been French president since 1969.

David A. Ciqueiros, a Mexican muralist.

Clapp, Margaret (1910-May 3), president of Wellesley College, Wellesley, Mass., from 1949 to 1966.

Coldwell, M. J. (James William) (1888-Aug. 25), who headed Canada's Cooperative Commonwealth Federation, now known as the New Democrat Party, from 1942 until 1960.

Colwell, Ernest Cadman (1901-Sept. 12), president of the University of Chicago from 1945 to 1951 and a leading New Testament scholar.

*** Condon, Edward U.** (1902-March 26), physicist who played a major role in the World War II atomic bomb and radar programs.

Connolly, Cyril (1903-Nov. 26), witty British literary critic and author.

Cooley, Harold D. (1897-Jan. 15), Democrat from North Carolina who served in the U.S. House of Representatives from 1935 until 1967.

*** Cornell, Katharine** (1893-June 9), one of the greatest actresses of the American stage. Her major triumphs included *The Barretts of Wimpole Street, Romeo and Juliet,* and *Candida.*

Cowan, Clyde L., Jr. (1919-May 24), professor of physics at Catholic University of America and co-discoverer in 1956 of the elusive neutrino particle.

Cox, James M. (1903-Oct. 27), chairman of the Cox Enterprises newspaper-publishing company and the Cox Broadcasting Corporation.

Crossman, Richard (1907-April 5), journalist and a leader of the British Labour Party. He first became a member of Parliament in 1946 and was minister of

Chet Huntley, a
TV newscaster.

Anne Klein, a designer of
casual, but elegant, clothes.

Peter Revson, a
top racing driver.

Cass Elliott, pop singer who
appeared often on television.

housing and local government from 1964 to 1966 and secretary of state for social services from 1968 to 1970.

Daley, Arthur J. (1904-Jan. 3), long-time sports columnist for *The New York Times*.

Danielou, Jean Cardinal (1905-May 20), a leading Jesuit theologian, defender of papal authority, and one of the best-known members of France's Roman Catholic hierarchy.

*__Daugherty, James H.__ (1889-Feb. 21), early non-objective artist who also was a distinguished writer and illustrator of children's books.

Davis, Adelle (1904-May 31), nutritionist whose message was "You are what you eat."

*__Dean, Dizzy__ (Jay Hanna Dean) (1911-July 17), baseball Hall of Fame pitcher with a 150-83 career record. When an injury ended his colorful playing career, he became a sportscaster and enriched the language with such phrases as "slud into third," and "The players returned to their respectable bases."

*__De Seversky, Alexander P.__ (1894-Aug. 24), pilot, aircraft designer, and member of the Aviation Hall of Fame. He was born in Russia.

*__De Sica, Vittorio__ (1902-Nov. 13), Italian motion-picture director of such classics as *Shoeshine* and *The Bicycle Thief*.

Dilworth, Richardson K. (1898-Jan. 23), two-term (1955-1962) Democratic mayor of Philadelphia.

Dunn, Alan (1900-May 20), most prolific of *The New Yorker* magazine cartoonists, with 1,906 drawings and 9 covers between Aug. 7, 1926, and May 6, 1974.

Durham, Carl T. (1892-April 29), North Carolina Democrat who served 11 terms in the U.S. House of Representatives.

Earle, George H. 3rd (1890-Dec. 30), former Republican governor of Pennsylvania.

*__Ellington, Duke__ (1899-May 24), one of the most important figures in the history of jazz. See MUSIC, POPULAR (Close-Up).

Elliott, Cass (1941-July 29), pop singer who first became a hit as a star of The Mamas and The Papas folk-rock group.

Esterel, Jacques (Charles Martin) (1917-April 14), French fashion designer and musical composer. His designs generally were considered novelties, such as his umbrella with a built-in light.

Ewing, W. Maurice (1906-May 4), pioneer in earth sciences research. He was director of the Lamont-Doherty Geological Observatory of Columbia University from 1948 to 1972, and chief of the Earth and Planetary Sciences Division at the University of Texas Marine Biomedical Institute since 1972.

Flynn, Joe (1924-July 18), actor best known for his portrayal of Captain Binghampton in the television series "McHale's Navy."

Fouchet, Christian (1911-Aug. 11), former French Cabinet member and ambassador who once was described as "more Gaullist than De Gaulle."

Garand, John C. (1888-Feb. 16), Canadian-born inventor of the .30-caliber M-1 rifle of World War II.

Gerber, Daniel F. (1898-March 16), head of the Gerber Products Company, the world's largest baby-food manufacturer.

Gloucester, Duke of (Prince Henry William Frederick Albert) (1900-June 10), uncle of Queen Elizabeth II and last surviving son of King George V.

Goldsmith, Alfred N. (1888-July 2), prolific inventor, electronics scientist, and engineer. His career reached from radio's early days to the present day of color television and satellite communications.

*__Goldwyn, Samuel__ (1882-Jan. 31), pioneer Hollywood producer and creator of grand-scale motion pictures. Born in Poland, he was known for his "Goldwynisms," such as "A man who goes to a psychiatrist should have his head examined."

Gruenberg, Sidonie M. (1881-March 11), director of the Child Study Association of America from 1923 to 1950 and editor in chief of the *Encyclopedia of Child Care and Guidance*. She was born in Vienna, Austria.

*__Gruening, Ernest__ (1887-June 26), Democratic senator from Alaska from 1959 to 1969.

Guttmacher, Alan F. (1898-March 18), leader in the family-planning movement and president of the Planned Parenthood Federation of America since 1962.

Handwerker, Nathan (1890-March 24), co-founder with his wife Ida of Nathan's Famous, Incorporated, the noted hot-dog, fast-food restaurant chain. Born in Poland, he opened his first stand on Coney Island, New York.

Hepburn, Commissioner Samuel (1901-Aug. 28), who retired in 1971 as national commander of the Salvation Army in the United States. Born in England, he served with the organization for 52 years.

Heyer, Georgette (1902-July 4), British writer of more than 50 books, most of them historical novels set in Regency England.

Hodges, Luther H. (1898-Oct. 6), Democratic governor of North Carolina from 1954 to 1960, and U.S. secretary of commerce from 1961 to 1964.

Hoffman, Paul G. (1891-Oct. 8), automobile executive who was the first administrator of the Marshall Plan for aid to Europe, from 1948 to 1950.

Homans, Abigail Adams (1879-February 4), great-great-granddaughter of John Adams, the second Presi-

Eagle
Of the
Skies

Charles A. Lindbergh
(1902-1974)

Charles A. Lindbergh was a tall, gangly, bashful 25-year-old when he captured the world's imagination in 1927 with the first solo flight across the Atlantic Ocean. Others had flown the Atlantic before, but his was the first flight from continent to continent, and the first by a lone man. The adulation that followed obscured the fact that his feat was a minutely planned project by an experienced pilot with 2,000 hours of flying time under his belt.

Lindbergh began thinking about going after aviation's biggest prize—$25,000 for the first solo flight between New York and Paris—while flying a mail plane between Chicago and St. Louis. Once he decided he could do it, he devoted all his energies to the project—getting financial backing, designing the plane, mapping the route, and planning for emergencies.

He took off from Roosevelt Field, near New York City, on May 20, 1927, in bad weather. Weighted down with fuel, his single-engine plane, the *Spirit of St. Louis*, barely cleared the phone wires at the end of the runway. For the next 33½ hours, he was alone. But the attention of the world was riveted on the slim young flier, and when he finally landed at Le Bourget Airport near Paris, thousands of cheering Parisians quickly surrounded him.

The cheering followed him back across the Atlantic. The small-town Minnesota youth, who began dreaming of flying as a boy, overnight became an international hero, the Lone Eagle. He was awarded the United States Medal of Honor, previously given only to military heroes, and the nation's first Distinguished Flying Cross. In New York City, 4 million people spilled into the streets to watch as ticker tape and confetti rained on a parade down Broadway. Other cities held triumphal parades and receptions, and Lindbergh eventually flew his plane to every state in the union. Songs were written about him and babies named after him.

The shouting and hysteria were to follow him for years, until he finally fled from the publicity that engulfed him. Throughout his life, he sought peace and privacy; instead, he was dogged by tragedy and controversy.

After returning from Paris, Lindbergh helped lay out transcontinental, transatlantic, and Caribbean air routes. He married Anne Morrow in 1929. Their life seemed idyllic, but the peace was shattered in 1932 with the kidnaping and murder of their first child, 20-month-old Charles A. Lindbergh, Jr. After one of the most sensational trials of the century, a carpenter, Bruno Hauptmann, was convicted of the crime and executed. Hounded by the press, Lindbergh finally packed up his family and moved to Great Britain.

While in Europe, he visited the air forces of Britain, France, and Germany. He was greatly impressed by Germany's air power and appalled by the unpreparedness of Britain and France. In 1939, he returned home, convinced that the United States should stay out of the impending war. For two years, he campaigned actively against American intervention in World War II. Despite charges of fascism and anti-Semitism, he never recanted his position.

But once the United States declared war after Pearl Harbor, Lindbergh tried to join the armed forces. He was turned down by President Franklin D. Roosevelt, who could not forgive his earlier opposition. Lindbergh then joined United Aircraft as a consultant. In that role, he managed to get to the Pacific, where he flew 50 combat missions—as a civilian.

After the war, he dropped out of the spotlight for more than 15 years. During this period, he worked on secret government projects, apparently in space rocketry and missiles.

A concern for the deteriorating environment thrust him back into the public eye in the 1960s. He worked to save the humpback and blue whales from extinction and studied monkey-eating eagles and primitive tribes in the Philippines. He also was an outspoken opponent of the supersonic transport, fearing its impact on the upper atmosphere.

On Aug. 26, 1974, Lindbergh died of lymphatic cancer at his home in Maui, Hawaii. The funeral, only a few hours after his death, was as simple and private as the man himself. At last, he found peace. Kathryn Sederberg

Katharine Cornell
was a noted actress.

Dizzy Dean, legendary pitcher
and colorful sportscaster.

Creighton Abrams
Army chief of staff.

Alberta King, the mother of
Martin Luther King, Jr.

dent of the United States, and great-granddaughter of the sixth President, John Quincy Adams.

Horton, Tim (1930-Feb. 21), defenseman with the Buffalo Sabres of the National Hockey League. A Canadian, he was the oldest regular in the league.

Howard, Bailey K. (1914-Aug. 12), chairman of the executive committee of Field Enterprises, Incorporated, parent corporation of 21 national and international divisions and subsidiary companies, including WORLD BOOK and THE WORLD BOOK YEAR BOOK.

*****Hunt, H. L.** (1889-Nov. 29), oil billionaire considered to be one of the world's richest men.

Huntley, Chet (1911-March 20), former television newscaster who teamed with David Brinkley on NBC's "Huntley-Brinkley Report" from 1956 to 1970. Their sign-off—"Good night, David." "Good night, Chet"—became a national catch phrase.

Hurok, Sol (1888-March 5), Russian-born impresario who brought many distinguished virtuosos and groups—American and foreign—to U.S. audiences.

Husseini, Haj Amin el- (1893-July 4), former Grand Mufti of Jerusalem and controversial Arab leader.

*****Jackson, Alexander Young** (1882-April 6), Canadian landscape painter and the last survivor of the Group of Seven, a school of Toronto artists who broke with European techniques in the 1920s and early 1930s.

Jonas, Franz (1899-April 23), president of Austria since 1965, and mayor of Vienna prior to that.

Jordan, B. Everett (1896-March 15), Democratic senator from North Carolina from 1958 to 1973.

Kaestner, Erich (1899-July 29), one of Germany's best-known authors. His most famous work was "Emil and the Detectives," a children's story that was translated into 24 languages.

Kahn, Louis I. (1901-March 17), one of America's foremost architects. Born in Estonia, he came to the United States in 1905. See ARCHITECTURE (Close-Up).

*****Kelly, George E.** (1887-June 18), playwright who won the Pulitzer Prize for *Craig's Wife* (1925).

King, Alberta (Mrs. Martin Luther King, Sr.) (1903-June 30), mother of the slain civil rights leader.

King, Cecil R. (1898-March 17), Democrat from California who served in the U.S. House of Representatives from 1942 to 1967.

Kirk, Norman E. (1923-Aug. 31), prime minister of New Zealand. He took office in November, 1972, after the Labour Party won a landslide majority in Parliament. He had become party leader in 1965, and was one of the youngest prime ministers in New Zealand history.

Klein, Anne (1922-March 19), influential dress designer who is credited with starting the trend toward casual, yet elegant, clothes.

*****Knowland, William F.** (1908-Feb. 23), publisher of the *Oakland* (Calif.) *Tribune*, who served in the U.S. Senate from 1945 to 1959 and was Senate Republican leader from 1953 to 1958.

Kominek, Boleslaw Cardinal (1903-March 10), archbishop of Wrocław (Breslau), Poland, since 1956.

Kowalski, Frank (1907-Oct. 11), Democratic congressman at large from Connecticut from 1959 to 1963.

Krips, Henry Josef (1902-Oct. 12), one of the last of the great Viennese conductors, whose career spanned 53 years.

*****Krishna Menon, V. K.** (1897-Oct. 6), controversial figure in Indian and world politics, who was defense minister from 1957 to 1962.

Krock, Arthur (1887-April 11), for 60 years a reporter, Washington bureau chief, and columnist of *The New York Times*. In 1968, his book *Memoirs: 60 Years on the Firing Line* became a best seller.

Kuznetsov, Admiral Nikolai G. (1902-Dec. 8?), commander of Russia's naval forces during World War II.

*****Lagerkvist, Pär Fabian** (1891-July 11), Swedish novelist, playwright, and poet who won the Nobel Prize for Literature in 1951. His two most famous novels are *The Dwarf* (1944) and *Barabbas* (1951).

*****Lenski, Lois** (1893-Sept. 11), author and illustrator of more than 50 children's books. She won the 1946 Newbery Medal for *Strawberry Girl*.

Leslie, Kenneth (1892-Oct. 7), Canadian poet and composer whose works reflected life in rural areas of Nova Scotia. He won the 1938 Governor-General's Literary Award for his book *By Stubborn Stars*.

Lewis, John Henry (1914-April 14), world light-heavyweight boxing champion from 1935 to 1939.

*****Lindbergh, Charles A.** (1902-Aug. 26), aviator who made the first solo flight across the Atlantic Ocean in the single-engine airplane *Spirit of St. Louis*. See Close-Up.

*****Lippmann, Walter** (1889-Dec. 14), dean of 20th century American political journalism. His widely read and respected newspaper columns won him two Pulitzer Prizes and other awards.

Loeb, Harold (1891-Jan. 20), publisher of the avant-garde literary magazine *Broom* from 1921 to 1924. A crony of Ernest Hemingway and other American expatriates, Loeb appeared as Robert Cohn in Hemingway's novel *The Sun Also Rises* (1926).

Lovejoy, Clarence E. (1894-Jan. 16), editor of the Lovejoy series of school and college guides.

Marsh, Bruce (1925-March 16), one of Canada's most popular broadcasters for some 20 years.

McCafferty, Don (1921-July 28), head coach of the Detroit Lions football team.

McGee, Frank (1921-April 17), newsman with the National Broadcasting Company since 1957 and host of the network's early-morning television show "Today" since 1971.

***McGuigan, James Cardinal** (1894-April 8), archbishop of the Roman Catholic archdiocese of Toronto, Canada, from 1934 to 1971.

McIntire, Clifford G. (1908-Oct. 1), Republican member of the U.S. House of Representatives from Maine from 1951 to 1965.

McKeldin, Theodore Roosevelt (1900-Aug. 10), Republican governor of Maryland from 1951 to 1959, and twice mayor of Baltimore.

Merrow, Chester E. (1906-Feb. 10), Republican congressman from New Hampshire from 1943 to 1963. He failed in attempts to return as a Democrat in 1970 and 1972.

Meyer, Karl F. (1884-April 27), Swiss-born viral scientist regarded as the most versatile microbe hunter since Louis Pasteur.

***Milhaud, Darius** (1892-June 22), French composer who helped overturn traditional ideas about music in the 1920s.

Molyneux, Edward H. (1894-March 22), British fashion designer whose basic theory was that "clothes must make us look our best, better than we really are."

Moorehead, Agnes (1906-April 30), actress who made about 100 motion pictures but who probably was best known as Endora, a witch in the "Bewitched" television series.

***Morse, Wayne L.** (1900-July 22), former senator from Oregon, a strong and early critic of the Vietnam War. He was trying to win re-election to the Senate seat he lost in 1968.

Muilenburg, James (1896-May 10), scholar who worked on the *Revised Standard Version of the Bible*, published in 1952. He was Gray Professor of Hebrew Exegesis and Old Testament in San Anselmo, Calif., from 1963 until he retired in 1972.

***Mundt, Karl E.** (1900-Aug. 16), former Republican senator from South Dakota, who figured prominently in the Alger Hiss and Army-McCarthy hearings. He was first elected to the House of Representatives in 1938 and moved to the Senate in 1949.

Munro, Sir Leslie (1901-Feb. 13), New Zealand diplomat, lawyer, and journalist who was president of the United Nations General Assembly in 1957 and 1958.

O'Brien, Kate (1897-Aug. 13), Irish novelist and playwright whose first novel, *Without My Clock* (1931), won two of the top British literary awards of the day.

Packer, Sir Frank (1906-April 30), chairman of the Australian Consolidated Press and a pioneer in Australian commercial television.

Pagnol, Marcel P. (1895-April 18), French film director and playwright. His greatest achievement was the trilogy about Marseilles waterfront life—*Marius*, *Fanny*, and *César*.

Parker, Ross (1915-Aug. 2), British lyricist and composer whose hits included "We'll Meet Again" and "There'll Always Be an England."

Partch, Harry (1901-Sept. 3), avant-garde composer who invented his own musical scales and his own bizarre instruments.

***Perón, Juan Domingo** (1895-July 1), one of the most controversial political figures in Latin America. He was president of Argentina from 1946 to 1955, then went into exile, but returned as president in 1973.

***Pompidou, Georges Jean Raymond** (1911-April 2), 18th president of the modern French republic. He served from 1969 until his death. Earlier he had been premier under President Charles de Gaulle.

Ed Sullivan was the host of TV's longest-running program.

Juan Perón was twice Argentina's president.

Darius Milhaud, an innovative French composer of the 1920s.

Sol Hurok was a top impresario.

Prouty, Olive Higgins (1882-March 24), author of several novels, including *Stella Dallas* (1922), which later became a Broadway play, a silent movie, a sound movie, and a long-running radio serial.

Pulitzer, Margaret Leech (1893-Feb. 24), award-winning historian whose books included *Reveille in Washington* (1941) and *In the Days of McKinley* (1959).

Radcliffe, George L. (1877-July 29), Democratic senator from Maryland from 1935 to 1947.

***Ransom, John Crowe** (1888-July 3), noted critic, editor, and poet.

Revson, Peter (1939-March 22), one of America's top road-racing drivers, who died when his car crashed during a practice run for the South Africa Grand Prix.

Ritter, Tex (1905-Jan. 2), country-music singer and guitar player who also made some 78 Western movies. Among his hit songs were "I've Got Spurs That Jingle, Jangle, Jingle" and the title song from the movie *High Noon*.

Roberts, William Goodridge (1904-Jan. 28), Canadian painter, best known for his landscapes and still lifes.

Rock, Lillian D. (1902-May 14), feminist leader who suggested in the 1930s that women fill high public offices. In 1935, she founded and became president of the League for a Woman President and Vice-President.

Ruby, Harry (1895-Feb. 23), popular-song composer and writer of movie scenarios and Broadway scores. With Bert Kalmar, he wrote such hits as "Three Little Words" and "A Kiss to Build a Dream On."

Jacqueline Susann wrote best sellers.

Erskine Childers had been the president of Ireland.

Jack Benny, famous for deadpan humor.

U Thant was secretary-general of the UN for nine years.

Russell, Louis B. (1925-Nov. 27), who had lived longer with a transplanted heart than anyone else—since Aug. 24, 1968.

Ryan, Cornelius (1920-Nov. 23), Irish-born author of the World War II books *The Longest Day, The Last Battle,* and *A Bridge Too Far.*

Santos, Eduardo (1888-March 27), president of Colombia from 1938 to 1942.

Sark, Dame of (Sibyl Hathaway) (1884?-July 14), hereditary feudal ruler of the British Channel island of Sark.

Seeley, Blossom (1891-April 17), song-and-dance star of vaudeville and burlesque. She teamed for many years with her husband, Benny Fields, using as theme songs "Melancholy Baby" and "Lullaby of Broadway."

Sexton, Anne (1928-Oct. 4), who won the 1967 Pulitzer Prize for Poetry.

Shaw, Clay L. (1914-Aug. 15), New Orleans businessman who was acquitted in 1969 of plotting to assassinate President John F. Kennedy.

*Shazar, Schneor Zalman** (1889-Oct. 5), who was born in Russia and served as Israel's third president, from 1963 to 1973.

Shelley, John F. (1905-Sept. 1), California state senator for 6 years, Democratic congressman for 13, and mayor of San Francisco from 1964 to 1967.

Simonds, General Guy G. (1903-May 15), leading Canadian field commander in the Mediterranean area of operations during World War II. He served as chief of staff from 1951 until his retirement in 1955.

Siqueiros, David A. (1896-Jan. 6), socially conscious Mexican muralist, recipient of his country's highest cultural award, the National Prize for Art.

*Spaatz, General Carl A.** (1891-July 14), first chief of staff of the Air Force. During World War II, he commanded U.S. strategic bombing forces in Europe and the Pacific.

Spottswood, Bishop Stephen Gill (1897-Dec. 1), board chairman of the National Association for the Advancement of Colored People since 1961 and a retired bishop of the African Methodist Episcopal Zion Church.

Starrett, Vincent (1886-Jan. 5), Chicago newspaperman, critic, poet, and novelist who in 1934 was a founder of the Baker Street Irregulars, a group devoted to the lore of Sherlock Holmes.

Strauss, Lewis L. (1896-Jan. 21), retired rear admiral who was a member of the Atomic Energy Commission from 1946 to 1950 and its chairman from 1953 to 1958.

Sullivan, Ed (1902-Oct. 13), Broadway columnist for the *New York Daily News* and host of the longest-running show in television history. His "really big shew" opened on June 20, 1948, and lasted for 23 years.

Susann, Jacqueline (1921-Sept. 21), former actress whose 1966 novel *Valley of the Dolls* became the all-time best seller, with more than 17 million copies sold.

Sutherland, Earl W., Jr. (1915-March 9), winner of the 1971 Nobel Prize in Physiology and Medicine for his discovery of the ways hormones act.

Tanaka, Kotaro (1890-March 1), chief justice of Japan's Supreme Court from 1950 to 1961 and a judge of the International Court of Justice from 1961 to 1970.

Taylor, Sir Hugh (1890-April 17), former dean of the Princeton University Graduate School and a prominent physical chemist. He was born in England.

Teague, Charles M. (1909-Jan. 1), California Republican serving his 10th term in the U.S. House of Representatives.

*Thant, U** (1909-Nov. 25), former United Nations secretary-general, who served longer in that post—from 1962 to 1971—than any other man. He was Burmese, but had stayed in New York City after retiring.

Torres Bodet, Jaime (1902-May 13), called the father of modern Mexican education, and director-general of the United Nations Educational, Scientific, and Cultural Organization from 1948 to 1952.

Trochta, Stepan Cardinal (1905-April 6), Czechoslovak cardinal sent to prison for "espionage" in 1954. His conviction was canceled and he was returned to office in 1968.

Vanderbilt, Amy (1908-Dec. 27), syndicated columnist and authority on etiquette.

Volkoff, Boris (1902-March 11), who founded a ballet school that for more than 20 years was synonymous with ballet in most of Canada. Born in Russia, he pioneered a form of Canadian self-expression based on Eskimo and Indian legends.

Vursell, Charles W. (1881-Sept. 21), Republican representative from Illinois from 1943 to 1959.

*Warren, Earl** (1891-July 9), chief justice of the United States from 1953 to 1969. In 1954, he wrote the majority opinion for the ruling outlawing racial segregation in public schools. See SUPREME COURT OF THE UNITED STATES (Close-Up).

Watson, Arthur K. (1919-July 26), International Business Machines Corporation executive.

*Zhukov, Marshal Georgi K.** (1896-June 18), greatest Russian hero of World War II. He organized the defense of Moscow in 1941 and the victory at Stalingrad in 1942 and 1943, and led the Red army into Berlin in 1945.   Wayne Wille

DELAWARE. See STATE GOVERNMENT.

DEMOCRATIC PARTY. The Democrats scored dramatic election victories in November, 1974, posting a net gain of 4 governorships, at least 3 U.S. Senate seats, and 43 seats in the House of Representatives. One Senate race was contested. The victory was sweeter because Democrats won governor's races in the two most populous states, with Hugh L. Carey ending 16 years of Republican control in New York and Edmund G. Brown, Jr., recapturing the California governorship from retiring Republican Ronald Reagan. See ELECTIONS.

Despite the size of the triumph, Democratic leaders muted the celebration with warnings that the voters would now expect the party to deliver in Congress and in the 36 state houses held by Democrats. At the midterm convention in December, Democrats moved to strengthen the party by bringing together the various factions fighting for control of the presidential nominating convention in 1976. The plight of the Watergate-scarred Republican Party and public dissatisfaction over the nation's economic troubles increased the scramble by individual Democrats hoping to win control of the White House.

Field of Candidates. Senator Edward M. Kennedy of Massachusetts, rated by polls as the most popular man in his party, announced on September 23 that he would not be a candidate for the presidency in 1976. Kennedy cited personal and family reasons for his withdrawal from the 1976 campaign.

This increased the chances for the party's many other potential contenders for the Democratic presidential nomination. Senators Henry M. Jackson of Washington and Lloyd M. Bentsen, Jr., of Texas and Alabama Governor George C. Wallace were among those frequently mentioned as hopefuls.

The sizable election victories by first-term senators John H. Glenn of Ohio and Dale Bumpers of Arkansas injected their names into presidential speculation. Reportedly, Chicago's powerful Mayor Richard J. Daley favored Sargent Shriver, the Democrat's 1972 vice-presidential candidate. Illinois Governor Daniel Walker also had presidential aspirations, as did Georgia Governor Jimmy Carter and Arizona Congressman Morris K. Udall.

A Gallup Poll taken between November 8 and 11 showed that none of the potential candidates had a large following among Democratic voters. Presented with a list of 32 contenders, 19 per cent of those surveyed chose Wallace; 11 per cent chose Senator Hubert H. Humphrey of Minnesota; 10 per cent, Jackson; and 6 per cent each went to Senators Edmund S. Muskie of Maine and George S. McGovern of South Dakota.

Charter Adopted. About 2,000 Democrats gathered in Kansas City, Mo., from December 6 to 8 for their midterm convention and to adopt the first

Senator Edward M. Kennedy announces on September 23 that he will not seek the presidency in 1976 because of family responsibilities.

national charter of any major U.S. political party. Many Democrats had feared that the reformist and regular factions would quarrel before the nation's television audience, further weakening the party.

Before the convention, the Democrats were divided over how best to ensure participation by minorities, women, and young people. A meeting of the charter commission broke up on August 18 when blacks and liberal members walked out to protest changes in the draft document that they charged would "drive women and blacks out of the party." The issue was referred to the miniconvention. The issue of a midterm convention between presidential election years itself divided the Democrats.

However, the fears of controversy were never realized. The delegates met in a spirit of cooperation and adopted a charter acceptable to most Democrats, from Southern conservatives to liberal labor unionists. "We have brought the national Democratic Party back to life," said Democratic National Chairman Robert S. Strauss.

The new charter required taking affirmative action to involve minorities, women, and young people in all party affairs "as indicated by their presence in the Democratic electorate." However, mandatory quotas, an issue that split the party during the 1972 presidential nominating convention, were banned. The delegates also abolished the *unit rule*, by which the winner of a state presidential primary would get all of that state's delegate votes.

Some labor representatives were disgruntled, however, because they wanted a stronger stand against quotas. One delegate noted that power had shifted within the party. "In 1964 and 1968," he said, "blacks raised issues, and white liberals wrote the rules. This year, blacks, women, and liberals wrote the rules, and labor raised issues." To placate the labor faction, Strauss made plans to meet with labor leaders.

Identifying the Issues. Eight seminars were held during the convention, and the points they addressed were passed on to committees drafting the 1976 party platform. Although the convention did not plan to deal with policy issues, the panels reported on foreign policy, law enforcement, the economy, and increasing the power of Congress.

The Democrats offered an alternative economic policy to that being followed by Republican President Gerald R. Ford. The Democratic program called for mandatory controls on wages, prices, rents, and profits, as opposed to Ford's appeal for voluntary restraint. It recommended that wages catch up to the inflation rate and that some prices be rolled back. The Democrats also called for national health insurance, tax reform, stronger antitrust laws, more public service jobs, and gas and oil rationing, if necessary. Senator Robert C. Byrd of West Virginia said that the Democrat-controlled Congress would try to pass some of these measures.   William J. Eaton

DENMARK. An industrial boom in 1974 brought with it a trade deficit that reached $1.6 billion, double that of 1973. Amid political instability, the government directed its efforts to keeping employment up and containing inflation, which continued to run at a rate of more than 10 per cent.

Stiff Tax Measures. The seven non-Socialist parties in the *Folketing* (parliament) united on May 15 in a vote of confidence that averted the downfall of Prime Minister Poul Hartling's five-month-old minority Liberal government. A bill that would raise taxes to slow inflation, curb imports, and protect currency reserves had precipitated the crisis. It was passed despite opposition by Danish workers and other member countries of the European Community (Common Market). The tax package increased retail automobile prices by 25 per cent and boosted taxes on alcoholic beverages, tobacco, and appliances. State spending was cut by $100 million.

Others Protest. The European Commission, the Common Market executive body, expressed displeasure over Denmark's unilateral tax measures because of their effects on the exports of other market countries. While the measures did not violate the Treaty of Rome, the commission regretted the lack of consultation with other member countries.

One-fourth of Denmark's industrial labor force staged a wildcat strike on May 13 to protest the tax proposals. On May 16, following passage of the bill, most docks, shipyards, breweries, newspapers, and industries were shut down by strikes. About 60,000 people took part in day-long demonstrations outside Christiansborg Palace in Copenhagen and smaller numbers marched in provincial towns.

Rising Unemployment. The May 15 tax package did not cure the government's political and economic ills, however. Measures to combat unemployment, running at 3.9 per cent, were announced on August 20. The government raised the ceiling on borrowing and reactivated certain public sector investment projects. On September 20, the government survived by narrow margins four no-confidence motions on a finance bill that reduces income taxes in 1975 by $1.35 billion. But on December 5, Hartling dissolved parliament and set an election for Jan. 9, 1975, to seek the people's views on plans to meet the economic crisis. These plans include a one-year wage freeze and price controls.

Party Leader Charged. Mogens Glistrup, leader of the antitax Progress Party, was charged on October 7 with fraud and tax evasion. Traditionally, Folketing members are immune from prosecution. Glistrup, a lawyer, had been under investigation by police for two years. He had stated on television that it was everyone's duty to pay as little in taxes as possible, because Danish taxes were unreasonably high. As a tax expert, he would be neglecting his duty if he paid tax himself, he said.   Kenneth Brown

See also EUROPE (Facts in Brief Table).

Striking Danish workers rally in front of Christiansborg Palace in Copenhagen after parliament passed a bill increasing sales taxes.

DENTISTRY. An appropriation by the Massachusetts legislature will eventually add Boston to the list of major cities in the United States having fluoridated water supplies. As planned by the Metropolitan District Commission, which serves 33 Boston communities, the move will swell the ranks of those receiving fluoridated water by 2 million persons. More than 100 million Americans now reside in communities with fluoridated water supplies. Only the water supplies of Los Angeles and Houston remain unfluoridated among the major cities, but efforts to start are underway in both cities.

Private Practice and National Health. Although the design of a national health insurance program remained uncertain in 1974, American Dental Association (ADA) officials maintained that the fee-for-service, private-practice system should be an integral part of any national health insurance proposal adopted by Congress. They said that its effectiveness has been demonstrated in the rapidly growing field of dental insurance. Such dental coverage was expanded on October 1 when 2.75 million members of the United Automobile Workers—who work for the auto industry's "Big Three," Ford Motor Company, General Motors Corporation, and Chrysler Corporation—were added to the ranks of insured.

Threat to Dental Education. The ADA warned in September that, unless Congress acts swiftly, the future of many of the nation's dental schools may be at stake. The quality of dental education may suffer greatly if the expired Health Manpower Education Act is not replaced, said the ADA, because the cost of dental education has been increasing steadily.

Immunity and Periodontal Disease. An immune mechanism involving the body's lymphocyte (white blood cell) system may play an important role in the development of periodontal (gum) disease, a Mayo Clinic dental researcher has suggested. Periodontal disease is a destructive process affecting the supporting structures surrounding the teeth, including the gums. More teeth are lost in adults because of this disorder than from any other cause. David L. Movius of Rochester, Minn., reported to the annual meeting of the International Association for Dental Research that gum-tissue cells incubated with lymphocytes from patients suffering from gum disease did not survive as well as similar cells incubated with lymphocytes from healthy patients.

Young Musicians and Dental Problems. Parents whose children plan to take up a musical instrument should consult the family dentist, warned New York dentist Ernest Herman. The wrong instrument for a particular child may lead to dental problems ranging from faulty alignment and tooth mobility to gum problems. Even stringed instruments can have an impact on the player's dental condition. In some violin players, the constant pressure on the jaw can lead to faulty bite. Lou Joseph

297

DETROIT. The Supreme Court of the United States on July 25, 1974, overturned a lower court order requiring school busing between Detroit and its suburbs. The landmark ruling stated that the U.S. District Court had erred in ordering a desegregation plan embracing Detroit and suburban school districts and ordered the lower court to formulate a plan for the central city only.

In its decision, the High Court said that multidistrict integration could be imposed only when all districts involved operate segregated school systems. The high court found no evidence that the Detroit suburban schools were not integrated.

Organized Crime. In February, a month after taking office, Detroit's first black mayor, Coleman A. Young, asserted that Detroit was involved in a gangland war "that makes the heyday of Al Capone look like small potatoes." The violence revolved around narcotics traffic and was partly responsible for giving Detroit the nation's highest homicide rate, 44.5 homicides per 100,000 citizens.

According to police records, the murder rate increased throughout the year, spurred on by a number of multiple, gang-style killings. Police records also showed a 20 per cent increase in vandalism during the first four months of 1974. To help combat street crime, Mayor Young planned a network of police ministations in high-crime areas. The first ministation opened in a housing project in May. Federal Bureau of Investigation reports released on October 4 showed that all serious crime in Detroit increased 13.5 per cent during the first half of the year.

A private study of the criminal justice systems of Baltimore, Chicago, and Detroit, issued by two political scientists in September, showed that Detroit courts in 1972 convicted an average rate of 57.5 per cent of persons accused of felonies but sent only 34.8 per cent of them to jail. Detroit was the most lenient of the three cities in sentencing convicted felons and also had the highest crime rate.

Racial Minorities in Detroit were receiving an appropriate share of jobs in city government, according to figures reported by the U.S. Equal Employment Opportunity Commission in October. Minorities, which make up 45.5 per cent of the city's population, held 46.3 per cent of the city's jobs.

Several hundred students battled each other at a Detroit high school on May 29 in what police described as a racial disorder. One student was stabbed, and classes were temporarily suspended.

The Cost of Living in Detroit rose 10.8 per cent between June, 1973, and June, 1974. Food costs rose 15.2 per cent during that period. However, wages of the average factory worker increased only 3.4 per cent during the year ending in July. Even so, blue-collar workers earned an above-average annual salary of $13,363.   James M. Banovetz

DICTIONARY. See Section Six, DICTIONARY SUPPLEMENT.

DISASTERS and human tragedy struck with especially brutal force in Bangladesh during 1974. Floods inundated half the country in July and August, killing at least 2,000 persons. In the wake of the floods, cholera and smallpox swept the nation, killing thousands more. Because the land was covered with water, crop planting was delayed, and this led to mass starvation. By October, in Dacca alone, welfare workers were finding the bodies of at least 25 famine victims a day in the streets. A World Health Organization official expected the nation's death toll would surpass 100,000 for the year.

Other major disasters in 1974 included the following:

Aircraft Crashes

Jan. 1—Turin, Italy. An Italian jet crashed while attempting to land in rain and fog, killing 39 persons.

Jan. 10—Southern Colombia. All 40 persons aboard were killed when an airliner crashed near the Andes.

Jan. 26—Izmir, Turkey. A jetliner crashed during take-off, killing 63 of the 73 persons aboard.

Jan. 31—Pago Pago, American Samoa. Ninety-two persons were killed when a Pan American World Airways (PanAm) jet, carrying 101 passengers and crew members, crashed during a landing attempt.

March 3—Near Paris. A Turkish DC-10 jumbo jet exploded and crashed in a forest when a cargo door blew off soon after take-off from Orly Airport. All 346 persons aboard were killed, making it the worst disaster in aviation history.

March 8—Hanoi, North Vietnam. Sixteen Algerian newsmen were killed when their plane crashed.

March 13—Near Bishop, Calif. A charter plane carrying television actors and a camera crew crashed into a mountain ridge, killing all 36 persons aboard.

March 15—Teheran, Iran. A Danish airliner caught fire on a runway, killing 16 persons.

April 4—Francistown, Botswana. A plane transporting gold miners to Malawi caught fire and crashed, killing 77 of the 83 persons aboard.

April 22—Near Denpasar, Indonesia. All 107 passengers and crew members of a PanAm jet were killed when the plane crashed on the island of Bali.

April 27—Leningrad, Russia. Western observers reported that an Ilyushin 18 turboprop crashed after take-off, killing at least 108 persons.

May 2—Andes Mountains, Ecuador. An airliner crashed in the mountains, killing 22 persons.

June 9—Near Cúcuta, Colombia. An airplane crashed in a mountainous area, killing all 43 persons aboard.

June 28—Northwestern Cambodia. An airliner crashed during take-off, killing 20 of the 25 persons aboard.

Aug. 12—Near Ouagadougou, Upper Volta. A Mali airliner crashed, killing 47 persons.

Aug. 14—Off Caracas, Venezuela. A Venezuelan airliner crashed on Margarita Island in the Caribbean Sea, killing 49 of the 50 tourists and crew members aboard.

Aug. 18—Near Kisangani, Zaire. A Zaire military transport crashed, killing 35 persons.

Sept. 7—Telukbetung, Indonesia. Thirty-five of the 39 persons aboard an Indonesian airliner were killed when high winds blew the landing plane off its runway-approach course and into an abandoned house.

Sept. 8—Ionian Sea off Greece. A Trans World Airlines (TWA) jet crashed, killing all 88 persons aboard.

Sept. 11—Charlotte, S.C. An Eastern Airlines jet crashed while attempting to land. Seventy-one of the 82 persons aboard were killed.

Sept. 18—Ponta Pora, Brazil. A military transport crashed, killing 22 Brazilian Army officers.

Survivors look for belongings amid the rubble of Choloma, Honduras, after Hurricane Fifi leveled the town and killed 8,000 in September.

Nov. 20—Nairobi, Kenya. A Boeing 747 jumbo jet crashed after take-off, killing 59 persons.

Dec. 1—Near Washington, D.C. A TWA jet crashed into a wooded hillside, killing all 92 persons aboard.

Dec. 4—Near Colombo, Sri Lanka. A jet carrying Moslem pilgrims crashed, killing 191 persons.

Dec. 12—South Vietnam. A military helicopter crashed, killing 54 soldiers.

Dec. 22—Maturín, Venezuela. A jetliner exploded after take-off, killing 77 persons.

Dec. 28—Northern Guatemala. Twenty-four persons died when a chartered plane crashed during take-off.

Bus and Truck Crashes

Jan. 24—Central Taiwan. A bus skidded off a mountain road, killing 49 passengers.

May 21—Southeastern Mexico. A tour bus plunged into the Carizales River, killing at least 32 persons.

July 9—Multan, Pakistan. Two buses collided and burned, killing 22 persons and injuring 24 others.

July 21—Near New Delhi, India. A truck rolled down a hill about 250 miles (400 kilometers) north of New Delhi, killing 38.

July 28—Near Belém, Brazil. A bus and a truck collided head-on, killing 69 persons.

July 29—San Mateo Atenco, Mexico. At least 29 persons were killed when a bus ran into a bridge.

August 11—Western Turkey. Two buses collided on the highway linking Ankara and Istanbul. Twenty-one persons were killed and 41 injured.

Dec. 9—Zambia. A bus accident killed 26 persons.

DISASTERS

Earthquakes

May 9—Central Japan. A violent earthquake killed 30 persons and injured 77 others.

Oct. 3—Lima, Peru. A violent earthquake killed 73 persons and injured more than 2,000 others.

Dec. 28-29—Near Rawalpindi, Pakistan. Earthquake destroyed 11 villages, killing about 5,300 persons.

Explosions and Fires

Jan. 23—Heusden, Belgium. Fire in a Roman Catholic school dormitory killed 23 boys.

Feb. 1—São Paulo, Brazil. A blaze in a new, 25-story bank building killed 189 persons.

June 1—Flixborough, England. Thirty persons were killed by an explosion in a chemical plant.

June 17—Lahore, Pakistan. Fire in a downtown building killed at least 40 persons.

June 30—Port Chester, N.Y. A flash fire set in a singles bar killed 24 patrons and injured 32 others.

Sept. 5—Southern Nigeria. Fire aboard a passenger-carrying riverboat killed 67 persons.

Nov. 3—Seoul, South Korea. Fire raged through a hotel, killing 88 persons.

Dec. 15—Nottingham, England. Fire in a nursing home killed 18 residents.

Floods

Feb. 17—Northwestern Argentina. At least 60 persons drowned when floodwaters inundated the area.

March 27—Tubarão, Brazil. Floods almost destroyed this city in southern Brazil, killing up to 1,500 persons.

July 4—Bombay, India. Forty-two persons were killed by a flood caused by heavy rainfall.

July and August—Bangladesh. Floodwaters inundated half the nation, killing more than 2,000 persons.

Aug. 11—India. About 260 persons were reported killed by floods caused by six weeks of rain.

Aug. 21—Luzon, the Philippines. Officials reported 78 persons were killed by floods following monsoon rains.

Hurricanes, Tornadoes, and Other Storms

March 25—Southern Coast of Bangladesh. A storm along the Bay of Bengal killed some 300 persons.

April 3-4—Central and Southern United States. A series of 100 tornadoes struck an 11-state area, killing a total of 336 persons. Half the town of Xenia, Ohio, was destroyed and 30 residents were killed. Ten states were declared national disaster areas: Alabama (87 dead), Georgia (17 dead), Illinois (2 dead), Indiana (31 dead), Kentucky (88 dead), Michigan (3 dead), North Carolina (7 dead), Ohio (45 dead), Tennessee (53 dead), and West Virginia (1 dead).

June 8-10—Midwestern United States. A series of tornadoes and flash floods killed 28 persons.

June 11—Luzon, the Philippines. A tropical storm struck the main island, killing 71 persons.

July 6-7—Japan and South Korea. Typhoon Gilda swept across most of Japan and southern South Korea, killing at least 88 persons.

July 10—Michoacán State, Mexico. Officials reported that torrential rains killed 20 persons.

Aug. 15—Southern Caribbean Sea. Officials reported that 48 persons were killed by Tropical Storm Alma.

Aug. 15—West Bengal, India. A cyclone swept across the coastal area, killing at least 20 persons.

Sept. 18-19—Honduras. Honduran officials estimated that Hurricane Fifi killed between 7,500 and 8,000 persons and left more than 300,000 homeless.

Sept. 28—Taiwan. A typhoon sank a Panamanian freighter, killing 31 of the 34 crewmen aboard.

Rescuers examine the remains of a Turkish jumbo jet that crashed near Paris on March 3, killing 346 persons in the world's worst air disaster.

Rescue workers and soldiers search wreckage for bodies after a train derailed in Zagreb, Yugoslavia, killing 121 passengers on August 30.

Shipwrecks

Jan. 5—Off the Philippines. A ferryboat sank in stormy seas, killing 82 persons.

Jan. 17—The English Channel. The worst gales in 20 years sank two ships, killing 26 crewmen.

Feb. 22—Off Ch'ungmu, South Korea. Two South Korean naval recruits were killed and 157 others were missing and presumed dead after a tugboat on which they were being transported capsized.

Feb. 26—Gulf of Mexico. A Mexican naval tugboat sank, drowning 43 men.

April 21—Off Burma. An estimated 100 persons were killed when a fishing schooner sank.

May 1—Off Dacca, Bangladesh. A passenger boat capsized, drowning an estimated 250 persons.

Aug. 21—Off Taiwan. A freighter sank, killing 31 crewmen.

Aug. 29—Off Korea. Five boats carrying 59 fishermen disappeared during a storm, and the men were presumed dead.

Sept. 26—The Black Sea. A Russian destroyer caught fire and sank, killing an estimated 200 sailors.

Sept. 28—Off Hong Kong. A Panamanian freighter sank during a typhoon, killing 31 crewmen.

Train Wrecks

Feb. 21—Uttar Pradesh, India. More than 40 persons were killed when a freight train collided with a passenger train.

March 27—Near Lourenço Marques, Mozambique. A passenger train and a freight train collided head-on, killing 60 persons.

Aug. 30—Zagreb, Yugoslavia. A speeding express train careened off the track as it entered Zagreb station, killing 121 passengers and injuring 97 others.

Other Disasters

Feb. 17—Cairo, Egypt. Soccer fans broke through barricades, trying to enter an already full stadium. In the stampede, 49 persons were trampled to death and 47 others injured.

April 25—Andes Mountains, Peru. Massive landslides killed 250 persons. In addition, an entire village was buried, and its 500 residents were missing and presumed dead.

April 27—Near Tokyo, Japan. A mud slide caused by heavy rains killed 17 persons.

June 28—Near Bogotá, Colombia. A massive landslide covered a section of highway, burying more than 20 vehicles—including six buses filled with passengers—and killing at least 200 persons.

July 27—Near Colombo, Sri Lanka. Police reported that heavy rains caused a landslide that killed 27 persons.

Sept. 29—Outskirts of Medellín, Colombia. Officials reported that 90 persons were killed in a landslide.

Sept. 30—Near Medellín, Colombia. A landslide killed at least 50 persons. On October 6, about 30 others were killed by another landslide in the area.

Oct. 10—Near Manila, the Philippines. At least 18 workmen were killed when scaffolding around a building under construction in a suburb collapsed.

Dec. 5—Teheran, Iran. Sixteen persons were killed and 11 injured when the roof of the Teheran airport terminal collapsed after a 12-hour snowfall.

Dec. 25—Darwin, Australia. A cyclone that devastated the city killed at least 48 persons and left 20,000 homeless.

Dec. 27—Liévin, France. An explosion and fire in a coal mine killed 41 miners.   Darlene R. Stille

DOMINICAN REPUBLIC. See LATIN AMERICA.

DRUGS. The Turkish government decided on March 9, 1974, to end a three-year ban on the cultivation of opium poppies. The decision caused serious concern in the United States because of the prospect of a worldwide rise in heroin addiction. After months of negotiation and U.S. threats to withdraw all economic aid to Turkey, the Turkish government announced in September that it would adopt a new method of harvesting the opium poppy to prevent its being diverted into illegal drug traffic. The U.S. Department of State expressed pleasure at the decision. Under the new procedure, the Turkish government will collect the whole poppy pod rather than opium gum. Traditionally, the opium gum was gathered and sold by the farmers, and a portion of this gum was illegally diverted.

Hard-core heroin use in the United States in the early months of 1974 was down 60 per cent from the 1969 to 1971 peak, according to John Bartels, Jr., head of the U.S. Drug Enforcement Agency. He told the United Nations Commission on Narcotic Drugs that worldwide traffic in drugs had also dropped sharply. He attributed the situation to Turkey's ban on growing the opium poppy.

The Methadone Controversy continued. On June 7, a federal district judge in Washington, D.C., struck down the December, 1972, regulations of the Food and Drug Administration (FDA) that limited distribution of the drug to methadone-maintenance clinics and hospital pharmacies. Unless overturned on appeal, the ruling would force the FDA either to withdraw the drug from the market or to allow it to be distributed to any pharmacy. According to Grasty Crews, the general counsel for the White House's special action office for prevention of drug abuse, withdrawal of the drug from the market would "have to be ruled out," because more than 100,000 persons are on methadone-maintenance programs in the United States.

Rockefeller Law. Hearings on New York state's tough drug law began on September 1, the first anniversary of its passage. The law was drafted by Governor Nelson A. Rockefeller in 1973, and the hearings were before the Temporary State Commission to Evaluate the Drug Law. The consensus was that the harsh drug penalties—the stiffest in the nation—have not cut down the state's drug traffic and have not forced addicts voluntarily to seek treatment. Neither, as was predicted, have the jails been crowded with drug abusers. Drug arrests have actually declined. However, Special Prosecutor Frank J. Rogers claimed that the new law had helped him send 155 drug pushers to jail during the year.

Alcohol Use. The proportion of U.S. adults who drink alcoholic beverages was at an all-time high in 1974, according to a Gallup Poll report released on June 8. The findings were based on interviews with 1,543 adults over 18 years of age. Of those surveyed, 68 per cent said they drank—nearly 25 per cent of them to excess—and 12 per cent said liquor had been a cause of trouble in the family. The poll also showed that the increase in drinkers since 1939, when the first Gallup survey was made, has been twice as great among women as among men.

Criticism of the FDA. The FDA was criticized both for approving some new drugs considered dangerous by staff doctors and for rejecting others considered beneficial. A number of doctors testified before a Senate panel on August 16 that the FDA frequently suppresses unfavorable reports on new drugs and disciplines the doctors who draft them. On the other hand, an editorial in the August issue of the *Journal of the American Medical Association* criticized the agency for being slow to accept three new drugs that were found helpful in treating high blood pressure in Great Britain. Applications for the approval of the three drugs—bethanidine, debrisquine, and propranolol hydrochloride—were submitted to the FDA "years ago," the editorial stated, but one has been disapproved and the other two have not been acted on.

During the year the FDA recalled 51 brands of aerosol sprays containing vinyl chloride. The chemical, which is used as a propellant in aerosol sprays, has been associated with a rare form of liver cancer found among industrial workers. The products containing vinyl chloride include many brands of medicated vaporizers and hair sprays.   Mary E. Jessup

DYLAN, BOB (1941-   ), made his first concert tour in eight years in January and February, 1974. Dylan had performed in public only for special benefits since a near-fatal motorcycle accident in 1966. His fans packed the 40 performances he gave in 21 cities to hear his recent works as well as the folk songs he composed and sang in the early 1960s that voiced their youthful protest against social wrongs. Promoters estimated that more than 2 million ticket requests went unfilled.

Dylan was born Robert Zimmerman on May 24, 1941, in Duluth, Minn. (He changed his last name in 1962 to honor the late poet Dylan Thomas.) Raised in Hibbing, a mining town, he taught himself to play guitar, piano, autoharp, and harmonica by the time he was 15. He attended the University of Minnesota briefly in 1960, performing in a local coffee house. Leaving Minnesota in the fall of 1960, Dylan eventually arrived in New York City, where he performed in Greenwich Village coffee houses. By the summer of 1961, he had signed a recording contract. Acclaimed by music critics, his songs gained even wider popularity through recordings by such polished performers as Joan Baez.

Dylan was influenced by Negro folk, white country, and rhythm-and-blues singers, and he especially patterned his music after that of folk musician Woody Guthrie.   Robert K. Johnson

EARTHQUAKES. See DISASTERS.

Archbishop Iakovos symbolically knocks on the church door to open the 22nd Biennial Congress of Greek Orthodox Christians in Oak Lawn, Ill.

EASTERN ORTHODOX CHURCHES. The expulsion from Russia on Feb. 13, 1974, of novelist Alexander Solzhenitsyn provoked a crisis in the Eastern Orthodox churches under the Moscow Patriarchate. When Metropolitan Seraphim of Krutitzy, the auxiliary to Patriarch Pimen, officially condemned Solzhenitsyn, Metropolitan Anthony Bloom, the Patriarchal Exarch in Western Europe, and Archbishop Basil Krivoschein of Brussels protested in letters to British and Belgian newspapers. Metropolitan Anthony resigned as exarch, while remaining the head of the Patriarchal parishes in Great Britain. Metropolitan Nikodim of Leningrad was appointed the new exarch for the Patriarchal Dioceses in Western Europe.

An official delegation of the U.S. National Council of Churches visited Russia in August and held theological discussions with representatives of the Russian church. Russian churchmen, headed by Patriarch Pimen, planned to visit the United States in February, 1975.

In Greece, rule by the military junta and its downfall in July resulted in a chaotic situation within the Orthodox Church. Bishops were removed and replaced so that the Diocese of Thessalonika now has three bishops instead of one, two of whom were forcibly retired but are still recognized by some members of clergy and laity as the canonical heads of the diocese. In February, the Patriarch Elias of Antioch attended the Second Islamic Summit Conference held in Lahore, India.

In the United States, the Cyprus warfare, which began in July with the ouster of President Archbishop Makarios III, had profound repercussions in Greek-American communities. Archbishop Iakovos of the Greek Orthodox Archdiocese of North and South America led a campaign to influence the policies of the U.S. government, which the Greek community considered to favor Turkey, and a mobilization of Greek churches for support for Greek Cypriots.

Archbishop Iakovos was also instrumental in setting up the first social concerns agency for the Greek Orthodox Church in July. It is charged with developing a program of social action for the church's 2-million members in the United States and Canada.

In September, the Russian Orthodox Church Outside Russia, the ecclesiastical group that opposes the Moscow Patriarchate, held its third convention at the Holy Trinity Monastery in Jordanville, N.Y. The convention received a letter from Solzhenitsyn in which he called on the various Russian Orthodox groups in exile to "forget the past and think of the future," and to put an end to a half century of divisions. As a result of this appeal, the bishops issued letters to various other groups inviting them to discuss a renewal of friendly relations among the branches of Eastern Orthodoxy. Alexander Schmemann

See also RELIGION.

ECONOMICS

The world began 1974 in the grip of a fuel and energy shortage caused by the Arab oil embargo. The year ended with the world economy in the midst of what promised to be the longest recession since the end of World War II and with many countries suffering from the most serious peacetime inflation in this century. Widespread drought significantly reduced the output of both bread and feed grains, sending some countries to the brink of starvation. See AGRICULTURE; FOOD; POVERTY.

The United States lived through a year so full of contradictions that analysis is difficult and likely to be misleading. Comparisons with prior years can be made only with great care. What is surprising is not the relatively poor performance of the economy, but rather that it performed as well as it did in the face of a series of shocks and uncertainties.

What has most concerned American citizens and profoundly disturbed economists is the simultaneous worsening of both inflation and recession. It has been a matter of economic faith that inflation is checked by recession. When the two appear to move forward together, as in 1974, the concern is obvious. The phenomenon has given birth to a new word, *stagflation*, indicating a tendency for the economy to stagnate while prices still rise rapidly.

The gross national product (GNP) in the United States was almost $1.4 trillion in 1974, up from $1.295 trillion in 1973. But with prices of all goods and services 10.2 per cent higher, the real output dropped to $1.26 trillion, a fall of 2.2 per cent.

Real output began dropping in the first quarter of 1974, and businessmen and economists do not anticipate any marked recovery until at least the middle of 1975. If so, the 1974-1975 recession would be the longest in the United States since World War II. Especially hard hit have been the home-building industry, with new housing starts down 26 per cent to 1.5 million, and automobile production, with output down from 9.7 million cars to about 7.3-million, a drop of 24 per cent.

But this relatively gloomy picture ignores the fact that by the end of the year 85.2 million Americans were gainfully employed, and that the unemployment rate was 7.1 per cent. When this is compared with the depths of the Great Depression of 1929-1933, when more than 24 per cent of the labor force was out of work, it is apparent that the 1974 recession still falls well short of a major depression, and that the performance of the economy is spottily bad, rather than solidly bad.

Price Rises. By the end of the year, U.S. consumer prices had risen more than 12 per cent and the more broadly based GNP price deflator by 10.2

per cent. Wholesale prices, after rising rapidly during the early part of the year, declined somewhat in the closing months and ended the year about 20 per cent above the level of a year earlier.

A considerable part of the 1974 rise in prices, for the United States and other oil-importing countries, was caused by the Arab oil embargo and the effects of the subsequent price increases imposed by the oil-exporting nations. Also contributing was the rise in food prices, initially caused by a low carry-over of supplies from the previous year and helped along by a relatively poor crop year in the United States. Plantings were delayed by rains, and excessively dry weather throughout the summer and an early frost in September reduced crop sizes. But

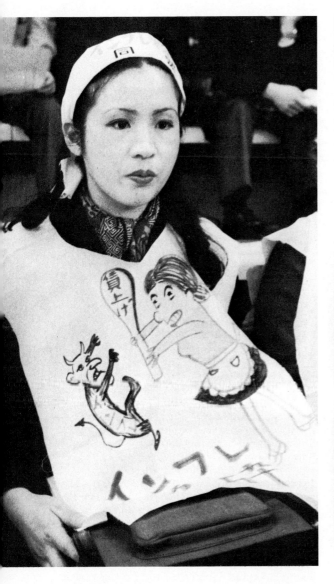

these elements accounted for only a relatively small portion of the total increase in prices, which showed an alarming tendency to rise across-the-board.

In an effort to choke off these increases, the U.S. Federal Reserve Board followed a restrictive monetary policy for most of the year. The money supply grew at an annual rate of only 6 per cent during the first nine months, though the rising unemployment rate in the final quarter led to some easing of the pressure. The net result was that the prime interest rate—the rate on loans made to top-ranked commercial customers—reached a record high of 12.25 per cent during July. By December, it had backed down to about 10 per cent, but this was still at a level that did little to expand home building.

Workers in Italy, Japan, and Great Britain were among those who used demonstrations and strikes to protest against rising prices.

Wage Settlements in the United States continued at high levels in an effort to keep up with the rising cost of living. The average increase in contracts negotiated during the second quarter was 10 per cent. This rose to 11.3 per cent during the third quarter. Even larger increases loomed ahead after the striking United Mine Workers settled in December for a three-year contract providing a 64 per cent boost in wages and benefits, with a 10 per cent pay boost the first year.

ECONOMICS

Soaring Consumer Prices

Percentage price increases for year ending on date indicated

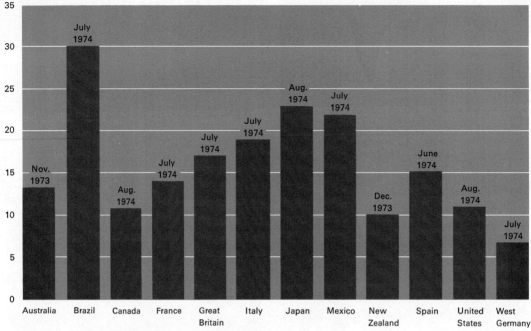

Source: *International Financial Statistics,* International Monetary Fund

Workers also sought to protect the dwindling purchasing power of their paychecks by bargaining for escalation clauses in their contracts. Such a clause provides an automatic increase in wages whenever the consumer price index rises by a given amount. During the first nine months of the year, more than 600,000 workers gained this coverage, bringing the total number of workers receiving such protection to more than 5 million.

Some economists view this situation as a prescription for permanent inflation. Every time prices move up, there is an upward adjustment of wages, which in turn is reflected in higher costs and higher prices. Even though such contracts cover only a small fraction of the work force, wages of all workers tend to reflect the increases. Social security payments also are geared to the cost of living. Other devices, such as "floating rate" mortgages and variable interest bonds or notes, also vary their payments according to changes in the cost of living or in interest rates.

Indexation. The advantages of pegging income payments and costs to the cost of living seem so obvious that some economists – most notably Milton Friedman of the University of Chicago – have seriously proposed that the system should be extended to a multitude of payments: government and private bond interest and capital, taxes, interest on savings and loan deposits, and a variety of long-

term contract payments. Such a system is known as *indexation.* This is a new word to most Americans, but it runs well back into the 1800s, when economists first proposed the idea to soften the impact of both inflation and deflation.

Other economists claim that the obvious advantages are offset not only by the built-in aspects of further inflation during a period of rapidly rising prices, but also by the enormous difficulties of instituting such a program for the economy as a whole.

Brazil has operated on such a system for more than 20 years, with some success in meeting an annual inflation rate ranging up to 25 per cent and more. But the example is scarcely appealing to most Americans. It involves massive government intervention in the entire economy to an extent that seems scarcely compatible with basic adherence to the U.S. free market system.

Furthermore, in the absence of Brazil's kind of direct controls, there is some doubt whether wages and prices would ever drop during a period of deflation. Workers covered by cost-of-living clauses have usually bargained successfully to get their past gains built into their wage base so that there is little prospect of a future decline. The political consequences and highly technical nature of indexation make it unlikely that it will be generally adopted, though such concepts may continue to appear in certain types of long-term contracts.

Wage and Price Controls. Congressional support increased toward the end of the year for giving the President stand-by authority to reimpose wage and price controls if inflation could not be checked otherwise. President Gerald R. Ford, however, continued to oppose controls. Although controls are politically appealing, the last U.S. experience with them, which ended in early 1974, showed that they can provide no permanent solution to the problems faced. To the extent that they are effective, they create distortions and shortages in the market place. And when they are relaxed, as they inevitably must be, prices surge upward as labor and business alike seek to correct the distortions.

No Simple Solutions. President Ford correctly called inflation "our number-one problem," and the Administration continued to emphasize the fight against inflation, even as the recession deepened. However, toward the end of the year, the Administration began taking more interest in ways of stimulating the economy. What makes inflation so alarming is the lack of ready or palatable solutions. The United States experience over the past decade seems to indicate that, when offered a choice between inflation and unemployment, most people will select inflation while at the same time complaining bitterly about high prices. There is apparently no general awareness that wages cannot increase more rapidly than productivity (which grew about 3 per cent in 1974) without forcing prices up or profits down. Since profits remain the major source of the new machinery and equipment necessary to increase productivity, wage increases continue to lead to further price increases.

The principal sufferers from unemployment at the present time appear to be minority groups and young, inexperienced workers, whose unemployment rates are from two to three times as high as the national average. As of November, only 3.3 per cent of married men were unemployed – though layoffs in the automobile industry doubtless increased that figure as the year ended.

Conflicting Pressures highlight all these issues. Efforts to produce a cleaner environment, for example, inevitably entail higher costs. Nearly 40 per cent of the increased prices for 1975 automobiles resulted from required antipollution and safety devices. Cleaner air will cost the utility industry billions of dollars over the next few years. Indeed, it threatens the use of the United States only remaining plentiful energy resource, coal, because there is yet no adequate way to reduce emissions from the high-sulfur fuel that makes up the bulk of the present U.S. coal supply. In the meantime, environmentalists steadfastly oppose the opening of new strip mines in Western states where a huge quantity of low-sulfur coal is waiting to be mined. Similar resistance to the rapid expansion of nuclear-fuel generating plants, largely on the grounds of alleged safety defects, hampers this method of expanding badly needed energy supplies.

More Vigorous Enforcement of the antitrust laws, with tougher prosecution of those believed to be engaged in price fixing or other monopolistic practices, is seen as one line of attack on rising prices. One sign of this was the filing of a suit in late November against the American Telephone and Telegraph Company seeking to divest the largest of all American corporations of its manufacturing subsidiary and of its long-lines division. Both economists and businessmen were divided over whether this would mean lower telephone rates or merely poorer service. But all the experts anticipated that it would take many years to fight all the legal issues and that no immediate impact on inflation could be expected. However, tangible evidence of stricter enforcement may deter collusive price-fixing efforts on the part of others. See TELEPHONE.

A more promising approach appeared immediately after Thanksgiving when several of the large food retailers indicated they were freezing prices on many food items. Voluntary action of this nature may discourage the expectation of ever-rising inflation and thus cool the upward price spiral.

The Good Side. Despite all the problems, the performance of the U.S. economy was not all dreary. More than 85 million Americans were at work during the closing months of the year, down somewhat from a record high 86.5 million in September. Weekly earnings of factory workers averaged $182.50 in October, and hourly earnings were at a record $4.55. Consumer spending was at a record $900 billion. Personal savings, for the first three quarters, were running at an annual rate of $72 billion, down slightly from the record $74.4-billion saved in 1973.

Investors fared less well, in spite of record corporate profits. Stock prices were down more than 20 per cent from their levels at the beginning of the year, though profits rose by 20 per cent to about $87 billion. However, a large part of this figure was made up of inventory profits – the rising value of inventories caused by inflation.

International Growth. The twin specters of inflation and recession bedeviled other countries as well as the United States. Growth rates in all major countries fell sharply from their buoyant 1973 levels, and, in light of inflation, all declined in real output. Growth rates for the first half of the year were 4.7 per cent in France, 2.1 per cent in Germany, 2.4 per cent in Italy, and 5.6 per cent in Canada. Great Britain declined 1.9 per cent, and Japan fell 8.1 per cent.

Most countries also experienced the soaring wage rates that have contributed to choking inflation, with wage increases ranging up to 30.8 per cent in the first half. Even more rapid rises occurred in the second half of the year.

Selected Key U.S. Economic Indicators

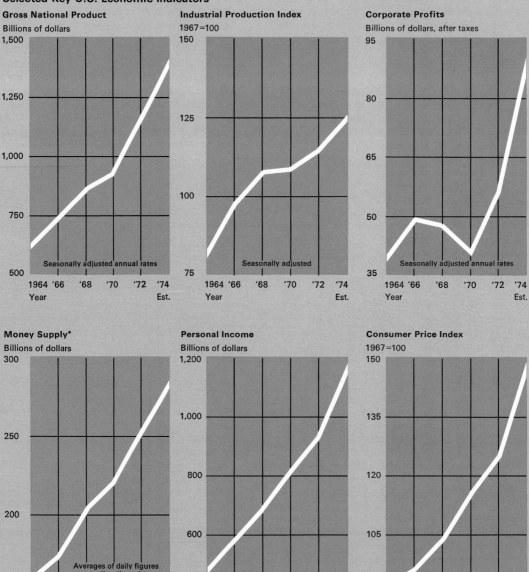

Gross National Product
Billions of dollars

Seasonally adjusted annual rates

1964 '66 '68 '70 '72 '74
Year Est.

Industrial Production Index
1967=100

Seasonally adjusted

1964 '66 '68 '70 '72 '74
Year Est.

Corporate Profits
Billions of dollars, after taxes

Seasonally adjusted annual rates

1964 '66 '68 '70 '72 '74
Year Est.

Money Supply*
Billions of dollars

Averages of daily figures
seasonally adjusted
*Revised in 1970

1964 '66 '68 '70 '72 '74
Year Est.

Personal Income
Billions of dollars

Seasonally adjusted annual rates

1964 '66 '68 '70 '72 '74
Year Est.

Consumer Price Index
1967=100

All items

1964 '66 '68 '70 '72 '74
Year Est.

The most comprehensive measure of the nation's total output of goods and services is the *Gross National Product* (GNP). The GNP represents the dollar value in current prices of all goods and services plus the estimated value of certain imputed outputs, such as the rental value of owner-occupied dwellings. *Industrial Production Index* is a monthly measure of the physical output of manufacturing, mining, and utility industries. *Corporate Profits* are quarterly profit samplings from major industries. *Money Supply* measures the total amount of money in the economy in coin, currency, and demand deposits. *Personal Income* is current income received by persons (including nonprofit institutions and private trust funds) before personal taxes. *Consumer Price Index* (CPI) is a monthly measure of changes in the prices of goods and services consumed by urban families and individuals. CPI includes about 300 goods and services. All 1974 figures are *Year Book* estimates.

World Inflation. The inflation that gripped the entire industrialized world threatened the economic stability of many countries. The inflation rate in Great Britain reached 20 per cent by the end of the year. Australian prices also were up 20 per cent, while New Zealand posted a 15 per cent rate. Canada reached 12 per cent in November. Consumer prices in France have been rising by more than 14 per cent, in Italy by 17 per cent, and in Japan by 24 per cent. The rates were even higher in the less developed areas of the world, with the pace set by Chile's 600 per cent increase at midyear.

Only West Germany among the major powers escaped the ravages of double-digit inflation. Yet, its rate of 7 per cent was high for a country that has prided itself since 1950 on maintaining virtually stable price levels. But in mid-December, West Germany dropped its anti-inflation program and turned its attention to fighting unemployment and recession. The new program will increase unemployment benefits and government spending and help unemployed persons find jobs. Stimulation of the West German economy, the strongest in Europe, is expected to bolster all of Europe.

Britain's Economy worsened during the year as the country fought a losing battle against chronic inflation and an immense trade deficit. The trade deficit in November was $1.3 billion, the worst in British history and up sharply from October. The oil picture improved, but trade in other products fell off. Britain's trade deficit for the year was $12.2 billion, possibly the world's highest.

Current government strategy is to try to head off recession and curtail unemployment through economic stimulation. But many businessmen and economists believe that curbing inflation should be the nation's first priority and that some increase in unemployment must be accepted as a necessary by-product. Business leaders grew increasingly critical of the government's economic policies in 1974, and unions freely ignored the "social contract" under which they agreed to moderate wage demands. A run on the pound began in mid-December and was expected to continue, possibly dropping its value as low as $2 in 1975.

Balance of Payments. The impact of the oil embargo and the high cost of food was minimal in the United States compared with the rest of the world. The U.S. basic balance of payments was expected to show a deficit of $6 billion or more for 1974. This was up from the 1973 deficit of $1 billion, but far less than the $11 billion deficit in 1972. After achieving a small surplus in 1973, the balance of trade again fell, showing a deficit of about $3-billion in 1974, primarily due to the cost of oil.

The balance-of-payments picture might have been much worse if the oil-exporting countries had not begun to invest heavily in the United States, considering it a safe place for their foreign reserve holdings, which have spiraled upward as a result of the prices set for their crude oil.

By contrast, Italy approached bankruptcy. It was unable to pay for needed oil imports, and only a substantial loan from its European partners enabled it to maintain even a semblance of solvency.

Long-Range Solutions to international balance-of-payments problems are merely in the discussion stage. At current price levels, oil-exporting countries will be achieving surpluses of from $50 billion to $60 billion annually, most of which will come from the industrialized world. Large portions of that will be reinvested in other countries, but there is no likelihood that such reinvestment will be distributed among the oil-importing nations in proportion to their oil purchases. To prevent any importing nation from being forced to exhaust its reserves to pay for energy, it has been proposed that the industrial nations establish a fund to aid countries experiencing serious payments problems.

The long-run success of any such venture would depend on the ability of all countries to attract a proportionate amount of Arab capital investment, or to achieve other compensating shifts in exports and imports. Unless this occurred, the fund would eventually be exhausted by those countries unable to offset oil imports.

Negotiating such an agreement will not be easy, but it is a measure of the extent of the oil crisis that the proposal was even made. At the best, Western Europe cannot expect self-sufficiency in energy for at least a decade, and many believe that even the United States cannot hope to achieve relative independence from Arab oil imports much before 1982.

Looking Ahead. As 1974 ended, the entire industrial world was gripped in a recession, serious in such countries as Britain and Italy and at least more than mildly bothering in the others. Such an unusual simultaneous decline had not occurred since World War II. It provoked some fears that the world might be on the brink of a depression similar to the one that gripped it from 1929 to 1933.

Most economists believe, however, that the improved monetary cooperation and institutions forged since 1950 will prevent such catastrophe and that 1975 could witness a return to the upward movement that has characterized the post-World War II period. For some countries, such as Britain and Italy, the road back to stability and prosperity may be long and bumpy. For others, such as West Germany, Canada, and the United States, an upturn seems possible no later than September, 1975. By then, the recession will have lasted 21 months, easily twice the average length of all other recent downward movements.   Warren W. Shearer

See also articles on individual countries; BANKS AND BANKING; ENERGY; INTERNATIONAL TRADE AND FINANCE; LABOR; PETROLEUM AND GAS; Section One, FOCUS ON THE ECONOMY.

ECUADOR. President Guillermo Rodriguez Lara's military government made it plain in 1974 that it intended to remain in power. On July 11, Rodriguez Lara suspended all political activities, including elections, for five years. He indicated that this would enable his administration to carry out a national development program. However, two opposition groups, the National Velasquista Federation and the Conservative Party, made it clear that they opposed the move, and in a secret national congress held on August 10, the federation announced it would pursue a policy of "belligerent and combative opposition" to the military regime and its policies. It was also reported that the congress had agreed to call on the Inter-American Commission on Human Rights of the Organization of American States to verify "violations of individual rights" allegedly being committed by the regime. However, as differences between conservatives and the economic nationalists in the high command surfaced, Rodriguez Lara finally came down on the side of the former, who supported a "Brazilian" policy of encouraging foreign investment.

Another Key Political Issue involved the treatment of the U.S. oil companies operating in Ecuador. On June 6, the state oil company took over a 25 per cent share of the Texaco-Gulf consortium operating in the northeastern jungle region. In so doing, it acquired one-fourth of the consortium's daily production of 210,000 barrels of crude oil, and it was expected that it would eventually acquire the controlling interest. Under the strongly nationalistic minister of energy, Gustavo Jarrín Ampudia, taxes on the oil companies were raised until Ecuador was taking more than 80 per cent of their gross income. However, in a major Cabinet reshuffle in November, Jarrín was replaced by Luis Salazar Landeta, a less political figure, and a number of left wing officials in the state oil consortium were removed.

Considerable Unrest was the result of Ecuador's 23 per cent inflation. On April 25, price increases and a severe shortage of such staples as sugar, corn, potatoes, and rice led housewives in Quito to stage a protest demonstration. Police were called to disperse the demonstrators, who were joined by students. On August 13, students in Quito went on a three-day spree of rioting to protest a bus-fare increase. Under pressure, Rodriguez Lara rescinded the increase.

Agriculture also continued to lag behind, partly because of confused direction; there had been five ministers of agriculture in 2½ years. Despite its rapidly increasing oil revenues, Ecuador continued to solicit foreign credits. One of these was a loan of $23.2 million granted by the World Bank for a water-supply project in Guayaquil. Also being planned was a new deepwater port at Posorja, about 35 miles (56 kilometers) southwest of Guayaquil. Robert Moss

See also LATIN AMERICA (Facts in Brief Table).

EDUCATION in the United States in 1974 faced critical problems arising from inflation of costs and deflation of enrollments. Economic uncertainties and a tightening job market shifted emphasis from academic concerns to specialized studies with greater promise of future employment. In the elementary schools, there was a marked trend back to the traditional concern with the "three R's."

In higher education, the new career orientation increased admission pressures on professional schools, particularly in law and medicine. Interest increased in journalism as well, possibly as a result of the media's role in the Watergate disclosures. After several years of declining enrollments, engineering schools also staged a comeback. In contrast, history enrollments declined by 12 per cent, following earlier, similar drops in foreign languages.

Conservative trends were also seen in greater competition for high grades, and a new interest in studies related to ethical and religious values. After a decade during which required courses in undergraduate education had been greatly reduced by the reforms that followed the student revolts of the 1960s, new programs across the country–from Berkeley, Calif., to Brooklyn College in New York City –re-emphasized broad general studies for freshmen and sophomores.

Total Enrollment in American schools and colleges declined for the second successive year, after almost three decades of constant growth. Although high school and college enrollments continued to increase, a drop of more than 700,000 in the elementary schools–following a 600,000 decline the year before–turned the overall enrollment curve down. At the start of the school year, communities that only a short time before had struggled with double sessions and lack of space actually had to cope with too much room for too few children. Some schools were shut down. Many colleges, overextended as a result of excessively optimistic enrollment forecasts, had fewer students than they could accommodate. High tuition costs, at a time of inflationary pressure on family budgets, turned increasing numbers from expensive private colleges and universities to relatively low-cost public institutions.

Campuses had an estimated 600,000 vacant places, even though top-ranked colleges still had to turn away some applicants. Many admissions offices resorted to extensive mailings to solicit interest, particularly among candidates with high academic achievements. For the first time, 400 colleges initiated a mass-recruiting effort by setting up booths during a college fair in New York City's Coliseum.

Busing and Books. While financial concern deepened, the general mood in the schools and colleges was quiet. There were fewer teachers' strikes than in previous years. The 20th anniversary of the 1954 ruling by the Supreme Court of the United States against school segregation was marked by declining controversy over school busing. An exception to that trend was Boston.

The trouble in Boston arose after a U.S. District Court ruling in June that the city integrate 94,000 public school students by busing. Violence marred the start of busing in September, and about 30,000 students stayed home on the first day of school. On October 15, Governor Francis W. Sargent of Massachusetts mobilized two National Guard military police units. The crisis continued through the year as the Boston school board refused to comply with a court order to desegregate. See BOSTON.

In Kanawha County, around Charleston, W. Va., schools were closed for several days in September amid sometimes violent protests against "filthy," "Godless," and "un-American" textbooks. The use of the language arts textbooks, which contain works by many contemporary authors, was generally supported by teachers. Under an agreement between county school officials and the textbook critics, led by several fundamentalist ministers, the books were withdrawn for review by a citizens' committee. See Section One, FOCUS ON EDUCATION.

Teachers and Enrollment. There were 3 million teachers at all levels of U.S. education, including 600,000 in colleges and universities. About 400,000 of the total were employed in private schools, half of them in higher education. There was still a substantial surplus of teachers, particularly in such areas as English and history. The National Education Association (NEA) reported a 1973-1974 supply of 234,550 newly graduated teachers but a demand for only 111,300.

The average teacher's salary for the 1973-1974 school year was $11,199 at all public school levels, and $10,337 for elementary-school teachers, a gain of about 4.7 per cent over the previous year. Averages ranged from Mississippi's $7,457 to Alaska's $15,547.

In higher education, the American Association of University Professors reported that faculty salaries rose 5.9 per cent in the 1973-74 academic year. But, for the first time in the history of the association's annual survey, the professors' purchasing power declined when measured against the increase in the cost of living. The Graduate Center of the City University of New York led the field with an average salary of $32,090, followed by the university's City College, at $26,209. Average pay at the nation's predominantly black colleges remained 10 per cent less.

The total enrollment in public and private institutions declined to 58.6 million in 1974-1975 from about 59 million the preceding year. The elementary grades (kindergarten through grade 8) enrolled 34.4 million, with 30.7 million in public schools. High schools (grades 9 through 12) enrolled

Louise Day Hicks, center, Boston City Council member, leads a march to the Massachusetts State House to protest against school busing.

15.6 million, with 14.3 million in public schools, an increase of 225,000 over the previous year.

The 1975 high school graduating class is expected to total slightly more than 3.1 million and will be the largest graduating class in the history of American education. An estimated 950,000 bachelor's degrees, 50,000 first professional degrees, 270,000 master's degrees, and 40,000 doctorates will be conferred during the academic year.

According to the United States Office of Education, education will be the principal occupation, as learners or teachers, of 29 per cent of the population, making it the nation's largest enterprise, both in the number of persons involved and in total expenditures. Moreover, an estimated 75 per cent of the 16- and 17-year age group will graduate from high school; 48 per cent of this group will enter an institution of higher learning; 25 per cent will earn a bachelor's degree; and 8 per cent and 1.5 per cent, respectively, will gain master's and doctor's degrees.

Education Expenditures at all levels in 1974-1975 were estimated by the Office of Education at $108-billion from local, state, and federal sources, compared with $97 billion the previous year. However, the increase is attributable to inflation rather than to growing support. About $68 billion of the total will be spent for elementary and high schools, with $6 billion of that amount going to private schools.

The $40-billion total for higher education represents $27 billion for public schools and $13 billion for private institutions. National educational expenditure remains fixed at just below 8 per cent of the gross national product. The average per-pupil outlay was $1,121, an 8.3 per cent increase over the previous year.

Teachers' Unions. The two largest U.S. teacher organizations—the NEA with 1.4 million members and the American Federation of Teachers (AFT) with about 400,000 members—failed to reconcile their differences and abruptly called off their merger talks. The AFT is affiliated with the American Federation of Labor and Congress of Industrial Organizations (AFL-CIO), and the AFT leadership's demand that all members of a merged organization also affiliate with the AFL-CIO was the major roadblock to agreement.

Underscoring the close relationship between the AFT and the AFL-CIO, Albert Shanker, president of New York's United Federation of Teachers, was elected national head of AFT shortly after he had been named a vice-president of the AFL-CIO. Shanker is also co-president of United Teachers of New York, the largest existing merger of NEA and AFL-CIO affiliates, with a membership of more than 200,000. The NEA is headed by Terry Herndon, a 35-year-old former Michigan teacher. Both

Compensatory education techniques, designed to help slow learners catch up with other children, are beginning to pay off in many U.S. schools.

men insist that eventual merger is in the teachers' interests.

The AFT leaders announced that they will give top priority to organizing college professors. An estimated 35,000 higher-education faculty members are union members.

Court Rulings. In a 5 to 4 ruling, the U.S. Supreme Court held in July that the Detroit school district, with 67 per cent of its enrollment black, could not be ordered to consolidate with the surrounding suburban districts in order to achieve better integration. Stressing local control of public education, it returned the case to the lower courts to seek remedies within the city's confines.

In another case involving questions of race in higher education, the court held in a 5 to 4 decision in April that a white student's complaint of discrimination against the University of Washington was moot because the student, attending the institution's law school under a special court order, was about to graduate. The landmark case was brought by Marco DeFunis, Jr., a Phi Beta Kappa Washington graduate. He charged discrimination when the law school rejected his application while admitting a number of black candidates with lower scores. In a widely noted dissent, Justice William O. Douglas argued that, while it is proper for a university to consider a student's personal background and past deprivations, it is unconstitutional to give preferential treatment solely on the basis of race.

Women's Rights. The Department of Health, Education, and Welfare (HEW) issued guidelines, to be implemented in the 1975-1976 academic year, that would bar sex discrimination in admission to vocational schools, high schools, and graduate schools. The order would not affect private women's colleges, but it would ban existing practices that limit home economics instruction to girls and shop courses to boys. It would also reduce sex discrimination in the administration and financing of athletic programs.

Other Developments. President Gerald R. Ford approved the omnibus school aid bill on August 21, authorizing a $25-billion expenditure over a four-year period for elementary and secondary schools. The measure is essentially a continuation of the Elementary and Secondary Education Act of 1965. In a major new provision, the law contains a "right to privacy" clause that gives students and parents the right to inspect their own and their children's school records and prohibits the release of such material without written consent by the interested parties, except for specified educational purposes.

A school-busing provision, included in the aid bill after much controversy, prohibits busing children beyond the school closest or next closest to their homes unless a court holds that the failure to bus a greater distance would violate the constitutional rights of the child. Fred M. Hechinger

EGYPT. The national euphoria released by military successes in the October, 1973, war with Israel carried over into 1974. The cease-fire agreement that ended fighting between Egyptian and Israeli forces along the Suez Canal in January added more laurels to President Anwar al-Sadat's crown. As Israeli forces withdrew from parts of occupied Egyptian territory, Sadat became a greater national hero than the late President Gamal Abdel Nasser.

With his popular mandate seemingly assured, Sadat started to liberalize and revitalize Egyptian society. An amnesty bill announced on January 28 applied to all political prisoners jailed during the Nasser and Sadat regimes. Among those released were journalist Mustafa Amin, sentenced in 1966 as a U.S. spy, and General Mahmoud Fawzi, leader of an attempt to overthrow Sadat in 1971. Amin's twin brother, Ali, subsequently returned from political exile and became editor of al-Ahram, Egypt's official newspaper, when editor Mohammed Heykal, a Nasser confidant, was dismissed for criticizing Sadat's policies. Press censorship ended on February 9. In November, Egyptian newspapers won the right to publish criticism of government mismanagement and corruption.

Guerrilla Attack. Liberalism was not without its risks. An opposition group calling itself the Islamic Liberation Organization attacked the Cairo Military Technical Academy on April 18. Eleven persons were killed and 27 injured in the attack, and 80 guerrillas were arrested.

The group claimed it planned to kidnap Sadat and proclaim a universal Islamic community. Sadat accused Libya of financing the plot. In a Cabinet realignment on April 25, the Ministry of Libyan Affairs was abolished.

Relations with Russia cooled. Although Russia pledged a $50-million loan on October 29, it delayed promised arms deliveries. The United States gained influence, in contrast; diplomatic relations were restored in February after a seven-year break. President Richard M. Nixon received a tumultuous reception in Egypt in June and pledged $250 million in aid, including a nuclear reactor. The aid bill passed the Senate in December. The October Arab summit conference in Rabat, Morocco, voted Egypt $1 billion in aid, and in November, Saudi Arabia approved $160 million for economic projects.

Yet Egypt's economic future remained clouded. In April, the government acknowledged that real economic growth had averaged only 4 per cent a year since 1967. But a new oil field with an estimated 600 million barrels was discovered in March in the Gulf of Suez. Clearing of the Suez Canal went ahead, and the canal was expected to be open early in 1975. The government announced in May that 61 per cent of the Russian loans for the Aswan High Dam had been repaid. William Spencer

See also MIDDLE EAST (Facts in Brief Table).

ELECTIONS

ELECTIONS. Inflation- and scandal-weary American voters went to the polls in November, 1974, and turned down most Republican candidates, giving the Democrats a sweeping victory. With gains of 43 seats in the U.S. House of Representatives and at least three seats in the Senate, the Democrats enjoyed their largest congressional majorities in a decade. One contested Senate race was unresolved at year-end. The Democrats also picked up four governorships, giving them a total of 36.

Despite the rebuff for the Republican Party, President Gerald R. Ford said that he "definitely" would be a candidate for a four-year term in 1976. Ford had campaigned in 20 states for Republican candidates, but most lost despite his aid.

Election specialists had predicted the trend far in advance of the November 5 balloting. Voters were disgruntled because of the steep rise in prices and mounting unemployment throughout 1974. The continuing revelations of the Watergate scandal, climaxed by President Richard M. Nixon's resignation on August 9, added to the poor climate for Republican candidates. Ford's pardon of Nixon on September 8 and his pre-election proposal for a 5 per cent surtax on middle and upper incomes also hurt Republican contenders. Many of the Republicans who managed to survive had separated themselves from the Nixon Administration on the Watergate case and from the Ford Administration's economic policy.

November winners include, *clockwise from left,* Ella Grasso, first woman governor of Connecticut; astronaut John Glenn, Ohio senator (watching TV returns with wife, Annie) ; Representative Edward Hutchinson (R., Mich.) of House Judiciary Committee, which held impeachment hearings ; James Longley, Independent governor of Maine.

Early Warning. The trend toward favoring Democrats was established early in the year in special elections called to fill six House seats left vacant by deaths or resignations. Riding the Watergate issue hard, Democrats won five of the six seats, all formerly held by Republicans.

The most startling upset occurred on February 18 in Grand Rapids, Mich., where Democrat Richard F. Vander Veen defeated a Republican candidate in a solidly Republican area for the congressional seat held by Ford before he became Vice-President. Democrats also won in Pennsylvania, Ohio, another Michigan district, and one of two special elections in California. The November elections confirmed all of these victories except one. In a rerun of their March race, Democratic Congressman Thomas A. Luken of Ohio lost to Republican Willis D. Gradison, Jr.

Primary Elections. The major surprise in the Democratic primary elections was the defeat on May 28 of Senator J. William Fulbright of Arkansas, chairman of the Senate Foreign Relations Committee, by Arkansas Governor Dale Bumpers. Fulbright, who had spent 30 years in the Senate, lost by a 2 to 1 margin.

Wayne L. Morse of Oregon on May 28 won the Democratic nomination to try to regain his Senate seat. But he died before the election. His replacement, state Senator Betty Roberts, lost to Republican Robert W. Packwood in November.

Former astronaut John H. Glenn defeated incumbent Senator Howard M. Metzenbaum in the Ohio Democratic primary on May 7. Glenn went on to win by a million votes against his Republican foe, Cleveland Mayor Ralph J. Perk.

Governors' Races. Democrats won 27 of the 35 governors' races, including eight of the 10 largest states. Republicans won seven governorships, and Maine elected an Independent, James B. Longley.

A young Democrat, 36-year-old Edmund G. Brown, Jr., won over Republican Houston I. Flourney to succeed retiring California Governor Ronald Reagan. California also elected Democrat Mervin Dymally, a black state senator, as lieutenant governor.

A little-known congressman from Brooklyn, Hugh L. Carey, united New York state Democrats to end 16 years of Republican control of the state house. Carey defeated Republican Governor Malcolm Wilson by an 800,000-vote margin.

Republican Governor William G. Milliken of Michigan barely defeated his Democratic opponent Sander M. Levin. Republican challenger James A. Rhodes managed a close victory over Democratic Governor John J. Gilligan in Ohio.

Democratic Congresswoman Ella T. Grasso won the governor's race in Connecticut. She is the first woman to win a state governorship on her own merits rather than by succeeding her husband.

Democratic state Senator Jerry Apodaca became the first Spanish-surnamed governor of New Mexico since 1921, and Democrat Raul H. Castro was elected governor of Arizona. Acting Governor George Ariyoshi, a Japanese American and a Democrat, was elected governor of Hawaii. Democrat David L. Boren, who used a broom as a symbol of clean politics, was swept into the Oklahoma governor's office.

In the Senate Races, Democrats retained all of their seats except one – in Nevada – and took at least three seats formerly held by Republicans. In New Hampshire, it first appeared that Republican Louis C. Wyman had defeated his Democratic opponent, John A. Durkin, in the Senate race. However, a recount showed that Durkin had won by 10 votes. Wyman challenged the recount, and the state Ballot Law Commission declared him the winner. Durkin, in turn, protested that the commission was controlled by Republicans, and the outcome of the election was undecided at the end of the year.

In Colorado, Republican Senator Peter H. Dominick was ousted by Democrat Gary W. Hart, who was national campaign director for Senator George S. McGovern (D., S. Dak.), the presidential candidate in 1972. McGovern himself, spending $1-million in sparsely settled South Dakota, was re-elected with 53 per cent of the vote over his Republican challenger, former Vietnam prisoner of war Leo K. Thorsness. In Kentucky, Democratic Governor Wendell H. Ford defeated the incumbent Senator Marlow W. Cook, a Republican.

Patrick J. Leahy scored a notable victory, becoming the first Democrat in more than a century to be elected to the Senate from Vermont. Leahy defeated Republican Congressman Richard W. Mallary to replace the retiring George D. Aiken.

Three Eastern Republicans with liberal to moderate voting records were re-elected: New York state's Jacob K. Javits, Maryland's Charles McC. Mathias, and Pennsylvania's Richard S. Schweiker. All three had endorsements from organized labor.

Former Republican National Chairman Senator Robert J. Dole survived a close re-election race in Kansas, while the party's elder statesman, Barry Goldwater of Arizona, easily won another Senate term. In Nevada, former Republican Governor Paul Laxalt took the seat of retiring Democratic Senator Alan Bible.

In the House, the Democrats scored their most significant gain in adding 43 seats to their majority. By replacing conservative Republicans with liberal or moderate Democrats, the voters moved the political center of gravity noticeably to the left in the new Congress.

A congressional race in Louisiana was rerun in January, 1975, after officials learned that voting machines had malfunctioned. Republican W. Henson Moore won the election.

Many senior Republican congressmen were defeated, including ranking Republicans William B. Widnall (N.J.) on the Banking Committee and William G. Bray (Ind.) on the Armed Services Committee. Both lost to young Democratic challengers. Some of Nixon's strongest supporters on the House Judiciary Committee were defeated, including Charles W. Sandman, Jr., and Joseph J. Maraziti, both of New Jersey.

The number of blacks in the House increased to 17 with the election of Harold E. Ford, a 29-year-old Democrat from Tennessee. Six women were elected to the House for the first time. This offset the departure of four others, bringing the total number of women in the House to 18.

In Other Contests. Democrat Susie Sharp, 67, was elected chief justice of the North Carolina Supreme Court, the first woman popularly elected to this post in any state. Janet Gray Hayes was elected mayor of San Jose, Calif., the first woman elected to run a city of more than 500,000 persons.

In a historic action that will affect future congressional and presidential contests, President Ford signed the Federal Election Campaign Act into law on October 15. It set limits on contributions and spending in national campaigns.   William J. Eaton

See also CONGRESS OF THE UNITED STATES; DEMOCRATIC PARTY; REPUBLICAN PARTY.

ELECTRIC POWER. See ENERGY.

ELECTRONICS. Inflation, materials shortages, and the energy crisis both hampered and spurred on the electronics industry in 1974. Firms intensified research efforts aimed at developing less-costly photovoltaic cells that convert sunlight directly into electricity. There were few dramatic innovations in sophisticated technology, and the widespread application of electronics to consumer products tapered off. But there were many developments in medical electronics, and *microprocessors* – low-cost data processors and memory units on single semiconductor chips – came into widespread use.

Photovoltaic cells that convert sunlight directly to electricity are being used in such small-scale applications as recharging hearing-aid batteries. The major drawback to large-scale use of photovoltaic cells is their cost. But breakthroughs announced by Tyco Laboratories, Incorporated, of Waltham, Mass., may bring costs closer to that of electricity produced from nonsolar sources.

Meanwhile, the MITRE Corporation of Bedford, Mass., is constructing a building that will use panels of photovoltaic cells mounted on its roof to provide 1 kilowatt of electric power during full sunlight. Under a program called Sunshine, Japan plans to operate a 1-megawatt solar plant in the early 1980s.

Medical Equipment improvements continued through the application of electronics. Survival

Technology, Incorporated, of Bethesda, Md., began marketing a portable heart monitor that attaches to the body with two small electrodes. The unit can transmit an electrocardiogram over a telephone. A team of scientists at the University of Southern California's medical school in Los Angeles displayed their prototype artificial pancreas for diabetics. It monitors the wearer's blood-sugar level and automatically dispenses small amounts of insulin into the blood stream as needed. In September, Miles Laboratories, Incorporated, of Elkhart, Ind., reported that a similar computerized device had been successfully tested.

Artificial vision for the blind came closer to realization at the University of Utah's Institute for Biomedical Research. Blind volunteers were able to "see" letters of the alphabet when electric signals stimulated nerve endings in their brains. The researchers envision future artificial-vision devices consisting of sensors mounted in the eye sockets, a miniature computer mounted in a dummy eyeglass frame, and permanently implanted electrodes.

The computer also revolutionized X-ray scanning techniques that physicians use to probe internally without resorting to surgery. R. S. Ledley and his associates at Georgetown University in Washington, D.C., developed a computerized X-ray scanner for examining cross sections of the human body. Physicians examine the color representations to detect internal diseases.

Computer Technology advanced steadily in 1974. Microprocessors established markets by finding use in such diverse applications as oscilloscopes, machine tools, chart recorders, and medical equipment. Spacelabs Incorporated, of Chatsworth, Calif., introduced a patient-monitoring system for hospitals that is made economically feasible by the microprocessor. It can simultaneously check the temperature, respiration, blood pressure, and heartbeat of eight patients.

Microprocessors are the first general-purpose circuits made using large-scale-integration (LSI) techniques. Previous LSI circuits had to be custom-designed for specific applications, often at great cost. Miniature computers that use a microprocessor plus additional circuitry are slower and less versatile than larger computers, but cost only 1 per cent as much.

Another cost-reducing technological development is the 4,000-bit random-access memory (RAM) for computer-data storage. A bit is the basic information unit in a binary digital computer. Previous RAM's held only 2,000 bits. Because the new RAM's can be manufactured for about the same cost as the old ones, twice as much storage is available at no extra cost.   Marilyn J. Offenheiser

EL SALVADOR. See LATIN AMERICA.

EMPLOYMENT. See ECONOMICS; EDUCATION; LABOR; SOCIAL SECURITY; SOCIAL WELFARE.

The world's largest nuclear power station, being built on the Rhine River in West Germany, produced its first electricity in June.

ENERGY. Threats to energy supplies remained a prime worry in all parts of the world throughout 1974. The year was studded with meetings of engineers, scientists, politicians, and concerned citizens, all aimed at finding both immediate and long-range solutions. Costs for fuel–coal, oil, natural gas, and gasoline–continued to rise, and shortages loomed in various parts of the world.

The World Energy Conference, held in Detroit in September, brought more than 4,000 concerned energy leaders from throughout the world to examine available supplies, rising energy costs, and the environmental and economic impact of current and long-range demands.

President Gerald R. Ford sounded the theme "Project Interdependence" in an address to the conference. This was a radical departure from "Project Independence," the policy established by President Richard M. Nixon in 1973. Ford stressed the need for the United States and other nations to work together in satisfying world energy needs. He proposed that all nations try to increase energy production, each according to its resources and level of technology. The world, he said, must use common sense, self-discipline, and new technology to reduce the rate of energy consumption. Ford proposed seeking global fuel prices that provide a strong incentive to producers while not seriously disrupting consumer economics. On December 16, Ford and President Valery Giscard d'Estaing of France called for a general conference of the oil-producing and oil-consuming countries to attempt to stabilize the world petroleum market.

The Arab View was outlined in Detroit by Sheik Ahmed Zaki Yamani, Saudi Arabia's minister of petroleum resources, who tried to show how the oil-producing Middle East nations set positive goals. He cited the need for oil conservation and the Arabs' need to ensure their future income. Oil is a depletable resource that was being undersold until recently, according to Yamani.

The Arabs want to trade off their rich oil resources, at a moderate pace, for technological know-how and equipment. Their goal is to develop the Arab nations into more advanced and self-sustaining technical and industrial centers.

A National Energy Policy. On October 29, Ford formed the Energy Resources Council, under Secretary of the Interior Rogers C. B. Morton, to shape national energy policy. He also named Frank G. Zarb to succeed John C. Sawhill as federal energy administrator. The Energy Research and Development Administration was created to replace the Atomic Energy Commission. In early November, the government published the Project Independence report, which called for stronger federal energy-conservation measures. Ford was reported to prefer voluntary conservation, and he repeatedly rejected proposals for a heavy gasoline tax to discourage the use of automobiles. Details of the Administration's energy policy were to be announced early in 1975.

Construction Delays in building power plants made a major dent in 1974 plans for growth in the United States. Inflation, the inability to borrow money, and a smaller demand than expected were at the root of the problem. Energy conservation efforts by both the public and industry contributed to the drop in demand. But even with current delays and cancellations of new nuclear plants, the Atomic Energy Commission predicted that the United States will have a generating capacity of 102,000 nuclear megawatts (Mw) by 1980 and 250,000 Mw by 1985.

A close look at the buying patterns of the electric utilities in late 1974 showed a dramatic decrease in unit sales of gas turbines to utilities. The key reasons for the downtrend appear to be:

- Potential shortages of oil and natural gas, which are generally burned in gas turbines.
- Expected high cost of such fuels in years to come.
- Less demand in some systems.

Spending Plans were slashed by the electric utilities during the year. In every case, utilities pointed to scaled-down predictions of energy consumption, reflecting the hope that consumers will continue to conserve energy. This is a reasonable assumption in light of the sharp increase in the cost of electricity and natural gas.

Shaken from its growth pattern by the Arab oil embargo, the U.S. economy emphasized energy conservation in 1974. The effect was felt immediately in terms of kilowatt-hour (kwh) sales. Less electricity was used throughout the year, and electric utility sales gained only about 0.7 per cent, principally because of a 2.4 per cent gain in customers. However, new industrial facilities being built to comply with air- and water-pollution control laws will use more power. Some added electric load will also be needed to comply with recent rulings on worker safety and health.

Many utility customers took a harder look at electricity conservation, as they complained bitterly about paying more for less electricity. The average rate for residential service in 1974 was 2.88 cents per kwh, a 20 per cent increase from 1973.

In the face of soaring fuel charges and the shortage of needed capital, the U.S. electric utility industry reported the following in terms of revenue, profit, and output:

	1973	1974	percent change
	(in millions)		
Total capability (kw)	437.6	475	8.5
Utilities generation (kwh)	1,870,000	1,830,000	−2.1
Utilities sales (kwh)	1,688,000	1,700,000	0.7
Utilities revenue*	$27,000	$34,500	27.8

*For investor-owned companies

The basic problem for electric utilities was financial. For example, 22 utilities—electric and combination companies that supply both gas and electricity—showed a gain of 32.4 per cent in revenues for the third quarter of 1974, but earnings were up only 2.9 per cent. Thus, with inflation and a lack of confidence in the utilities' earnings growth, the year ended on a downbeat. Another important segment of the U.S. energy picture, the major oil companies, continued to show vigorous growth and earnings despite the increased costs of imported petroleum.

Russia Expanded its pursuit of nuclear energy, declaring that nuclear power is most economically attractive and justified in the far northern and northeastern parts of the Soviet Union. Nuclear plants of the pressurized-water type, rated at 1,000 Mw, are being developed and one such unit is being installed at the Novovoronezh atomic power station. This plant is now equipped with two 550-Mw turbines. Future plants will feature a single 1,000-Mw turbine generator to be supplied from a single nuclear reactor steam supply system. Russia made noticeable progress in tests of its sodium-cooled breeder reactor in the town of Shevchenko in Kazakhstan. Construction is also underway on another breeder reactor at the Beloyarsk nuclear power station in the Ural Mountains.

New Energy Sources were given close scrutiny in many countries during 1974. Fuel cells, *magnetohydrodynamics* (converting ionized particles into electric current), *geothermal* (underground heat), and solar energy sources were all examined anew. Tidal power, previously ignored as a power source, showed promise. Engineers contemplated harnessing the enormous energy developed in the rise and fall of ocean tides to generate electricity during periods of peak demand. Sites suitable for tidal development have been found in 23 countries. So far, only La Rance, on France's Brittany coast, is producing commercial power from the tides. In the early 1930s, President Franklin D. Roosevelt requested $2.5 million for a tidal-system study at Passamaquoddy Bay in the Bay of Fundy between Maine and Canada, where tides sometimes rise as much as 27 feet (8 meters). However, Congress refused to approve the project, contending that it was not economical. Canada is expected to approve the construction of a tidal power station that will cost between $2 billion and $3 billion in the Bay of Fundy, between Nova Scotia and New Brunswick. The Bay of Fundy has the world's highest tidal rise and fall, about 53 feet (16 meters). To harness the Fundy tides, engineers plan to build a dam behind which water would build up during incoming tides. By means of a series of storage basins behind the dam, the penned-up water could then be released during peak demand periods to generate supplementary electricity by means of spinning turbines.   James J. O'Connor

ENGINEERING. See BUILDING AND CONSTRUCTION.

ENVIRONMENT. Scientists throughout the world expressed concern in 1974 over the pollution of the atmosphere by man-made aerosols. They feared that these chemicals might adversely affect the weather and even produce cancer because of their effect on atmospheric ozone. See WEATHER.

Meanwhile, efforts to clean up the U.S. environment were battered by the energy crisis and an industry-oriented approach to environmental issues. The pace of environmental progress slowed and some safeguards were weakened, but the basic framework of environmental legislation withstood the most potentially damaging attacks.

Early in the year, the fuel shortage resulting from the Arab oil embargo triggered attacks by industry spokesmen on environmentalist opposition to the construction of the Alaska oil pipeline, the location of new power plants, and the use of high-sulfur coal by electric utilities. At the same time, the Nixon Administration weakened or withdrew its support for such key conservation measures as land use and strip-mining controls. A policy of moderate compromise between the Environmental Protection Agency (EPA) and environmental groups seemed to have succeeded by late summer. However, opponents renewed their attacks on environmental programs in the fall, charging they were inflationary.

Energy Needs or Environment? Conservation groups were concerned over the attitude of President Gerald R. Ford, who seemed to give economic growth priority over preservation of environmental safeguards. In an August 15 address, he attacked "a zero growth philosophy," and asserted that there must be reasonable compromise where environmental considerations conflict with other needs. Conservationists viewed Ford's October 8 proposal of an "inflation impact" statement to accompany new governmental actions as offsetting the "environmental impact" assessment required under the National Environmental Policy Act of 1970. Conservation groups focused their criticism on President Ford's proposal for relaxing clean-air standards and requiring many power plants to convert from oil and gas to coal. They said this could lead to increased air pollution and wholesale coal-stripping operations in the West.

Alaska Pipeline. The U.S. Department of the Interior issued a right-of-way permit for the 789-mile (1,270-kilometer) Trans-Alaska Pipeline on January 23. The pipeline will deliver crude oil from Prudhoe Bay on the Arctic Ocean to Valdez on the Gulf of Alaska. Conservationists who had threatened to challenge the constitutionality of legislation permitting the construction of the pipeline decided to forego a court battle. As the Arctic winter arrived in October, barely five months after construction began, the final link-up was completed in a 360-mile (580-kilometer) construction road from the Yukon River north to Prudhoe Bay. The $4.5-billion project is expected to begin delivering 1.2-million barrels of oil daily to Valdez by June, 1977.

Air Pollution Legislation. The Energy Supply and Environmental Coordination Act of 1974 was signed into law by President Richard M. Nixon on June 22. The legislation amended the Clean Air Act of 1970 by extending for up to two years the present emission standards for automobiles. It also provided a limited program to convert power plants to burn coal rather than oil or natural gas. The National Clean Air Coalition, a private conservation group, said the bill as enacted constituted a defeat for the efforts of the coal and electric utility industries "to use the short-term energy situation as a justification for gutting the Clean Air Act."

In October, however, President Ford renewed the call for softening the Clean Air Act to permit continued use of high-sulfur coal. The Environmental Policy Center said on October 9 that one of the greatest debates in Congress in 1975 will be "whether clean air—not just the Clean Air Act—is going to be sacrificed."

Land Programs. Legislation to control haphazard land use, long advocated by environmental groups, was defeated by the opposition of real estate groups, the U.S. Chamber of Commerce, and the Nixon Administration, which switched its previous position of support for the legislation. On June 11,

One of four bronze horses at Saint Mark's Cathedral in Venice is removed for treatment against decay caused by city's air pollution.

by a vote of 211 to 204, the House of Representatives defeated the legislation that would have allowed the states $100 million in annual grants for eight years to develop comprehensive land-use planning programs.

However, the House approved legislation on July 25 to impose strict controls on the strip mining of coal. The House vote was hailed as a victory by environmentalists, but coal interests called it "unworkable." It established a federal-state program with stringent environmental controls to regulate surface mining and the reclamation of strip-mined land. The bill was approved by a House-Senate Conference Committee in November and passed on December 16, but Administration spokesmen called its key provisions "unacceptable" because they would hamper the output of coal.

Water Pollution. Environmentalists and some city administrators charged that EPA programs were undermined by the Nixon Administration policy of impounding funds appropriated by Congress for a water cleanup program. But spokesmen for the agency said there were signs EPA had "turned the corner" on pollution levels, though it would take three to four years for the public to notice the difference.

In a landmark environmental case, the Supreme Court of the United States refused on July 10 to order the Reserve Mining Company of Silver Bay, Minn., to stop dumping 67,000 tons of rock waste daily into Lake Superior. The Minnesota Environmental Protection Agency had charged that the discharges, which contain asbestos fibers, posed health hazards to those drinking the lake water. The court case, the longest and most expensive environmental suit on record, was heard before U.S. District Judge Miles Lord of Minneapolis, who ordered the plant closed. But two days later, it was reopened when an appeals court ruled there was not sufficient evidence of a health hazard. The Supreme Court said state and federal agencies could renew their request to stop the dumping if the U.S. Circuit Court in St. Louis did not decide the health issue by Jan. 31, 1975.

Recycling Solid Wastes. Spurred by the rising costs of energy and materials, several cities and states launched more intensive efforts to recycle trash. The United States generates an estimated 130 million short tons (118 million metric tons) of municipal solid waste each year, and cities are finding it increasingly difficult to dispose of this because of a shortage of landfill sites and more stringent environmental rules. The EPA reported in June that America's trash could supply 1 per cent of current energy needs. Andrew L. Newman

EQUATORIAL GUINEA. See Africa.

Krokodil/Moscow

"Comrade Director, on the occasion of your anniversary, allow us to present you with a working model of your factory!"

ETHIOPIA. Emperor Haile Selassie I, the 82-year-old Lion of Judah, was deposed in 1974, after 58 years as absolute ruler. Selassie was led from his palace on September 12 and held at a palace outside the capital, Addis Ababa. He was charged with abusing his power and failure to aid starving victims of Ethiopia's drought and famine.

International aid agencies had revealed in October, 1973, that famine had killed between 50,000 and 100,000 Ethiopians. Ethiopian authorities were still trying to keep the disaster secret when a United Nations report disclosed in January, 1974, that 1,000 people were dying each week.

The chain of events leading to Selassie's downfall began in February with a cabdrivers' strike. This escalated into riots and demonstrations against inflation and unemployment. In March, 10 persons were killed when peasants tried to take land that had been given to landlords who lived elsewhere. Four were killed in police-student clashes. A wave of strikes brought 4,000 demonstrators to union buildings in Addis Ababa. The Eritrean Liberation Front, fighting a guerrilla war to liberate its Moslem area in northeastern Ethiopia, stepped up operations.

The Army Moves. In February, junior officers and sergeants in Asmara, capital of Eritrea, started political study groups that formed the basis for the Armed Forces Coordinating Committee for Peaceful Solutions, the group that ended imperial rule.

After the strikes and demonstrations, the emperor handed over many powers to Prime Minister Endalkachew Makonnen. Meanwhile, the military gradually began to isolate Selassie. Troops seized key points in Addis Ababa on June 30 and arrested a number of officials in an anticorruption campaign. On July 6, the emperor agreed to an amnesty, swift constitutional reform, and a greater voice for the military in government affairs. Makonnen was dismissed on July 22 and arrested the next day. His successor, Michael Imru, a cousin of Selassie, named a new Cabinet that contained only two army men, and published a new Constitution on August 8 that made the emperor a figurehead. On the same day, Selassie's personal aide, Lieutenant General Assefa Demissie, was arrested on the palace grounds and held with some 140 governors, judges, and other officials pending the results of an inquiry into charges of corruption.

Empire's End. The army abolished the crown council, the emperor's court of justice and military committee, on August 16. The following day, his bodyguard, Major General Tafesse Lemma, was arrested. On August 27, Selassie was ordered not to leave the capital. When the aged emperor was finally deposed on September 12, the army banned strikes and demonstrations.

The ruling 121-man Armed Forces Coordinating Committee was led by popular Lieutenant General Aman Andom. The committee ranged from almost illiterate sergeants to internationally experienced senior officers. The army proclaimed a military government in late September, and General Aman was named head of the Cabinet.

Eritrea's Status and questions of government reform caused serious disputes among the members of the Coordinating Committee. Eritrean members of Parliament had resigned in August to protest government refusal to give the province freedom or federal status. General Aman, an Eritrean, was believed to favor compromise on Eritrea. On November 23, hard-line committee members seized power. They executed Aman and 59 others – aristocrats and army and government officials, including two former prime ministers. Ethiopia's new strongman appeared to be a 36-year-old major, Mengistu Haile Miriam. The executions provoked renewed unrest in Eritrea in December.

The military government announced on December 20 that the country would turn to socialism, that it would have only one political party, and that collective farms would be established. Meanwhile, famine continued and disputes arose over Ethiopia's needs. The government was reported reluctant to use its own monetary resources to buy much-needed grain. Instead, it was reported planning to buy military equipment.   John Storm Roberts

See also AFRICA (Facts in Brief Table).

Emperor Haile Selassie I, the Lion of Judah, was deposed in September by army officers who ended the ancient feudal monarchy.

EUROPE

EUROPE was in disarray in 1974. Sharply higher prices for Arab petroleum led to widespread double-digit inflation and trade imbalances. The nine member countries of the European Community (Common Market) disagreed over how to ease the impact of high oil prices and over other common economic and monetary policies. The market's agricultural policy crumbled when farmers in all nine countries protested low produce prices. Relations with outside powers, especially the United States, were strained by disagreements over political, economic, and military cooperation.

It was a year marked by startling leadership changes in major European countries. Willy Brandt resigned as West German chancellor on May 6 and was succeeded by Helmut Schmidt (see GERMANY, WEST). President Georges Pompidou of France died on April 3, and Valery Giscard d'Estaing succeeded him after winning a close run-off election against Socialist candidate François Mitterrand. The election marked the end of Gaullism in France. See FRANCE.

Mounting economic problems produced political changes in the two hardest-hit European countries. British Prime Minister Edward Heath resigned in March and was succeeded by Labour Party leader Harold Wilson (see GREAT BRITAIN). The shaky coalition governments of Italy's Prime Minister Mari-

ano Rumor resigned three times during the year, and, in October, President Giovanni Leone asked first Amintori Fanfani, then Aldo Moro to forge a new coalition. See ITALY.

Portugal and Greece turned toward democracy during 1974. In a dawn coup in Lisbon, Portugal, on April 25, liberal army rebels overthrew the civilian dictatorship of Marcello Caetano. They ended press censorship, promised elections within a year, and pledged independence for Portugal's African colonies (see AFRICA). On July 23, the seven-year-old Greek military junta resigned and called in professional politicians. Former Prime Minister Constantin Karamanlis returned from exile in Paris to head a provisional government. His party won a majority in Parliament in November elections. See GREECE.

The resignation of the military government in Greece resulted from that country's struggle with Turkey for control of the Mediterranean island of Cyprus. The conflict between the two North Atlantic Treaty Organization (NATO) countries posed a problem for that group during its 25th anniversary year, especially when Greece withdrew its forces from NATO in August. See CYPRUS; TURKEY.

Common Market Disunity developed in January on tackling common economic problems produced by oil price rises. West Germany sided with

Mitchell Sharp, left, Canada's external affairs secretary, and NATO Secretary-General Josef Luns cut NATO's 25th birthday cake in Ottawa.

the United States in pushing for concerted action by oil-consuming countries to persuade oil producers to lower prices. They viewed bilateral trade agreements by France and Britain as adding to international difficulties.

France split from the rest of the Common Market at an energy conference of 13 major industrial nations in Washington, D.C., on February 11. French Foreign Minister Michel Jobert repudiated the conference as an attempt by the big consuming countries to impose their will on the rest of the world. He wanted the discussion moved to the United Nations.

In September, the remaining 12 oil-consuming nations formally agreed on a comprehensive and binding emergency oil-sharing scheme. Members would cut back demand by from 7 to 10 per cent if oil supplies of the whole group fell by the same figure. Supplies would be shared. France softened its position somewhat at a weekend meeting in Martinique in December between President Giscard d'Estaing and President Gerald R. Ford. While France would not join the U.S.-led agency of oil importers, it did agree to coordinate policy. In return, the United States agreed to participate in French-backed conferences between oil producers and oil consumers in 1975. As a further sign of unity, the nine market energy ministers, meeting in Brussels, Belgium, on December 17, agreed on reduced energy growth and energy conservation as the cornerstone of their common oil policy.

A general election victory for a Labour minority government on February 28 brought into question a campaign pledge to renegotiate Britain's Common Market treaties. On April 1, Foreign Secretary James Callaghan emphasized that if renegotiations of agricultural policy and reduction of Britain's share of costs should fail, Britain might withdraw. France rejected renegotiation.

New Leaders Meet. On May 31, the new French president, Valery Giscard d'Estaing, welcomed the new German chancellor, Helmut Schmidt, to Paris in an effort to solve common problems. Franco-German conflicts eased, though West Germany retained its reservations about French plans for a European economic and monetary union with the goal of a confederate organization by 1980. On June 4, internal market tensions eased further when Britain softened its treaty renegotiation demands.

More harmony was restored on September 15 when Giscard d'Estaing hosted a Paris dinner for the eight other heads of government and François-Xavier Ortoli, president of the European Commission, a Common Market executive group. They discussed the market's problems and agreed to hold similar, informal summits to avoid the build-ups and disappointments of formal summits. The seventh, and last, formal summit was held in December in Paris, where the nine heads of state pledged easier terms for Britain.

French President Valery Giscard d'Estaing, right, and West German Chancellor Helmut Schmidt meet in Paris in September for talks on Europe.

The Economic Crises. The oil crisis dashed hopes of completing economic and monetary union by the end of the decade. France floated the franc on January 20, effectively ending the Common Market system of closely tied currencies. The system required all of the market's currencies to fluctuate jointly within a margin of 2.25 per cent.

The energy crisis and rampant inflation bedeviled Europe's economic progress. The European Commission forecast in February an average growth of 2 per cent and a balance-of-trade deficit of about $8 billion. Before the 1973 Middle East War, an $8-billion surplus had been forecast. By year's end, the trade deficit had nearly doubled.

A monetary crisis, with fears of total bankruptcy, forced Italy to impose a 50 per cent surcharge on most imports on April 30. The other market countries protested, but the commission agreed.

The European Commission proposed a 1975 budget on September 5 of $8.7 billion, up 37 per cent from 1974. The farm fund total was up 14.6 per cent to $5.4 billion, and 10 per cent of the total was earmarked for a projected regional fund. Hopes of self-financing the budget had been dashed on July 2, when the nine finally and formally abandoned plans to implement a common value-added tax system. After a 14-hour pruning session on September 24, the nine, led by West Germany, cut the 1975 budget by about one-third.

Facts in Brief on the European Countries

Country	Population	Government	Monetary Unit*	Foreign Trade (million U.S. $) Exports	Imports
Albania	2,502,000	Communist Party First Secretary Enver Hoxha; Premier Mehmet Shehu; People's Assembly Presidium Chairman Haxhi Lleshi	lek (10.25 = $1)	80	143
Andorra	25,000	The bishop of Urgel, Spain, and the president of France	French franc and Spanish peseta	no statistics available	
Austria	7,603,000	President Rudolf Kirchschlaeger; Chancellor Bruno Kreisky	schilling (17.8 = $1)	5,287	7,119
Belgium	9,856,000	King Baudouin I; Prime Minister Leo Tindemans	franc (37.5 = $1)	22,459 (includes Luxembourg)	21,987
Bulgaria	8,761,000	Communist Party First Secretary & State Council Chairman Todor Zhivkov; Premier Stanko Todorov	lev (1.65 = $1)	2,752	2,689
Czechoslovakia	14,654,000	Communist Party First Secretary Gustav Husak; President Ludvik Svoboda; Premier Lubomir Strougal	koruna (12.5 = $1)	5,014	4,755
Denmark	5,096,000	Queen Margrethe II; Prime Minister Poul Hartling	krone (5.9 = $1)	6,248	7,682
Finland	4,658,000	President Urho Kekkonen; Prime Minister Kalevi Sorsa	markka (3.7 = $1)	3,828	4,333
France	53,129,000	President Valery Giscard d'Estaing; Prime Minister Jacques Chirac	franc (4.5 = $1)	36,659	37,727
Germany, East	17,012,000	Communist Party First Secretary Erich Honecker; State Council Chairman Willi Stoph; Prime Minister Horst Sindermann	mark (1.78 = $1)	7,928	7,871
Germany, West	63,075,000	President Walter Scheel; Chancellor Helmut Schmidt	Deutsche mark (2.5 = $1)	67,502	54,552
Great Britain	56,427,000	Queen Elizabeth II; Prime Minister Harold Wilson	pound (1 = $2.32)	30,535	38,847
Greece	8,885,000	President Michael Stassinopoulos; Prime Minister Constantin Karamanlis	drachma (30 = $1)	1,440	3,456
Hungary	10,525,000	Communist Party First Secretary Janos Kadar; President Pál Losonczi; Premier Jenö Fock	forint (24.9 = $1)	3,558	3,409
Iceland	217,000	President Kristján Eldjárn; Prime Minister Geir Hallgrimsson	króna (98.6 = $1)	291	359
Ireland	3,065,000	President Cearbhall O Dalaigh; Prime Minister Liam Cosgrave	pound (1 = $2.33)	2,134	2,736
Italy	55,500,000	President Giovanni Leone; Prime Minister Aldo Moro	lira (666 = $1)	22,224	27,796
Liechtenstein	23,000	Prince Francis Joseph II	Swiss franc	no statistics available	
Luxembourg	361,000	Grand Duke Jean; Prime Minister Gaston Thorn	franc (37.5 = $1)	22,459 (includes Belgium)	21,987
Malta	321,000	President Sir Anthony Mamo; Prime Minister Dom Mintoff	pound (1 = $2.60)	98	240
Monaco	24,000	Prince Rainier III	French franc	no statistics available	
Netherlands	13,816,000	Queen Juliana; Prime Minister Johannes Martin den Uyl	guilder (2.6 = $1)	24,072	24,736
Norway	4,025,000	King Olav V; Prime Minister Trygve Bratteli	krone (5.4 = $1)	4,765	6,241
Poland	33,870,000	Communist Party First Secretary Edward Gierek; State Council Chairman Henryk Jablonski; Premier Piotr Jaroszewicz	zloty (33.2 = $1)	5,495	5,943
Portugal	8,514,000	President Francisco da Costa Gomes; Prime Minister Vasco dos Santos Gonçalves	escudo (24.7 = $1)	1,836	3,007
Romania	21,463,000	Communist Party General Secretary & President Nicolae Ceausescu; Prime Minister Manea Manescu	leu (4.9 = $1)	2,877	2,893
Russia	255,543,000	Communist Party General Secretary Leonid I. Brezhnev; Premier Aleksei N. Kosygin; Supreme Soviet Presidium Chairman Nikolai V. Podgorny	ruble (1 = $1.29)	16,510	17,290
San Marino	19,000	2 regents appointed by Grand Council every 6 months	Italian lira	no statistics available	
Spain	35,664,000	Chief of State (El Caudillo) Francisco Franco; President Carlos Arias Navarro	peseta (56.8 = $1)	5,164	9,521
Sweden	8,292,000	King Carl XVI Gustaf; Prime Minister Olof Palme	krona (4.3 = $1)	12,171	10,625
Switzerland	6,654,000	President Pierre Graber	franc (2.7 = $1)	9,477	11,613
Turkey	39,896,000	President Fahri Koruturk; Prime Minister Sadi Irmak	lira (15 = $1)	1,318	2,091
Yugoslavia	21,399,000	President Josip Broz Tito; Prime Minister Djemal Bijedic	dinar (17.3 = $1)	3,024	4,776

*Exchange rates as of Dec. 2, 1974

In Paris, on September 8, the market finance ministers adopted measures to reduce inflation without cutting output or undermining employment. They agreed on October 21 to guarantee loans from oil-producing countries of as much as $3-billion to cover balance-of-payments deficits – each loan to be approved on an individual basis by the nine ministers and not to be used for any other purpose. West Germany, with the strongest economy in the Common Market, insisted that countries receiving such loans must agree to domestic austerity guidelines laid down by the nine ministers.

Farm Crises. The Common Market's biggest problem was its agricultural policy. Throughout Europe, farmers protested against low prices and high feed and fertilizer costs. A market beef surplus reached 70,000 short tons (64,000 metric tons) on April 24, as farmers began slaughtering cattle they could not afford to feed. By June 27, the surplus topped 100,000 short tons (91,000 metric tons), and some was sold to Russia in a cut-price deal.

After a day of concerted farmers' protests during which they blocked roads with their tractors, the market on September 20 raised all farm prices by 5 per cent, effective October 1, and changed the system of border taxes on farm products. The West German Cabinet shocked its partners by vetoing the increase on September 25, but later accepted it when the other countries agreed to reform the entire policy. Britain said it would offset price rises by subsidizing milk, butter, and cheese.

Common Market countries also clashed in January over a planned regional fund to help member countries with underdeveloped areas. Britain, France, West Germany, and Italy all put forward proposals that differed widely on size and distribution of the fund, which the commission had suggested should total $2.5 billion. In December, the nine agreed to a $1.5-million fund at the Paris summit, with Italy to receive 40 per cent and Britain about 30 per cent.

U.S. Relations. The precarious state of United States-European relations led President Richard M. Nixon to threaten on March 15 to withdraw U.S. troops from Europe. The rift widened on March 27 when President Pompidou said France would not consent to U.S. participation in decisions by European countries concerning their future. On April 7, President Nixon consulted with European heads of state in Paris following Pompidou's funeral. Tensions eased further on April 21 after a meeting of the nine market foreign ministers in Bonn. They compromised by agreeing to consultations between Europe and the United States on a "pragmatic, case-by-case basis." The Cyprus emergency in July provided an example of concerted crisis management by the nine market nations. European efforts to solve the crisis were in step with those taken by U.S. Secretary of State Henry A. Kissinger.

Other Relations. The Danish Faeroe Islands decided not to join the Common Market by the end of 1975 as planned under the terms of Denmark's entry. The Faeroese stayed out to protect their fishing interests.

The nine market members took first steps toward long-term cooperation with the Arab world on March 4. However, they united on November 20 in urging a solution to the Middle East problem that would guarantee the continued existence of Israel as a nation. They also continued trade, aid, and cooperation negotiations with 44 developing countries. Plans call for a development fund of $4.5-billion by February, 1975, with stabilization of the export earnings of the 44 countries. Negotiations opened in September with Algeria, Morocco, Tunisia, Spain, Israel, and Malta on a European-Mediterranean free trade area.

NATO observed its 25th anniversary in muted style on April 4. A new declaration of principles binding the alliance went unsigned. The anniversary was marked at the Brussels, Belgium, headquarters by some military music and a fly-by of 36 assorted NATO planes. Secretary-General Josef Luns warned that the margin of safety to the West afforded by NATO forces had been reduced by the expansion of Warsaw Pact forces. Meeting in Ottawa on June 18, NATO ministers pledged closer consultation, particularly between the United States and Europe. On June 26, President Nixon flew to Brussels to sign the Declaration of Atlantic Principles at a summit meeting.

The Conference on Security and Cooperation in Europe reconvened in Geneva, Switzerland, on January 15. Representatives of 35 nations met to try to ease East-West tensions by improving relations between participating states. By midyear, however, the conference had stalled on all key issues. In December, France and Russia jointly called for a summit conference of heads of state.

Eastern European Unity. In contrast with the Common Market, the nine countries of the Council for Mutual Economic Assistance (COMECON) acted in unity during 1974. They pooled resources to develop energy and deliver oil and electricity behind the Iron Curtain. COMECON, 25 years old, was described by Premier Aleksei N. Kosygin of Russia as "the most dynamic force in the world" at a four-day summit meeting in Sofia, Bulgaria, in June. The nine prime ministers resolved to integrate their economies more closely and to coordinate five-year plans taking them into the next decade. Energy was given top priority in agreements on "qualitative cooperation." COMECON Secretary-General Nikolai Feddeyev held informal discussions on proposals for economic ties with the Common Market, but no progress was made.   Kenneth Brown

See also INTERNATIONAL TRADE AND FINANCE.

EXPLOSION. See DISASTERS.

Spokane Celebrates Renewal

Expo '74, the international world's fair in Spokane, Wash., was a success even before it opened on May 4, 1974. In five years time, preparations by Spokane's business community had sparked renewal of the decaying inner city, reclamation of the polluted Spokane River that runs through the center of town, and construction of a multimillion-dollar park and convention center.

The idea for Expo '74 grew out of a problem that many cities have faced—Spokane's downtown businesses were fleeing to the suburbs. To stop the exodus, a plan was drawn up to turn a railroad yard and dilapidated buildings into a 50-acre (20.2-hectare) park spread over two islands and the riverbank. Hopefully, people would be drawn back into the city, revitalizing the downtown area.

To make the plan work, Spokane's merchants taxed themselves to retire a $6-million private bond issue. In addition, nearly $5 million in federal funds was used to develop the site. When the Bureau of International Exhibitions officially approved Expo '74, in November, 1971, the developers felt relieved despite the work ahead. They estimate that the reclamation could have taken at least 25 years and cost far more without the fair. Over 10 years, Expo '74 will have pumped $700 million into the Spokane region's economy.

Despite gloomy spring predictions based on fears of a fuel shortage, visitors turned out in large numbers when Expo '74 opened on May 4. By closing day, November 3, about 5.2-million tourists had wandered through the 30-odd exhibits, witnessing varied expressions of the fair's theme: "Celebrating Tomorrow's Fresh New Environment."

Of the 10 national exhibits, the $3-million Soviet Pavilion was the most popular. It included Armenian folk artifacts, three movie theaters, and a riverfront restaurant that featured, of course, chicken Kiev and Russian vodka.

Canada and its two western provinces, Alberta and British Columbia, built a children's park and indoor and outdoor theaters on an island, which was renamed Canada Island.

The $11.5-million U.S. Pavilion dominated the fairgrounds. Supported by 4½ miles (7.2 kilometers) of steel cable and covered by a translucent vinyl canopy that does not touch the ground, the giant tepee covers an area the size of two football fields. Inside, an 800-seat theater treated visitors to an environmental film that included a dizzying aerial sweep of the Grand Canyon and a raft ride through Colorado River rapids—all projected on a 65-by-95-foot (20-by-30-meter) screen.

The structure remained after the fair as a federal information center, along with the $12-million Washington State Pavilion (opera house and convention center), an outdoor 1,000-seat amphitheater, and the park built by Canada. All the other buildings, equipment, and such items as flagpoles were "recycled"—sold to various universities and neighboring communities.

Australia featured its geography and wildlife, in sharp contrast to strong emphasis by other nations on industrial and governmental solutions to pollution. Iran, Japan, the Philippines, South Korea, Taiwan, and West Germany also exhibited.

Some commercial exhibitors had a tough time balancing promotion against the fair's environmental theme. But Boeing Corporation's permanent amphitheater and the "reusable" Kodak Pavilion were applauded by environmentalists.

Expo '74 also featured a $4-million art exhibit assembled by Alfred Frankenstein, a San Francisco art critic. Landscapes by Canadian, Hawaiian, and mainland U.S. painters were on display.

Spokane's fair was small when compared to previous expos, but it was highly ambitious for a city of Spokane's size (about 170,000 population). Perhaps Expo '74 realized its environmental theme most fully in the Spokane River. Cleaned by new settling tanks and an upstream sewage-treatment plant, its sparkling waters now rush past the once-blighted islands and riverbanks in downtown Spokane, bearing witness that tomorrow's environment can be made fresh and new. Robert K. Johnson

expo'74.

Spokane, Wash., world's fair symbol—the Möbius strip, a closed ribbon with only one surface.

FAIRS AND EXPOSITIONS. Despite the fuel crisis and such hazards as occasional bombing threats by terrorist groups, more than 700 international and 200 United States trade fairs were held in 1974. These ranged from general fairs to highly specialized events designed around specific products, such as children's books and prestressed concrete. Some of the biggest trade fairs were the Hannover Fair in West Germany, which was held from April 25 to May 3; the Paris Fair, April 27 to May 14; and Italy's ever-popular Milan Fair, April 14 to 25. The Hannover Fair, a showplace for new products, had nearly 6,000 exhibitors, and the Milan Fair, about 11,000 exhibitors and more than 3 million visitors. More than 1.5 million people crowded the Paris Fair's 50-acre (20-hectare) site.

World Exhibits. Polymer 74, Russia's first international commercial plastics exhibition, was held in Moscow in September. Included among the exhibitors were 36 American companies, new to the Russian market. They competed with concerns from Western and Eastern Europe in a display of chemical-processing equipment, plastics technology, and finished goods. A fire that destroyed one of the exhibition pavilions several days before Polymer 74 opened damaged some of the exhibits of American and French plastics manufacturers.

More than 300 exhibitors and thousands of oilmen gathered early in September in Stavanger, Norway, for that nation's first oil fair. The event featured the vast oil finds that have been made recently in Norwegian waters.

The revived interest in jazz music generated a number of major festivals throughout the world. The Newport Jazz Festival, which moved to New York City in 1972, was held from June 28 to July 7. A new jazz festival was launched in Nice, France, on July 15.

U.S. Exhibits. The 10-day International Machine Tool Show in Chicago brought about 10,000 potential foreign buyers together with U.S. and foreign manufacturers in September. There were hundreds of state and county fairs and countless thousands of festivals held in the United States in 1974, among them more than 300 rodeos. The biggest of these, the 89th Texas State Fair, was held in Dallas from October 4 to 21. It attracted more than 3 million visitors.

Expo '74 in Spokane, Wash., the decade's only world's fair, opened on May 4. It attracted nearly 5-million visitors before it closed. See Close-Up.

Bicentennial Plans. After a desultory start, public and private support began to grow in 1974 for the U.S. bicentennial celebration, to be held in 1976. John W. Warner, former secretary of the Navy, became the administrator of the newly created American Revolution Bicentennial Administration on April 11. This agency replaced the original Bicentennial Commission, which was established in 1970.

The new commission continued to emphasize the federal government's role in counseling, coordinating, and financially supporting state and local observances. Some 1,900 communities have been awarded Bicentennial Community designations.

Warner announced two new bicentennial projects. "American Issues Forum," a calendar of topics for discussion during 1975 and 1976, is designed to develop a better understanding of America's history. The other project is an exhibit, "The Age of Franklin and Jefferson." It will contain artifacts, paintings, manuscripts, photo reproductions, and other reconstructions of that era. It will be shown in Paris, Warsaw, and London before the exhibit begins a tour of the United States in 1976.

Philadelphia celebrated the 200th anniversary of the First Continental Congress in September. Governors and representatives of the 13 original states were on hand for a re-enactment of that historic event in Carpenter's Hall. Boston was scheduled to officially launch its bicentennial festivities on Patriot's Day, April 18, 1975.

The American Freedom Train, a four-car train carrying bicentennial exhibits scheduled for a 21-month journey across the United States in 1976, made a preliminary five-month tour of 76 cities in 1974. *Lynn Beaumont*

See also BICENTENNIAL CELEBRATION.

FARM MACHINERY. See MANUFACTURING.

FASHION. The winds of change swept through the workrooms of designers in 1974 and tried to blow away the skinny, skimpy, body-hugging clothes of the last 10 years. The biggest news in fashion was the very bigness of fashion. Voluminous. Wide. Massive. Soft. These were the words to describe the emerging silhouette, which was characterized by amply cut tops, fuller skirts, and longer hemlines. Promoted as The Big Look or denounced as The Droop, this radically different fashion, designers hoped, would send inflation-weary consumers back to the stores and, specifically, back to dresses.

Even if dresses were to fail to make a comeback, couturiers reasoned, the latest look could revitalize an industry saturated with trusty sweaters and pants. It was an enormous gamble. The midi debacle of 1970, compounded by the coinciding economic recession, forced several venerable couture houses, retailers, and small manufacturers to either fold, merge, or verge on bankruptcy.

Such respected designers as Halston, Oscar de la Renta, and Kasper of Joan Leslie made a point not to rock the boat too much in 1974 by presenting several choices of hemlines. As a result, the winds of change hardly swept away everything in their path. There were still plenty of pants and layers of sweaters in most women's wardrobes. The new pants were more refined, cut of quality fabrics. The latest sweaters were sweat-shirt styled, burly

The lowly T-shirt, sporting slogans or pictures to reflect a wearer's every whim, became one of the year's hot fashion trends.

peasantlike coats, fur-lined or fur-topped cardigans, boleros with rolled and padded edges. It was the year of the blouse: fragile laces, Russian tunics, silken see-through prints.

The denim saga continued to enchant the young. Well-worn blue jeans of cow-country-to-campus fame were most frequently paired with T-shirts emblazoned with political slogans, product endorsements, or sentiments such as "Don't bug me." Other youth fads were a late-summer bloom of flower-splashed skirts and The String, a minimal bikini consisting of four smidgen triangles held to the body by the slenderest of straps.

The Big Look differed from the midi in that it brought the fabric flowing in immense yardages about the body. It meant very little inner construction, very few seams. Linings, interfacings, and even turned-under hems were practically eliminated. As a result, the clothes could be piled on top of each other in layers without making the wearer look enormous.

The look was pioneered in Paris in the spring by two young leaders of French ready-to-wear fashion, Carl Lagerfeld, of Chloe, and Kenzo Takada, the first of several current Japanese designers to triumph in Paris. The initial shapes were absurdly full, reminiscent of suffragettes' costumes. By fall, Givenchy, Ungaro, and especially Yves Saint Laurent with his beltless Naïve Chemise gave the

look the stamp of haute couture. In the United States, Calvin Klein was cheered for his wearable, toned-down, Americanized versions.

Typical of The Big Look was the circular cape, tossed over a bulky sweater and a skirt swirling to below the knee. Coats were tentlike and full. Standouts were the steamer coat—raglan-sleeved, swinging to width in the back—as well as cardigans or kimonos of dressing-gown proportions with yokes, smocking, capelets, and drop-shoulders.

Suits were actually sportswear-concept turnouts, linked by pattern and color. Dresses were soft, limp; bloused, gathered, pleated, smocked; falling in supple fullness to anywhere below the knee.

The fabric message was played out in gentle tones: fluffy mohairs, cashmere, angora jerseys, velvets, wool challis, crepe, and pure silk in subdued burgundy, muted greens, earth hues, heather, slate, and smoke blues. There were flashes of true violet and fire-engine red. Black remained the strongest color by night for silky evening pajamas, lingerie-look gowns with lace insets and underwear straps, and covered-up dresses starred with diamantés and sequins.

Accessories. Berets, miles of muffling scarves, and high-heeled, baggily crushed boots were essentials to The Big Look. Also, "that little something extra" could turn last year's dress into an attention-commanding outfit. Newest of these were understated leather belts, slender neck chains, delicate rhinestone ropes, lace-edged chiffon kerchiefs, silk flowers, high-heeled T-strap shoes, or low-heeled ballerina pumps. Barrettes, combs, and ornamental clasps marked the wave of curlier coiffures.

Menswear. The wavering line between sportswear and tailored suits blurred further with the introduction of the so-called "leisure suit" – matched sets with shirt-styled jackets. While they were intended for the country, they appeared everywhere short of the office.

The country influence carried over to traditionally styled suits in the year's favorite fabrics: camel's hair, Donegal tweed, corduroy, and denim. Western shirts, shearling jackets, and pile-lined, pile-collared "ranch coats" were the warmest gear a man could own, while camel-colored plaids and subtly striped banker's grays with notched lapels and center-vented jackets suited the business of dressing for business.

The Coty Awards. The fashion industry gathered on October 17 to watch Geoffrey Beene and Halston elected to the Coty Hall of Fame. Calvin Klein accepted a Return Award and Ralph Lauren received the Winnie as best designer of the year. Five special awards were presented to designers responsible for the "lingerie renaissance": Stephen Burrows, John Kloss, Stan Herman, Fernando Sanchez, and Bill Tice.   Kathryn Zahony Livingston

FINLAND. A wage agreement effective until January, 1976, was signed on March 30, 1974, as a continuation of the incomes policy initiated in 1968. A high rate of inflation made the new pact imperative. Total labor costs to industry had risen 16 per cent. The new agreement called for four wage hikes totaling 10 per cent in both 1974 and 1975.

An agreement signed with Russia on April 1 increased the value of Finnish exports to the Soviet Union by $230 million, or 25 per cent. This rise partially offset the tripling of Russian oil prices, which cost Finland $1.1 billion in 1974. Finland imports 65 per cent of its crude oil from Russia. The export deal covers manufactured goods, agricultural products, and ships. Foreign Trade Minister Jermu Laine said the agreement would not affect deliveries of goods to Finland's other trading partners.

Overall exports were up 48 per cent during the first half of 1974, but imports increased 52 per cent, hiking the trade gap by $20 million. The Finnish paper and board industry had a record output due to a worldwide newsprint shortage. Deliveries rose 14 per cent to a gross value of $228 million.

The biggest shipping orders Finland has ever had, worth $310 million, were received for six tankers from Russia and seven ammonia carriers from Norway.   Kenneth Brown

See also EUROPE (Facts in Brief Table).

FIRE. See DISASTERS.

FISHING. The United States Fish and Wildlife Service issued reports in May, 1974, confirming what many Americans already knew: Sport fishing ranks as a major American pastime. The service reported that more than 26 million persons bought fishing licenses in 1973. California is by far the fishing capital of the nation, with sales of 5.5 million licenses and permits. Runners-up are Michigan and Texas, each with 1.6 million active fishermen. Wisconsin attracts the most out-of-state fishermen, with nearly 500,000 visitors buying licenses.

Recent surveys place the number of U.S. saltwater anglers, who do not require licenses, at 9 million, and oceanic game-fish authorities expect that there may be 27 million salt-water fishermen in less than 20 years. To help meet the need for information to aid ocean anglers, the National Oceanic and Atmospheric Administration has expanded its research on the viability of oceanic game-fish species. In its *Oceanic Gamefish Investigations Newsletter*, the agency compares fishing effort to catches, and cites the best fishing hours for blue marlin (after 4 P.M.), white marlin (between 10 A.M. and 1 P.M.), and sailfish (6 to 7 A.M.).

The American League of Anglers, Incorporated, launched in March, seeks to unify sports fishermen into a political force to work against the degradation of fish habitats. It has the support of a number of major fishing organizations.   Andrew L. Newman

FISHING INDUSTRY. The third United Nations Conference on the Law of the Sea, held in Caracas, Venezuela, in July and August, 1974, failed to reach any agreements. Among unresolved issues were control of coastal sea resources, including those crucial to the fishing industry. See OCEAN.

Following the conference, the Ford Administration told the United States Congress it would impose tight controls on foreign fishing off U.S. shores while awaiting an international treaty to extend economic jurisdiction over coastal waters. The Department of State, however, opposed unilaterally extending the domestic fishing zone from the present 12 nautical miles to 200 nautical miles because it would endanger the effort to achieve an international treaty. The U.S. fishing industry was divided. New England fishermen said their industry might face extinction unless foreign fishers were excluded, but shrimp and tuna fishermen said such action would lead other countries to retaliate.

The urgency of a solution to world fishing problems was underlined on September 17 when John Norton Moore, chairman of the U.S. Law of the Sea Task Force, said: "Fishing pressure has increased so dramatically that by the end of this decade we will reach or exceed the maximum sustainable yield for most species now on the market."

The Cod War. The World Court ruled on July 25 that Iceland's 1972 decision to extend its fishing

Workmen at a mainland China fish-breeding farm spread a net to gather fish. Farming produced 7.5 billion frying fish between 1967 and 1973.

limits from 12 to 50 nautical miles could not apply to either Great Britain or West Germany. However, Iceland rejected the court's decision and said it would continue to ban fishing in the area.

The U.S. Fishing Industry. United States commercial fishermen caught about 4.7 billion pounds (2.1 billion kilograms) of fish and shellfish in 1973, almost the same as in 1972. But the value was up to a record $907.4 million, about 29 per cent higher than in 1972, because of higher prices. However, fishermen complained that 1974 dockside prices dropped as much as 15 per cent, while retail prices remained high.

Alaska banned commercial fishing for red salmon for the first time since the industry was started in 1893. The action was an attempt to rehabilitate the species, depleted by overfishing and by two unusually cold winters.

The International Whaling Commission held its 26th session in London in June, but failed to approve the 10-year moratorium on all commercial whaling sought by the United States. However, participants agreed to lower quotas for those whale species that are most endangered.   Andrew L. Newman

See also Section Two, DOOM FOR THE GIANTS OF THE SEA?

FLOOD. See DISASTERS.

FLORIDA. See STATE GOVERNMENT.

FLOWER. See GARDENING.

FOOD. World hunger problems, rising food prices, nutrition, and the proliferation of "natural" foods dominated developments in the food industry in 1974. Government officials sought aid for an estimated 460 million people imperiled by hunger in various parts of the world. See AFRICA; INDIA.

In a search for ways to ease the worldwide shortage of food, delegates from 130 countries met in Rome at the United Nations World Food Conference in November. After 11 days of debate, negotiation, and compromise, they called for a World Food Council to coordinate the work of various international agencies. See POPULATION, WORLD.

Other meetings held throughout the year discussed long-range solutions to the world food problem. The complexity of the problem was demonstrated by the variety of people participating. They included food technologists, nutritionists, home economists, plant geneticists, and consumers, and all agreed that any solution would require a coordinated attack from many directions.

Food Prices. Retail food prices in the United States rose 12 per cent during the year ending Oct. 31, 1974. However, the annual rate was an estimated 15 or 16 per cent by the end of the year.

Processed and packaged foods accounted for a large share of the price increases in the supermarkets. Food processors defended them on the grounds that they were simply passing on sharp increases in the cost of ingredients and packaging materials. For example, they cited these wholesale price increases: flour, 7 per cent; cocoa, 25 per cent; tin plate, 50 per cent; and cottonseed oil, 100 per cent.

The most dramatic price rise was the more than 300 per cent increase in the cost of sugar on both the retail and wholesale markets. At its peak in December, a 5-pound (2.3-kilogram) bag sold for as much as $3.49 in Chicago and even more in some other cities. This price spiral led to consumer boycotts, and some supermarket chains used advertisements to urge consumers not to buy sugar. In addition, the President's Council on Wage and Price Stability held public hearings on the price of sugar on October 31 and November 1. Early in December, the wholesale price dropped 5 cents per pound (0.45 kilogram), partly as a result of government pressure. Retail prices dropped slightly.

Interest in Nutrition. Because of the rising food prices and new information on the state of the nation's nutritional health, more Americans became interested in obtaining the best nutrition for the least cost. Finding ways to attain this was a goal of hearings by the U.S. Senate's Select Committee on Nutrition and Human Needs in June.

Among the working papers prepared for the hearings was "Guidelines for a National Nutrition Policy," submitted by the National Nutrition Consortium—made up of representatives from the Institute of Food Technologists, the American Dietetic Association, the American Institute of Nutrition, and the American Society for Clinical Nutrition.

The guidelines emphasized the need for an adequate diet at a reasonable cost for every American. Programs needed to meet this objective were also described. However, at year's end, no action had been taken on the guidelines.

Nutrition labeling and 41 other food relabeling rules were to have become effective on Dec. 31, 1974. However, the Food and Drug Administration (FDA) extended the deadline to June 30, 1975. The FDA said that some companies would be compelled to destroy valuable food, expensive labels, and containers if forced to meet the December 31 deadline, incurring expenses that would be passed on to the consumer.

In another development, the Federal Trade Commission proposed rules requiring that advertisements making nutritional claims also contain detailed information to back up the claims. These rules also would drastically limit the claims advertisers could make in comparing the nutritional quality of one food to another.

Natural Foods. New-food-product introductions broke records in 1974, and "natural" foods set the pace. Natural foods are defined as those foods that are made entirely from natural ingredients. They contain neither synthetic additives nor chemically modified ingredients. They include ice cream, candy, bakery products, fruit drinks, breakfast cereals, snacks, and yogurt. Breakfast cereals were by far the most successful of the natural products in 1974, with the major cereal manufacturers getting on the natural food bandwagon with a variety of granola products.

Food Additives. Stimulated by the public furor over the safety of cyclamates in 1969 and a continuing barrage of publicity by consumer activists, U.S. consumers have developed a deep-seated suspicion of food additives. Many scientists now claim that the study on which the cyclamate ban was based was scientifically unsound. Researchers around the world have been unable to confirm the original findings of the study, and new studies have reaffirmed the safety of cyclamates. At year's end, however, appeals by the major manufacturer for the reinstatement of cyclamates were denied, and the FDA has called for further tests of the sweetener.

Another sweetener, Aspartame, received FDA approval for use in certain classes of foods on July 26, 1974. However, certain objections to the clearance were filed in September. At year's end, the FDA was attempting to persuade the objectors to agree to a board of inquiry to study the safety of the sweetener.   John B. Klis and Howard W. Mattson

See also NUTRITION.

Garden plots provide lunchtime exercise and food for Lederle Laboratories employees in Pearl River, N.Y. The practice has spread with inflation.

FOOTBALL

FOOTBALL. The blissful, relatively unharried growth of professional football in the United States hit several snags in 1974. Attendance and television ratings were down. A six-week strike by players in July and August upset training-camp routine. A federal court ruling the week before Christmas struck down the standard professional player contract and left the game's structure in doubt. And a new league, the World Football League (WFL), appeared and suffered the greatest financial disaster in the history of American professional sports. At year's end, it was planning for another try in 1975.

There were sour notes in college football, too, where attendance also fell and costs rose dramatically. As usual, Ohio State and Michigan were involved in battles on and off the field for a Rose Bowl berth. And there was a serious divergence of opinion over picking a national champion.

The most successful teams in the National Football League (NFL) were the Minnesota Vikings and Pittsburgh Steelers. The Vikings won the National Football Conference (NFC) title for the third time in six years, and the Steelers gained the American Football Conference (AFC) title.

The Steelers won the Super Bowl game in New Orleans on Jan. 12, 1975, beating the Vikings 16-6 to win the club's first NFL title in its 42-year history. The Steelers limited the Vikings to 17 yards rushing, while Pittsburgh running back Franco Harris gained 158 yards in 34 carries.

The Miami Dolphins, winners of the two previous Super Bowls and three previous AFC championships, were eliminated in the first round of the AFC play-offs. The Oakland Raiders beat them, 28-26, on a touchdown pass with 26 seconds left. The Steelers defeated the Buffalo Bills, 32-14, in their first play-off game, then upset the Raiders, 24-13, in the AFC final.

Defense made the difference for the Steelers. Defense was also the strong point for the Vikings, who opened the NFC play-offs with a 30-14 victory over the surprising St. Louis Cardinals. The Los Angeles Rams beat the Washington Redskins, 19-10, in the other NFC play-off elimination. In the NFC final, the Vikings got by the Rams, 14-10.

Player Relations. The most significant development of the year may have been the ruling by William T. Sweigert, a United States District Court judge in San Francisco, in the Joe Kapp case. Kapp had sued the NFL because it had barred him from playing unless he signed a standard player contract. Sweigert upheld Kapp's contention that the NFL contract violated antitrust laws. He ruled, among other things, that the so-called *Rozelle rule*, part of the standard contract, was illegal. The rule requires a team signing a player who has played out his option to compensate the player's former team.

For more than half a century, baseball had been exempt from federal antitrust laws because of a ruling by the Supreme Court of the United States, but no other sport enjoyed such exemption. The NFL contended that if players were free to move at will from one team to another, chaos and unbalance would result. The league awaited instructions from the judge on what it had to do to conform to the law, but in any case, it said, it would appeal.

The NFL Players Association had attempted in the spring and summer to negotiate the abolition of the Rozelle rule, the option clause, and other provisions it considered restrictive. Its contract with the NFL, covering almost everything except playing rules and individual salaries, had expired after the 1973 season. When no agreement was reached, the players struck on June 30.

Training camps opened with rookies, free agents, and a few veterans, and they played the first few exhibition games. On August 11, the players suspended the strike for two weeks while negotiations continued. No agreement was reached, but they stayed in camp. Ed Garvey, the executive director of the players association, said later, "The strike collapsed and we lost."

The WFL. While the NFL and its players were squabbling, the World Football League was playing. The new league consisted of 12 teams staffed mainly by veteran players weaned from or cut by NFL teams. Each team was scheduled for 20 regular-season games (but no exhibitions) from July to November.

At first, few football people took the WFL seriously. That changed on March 31 when the Toronto Northmen of the WFL signed fullback Larry Csonka, halfback Jim Kiick, and wide receiver Paul Warfield of the Miami Dolphins for a total of $3,884,000 over three years, starting in 1975. The money supposedly was guaranteed, even if the league did not survive. Tom Origer, owner of the WFL's Chicago franchise, called the signing "crazy, insane, idiotic," and said, "We don't have to throw away millions of dollars to get players."

The WFL soon signed many other NFL stars, mostly for 1975 and 1976, when they will have played out the options in their contracts. Among them were Calvin Hill, Ken Stabler, Daryle Lamonica, Craig Morton, Ted Kwalick, and Bill Bergey. Later, some tried to have the WFL contracts ruled invalid, saying that cash payments had not been made on schedule. Stabler succeeded.

The WFL attendance figures were impressive for the first few weeks of the season. Then came disclosure that stadiums had been filled with free tickets—that of the 119,000 who saw Philadelphia's first two games, only 19,000 had paid for their tickets.

Next came financial disaster for most teams. The Detroit and Jacksonville teams folded in midseason. The New York franchise was moved to Charlotte, N.C.; the Washington, D.C., franchise moved to Norfolk, Va., and then to Orlando, Fla., as the

Florida Blazers; and the Houston franchise moved to Shreveport, La. Most teams fell behind in paying players, and most never caught up. The Internal Revenue Service filed tax liens against several teams. Uniforms were impounded. Commissioner Gary Davidson resigned. In all, the WFL teams lost about $10 million.

The championship game, called the World Bowl, was played on December 5 in Birmingham, Ala., and the Birmingham Americans beat the Florida Blazers, 22-21. Birmingham had missed its last three paydays. Florida players had not been paid since September.

The New Rules. The WFL introduced rules changes designed to enliven the game. They included a touchdown worth 7 points rather than 6 and an action point (a run or pass from the 2½-yard line) after each touchdown. The NFL, responding to charges of dullness and perhaps to the WFL challenge, introduced nine rules changes, some similar to those of the WFL.

The NFL changes included sudden-death overtime to break ties, goal posts at the rear of the end zone rather than on the goal line, and the return of long, unsuccessful field goals to the line of scrimmage rather than the 20-yard line. The changes resulted in more touchdowns, fewer field-goal attempts, fewer successful field goals, longer punt returns, and more punts kicked out of bounds. In general, the public liked the changes.

Standings in National Football Conference

Eastern Division	W.	L.	T.	Pct.
St. Louis	10	4	0	.714
Washington	10	4	0	.714
Dallas	8	6	0	.571
Philadelphia	7	7	0	.500
New York Giants	2	12	0	.143

Central Division	W.	L.	T.	Pct.
Minnesota	10	4	0	.714
Detroit	7	7	0	.500
Green Bay	6	8	0	.429
Chicago	4	10	0	.286

Western Division	W.	L.	T.	Pct.
Los Angeles	10	4	0	.714
San Francisco	6	8	0	.429
New Orleans	5	9	0	.357
Atlanta	3	11	0	.214

Standings in American Football Conference

Eastern Division	W.	L.	T.	Pct.
Miami	11	3	0	.786
Buffalo	9	5	0	.643
New England	7	7	0	.500
New York Jets	7	7	0	.500
Baltimore	2	12	0	.143

Central Division	W.	L.	T.	Pct.
Pittsburgh	10	3	1	.769
Cincinnati	7	7	0	.500
Houston	7	7	0	.500
Cleveland	4	10	0	.286

Western Division	W.	L.	T.	Pct.
Oakland	12	2	0	.857
Denver	7	6	1	.538
Kansas City	5	9	0	.357
San Diego	5	9	0	.357

National Conference Individual Statistics

Scoring	TDs.	E.P.	F.G.	Pts.
Marcol, G.B.	0	19	25	94
Mann, Det.	0	23	23	92
Foreman, Minn.	15	0	0	90
Moseley, Wash.	0	27	18	81

Passing	Att.	Comp.	Pct.	Yds.	TDs.
Jurgensen, Wash.	167	107	64.1	1,185	11
Harris, L.A.	198	106	53.5	1,544	11
Kilmer, Wash.	234	137	58.5	1,632	10
Tarkenton, Minn.	351	199	56.7	2,598	17

Receiving	No. Caught	Total Yds.	Avg. Gain	TDs.
Young, Phil.	63	696	11.0	3
Pearson, Dall.	62	1,087	17.5	2
Carmichael, Phil.	56	649	11.6	8
Jessie, Det.	54	761	14.1	3

Rushing	Att.	Yds.	Avg. Gain	TDs.
McCutcheon, L.A.	236	1,109	4.7	3
Brockington, G.B.	266	883	3.3	5
Hill, Dall.	185	844	4.6	7
Foreman, Minn.	199	777	3.9	9

Punting	No.	Yds.	Avg.	Longest
Blanchard, N.O.	88	3,704	42.1	71
Wittum, S.F.	68	2,800	41.2	67
James, Atl.	96	3,891	40.5	61
Jennings, N.Y.	68	2,709	39.8	64

Punt Returns	No.	Yds.	Avg.	TDs.
Jauron, Det.	17	286	16.8	0
Morgan, Dall.	19	287	15.1	1
Tinker, Atl.	14	195	13.9	1
Metcalf, St. L.	26	340	13.1	0

American Conference Individual Statistics

Scoring	TDs.	E.P.	F.G.	Pts.
Gerela, Pitt.	0	33	20	93
J. Smith, N.E.	0	42	16	90
Leypoldt, Buff.	0	25	19	82
Branch, Oak.	13	0	0	78

Passing	Att.	Comp.	Pct.	Yds.	TDs.
Anderson, Cin.	328	213	64.9	2,667	18
Stabler, Oak.	310	178	57.4	2,469	26
Johnson, Den.	244	136	55.7	1,969	13
Griese, Mia.	253	152	60.1	1,968	16

Receiving	No. Caught	Total Yds.	Avg. Gain	TDs.
Mitchell, Balt.	72	544	7.6	2
Branch, Oak.	60	1,092	18.2	13
Podolak, K.C.	43	306	7.1	1
Odoms, Den.	42	639	15.2	6

Rushing	Att.	Yds.	Avg. Gain	TDs.
Armstrong, Den.	263	1,407	5.3	9
Woods, S.D.	227	1,162	5.1	7
Simpson, Buff.	270	1,125	4.2	3

Punting	No.	Yds.	Avg.	Longest
Guy, Oak.	74	3,124	42.2	66
Wilson, K.C.	83	3,462	41.7	64
Green, Cin.	66	2,701	40.9	53
Cockroft, Cleve.	90	3,643	40.5	64

Punt Returns	No.	Yds.	Avg.	TDs.
Parrish, Cin.	18	338	18.8	2
Herron, N.E.	35	517	14.8	0
Swann, Pitt.	41	577	14.1	1
B. Johnson, Hous.	30	409	13.6	0

Receiver Shelton Diggs triumphantly displays ball after catching 2-point conversion pass that gave Southern California an 18-17 Rose Bowl victory.

Canadian Football. The Canadian Football League (CFL) spent an apprehensive year. First, it feared that WFL teams in Canadian cities would destroy the CFL, and it exerted so much pressure that the Toronto Northmen (the team that signed Csonka, Kiick, and Warfield) moved to the United States and became the Memphis Southmen. Then it endured a player strike during training camp. It also fought to keep solvent as attendance declined 6 per cent and player salaries rose.

The highest-salaried player was Johnny Rodgers of the Montreal Alouettes, the second-year running back from the University of Nebraska. He was earning $100,000 a year, the most in CFL history, but he was talking of playing out his option and trying the NFL. The Alouettes gave him a seven-year contract worth more than $1 million.

The Alouettes beat the Edmonton Eskimos, 20-7, in the Grey Cup championship game on November 24 in Vancouver, British Columbia. Quarterback Tom Wilkinson of Edmonton was voted the CFL's most valuable player. He completed 173 of 262 passes for 2,169 yards and 13 touchdowns during the season. Second in the voting was Rodgers, who ran for 492 yards and caught 60 passes for 1,024 yards.

The College Season. There is no official college champion, but most people recognize the winners of the Associated Press and United Press International (UPI) polls. Usually they are the same team.

But in 1974, the Associated Press panel of sportswriters and broadcasters chose Oklahoma, and the United Press International panel of 35 coaches picked Southern California.

Oklahoma and Alabama were the only major teams undefeated and untied during the regular season, but Oklahoma was never picked at any time during the year in the UPI poll. The American Football Coaches Association had recommended that all teams placed on probation by the National Collegiate Athletic Association (NCAA) be barred from the polls, and the 35 UPI coaches, all members of the association, went along. Oklahoma was on NCAA probation because the high school transcript of a prospective player had been changed.

Oklahoma led all major colleges in per-game scoring (43 points), total offense (507.7 yards), and rushing offense (438.8 yards). Alabama's unbeaten regular season was its third in four years, and it won its fourth straight Southeastern Conference title. But when it lost to Notre Dame, 13-11, in the Orange Bowl on New Year's night, it also lost its number-one ranking in the UPI poll. Oklahoma was barred from bowl games as part of its NCAA probation.

With the defeat of Alabama, the UPI voters turned to Southern California (USC), winner of its last two games in spectacular fashion. In its last game of the regular season on November 30 at Los

Angeles, Southern California fell behind Notre Dame, 24-0. Then USC reeled off seven touchdowns in 17 minutes and won, 55-24. In the Rose Bowl, Southern California upset Ohio State, 18-17, on a touchdown pass with two minutes left followed by a 2-point conversion pass. During the year, USC lost only to Arkansas and was tied by California.

Ohio State was in the fight for the national championship until its November 9 upset loss to Michigan State, 16-13. Two weeks later, in the regular-season finale for both, Ohio State defeated Michigan, 12-10, on four field goals by Tom Klaben. That left Ohio State and Michigan tied for the Big Ten title, and the next day the conference athletic directors met to choose a Rose Bowl representative.

In the secret vote, Ohio State was named on five ballots, Michigan on four, and Michigan State on one (its own). For the second straight year, the vote touched off bitter reaction, and 10 days later the Big Ten changed the method of naming its Rose Bowl team to automatic procedures.

The Player of the Year and winner of the Heisman Trophy was tailback Archie Griffin, an Ohio State junior. Anthony Davis of Southern California and Joe Washington of Oklahoma, also running backs, were next in the Heisman voting.

After 20 straight years of increased attendance, there was a slight drop — two-tenths of 1 per cent. Total attendance for college games was 31,234,855. Costs continued to rise, and the University of Vermont found the ultimate solution by dropping football, the first state university to do so. Other colleges yearned for a return to one-platoon football and limited substitutions, which would require fewer players and thus lower costs.

Coaching Changes began early in the season with a tragedy. Detroit Lions coach Don McCafferty died after suffering a heart attack on July 28. Rick Forzano was named to succeed him on August 3. Coach Jim Garrett of the WFL Houston Texans (later Shreveport Steamer) was suspended on September 18 for "conduct detrimental to the league." On September 29, Baltimore Colts owner Robert Irsay went to the sidelines to fire coach Howard Schnellenberger. Norm Van Brocklin, coach of the Atlanta Falcons since 1968, was dismissed on November 5.

Ara Parseghian astonished the football world and set off a chain reaction of changes when he resigned after 11 successful years as Notre Dame coach. Parseghian said he would not coach for at least a year. The day after he quit, Dan Devine resigned as coach of the Green Bay Packers and took the Notre Dame job. Former Packer quarterback Bart Starr was named to succeed Devine at Green Bay. The Cleveland Browns fired Nick Skorich, and the Chicago Bears fired Abe Gibron. Jack Pardee, coach of the WFL's Florida Blazers, was named to succeed Gibron.

Frank Litsky

1974 College Conference Champions

Conference	School
Atlantic Coast	Maryland
Big Eight	Oklahoma
Big Sky	Boise State
Big Ten	Michigan-Ohio State (tie)
Ivy League	Harvard-Yale (tie)
Mid-American	Miami (Ohio)
Missouri Valley	Tulsa
Ohio Valley	Eastern Kentucky
Pacific Eight	Southern California
Southeastern	Alabama
Southern	Virginia Military Institute
Southwest	Baylor
Western Athletic	Brigham Young
Yankee	Maine-Massachusetts (tie)

The Bowl Games

Bowl	Winner	Loser
Astro-Bluebonnet	Houston 31 (tie)	N.C. State 31 (tie)
Blue-Gray	North 29	South 24
Camellia	Central Mich. 54	Delaware 14
Cotton	Penn State 41	Baylor 20
East-West	East 16	West 14
Fiesta	Oklahoma State 16	Brigham Young 6
Gator	Auburn 27	Texas 3
Liberty	Tennessee 7	Maryland 3
Orange	Notre Dame 13	Alabama 11
Peach	Vanderbilt 6 (tie)	Texas Tech 6 (tie)
Rose	USC 18	Ohio State 17
Sugar	Nebraska 13	Florida 10
Sun	Mississippi State 26	North Carolina 24
Tangerine	Miami (Ohio) 21	Georgia 10

All-America Team (as picked by UPI)

Offense

Ends—Pete Dommerle, Notre Dame; Bennie Cunningham, Clemson.
Tackles—Kurt Schumacher, Ohio State; Marvin Crenshaw, Nebraska.
Guards—John Roush, Oklahoma; Gerry Dinardo, Notre Dame.
Center—Steve Myers, Ohio State.
Quarterback—Steve Bartkowski, California.
Running backs—Archie Griffin, Ohio State; Joe Washington, Oklahoma; Anthony Davis, Southern California.

Defense

Ends—Van DeCree, Ohio State; Pat Donovan, Stanford.
Tackles—Randy White, Maryland; Mike Hartenstine, Penn State.
Middle guard—Rubin Carter, Miami (Fla.).
Linebackers—Rod Shoate, Oklahoma; Richard Wood, Southern California; Woodrow Lowe, Alabama.
Defensive backs—Neal Colzie, Ohio State; Dave Brown, Michigan; Randy Hughes, Oklahoma.

World Football League Standings

Eastern Division	W.	L.	T.	Pct.
Florida	14	6	0	.700
Charlotte	10	10	0	.500
Philadelphia	9	11	0	.450
Jacksonville	4	10	0	.286
Central Division				
Memphis	17	3	0	.850
Birmingham	16	5	0	.760
Chicago	7	13	0	.350
Detroit	1	13	0	.071
Western Division				
Southern California	13	7	0	.650
Hawaiians	8	11	0	.421
Portland	7	11	1	.388
Shreveport	7	12	1	.368

President Ford's wife, Betty, recovering from September breast-cancer surgery, passes a football given to her by the Washington Redskins.

FORD, GERALD RUDOLPH (1913-   ), became the 38th President of the United States on Aug. 9, 1974, following the resignation of Richard M. Nixon. Nixon was forced to resign from office after releasing information that showed he was involved in the Watergate scandal cover-up. See NIXON, RICHARD M.; PRESIDENT OF THE UNITED STATES; UNITED STATES CONSTITUTION; WATERGATE; Section Two, FROM TRIUMPH TO TRAGEDY.

As Vice-President, Ford staunchly defended Nixon's innocence, traveling around the country to rally support for the President. In a hard-hitting speech in Atlantic City, N.J., on January 15, Ford denounced Nixon's Watergate critics as "a few extreme partisans . . . bent on stretching out the ordeal of Watergate for their own purposes." Ford also said he did not believe the House Judiciary Committee would recommend Nixon's impeachment. Two days later, during a visit to his hometown of Grand Rapids, Mich., Ford said the speech was based on a White House draft.

After revelations of high-level involvement in Watergate, Ford's support for the Nixon Administration became less enthusiastic. But he continued to believe in Nixon's innocence. In March, Ford told a gathering of Republican leaders in Chicago that the Committee to Re-Elect the President was "an arrogant, élite guard of political adolescents" who had by-passed the regular Republican Party.

In May, Ford denounced the "corruption, malfeasance, and wrongdoing," at high levels of government. He first criticized, then supported, Nixon's refusal to turn over tape recordings subpoenaed by the House Judiciary Committee.

On August 5, when Nixon released evidence showing his early involvement in Watergate, Ford announced he would make no further statements on the impeachment issue. He said that "the public interest is no longer served by repetition of my previously expressed belief that . . . the President is not guilty of an impeachable offense . . . ." Three days later, Nixon announced his resignation. And at noon on August 9, Ford was sworn in as the new President. He soon shocked the American people by pardoning Nixon for any crimes he committed or may have committed while in office.

With Ford President, he, his wife, Betty, and their children immediately received the focus of national attention. For the most part, they seemed to accept the limelight without much change in their personal lives. On August 19, the Fords moved from their home in suburban Alexandria, Va., where they had lived for nearly 20 years, to the White House.

Ford disliked having to give up his private swimming pool and considered collecting $300,000 in public donations to build a swimming pool on the South Lawn of the Executive Mansion. But he later shelved the idea in keeping with his call for personal sacrifice to fight inflation.

Betty Ford's Surgery. Less than two months after becoming first lady, Betty Ford underwent surgery for removal of a cancerous right breast on September 28 at the Bethesda (Md.) Naval Medical Center. Doctors were hopeful for the total recovery of the 56-year-old Mrs. Ford.

Just before the operation, Mrs. Ford conducted her first news conference. She surprised many observers by her outspoken comments on such traditionally taboo subjects as abortion and the possible use of marijuana by her children.

New First Family. The Fords' only daughter, 17-year-old Susan, a senior at a private high school in Bethesda, was the only one of the Ford children living at home. Michael, 24, was studying at a theological seminary in Massachusetts. He had married Gayle Brumbaugh, 23, on July 5.

John, 22, was studying forestry at Utah State University, and worked as a forest ranger in Yellowstone National Park during the summer. Steven, 18, graduated from public high school in Alexandria in June. He then decided to work on a ranch in Montana for about a year before enrolling at Duke University. William J. Eaton

See also Section One, FOCUS ON THE NATION; Section Five, FORD, GERALD RUDOLPH.

FOREST AND FOREST PRODUCTS. The sharp decline in housing starts in 1974 severely depressed the United States pulpwood and lumber industry. In August, forest industry leaders asked President Gerald R. Ford for federal action to aid the housing industry. Lumber and plywood prices rose faster than expected early in 1974, due to strong housing starts in February, a shortage of railroad boxcars, and a holding of inventories by producers. However, the continued decline in the housing demand later in the year forced down prices and squeezed producers faced with high costs. See HOUSING.

Congress banned exports of unprocessed timber from Western national forests on March 8. Sale of timber from the forests to replace private timber exports was also barred.

President Ford signed the Forest and Rangeland Renewable Resources Planning Act on August 17. The act provides for long-range planning to ensure adequate future supplies of forest resources. Regulations went into effect on September 1 requiring miners on national forestlands to provide a bond to cover the cost of rehabilitation after prospecting or mining. Andrew L. Newman

FORMOSA. See TAIWAN.

FOUR-H CLUBS. See YOUTH ORGANIZATIONS.

FUTURE FARMERS OF AMERICA (FFA). See YOUTH ORGANIZATIONS.

President Ford, an avid skier and swimmer, exercises at his home in Alexandria, Va., before moving into the White House, which has no pool.

FRANCE

France moved away from Gaullism in 1974 with the election of Valery Giscard d'Estaing, 48, as president on May 19. He succeeded Georges Pompidou, who died on April 2 after five years in office. Giscard d'Estaing, the Independent Republican candidate and former finance minister, ran against Jacques Chaban-Delmas, the Gaullist former prime minister, and Socialist candidate François Mitterrand, who had Communist Party support. See GISCARD D'ESTAING, VALERY.

In the first ballot on May 5, Mitterrand received 43 per cent of the vote, Giscard d'Estaing 33 per cent, and Chaban-Delmas about 15 per cent. In a run-off election two weeks later, Giscard d'Estaing received 51 per cent (13,396,203) of the votes cast and Mitterrand 49 per cent (12,971,604). Because Independent Republicans hold only 55 of about 500 seats in the National Assembly, Giscard d'Estaing's victory was seen as a personal endorsement by the electorate.

Accepting defeat, Mitterrand made it clear he would maintain his alliance with the Communists. His narrow defeat was welcomed by members of the European Community (Common Market) and the North Atlantic Treaty Organization, which did not wish to share secrets with a partially Communist government.

New Cabinet. In keeping with his youthful, innovative image, Giscard d'Estaing walked to the Elysée Palace in Paris on May 27 to inaugurate his seven-year term as president. His first act was to appoint Jacques Chirac, 41, a former Gaullist interior minister, as prime minister (see CHIRAC, JACQUES). He then announced a new Cabinet that was youthful, technically competent, and surprisingly nonpolitical. Only three of the 16 ministers from the Pompidou Cabinet were held over and, apart from Chirac, only five were Gaullists.

Giscard d'Estaing appointed a number of opposition reformers including Jean-Jacques Servan-Schreiber, former Radical Socialist Party leader as minister of reforms. But on June 9, Servan-Schreiber was dismissed for criticizing a government decision to resume nuclear testing. The opposition balance was restored July 16 by the appointment of feminist writer Françoise Giroud, 58, to the newly created post of junior minister in charge of women's affairs. Giroud cofounded the weekly news magazine *l'Express* with Servan-Schreiber.

Combats Inflation. Faced with a cost of living that was rising at an annual rate of 16.5 per cent, Giscard d'Estaing introduced an austerity program on June 12. It increased corporate taxes 18 per cent and individual income taxes 5 to 15 per cent, in-

Valery Giscard d'Estaing, out campaigning in May for president of France, greets crowd on Corsica with a Kennedy-like style.

creased gasoline prices, and tightened credit. Part of the income tax was to be reimbursed in 1975.

On September 2, the government launched "operation price brake" to mobilize support for voluntary price rollbacks. Under the 90-day program, one-third of France's retailers sold 40 consumer items at 5 per cent below July 31 prices.

On January 19, Giscard d'Estaing, then finance minister, announced that the franc would join the British pound and the Italian lira outside the Com-

mon Market's requirement that member nation currencies fluctuate within a margin of 2.25 per cent. The decision was taken to safeguard French gold and dwindling foreign exchange reserves. Along with inflation, France was plagued by an enormous balance-of-trade deficit of about $6.5-billion. On February 7, France negotiated a $1.5-billion loan on the Eurodollar market to help finance the deficit caused primarily by increased oil prices.

Oil Policy. France chose to act independently from other Western nations in dealing with the devastating impact of the fourfold increase in prices by petroleum-producing states.

In June, France and Iran signed a $4-billion trade agreement calling for France to build five 1,000-megawatt nuclear reactors in Iran. Iran agreed to make an advance deposit of $1 billion in the Bank of France and to pay most of the remaining cost within five years.

On September 25, the French Cabinet set a limit on spending for oil imports of about $10.6 billion for 1975. At current oil prices, this figure represented a 10 per cent drop in imports from 1973. Home and industrial conservation measures were to bring demand into line with the reduced supply.

In December, France relaxed its go-it-alone oil policy at a meeting between Giscard d'Estaing and President Gerald R. Ford on Martinique in the West Indies. See EUROPE.

A public garden will be built on the site of the demolished Les Halles, Paris' famous central market, which has moved to a southern suburb.

Social Reform. To offset the bitter pill of the new austerity program, the Cabinet adopted a social welfare program on June 19 that may cost as much as $1 billion. The program raised the minimum wage, family allowances, and retirement benefits. On September 1, the minimum wage was again raised, to 26 per cent above the 1973 level. On October 14, French trade unions signed an agreement with the employers group that guarantees the nation's workers a year's pay if they are laid off.

Such liberal social reforms did not prevent widespread strikes. A six-week strike by Paris mail sorters ended in late November after the government refused the strikers' demands for more pay. Their strike triggered shorter work stoppages by railway workers, utility workers, and garbage collectors.

Atomic Tests. France conducted a series of six atmospheric nuclear tests from June to September at Mururoa Atoll in French Polynesia. Australia, Canada, Japan, and New Zealand protested.

Lower Voting Age. The National Assembly voted nearly unanimously on June 25 to lower the voting age from 21 to 18 and grant full civil rights to an estimated 2.5 million French youths. Following bitter debate, the Assembly voted 284 to 189 on November 29 to legalize abortion.   Kenneth Brown

See also EUROPE (Facts in Brief Table).

GABON. See AFRICA.

GAMBIA. See AFRICA.

GAMES, MODELS, AND TOYS. The ancient game of backgammon, which dates back 2,000 years to the days of the Roman Empire, swept the United States and other Western nations like an epidemic in 1974. What appeared to be attaché cases were actually backgammon sets that folded out to form playing boards. Sets packaged in gold-tooled leather and special sets for travelers, containing markers held to the playing board by magnets, sold for about $140. A London gambling club reserved a special room for backgammon, and the ocean liner *Queen Elizabeth II* offered a backgammon cruise.

Fewer New Items. A plastic shortage and the uncertain economic conditions caused toy manufacturers to restrict their lines to market-tested products. Mattel, Incorporated, the largest toy manufacturer, offered a total of 250 items in 1974, compared with 550 in 1972. Because of inflation, industry representatives predicted that 1974 Christmas toy prices would be about 15 per cent higher than those of Christmas, 1973.

The Watergate scandal continued to influence toy and game manufacturers. "The Watergate bug," a doll wearing earphones on a large head that bounced on springs, was a popular item on the West Coast. Other topical best sellers included a model of Evel Knievel's Skycycle, introduced before his Snake River Canyon jump. One company projected sales of $18 million in Knievel items.

The first wave of U.S. bicentennial-oriented toys began to appear during the year. They included Betsy Ross costumes, a board game based on Revolutionary War battles, and a noiseless replica of a rifle used by George Washington's troops.

Consumer groups pressed the toy industry to eliminate what they termed sexist products, labeled as "for boys" or "for girls." The Lionel train division of the Model Products Corporation responded with a new advertising line, "Whoever said Lionel was only for boys?"

Lead toy soldiers gained popularity with adults, who were using them to play war games. A toy soldier that cost 20 to 25 cents in 1966 brought as much as $3 in England in 1974, according to Jack Scruby of Cambria, Calif., who manufactures lead soldiers. "War gaming is the number-one hobby in England," said Scruby, "and it isn't far behind in the United States."

Model Making. Mark Valerius of Houston, Tex., won both the grand national and the open national titles at the National Miniature Aircraft Championships held in Lake Charles, La., from August 5 to August 15. Kenneth Bauer of Orange, Calif., won the senior national championship, and the junior championship went to Jimmy Clem of Dallas. The national team championship was again won by the Dixie Whiz Kids and the club team championship by the Chicago Aeronuts. Theodore M. O'Leary

GARDENING. With food prices rising, vegetable and fruit gardening continued to gain in popularity in the United States in 1974. Some of this interest also found its way into ornamental gardening.

An increasing number of companies, cities, and other institutions encouraged vegetable gardening. The RCA David Sarnoff Research Center in Princeton, N.J., had plots for 300 employees, and Dow Chemical Company of Midland, Mich., provided garden plots for lunchtime employee gardeners. Rutgers University in New Jersey allocated gardening space for married students. The city's Department of Human Resources encouraged Chicagoans to garden on open urban renewal land.

Two major horticultural organizations moved to new homes in 1974. The American Rose Society moved its headquarters from Columbus, Ohio, to Shreveport, La., where it is building extensive trial and demonstration gardens. The American Horticultural Society moved to River Farm, once the property of George Washington, in Mt. Vernon, Va.

New Plants included six All-America Award-winning flowers and two vegetables. A gold medal was awarded to the hybrid zinnia "Scarlet Ruffles." Another zinnia, "Peter Pan Orange," won a bronze medal, while "Showboat" marigold won a bronze medal and awards in the new All-Britain Trials and the European Fleuroselect trials. Celosia "Red Fox," dianthus mixture "Magic Charms," and

cosmos "Diablo" also won bronze medals. The new bush acorn squash "Table King" was given a silver medal, and the disease-resistant wax bean "Goldcrop," a bronze medal. All-America Gladioli were tall, striking "Fire Chief" and "Navy Blue."

Other new plants of note included two superhardy hollies, hybrids of *Ilex aquifolium* and *rugosa*, "Blue Princess" and "Blue Angel" (both female berry-producing plants), as well as 12 new chrysanthemums, the "Masterpiece Series."

Awards. The Arthur Hoyt Scott Medal and $1,000 award went to George S. Avery, Jr., director emeritus of Brooklyn Botanic Garden. Britain's Royal Horticultural Society awarded Avery its Vietch Memorial Medal.

Boston's Massachusetts Horticultural Society, celebrating its 145th year, presented the following awards: the George Robert Medal of Honor to Leon C. Snyder for developing the University of Minnesota's Landscape Arboretum; and the Thomas Roland Medal for exceptional horticultural skill to Ernesta Ballard, president of the Pennsylvania Horticultural Society.

The Liberty Hyde Bailey Medal, highest award of the American Horticultural Society, went to plant scientist Francis L. O'Rourke of Colorado State University, Fort Collins, Colo. Edwin F. Steffek

GAS AND GASOLINE. See ENERGY; PETROLEUM.

Seed sales zoomed to record levels in 1974 as home gardening spread among Americans troubled by inflation and high food prices.

GEISEL, ERNESTO (1908-   ), a retired army general, was elected president by Brazil's electoral college on Jan. 15, 1974, and took office on March 15 (see BRAZIL). He is the fourth successive general to hold the office since the 1964 military overthrow of João Goulart's civilian government. Virtually unknown to the public, Geisel is the first Protestant president of the mostly Roman Catholic country.

He is expected to direct Brazil's continued economic growth in the face of shortages and inflation.

Geisel was born on Aug. 3, 1908, in Bento Gonçalves, a town in Brazil's southernmost state. He graduated from the Realengo Military School in 1928, and became secretary-general of the state government of Rio Grande do Norte in 1931. Geisel held numerous other government posts as he rose through the military ranks, becoming a general in 1960.

Geisel headed the military Cabinet of President Ranieri Mazzilli in 1961 and that of Brazil's first military president, General Humberto de Alencar Castelo Branco, in 1964. From 1967 to 1969, he was minister of the Superior Military Court. He retired from the army in 1969 to become president of Petrobas, the state oil monopoly.

Geisel and his wife, Luci, whom he married in 1940, have one daughter, a high-school teacher. For relaxation, Geisel plays chess.   Robert K. Johnson

Divers stand on the deck of *Alvin,* one of the research vessels that probed the Atlantic Ocean floor, as it approaches the mother ship, *Lulu.*

GEOLOGY. Scientists conducted the first manned exploration of the Mid-Atlantic Ridge, a geologic formation that bisects the Atlantic Ocean floor, in 1974. The joint French-American project, which used three oceanographic submarines and one surface drilling vessel, provided firm evidence that the ocean bottom at the ridge is separating at the rate of about 1 inch (2½ centimeters) each year. Geologists had suspected this for a long time on the basis of the distribution and depths of earthquakes and the pattern of magnetic irregularities in the rocks that form the ocean bottom. However, they now have rock samples and other evidence that proves sea-floor spreading.

The French-American Mid-Ocean Undersea Study (FAMOUS) used the French oceanographic submarines *Archimede* and *Cyana* (designed by Jacques-Yves Cousteau) and the U.S. deep-diving submarine *Alvin* to probe the ridge system on the Atlantic floor. In some cases, the vessels went far below the depths ordinary submarines could reach – more than 9,000 feet (2,700 meters) deep. They collected rock samples and took photographs.

The pictures showed steep cliffs and high mountains that rise abruptly from the ocean bottom. Among the youngest formations, Mount Venus and Mount Pluto are much alike in shape and about a half-mile (0.8 kilometer) on either side of the ridge center line. They are both partly encrusted with staghornlike formations of volcanic glass. The U.S. surface ship *Glomar Challenger* used a large drilling rig to take core samples from the ocean floor in the area from which the submarines took rock samples.

Geologist Wilfred B. Bryan of the Woods Hole Oceanographic Institute in Massachusetts said that the Mid-Atlantic Ridge represents the suture, or master fracture, that separates several of the 20 giant plates that form the earth's outer shell. In this case, the ridge separates the American Plate, which contains the continent of North America, from the Eurasian and African plates on the east, which contain the European and African continents. As the plates slowly separate, molten material rich in minerals rises from the interior of the earth into this fracture zone. Geologists hope to find a way to recover this mineral wealth.

In another part of the Atlantic, geologists found a submerged land area that once joined the tips of Africa and South America. The region is a finger-like extension of the Falkland Plateau surrounding the Falkland Islands off Argentina. According to Ian W. D. Dalziel of Columbia University, the newly identified area provides the last jigsaw fragment required to complete the fit for the joining of the two continents. See OCEAN.

Geologic Evolution. Geologist Thomas J. M. Schopf of the University of Chicago related the movement of the earth's giant plates to changes in evolutionary history. He pointed out that about 275

to 270 million years ago, during the Permian Period, many animal species disappeared, especially species of marine invertebrates. Only their fossil record remains. This abrupt disappearance has puzzled geologists and paleontologists for years and has been given such names as the "time of the great dying" and "faunal crisis in earth history."

Schopf says that the movement of the earth's giant plates during the Permian Period caused the continents to move together and form one large supercontinent, which geologists call Pangea. Pangea later split and formed two supercontinents, Gondwanaland and Laurasia, and then the present continents. The construction of Pangea is in part reflected in the formation of the Appalachian Mountains along the East Coast of North America. These were pushed up by the collision of the plates that now contain North America, Europe, and Africa. The withdrawal of the shallow continental seas that resulted from the formation of Pangea drastically reduced the living space available to marine invertebrates. This also created "life islands," or small, restricted habitats, in which the competition to survive became acute. As a result, according to Schopf, a great number of species became extinct.

Earthquake Prediction. Scientists of the U.S. Geological Survey reported that they hope soon to be able to predict where an earthquake will strike, its magnitude, and roughly when to expect it. They successfully predicted a few quakes in 1973. Their optimism is based on a new theory, the dilatancy-diffusion model, which geologists have recently developed. It is said to be the most convincing explanation that has ever been advanced about what happens miles or kilometers beneath the earth's surface as tremendous stresses in the rock build toward an earthquake.

To predict an earthquake, the geologists measure changes that occur in one kind of seismic wave, the pressure wave. Scientists have found that this wave slows down and then returns to normal just before an earthquake occurs. They have found that the longer the abnormality in the pressure wave, the heavier the shock.

According to geologist Clarence Allen of the California Institute of Technology, rocks begin to develop tiny cracks and fissures as stress from the pressure on the rocks in a fault builds toward the critical point. Ordinarily, ground water flows into such cracks as soon as they form and permits the pressure wave to travel at its normal speed. But in this case, the new cracks open faster than the water can fill them and the wave slows down. Then, when water finally fills the cracks, the wave speed returns to normal. The rocks are weakened by the many new cracks that have opened, however, and the earthquake occurs.   Thomas X. Grasso

GEORGIA. See STATE GOVERNMENT.

GERMANY, EAST, celebrated its 25th anniversary on Oct. 7, 1974, with a military parade through the streets of East Berlin. Russian Communist Party General Secretary Leonid I. Brezhnev reviewed the parade, while the United States joined Great Britain and France in protesting it. The United States established formal diplomatic ties with the Democratic Republic of Germany on September 4, but it does not recognize the country's right to have armed forces in East Berlin.

East-West Relations were both normalized and strained during the year. On June 18, Günter Gaus became West Germany's first permanent representative in East Berlin. Michael Kohl will represent East Germany in Bonn in an exchange that was arranged in 1972 but was delayed by friction between the two countries. Kohl was not received as a full ambassador by West Germany.

On July 25, the Bonn government opened a Federal Environment Protection Office in West Berlin, defying East Germany's wishes. Britain, the United States, and France stated that the office did not violate the 1971 four-power agreement on Berlin. But East Germany disagreed, and began disrupting the flow of traffic across the border. Following independent protests by France, Britain, and the United States to Russia on August 5, the harassment ceased. Despite the trouble, East and West Germany resumed talks on August 29 on such mutual problems as water supplies and rescue of accident victims on their border.

Border Arrests. Heinz Morgenstern, West Germany's undersecretary for inter-German relations, reported on August 9 in Bonn that East Germany had arrested 221 persons attempting to escape since June, 1972. On August 12, the East German news agency, ADN, announced that 52 West Germans and West Berliners had been convicted of helping East Germans escape since July 11. Sentences ranged up to 15 years imprisonment.

Trade Gains. East Germany substantially increased its trading with both Western and Eastern European nations during the first six months of 1974. On September 3, East Germany's Foreign Trade Minister Horst Solle reported trade with the West had increased 8 per cent, and with other members of the Council for Mutual Economic Assistance by 11 per cent. British exports alone tripled to $7-million. Trade with Italy, Switzerland, the Netherlands, the United States, and especially West Germany produced an East German trade deficit of about $800 million for 1974. Imports of plant equipment that was badly needed to improve industrial productivity reportedly accounted for the country's trade imbalance.

According to the North Atlantic Treaty Organization, Russia built up its forces in East Germany in 1974 to 400,000 men.   Kenneth Brown

See also EUROPE (Facts in Brief Table).

Chancellor Willy Brandt of West Germany, right,
quit in May when an aide, Günter Guillaume,
far left, was unmasked as an East German spy.

GERMANY, WEST. Helmut Schmidt, 55, became
the fifth and youngest chancellor of the Federal
Republic of Germany on May 16, 1974. The Bundestag (lower house) elected him to succeed Willy
Brandt, who resigned on May 6. Schmidt was formerly the finance minister. See SCHMIDT, HELMUT.

Brandt's departure first became a possibility in
February, when an 11 per cent union wage settlement ruined his administration's incomes policy.
The pact ended two days of strikes by 800,000 public
service employees. He was also worried about the
state of the European Community (Common Market), which he described on March 28 as "critical."

Spy Scandal. But a spy scandal precipitated
Brandt's resignation. Günter Guillaume, Brandt's
personal adviser on political party matters, was arrested on April 24 as a spy for East Germany. He
reportedly confessed to being an agent of the East
German Ministry of State Security and an officer
on the East German Army's active list. In his letter
of resignation to President Gustav Heinemann,
Brandt took full responsibility for "negligence."

Under the Constitution, Brandt's Cabinet resigned with him. Schmidt chose Hans-Dietrich
Genscher, former minister of the interior, as his
deputy and foreign minister. In a policy statement
on May 17, Schmidt said West Germany's foreign
and defense policy positions remain unaltered. He
declared his administration favored the political

unification of Europe in partnership with the
United States.

25th Anniversary. President Gustav Heinemann
led a solemn commemoration ceremony on May 24
to mark West Germany's 25th anniversary. He reminded members of parliament that their Constitution, or Basic Law, was originally conceived as a
provisional constitution. Yet it had survived many
crucial tests during its 25-year history.

Deputy Chancellor Walter Scheel, 55, took office
on July 2 as West Germany's fourth and youngest
president. He succeeded Heinemann, who resigned
on June 30 after a five-year term of office.

Trade Surplus. Almost alone among European
nations, West Germany was not gravely threatened
by inflation or a high balance-of-payments deficit.
In fact, the country reported a trade surplus of
nearly $10 billion and a balance-of-payments sur-
plus of $5.4 million for the first half of 1974. Exports
rose, while imports were stable. German economic
research institutes called for revaluation of the
Deutsche mark to cut the surplus. The cost of living
index rose at an annual rate of 7.2 per cent, and
unemployment was a low 2.4 per cent in September, but was expected to rise to about 4 per cent at
year's end.

Schmidt was generally given credit for Germany's
remarkable economic health, but he had been
helped by a public willingness to cut consumer borrowing and increase personal savings. And he had
suffered occasional defeats. Farmers blocked roads
on August 7 to protest low prices for farm products.
A bill designed to stimulate consumer spending by
easing some of the tax burden for middle- and low-
income groups ran into opposition in the Bundesrat
(upper house). On July 18, Chancellor Schmidt told
newsmen that he would accept a compromise
plan whereby taxes would be cut by an additional
20 per cent.

Many observers believed that Germany's prosperity was at the expense of fellow Common Market
partners. Schmidt, however, urged the other nations to follow Germany's lead in keeping interest
rates high, raising taxes, and taking other unpopular measures to control inflation. He discussed
France's anti-inflation programs and international
political and economic matters in Bonn with French
President Valéry Giscard d'Estaing on July 8 and 9.
It was the first in a series of semi-annual Franco-
German meetings.

Schmidt met Italian Prime Minister Mariano
Rumor at Bellagio, Italy, during the last two days
of August. They discussed financing for the Common Market's ailing economies. Germany agreed
to loan Italy $2 billion.

At year's end, the anti-inflation program was
working too well, and interest rates were lowered
to stimulate the economy.   Kenneth Brown

See also EUROPE (Facts in Brief Table).

GESELL, GERHARD ALDEN (1910-   ), United States District Court judge for the District of Columbia, issued rulings in 1974 that helped to shape the course of important Watergate trials. On May 24, he ruled out national security as a defense by presidential aides John D. Ehrlichman and Charles W. Colson. They were charged, along with others, with violating the civil rights of Daniel Ellsberg's psychiatrist. Ellsberg had leaked top-secret documents on the Vietnam War in 1971.

Gesell also threatened to dismiss the case when President Richard M. Nixon, claiming executive privilege and national security, withheld personal documents that Ehrlichman and Colson had subpoenaed. Ehrlichman was given access to notes on his White House discussions with President Nixon after Colson pleaded guilty on June 3, but only after a series of confrontations between Gesell and President Nixon's lawyers.

Gesell was born on June 16, 1910, in Los Angeles, the son of a well-known pediatrician. He earned a B.A. degree from Yale College in 1932 and an LL.B. degree from Yale Law School in 1935. He married Peggy Holliday Pike in 1936, and they moved to Washington, D.C., where he became an attorney with the Securities and Exchange Commission. He entered private practice there in 1941. President Lyndon B. Johnson appointed him to the bench in 1967. See WATERGATE.   Robert K. Johnson

GHANA enjoyed a peaceful year politically in 1974. However, the nation's three universities were temporarily closed in February, when students demonstrated against alleged army brutality. Four politicians were sentenced to death in February for their role in a 1973 attempted coup. In April, their sentences were commuted to life imprisonment. Secessionists in the Volta Region stepped up demands to join neighboring Togo, but Ghana rejected their demands, and Togo supported Ghana.

The government continued to struggle with its enormous debt, accrued largely during the rule of Kwame Nkrumah, who was overthrown in 1966. In early May, the ruling National Redemption Council (NRC) announced that payments on term debts of $294 million were being rescheduled.

A Ghana Tourist Development Company was established during the year to promote tourism. The government reported that 1973 tourist earnings were up about 33 per cent to $7 million.

Ghana's tenuous balance of trade was threatened by rising oil prices. In June, the NRC withdrew subsidies on other consumer imports, which had cost the government $42 million over the previous two years. It hoped that by discouraging imports it would aid national self-reliance.   John Storm Roberts

See also AFRICA (Facts in Brief Table).

GIRL SCOUTS. See YOUTH ORGANIZATIONS.
GIRLS' CLUBS. See YOUTH ORGANIZATIONS.

GISCARD D'ESTAING, VALERY (1926-   ), was elected president of France on May 19, 1974, defeating Socialist François Mitterrand in a hotly contested election. He succeeded President Georges Pompidou, who died on April 2.

Giscard d'Estaing was born on Feb. 2, 1926, in Koblenz, Germany, where his father was serving in the French High Commissariat. He attended the distinguished Polytechnical School and the National School of Administration, both in Paris. After serving in the French resistance during the Nazi occupation of World War II, he joined the French First Army of Liberation in 1944.

The new president began his government career in the finance ministry in 1952 and has specialized in finance since then. He was elected to the National Assembly in 1956, and also served as a member of the French delegation to the United Nations General Assembly from 1956 to 1958. He was named secretary of state for finance in 1959. He served as minister of finance and economic affairs from 1962 until he left the Cabinet in 1966 and from 1969 until his election as president.

Wealthy, aristocratic, and intellectual, Giscard d'Estaing has deliberately cultivated a public image of youthful vigor. He skis, hunts, plays football, and flies his own plane. He and his socially prominent wife, Anne-Aymone de Brantes, have four children.   Edward G. Nash

GOLF. Gary Player was obsessed with practice and Johnny Miller avoided it. Each followed his path to golf glory and riches in 1974. Player won the Masters and British Open, two of the four major tournaments, and Miller won more tournaments (eight) and more prize money ($353,030) than any other professional, and was voted Player of the Year by the Professional Golfers' Association (PGA).

Miller, a 27-year-old Californian, won the first three tournaments of the year–the Bing Crosby Pro-Amateur, the Phoenix Open, and the Dean Martin-Tucson Open, all in January. He won the Heritage Classic in March, the Tournament of Champions in April, the Westchester Classic in August, and the World Open and Kaiser International Open in September. He broke Jack Nicklaus' 1972 earnings record of $320,542, and he won more tournaments than anyone since Arnold Palmer won eight in 1960.

He seldom practiced except to loosen up before a round. "My game doesn't require a lot of maintenance," he said. "My swing is grooved, for good or bad. Most guys who practice too much fiddle with their swings and then screw up. All the practice is doing is confusing their memory muscle."

Player, a 37-year-old South African, took an opposite approach, saying, "The more dedicated you are, the more sacrifices you make, the more you appreciate winning a major championship."

For Johnny Miller, 27, it was a very profitable year. He won eight tournaments, and his total earnings, $353,030, set a single-season record.

Player won his second Masters title by two strokes in April at Augusta, Ga., and the British Open – his third triumph there – by four strokes in July at Lytham St. Annes, England. He was seventh in the PGA championship, he tied for eighth in the United States Open, and he lost to Hale Irwin in the final of the Piccadilly world match-play tournament.

Irwin, a former defensive back at the University of Colorado, surprisingly won the U.S. Open by two strokes in June at Mamaroneck, N.Y. The Winged Foot Golf Club course had so many pitfalls that Will Grimsley of the Associated Press called it an "Anzio beachhead." After conquering it, Irwin said, "This will do a lot of good for my ego."

Lee Trevino of El Paso, Tex., won the PGA championship in August at Clemmons, N.C., beating Nicklaus by a stroke. Nicklaus won the Hawaiian Open and the first Tournament Players Division championship, finished third in the British Open, tied for fourth in the Masters, and tied for 10th in the U.S. Open.

Trevino also won the Greater New Orleans Open and the four-man World Series of Golf, and he was runner-up to Miller in voting for Player of the Year. Hubert Green was third and Nicklaus fourth in the voting. Green won four tournaments (Bob Hope Desert Classic, Greater Jacksonville Open, IVB-Philadelphia Golf Classic, and, with Mac McLendon, the PGA team championship). Dave Stockton won three (Glen Campbell-Los Angeles Open, Quad Cities Open, and the Sammy Davis-Greater Hartford Open). Bobby Nichols won two (Andy Williams-San Diego Open and the Canadian Open). Brian (Bud) Allin, a former artillery officer in Vietnam, also won two (Doral-Eastern Open and the Byron Nelson Classic).

Lee Elder, a black, qualified for the 1975 Masters by winning the Monsanto Open in April at Pensacola, Fla. No black has ever played in the Masters. Charlie Sifford (in 1967 and 1969) and Pete Brown (in 1970) had won on the PGA tour, but that was before tournament victories meant automatic invitations to the Masters.

Elder was a high school dropout, the son of a Dallas truckdriver. He did not play his first 18-hole round until he was 16, and he spent most of his professional career playing against other blacks on municipal courses for tiny purses. He often had to *hustle* (play for side bets) to earn a living.

The Women's Tour. The star of the Ladies Professional Golf Association (LPGA) tour was 35-year-old JoAnne Gunderson Carner, who won six tournaments. Her sixth victory in Portland, Ore., in September broke Kathy Whitworth's one-year earnings record ($85,209 in 1973). She earned $87,094 during the year. Sandra Haynie of Dallas won the women's U.S. Open and LPGA championships. Frank Litsky

GONÇALVES, VASCO DOS SANTOS (1921-), an army colonel, was named prime minister of Portugal by provisional President António de Spínola on July 13, 1974. He was the ideological leader of the Armed Forces Movement that overthrew Portugal's civilian dictatorship on April 25. He vowed to bring democracy to Portugal by the spring of 1975 and to end the wars in Portugal's African territories as quickly as possible. See AFRICA; PORTUGAL.

Assuming office in Lisbon, Gonçalves took note of the prevailing climate of anarchy and warned that "we all have to live now in a true period of austerity." Without "hard work by all the Portuguese at all levels," he asserted, "the development of the nation will never be accomplished."

Gonçalves was born in Lisbon, the son of Victor Gonçalves, a well-known soccer player for Lisbon's leading team, Bonfica. He graduated from the Portuguese Military Academy in 1942, and has spent his military career in the Army Engineering Corps. His experiences made him one of the war-weary generation of professional soldiers who watched Portugal become caught in the seemingly never-ending colonial warfare.

Gonçalves is married and has two children, Victor Alfonso, a 23-year-old engineering student, and Maria, an architectural student.   Foster Stockwell

GOVERNORS, U.S. See STATE GOVERNMENT.

GREAT BRITAIN. As the gathering economic gloom thickened in 1974 – with the prospect of runaway inflation and massive unemployment growing more imminent by the month – the British people recoiled from making the hard political choices that their economic predicament demanded. Great Britain last had two elections in the same year in 1910, and both had produced the same indecisive results. History virtually repeated itself when Britain went to the polls in February and October, 1974.

On both occasions, voters remained stubbornly reluctant to give a safe working majority to either the Conservatives or Labour. Instead, an increasing number of voters flirted with third parties. When the national coal miners strike prompted the Conservatives to go to the country in February, Labour ended up with the most seats in Parliament, but without an overall majority. The October election gave Labour a three-seat edge, a majority that could easily disappear after a few by-elections.

Miners' Troubles. Prospects from the start were the bleakest in more than 25 years. Britain's workers went on a three-day workweek on January 1 as part of the Conservative government's energy-saving measures to combat the Middle East oil embargo and the coal miners' ban on overtime work. But oil supplies still got through, and it soon became apparent that the government's real battle – one that it was to lose – was with the miners. Prime Minister Edward Heath maintained that to give in to the miners' wage demands would destroy the government's counterinflation policy. The miners wanted a pay hike of from 30 to 40 per cent, and the government offered a raise of about 16 per cent.

On February 4, Britain's 260,000 miners voted to call a strike, to start on February 10. Heath replied by setting a general election for February 28.

The Campaign. Heath campaigned on the theme that inflation could be controlled only if the government stood up to the union militants. Conservatives warned of the dire consequences of allowing a small left wing minority to thwart the will of a democratically elected government and pointed to Communists on the mining union executive who made no secret of their desire to have a strike to bring down the government. The opinion polls gave the Conservatives a comfortable lead, and Heath was quietly confident as his whistle-stop tour of the country gathered momentum.

Labour Party leader Harold Wilson concentrated on the steep rise in prices under the Conservatives. He offered the country a social contract under which the unions would voluntarily hold the line on wages in return for action by a Labour government to establish a socialist society. Toward the end of the campaign, the polls started to show a

Prime Minister Harold Wilson, center, launches the campaign for Britain's second 1974 election in September. His Labour Party won a slim majority.

Smoke and flames pour from London's Westminster Hall after an Irish terrorist bomb exploded in the Houses of Parliament on June 17.

Liberal Party surge, mainly at the expense of the Conservative Party.

Election Results. Labour emerged with 301 seats in the 635-seat House of Commons, 5 ahead of the Conservatives. Yet Labour had finished second in the popular vote with 11.6 million votes, 200,000 votes behind the Conservatives. The Liberals won 6 million votes, but gained only 14 seats. The Liberals, however, together with 7 Scottish Nationalists, 2 Welsh Nationalists, 11 Ulster Unionists, and 4 others, were in a key position because neither of the two big parties could govern without their support.

Heath offered Liberal leader Jeremy Thorpe three positions in a Conservative Cabinet, plus a change in the electoral system to benefit the Liberals, as part of a deal to form a Conservative-Liberal coalition. Thorpe rejected the offer, and Heath resigned as prime minister. Harold Wilson became head of a minority Labour government on March 4.

Labour's Program. The first act of Britain's first minority government in over 40 years was to settle the miners' dispute. On March 6, the miners accepted a $200-million wage offer, a 35 per cent increase, that gave them nearly all they had asked for, and the strike was called off.

Wilson on March 12 outlined a program that promised a fundamental renegotiation of Britain's terms of entry into the European Community (Common Market), rigid price controls, massive food subsidies, a rent freeze, land nationalization, an increase in retirement pensions, redistribution of income and wealth, and repeal of the Industrial Relations Act regulating union activities.

Chancellor of the Exchequer Denis Healey introduced his first budget on March 26, and its broadly antibusiness outlook pleased his own party. Taxes were raised by $3.2 billion, partly through a 3 per cent increase in income taxes and a 2 per cent increase in corporation taxes. Companies also had to bear the brunt of the cost of increased pensions (which rose to $23 a week for single persons and $37 a week for married couples). Over $1 billion was laid aside for food subsidies. Those on low incomes were given tax relief, while the rich were hit the hardest with an 8 per cent income tax boost and a 98 per cent tax rate on investment income. Wealth and gift taxes were also promised.

A Deteriorating Situation. By the summer, the government's legislative program was badly mauled. Liberals, Scottish Nationalists, and Ulster Unionists joined with the Conservatives on June 19 to defeat a government attempt to refund the unions with $23 million in lost tax relief. The following day, they joined again in a sweeping condemnation of nationalization. Regular defeats on trade union and financial matters followed.

Meanwhile, the economic situation continued to deteriorate. With the abolition of wage controls, inflation neared an annual rate of 20 per cent, unemployment rose, investment remained sluggish, and the country headed for a $10-billion balance-of-payments deficit. By July, Healey realized that his first budget had deflated demand just when the economy was already heading for a recession. A second budget on July 22 included a 2 per cent cut in the value-added tax, property tax relief, softer dividend controls, and a doubling of the employment subsidy for companies in depressed regions.

The Second Election. Wilson called an election for October 10. The social contract with the unions became the centerpiece of his anti-inflation strategy, and he contrasted it with the Heath approach of confrontation and statutory wage controls. Heath replied by claiming that the summer's wage demands had already shown the contract to be a charade and said that the nation's problems were so grave that only a government of national unity could tackle them.

This time, Labour scraped home with a narrow overall majority. It won 319 seats, the Conservatives 276, the Liberals 13, the Scottish Nationalists 11, the Ulster Unionists 10, and others 6. Labour went after most of the socialist measures it had been unable to pursue while it was still a minority government: nationalization of land, shipbuilding, and aircraft industries; state control of the private sector through a national enterprise board; and the $23-million tax refund for the unions. But Healey annoyed the Labour left wing with his third budget of the year, which increased company liquidity by $3.7 billion. Pensions and family allowances were also increased.

By winter, however, the social contract was looking distinctly tattered. Scotland was crippled by 25 unofficial strikes, many resolved only by conceding wage demands far in excess of the contract. English workers increased their wage demands as a result of union successes in Scotland. The pound headed for an all-time low.

Other Action. On December 3, Britain announced major cuts in its defense budget that mean giving up its worldwide military role. Cuts will be achieved by reducing military manpower, ending new programs, closing bases, and recalling forces from Singapore and Hong Kong. Defense spending will drop by about $700 million in 1975-1976 and by $11 billion over the next 10 years.

A mandatory energy-saving program went into effect on December 9, including lower speed limits and lower temperatures.

The major foreign issue was whether Britain should continue its membership in the European Community. Foreign Secretary James Callaghan began to renegotiate the terms in March. A referendum on continued membership was promised after the negotiations were complete. The Paris summit of Common Market leaders in De-

cember raised hopes of a successful renegotiation, and, much to the anger of the anti-Market Labour left, Wilson said that if the terms were right, he would recommend that Britain stay in. See EUROPE.

North Sea Oil offered the one gleam of light shining through the economic gloom. Britain hopes to be self-sufficient in oil by 1980. Proven recoverable reserves in the British sector were estimated at 895 million short tons (810 metric tons).

North Sea oil discoveries, however, posed a new threat to British unity. Most of the oil fields are off the Scottish coast, and the Scottish Nationalist Party (SNP), which wants an independent Scotland, made great progress in both elections campaigning on the theme of "It's Scotland's oil." In February, the SNP increased its seats from 1 to 7, and in October, the number rose to 11. With 30 per cent of the Scottish vote, they are now Scotland's second party.

Terrorism in Ulster continued to spill over into the rest of Britain. Since 1972, bombing outrages have killed more than 50 persons in England. The worst atrocity was a bomb attack on two Birmingham pubs in October that killed 21 persons. This led Parliament to ban the Irish Republican Army and institute tough new antiterrorism laws. But a move to reintroduce the death penalty was defeated.   Andrew F. Neil

See also EUROPE (Facts in Brief Table).

British coal miners demonstrate outside union headquarters in London in January, demanding higher wages. They went on strike in February.

GREECE

GREECE. Democracy returned to Greece on July 23, 1974, when the military junta resigned after seven years in power and called on professional politicians to form a government of national unity. Former Prime Minister Constantin Karamanlis flew back from exile in Paris to head the new government (see KARAMANLIS, CONSTANTIN). The changeover was greeted with celebrations throughout Greece. The junta had supported a military take-over in Cyprus, but when Turkish forces invaded the island, the colonels resigned.

Prisoners Released. Minutes after returning to a hero's welcome, Karamanlis announced measures for the "immediate restoration of democratic legality." These included the release of all political prisoners, restitution of citizenship to opponents of the junta who had been deprived of their nationality, and abolition of all orders restricting movement to and from Greece. Karamanlis formed a broadly based Cabinet that included Greeks who had been directly associated with resistance against the dictatorship. The 1952 Constitution, abolished by the military regime in 1968, was reinstated on August 1.

Relations with Turkey. Tension between Greece and neighboring Turkey had been building since January over ownership of the potentially oil-rich Aegean Sea continental shelf. On March 31, the Greeks pulled out of a North Atlantic Treaty Organization (NATO) naval exercise in the Aegean because, they said, Turkey had violated Greek air space. Because both countries were NATO members, the United States urged them to avoid confrontation that would jeopardize NATO's flank.

Makarios Goes. The first signs of trouble in Cyprus came on July 7 with a letter from the island's president, Archbishop Makarios III, to Greek President Phaidon Gizikis, accusing the Athens regime of conspiring to seize power in Cyprus and even to assassinate him. He demanded immediate withdrawal of 650 Greek Army officers controlling the Cypriot National Guard. His plea was ignored, and, on July 15, the National Guard seized control of Cyprus. Makarios escaped to Malta and then London.

Negotiations bogged down among Britain, Turkey, and Greece – which were bound by a 1960 treaty to guarantee the Cypriot Constitution. Turkey invaded the island on July 20, and in two months took control of the northeastern third. See CYPRUS.

Withdrawal from NATO. Greece pulled its armed forces out of NATO on August 14 when Turkey renewed its offensive in Cyprus after peace talks sponsored by the United Nations broke down. A government statement said NATO had "demonstrated its inability to prevent Turkey from creating a state of conflict between two allies." Greece promised to retain NATO political ties and was thought to be ready to renegotiate U.S. use of Greek military bases.

Prime Minister Constantin Karamanlis returns to power in Greece in July following the collapse of a military junta that ruled seven years.

Karamanlis described the decision to pull out of the military structure of NATO as "firm and final." But it did not mean that Greece would "sever her political and moral links with Europe, to whom she belongs and wishes to belong." In his first public speech since his recall from exile, Karamanlis reproached the United States and Britain for "crimes of omission or commission" over Cyprus.

Military Rulers Exiled. On October 23, the government arrested fallen dictator George Papadopoulos and four other junta leaders who helped him seize power in 1967. The five were sent into exile on the small Aegean island of Kea.

Greek ministers met European Community (Common Market) officials in Brussels, Belgium, on August 28 to re-establish relations. Greece hopes to become a full member "in four years," said Foreign Minister George Mavros.

Free Elections, Greece's first in over a decade, were held on November 17, and Karamanlis and his New Democracy Party won about 55 per cent of the vote. The Center Union-New Forces Party, led by Mavros, placed second with about 20 per cent.

Three weeks later, the Greeks voted 2 to 1 to replace the 142-year-old monarchy with a republican form of government. Michael Stassinopoulos was elected provisional president by the Parliament on December 18.   Kenneth Brown

See also EUROPE (Facts in Brief Table); TURKEY.

GRENADA, the southernmost of the Windward Islands, and only 133 square miles (344 square kilometers) in area, became the smallest independent nation in the Western Hemisphere on Feb. 7, 1974. The independence ceremonies, which had been preceded by a week of celebrations, ended 200 years of British colonial rule. The festivities were attended by representatives of 38 countries.

Prime Minister Eric M. Gairy, in his independence day address, urged an end to the conflict that had divided the island nation since November, 1973. This conflict pits two groups against the Gairy regime. The Committee of 22 consists of religious, business, and union leaders; the New Jewel Movement's membership includes such diverse groups as farmers, shopkeepers, high officials in the Roman Catholic Church, and young black radical socialists.

Both groups complained about a 500-man secret police force known as the Volunteers for the Protection of Fundamental Human Rights. They accused Gairy of recruiting the force from criminal elements and prison inmates.

The independence celebrations were marred by strikes affecting electricity and telephone services. A longshoremen's strike also in progress seriously disrupted the shipping industry.   Paul C. Tullier

See also LATIN AMERICA (Facts in Brief Table).

GUATEMALA. See LATIN AMERICA.

GUINEA. See AFRICA.

GUINEA-BISSAU, Portugal's smallest African territory, became an independent nation on Sept. 10, 1974. The last Portuguese troops withdrew on October 31. The African Party for the Independence of Guinea-Bissau and the Cape Verde Islands (PAIGC) had won control of most of the country after 11 years of guerrilla warfare. Portugal agreed to grant independence after an April coup ousted the Portuguese government. See PORTUGAL.

Talks between PAIGC leaders and Portuguese officials deadlocked over the status of the Cape Verde Islands, which are important to Portugal's military and telecommunications network. In July, there was also disagreement within the PAIGC about the importance of including the islands in the new nation. The settlement separated the islands, but Portugal promised a referendum to determine if the islanders want to join Guinea-Bissau.

The new PAIGC government, though strongly Marxist, declared it would cooperate with Portugal in cultural, economic, and technical areas. Government officials also stressed the nation's development needs, particularly in the battle-scarred north. The PAIGC's first major goals were to bring water systems and electric power to rural villages. In September, Medina de Boa replaced Bissau as the nation's capital.   John Storm Roberts

See also AFRICA (Facts in Brief Table).

GUYANA. See LATIN AMERICA.

HAITI. President Jean-Claude Duvalier emphasized the need to solve critical economic and social problems in 1974. Although the 22-year-old leader refused to permit opposition parties to function, he began to gain the approval of representatives of foreign countries and international development agencies. He seemed determined to reverse the trend that had set in during his father's 14-year dictatorship.

An upturn in the economy gave Haiti a much needed boost toward financial stability. In the three years since President Duvalier had succeeded his father, the economy had grown by about 5 per cent. New assembly plants, financed largely by U.S.-owned companies, were being built along the road to François Duvalier Airport. Construction was underway on hotels and residences in the hills overlooking Port-au-Prince. Tourism was increasing.

The construction boom and a rise in tourism, however, did little to ease the poverty of the majority. About 80 per cent of Haiti's people continued to exist at bare subsistence levels. Agricultural production had not kept pace with population growth, and food shortages were acute in many regions. International assistance agencies, including the U.S. Agency for International Development and the U.S.-sponsored CARE program, provided food and other relief.   Paul C. Tullier

See also LATIN AMERICA (Facts in Brief Table).

HANDICAPPED. A two-year study by the Rand Corporation, released in February, 1974, showed that federal, state, and local programs to help handicapped youth in the United States lack direction and coordination. The study also found that the programs, which cost taxpayers about $5 billion each year, often fail to identify those eligible for aid and unfairly serve those they find. The study was authorized by the U.S. Department of Health, Education, and Welfare (HEW).

According to James S. Kakalik, director of the study, more than one-third of the handicapped children between the ages of 5 and 17 are not enrolled in the special educational programs to which they are entitled. By Rand's criteria, about 9 million American youths are handicapped, or about 1 in 10 of those under 21. Rand defined handicapped youths as persons under 21 with physical or mental impairments for which they need help not required by normal youths. This definition does not include the disadvantaged whose problems come mainly from social or economic conditions.

Because some states have no schools for deaf youths or educational programs for the hard of hearing, a few families have had to move to other states to fulfill their needs, according to Kakalik. "In one instance," he said, "we also found that a child with a hearing defect had been enrolled for nine years in a school for the deaf before educators admitted he would fare better in a more normal educational environment."

The study cited the need for more funds and emphasized the need for complementing coordination to use existing resources better. It also noted the lack of planning and an agency to provide such devices as hearing aids, glasses, and artificial limbs. Kakalik said that many children could be placed in a normal school setting if fitted with such aids.

Handicapped Office. On July 8, HEW announced a $200,000 grant to establish an office in Washington, D.C., for the newly created National Industries for the Severely Handicapped. The organization, which was started in 1973, is a counterpart of one that served the blind for many years. It is to assist in obtaining government contracts for sheltered workshops employing severely handicapped persons.

HEW's Rehabilitation Services Administration will coordinate the work of the six participating agencies, all of which have workshop affiliates. They are Goodwill Industries of America, Incorporated; International Association of Rehabilitation Facilities; Jewish Occupational Council for Jewish Vocational Services; National Association for Retarded Citizens; National Easter Seal Society for Crippled Children and Adults; and United Cerebral Palsy Associations, Incorporated.

"Sight" for the Blind. Medical researchers at the University of Utah at Salt Lake City and the University of Western Ontario at London, Ontario, Canada, announced in February that they had successfully stimulated artificial sight in two blind patients. By the stimulation of an array of electrodes implanted in their brains, the two patients, one 28 years old and the other 43, were able to "see" dots of light. The electrodes were implanted in the visual cortex region at the back of the head and linked by means of a cable to a computer. The system bypassed the retina, optic nerve, and other parts of the nervous system enabling a normal person to see.

In their report, William H. Dobelle and Michael G. Mladejovsky of Utah and John P. Girvin of Ontario said, "Our long-term objective is to build a visual prosthesis to give artificial vision. We're trying to devise a way that will allow a blind person to walk out of a room without bumping into things."

The two patients have been involved with the project for at least four years. Grids of 64 electrodes each were implanted in their brains. A few of the electrodes were stimulated for seconds at a time, creating patterns of dots called *phosphenes* that resembled squares or alphabet letters. One patient reported that he could see only the dots, but the other could make out the patterns. Joseph P. Anderson

See also Section Two, LEARNING FOR LIVING IN A SILENT WORLD.

HARNESS RACING. See HORSE RACING.

HAWAII. See STATE GOVERNMENT.

HEALTH AND DISEASE. A smallpox epidemic hit India, Bangladesh, Nepal, Pakistan, and Ethiopia in 1974, and a meningitis epidemic caused alarm in Brazil. Health officials rushed preventive vaccines to the infected areas and conducted widespread health campaigns. At the same time, officers of the World Health Organization (WHO) optimistically predicted the worldwide eradication of smallpox by the end of 1975.

In India, the smallpox epidemic spread from the state of Bihar to Uttar Pradesh and other states. By July, Bihar reported 91,400 cases; Uttar Pradesh, 28,000; West Bengal, 9,000; and Assam, 4,000. About 26,000 Indians died from smallpox. Bangladesh reported 13,000 cases; Pakistan, 7,000; and Nepal, 1,000. Ethiopia, the only nation outside the Asian subcontinent reporting smallpox, had 3,000.

Donald A. Henderson, a U.S. Public Health Service officer stationed in New Delhi, India, said in July that the epidemic was under control and that all health personnel were working to keep the disease from spreading. Henderson heads WHO's smallpox-eradication program. "If this interest and concern about ending smallpox can be maintained for the next few months," Henderson said, "it's all over. We don't think we're overconfident, but everything looks good. By June of 1975, we hope we'll be finished with smallpox in Asia."

Who Gets a Cold, and When

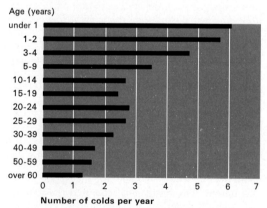

When colds begin in young people (age 5-19 years)

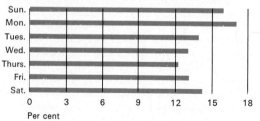

Source: *Journal of American Medical Association*

In Brazil, more than 1,000 people died in 10,572 cases of meningitis reported from January through August. São Paulo, the country's industrial capital, was hit the hardest. The disease claimed 67 lives there in the first week of August alone. Health officials said that the disease was difficult to control because most cases were caused by meningococcus bacterium, type A, which had seldom occurred previously. As a result, there had been no mass vaccinations in the past.

U.S. Health Trends. Statisticians for the U.S. Department of Health, Education, and Welfare reported in May that death rates from heart disease, stroke, peptic ulcers, and even suicides have declined during the past two decades. Among the diseases studied, only cancer and cirrhosis of the liver caused more deaths.

The experts said that the figures showed that some important changes in national life styles, behavior, or environment have led to the decline, but they could not identify the crucial changes.

Effects of Soft Water. Andrew G. Shaper, a British physician, reported a striking statistical correlation between soft water and heart disease in 1974. He said that a study of geographical regions in both England and the United States revealed a significantly higher incidence of heart attacks and fatal heart attacks among persons who regularly drank large amounts of soft water.

Shaper, a member of the scientific staff of the United Kingdom Medical Research Council's Social Medicine Unit in London, cited a U.S. study involving 7.5 million persons in 140 counties along the Ohio and Columbia rivers (soft-water areas) and the Missouri and Colorado rivers (hard-water areas). In all four river basins, he said, death rates from causes other than heart disease were virtually the same, but death rates from heart disease were much lower in the hard-water regions.

In Monroe County, Florida, the water supply was changed from rainwater, with a hardness of 0.5 parts per million, to deep-well water, with a hardness of 200 parts per million. Death rates from cardiovascular disease dropped dramatically, from a range of between 500 and 700 persons a year in the county to a range of between 200 and 300, only four years after the increase in water hardness.

Shaper admits that the British researchers are still far from pinpointing the precise cause – if any – of soft-water-related heart disease. However, they believe that minerals in the water (calcium, magnesium, and sodium) may play a role. For example, some soft water carries metal contaminants such as lead from pipes or soil. Shaper says the hardness or softness of water probably determines its ability to extract other trace elements from rocks, food, and even cooking utensils. Richard P. Davies

HIGHWAY. See BUILDING AND CONSTRUCTION; TRANSPORTATION.

HOBBIES. Letters by political figures were expensive collectors' items in 1974. The autograph collection of Harry J. Sonneborn, founder of the McDonald's hamburger chain, was auctioned for $314,450 in New York City in June. From his collection, a first edition of George Washington's 1796 address announcing his retirement from public life brought the top price of $12,000. Abraham Lincoln's last letter, written on April 14, 1865, went for $8,000. An 1861 correspondence between former Presidents Franklin Pierce and Martin Van Buren brought $8,000. Caustic 1949 letters between President Harry S. Truman and labor leader John L. Lewis sold for $5,000. And President John F. Kennedy's autograph went for $700, while that of his assassin, Lee Harvey Oswald, sold for $1,600.

On January 30, a letter written by Benjamin Franklin discussing events leading to the American Revolution was auctioned in New York City for $7,500. Two letters written by Thomas Jefferson brought $4,200 and $3,500 on July 25.

Record Prices. Earl Clark of Lancaster, Pa., paid a record price for a classic motor car on January 5. He bid $180,000 for a gold-plated 1920 Pierce Arrow opera coupé owned by Kenneth Mausolf of Denver at an auction in Scottsdale, Ariz. At Lake George, N.Y., on May 25, James H. Southard of Smyrna, Ga., bid $60,000 for a 1936 Duesenberg.

A record price for a work of art other than a painting was the $1,003,800 paid for a Chinese vase by Helen Glatz, a London art dealer, on April 2. She purchased the Ming bottle-shaped vase, dating to the 1400s, in London for an unidentified client. A Mei P'ing jar made in the 1300s brought the second highest price for a nonpainting, $554,000. Frederic M. Mayer of New York City sold the jar to a Japanese art dealer in London on June 24.

A gold snuff box, which had been made for Frederick the Great of Prussia in the 1700s, sold for $206,400 at auction in London on June 10. It was owned by a descendant of Frederick – Queen Frederica, former queen mother of Greece.

Total sales at a January auction of Americana in New York City brought in $1.5 million. A New York dealer paid $62,000 for a hand-carved wood cupboard dated 1683 and made in Ipswich, Mass.

A New York dealer, Lew D. Feldman, paid $216,000 for a 15th-century illuminated, hand-written manuscript of Chaucer's *The Canterbury Tales* in London on June 5.

Something of a collectors' boom in old alarm clocks developed during the year. Clocks that formerly sold for 50 cents to $1 brought $15 to $20 each, particularly if they were made between 1912 and 1930 or in the early 1940s. In August, the U.S. Federal Trade Commission proposed a rule that would protect collectors of political memorabilia by requiring that buttons and such items show the year in which they were produced. Theodore M. O'Leary

Standings in National Hockey League

East Division

	W.	L.	T.	Points
Boston	52	17	9	113
Montreal	45	24	9	99
N.Y. Rangers	40	24	14	94
Toronto	35	27	16	86
Buffalo	32	34	12	76
Detroit	29	39	10	68
Vancouver	24	43	11	59
N.Y. Islanders	19	41	18	56

West Division

	W.	L.	T.	Points
Philadelphia	50	16	12	112
Chicago	41	14	23	105
Los Angeles	33	33	12	70
Atlanta	30	34	14	74
Pittsburgh	28	41	9	65
St. Louis	26	40	12	64
Minnesota	23	38	17	63
California	13	55	10	36

Scoring Leaders

	Games	Goals	Assists	Points
Phil Esposito, Boston	78	68	77	145
Bobby Orr, Boston	74	32	90	122
Ken Hodge, Boston	76	50	55	105
Wayne Cashman, Boston	78	30	59	89
Bobby Clarke, Philadelphia	77	35	52	87
Richard Martin, Buffalo	78	52	34	86
Syl Apps, Pittsburgh	75	24	61	85
Darryl Sittler, Toronto	78	38	46	84
Lowell MacDonald, Pittsburgh	78	43	39	82
Brad Park, N.Y. Rangers	78	25	57	82
Dennis Hextall, Minnesota	78	20	62	82

Leading Goalies

	Games	Goals against	Avg.
Bernie Parent, Philadelphia	73	136	1.89
Bobby Taylor, Philadelphia	7	26	4.26
Philadelphia Totals	78	164	2.10
Tony Esposito, Chicago	70	141	2.04
Mike Veisor, Chicago	10	20	2.23
Chicago Totals	78	164	2.10
Ross Brooks, Boston	21	46	2.36
Gilles Gilbert, Boston	54	158	2.95
Ken Broderick, Boston	5	16	3.20
Boston Totals	78	221	2.83

Awards

Calder Trophy (best rookie)—Denis Potvin, N.Y. Islanders
Hart Trophy (most valuable player)—Phil Esposito, Boston
Lady Byng Trophy (sportsmanship)—John Bucyk, Boston
Norris Trophy (best defenseman)—Bobby Orr, Boston
Art Ross Trophy (leading scorer)—Phil Esposito, Boston
Smythe Trophy (most valuable player in Stanley Cup play)—
  Bernie Parent, Philadelphia
Vezina Trophy (leading goalie)—Bernie Parent, Philadelphia,
  and Tony Esposito, Chicago
Masterton Trophy (perseverance, dedication to hockey)—
  Henri Richard, Montreal

Standings in World Hockey Association

East Division

	W.	L.	T.	Points
New England	43	31	4	90
Toronto	41	33	4	86
Cleveland	37	32	9	83
Chicago	38	35	5	81
Quebec	38	36	4	80
New Jersey	32	42	4	68

West Division

	W.	L.	T.	Points
Houston	48	25	5	101
Minnesota	44	32	2	90
Edmonton	38	37	3	79
Winnipeg	34	39	5	73
Vancouver	27	50	1	55
Los Angeles	25	53	0	50

Scoring Leaders

	Games	Goals	Assists	Points
Mike Walton, Minnesota	78	57	60	117
Andre Lacroix, New Jersey	78	31	80	111
Gordie Howe, Houston	70	31	69	100
Bobby Hull, Winnipeg	75	53	42	95
Wayne Connelly, Minnesota	78	42	53	95
Wayne Carleton, Toronto	78	37	55	92
Bryan Campbell, Vancouver	76	27	62	89
Danny Lawson, Vancouver	78	50	38	88
Serge Bernier, Quebec	74	37	49	86
Larry Lund, Houston	75	33	53	86

Leading Goalies

	Games	Goals against	Avg.
Ron Grahame, Houston	4	5	1.20
Don McLeod, Houston	49	127	2.56
Wayne Rutledge, Houston	25	84	3.34
Houston Totals	78	216	2.74
Al Smith, New England	55	164	3.08
Bill Berglund, New England	3	10	3.33
Bruce Landon, New England	24	82	3.55
New England Totals	78	256	3.23
Gerry Cheevers, Cleveland	59	180	3.03
Bob Whidden, Cleveland	22	80	3.90
Cleveland Totals	78	260	3.26

Awards

Gary L. Davidson Trophy (most valuable player)—
  Gordie Howe, Houston
W.D. (Bill) Hunter Trophy (leading scorer)—
  Mike Walton, Minnesota
Lou Kaplan Award (best rookie)—Mark Howe, Houston
Ben Hatskin Trophy (leading goalie)—Don MacLeod, Houston
Dennis A. Murphy Award (best defenseman)—
  Pat Stapleton, Chicago
Howard Baldwin Award (coach of the year)—
  Billy Harris, Toronto

HOCKEY. In 1974, for the first time in National Hockey League (NHL) history, an expansion team won the Stanley Cup play-offs. The team was the Philadelphia Flyers, who believed in playing rough, and they alienated purists who revered hockey as a game of finesse. The Flyers, according to hockey writer Stan Fischler, put "blood on the ice."

The Flyers' coach, Fred Shero, preached that the team that intimidated was the team that won. "If the other team doesn't fight back, beautiful," he said. "If they do, then you've got a hockey game." Dave Schultz, the roughest of the Flyers, said, "We're not a ballet show or follies on the ice."

During the regular season, the Flyers won the West Division title and the Boston Bruins won in the East. They met in the play-off finals, with the Flyers winning in six games. The Most Valuable Player in the play-offs was Bernie Parent, the Flyers' goalie, who had been the first player to jump from the NHL to the rival World Hockey Association (WHA) and the first to jump back.

Shero, who earned $35,000 a year, accepted a $5,000 raise and rejected an offer to become part owner, general manager, and coach of Minnesota of the WHA for $100,000 a year. Armand (Bep) Guidolin, coach of the Bruins, quit when Boston refused to give him a five-year contract.

The Bruins. Guidolin was unhappy with some of his players. He said Phil Esposito's mind seemed to be on negotiations with the WHA rather than the play-offs. Esposito disagreed and called the Bruins "the worst a team of mine has ever been prepared." Guidolin suspended colorful Derek Sanderson for fighting with a teammate, and Sanderson was later exiled to the New York Rangers.

The four highest scorers in the league were Bruins –Esposito (145 points in 78 games), Bobby Orr, Ken Hodge, and Wayne Cashman. Esposito was voted Most Valuable Player in the league, Orr the outstanding defenseman. The All-Star team had Parent in goal, Orr and Brad Park of the Rangers on defense, Esposito at center, and Hodge and Buffalo's Richard Martin on wing.

The NHL played the season with 16 teams, then added the Washington Capitals and the Kansas City Scouts for 1974-1975 and voted franchises to Denver and Seattle for the 1976-1977 season. It switched to four divisions for the 1974-1975 season. After long and tumultuous negotiations, the league bought back the California Golden Seals from Charles O. Finley for $6,585,000.

In the WHA, there was realignment after the 12 teams lost $15 million in their first season (1972-1973). The Philadelphia team moved to Vancouver, Ottawa to Toronto, and, in midseason, New York moved to Cherry Hill, N.J., and became the Jersey Knights. After the season, the Los Angeles team became the Michigan Stags and Jersey moved to San Diego. The WHA switched to three divisions for 1974-1975, with new teams in Phoenix and Indianapolis. The league continued to lure NHL players, then agreed to mutual recognition of contracts.

In the WHA's first year, its major attraction was Bobby Hull of the Winnipeg Jets, previously one of the NHL's great scorers. In 1973-1974, the attraction was Gordie Howe and family, who joined the Houston Aeros and led them to the championship. Houston and the New England Whalers won the division titles; and in the play-off finals, Houston beat the Chicago Cougars in four games.

The 46-year-old Howe, rated by many the greatest player in hockey history, had played 25 years for the Detroit Red Wings and held every NHL lifetime scoring record. He had retired, but Houston brought him back with a million-dollar contract. Houston also signed his sons Mark and Marty.

Howe's skills and elbows were as sharp as ever. He was third in the WHA in scoring with 100 points in 70 games (Mike Walton of Minnesota was first with 117), he was named the league's Most Valuable Player, and he made the All-Star team at right wing. Son Mark, 19, was Rookie of the Year.

The Soviet Union's national team retained the world amateur championship in April and played Team Canada, made up of WHA stars, in September and October. Russia won the eight-game series, 4 games to 1. Three games ended in ties. Frank Litsky

HOME FURNISHINGS. See INTERIOR DESIGN.

HONDURAS. See LATIN AMERICA.

HORSE RACING. Dahlia was the star of world horse racing in 1974, traveling widely from her base in France. By year's end, the 4-year-old filly, bred in Kentucky and owned by Texan N. B. Hunt, had career earnings of $1,216,705 to rank as the richest female thoroughbred in history.

After winning major stakes in France and England, Dahlia won the Man o' War at Belmont Park in New York in October and the Canadian International Championship at Woodbine, both against males. In her last 1974 race, she lost by a length and a half, finishing third in the Washington, D.C., International at Laurel, Md., in November.

The 2-year-old division in the United States had an outstanding filly and an equally outstanding colt. Ruffian won all five of her races and was judged the best young filly in years, but a minor fracture in September curtailed her competition until 1975. Her male counterpart, Foolish Pleasure, won the Champagne and six other races to remain undefeated.

The Kentucky Derby attracted a large field to Churchill Downs on May 4, but quantity did not equal quality. The winner, Cannonade, did not live up to his promise in succeeding races. Little Current won the other Triple Crown races, the Preakness and Belmont. However, he was injured soon afterward and retired to stud.

Major U.S. Horse Races of 1974

Race	Winner	Value to Winner
Alabama Stakes	Quaze Quilt	$33,660
Arlington-Washington Futurity	Greek Answer	122,505
Belmont Stakes	Little Current	101,970
Brooklyn Handicap	Forego	66,600
Coaching Club American Oaks	Chris Evert	68,520
Hollywood Derby	Agitate	90,000
Hollywood Gold Cup	Tree of Knowledge	90,000
Jockey Club Gold Cup	Forego	67,140
Kentucky Derby	Cannonade	274,000
Man o' War Stakes	Dahlia	71,700
Marlboro Cup Handicap	Big Spruce	150,000
Preakness Stakes	Little Current	156,500
Santa Anita Derby	Destroyer	85,200
Santa Anita Handicap	Prince Dantan	105,000
United Nations Handicap	Halo	65,000
Washington, D.C., Int'l.	Admetus	100,000
Woodward Stakes	Forego	69,240

Major U.S. Harness Races of 1974

Race	Winner	Value to Winner
Cane Pace	Boyden Hanover	$51,165
Hambletonian	Christopher T.	80,075
Kentucky Futurity	Waymaker	32,500
Little Brown Jug	Armbro Omaha	48,073
Messenger Pace	Armbro Omaha	75,521
Roosevelt International	Delmonica Hanover	100,000
Yonkers Trot	Spitfire Hanover	37,746

Delmonica Hanover noses out Canada's Keystone Gary to win the $200,000
Roosevelt International Trot at New York's Roosevelt Raceway in July.

The most consistent 3-year-old was a filly, Chris Evert, who won the "Triple Crown for Fillies" at the New York tracks—the Acorn, Mother Goose, and Coaching Club American Oaks. Chris Evert met a challenge to race against California's best filly, Miss Musket, in a winner-take-all $350,000 match race at Hollywood Park in July. The East Coast champion won by 50 lengths, with Miss Musket eased up by her jockey in defeat.

Forego and Big Spruce emerged as the best older horses, each winning several important stakes. Late in the year, Desert Vixen returned to the form that made her 1973's best filly. Forego was named horse of the year in thoroughbred racing.

Jockey Chris McCarron, 19, who rode in his first race on January 29, set a new one-year record for victories when he rode his 516th winner on December 17 at Laurel.

Harness Racing. In October in Lexington, Ky., a colt, Alert Bret, paced the mile in 1 minute, 55⅘ seconds, and a filly, Handle With Care, did it in 1:54⅖ to become the fastest 2-year-olds in history. The filly's mile was the third fastest ever run by a pacer.

Hervé Filion became the first North American driver to win more than 5,000 races.

Quarter Horse Racing. Easy Date earned $330,000 when she won the All-American Futurity for 2-year-olds at Ruidoso, N. Mex.   Jane Goldstein

HOSPITAL. Under the federally mandated cost containment program known as the Economic Stabilization Program (ESP), U.S. hospital costs, for the first time in history, rose less than the general rate of inflation for the economy as a whole in 1974. Hospital service charges increased only 7.9 per cent by May, 1974, while the economy jumped 11.1 per cent. But by the time ESP ended in April, hospital operating margins had slipped from 2.2 per cent in 1971 to less than 1 per cent, and the percentage of hospital funds spent for expansion and improvement of services had declined considerably. As a result, hospitals began increasing charges when ESP ended, in order to cover higher costs.

Legislation lifting the exemption of employees of not-for-profit hospitals from provisions of the National Labor Relations Act (NLRA) was signed into law by President Richard M. Nixon on July 26. The NLRA change gave the employees of nearly 3,500 community hospitals the right to establish unions and conduct negotiations as do other workers protected by the NLRA.

The American Hospital Association registered 7,123 hospitals with 1.54 million beds in 1973. The hospitals reported 34.4 million inpatient and 233.6-million outpatient admissions in 1973, representing 3.3 and 6.6 per cent increases, respectively. They had more than 3 million full- and part-time employees in 1973.   Madison B. Brown

HOUSING. Disaster hit the U.S. housing industry in 1974 as rising inflation and tight credit cut drastically into the level of new construction and drove up building and financing costs. In an effort to stem the growing crisis, Congress passed the nation's first major housing bill since 1968, and the government pumped money into the ailing mortgage market.

New housing construction plummeted to its lowest level in 4½ years in August when the adjusted annual rate of new housing starts dropped to 1.12-million. This was 45 per cent below the August, 1973, level of 2.03 million starts. In September, the rate of housing starts increased slightly, but the adjusted annual rate of building permits issued – an indicator of future construction activity – fell to 825,000 units, the lowest level in eight years.

Cost Plus Interest. Construction costs increased sharply during a 14-month period ending in August, 1974. The average cost of a single-family home rose 21 per cent to $35,000, while the average house payment increased 35.6 per cent to $278 per month.

Mortgage interest rates rose steadily. The government gradually raised the ceiling on federally insured Federal Housing Administration (FHA) and Veterans Administration mortgages until it reached 9.5 per cent by August 13. There were 8 per cent more home-mortgage defaults during the first quarter of the year than in the same period of 1973.

Government Response. President Richard M. Nixon's Administration tried to bolster the housing industry by subsidizing interest rates so that some home buyers could borrow at less than the market rates. In January, the government committed $6.6-billion for this purpose. In May, it provided $10.3-billion to increase the mortgage-money supply.

President Gerald R. Ford essentially carried on the Nixon Administration's policies. In his October 8 message on inflation, Ford asked Congress to appropriate $3 billion more in home-mortgage funds. Congress passed a bill on October 15, authorizing the government to spend $7.75 billion a year for this purpose. But Ford indicated he would initially release only the $3 billion he requested.

Housing Act. The Housing and Community Development Act of 1974 was signed into law by President Ford on August 22. It was designed to stabilize federal housing and community development programs and ease the worsening mortgage credit market. The $11.3-million omnibus housing bill established a new rental-assistance program for low- and moderate-income groups, while continuing existing housing subsidy programs. See CITY.

The act authorized $1.23 billion to be spent for public housing in fiscal 1975 (June 30, 1974, to July 1, 1975). This included funds for the new rental-leasing subsidy program. Under the new program, strongly backed by the U.S. Department of Housing and Urban Development (HUD), the govern-

ment will subsidize rental payments so that poor families can lease housing from private landlords. It will also finance about 400,000 units of new or rehabilitated housing and 30,000 new units of conventional public housing for low-income subsidy rentals. This program was inspired by a HUD report, "Housing for the Seventies," distributed in February, which indicated that conventional public housing programs have failed to help the poor while providing profit-making opportunities for others.

According to the report, financial institutions profited from tax-free public housing bonds. Builders profited by erecting poorly constructed housing at excessively high cost. Corruption scandalized the FHA home-mortgage program, as real estate dealers charged low-income families high prices for buildings in need of extensive repair.

Upgrading Housing. The federal government also tried to improve the quality of existing housing. The Federal Home Loan Bank Board in April announced a $2.75-million experimental program to help stop the deterioration of neighborhoods. In June, HUD announced that it would spend $100-million to upgrade public housing in 32 cities. The Federal Trade Commission announced on July 4 that it was starting an investigation of condominiums to determine if developers used unfair or deceptive practices, such as forcing buyers to lease recreational facilities.   James M. Banovetz

HOUSTON fared better than the nation as a whole in economic areas during 1974. The cost of living increased by only 9.7 per cent between April, 1973, and April, 1974. The income of the average factory worker increased by 11 per cent, reaching an annual average of $10,829 by July. Even this income, however, was insufficient to provide an average family of four with the $12,000 that the U.S. Department of Labor said was required to live in moderate comfort in the city. A minimum livable income for such a Houston family was set at $7,900, below the estimated national minimum-income average of $9,100.

According to the U.S. Department of Commerce, employment in Houston rose 4.4 per cent between August, 1973, and August, 1974. Construction activity, in turn, was up 1.7 per cent, and department store sales were up 7.9 per cent over July, 1973, levels. Food costs, however, rose 12.6 per cent in the year ending in June, 1974.

Henley Trial. Elmer Wayne Henley, Jr., 18, was convicted on July 15 and sentenced to a total of 594 years in prison for the murder of six youths. Henley confessed to being part of a ring that tortured and killed 27 boys. The trial had been moved to San Antonio, Tex., because of fear that pretrial publicity in the Houston area might have prejudiced the outcome.

Another notable crime in Houston involved the

bishop of the Roman Catholic diocese of Houston-Galveston, who was pistol-whipped by two bandits in his chapel on March 8. Bishop John L. Morkovsky permanently lost the sight in his left eye as a result of his injuries.

Despite such incidents, crime in the Houston area increased at a lower rate than in the nation as a whole. According to Federal Bureau of Investigation reports released on October 3, crime in the Houston area increased 12 per cent during the first six months of 1974. The national increase was 16 per cent for the same period.

Two Tank Cars Exploded in a Houston railroad yard on September 21, shattering windows and damaging buildings within a 4-mile (6.4-kilometer) area. Ninety-six persons were injured, and 3,000 others were evacuated from the area because of the danger of more explosions. Fires caused by the explosion burned for several days.

More than 100 tank cars and boxcars, some loaded with highly flammable materials, were destroyed in the blast. The explosion was caused by a chemical that leaked from the tank cars.

Houston was the site of several important meetings, including two women's gatherings—the National Organization for Women Convention in May and a meeting of 600 nuns in August. The nuns called on the Roman Catholic Church to ordain women as priests.   James M. Banovetz

HUNGARY continued to tighten domestic political control in 1974 while expanding its trade with the West. On March 20, the Central Committee demoted four senior Communist Party leaders including Rezso Nyers, architect of Hungary's 1968 economic reform. Nyers became director of an economic institute. The second most important member of the group, György Aczel, who had guided Hungary's relatively permissive cultural and ideological policy since 1969, became a deputy premier.

Foreign Relations. Communist Party First Secretary Janos Kadar made a speech on September 2 stressing Hungary's continuing loyalty to Russia. Nyers' successor as Central Committee secretary, Karoly Nemeth, met with Russian officials in September, and Kadar followed with a full delegation.

Hungary appointed its ambassador to West Germany in January, and Foreign Minister Walter Scheel of West Germany visited Budapest in April. In May, the first joint commercial venture with a Western firm on Hungarian soil began with Siemens of West Germany. In July, a similar joint venture was set up with Volvo of Sweden, once again with 51 per cent Hungarian participation in the motor-manufacturing project.

In February, Hungary gave Yugoslavia a $50-million credit to help finance the $350-million Adriatic Sea oil pipeline, about 420 miles (680 kilometers) long, which will link Yugoslavia, Hungary,

The Brown Pavilion, an addition to Houston's Museum of Fine Arts designed by architect Ludwig Mies van der Rohe, opened in January.

and Czechoslovakia. The pipeline project was signed on February 12.

The Economy. Industrial productivity rose 9.1 per cent during the first nine months of 1974. Imports from the West increased 69 per cent over the first nine months of 1973. Hungary's corn and sugar beet crops were badly hit by floods in October. The government spent $803 million (10 per cent of the 1974 budget) on subsidies to shield the consumer and industry from the effects of rising world prices. Hungary's exports to the West were hit by the European Community's July 16 ban on beef imports.

A reshuffle of Roman Catholic bishops took place in February to coincide with Pope Paul VI's removal of exiled Joseph Cardinal Mindszenty from his post as primate of Hungary. In October, it was announced at the bishops' synod in Rome that the Hungarian government had agreed to religious teaching for small groups of schoolchildren.

Three prominent writers who had associated with liberal Marxist sociologists were arrested in October, then released and advised to emigrate to the West. Two of them, György Konrad and Ivan Szelenyi, had testified for the defense at the trial of a young left wing poet, Miklos Haraszti, who received an eight-month conditional sentence in January for criticizing working conditions.   Chris Cviic

See also EUROPE (Facts in Brief Table).

HUNTING. The U.S. Fish and Wildlife Service published proposed regulations in July, 1974, that would ban the use of lead shotgun ammunition in the Atlantic Flyway in 1976, the Mississippi Flyway in 1977, and in parts of the Central and Pacific flyways in 1978. The controversial proposal is designed to stop the dropping of lead pellets in waterfowl habitat. The service says that spent pellets eaten by ducks and geese cause lead poisoning, which kills "tens of thousands" of birds each year. Steel is the only practical nontoxic substitute available.

Opposition to steel shot has been based on claims that it would increase crippling losses of birds, because lead pellets have more killing power than steel shot. Opponents of the proposal also contend that steel shot will damage shotgun barrels.

The U.S. Court of Appeals for the District of Columbia on July 8 upheld hunting on national wildlife refuges as one method of wildlife management to control surplus animal populations. The Humane Society had charged that scheduled hunts on three refuges were not compatible with the primary purposes of the refuges and sought a permanent injunction. Hunting is permitted in about half of the 356 U.S. national wildlife refuges.

Hunters in most states enjoyed good waterfowl hunting. Breeding grounds in the north-central United States were the wettest since 1955, and the outlook for 1975 was favorable.   Andrew L. Newman

ICE SKATING. For the first time in history, Eastern European nations swept the four events of the world figure-skating championships in March, 1974, in Munich, West Germany. The singles titles were won by 17-year-old East Germans, the pairs titles by Russian skaters.

Christine Errath won the women's title, with Dorothy Hamill of Riverside, Conn., second and Diane De Leeuw of Paramount, Calif., representing the Netherlands, third. Jan Hoffmann, who had been skating since the age of 5, became men's champion, a great improvement on his last-place finish in the 1972 Olympics. Gordon McKellen of Lake Placid, N.Y., was the leading American man, finishing sixth. The 22-year-old McKellen and the 17-year-old Hamill had won the U.S. championships in February at Providence, R.I.

Irina Rodnina and Alexander Zaitsev won the world pairs figure title for the second straight year. Ludmilla Pakhomova and Alexander Gorshkov, husband and wife, took the pairs dance title.

Speed Skating. Sheila Young of Detroit, a 1973 world sprint champion in speed skating and bicycle racing, inadvertently helped Leah Poulos of Northbrook, Ill., take one of her titles in 1974. Young, 23, and Poulos, 22, competed in the world speed-skating sprint championships on February 16 and 17 in Innsbruck, Austria. The competition consisted of a

Christine Errath, petite 17-year-old from East Berlin, captured the world women's figure-skating title in Munich in March.

500-meter race and a 1,000-meter race each day.

In the first 500-meter race, Young fell and lost any chance to retain her overall title. About to cross from the outside lane to the inside lane in the second 1,000-meter race, Young was blocked by Tatyana Averina of Russia. Averina was disqualified, and the overall title went to Poulos.

All-Around Championships. On the following weekend, Young competed in the world all-around championships for women at Heerenveen, the Netherlands. There were four races—500, 1,000, 1,500, and 3,000 meters. Young won the 500-meter title, and after the first day, she was the overall leader. The next day, she faded to fourth as Atje Keulen-Deelstra of the Netherlands won.

The men's world champions were Norwegians— Sten Stensen (all-around) and Per Broerang (sprint). Leigh Barczewski of West Allis, Wis., and Mike Passarella of Chicago tied for the United States outdoor championship. The United States women's outdoor champion was Kris Garbe of West Allis, Wis.   Frank Litsky

ICELAND. See EUROPE.

IDAHO. See STATE GOVERNMENT.

ILLINOIS. See CHICAGO; STATE GOVERNMENT.

IMPEACHMENT. See WATERGATE; Section Two, FROM TRIUMPH TO TRAGEDY.

INCOME TAX. See TAXATION.

INDIA. In the days of drought and despair in 1972 and 1973, it seemed as if life in India could not get worse. But events in 1974 proved they could. It was the harshest year in modern India's history, a year of hunger, violence, and an atomic blast.

The monsoon rains were cruel to India. They left many states dry, while bringing devastating floods to others. The autumn harvest produced only 60 million short tons (54 million metric tons) of grain, instead of the expected 69 million (63 million metric). The year's total grain yield was expected to drop below 100 million short tons (91 million metric tons), while the country needed a minimum of more than 115 million (104 million metric). These were the harbingers of famine—and in September, swallowing its pride, the government informally asked the United States for help.

Economic Crisis. Inflation racked the nation. With farmers hoarding grain, and with kerosene, soap, sugar, and vanaspathi (cooking oil) short, prices rose at a rate of 36 per cent a year. And for the third year in the last four, per-capita income sagged. In a nation in which perhaps 230 million of some 600 million people earn less than $60 a year, this meant mass suffering. Industry lay stagnant.

As if this were not enough, the Arab oil squeeze in late 1973 hurt India perhaps more than any other country. The Indians need oil for kerosene to light

"Rejoice . . . we have finally conquered the atom."

Strike by railway workers in May hurt India, a nation already wracked with crippling economic problems and a severe food shortage.

their village huts, for chemical fertilizer, for irrigation pumps, and for electric power, industry, and transport. New Delhi planned to buy 17.5 million short tons (16 million metric tons) of oil in 1974. It was compelled to trim this to 12.6 million (11 million metric), with cruel effect on the economy and on private lives.

Violence was a natural by-product of the economic crisis. Bloody riots, such as those that toppled the corrupt state government of Gujarat in February, kept exploding in hungry West Bengal, in New Delhi, and, especially, among the 60 million or so persons of restless Bihar state. There were crippling strikes, especially the walkout of 2-million railway workers in May. Prime Minister Indira Gandhi broke it (according to union accounts) by arresting 50,000 strikers, firing 10,000, and evicting 30,000 from their company homes.

Political Developments. Even Gandhi's enemies conceded no one else could deal any better with the terrifying problems. But she was accused of a highly personal and intuitive style of governing; of tolerating inept men around her; of condoning corruption so as not to rock her Congress Party machine; and of letting Socialist rhetoric lead her into disasters.

The only real challenge to her came from a 72-year-old pacifist and former associate of Mahatma Gandhi, Jayaprakash Narayan. He is widely known in India as "J. P." or as *Loknaik* (People's Hero). The frail old man set Bihar afire with demands that the state government quit. He blamed its inaction for the death of 20,000 people in a smallpox epidemic. He called protest strikes, urged the people not to pay taxes, and counseled students to take a year off to make "moral revolution."

Fakhruddin Ali Ahmed, former food minister and a wealthy Moslem, was elected fifth president of India in August. He was Gandhi's choice.

In September, after 16 months of turmoil, India's tiny protectorate of Sikkim became an associate state of India. With this development, the powers of Sikkim's ruler, Palden Thondhup Namgyal, were trimmed. His American wife, Hope Cook, has been in New York City since 1973.

The Atomic Bomb. A nuclear device was exploded on May 18 under the sands of the state of Rajasthan. Gandhi said the atomic test, which made India the sixth member of the nuclear club, was for peaceful purposes. Nevertheless, it brought protests from Canada (which supplied the reactor from which the plutonium was extracted), Pakistan, Japan, the United States, and the 25-nation disarmament conference in Geneva.

Opinion polls showed the atomic blast as the year's only event to bring pride to most Indians. All the other news was dismal.   Mark Gayn

See also Asia (Facts in Brief Table).

INDIAN, AMERICAN. Efforts by American Indians to win greater control over their own affairs gained momentum in 1974. United States Secretary of the Interior Rogers C. B. Morton announced on August 15 that the Administration of President Gerald R. Ford would fully support the Indian self-determination policy set forth by President Richard M. Nixon in July, 1970.

However, some Indian spokesmen complained that after four years of so-called self-determination only two tribes, the Miccosukees of Florida and the Zuñis of New Mexico, had won more than limited control of their affairs. More moderate spokesmen pointed out that, while progress was slow, it was based on the firmer ground of legal and governmental action than on the militancy that led to the 1973 occupation of Wounded Knee, S. Dak.

Wounded Knee Trial. On September 16, Judge Fred J. Nichol of the U.S. District Court in St. Paul, Minn., dismissed charges of assault, conspiracy, and larceny against American Indian Movement leaders Russell C. Means and Dennis J. Banks for their part in the 71-day occupation of Wounded Knee. The U.S. Department of Justice would not permit the case to be decided by an 11-member jury, and ordered its prosecutors to call for a mistrial after one of the jurors became ill. In dismissing the case, Judge Nichol castigated the Justice Department for being more interested in conviction than justice. He accused the Federal Bureau of Investigation of "misconduct" in giving untrue testimony, falsifying documents, and paying its star witness.

Other Court Actions. The Supreme Court of the United States ruled on February 20 that the federal government cannot limit general welfare assistance for Indians to those living on reservations. Since nearly half the nation's 800,000 Indians live in urban areas, the decision could have a far-reaching impact on their relations with the government.

The Supreme Court on June 17 upheld the policy of giving Indians hiring and promotion preference in the Bureau of Indian Affairs (BIA), holding that this did not constitute racial discrimination. The unanimous ruling reversed a district court decision that the 1972 Equal Employment Opportunity Act should take precedence over earlier Indian-preference laws.

During the year, the BIA reduced its Washington, D.C., headquarters staff from 1,315 to 787. Although the cuts were challenged at a congressional hearing in August, further BIA personnel reductions were scheduled for 1975. This resulted from an Administration effort to force the BIA to turn more functions over to individual tribes.

In a landmark decision on February 12 in Tacoma, Wash., U.S. District Judge George H. Boldt ruled that the fishing activities of 14 Indian tribes in western Washington could not be regulated by state agencies, except to preserve stocks of salmon and steelhead trout.

Disputes Settled. The U.S. Interior Department made several decisions supporting Indian land rights and resolving long-standing controversies. In June, the department canceled some leases and exploratory permits for the strip mining of coal on the Northern Cheyenne Indian reservation in Montana. The Indians claimed they had been cheated by the original negotiations. The department also determined that the Fort Mohave Indian tribe owns 3,500 acres (1,416 hectares) claimed by the Bureau of Land Management near the Colorado River in California, and that the Colville and Spokane tribes have exclusive rights to hunt and fish in the so-called Indian zone of Lake Roosevelt in Washington state. In August, the department ruled that the Chemehuevi tribe has title to 18 miles (29 kilometers) of shoreline along Lake Havasu in California.

President Ford signed legislation on January 4, 1975, turning over 185,000 acres (75,000 hectares) of Grand Canyon National Park land on a plateau below the south rim of the canyon to the Havasupai tribe. The Indians want the plateau for grazing land. The Sierra Club opposed the legislation, fearing that it would set a dangerous precedent for disposing of national parklands.   Andrew L. Newman

INDIANA. See STATE GOVERNMENT.

INDONESIA. Agents of the Indonesian military security command brought word to government officials early in January, 1974, that demonstrations were being planned by restive students during the visit of Japan's Prime Minister Kakuei Tanaka. The students were cautioned, and the police were alerted. But trouble broke out on January 15, and its fury and scale stunned the nation. The students began their demonstrations by ripping down Japanese flags and wrecking Japanese cars in Djakarta. But before the day ended, many Japanese shops had been gutted.

Tanaka and President Suharto signed a $200-million loan agreement while the roar of the rioting crowds could be heard outside the presidential palace. When the riots finally ended after 48 hours, 11 people were dead, and hundreds had been arrested. Within a week, half a dozen periodicals had been banned, army censorship was tightened, and army tribunals had begun their months of investigations and courts-martial.

Behind the Riots lay the belief that the country was being "sold out" to foreign investors, especially the Japanese. There are about 3,000 Japanese businessmen in the capital, and Japanese investment in Indonesia accounts for 15 per cent of foreign investments in the country.

After the fall of President Sukarno in 1967, the country was governed by an army junta, with the

Students in Djakarta commandeer a truck during January anti Japanese riots that protested the visit of Japan's Prime Minister Kakuei Tanaka.

help of a group of professors educated at the University of California, who have sometimes been called the Berkeley Mafia. The regime had not done badly. Inflation, running at 600 per cent a year under Sukarno, had become manageable. Foreign businessmen had come back in droves to bring the total investment to $3 billion.

But the odor of corruption also returned to the land. Import licenses and "non-Communist" police certificates were for sale on the black market. Kickbacks to army officers became a way of doing business. Military men were smuggling vast quantities of oil to Singapore for illicit sale.

While army officers and top officials lived in luxury, the poor became poorer. The per-capita income stood at $95 a year, but tens of millions lived on less. At year's end, 11 million people, or one-fourth of the labor force, were seeking jobs. And if the oil boom boosted Indonesia's income at the annual rate of $6 billion by late 1974, little of the money seeped down to the population.

General Suharto was still in control. But lesser generals under him fought for power. And the army remained a state within the state. It controlled the secret police, speculated in industry and trade, and sold "protection" to the resident Chinese. All this led one study to predict a "cataclysmic" upheaval in the next 5 to 10 years.   Mark Gayn

See also ASIA (Facts in Brief Table).

INSURANCE. President Gerald R. Ford signed the Employee Retirement Income Security Act on Sept. 2, 1974, providing the first federal standards for more than 300,000 private pension plans covering about 35 million American workers. Most existing plans will need to be amended to conform with the new standards, under a timetable that will provide an orderly transition.

The law calls for *vesting* (ownership of pension funds by the individual worker after a specified period of service) and the ability to transfer vested funds when moving to a new job. In other words, a worker will no longer sacrifice his pension if he leaves a job before reaching retirement age. The law also provides standards for the investment of the estimated $160 billion in pension funds, and it sets up the Pension Benefit Guaranty Corporation, an agency similar to the Federal Deposit Insurance Corporation, to insure the solvency, or ability to pay, of private pension plans.

Workers not covered by private pension plans may take 15 per cent of their salaries, up to $1,500, tax free, to establish individual retirement accounts. Such accounts may be invested in long-term annuities or endowment plans through insurance companies, special U.S. Treasury bonds, or trust funds administered by banks.

No-Fault Insurance. The U.S. Senate, after a four-year struggle, passed a no-fault auto insurance bill on May 1, and hearings began in the House in July. The bill sets federal minimum standards for state no-fault laws, under which accident victims are reimbursed by their own insurance companies. At present, no state meets the criteria. President Ford showed little interest in the issue, and Congress adjourned without acting.

Four states joined the no-fault ranks in 1974. Laws became effective October 1 in Georgia and South Carolina, and were due to take effect July 1, 1975, in Kentucky and Pennsylvania.

Several state no-fault laws encountered constitutional challenges in 1974. The Florida Supreme Court on April 17 upheld the constitutionality of the personal injury segment of the state's no-fault law. A Michigan county circuit court ruled that state's no-fault law unconstitutional in August, but it was to remain in force until a final decision by the Michigan Supreme Court. The Kansas Supreme Court upheld the constitutionality of a no-fault law, but the legislature had already amended the law to overcome a lower court's objections.

Flood Protection. The Flood Disaster Protection Act, amending the Flood Insurance Act, went into effect July 1. It allows U.S. homeowners, businessmen, and others to buy significantly increased amounts of flood insurance at reduced rates under a joint federal-private industry program. Property owners and local communities in designated flood-prone areas must undertake preventive measures, based on minimum land-use standards, by July 1, 1975. Otherwise, they lose the right to buy the low-cost insurance, or to get construction or mortgage loans from any federally regulated bank or savings and loan association.

Financial Results. Property and liability insurance companies in the United States suffered a disastrous $1-billion underwriting loss in the first half of 1974. Inflation and the worst tornado season on record contributed to the loss, the largest in history. The underwriting loss for the entire year was expected to reach $2 billion.

Equity Funding Scandal. The insurance commissioners of Illinois and California in September announced a court-approved settlement agreement governing the scandal-ridden, defunct Equity Funding Life Insurance Company. The agreement transfers all policyholders to the Northern Life Insurance Company of Seattle, provides for the payment of other creditors, and establishes a $2-million fund to pay shareholders in the parent Equity Funding Corporation of America.

The parent company filed for bankruptcy in 1973 after it was accused of engaging in a multimillion-dollar fraud involving nonexistent assets, bogus life insurance policies, and forged bonds and death certificates. In October, Stanley Goldblum, former chairman of the parent company, pleaded guilty to five felony counts in Los Angeles.   Emanuel Levy

Decorators stressed U.S. bicentennial themes. For example, they stenciled golden eagles and stars and stripes on folding rocking chairs.

INTERIOR DESIGN. Fashions in furniture and home decoration reflected the influence of nature in 1974. The interior design of rooms and homes was orderly and restful in appearance. The big, massive stylings of past years were replaced by chairs, sofas, and tables with clean, simple lines. Dining and bedroom furniture was refined in size and scaled down for today's smaller rooms and lower ceilings.

Designs in the major categories–modern, traditional, and Early American–all leaned toward functionalism and practical appeal. Shortages of wood, plastic, and man-made fibers led manufacturers to eliminate heavy carvings, ornate detailing, and bold scalings in furniture.

Popular Styles. The colonial-Early American category had the greatest overall customer appeal, according to *Home Furnishings Daily*. Much of the interest was attributed to the approaching 1976 American Revolution Bicentennial celebration.

Retailers and furniture dealers considered contemporary and modern styles to be the fastest-growing categories. Modern dining-room selections were shown with glass tops and polished chrome or aluminum bases and legs. Metal was also shown in combination with warm wood-tone veneers, and it appeared on upholstered furniture as trimming.

Homemakers made growing use of sectional, or component seating, selections. These sofas and love

seats were available armless, or with one or two arms. They were used in combination with chairs and an ottoman to create various arrangements.

Man-Made Fibers were stressed by upholstered-furniture manufacturers, as well as by carpeting and soft-surface floor-covering mills. Especially popular were nylon and olefin fiber upholsteries and carpeting. Nylon's durability, plus its ability to hold color dyes and its availability in a wide price range, made it desirable. Olefin is also long-wearing and attractive, with the look of natural fibers.

Many print and floral upholstery patterns were featured in nylon in soft, natural colors such as bittersweet, coral, apple-green, terra-cotta, and soft, earth-tone browns. Popular patterns included the flame stitch, herringbone, and chevron. Vinyl coverings were shown on all types of seating selections. Leather appeared on traditional and Early American designs.

The shag texture was popular in carpeting. It was available in many solid colors and tweeds, and in various loop lengths. Pattern and print carpeting with nature and Americana motifs were among the new offerings. Natural fiber coverings included loosely woven carpeting of sisal hemp and *coir* (a fiber from the outer husk of coconuts).

Motifs from Nature, along with American-history themes, dominated designs for decorative accessories. Early colonial folk art and red, white, and blue color combinations were plentiful. Pewter, considered a "new find" metal, was fashionable in tableware. Animals of all types were used in designs for pottery, wall decorations, and pictures. Terrariums and planters of wood, plastics, pottery, ceramics, and glass were popular. Denim and gingham linens were also favored.

Professional Plans. Interior designers completed plans to consolidate two professional societies, the American Institute of Interior Designers and the National Society of Interior Designers. The new society, the American Society of Interior Designers, is considered the world's largest association for interior designers.

The Copper Development Association, Incorporated, in conjunction with building and home products companies, announced plans for the first practical solar home. The home, to be built near Tucson, Ariz., is designed to show the availability and use of power from stored-up solar energy. The four-bedroom home will contain about 3,000 square feet (280 square meters) of space, and will feature a number of innovative ideas in architecture and furnishings.

Home-furnishings industries started the year with good sales and profits. But shortages and price increases caused production problems as the year continued. Consumer purchases dropped markedly during the second half.　　　　　　　Helen C. Schubert

INTERNATIONAL LIVE STOCK EXPOSITION. A
new record price of $30 a pound (0.45 kilogram) was paid for the grand champion lamb at the Diamond Jubilee International Live Stock Exposition, held in Chicago from Nov. 25 to Dec. 3, 1974. The Suffolk was owned by Charles Hunter of Blanco, Tex., and weighed 125 pounds (57 kilograms). The reserve grand champion lamb was an entry of Richard Roe of St. Ansgar, Iowa. Donna Bolin, 14, topped the junior show, with a crossbreed.

The grand champion steer Mainliner, a crossbred Maine-Anjou-Angus weighing 1,350 pounds (612 kilograms) was owned by Curt Robertson, 15, of Bayard, Iowa. It sold at $15 a pound (0.45 kilogram) to National Food Stores. The reserve grand champion steer (runner-up) was a Hereford weighing 1,335 pounds (606 kilograms) shown by Kevin Newman, 10, of Stanton, Tex. Jerry Adamson of Cody, Nebr., exhibited the champion pen of feeder calves.

In the swine department, the Duroc barrow grand champion hog entry of Marvin Larrick of Leesburg, Ohio, weighed 209 pounds (95 kilograms) and sold to American Meat Packing for $14.25 a pound (0.45 kilogram). The reserve grand champion was a Hampshire entry of William G. Nash & Sons of Sharpsville, Ind. Champion truck-lot of hogs were Durocs from LaVerne Weller & Sons of Dwight, Ill.　　　　　　　Morris E. Rogers

INTERNATIONAL TRADE AND FINANCE was
dominated by oil in 1974. A successful cartel called the Organization of Petroleum Exporting Countries (OPEC) had managed to quadruple the world price of oil in late 1973, and the financial and economic repercussions were felt throughout 1974.

Not only did the higher oil price contribute to the serious inflation that afflicted almost every country in the world, but, more important, it threw into deficit the balance of trade and payments of nearly all the oil-importing countries. The issue of how to pay for oil was still bedeviling governments as the year ended.

Economic Strain. Although the world managed to survive without a major crisis, and employment generally remained high, world leaders regarded the situation with uneasy apprehension.

While many of the poorest countries faced near-disaster, a few industrial countries were scarcely touched. Canada, as an oil exporter, benefited from the higher price. West Germany continued to expand its exports enough to cover its higher oil bill. But for the rest, including the United States, paying for oil meant going into debt.

The Oil Debt. A handful of oil producers, such as Saudi Arabia, Kuwait, and Iran, increased their monetary reserves in 1974 by an estimated $55-billion. These revenues were recycled back to the rest of the world in one fashion or another. A typical mechanism was the deposit of "petrodollars," as they were called, in European banks, which in turn loaned them to such countries as Italy, Great Britain, Japan, and France. But most bankers said that this process could not continue as the borrowing countries became over-indebted.

The problem was less severe in the United States. Petrodollars coming to the United States were invested mainly in government securities such as treasury bills. This, too, was debt, but if foreigners had not purchased the bills, Americans would have had to buy them. What ultimately will happen to this external debt is not known, but there were no serious problems in 1974.

OPEC Offers Help. In a relatively small way, the OPEC countries cooperated with international efforts to deal with the financial problem. The International Monetary Fund borrowed about $3.4 billion from seven OPEC countries and in June established a new "oil facility," a special fund to provide loans to oil-importing countries, especially the less developed ones.

The European Community (Common Market) in October also planned a joint loan of up to $3-billion from the Arab oil countries. The funds were to help those members with the worst economic problems meet balance-of-payments deficits. Italy would be a likely first candidate.

The oil-producing countries also bought more than $1 billion in bonds from the World Bank,

International Harvester tractors unloaded on the docks of Murmansk,
Russia, are evidence of the increasing American-Soviet trade.

which provides loans for development projects in the poorer countries. Finally, the OPEC countries gave direct aid to the importing countries. For example, Iran made investments or loans in Great Britain, West Germany, and the United States. The OPEC countries also planned to help less developed nations, particularly those Arab countries that do not produce oil.

The Problem Continues. Eventually, the Arab countries will develop their own industry and be able to spend their riches on real goods and services from the industrial countries. But until then, they will go on piling up monetary reserves as long as the high oil prices continue. And the OPEC countries showed both the determination and the ability to maintain the price. As world demand declined somewhat in response to the high prices, the OPEC countries simply reduced production.

The Committee of 20–the nations negotiating world monetary reform–recognized in January that nearly all countries would have to live with balance-of-payments deficits for a while, and that no one would gain by restricting imports or subsidizing exports. Their pledge to avoid trade restrictions was generally adhered to, though a desperate Italy imposed mild import restraints in May.

World Trade continued to expand. In the second quarter, exports of the industrial countries were running at an annual rate of $516 billion, up from a rate of $438 billion in the first quarter. Much of this increase simply reflected inflation–higher prices for each item shipped–but real volume increased as well. United States exports continued to expand, though the higher cost of imported oil threw the dollar trade balance into deficit. From a small 1973 surplus, the U.S. balance of trade slipped quickly, reaching a deficit of $2.35 billion for the first three quarters, due entirely to oil imports. Japan's deficit also reflected the high cost of oil. But a few countries, such as Italy and Britain, had a nonoil trade deficit to go with their oil deficit and had to borrow heavily to stay afloat.

The outlook for world trade was uncertain as the year ended. Partly because of the impact of higher oil prices–which reduced consumer purchasing power–and partly because of government measures to slow inflation, the world economy entered a general slowdown in 1974. If economic growth continued to slow down or drop, world trade would suffer. But some world leaders argued that only a sustained period of reduced growth could conquer world inflation.

Preparations went on for a major new round of international trade negotiations, but everything hinged on congressional passage of the U.S. Trade Reform Act giving the President broad new authority in trade negotiations. The bill, stalled by a dispute over linking trade concessions to Russia with a relaxation in Russian emigration policies, finally cleared Congress on December 20 and was signed by President Ford.

Monetary Reforms. The Committee of 20 recognized at its January meeting in Rome that the new situation created by higher oil prices made its search for a fully reformed international monetary system temporarily irrelevant. The committee agreed that exchange rates would have to *float* (fluctuate) indefinitely with supply and demand. However, central banks could intervene in foreign exchange trading to prevent large exchange rate movements.

The system worked remarkably well in 1974. Despite all its other troubles, the world did not experience the financial crises that had characterized the last years of fixed exchange rates, when huge volumes of money flowed out of one currency into another in expectation of rate changes. The world's business continued, though traders could no longer count on a fixed relationship among currencies. As the year went on, the fluctuations of the dollar against other leading currencies became smaller and exchange rates for all currencies became more stable.   Edwin L. Dale, Jr.

See also ECONOMICS; Section One, FOCUS ON THE ECONOMY.

IOWA. See STATE GOVERNMENT.

"Just how serious are these foreign investments in American properties?"

IRAN. A steady flow of oil revenues estimated at over $1 billion a month quadrupled Iran's national income in 1974. The oil revenues enabled the government of Shah Mohammed Reza Pahlavi to pursue the twin objectives of military preparedness and rapid economic development.

The country's improving cash position also placed it in the role of a provider, rather than recipient, of foreign aid. Thus, in May, Iran signed an agreement to give Egypt more than $1 billion in loans and credits. It made Iran Egypt's principal source of foreign investment. On July 22, the government loaned $1.2 billion to Great Britain, its largest single loan to any country and an ironic reversal of roles, and $580 million to Pakistan to cover its balance-of-payments deficit. The shah also proposed a multibillion-dollar fund to help developing countries adversely affected by high oil prices. He promised a $1-billion Iranian contribution. Iran also paid off its $1.7-billion foreign debt.

In Related Developments, Iran loaned $100 million to Syria and $30 million to Morocco in May, and purchased a 25 per cent interest in the steel and engineering division of West Germany's Krupp Group in July. The agreement provides for building a steel industry in Iran. Iran also concluded a $4-billion, 10-year agreement with France in June by which it will get five nuclear reactors.

During the year, the shah ordered 80 U.S. F14-A Tomcat fighter aircraft costing nearly $2 billion from the financially troubled Grumman Aerospace Corporation. Altogether, the shah's shopping list for military equipment totaled $4 billion, which represented one-half of all U.S. 1974 arms sales.

Border Fight Erupts. A long-standing border dispute with Iraq broke out in open conflict again in February. Each country accused the other of aggression, and Iraq called a special session of the United Nations (UN) Security Council. A cease-fire was arranged on March 7, and both countries agreed to accept a final UN border settlement.

There were some strains on the economy despite the oil wealth, as Iran struggled to absorb the increased revenues. Prices of staple foods and textile products doubled during the year, and the government faced a serious skilled-manpower shortage. An industrial training program to provide the 500,000 skilled workers needed under the revised five-year plan began in September. The shah introduced a welfare program with free medical care for all Iranians and the distribution of 20 per cent of net factory profits to workers. A major Cabinet reshuffle added new departments of welfare, planning, and vocational education in May to cope with the changes in Iranian life. A new offshore gas field was discovered in the Persian Gulf with reserves of 70-trillion to 100 trillion cubic feet (2 trillion to 3-trillion cubic meters).   William Spencer

See also MIDDLE EAST (Facts in Brief Table).

IRAQ. Civil war between government and Kurd forces resumed in March, 1974. The shaky four-year cease-fire collapsed as the Kurdish leader, Mustafa Barzani, refused to accept a government plan for Kurdish self-rule in northern Iraq. On March 11, Iraqi President Ahmad Hasan al-Bakr had proclaimed Kurdish autonomy based on the 1970 cease-fire agreement. The proclamation defined Kurdistan (those areas in northern Iraq where Kurds constitute a majority of the population) as an autonomous province within Iraq. It gave the province an elected legislative assembly, responsible to an executive council whose chairman would be appointed by the Iraqi president. It also specified Kurdish and Arabic as official languages.

However, Barzani, the head of the Democratic Party of Kurdistan (PDK), representing Iraq's 2-million Kurds, claimed the plan violated pledges made to the Kurds by excluding the oil-rich Kirkuk district from the province. He also charged that it did not provide an adequate share of oil revenues or sufficient Kurdish representation in key Iraqi government ministries. Fighting resumed after Barzani's forces ignored a government peace offer.

Resumption of Hostilities caused a split in the PDK. Barzani's eldest son, Abaydullah, and other leaders sided with the government. Abaydullah was appointed minister of state, and another prominent Kurd was named a vice-president. The Iraqi Army, equipped with Russian jets and artillery, drove Barzani's Pesh Merga guerrillas deep into the mountains of northeastern Iraq. Iraqi bombing of Kurdish villages caused nearly 2,000 casualties. Syria and Turkey closed their borders with Iraq, a further hardship for the Kurds. Only Iran provided military equipment and the sanctuary of an open border to the Kurds. Nevertheless, the Kurds still controlled the northern Iraqi mountains in late October, though Iraqi regulars held most of the towns and cities.

The Iraqi regime had more success elsewhere. On the sixth anniversary of its seizure of power, in July, the government announced a record $4-billion development program, including $300 million for Kurdistan. The $210-million Kirkuk irrigation project was inaugurated on June 21. The government also completed the first stage of a rural electrification program to bring electricity to 9,000 villages.

Despite its criticism of Egyptian policy toward Israel, Iraq loaned Egypt $16 million in August. A 10-year, $3-billion pact with Italy was concluded July 26. Italy would provide technical assistance for industries in return for Iraqi crude oil shipments. Japan agreed in August to build industrial plants in exchange for petroleum. William Spencer

See also MIDDLE EAST (Facts in Brief Table).

Kurdish children find safety at one of a dozen refugee camps set up in Iran to aid an estimated 80,000 Kurds fleeing Iraqi military attacks.

IRELAND. The collapse of Northern Ireland's power-sharing executive body in May, 1974, canceled an agreement on Ulster between Great Britain and the Republic of Ireland before it could be ratified. The executive body of Roman Catholics and Protestants had been the cornerstone of that agreement. The Irish government was to recognize Ulster as part of Britain and to introduce tougher laws against terrorism. Also proposed was a Council of Ireland, consisting of seven ministers from Ulster and the republic.

The agreement was beset by problems from the start. Recognition of Ulster as part of Britain conflicted with the Irish Constitution, which claimed sovereignty over all of Ireland, and Prime Minister Liam Cosgrave's coalition of *Fine Gael* (Gaelic People) and Labour parties came under attack from the *Fianna Fáil* (Soldiers of Destiny) Party.

A Further Setback came with the report of the Anglo-Irish law commission on May 23. The Irish rejected the British plan for the extradition of terrorists from the republic, while the British rejected Ireland's proposal for an all-Ireland court. The compromise of extraterritorial courts did not please Ulster's chief executive, Brian Faulkner. Cosgrave pressed the British to ratify the Anglo-Irish agreement and establish the council, but the British wanted action by Dublin on security and recognition first.

New Violence. Cosgrave blamed the collapse of the Ulster government in May on continuing violence by the Irish Republican Army. He said this had provoked a sectarian backlash. Death came to Dublin on May 17 when car bombs exploded without warning in a main city street, killing 23 people and maiming scores of others. A similar explosion in Monaghan killed five men and injured 30.

Tension between the coalition government's members came to a head over the "contraceptive crisis." On July 16, Cosgrave and six Fine Gael Parliament members voted against their own party's bill to legalize the sale of contraceptives, which was defeated by 75 to 61 votes. At its conference in October, however, Labour decided to stay in the coalition.

Economic Growth reached 7 per cent in 1973, but rising oil prices added $230 million to Ireland's import bill, and the unions' rejection of a national pay agreement stoked inflation. Because this threatened further growth, Finance Minister Ritchie Ryan took a number of expansionary measures in his April budget, including a 20 per cent rise in capital expenditure, increased unemployment benefits and pensions, and tax cuts.

Erskine Childers, president since June, 1973, died November 17. Cearbhall O Dalaigh was elected to succeed him on December 18.   Andrew F. Neil

See also EUROPE (Facts in Brief Table); GREAT BRITAIN; NORTHERN IRELAND.

ISRAEL. A new generation of leaders took charge in Israel in 1974 as the nation faced mounting economic problems and continuing threats from the Arab world. Prime Minister Golda Meir resigned on April 10 because of deep divisions in her own Labor Party, ending a three-month political crisis. Her party won only a narrow margin in the Dec. 31, 1973, national elections, which had been postponed by the October, 1973, Arab-Israeli war. She tried forming a coalition government, but criticism of the cease-fire agreement with Egypt and demands that Defense Minister Moshe Dayan resign finally led to her resignation.

The crisis began when Meir's Labor coalition won only 51 of the 120 seats in the Knesset (parliament) to 39 for the right wing opposition Likud Party and 10 for the National Religious Party (NRP). After considerable political infighting, related as much to Israel's internal economic difficulties as to the controversial agreement to withdraw from the Suez Canal, Meir won a vote of confidence in the Knesset on March 10.

But the new government's troubles were far from over. The Agranat Commission Report, released on April 2, blamed Israel's initial failures in the October war on faulty intelligence and overoptimism regarding Arab military capabilities. A wholesale shakeup of the high command followed, and demands for Dayan's resignation continued, though he was cleared of blame by the report. A weary Meir resigned after five years as prime minister and gave up the Knesset seat she had held for 25 years.

The crisis continued until a compromise brought Yitzhak Rabin in as prime minister on April 23 (see RABIN, YITZHAK). Rabin's new 18-member Cabinet was approved by the Knesset on June 3, and Shimon Peres replaced Dayan as defense minister. On October 24, the NRP voted to join the Rabin government, giving it a solid majority in the Knesset.

Less Terrorism. The establishment of border agreements with Syria and Egypt and a visible United Nations presence resulted in less internal terrorism. But on April 11, 18 persons were massacred in Qiryat-Shemona village, and 20 children held as hostages by Palestinian guerrillas in a school in Maalot died on May 15 when Israeli forces stormed the school. On November 19, four Israelis and three Arab raiders died when guerrillas attacked the town of Bet Shean. The Maalot incident aroused intense criticism of the government.

Israeli concern about the future of the West Bank of the Jordan River was heightened on November 22 when the United Nations approved two resolutions on the Middle East. One declared that the Palestinian people have a right to national independence and sovereignty. The other granted the Palestine Liberation Organization permanent observer status in the General Assembly. See MIDDLE EAST; UNITED NATIONS.

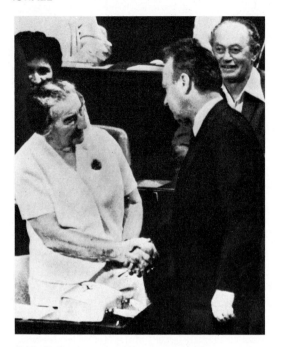

Golda Meir congratulates her successor, Prime Minister Yitzhak Rabin, after he was sworn in at a June 3 Knesset meeting in Jerusalem.

ITALY was rocked by economic and political crises and a wave of neo-Fascist terrorism during 1974. Higher Mideast crude oil prices hoisted the trade deficit to nearly $9 billion. Outstanding international debts totaled nearly $20 billion, and inflation was running at over 20 per cent annually. Fearing bankruptcy and mass unemployment, the government took drastic steps.

Imports Surcharge. A 50 per cent, six-month deposit surcharge on all imports except raw materials and capital investment goods was announced on April 30. Italy's European Community (Common Market) partners protested that this breached the principle of free movement of goods as spelled out in the Treaty of Rome. The Italians cited a treaty article that allows member states to take "necessary measures" to meet a sudden payments imbalance.

On June 28, the Chamber of Deputies passed Prime Minister Mariano Rumor's austerity package designed to take $5 billion out of the economy. It included increased value-added taxes ranging from 18 to 30 per cent on luxury items; additional beef and gasoline taxes; and a onetime levy on motorists and property owners. The tough measures failed to rescue the economy. Following a two-day summit meeting in Bellagio on August 30 and 31, West Germany agreed to lend $2 billion against Italian gold. On September 24, the International Monetary Fund

Economic Problems. The continued cost of military preparedness plus soaring inflation hit the Israeli economy hard. The government slashed basic commodity subsidies in January, causing a 30 per cent jump in food prices. Earnings from tourism dropped 20 per cent. Cost-of-living salary increases for civil servants negotiated in 1973 added an inflationary push. The new budget, for $8.6 billion, included a supplementary budget of $4.75 billion for defense purchases. Faced with declining reserves and continuing deficits, the government announced an austerity program on November 10. It included a 43 per cent devaluation of the Israeli pound, higher taxes, restrictions on imports, and price increases.

There were some economic bright spots. In July, the United States waived payment on $500 million in Israeli arms purchases made since October, 1973. Congress also voted $250 million in nonmilitary aid on August 6. Israel's association agreement with the European Community (Common Market) established progressive tariff reductions on Israeli agricultural exports to Common Market countries leading to their elimination in four years. Expanded agricultural export earnings and the resumption of normal production in the industrial diamond industry cut Israel's trade deficit by $200 million to just under $3 billion.   William Spencer

See also MIDDLE EAST (Facts in Brief Table).

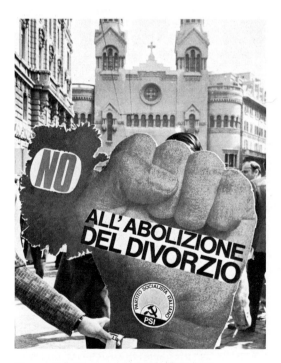

Sign reading "No to the abolition of divorce" urges Italian voters to retain a 1970 law permitting divorce, and they did in a May vote.

agreed to loan Italy an additional $855 million. The Common Market established a $3-billion loan pool in October to help its members in need. In November, it gave Italy 3½ years to repay a $2-billion loan made in March.

Political Crises. Rumor resigned on March 2 following the Republican Party's withdrawal from his four-party coalition in a disagreement over economic policy. He formed his fifth government, and Italy's 36th since the end of World War II, 14 days later from the Christian Democrat, Socialist, and Social Democrat parties. Rumor resigned again on June 10 over economic policy disagreements, but President Giovanni Leone refused to accept the resignation. The shaky coalition collapsed again on October 3, and Amintore Fanfani was asked to form a new government. When Fanfani failed, Aldo Moro formed a government on November 20.

Fascist Revival. Six persons were killed and 60 injured in a bomb attack during an anti-Fascist rally in Brescia on May 28. The neo-Fascists claimed responsibility for placing a time bomb on the Rome-Munich express that killed 12 persons on August 4.

In a May referendum, Italians voted 3 to 2 in favor of keeping a law that allows divorce. Originally passed in December, 1970, the law was opposed by the Roman Catholic Church.   Kenneth Brown

See also EUROPE (Facts in Brief Table).

IVORY COAST. See AFRICA.

JACKSON, GLENDA (1936-   ), won the 1974 Academy of Motion Picture Arts and Sciences Award for best actress for her bittersweet performance as a newly divorced London fashion designer in the 1973 film *A Touch of Class*. Jackson also won an Oscar for her 1970 work in *Women in Love*.

Jackson was born in Birkenhead, across the Mersey River from Liverpool, England, on May 9, 1936. Leaving school at the age of 16 to join an amateur theater group, she later won a two-year scholarship to the Royal Academy of Dramatic Art. Her first stage appearance was in *Separate Tables* in 1957. After working in repertory companies, she joined the Royal Shakespeare Company in 1964. For her New York City debut in 1965, she re-created her stunning characterization of Charlotte Corday in *Marat/Sade*, a role she had performed in London.

The English actress has appeared in a number of films since 1968. She won critical acclaim for her roles in *Sunday, Bloody Sunday* and *The Music Lovers*.

Her television career began in 1960. Perhaps her best-known television role was a remarkable portrayal of Queen Elizabeth I from a spirited young girl to an aging, dying monarch in *Elizabeth R*.

Jackson is married to Roy Hodges, who runs a small art gallery. With their young son, they live in a London suburb.   Edward G. Nash

JAMAICA. See WEST INDIES.

JAPAN. Domestic politics, continuing economic problems, and related foreign policy issues dominated events in Japan in 1974. A record 73 per cent of the electorate voted on July 7 to fill 130 of the 252 seats in the House of Councillors (upper house). The dominant Liberal-Democratic Party (LDP) won 62 seats, giving it 126, down slightly from its pre-election total of 134. It maintained a bare majority, however, because two independents lined up with the LDP. The Communist Party won 13 seats for a total of 20, while the Socialist Party gained 3 seats to reach 62.

The LDP won 42 per cent of the total vote, a slight drop from 1971. The Socialists won about 21 per cent, a somewhat greater loss, and the Communists received about 9 per cent, a slight gain.

The elections were a political setback for Prime Minister Kakuei Tanaka, the LDP president. Big corporations, because of public criticism and their disappointment with the election results, announced that they were either stopping or substantially reducing their political contributions. Tanaka's support in opinion polls dropped to less than 20 per cent. On July 16, Finance Minister Takeo Fukuda and Minister of State Shigeru Hori resigned, demanding a fundamental change in the strife-torn LDP. On November 26, soon after a visit to Japan by U.S. President Gerald R. Ford, Tanaka resigned and was replaced by Takeo Miki, a veteran LDP politician and a Tanaka critic.

Economic Woes. Contributing to the political difficulties of Tanaka and his party was widespread public concern over the economy. The economic gloom focused on Japan's inflation – the highest rate among the industrialized nations – the energy crisis, rising world prices of basic foodstuffs and raw materials, and a falling Tokyo stock market. In August, the Organization for Economic Cooperation and Development (OECD) announced that Japanese inflation had reached "unprecedented and clearly intolerable rates." The OECD pointed out that Japanese consumer price increases were at a yearly rate of 24.5 per cent in the first quarter of 1974. The average annual wholesale price increase was set at a 35.5 per cent rate for the same period. The overall deficit in the international balance of payments for the first half of the fiscal year (ending September 30) was $3.6 billion.

There were a few bright spots in the economic picture. Salary rates were almost keeping pace with prices. In September, foreign exchange reserves totaled $13.7 billion, only a slight drop from a year earlier. The gross national product surpassed $400-billion for the first time in 1973, and average per capita income was $3,020. Although the Economic Planning Agency in Tokyo predicted no growth in 1974, economic experts were cautiously optimistic, predicting an annual economic growth rate between 6 and 8 per cent for the rest of the 1970s.

Japanese fishermen, fearing radioactive leaks, blockade that nation's first nuclear ship, *Mutsu*, preventing its test runs.

Personal Diplomacy. Prime Minister Tanaka continued his personal diplomacy, attempting to bolster his waning political popularity and to ease the economic crisis. In January, he visited the Philippines, Thailand, Singapore, Malaysia, and Indonesia to confer with government leaders. The visits were marred by anti-Japanese demonstrations in Thailand and Indonesia. Demonstrators virtually forced Tanaka to flee from Indonesia.

In September, Tanaka visited Brazil, Mexico, Canada, and the United States. He paid a courtesy call on President Ford on September 21. In Brazil, he signed agreements to establish an aluminum industrial complex in the Amazon River Basin and cellulose and paper industries in Brazil's Espírito Santo state.

President Ford's visit to Japan in November was part of an eight-day trip that also took him to South Korea and Russia. Although there were some anti-American demonstrations during the Japanese visit, police kept the demonstrators under strict control.

An Agreement in Peking, signed on April 20, established regular air service between Japan and China. The service started on September 29, the second anniversary of the establishment of Japanese-Chinese diplomatic relations. Each country scheduled one round-trip flight between Tokyo and Peking each week. When the agreement was signed,

Taiwan's Nationalist government banned Japanese planes from landing there, thus ending Japan Air Line's busiest and most profitable route. Trade between Japan and the People's Republic of China was expected to reach $2.5 billion in 1974, about 25 per cent more than in 1973.

Relations with South Korea were unsettled. In July, two Japanese were convicted and given 20-year sentences by a Korean military court on charges of complicity in an antigovernment underground movement. On August 15, a Korean resident of Japan murdered the wife of Korea's President Chung Hee Park while trying to assassinate President Park. The Korean government charged that Japanese authorities were lax in failing to prevent the man from obtaining a forged Japanese passport and the murder weapon. Prime Minister Tanaka attended Mrs. Park's funeral, and the Japanese government sent both written and oral messages expressing its regret to the Korean government.

On August 30, the Mitsubishi Heavy Industries building in downtown Tokyo was damaged by a bomb that killed eight people and injured 330. On October 14, the home office of the giant Mitsui & Company was also bombed, but telephoned warnings kept casualties to 16 injured.   John M. Maki

See also ASIA (Facts in Brief Table); NOBEL PRIZES.

JAWORSKI, LEON (1905-   ), resigned as special prosecutor in the Watergate affair on Oct. 12, 1974, a few hours after the Washington, D.C., jury in the cover-up conspiracy trial of five defendants had been selected and secluded from public contact.

Jaworski, a Texas lawyer and a former president of the American Bar Association, was appointed in November, 1973, succeeding Archibald Cox.

His persistent attempts to gain access to tapes and documents led to a running series of legal battles with White House lawyers. The conflict ended in arguments before the Supreme Court of the United States by Jaworski and President Richard M. Nixon's lawyer, James D. St. Clair, in July. On July 24, the court unanimously upheld Jaworski's right to the tapes of 64 White House conversations. The public impact of some of these conversations brought about President Nixon's resignation.

In his 11 months as special prosecutor, Jaworski and his aides produced indictments of, or guilty pleas from, 14 major officials of the Nixon Administration and the Committee to Re-elect the President, as well as a dozen corporations and 17 of their executives for illegal campaign contributions.

Jaworski was born in Waco, Tex., on Sept. 19, 1905. He holds law degrees from Baylor University and George Washington University. He and his wife Jeanette have three children.   Edward G. Nash

See also WATERGATE.

JEWS. Hostilities between Israel and the Arab countries continued to hold the attention of Jews throughout the world in 1974. Three Arab terrorists made the most severe attack upon Israel in recent years in May, murdering 26 Israeli citizens in Maalot. The terrorists were killed by the Israeli Army. See ISRAEL.

In Syria, Jews continued to live under severe government restrictions and suffered frequent harassment. Emigration was forbidden, and four Jewish women were murdered in March near the Syrian-Lebanese border when they attempted to flee the country. In June, two prominent members of the Syrian Jewish community were charged with their murder. Despite international protests, they were placed on trial with two other defendants.

In Russia, about 120,000 Jews had applied for exit visas, with 6,000 applying each month. But it appeared that emigrants would total only about half the 35,000 that left the country in 1973. Despite this reduction, Western Jewish leaders were guardedly optimistic as a result of an accord reportedly reached between the U.S. Congress, the Ford Administration, and Russia on U.S. trade credits and Jewish emigration that would permit 60,000 Jews to leave Russia each year.

U.S. Civil Rights. On April 23, the Supreme Court of the United States declared "moot" an appeal by Marco DeFunis, Jr., of a lower court ruling on his suit against the University of Washington Law School. DeFunis, who is Jewish and had completed his studies elsewhere, accused the school of denying him admission in 1971 in favor of a less qualified black candidate. Despite the court's refusal to rule, the case became the subject of heated controversy because of its implications for Jews.

While the DeFunis case heightened tensions between the Jewish and black communities, there were also indications of renewed harmony between the two groups. Two prominent black spokesmen – Vernon E. Jordan, Jr., executive director of the National Urban League, and Jesse Jackson, founder of People United to Save Humanity (PUSH) – called for a working black-Jewish alliance. Jordan made his remarks in June before the American Jewish Committee in Atlanta, while Jackson spoke before the Urban League's San Francisco convention in July.

U.S. Affairs. Controversy surrounded Rabbi Baruch Korff of Providence, R.I., who served as founder and president of the Committee for Fairness to the Presidency. Prior to President Richard M. Nixon's resignation in August, Korff wrote a book defending Nixon, and he was one of Nixon's most vocal supporters.

In June, Representative Elizabeth Holtzman (D., N.Y.) charged that the U.S. Immigration and Naturalization Service had "failed to conduct a thorough investigation" of alleged Nazi war criminals who had taken refuge in the United States. She charged that 60 of 73 reported war criminals were still living in the United States. The Immigration and Naturalization Service replied that it was investigating 37 of the 60 people named by Congresswoman Holtzman, and that the other 23 were outside its jurisdiction.

Jewish communities throughout the United States were hosts during 1974 to three renowned rabbis. Moshe Rosen, chief rabbi of Romania, toured the country in February. Israel's Sephardic chief rabbi, Ovadia Yosef, visited in April, as did his Ashkenazic counterpart, Shlomo Goren, in June. The visits by Rabbis Yosef and Goren marked the first by Israeli chief rabbis to the United States.

The Union of Orthodox Jewish Congregations of America suspended its participation in the Synagogue Council of America, which includes the Reform and Conservative branches of Judaism, but later agreed to postpone until March, 1975, any decision about whether to formally withdraw.

Three prominent Jewish leaders died in Israel in 1974. Rabbi Amram Blau, the leader of the ultra-Orthodox Neturai Karta sect of Jerusalem, died on July 5. Ted Lurie, editor of the *Jerusalem Post*, died on June 1, and was succeeded by Lea Ben-Dor. And the former president of Israel, Schneor Zalman Shazar, died on October 5.   Judah Graubart

Ballet dancers Valery and Galina Panov, center, who themselves fled Russia, join in a London protest against the Moscow trial of a friend.

JORDAN. King Hussein I's claims to represent Palestinians on both banks of the River Jordan were shattered by Arab leaders in 1974. They voted at a summit conference in Rabat, Morocco, in October to recognize the Palestinian Liberation Organization (PLO) as the sole representative of the Palestinian people. Hussein then began a reorganization of the government. On November 10, Parliament passed constitutional amendments to allow Hussein to dissolve it and defer elections for a year until West Bank voters were disenfranchised.

Army Protests in February dramatized dissatisfaction with rising prices, pay inequities, and alleged corruption. Some junior officers were also frustrated by Jordan's limited role in the October war with Israel in 1973. They felt that a strong showing would have demonstrated Jordanian effectiveness in the eyes of other Arab states. Hussein met the situation by granting a 10 per cent pay raise for the armed forces to match that given to civil servants. He also retired 10 senior officers.

President Richard M. Nixon visited Jordan in June. Nixon and Hussein agreed to form a joint commission to review economic and military aid. In August, Hussein was the first chief of state to visit President Gerald R. Ford in the White House. American aid to Jordan was pegged at $233 million, about half of it in military equipment.

Economy Improves. Phosphate production reached 1.8 million short tons (1.6 million metric tons), a 15 per cent increase. Other favorable economic developments included sales of $480,000 worth of Jordanian industrial products to Egypt. Tonnage handled at the port of Aqaba, Jordan's only seaport, reached the prewar level of 1967 at 1.25 million short tons (1.13 million metric tons). Encouraged by Jordan's relative political stability and its prospects, the First National City Bank of New York City opened a branch in Amman, the Jordanian capital.

Kuwait and Saudi Arabia continued their annual subsidies, and Taiwan loaned Jordan $5 million in April to finance industrial projects in the current three-year plan. In July, the Kuwait Fund for Arab Economic and Social Development underwrote Jordan's Industrial Development Bank with $2.85-million. As an Arab "confrontation country" against Israel, Jordan received a $15 million gift from Abu Dhabi.

In April, the King Talal Dam project on the Jordan River and the paved highway from El Azraq to the Jordan-Saudi Arabian border went into operation. The latter will provide a much-needed transport link with Saudi Arabia's developing road network.   William Spencer

See also MIDDLE EAST (Facts in Brief Table).

JUNIOR ACHIEVEMENT (JA). See YOUTH ORGANIZATIONS.

KANSAS. See STATE GOVERNMENT.

KARAMANLIS, CONSTANTIN E. (1907-   ), prime minister of Greece from 1956 to 1963, returned from self-imposed exile in Paris on July 24, 1974, to become prime minister of a provisional Greek government. The day before, the military junta that had ruled Greece for seven years resigned. Greek voters gave Karamanlis' New Democracy Party 214 of 300 parliamentary seats in November general elections, and he quickly turned his attention to solution of the Cyprus question, which had precipitated the junta's fall and had plagued Karamanlis in 1956 during his first term as prime minister. See CYPRUS; GREECE.

Karamanlis was born in 1907 in a small hamlet near Sérrai, Macedonia. He received a law degree in 1932 from the University of Athens, was elected to Parliament in 1935, and became a Cabinet minister in 1946. He was elected prime minister on Feb. 19, 1956, after holding seven Cabinet posts.

A staunch anti-Communist, Karamanlis pushed progressive domestic programs that, with sizable U.S. assistance, produced an economic boom. Re-elected in 1958, he endorsed an agreement with Turkey and Great Britain guaranteeing the independence of Cyprus, and brought Greece into the European Community (Common Market) as an associate member. A quarrel with the monarchy led him to flee the country in 1963.   Robert K. Johnson

KENTUCKY. See STATE GOVERNMENT.

KENYA. Voters turned out about half the incumbents, including four government ministers and several assistant ministers, in parliamentary elections in October, 1974. More than 700 candidates vied for the 158 seats, even though the election was open only to Kenya African National Union (KANU) candidates. Inflation, unemployment, uneven distribution of land and wealth, and a housing shortage were major election issues.

Former Vice-President Oginga Odinga, leader of government opposition since the mid-1960s, and nine former members of his banned Kenya People's Union Party were forbidden to run for office, even though they had all rejoined KANU. So Odinga urged his supporters to vote against incumbents.

Strikes Banned. On August 16, President Jomo Kenyatta issued a ban on all strikes. The nation had been swept by a wave of industrial unrest involving strikes by railroad, airport, and bank employees. There were also strikes by high school and university students. Student boycotts at the University College in Nairobi, protesting inadequate instruction and poor living conditions, forced the government to close the school in February.

President Kenyatta warned that severe disciplinary action would be taken against students and workers who violated the strike ban. One labor leader expressed fears that the ban would lead to the end of trade unionism in Kenya.

The Economic Picture. Figures released in 1974 showed that production increased 20 per cent during 1973. Kenya's trade deficit was reduced to $29 million during the first half of 1973, compared with $89 million for the same period of 1972.

Foreign exchange reserves reached a new high of $300 million in 1974. As a result, Kenya relaxed import restrictions. However, the tourist industry suffered because of the international oil crisis and unrest in neighboring Uganda.

Canada, Great Britain, and the United States announced in October they would put $36 million into a project to help develop Kenya's beef industry. The World Bank loaned $10.4 million to Kenya's tea industry. In July, Kenya agreed to allow U.S. oil interests to look for oil in northeastern Kenya.

About 2 million citizens of Kenya were affected by the general sub-Sahara drought, which reduced food production. A Chase Manhattan Bank publication in April suggested this would make it difficult for Kenya to achieve even half its usual annual growth rate. The government forbade the export of certain grains and grain products.

Kenya may be rethinking its pro-Arab position. In June, a government official complained that Kenya had suffered from its break with Israel. The Arabs did not provide aid, as Israel had, and would not sell oil at cut-rate prices.   John Storm Roberts

See also AFRICA (Facts in Brief Table).

Khmer troops recapture a badly damaged temple in Oudong in July during a battle with the Khmer Rouge insurgents north of Phnom Penh.

KHMER. President Lon Nol's government proposed unconditional negotiations with its enemies on July 9, 1974, dropping previous demands for a cease-fire and withdrawal of North Vietnamese troops before talks could begin. But both Prince Norodom Sihanouk, the deposed leader who now lives in Peking, China, and the Khmer Rouge leaders fighting inside the country rejected the offer.

All elements opposing Lon Nol made efforts to give Khmer's United Nations seat to Sihanouk's government-in-exile. The United States and Japan led the successful opposition to this move. Opponents of Lon Nol, however, were basically disunited. Sihanouk admitted conflicts with the Khmer Rouge, a Communist-led movement, while some elements within that movement accepted North Vietnamese leadership and some pursued more nationalistic aims. The apparent leader of the nationalistic group, Khieu Samphan, made a two-month trip to 11 countries in April and May to seek aid and to enhance his status.

War Continues. In January, a major attack on Phnom Penh, Lon Nol's capital, was beaten back. Several times during the year the enemy put captured U.S.-made artillery and Communist rockets within range of the city and bombarded it. Only two surface routes into the capital were kept open, both by river, as the enemy held much of the countryside. Possible tension within the enemy camp was shown by North Vietnam's failure to supply enough heavy weapons to make attempts to isolate Phnom Penh more effective.

There was uncertainty about the government's future ability to defend its enclaves because of cuts in military aid by the U.S. Congress. The cost of U.S.-supplied ammunition had soared from $169.2-million between 1970 and June 30, 1973, to $288.7-million in the next 12 months, largely because the August, 1973, halt in U.S. bombing meant Khmer forces needed more firepower of their own.

Imports of U.S. food and other civilian aid also increased. In July, the Khmer Rouge stopped letting any rubber grown in its area cross to the government side. This cut the main export left to Phnom Penh and increased Lon Nol's dependence on the United States.

Dean's Influence. This dependence enhanced U.S. influence. The new U.S. ambassador, John Gunther Dean, used the influence more openly to try to reduce corruption and governmental inefficiency. Dean worked closely with the Cabinet headed by Prime Minister Long Boret, who remained in this post after Cabinet changes in June.

With inflation running at about 250 per cent a year in Phnom Penh, the government adjusted rice prices and raised salaries on September 15. But economic distress continued.   Henry S. Bradsher

See also ASIA (Facts in Brief Table).

KIRCHSCHLAEGER, RUDOLF (1915-   ), was elected president of Austria on June 23, 1974. He succeeded Franz Jonas, who died in April, in the largely ceremonial office. Kirchschlaeger was picked for the post by Chancellor Bruno Kreisky over the opposition of some other Socialist leaders.

Kirchschlaeger was born in Obermühl, Austria, on March 20, 1915. He graduated from college in 1935 and received his law degree from the University of Vienna in 1940. After military service in World War II, he entered the judiciary system, working first for the public prosecutor's office in the city of Krems, near Vienna. By January, 1954, he was a judge in Vienna.

In mid-1954, Kirchschlaeger joined the ministry for foreign affairs. In 1956, he was appointed a member of the Austrian foreign service and became legal adviser to the minister for foreign affairs. He helped write the constitutional law that established Austria's permanent neutrality. From 1956 to 1965, he was a member of Austria's United Nations delegation. He headed Austrian delegations to several important international conferences, including the Second Geneva Conference on the Law of the Sea in 1960. Kirchschlaeger was appointed envoy extraordinary and minister plenipotentiary to Czechoslovakia in 1967. He became foreign minister in 1970. Kirchschlaeger married Herma Sorger in 1940. They have two children.   Edward G. Nash

KISSINGER, HENRY ALFRED (1923-   ), U.S. secretary of state, continued his highly personal style of diplomacy in 1974. After difficult negotiations, Kissinger concluded pacts between Egypt and Israel in January and Israel and Syria in May that provided for troop pullbacks and United Nations buffer zones on both fronts of the October, 1973, Arab-Israeli war.

Perhaps Kissinger's greatest service was to provide continuity in foreign affairs during the transfer of power from the Administration of President Richard M. Nixon, collapsing under the Watergate affair, to that of President Gerald R. Ford.

Kissinger was born in Fürth, Germany, on May 27, 1923. He and his family fled the Nazi persecution of Jews in 1938, settling in New York City. He attended Harvard University, then served on the Harvard faculty and also as a consultant to Presidents Dwight D. Eisenhower, John F. Kennedy, and Lyndon B. Johnson.

He became a presidential assistant in 1969, and was named secretary of state in 1973. He was instrumental in re-establishing diplomatic contacts with the People's Republic of China, and in ending the U.S. involvement in Vietnam, for which he won the 1973 Nobel Peace Prize. Kissinger married Ann Fleischer in 1949; they divorced in 1964. He has two children by that marriage. On March 30, 1974, he married Nancy Maginnes.   Edward G. Nash

KIWANIS INTERNATIONAL delegates to the 59th annual convention, held in Denver in June, 1974, disapproved a proposal that would have allowed women to become active or honorary Kiwanis members. They also decided that Kiwanis clubs cannot use lotteries, drawings, raffles, or other games of chance to raise public funds, even where they are permitted by local law.

Delegates confirmed the election of Roy W. Davis of Chicago as president and Ted R. Osborn of Lexington, Ky., as president-elect. They also adopted an administrative resolution that calls on the board of trustees to begin preliminary exploration of a worldwide Kiwanis structure.

The delegates accepted two major service programs for Kiwanis members during the 1974-1975 service year: The Younger Years, on behalf of children with learning disabilities; and The Greater Years, on behalf of the aging and those in their pre-retirement years.

The constitution and bylaws were amended to raise the overseas extension dues allocation to $1 and the per-capita dues each club pays to Kiwanis International to $6 per year. Convention delegates also eliminated the requirement of a meal function at regular weekly club meetings and changed the name of the committee on membership development to the committee on membership growth and education.   Joseph P. Anderson

KOREA, NORTH. Trade contacts with Japan and Western Europe expanded during 1974. The national industrialization effort apparently had advanced enough to require more technically sophisticated equipment than could be supplied by Russia, North Korea's main trading partner. Relations with Moscow were strained by Russian efforts to align North Korea against China. President Kim Il-song held a middle position in the Chinese-Russian dispute by maintaining good relations with Peking, too.

The Supreme People's Assembly abolished taxes on March 25. Hailed as a major step toward pure Communism, this was made possible by controlling production and sale prices so that government profits replaced taxes.

An official statement on October 8 reported "no progress has been made in the dialogue between the North and the South [Korea], and North-South relations are returning to those before the announcement of the North-South joint statement," July 4, 1972. That announcement established a committee to work toward reunification of Korea.

North Korea blamed the United States for lack of progress, and it asked the United Nations (UN) to remove the UN military command from South Korea. The military command is primarily composed of U.S. troops.   Henry S. Bradsher

See also Asia (Facts in Brief Table).

Children of Mrs. Chung Hee Park place flowers beneath her picture during her funeral. The wife of South Korea's president was slain August 15.

KOREA, SOUTH. Political unrest and tension gripped South Korea in 1974. Opposition to the constitutional changes made in 1972 by President Chung Hee Park, which increased his personal power, continued to cause demonstrations and protest meetings. The resistance had been heightened by the kidnaping from Japan on Aug. 8, 1973, of opposition leader Kim Dae-jung.

Park proclaimed emergency measures on January 8, banning criticism of the Korean Constitution. They provided up to 15 years' imprisonment for any violations. But college students, Christian groups, and some intellectuals continued to oppose Park. On April 3, Park decreed the death penalty for dissent, in an effort to check demonstrations.

The decrees were lifted on August 23, but the 194 convictions and nine death sentences enacted under the emergency measures remained valid. Those sentenced included Bishop Daniel Chi Hak Sun, leader of the nation's 800,000 Roman Catholics, who was imprisoned for 15 years, and a noted poet, Kim Chi Ha. Demonstrations flared again in October despite repressive measures under other laws.

Mrs. Park Killed. On August 15, a Korean resident of Japan tried to shoot Park in Seoul. He missed, but killed Mrs. Park. The government charged that the assassin, Mun Se-kwang, had been sent to Seoul by a North Korean organization based in Japan. Mobs attacked the Japanese Em-

bassy in Seoul, and the government tried to force Japan to suppress the North Korean organization. Observers thought this was partly intended to halt Japanese complaints that South Korea had failed to carry out a promise to let Kim Dae-jung return to Japan. Kim was put on trial on old election-fraud charges instead.

The opposition New Democratic Party elected Kim Young-sam as its leader on August 23. He launched a more vigorous public attack on Park's regime than had been possible for some time. He called it a "one-man dictatorship in defiance of democracy" and threatened to lead demonstrations. Kim also called for Park to resign.

Ford Visits. South Korea continued to rely on U.S. military forces stationed in the country for protection against invasion by North Korea, though the North called for their removal. The U.S. forces were expected to remain indefinitely. President Gerald R. Ford visited Seoul in November, and political opponents denounced this implied U.S. endorsement of Park's government.

The increase in oil prices and worldwide inflation hurt South Korea's economy. Inflation and trade deficits rose. But the growing proficiency of Korean industry, moving from simple products to advanced equipment, offered hope of continued economic growth.   Henry S. Bradsher

See also ASIA (Facts in Brief Table).

KUWAIT influenced Arab affairs in 1974 with funds from its enormous oil-based treasury. On April 20, the National Assembly allocated $437 million to the Arab countries confronting Israel. Syria received $100 million of this sum. The government also continued its subsidy to Jordan and provided emergency aid to Lebanon in June for reconstruction of villages hit in Israeli bombing raids. Kuwait tried unsuccessfully to mediate the dispute between Oman and Yemen (Aden) over Yemeni aid to rebels opposing Oman in Dhofar Province.

The Assembly on May 14 approved an agreement with the British Petroleum Company and Gulf Oil Corporation, owners of Kuwait Oil Company (KOC), which gave Kuwait a 60 per cent interest in KOC operations. Each company received $56-million in compensation. On October 1, Kuwait boosted tax and royalty rates on oil produced by the companies for their own accounts. The increase helped hike Kuwait's total oil revenues 3.5 per cent.

There was a 13 per cent rise in Kuwait's cost of living. Bank employees struck for higher pay in June. Along with 95,000 civil servants, they were granted a 25 per cent pay raise.

Kuwait loaned $100 million to Yugoslavia on June 24 to expand its shipbuilding industry. On June 28, a cultural exchange agreement with Russia was approved by the Assembly.   William Spencer

See also MIDDLE EAST (Facts in Brief Table).

About 2,000 women meet in a Chicago hotel in March for the founding
of the Coalition of Labor Union Women, dedicated to ending job sex bias.

LABOR. Inflation and unemployment, twin enemies of workers, dominated the labor scene in the
United States in 1974. Attempts to control inflation
created recessionary conditions that led to spiraling
unemployment. In December, the national unemployment rate reached 7.1 per cent, its highest level
since May, 1961. A total of 6.5 million workers were
unemployed, an increase of more than 2 million
since December, 1973. By the end of 1974, the
unemployment picture was even bleaker, because
of widespread layoffs, most of them in the automobile industry, after the December jobless rate was
compiled by the U.S. Bureau of Labor Statistics
(BLS).

Wages Versus Inflation. The BLS Consumer
Price Index rose 12.2 per cent in the one-year period
ending in October. This was the largest rise during
a 12-month span since 1947. This compared to an
average annual rise of 6.2 per cent in 1973 and 3.3
per cent in 1972, when controls were still in effect.

Double-digit inflation ate into workers' purchasing power by diminishing their real earnings 4.1 per
cent between October, 1973, and October, 1974. An
8.8 per cent rise in average weekly earnings was offset by the 12.2 per cent rise in the cost of living. Real
spendable earnings, after social security and federal income taxes were deducted, declined 4.9 per
cent.

Preliminary BLS estimates given in the following
table summarize major employment changes in
1974:

	1973	1974*
	(in thousands)	
Total labor force	**91,040**	**93,077**
Armed forces	2,326	2,234
Civilian labor force	88,714	90,843
Unemployment	4,304	4,796
Unemployment rate	4.9%	5.3%
Change in real weekly earnings	−1.4%	−5.2%†
(Workers with 3 dependents—		
private nonfarm sector)		
Change in output per man-hour	2.7%	−2.9%‡
(Private nonfarm sector)		

*January to September average, seasonally adjusted, except for
armed forces data.
†For 12-month period ending Sept. 30, 1974.
‡Third quarter of 1974, compared with third quarter of 1973.

New Stabilization Program. On August 24,
President Gerald R. Ford signed a bill creating the
Council on Wage and Price Stability, which would
use persuasion, instead of controls, to limit wage
and price increases. In September, Ford also revealed the creation of a White House Labor-Management Committee, a presidential advisory group.

The stabilization program of President Richard
M. Nixon had been gradually dismantled during
the first half of 1974. The Cost of Living Council
formally abolished itself on July 1.

Wage and Unemployment Acts. On April 8,
President Nixon signed legislation increasing the

minimum wage from $1.60 to $2.30 an hour by 1976. The act extended coverage of the Fair Labor Standards Act to an additional 7.4 million workers, including household, retail, and service workers and federal, state, and local government employees.

On December 31, President Ford signed a bill providing $2.5 billion for public-service jobs in high-unemployment areas. The bill also extended the duration of unemployment benefits and covered an additional 3 million workers. In 1974, the government had provided $415 million for 85,000 jobs.

Collective Bargaining. Some 5.2 million workers were covered by major collective bargaining agreements that expired or were reopened in 1974. For the first nine months of 1974, the BLS estimated an average increase of 9.6 per cent in the first year of the contract and 7.2 per cent a year over the life of the agreements. This compares to 5.8 per cent for the first year and 5.1 per cent over the life of contracts negotiated in 1973.

The 5.5 per cent federal wage guideline, a focus on nonwage issues, and an end to the cost-of-living catch-up cycle had limited 1973 wage demands. But by 1974, union negotiators were responding to renewed inflation. The number of workers covered by cost-of-living escalator clauses to protect against price increases rose to 5 million in 1974. More than 600,000 workers benefited from settlements adopting such clauses during the first nine months of the year.

Coal Strike. The United Mine Workers (UMW) struck for 24 days in November and December, causing some layoffs in the automobile and steel industries. About 120,000 miners walked off their jobs on November 12. Negotiators for the UMW and Bituminous Coal Operators Association agreed on a tentative new contract on November 14, but the bargaining council, made up of local union officials, rejected it. The two sides finally reached a new agreement that was officially accepted on December 5. See COAL.

The miners, who previously earned $42 to $50 a day, received a 17 per cent wage hike over the three-year contract period, beginning with 10 per cent the first year. The pact also established a cost-of-living escalator clause. The prior flat $150-a-month pension was increased in steps to $250 a month, and the pension for future retirees would range up to more than $550 a month. Disability and widow's benefits were increased, and a sickness and accident program was established providing $100 a week for up to 52 weeks. The miners also gained five days paid sick leave and improved vacation, safety, training, grievance, and seniority provisions.

Other Strikes. Strike activity mounted in 1974. The BLS reported 38 million days of idleness, nearly double the amount in 1973. In addition to

Taxi drivers park their cabs on a busy thoroughfare in Rome, blocking rush-hour traffic on June 12 to dramatize demands for fare increases.

Picketing printers, fearful computer typesetting will take their jobs away, tear up copies of the New York *Daily News* produced by automation.

the coal strike, there was labor unrest in the construction, copper, and men's apparel industries, and among Greyhound bus drivers, United Parcel Service workers, and some auto workers. A three-year pact reached in July ended a four-month work stoppage by 5,500 steelworkers at the Dow Chemical Company's Midland, Mich., plant. A two-year strike and boycott by the Amalgamated Clothing Workers of America against the Farah Manufacturing Company of El Paso, Tex., ended on February 24, when the clothier recognized the union.

New Steel Pact. The United Steelworkers of America reached a three-year settlement with the United States Steel Corporation and nine other major steel producers 3½ months before the August 1 expiration of their agreement. The pact, ratified on April 12, raised the wages and benefits of 365,000 steelworkers by about 40 per cent over the three-year period. The cost-of-living escalator was increased, and a dental-insurance plan was established. The workers also gained a 10th paid holiday and improvements in vacations, sick days, pensions, and accident and medical benefits.

The union and companies cited the Experimental Negotiating Agreement (ENA), accepted in March, 1973, as a major factor in allowing them to reach a peaceful accord. Under ENA, both sides pledged to bar strikes or lockouts on the national level, instead accepting arbitration of any unresolved issues. In return for the steelworkers' cooperation, ENA had guaranteed 3 per cent minimum wage increases for three years; continued the cost-of-living clause; and allowed a one-time $150 bonus.

In February, the steelworkers' union concluded agreements with the major aluminum and can producers that generally paralleled the provisions in the steel settlements. However, the aluminum and can pacts provided a historic first by tying pension benefits to automatic cost-of-living adjustments.

Telephone Contract. A three-year accord reached on August 4 with the American Telephone & Telegraph Company (A.T. & T.) covered some 500,000 members of the Communications Workers of America. First-year wage increases ranged from 7.1 to 10.7 per cent, depending on the job grade, with 3.3 per cent wage hikes in the second and third years. The pact also provided an improved cost-of-living escalator clause, a 10th paid holiday, improved pension and health insurance benefits, and a company-financed dental plan.

This was the first A.T. & T. agreement reached on a companywide basis. The prior system of bargaining separately with Bell System affiliates had been altered early in 1974. As a result, the new contract contained a uniform expiration date of Aug. 6, 1977. Similar terms were extended to 206,000 members of the International Brotherhood of Electrical Workers and independent unions.

Other Settlements included an 11-year agreement reached in May between Local 6 of the International Typographical Union and *The New York Times* and the New York *Daily News*. The newspapers won the right to use automated typesetting equipment in return for lifetime job protection for their typesetters. An average 5.5 per cent pay hike was granted to 3.5 million federal civilian and military personnel in October, after Congress rejected President Ford's proposal to delay the increase 90 days as an anti-inflationary measure.

A walkout by professional football players in July and August hampered the National Football League's preseason play. Baltimore municipal employees, including about half the city's policemen, went on strike in July. See BALTIMORE.

Pension Reform highlighted the year's labor legislation. On September 2, President Ford signed into law the Employee Retirement Income Security Act of 1974. The law protects the pension rights of workers if they quit or are dismissed after lengthy service, or if their employer goes out of business.

Employers were given three options to achieve *vesting* (the guaranteeing of workers' rights to their accumulated pension benefits). The first provides 100 per cent vesting after 10 years of service. The second calls for 25 per cent vesting after 5 years, with 5 per cent raises a year to 50 per cent vesting by the 10th year and 100 per cent after 15 years. The third option guarantees 50 per cent vesting when a worker's age plus years of service total 45–if the employee has a minimum of five years' service–with full vesting assured after 15 years of employment, regardless of age.

The act does not force an employer to establish a pension plan, but it establishes regulations for company or union plans. It also establishes a Pension Benefit Guarantee Corporation to pay workers whose pension plans collapse.

Job Discrimination. In the largest back-pay award on record, nine major steel companies and the steelworkers' union agreed on April 15 to pay $30.9 million to 40,000 women and minority workers. A federal district judge on January 31 ordered the Georgia Power Company to pay $2.1 million in back wages and benefits to black employees, and A.T. & T. on May 30 agreed to change its pay system for managerial employees to prevent pay bias.

Both the Bank of America and the B.F. Goodrich Company acted during the year to eliminate sex discrimination. The Standard Oil Company of California on May 16 agreed to pay $2 million to alleged victims of age bias.

On April 11, former UMW President W. A. (Tony) Boyle was convicted of first-degree murder in the 1969 slaying of union rival Joseph A. Yablonski and his wife and daughter. Leon Bornstein

See also ECONOMICS; Section One, FOCUS ON THE ECONOMY.

LAOS. Two groups of men in white jackets and blue sarongs filed into the royal palace at Luang Prabang on April 5, 1974. In the first, 72-year-old Prince Souvanna Phouma led his new Cabinet of 12. The other group of 42 was the Joint National Political Council (JNPC) headed by Souvanna's 62-year-old half brother Prince Souphanouvong. Souvanna has been known as a neutralist, leaning toward the West. His half brother took part in the 1950 meeting in which the pro-Communist Pathet Lao movement was born.

After a swearing-in ceremony led by King Savang Vatthana, the men flew to the political capital, Vientiane, to begin governing this nation of 3.2-million people. Thus, 13½ months after the signing of a cease-fire accord, the 20-year civil war ended, and the rivals were joined in a coalition regime.

Many Uncertainties. The new arrangement was fragile. When the cease-fire began, the Pathet Lao, aided by the North Vietnamese, controlled two-thirds of the countryside, while Souvanna's regime of neutralists and rightist generals in Vientiane controlled two-thirds of the population. The new accord gave the two foes a scrupulous 50-50 ratio.

The first major action of the new government was to announce acceptance, April 30, of a $30-million economic-aid offer from the United States, France, Great Britain, Australia, and Japan. The funds were to purchase food and stabilize the Laotian currency.

Souvanna Phouma stayed on as prime minister. The Pathet Lao took over the Cabinet ministries of economy, foreign affairs, and information. Souvanna's own men took the interior, defense, and finance portfolios. But, on the Pathet Lao's insistence, a National Political Council was formed in which the JNPC controlled half the representatives; the National Political Council was given powers equal to the Cabinet's. This was a formula for continued friction. The Pathet Lao confirmed this in May by forcing the dissolution of the 60-member, rightist-dominated National Assembly. Not until July did the demoralized neutralists and rightists form a political grouping to block Communist moves and prepare for the 1976 elections. But they lacked the drive and ingenuity of their Communist rivals. The Pathet Lao supported labor and school strikes in the Vientiane area. And as the year ended, there were charges of armed intrusions, U.S. air raids, and attempted coups d'état.

Souvanna Phouma, the superb compromiser, was the key man in the picture. Therefore, when he suffered a heart attack on July 12, it threw the rival camps into consternation. Sensitive problems remained unsolved until he returned in November. He immediately appealed to the feuding factions to end the hostilities and strikes, and he predicted it would take up to five years to have "complete understanding." Mark Gayn

See also ASIA (Facts in Brief Table).

COLOMBIA   MEXICO   ARGENTINA

LATIN AMERICA

It was a time of testing in Latin America, where the big questions in 1974 were: Can the few remaining democracies survive? Will the military regimes in power throughout most of the continent swing to the political right or to the left?

To the surprise of most people, Argentina struggled through to the end of the year under President María Estela (Isabel) Martínez de Perón, in the teeth of rising terrorist violence. The right wing junta set up in Chile in 1973 held on despite economic troubles, but military regimes elsewhere—notably those in Peru, Panama, and Ecuador—displayed a growing tendency to flirt with radical ideas. It was obvious in 1974 that in Latin America the armed forces were by no means synonymous with conservative reaction. At the same time, the worldwide oil crisis had a marked effect on the economic and political balance of the region. Venezuela, under a new president, emerged as a force with which to reckon. Terrorism and kidnapings for ransom were equally potent forces, especially in Argentina and Mexico.

U.S.-Russian Policy. The decline of United States influence over Latin American affairs continued. This was best exemplified by the growing support for lifting sanctions against Cuba. Accusations of U.S. Central Intelligence Agency (CIA) involvement in the overthrow of the late Salvador Allende Gossens' regime in Chile—fed by reports that CIA Director William E. Colby had admitted to the use of $8 million in clandestine funds to support anti-Allende media and political groups—added to a "hands-off" trend in Washington, D.C. United States Secretary of State Henry A. Kissinger was clearly preoccupied by crises elsewhere but appeared to be wavering toward a policy of détente toward Cuba. The new assistant secretary of state for inter-American affairs, William Rogers, who was appointed in September, believed firmly in a less interventionist U.S. policy.

The publication on October 16 of a major report issued by the Commission on United States-Latin American Relations (a group closely related to Kissinger) provided some important clues to the drift of U.S. policy, though it was not an official document. The report stressed the principle of nonintervention within the Western Hemisphere, détente with Cuba, regional arms limitation, increased bilateral aid, and a less dominant role for the United States in international lending bodies such as the Inter-American Development Bank.

Russia, chastened by the failure of the Marxist experiment it had supported in Chile under President Allende, now stressed the chances for cooperation with well-established "progressive" regimes, notably in Peru and Argentina. Soviet arms sales to Peru, the presence of Soviet military advisers, and the large Soviet Embassy in Lima (the largest in Latin America apart from Cuba) were a source of increasing alarm for neighboring Chile. In 1974, Aeroflot, the Russian airline, also received permission to start Moscow-Lima flights. The Russians signed major trade and economic cooperation agreements with Argentina in February; and José Ber Gelbard, then economics minister, received the highest honors when he visited Moscow in May.

At the same time, Russian trade and diplomatic contacts with right wing regimes continued to increase. Brazil's exports to Russia, for example, rose to over $100 million. The only government that the Russians seemed determined to quarantine was Chile's; after diplomatic relations were suspended on Sept. 21, 1973, the Russians directly supported the propaganda campaign against the Chilean junta.

The Cuba Issue. The Organization of American States (OAS) came within a hair's-breadth of dropping sanctions against Cuba at the foreign ministers' meeting in Quito, Ecuador, on November 8, but the pro-Castro resolution was finally defeated by 14 votes to 12. The trend toward unilateral recognition of Cuba, however, continued to gather strength. Two U.S. senators, Jacob K. Javits (R., N.Y.) and Claiborne Pell (D., R.I.), visited Cuba in September for talks with Prime Minister Fidel Castro. There were signs of Russian pressure on Castro to accept détente with the United States, influenced partly by the Soviets' broader foreign policy goals and also by the desire to save freight costs on their petroleum shipment to Cuba by gaining access to the Venezuelan oil market. See CUBA.

Oil and Geopolitics. Successive price rises, by the Organization of Petroleum Exporting Countries (OPEC), transformed the world's economic balance and potentially its political balance, in Latin America as in the rest of the world. The region is a net exporter of oil; exports in 1974 were worth $12 billion, as against imports worth only $4.5 billion. But the situation varied dramatically from country to country.

The oil exporters, notably Venezuela and Ecuador—but also including Bolivia, Colombia, and (since June) Mexico—saw their payments problems eased and their capacity to influence

Argentina's Alberto Vignes addresses the first meeting of the Organization of American States held in the United States, in Atlanta, Ga., in April.

383

neighboring countries substantially increased. Peru and Argentina, though less favorably placed, were well on the way to self-sufficiency in oil. In contrast, Brazil, the continent's industrial giant, had to spend $2.5 billion on oil imports. Chile was also adversely affected. Those who suffered most, however, were the weaker republics of Central America and the Caribbean (excluding Trinidad and Tobago), and Uruguay and Paraguay. None had any oil. Furthermore, these smaller countries lacked the financial reserves and international credit standing of such giants as Brazil and were forced to try to organize producers' cartels to defend the prices of their major export commodities.

The New Cartels. Attempts were made to organize a number of new producers' associations on the lines of OPEC. On September 17, after protracted efforts, a Banana Exporters' Union (UPEC) was formally set up by Colombia, Costa Rica, Guatemala, Honduras, and Panama. It was weakened, however, by the fact that Ecuador, the biggest Latin American producer, declined to join. Jamaica's Prime Minister Michael N. Manley was the driving force behind the International Bauxite Association that was set up in Guinea earlier in the year. Jamaica then imposed new levies and royalties on the U.S.-owned companies taking bauxite out of the country, thus increasing its revenues enormously.

In September, the International Coffee Organization met in London. The Latin American producers attending it agreed to withhold stocks from the world market until prices returned to an acceptable level. There were later charges, however, that Central American producers had sabotaged this scheme by releasing 400,000 short tons (363,000 metric tons) for sale without getting the prior consent of other producers. Iron-exporting countries, including Brazil and Venezuela, met in Geneva, Switzerland, in early November to discuss the chances of setting up yet another cartel.

The Andean Pact was strained during the year. Five members—Colombia, Venezuela, Bolivia, Peru, and Ecuador—claimed that the sixth, Chile, had violated an article of the pact with its new decrees encouraging foreign investment. It seemed increasingly doubtful, however, that those members not exporting oil would be willing to enforce tough restrictions subsequently imposed on foreign investors. This was due as much to their urgent need for capital and technology as to the growing reluctance of many American companies to run the political risks involved in many Latin American countries.

Central America
Costa Rica. The results of the February 3 presidential elections broke a 25-year Costa Rican tradition: that a party does not succeed itself in office. Largely because the opposition was hope-

lessly divided, Daniel Oduber Quirós, the candidate of the ruling National Liberation Party, romped home with about 44 per cent of the vote. He took over from President José Figueres Ferrer on May 8. See ODUBER QUIRÓS, DANIEL.

A cloud of scandal hovered over the Figueres regime throughout the year. In March, President Figueres rushed through a new law regulating extradition, a move widely regarded as a naked attempt to protect American financier Robert L. Vesco from attempts to return him to the United States for trial on fraud charges. In September, a former minister of industry, Gaston Kogan, admitted that he had helped to operate an illegal campaign fund to help Oduber in the March election.

El Salvador. Tension between El Salvador and Honduras continued to run high, delaying the summit meeting of Central American leaders that had been tentatively scheduled for May, 1974. The ruling Salvadorean National Conciliation Party increased its majority in the congressional elections on March 10; a major factor was the patriotic, anti-Honduran sentiment drummed up by President Arturo Armando Molina Barraza. The government faced serious economic problems during the year. The rate of inflation rose to between 30 and 40 per cent because of the higher cost of imported oil and foods and the reckless expansion of the monetary supply. Faced with a worsening trade deficit, the Salvadoreans made a determined attempt to find new markets for traditional exports, mostly cotton and coffee; new trade agreements with Eastern Europe were signed.

Guatemala. General Kjell Eugenio Laugerud García won the presidential election held on March 3. The early results showed that his rival, General Efrain Rios Montt, who represented the National Opposition Front, was clearly in the lead. Electoral officials, however, then stopped giving results and pronounced General Laugerud the victor even before all the results were in. Congressmen on the board of scrutineers resigned, alleging fraud, and Rios was sent to Madrid as military attaché after calling on his supporters to practice "passive resistance." See LAUGERUD GARCÍA, KJELL EUGENIO.

Honduras. Officials estimated that it would take Honduras at least five years to recover from the effects of Hurricane Fifi, which hit the country on September 18 and 19. The storm killed about 8,000 persons; destroyed 80 per cent of the 1974 banana crop, most of the Honduran fishing fleet, and the main facilities of Puerto Cortes, the most important port; and drowned two-fifths of the country's cattle. The total damage, estimated at about $900-million, was devastating. The national income was expected to fall by 30 per cent in 1975.

President Oswaldo López Arellano was under fire from both the left and the right during the year. Conservatives objected to his reformist proposals for a national development plan and to such nationalization moves as the take-over of the country's timber industry that involved 119 companies—83 of them foreign-owned.

Nicaragua. No one was surprised by the outcome of the presidential election held on September 1. The opposition Conservative candidate, Edmundo Paguaga-Irias, declared himself defeated before the results were even announced. Former President Anastasio Somoza Debayle, the Liberal candidate, was the winner. He had resigned in 1971 to comply with a constitutional provision prohibiting a president from succeeding himself, turning the government over to a triumvirate he controlled. After his

inauguration on December 1, he dismissed the triumvirate. All stirrings of opposition and especially press criticism continued to be ruthlessly suppressed by the regime.

Caribbean Islands

Dominican Republic. Strikes, demonstrations, and terrorism accompanied the re-election of President Joaquín Balaguer on May 16. There was also widespread voter abstention when the opposition parties, including a coalition group known as the Santiago Agreement, indicated that the Balaguer government no longer had a popular base. Three of the four opposition candidates withdrew from the race during the violent election campaign.

Robert Moss

Facts in Brief on Latin American Political Units

Country	Population	Government	Monetary Unit*	Foreign Trade (million U.S. $) Exports	Imports
Argentina	25,013,000	President María Estela (Isabel) Martínez de Perón	peso (9.8=$1)	1,941	1,905
Bahamas	216,000	Governor General Sir Milo B. Butler; Prime Minister Lynden O. Pindling	dollar (1=$1)	265	508
Barbados	240,000	Governor General Sir Arleigh Winston Scott; Prime Minister Errol W. Barrow	dollar (2.06=$1)	54	169
Belize	142,000	Governor General Richard Neil Posnett; Premier George Price	dollar (1.72=$1)	17	30
Bolivia	5,606,000	President Hugo Banzer Suarez	peso (20=$1)	209	186
Brazil	107,702,000	President Ernesto Geisel	cruzeiro (7.14=$1)	6,198	6,855
Chile	9,506,000	President (of military junta) General Augusto Pinochet Ugarte	escudo (990=$1)	1,231	1,480
Colombia	24,719,000	President Alfonso Lopez Michelsen	peso (27=$1)	743	857
Costa Rica	2,022,000	President Daniel Oduber Quirós	colón (8.5=$1)	339	476
Cuba	9,286,000	President Osvaldo Dorticos Torrado; Premier Fidel Castro	peso (1=$1.25)	1,031	1,662
Dominican Republic	4,699,000	President Joaquín Balaguer	peso (1=$1)	442	486
Ecuador	7,197,000	President Guillermo Rodriguez Lara	sucre (25=$1)	558	532
El Salvador	4,193,000	President Arturo Armando Molina Barraza	colón (2.5=$1)	352	377
Grenada	104,000	Governor Leo V. DeGale; Prime Minister Eric M. Gairy	East Caribbean dollar (1.92=$1)	8	17
Guatemala	6,173,000	President Kjell Eugenio Laugerud García	quetzal (1=$1)	436	431
Guyana	803,000	President Raymond Arthur Chung; Prime Minister L. F. S. Burnham	dollar (2.2=$1)	136	164
Haiti	5,380,000	President Jean-Claude Duvalier	gourde (5=$1)	43	64
Honduras	2,948,000	President Oswaldo López Arellano	lempira (2=$1)	237	262
Jamaica	2,002,000	Governor General Florizel Glasspole; Prime Minister Michael Norman Manley	dollar (1=$1.10)	392	672
Mexico	58,363,000	President Luis Echeverría Alvarez	peso (12.49=$1)	2,631	4,146
Nicaragua	2,374,000	President Anastasio Somoza Debayle	córdoba (7.1=$1)	270	327
Panama	1,661,000	Supreme Revolutionary Leader Omar Torrijos Herrera; President Demetrio B. Lakas	balboa (1=$1)	133	489
Paraguay	2,852,000	President Alfredo Stroessner	guaraní (126=$1)	127	122
Peru	15,847,000	President Juan Velasco Alvarado; Prime Minister Edgardo Mercado Jarrín	sol (42.5=$1)	1,039	810
Puerto Rico	2,929,400	Governor Rafael Hernández Colón	dollar (U.S.)	2,436	3,324
Trinidad and Tobago	1,084,000	Governor General Sir Ellis Clarke; Prime Minister Eric Eustace Williams	dollar (2.1=$1)	658	776
Uruguay	3,068,000	President Juan María Bordaberry Arocena	peso (1,448=$1)	322	285
Venezuela	12,127,000	President Carlos Andrés Pérez	bolívar (4.2=$1)	3,714	2,436

*Exchange rates as of Dec. 2, 1974

LAUGERUD GARCÍA, KJELL EUGENIO

LAUGERUD GARCÍA, KJELL EUGENIO

LAUGERUD GARCÍA, KJELL EUGENIO (1930-
), was elected president of Guatemala in a
hotly contested election on March 3, 1974. He was
inaugurated on July 2. Laugerud's chief opponent,
General Efrain Rios Montt, claimed victory and
charged there were massive vote frauds by the government, which had supported Laugerud's candidacy. The official announcement proclaiming Laugerud the winner triggered widespread protests.
The official returns gave the conservative General
Laugerud 41 per cent of the vote against Rios
Montt's 31 per cent. Some diplomatic observers
believe that the returns bore little relation to the
actual electoral results.

Laugerud was born in Guatemala City on July
24, 1930. His father was a Norwegian immigrant and
his mother a native-born Guatemalan. He graduated from the Politechnica, Guatemala's military
academy, in 1949 and served in a variety of military
assignments, including platoon commander and
chief of plans and operations for the General Staff.
After training in the United States, he became
superintendent of the Politechnica in 1965. He was
military attaché in Washington, D.C., before being
appointed army chief of staff in July, 1970. Laugerud was defense minister from July, 1972, until he
ran for the presidency.   Edward G. Nash

LAW. See CIVIL RIGHTS; COURTS AND LAWS;
CRIME; SUPREME COURT OF THE UNITED STATES.

LEBANON. A rising crime rate, the failure to curb
rising prices, and clashes between armed members
of opposing political parties caused Prime Minister Takieddin Solh to resign on Sept. 25, 1974.
Solh quit after a battle in a mountain village between right wing Phalangists and Progressive
Socialist Party members on September 22 in which
three were killed and several injured. Solh was
criticized for failing to cope with this and other
cases of public violence, as well as increased crime.

President Suleiman Franjieh then asked Saeb
Salaam, a former prime minister, to form a government. But Salaam could not muster enough support
among Lebanon's numerous parties to form a coalition Cabinet. On October 24, Franjieh named
Rashid Solh interim prime minister. The new government was approved on October 31.

Lebanon's Difficulties were compounded by
student unrest and raids by Palestinian guerrillas
on Israel from bases in southern Lebanon, which
provoked Israeli retaliation against Lebanese villages. In addition, Lebanese religious groups re-
sisted needed administrative reforms. A civil service
reform plan was launched in February to make appointments on the basis of ability rather than ethnic,
religious, or family background. It would have increased the number of government posts allotted to
Shiite Moslems and members of other minority
sects. However, the National Liberal Party, repre-

senting the dominant Maronite Christian majority,
withdrew its Cabinet ministers in protest, and the
reforms were tabled.

Student strikes occurred intermittently. The
American University of Beirut was shut down in
March for 10 weeks as students protested a 10 per
cent tuition increase. Lebanese police were called in
several times to evict strikers from occupied buildings. In the end, the tuition increase was canceled.

The destruction of Lebanese villages by Israeli
retaliation bombing raids brought help from other
Middle East countries. Following June raids by
Israel, Kuwait and Saudi Arabia gave $5 million
and Iraq pledged $2,800 per victim for compensa-
tion and resettlement.

The Lebanese Economy continued its progress
despite the unstable political climate. The 1974
budget was $630 million, up 13.8 per cent.

Lebanon received $64.8 million from the United
Arab Emirates in May to finance the Litani River
hydroelectric project. In August, the World Bank
loaned $3.9 million to enlarge the Amchit textile
factory to produce 3,000 short tons (2,700 metric
tons) of cotton yarn annually.

The government announced in June that 178
new enterprises valued at $45.5 million and creating
6,000 new jobs had been established during the first
half of the year.   William Spencer

See also MIDDLE EAST (Facts in Brief Table).

LÉGER, JULES (1913-   ), was installed as Canada's governor general at a ceremony in Ottawa on
Jan. 14, 1974. He is the 21st governor general since
Confederation and the 64th since Samuel de Cham-
plain founded Quebec, Canada's first permanent
settlement, in 1608. He succeeded Roland Michener, who retired after almost seven years in the
post. Léger is a scholarly French-Canadian diplomat, deeply interested in the arts. He is the fourth
Canadian to serve as the queen's representative.

Léger spent the first months of his term visiting
most of the Canadian provinces. While receiving an
honorary doctorate at the University of Sherbrooke
in Quebec on June 8, in company with his brother,
Paul-Émile Cardinal Léger, he suffered a stroke.
After being hospitalized for two weeks in Sherbrooke, the governor general returned to Rideau
Hall, his Ottawa residence, where he gradually
regained his strength. He resumed his duties on
December 6. While he was recovering, they were
handled by Bora Laskin, who had been installed as
chief justice of Canada only a week before Léger
took office. Laskin was named administrator of the
government of Canada.

During 1974, the Légers or Laskin entertained
the following visitors: Princess Anne of Great
Britain and her husband, Mark Phillips; King
Hussein and Queen Alia of Jordan; and Prime
Minister Kakuei Tanaka of Japan.   David M. L. Farr

LEMMON, JACK (1925-   ), received the Academy of Motion Picture Arts and Sciences Award as best actor of 1973 for his performance as a morally corrupted garment manufacturer in *Save The Tiger*. It was Lemmon's second Oscar. He was judged best supporting actor in 1955 for his amusing portrayal of Ensign Pulver in *Mister Roberts*.

John Uhler Lemmon III was born in Boston on Feb. 8, 1925, and by the time he was 15 he was acting in summer stock. He attended Phillips Academy in Andover, Mass., and graduated from Harvard University in 1947.

He began working in radio, and appeared in several television series in the early 1950s. Lemmon played in *Room Service* on the Broadway stage in 1953. He returned in 1960 in *Face of a Hero*.

But it is in films that Lemmon has achieved his greatest success. He is best known for light comic roles and has appeared in many in the past 20 years. Such motion pictures as *Phffft, My Sister Eileen, The Apartment, Mister Roberts, Some Like It Hot*, and *The Odd Couple* are triumphs of his comic style. He has also played a number of serious roles, as in *Days of Wine and Roses* and *Save The Tiger*.

Lemmon is married to actress Felicia Farr; they have one daughter. He has a son by a previous marriage.   Edward G. Nash

LESOTHO. See Africa.

LIBERIA. See Africa.

A series of four band concerts conducted at the New York City Public Library raised funds for the library's research facilities

LIBRARY. Revenue sharing, state and local funds, endowments, and fund-raising campaign receipts contributed to a wide range of new building projects in the United States in 1974, despite warnings that federal funding for library construction would end. A contract was awarded for the construction of a 3.25-million-volume central research library at the University of Texas in Austin. The building will seat 2,800 students. Ground was also broken for a new $14-million library at Ball State University in Muncie, Ind. The South Dakota State Library appropriated $2 million for a building that will house the State Historical Society as well as the State Library. Residents of Lawton, Okla., dedicated a new $1.3-million public library building.

A $1,265,000 grant for a new library was given to Lawrence University in Appleton, Wis., by the Seeley G. Mudd Fund. The building will house 500,000 volumes.

Information Network. The National Commission on Libraries and Information Service proposed a unified program of library and information service in the United States in 1974. The program advocates federal funding for the national elements of the program and funding by the states for their shares. The commission wants a vastly increased use of computer and telecommunications technologies in the national network. The goal of the program is to give everyone in the country, regardless of social or economic condition, equal access to national information resources.

National Library Week. "Get It All Together . . . at Your Library" and "Grow with Books" were the themes for National Library Week, from April 21 through April 27. The former highlighted the use of audio-visual materials by libraries, while the latter focused on the role of libraries and reading in intellectual growth throughout an individual's lifetime.

Library Conferences. More than 11,000 librarians gathered in New York City from July 7 to 13 for the 93rd annual conference of the American Library Association. "The Nature of the Profession" was the conference theme. Many of the individual meetings discussed the problems of providing improved library service to cultural and ethnic minorities.

A 1969 tax law revision to prevent tax deductions for donated personal papers has sharply reduced donations of manuscripts and other important documents, library officials say. The Library of Congress has not received a single significant collection since the law was passed.

After serving 20 years as the director of the world's largest library, the librarian of Congress, L. Quincy Mumford, announced his retirement in 1974.   Robert J. Shaw

See also AMERICAN LIBRARY ASSOCIATION; CANADIAN LIBRARY ASSOCIATION.

LIBYA. Revolutionary Command Council President Muammar Muhammad al-Qadhaafi tried to merge Libya with neighboring Tunisia in 1974. In January, Qadhaafi and Tunisian President Habib Bourguiba signed a merger agreement. However, Tunisia's National Assembly shelved the merger proposal soon after it was announced, and Bourguiba withdrew his support in March.

In April, the Revolutionary Command Council announced a reshuffle of the responsibilities of Qadhaafi and Prime Minister Abd al Salam Jallud. Jallud took charge of all administrative, executive, and protocol affairs. Qadhaafi was responsible for ideological and popular leadership.

Serious Disagreements developed between Libya and other Arab nations. In April, Egypt accused Libya of complicity in a plot to overthrow Egyptian President Anwar al-Sadat. The plot was linked with an Egyptian youth organization allegedly financed by Libya. In August, Sadat accused Qadhaafi of plotting to blow up the Egyptian president's Mediterranean retreat. The Sudanese president also charged Qadhaafi with supporting subversive elements in Sudan.

Another reason for Libya's increasing isolation in the Arab world was the improvement in Libya's relations with Russia, while other Arab-Russian relations continued to be tense. A delegation led by Prime Minister Jallud visited Moscow in May. As a result of the visit, Libya ordered an estimated $1.5-billion worth of Soviet arms. At a parade in September, marking the fifth anniversary of the coup that brought Qadhaafi to power, the armed forces displayed 200 Russian-made tanks and a number of ground-to-air missiles.

Libya's popularity in Africa also declined, even though Libya sponsored the fourth Pan-African Youth Congress in March and sent financial aid to various African nations. The new military government of Niger on May 22 canceled a defense treaty with Libya, and Gabon's President Omar Bongo criticized the Libyan government for not honoring treaties or financial commitments.

Oil Revenues continued to flow into Libya at record levels. A new oil field discovered on March 17 promised to bring even greater wealth.

In February, the government nationalized all Libyan interests of Texaco, Standard Oil of California, and the Atlantic Richfield Company. In October, Libya shut down all of Exxon Corporation's oil production in Libya, of which the government owns 51 per cent. However, the loss of 110,000 barrels of oil a day had hardly any effect on Libya's financial position. As of March, Libyan bank assets totaled $3.67 billion.   William Spencer

See also AFRICA (Facts in Brief Table).

LIECHTENSTEIN. See EUROPE.

LIONS INTERNATIONAL held its 57th International Convention in San Francisco in July, 1974. More than 35,000 Lions and their families attended the convention, and many delegates participated in seminars and workshops designed to help them carry out their service programs more effectively. Seminar topics included work for the blind and deaf, youth, community analysis, and international relations. Johnny Balbo of Oak Brook, Ill., was elected president for 1974-1975.

A total membership of 1,065,000 was reported at the convention. These members are part of 2,700 Lions clubs located in 146 nations.

Delegates to the convention agreed to amend their constitution and bylaws to raise annual dues by 75 cents, increase the subscription price of *Lion* magazine by 25 cents per issue, select convention sites seven years in advance, and fill vacancies in district governor positions whether they result from failure to elect, refusal to serve, or death.

Two membership drives were launched. Under the 1974-1975 Membership Development and Retention Program, those clubs that retain current membership levels through April, 1975, will receive an award. The Founders' (Melvin Jones) Membership Growth Program is designed to recruit new members from among a community's civic-minded citizens. A kit was distributed to help with the two programs.   Joseph P. Anderson

Libyan President Muammar al-Qadhaafi speaks at the February meeting in Lahore, Pakistan, of leaders of 38 Islamic nations.

LITERATURE. Hard-cover book publishers throughout the world – from London and Paris to New York City and Tokyo – were caught in an inflationary spiral in 1974. It forced them to pay more for paper, printing, labor, and all the essentials that go into the publishing of books – best sellers or otherwise. Consequently, as the cost of producing books mounted inexorably and sent book retail prices soaring, many bookmen feared that the spiral would almost inevitably result in a drastic reduction in the number of books published, especially first novels. One prestigious casualty of the cost rise in the United States was the 20-year-old National Book Award Committee, which is funded principally by publishers' contributions. Late in the year, the committee announced that it would disband because of reduced funds, maintaining only a skeleton operation so that the 1975 book awards could be made.

It was a year when so few American books of substance could be found that the trade was given to touting as gripping – even significant – such books as Richard Adams' *Watership Down*, a juvenile English fantasy about a family of rabbits. Other examples included Mary Daniels' *Morris*, billed by *Publishers' Weekly* as "the intimate life story of the feline superstar of TV cat food ads"; Kenneth Tynan's and Stephen F. Zito's *Sinema: American Pornographic Films and the People Who Make Them;* and two gruesome

narratives – Vincent Bugliosi's and Curt Gentry's *Helter Skelter: The True Story of the Manson Murders* and Tracy Kidder's *The Road to Yuba City*, the story of mass murderer Juan Corona.

The Novels. Of the hundreds of American novels published during the year, the two most talked about came from Joseph Heller and James A. Michener. The most attention went to Heller's *Something Happened*, a portrait of a business executive pondering the meaning of his life amidst the uncertainties of middle age. Michener's *Centennial*, on the other hand, met the usual chilly reception accorded his plodding narratives by the critics, but popular support made it a best seller.

Most of the remaining fiction was dominated by writers well known to the reading public. One of the more amusing novels was Vladimir Nabokov's *Look at the Harlequins!*, a scintillating *tour de force* in which the Russian-born novelist employed an alter ego to parody his own career as professor and master of fiction. A similarly light-fingered touch was the hallmark of Gore Vidal's *Myron*, which brought back his fictional creation Myra Breckinridge.

A younger novelist who has been making strides with weird fiction, Richard Brautigan, came up with a Western story unlike any Western ever written in *The Hawkline Monster*. It dealt with a monster living in the fantastic ice caves beneath a turn-of-

THE PHILADELPHIA INQUIRER
AUTH

"May I have your autograph, please . . . ."

the-century Oregon house. Peter DeVries' *The Glory of the Hummingbird* dealt with the rise and fall of one Jim Tickler, a lively participant in many wild adventures.

In a more serious vein, Louis Auchincloss was back with another novel, *The Partners*, which was about the members of a law firm. Robert Stone, the author of one well-regarded novel, *A Hall of Mirrors*, came back with *Dog Soldiers*, a tightly written adventure story about a cache of heroin.

From the black contingent came two novels of considerable appeal. James Baldwin, writing in *If Beale Street Could Talk* from the viewpoint of his heroine, told a love story of a young woman whose sweetheart is in prison. Ishmael Reed continued the adventures of his "hoodoo" detective, Papa Lamas, in *The Last Days of Louisiana Red*.

The most impressive first novel of 1974 was *Winter in the Blood* by James Welch, an American Indian poet living in Montana. It was a short, vivid, bleak tale of reservation Indian life with a surprise ending.

Among the books from abroad was *The Abbess of Crewe*, a substantial fantasy from English novelist Muriel Spark. A more orthodox novel with political overtones was C.P. Snow's *In Their Wisdom*, a tale of some wealthy Englishmen engaged in a spirited contest over a will.

High among the other importations of the year were Louis-Ferdinand Céline's abrasive *Rigadoon* and the late Yukio Mishima's *The Decay of the Angel*. *Rigadoon* was the final installment of Céline's trilogy about Europe at the end of World War II. *The Decay of the Angel* completed the Yukio tetralogy.

Short Stories. The year was especially good for the short story, with impressive collections from several distinguished pens. Two of the best by Americans were *The King's Indian* by John Gardner and *The Goddess and Other Women* by the prolific Joyce Carol Oates. Tennessee Williams and Brendan Gill offered notable new works—Williams with a collection of six tales entitled *Eight Mortal Ladies Possessed* and Gill with *Ways of Loving*, a group of 18 stories and two novellas. Maeve Brennan also published a fine collection in *Christmas Eve: Stories*.

Grace Paley was back again with another collection of exceptional short stories, *Enormous Changes at the Last Minute*. Despite Donald Barthelme's claim that *Guilty Pleasures* was nonfiction, the book was classified as a collection of antic short stories written by a craftsman who knows exactly what he is doing.

From England came three fine story collections—Alan Sillitoe's *Men, Women and Children*, which dealt with the working-class people of Nottingham; V.S. Pritchett's *The Camberwell Beauty*, which again exhibited that veteran critic's undiminished gifts as a storyteller; and *The Ebony Tower* by John Fowles. One other noteworthy import in the short-story field was Samuel Beckett's *First Love and Other Shorts*, which also included his new dramatic work, *Not I*.

Biography and Autobiography. As is usually the case, statesmen and literary personalities were prominent among the subjects of the year's outstanding books of serious biography. Dumas Malone published the fifth and penultimate volume of his definitive life of Thomas Jefferson in *Jefferson the President: Second Term, 1805-1809*. Two other early American statesmen, George Washington and Benjamin Franklin, were the subjects of absorbing new studies. The first of these was *Washington: The Indispensable Man* by James Thomas Flexner. The second was *The Most Dangerous Man in America: Scenes from the Life of Benjamin Franklin* by Catherine Drinker Bowen. One of the most popular and readable books of the year was *Plain Speaking: An Oral Biography of Harry Truman*, edited by Merle Miller from taped interviews with the former President.

In the literary area, the most impressive contribution was Richard B. Sewall's two-volume work, *The Life of Emily Dickinson*, a fascinating portrait of the New England recluse who was the most distinctive American poet of the 1800s. Wallace Stegner provided a sympathetic account of the life and times of the irascible critic, essayist, and historian Bernard DeVoto in *The Uneasy Chair*.

Other titles of literary interest included Gordon N. Ray's *H. G. Wells and Rebecca West*, an account of their tempestuous 10-year love affair; another segment in *The Diary of Anaïs Nin*, covering the years 1947-1955; James R. Mellow's *Charmed Circle: Gertrude Stein & Company;* the French novelist Colette's *The Evening Star: Recollections*, written when she was in her 70s; and Margaret Drabble's *Arnold Bennett*, a fine portrait of a neglected English novelist of a generation ago. There were also Sybille Bedford's highly readable *Aldous Huxley*, a sympathetic portrait; Graham Greene's *Lord Rochester's Monkey*, a biography of the Restoration rake John Wilmot; and Joseph Blotner's 2,115-page *Faulkner*.

There were several biographical works of value in other fields, among them Cass Canfield's *The Incredible Pierpont Morgan: Financier and Art Collector;* Laura Wood Roper's excellent *F.L.O.*, the life of Frederick Law Olmsted, the landscape architect; Robert Lacey's *Sir Walter Ralegh*, a superb portrait of the great English navigator and pioneer in America; and Anne Morrow Lindbergh's *Locked Rooms and Open Doors*, the third volume of her autobiography, covering the period from 1933 to 1935.

History. Two major historical works were concluded in 1974. Admiral Samuel Eliot Morison published *The European Discovery of America: The Southern Voyages*, the second volume of his magnificent work on the New World that had begun with *The Northern Voyages*. Shelby Foote's *The Civil War, A Narrative: Red River to Appomattox* was the third and final volume of a history of the War Between the States.

Pre-Civil War history of the institution of slavery was the subject of two major contributions. The

Banished: Russia's Conscience

A literary *cause célèbre* filled with political overtones and human drama burst upon the world in 1974. At its center stood Alexander Isaevich Solzhenitsyn, winner of the 1970 Nobel Prize for Literature and Russia's most famous living novelist. The immediate cause of the furor was his book *The Gulag Archipelago*.

Solzhenitsyn had revealed the existence of his book—a huge, nonfiction exposé of Russia's secret slave-labor organization—late in 1973. For years, Solzhenitsyn had refused to publish the book in the West, primarily to protect his sources. But in August, 1973, the Russian secret police had arrested Elisaveta Voroyenskaya, a friend of his who possessed a copy of the manuscript. After five days of brutal interrogation, she had turned it over to the police. Solzhenitsyn, his hand forced, decided to spirit his own copy out of Russia.

The first two parts of *The Gulag Archipelago* were published in Paris in December, 1973, and its revelations immediately staggered the world. A nightmarish fresco of repression and terror in Russia's "archipelago" of concentration camps, the book described not only Solzhenitsyn's own experiences, but also those of more than 200 victims he had known.

To the Kremlin, the existence in Russia of such a powerful critic was intolerable. But to imprison Solzhenitsyn or consign him to a mental institution (the fate of many Soviet dissidents during and after the Stalin regime) would invite the wrath of an already aroused world opinion. A new technique was needed.

Early in January, 1974, the state-controlled Soviet press launched a campaign of calumny against "the traitor Solzhenitsyn." Then, on the night of February 12, came the dreaded knock at the door, and seven secret policemen dragged the Nobel medalist from his apartment. Within 24 hours, Solzhenitsyn had been banished—deported to Frankfurt, West Germany.

The West welcomed him as a literary hero, a free spirit who had struggled heroically for the right to write the truth. Copies of his book were printed by the thousands.

Scores of Western nations offered him citizenship. But Solzhenitsyn chose the neutrality of Switzerland and settled in Zurich, where he was joined by his family in March. They brought with them the rest of *The Gulag Archipelago*.

Subsequently, Solzhenitsyn released the text of an astonishing and puzzling "Letter to the Soviet Government," which he had sent to the Kremlin in the fall of 1973. In it, he had offered a prescription for Russia's future. Russia could save itself, Solzhenitsyn wrote, only by turning inward and becoming isolationist. Communism, he said in effect, is unworkable.

He was equally critical of Western democracy. "In perhaps its last decline," he said, "democracy is devoid of ethical foundation, little more than a framework in which political parties and social classes battle for their self-interest." Solzhenitsyn advocated a return to the land, which he envisioned as a rural paradise in which the internal combustion engine would be outlawed—going back to the horse and buggy if necessary.

This remarkable letter shows Solzhenitsyn as a mystic, conservative man with a deeply isolationist and even religious view of his country and its history. Of this there was no doubt. Less certain was Solzhenitsyn's stature as an artist. Some Western literary critics complained that those who call him Russia's greatest living writer were confusing his political symbolism with his art. Much of his work, they pointed out, is ponderous, and excessively preachy.

But Solzhenitsyn's own view of his mission could not be faulted. As he said in his Nobel lecture, he wanted to give back to Mother Russia the missing chapters of her history. "Woe to that nation whose literature is disturbed by the intervention of power. Because that is not just a violation against freedom of print," he wrote. "It is the closing down of the heart of the nation, a slashing to pieces of the memory."

His words rang true; throughout the year, *The Gulag Archipelago*, nourished by the underground press, circulated in Russia.   Henry Kisor

Solzhenitsyn

Jill Krementz

Joseph Heller, author of *Catch 22*, autographs unbound flyleaves of his second novel, *Something Happened*. It took him 12 years to write it.

American Marxist historian Eugene D. Genovese pursued in depth the part played by Christianity in the slave culture in *Roll, Jordan, Roll: The World the Slaves Made*. Robert W. Fogel's and Stanley L. Engerman's two-volume study, *Time on the Cross*, analyzed with statistical research the economics of the slave system. Another type of slavery was the subject of the year's most widely publicized work of history, Alexander I. Solzhenitsyn's *The Gulag Archipelago, 1918-1956*. See Close-Up.

Letters and Journals. The letters of two important literary figures made news in 1974. Henry James's industrious biographer, Leon Edel, launched a projected four-volume series of the great novelist's correspondence in *The Letters of Henry James, 1843-1875*. In an ongoing series, Leslie A. Marchand published the third volume of *Byron's Letters and Journals*, this one subtitled *Alas! The Love of Women* and embracing the flamboyant poet's love affairs. The University of California Press launched a new series of Samuel Clemens' writings with the first two volumes of *Mark Twain's Notebooks and Journals*. Another notebook of importance made its first appearance in Howard E. Gruber's and Paul H. Barrett's *Darwin on Man*, which included the young scientist's notes from 1837 to 1839, years in which he was toying with the ideas that led years later to the classic theory of evolution enunciated in *The Origin of Species*.

Current Affairs. The scandal that brought the downfall of President Richard M. Nixon resulted in more than a dozen books. The most widely read and discussed titles were Carl Bernstein's and Bob Woodward's *All the President's Men* by the two newsmen who exposed the cover-up by Nixon and his aides; novelist Mary McCarthy's report in *The Mask of State* on the 1973 Watergate hearings before the Senate's investigative committee; and Dan Rather's and Gary Gates's *The Palace Guard*, about the White House conspirators and their roles.

Despite the convulsive nature of the crisis in Washington, D.C., there were other national concerns exhibited in books of more than passing value. One such was the situation at the close of the American war experience in Vietnam, vividly recorded in novelist James Jones's *Viet Journal*, the diary of a five-week stay in that troubled land. The continuing struggle of blacks for a more just place in American society was the inspiration for one of the year's more remarkable books: Theodore Rosengarten's *All God's Dangers; The Life of Nate Shaw*, recollections (under a pseudonym) of an elderly black man relating via a tape recorder his experiences with the Sharecropper's Union in Alabama in the early part of the century. Another tape-recorded book of conversations was Studs Terkel's *Working*.

Miscellaneous. The combination of text and picture in a pre-Christmas publishing stereotype known to the trade as the "gift" or "coffee table" book produces works of significance on a hit-or-miss basis, and 1974 was a better than average year for hits. Putnam's came up with *The Exploration of North America, 1630-1776*, a book of pictures and journals kept by early explorers and frontiersmen. Richard M. Ketchum's *The World of George Washington* is a series of historical essays on the Revolutionary War general.

The arts of the photographer were, of course, predominant among the fall gift books. Among the best were *Ansel Adams: Images 1922-1974*, an exhibit of his photographic achievement edited by the novelist Wallace Stegner; Gordon Hendricks' *Albert Bierstadt: Painter of the American West;* Harold G. Davidson's *Edward Borein: Cowboy Artist;* collector David R. Phillips' photographic album *The Taming of the West;* and the National Geographic Society's *The World of the American Indian*. Some other picture-and-text volumes of special interest included Scottie Fitzgerald Smith's *The Romantic Egoists*, a scrapbook-album about her parents – F. Scott and Zelda Fitzgerald – and Otto L. Bettmann's *The Good Old Days – They Were Terrible!*, an amusingly cynical look at the past by the master of the famed Bettmann Archive. Van Allen Bradley

See also AWARDS AND PRIZES (Literature Awards); LITERATURE FOR CHILDREN; NOBEL PRIZES; POETRY. **LITERATURE, CANADIAN.** See CANADIAN LIBRARY ASSOCIATION; CANADIAN LITERATURE.

LITERATURE FOR CHILDREN.

There were indications that children's literature was becoming an "in thing" in 1974. Numerous colleges were adding or expanding courses in the field, and the number of students interested in the subject was increasing. The rising interest in this branch of literature prompted the United States and several European countries to hold various seminars, workshops, and conferences on the subject, and all drew large and enthusiastic audiences.

An unusually large number of good "how to" books appeared in 1974; young readers interested in crafts could find dozens of books offering suggestions and instructions for making items that ranged from the simplest things to those quite complicated and very professional in appearance.

Here are some of the outstanding books published in 1974:

Picture Books

How Tom Beat Captain Najork and His Hired Sportsmen, by Russell Hoban, illustrated by Quentin Blake (Atheneum). A delightful bit of nonsense that indicates the virtues of fooling around, as Tom (who lives with an aunt named Miss Fidget Workham-Strong, who "wore an iron hat and took no nonsense from anyone") demonstrates. The pictures are as imaginative as the text. Ages 5 to 9.

Alfred Goes House Hunting, by Bill Binzen (Doubleday). Appealing color photographs show a tiny teddy bear looking for a new home; an ingenious solution brings a happy ending. Ages 3 to 8.

Little Mops and the Butterfly, by Elzbieta (Doubleday). A picture book without words that shows Little Mops as he finds a tiny, tiny shoe and then discovers what goes with it. Ages 3 to 7.

The History of Mother Twaddle and the Marvelous Achievements of Her Son Jack, by Paul Galdone (Seabury). Using a verse rendition of Jack and the Beanstalk adapted from an 1807 version, Galdone has added vigorous full-color illustrations to make this a lively and delightful addition to the nursery rhyme library. Ages 4 to 8.

Walk Home Tired, Billy Jenkins, by Ianthe Thomas, pictures by Thomas DiGrazia (Harper). The wonderfully expressive illustrations of two black children walking big-city streets provide exactly the right touch of poetic realism to this simple appeal of a big sister to a little brother's imagination. Ages 3 to 7.

The Halloween Party, by Lonzo Anderson, illustrated by Adrienne Adams (Scribners). Unusual illustrations show a properly spooky atmosphere when a boy stumbles into a Halloween party of witches, gremlins, and ogres. Ages 4 to 8.

Why the Sky is Far Away, by Mary-Joan Gerson, illustrated by Hope Meryman (Harcourt). This tale from the Bini people of Nigeria explains why the sky, which once supplied all the food people needed, moved out of reach. Woodcut illustrations in blue and dark brown add interest and distinction. Ages 4 to 8.

All for Fall, by Ethel Kessler, illustrated by Leonard Kessler (Parents' Magazine Press). Double-page, full-color pictures show various fall-season activities, and both text and illustrations identify and emphasize the colors one might associate with each. Ages 4 to 8.

Just for Fun

Let's Marry Said the Cherry, and Other Nonsense Poems, written and illustrated by N. M. Bodecker (McElderry/Atheneum). Delightful verses matched with delightful pictures that enhance and extend the humor of the poems make an altogether charming little book that should prove a happy introduction to nonsense for the young reader (or listener). Ages 9 and up.

What? A Riddle Book, by Jane Sarnoff and Reynold Ruffins (Scribners). Page after page of funny puns and riddles interspersed with full-color pictures should make this book a great favorite with anyone from ages 9 and up.

A Comick Book of Sports, by Arnold Roth (Scribners). Covering some 56 sports ranging from football to curling, this author-illustrator has created many ridiculous and some wildly funny cartoons dealing with a variety of sports terms, plays, and situations. Ages 9 and up.

Things to Do

Boomerangs: How To Make and Throw Them, by Bernard S. Mason (Dover). This includes a history of boomerangs and detailed instructions for making and learning how to throw them. Ages 10 and up.

Printmaking, by Anne and Harlow Rockwell (Doubleday). One in the Crafts for Children Series, this tells about–and illustrates–such things as hand, styrofoam, or glue prints in simple terms, and then goes on to the more complicated linoleum and woodcut prints. Ages 6 and up.

Candies, Cookies, Cakes, by the authors of *Kids Cooking*, Aileen Paul and Arthur Hawkins (Doubleday). This clear, step-by-step approach to cooking (in such a popular category) should start many a young cook on the way. Ages 8 and up.

Christmas Crafts, Things To Make the 24 Days Before Christmas, by Carolyn Meyer, pictures by Anita Lobel (Harper). This book gives full directions in text and illustrations for making such things as an Advent banner, a gingerbread cottage, and a bread-dough manger. Ages 10 and up.

Professional Magic For Amateurs, by Walter B. Gibson (Dover). Covering such categories as Simplified Card Tricks, Mental Magic, and Famous Stage Illusions, this book gives complete explanations and instructions on how famous tricks and illusions are accomplished. Ages 10 and up.

Latin American Crafts and Their Cultural Backgrounds, by Jeremy Comins (Lothrop). Five traditional crafts of Latin America are discussed; illustra-

Margot Zemach won the Caldecott Medal for illustrating *Duffy and the Devil*, a tale of a Cornish servant girl and a particularly impish devil.

tions and detailed instructions are included so the young reader can try them himself. Ages 10 and up.

Zooming In: Photographic Discoveries Under The Microscope, by Barbara J. Wolberg and Lewis R. Wolberg (Harcourt). A whole new world is opened up in these photomicrographs of microscopic plants and animals. The book also includes a detailed explanation of how to take such photographs. Ages 10 and up.

Kicking the Football Soccer Style, by Pete Gogolak, edited by Ray Siegener (Atheneum). Newly available in paperback, this readable account tells the young kicker that "regardless of your physical size, you can become a valued member of your team," and gives much information and many suggestions. Ages 10 and up.

Making Costumes for Parties, Plays, and Holidays, by Alice Gilbreath, pictures by Timothy Evans (Morrow). Instructions for making 21 costumes, arranged in order of difficulty from ghost to dragon, are given in a clear, understandable manner that should encourage the child to try making them himself. Ages 8 to 12.

Science, People, and Things

Hearts, Cupids, and Red Roses; the Story of the Valentine Symbols, by Edna Barth, drawings by Ursula Arndt (Seabury). Starting with various theories about the origin of St. Valentine's Day, this book then goes on to discuss the history of valentines and the meaning

and origin of the symbols associated with the holiday. Attractive line drawings touched with red or pink illustrate the text. Ages 9 and up.

Black Cop: A Biography of Tilmon O'Bryant, Assistant Chief of Police, Washington, D.C., by Ina R. Friedman (Westminster). This is an exciting account of one man's successful climb to prominence despite prejudice and poverty. O'Bryant's commitment to fair treatment under law for all men and the sense of genuine dedication to unselfish service to others are inspiring. Ages 11 to 14.

Looking at Architecture, by Roberta Paine (Lothrop). Covering major milestones of interest from ancient Egypt to present-day New York City, this book discusses architecture throughout history and around the world. An interesting and informative text is supplemented by photographs. Ages 8 to 12.

Famous Custom and Show Cars, by George Barris and Jack Scagnetti (Dutton). Pictures, descriptions, and some technical information about more than 75 unique cars are given here. Such custom specials as a hardhat mobile complete with 4-foot (1.2-meter) hardhat and an oversized lunch box should fascinate the car enthusiast. Ages 12 and up.

Beat It, Burn It, and Drown It, by Suzanne Hilton (Westminster). A fascinating account of the ways various products are tested for the market, this is written in a clear style with a touch of humor. It is illustrated with photographs. Ages 10 and up.

A Snail's Pace, by Lilo Hess (Scribners). Excellent photographs and an informative text interestingly portray the land snail and his relatives. Information on keeping snails as pets is included. Ages 6 to 10.

The Doubleday Nature Encyclopedia, by Angela Sheehan (Doubleday). Although not really an encyclopedia, this book still has much general information about plants and animals and more than 1,000 excellent full-color illustrations. It is indexed, and can be read aloud to children under 10.

How to Make Your Science Project Scientific, by Thomas Moorman (Atheneum). A book for the serious reader, this explains clearly and understandably some of the basic approaches to scientific reasoning. Ages 11 and up.

Indian Scout Craft and Lore, by Charles A. Eastman ("Ohiyesa") (Dover). These talks by an Indian on such things as How to Make Friends with Wild Animals, The Language of Footprints, and How to Make and Handle Indian Canoes are fascinating to read and give a real insight into Indian attitudes and skills. Ages 10 and up.

Fiction

The Jargoon Pard, by Andre Norton (McElderry/Atheneum). This exciting and compelling fantasy tells the story of Kethan and the strange fate that mysteriously unfolds before him after he is given the gift of a leopard-skin belt with a jeweled clasp. Ages 11 and up.

Jason and the Money Tree, by Sonia Levitin, illustrated by Pat Grant Porter (Harcourt). Jason finds that his grandfather's legacy–a $10 bill that starts to grow and bear other $10 bills when it is planted–brings unexpected and sometimes humorous difficulties. Ages 8 to 12.

The Mushroom Center Disaster, by N. M. Bodecker, pictures by Erik Blegvad (McElderry/Atheneum). Delightful pen-and-ink drawings depicting the inhabitants and the insides of some of their snug little mushroom homes add much to this story of a tiny town and how it coped imaginatively with the disaster that befell it. Ages 6 to 9.

Tough Chauncey, by Doris Buchanan Smith (Morrow). A rather tough story about a 13-year-old boy who wants to stop being a troublemaker but doesn't know how. Finally, his love for a kitten he protects from his grandfather's cruelty gives him the courage to take the steps necessary to get away from his old life. Ages 10 to 14.

Cross-Country Runner, by Leon McClinton (Dutton). When the senior football star decides to give up football for cross-country running, he runs into trouble all around. A sports book dealing with one of the less popular sports, this gives the reader a feeling for the difficulties and rewards of the sport in what seems a very authentic way. Ages 9 to 14.

Gabriel, by Jean Slaughter Doty, illustrated by Ted Lewin (Macmillan). Beginning with a very satisfactory account of the rescue and raising of a lost newborn puppy, this moves on into the world of the dog-show ring when it is discovered that the puppy is the grandson of a champion keeshond. A dog book written from a slightly different point of view, it should be interesting to dog lovers and to those interested in showing dogs. Ages 8 to 12.

The Strange but Cosmic Awareness of Duffy Moon, by Jean Robinson; drawings by Lawrence DiFiori (Seabury). Because Duffy Moon was small, he felt he was a nobody until he sent for a course in Cosmic Awareness. The adventures that the new Duffy brings upon himself and his friend Peter are entertaining and amusing. Ages 8 to 12.

Toolmaker, by Jill Paton Walsh, illustrated by Jeroo Ray (Seabury). This is the story of how Ra, a prehistoric boy, gradually became a toolmaker. One gets the feeling of the primitive way of life and thought that must have been typical of that time. The simple, rough illustrations add to the atmosphere of the book. Ages 9 to 12.

The Girl in the Grove, by David Severn (Harper). A teen-age girl in England is attracted to a boy who, sullen and hard to understand, has made friends with the ghost of a girl whose hold over him seems hard to break. Ages 12 and up.

William and Mary, by Penelope Farmer (McElderry/Atheneum). Mary, alone between terms at the school her parents run, finds her summer taking a very unusual turn when William, a student who comes to stay until term starts, shows her his magic sea shell. Together, they share some exciting underwater adventures. Ages 10 to 14.

Awards in 1974 included:

American Library Association Children's Service Division Awards: The *Newbery Medal* for "the most distinguished contribution to American literature for children" was awarded to Paula Fox for *The Slave Dancer*, illustrated by Eros Keith (Bradbury). The *Caldecott Medal* for "the most distinguished American picture book for children" was presented to Margot Zemach for her illustrations for *Duffy and the Devil* (Farrar), by Harve Zemach. The *Mildred L. Batchelder Award* for "a book considered to be the most outstanding of those books originally published in a foreign country and subsequently translated and published in the United States" went to E. P. Dutton for Alki Zei's *Petros War*, translated by Edward Fenton.

British Book Awards: The *Carnegie Medal* for "the most outstanding book of the year" went to Penelope Lively for *The Ghost of Thomas Kempe* (Dutton). The *Kate Greenaway Medal* "for the most distinguished work in the illustration of a children's book" was given to Raymond Briggs for *Father Christmas* (Coward). Lynn de Grummond Delaune

LIVESTOCK. See AGRICULTURE; INTERNATIONAL LIVE STOCK EXPOSITION.

LONG BEACH, CALIF. See LOS ANGELES–LONG BEACH.

LOPEZ MICHELSEN, ALFONSO (1913-   ), was elected president of Colombia on April 21, 1974, and took office on August 7 (see COLOMBIA). He promised to work for constitutional reform, equal rights for women, regulation of monopolies, and reorganization of the Agrarian Reform Institute.

He also promised that the Conservatives would continue to share in the government with his own Liberal Party. To eliminate bloody party rivalry, Colombia has been governed for the last 16 years by a coalition of Liberals and Conservatives, with the two parties alternating in the presidency. The 1974 election was the first since 1958.

Lopez Michelsen was born in Bogotá, and attended primary school there. He then attended schools in Paris, London, and Brussels. After obtaining his law degree at the University of Chile, he taught administrative law at Bogotá National University. He also practiced law in Bogotá.

In 1958, he broke with the Liberal Party to help found a splinter group – the Liberal Revolutionary Movement. Four years later, he ran unsuccessfully for president. Later, he was elected to the Senate. In 1967, he returned to the Liberal Party and he served from 1967 to 1968 as governor of the department, or district, of César. He was minister of foreign affairs from 1968 to 1970.

Lopez Michelsen and his wife, Cecilia, have three married sons. *Kathryn Sederberg*

LOS ANGELES-LONG BEACH. A series of bombings and explosions rocked Los Angeles during 1974. On August 6, a bomb exploded in a busy ticket section at Los Angeles International Airport, killing two persons and injuring 26 others. Officials termed it the "deadliest civil airport bombing in U.S. history."

The bombing was attributed to the so-called "Alphabet Bomber." A man, who identified himself as Isaac Rasim, sent taped messages to the *Los Angeles Times* claiming he would write "Aliens of America," letter by letter, in similar bombings. The bomber then alerted the newspaper on August 16 to a bomb he set in a bus-terminal locker. Police disarmed the bomb before it exploded.

While the city waited in fear, the biggest explosion in Los Angeles history demolished a downtown industrial district, creating a 10-story-high ball of fire and devastating a square block of buildings. However, police said the explosion was not the work of the Alphabet Bomber, who was finally captured on August 20. The alleged bomber was a 31-year-old Yugoslav immigrant, Muharem Kurbegovic.

A May explosion caused by defective electric equipment destroyed several sound stages and storage buildings at the Metro-Goldwyn-Mayer motion-picture studio. Three persons were injured. Another bombing on October 6 caused extensive damage to a Sheraton Motor Inn.

Other Crimes. Six members of the Symbionese Liberation Army (SLA) were killed on May 17 in a shoot-out with Los Angeles police. The SLA kidnaped San Francisco newspaper heiress Patricia Hearst in February. See CRIME (Close-Up).

An arsenal of weapons, including machine guns and grenade launchers, was stolen from a National Guard Armory in suburban Compton on July 4. The thieves took enough weaponry to equip an army combat unit. The Federal Bureau of Investigation reported that crime in the Los Angeles area increased 6 per cent during the first half of 1974.

In December, police arrested two men for attempting to defraud Los Angeles of millions of dollars by rigging a city computer to issue checks to nonexistent corporations.

The Cost of Living rose 10.4 per cent in the Los Angeles area between June, 1973, and June, 1974. Wages of the average factory worker increased only 3.3 per cent during a one-year period ending in July, to an average of $9,250 a year. The U.S. Department of Labor estimated that $9,377 per year was the minimum necessary to maintain a family of four. Employment in the area rose only 0.7 per cent during the year ending in July, while department store sales increased 12 per cent, and construction activity fell 31.6 per cent. *James M. Banovetz*

LOUISIANA. See NEW ORLEANS; STATE GOV'T.

LUMBER. See FOREST AND FOREST PRODUCTS.

LUXEMBOURG. The smallest parliamentary democracy in the world changed to a Liberal-Socialist coalition in 1974 as a result of general elections on May 26. The elections ended 55 years of uninterrupted rule, alone or in coalition, by the conservative Christian Social Party. Headed by Pierre Werner, it lost 3 of its 21 seats. The Socialists won 17, a gain of 5, and the Liberals took 14, a gain of 3. Werner's Cabinet resigned May 27, though his party still held more of the 59 Chamber of Deputies' seats than any other single party. The elections were the first since the voting age was lowered to 18.

Gaston Thorn, Liberal foreign minister, became the new prime minister on June 18. His government, a coalition Cabinet of four Liberals and four Socialists, reduced the value-added tax on certain manufactured items on July 5. The tax was reduced to counter a 6.1 per cent rate of inflation.

The economic upswing, which began in 1972, became more pronounced in 1974, with chemicals output up 14.9 per cent and iron and steel production up 10.9 per cent. Extremely large steel price increases, a buoyant domestic consumer demand, and an influx of 3,000 foreign workers fueled the booming economy. But the Organization for Economic Cooperation and Development reported in July that foreign demand was unlikely to grow because of high oil prices. *Kenneth Brown*

See also EUROPE (Facts in Brief Table).

MAGAZINE. The U.S. magazine industry continued to grow in 1974, despite increased postal costs, paper shortages, and general inflation. Advertising revenues rose during the year, except in April. According to a Publishers Information Bureau estimate, magazine publishers received a record $1.35-billion in advertising revenue in 1974.

Americans continued to buy consumer magazines at the annual rate of about 5.5 billion copies, despite higher subscription rates and newsstand prices. For example, *Newsweek*'s newsstand price rose from 50 cents to 75 cents a copy, while the price of *Playboy* went from $1 to $1.25. Increased costs for paper, printing ink, and distribution were generally blamed for the higher prices.

On June 30, President Richard M. Nixon signed into law postal legislation that extends the period over which magazines and newspapers must adjust to substantially higher postal rates mandated by the Postal Reorganization Act of 1970. Regular-rate publications have three additional years to adjust to the increases; nonprofit publications have six.

New Magazines were launched in substantial numbers, while a much smaller number ceased publication during 1974. *People*, a weekly published by Time Incorporated, debuted March 4 at the newsstands. Richard J. Durrell is publisher and Richard B. Stolley is managing editor. *Women-*

Sports became the first major sports magazine written for, and sold primarily to, women. Launched by tennis pro Billie Jean King in June, it reflects her belief that the time is right for a successful monthly magazine for physically active women.

Country Journal, published by William S. Blair and edited by Richard M. Ketchum, is a new magazine about life in rural New England. Written with the active homeowner in mind, it appears 11 times a year. Nicholas H. Charney and John J. Veronis began a new magazine, *Book Digest*, that will be published bimonthly. It contains abridgments of leading new nonfiction and fiction books.

Among the magazines that ceased publication are *Architectural Forum*, an 82-year-old trade journal previously published by Billboard Publications, Incorporated; *Saturday Night*, an 87-year-old Canadian magazine that had offered a perspective on a wide range of national issues and cultural events; *Homelife*, a digest-size television-listing magazine, started in 1973, that contained home-and-family articles, published by In-Store Publications; *The Lamp/A Christian Unity Magazine*, which was a 71-year-old religious publication of the Graymoor Ecumenical Institute; and *Chicagoan*, a 1-year-old monthly that was absorbed by *Chicago Guide*.

Modern Photography and *High Fidelity* were bought by the American Broadcasting Company from Billboard Publications Incorporated. *True* magazine, which was published by Fawcett Publications, Incorporated, for 37 years, was purchased by Petersen Publishing Company. *The New Republic*, a weekly journal of politics and the arts, was purchased by Martin Peretz, a lecturer at Harvard University.

Publishing Milestones. Billboard Publications celebrated its 80th anniversary. *American Legion*, first published in 1919, celebrated its 55th year, as did *True Story*. *Saturday Review/World*, edited by Norman Cousins, celebrated the 50th anniversary of the parent magazine *Saturday Review*. *Glamour* magazine celebrated its 35th year, and *Sports Illustrated* marked its 20th year on August 16.

Awards. The Magazine Publishers Association selected a family as the recipient of the 1974 Henry Johnson Fisher Award as Publisher of the Year. Named as winners were Laurence W. Lane, Jr., Melvin B. Lane, and Mrs. Laurence W. Lane, Sr., all of Lane Publishing Co., Menlo Park, Calif., publishers of *Sunset*. Winners of the National Magazine Awards, administered by the Columbia University Graduate School of Journalism, were *The New Yorker* for fiction, *Scientific American* for public service, *The New Yorker* for reporting excellence, *Newsweek* for visual excellence, *Sports Illustrated* for service to the individual, and *Texas Monthly* for specialized journalism.
                                        Gloria Ricks Dixon

MAINE. See STATE GOVERNMENT.
MALAGASY REPUBLIC. See AFRICA.
MALAWI. See AFRICA.

People, a new weekly magazine that focuses on personalities, made its debut in February. It sells at newsstands as well as by subscriptions.

MALAYSIA. Prime Minister Abdul Razak's carefully worked out strategy produced a landslide victory for his National Front Coalition in August, 1974, elections. It captured 135 of the 154 seats in the Malaysian Parliament, while the opposition Democratic Action Party secured only nine seats.

Razak and his supporters hailed the victory as proof that the people had voted for multiracial harmony and national unity. But opposition critics said it showed that the people voted for racial disharmony and polarization. They also charged that the prime minister was trying to create an authoritarian one-party government.

The roots of this disagreement lay in Malaysia's mix of racial groupings, which includes Malays, Chinese, and Indians. When the state was born in 1957, it was based on a triple alliance that gave the Malays the greatest political power while the Chinese retained their economic supremacy. The Indians got little or nothing. The compact lasted until May, 1969, when it was drowned in the blood of racial riots. Ever since, the Malays have pursued a policy aimed at Malaynizing the civil service system and pushing to increase their slice of the income pie.

Wily Policy. Razak, in his strategy for the elections, expanded the old triple alliance by wooing minority parties into his catchall coalition. Opposition parties survived but were forbidden by new sedition laws to discuss "sensitive" issues, such as his pro-Malay policies. Thus, the law was invoked to ban an election poster in which the Democratic Action Party promised to protect Chinese culture.

But there were other elements in Razak's triumph. To a nation that still remembered the bloodshed of 1969, he stood for order and stability. He was also aided by a buoyant, if spotty, economy. He also scored a coup in May when he journeyed to Peking, China, to open diplomatic relations. In the election, his Chinese partners used a photo of this onetime fervent anti-Communist shaking hands with China's Mao Tse-tung.

Bad Omens. The government spoke of "the economic storms ahead," but Malaysia seemed well equipped to weather them. The gross national product grew by 6.3 per cent in 1974. Many of Malaysia's raw materials still commanded high prices abroad. Most important, its oil wells yielded 90,000 barrels each day.

But unemployment was up and inflation continued, while world prices on rubber and timber dropped. Not the least sign of distress was student unrest. In December, word of starvation deaths among Malaysian rubber workers set off demonstrations by villagers and students.   Foster Stockwell

See also ASIA (Facts in Brief Table).

MALDIVES. See ASIA.
MALI. See AFRICA.
MALTA. See EUROPE.

MANESCU, MANEA (1916-   ), was named prime minister of Romania on March 26, 1974. He succeeded Ion Gheorghe Maurer, who quit because of ill health. Manescu's appointment was part of a major government reshuffle by the Romanian Communist Party's Central Committee. However, the real power remains with President Nicolae Ceausescu, head of the party. See ROMANIA.

Manescu was born in Brăila, Romania, and joined the Communist Party in 1936. He had been serving as a deputy premier and minister of the Committee for State Planning before being named prime minister.

Manescu has held a variety of senior economic posts. He was general director of the Central Statistical Office from 1951 to 1955 and minister for finance from 1955 to 1957. In 1957, he was named chairman of the Labor and Wages State Committee and first vice-president of the State Planning Committee. From 1961 to 1969, he served as the chairman of the Economic and Financial Standing Committee of the Grand National Assembly.

Manescu became a member of the Romanian Communist Party Central Committee in 1960. He became a member of the executive committee in 1968 and a member of the policy-making Standing Presidium in 1971.   Kathryn Sederberg

MANITOBA. See CANADA.

MANUFACTURING. Industry in the United States reeled in 1974 under the pressure of declining sales, excessive inventories, reduced backlogs, high materials costs, declining productivity, mounting layoffs, and tight money. The crude oil shortage that ushered in the year was over, temporarily, but it left a residue of higher prices for oil-based products. The severe materials and parts shortages in the metalworking, paper, lumber, and other basic industries also eased, but prices soared.

The White House finally admitted in November that the nation was in the grip of a recession. This came months after economic forecasters of every theoretical cast had indicated that the 1974 recession could become the longest and most severe post-World War II slump.

New Factory Orders for durable goods fell in November by $1.37 billion, to $43.72 billion, following an October drop of $864 million and a September decline of $3.16 billion, the sharpest drop in 6½ years. November declines were across-the-board, affecting metals, machinery, and transportation equipment. For October, the capital goods sector showed a marked weakness, with nondefense orders off by $482 million from September. At $11.5 billion, they were down $1.5-billion from the summer's high-water mark. October shipments of hard-goods manufacturers were up $1.7 billion, to $46.8 billion. But shipments were ahead of new orders, and for the first time in three years, order backlogs declined.

Manufacturers' inventories rose rapidly, always a bad sign in the face of falling sales. A survey of manufacturers' inventory expectations in August showed that 29.7 per cent of those replying feared that their inventories were too high, up from 22.8 per cent in the first quarter. Inventories in the final quarter were expected to reach an adjusted $151.3 billion, up from $141.8 billion in the third quarter when inventories expanded 6.2 per cent.

Industrial Production in the third quarter fell at an annual rate of 0.3 per cent, to 125 per cent of the 1967 average. This compared to a rise of 1.9 per cent, to 125.3 per cent of the 1967 average during the second quarter, and a 6.6 per cent decline in the first quarter. Auto production, which had declined steadily since December, 1973, was expected to end the year with a drop of about 24 per cent (see AUTOMOBILE). Production of other durable goods, mainly appliances and furniture, and nondurable goods also declined.

Worker productivity also fell, and unit labor costs spurted. The U.S. Department of Labor reported that productivity, or output per man-hour, in the private economy declined at an annual rate of 2.4 per cent in the third quarter, marking the sixth consecutive quarter of decline or no growth. Unit labor costs in manufacturing rose at an annual rate of 12.2 per cent in the third quarter. After adjustments for inflation, paychecks in manufacturing were worth 0.9 per cent less, at an annual rate, than in the second quarter. Manufacturing work hours declined at a 1.3 per cent annual rate despite a longer workweek.

Capital Investment. Obsolete plants and equipment continued to plague U.S. industry. A McGraw-Hill survey of capital obsolescence revealed that 20 per cent of U.S. industrial plants are 20 years old or older. Equipment that old now accounts for 21 per cent of the total, up from 17 per cent in 1970. Manufacturers claimed that 14 per cent of their plants and equipment were outmoded, a rise of 12 per cent since 1972. All this occurred in the face of $382 billion invested by industry in new plants and equipment since 1970. Inflation was the culprit, eroding the impact of this huge outlay. It would cost an estimated $14.3 billion to modernize the steel industry completely, $13.6 billion for machinery makers, and $1.3 billion for aerospace.

Capital spending reflected the joint problems of recession and inflation. Higher prices ate up most of the record outlay of $112.1 billion. There was little, if any, real growth. Many manufacturers reported significant cutbacks in capital spending in 1974, with 54 per cent indicating they had canceled or delayed capital improvements since the spring of 1974.

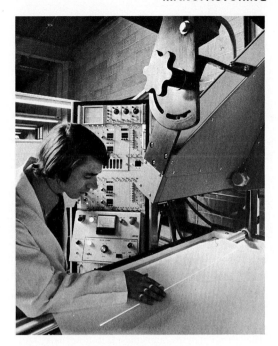

Laser scanning systems outperform humans in detecting tiny flaws in continuous sheets of material speeding down production lines.

Unemployment became a national issue as the year drew to a close. About 7.1 per cent of the work force was unemployed in December, up from 6.5 per cent in November. In the auto industry alone, nearly 180,000 employees were out of work in December. Layoff notices were also posted in steel, textiles, appliances, metalworking, rubber, glass, electrical and electronics, chemicals, aluminum, photographic, and just about every other category of manufacturing. The situation was made even worse by a coal strike, which lasted from November 12 until December 5.

Energy Conservation emerged as a prime goal for industry because of the high costs and shortage of fuel. Companies throughout the nation started energy conservation programs that resulted in substantial savings of fuel and dollars. A typical example was Wang Laboratories, an electronics firm in Tewksbury, Mass., which established a program that included lowered thermostats, fewer lights, and selected equipment shut-downs. Use of electric energy was slashed to 61 per cent of the amount used in January, 1974. Natural gas consumption was cut to 49 per cent of the former level. And peak electrical demand was reduced to less than 80 per cent of its former level.

The Hartford Insurance Company began constructing a nine-story building that will use recycled heat from a computer to heat the building.

MANUFACTURING

The heat-recovery equipment will cost more to install than conventional equipment, but first-year operations are expected to save 81,000 gallons (307,000 liters) of fuel oil in 1976.

New Technology and new products were geared primarily to finding alternative materials to those in short supply, conserving existing materials, and reducing waste. A prime concern was to find a way to extract a liquid fuel from coal. Universal Oil Products of Des Plaines, Ill., appeared to have solved the problem that stymied all efforts – separating an ashlike substance from the pulverized coal. By successfully separating the ash, Universal changed the asphaltlike fluid to a coal-derived liquid that can be refined into other fuels.

Union Carbide Corporation developed a new membrane that could prove important in conserving process waste. Applied to filtration systems, the membrane could help to recover such materials as protein from cheese whey, sizing from textile mills, and oil emulsions from metal-finishing processes.

Du Pont Company developed a new fiber it claimed is stronger than steel. The new fiber, called Kevlar, is said to have unusually high resistance to stretch and high temperatures and, pound for pound, is five times stronger than steel. It is being used as an alternative to steel in radial tires. The company also claims the new fiber is

strong enough to anchor oil rigs at sea and could be used for such applications as fan belts for automobile engines, hose for unloading oil from tankers, rope to replace steel cables, and also as a reinforcement for plastics in products ranging from planes to golf clubs.

Machine Tools, a bedrock of the economy through most of the year, faltered in October and plunged in November when new orders dropped 53 per cent from October and 63 per cent from November, 1973. The decline began during the second quarter. New orders for the first 11 months were slightly ahead of the previous year, $2.42 billion to $2.38 billion. More significant than the drop in orders, November shipments exceeded orders by $99.5 million, reducing the industry backlog to $2.69 billion. The National Machine Tool Builders Association reported that order cancellations for November rose to $64.1-million, 61 per cent above October's unusually high $39.7 million and more than triple the more typical $18.6 million for November, 1973.

Electrical Products shipped during the year increased in value by 10 per cent over 1973, to $64.4-billion. But real physical growth was only 2 per cent, because of the general softening of the economy, particularly the slump in residential housing. Shipments of industrial electrical equipment were up 15 per cent to $9.7 billion, and power equipment shipments were up 16 per cent to $7.1-billion. Electrical consumer products were hardest hit, rising only 3 per cent, to $13.7 billion.

The Rubber Industry suffered from the drop in auto sales. Tire shipments were expected to fall to 182 million, from 1973's total of 205 million. Most of the decline came in tires for new cars, which were expected to drop 13 million units below the 57-million shipped in 1973. To make up for the slack, the more diversified manufacturers began producing more industrial rubber products such as conveyor belts, tubing, and hoses. But that was not enough to keep projected capital spending plans on course. Goodyear Tire and Rubber Company, the industry leader, trimmed its planned capital expenditures by 10 per cent (about $30-million) by slowing its conversion to radial tire manufacturing equipment.

Farm Equipment, on the other hand, could not keep pace with demand. Hampered by shortages in steel, castings and forgings, and hydraulic components, manufacturers were expected to fall 5 to 25 per cent below their material requirements for the year. This would cause a production drop of about 10 per cent from 1973.   George J. Berkwitt

MARINE CORPS, U.S. See NATIONAL DEFENSE.
MARYLAND. See BALTIMORE; STATE GOV'T.
MASSACHUSETTS. See BOSTON; STATE GOV'T.
MAURITANIA. See AFRICA.
MAURITIUS. See AFRICA.

Machine on an automated production line turns out an endless chain of plastic pencils, and it also cuts and paints each of them.

MEDICINE. New pain-killing drugs and artificial blood were developed by medical researchers in 1974. In the United States, the number of doctors increased, and the nation's leading medical organization changed its attitude toward the regulation of medical standards.

The Pan-American Congress on Rheumatic Diseases, meeting in Toronto, Canada, heard reports in July on several new drugs designed to relieve both the pain and inflammation of rheumatoid arthritis. The drugs – ibuprofen, tolmetin, fenoprofen, and naproxen – are now licensed for use in several countries, and at least one is likely to be licensed in the United States sometime in 1975, according to researchers.

All four drugs apparently produce fewer side effects, such as bleeding and gastrointestinal upsets, than aspirin. Aspirin and the new drugs are equally effective in reducing joint pain and swelling, according to the research reports.

Despite the reduction of side effects, some doctors said they still prefer to use aspirin because of its recognized efficacy and safety for short-term treatment of rheumatoid arthritis. Aspirin is also much cheaper than the new drugs.

Artificial Blood. A silicone-oil/oxygen solution was produced by Leland Clarke, Jr., of the University of Cincinnati for use as a form of artificial blood in organ transplantation. Clarke disclosed his development in June, 1974. He said it can keep kidneys alive for several days.

Clarke said that the artificial blood's early use may be in organ preservation, but that eventually it will undoubtedly be used in kidney transplant surgery. The liquid can be stored easily and has no blood type. Unlike natural blood, which sometimes carries hepatitis and other diseases, it can be sterilized.

The oxygenated fluorocarbon can also be breathed by submerged animals or humans, leading to further possible medical uses. Cats and mice fared well in breathing the solution. This function has not yet been extensively tested on humans.

If clinical tests in other laboratories bear out Clarke's results, he predicts that the artificial blood could be used to treat sickle cell anemia and eradicate deep-sea bends.

On November 25, heart transplant pioneer Christiaan N. Barnard implanted a second heart in a 58-year-old man in Cape Town, South Africa. It was the first time such an operation was ever performed without first removing the patient's diseased heart, and following the operation, both hearts were said to be beating together.

New Doctors. More than 16,000 new doctors received licenses to practice medicine in the United

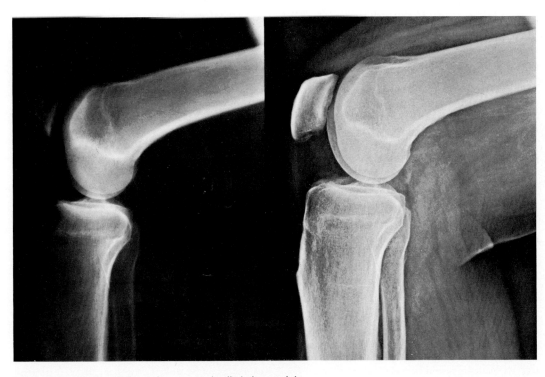

A new X-ray process, XRG, produces more detailed picture, *right*, and exposes the body to less radiation than standard X ray, *left*.

States during 1973, according to the American Medical Association (AMA). This was the largest one-year gain in medical manpower in U.S. history. AMA officials predicted that 1974 figures would also show gains.

The number of new doctors in 1973 – 16,689 – was 15 per cent greater than the 14,476 doctors newly licensed during 1972. The net increase, after deaths and the departure of foreign doctors for their homelands, was 12,306 doctors, raising the total number of physicians in the United States to 326,933.

The AMA also reported that American women are entering the medical profession in dramatically increasing numbers. In just three years, the number of women enrolled in U.S. medical schools has more than doubled, rising from 3,894, or 9.6 per cent of total enrollment, to 7,824, or 15.4 per cent.

Peer Review. The AMA House of Delegates voted overwhelmingly on June 26 to cooperate with the federal government in operating a system by which doctors will review each other's work. The surprise move rejected a six-month campaign by some AMA members seeking repeal of the federal law on peer review. Instead, the delegates agreed to work to amend portions of the law, which was established to monitor care given to 50 million U.S. citizens under the Medicare and Medicaid programs. The law provides for the creation of professional standards review organizations that would be set up and run by local physicians under government guidelines and with federal money.

Common Cold. University of Illinois researchers reported the development of an experimental drug that significantly increases the body's defenses against the common cold. The drug, propanediamine, stimulates the body to increase its natural production of interferon, a protein produced by the interaction of animal cells with viruses. Interferon can keep viruses from multiplying.

Since interferon is effective against all viruses, it has been considered promising in the control of respiratory infections, such as the cold. Because colds are caused by various types of viruses, a vaccine against all of them is thought to be impracticable.

The research team at the university's medical school in Chicago, which was headed by Charoen Panusarn, administered the drug in the form of nose drops to 15 subjects. The patients were then exposed to cold-causing viruses. The team reported that the exposed subjects developed no cold symptoms. Twenty-four other patients not given the drug, but exposed to the same viruses, developed severe colds.

Panusarn noted that the increase in interferon production also reduced the production of viruses in the subjects receiving the drug, meaning that the injected patients would be less likely to spread their contagion. *Richard P. Davies*

See also HEALTH AND DISEASE.

MENTAL HEALTH. A group of physicians and scientists established the Society to Conquer Mental Illness in 1974, through which they hope to focus attention on the need for more refined scientific research into the causes and treatment of serious mental illness. The group was formed in New York City on May 3.

In describing plans for the new society, Seymour Kety, professor of psychiatry at Harvard Medical School, and Paul Wender, professor of psychiatry at the University of Utah, cited recent studies indicating that schizophrenia, a severe mental disorder, was largely determined by human genetics and was a result of a distortion in the chemistry of the brain.

"Evidence for the notion that children become schizophrenic because of the way their parents raised them just does not exist," Kety said. He added that he was distressed by people working for civil rights of the mentally ill who suggested that there was no such thing as mental illness, only a sick society with a distorted view of people.

Psychiatric Definition. In April, the American Psychiatric Association (APA) agreed to uphold its board of trustees' decision to drop homosexuality from its list of mental disorders. The vote changed an association position held for nearly 100 years, that homosexuality is a condition that merits psychiatric treatment. The association's new position, in effect, is that homosexuality needs to be treated only if the individual wants to change.

Effects of Weather. Delegates to the annual APA meeting in Detroit in May heard reports on research into the causes of various mental disturbances. John H. Valentine of the University of Pennsylvania School of Medicine in Philadelphia reported on his studies on the effects of weather conditions and air pollution on mental health.

Valentine and his co-workers found that more people sought help for states of depression during periods of high barometric pressure, while more cases of intoxication occurred during times of low pressure. Days with more sunshine showed a decrease in the number of homicides. The researchers found that pollution from rising levels of sulfur dioxide, oxidants, suspended dust particles, and smoke and haze was associated with increased violence, violent deaths, drug use, psychiatric emergencies among children, and nervous disturbances. Irritation of the lungs from air pollution may cause anxiety leading to drug use and a violent acting out of feelings, Valentine suggested. Higher carbon monoxide levels in the atmosphere brought more reports of people suffering various types of organic brain damage.

Coffee Nerves. Some anxiety neuroses start at the kitchen table, according to another report at the Detroit meeting. John G. Greden, associate director of psychiatric research at Walter Reed Army Medical Center in Washington, D.C., reported on the effects of caffeine toxicity. He described patients he had treated who were anxious and did not sleep well. "Before we discuss their nerves," he said, "it might be well to ask them how much coffee, tea, and cola they drink."

Coffee and tea are often advertised as promoting clear thinking, quick energy, and decreased drowsiness or fatigue. However, Greden said they can also bring on central nervous system reactions that include general nervousness, breathlessness, irritability, lethargy, and insomnia. "Furthermore," he said, "caffeine can cause cardiovascular reactions such as palpitations, *extrasystoles* [skipping heartbeats], *tachycardia* [fast pulse], *arrhythmia* [irregular heartbeat], and flushing [feeling warm]; and gastrointestinal symptoms like nausea...[and] vomiting."

More than 250 milligrams (0.0088 ounce) of caffeine a day is considered a large amount, but, Greden pointed out, many people exceed this. For instance, a person who consumes three cups of coffee, two "headache tablets," and a cola drink before lunch has ingested about 500 milligrams (0.0176 ounce) of caffeine. "From the clinical perspective," he said, "many individuals complaining of anxiety will continue to receive substantial benefit from psychopharmacological agents. But for an undetermined number of others, subtracting one drug—caffeine—may be of greater benefit than adding another."   Richard P. Davies

MEXICO. President Luis Echeverría Alvarez seemed increasingly lonely in 1974 as he served out his fourth year in office. The 12 gubernatorial elections held during the year in no way reflected the deepening political divisions that in themselves drove the president to complain that right wing elements were conspiring to bring about a coup d'état. Only one state, Chihuahua, had an opposition candidate and even there, the ruling Institutional Revolutionary Party (PRI) was returned with its habitual sweeping majority. President Echeverría, under attack from both left and right, could find solace only in the major oil discoveries reported in the "La Reforma" area of southeast Mexico in October.

Foreign Relations. One of the high points of the year was President Echeverría's meeting with President Gerald R. Ford on October 21 in Nogales, Ariz., and Magdalena, Mexico. The talks were cordial, but they did not lead to a formal agreement on a long-term contract for Mexico to sell oil to the United States. The Mexicans failed, too, to get more generous terms for migrant laborers who enter the United States either legally or illegally, though President Echeverría acknowledged publicly that it fell to the government to improve conditions so that peasants would stay at home.

In July, Echeverría visited Peru, Argentina, and Brazil to promote trade cooperation and his proposal for an exclusively Latin American organization to supplant the Organization of American States (OAS). The usefulness of the OAS, he claimed, had "practically disappeared."

Revolutionary Violence became a more direct threat to civil order than in any other Latin American state, excluding Argentina. Two spectacular guerrilla actions stood out. One was the kidnaping on June 27 of Senator Ruben Figueroa, the PRI's candidate for governor in Guerrero. The second involved 83-year-old José Guadalupe Zuno Hernández, the president's father-in-law and a former governor of Jalisco state. The conditions of Zuno's release on September 7 exposed the government to general derision. For a while, it was feared that Zuno, who was recovering from surgery, might die in captivity. But his captors, who were members of the People's Revolutionary Armed Forces, released him without issuing a ransom demand. Instead, they settled for a tape-recorded statement from Zuno, praising them and denouncing the Echeverría administration. Zuno later denied that the statement had been extracted from him under duress. The Mexican Army, however, salvaged some of the government's honor the following day, when it freed Figueroa after a bloody shoot-out in the hills with guerrilla followers of Lucio Cabañas, an almost legendary guerrilla chieftain. For years, Cabañas had led his followers in sorties that included kidnaping, bank robberies, and assassinations of government officials. Cabañas and a large part of his group were killed on December 2 by troops in the Sierra Madre del Sur region.

The Oil Discoveries. Oil was first discovered in the southeastern states of Chiapas and Tabasco in 1972, but Mexico did not become an oil exporter until June, 1974. By the end of the year, the 40 major wells in the La Reforma area were producing more than 230,000 barrels a day, and it was confidently predicted that production would reach 1-million barrels a day by the end of 1975. President Echeverría announced in a major speech on September 1 that Mexico's export policy would be "profoundly nationalist and anti-imperialist." Despite the rhetoric, it was clear that the two main markets would be the United States and Brazil, which signed a long-term contract to buy Mexican oil in November. It appeared likely, according to experts, that the flow of oil would help turn the country's chronic trade deficit into a surplus within two years.

Labor Relations. Fears that union demands for a 35 per cent overall wage increase would result in a general strike were allayed in September. Echeverría persuaded Fidel Velázquez, the extremely influential veteran leader of the Mexican Workers' Confederation, to settle for 22 per cent.   Robert Moss

See also LATIN AMERICA (Facts in Brief Table).

MICHIGAN. See DETROIT; STATE GOV'T.

MIDDLE EAST

Israel and the Arab states spent 1974 still locked in a state of "no war, no peace," despite efforts on the part of other powers to bring about a peaceful settlement of their 25-year-old conflict. As the first anniversary of the October, 1973, war passed, the region remained the focal point of international tension.

Two small wars that broke out during the year in Iraq and Cyprus, though localized, added to the tension. And Arab oil policies and price manipulations had a profound impact on the generally unsettled world economy. Although the Arabs applied some of their vast new oil wealth to development projects in less fortunate nations, the bulk of it went for arms or continued to pile up as reserves.

The year began with some optimism, though there was no move to reopen the peace talks once scheduled between Israeli and Arab representatives in Geneva, Switzerland, following the 1973 cease-fire. Largely due to U.S. Secretary of State Henry A. Kissinger's "shuttle diplomacy," Israel and Egypt agreed on January 17 to separate their forces along the Suez Canal, and Israel and Syria agreed on May 31 to separate their forces on the Golan Heights.

The Disengagement. The Israeli-Egyptian pact, signed on January 18 in a tent at Kilometer 101 on the Suez-Cairo Road, called for Israeli forces to withdraw in stages to new positions from 13 to 20 miles (21 to 32 kilometers) east of the Suez Canal but still west of the strategic Sinai mountain passes. A buffer zone manned by the United Nations (UN) Emergency Force was established between the Israeli and Egyptian forces along the canal's east bank. The operation was completed March 5, and there were no further incidents on the Sinai front.

The Israeli-Syrian disengagement was more difficult to accomplish. Syria insisted that Israel guarantee that it would completely evacuate the Golan Heights. Israel refused to give up land beyond the cease-fire line established in 1967. Meanwhile, the two sides fought intense artillery and air battles along the front. Israeli Prime Minister Golda Meir's troubles in forming a coalition government also probably encouraged Syria to continue its "talk while we fight" policy. However, Kissinger persevered, and the agreement was finally signed in Geneva. See EGYPT; ISRAEL; SYRIA.

Both sides agreed to withdraw from previous positions with a narrow buffer zone along the crest of the Golan Heights, manned by a UN force, separating them. The ruined town of Al Qunaytirah was returned to Syria, and 68 Israeli prisoners were exchanged for 392 Syrians. The disengagement was completed on June 25, and, despite gloomy predictions, the cease-fire held up.

Guerrilla Raids. With Israel's Syrian and Egyptian borders stabilized, activity shifted to the Lebanese border. Infiltration raids into Israel by Palestinian guerrillas from southern Lebanon killed 40 persons and injured scores more in April and May. The most serious were the attack on Qiryat Shemona kibbutz on April 11, where 18 persons died,

Israeli delegation's seats, left, are empty as Yasir Arafat of the Palestine Liberation Organization addresses the United Nations.

and the Maalot massacre on May 15, in which 26 Israeli citizens and also three Arab guerrillas were killed. Reprisal raids by Israeli forces into Lebanon and the bombing of Lebanese refugee camps killed more than 25 persons and provoked a UN Security Council resolution censuring Israel.

Palestinian Gains. Far more effective than their guerrilla tactics against Israel, however, was the new-found ability of the Palestinians to attract international recognition for their cause. Ironically, the start of their success came in the same year as the death, on July 4, of Haj Amin el-Husseini, the former Grand Mufti of Jerusalem, who had led the Palestinian fight against Great Britain during two decades of the British Mandate. The drumfire in-

sistence by the Palestine Liberation Organization (PLO) on its right to represent the Palestinians and to participate in Arab-Israeli settlement talks finally produced results. After years of dodging the issue, Arab leaders meeting in October for their eighth summit conference in Rabat, Morocco, voted over Jordanian opposition in favor of a separate Palestinian state on the West Bank. They also recognized the PLO as the sole representative of the Palestinian people. Arab leaders agreed to establish a $2.35-billion fund for arms to build up the Arab military arsenal. On November 4, King Hussein I of Jordan declared himself ready to recognize a PLO government-in-exile, though he continued to insist on his right to negotiate with Israel for the Palestinians.

Arab-Israeli Buffer Zones

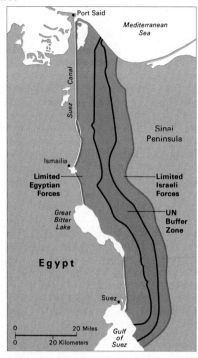

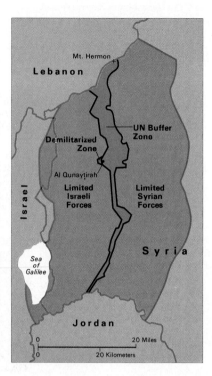

Then, on October 14, the UN General Assembly voted 105 to 4 to invite PLO observers to participate in the November debate on Palestine. Yasir Arafat, head of the PLO, addressed the UN General Assembly in New York City on November 13. Israel's right to rebuttal was restricted by a 75 to 23 vote on November 15, and on November 22, the UN approved resolutions declaring that the Palestinians have a right to national independence and granting the PLO permanent observer status in the General Assembly.

Israel, insisting on its refusal to deal with any terrorist organization dedicated to its destruction, found itself increasingly isolated and identified as the obstacle to peace in the Middle East.

Other Conflicts. The complexities and rapid shifts in Arab-Israeli relations diverted the world's concern from two lesser conflicts that might in other times have produced dangerous consequences. In March, Iraq announced a self-rule plan for its Kurdish population, in fulfillment of a 1970 pact ending a civil war. However, the plan was rejected as inadequate by Kurdish leader Mustafa Barzani, and the civil war resumed. The Iraqi Army, equipped with new Russian arms, sought a military solution to the Kurdish question. The conflict remained localized because Syria and Turkey closed their borders with Iraq. Only Iran provided limited aid to the Kurds. See IRAQ.

A more serious threat to peace in the Middle East developed when a revolt by the Cypriot National Guard, supported by the ruling military regime in Greece, overthrew Cypriot President Archbishop Makarios III on July 15. Negotiations involving Turkey, Greece, and Great Britain–the three guarantors of Cyprus' independence under the 1960 Zurich Accords–broke down, and Turkish forces invaded the island. Enjoying total air superiority, the invasion forces quickly occupied the northern third of Cyprus and then accepted a UN-sponsored cease-fire. The U.S. House of Representatives, angry at Turkey anyway over its resumption of opium-poppy cultivation, protested Turkey's use of U.S. arms for aggression by voting to ban all military aid to Turkey after December 10. In December, it extended the aid until Feb. 5, 1975. See CYPRUS; TURKEY.

Archbishop Makarios, who fled Cyprus during the revolt, returned in early December. While he offered to compromise with the Turkish Cypriots, the parties concerned were still far from agreement.

The Money Weapon. The difficulty of separating economic from political policy was effectively illustrated by developments in the Middle East's oil industry. The embargo on oil shipments to the United States imposed by the Arab oil-producing states as a consequence of U.S. support for Israel during the October, 1973, war was lifted on March

Facts in Brief on the Middle East Countries

Country	Population	Government	Monetary Unit*	Foreign Trade (million U.S. $) Exports	Imports
Bahrain	240,000	Amir Isa bin Salman Al Khalifa; Prime Minister Khalifa bin Salman Al Khalifa	dinar (1 = $2.53)	53	168
Cyprus	672,000	President Archbishop Makarios III; Vice-President Rauf Denktash	pound (1 = $2.70)	179	447
Egypt	37,519,000	President Anwar al-Sadat; Prime Minister Abdul Aziz Hegazi	pound (1 = $2.56)	1,119	905
Iran	33,383,000	Shah Mohammed Reza Pahlavi; Prime Minister Amir Abbas Hoveyda	rial (71.4 = $1)	6,943	3,442
Iraq	11,100,000	President Ahmad Hasan al-Bakr	dinar (1 = $3.38)	2,331	898
Israel	3,356,000	President Ephraim Katzir; Prime Minister Yitzhak Rabin	pound (6 = $1)	1,444	4,240
Jordan	2,739,000	King Hussein I; Prime Minister Zayd Rifai	dinar (1 = $3.11)	64	328
Kuwait	1,208,000	Emir Sabah al-Salim al-Sabah; Prime Minister Jabir al-Ahmad al-Sabah	dinar (1 = $3.40)	3,790	1,042
Lebanon	3,401,000	President Suleiman Franjieh; Prime Minister Rashid Solh	pound (2.3 = $1)	355	850
Oman	763,000	Sultan & Prime Minister Qabus bin Said	Saidi rial (1 = $2.89)	239	106
Qatar	94,000	Amir & Prime Minister Khalifa bin Hamad Al-Thani	riyal (3.9 = $1)	27	16
Saudi Arabia	8,861,000	King & Prime Minister Faisal	riyal (3.6 = $1)	6,474	1,345
Sudan	17,862,000	President Sayed Gaafar Mohamed Nimeiri	pound (1 = $2.87)	434	436
Syria	7,363,000	President Hafiz al-Asad; Prime Minister Mahmud al-Ayyubi	pound (3.7 = $1)	339	595
Turkey	39,896,000	President Fahri Koruturk; Prime Minister Sadi Irmak	lira (15 = $1)	1,318	2,091
United Arab Emirates	215,000	President Zayid bin Sultan al-Nuhayan; Prime Minister Maktum ibn Rashid al-Maktum al-Falasa	dirham (3.9 = $1)	74	130
Yemen (Aden)	1,650,000	Presidential Council Chairman Salim Ali Rubayya; Prime Minister Ali Nasir Muhammad Hasani	dinar (1 = $2.90)	105	158
Yemen (Sana)	6,564,000	Command Council Chairman Ibrahim Mohamed al-Hamdi; Prime Minister Muhsin bin Ahmad al-Ayni	rial (4.6 = $1)	4	35

*Exchange rates as of Dec. 2, 1974

18. The United States had received good marks from the Arab states for its efforts toward achieving a peaceful settlement. Algeria, Egypt, and Syria reopened relations with the United States.

But the spiraling effects of oil industry nationalization in country after country and of consequent price increases not only gave the oil producers unexpected political leverage, but also threatened economic disaster for industrial and developing nations. Saudi Arabia, Kuwait, Abu Dhabi, and Bahrain joined the list of countries acquiring 60 per cent majority interest in oil operations as a prelude to total control of oil production in their territory. Added revenues from higher taxes and royalties were only part of the story, however.

The shah of Iran and Saudi Arabia's Oil Minister Sheik Ahmad Zaki Yamani, leaders in the fight for higher returns for the oil-producing states, insisted that oil prices would stay up until oil-company profits came down. Prices that reached $11.65 per barrel for Arab and Iranian oil contributed heavily to inflation among the oil-consuming states. By September, Saudi Arabia had acquired an astonishing $11.5-billion surplus; Iran's reserves were $6.3 billion; Libya's, $3.7 billion; Algeria's, $2-billion; and Kuwait's, $1 billion. Arab financial experts proved wary of making long-term investments with these reserves. Much of the money was placed in short-term deposits in European and U.S. banks. The short-term nature of these "petrodollar" deposits caused an added strain on already hard-pressed central and international banks (see INTERNATIONAL TRADE AND FINANCE). There were some longer-term investments by Middle Eastern countries. Iran invested in an iron and steel company controlled by the Krupp interests of West Germany and Kuwait bought a substantial share of Daimler-Benz, the West German automaker.

Apart from greatly increased arms expenditures, the producing states seemed either unable or unwilling to channel much of their surplus into regional-development projects or aid to other, less-fortunate developing nations. Saudi Arabia established a $2.8-billion fund for loans to developing states in August, and, with Kuwait and Abu Dhabi, set up the Islamic Development Bank.

Work started on clearing the Suez Canal, which had been blocked since the 1967 Arab-Israeli war. The original estimates called for the canal to be reopened to ship traffic within six months, but the international team of divers and engineers was slowed by mines and salvage difficulties. By late November, some vessels were moving in the canal, but extensive dredging operations would delay its full use until early 1975. With Egypt facing a huge budget deficit, the canal's complete reopening could not come too soon.   William Spencer

See also UNITED NATIONS.

MIDLER, BETTE (1945-   ), won a Grammy Award in March, 1974, as the best new recording artist of 1973. Billed as "the divine Miss M," she released her first album on the Atlantic label in November, 1972.

She was born in Honolulu, where her father was a house painter for the U.S. Navy. After a year as a drama major at the University of Hawaii, she obtained a bit part in the movie *Hawaii*, and earned enough to pay her way to New York City. There she sold gloves in a department store while she took voice, dance, piano, and acting lessons.

Her first break came when she got a chorus part in Broadway's *Fiddler on the Roof*. In a three-year stint, she eventually worked her way up to the role of the daughter Tzeitel. After hours, she sang in small nightclubs, but without great success. In early 1971, she began singing at Manhattan's Continental Baths. There she developed the style that has become her trademark – an exuberant parody of camp, nostalgia, and vulgarity. She soon became a pop star, and her recording of "Boogie Woogie Bugle Boy of Company B" was a big success.

On stage, Midler garbs herself in bizarre outfits of satins and sequins, and struts across the stage at triple speed. But all that spontaneous energy is carefully planned and staged for maximum effect. She lives in an apartment in New York City's Greenwich Village.   Kathryn Sederberg

MINES AND MINING. The United Mine Workers (UMW) and coal industry representatives proposed a new three-year contract on Nov. 13, 1974, two days after 120,000 UMW members who mine about 70 per cent of the United States coal went on strike. The agreement was subsequently changed, then ratified on December 4 and 5. See COAL; LABOR.

Although the United States has vast coal reserves, it continued to count heavily on imports to supply other mined metals and minerals. More than 90 per cent of the manganese, platinum, cobalt, graphite, chromium, and bauxite (the ore from which aluminum is made) that U.S. industries use is imported. Also high on the list of imports are tin, nickel, antimony, bismuth, mercury, and zinc.

Government officials worry that such dependence on imports of vital industrial minerals could make the United States economically vulnerable to cartels. Mineral producers could band together and raise prices in much the same way that oil producers raised prices fourfold in 1973.

Copper Cartel. Indeed, four major copper-exporting countries – Chile, Peru, Zaire, and Zambia – imposed a fixed minimum price on copper during 1974. Meeting in Zambia in June and October, the four countries formed a cartel called the Intergovernmental Council of Copper Exporting Countries. In November, the group announced it would cut production by 10 per cent to boost sag-

ging prices. Although the United States is the world's largest copper producer, it still must import about 400,000 short tons (363,000 metric tons) annually.

Possibly of even greater concern to U.S. industry were Jamaica's plans to almost quadruple the taxes and royalties on bauxite that is mined by foreign aluminum companies. See WEST INDIES.

Ocean Mineral Discoveries intensified interest in mining the ocean floor. Kennecott Copper Corporation and British, Canadian, and Japanese mining companies announced joint plans in January for a $50-million, five-year research and development program on the recovery of manganese-rich nodules from the ocean floor. The nodules also contain copper and nickel. In July, French participants in the French-American Mid-Ocean Undersea Study (FAMOUS), which is exploring the Mid-Atlantic Ridge rift valley floor, announced the discovery of a manganese-spewing geyser at a depth of about 9,000 feet (2,740 meters). Earlier, U.S. Navy scientists participating in FAMOUS found manganese and other deposits elsewhere on the ocean floor. See OCEAN.

Challenge of the Yukon. The lure of metals drew prospectors in increasing numbers to Canada's Yukon Territory. With retail gold prices reaching $190 a troy ounce (31 grams) in November, gold prospecting was particularly attractive. However, gold mining will be insignificant in comparison with the territory's total mineral production according to *The Northern Miner*, the Canadian mining industry newspaper. Can Ogilvy, manager of the Yukon Chamber of Commerce, estimates that known metal deposits are worth $800 million at current prices. Meanwhile, actual output of Yukon metals rose from $10 million in 1968 to $145.5 million in 1973, according to government sources.

U.S. Government. In January, Thomas V. Falkie was named director of the U.S. Bureau of Mines. He was formerly head of the Department of Mineral Engineering at Pennsylvania State University, in State College. In July, specialists in the bureau announced the discovery of a more efficient method of recovering gold from ore.

The U.S. General Services Administration began accepting bids on its sale of government-surplus copper in February. The sale was the first under a law signed in January that authorized the sale of about $900 million in stockpiled copper, aluminum, zinc, silicon carbide, and molybdenum.

A federal judge ruled in July that Reserve Mining Company was violating the federal 1899 Refuse Act and two Wisconsin water-quality laws by dumping wastes into Lake Superior from its taconite processing plant at Silver Bay, Minn. An appeals court reversed the judge's April order closing the plant, pending a full review in December. See ENVIRONMENT.   Mary E. Jessup

MINNEAPOLIS-ST. PAUL. Lawrence Cohen was re-elected mayor of St. Paul on April 30, 1974. His Democratic Farmer Labor Party won all seats on the city council.

Art Mecca. There was a great deal of fine arts activity in the Twin Cities during the year. On October 21, the $7.2-million Orchestra Hall opened in downtown Minneapolis. The new concert hall was widely acclaimed for its excellent acoustics. Giant cubes in the ceiling and behind the stage diffuse the sound.

The Minneapolis Institute of Arts reopened on October 6. It had been closed for a two-year, $32-million renovation project that transformed the institute into the Minneapolis Society of Fine Arts Park. The new 17-acre (6.9-hectare) complex, designed by Japanese architect Kenzo Tange, includes a museum, the Minneapolis College of Art and Design, and a children's theater.

On January 15, the art museum was given the late Richard P. Gale's collection of Japanese ukiyo-e prints and paintings, one of the most important privately owned collections of its kind in the world. The collection includes about 100 scroll paintings and more than 200 prints dating from the 1600s and 1700s.

A Ford Foundation survey released in October rated the Minneapolis-St. Paul area as second only to New York City in offering motion pictures and the performing arts. The Twin Cities ranked highest of 26 metropolitan areas surveyed in terms of movies shown on television and in theaters; live amateur plays; jazz, rock, and folk music on radio, television, and records; live concerts by amateur orchestras; and live amateur opera.

Milwaukee Avenue, a two-block street in south Minneapolis dating from 1880, was designated a national historic site by U.S. Secretary of the Interior Rogers C. B. Morton. The area's 48 homes had been scheduled for demolition as part of an urban renewal project.

The Cost of Living jumped sharply in the Twin Cities area, increasing 11 per cent between April, 1973, and April, 1974. Food prices rose 16 per cent in the year ending in June. The wages of the average factory worker in the area rose only 7.2 per cent between July, 1973, and July, 1974. During the same period, department store sales rose 12.4 per cent, employment was up 4.4 per cent, and construction activity was up 0.5 per cent. The rate of serious crimes in Minneapolis fell 5 per cent during the first six months of 1974.   James M. Banovetz

MINNESOTA. See MINNEAPOLIS-ST. PAUL; STATE GOVERNMENT.

MISSISSIPPI. See STATE GOVERNMENT.

MISSOURI. See SAINT LOUIS; STATE GOV'T.

MONACO. See EUROPE.

MONGOLIA. See ASIA.

MONTANA. See STATE GOVERNMENT.

MOROCCO. The sudden death of Istiqlal Party leader Allal al-Fassi on May 13, 1974, in Romania ended an era in Moroccan politics and reduced the effectiveness of political opposition to King Hassan II. Fassi, who had run the party since the 1930s, was succeeded by Mohammed Boucetta.

The opposition's lack of another leader of Fassi's stature enabled Hassan to retain firm control. Hassan also gained considerable popular support by pressing Morocco's dispute with Spain over the Spanish Sahara, which Morocco claims. In July, Spain announced plans to grant self-rule to the large territory adjoining Morocco, which has enormous phosphate deposits. Opposition to the proposal united all Moroccan political elements behind the monarchy for the first time since the early 1960s. A Moroccan proposal to submit the dispute to the World Court for arbitration was rejected by Spain in October. Morocco's arms inferiority made military action unlikely, but the issue gave Hassan domestic leverage in his efforts to develop representative government.

The Cabinet was enlarged in April. Eight new secretaries of state, all young technical experts, were appointed, underscoring Hassan's promises of rapid industrial development. In April, imprisoned opposition leaders of the National Union of Popular Forces (UNFP) were released. The king met with UNFP head Abdurrahim Bouabid on June 15 and promised an end to political repression, and elections in the fall, but he refused to set a date.

The Economy. Pending the return of parliamentary government, the best news for Moroccans was economic. On March 3, the king announced the discovery of a massive deposit of shale oil in the Middle Atlas Mountains. Although extracting the oil poses serious technical problems, the discovery promised long-term gains for Morocco's economy.

France resumed economic aid to Morocco in February; it had been suspended for a year because Morocco had refused to specify the amount of compensation due French landowners for their nationalized properties. A French-Moroccan agreement released more than $40 million in loans and French investments in Morocco. Morocco also received $30 million from Iran in March and $50 million from Saudi Arabia in May for agricultural projects. On March 21, the government signed a 30-year aid agreement with Russia for the Loukkos Dam project near Tangier and for phosphate exploitation. The World Bank continued its Moroccan aid with $32 million for the flood-control phase of the Sebou Basin project.

King Hassan inaugurated the new phosphate port of El Jadida in May and the Russian-built Ksar el-Kebir Dam on the Loukkos River. The dam will help irrigate 56,000 acres (23,000 hectares) of land.   William Spencer

See also AFRICA (Facts in Brief Table).

MOTION PICTURES. The year 1974 will be remembered as the one in which mass audiences came back to the movies. The trend was worldwide in scope, and film houses in Europe, Great Britain, Canada, and Japan did a rousing box-office business. In the United States, the industry was ecstatic because all through winter, spring, and summer, receipts soared. By fall, the total 1974 box-office gross promised to equal the record high of $1.65-billion set in 1946. Of course, this did not mean that the number of weekly moviegoers came anywhere close to 1946's 80 million. Inflation had more than quadrupled ticket prices. Still, 1974's estimated 20 to 21 million weekly admissions represented a significant increase over the 15-million yearly average recorded during the early 1970s.

The key question for the elated U.S. movie industry was what caused this apparent renewal of the moviegoing habit. Was it disenchantment with television? Or was it the new trend of building movie theaters in shopping centers with convenient parking facilities, the fuel shortage that lessened leisure-time options, or a depression mentality brought about by a frightening economic situation? All of these probably played some role in the increased movie attendance, but perhaps the most crucial factor was the year's movies themselves. For 1974 was the year of *The Exorcist*, a film that set box-office records all over the world. *The Exorcist* grossed a staggering $180 million in the United States alone after its release in late December, 1973 – $55 million more than *The Godfather* garnered in its first year and $100 million more than *The Sound of Music*.

The Exorcist was produced and adapted for the screen by William Peter Blatty from his best-selling novel of the same name and directed by Academy Award winner William Friedkin (*The French Connection*). It opened to, and continued to play amidst, heated controversy. Its terrifying story described the demonic possession of a 12-year-old girl, and its sensational treatment showed her uttering startlingly foul language and performing profane and obscene acts. This resulted in a film that was immoral and insulting to many and a brilliant tour de force to others.

Intensifying the conflicting feelings surrounding the film was the fact that it appeared to have church approval because two Jesuit priests had served as Friedkin's technical advisers and also appeared in the film as actors. The controversy produced a great deal of publicity that made *The Exorcist* a major event in which nearly everyone wanted to participate – especially since rumors circulated that the film's horrors caused members of the audience to faint and vomit. "I want to see

The Exorcist, a box-office sensation, had moviegoers waiting in long lines wherever it was shown in the United States and other countries.

what everyone's throwing up about," the trade journal *Variety* reported some patrons as saying.

The Nostalgia Wave. Interestingly enough, there were no big-name stars to attract audiences to *The Exorcist* as there were to the year's other huge blockbuster, *The Sting*, which starred Paul Newman and Robert Redford. *The Sting*, directed by George Roy Hill, reunited the team that had made 1969's highly successful *Butch Cassidy and the Sundance Kid*. If many considered *The Exorcist* to be potentially harmful movie fare, *The Sting*, which grossed over $100 million, was considered by nearly everyone to be absolutely harmless—just golden entertainment. The plot concerned a large-scale confidence game set in the 1930s. In addition to its other ingredients for success (not least of which was Scott Joplin's music), *The Sting* was clearly riding the commercially viable nostalgia wave.

So, too, were some of the year's other top-grossing films. The critical failure, *The Great Gatsby*, which starred Redford, re-created the flapper world of the 1920s in lush detail. Roman Polanski's highly praised *Chinatown*, starring Jack Nicholson and Faye Dunaway, set its mystery and murders in a carefully reconstructed Los Angeles of the 1930s. Such atmospheric effects characterized several of the year's late releases, as well. These included a star-studded treatment of Agatha Christie's detective classic, *Murder on the Orient Express*, which was ripe with Art Deco decor, and a remake of Ben Hecht and Charles MacArthur's *Front Page*, which revived the Chicago newspaper world of the 1930s. Even *Lenny*, a sentimentalized biography of the late satirist Lenny Bruce, which starred Dustin Hoffman in the title role and Valerie Perrine as his wife, made its evocation of the styles of the 1950s and 1960s crucial to its appeal.

But perhaps the clearest indication of nostalgia's box-office value was the immensely profitable release of *"That's Entertainment!"*, a compilation of excerpts from the great Metro-Goldwyn-Mayer musicals of the 1930s, 1940s, and 1950s. Made at a total cost of about $2 million, including expenditures for publicity, *"That's Entertainment!"* grossed over $18 million. (*The Exorcist*'s production costs alone were over $10 million.)

Disaster as Entertainment. To many in the industry, *"That's Entertainment!"* held another key to the general upswing in movie profits—the word *entertainment* itself. "This is an entertainment industry; if you have a message, send it by Western Union" had been Hollywood's golden rule during its richest years, and promised to become the industry's golden rule once again.

Such American "art films" as Francis Ford Coppola's *The Conversation*, a perceptive study of dehumanization and loss of privacy starring Gene Hackman as a professional surveillance man, may have garnered prizes at the prestigious Cannes

Ingmar Bergman's film *Scenes from a Marriage* starred Liv Ullmann and Erland Josephson in what was originally a European television series.

Film Festival in France, but the acclaim made no impact at the box office. What had, in recent years at least, were such mindless offerings as *Airport* and *The Poseidon Adventure*. Each of these films offered a huge cast of stars, dramatized a major calamity, and used special cinematic effects extensively.

This same formula characterized the great string of star-studded disaster films released late in 1974 that promised to attract huge audiences. *Airport 1975*, concerning a midair collision and starring Charlton Heston and Gloria Swanson, was one of these. *Earthquake* introduced a new process called *sensurround* that offered kinetic sensations to its audiences, and it starred Charlton Heston and a host of celebrities. *The Towering Inferno* visualized the incineration of the world's tallest office building, which was populated by some of Hollywood's most famous personalities.

A new kind of violence, then, seemed to be asserting its appeal among moviegoers, while the more traditional cops-and-robbers variety seemed to be on the wane. This was especially true in black films, where blood and gore had predominated for several years. In 1974, however, the black family film became popular. Such films included *Claudine*, a light romantic comedy starring James Earl Jones and Diahann Carroll, and *Uptown Saturday Night*, distinctive not only in its cast of black actors but also in having been produced, directed, and written by blacks. It starred Harry Belafonte and Sidney Poitier.

Imports. If U.S. films gave viewers entertainment in 1974, European films gave them art. The most noteworthy of the continental films were Ingmar Bergman's *Scenes from a Marriage*, an emotionally overwhelming film version of what had originally been presented abroad as a television series, and Federico Fellini's bittersweet reminiscences of his youth, *Amarcord*. Other European pictures that won wide acclaim were 74-year-old Luis Buñuel's hilarious surrealist masterwork *The Phantom of Liberte*, and *Lacombe, Lucien*, a sensitive study of French collaboration during World War II directed by Louis Malle.

Lacombe, Lucien and *The Phantom of Liberte* had premièred at 1974's New York Film Festival, which, not insignificantly, included among its offerings only one American feature – John Cassavetes' *A Woman Under the Influence*. In earlier years, this festival had included as many as five U.S. films. But in 1974, the U.S. film industry clearly was not addressing itself to the heady patrons of festivals and art houses. Instead, it was courting and winning back its long-lost mass audience. Joy Gould Boyum

See also AWARDS AND PRIZES (Theater and Motion Picture Awards); JACKSON, GLENDA; LEMMON, JACK.

MOZAMBIQUE. The Mozambique Liberation Front (FRELIMO) and Portugal signed a peace treaty on Sept. 7, 1974, ending a decade of guerrilla warfare. The pact set June 25, 1975, as the date for Mozambique's independence. An interim government appointed by FRELIMO and the Portuguese high commissioner was set up on September 20. Portugal's decision to end colonial rule followed a coup that overthrew the Lisbon government. See PORTUGAL.

The agreement and the inclusion of blacks in the interim government led to white riots. After the agreement was signed, a group of whites took over the radio station in Lourenço Marques, the capital, and called for independence without FRELIMO. Rioting then broke out in the streets. At least 100 persons were killed and 250 injured before order was restored by the Portuguese Army. An additional 30 deaths were reported in Beira.

More rioting occurred on October 21, sparked by an outbreak of shooting in the capital between a group of FRELIMO guerrillas and Portuguese commandos. In the clashes that followed between blacks and whites, at least 47 persons were killed.

For the remainder of the year, tension continued between the country's 9 million blacks and 200,000 whites. Darlene R. Stille

See also AFRICA (Facts in Brief Table).

White rebels seize a radio station in Mozambique and display their own flag to protest Portugal's independence pact with guerrilla forces.

The ship shaped Maritime Science Museum in Tokyo will exhibit models of old and new ships. Its observation tower is more than 20 stories high.

MUSEUMS. Noted Mexican artist Rufino Tamayo formally opened the Rufino Tamayo Museum of Pre-Hispanic Art on Jan. 24, 1974, in his native city of Oaxaca, Mexico. The museum, a restored late-17th-century palace, houses Tamayo's remarkable collection of Mexican sculptures.

Displaying artifacts uncovered by World War II bombing raids and in postwar construction projects, a museum celebrating the Roman heritage of the ancient city of Cologne, West Germany, opened there on March 4. On October 4, the Joseph H. Hirshhorn Museum and Sculpture Garden, a part of the Smithsonian Institution, opened its extensive collection of 6,000 modern paintings and sculptures to the public in Washington, D.C. See Section Two, To Increase Knowledge Among Men.

Through the National Endowment for the Arts, 101 American museums received grants totaling $4.6 million. A National Conservation Advisory Council linked to the President's Advisory Council on Historic Preservation began to coordinate resources for the scientific care of specimens.

Building Plans. The citizens of Anchorage, Alaska, voted a $1.2-million bond issue to double the size of the Anchorage Historical and Fine Arts Museum. Norfolk, Va., allotted $1 million of its revenue-sharing money for an addition to the Chrysler Museum. Revenue-sharing funds also enabled the Greensboro (N.C.) Historical Museum to provide a safer environment for its collections. The Museum of Fine Arts in Houston completed a $4-million extension designed by the late Ludwig Mies van der Rohe.

In New York City, the American Museum of Natural History inaugurated the Alexander M. White Natural Science Center to show children how ecological processes work in the inner city. The Metropolitan Museum of Art received $1 million to endow scholarly uses of its collections.

Energy Crisis. When schools stopped sending classes on field trips to museums in order to save bus fuel, museum teachers began taking specimens to schools. The Indianapolis Children's Museum readjusted its school services to provide as many in-school programs as possible. Old Sturbridge Village, Mass., provided new resource kits for classroom use on New England life in the 1800s, which the museum interprets. The Canal Museum in Syracuse, N.Y., with the aid of the Syracuse University faculty, offered a brief evening course on ways to conserve energy and installed a special exhibition on energy problems.

Administrative Problems. Trustees and directors encountered growing staff pressures. Employees, particularly in large urban museums, continued to organize unions for collective bargaining on pay, personnel policies, and other issues, including a role in policy formulation. Ralph H. Lewis

Soprano Maria Callas, one of the finest operatic actresses of her time, made a long-awaited return to New York City's Carnegie Hall in March.

MUSIC, CLASSICAL. The mix of trouble, pessimism, and hope that saturates the atmosphere wherever classical music is performed in the United States was sharply reflected by three events in 1974. They showed the burden under which most U.S. musical organizations must operate.

The Dallas Symphony temporarily collapsed in March, beleaguered by internal strife, minimal civic support, and, most of all, unpaid bills and $850,000 in loans. In the ensuing squabbles, music director Max Rudolf left, followed by others crucial to the orchestra's operation. Some concerts were restored later in an effort to keep the group alive. The debacle revealed the desperate straits in which the Dallas Symphony, like many other orchestras, found itself. In most cities, deficits piled up and, in a society pounded by inflation and recession, the increasing gap between income and expenditures became more difficult to fill.

New York City's Metropolitan Opera opened its 90th season in September with a projected deficit of $9 million. The National Endowment for the Arts had provided a $1-million emergency grant in early March, but such governmental generosity went only a small way toward meeting financial goals. The Met, like its counterparts in Chicago, San Francisco, and elsewhere, was scratching for funds, and the funds were harder to come by.

In Minneapolis, the Minnesota Orchestra and its conductor, Stanislaw Skrowaczewski, played a concert of Bach, Ives, Stravinsky, and Beethoven on October 21 to open their new $7.2-million Orchestra Hall. The orchestral association raised more than $13 million for the project, which will include a multilevel parking facility and park when completed. The event symbolized the continuing determination of arts organizations to survive, moved by the growing realization that the arts are vital to sane well-being in a complex and troubled urban society.

Two Centenaries. The Minnesota concert quite appropriately included Charles Ives's *Decoration Day*, in observance of the 100th anniversary of his birth. It was also pioneer 12-tonalist Arnold Schönberg's centenary. Schönberg, an Austrian who made the United States his home, was also honored in numerous performances by the nation's orchestras. See CELEBRATIONS.

A representative sampling of Ives performances during the centennial included his *Symphony No. 1* (San Francisco), *Symphony No. 2* (Rochester), *Symphony No. 3* (Minnesota), *Central Park in the Dark* (Boston), *Psalm* (Los Angeles), and *Three Places in New England* (Philadelphia and Detroit). There were Ives festivals in Miami, Fla.; New Haven, Conn.; and New York City.

Schönberg's music turned up virtually everywhere, including Milwaukee, Wis.; Minnesota; and

Tanglewood, Mass. (*Gurrelieder*); Chicago and Philadelphia (*Survivor from Warsaw*); Cincinnati (*Pelleas and Melisande*); Boston (*Modern Psalm* and *Accompaniment to a Film Sequence*); and Los Angeles (*De Profundis*).

Old and New. Two old works were unearthed to spice repertory. The Baltimore Symphony found Niccolò Paganini's *Sonata per la grand viola* and played it for the first time anywhere in March. The National Symphony came upon the late Zoltán Kodály's *Old Hungarian Soldiers' Tunes* and premièred them in October.

New music was being performed everywhere. The American Society of Composers, Authors, and Publishers honored 15 orchestras for adventuresome programming of contemporary music. Highest awards were given to the Los Angeles Philharmonic, the Minnesota Orchestra, and the National Symphony in Washington, D.C.

Among the many world premières were: Robert Starer's *Piano Concerto No. 3* (Baltimore); William Schuman's *Concerto on Old English Rounds for Viola, Women's Chorus, and Orchestra* (Boston); Oliver Knussen's *Symphony No. 3* (Buffalo); Felix Labunski's *Primavera* (Cincinnati); Bruno Maderna's *Quadrivium for Four Orchestras* (Cleveland); Richard Rodney Bennett's *Concerto for Orchestra* (Denver); Benjamin Lees's *Études for Piano and Orchestra* (Houston); Paul Chihara's *Ceremony IV* and Morton Subotnick's *Two Butterflies for Orchestra* (Los Angeles); Robert Moevs' *Main-Travelled Roads* (Milwaukee); Peter Mennin's *Symphony No. 8* and Charles Wuorinin's *Concerto* for piano (New York); Alberto Ginastera's *Turbas: Gregorian Passion for Chorus and Orchestra* (Philadelphia); Robert Suderburg's *Concerto* for piano (Seattle); and Vladimir Ussachevsky's *Colloquy for Symphony Orchestra, Electronic Tape, and Various Chairs* (Utah).

United States premières were frequent, too. Michael Tippett, the noted British composer, was on hand as the Boston Symphony introduced his *Symphony No. 3* in February. He later conducted the work himself in Chicago and was a very active observer as his opera, *The Knot Garden*, had its U.S. première at Northwestern University in nearby Evanston.

Opera companies also sponsored new works. Thomas Pasatieri's excursion into Chekhov, *The Sea Gull*, was commissioned and then premièred by the Houston Opera in March. Richard Owen's *Mary Dyer* was performed for the first time in June on the Boston Commons.

The famed Chautauqua Institution's centennial celebration was climaxed in July by the première of Seymour Barab's *Philip Marshall*, a work about a Confederate soldier who returns home a pacifist unable to relate to other people. The Lake George Opera in New York introduced José Raul Bernardo's *La Nina*, based on a poem by the Cuban patriot José Martí. William Grant Still's *Bayou Legend* was premièred by Opera South in Jackson, Miss., in November.

Among U.S. opera premières were the first staging of Busoni's *Doktor Faust* by the Nevada Opera Guild and Werner Egk's *Engagement in San Domingo* by the St. Paul Opera. In Portland, Ore., Ernst Křenek was honored on his 75th birthday with the U.S. première of *The Life of Orestes*, written in 1930. Sergei Prokofiev's *War and Peace* was produced by the Opera Company of Boston. In Washington, D.C., the Opera Society did Claudio Monteverdi's *Il Ritorno d'Ulisse in Patria*. The Met turned to Benjamin Britten's *Death in Venice*.

The varied repertory in Santa Fe, N. Mex., encompassed both Alban Berg's *Lulu* and *Egisto*, a 17th-century piece by Pietro Francesco Cavalli, never before done in this country. In Boston and at Chicago's Lyric Opera, *Don Quichotte*, the Jules Massenet version of *Man of La Mancha*, was revived. Another Massenet opera, *Esclarmonde*, was unearthed in San Francisco.

Among major opera premières around the world were Thea Musgrave's *The Voice of Ariadne* at Aldeburgh, England; Sándor Szokolay's *Samson* in Budapest, Hungary; Ian Hamilton's *The Cataline Conspiracy* in Stirling, Scotland; and Ján Cikker's *Coriolanus* in Prague, Czechoslovakia. In East Berlin, Paul Dessau's *Einstein* was premièred. It recounts Albert Einstein's contribution to the development of the atomic bomb and the scientist's later worry about the bomb. The opera had a distinct anti-American tone.

Mixed Bag. The year had a mixed bag of other events, serious and silly, major and minor. Sol Hurok, the greatest of the impresarios, died March 5, leaving the kind of void that usually only the most important musicians leave.

The Cleveland Orchestra toured Japan, and the New York Philharmonic traveled through New Zealand and Australia. The Chicago Symphony went to Europe again, and Milan's La Scala visited Moscow. The International Verdi Congress convened in Chicago, its first U.S. site. The San Francisco Opera initiated Brown-Bag Opera, a twice-weekly series of short works and excerpts for a 50-cent admission. The brown-bag lunches could be either brought or bought. An Anton Bruckner Center opened in Linz, Austria, to mark the 150th anniversary of his birth.

In Rio de Janeiro, Brazil, a production of *La Traviata* showed Violetta in delirium, dreaming the whole opera and surrounded by dancers representing the vices of her life. In Kassel, West Germany, a new *Ring* cycle had Rhine maidens as scuba divers on underwater scooters and gods in space suits.

Maria Callas reappeared in Chicago, Philadelphia, and New York City to the adoring cheers of her fans. Critics generally agreed the voice was

Russian cellist Mstislav Rostropovich lands
in England to start a two-year tour. Friends
fear the dissident musician may be exiled.

MUSIC, POPULAR.

Effects of the energy crisis reached into the popular music world in 1974. Due to the fuel shortage, many U.S. artists were forced to cancel British and European tours, including the Allman Brothers, Steely Dan, and others.

British-born singer Elton John, after three years of moderate popularity, became a superstar both in his home country and in the United States. In a typical case, all 75,000 tickets for his four appearances at the Forum in Inglewood, Calif., in October were purchased within hours after they were put on sale to the public.

Old Favorites Return. One of the most publicized events of the year was the return of 32-year-old Bob Dylan in January, his first concert tour since a near-fatal motorcycle accident in 1966. Backed up by a group billed as The Band, he opened in Chicago and performed to packed houses in 39 shows in 21 cities. His talent was undimmed by his long absence. Many in the audience were youths in their teens or early 20s who were only from 5 to 15 years old when Dylan created his most-acclaimed works during the mid-1960s. See DYLAN, BOB.

Frank Sinatra, resuming public appearances after a two-year absence, was another long-established favorite who returned to the scene in 1974. Sinatra's first major appearance, in a Las Vegas, Nev., casino, was before an audience that paid a record-breaking $30 each to attend the dinner show. A nine-city tour, starting in New York City in April, was his first tour in six years. Sinatra also visited Australia in July and stirred up a dispute with the Australian press that threatened to curtail his tour. The tour was continued after he mollified the Australian unions.

Herb Alpert also returned to recording and public performing after an absence of many years. He appeared with a reorganized version of his Tijuana Brass group, using several of his original musicians. During the fall, they toured Europe with great success. Also reorganized were Crosby, Stills, Nash & Young, who got back together in June after each had tried working on his own.

New Trends. Black artists gained an unprecedented hold in the mass popular music market. Roberta Flack remained the best-selling artist. Stevie Wonder, back on tour after recovering from a serious accident, scored heavily with his album "Innervisions."

Gladys Knight and the Pips became the most successful new vocal group. Among their best-known single hits was "Neither One of Us Wants To Be the First to Say Goodbye." The single "Midnight Train" achieved success in rhythm and blues circles. An album they recorded of the musical sound track for the film *Claudine* also sold well.

The "glitter rock" movement, represented by such performers as David Bowie and Alice Cooper,

diminished, but the capacity to excite remained. Pianist Vladimir Horowitz also returned, and for him there were cheers and critical praise.

The San Francisco Symphony was embroiled in bitter controversy. Its conductor, Seiji Ozawa, had previously hired a black woman timpanist and an American-born male bassoonist of Japanese ancestry. At contract-renewal time, a players' committee decided they should not be kept on, causing a clear authority conflict between the conductor and his musicians. The two players later were reinstated for a year, but the dispute was far from solved. In a more gentle dispute, Metropolitan Opera musical director Rafael Kubelik resigned in February, unable to come to terms with management about duties and production conditions. Because of continuing trouble with his government, Russian cellist Mstislav Rostropovich, now on a two-year tour, may be refused permission to return to Russia.

In Atlanta, electronically controlled explosives installed to simulate cannon sounds for the *1812 Overture* triggered the automatic fire alarm and brought firemen to the arts center during a performance in June. In China, the press called Beethoven a villain for "propagating the capitalist theory of human nature." And in London, film maker Ken Russell announced he would make a movie of Franz Liszt's life, featuring rock star Mick Jagger as the tempestuous Liszt.   Peter P. Jacobi

Farewell
To the Duke

In 1917, 18-year-old Edward Kennedy Ellington was offered an art scholarship to the Pratt Institute in New York City. Fortunately, he turned it down to concentrate on music. When death ended his performance on May 24, 1974, Duke Ellington ranked as one of America's most important composers and most influential jazz musicians.

Millions of people will always associate Duke Ellington with jazz. But he preferred to describe his work as "American music." He played it everywhere, from Harlem's Cotton Club to London's Westminster Abbey.

Ellington spent most of his life at the piano. The son of a Washington, D.C., butler and blueprint maker, he began studying piano in 1906, at the age of 7. By 1916, he was earning money playing at night.

He played and organized bands in Washington until 1922, when he went to New York City. He failed to find work there, but returned in 1923 with a small combo that included drummer Sonny Greer. Success did not come easily. "Every day we'd go play pool until we made $2," Duke recalled later. "With $2, we'd get a pair of 75-cent steaks, beer for a quarter, and have a quarter for tomorrow." Finally, the Cotton Club hired him in 1927, and he expanded the combo to an 11-piece band.

Ellington maintained his own big band for the next 47 years and toured with it until his final illness. He made his first tour of Europe in 1933. He also toured the Middle East, the Far East, Russia, Africa, and South America.

On tour or at home, Duke composed constantly. "You know how it is," he said. "You go home expecting to go right to bed. But there, on the way, you go past the piano and there's a flirtation. . . . So you sit down and try out a couple of chords, and when you look up, it's 7 A.M."

His early music had an exotic quality, a jungle style, but it gradually became more sophisticated. Duke composed mainly for the great instrumentalists that joined his band—such men as saxophonists Johnny Hodges and Paul Gonsalves, trumpeter Cootie Williams, and clarinetist Barney Bigard.

"Their sound is an instrument," he said. "It's the total personality of the person playing, and that's what I write for, that's how I hear music. Before you can play anything or write anything, you have to hear it. My reward is hearing what I've done, unlike most composers, immediately. That's why I keep these expensive gentlemen around."

Duke Ellington wrote more than 6,000 musical pieces, including symphonies, sacred music, music for jazz groups, a ballet, and scores for five motion pictures. His songs include "Satin Doll," "Mood Indigo," "Solitude," "Sophisticated Lady," "In a Sentimental Mood," "Do Nothing 'Til You Hear from Me," and "Don't Get Around Much Anymore."

He pioneered in extending jazz composition beyond the customary 12- or 32-bar chorus. He wrote "Reminiscing in Tempo," a 12-minute work, in 1934; and "Blue Belles of Harlem," a concert piece, in 1938. He composed *Black, Brown, and Beige*, a 50-minute work, for the first of his annual Carnegie Hall concerts in 1943. He also composed *New World a-Comin'*, *The Deep South Suite*, *The Perfume Suite*, *The Liberian Suite*, and *Togo Brava*.

In 1965, he turned to sacred music, presenting a Concert of Sacred Music in Grace Cathedral in San Francisco. In 1968, he presented a Second Sacred Concert at the Cathedral Church of St. John the Divine in New York City. His Third Sacred Concert was performed in 1973 in Westminster Abbey.

Honors came slowly to this elegant, suave man. When judges rejected a recommendation that he receive the 1965 Pulitzer Prize in Music, he said only: "Fate is being kind to me. Fate doesn't want me to be famous too young." But, inevitably, the honors came. He received the Presidential Medal of Freedom in 1969, was elected to the Royal Swedish Academy of Music in 1971, and received the French Legion of Honor in 1973.

But Duke Ellington needed only his music. "Music is my mistress," he wrote, "and she plays second fiddle to no one." Joseph P. Spohn

Duke Ellington
(1899–1974)

417

The last "Grand Ole Opry" show in Nashville's Ryman Auditorium featured Johnny Cash and Maybelle Carter. Opry moved to new quarters in March.

began to diminish in popularity as some of the better-known artists leaned toward a simpler and less ostentatious approach.

Festivals. A marathon 12-hour rock show attracted more than 200,000 fans to the Motor Speedway in Ontario, Calif., on August 3. Grossing over $2 million, it was the most lucrative single rock event in history. Among the acts presented were Seals & Crofts, the Eagles, and radio personality Don Imus.

The first American Song Festival was presented in the Performing Arts Center at Saratoga Springs, N.Y., in August. Amateur entries outnumbered professional ones by more than 6 to 1 among the more than 60,000 songs submitted. Prizes of $30,500 were awarded to the best amateur song, "Natural Ways" by Barry Blackwood, and to the best professional song, "Lonely Together" by Rod McBride and Estelle Levitt. Attendance was poor, but the event received wider exposure when it was later shown on television. Plans are to hold it annually.

Still Popular groups and singers included John Denver, Charlie Rich, Paul Williams, Olivia Newton-John, Helen Reddy, Tony Orlando and Dawn, Barry White, and the Osmonds. Jim Croce, the singer and composer who died in September, 1973, was still prominent with three albums among the best sellers.

Popular performers who died during the year included "Mama" Cass Elliott; Vinnie Taylor, the lead guitarist of the Sha-Na-Na group; and trumpeter Bill Chase and three members of his jazz-rock group.

The Jazz Scene. A strong trend in jazz was the conversion of many artists to a jazz-rock or straight rock format that helped to expand their areas of impact. One of the notable proponents of this style was pianist-composer Herbie Hancock, whose group featured electronic keyboards and synthesizers. Moving along similar lines were trumpeter-composer Freddie Hubbard, vibraphonist Roy Ayers, and saxophonist Lou Donaldson.

The Newport Jazz Festival, held in New York City for 10 days in June and July, attracted 200,000 listeners. Along with a festival in Monterey, Calif., in September, it was one of the most successful domestic jazz festivals. In Nice, France, scene of the world's first jazz festival in 1948, American and European artists took part in a weeklong Festival of Traditional Jazz and Blues in July.

The jazz world sustained its greatest loss in May with the death of composer-bandleader Duke Ellington (see Close-Up). Many of Ellington's albums were reissued and his orchestra continued under the direction of his son Mercer, a talented composer himself. Leonard Feather

See also RECORDINGS.

NAMIBIA. See AFRICA.

NATIONAL DEFENSE. President Gerald R. Ford announced a controversial conditional amnesty program on Sept. 16, 1974. He said it would permit an estimated 28,000 to 50,000 Vietnam-era draft evaders and military deserters to obtain "earned re-entry" into American society.

Eligible men could avoid criminal penalties by turning themselves in to federal officials by Jan. 31, 1975, reaffirming their allegiance to the United States, and agreeing to up to 24 months of alternate service in low-paying jobs that "promote the national health, safety, or interest." In return, draft evaders would be granted immunity from prosecution, while deserters would be given undesirable discharges that would be replaced by "clemency discharges" on completion of alternate service. A national clemency review board, headed by former Republican Senator Charles E. Goodell of New York, was created to review the cases of those already convicted or given undesirable discharges.

The program was denounced by veterans' organizations as too lenient and by many evader and deserter organizations as too punitive. By December 31, 2,521 deserters and 155 evaders had taken advantage of the program.

Military Strength. The United States trimmed its military forces to 2,153,914 troops as of November 30, the lowest level in 24 years. However, a scheduled round of major personnel reductions and domestic military base closings was canceled because of the adverse impact such cutbacks would have had on the sluggish national economy. Nevertheless, the Pentagon continued to streamline its command structure in an effort to offset rising personnel and weapons costs. Secretary of Defense James R. Schlesinger ordered a 15 per cent reduction in the size of his staff and that of the Joint Chiefs of Staff by mid-1975.

After failing to meet its recruiting goals for several months, the Army's all-volunteer program was declared a success on July 1, when troop strength was more than 1,000 over the Army's authorized strength. However, critics claimed that the Army had lowered its standards to meet its quotas.

Defense Budget. Despite further declines in U.S. troop strength, elimination of several military headquarters, and efforts to achieve further détente with Russia and China, defense spending continued its steady rise. In 1974, it exceeded the World War II peak of $79.8 billion. Defense officials predicted even higher expenditures in 1975. Rising costs were attributed to a new round of pay increases, inflation, higher petroleum costs, and continued cost overruns in developing and manufacturing new weapons systems.

The Department of Defense's budget for fiscal

President Ford, in an August 19 speech in Chicago, tells Veterans of Foreign Wars he favors leniency for deserters and draft dodgers.

Russia's Communist Party leader Leonid Brezhnev and President Richard
Nixon sign communiqué after their June meeting in San Clemente, Calif.

1975 (July 1, 1974, to June 30, 1975) was set by
Congress at $82.1 billion, exclusive of military
assistance, military construction, and civil defense
funds. This was a $5-billion reduction from the
Pentagon budget request submitted in March.
The appropriation supported 13⅓ Army and 3
Marine divisions, 22 Air Force tactical wings, 17
Navy and Marine air wings, 17 strategic airlift
squadrons, and a Navy fleet of 508 vessels. Strategic
strength remained virtually unchanged. It included
1,054 intercontinental ballistic missiles (ICBM's),
656 submarine-launched ballistic missiles, 27 strategic bomber squadrons, and 6 fighter interceptor
squadrons.

The Navy received the largest share of the
budget, $27.1 billion; the Air Force, $25.4 billion;
and the Army, $20.4 billion.

The Navy received $2.1 billion for the Trident
missile-submarine program, $457.1 million for
DD-963 destroyers, $502.5 million for SSN-688 submarines, $429.4 million for the S-3A Viking antisubmarine aircraft, $186 million for patrol frigates,
$135.4 million for the Mark 48 torpedo, and $617.3-
million for the F-14A Tomcat jet fighter. The Tomcat program remained in trouble, however; despite
threats by the F-14 contractor, Grumman Aerospace Corporation, to halt production because of
continued cost overruns, Congress rejected a Navy
plan to provide $100 million in advance payments.

The Air Force received $930.6 million for the F-15
Eagle jet fighter, $615 million for the AWACS airborne radar system, $445 million for the B-1 strategic
bomber, and $219.4 million for the A-10 battlefield
support fighter. The first production order of 52
A-10 aircraft was approved after the plane won in a
competition flyoff with the A-7D fighter. Engine
problems with the F-15 fighter were corrected, but
more technical problems with the B-1 program
forced the Air Force to increase the number of B-1
prototypes from three to five; delay the first B-1
flight by several months, until December 23; and
postpone a production decision for the second time,
until November, 1976.

The Army received $118 million for an advanced
"site defense" ABM system, $104.6 million for the
TOW antitank missile, $104.2 million for the
SAM-D missile, $65 million for advanced tank development, and $52.7 million for a new utility helicopter. The Heavy Lift Helicopter program was
delayed for 10 months because of technical problems. Similar difficulties with the SAM-D missile
forced the Army to reduce the program in favor of
a cheaper and less complex surface-to-air missile.

SALT II Agreement. Meeting in the Russian
port city of Vladivostok in late November, President Ford and Russian leader Leonid I. Brezhnev
reached a broad tentative agreement supplementing the Strategic Arms Limitation Treaty (SALT)

signed in 1972. Secretary of State Henry A. Kissinger called the agreement a major breakthrough in arms negotiations. The new pact extends the SALT agreement from 1977 to 1985 and sets upper limits on the number of delivery vehicles (planes and ICBM's) and nuclear warheads for each country. SALT II will require congressional approval, and critics in Congress were quick to point out that the agreement will actually allow increases in the nuclear arsenals of both countries, thus hiking defense spending for some years to come. Previously, negotiators signed a protocol on July 3 limiting each nation to a single site for antiballistic missile (ABM) systems; the 1972 treaty had permitted two.

Both superpowers, however, continued developing a variety of new weapons systems. The Pentagon worked on the B-1 strategic bomber, the "site defense" advanced ABM system, and a strategic submarine-launched cruise missile. Construction also began in July on the first of 10 Trident submarines, which will carry advanced ICBM's with multiple warheads (MIRV) having an estimated range of 6,000 miles (9,700 kilometers).

New strategic programs begun in fiscal 1975 included a more accurate version of the Minuteman land-based ICBM, a larger and more accurate Minuteman warhead, and a maneuverable warhead that can change trajectory after launch.

In a major change in U.S. nuclear strategy, Schlesinger revealed in January that the United States was switching from an "assured destruction" approach to a "counterforce" concept in which some strategic missiles aimed at Russian cities were being retargeted against military targets such as missile silos. Schlesinger said the policy change was needed to counter continuing improvements in Russian strategic weapons and to provide the United States with a more favorable negotiating position at the SALT talks.

Command Changes. Admiral Thomas H. Moorer retired as chairman of the Joint Chiefs of Staff. He was succeeded on July 1 by General George S. Brown, who was replaced as Air Force chief of staff by General David C. Jones. Admiral Elmo R. Zumwalt, Jr., retired on May 30 and was replaced as chief of naval operations by Admiral James L. Holloway III.

Army Chief of Staff General Creighton W. Abrams, Jr., died on September 4. He was succeeded by General Frederick C. Weyand.

General Alexander M. Haig, Jr., the White House chief of staff, returned to active duty in September and became commander-in-chief of U.S. troops in Europe and supreme commander of Allied forces in Europe. Haig replaced retiring General Andrew J. Goodpaster.   Thomas M. DeFrank

NATIONALIST CHINA. See TAIWAN.

NAVY, U.S. See NATIONAL DEFENSE.

NEBRASKA. See STATE GOVERNMENT.

NEFF, FRANCINE IRVING (1924-), was sworn in as treasurer of the United States on June 21, 1974. She is the seventh woman to hold the post.

Francine Irving was born on Dec. 6, 1924, in Albuquerque, N. Mex., and grew up near Mountainair, N. Mex., where her family had a vegetable farm. She graduated from the University of New Mexico in 1948.

Neff became an active Republican in 1964. She had been a Democrat, but she became increasingly unhappy with the Democratic Party. When a friend urged her to stop complaining and start working for what she wanted, she joined Barry Goldwater's unsuccessful presidential campaign against Lyndon B. Johnson.

She continued her volunteer political activities after the campaign. In 1967, she was named to the New Mexico State Central Committee, and in 1968 she was chairman of the New Mexico Women for Nixon. A year later, she became a member of the State Executive Committee. In 1970, she was named the national Republican committeewoman for New Mexico. From 1972 until her appointment as treasurer, she was a member of the executive committee of the Republican National Committee. She resigned all her active political posts when she was sworn in as treasurer.

Neff and her husband, Edward, have a daughter and a son.   Kathryn Sederborg

NEPAL. Astrologers in 1974 finally picked a day in February, 1975, for the coronation of King Birendra Bir Bikram Shah Deva, who has ruled this tiny kingdom since 1972. In November, 10,000 sheep and goats were imported from Tibet for sacrifice to the gods. Both Nepal and the king needed all the divine help they could get. Not only is this landlocked kingdom of 12 million regarded as the poorest state in Asia, but it also lives in constant fear of being taken over by its two huge neighbors, India and China. It dreads them, even as it must depend on them for essential goods in order to survive.

Nepal had reasons for anxiety in 1974. The kingdom of Sikkim was forced to become an associate state of India in September. This provoked critical exchanges between the governments of Nepal and India, as well as violent anti-Indian demonstrations in Nepal's capital, Katmandu. As the year ended, India was offering asylum to leaders of the Nepal Congress Party, who were actively fighting the king.

In the Himalaya to the north, the government had to contend with thousands of heavily armed Khampa refugees from Tibet. Nepal tried in vain to force these refugees south lest China intervene. At the same time, inflation, shortages, and the feudal regime of King Birendra produced student unrest, assassinations, and arson.   Mark Gayn

See also ASIA (Facts in Brief Table).

NETHERLANDS. The Arab oil nations lifted their oil embargo on July 10, 1974. The ban, which had been imposed in October, 1973, for Dutch support of Israel during the Middle East war, cost the port of Rotterdam, Europe's largest oil terminal, about $10 million in lost duties. Ironically, the Foreign Ministry reported an increase of 30 per cent in Dutch oil reserves during the embargo, due largely to mild winter weather, governmental conservation measures, and rerouting of non-Arab oil.

To counter the embargo's effects, the government passed a Special Powers Act in early January. The act permitted control of wages, prices, rents, dividends, and other economic factors. Gasoline was rationed from January 12 to February 4, each driver receiving about 16 gallons (60 liters) for the three-week period. Many garages ignored the limit, and motorists filled their tanks in bordering West Germany and Belgium. A Sunday ban on pleasure driving replaced the rationing effort.

Natural Gas Revenues will finance additional expenditures for welfare, pensions, and health care in 1975. Increased revenue from the Slochteren natural gas field in Groningen province, Europe's largest single energy source, makes possible the 20 per cent increase.

In her speech from the throne at the opening of parliament on September 17, Queen Juliana said the Special Powers Act would not be renewed. She promised equal pay for women by Jan. 1, 1975.

Defense Cuts. A 10-year defense plan, announced on July 9, included an 18 per cent cut in the Dutch armed forces. The plan could save the government $300 million over the next four years, and help offset the cost of modernizing a smaller navy and air force. National service will be shortened from 16 to 11 months by 1977. From its Brussels, Belgium, headquarters, North Atlantic Treaty Organization (NATO) officials attacked the Dutch plans, saying they would severely weaken NATO.

Provincial Elections. On March 27, smaller parties in the 14-party parliamentary system lost votes to the two large parties. The Liberals' share of the vote advanced from 14.45 per cent to 18.99 per cent. The Labor Party of Prime Minister Johannes Martin den Uyl, the largest party, won 27.9 per cent. Control of inflation remained a major problem for Den Uyl's government. The Organization for Economic Cooperation and Development cautioned in June that the probability of substantial natural gas revenues did not eliminate the need for careful planning of public spending.   Kenneth Brown

See also EUROPE (Facts in Brief Table).

NEVADA. See STATE GOVERNMENT.

NEW BRUNSWICK. See CANADA.

NEW GUINEA. See PACIFIC ISLANDS.

NEW HAMPSHIRE. See STATE GOVERNMENT.

NEW JERSEY. See NEWARK; STATE GOVERNMENT.

NEW MEXICO. See STATE GOVERNMENT.

NEW ORLEANS citizens faced a unique problem in 1974. A private organization, the Environmental Defense Fund, announced in November that the city's drinking water may cause cancer and account for the high incidence of that disease among white New Orleans males. Also in November, the federal Environmental Protection Agency (EPA) reported finding 38 toxic chemicals in the water supply, some of which are known to cause cancer in animals.

Many city officials criticized the methods used in the private study and regarded the EPA investigation as incomplete. Nevertheless, sales of bottled water soared to from 15 to 30 times their normal rate after the reports were released.

New Orleans City Council members in early 1974 began serving an unusual fifth year in office, even though they had been elected to four-year terms. The situation arose when a federal court in March, 1974, postponed new elections until reapportionment of the city's voting districts was resolved.

Architectural Preservation. Mayor Moon Landrieu imposed a temporary moratorium on all demolition permits for razing buildings in the downtown business district adjacent to New Orleans' famed French Quarter. The moratorium was to be in effect from April to January, 1975, while plans for growth management in the area were being developed. Critics of the land developers had claimed that many noteworthy old buildings were being razed and that the city was treating the area around the French Quarter as a "business bonanza" rather than an architectural trust.

The architect of the Louisiana Superdome announced on July 1 that completion of the city's huge domed stadium would be delayed until March, 1975. Strikes by construction workers had put the project six weeks behind schedule. Consequently, the January, 1975, Super Bowl game had to be played in Tulane Stadium.

Serious Crimes rose about 2.5 per cent in New Orleans during the first half of 1974, well below the national increase of 16 per cent reported by the Federal Bureau of Investigation on October 3. On June 12, two gunmen hijacked a bus, robbed the driver and passengers, and then abducted and raped a woman. As a result, city police assigned security officers to ride on public transit buses.

New Orleans District Attorney Jim Garrison was found innocent of income tax evasion on March 26. Garrison, however, had lost his 1973 re-election bid and was replaced by Harry Connick on April 1, 1974.

Economic Conditions deteriorated in the city during the first half of the year. In June, the U.S. Department of Labor announced that the unemployment rate had risen to 8.5 per cent. Department store sales fell 6 per cent, and construction activity was off 2 per cent.   James M. Banovetz

NEW YORK. See NEW YORK CITY; STATE GOV'T.

NEW YORK CITY. The construction industry in New York City fell into a serious slump in 1974, the worst since the 1950s. As a result, 15,000 construction workers were laid off, and the number of architectural contracts signed fell to only 55 per cent of those awarded in 1969. Meanwhile, living costs rose 10.6 per cent between June, 1973, and June, 1974. In terms of living costs, New York ranked 10th highest out of 47 of the world's largest cities that were surveyed by Business International Corporation.

There was substantial unemployment, according to the U.S. Department of Labor. The number of jobs decreased by 0.6 per cent during the year ending in July, when the State Department of Labor reported unemployment in the city at 7.5 per cent. The average factory worker's pay increased only 5.4 per cent, to $8,434 a year. This was considerably less than the $9,353 annual income required to support a family of four in the city on a minimum budget.

City Hall. Abraham D. Beame was sworn into office on Dec. 31, 1973, six hours before he officially took office at midnight. He appointed the city's first black deputy mayor, Paul F. Gibson, Jr., who was sworn into office on January 17. On May 15, Beame submitted his first city budget, an $11.1-billion spending plan.

During his first year in office, Beame faced the usual problems of a New York City mayor. A strike by school maintenance workers in January left schools without heat or janitorial services and forced some to close. A $300-million budget deficit forced Beame to impose a freeze on hiring in February. In November, he laid off 1,500 city workers, and cut city services costing $100 million.

A federal district court judge ruled on January 28 that local, state, and federal housing authorities must help desegregate a high school in Brooklyn. This was the first school desegregation order ever directed at housing authorities. The judge noted that racially imbalanced housing contributed to school segregation.

Crime and Corruption. Federal Bureau of Investigation figures showed that the crime rate in New York City rose 4 per cent during the first six months of 1974. More instances of police corruption were reported. Eleven city narcotics detectives were indicted on March 8 on charges of selling narcotics seized during arrests. Ten police sergeants were charged on August 8 with accepting bribes.

Beame announced in November that an investigation had uncovered widespread corruption in the construction industry and the city's buildings department. Bribes accepted by building inspectors could be more than $25 million.   James M. Banovetz

While his wife, Mary, looks on, Abraham D. Beame is formally inaugurated as mayor of New York City at a ceremony outside City Hall on January 1.

NEW ZEALAND. After two years of record export income and the building up of relatively large reserves, New Zealand's trade status changed dramatically in 1974. The slump in world demand for beef and wool reduced export income, while the volume and cost of New Zealand's imports rose markedly due to the higher prices paid for oil, of which the country imports nearly all its needs.

New Zealand's trading situation was its principal problem. It also suffered from domestic inflation of about 10 per cent, somewhat less than the rate of its neighbor, Australia. The New Zealand dollar was devalued by 9 per cent on September 25, following an Australian devaluation of 12 per cent.

Prime Minister Dies. The Labour government continued in office following the death of Prime Minister Norman E. Kirk on August 31. Kirk's son later won his Parliament seat at a by-election. The new prime minister and minister for foreign affairs was Wallace E. Rowling, formerly minister for finance. See ROWLING, WALLACE E.

Determined to counter inflation and to reduce the demand for imports, Rowling's government instituted a system of forced, or involuntary, loans, following earlier controls on prices and profits. New criteria for British immigrants were announced in April, based on the country's capacity to absorb them.

Foreign Affairs. New Zealand continued on the course mapped out after the election of the Kirk government in December, 1972. It withdrew all military support from Vietnam, recognized the People's Republic of China, and also recognized North Vietnam and East Germany. It was closely associated with Australia in restructuring the Southeast Asia Treaty Organization to diminish its preoccupation with military affairs and give it more of a political and economic character.

New Zealand's interest in the Middle East, dormant for almost 20 years, again became apparent through a government good-will mission to Lebanon and other Arab countries in February and the appointment of New Zealand's first ambassador to Egypt in June. The shah of Iran visited in September and signed a trade agreement with New Zealand. It was announced that New Zealand would set up an embassy in Teheran for the first time in 1975.

Kirk returned on January 8 from a month-long visit to Papua New Guinea, Indonesia, Singapore, India, and Bangladesh. The main purpose of his trip was to explain a shift in New Zealand's foreign policy. In the future, New Zealand plans to take a position more independent of the major Western powers and cooperate more closely with other Pacific countries to shape policy in the area. Kirk also attended the South Pacific Forum on the island of Rarotonga in March. New Zealand, like Australia, continued to protest in vain against French nuclear tests in the Pacific. J. D. B. Miller

See also ASIA (Facts in Brief Table).

Wallace E. Rowling was selected by the ruling Labour Party to become prime minister of New Zealand after Norman E. Kirk died in August.

NEWARK Mayor Kenneth A. Gibson easily won a second term by defeating State Senator Anthony Imperiale in the May 14, 1974, election. Gibson, whose first-term election in 1970 made him the first black mayor of a major Eastern city, received 55 per cent of the votes cast.

Gibson campaigned on his record in dealing with the problems of the predominantly black city and pointed to a decreasing crime rate. Imperiale, a leader of Newark's white minority who organized white street patrols after the 1967 race riots, charged that Gibson was unable to guarantee stability.

On March 29, a federal jury in Newark convicted Nelson G. Gross, former New Jersey Republican Party chairman, of conspiracy to commit tax fraud in connection with former Governor William T. Cahill's 1969 political campaign. Gross was found guilty of establishing a scheme that permitted campaign contributors to take illegal tax deductions.

September Riots. The first major disturbance since Gibson took office occurred in September. Four days of violence and disorder erupted in a predominantly Puerto Rican community on September 1, when police attempted to break up an illegal dice game during a Spanish festival. Two persons died during the disturbances, three were wounded, and at least 60 others were injured. Demonstrators stormed City Hall on September 2, smashing windows.

On September 3, the city imposed a ban on street

demonstrations and a 10 P.M. to 6 A.M. curfew on teen-agers in the area after sporadic looting and rock-throwing broke out. Mayor Gibson had leaflets distributed in the community inviting citizens to bring their concerns to him.

Ineffective Education. A task force report issued on November 2 claimed there was little improvement in the quality of education in Newark public schools, despite special programs aimed at developing basic academic skills. In fact, reading and mathematics achievement scores declined during the 1972-1973 school year. The task force recommended a bilingual program for Newark's Spanish-speaking students and new programs aimed at increasing reading, writing, and verbal skills.

The Cost of Living in the area rose 10.6 per cent between June, 1973, and June, 1974. But the income of factory workers rose only 6.7 per cent during the same period. By mid-1974, Newark had substantial unemployment, according to the U.S. Department of Labor. Jobs had declined 0.1 per cent between July, 1973, and July, 1974.

A four-year rent strike by tenants in a deteriorated public housing project ended on July 17. The tenants won an agreement that calls for rehabilitation of the buildings and gives tenants a voice in managing the project.   James M. Banovetz

NEWFOUNDLAND. See CANADA.

NEWSPAPER. Daily and weekly newspapers around the world suffered from tight newsprint supplies and soaring paper prices in 1974. The situation was especially severe in developing countries such as India, where the government began rationing supplies to newspapers. In Great Britain, Beaverbrook Newspapers, Limited, cited the high cost of newsprint as one reason for closing the three newspapers it owned in Scotland.

Tight supplies eased somewhat in the United States late in the year, but tonnage costs continued to rise. Added to the gloomy picture was the decision by several paper mills to produce pulp rather than newsprint. Other mills abandoned newsprint production to manufacture heavier stocks for magazines. Those mills that continued to produce newsprint switched to a lighter stock. This brought newspaper complaints that imperfections in the rolls caused paper breaks while the presses were running.

U.S. Newspapers exercised caution in purchasing new equipment and building new facilities, but increased advertising sales led to improved earnings for most companies. Employment remained stable, with few layoffs except where the still-new electronics technology took over. Even here, the mortality rate for printing craftsmen caused little alarm, because most younger employees were willing to retrain to keep their jobs.

The *National Star*, a new national paper, was launched in February. But *Chicago Today* put out its last issue on Friday, September 13.

Most publishers and their finance officers saw only a slight further slowing in activity through the first half of 1975. They believed that, with good management, the industry could find its way back to economic stability.

The financially troubled *Washington* (D.C.) *Star-News* adopted a four-day workweek and 20 per cent pay cuts on December 10 as an alternative to massive layoffs.

For the first time in U.S. newspaper history, the number of daily papers printed by the offset process outnumbered those produced by letterpress, or hot type. A survey showed that 976 dailies, or 55 per cent of a total 1,774, were printed by offset.

The afternoon *Chicago Today* stopped publishing on September 13. Many of its features and part of its staff were absorbed by the morning *Chicago Tribune*, which became a 24-hour paper on September 16. Australian publisher Rupert Murdoch in February launched the *National Star*, a new national weekly newspaper, in the United States.

Knight Newspapers and Ridder Publications merged November 30. The new company, Knight-Ridder Newspapers, publishes 33 dailies with a total daily circulation of 3.5 million.

Advertising revenue in U.S. newspapers now exceeds $7.6 billion annually, with more than half of the total coming from retail ads.   Gerald B. Healey

NICARAGUA. See LATIN AMERICA.

NIGER. President Hamani Diori, who led the country to independence in 1960, was overthrown on April 15, 1974, by a military coup headed by Lieutenant Colonel Seyni Kountche. Kountche became head of a 12-man military junta. Reportedly, the rebel officers placed Diori under arrest. The new regime said that 10 persons, including Diori's wife, were killed in the coup. But other reports claimed 100 persons were killed.

The officers charged that Diori's government had failed to deal with the effects of the six-year drought ravaging Niger and other nations south of the Sahara. However, many observers suspected French involvement in the coup. France had been displeased because Diori reportedly tried to attract other foreign investment in Niger's large uranium deposits.

Kountche denied that the coup had foreign backing. The military government said it would review Niger's 1960 defense agreement with France, and in May, it ordered French troops to leave Niger.

The new regime reopened uranium-development negotiations with France and concluded investment agreements with Germany and Japan. Negotiations were also underway with Spanish and U.S. uranium interests.

The people continued to suffer from the African drought, though substantial rains fell in June for the first time in years.   John Storm Roberts

See also AFRICA (Facts in Brief Table).

NIGERIA. President Yakubu Gowon postponed in October, 1974, the return to civilian rule scheduled for 1976. Gowon said he feared a return to "the old cutthroat politics that once led this nation into serious crisis." He also continued the ban on political activity. Some observers believed his decision resulted from unrest in the northern part of the country in September, which was aggravated by the publication of controversial census results.

The Census. Provisional 1973 census figures issued in May, 1974, indicated that Nigeria's population had reached nearly 80 million persons, an increase of about 24 million since the 1963 census was taken.

The greatest population increase was in northern Nigeria, which appeared to have doubled its population. Other regions charged the northerners with rigging the census, but the northerners claimed they had been undercounted in the 1963 census. Census is a sensitive political issue, because political representation and distribution of development funds are based on population. President Gowon announced in July that a mini-census would be held to check disputed figures. He was anxious to play down the controversy because allegations of rigging in 1963 fueled much of the dissension that led in 1967 to the Nigerian civil war.

After the census figures were released, those who advocated an increase in the number of states from 12 to as many as 24 stepped up their demands. They claimed this would allow greater representation of minority ethnic groups. Opponents of the idea feared this would polarize Nigeria's 250 ethnic groups. There was also debate on how new states should be created. Some suggested that the government issue a decree. Others wanted the matter settled by a constitutional convention.

The Schools. Nigeria prepared for its first year of free primary education beginning in 1976. In September, a crash course was launched to train about 44,000 teachers. The government expected an enrollment of up to 3 million children the first year.

Student unrest forced four universities to shut down in February. The student rioting began at Ibadan University, where police and students clashed during a memorial service for a student killed during a demonstration three years before.

The Economy. As of April 1, Nigeria took a 55 per cent interest in foreign oil companies. In July, Nigeria decided to sell its oil at a cut-rate price to other African nations. There was a record trade surplus for the first half of 1974, with oil producing 90 per cent of Nigeria's revenue.

The African drought hurt northern Nigerian states, cutting down on the peanut harvest. So in February, Nigeria, the world's largest peanut exporter, cut off all peanut shipments for the year. A report issued in April said that $75 million worth of livestock had perished.   John Storm Roberts

See also AFRICA (Facts in Brief Table).

NIXON, RICHARD MILHOUS (1913-   ), 37th President of the United States, faced his bitterest crisis in 1974, the loss of his high office. He was forced to resign the presidency at noon on August 9. Nixon then secluded himself at San Clemente, Calif., facing legal battles, financial difficulties, and a serious phlebitis condition that threatened his life.

The Fall. Throughout 1974, Nixon lived in the shadow of the Watergate scandal. Secretly taped White House conversations with his closest aides provided evidence that he was involved in the Watergate cover-up. He withheld this incriminating evidence until a decision by the Supreme Court of the United States in July forced him to release the tapes. He made the evidence public on August 5 and was forced to announce his resignation three days later. Former Vice-President Gerald R. Ford took office on August 9. See PRESIDENT OF THE UNITED STATES; WATERGATE; Section Two, FROM TRIUMPH TO TRAGEDY.

On October 2, a Senate subcommittee reported that the government had spent $415,000 to support Nixon during his first six weeks out of office. Ford requested $850,000 from Congress to cover Nixon's expenses through June, 1975. But in December Congress voted Nixon only $200,000.

The Pardon. On September 8, President Ford granted, and Nixon accepted, a pardon for any fed-eral crimes Nixon committed or may have committed while in office. This created a national furor, but Ford stated that Nixon's acceptance of the pardon clearly implied his guilt.

President Ford, in August, also agreed to give Nixon sole control over more than 350,000 presidential documents and 950 White House tapes. But there was strong congressional and judicial opposition to the agreement.

On November 11, the White House agreed to give special Watergate prosecutor Henry S. Ruth, Jr., access to all of Nixon's records. On December 9, Congress passed a measure giving the government complete and permanent custody of all of Nixon's tapes and presidential papers. Nixon will have access to, but not control over, the material.

Failing Health. After his resignation, Nixon was reported to be worn, withdrawn, and depressed. Meanwhile, lawyers for defendants in the Watergate cover-up trial in Washington, D.C., tried to force the former President to testify. However, it became increasingly apparent that Nixon was seriously ill.

On September 23, he entered Memorial Hospital Medical Center in Long Beach, Calif., for treatment of chronic phlebitis and blood clots in his left leg. On September 25, his physician, John C. Lungren, revealed that part of a blood clot in his left leg had traveled to the lung, damaging an area the size of a

The Nixons, flanked by Edward and Tricia Cox, left, and Julie and David Eisenhower, pose for their last White House family picture on August 7.

With wife, Pat, and daughter Tricia, Richard
Nixon leaves a Long Beach, Calif., hospital
in October after treatment for phlebitis.

dime. Nixon left the hospital on October 4 but re-entered on October 23.

On October 29, he underwent surgery to block off a vein in his left leg and thus prevent more blood clots from traveling to his heart or lungs. He went into shock after the surgery and was in critical condition for several days.

Nixon improved slowly and left the hospital on November 14. However, a team of doctors appointed by U.S. District Judge John J. Sirica determined that Nixon was too ill to testify in 1974.

Tax Problems. In December, 1973, Nixon had requested the congressional Joint Committee on Internal Revenue Taxation to rule on his tax deductions. In January, the Internal Revenue Service (IRS) began rechecking his tax returns.

Subsequently, the IRS disallowed his $576,000 tax deduction for giving his vice-presidential papers to the nation. The IRS also ruled that he had to pay capital gains taxes on two real estate deals.

The Joint Committee on Internal Revenue Taxation made its report public on April 3. It criticized the President's use of public funds for his personal benefit and concluded that he owed $444,022 in federal income taxes from 1969 to 1972. On April 3, Nixon announced he would pay an IRS assessment of $432,787.13 in back taxes plus interest.

Nixon faced more than 30 private lawsuits growing out of the Watergate scandal.   Carol L. Thompson

NOBEL PRIZES in peace, literature, economics, and science were presented in 1974. The formal ceremony in Stockholm, Sweden, was marked by the appearance of Alexander Solzhenitsyn to receive the prize for literature awarded to him in 1970. He did not receive it then because he feared Russian authorities would not allow him to return to his home. See LITERATURE (Close-Up).

Peace Prize was given to former Prime Minister Eisaku Sato of Japan and Sean MacBride of Ireland, the United Nations (UN) commissioner for Namibia (South West Africa). Sato, 73, was cited for policies that led Japan to pledge, through signing a treaty to stop the spread of nuclear weapons, never to acquire such arms of its own. The citation also said his policies contributed to stabilizing conditions in the Pacific area. MacBride, 70, was honored for his work on behalf of human rights. He supervises UN efforts to gain independence from South Africa for the territory of Namibia. His citation, however, covered work in such organizations as Amnesty International, a group of which he is chairman, that works on behalf of political prisoners.

Literature Prize was shared by two Swedish writers regarded as literary giants in their own country but virtually unknown elsewhere. Eyvind Johnson, 74, has written novels and short stories based on his early, hard life in northern Sweden. He was cited for "a narrative art, far-seeing in lands and ages, in the service of freedom." Harry Edmund Martinson, 70, is a poet, novelist, essayist, and dramatist whose best-known work outside Sweden is a long narrative poem called "Anaira." He was praised for writings "that catch the dewdrop and reflect the cosmos."

Economic Science Prize was jointly awarded to Swedish economist Gunnar Myrdal, 75, and Austrian economist Friedrich August von Hayek, 75, for "their pioneering work in the theory of money and economic fluctuations and for their penetrating analysis of the interdependence of economic, social, and institutional phenomena." The two economists have usually taken opposite positions on the ways to solve world problems, however. In 1944, Myrdal published a 1,438-page study of race relations in the United States, *An American Dilemma: The Negro Problem and Modern Democracy*, which is considered a classic in the field of social studies. Von Hayek is well known for his book *The Road to Serfdom*, which held that mild, piecemeal reforms lead inevitably to evil forms of totalitarianism.

Chemistry Prize was awarded to Paul J. Flory, 64, professor of chemistry at Stanford University in California. He received the award for his work in polymer chemistry, which he began more than 30 years earlier at the Du Pont Experimental Station in Wilmington, Del. He was a member of the team of researchers that developed nylon, one of the earliest synthetic polymers to receive wide application.

Physics Prize was given jointly to two British radio astronomers, Sir Martin Ryle, 56, and Antony Hewish, 50, both of Cambridge University, for their pioneering research in radio astrophysics. Ryle was cited for devising a technique known as aperture synthesis, in which several small radio telescopes can be operated in concert to achieve the observational power of a single, large radio telescope with a dish-shaped antenna several miles or kilometers in diameter. Hewish was honored for his decisive role, using radio telescopes, in the discovery of pulsars.

Physiology and Medicine Prize went to three pioneers in cell biology who have made many contributions to the understanding of how living cells work. They are Albert Claude, 75, who heads the Jules Bordet Institute in Brussels, Belgium; George Emil Palade, 61, of Yale University, New Haven, Conn.; and Christian Rene de Duve, 57, who holds appointments at both Rockefeller University in New York City and the University of Louvain in Belgium. Claude was born in Luxembourg, and Palade was born in Romania, though both are now American citizens. De Duve, born in England of Belgian parents, is a Belgian citizen.   Foster Stockwell

NORTH ATLANTIC TREATY ORGANIZATION (NATO). See EUROPE.

NORTH CAROLINA. See STATE GOVERNMENT.

NORTH DAKOTA. See STATE GOVERNMENT.

NORTHERN IRELAND entered 1974 with hopes for peace and reconciliation higher than at any time since the present troubles started in 1969. The year ended with the ominous smell of an impending civil war in the Ulster air. An event unique in the history of Ulster took place on Jan. 1, 1974. Protestant and Roman Catholic politicians formed a government to run the province together. But the dreams of the moderates were shattered in May when militant Protestant loyalists, opposed to sharing power with republican Catholics, organized a general strike that brought the province to its knees and forced the collapse of the power-sharing Executive. The British government, its policy in ruins, had no alternative but to resume direct rule.

Loyalist Opposition. The 11-man executive body was part of an Anglo-Irish deal on Ulster. The first blow to that agreement came only a week after the executive body took power when the Unionist Party rank and file refused to accept the agreement. Brian Faulkner, the Unionist Party leader and executive body chief, was forced to resign as party leader. The Unionist Party joined with Protestant hard-liners Ian Paisley and William Craig in a loyalist coalition that bitterly opposed the work of the executive body in the Assembly.

Faulkner's moderate line cost him the support of most Protestants, who resented sharing power with

East Belfast Protestants celebrate the news that the Executive, a joint Protestant-Roman Catholic ruling body, has collapsed.

a party (the Catholic Social Democratic and Labor Party) committed to a united Ireland. As a result, there was a loyalist landslide in the February general election, with 11 of Ulster's 12 seats in the British Parliament going to the Protestant militants.

Meanwhile, the Irish Republican Army continued to kill, maim, and destroy. In April, Ulster's terrorist death toll since 1969 passed the 1,000 mark. Power sharing had not brought peace.

The General Strike was called by the Ulster Workers' Council (UWC) in May. Industrial and commercial life ground to a halt, serious food and power shortages developed, and Protestant paramilitary groups threw up barricades in loyalist areas. The crunch came when the UWC stopped gasoline and oil supplies. On May 28, Britain's secretary of state for Ulster, Merlyn Rees, refused Faulkner's request for negotiations with the strikers. Faulkner and his Unionist ministers then resigned, bringing down the government. The strike ended the next day.

In July, Rees proposed elections for a constitutional convention to decide the future government of the province. However, in the October general election, the loyalists increased their share of the vote from 52 to 58 per cent. Any constitutional convention was bound to produce a large loyalist majority opposed to power sharing, and so be unacceptable to the British. Andrew F. Neil

See also EUROPE (Facts in Brief Table).

NORWAY announced plans on Sept. 26, 1974, to extend its offshore fishing limits off the northern coast to 50 nautical miles in 1975 and to 200 nautical miles at a later date. Minister of Fisheries Eivind Bolle had said in August that the inconclusive international Law of the Sea Conference in Caracas, Venezuela, "cannot prevent us from taking measures on a national basis." See OCEAN.

In November, Norway discussed with Russia their conflicting claims to offshore oil-exploration rights on the Arctic Sea floor, north of the 70th parallel. This region is an extension of the continental shelf where large quantities of oil have been found. Russia's claim to a share comes from possession of the Novaya Islands, north of the Russian mainland.

Labor Party Woes. Leadership problems plagued the Labor Party, which has dominated Norway's politics since the 1930s. Secretary-General Ronald Bye announced his resignation on August 29, and Prime Minister Trygve Bratteli said he would not continue as party chairman in 1975. Feuds over European Community (Common Market) membership precipitated the leadership crisis.

On April 21, the Communists, Socialist People's Party, Independent Laborites, and Independent Socialists formed a left wing Radical Party.

Stable Growth characterized Norway's economy despite inflationary pressures from abroad. Increasing offshore oil production minimized the effects of the energy crisis. In fact, Norwegian oil production was expected to match total domestic oil and natural gas use in 1975.

Integrating the new wealth from oil into the economy poses a major problem. The Ministry of Finance plans to limit oil production and hold annual increases in domestic spending for consumer goods and services to $1.05 billion – about 50 per cent of the expected oil revenue in 1980 when production is expected to peak. The plan encourages foreign offshore exploration and drilling investments north of the 62nd parallel, but only under strong government control. Norway shocked the oil companies in early December by proposing a 90 per cent tax on North Sea oil profits.

Finance Minister Per Kleppe presented the 1975 budget to the Storting (parliament) on October 4. It reduces income taxes from 7 to 9 per cent for those earning between about $8,000 and $33,000. The lost revenue will be partially made up through increased public service charges and alcohol taxes, and by borrowing against future oil earnings.

In a speech from the throne, on October 2, King Olav V promised large tax cuts, fairer tax systems, and a shorter workweek for shift workers. Norway will also work to strengthen its ties with Western Europe and North America, he said. Kenneth Brown

See also EUROPE (Facts in Brief Table).

NOVA SCOTIA. See CANADA.

NUTRITION. The reports of Nutrition Canada, the largest national survey of nutrition ever undertaken, were published in 1974. The Canadian government project, which surveyed 19,000 people, began in 1969. It revealed no major health problems resulting from poor nutrition in the general population, but identified many areas for dietary improvement. According to the report, many Canadians are overweight – 40 per cent of those between 20 and 39 years of age and 60 per cent of those 40 or older. The data confirmed smaller studies that had indicated that obese people do not appear to consume greater amounts of food than lean people.

The Canadian survey also revealed that the lower caloric intake of women resulted in their getting less protein, vitamins (except ascorbic acid), and minerals. Figures for Indians and Eskimos revealed the effects of social deprivation, though data for the general population indicated that level of income is not a strong factor in determining diet quality.

Children in Danger. Adequate diet is a critical issue around the world. Protein supplies for people in the developing countries are especially inadequate.

The World Health Organization (WHO) says that 1 million children in Latin America are suffering from severe malnutrition and 10 million more are only slightly better off. Africa has 3 million children with severe cases of malnutrition and 16-million with less severe symptoms. About 6 million

"Here you've just had a nice low-cholesterol, low-cal breakfast of egg white, corn oil, skim milk, lecithin, mono- and diglycerides, propylene glycol monostearate, cellulose and xantha gums; trisodium and triethyl citrate, fortified with thiamin, riboflavin, and vitamin D; decaffeinated coffee with nutritive lactose and soluble saccharino . . . and you're still not happy?"

Drawing by Stan Hunt; © 1974 The New Yorker Magazine, Inc.

Asian children do not have enough food and another 64 million have barely enough. WHO estimated that 10 million children in the world are in danger of dying from malnutrition, and more than one-third of them experienced such deprivation that they will die even if food could now be furnished. Another 90 million children, their young bodies made defenseless by prolonged malnutrition, could hardly survive common infectious diseases.

Protein Supply. Much malnutrition is caused by the lack of protein in the diet. Traditional sources of protein such as meat and fish are presently in short supply and what is available is extremely expensive. Smaller corn and soybean crops in 1974 aggravated an already serious world protein shortage.

Soybean protein is now being used to produce inexpensive meat substitutes. It supplied 96 million pounds (44 million kilograms) of such products during 1974 in the United States alone. But, even though making meat and cheese substitutes from the soybean is less wasteful than using the beans as animal feed, these products are still too expensive for poor people in developing countries.

The world's poor have eaten other legumes for a long time. But recently they have ignored other beans and peas in favor of the soybean and such startlingly productive crops as the new hybrid wheat and rice varieties. Samuel Kon and his colleagues at the U.S. Department of Agriculture's Regional Re-

search Laboratory in Berkeley, Calif., have examined the possibility of using such crops as garbanzo, fava, lima beans, and lentils, as well as winter and garden peas, to make a high-protein product. Careful nutritional studies of the California small white and pinto beans revealed the possibility of making a product with nearly the same nutritional value as the original bean sources. Fortification with other forms of protein could increase the value almost to that of the milk proteins. While more research must be done before such products can be used, the recent loss of much of the soybean crop indicates that it is unwise to depend on only one protein source.

Foolish Food Fads. Many nutritionists have become alarmed at the popularity of unsound dietary fads and practices. Edward H. Rearson, emeritus professor of medicine at the Mayo Clinic and Mayo Foundation, surveyed various practices, ranging from those propounded by the late Adelle Davis to Zen macrobiotics. Checking references to the scientific literature from Davis' books *Let's Get Well* and *Let's Eat Right to Keep Fit*, he found few articles that could be verified. Moreover, when researching the reported testimonials of noted nutritionists, Rearson said that none had been contacted by Davis and that most felt they had been quoted out of context. He also debunked current fads involving vitamin E, hypoglycemia, and Zen macrobiotic foods. Paul F Araujo

OAKLAND, CALIF. See SAN FRANCISCO-OAKLAND.

OCEAN. During the summer of 1974, a joint expedition named FAMOUS (French-American Mid-Ocean Undersea Study) explored a section of the Mid-Atlantic Ridge ocean floor about 200 miles (320 kilometers) southwest of the Azores. Three manned deep-ocean research craft–the French bathyscaph *Archimede*, America's deep-diving submarine *Alvin*, and the French *Cyana*–roamed across a major rift valley that splits the ridge some 1.6 miles (2.6 kilometers) below the ocean surface. The rift marks the border along which the African and North American plates of the earth's crust are inching apart, and material flows upward to fill the gap.

The scientists mapped the ocean floor's topography and geology and brought up samples that would help determine the origin of the earth's crust, conditions under which metallic ores are formed, and the nature of mid-ocean earthquakes. These subjects are related to the mid-ocean ridge system, which winds some 40,000 miles (64,000 kilometers) beneath the world's oceans. See GEOLOGY.

The Missing Piece. Scientists on the U.S. Deep Sea Drilling Project (DSDP), searching the floor of the South Atlantic Ocean in April and May, found the last piece in the great South America/Africa continental jigsaw puzzle. They located the finger-shaped extension of the Falkland Plateau that reaches eastward to a point about 1,600 miles (2,600 kilometers) from the South American mainland. This filled a gap in scientists' reconstruction of Gondwanaland, the ancient southern supercontinent. The rocks that proved the piece's origin are believed to be more than 600 million years old – the oldest ever brought up from the bottom of any ocean.

Operating within 20 miles (32 kilometers) of the project FAMOUS site, the DSDP surface ship *Glomar Challenger* later drilled a record 1,910 feet (580 meters) into oceanic basement rock. In hundreds of previous samplings of the oceanic crust throughout the world, the *Challenger* had penetrated only 260 feet (179 meters) into the volcanic rocks beneath the ocean floor. The record drill core samples revealed alternate layers of deep-sea sediments and volcanic rocks that probably formed some 3.5 million years ago on what was then the floor of the Mid-Atlantic Ridge rift valley.

A 10-month expedition in the Pacific Ocean by the research vessel *Melville*, seeking a detailed understanding of the stirring and mixing processes at work in the Atlantic and Pacific oceans, was completed in June. It was the second phase of the Geochemical Ocean Section Study.

Scientists confirmed that cold, dense Antarctic bottom water flows north in the deep Pacific beneath a 4-million-square-mile (10-million-square-kilometer) sloping surface. The flow creates a *benthic front* – similar to weather fronts marking the interface of cold and warm air masses in the atmosphere. The front begins about 2,300 miles (3,700 kilometers) east of New Zealand at a depth of about 8,000 feet (2,400 meters) and extends northward, marking the boundary between the Central Pacific deep-water mass and the Antarctic bottom-water mass. Beyond the latitude of Hawaii, the subsurface front could no longer be detected.

Laws and Policies. The Third United Nations Conference on Law of the Sea was held in Caracas, Venezuela, from June 20 through August 29. The session ended without agreement on terms of a new international treaty to replace the current law covering the oceans. The concept of a 12-nautical-mile territorial sea limit and a 200-nautical-mile economic zone limit was all but formally agreed to, however, subject to the acceptable resolution of such thorny issues as transit of merchant and military vessels through straits, total freedom of scientific research, and seabed mining.

The U.S. National Advisory Committee on Oceans and Atmosphere, in its third annual report in June, reflected concern for food production and pollution. By understanding the behavior of the oceans and the atmosphere and their relationship, the report says, scientists can relate them, through climate, to agricultural productivity and the capacity to absorb waste heat and materials from industrial enterprises.

Arthur G. Alexiou

Missing Continental Interlock Found

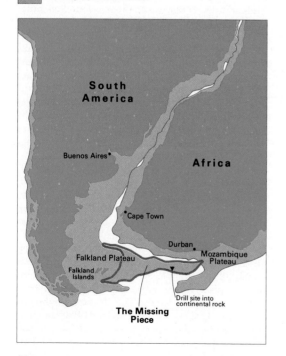

☐ Submerged parts of continents

South America

Africa

Buenos Aires

Africa

Cape Town

Durban

Falkland Plateau

Mozambique Plateau

Falkland Islands

Drill site into continental rock

The Missing Piece

ODUBER QUIRÓS, DANIEL (1921-   ), was elected president of Costa Rica on Feb. 3, 1974, and took office on May 8. He called for constitutional reform to strengthen the executive branch, and promised continuation of the government's liberal policies.

Oduber Quirós was born in the capital city of San José and worked his way through law school by working in the local telegraph office. He practiced law briefly in San José, then studied at McGill University in Montreal, Canada, and the Sorbonne in Paris.

At 19, he helped form the Center for the Study of National Problems, a group that eventually provided the momentum for a revolution in 1948. The National Liberation Party was founded in 1951, and Oduber became its secretary general in 1956.

Oduber made his first unsuccessful bid for the presidency in 1961. From 1962 to 1966, he was foreign minister and strongly supported Alliance for Progress. In 1966, he tried again for the presidency, narrowly losing the election. From 1970 to 1973, he served as president of the Legislative Assembly.

Oduber is known as a quiet politician and a behind-the-scenes negotiator. He and his wife, Marjorie Elliot of Canada, have one son, Luis Adrian. Oduber devotes his free time to a cattle ranch in the north of Costa Rica.

Kathryn Sederberg

OHIO. See CLEVELAND; STATE GOVERNMENT.

OKLAHOMA. See STATE GOVERNMENT.

OLD AGE. President Gerald R. Ford signed the Employee Retirement Income Security Act of 1974 on Labor Day, September 2. The act establishes federal standards for private pension plans and prevents loss of benefits. Although some economists criticized the law, Bernard E. Nash, executive director of the American Association of Retired People, favored it. "This legislation represents the greatest single achievement since the enactment of social security for the income security of millions of Americans in their retirement years," he said.

The act substantially repairs two notable weaknesses in private pension plans that cover more than 30 million persons. It protects retired employees against deterioration of a particular company pension fund because of company bankruptcy or mismanagement of the money in its fund. The law sets up a government-supervised Pension Benefit Guarantee Corporation that is, in effect, an insurance agency to guarantee pension payments if a particular pension fund runs into difficulties. The new agency is patterned after the Federal Deposit Insurance Corporation, which insures bank depositors.

The pension law also provides *portability* to workers who change jobs. A person who leaves a job before reaching retirement age is nevertheless eligible to receive whatever benefits he has earned when he reaches retirement age. If the new employer agrees, the worker's credits can be transferred from the old to the new pension fund when the worker moves from one job to another.

The combination of social security benefits and private pension plan payments will place from one-third to one-half of elderly Americans in a reasonably secure economic position. But the majority of elderly Americans will not be covered by private pension plans unless such plans are substantially expanded in the future. See SOCIAL SECURITY.

Social Services. The Administration on Aging put into action a national plan for coordinating social services for the elderly through state and local agencies. Under the plan, each state will have a Department of Aging, with a number of area agencies, each serving a dozen or more rural counties or a large city. These agencies will plan and coordinate the services of private and public service organizations so as to meet housing, nutrition, health, and social assistance needs.

In May, Congress established a National Institute on Aging at the government-supported National Institutes of Health (NIH) in Bethesda, Md. The institute will support research on the biomedical and social aspects of aging, much as the other NIH agencies deal with cancer, mental health, and child development. In October, the House of Representatives established a permanent Committee on Aging for investigative purposes.   Robert J. Havighurst

Margaret Kuhn, right, leads Gray Panthers, the group she organized to fight discrimination against the elderly, in a Chicago protest.

OLYMPIC GAMES. The International Olympic Committee (IOC), meeting in Vienna, Austria, in October, 1974, awarded the 1980 Olympic Summer Games to Moscow and the 1980 Winter Games to Lake Placid, N.Y. Moscow and Los Angeles, the 1932 host, were the only candidates for the Summer Games. Moscow won by about a 2-to-1 vote margin, partly because a North American city (Montreal) had already been awarded the 1976 games and partly because an Eastern European city never had been an Olympic host. As Comte Jean de Beaumont of the IOC, said, "It's good that the ideal of the Olympic movement opens a new country."

At first, five cities sought the 1980 Winter Games, but four dropped out. When Vancouver, Canada, withdrew two weeks before the voting, only Lake Placid remained. The town of 3,000 in the Adirondack Mountains of upstate New York had been host of the 1932 Winter Olympics. Before the voting, many feared that the IOC would discontinue the Winter Games because of overcommercialization or refuse to give them to an American city because Denver had accepted the 1976 Winter Games, then rejected them when financing fell through. The 1976 games were later awarded to Innsbruck, Austria.

São Paulo, Brazil, scheduled to stage the 1975 Pan American Games, withdrew because of financial problems and a meningitis epidemic. Mexico City quickly accepted the role of host.   Frank Litsky

OMAN. The government of Sultan Qabus bin Said made considerable progress in 1974 toward ending the nine-year rebellion in Dhofar Province. The government pressed several campaigns against the rebels, the Popular Front for the Liberation of Oman and the Arab Gulf (PFLOAG), who receive arms and sanctuary from neighboring Yemen (Aden). In March, British-trained Omani forces drove the rebels from their nearby mountain hideouts, ending the siege of Salalah, Dhofar's main city.

Official support for Qabus came from Saudi Arabia and Sudan, and Iran provided equipment and training advisers. An Arab League mediation mission met with Omani and Aden Yemeni representatives in May, but it failed to resolve their differences. Meanwhile, an electrified barrier along the Oman-Yemen border sealed off the rebels from their sanctuary. Government forces launched a major campaign against their strongholds in October.

Oman's oil-based economic boom continued. The budget issued in April envisaged revenues of $636-million and expenditures of $581 million. To aid nomadic tribesmen affected by the rebellion, the government opened community centers to provide food, medical services, and schools. William Spencer

See also MIDDLE EAST (Facts in Brief Table).

ONTARIO. See CANADA.

OPERA. See MUSIC, CLASSICAL.

OREGON. See STATE GOVERNMENT.

Tribesmen in colorful costume welcome Queen Elizabeth II to New Guinea, one stop on her tour of the Pacific Islands in February.

PACIFIC ISLANDS. A number of island territories in the Pacific Ocean moved closer to independence in 1974, against a background of rapid population increases and a search for foreign investment to raise incomes. The excitement engendered a year earlier by French nuclear tests subsided, even though France exploded another nuclear device over Mururoa Atoll on June 17. That issue remained before the International Court of Justice.

Independence Gains. The anticipation of full independence for Papua New Guinea by December 1 faded as the year went on. Papua New Guinea, an Australian territory, had gained full internal self-government on Dec. 1, 1973, and the goal of complete independence had the full support of the Australian government. Delay arose, however, from controversy within Papua New Guinea about its future constitution. A majority of the constitutional planning committee, which reported in July, wanted a parliamentary system with no head of state. A minority of the committee, including Chief Minister Michael Somare, favored a presidential system. There were also disputes over the role to be played by provincial assemblies and the eligibility for citizenship of Europeans and people of mixed ancestry.

Discussion continued between the United States and Micronesia over that territory's future status. A joint compact, applying to the Caroline and Marshall island groups, was announced on August 8; the Marianas were to be treated separately. Subject to approval at a plebiscite, the compact provided that the new government of the area would have full responsibility for internal affairs. The United States would be responsible for foreign affairs and defense, and would have the right to continue its military installations. It would also provide postal and aviation services, and much greater financial assistance than it had previously offered. United States currency would continue to circulate.

Some British islands also moved toward self-government. The first chief minister in the Solomon Islands, Solomon Mamaloni, took office on August 27. The Gilbert and Ellice Islands began to operate under a new and more representative Constitution, though there were doubts whether the Ellice islanders would want to remain linked to the Gilberts.

There were two exceptions to the general independence movement. The voters of American Samoa on June 18 rejected for the third time proposals for an elected governor and lieutenant governor. The majority continued to prefer U.S. appointees. And Sir Albert Henry, chief minister of the Cook Islands, a New Zealand dependency, announced at one stage that he was seeking independence, but later said he would prefer integration with New Zealand.

Pacific Organizations. There were moves toward merging the South Pacific Conference and the South Pacific Commission, with some of the newly independent states feeling that the latter did not provide them with sufficient scope. The fifth annual meeting of the South Pacific Forum in Rarotonga in March was the first attended by Papua New Guinea as a full member. The area's independent diplomacy was illustrated at this meeting by a dispute over regional airline policy. Certain states wished to set up national airlines to compete with Air Pacific, which is primarily Fijian, but also serves other governments. In addition, Australia and New Zealand were criticized for not providing more opportunities for immigrants from the island states.

Economic Change. All the major Pacific islands were involved in the quest for economic growth. The New Hebrides, known as a tax haven, benefited increasingly from foreign investment. An announcement by Rogers C. B. Morton, U.S. secretary of the interior, that Micronesia would be opened to business and commercial investment from all countries raised the prospect of greatly increased Japanese investment in the territory.

The problems of massive foreign investment were underlined by the response of Papua New Guinea to the declaration of Bougainville Copper's profit of $145.8 million in 1973. Protracted negotiations with the government followed, resulting in a new agreement that greatly increased the government's income from this mining venture. J. D. B. Miller

PAINTING. See VISUAL ARTS

PAKISTAN. Prime Minister Zulfikar Ali Bhutto seemed to be in perpetual motion in 1974. He restlessly crisscrossed the four provinces left to Pakistan after the war of 1971 haranguing thousands at meetings and holding *katchery* (court) to hear their grievances. He told his listeners that, despite the loss of Bangladesh, Pakistan was still a dynamic nation whose voice was heard throughout the world with respect.

But Bhutto's ability to inspire the people had lost much of its earlier luster. Slogans now appeared on the walls demanding the release of political prisoners, and the government tried to silence opposition by rigidly censoring radio, television, and newspapers. Opposition leaders were denied the right to address mass meetings, and some were arrested. Many people still agreed, however, that no one else could hold the troubled nation together better than Bhutto did.

The Woes. The war had left Pakistan with less than half its original population and with its morale shattered. In 1973 there were disastrous floods, and 1974 brought the oil crisis, a severe drought, and a disastrous earthquake that took at least 5,300 lives (see DISASTERS). Also, the market for Pakistan's raw cotton and textiles shrank in the global recession, while its oil bill soared from $60 million in fiscal 1973 to nearly $400 million in fiscal 1975. Prices went up 25 per cent, and the state had to subsidize essentials. The government tightened its control over the eco-

nomic life of the country in January by nationalizing Pakistan's 15 private banks as well as its shipping and oil-distributing industries.

Separatist Movements in the provinces of Baluchistan and the North-West Frontier were openly backed by Afghanistan, which apparently dreamed of carving the state of Pakhtunistan out of Pakistan's western flank. Bombs exploded in Quetta, capital of Baluchistan, and rebel tribesmen went into the hills to wage guerrilla war in the North-West Frontier. Bhutto used his troops, played one chieftain against others, and imprisoned some of the rebels. But it was to no avail. In September, he took away the last vestige of independence from the mountain state of Hunza in the disputed Kashmir boundary area between India and Pakistan, which has been under the protection of Pakistan.

Bhutto was only a little more successful in dealing with the small Ahmadi Moslem sect, which the Islamic clergy wanted excommunicated. After calling out troops in July to stop religious riots, he finally bowed to the clergy.

Peace Returns. Bhutto recognized the independence of Bangladesh, but his visit there in June yielded only discord. Things went better with India. He reacted with fury to the Indian nuclear test in May. But in the fall, he approved trade, postal, telephone, and air links with India. Mark Gayn

See also ASIA (Facts in Brief Table).

PANAMA. The government cracked down on alleged subversive groups early in 1974. On January 16, five members of the National Civilista Front were arrested and charged with trying to change Panama's form of government and subvert public order. The organization's activities were allegedly financed by Panamanian exiles in the United States.

The government also moved against two other elements of opposition in January. One of these was the National Civic Movement (NCM), which met in the Panama City Chamber of Commerce Building. The government warned the chamber as well as proprietors of other public halls to deny access to the NCM. The government also barred publication of the new newspaper *Quiubo* because of antigovernment bias.

A new treaty covering the continuing use by the United States of the Panama Canal and Zone was discussed in 1974. On February 7, U.S. Secretary of State Henry A. Kissinger and Panamanian Foreign Minister Juan Antonio Tack signed a pact in Panama City setting forth eight principles that would serve as guidelines in negotiations for a new treaty. Under its provisions, the United States would eventually transfer sovereignty over the waterway to Panama.

However, strong opposition developed in the U.S. Congress. On March 29, nearly one-third of the Senate publicly opposed surrendering U.S. sovereignty rights. Paul C. Tullier

See also LATIN AMERICA (Facts in Brief Table).

PARAGUAY. On Aug. 14, 1974, President Alfredo Stroessner called upon the nation's various political parties to hold "a national dialogue" in the interests of "harmony within the country." He suggested that cooperation might lead to the easing of some restrictive government policies, including press censorship and tight controls over political gatherings.

Most groups indicated a willingness to cooperate, but the Radical Liberal Party – the largest opposition group in Paraguay – expressed reservations. It indicated that its members might participate, but only if the government proved its good faith by first easing its restrictions.

Political Prisoners and the high cost of living aroused dissatisfaction during the year. In late February, hundreds of students and peasants demonstrated in Asunción, demanding the immediate release of many who have been in jail since 1958, when the Paraguayan Communist Party was outlawed. The government, however, considered the demonstrations subversive, and about 100 students were arrested and turned over to military tribunals for trial and sentencing.

Another source of unrest was the soaring cost of living, which rose 60 per cent during the last eight months of 1973 and 20 per cent in the first quarter of 1974. One consequence was a demand by the Paraguayan Workers Confederation (PWC), the nation's only legal labor organization, for a wage increase from the government. It was the first such demand made by the PWC in several years.

Economic Development. Texaco, Incorporated, an American-owned firm, signed an agreement with the government in January covering all exploration and exploitation rights in the Chaco region in northwestern Paraguay. In February, bids were accepted for the building of a cement plant that would supply 1,000 short tons (907 metric tons) a day for the massive Itaipu and Apipe-Yacireta hydroelectric projects under construction. The Itaipu project, being built at an estimated cost of $2 billion, was a joint venture with Brazil. Apipe-Yacireta was being carried out as a joint venture with Argentina.

In March, Paraguay signed a pact under which Argentina agreed to supply oil for domestic consumption. It marked an effort by the Stroessner regime to ease an oil shortage during which gasoline had risen to $1 a gallon (3.8 liters). In November, an agreement covering purchases of wheat and industrial products was signed with Argentina.

In other developments, work began early in the year on a new $17.2-million airport at Asunción. The facility was being financed almost entirely through a $15.4-million loan provided by the Argentine Central Bank. In March, the government announced plans to modernize 93 miles (150 kilometers) of railroad connecting Asunción and Villarica at a cost of about $47 million. Paul C. Tullier

See also LATIN AMERICA (Facts in Brief Table).

PARENTS AND TEACHERS, NATIONAL CONGRESS OF (PTA), named five priority goals at its 78th annual convention held in San Antonio, Tex., from May 19 to 22, 1974. The five areas are decision-making, improving child health, developing effective leadership, increasing membership, and improving relationships between parents, teachers, students, administrators, and the community. Action in these areas will receive priority attention.

Convention delegates also approved a national dues increase of 10 cents a year, effective in 1975. Other new amendments to the national bylaws are intended to strengthen the organizational structure and achieve greater financial stability. Delegates elected the following to two-year terms: Madelyn H. Wills, Lake Charles, La., secretary; and Martin W. Essex, Columbus, Ohio, treasurer.

The National PTA received a grant of $97,765 from the National Institute on Alcohol and Alcoholism to finance a project on alcohol education. The project will provide opportunities for parents and school-aged youths to learn about the responsible use or the nonuse of alcoholic beverages, increase parents' awareness of their role in influencing their children's drinking behavior, and help students develop and carry through their own information programs for other children. Joseph P. Anderson

PENNSYLVANIA. See PHILADELPHIA; STATE GOVERNMENT.

PÉREZ, CARLOS ANDRÉS (1923-   ), was sworn in as president of Venezuela on March 12, 1974 (see VENEZUELA). His 11-month presidential campaign featured walks – he traveled about 3,000 miles (4,800 kilometers) on foot to communicate personally with his constituents.

Pérez, the 11th of 12 children, was born in the Andean state of Tachira where his father was a coffee grower. After completing his primary studies in his hometown of Rubio, Pérez entered the Liceo Andrés Bello in Caracas. As a student, Pérez became interested in politics, joining the clandestine Democratic National Party (later Acción Democratica) at the age of 15. He remained politically active while studying law at the Central University of Venezuela from 1944 to 1947.

Following a military coup in 1948, Pérez and other political leaders sympathetic to the ousted regime were imprisoned and subsequently exiled. He did not return until 1958, following the return of civilian government. Re-entering politics, he served as a director-general in the ministry of interior and as secretary-general of the National Executive Committee of Acción Democratica. He was a deputy to the National Congress when he was elected president.

Pérez has been married for 26 years to his cousin, the former Blanca Rodriguez. They have six children and one grandchild. Pérez and his family live in a suburb of Caracas. Paul C. Tullier

PERÓN, MARÍA ESTELA (ISABEL) MARTÍNEZ DE

(1931-   ), assumed the presidency of Argentina on July 1, 1974, when her husband, President Juan Domingo Perón, died. She had served as vice-president since their election on Sept. 23, 1973. She is the first woman chief of state in the Americas. See ARGENTINA.

Isabel Perón was born in La Rioja province, northwest of Buenos Aires. The youngest of six children, she ended her formal education with the sixth grade. However, she studied piano and dance and became an entertainer. She met General Perón while on a dance tour of Central America in 1956, and became his secretary. The military had forced Perón out of the presidency in 1955. They were married in 1961 in a suburb of Madrid, Spain.

Isabel Perón first gained public attention in 1971 when she returned to Argentina from Spain to help unify her husband's political support. Following his return in 1973, he shocked his supporters by naming his politically inexperienced wife as running mate.

As vice-president, Mrs. Perón presided over Cabinet meetings and delivered speeches supporting her husband's controversial economic policies. She became acting president on June 29, after he had become seriously ill. Upon Perón's death, most political and military leaders pledged support for his widow. However, she lacks the support of the young socialistic faction of Peronists.   Robert K. Johnson

PERSONALITIES OF 1974.

United States Secretary of State Henry A. Kissinger was the man Americans most admired in 1974, according to the Gallup Poll. It was the second consecutive year he received that honor. Following in order were evangelist Billy Graham, President Gerald R. Ford, Senator Edward M. Kennedy (D., Mass.), Governor George C. Wallace of Alabama, Vice-President Nelson A. Rockefeller, former President Richard M. Nixon, Senator Barry Goldwater (R., Ariz.), former Governor Ronald Reagan of California, and Senator Henry M. Jackson (D., Wash.). Dropped from the 1973 list were consumer activist Ralph Nader and Pope Paul VI.

Golda Meir, former prime minister of Israel, topped the list of most admired women for the second straight year. She was followed by Betty Ford, wife of President Ford, a newcomer to the list. Others on the list were Mrs. Richard M. (Pat) Nixon, Mrs. Joseph (Rose) Kennedy, Mrs. Nelson (Happy) Rockefeller, U.S. Representative Shirley Chisholm (D., N.Y.), and Indian Prime Minister Indira Gandhi (tied for sixth), Mrs. Martin Luther (Coretta) King, Mrs. Lyndon B. (Lady Bird) Johnson, Mrs. Aristotle (Jacqueline Kennedy) Onassis, and Mrs. Dwight D. (Mamie) Eisenhower. Dropped were Great Britain's Queen Elizabeth II, Mrs. Robert (Ethel) Kennedy, and former Maine Senator Margaret Chase Smith.

King Faisal of Saudi Arabia was chosen as *Time* magazine's Man of the Year.

Beaumont, Michael, 47, became the 22nd seigneur of Sark in July. The tiny island in the English Channel is Great Britain's oldest and smallest dependency. Beaumont promised to continue the ways of his late grandmother, Dame Sybil Hathaway, who tried to keep the island unspoiled by the 20th century. Like her, he will allow no automobiles, no divorce, no labor unions, and no taxes on income, liquor, or cigarettes on the island.

Bernstein, Leonard, conductor and composer, joined the Massachusetts Institute of Technology faculty as a lecturer. Officials set up a special faculty seminar to study musical structure in relation to linguistics and aesthetics.

Bradley, Omar N., the United States only living general of the Army, returned to West Point on April 2 for the dedication of a library named for him. The 81-year-old, five-star general graduated from the academy in 1915. The Bradley Library will house the general's correspondence and diaries he kept while he was commander of the 12th Army Group in World War II, administrator of veterans affairs during the postwar demobilization, and chairman of the Joint Chiefs of Staff.

Brown, Lionne Kim, 22, became the first woman floor trader on the Midwest Stock Exchange in Chicago when she bought 400 shares of a utility stock in January. She is the daughter of the president of K. J.

Alan Osmond, of the singing Osmond family, hugs his fiancée, Suzanne Pinegar, a college cheerleader. The two were married in July.

Actor James Cagney, noted for 40 years of movie tough-guy roles, received the American Film Institute's Life Achievement Award in March.

Brown & Company, a brokerage firm in Muncie, Ind. Her first venture into the market came when she was 14 and traded short in rye on the commodities exchange. She started at the minimum salary for floor traders, $16,000.

Charles, Prince, of Great Britain, made his maiden speech in the House of Lords in June, but was nearly upstaged by the blond daughter of a U.S. admiral, Laura Jo Watkins, who sat in the gallery as a guest of the prince. She met Charles in March when the British Navy ship he was serving on docked in San Diego. In his speech, the prince urged more government action to promote recreation.

Cleves, Virgil, 67, of Lima, Ohio, and a female companion were arrested on March 8 for strolling in the city's public square in the nude. They were charged with public indecency. Cleves told police that he was too old for streaking; for older people, he said, it should be termed "snailing."

Dacosta, Michael, of London, found a practical use for streaking in the spring when a suit he bought began to come apart at the seams. When the store refused to replace it, Dacosta lost his temper. "I took the suit off and ran around the store naked, shouting at people not to buy anything there," he said. "That did it. They gave me a new suit immediately."

Davis, Peter, of Hockliffe, England, has earned the thanks of dozens of motorists with his ingenious use of nylon stockings. The road past his house is straight and downhill, and has caused many a fan belt to snap as the driver steps on the brake. Davis discovered the old nylons will function as a substitute fan belt until the driver can reach the nearest garage. The Davises often have five or six callers a week.

Downer, Dan, 21, an unemployed Canadian truckdriver from Nanaimo, B.C., became the 1974 world champion bathtubber in July. He crossed the 36-mile (58-kilometer) Strait of Georgia from Nanaimo to Vancouver in 1 hour 53 minutes in the Great International Bathtub Race. Over 250 craft—all remodeled bathtubs—started the race; 100 finished.

Dugan, Daniel A., 46, of Arlington, Va., has become disgusted with the government's persistence in sending out his death notice. In 1944, the Navy sent his wife a Purple Heart and a notice that he had "died in the service of his country." Then, in June, 1974, the Veterans Administration (VA) sent Mrs. Dugan condolences on his death after he applied for an allowance to buy a burial plot. On top of that, the government stopped sending his combat disability benefits. A VA spokesman called the case "unfortunate," and added: "You're bound to have these clerical errors occur."

Du Pont, Pierre S., IV, Republican congressman from Delaware, believes that political candidates should get their financial support from the people, even though he's a member of a famous family of millionaires. Facing a re-election campaign, he raised $77,000 from 4,800 contributors, none of whom gave more than $100. He said he hoped his example would embarrass members of Congress who continue to depend on business, labor, and other special-interest groups for funds.

Eustis, Brian, a Colorado college freshman from Winnetka, Ill., discovered a self-portrait of Flemish artist Jan van Eyck that had gone unrecognized for 500 years. The portrait was painted as a reflection in a pearl that appears in the crown of God in a painting over the altar of the Cathedral of St. Bavon in Ghent, Belgium. Eustis found the portrait while he was viewing slides for an art history course; he received a "B" in the course.

Frederick, Pauline, one of the first television newswomen, retired from NBC News in January. NBC's United Nations correspondent since 1953, she was the first woman to be elected president of the United Nations Correspondents Association. She plans to lecture and write in her retirement.

Getty, J. Paul, one of the world's richest men, announced in September that he would leave Great Britain and move to his estate in Malibu, Calif. His decision came after the British government announced it would tax the worldwide income of foreign residents. Getty, who has lived in England for 20 years, objected to the tax on the grounds that his income is not earned in Britain, that he employs 600 Britons, and that he spends more than $1.4 million there annually.

Hicks, Garnetta, of Covington, Ky., found a potential supply of free beef in her basement in March. A steer, escaping from a packing house, had crashed through her door and ducked down the stairs. It was soon joined by pursuing police, intent on returning it to the packing house. "The cost of beef being what it is, I was tempted to invite the steer upstairs to jump into the freezer," Hicks said later.

Horie, Kenichi, 35, returned triumphantly to Japan in May after completing a nonstop solo voyage around the world. His wife and thousands of well-wishers welcomed him as he sailed his 25-foot (7.6-meter) sloop into the harbor at Osaka on May 4. He covered 31,000 miles (50,000 kilometers) during his 276-day journey.

Jones, James, 53, American novelist, decided in February to return to the United States after 16 years in Paris. The author of *From Here to Eternity* took a year's lease on a house in Key Biscayne, Fla. "I'm tired of Europe, the French," said Jones, explaining why he was coming home. "The United States is where it's all happening today."

Knievel, Evel, daredevil motorcyclist, survived unhurt an unsuccessful attempt to rocket over the Snake River Canyon in Idaho in September. His much-publicized attempt failed when a tail parachute was released prematurely at his steam rocket's take-off. The rocket floated down into the canyon to land nose-down on a rocky bank at the river's edge. A helicopter rescued Knievel a few minutes later.

Kudirka, Simas, a Lithuanian seaman serving a 10-year sentence for trying to defect to the United States in 1970, was freed by Russian authorities in August and entered the United States on November 5. Kudirka became the focus of an international incident when he was returned to Russian authorities after he attempted to leap onto a U.S. Coast Guard cutter. His release came after it was learned that he was an American citizen because his mother had been born in New York City.

Kunst, David, 35, returned home to Waseca, Minn., in October after spending 4½ years walking around the world. During his trek, he crossed 13 countries and wore out 21 pairs of shoes. His brother John was killed by bandits in Afghanistan in 1972, but David continued the hike. On his return home, he toasted the United States as "the best damn country I've ever been in."

Lyons, Leonard, 67, stopped writing his Broadway column in May after 40 years of celebrity name-dropping. As a young lawyer, he wrote a column for the *Jewish Daily Forward* and fed items to such noted Broadway columnists as Walter Winchell and Mark Hellinger. A scrapbook of these items won him a post as their competitor on *The New York Post* in 1934. At its peak, his column, "The Lyons Den," appeared in

In the limelight: Morris, TV cat-food salesman and subject of a biography. In the money: tennis world champion John Newcombe of Australia.

about 100 newspapers with combined circulation of 13 million.

Maharaj Ji, the 16-year-old Indian guru who is said to be the spiritual leader of an estimated 6 million people associated with his Divine Light Mission, needed a court order in May when he decided to marry his secretary. He was too young to obtain a marriage license in Colorado without parental consent. The guru was married to Marolyn Lois Johnson, 24, in his Denver home.

McCoy, Danny, of Fort Worth, Tex., organized "Uglies Unlimited" in June to fight discrimination against ugly people. He said he was appalled by job application forms that require "a well-proportioned figure." Said McCoy: "The blacks, the Chicanos, and the American Indians have all had their days in the sun. Now it's time for ugly people."

Medvedev, Zhores A., exiled Russian geneticist, in August dismissed as a myth the claims that people in the Caucasus region of Russia live to be well over 100, sometimes as old as 165. He cited the lack of documented statistical records and said Russian scientists simply accepted the word of the elderly people themselves.

Mesta, Perle, Washington's "hostess with the mostest," moved to Oklahoma City in February to live with her brother. Mesta, who lived and entertained in Washington for nearly 50 years, was a tireless Democratic Party fund-raiser, and was ambassador to Luxembourg under President Harry S. Truman.

Onoda, Hiroo, 52, a Japanese lieutenant, emerged from a Philippine jungle in March after 29 years in hiding. In a formal surrender, he presented his samurai sword to Major General José Rancudo, commander of the Philippine Air Force. Onoda, an intelligence officer during World War II, told newsmen he had not come out earlier because "I had not received the order." Several searches had been conducted for him, and twice he had been declared dead. Japanese officials estimate that hundreds of other soldiers may still be hiding in the jungles.

Palmgren, Jerry, a janitor at the University of Washington in Seattle, sat down to play a "piano" in the wee hours of a January morning, and promptly aroused angry residents for miles around. While cleaning the music building, Palmgren twisted a few dials on a keyboard and started playing. But it turned out that the keyboard was connected to the university's electronic carillon, and he had it turned on full volume. His song? "The Sounds of Silence."

Petit, Philippe, French high-wire artist, tiptoed back and forth for 45 minutes on a tightrope about 1,300 feet (400 meters) above the street in New York City in August before police finally persuaded him to come down. Spectators created an early-morning traffic jam as they watched the slender Frenchman perform on a cable he and friends had secretly stretched between the twin towers of the World Trade Center overnight. "When I see two towers, I have to walk," explained Petit. Charges were dropped when he agreed to repeat his stunt at a much lower level in a city park for New York City children.

Salmon, Thomas, governor of Vermont, felt he vindicated his name in June when he caught three large salmon during a fishing trip off the coast of the state of Washington. Perhaps now people would stop teasing him about his name, he said hopefully.

Sargent, Francis W., governor of Massachusetts, tried to set a good example when he offered his official state car, a 1974 Lincoln, as guinea pig for a new machine that checks automotive emissions. But the car flunked the test, which will be required for all automobiles garaged in Boston starting in 1975.

Schaefer, Robert, of Brookfield, Wis., found an old-fashioned solution to the energy problem. He erected a tall windmill in his back yard in May. Schaefer says the windmill will provide 2,000 watts of power, enough to supply about one-third of his family's electrical needs.

Shepard, Alan B., 50, the first American in space, retired from the space program on August 1. Shepard, a rear admiral in the Navy, was one of the first seven astronauts. On May 5, 1961, he was in the cockpit of a Mercury capsule that was shot into space to begin the U.S. space program. As commander of the *Apollo 14* lunar mission in 1971, he was the fifth American to walk on the moon. He joined the Marathon Construction Company, a real estate development company in Houston, as partner and chairman.

Silverheels, Jay, the Mohawk Indian who rode with the Lone Ranger as his sidekick Tonto, began riding in a sulky behind harness horses. He obtained a license to drive in qualifying races at the Red Mile track in Lexington, Ky., and began working toward his regular license.

Streeter, Fred, celebrated his 97th birthday in June with a cake topped by his favorite flower, the primrose. Streeter, Great Britain's oldest and perhaps best-loved radio star, has been giving a regular broadcast on gardening for the British Broadcasting Corporation since 1935. He said his first contact with gardens came at the age of 2, when he fell from a window into a bed of pink carnations.

Zworykin, Vladimir K., inventor of the first practical television tube, confessed on his 85th birthday in July that the part of a TV set he likes best is the "off" switch. "When broadcasting began to develop," he said from his home in Los Angeles, "I hoped TV would be used for educational purposes, especially so that different cultures could learn to understand each other. Instead, most of the time when I turn on the TV – bang, bang, bang." The Russian-born scientist was working for Westinghouse Electric Corporation when he invented a crude TV picture tube in 1923. But when Westinghouse ignored his device, Zworykin moved over to RCA Corporation, where he remains as a consultant.   Kathryn Sederberg

PERU. Despite his failing health, President Juan Velasco Alvarado in 1974 clamped down on opposition elements in an effort to swing Peru still further to the left. He ruthlessly purged senior military officers who dissented. The navy commander, Vice-Admiral Luis Vargas Caballero, was sacked on May 31 for making critical remarks about government attempts to muzzle both the press and the Acción Popular Party, which had ruled the country until the coup in 1968.

The conflict between the regime and its critics was further aggravated on June 27, when Velasco ordered all newspapers with a circulation of over 20,000 taken over by the government. This move involved the take-over of the six major Lima dailies. Luis Miró Quesada, owner of the long-established *El Comercio*, was placed under house arrest. In due course, according to the government, the newspapers would be handed over to "organized sectors of society" such as the peasants' syndicates. The seizures prompted violent demonstrations, in which more than 500 people were arrested.

Foreign Relations. President Velasco maintained close relations with Cuba and the Russian bloc during the year. On February 25, teams of Russian military instructors entered Peru along with T-52 medium tanks, and the Russian Embassy in Lima became the largest in Latin America, excluding Havana. Raúl Castro, the Cuban defense minister, attended a big military parade in Lima on July 29.

Nationalization Program. In a speech on July 28, President Velasco revealed the details of Plan Inca—supposedly a blueprint that had been drawn up for the country by a military study group before the 1968 coup but kept secret. It stressed an accelerating process of nationalizing all private banks, financial houses, insurance firms, shipping lines, airlines, and medium-sized mining companies. The major foreign mining enterprise, the Cerro de Pasco Corporation, had been nationalized on Dec. 31, 1973.

It was a reassuring sign for some foreign investors that a compensation agreement for the Cerro Corporation and other expropriated American firms was concluded on February 15. The agreement provided for the immediate payment of $76 million to the U.S. government for distribution to the firms affected and for the payment of $74 million directly to the firms.

The Domestic Economy suffered from rising inflation that resulted from hikes in world petroleum and cereal prices. Inflation rose to an annual rate of about 30 per cent, while the foreign debt soared to more than $1.8 billion. There were serious allegations of corruption and incompetence in the official food-import organization and the state-run fish-meal industry.   Robert Moss

See also LATIN AMERICA (Facts in Brief Table).

Peru's President Juan Velasco Alvarado dons an Indian headdress to show Andean tribes his government is concerned with their needs.

PET. A growing overpopulation of pets, particularly cats and dogs, and a shortage of veterinarians caused concern in the United States in 1974. With the U.S. cat population numbering about 38 million and dogs 33 million, at least 10,000 more veterinarians are needed, according to a report by the National Academy of Sciences. Because of limited educational facilities, only 1 out of 10 applicants can be accepted into veterinary colleges. So only about 1,600 animal doctors graduate each year.

Pet Problems. The U.S. news media exposed widespread underground dog-fighting rings that sponsored fights for wagering and other commercial purposes. The revelations prompted Congress to begin considering federal legislation in September that would outlaw such fights. Dog fights are illegal in most states.

John A. Hoyt, president of the United States Humane Society, in March charged the $310-million pet-breeding industry with irresponsible practices. He said that "puppy mills" were producing too many dogs with too little regard for their quality and health. Hoyt called for strict government regulation of breeders, wholesalers, and pet shops. He also called for legislation requiring that breeders issue a health certificate for each dog and cat they sell.

Top Dogs. Ch. Gretchenhof Columbia River, a German short-haired pointer owned by Richard P. Smith of Hayward, Calif., was named best of the 3,146 dogs in the Westminster Kennel Club's 98th show held on February 11 and 12 in New York City. It was the 28th best-in-show award for the 5-year-old dog. Ch. Saliyn's Classic, an English springer spaniel owned by Julie Gasow and Barbara Gates of Birmingham, Mich., was chosen best-in-show of the 3,581 dogs at the International Kennel Club show in Chicago in March.

For the 14th consecutive year, poodles were the most popular dogs in the United States, according to registration figures released by the American Kennel Club (AKC) in April. Following in order were German shepherds, Irish setters, beagles, dachshunds, miniature schnauzers, Saint Bernards, Doberman pinschers, Labrador retrievers, and cocker spaniels, the only newcomer to the top 10. Collies dropped from 9th to 11th place. On October 1, Staffordshire bull terriers became the 121st AKC registered breed.

Top Cats. Kalico's Mary Poppins of Marvonak, a blue British shorthair female, owned by Jack and Yvonne Patrick of Vancouver, Canada, received the All-America *Cat of the Year* award of *Cats* magazine.

Best Kitten was The Island's Merryelle, a blue-point Himalayan female owned by Shirley and Don Johnes of Pottersville, N.J. *Best Alter* went to Playwickey's Sugar Ray O'Char-Fae, a black Persian neuter, owned by Charles and Fay Afflerbach of Bangor, Pa.   Theodore M. O'Leary

PETROLEUM AND GAS. The nations of the world tried to cut petroleum consumption and stepped up their search for new oil sources in 1974. The urgency in their efforts stemmed from the Arab oil embargo that started in November, 1973, and lasted until March, 1974. Even though the shortage eased after the embargo was lifted, steep increases that sent posted oil prices from $3 a barrel on Oct. 1, 1973, to $11.65 on Jan. 1, 1974, made solutions mandatory.

Most of the restrictions that many nations put on the use of petroleum products late in 1973 remained in force early in 1974. In the United States, mandatory Sunday closing of gasoline stations was in effect until March, and many stations struggled with short supplies, limiting sales to a few gallons or liters per customer. A speed limit of 55 miles (89 kilometers) per hour produced better fuel mileage.

Despite an inauspicious start, the worldwide ratio of oil supplies to oil demand improved in 1974. Instead of rising sharply as predicted, demand remained at or slightly lower than the 1973 level as a result of conservation measures and greatly increased prices for gasoline, fuel oil, and other petroleum products. Supplies increased after seven of the nine Arab oil-exporting countries at a conference held in Vienna, Austria, ended their ban on oil shipments to the United States in March. Only Libya and Syria refused to join the majority. At a second Vienna meeting in September, advisers to the Organization

Ch. Gretchenhof Columbia River, a German short-haired pointer, takes top honors in the Westminster Kennel Club show in February.

of Petroleum Exporting Countries (OPEC) recommended that crude-oil prices remain frozen at $11.65 a barrel until the end of 1974. They also urged the 12 OPEC member nations to cut back production to prevent a surplus that would push prices down. In December, OPEC raised 1975 oil prices by 4 per cent.

The long-range forecast was far from reassuring. Stringent taxes will be the only way to reduce the use of gasoline in the years to come, according to researchers at the Rand Corporation, Santa Monica, Calif. The Rand findings were released in October in a 250-page study, part of a $500,000 research program conducted for the National Science Foundation. Surtaxes of from 15 to 45 cents a gallon (3.8 liters), the study indicates, could cut gasoline use by from 16 to 40 per cent by 1980, a saving of from 11 to 27 billion gallons (42 to 102 billion liters) a year.

New Supplies Sought. As a result of such predictions and the fourfold increase in oil prices that nearly ruined many national economies, a stepped-up search got underway for alternatives to the Middle East supply. Every available drilling rig was either in action or on its way to a new location. In the United States alone, 1,500 drilling rigs were in operation, a 25 per cent increase over 1973.

Oil will be increasingly harder and more costly to tap as the search moves offshore and to some of the most remote areas of the world. Proven world reserves in 1974 were estimated at about 600 billion barrels, with about two-thirds of it in the Middle East. At the present consumption rate of about 21 billion barrels a year, this would last for less than 30 years.

The *British Petroleum Statistical Review* forecasts likely finds of about 760 billion barrels. One of the most promising recent discoveries has been made in the Reforma fields in the southeastern Mexican states of Chiapas and Tabasco, operated by the Mexican state oil company, Petroleum Mexicanos. Production there has grown in a year from less than 20,000 barrels a day to over 230,000 barrels a day. The Amazon Basin areas of Ecuador, Peru, and Colombia are the principal South American research regions. Oil reserves in the North Sea off Great Britain and Norway may contain up to 40 billion barrels. Present production is about 50,000 barrels a day.

The world's best hope for finding oil fields comparable to those of the Middle East, however, lies in the frozen lands of the American, Canadian, and Russian Arctic regions. North America's largest discovery, for instance, is on the Arctic coast of Alaska at Prudhoe Bay. Although production there is very difficult and costly, the geologic formations of the area are similar to those in the Middle East.

A newcomer in oil production is China, which is expected to produce about 2.4 million barrels a day from new finds on the mainland and in the Yellow Sea. Much of this oil will be exported because of China's low domestic consumption.

The United States is the world's most explored and

Fuel shortages and consumer panic stemming from the Arab oil embargo created long waiting lines at service stations in January and February.

drilled area, but the U.S. Geological Survey estimates that it still has between 110 billion and 214-billion barrels of undiscovered recoverable oil. There are hopes for major offshore discoveries in the Gulf of Mexico, in the Santa Barbara Channel off the California coast, in the Baltimore Canyon south of Long Island, and off Cape Cod.

Research in methods of extracting oil from shale were also intensified in 1974. Since 1972, the Garrett Research and Development Company, a subsidiary of the Occidental Petroleum Company, has been experimenting on a tract of about 4,000 acres (1,600 hectares) in western Colorado. The company is using a patented underground process based on earlier work by the U.S. Bureau of Mines. In simplified terms, the process involves fragmenting the solid shale with explosives, then heating it until the oil can be drained from it. If the United States could exploit all of the oil locked in shale formations in six government-owned areas in Colorado, Utah, and Wyoming, it could produce nearly 2 trillion short tons (1.8-trillion metric tons) of oil, several times the total world reserve. The process would be slow, difficult, and very costly, but it may be necessary in the long run.

Natural Gas. Federal, state, and industry officials warned Americans in September that the United States faces a natural gas crisis. Although shortages were expected in various parts of the country, officials said the cold Northeast would be the most seriously

Leaders of the Arab oil-producing nations agreed in March to end the oil embargo against the United States, but they did not roll back prices.

affected. The shortages will be still greater in 1975-1976, according to the experts.

Of the 42 principal interstate pipeline companies, 17 told the Federal Power Commission that they would be unable to meet 11 per cent of their delivery commitments during the November, 1974, to March, 1975, heating season, compared with a 7.2 per cent shortfall during the same 1973-1974 period. The estimated shortage of 768 billion cubic feet (22 billion cubic meters) was 61 per cent greater than a year earlier. Although deliveries to homes were not greatly affected, schools, offices, factories, and stores faced the greatest problem.

Canadian Plans. A group of Canadian companies asked the Canadian National Energy Board in October for permission to build a $2-billion domestic pipeline to natural gas fields in the Canadian Arctic. The pipeline was offered as an alternative to a proposed Canadian-American line 2,625 miles (4,224 kilometers) long and costing $6 billion that would carry Canadian and Alaskan gas to consumers in both Canada and the United States. The pipeline would carry natural gas from the Prudhoe Bay field and the Mackenzie River Delta.

Meanwhile, Canada announced that oil exports to the United States would be reduced to 800,000 barrels a day at year's end, down from 1.15 million barrels in 1973. Mary E. Jessup

See also CANADA; ENERGY.

PHILADELPHIA. The nation's bicentennial celebrations began in Philadelphia on Sept. 5, 1974, when delegates from the 13 original colonies reconvened the First Continental Congress in historic Carpenters' Hall. On Sept. 5, 1774, the original Congress had convened in the same hall, later moving its meetings a block east to the building now known as Independence Hall.

Pennsylvania Governor Milton J. Shapp hosted the two-day meeting, and President Gerald R. Ford addressed the gathering. While the delegates met inside discussing the purpose of the original Congress, a group of citizens objecting to taxation of nonresidents working in Pennsylvania demonstrated outside the hall.

The September celebration was marred by an unusual crime. Bronze plaques marking the graves of nine historic figures, including Benjamin Franklin, were stolen from the Christ Church burial grounds.

Police Corruption. The Pennsylvania Crime Commission charged on March 10 that corruption in the Philadelphia Police Department was "ongoing, widespread, systematic, and occurring at all levels." Police Commissioner Joseph O'Neill retorted that the commission's charges were not substantiated by facts and that the commission did not have the evidence necessary to initiate a major investigation. Mayor Frank L. Rizzo, a former police commissioner, said that he deplored any attempt to smear the entire police department with undocumented allegations.

According to the Federal Bureau of Investigation, serious crimes in Philadelphia increased at a rate of 6.9 per cent during the first six months of 1974. This was well below the 16 per cent rate increase experienced by the nation as a whole.

The Cost of Living in Philadelphia rose 12.2 per cent between June, 1973, and June, 1974, the second highest living cost increase among major U.S. cities. Food costs rose 16 per cent during that period, but the average factory worker's wages increased only 3.9 per cent during the year ending in July. The U.S. Department of Labor rated unemployment as "substantial," and the total number of jobs in the area declined 0.1 per cent as of July. During the same period, construction activity declined 2.6 per cent, while department store sales increased 16.9 per cent. Energy was also a problem. On January 26, Texaco, Incorporated, began rationing home heating oil in the city.

Women's Rights. Eleven women were ordained as Episcopal priests in Philadelphia's Church of the Advocate on July 29, touching off a controversy. The ordinations were not authorized by the church, and the Episcopal House of Bishops termed them invalid. See PROTESTANT.

The Pen and Pencil Club of Philadelphia, the oldest newspaperman's club in America, voted in February to accept women members.   James M. Banovetz

PHILIPPINES. Opposition to President Ferdinand E. Marcos' martial law regime increased during 1974. The main opponents were Moslem separatists in the southern islands, Maoist guerrillas, and the Roman Catholic Church, to which most Filipinos belong.

Under the banner of the Moro National Liberation Front, Moslems increased guerrilla warfare. In February, they captured the city of Jolo in the Sulu Archipelago. It was destroyed as the Philippine Army and Navy retook it. Balabagan on Mindanao Island was similarly ravaged in August. Numerous small clashes contributed to the sporadic fighting.

Libya admitted aiding the separatists, apparently through the Malaysian state of Sabah, adjacent to the Sulu Islands. Islamic nations tried to mediate the civil war, but no end was in sight.

Opposition Seethes. Twenty-seven leaders of the old Philippine Communist Party surrendered in October, after decades of fighting the government. They pledged support to Marcos. But a Maoist faction, the New People's Army, continued its guerrilla campaign on Luzon Island and expanded into the central islands.

Some Protestant protest leaders were arrested on June 26. Trying to catch Maoists, the army also raided a Jesuit novitiate on August 24. Many Catholic Church leaders had long been in conflict with the government by leading movements to reduce social and economic inequalities, but this raid brought the

Catholic hierarchy into more direct collision with Marcos. Archbishop Jaime L. Sin of Manila, the nation's leading Catholic, called for prayers for a chance to "live under a regime of truth and justice, peace and freedom." This was interpreted as a direct slap at the president and the martial law system he established in 1972.

On his 57th birthday, September 11, Marcos released five prominent men who had been detained under martial law. But a main opponent, Senator Benigno S. Aquino, Jr., and several others were still held. Marcos said in June that martial law might have to continue for five more years. In November, he offered amnesty to those persons he considers ideological subversives.

Floods in August and typhoons in October killed about 215 persons and left 1.25 million homeless. Imelda Marcos, the president's wife, led flood relief work, part of her widely publicized political and social activities. She visited China in September to pave the way for establishing diplomatic ties.

Harvests improved, but the nation continued to import its main food, rice. An International Labor Organization report warned that unbalanced economic growth would lead to "social and political unrest." Foreign investment increased, encouraged by reduced crime and other signs of stability under martial law.   Henry S. Bradsher

See also ASIA (Facts in Brief Table).

PHOTOGRAPHY saw gains in technology and artistic prestige in 1974 but suffered business setbacks that reflected the world's economic unrest. A daguerreotype of Edgar Allan Poe sold for a reported $38,000, by far the most ever paid. New York City welcomed its first museum devoted exclusively to photography, the International Center of Photography, headed by photojournalist Cornell Capa. And Minox added 110 (a new pocket film size introduced in 1973) and full-frame 35-mm cameras to its traditional precision subminiature camera.

New Products dominated the photo year. The biennial *photokina* (World's Fair of Photography) in Cologne, West Germany, brought major new cameras, lenses, and other photographic equipment to public attention in October.

Germany's Zeiss announced cooperation with Japan's Yashica in producing the Zeiss-designed, Yashica-manufactured Contax RTS, an advanced 35-mm SLR camera backed by a wide array of lenses and other accessories. Also introduced was the Minox 35 EL, a tiny 35-mm camera with an electronically controlled shutter.

An interesting new 10-bladed focal-plane shutter, the CLS (Copal/Leitz Shutter), appeared in the Minolta XE-7 camera at the German exhibition. The electronically controlled shutter, an adaptation of a Leitz design, has speeds from 4 seconds to 0.001 second. It permits cameras with a lower height to be

The first complete photo map of the United States is a mosaic of photographs taken by the Earth Resources Technology Satellite.

designed, because it is not as high as the Copal Square shutter currently used in many cameras.

Both European and Japanese manufacturers showed direct-sound, high-performance Super-8 movie cameras. As a definite design trend in motion picture equipment, they may be a further step toward putting the Super-8 format into professional use.

Several projectors for pocket-format slides were introduced. This may mean that manufacturers expect an upswing in pocket color slides with the appearance of more sophisticated 110 cameras. So far, more than 90 per cent of the pocket-camera picture-taking is done with color print film.

New Lenses were introduced by the score. One especially interesting one was Minolta's 24-mm variable field curvature (VFC) lens. The field of focus of this lens can be varied to give sharp images of objects at varying distances that would otherwise be out of focus.

Other interesting introductions were the Vivitar solid catadioptric (combined lens-and-mirror optics) lenses. The lenses use all solid optics, with virtually no air spaces between lens elements, and are physically strong and remarkably compact.

Many makers offered resin-coated enlarging papers that shorten processing times and should soon replace conventional paper types. Both Eastman Kodak and Ilford introduced papers and chemicals for home darkrooms that can produce color prints

directly from color transparencies in 12 minutes. Most other home color processes require color negatives to make prints. Ilford also introduced a special system and paper in six contrast grades for home darkrooms. The system can produce a dry black-and-white print in four minutes.

Film Improvements. Kodak introduced several new films in March. Kodachrome 25 replaced Kodachrome II in 35-mm and 126 still films and 8-mm and 16-mm movie films. Kodachrome 64 replaced Kodachrome-X. Kodak also introduced Kodachrome 40, in 8-mm and 16-mm movie films, replacing Kodachrome II, Type A, for artificial light.

A new high-speed universal movie film, Kodak's Super-8 Ektachrome Type G, allows movies to be made without using special filters, regardless of the light source.

Economic Clouds. Despite the cornucopia of product introductions, the industry had problems. Yashica, after completing the agreements with Zeiss to produce the Contax RTS, retrenched with the layoff of 900 workers in the fall. Polaroid, beset by problems with its SX-70 camera, saw its stock plunge below 15 points a share at one point. Even the giant Eastman Kodak Company temporarily laid off several hundred workers, a clear indication that the unsettled economic weather was beginning to cloud the sunny skies under which the photo industry has basked for many years.

Kenneth Poli

PHYSICS. Physicists stumbled onto a new elementary particle in November, 1974. Waves of excitement spread from Stanford Linear Accelerator (SLAC) in Palo Alto, Calif., to the Brookhaven National Laboratory in Long Island, N.Y., the two experimental facilities where the particle was independently discovered. The news quickly spread overseas, where researchers at Frascati, near Rome, confirmed the discovery.

In recent years, theoretical physicists have told experimenters to look for new particles where classification schemes had missing members. But the new particle, called the psi-particle in California and the J-particle in New York, completely surprised both theorists and experimenters. Because it carries no electric charge, physicists do not think it is a quark, a tiny, fractionally charged fundamental particle suggested by physicist Murray Gell-Mann to explain the regular patterns in his Eightfold Way elementary particle classification scheme. However, its well-defined mass and extremely long lifetime indicate that it may carry the weak force, just as the photon is said to carry the electromagnetic force. Unfortunately, the new particle is far lighter than predicted by existing weak force theory.

Electron-Positron Annihilation. The new particle was discovered at SLAC as experimenters studied what happens when beams of electrons and their antiparticles, positrons, collide at high energies and are annihilated, or destroyed. Their destruction releases vast amounts of energy from which new and different forms of matter emerge. Occasionally, a violent annihilation produces a burst of *hadrons*, much heavier particles such as protons, neutrons, and pi-mesons. The SLAC experimenters reported in February that the number of hadron-producing interactions remained about the same as they raised the beam energies. Completely unexpected from a theoretical point of view, this result confirmed earlier experiments at the now-defunct Cambridge Electron Accelerator in Massachusetts.

Electrons and positrons interact at high energy according to the electromagnetic theory called quantum electrodynamics (QED). It is an extremely accurate and successful interaction theory, whose predictions agree with measurements to one part in a billion. Hadron interactions are not as well understood, but recent evidence indicates that hadrons are composed of even tinier pointlike constituents, quarks. By combining quark theories with QED, physicists calculated that the number of hadrons produced when electrons and positrons annihilate should have decreased with increasing energy, instead of remaining constant as in the SLAC experiment.

The quark theorists were forced to begin a major reappraisal of their understanding of QED and hadron structure and the experimenters rechecked their results. At about noon on November 10, the SLAC researchers set the beam energies at just the right value to produce the new particle. Now, two puzzles face the world's physicists, who have not been so excited in nearly a decade.

Elegant Spectroscopy. Experimental groups at the University of Paris, Harvard University, and Stanford University independently announced an elegant and flexible way of distinguishing between closely spaced atomic energy levels. They use two laser beams to improve by a factor of 100 their measurements of an atom's energy structure.

Because electrons in an atom obey the laws of quantum mechanics, they can have only a fixed amount of energy as they orbit the atom's nucleus. Physicists measure the quantized energy structure of atoms by boosting electrons to higher energy orbits with energy from a laser beam. When the electron returns to a lower energy level, the atom emits radiation, which can be recorded as lines on a strip of photographic film in a spectrometer.

An effect called *Doppler broadening* widens these lines, blurring together two or more closely spaced lines. The effect is similar to the familiar change in pitch of a moving train whistle or automobile horn. By using two opposing laser beams to excite the atoms, the researchers eliminate slight frequency shifts that would result from the atom's relative motions. Lines that formerly appeared as one become distinguishable. Thomas O. White

PITTSBURGH Mayor Peter F. Flaherty, who was inaugurated for his second term on Jan. 7, 1974, ran for the U.S. Senate and defeated incumbent Republican Richard S. Schweiker, Jr., in the November 5 election. Flaherty won the Democratic nomination for the Senate by defeating Herbert S. Denenberg in the May 21 primary. In his bid for a second term as mayor, he had won both the Republican and Democratic nominations.

On September 9, President Gerald R. Ford encountered his first major public protest while visiting Pittsburgh. His visit came just after he announced a pardon for former President Richard M. Nixon. Polish Communist Party leader Edward Gierek also visited Pittsburgh, on October 10 during a tour of Western industrial nations.

The Supreme Court of the United States ruled unanimously on June 10 that Pittsburgh could levy high taxes on private parking lots and garages in an effort to reduce urban congestion and encourage commuters to use public transportation. This reversed a lower court ruling invalidating a 20 per cent tax on private parking-lot operators as unconstitutional. The lower court had claimed that the high tax made some private lots unprofitable and was enacted by a city government that operated competitive parking facilities.

Energy-Saving Building. The first commercial building to use solar energy for heating and cooling will be developed in the Pittsburgh area. Plans for the building were announced on August 27 by Standard Oil of Ohio.

A mock-up structure, 2½ stories high, was scheduled to be built in early 1975. Its cost was estimated at $90,000. Another experimental structure was estimated at $30,000. The actual building, from six to 10 stories high, is expected to provide operational savings that will justify the more expensive energy-saving construction.

Economic Conditions. Blue-collar wages kept up with inflation in the first half of 1974. The average earnings of factory workers increased 14.4 per cent between July, 1973, and July, 1974, while the cost of living rose only 9.9 per cent over the April, 1973, level. The cost of food, however, was up 18 per cent during the year ending in May.

The average factory worker in Pittsburgh was earning $11,756 a year by mid-1974. However, U.S. Department of Labor statistics indicated that an average family of four needed more than $13,300 to live in moderate comfort in Pittsburgh.

A newspaper workers strike deprived the city of the *Pittsburgh Press* and the *Pittsburgh Post-Gazette* for 46 days. The strike was settled on May 16.

Crime in the Pittsburgh area rose 8 per cent during the first six months of 1974, according to figures released by the Federal Bureau of Investigation in October.   James M. Banovetz

PLUMMER, CHRISTOPHER (1929-   ), won a Tony Award in 1974 as the best actor in a Broadway musical play. He played the title role in the musical *Cyrano*, based on the play *Cyrano de Bergerac* by Edmond Rostand. The role was his first Broadway appearance since 1965.

Plummer was born in Toronto, Canada, and educated in Montreal. He made his professional stage debut in 1950 as Faulkland in *The Rivals* at the Ottawa Repertory Theatre. During the next two years, he appeared in over 75 productions.

He made his Broadway debut in *The Starcross Story* in 1954. In 1956, he made his first appearance at the Stratford (Ont.) Shakespeare Festival in the title role in *Henry V*, and played the title role in *Hamlet* the following year.

Plummer made his debut in Great Britain in 1961, acting the title role in *Richard III* in Stratford-on-Avon. He also played Henry II in *Becket* in London, and won the Evening Standard Award for the portrayal. In 1963, he made his first appearance as Cyrano in Rostand's play in Stratford, Ont.

He has made numerous appearances on the stage in the United States and Canada and has been a leading actor in the National Theatre Company of Great Britain since 1971. He first appeared on television in 1953 and made his first film in 1957.

Plummer has been married three times and has one daughter.   Kathryn Sederberg

POETRY. Several deaths depleted the poetry scene in 1974. American poetry lost its most accomplished man of letters in the old, grand tradition when John Crowe Ransom died on July 5 at 86. Critic, teacher, and editor, he was known for the civilized, dry wit with which his poems confront the absurdities and vagaries of the human situation. David Jones, the Welsh-English epic poet and artist, died on October 28 at 78. Anne Sexton, a Pulitzer Prizewinning poet, died at 45 on October 4.

Among the Finest Books of 1974 were Philip Levine's *1933*, tough, tender lyrics that often involved family scenes; and Alan Dugan's *Poems 4*, described by Stanley Kunitz as "spare, quirky, fierce, unconcessive, grudging, loving, and terribly real." Other books that received wide discussion included James Schuyler's *Hymn to Life;* Galway Kinnell's *The Avenue Bearing the Initial Christ into the New World;* Frank O'Hara's *Selected Poems;* and Muriel Rukeyser's *Breaking Open.*

Good volumes by younger poets included Bill Knott's intense, comic, heartbreaking *Love Songs to Myself.* William Hunt's *Of the Map that Changes* contained the best titles since Wallace Stevens. Other works were Andrei Codrescu's often electrifying *The History of the Growth of Heaven;* Charles Simic's *Return to a Room Lit by Milk;* Marvin Bell's *Residue of Song;* Diane Wakowski's *Trilogy;* and Michael Ryan's *Threats Instead of Trees.*

The National Book Award went to Adrienne Rich's *Diving into the Wreck*, modest, careful poems about inner perceptions and external scenes; and Allen Ginsberg's *The Fall of America: Poems of These States*, an inferior, rhetorically plagued work by a potentially major American poet. Robert Lowell won the Pulitzer Prize for poetry. *After Our War* by John Balaban won the important Lamont Poetry Selection as the finest first book.

Valuable Translations continued to appear in profusion. Most important was Robert Fitzgerald's muscular version of *The Iliad*, which took its place beside his Bollingen Prizewinning translation of *The Odyssey.* Other excellent translations included *The Old Man Who Does as He Pleases: Selections from Lu Yu*, translated by Burton Watson; *Poetry from the Russian Underground*, translated by Joseph Langland and others; *Selected Poems of Josip Brodsky*, translated by George Kline; Raphael Alberti's *The Owl's Insomnia*, translated by Mark Strand; and *Mystical Poems of Rumi*, translated by A. J. Arberry.

John Ashbery's long, sober, funny, philosophical "Grand Galop" was published in the April issue of *Poetry.* It is a brilliant poem.

The American Poetry Review featured such works as Joseph Bruchac's translation of drum songs by Vinorkor Akpalu, an 84-year-old West African poet of genius; poems and calligraphy by Mao Tse-tung; and a fascinating supplement, "Poetry in the Schools."   Paul Carroll

POLAND rapidly expanded its business ties with the West in 1974, without modifying its orthodox ideological stance at home. Imports from the West increased by 59 per cent in the first half of 1974 while imports from Communist countries increased only 17 per cent. Despite high prices for such Polish exports as coal, the trade deficit widened from $1.3-billion at the end of 1973 to about $1.5 billion at the end of 1974.

U.S. Visit. Communist Party First Secretary Edward Gierek visited the United States in October and announced that Poland would buy $1.5 billion worth of U.S. industrial equipment and technology by 1980. During his visit, Poland and the United States signed agreements on cooperation in health, coal mining, and environmental protection; a taxation agreement; and a joint statement on trade in agricultural produce. Also in October, a consortium of six U.S. and Canadian banks granted Poland a $100-million loan for the development of its copper industry. Poland's largest Western trade deal was a $360-million agreement with a British-Canadian firm for the production of tractors and diesel engines in Poland. About 75,000 tractors and 100,000 engines would be produced annually by 1980.

Relations with Russia remained the cornerstone of Poland's foreign policy. Gierek visited Russia in July, and Russian Foreign Minister Andrei Gromyko visited Poland on the eve of Gierek's visit to the United States. Poland hosted a consultative Communist Parties Conference of 20 Western and eight Eastern European parties in October.

Relations with West Germany improved little. Poland demanded social security payments for Polish workers who had been deported to Germany during World War II. The government also sought additional trade credits. West Germany insisted on more visas for Germans wishing to emigrate from Poland. Chancellor Helmut Schmidt and Gierek exchanged letters in July, but failed to break the deadlock.

On June 25, the Polish Communist Party Central Committee removed its secretary, Franciszek Szlachcic, allegedly for his doubtful loyalty to the Russian alliance. Szlachcic, who had been Poland's second most powerful official, was demoted to a low-ranking government post but retained his seat on the party's Politburo.

Kazimierz Kakol, a hard-line official, was put in charge of church affairs in May, but relations with the Vatican continued to improve. The Vatican's chief diplomat, Archbishop Agostino Casaroli, visited Warsaw in February and took the first step toward eventual full diplomatic relations. Poland's bishops, however, remained skeptical of the government's conciliatory policy.   Chris Cviic

See also EUROPE (Facts in Brief Table).

POLLUTION. See ENVIRONMENT.

POPULATION, WORLD. A continuing upward spiral in world population and dwindling food supplies were international concerns in 1974. Demographers worried especially about the global growth rate. If it continued at the present 2.2 per cent a year, the present overall population of 4.1 billion would be increasing by 90 million people a year – the highest annual growth rate in history.

The United Nations (UN) sponsored a 12-day World Population Conference in August in Bucharest, Romania, to formulate policies aimed at reducing the growth rate substantially by 1985. The first global intergovernmental parley on population, it was attended by about 1,250 delegates from 135 nations.

World Plan of Action. There were 340 items on the agenda. After extended, often rancorous, debate, 108 were adopted as guidelines that, it was hoped, if followed might ease population pressures. The items were known as the World Plan of Action.

Most demographic experts were disappointed at the outcome, believing that the documents provided little hope for a quick, urgently needed solution to the looming population crisis. They believed the plan reflected only too accurately the divisiveness among the conferees. The developed nations believed it essential to curb population growth; the United States, for example, proposed two-child families as the ideal way to stabilize the growth rate. The developing nations, however, insisted that the population

Leonid I. Brezhnev, Russia's Communist Party leader, joins in a Warsaw celebration of 30 years of Communist rule in Poland.

Worldwide concern over soaring populations brought delegates from 135 nations to a United Nations conference in Bucharest, Romania, in August.

problem should be viewed within a framework of social, economic, and cultural policy; they maintained that only by first solving problems in these areas could population growth be brought under control. India's chief representative emphasized that only by eradicating poverty and raising living standards would overpopulation be staved off.

Other nations, including Argentina, Brazil, and various other Latin American and African countries, contended that population growth was necessary for economic development. China and its adherents insisted that fuller exploitation of natural resources would comfortably support 10 times the world's present population.

Food Conference. At several points, the World Plan of Action referred to a shortage of food as the most pressing problem related to population. Subsequently, a 10-day, UN-sponsored World Food Conference opened in Rome on November 5, with 1,000 governmental and private delegates from 130 countries attending. Their immediate concern was a serious food shortage in South Asia and in Africa south of the Sahara. More than 500 million people on the two continents were already trapped in a "famine zone." Very poor crop yields due to drought and to fertilizer and energy scarcities caused the crisis. Huge food reserves, such as those that had helped avert famine in India in 1966 no longer existed. It was the conference's task to organize a relief effort

to avert a potential catastrophe in which millions might die of starvation by June, 1975. See AFRICA.

Food Council Established. Delegates unanimously agreed to establish a World Food Council to supervise and coordinate a number of new programs to boost food production. Three major plans, whose details would be worked out at subsequent meetings, set up an International Fund for Agricultural Development, created an "early-warning system" to provide information that could help avert serious food crises in specific areas of the world, and established, through pledges of commodities and financing, a minimum food-aid reserve of 10 million tons of cereal grains per year. See FOOD.

Family-Planning Programs were being carried on in about 60 countries in 1974. Many of them were financed by the U.S. Agency for International Development, which distributed $104 million.

In the United States, organized family-planning programs were serving an estimated 32 million women – a fourfold increase from 1968, according to U.S. Secretary of Health, Education, and Welfare Caspar W. Weinberger. In South Korea, one-fourth of all married couples were practicing birth prevention; in India, an estimated 25 million couples were following family-planning programs. France, a Roman Catholic country, was the scene of a historic development in December when its National Assembly voted to legalize abortion.　　Robert C. Cook

PORTUGAL. In an almost bloodless dawn coup, a group of army officers called the Armed Forces Movement (AFM) overthrew the government of Prime Minister Marcello Caetano on April 25, 1974. Caetano, President Américo Thomaz, and four Cabinet ministers were exiled to Madeira and later to Brazil. The coup ended 40 years of civilian dictatorship in Portugal.

The AFM leaders named General António de Spínola as provisional president. He promised elections within a year, release of political prisoners, an end to press censorship, and self-determination for Portugal's African territories of Mozambique, Angola, and Guinea-Bissau. The last resistance to Spínola and his military junta of seven AFM leaders crumbled on April 26 with the surrender of 300 secret police at their besieged headquarters in Lisbon.

Opposition Leader Home. Socialist leader Mario Soares returned from exile in Paris on April 28 to become foreign minister and help shape a democratic future for Portugal. Spínola formally became president on May 15 and named a civilian provisional Cabinet that included two Communists for the first time in the country's history. Adelino da Palma Carlos, a right-of-center Democrat, was chosen as prime minister.

The jubilance of the people quickly dimmed, however, as the new regime ran into economic and political difficulties. To slow an inflation rate of nearly 30 per cent, the government imposed wage and price controls on May 26. Two days later, postmen, bankers, and transit workers went on strike.

Spínola warned on May 29 that "counter-revolutionaries and anarchists" threatened the country's new freedom. More strikes and internal strains forced Palma Carlos and four of his moderate ministers to resign on July 9. Two days later, Spínola dismissed the rest of the Cabinet. On July 14, he named Vasco dos Santos Gonçalves, a left wing veteran colonel of African campaigns and principal leader of the AFM, as prime minister. He installed military men in seven key posts. See GONÇALVES, VASCO DOS SANTOS.

Spínola Resigns. Threat of a clash between left and right wing elements was narrowly averted on September 29 after the government banned a demonstration by reactionaries in Lisbon. On September 30, Spínola resigned and General Francisco da Costa Gomes, former armed forces chief of staff, replaced him. Spínola said that conditions had made it impossible for Portugal to adopt true democracy.

Spínola also attacked the handing over of political power to black liberation forces as an "antidemocratic" way of ending four centuries of colonial rule in Africa. He held that the Africans are not yet ready to decide their own future. In Guinea-Bissau, with a single independence movement and few white settlers, an early agreement was reached. The European Community (Common Market) recognized Guinea-Bissau as a new nation on August 12, and the independence pact was signed in Algiers on August 26 (see GUINEA-BISSAU). Talks with the Mozambique Liberation Front (FRELIMO) began in Lusaka, Zambia, on June 5 with a speedy cease-fire and maintenance of law and order as immediate objectives. A "white movement for a free Mozambique" tried to take over the capital, Lourenço Marques, on September 9, leading to rioting by blacks. The Marxist FRELIMO took over the government on September 20 (see MOZAMBIQUE). The third African territory, Angola, tried to unify its nationalist movements in order to negotiate freedom. See ANGOLA.

Economic Problems. Gonçalves announced higher prices on August 19 as the balance-of-payments deficit topped $340 million. The Organization for Economic Cooperation and Development advised the regime on September 18 to run budget deficits to maintain high economic activity and employment. In October, workers responded to an appeal by Gonçalves to "do a day's work for the nation" by working on Sundays.

In October, President da Costa Gomes addressed the United Nations General Assembly in New York City and later met with President Gerald R. Ford in Washington, D.C. Russia pledged economic support to Portugal on November 2 "with regard to available resources." Kenneth Brown

See also EUROPE (Facts in Brief Table).

Parading Portuguese in Lisbon call for "public justice for Fascist criminals" after an April coup ended 40 years of civilian dictatorship.

The last U.S. highway post office loads for its final run on June 30.
Workers sorted the mail during the run from Cleveland to Cincinnati.

POSTAL SERVICE, U.S. Congress intervened in 1974 to put off from 1976 until 1979 the full impact of scheduled U.S. postal rate increases for newspapers, magazines, books, and records. The new law, signed by President Richard M. Nixon on June 30, also deferred the full increases for weekly newspapers and nonprofit organizations' mail from 1981 until 1987. The delays will cost the U.S. Postal Service an estimated $754 million in anticipated revenue over the next dozen years and require the federal subsidy to be enlarged by that amount.

Opponents charged that the measure was a "rip-off" to benefit wealthy publishers. But supporters of the measure argued that postal rates for newspapers and magazines had risen 74 per cent since 1974 and that some relief was in order. Some publications said the postal rate increases threatened their survival.

The Senate approved the delay 71 to 11, and the House adopted it without change by a vote of 277 to 129. The congressional move illustrated the problems the U.S. Postal Service faced in trying to run the mails as a business and charging the rates needed to recover its costs.

First-Class Mail Rates went up on March 2. The price of a stamp for an ordinary letter went up from 8 to 10 cents, airmail from 11 to 13 cents, and postal cards from 6 to 8 cents. International airmail rates increased by an average of 20 per cent and surface-air parcel rates rose about 15 per cent. Postal Service officials said, however, that an eight-week delay in the rate increases ordered by the Cost of Living Council would raise 1974 losses by $236 million.

Without the new rates, the Postal Service had forecast a 1974 deficit of $1.3 billion, but it said this would be cut to $621 million with the additional revenue from first-class mailings. Congress approved a subsidy of $920 million for fiscal 1974.

Preliminary figures showed that operating revenues went up by 7.4 per cent in 1974, rising from $8.3-billion to $8.9 billion. Mail volume edged up 0.2 per cent to 89.9 billion pieces. Employment, which had been declining for years, climbed by 1.3 per cent to about 710,000.

Response to Complaints. Despite widespread customer criticism of slow service, Postmaster General Elmer T. Klassen insisted that 95 per cent of all local first-class mail is delivered the day after it is mailed. He added that 90 per cent of all first-class mail to any point in the United States is delivered by the third working day and that 99 per cent has arrived by the fourth working day.

Responding to complaints from utilities and department stores, the Postal Service on November 17 began returning mail to the sender or forwarding it to the dead-letter office if it carries no postage. In another change, the maximum value for parcels that can be sent collect on delivery was raised from $200 to $300.   William J. Eaton

POVERTY constitutes a global emergency, Secretary-General Kurt Waldheim told a special United Nations (UN) General Assembly meeting in April, 1974. Waldheim told the delegates, called to discuss raw materials and world development, that mass poverty is a devastating indictment of current world civilization. Two-thirds of the world's people live in stark poverty that permeates every phase of life in developing countries, he said.

Robert McNamara, president of the World Bank, warned that the deteriorating world economic situation has had the hardest impact on the "have-not" nations and threatens the lives of hundreds of millions of people. McNamara appealed to industrialized and developed countries to renew their lagging assistance to the "have-nots."

Before the session ended on May 2, the delegates approved two resolutions characterized by some observers as weak. One established an emergency plan to help the world's poorest countries maintain essential imports during the year. The other set up an emergency fund under UN auspices, with voluntary contributions from industrialized nations and others. The fund is to be used to provide emergency relief and development assistance to needy countries. But there were few firm promises of financial aid from the wealthy countries and, on December 17, the United States announced that it would not contribute to the fund and would not serve on the board of governors of the fund. However, U. S. aid would continue through existing channels. See UNITED NATIONS.

Poverty Agency Closes. The Office of Economic Opportunity (OEO), created by President Lyndon B. Johnson to lead the Great Society's war against poverty, ceased to exist when the Economic Opportunity Act of 1964 expired on June 30. OEO's fate was similar to 900 other antipoverty agencies across the country that have begun to wind down.

Critics of OEO suggested that revenue sharing – a massive redistribution of money from Washington, D.C., to local communities – would provide the poor with better benefits. Supporters of the agency insisted that the poor and powerless need a federal advocacy agency.

The House of Representatives completed the disbanding of the OEO on May 29 but created a new administration in the Department of Health, Education, and Welfare (HEW) to run community action programs. The House also extended other OEO programs and transferred them to other departments, with nearly $4 billion in funding. In effect, the House voted to kill OEO in name but not in spirit.

Among the former OEO programs that will continue to receive federal money are Head Start, which provides classes, recreation, and meals for preschool children; Community Action, which helps local groups to aid the poor in obtaining jobs and education; and Follow Through, which assists children going from Head Start into grade school. Other programs will continue to help American Indians, migrant workers, pregnant women, and the elderly.

Transport Aid to the Poor. The Washington Center for Metropolitan Studies says that many rural families earning as little as $4,000 or $5,000 a year spend 25 to 40 per cent of their income on automobiles, primarily for gas to get to and from work. Only about half of all poor families have cars, but those who do use them almost entirely for work-related purposes.

Some government agencies began testing a transportation stamp program in West Virginia that is modeled after the government food stamp program. Low-income persons who are handicapped or 60 years old or more can buy discount tickets for bus, taxi, train, and airplane travel. They can purchase $8 worth of transportation stamps a month at prices ranging from $1 to $5 depending on their income.

This is much more ambitious than the projects that use local or state subsidies to provide discount rides for the elderly or disabled in many major cities. The West Virginia stamps are good for all modes of transportation, public and private, as long as the carrier agrees to accept the stamps.

The transportation stamp experiment has stimulated both deep opposition and strong support. Some opponents challenge the experiment as a step toward potentially huge commitments of federal funds to travel. Supporters insist some kind of transportation aid for the poor is essential – especially in rural areas. In many cases, an individual cannot obtain adequate health care, vocational training, or even food and other necessities without transportation.

If the pilot transportation stamp program is a success, it could lead to testing a more comprehensive food stamp program that would enable the poor to buy gas and even heating oil at reduced prices.

The Poor Get Poorer. Despite greater federal and state spending on food programs, the poor in the United States are needier and hungrier than they were in 1964, experts told the Senate Select Committee on Nutrition and Human Needs at June hearings. A major reason for this is inflation. Higher-income families can combat rising food prices by "spending down" – buying cheaper kinds of food. But the poor, who are already buying the cheapest kinds of food, do not have this option.

Food Stamp Suits. On September 23, various legal public service groups filed suits in federal courts against 17 states, charging failure to promote and expand food stamp programs. The suits said that only 13.5 million people were taking part in the food stamp programs, out of an estimated 37 million who are eligible. Under a January, 1971, amendment to the Food Stamp Act, each state is required to inform the poor of their eligibility and "ensure" their participation in the program.   Joseph P. Anderson

PRESIDENT OF THE UNITED STATES

A year of grave crisis beset the United States presidency in 1974. First President Richard M. Nixon, then his successor, President Gerald R. Ford, emphasized foreign policy in an effort to turn attention away from their serious domestic problems.

President Nixon toured the Middle East and met with Soviet Communist Party leader Leonid I. Brezhnev in Russia in June. In November, President Ford crossed the Pacific Ocean to Japan and South Korea and also met with Brezhnev in Vladivostok, Russia. But no diplomatic success could overshadow the Watergate scandal or chase away the rampant inflation and recession that threatened the U.S. economy.

As the year began, President Nixon struggled to retain the presidency and to conceal his knowledge of the Watergate scandal. In his State of the Union message on January 30, Nixon declared that he would not "walk away from the job the people elected me to do." He assured Congress and the

Gerald R. Ford takes the oath as President, *left*, at noon on August 9 after Richard M. Nixon bids his aides an emotional farewell, *right*.

American people that he had surrendered to special Watergate prosecutor Leon Jaworski "all the evidence that he needs to conclude his investigation" of the Watergate cover-up. But, in a historic case, the Supreme Court of the United States ruled unanimously on July 24 that the President had to surrender 64 tapes to U.S. District Court Judge John J. Sirica. On August 5, the President released the incriminating transcript of a June 23, 1972, conversation that revealed he knew about the cover-up almost from the beginning. In a public statement, he acknowledged that portions of the tape were "at variance" with some of his earlier claims and admitted that he had withheld this evidence.

In the next few days, the President's former supporters in Congress informed him that they would vote to remove him from office. Faced with certain impeachment by the House of Representatives and probable conviction by the Senate, he announced on August 8 that he would resign the next day. At noon on August 9, Ford was sworn in as the 38th President of the United States. Ford's vice-presidential nominee, Nelson A. Rockefeller, took office in December. See FORD, GERALD R.; ROCKEFELLER, NELSON A.; WATERGATE; Section Two, FROM TRIUMPH TO TRAGEDY.

For the first time in the nation's history, neither the President nor the Vice-President had been elected to their high office by the people. In accordance with the 25th Amendment to the U.S. Constitution, Ford had been appointed Vice-President in December, 1973, by Nixon after Spiro T. Agnew resigned in October, 1973. Subsequently, Nixon's resignation left Ford as President and gave him the authority to choose his own Vice-President.

The Nixon Administration. Perhaps President Nixon's most successful action in 1974 was his trip to the Middle East in June, following Secretary of State Henry A. Kissinger's negotiation of a cease-fire between Arabs and Israelis. See KISSINGER, HENRY A.

From June 12 to 14, President Nixon conferred in Cairo with Egyptian President Anwar al-Sadat, and millions of Egyptians lined the streets to cheer him. In a declaration of friendship and cooperation between the two nations, Nixon promised to supply Egypt with nuclear technology for peaceful purposes.

Then he flew to Saudi Arabia, Syria, Israel, and Jordan. His visit to the Saudi Arabian capital of Riyadh was the first ever made by a U.S. President. On June 16, Nixon announced the resumption of diplomatic ties with Syria, broken since the 1967 Arab-Israeli war. After a stop in the Azores to talk to Portuguese President António de Spínola, he returned to Washington on June 19.

On June 25, President Nixon left for a summit meeting with Brezhnev in Moscow. On the way, Nixon stopped in Brussels for talks with North Atlantic Treaty Organization (NATO) leaders.

Nixon and Brezhnev signed a 10-year economic agreement on June 29. On July 3, after six days of conferences in Moscow and Yalta, the President and Brezhnev pledged their nations to negotiate an interim arms limitation agreement that would be in effect until 1985. After returning from Moscow, President Nixon told the nation that the chances for world peace were the "brightest in a generation."

Before the President left for Russia, Americans learned that he was suffering from chronic phlebitis and blood clots in his left leg. The illness flared up

455

President Gerald R. Ford confers with Donald Rumsfeld, whom he appointed
as a presidential assistant in charge of administration and coordination.

before he left for his Middle East trip, and it hospitalized him in September and October.

In April, Nixon went to France for the funeral of French President Georges Pompidou. He was warmly received by crowds in Paris and also conferred with Japanese, European, and Russian leaders.

The Ford Administration. The day he was sworn in, President Ford named a four-man committee— William W. Scranton, Donald M. Rumsfeld, Rogers C. B. Morton, and John O. Marsh—to make recommendations for an orderly transition of government. Ford named Jerald F. terHorst press secretary. The next day, at a full Cabinet meeting, the President asked all Cabinet members and the heads of all federal agencies to remain in office in the name of "continuity and stability." See CABINET, U.S.

On August 15, President Ford named his former law partner, Philip W. Buchan, as presidential counsel in charge of all legal matters. Buchan was promoted to Cabinet rank on September 12. Rumsfeld became assistant to the President, with Cabinet rank, on September 24.

On September 16, General Alexander M. Haig, Jr., was named Supreme Allied Commander in Europe and assumed the NATO post in December.

The President on October 8 named Secretary of the Interior Rogers C. B. Morton to head the new national energy board and the U.S. energy program. On October 29, Ford announced the forced resigna-

tion of John C. Sawhill as administrator of the Federal Energy Office and named Andrew E. Gibson to succeed him (see SAWHILL, JOHN C.). The President withdrew Gibson's name on November 12, because of Gibson's continuing ties with a major oil company. Finally, Frank G. Zarb was named head of the energy office on November 25.

On September 16, President Ford offered clemency to about 28,000 persons who had evaded the draft or deserted the military during the war in Vietnam. They were given a chance to earn re-entry into the United States by taking an oath of allegiance and performing alternative service.

Nixon's Pardon. In his first news conference as President, on August 28, Ford indicated that he was considering clemency for former President Nixon, who faced charges of criminal obstruction of justice in the Watergate cover-up. However, Ford declared that he would not grant clemency until legal processes had gone forward in the courts.

Then, in a dramatic change of heart, on September 8, President Ford granted an unconditional pardon to Nixon for all federal crimes that he "committed or may have committed or taken part in" during his term of office, from Jan. 20, 1969, through Aug. 9, 1974. Nixon accepted the pardon, declaring that he was "wrong in not acting more decisively and more forthrightly in dealing with Watergate" but not admitting any guilt.

Ford was severely criticized for pardoning Nixon before he was formally accused of any crime. Presidential press secretary terHorst resigned in protest. After terHorst resigned as press secretary, the President named Ronald H. Nessen, a television newsman, as his press secretary.

On October 17, Ford appeared personally before a subcommittee of the House Judiciary Committee to answer questions about the pardon. In this unprecedented, televised appearance of a President before the subcommittee, Ford assured the American people that there was "no deal, under no circumstances" connected with the pardon. On the contrary, the President said, he had acted in what he perceived as the best interests of the country and because he believed that Nixon had suffered enough. Out of compassion for the former President, Ford asked Congress to appropriate $850,000 to help Nixon in the transition to private life until June 30, 1975. However, Congress voted only $200,000.

The Ford Administration also agreed to give Nixon control of his presidential tapes and papers. But Congress objected, and on December 9 voted to give the government permanent custody of the tapes. See NIXON, RICHARD MILHOUS.

The Economy. In 1974, runaway inflation coupled with recessionary conditions became an unhappy fact of American life. Unemployment reached 7.1 per cent in December, with about 6.5 million persons unemployed. See LABOR.

President Ford followed the conservative economic doctrines of the Nixon Administration. He declared on August 28 that he could "foresee no circumstances under which I can see the reimposition of wage and price controls to curb inflation."

On September 27 and 28, after a series of preliminary meetings, the President held a televised two-day summit meeting on inflation in Washington, D.C., attended by about 800 delegates representing both business and labor. At the close of the meeting, President Ford announced the creation of an Economic Policy Board, chaired by Treasury Secretary William E. Simon, and a White House Labor-Management Committee, coordinated by John T. Dunlop, former director of the defunct Cost of Living Council. Ford named Princeton University economist Albert Rees to head an advisory Council on Wage and Price Stability. Addressing a joint session of Congress on October 8, President Ford suggested a broad economic program to "Whip Inflation Now," with the slogan "WIN."

President Ford hoped to hold federal spending in fiscal 1975 to $302.2 billion and proposed a 5 per cent surtax on family incomes of more than $15,000. He was unable to impound funds already appropriated by Congress, as President Nixon had done to

President and Mrs. Ford welcome King Hussein I and Queen Alia of Jordan to the White House in August for Ford's first official state dinner.

Emperor Hirohito and Gerald R. Ford stand side by side during a
ceremony welcoming the U. S. President to Japan on November 19.

keep the federal spending down. This power was
eliminated by the Congressional Budget and Impoundment Control Act of 1974. See CONGRESS.

Foreign Policy. Immediately after Nixon resigned, Ford announced that Kissinger would remain
as secretary of state, indicating that there would be
no change in foreign policy. On August 9, Ford and
Kissinger began meeting with foreign envoys to
assure them that the new Administration would
carry out Nixon's policies.

Ford attended the Ninth World Energy Conference in Detroit on September 23 and warned of the
dangers of spiraling oil prices. He made his first
address to the United Nations on September 18,
urging a global strategy to ensure adequate supplies
of food and energy.

Early in his Administration, President Ford was
embarrassed by a report that the Central Intelligence
Agency (CIA) had interfered in Chile's internal
affairs between 1970 and 1973. At a press conference
on September 16, the President admitted the CIA
had intervened in Chile in 1970 to protect U.S.
interests. Late in 1974, there were reports that the
CIA had engaged in domestic spying.

On October 21, President Ford conferred with
Mexican President Luis Echeverría Alvarez in
Nogales, Ariz., and Magdalena, Mexico.

In November, President Ford made a 14,600-mile
(23,500-kilometer), nine-day journey to the Far

East. He flew to Japan on November 18 and to South
Korea on November 22. The next day, he began to
confer with Soviet Communist Party leader Brezhnev
at a spa on the outskirts of Vladivostok, Russia. The
two superpower leaders reached tentative agreement
there on a limitation of offensive nuclear arms. In
December, Ford met with French President Valery
Giscard d'Estaing on the Caribbean island of
Martinique.

President Ford had many foreign visitors during
his first months in office, including the foreign ministers of Egypt, Jordan, Syria, and Russia. Jordan's
King Hussein I visited Ford at the White House from
August 16 to 18; Israeli Prime Minister Yitzhak
Rabin, from September 9 to 13; Italian President
Giovanni Leone, on September 25; and Polish Communist Party leader Edward Gierek, on October 8
and 9.

Politics. As President of the United States, Gerald
Ford also became the titular head of the Republican
Party. Before the November elections, the President
campaigned as if he himself were running for office.
In October, he traveled 16,000 miles (25,750 kilo-
meters) across 20 states. But he could not prevent a
Democratic sweep in the November elections (see
ELECTIONS). On November 15, Ford revealed that
he would be a candidate for a full term as President
in 1976.   Carol L. Thompson

PRINCE EDWARD ISLAND. See CANADA.

PRISON. An unusual number of court rulings helped to define the rights and privileges of inmates in United States federal and state prisons during 1974. The general thrust of the decisions was to widen prisoner rights through judicial decree, continuing a recent trend.

In a major decision, U.S. District Judge John W. Oliver on July 31 declared unconstitutional the procedures used by federal prison officials in transferring prisoners into a behavior modification program at a Springfield, Mo., facility. Although the Bureau of Prisons had abandoned the program after inmates filed suit, Judge Oliver ruled that it was "capable of repetition" and held that no prisoner should be involuntarily placed in such a program without a formal hearing.

The Supreme Court of the United States also issued a series of rulings advancing prisoners' rights. The court on April 29 ruled unconstitutional the methods used by California officials to censor prisoners' mail. It also directed that prisoners be allowed to seek legal help from law students and paraprofessionals as well as attorneys. On June 26, the court held that prisoners facing disciplinary proceedings must be informed of all charges against them and be allowed to present contrary evidence. But in a 5 to 4 vote on June 24, the court ruled that prison officials could constitutionally deny journalists the right to interview specific prisoners.

Prisoner Population in state and federal institutions declined slightly to about 221,800. About 199,000 inmates were held in 550 major adult and juvenile facilities in the District of Columbia and 50 state prison systems, and 22,800 inmates were in the 35 federal correctional institutions. An additional 141,000 persons were housed in the 3,921 county and municipal jails on a typical day.

Attorney General William B. Saxbe caused a furor among correctional officials when he attacked the rehabilitative potential of the nation's prisons at a national police chiefs convention on September 23. Saxbe modified his remarks on November 15 to suggest that rehabilitative efforts should be concentrated on youthful and first-time offenders.

Jailbreaks. The year's longest and most dramatic jailbreak attempts ended in failure. Two convicts seized seven hostages on July 11 and barricaded themselves in a cell block in the U.S. District Courthouse in Washington, D.C. But the hostages escaped via a courthouse elevator three days later, and the two convicts were forced to surrender on July 15.

Three inmates at the Huntsville, Tex., state prison captured 12 hostages in the prison library on July 24. After negotiations failed, two inmates and two hostages were killed by gunfire when the prisoners attempted to escape on August 3.   David C. Beckwith

PRIZES. See Awards and Prizes; Canadian Library Association; Canadian Literature; Nobel Prizes; Pulitzer Prizes.

PROELL, ANNEMARIE (1953-   ), won an unprecedented fourth consecutive World Cup title in skiing in 1974. The title is based on total points gained in the season; she finished with 288 points for the 17-race 1974 series.

Annemarie was born near Salzburg, Austria, the sixth of eight children in a poor mountain farm family. Her father whittled her first pair of skis when she was 4 and, from then on, she spent every spare moment on the slopes. Often, she skipped breakfast to ski before school.

She burst onto the international ski scene in 1969 as a freckled, blonde 15-year-old, the youngest member of the Austrian ski team. Since then, she has won more World Cup races than any other skier. By the end of the 1973-1974 season, she had a record 31 victories, including 19 downhill trophies. In the 1972-1973 season, she won all eight women's downhill races, becoming the first skier to score a sweep in an Alpine skiing event.

She has an aggressive drive to win and is content with nothing less than first. Her greatest disappointment came in the 1972 Winter Olympics in Sapporo, Japan, when she won only two silver medals.

She was married in the fall of 1973 to Herbert Moser, a ski salesman. Her ambition is to win the championship gold medal in skiing in the 1976 Olympic Games in Innsbruck, Austria, and then start raising a family.   Kathryn Sederberg

PROTESTANT. Inner tensions among denominations, coupled with outer pressures caused by political changes, were a global concern to Protestants in 1974. In some countries, particularly Canada, there was a precipitous drop in Sunday school attendance. The *Toronto Star* called the decline "catastrophic," since it has reached the near 50 per cent point in just a few years. The United Church of Canada and the Anglican Church experienced the greatest losses.

South Korea, one of the more strongly Protestantized nations in Asia, saw both religious revivals and repressions during 1974. Evangelists from the United States, among them Campus Crusade International leader Bill Bright, spoke to hundreds of thousands of evangelicals in Korea. Bright and other American evangelicals who make rigid distinctions between religious and political dissent praised President Chung Hee Park's imprisoning of religious dissenters. They claimed that the Koreans had complete religious freedom.

But those who spoke against political repression in Korea in the name of religion did suffer. While much of the call for freedom came from Korea's small but assertive Catholic community, Protestants were also jailed. South Korean churchmen also continued to disappear, evidently victims of Park's purges.

Northern Ireland remained a consistently tense area where religion both motivated and reinforced economic and other problems that divided Protestants and Catholics. The Irish Republican Army, an underground Catholic group in Northern Ireland, claimed credit for terrorist activities in England during the year. These included vandalism in King's College Chapel at Cambridge University and the bombing of Westminster Hall in London.

Women Priests. Most Protestant denominations now ordain women. But the Episcopal Church has not done so to date, in part because of its own traditions and in part because it would like to keep the door open to accommodation with Roman Catholicism, which also still has an all-male clergy. But on two occasions since 1969, Episcopal bishops, priests, and lay delegates have moved toward voting their permission to ordain women. The General Convention majorities did not prevail, however, because of a procedural complication.

On July 29, four bishops – three of them retired and one active in Costa Rica – did ordain 11 women candidates at the Episcopal Church of the Advocate in Philadelphia. Their act violated the canons of the Episcopal Church, and the House of Bishops condemned it at a meeting in Chicago on August 15 and declared the ordinations invalid. A number of the ordained women announced they regarded the ordinations as valid and would pursue their priesthoods.

As the months passed, tensions grew within the church. The women argued that they were merely acting out an idea whose time had come, that they were in the vanguard of tomorrow's church, and that the Christian church needed new symbols to demonstrate that it regarded both sexes equally. Their opponents for the most part did not take a hard line on ordination of women, but expressed concern about the violation of canons and the integrity of church order. On November 10, one of the newly ordained women priests was permitted to serve Communion at St. Stephen and the Incarnation Church in Washington, D.C.

Evangelical Developments. The major evangelical event of the year was a huge Congress on World Evangelization, held in July at Lausanne, Switzerland. With Roman Catholics and some traditionally ecumenical Protestants as their guests, the mission-minded evangelicals met not far from the Geneva headquarters of the World Council of Churches. The evangelicals continued their well-publicized attacks on that organization, charging that its original zeal for evangelism and conversion had been displaced by preoccupation with social change.

Another evangelical phenomenon was the rise of movements that combined theologically conservative and somewhat radical political expressions. Some of these were based on the 1973 Chicago Declaration of Evangelical Social Concern. *The Post American*, a biweekly published in Chicago, and a book, *The*

His image on a huge screen, evangelist Billy Graham addresses delegates to the July Congress on World Evangelization in Lausanne, Switzerland.

Young Evangelicals by Richard Quebedeaux, showed that the evangelical front was no longer politically homogeneous, and that a critical social movement was developing in many campus evangelical centers.

The declaration by the U.S. Congress of a "Day of Humiliation, Fasting, and Prayer" on April 30, which was strongly supported by evangelical Christians, did not receive much attention, particularly in urban centers. Motivated by efforts centering around Senator Mark Hatfield (R., Ore.), the day was to have called America to its religious roots.

World Anglicanism saw an evangelical bishop rise to primacy when the Most Reverend Donald Coggan succeeded the Most Reverend Michael Ramsey as Archbishop of Canterbury in December. The 65-year-old primate was described as a "caretaker," a term he gladly accepted. See COGGAN, DONALD.

Denominations. The most battle-ridden Protestant denomination in America was the 2.8-million-member Lutheran Church–Missouri Synod. It made headlines because of its conflicts for the fifth straight year, ever since the intransigently conservative Jacob A. O. Preus was elected its president. He brought with him a tradionalist administration and new policies, initiated by Preus-favoring convention majorities, that exacted doctrinal pledges from the synod's members.

Missions became an area of controversy. The Preus element elected a Board of Missions that wanted to retreat from ecumenical and social commitments on the world mission front. The previously appointed missionary staff unanimously opposed the new policies, and most of the staff members resigned in 1974. The Asian member churches, having listened to both sides, held a summer conclave and adopted angry resolutions against the synod's administration and its board.

The synod's major seminary, Concordia in St. Louis, was divided by the controversy. In a move unprecedented in American church history, its majority went into exile. All but four or five professors on a faculty of nearly 50 followed their suspended President John H. Tietjen away from the historic campus. So did the bulk of the student body. With the help of Roman Catholic St. Louis University and the United Church of Christ's Eden Seminary, Concordia Seminary in Exile–or Seminex–thrived, while the old Concordia had to begin a process of organizing its school almost from the beginning again.

The Presbyterian Church in the United States, a largely Southern-based church that lost some of its million members in 1973 through a schism that led to the founding of the National Presbyterian Church, elected its first black moderator, Lawrence W. Bottoms. Race was one of the issues that had led to the traditionalists' 1973 breakaway. The traditionalists also criticized moves that might lead to merger with the somewhat more liberal (and more Northern) United Presbyterian Church in the U.S.A.

The fast-growing Church of Jesus Christ of Latter-day Saints, or Mormons, saw a change of leadership upon the death of Harold B. Lee. His successor was Spencer Woolley Kimball.

Religious Movements and the Young. The charismatic, or Pentecostal, movement continued to make headlines. Many Protestants were in the audience of 30,000 at the annual Catholic Pentecostal meeting in June at Notre Dame University in South Bend, Ind. Lutherans held a summer conclave in Minneapolis to celebrate "Spirit" movements, with 10,000 present. The prospering Pentecostal publishers contributed to the cause's progress with a steady stream of magazines and books, and few denominations were untouched by the trend. Many local congregations were filled with tension between the traditional churchgoers and the "Spirit-filled" people who made much of speaking in tongues and spiritual healing.

Gaining in popularity on the evangelistic front was Bill Gothard, 39-year-old leader of Basic Youth Conflict seminars. His series of 28-hour lecture sequences for which hundreds of thousands of Protestants–most of them white suburbanites–willingly paid, combined Biblical fundamentalism with authority-minded and hierarchical rules for family living. Gothard outlined an ordering of life from God through the husband to the wife, and then from parents to children–an inviolable sequence. Martin E. Marty

See also RELIGION.

PSYCHOLOGY. Psychologists at the Boston University Medical Center carefully examined the response of infants to human speech in 1974. They concentrated particularly on speech rhythms, the perception of which may be a uniquely human ability. Some animals, such as chimpanzees, have abilities that are similar to man's and provide the basis for the development of artificial languages. But man's conscious enjoyment of the rhythms of speech, as shown by his poetry, may underlie his unique ability to learn a language readily.

The scientists, William S. Condon and Louis W. Sander, studied many infants, including some who were only 12 hours old. Using motion-picture cameras and making exact observations, they showed that the spontaneous movements of infants became coordinated to the patterns of adult speech. Although the infants moved in response to many sounds, their movements showed synchronization only with true speech. Moreover, they responded rhythmically as well to spoken Chinese as to English, and to tape recordings of speech. The use of tape recordings proved that the infants were not responding to the speaking adult's body movements and that the adult was not speaking in time with the infant's movements.

The work is important as a demonstration of the interplay between speech and rhythmical perception, and because of the opportunity it provides for early detection and treatment of developmental disorders. For example, infants that fail to respond to speech, or do not respond in a coordinated way, may have brain malfunctions that cannot otherwise be detected or diagnosed at early ages. Early diagnosis might offer new opportunities for treatment.

Psychological Pest Control. University of Utah studies reported in May indicate that sheep owners may be able to keep coyotes from preying on their flocks by "turning off" the coyotes' taste for lamb. In experiments directed by psychologist Carl R. Gustavson, researchers gave coyotes lamb laced with a chemical that made the coyotes vomit. After just one such meal, most of the coyotes refused to eat any more lamb. Some coyotes that had eaten the treated meat actually hid, rather than attack, when a lamb was placed in the same pen.

The experiments were based on a well-established behavioral principle of mammals in which the palatability of food is defined by its aftereffects. In making their report, the psychologists pointed out that the same effect explains why people dislike the food they eat just before getting seasick.

The scientists said it was possible that a coyote mother would pass on its distaste for lamb to her pups. Such an effect has been established in rats. They also suggested the procedure might be reversed to get an animal to enjoy specific food. Robert W. Goy

PUBLISHING. See CANADIAN LITERATURE; LITERATURE; MAGAZINE; NEWSPAPER; POETRY.

PUERTO RICO was plagued by a rash of strikes early in 1974. On February 12, the island's gasoline stations shut down in a two-day protest against government fuel-rationing policies. They were joined by about 5,000 jitney drivers, most of whom operate outside metropolitan San Juan. The city's bus service was also curtailed briefly during the shutdown after several vehicles were stoned by the strikers.

Economic self-reliance and less dependence on the United States continued to be a major objective of Governor Rafael Hernández Colón. In July, the governor announced that the Puerto Rico Telephone Company, a subsidiary of International Telephone and Telegraph Corporation (ITT), was being transferred to the newly created Puerto Rico Telephone Authority. The authority agreed to pay ITT about $165 million in cash, bonds, and notes.

On December 1, four Puerto Rican cities were damaged by bomb explosions in the worst sabotage attack in the island's recent history. One blast in San Juan shattered the façade of a building housing offices of ITT, but many of the bombs were planted in or near water mains. Authorities attributed the sabotage to left wing elements who sympathized with water and sewage authority workers who had gone out on strike early in November. About 2,500 National Guard men were called up to guard the water supply system. Paul C. Tullier

See also LATIN AMERICA (Facts in Brief Table).

PULITZER PRIZES in journalism, letters, and music were announced in New York City on May 6, 1974. The distinguished awards have been given for 58 years. The following awards were made:

Journalism

Public Service. A gold medal to *Newsday*, Garden City, N.Y., for a 32-part series, "The Heroin Trail," which traced the route heroin takes on its journey from the poppy fields of Turkey, through France, to the streets of Long Island. Under senior editor Robert W. Greene, 14 *Newsday* reporters researched the stories, including reporters Leslie Payne and Knut Royce, who worked for six months in Turkey and Europe. The award was the third Pulitzer gold medal for public service won by *Newsday* since it began publishing in 1940.

General Local Reporting. $1,000 to Hugh F. Hough, 50, and Arthur M. Petacque, 49, of the *Chicago Sun-Times*, for investigative reporting that led to the reopening of the 1966 case in which Valerie Percy, the daughter of Senator Charles H. Percy (R., Ill.), was murdered. The reporters charged that the murder was committed by a burglar now serving a 30-year prison sentence in the Iowa State Penitentiary. The man denied the charges, but implicated three other members of his burglary ring and named one of them, now dead, as the murderer.

Special Local Reporting. $1,000 to William Sherman, 27, reporter for the *New York Daily News*, for 14 articles detailing abuses in New York City's Medicaid program. Posing as a Medicaid recipient, Sherman uncovered flagrant abuses of the program, including one doctor who claimed to have treated 300 patients in a single day, and psychiatrists who billed the city for more than 24 hours of client visits a day. Sherman's investigations have resulted in prosecutions and the repaying of $1 million in fraudulent charges.

National Reporting. $1,000 each to James R. Polk, 36, of the *Washington Star-News*, and to Jack White, 32, of the *Providence* (R.I.) *Journal-Bulletin*. Polk won his award for disclosing irregularities in the 1972 campaign funds of President Richard M. Nixon, including financier Robert L. Vesco's secret $200,000 contribution. White revealed Nixon's 1970 and 1971 federal tax returns in stories that led to the reassessment of Nixon's tax liabilities and his payment of back taxes. White's award prompted some concern among the trustees of Columbia University, which administers the prizes, because the tax returns were confidential documents of the Internal Revenue Service. White refused to explain how he obtained them.

International Reporting. $1,000 to Hedrick Smith, 41, chief of the Moscow bureau of *The New York Times* since 1971, for his reporting of events in Russia and Eastern Europe. Before his Moscow assignment, Smith worked in the *Times* Washington bureau. He was among the journalists whose phones

Distinguished Criticism. $1,000 to Emily Genauer, 63, art critic for the *Newsday* syndicate. Genauer has been an art critic for various New York newspapers since 1929. For four years she was a commentator on art for public television.

Editorial Cartooning. $1,000 to Paul Michael Szep, 32, cartoonist for the *Boston Globe*. The young Canadian has worked for the *Globe* since 1966. The prize honored his work, which appears five times a week, throughout 1973. He is a graduate of the Ontario College of Art in Toronto. Three volumes of his cartoons have been published.

Letters

For the second time in three years, no prize was awarded for drama. None was given for fiction, the second time in four years.

Biography. $1,000 to Louis Sheaffer, 62, for *O'Neill, Son and Artist*, the second part of Sheaffer's two-volume biography of American playwright Eugene O'Neill. The first volume, *O'Neill, Son and Playwright* was published in 1968. The work is the result of more than 16 years of research and writing, supported in part by three Guggenheim fellowships and two grants from the Council of Learned Societies. Sheaffer was formerly drama critic of the *Brooklyn Eagle*, which ceased publication in 1955.

General Nonfiction. A posthumous award to Ernest Becker for *The Denial of Death*, in which the cultural anthropologist wrote that "fear of life and fear of death are mainsprings of human activity." Becker, who had been teaching at Simon Fraser University in Vancouver, Canada, died of cancer on March 6, 1974, at 49.

History. $1,000 to Daniel J. Boorstin, 60, for *The Americans: The Democratic Experience*, the third volume in his history of the United States. Boorstin, who has taught at Harvard University, Swarthmore College, and the University of Chicago, recently resigned as director of the Smithsonian Institution's National Museum of History and Technology, but remains there as senior historian.

Poetry. $1,000 to Robert Lowell, 57, for his collection of poems *The Dolphin*. The award is Lowell's second Pulitzer Prize; he won his first in 1947. Lowell is generally considered the most important living American poet. He is best known for his book *Lord Weary's Castle*.

Music. Special Citation to American composer Roger Sessions for his life's work. The 77-year-old composer-teacher lives in Princeton, N.J. He has taught at Boston University, Princeton University, the University of California, and the Juilliard School of Music. $1,000 to Donald Martino, 43, for his chamber-music piece "Notturno," commissioned by the Walter W. Naumburg Foundation. Martino is chairman of the Composition Department at the New England Conservatory of Music in Boston. His composition teachers include Roger Sessions, Ernst Bacon, Milton Babbit, and Luigi Dallapiccola. Edward G. Nash

Canadian Paul Szep works at his *Boston Globe* drawing board after winning a Pulitzer Prize for his penetrating editorial cartoons.

were tapped by the Nixon Administration in its attempt to discover news leaks.

Editorial Writing. $1,000 to F. Gilman Spencer, 49, editor of the *Trenton* (N.J.) *Trentonian*, for a series of editorials attacking scandals in the New Jersey state government. Jonathan L. Goldstein, acting U.S. attorney for the district of New Jersey, nominated Spencer for the prize. Investigation of the scandals led to federal indictments.

Spot News Photography. $1,000 to Anthony K. Roberts, 33, for his photo coverage of an alleged attempted kidnaping and the subsequent slaying of the kidnaper by an armed guard in a Hollywood, Calif., parking lot. Roberts, a free-lance photographer, chanced on the scene. The photos, his first attempt at news photography, were published by the *Los Angeles Times* and the Associated Press (AP), which nominated him for the prize.

Feature Photography. $1,000 to Slava Veder, 47, photographer for the AP bureau in San Francisco, for a single photo, "Burst of Joy." The photo captured the emotional meeting of an American prisoner of war, Air Force Lieutenant Colonel Robert L. Stirm, and his family, on his return from five years in a North Vietnamese prison camp.

Distinguished Commentary. $1,000 to Edwin A. Roberts Jr., 42, columnist for the *National Observer*. Roberts has been writing his wide-ranging column of opinion, "Mainstreams," since June, 1969.

463

PYNCHON, THOMAS (1937-   ), writer, won the 1974 National Book Award for his World War II novel *Gravity's Rainbow* (1973). The novel, set in London during the blitz bombing, is about a U.S. soldier who can predict German rocket launchings, and how he tries to escape being swallowed up by the Allied intelligence community. Pursued by technology, he makes a symbolic flight through war-devastated Europe. Some critics described the book's central theme as the sexual love of death.

Controversy over the book developed in May, after the Pulitzer fiction jury unanimously recommended it for the Pulitzer Prize, but was turned down by the advisory board. The jury claimed it received no explanation for the rejection. However, some members of the board reportedly regarded the 760-page book as unreadable and, in parts, obscene.

Little is known about Pynchon, a deeply private man. He was born in Glen Cove, N.Y., served in the U.S. Navy, and graduated from Cornell University in 1958.

After graduating, he stayed with friends in New York City's Greenwich Village, writing his first novel, *V* (1963). He worked briefly for a Boeing Aircraft publication in Seattle. After *V* was accepted for publication, Pynchon sought anonymity by moving to Mexico. His second novel, *The Crying of Lot 49*, was published in 1966. Pynchon has also written several short stories.   Darlene R. Stille

QATAR used the wealth from its ever-growing oil revenues to continue its economic expansion in 1974. Along with other oil-producing Arab countries, it also exerted increasing force in world money markets. In February, Qatar gained a controlling 60 per cent interest in Shell Oil Company of Qatar and the Qatar Petroleum Company.

The government reached an agreement with Iran in May to purchase $2 billion worth of Iranian oil to supplement its own oil stocks. Also in May, a new bank, Qatar Commercial Bank, began private lending operations to finance both domestic development projects and those in other Arab countries. A Qatari subsidy of $6.5 million was given to the new Cairo-based Arab International Bank in August, and Qatar loaned $21 million to Jordan to finance agricultural programs. The government budget, which was issued in June, envisaged a 50 per cent increase in expenditures to $150 million.

Other developments affected the life style of Qatari citizens. For example, a new television complex with a 750-kilowatt transmitter went into operation at Doha, the capital, on July 1, as did Qatar's first weekly Arab-language newspaper, *Al-Ahad*. On August 23, the government announced the establishment of a university in Doha, with an initial allocation of $25 million.   William Spencer

See also MIDDLE EAST (Facts in Brief Table).

QUEBEC. See CANADA.

RABIN, YITZHAK (1922-   ), a soldier and diplomat, succeeded Golda Meir as prime minister of Israel on June 3, 1974. The change stemmed from controversy over who was responsible for Israel's lack of preparedness for the Arab attack in October, 1973. See ISRAEL.

Although Rabin had little prior political experience, the Labor Party called on him to form a new coalition government of leftist and liberal groups. His lack of experience proved to be an asset, however, because he could not be blamed for any of the decisions made during the war.

Rabin was born of Russian Jewish parents in Jerusalem on March 1, 1922. He attended an agricultural school in Galilee, but joined the Haganah, an underground Jewish militia group, during the late 1930s.

He fought with British forces during World War II, but after the war he fought to end British control over Palestine and to establish a Jewish state there. His exploits inspired several episodes in Leon Uris' novel *Exodus*.

Rabin served as a brigade commander during the 1948 Arab-Israeli war and as a general and chief of staff during the 1967 hostilities. He retired from the military in 1968, and served as ambassador to the United States until 1973. Rabin and his wife, Lea, have two children.   Darlene R. Stille

RACING. See AUTOMOBILE RACING; BOATING; HORSE RACING; SWIMMING; TRACK AND FIELD.

RADIO in the United States, unfettered by television's time restrictions and need for visual impact, provided better in-depth coverage of at least one key happening in 1974's historic Watergate chronicle – the release of the explosive White House tape transcripts in April. The medium went all-out on the story. The National Public Radio Network even aired a marathon weekend reading of the massive, 1,308-page document in its entirety on its 164 noncommercial stations.

Radio also had the somewhat dubious distinction of being the favorite message medium for various terrorist groups. For example, the Symbionese Liberation Army, after kidnaping Patricia Hearst, communicated with her family and the public via tapes and written messages sent to KPFA-FM in Berkeley, Calif., and KPFK-FM in Los Angeles.

License renewals continued to be troublesome, as minorities and other citizen groups filed license challenges against stations. The Federal Communications Commission (FCC) held up some license renewals and station sales pending investigation of listener protests against proposed music format changes, such as from classical to rock.

Format Changes. The FCC's 1973 inquiry into the controversial sex-oriented talk shows prompted many stations to drop the so-called "topless radio" programs. In many cases, there was a corresponding drop in the station's ratings. The original "topless"

Radio
Rides
Again

Millions of Americans over 35 remember Titus Moody. He was a crusty, dour, laconic New England farmer whose neighbors included a bombastic Southern senator named Claghorn; a New York Jewish housewife, Pansy Nussbaum; and the hard-drinking, hard-fighting Ajax Cassidy. These were the inhabitants of Allen's Alley, a street as famous in the 1940s as Hollywood Boulevard or Broadway.

But Allen's Alley was an imaginary street, created by comedian Fred Allen for his weekly radio show. It existed not in the mind's eye, but in the mind's ear. Each week, Allen, perhaps the funniest man on radio, would amble down the Alley and discuss the events of the day with its denizens. Moody, though he owed his existence to radio, never approved of it. He once said, "I don't hold with furniture that talks." But millions of Americans, searching for something that television fails to give them, began turning back to radio in 1974. And radio answered by resurrecting such old favorites as "Dragnet" and "Our Miss Brooks."

From the mid-1920s to the early 1950s, radio was the major form of home entertainment. Hundreds of comedy shows, dramas, adventure stories, and musical programs crowded the airwaves. Nearly every prominent comedian had a radio show at one time or another. Allen, Jack Benny, Eddie Cantor, Bob Hope, Fanny Brice, Edgar Bergen and Charlie McCarthy, George Burns and Gracie Allen, and Fibber McGee and Molly brought wit and laughter.

Orson Welles presented the famous *War of the Worlds* in 1938 that created near-panic among listeners who thought that Martians had invaded New Jersey. He also broadcast Shakespeare on "The Mercury Theater." There were adventure shows and children's shows, such as "Little Orphan Annie," "Jack Armstrong," and "Captain Midnight." Suspense shows such as "Suspense," "The Shadow," and "Inner Sanctum" used sinister voices and eerie sound effects with telling impact. Millions danced to the "big bands" of Paul Whiteman, Glenn Miller, Benny Goodman, and Tommy and Jimmy Dorsey and listened to such singers as Bing Crosby, Dinah

The Shadow

Shore, Frank Sinatra, and the Andrews Sisters.

Then, suddenly, in the early 1950s, it ended. Radio's technological child, the "big eye," defeated the ear, and the Age of Television began.

No longer master in the home, radio tried specializing, aiming at specific market and interest groups. There were pop-music, hard-rock, country-and-Western, all-talk, and all-news stations. Some played only the "top 40 records" over and over. Once a treasure of delights for the imagination, radio became for many people a tundra of tedium, the fitting junior partner to the wasteland of television.

But recently, some stations began playing tape recordings of such old shows as "The Lone Ranger" and "The Green Hornet." They were astonished by the enthusiastic audience response. Now, station WLTD in Evanston, Ill., for one, broadcasts more than 20 hours of old-time radio each week. The recordings come from the collection of station manager Chuck Schaden, who has accumulated more than 12,000 old radio tapes. Schaden figures he can continue broadcasting until the middle of 1977 without repeating a show.

Radio clubs have sprung up in some parts of the United States. Enthusiasts meet to listen, discuss their favorite shows, and trade tapes. A San Francisco teacher, Roger Hill, has founded the North American Radio Archives, a nonprofit organization to preserve and circulate recordings of old shows.

Even the networks have revived radio drama and comedy. "CBS Radio Mystery Theater" began broadcasting original drama in January, 1974. The National Broadcasting Company has a science-fiction series, "X Minus One," and Mutual Radio broadcasts detective stories on "Zero Hour."

Nostalgia certainly plays a big part in the renewed interest in radio, but there are other reasons for its new popularity. A radio program requires the listener's active participation. Faces and places have to be imagined; sounds must be translated into action. No radio show "looks" the same to any two listeners. One veteran radio producer put it well: "TV just feeds you. Radio involves you."   Edward G. Nash

talk host, Bill Ballance, whose syndicated "Feminine Forum" originated on KGBS in Los Angeles, left that station in October. The outlet now features "gentle country music."

Rock music continued to dominate the disk-jockey scene, but a growing number of pop stations switched to country music formats. More than 1,000 broadcasters were playing the "Nashville Sound" exclusively in 1974, compared to 80 in 1961. The nation's number-one country music station, with an audience of 1.2 million, was WHN in New York City.

News Service. AP Radio, Associated Press's new audio news service, debuted on 210 stations on October 1, even though the Mutual Broadcasting System asked the FCC in August to classify AP Radio and UPI Audio (United Press International's voice-news operation) as networks and regulate them accordingly. AP and UPI filed separate petitions in September opposing the request, which would limit them to only one subscriber in each market area. UPI Audio has 750 station subscribers.

The best indicator of FM radio's steady growth in 1974 was the number of multimillion-dollar sales of FM stations. WBCN-FM, Boston, was sold in January to RBC, Incorporated, for $3.2 million. In the spring, First Media Corporation paid $5.8 million for WPGC-AM-FM in Washington, D.C. *Broadcasting Magazine* attributed at least three-quarters of the price to the FM channel. June Bundy Csida

Train derailments increased substantially in 1974. This Amtrak train jumped the track in Kansas in July, killing one and injuring 45.

RAILROAD systems throughout the world took on new importance in 1974. Government planners in an energy-short world focused greater attention on the railroads' fuel consumption advantages in moving certain types of freight.

U.S. Railroads experienced a sudden warming trend in the regulatory climate. The Interstate Commerce Commission (ICC) authorized nine freight-rate increases during the year, totaling 18.2 per cent. United States railroads set records in traffic and revenues.

Traffic growth of 1 per cent along with the rate increases pushed operating revenues to a record $17-billion, exceeding 1973's $14.8 billion by 15 per cent. Rail earnings improved significantly despite record expenses of $16 billion. They rose to $1 billion, doubling 1973's earnings.

The rate of return on net investment rose to 4 per cent, but rail executives believe this profitability is still too low to enable the industry to purchase new equipment and maintain worn tracks.

With the ICC's June 4 freight rate increase of 10 per cent, railroads were required to report their deferred maintenance, which totaled several billion dollars. On August 1, the Department of Transportation closed a 67-mile (108-kilometer) section of track between Chicago and Louisville, Ky., until it could be repaired and made safe.

On December 10, the House of Representatives voted to guarantee $2 billion in loans for railroads to buy cars and upgrade tracks. But the Senate Commerce Committee killed the bill for 1974 on December 17, objecting to a provision allowing rate changes without immediate ICC action.

Rail Reorganization. President Richard M. Nixon signed legislation on January 2 that set in motion a lengthy process of reorganizing seven bankrupt Northeastern railroads into one federally backed private corporation. The legislation, the Regional Rail Reorganization Act of 1973, created a United States Railway Association to plan and finance a rail network for the 17-state region, to be operated by a new Consolidated Rail Corporation.

Representatives of some of the affected railroads filed suits challenging the new law's legality. On December 16, the Supreme Court of the United States upheld the reorganization act.

Congress overrode a veto by President Gerald R. Ford on October 16 and passed into law a $7-billion railroad retirement bill. The law will restructure the Railroad Retirement System, currently in debt by $4 billion, and pump $285 million into it annually over the next 25 years.

Travel on trains being operated by the National Railroad Passenger Corporation (Amtrak) was up 9.7 per cent over 1973 to almost 19 million passengers. The fiscal 1975 operating deficit was estimated at $238 million. Kenneth E. Schaefle

RECORDINGS. A precedent-setting agreement in 1974 between Columbia Broadcasting System (CBS) Records and Russia's cultural and commercial authority cleared the way for U.S. recordings to be distributed in the Soviet Union. The agreement also made CBS the prime distributor of the Soviet national record label in the United States and Canada. Recordings by Miles Davis, Ray Conniff, Igor Stravinsky (conducting his own music), Duke Ellington, Ella Fitzgerald, and Blood, Sweat & Tears were reportedly among the first releases that were scheduled for distribution in Russia.

A federal trial in Los Angeles in August resulted in the first convictions for tape bootlegging. Richard Taxe, owner of a tape-duplicating company that copied and undersold popular tape recordings, and three others were convicted of tape piracy and given jail sentences and fines.

Broken Record. Total sales of all prerecorded music on records and tapes topped the $2-billion mark for the first time in 1973. Records led tapes in sales by $1.43 billion to $581 million. Among disk sales, albums provided 87 per cent of the dollar volume. Recordings of pop music accounted for 65.6 per cent of sales. In not-very-close second place was soul music with 14.6 per cent, followed by country music, 10.5 per cent; classical music, 6.1 per cent; and jazz, 1.3 per cent.

Anne Murray, Canada's female vocalist of the year for the fourth time, also had a new hit record album, "Love Song."

Lena Zavaroni's recording of "Ma! (He's Making Eyes at Me)" sold a million copies. Only 10 years old, the Scottish songstress also was a big TV hit.

Recording Trends. Country music continued merging with pop and soul and gaining great popularity in metropolitan areas. In New York City, sales of country music were estimated to be up 35 per cent during 1974.

What may be the most lucrative artist's recording contract in history was concluded when Elton John signed an $8-million agreement tying him for five years to MCA Records. Bob Dylan, after a year with Asylum Records, returned to CBS Records under a five-year contract at an undisclosed figure.

Chicago, the pop group, enjoyed immense popularity during the summer when all seven of its LP's were listed among the best-selling pop albums.

Classical and Semiclassical. The resurgence of ragtime received great impetus from the popularity of the movie *The Sting.* Its sound track, the work of Marvin Hamlisch, was a major hit (see Music, Popular). In September, the first five albums on the classical sales lists all featured the music of ragtime composer Scott Joplin (1868-1917). Four other albums that contained Joplin's music appeared lower on the lists. A series featuring music by William Grant Still and other black composers was successfully launched by CBS Records.

Recordings by Jean-Pierre Rampal of Bach's flute sonatas and Handel's sonatas for flute and harpsichord were among other well-received classical releases.   Leonard Feather

RED CROSS. The American Red Cross and other private organizations began 1974 by celebrating congressional adoption of new flood-disaster legislation. President Richard M. Nixon signed the Flood Disaster Protection Act of 1973 into law on Dec. 31, 1973. This legislation amended the Disaster Relief Act of 1970 by extending the federal assistance available to states and local communities suffering from the effects of such disasters as tornadoes.

The American Red Cross and the League of Red Cross Societies of Geneva, Switzerland, jointly sponsored a 10-day seminar in first-aid and basic water-safety instruction techniques in San Juan, Puerto Rico, beginning April 28. The meeting was to help Latin American Red Cross societies deal with the growing problem of accidental deaths and injuries. Representatives from Red Cross societies in 17 Latin American countries and Spain attended the seminar. Each participating Red Cross society was provided instructional material, such as films and manuals, to aid first-aid education programs in their countries. The American Red Cross was also developing an audio-visual method of teaching basic first aid to persons with limited or no reading ability.

The 49th American Red Cross National Convention was held in Minneapolis from May 19 to 22. The meeting focused on ways to strengthen the Red Cross role as a voluntary emergency response organization in local communities.   Joseph P. Anderson

RELIGION. The political interests of the Islamic world were manifest at the fifth Islamic Conference of Foreign Ministers, held in Kuala Lumpur, Malaysia, in June, 1974. The statements of the conferees showed that there is no concept in the Moslem world analogous to Western Christianity's "separation of church and state." At the same time, it was also evident that few wholly Islamic nations exist, though the faith remains the bond for half a billion North Africans, Middle Easterners, and South Asians.

The most militant Moslem leader in the Arab world, Libya's President Muammar Muhammad al-Qadhaafi, was sometimes an embarrassment to his neighbors because of his fanatic religious consistency. He successfully thwarted attempts to give women more freedom. But his own status in Libya became ever less secure, in part because of the rigidity of his religious practices.

In Africa. Religious traditionalism suffered a setback in Ethiopia, where Emperor Haile Selassie fell from power. He was removed by a reformist military coup that ended the Coptic Church-sanctioned feudalism in that increasingly pluralistic African nation in September.

Religion made hostilities worse in troubled Uganda, which is ruled by a ruthless and eccentric general, President Idi Amin Dada. Amin is a Moslem in a nation where over 90 per cent of the people

U.S. Church Membership Reported for Bodies with 150,000 or More Members*

African Methodist Episcopal Church	1,166,301
African Methodist Episcopal Zion Church	1,024,974
American Baptist Association	1,003,695
American Baptist Churches in the U.S.A.	1,502,759
The American Lutheran Church	2,465,584
Armenian Church of America, Diocese of the (Including Diocese of California)	372,000
Assemblies of God	1,177,116
Baptist Missionary Association of America	203,903
Christian Church (Disciples of Christ)	1,330,747
Christian Churches and Churches of Christ	1,034,047
Christian Methodist Episcopal Church	466,718
Christian Reformed Church	210,000
Church of God (Anderson, Ind.)	157,828
Church of God (Cleveland, Tenn.)	313,332
The Church of God in Christ	425,000
The Church of God in Christ, International	501,000
The Church of Jesus Christ of Latter-day Saints	2,208,045
Church of the Brethren	179,333
Church of the Nazarene	417,732
Churches of Christ	2,400,000
Conservative Baptist Association of America	300,000
The Episcopal Church	2,917,165
Free Will Baptists	214,104
General Association of Regular Baptist Churches	225,000
Greek Orthodox Archdiocese of North and South America	1,950,000
International General Assembly of Spiritualists	164,072
Jehovah's Witnesses	472,662
Jewish Congregations	6,115,000
Lutheran Church in America	3,017,778
The Lutheran Church—Missouri Synod	2,776,104
National Baptist Convention of America	2,668,799
National Baptist Convention, U.S.A., Inc.	5,500,000
National Primitive Baptist Convention, Inc.	1,645,000
Orthodox Church in America	1,000,000
Polish National Catholic Church of America	282,411
Presbyterian Church in the U.S.	946,536
Progressive National Baptist Convention, Inc.	521,692
Reformed Church in America	360,746
Reorganized Church of Jesus Christ of Latter Day Saints	157,131
The Roman Catholic Church	48,465,438
The Salvation Army	361,571
Seventh-day Adventists	464,276
Southern Baptist Convention	12,295,400
Unitarian-Universalist Association	200,405
United Church of Christ	1,867,810
The United Methodist Church	10,192,265
United Pentecostal Church, International	270,000
The United Presbyterian Church in the U.S.A.	2,808,942
Wisconsin Evangelical Lutheran Synod	387,286

*Majority of figures are for the years 1973 and 1974.
Source: National Council of Churches, *Yearbook of American and Canadian Churches* for 1975.

Devout Hindus bathe in the Ganges River in India during a sacred festival
to wash away their sins and ensure better life in their next reincarnation.

are not. Most of them are either Christian or non-Moslem, non-Christian tribesmen. Amin was believed to have provoked a rebellion, led in part by General Charles Arube, a Christian. The rebellion gave Amin an excuse to clamp down more fully on the suppressed majorities.

In Asia, Buddhists gained Western attention through a 10-nation European tour in 1973 and 1974 by the Tibetan Dalai Lama. He met religious leaders, but was snubbed by many government officials. His visit called attention to the dreams of many followers that he might one day return to Tibet, a dream hard to realize because of effective Chinese control of that historic Buddhist stronghold.

When the world's youngest monarch, 18-year-old King Jigme Singhi Wangchuk, was crowned in the tiny Himalayan country of Bhutan, traditional religious customs were honored. Astrologers set the date and Buddhist monks played significant parts in the ceremonies. But the show of tradition could hardly screen off Bhutan's problems. Not least of these were threats to assassinate the king by Tibetan refugees who hoped to use Bhutan as a means of regaining Tibet from China.

Religious loyalties were strongly evident in Indian elections in March, when Prime Minister Indira Gandhi's party won in her home state, Uttar Pradesh. The voting patterns clearly followed caste and religious outlines. The untouchables elected un-touchables, Brahmans chose Brahmans, and Moslems elected Moslems. Gandhi's Congress Party survived on the basis of this recognition of tense pluralism, though the outcome showed how tenuous religious and civil alliances are in India.

Religious Influences. The Eastern religions, because of the widely publicized visits of their leaders, continued to make an impact on the West, where increasing numbers – particularly of young Americans – adopted their methods. The Maharaj Ji, 16-year-old leader of the Divine Light Mission, married his secretary in June in Denver, Colo. This was only one of the highly visible moves by various Hindu gurus and swamis with U.S. followers.

Alexander I. Solzhenitsyn, who was exiled from Russia to the West, became a major religious voice with the publication in Western countries in March of his 15,000-word letter to Russia's political leaders. The author, who won a Nobel Prize in 1970, commented on the spiritual and moral crises of freedom in both Russia and the West, and exposed for millions the extent of oppression during more than half a century of Soviet rule. His comments fit no conventional Western democratic ideas, but his manifesting of faith in Christianity stirred many who had forgotten the religious dimension of East-West issues. See Literature (Close-Up). Martin E. Marty

See also Eastern Orthodox Churches; Jews; Protestant; Roman Catholic Church.

REPUBLICAN PARTY. Republicans suffered their worst election losses in a decade in 1974. The Watergate scandal and the nation's economic troubles cut the party's strength in the Senate, in the House of Representatives, and on state and local levels. The Democratic sweep cut Republican strength in the House by 43 seats and in the Senate by at least 3 seats, with 1 contested. In addition, the Republican Party lost the governorships of both New York and California. See ELECTIONS.

The resignation of President Richard M. Nixon on August 9, three months before the November elections, together with rapidly rising prices and unemployment, contributed to a near-rout of Republican Party candidates. Then the new Republican President, Gerald R. Ford, on September 8 unexpectedly pardoned Nixon for crimes he committed or may have committed while in office, and this apparently added to the Republican Party's troubles. President Ford was unable to stem the anti-Republican tide despite ardent campaigning in 20 states. Some Republican candidates blamed Ford's preelection request for a 5 per cent surtax on middle- and upper-income Americans for part of the Republican losses. See FORD, GERALD RUDOLPH; NIXON, RICHARD MILHOUS; PRESIDENT OF THE UNITED STATES; WATERGATE; Section Two, FROM TRIUMPH TO TRAGEDY.

Mary Smith takes over the gavel from outgoing Republican Party Chairman George Bush, center, while party Vice-Chairman Ray Bliss looks on.

The 1976 Hopefuls. Despite his party's poor showing, Ford announced in mid-November that he definitely would be a Republican candidate for President in 1976. However, Ford's popularity dropped sharply after his first month in office, and this encouraged former California Governor Ronald Reagan and others to keep alive their 1976 hopes for the Republican candidacy. But Senator Charles H. Percy of Illinois, one of the potential contenders, announced in August that he had put his presidential plans into a "deep freeze" after Nixon yielded his office to Ford.

Some conservative Republicans were dismayed over Ford's selection of former New York Governor Nelson A. Rockefeller, a moderate, to be Vice-President. During Rockefeller's Senate confirmation hearings, there was criticism of his loans and gifts to public officials and skepticism about the Rockefeller family's great wealth. This and Rockefeller's backing of a critical biography of former U.S. Supreme Court Justice Arthur J. Goldberg during their 1970 contest for the New York governorship seemed to dim his chances of seeking the presidency in the future. Nevertheless, Congress confirmed him as Vice-President in December. See ROCKEFELLER, NELSON.

Within the Party, Ford selected Mary Louise Smith, an Iowan, to be the first chairwoman of the Republican National Committee. On September 16, the Republican National Committee ratified her nomination to succeed George Bush, whom the President appointed U.S. envoy to the People's Republic of China on September 4.

Smith, party cochairman for six months before her promotion, was an alternate delegate to the 1964 Republican convention and a member of the national committee since 1964. Richard D. Obenshain, chairman of the Virginia State Republican Party, was named national vice-chairman. Smith was considered a moderate; Obenshain, a conservative.

After the election setback, Smith set in motion a shakeup in Republican National Headquarters and announced that a conference of 1,500 leaders would be held in March, 1975, to rebuild the party. "Watergate probably hurt us, certainly more than I anticipated," she said. She speculated that Republicans who survived "perhaps separated themselves to a greater extent from the Watergate situation."

She also announced a two-year public-relations program to improve the party's image and attract more Republican supporters. She noted with dismay that only 23 per cent of Americans identify themselves with the Republican Party, though a majority say they are conservatives.

The party suffered a legal setback on January 11, when a U.S. District Court judge ruled that part of the plan for selecting delegates to the 1976 convention was unconstitutional. The judge declared that a flat bonus system of awarding extra delegates to states that voted Republican unduly favored smaller states. However, he approved the idea of awarding a varying number of extra delegates based on the percentage of Republicans voting in a state.

Reform Rules. On December 8, a special committee of the Republican Party proposed a set of rules that would encourage wider participation of minority groups and women in the party and prevent future campaign abuses such as occurred during Nixon's 1972 re-election effort. The committee proposed that all state party organizations submit summaries of activities designed to open opportunities within the party to minorities and women. The conservatives emphasized that this rule, if adopted, would not be binding and did not impose a quota system for minority and women delegates to the 1976 convention.

The committee also proposed a rule to give the national committee greater control over presidential campaigns. It would require that the presidential campaign committee submit periodic reports to the Republican National Committee and that a national committee member be assigned to the presidential campaign. The Republican national chairman would also have to approve all campaign expenditures of more than $1,000. "We are not going to go down the road of the 1972 independent, candidate-oriented committee to re-elect anybody," said Congressman William A. Steiger of Wisconsin, chairman of the special committee.   William J. Eaton

RETAILING. Total United States retail sales of all products other than automotive products rose nearly 11 per cent during the first three quarters of 1974. But they dipped to close to the break-even point in the final quarter. It was the most difficult and challenging year for retailers in more than two decades. Inflation and shortages of materials and foods caused substantial price rises and reduced the real purchasing power of American families. Fearing continued price rises, many consumers anticipated purchases earlier in the year. Many stores did the same, and became overstocked. However, as a recession psychology spread in the last quarter, both customers and stores began to limit purchases to actual needs.

Despite early sales gains of close to 12 per cent in food stores and 8 per cent in general merchandise stores, unit sales showed little overall growth because of higher prices. Furniture, appliance, and other "big ticket" item sales slowed considerably as the year progressed, in reaction to record high interest rates and pressures exerted on family budgets by costlier groceries, gasoline, home-heating oil, and utility bills.

Surprisingly, the seven-year decline in the total number of retail outlets, other than gas stations, was reversed in 1974. But nearly 10 per cent of the nation's gas stations closed as a result of the energy crisis. Food outlets also decreased by an estimated 2.7 per cent.

Troubled Discount Houses. A few very large discount department-store chains went into bankruptcy, and others were in a shaky position. Yet, the number of discount stores in operation grew by more than 6 per cent. But the mood for rapid expansion was greatly tempered in most retail operations because of uncertain economic conditions and discouragingly high interest rates for capital expenditures, credit operations, and peak-season inventories. Many chains looked for opportunities to close unprofitable units, and some financially squeezed chains sold locations to stronger firms. Burdensome leases and overexpansion were major causes of failure.

At year's end, there were some signs that the inflation rate for apparel and home furnishings might be slowing. Polyester-fiber producers cut prices nearly 8 per cent in October. With sales slumping, many furniture makers were offering better values.

In order to avoid heavy overstocks at January inventory time, stores entered the Christmas season with tighter inventory controls. Despite increases in dollar-volume sales, most retailers would be happy to equal their 1973 profits. Should disposable consumer income continue to shrink in a tight-credit, sluggish economy in 1975, many retailers may not survive. As always, stores with entrenched positions and more capable management will retain and even expand their share of market.   Joseph R. Rowen

RHODE ISLAND. See STATE GOVERNMENT.

RHODESIA. The white-minority government made significant moves to negotiate with black nationalists in December, 1974. Rhodesian Prime Minister Ian D. Smith announced a cease-fire agreement with black guerrillas on December 11. As part of the agreement, blacks being held in detention were released to pave the way for a black-white conference on attaining black majority rule. The December developments reportedly resulted from secret talks between Smith and black African leaders.

Toward Black Unity. Three black nationalist factions met in Zambia on December 8 and agreed to unite within the African National Council (ANC) in future negotiations. Deep divisions remained. One group was reluctant to participate in any conference unless immediate black rule was guaranteed.

Then, observers reported on December 16 that South Africa's Prime Minister Balthazar Johannes Vorster had suggested a plan for universal franchise that would bring black majority rule to Rhodesia, perhaps in five years. During the transition period, blacks with at least one year of secondary school would be allowed to vote, thus increasing black representation in an interim parliament. Observers believed Vorster was trying to win agreements from black nations to curtail guerrilla activity against South Africa.

White Anxiety. All of white southern Africa became vitally interested in solving the Rhodesian problem after Portugal abandoned its colonial holdings, particularly Mozambique, which borders Rhodesia on the west and northwest. Except for its southern border with South Africa, Rhodesia will be surrounded by black nations, and black nationalist guerrillas would have a much broader base for attack. See PORTUGAL; MOZAMBIQUE.

The Rhodesian government stopped describing the guerrilla war, which was causing an average of one death a day, as a minor problem. However, the government dismissed reports about low morale among its troops and about atrocities committed against African civilians.

During the spring, 8,000 people were removed from an area near the Mozambique border to create a "free-fire" zone. In July, the government announced plans to move 60,000 Africans to 21 new "protected villages," which a black nationalist spokesman denounced as concentration camps.

Even before the changes in Mozambique, Rhodesia's uncertain political situation and the increasing danger of guerrilla attack had caused a major drop in white immigration. There was a net inflow of 2,130 persons in 1973, but 7,000 left the country.

Smith's ruling Rhodesian Front won all the white parliamentary seats in July elections. The ANC boycotted the elections to protest the arrest and detention in June of an ANC official.   John Storm Roberts

ROADS AND HIGHWAYS. See TRANSPORTATION.

ROCKEFELLER, NELSON ALDRICH (1908-   ), former Republican governor of New York and member of one of the richest families in America, was nominated to be the 41st Vice-President of the United States on Aug. 20, 1974, by President Gerald R. Ford. He was confirmed by the Senate on December 10. The House of Representatives confirmed him on December 19, and he was sworn into office that same day.

Congressional hearings on Rockefeller's nomination, which extended from August into December, were probably the most thorough investigation of a potential officeholder ever. Among the revelations that came from the hearings was the fact that Rockefeller's private wealth includes total holdings of $218 million, mostly in trusts, and that his average annual income over the past 10 years was $4.6-million before taxes. The investigators expressed concern over gifts totaling nearly $2 million that he made to political and staff associates, his handling of the 1971 riot at Attica (N.Y.) Prison while he was governor, and his role in the publication of a derogatory biography of Arthur J. Goldberg, his opponent in the 1970 campaign for governor.

Rockefeller was born July 8, 1908, in Bar Harbor, Me., the second son of John D., Jr., and Abby Greene (Aldrich) Rockefeller. He served as director of Rockefeller Center, Incorporated, in New York City from 1931 to 1958. From 1935 to 1940, he was also a director of the Creole Petroleum Corporation, a Standard Oil of New Jersey affiliate with large holdings in Venezuela. In 1940, President Franklin D. Roosevelt created the Office of the Coordinator of Inter-American Affairs and appointed Rockefeller to the post.

Rockefeller served from December, 1944, to August, 1945, as assistant secretary of state for Latin America. On Nov. 24, 1950, he became chairman of the 13-member Advisory Board on International Development, created as part of President Harry S. Truman's Point Four Program for aid to underdeveloped nations. He conducted a study for President Dwight D. Eisenhower that resulted in the creation of the Department of Health, Education, and Welfare (HEW) and served as HEW undersecretary from 1953 to 1954.

Rockefeller was elected governor of New York in 1958, defeating incumbent W. Averell Harriman, and was re-elected in 1962, 1966, and 1970. He resigned in December, 1973, to devote his time to two commissions studying problems of the future and water pollution. Rockefeller campaigned unsuccessfully for the Republican presidential nomination in 1964 and 1968.

His first marriage to Mary Todhunter Clark ended in divorce. They had five children. In May, 1963, he married Margarette (Happy) Fitler Murphy. They have two children.   Foster Stockwell

ROMAN CATHOLIC CHURCH. The organizational vitality of the church declined perceptibly in 1974, but there were no dramatic losses in personnel. At the same time, there was less factional friction between conservatives and progressives.

On May 22, Pope Paul VI addressed the United Nations Special Committee on Apartheid, which was then meeting in Rome. He condemned violence as a solution to problems of discrimination and deplored discrimination against women, migrant workers, "and all who live at the margin of society and are without voice." This set the tone for the Catholic Church's general program of social action without downplaying evangelism. The World Synod of Bishops began deliberations in Rome on September 27 that lasted for more than a month on "The Evangelization of the Modern World." On October 26, the pope, speaking at the final session of the synod, pronounced its work "positive" and then rejected many of the principal proposals made by the bishops. He said that some points "demand a refining" and that the proposals "need to be placed in proper proportion."

On February 5, the Vatican Press Office announced that the pope had relieved Joseph Cardinal Mindszenty as primate of Hungary and archbishop of Esztergom. The action was expected to promote better relations with the Communist governments of Eastern Europe. Many other sociopolitical prob-

Pope Paul VI concelebrates Mass in the Sistine Chapel in Vatican City at ceremonies opening the fourth World Synod of Bishops in September.

lems received the Vatican's attention. On February 9, Pope Paul gave an audience to President Luis Echeverría Alvarez, the first Mexican chief of state ever to visit the Vatican. This was an encouraging development, in view of the Mexican government's traditional anticlericalism. In early June, the Vatican re-established diplomatic relations with Cuba. United States Secretary of State Henry A. Kissinger met with the pope in Rome on July 6 to discuss world peace, the Middle East, and President Richard M. Nixon's conversations with Russian leaders.

World Freedoms. Chile's 28 bishops issued a pastoral letter on April 24 dealing mainly with the 1975 Holy Year observance. But the letter also directly attacked the military junta that controls the country, protesting its educational and economic policies as well as its repressive tactics. The bishops of the administrative board of the U.S. Catholic Conference also protested violations of human rights in Chile and Brazil in mid-February. They urged the U.S. government to consider ending financial aid to these countries unless human rights policies there are changed. These events tended to show the church's trend, since Vatican Council II, away from exclusive concern with spiritual matters and toward problems relating to the freedom and welfare of human beings.

The Vatican focused strong attention on the Middle East, not only because of the explosive Arab-Israeli tensions, but also because of Christian concerns in Jerusalem. On August 18, Archbishop Hilarion Capucci, patriarchal vicar of the Greek Catholic Church in Jerusalem, was arrested by Israeli police on suspicion of smuggling arms to Palestinian terrorists. After trial in Jerusalem, he was sentenced on December 9 to 12 years in prison.

Another area of concern was Northern Ireland, where a five-month-old coalition government collapsed on May 28. Failure of the coalition represented a victory for the Protestant extremists. See NORTHERN IRELAND.

The Abortion Issue was the liveliest topic of discussion among U.S. Catholics in 1974. On March 7, four cardinals – John Krol of Philadelphia, Timothy Manning of Los Angeles, Humberto Medeiros of Boston, and John Cody of Chicago – testified before the Senate Judiciary Constitutional Amendments Subcommittee in Washington, D.C. They supported amending the U.S. Constitution to provide due recognition of the right of the unborn child to life. They did not endorse any particular form of amendment. A noted liberal Catholic magazine, *Commonweal*, urged Catholics on May 31 to abandon hope for a total legal ban on abortion and to join with other moderates, Christian and Jew, to stop the rising tide of "abortion on demand." Even the National Conference of American Bishops on July 15, conceded that there is a tendency among U.S. Catholics to adopt a permissiveness toward birth control and abortion.

Most of the U.S. bishops appointed during 1974 were progressively oriented, including Robert Sanchez, archbishop of Santa Fe, N. Mex., the first Mexican-American archbishop. *The National Catholic Reporter* attributed the change largely to the significant role played by Archbishop Jean Jadot, the new apostolic delegate in the United States, in the selection of new bishops.

Pentecostal Trends. The most vigorous spiritual movement in U.S. Catholicism continued to be the Pentecostal movement. While the worldwide total of Catholic Pentecostals is estimated at 350,000, most are in the United States. A new facet of the movement appeared at the International Conference on Charismatic Renewal in the Catholic Church, held at Notre Dame University in June. About 50 persons reported healing of auditory, visual, and other ailments at a four-hour service attended by 33,000 charismatics. Some charismatics, however, believed that the reported healings might hurt the growth of the Pentecostal movement.

Sentiment favoring the ordination of women to the priesthood increased, though it was slow and without official encouragement. On August 31, 600 nuns attending the Leadership Conference of Women Religious in Houston approved a resolution calling implicitly for the ordination of women priests. However, Sister Gloria Fitzgerald was dropped from the campus ministry of Boston University for an alleged attempt to celebrate Mass on March 15.

Recognition of the rights of homosexuals in the Catholic Church also moved slowly. On May 5, 28 members of the Woodstock College academic community protested against the New York Archdiocese's opposition to a homosexual civil rights bill in New York City. Members of a Catholic homosexual organization, called Dignity, partook of Communion at St. Patrick's Cathedral in New York City.

Ecumenism. Catholic and Lutheran theologians, members of a joint national dialogue, issued a statement in March agreeing that a "renewed" papacy might well become the focus of unity. This confirmed the belief of many ecumenists that it was the historical style, not the basic concept of the papacy, that has obstructed Catholic-Protestant unity.

Richard McCormick, Jesuit research scholar at the Kennedy Institute of Human Reproduction and Bioethics, in Washington, D.C., surprised many when he wrote in the July 13 issue of *America* that severely deformed infants who have no potential for human relationships should be allowed to die. Several other priests also figured dramatically in the news. Robert F. Drinan (D., Mass.), a Jesuit, was a member of the House Judiciary Committee that investigated charges against President Richard M. Nixon and voted articles of impeachment. John McLaughlin, aide and speechwriter for President Nixon, was called to account by his Jesuit provincial, Richard Cleary, for defending Nixon's moral leadership. However, McLaughlin remained at his White House post until his resignation in October.

Bishop Bernard Flanagan of Worcester, Mass., acknowledged in October that the 1953 excommunication of a Boston Jesuit priest, Leonard Feeney, had been secretly lifted by the Vatican in November, 1972, without Feeney's recantation of error. Feeney held a rigid interpretation of the maxim, "Outside the Church, no salvation." At their annual meeting in Washington, D.C., the American bishops on November 21 departed from precedent in voting to oppose capital punishment.

In December, the Vatican announced that Elizabeth Ann Bayley Seton would be one of seven saints canonized during the 1975 Holy Year. Mother Seton, who was born in 1774, founded the Sisters of Charity of St. Joseph. She will be the first U.S.-born Catholic to become a saint.

Catholic Membership. The *Official Catholic Directory* for 1974 reported an increase in the number of Catholics in the United States of 5,011, making a national total of 48,465,438 Catholics. There were 56,712 priests as compared to 56,969 in 1973, and 139,963 sisters, as against 143,054 in 1973. The total of high school students decreased from 929,674 in 1973 to 911,730 in 1974, and elementary school students dropped from 2,872,875 in 1973 to 2,717,898 in 1974.

John B. Sheerin

See also RELIGION.

ROMANIA maintained its detached, independent position within the Warsaw Pact in 1974. In June, Russia reportedly demanded greater Romanian participation in the pact's defense integration program and the right of passage for Russian troops bound for Bulgaria. Both requests were rejected. In return, Russia snubbed Romania in August by sending only Premier Aleksei N. Kosygin to celebrations commemorating Romania's 1944 liberation. Romania vigorously opposed anti-Chinese proposals at the Russian-sponsored preparatory meeting for a European Communist Conference in Warsaw, Poland, in October.

President Nicolae Ceausescu strengthened his position by reshuffling party and government posts in March. Manea Manescu, a Ceausescu nominee, became prime minister, while a number of other leaders were demoted. Ceausescu became president of the republic on March 28, instead of merely president of the Council of State. Consequently, he now has the power to rule by decree when the Grand National Assembly is not sitting and to dismiss and appoint ministers without its approval. Ceausescu visited Argentina, Libya, and Guinea in February and March. In July, he met with Yugoslav President Josip Broz Tito in Bucharest and in November with U.S. Secretary of State Henry A. Kissinger.

Marxist and Nationalist Indoctrination continued in all spheres of public life. The "Romanian way to socialism" was spelled out in November at the Communist Party Congress, which re-elected Ceausescu as party general secretary for another five years. But concern over efficient management in the economy remained a key issue. To help Romania increase its agricultural production for exports, the World Bank granted a $60-million loan for a $200-million fertilizer factory. In June, however, negotiations to build Volkswagen cars in Romania ended in failure.

Ceausescu continued to press for rapid industrialization at the expense of an improved standard of living for Romanians. The forced pace took its toll in terms of serious accidents at key chemical, truck-manufacturing, and electrical engineering plants. On November 1, the government tempered its economic policy by raising the wages of skilled workers and increasing welfare allowances.

Romania's foreign trade system was reorganized in May to put all export activities under stricter government control. In April, the Manufacturers Hanover Trust Company of New York City opened an office in Bucharest, the first Western bank to do so. On August 8, the U.S. Senate voted Romania most-favored-nation status, and the two countries signed a five-year cooperation pact on December 14, the first political agreement between them. Chris Cviic

See also EUROPE (Facts in Brief Table); MANESCU, MANEA.

ROTARY INTERNATIONAL turned its attention to the problems of ecology at its 65th annual convention in Minneapolis-St. Paul in June, 1974. The central theme of the convention was "Quality of Life," with panel discussions on preservation of natural environment, conservation and use of energy, expanding educational opportunities, innovations in urban government, health care, world food supply, foundation of faith, and influence of the arts.

A seven-member committee was named to counsel the Rotary board of directors on environmental matters. The committee chairman is Charles Simeons of London, England. The other members are Gordon A. Knox of Toronto, Canada; Claude Romeiu of Montpelier, France; Vernon J. Heaslip of Ontario, Canada; Kamejero Saiki of Hemeki, Japan; and Cesar A. Tognoni of Buenos Aires, Argentina. Rotary clubs that seek advice on such programs can contact the general secretary.

William R. Robbins of Fort Lauderdale, Fla., became president of Rotary International on July 1. There were 16,079 clubs and an estimated 758,750 Rotarians in 151 countries and geographical regions. There also were 1,882 Rotaract Clubs (for 18- to 28-year-olds) with an estimated membership of 37,640 in 60 countries, and 3,226 Interact Clubs (for pre-university students) with an estimated membership of 70,962 in 68 countries. Joseph P. Anderson

ROWING. See SPORTS.

ROWLING, WALLACE E. (1927-   ), was named prime minister of New Zealand on Sept. 6, 1974, succeeding Norman E. Kirk, 51, who died of a heart attack on August 31. Rowling was expected to continue Kirk's policies. See NEW ZEALAND.

Rowling, a member of the Labour Party, is the youngest government chief in New Zealand's history. He was born in Motueka on the South Island, where his father was a fruit grower. He earned a master's degree in economics at Canterbury University in Christchurch and taught for 13 years before becoming an education officer with the New Zealand Army. In 1955, he spent several months in Seattle on a Fulbright teaching scholarship.

He first entered Parliament at the age of 35 in a 1962 by-election. He was elected vice-president of the Labour Party in 1969, and president shortly after. He has a keen interest in the European Community (Common Market) and traveled to Great Britain and Europe in 1971 to present his party's views on Britain's entry into the market. He became minister of finance in 1972 and has represented New Zealand at international finance meetings. As finance minister, his major legislative effort was introducing a government pension plan for all workers.

Rowling reputedly is a shy man and a middle-of-the-road politician. He and his wife have two sons and two daughters. Kathryn Sederberg

RUBBER. See MANUFACTURING.

RUMSFELD, DONALD (1932-   ), United States ambassador to the North Atlantic Treaty Organization (NATO) since December, 1972, was named assistant to the President on Sept. 24, 1974, by President Gerald R. Ford. He succeeded General Alexander M. Haig, Jr.

Rumsfeld was born in Chicago on July 9, 1932, and graduated from Princeton University in 1954. He then served as a U.S. Navy jet pilot and as an assistant to two Republican congressmen, David Dennison of Ohio and Robert R. Griffin of Michigan, and served briefly with a banking firm in Chicago. In 1962, he was elected to the House of Representatives from the 13th District of Illinois. He was re-elected to this post three times.

Rumsfeld supported Richard M. Nixon in the 1968 campaign, and was one of the delegates to make nomination speeches for Nixon at the Republican National Convention. The new President appointed Rumsfeld director of the Office of Economic Opportunity. In 1970, he became a counselor to the President, with Cabinet rank. Rumsfeld was also director of the Cost of Living Council, which was established to control inflation as part of the Nixon wage-price program.

Rumsfeld is married to the former Joyce Pierson, his high school sweetheart, and they have three children, Valerie Jeanne, Marcy Kay, and Donald Nicholas. Foster Stockwell

RUSSIA

Russia continued to expand its business ties with the West in 1974. Despite some new problems in their détente, Russia and the United States agreed to limit their nuclear arms race. Relations with China remained hostile. At home, the government pursued its campaign against political dissidents and other nonconformist elements with greater flexibility.

Nuclear Arms Agreement. President Richard M. Nixon visited Russia from June 27 to July 3, and his successor, Gerald R. Ford, met Communist Party General Secretary Leonid I. Brezhnev in Vladivostok on November 23 and 24. At the June meeting, the two countries confirmed the desirability of limiting strategic arms. The June summit also produced an agreement to limit underground nuclear explosions and antiballistic missile systems. But the Ford-Brezhnev meeting in November produced a tentative agreement to limit offensive nuclear weapons and delivery vehicles through 1985. United States Secretary of State Henry A. Kissinger termed the pact a "breakthrough." Negotiations to hammer out the details were to begin in Geneva, Switzerland, in January, 1975, with a final document possibly ready for initialing during Brezhnev's proposed visit to the United States in mid-1975. See NATIONAL DEFENSE.

Despite the friendly atmosphere at the November Vladivostok meeting, Russia and the United States remained at odds on other issues. Kissinger had visited Moscow at the end of October to discuss differences over the Middle East and Cyprus as well as to prepare for President Ford's November visit. President Ford's October 4 decision to halt Russia's purchase of 3.4 million short tons (3.1 metric tons) of corn and wheat angered the Russians. So did the publicity that surrounded an October 18 announcement by Senator Henry M. Jackson (D., Wash.) that Russia would allow 60,000 Russian Jews to emigrate annually in return for better trade terms.

The U.S. Congress passed the favorable trade bill in December despite a last-minute Russian disavowal of any deal. The official press agency Tass said on December 18 that Russian leaders "flatly reject as unacceptable" any attached conditions or other interference with the country's internal affairs. The lower U.S. tariffs on Russian imports will be reviewed after 18 months, and may be ended then if emigration policies have not eased.

In the Middle East, Russia continued its strong support of the Palestine Liberation Organization (PLO), and the PLO opened a mission in Moscow in August. On the Cyprus issue, Russia backed deposed President Archbishop Makarios III. But it also sided with Turkey over Greece when Turkish forces invaded Cyprus in July. See CYPRUS.

In Asia, Russian diplomacy backed the April 9 tripartite agreement between India, Pakistan, and Bangladesh. India's Foreign Minister Swaran Singh visited Moscow in September, and Pakistan's Prime Minister Zulfikar Ali Bhutto visited the Russian capital in October.

Relations with China deteriorated in March after a Russian military helicopter, which had strayed over the Chinese border, was forced to land and its three crewmen were arrested. Russia claimed the helicopter was on a medical mission, but the Chinese charged it had "intruded into China for espionage." On July 25, Soviet Deputy Foreign Minister Leonid Ilyichev ended a month of fruitless efforts in Peking aimed at settling border disputes and gaining the

Moscow's Red Square undergoes refurbishing as workers repair the pavement blocks and Lenin's tomb, right foreground, in front of St. Basil's Church.

crew's release. China's Deputy Premier Teng Hsiao-ping said in October that the crewmen would be tried for spying. Although 1974 produced no genuine reconciliation, China and Russia increased trade about 12 per cent above the 1973 level of $270 million.

China and its European ally, Albania, criticized Russian plans for a World Communist Party Conference in 1975 that would exclude the Chinese Communists. Albania boycotted a preparatory meeting attended by delegates from 28 European Communist parties in Warsaw, Poland, in October. Delegates from Hungary, Italy, Romania, and Yugoslavia strongly opposed the condemnation of any single party. But the delegates agreed to hold the conference in 1975, probably in East Berlin.

The Communist Bloc countries of southeastern Europe drew renewed Russian interest in the summer and autumn. In June, a top Russian Army commander visited Sofia, Bulgaria, for nearly two weeks without any official explanation. Reportedly, he also visited Bucharest, Romania, and he demanded the right for Russian troops to pass through the Romanian Black Sea province of Dobruja as well as closer military integration of Romania with the other Warsaw Pact countries. Russia snubbed Ro-

477

mania's celebration of its 30 years of Communist rule on August 22. The Russians sent Premier Aleksei N. Kosygin, not party leader Brezhnev, who had attended similar celebrations in Bulgaria and Poland (see ROMANIA). In September, Yugoslav authorities announced the arrest and trial of a group of pro-Russian Communists who had been "helped from abroad" (see YUGOSLAVIA). Elsewhere in Eastern Europe, Russia's control was reinforced by the world oil crisis. These countries have few natural resources and petroleum reserves.

Dissent at Home. Western public opinion continued to force the Russian government to tread carefully at home so as not to upset its policy of détente with the West. Alexander I. Solzhenitsyn, Russia's leading writer and winner of the Nobel Prize, was deported on February 13. See LITERATURE (Close-Up).

Novelist Vladimir Maximov was exiled in February. Ballet dancers Valery Panov and his wife, Galina Ragozina, emigrated to Israel on June 9. Former General Pyotr Grigorenko, a human rights campaigner who had spent five years in mental prison-hospitals, was released on June 26. Despite such actions, the number of Jews allowed to emigrate dwindled to less than one-half of 1973's total, presumably in anticipation of a Kissinger-Brezhnev bargain of more emigration for better trade terms.

The underground publication *Chronicle of Current Events*, suppressed by the secret police in 1972, resumed publication on May 12. But its former publisher, Garik Superfin, was sentenced on May 14 to five years in a labor camp followed by three years in exile for anti-Russian activities.

Police with bulldozers broke up an open-air art show in Moscow on September 15 and roughed up some Western correspondents present. The show was held on September 29, following worldwide protests against police behavior. But in a speech on November 10, Supreme Soviet Presidium Chairman Nikolai V. Podgorny warned the Russian public that only "socialist realism" was permitted in Russia.

Foreign Trade Agreements. On June 20, Russia signed a $200-million deal with the Chemical Construction Corporation for the construction of four ammonia-producing plants at the Volga River fertilizer and natural gas complex. Eight days later, another U.S. firm, the Occidental Petroleum Corporation, concluded a $20.3-billion, 20-year barter deal that was first agreed to in April, 1973. Occidental will equip the ports of Ventspils on the Baltic Sea and Odessa on the Black Sea to handle 4 million short tons (3.6 million metric tons) of ammonia, urea, and potassium chloride from the Volga River complex. Russia agreed to trade these chemicals annually for 1 million short tons (0.9 million metric ton) of

Russian workmen use U.S. equipment to lay part of a new transcontinental pipeline that will carry natural gas through the Kara Kum Desert to Moscow.

Muscovites read a poster that calls Alexander Solzhonitsyn a "traitor" and "anti-Communist slanderer." He was deported on February 13.

withdrew from a joint oil exploration program in November.

The Russian Economy easily reached its planned growth targets in the first half of 1974. The goals had been reduced in 1973. The government reported industrial production up 8.3 per cent over the first half of 1973 and labor productivity up 6.8 per cent. The largest gains were posted by engineering (up 12 per cent), chemical and petrochemical industries (up 11 per cent), and the food industry (up 10 per cent). Growth in the production of consumer goods rose about 4 per cent overall, but the output of such items as shoes, radios, and washing machines fell below government goals. In the first nine months, 829,000 cars were built, 23 per cent more than in the corresponding period of 1973.

On December 18, the chairman of the state planning agency reported a grain harvest of 195 million short tons (178 million metric tons), about 10 million short tons (9 million metric tons) short of the planned target, and well below Russia's record 1973 harvest. On October 19, U.S. Treasury Secretary William E. Simon, who had visited Moscow earlier in the month, announced that Russia would be allowed to purchase up to 1.3 million short tons (1.2 million metric tons) of U.S. wheat and 1.1 million short tons (1 million metric tons) of corn through June 30, 1975. Chris Cviic

See also Europe (Facts in Brief Table).

RWANDA. See Africa.

superphosphoric acid from Occidental. Deals with West Germany in October and November included an agreement to supply 2.1 trillion cubic feet (60 billion cubic meters) of Russian natural gas between 1978 and 2000; an agreement to deliver 10,000 special-purpose Magirus trucks to Russia with the aid of a $300-million loan provided by a group of German banks; and a $379-million deal to supply Russian nuclear fuel until 1990 to the West German firm that produces 40 per cent of Germany's electricity.

No Energy Crisis. While industrialized Western nations were reeling from the impact of skyrocketing oil prices, Russia became the world's leading oil producer, pumping 9.02 million barrels a day for the first six months of 1974. Despite Russia's relative abundance of energy, the Communist Party Central Committee urged workers in October to conserve gasoline, electricity, and materials.

In February, the first of six sulfur-recovery plants began operating at the Orenburg natural gas fields. Built with French help, the unit can process 175-billion cubic feet (4.9 billion cubic meters) of gas annually and recover over 100,000 short tons (91,000 metric tons) of sulfur. A 2,000-mile (3,200-kilometer) pipeline is under construction to pipe the gas to Russia's Eastern European neighbors. In November, a 2,000-mile pipeline began supplying Moscow with gas from fields in Siberia. But plans for further development there suffered a severe blow when Japan

SAFETY. Motor-vehicle-accident fatalities in the United States declined in 1974. Safety officials said the drop, which amounted to 8,000 lives saved in the first nine months of the year, could be attributed mainly to the mandatory speed limit of 55 miles (89 kilometers) per hour that was in effect during the year. Fuel conservation also played a part in the reduction of accidents, because it resulted in less traffic and particularly less nighttime and weekend driving. The National Safety Council's (NSC) projected annual rate for motor-vehicle deaths was 3.5 deaths per 100 million vehicle miles (161 million vehicle kilometers), the lowest on record.

There were also 2 per cent fewer deaths – 19,600 – in public places during the first nine months of 1974. Fatal home accidents dropped 4 per cent to 18,500, and fatal work accidents dropped 3 per cent to 10,400. The total death decline for the nine-month period in all classes was measured at 11 per cent.

Accident Costs. The cost of all accidents in 1973 rose, however, to $41.5 billion from $37 billion in 1972. Costs include wages lost due to temporary inability to work, lower wages upon returning to work because of some permanent impairment, and the value of future earnings lost by those totally incapacitated or killed.

Wage losses totaled $13.3 billion, and medical fees and hospital expenses came to $5.4 billion. Insurance and administrative costs reached $7.5 billion; property damage in motor-vehicle accidents, $6.3 billion; and property destroyed by fire, $2.6 billion. The money value of time lost by workers other than those with disabling injuries, who are directly or indirectly involved in accidents, was estimated at $6.4 billion.

In responding to President Gerald R. Ford's attack on inflationary factors late in 1974, the NSC pointed out that elimination of accidents could reduce by one-sixth the nation's 12 per cent rate of inflation. About 1 million productive man-years were lost in 1973 because of work accidents.

Accidental Deaths and Death Rates

	1973		1974†	
	Number	Rate††	Number	Rate††
Motor Vehicle	55,800	26.6	47,400	22.4
Work	14,200	6.8	13,900	6.6
Home	26,000	12.4	25,000	11.8
Public	25,000	11.9	24,500	11.6
Total*	117,000	55.8	107,000	50.6

†For 12-month period up to Oct. 1, 1974.
††Deaths per 100,000 population.
*The total does not equal the sum of the four classes because *Motor Vehicle* includes some deaths also included in *Work* and *Home*.

Source: National Safety Council estimates.

Legislation Stalled. The U.S. House of Representatives in August killed legislation calling for a mandatory seat-belt interlock system that would have required auto manufacturers to install such passive restraints in 1975 models. According to the NSC, the move "left a gaping void in the area of occupant protection that could have meant the saving of thousands of lives annually."

At the same time, legislation covering new air-bag restraint systems also was shelved, delaying installation of these passive-restraint devices, which were to have been installed in 1977-model cars. Safety officials viewed the action as a serious blow to the development of passive-restraint systems for motorists in the United States.

The NSC and other safety leaders called upon the states to pass mandatory seat-belt legislation and to otherwise strengthen seat-belt usage. They said this would help safeguard automobile travelers until proper passive restraints could be installed in all cars.

Youth Camp Safety was urged in June testimony before the House Select Committee on Labor. The committee was considering a safety act relating to recreation camps in the United States. The NSC, one of the groups that presented testimony, called for a larger and more representative number of members on the proposed Advisory Council on Youth Camp Safety, as well as new measures regulating camp standards, consultative services, education and training, travel camps, federal recreation camps, research, and finance. The legislation is expected to receive a more complete review in 1975.   Vincent L. Tofany

SAILING. See BOATING.

SAINT LOUIS voters twice rejected a proposed 66-cent increase per $100 of property valuation for the city's public school tax in 1974. Voters first rejected the proposed increase on June 6, prompting the school board president to warn that the school budget would have to be cut by $11 million. The second defeat, in the November 5 general election, was especially critical. It jeopardized an agreement reached on October 6 between the teachers and the school board providing increased salaries and decreased class sizes. The pact, which contained a no-strike promise by teachers, called for a starting salary of $8,850 and elementary class sizes of no more than 38 students.

City water workers and garbage collectors went on strike on June 12. The work stoppage ended on June 21 after the Board of Aldermen approved a $29.03 per month pay raise.

Electric Trash. The Union Electric Company, which serves the St. Louis area, on February 28 announced plans to construct a $70-million power plant that will produce electricity by burning trash. The new facility, scheduled to be completed by mid-1977, is expected to dispose of all trash collected in St. Louis and six surrounding counties in Missouri and Illinois. It will produce about 6 per cent of the utility's total power output.

A new $20-million river-rail terminal will be built

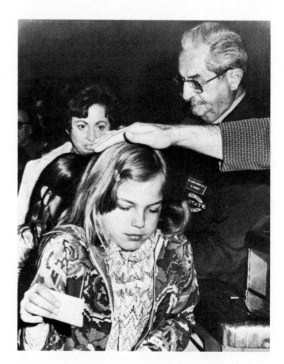

Nine-year-old Yonda Clark of Shipman, Ill., in May becomes the 5-millionth visitor to ride to the top of the Gateway Arch in St. Louis.

in the Columbia Bottoms industrial area of north St. Louis County by 1976. It will handle up to 20 million short tons (18 million metric tons) of coal annually. The facility will serve as a transportation hub for coal being shipped from Wyoming and Montana to electricity-generating facilities on the Mississippi and Ohio river systems.

The Federal Aviation Administration recommended on January 4 that a major new airport for the St. Louis area be built near Columbia, Ill. Efforts to win consensus for building the facility in Illinois have been underway since 1970.

Official Corruption. A grand jury subpoenaed more than 50 persons in September for its investigation into alleged kickbacks on public construction contracts by officials of five cities and two school districts in the Illinois portion of the St. Louis metropolitan region. The investigation involved officials from Alorton, Brooklyn, Centreville, Cahokia, and East St. Louis. Meanwhile, the Federal Bureau of Investigation reported that crime in the city dropped 4.3 per cent during the first six months of 1974.

The cost of living in St. Louis rose 10.4 per cent between June, 1973, and June, 1974. By midyear, the average take-home pay of factory workers had risen by only 7.4 per cent to $10,547 per year. During a one-year period ending in July, the number of jobs declined 2.2 per cent. James M. Banovetz

SAINT PAUL. See Minneapolis-St. Paul.

SALVATION ARMY officers and equipment served in a 10-state area in early April, 1974, after the worst tornadoes in nearly 50 years caused widespread death and destruction over an area stretching from Georgia to Ontario. In cooperation with the U.S. Federal Disaster Assistance Administration (FDAA), the Salvation Army provided food service at several evacuation centers. The army also coordinated the distribution of food, blankets, and clothing in the disaster areas.

The Salvation Army and other organizations such as American Red Cross and Goodwill Industries and the FDAA signed an agreement providing that the FDAA will coordinate the work of private and voluntary relief organizations. The new agreement was signed in Washington, D.C., on April 24. The agreement represented a major step forward in federal efforts to ease problems faced by individuals, communities, and states following disasters.

In June, the High Council, composed of 40 territorial commanders from all parts of the world, elected Commissioner Clarence D. Wiseman to replace the retiring international leader, General Erik Wikberg, as the army's 10th general. He was territorial commander for Canada and Bermuda. In November, William E. Chamberlain was installed as commander of the Salvation Army in the United States. His wife, Ethel, became president of the army's women's organizations. Joseph P. Anderson

SAN FRANCISCO-OAKLAND. San Francisco was thrown into chaos on March 8, 1974, when thousands of city employees walked off their jobs in a dispute over pay increases. The strike stopped the city's transit system, closed sewage-treatment plants, forced hospitals to turn patients away, shut down the city's port facilities, and caused garbage to pile up in streets and alleys. A separate strike by half the city's 4,500 public-school teachers all but closed the schools during the same period.

The courts ordered striking city employees back to work on March 12. The employees ignored the order and the court then ordered police to arrest picketing strikers. However, Mayor Joseph L. Alioto announced a 5¼ per cent wage-increase settlement on March 15. The school strike lasted until March 28, when teachers and the school board reached a separate settlement. Hospital care again suffered in June, when 4,000 registered nurses went on strike.

Crime made major news in the city during the year. The city was shaken by the "zebra" slayings – named for a police-radio band – of 12 white persons between October, 1973, and April, 1974. To find the killers, police used stop-and-question tactics that were widely criticized in the black community. In May, four Black Muslims were arrested and indicted for three of the murders. Patricia Hearst, daughter of the *San Francisco Chronicle*'s publisher, was kidnaped by the Symbionese Liberation Army on February 4. See Crime (Close Up).

Despite these dramatic events, crime in the metropolitan area dropped significantly during the first six months of 1974. A Federal Bureau of Investigation report released on October 4 indicated that the crime rate had declined 5 per cent in San Francisco and 9 per cent in Oakland.

The Economy. San Francisco was rated the 16th most expensive of the world's 47 major cities in a survey released by the Business International Corporation in September. According to the U.S. Department of Labor, living costs in the city increased 10.3 per cent between June, 1973, and June, 1974. The cost of food increased 18 per cent during that period, but the average factory worker's income increased by only 6.7 per cent during the year ending in July. Construction activity was down 20.9 per cent; and employment, 0.1 per cent. The economy was further hurt by the closing of the Hunters Point Naval Shipyard in June. The yard employed 5,600 civilians.

The $1.6-billion Bay Area Rapid Transit System (BART) – 75 miles (120 kilometers) long – was completed on September 16, when the tunnel under San Francisco Bay opened. However, BART ran out of money, so the California legislature extended the Bay Area's half-cent sales tax through 1978 to help eliminate the system's multimillion-dollar deficits. James M. Banovetz

SAN MARINO. See Europe.

SASKATCHEWAN. See Canada.

Secretary of State Henry Kissinger and Saudi Arabia's Prince Fahd Ibn
Abdel Aziz celebrate new economic and military pact at signing in June.

SAUDI ARABIA acquired a 60 per cent majority interest in the Arabian-American Oil Company (Aramco) in June, 1974, and immediately began negotiating for complete nationalization of the company. Aramco produces over 90 per cent of Saudi Arabia's oil. In December, the owners of Aramco–Standard Oil Company of California; Texaco, Incorporated; Exxon; and Mobil Oil Company–reportedly agreed to full Saudi ownership.

The 60 per cent interest generated vastly increased revenues for King Faisal's government, producing in September an $11.5-billion surplus. The budget approved by the Council of Ministers on July 20 was $26.7 billion, an increase of $9.6 billion over 1973. The major problem, especially after the oil embargo against some Western nations was lifted, was how to spend the funds. Saudi Arabia gave $50 million to the World Food Program on March 25, thus becoming the second largest contributor after the United States. The Saudi government loaned the International Monetary Fund $1.2 billion in August.

On June 8, the United States and Saudi Arabia signed an accord agreeing to establish two joint commissions. One, a military commission, would "review programs already underway for modernizing Saudi Arabia's armed forces." The other would help plan programs designed to increase industrialization and agricultural development. William Spencer

See also MIDDLE EAST (Facts in Brief Table).

SAWHILL, JOHN C. (1936-   ), became director of the U.S. Federal Energy Office in April, 1974, then resigned the post on October 29. He succeeded William E. Simon, who resigned to become U.S. secretary of the treasury. See SIMON, WILLIAM E.

Sawhill served as deputy director of the energy office during the 1973-1974 fuel oil and gasoline shortages and earned a reputation as a tough but fair-minded manager. After becoming director, one of his top priorities was straightening out internal management problems to make the agency more efficient. See ENERGY.

Sawhill was born on June 12, 1936, in Cleveland. He received his early education in private schools and graduated from Princeton University in 1958. In 1963, he earned a Ph.D. in business administration from New York University. While studying for his doctorate, Sawhill also worked as an assistant dean and professor of finance at the university. At the same time, he served as a consultant to the U.S. House of Representatives Committee on Banking.

Between 1963 and 1973, he worked for private financial and management consultant firms, rising to the post of senior vice-president with the Commercial Credit Company. In April, 1973, he became assistant director for natural resources, energy, and science in the U.S. Office of Management and Budget. He joined the Federal Energy Office in December, 1973. Sawhill and his wife have one son. Darlene R. Stille

SCHEEL, WALTER (1919-   ), was elected president of West Germany on May 15, 1974. As foreign affairs minister and vice-chancellor under former Chancellor Willy Brandt, Scheel had helped West Germany establish diplomatic ties with East European nations.

Scheel took over as acting chancellor on May 6, when Brandt resigned after a spy was discovered working in his office. He served until May 16, when Helmut Schmidt was elected to that office. Scheel is reportedly in poor health. His election to the largely honorary office of president was viewed as a graceful way for him to retire. See SCHMIDT, HELMUT; GERMANY, WEST.

Scheel was born on July 8, 1919, in Solingen, Germany, and studied to be a banker. During World War II, he was a fighter pilot in the German Air Force, flying missions over France and Russia. He entered politics in 1948 and was first elected to the Bundestag, one of West Germany's two houses of parliament, in 1953.

Scheel served as minister for economic cooperation from 1961 to 1966, as vice-president from 1967 to 1969, as foreign minister from 1969 to 1974, and chairman of the Free Democratic Party since 1967.

Scheel has been married twice. His first wife, by whom he had one son, died in 1966. In 1969, he married radiologist Mildred Wirtz. The Scheels have a daughter and an adopted son.   Darlene R. Stille

SCHMIDT, HELMUT (1918-   ), economist and political leader, became West Germany's fifth chancellor on May 16, 1974. He replaced Willy Brandt, who resigned because of a scandal involving a spy working in his office. See GERMANY, WEST.

Schmidt, who had been Brandt's minister of finance, pledged to continue West Germany's policy of improving relations with Eastern Europe. However, he believed that greater attention should be given to West Germany's internal affairs. Schmidt was regarded as friendly toward the United States and the North Atlantic Treaty Organization.

Schmidt was born in Hamburg, Germany, on Dec. 23, 1918, and studied economics at the University of Hamburg.

He entered politics in 1946 as a member of the Social Democratic Party and was a local transportation official from 1949 to 1953. He served in the Bundestag, one of Germany's houses of parliament, from 1953 to 1962 and was minister for domestic affairs in Hamburg from 1962 until 1965. He was again elected to the Bundestag in 1965.

Schmidt was the Bundestag floor leader of the Social Democrats from 1967 to 1969 and was elected party vice-chairman in 1968. In 1969, he became defense minister, a post he held until 1972, when he became finance minister.   Darlene R. Stille

SCHOOL. See CIVIL RIGHTS; EDUCATION; Section One, FOCUS ON EDUCATION.

SCIENCE AND RESEARCH. Scientists of many nations cooperated on projects in geology, oceanography, food production, population control, and space research in 1974. But perhaps the most unusual effort was the international expedition that set out on October 9 to traverse the 2,718 miles (4,374 kilometers) of the Congo River in Africa. The expedition came just 100 years after Henry Morton Stanley led an ill-starred expedition down the turbulent river.

Experts from Australia, England, Finland, France, Nepal, New Zealand, the United States, and Zaire were among the 140 scientists who took part in various phases of the program. The trip was expected to last four months. One of its purposes was to study river blindness, a disease transmitted by a fly-borne parasite that has blinded an estimated 3 million Africans living south of the Sahara.

Sakharov Campaign. Scientists in many countries expressed concern over Russia's actions toward its political and religious dissidents, particularly its denunciation of physicist Andrei D. Sakharov, who has criticized the Soviet government for destroying civil liberties. In the summer of 1973, the Russian press began denouncing Sakharov, and many members of the Soviet Academy of Sciences later joined the attack. Through the National Academy of Sciences, American scientists sent a telegram to the Soviet Academy warning that, if Sakharov were arrested or further harassed, it would be ". . . extremely difficult to imagine successful fulfillment of American pledges of binational scientific cooperation. . . ." After this and other international protests, the Russian government ceased its verbal abuse of Sakharov.

U.S. Energy Research. Research to develop alternate supplies of energy was a major concern of U.S. scientists in 1974. President Richard M. Nixon's budget for fiscal 1975 sought $1.8 billion for energy research, up from $999 million. This was one of the largest jumps in research funding since the early days of the space program. The budget also asked nearly $1 billion in additional funds for weapons research and development. Altogether, the federal research and development budget rose almost $2 billion to $19.56 billion.

About 40 per cent of the energy funds were slated for nuclear fission research, both to improve existing reactor technology and to continue development of a Liquid Metal Fast Breeder Reactor (LMFBR). The LMFBR is designed to combine the plentiful 233 isotope of uranium with a rare and extremely dangerous isotope of plutonium. It will produce both energy and more plutonium. The remainder of the energy research money was targeted for areas such as solar and geothermal conversion and the development of more efficient uses of coal and oil.

Nuclear Power Debate. The argument continued over whether depending on nuclear reactors to produce most of the country's electricity will pose a threat to the public. In January, the Joint Congressional Committee on Atomic Energy held hearings on the subject at which consumer advocate Ralph Nader criticized the committee as well as the Atomic Energy Commission (AEC) for what he said was a failure to alert the public to the dangers of radiation leaks and potential reactor accidents.

In March, the AEC issued an environmental impact statement declaring that the LMFBR posed only the most miniscule threat. But it was revealed in October that the AEC had years earlier suppressed the opinions of some of its own scientists, who had questioned certain safety features in conventional reactors.

On March 13, the Ford Foundation released the results of a $4-million study that concluded that the United States could achieve energy self-reliance without using such controversial energy sources as nuclear reactors, offshore oil drilling, oil from Rocky Mountain shale, or massive strip-mining of coal. The report, which called for strict conservation measures, was disputed by several oil industry representatives.

As it had in previous years, President Nixon's budget for fiscal 1975 allocated large increases for cancer and heart research, while leaving the funding for most other areas of biomedical research relatively static. Meanwhile, Congress responded to protests from scientists by tacking additional funds for basic research onto the fiscal 1974 budget.

The space budget was cut by $200 million, largely because of the demise of the Apollo and Skylab projects. The National Aeronautics and Space Administration (NASA) did get funds for the Venus Pioneer Program, two unmanned missions to that planet in 1978, and for a huge infrared telescope, to be built on Mauna Kea in Hawaii.

Research Act. President Nixon signed the National Research Act on July 12. Among other things, the act instituted a temporary ban on all research using live human fetuses. Such research had been the focus of widespread criticism, particularly from opponents of abortion. The act also established an 11-member commission consisting of scientists, clergymen, and legal experts that will set guidelines for all aspects of research on human subjects.

Biologists Take Stand. A group of eminent molecular biologists, backed by the National Academy of Sciences, published an unprecedented promise in the July 26 issues of the noted U.S. and British scientific journals *Science* and *Nature*. The scientists said they would refrain from further research into the effects of inserting particular genes into bacterial cells. They said they were afraid of possible long-range harm to humanity and called on others in the field to abandon such studies.

The biologists said that a new technique for inserting specific genes—or units of cellular informa-

tion—into bacterial cells should not be used to put viral genes, genes concerned with antibiotic resistance, or those regulating toxin production into bacteria. They warned that this type of "genetic engineering" might produce a deadly new bacterial mutant that could not be controlled by any form of antibiotic treatment. See BIOLOGY; Section One, FOCUS ON SCIENCE.

The Sloan-Kettering Institute for Cancer Research in New York City was rocked in May by one of the most serious scientific scandals in memory. It was alleged that William T. Summerlin, a prominent young researcher, had falsified his research findings. Summerlin was said to have painted black patches on the backs of white mice to make it appear that skin grafts were growing successfully. Summerlin was suspended and given a one-year leave of absence to seek psychiatric help. Many scientists believe the incident reflected some of the problems surrounding the current cancer research program, such as the intense competition for government funds and the pressure on scientists to make spectacular discoveries.   Robert J. Bazell

See also the various science articles.

SCULPTURE. See VISUAL ARTS.

SENEGAL. See AFRICA.

SERVICE CLUBS. See KIWANIS INTERNATIONAL; LIONS CLUBS, INTERNATIONAL ASSOCIATION OF; ROTARY INTERNATIONAL.

SHIP AND SHIPPING. Ship launchings throughout the world rose for the ninth straight year in 1974. According to Lloyd's Register of Shipping, there were 2,333 merchant ships under construction on September 30, an 8 per cent increase over the same date in 1973. Shipbuilding orders, including those ships under construction, increased to 5,304 from 4,678 in 1973.

Gross tonnage of vessels on order on September 30 increased to 127.7 million gross tons from 114.3 million gross tons in 1973. Although this figure was higher, it did not reflect a decline in world orders for two consecutive quarters during 1974. Orders had reached an all-time peak at the end of March with 133.4 million gross tons on order. Lloyd's explained that the decline resulted from cancellations of contracts for crude-oil supertankers.

U.S. Shipbuilding. In spite of economic, political, and energy uncertainties and shortages of certain materials, United States shipbuilders continued to enjoy a record peacetime order book of roughly $6.5-billion, slightly higher than at the close of 1973. The Shipbuilders Council of America, a trade group, estimated that the dollar volume of orders for commercial vessels in private yards was $4.2 billion, up from about $3.8 billion in 1973.

Some 87 ocean vessels were scheduled for completion by 1978. The ships will be able to haul about 6.2 million long tons (6.3 million metric tons), or a

Port Said citizens in July welcome the first ship to enter that Suez Canal port in seven years. The canal was expected to be open to traffic in 1975.

total equal to about one-half that of the 569 active ships in the U.S. merchant fleet.

A contract to build three ultralarge crude-oil carriers was placed at midyear, the Maritime Administration announced. To be built by the Newport News Shipbuilding and Dry Dock Company in Newport News, Va., the tankers will measure 1,204 feet (367 meters) long, and will be the largest ever built in the United States. Each will be able to haul 390,770 long tons (397,022 metric tons) of oil.

Still more supertankers were to be built under terms of the Energy Transportation Security Act of 1974. It would have required 20 per cent of imported oil to be hauled in U.S.-built ships by U.S. crews and 30 per cent by mid-1977, as against 6 per cent today. President Gerald R. Ford vetoed it.

Besides oil tankers, much of the 1974 order book for U.S. shipbuilders consisted of offshore drilling units, liquid natural gas carriers, and U.S. Navy ships. Navy contracts totaled $2.3 billion. Of these, half were for nuclear-powered ships, including 3 aircraft carriers, 4 guided-missile frigates, and 27 submarines. Work started in 1974 on a new generation of Trident nuclear-powered submarines as well as gas-turbine patrol frigates, intended as a part of the Navy's strategy for the 1980s.   Kenneth E. Schaefle

SHOOTING. See HUNTING; SPORTS.

SIERRA LEONE. See AFRICA.

SIKKIM. See INDIA.

SIMON, WILLIAM E. (1927-   ), became U.S. secretary of the treasury on April 30, 1974, succeeding George P. Shultz. Formerly, Simon headed the Federal Energy Office (FEO), an agency created in late 1973 to deal with the energy crisis. He also had served as deputy treasury secretary since December, 1972.

During 1973, before becoming director of the FEO, Simon had chaired the Nixon Administration's Interagency Oil Policy Committee. This made him familiar with the oil industry, the 60 or more government agencies dealing with the oil industry, and the causes of the energy shortage. As deputy secretary of the treasury, he handled the routine operations of the treasury department.

Simon was born in Paterson, N.J., on Nov. 27, 1927. His mother died when he was 8 years old, so he, his brother, and two sisters were raised by their father, an insurance broker.

After graduating from high school in 1946, Simon joined the U.S. Army and served for two years in Japan. He then attended Lafayette College in Easton, Pa., as a prelaw student, graduating in 1952. But, instead of pursuing law, Simon worked in various Wall Street financial firms until 1972, becoming an expert in municipal bonds and government securities and building a fortune of about $3 million.

Simon was married in 1951 to Carol Girard. They have seven children.   Darlene R. Stille

SIMPSON, O. J. (1947-   ), running back for the Buffalo Bills professional football team, was named Athlete of the Year by the Associated Press in January, 1974. Simpson was honored after he broke the National Football League's single-year rushing record by gaining a total of 2,003 yards from scrimmage during the 1973 season.

Orenthal James Simpson was born July 9, 1947, in San Francisco and grew up in Potero Hill, a ghetto neighborhood in that city. He attended Galilee High School, where he was an all-city schoolboy runner. He was also the leader of a street gang called the Superiors and was often in trouble with the school authorities.

Simpson did not have high enough scholastic marks to enter a major college, but he qualified for a junior college. At the City College of San Francisco, he scored 54 touchdowns in two seasons and twice was a junior college all-American selection. Then he transferred to the University of Southern California, where he emerged as a superstar. He won the Heisman Trophy in his senior year as the nation's outstanding college player. He was also an all-America selection in both his varsity seasons and was regarded by many as the best runner in college football history. He joined the Buffalo Bills in 1969.

Simpson married Marguerite Witley. They have two children, Arnella and Jason.   Foster Stockwell

SINGAPORE. See ASIA.

SINGER, ISAAC BASHEVIS (1904-   ), a Polish-born author who writes in Yiddish, was co-winner of the 25th annual National Book Award for the best book of fiction published in 1973, *A Crown of Feathers and Other Stories*. He shared the $1,000 prize with Thomas Pynchon, the author of *Gravity's Rainbow*. See PYNCHON, THOMAS.

Singer won the 1970 National Book Award for the best children's book of the year, *A Day of Pleasure: Stories of a Boy Growing Up in Warsaw*. Many of his writings combine modern realism with traditional Jewish folklore and fantasy. Imps and demons narrate many of his stories. His best-known collections of short stories are *Gimpel the Fool* (1957), *The Spinoza of Market Street* (1961), *Short Friday* (1964), and *A Friend of Kafka* (1970). His novels include *Satan in Goray* (1935), *The Family Moskat* (1945), *The Magician of Lublin* (1960), *The Slave* (1962), *The Manor* (1967), and *The Estate* (1969).

The son of a rabbi, Singer was educated in a rabbinical seminary. He was born in Radzymin, Poland, and grew up in Warsaw, where he wrote in Hebrew. He moved to the United States in 1935 and took a job with the *Jewish Daily Forward*, a Yiddish newspaper published in New York City. Singer then began to write in Yiddish. Most of his works have since been translated into English. His brother, Israel Joshua Singer, was also a noted author.   Foster Stockwell

SKATING. See HOCKEY; ICE SKATING.

SKIING. American skiing fortunes, which had been shaky for years, hit bottom in 1974. The Americans failed to win a medal in the quadrennial world championships, held in February in St. Moritz, Switzerland.

The best performance by an American woman was a sixth in the giant slalom by Barbara Ann Cochran of Richmond, Vt., a 1972 Olympic champion. The best by American men were 14th places by Bob Cochran, Barbara Ann's brother, in the downhill and Gary Adgate of Boyce City, Mich., in the giant slalom.

The most successful nations in the world championships were Austria with eight medals, France with four, and Italy and Liechtenstein with three each. Gustavo Thoeni of Italy won the men's special slalom and giant slalom; David Zwilling of Austria, the men's downhill; Annemarie Proell of Austria, the women's downhill; Fabienne Serrat of France, the women's giant slalom; and Hanni Wenzel of Liechtenstein, the women's special slalom.

World Cup. The world championships came in the middle of the annual World Cup competition, which consisted of 21 races for men and 17 for women from December, 1973, to March, 1974, all in Europe. Piero Gros, a 19-year-old Italian, won the men's overall title on the next-to-last day. Proell won the women's title for the fourth time. See PROELL, ANNEMARIE.

The Americans did poorly again. Barbara Ann Cochran finished 14th and Cindy Nelson of Lutsen, Minn., 15th, for the best women's showings. Bob Cochran's tie for 26th place was the highest by an American man. Nelson won the women's downhill on January 13 at Grindewald, Switzerland, the season's only individual victory by an American.

When the season started, the head of the American team was Gordon (Mickey) Cochran, father of four members of the American team (Barbara Ann, Marilyn, Lindy, and Bob Cochran). He resigned in January to return to his job as a design engineer. He was replaced by Hank Tauber.

In Nordic competition (cross-country and jumping), East Germany won five of the 10 world championships. Galina Kulakova of Russia won or shared in all three women's victories. Martha Rockwell, 29, of Putney, Vt., who held every American Nordic title for women, finished 10th in the world 10-kilometer championship, the best ever by an American in an international Nordic race.

Professional Skiing thrived despite the absence of two key men. Jean-Claude Killy of France, the 1973 champion, missed the season because of a stomach disorder, and Karl Schranz remained in Austria to attend a school for ski instructors.

The pro series ran from December to April and consisted of head-to-head races over parallel courses in special slalom and giant slalom. Hugo Nindl, an Austrian living in Hunter, N.Y., was the leading money winner with $89,200, including a $50,000 bonus as series champion.   Frank Litsky

SOCCER. Every four years, the best national soccer teams in the world gather for almost a month to compete for the World Cup. In 1974, the winner was West Germany, a 2 to 1 victor over the Netherlands in the championship game.

Soccer claims to be the world's most popular sport, with 142 nations belonging to its international federation and other nations that play the game but not internationally. The World Cup final, played July 7 in Munich, was seen on television by more than 800-million people around the world. In the United States, the game was shown on closed-circuit television in theaters that charged up to $20 a seat.

The competition was held in nine West German cities from June 13 to July 7. There were 16 teams—defending champion Brazil; West Germany, the host nation; and 14 others that had survived two years of eliminations among 99 nations. The United States, not yet a world soccer power, failed to qualify. England, which was a soccer power, also did not qualify. Italy qualified but was surprisingly eliminated in the first round, and more than 500 angry Italian fans attacked their team as it left the stadium.

The 16 teams were divided into four groups. In each group, each of the four teams played one game against each of the other three. The two leaders in each group advanced to the next round, leaving eight survivors—East Germany, West Germany, Yugoslavia, Brazil, the Netherlands, Sweden, Poland, and Argentina. Two four-team groups were then set up, and again each team played each other team in its group. The winner of each group advanced to the final.

The Championship Game pitted West Germany, a team strong on defense, against a Dutch team with a strong offense. The Netherlands scored in the first minute, but West Germany scored in the 20th and 43rd minutes and won the championship.

It was a lucrative competition. Ticket sales reached $14 million, and the organizers' total income from tickets, television rights, souvenirs, and other sources totaled $27 million and their profits $20 million.

It was big business for the West German players, too. Each of the 23 players earned $23,500, and some made much more from commercial endorsements and promotions.

U.S. Pro Soccer. The North American Soccer League continued to grow as more teams used more American players. The 15 teams (there were nine in 1973) played from April to August. The division winners were Boston, Miami, Dallas, and Los Angeles. In the nationally televised final, the Los Angeles Aztecs defeated the Miami Toros, 4-3, in overtime on August 25 at Miami. Season attendance totaled 1,181,630, an average of 7,825 per game. That was a 24 per cent increase over 1973.

Winning goal by Gerd Müller, left, barely eludes a stretching Arie Haan as West Germany beats the Netherlands 2-1 to win the World Cup title.

The $50,000 franchise price was raised to $250,000. More teams were admitted for 1975, when the league planned an indoor season from January to March and an outdoor season extending into September.

It was a bad season for Kyle Rote, Jr., of the Dallas Tornado, the league's best-known player. The league's 1973 scoring champion, he had a salary of $1,500 for that season. Then he gave American soccer an identity when he won the televised superstars competition and $53,400, competing against the superstars of other sports in Florida in March. He held out for $15,000 in 1974 and did not sign until 4:20 A.M. on the day of the opening game. But he spent much of the season on the bench.

Other Champions. For the fourth time in eight years, the New York Greek-Americans won the United States Challenge Cup, symbolic of supremacy among American semipro and amateur teams. Overseas, Feyenoord of the Netherlands won the European Union Cup; Magdeburg of East Germany, the European Cup Winners Cup; Liverpool, the English Football Association Cup; Wolverhampton, the English League Cup; Leeds United, the English League first division; and St. George-Budapest, Australia's most important championship. Glasgow Celtic won the Scottish first division (for the ninth straight year) and the Scottish Football Association Cup, and lost to Dundee, 1-0, in the final for the Scottish League Cup.   Frank Litsky

Ida Fuller, who received the first U.S. social security check, in 1940, celebrates her 100th birthday in Brattleboro, Vt., on September 6.

SOCIAL SECURITY. In one of the last acts before his resignation, President Richard M. Nixon signed a tariff bill on Aug. 8, 1974, that contained amendments to the supplemental security income (SSI) program. One change provided for cost-of-living increases in SSI benefits. The others were minor amendments affecting Medicare and social security.

Cost-of-Living Increases. The bill provides for automatic cost-of-living increases in SSI benefit levels in coordination with automatic cost-of-living increases in social security cash benefits. The change was made to ensure that the tax payments would increase at the same time that the benefits did. Cost-of-living increases under this provision, however, will not be effective until July, 1975.

The bill also authorized the Secretary of Health, Education, and Welfare to repay a state directly for interim assistance payments advanced to SSI applicants while their eligibility for SSI was being determined. Repayment would be made out of SSI funds.

Medicare Provisions. The bill extended from July 1, 1975, to March 1, 1976, the due date of a final report on a study of teaching physicians being conducted by the National Academy of Sciences. The study covers all aspects related to payment under Medicare and Medicaid for professional services in medical schools and teaching hospitals. Until the completion of this study, the services of a teaching physician may be reimbursed under Medicare on a cost basis, provided the hospital elects to receive such payment and all physicians in the hospital agree not to bill charges for professional services rendered Medicare patients.

The bill also included a minor change in the coverage provisions that apply to farm rental income. Such income is covered under social security only if the rental arrangement provides that the farm landowner actually helps to produce agricultural commodities on his land. The new regulations deny a landowner coverage if he employs a professional farm-management company or another person to manage and supervise the farm.

Tax and Income Limits. Beginning on Jan. 1, 1975, the maximum amount of earnings in a year that count for social security was to automatically increase to $14,100, up from 1974's maximum of $13,200. The maximum amount that a beneficiary can earn in a year and still get all of his social security checks increased to $2,520, from $2,400.

Those who earn more than $2,520 in 1975 may still get some social security benefits, but every dollar they earn above $2,520 may cause a loss of 50 cents in their social security benefits. No matter how much they earn during the entire year, they can get their benefits for any month in which they earn no more than $210. A person hospitalized under Medicare will be responsible for the first $92 of his hospital bill.   Joseph P. Anderson

SOCIAL WELFARE. A significant new study of the poor released by the Rand Institute in October, 1974, showed that 95 per cent of all adult newcomers to New York City failed to seek welfare in their first two years in the city, even though many of them were eligible. The $150,000 study, which was conducted by the institute over a period of several years, showed that two-thirds of those over 65 years of age in New York City and eligible for welfare were not getting it. The report also showed that there were no substantial numbers of persons on welfare who could be working and were not.

The study challenged theories that the poor were attracted to the city by "the prospect of the city's generous welfare allowance." It emphasized the heavy part children play in the welfare picture, showing the median age of welfare recipients in 1970 was 16.2 years compared with 32.4 years as the median age for the city's population as a whole.

About half of those eligible for welfare who did not go on welfare rolls in 1970 were described as families with children. One-fourth were elderly. By contrast, elderly comprise nearly 60 per cent of the city's population.

The report also showed that more than one-fifth of those aided by welfare during a year no longer required assistance at the end of that period. As newcomers stayed in the city and tried to make their own way, the incidence of eligibility for welfare dropped significantly from 23 per cent for those with under two years of residence. Eligibility leveled off at about 18 per cent after three years and settled at 15 per cent for those living in the city 10 years or more.

New Welfare Plan. At the request of President Gerald R. Ford, Caspar W. Weinberger, secretary of the U.S. Department of Health, Education, and Welfare (HEW), began developing a revised welfare plan for the nation's poor. The preliminary details of the plan showed that it would guarantee $3,600 a year to a family of four with no other income. It also would provide support to every low-income individual and family, including the working poor. In addition, eligible persons would not be required to pay any federal income tax.

The proposed income supplement program would provide every needy family with a single tax-free allotment. States would have the option of adding to the check, but they would not be encouraged to do so. It was estimated that the program would provide payments of $21.6 billion yearly to 42 million low-income families.

The HEW proposals would also abolish other public assistance programs such as the food stamp program, housing allowance program, and the Aid to Families with Dependent Children program. It would further facilitate establishment of a fair and equitable welfare system, replace the present variety of eligibility factors, and install a single income-based standard to cut administrative costs substantially.

Every able-bodied recipient would be required to sign up for work and take a job if it was offered. For every dollar earned, 50 cents of public support would be subtracted up to an earned income of $7,200 a year. HEW hoped the new welfare plan would be administered by the Internal Revenue Service or some new branch of the Treasury Department.

Decline Continues. Weinberger also reported that the decline in Aid to Families with Dependent Children first noted in 1973 had continued in 1974. He termed this first such yearly decline in recent memory as encouraging because it represents the movement of more than 250,000 Americans from dependence to self-sufficiency.

The secretary gave the state administrations much of the credit for the decline and reduced spending in Aid to Families with Dependent Children, citing their greatly improved management of the massive aid programs during the year. Equally significant was the fact that the majority of eligible welfare recipients were receiving more generous cash assistance while errors in the welfare rolls were being corrected.

This overdue reform has permitted 25 states to increase their welfare payments to the truly needy and fully eligible, using the money saved by weeding out ineligible persons, correcting the payments, and adopting practices that prevent ineligible persons from getting onto welfare rolls.   Joseph P. Anderson

SOMALIA. See AFRICA.

SOUTH AFRICA. The end of Portuguese colonial rule in Angola and Mozambique caused South Africa considerable anxiety in 1974. The white South African regime emphasized its friendship toward black African nations, particularly the future black governments of Angola and Mozambique. There was speculation that South Africa might abandon its support of white-ruled Rhodesia if that became necessary to ensure peaceful relations with black countries. See ANGOLA; MOZAMBIQUE; PORTUGAL.

However, in September, the South African government began arresting black militants who supported the successful Mozambique guerrillas. Reportedly, there was a nationwide wave of arrests and interrogations, particularly involving the South African Students Organization and the Black People's Convention.

Slow Change. In the April elections, the ruling National Party won three additional seats in Parliament and the major opposition, the Union Party, lost five. But the Progressive Party, which wants to end *apartheid* (separation of the races), increased its foothold from one to six seats.

There were moves during the year to ease petty apartheid rules. Several cities, including Capetown, Durban, and Johannesburg, allowed blacks in public parks and stopped reserving separate facilities, such as waiting rooms, for blacks. The army began accepting blacks. However, *grand apartheid*, the separate development of the races, was unaffected.

For the first time, leaders of South Africa's *Bantustans* (black homelands) met with Prime Minister Balthazar Johannes Vorster in March. Reportedly, they discussed land issues and black pay scales. Also in March, the Transkei Bantustan voted to ask for independence within five years.

Black labor unrest continued. In January, 10,000 black textile workers went on strike in Durban and won wage increases. Between March and June, 46 black workers were killed in gold mine riots. The miners received a 33 per cent pay hike in October.

UN Issue. In October, the United Nations (UN) General Assembly, for the first time, asked the Security Council to consider expelling South Africa because of its racial policies. Ten Council members voted to expel, two abstained, and three – France, Great Britain, and the United States – vetoed the measure. Nevertheless, South Africa was suspended from the session. See UNITED NATIONS.

South Africa had hoped to prevent difficulties at the UN by sending its first multiracial delegation and by announcing interracial discussions on the future of Namibia (South West Africa). John Storm Roberts

See also AFRICA (Facts in Brief Table).

SOUTH AMERICA. See LATIN AMERICA and articles on Latin American countries.

SOUTH CAROLINA. See STATE GOVERNMENT.

SOUTH DAKOTA. See STATE GOVERNMENT.

SPACE EXPLORATION. Ground controllers sent the last command to the United States *Skylab* Earth-orbiting space laboratory on Feb. 9, 1974. This marked the end of a nine-month program that demonstrated man's ability to live and work effectively in space for months at a time. The previous day, *Skylab* astronauts Gerald P. Carr, Edward G. Gibson, and William R. Pogue had splashed down in the Pacific Ocean, completing an 84-day space flight, the longest in history. They and two previous three-man crews spent a total of 171 days aboard *Skylab*, which is 117 feet (36 meters) long.

The nine men conducted 822 hours of medical experiments. Observations of the Sun, stars, and Earth's surface during 2,476 revolutions of the earth yielded more than 180,000 photographs and 45 miles (72 kilometers) of magnetic tape filled with data. Manufacturing experiments conducted in near-zero gravity produced such promising results that they will be continued on future manned missions. The crews spent 28, 59, and 84 days in orbit, respectively, and each crew returned in better physical condition than the previous one. Physicians attributed this to increased exercise and more time to adapt to weightlessness. None of the astronauts experienced major difficulties in readjusting to earth's gravity.

U.S.-Russian Flight. Training of crews and technical specialists, and testing of equipment, continued in anticipation of a joint United States-Russian space mission in July, 1975. The main goal of the Apollo Soyuz Test Project (ASTP) involves testing a docking system that will permit the transfer of men and equipment between the *Apollo* and *Soyuz* craft during the two days that they are docked. This mission could form the basis for future joint scientific and rescue missions. Astronauts and cosmonauts also plan to conduct joint experiments in astronomy, biology, physics, and welding.

Spacemen, technicians, and engineers exchanged visits to the space facilities near Moscow and the Johnson Space Center near Houston during the year. Both English and Russian were spoken during joint crew-training sessions, and no language difficulties occurred, according to the National Aeronautics and Space Administration (NASA). In September, U.S. ground controllers spent 12 days learning Russian space flight procedures.

***Soyuz* and *Salyut*.** Russia launched three manned missions in 1974. *Soyuz 14* cosmonauts docked with a *Salyut* space laboratory in July and spent two weeks aboard the laboratory testing equipment and conducting scientific and medical experiments. Cosmonauts aboard *Soyuz 15* attempted to dock with the same *Salyut* on August 27, but they failed when an automatic docking system malfunctioned. The cosmonauts then made an unusual night landing on August 29, indicating an emergency had occurred. Russian officials denied this, and said there was no connection between the docking problems of *Soyuz 15* and ASTP. *Soyuz 16* made a successful six-day flight, a rehearsal for the joint mission, in December. It flew with a new low-pressure atmosphere containing more oxygen.

Mars and Jupiter. Two of four unmanned Russian spacecraft launched toward Mars in 1973 missed their target in February and March, 1974. A third probe, *Mars 5*, orbited Mars and returned some photographic data. The Russians had planned for *Mars 5* to serve as a radio relay for *Mars 4* as the latter broadcast data from the Martian surface. However, contact with *Mars 4* was lost as it descended by parachute. United States experts speculated that high winds wrecked the spacecraft.

Astronomers analyzed data in 1974 from the United States *Pioneer 10*, the first probe to explore the outer part of the solar system when it flew within 81,000 miles (130,000 kilometers) of Jupiter in December, 1973. Scientists now believe that Jupiter is a huge sphere of liquid hydrogen with temperatures of 54,000° F. (29,700° C) at its center, which may be a small rocky core. Massive wind systems encircle the planet, producing bands of ascending gray-white clouds alternating with orange-brown troughs of descending air. The mysterious Great Red Spot is now believed to be a storm of whirling clouds 25,000 miles (40,000 kilometers) long and several hundred years old. *Pioneer 10* also returned new information about the four inner moons of Jupiter.

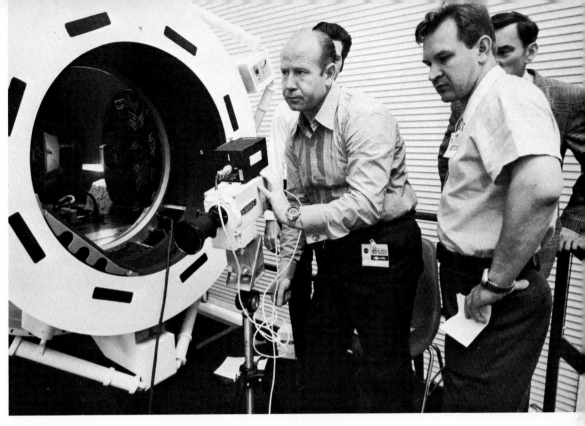

Cosmonaut Aleksei A. Leonov, center, trains at the Johnson Space Center near Houston for the Russian-U.S. *Apollo-Soyuz* space mission in 1975.

Pioneer 10 found Jovian magnetic fields much larger, and radiation belts more intense, than previously believed. Engineers were concerned that intense radiation, extending millions of miles or kilometers from Jupiter, would cause problems with instruments aboard the 570-pound (245-kilogram) probe. This did not occur, and NASA maneuvered *Pioneer 11* to within 26,000 miles (42,000 kilometers) on December 3. Both *Pioneer* spacecraft passed through the asteroid belt without damage, eliminating concern that some of the thousands of small planets that comprise the belt would strike and damage the spacecraft.

Venus and Mercury. *Mariner 10*, the first spacecraft to approach two planets on a single flight, sent back data from Venus in February, 1974, then gave scientists their first close-up look at Mercury in March. Ground controllers took advantage of the increase in speed produced by the pull of Venusian gravity to curve *Mariner* around Venus and bring it to a point 431 miles (690 kilometers) from Mercury. Photographs showed Mercury's surface to be heavily cratered and broken by long scarps or faults. Scientists believe the scarps formed as Mercury cooled and its outer crust shrank, causing slabs of rock to buckle and override each other. *Mariner 10*'s orbit took it on a second close approach to Mercury in September, 1974, and a third encounter is expected in March, 1975. See ASTRONOMY. William J. Cromie

SPAIN. Carlos Arias Navarro was sworn in on Jan. 2, 1974, as General Francisco Franco's first civilian president and promptly surprised the nation with his Cabinet appointments. He excluded from the Cabinet all members of Opus Dei, a Roman Catholic lay organization whose members have long dominated Spanish politics and business. A month later, he promised Spaniards more freedom and greater representation in government.

Franco, the chief of state, was hospitalized on July 9 with phlebitis. When his health worsened on July 19, he provisionally turned over his powers to Prince Juan Carlos. However, Franco was well enough to resume his position as head of state on September 2.

Labor Troubles. Although in the grip of a 14 per cent rate of inflation, the government lifted all wage controls on August 15 to prevent strikes by the Workers' Commission, the clandestine trade union organization. But with 32,000 workers on strike, police raided a Madrid church on October 6 and arrested 200 of the factory workers who were meeting there. The government broke up similar meetings in Valladolid, Seville, Barcelona, Bilbao, and Vitoria. The strikers demanded the right of free assembly and higher wages to compensate for inflation.

Church-State Conflict. A simmering conflict between church and state boiled up on February 27 with the house arrest of the bishop of Bilbao, Antonio Añoveros Ataún. He was accused of sympathizing with rebel priests from the Basque region of northern Spain. When the Vatican and Spain's Roman Catholic hierarchy closed ranks to support the bishop, the government dropped its plan to exile him. In March, the church asked the government not to interfere with its "freedom to promote greater justice among men. . . ."

The Franco government's struggle continued with the outlawed Basque Homeland and Liberty separatist movement. Four members, who claim responsibility for the assassination of Arias Navarro's predecessor, Admiral Luis Carrero Blanco, in December, 1973, detailed their plot in a book published in September. Twelve people died and 70 were injured in a terrorist bomb explosion in a Madrid restaurant on September 13.

Africa Colony. The government told the United Nations (UN) that it will hold a referendum in 1975 in Spain's colonial territory, Spanish Sahara, in West Africa. Morocco, Algeria, and the UN had demanded self-determination for the 70,000 nomads who occupy the phosphate-rich province.

Spain's negative trade balance could no longer be offset in 1974 by tourist revenues. Higher vacation costs caused by the oil crisis and failure of two major British travel agencies ended a tourist boom that began in the 1950s.   Kenneth Brown

See also ARIAS NAVARRO, CARLOS; EUROPE (Facts in Brief Table).

SPORTS. The boom in professional sports in the United States slowed somewhat in 1974, but more people put more money into new teams and new leagues. The World Football League made its debut with 12 teams, supposedly ready to lose $15 million the first year. But by midseason two teams had ceased operations, two had moved, others were unable to pay players, and the future of the league was shaky (see FOOTBALL). World Team Tennis played its first season with 16 teams and enjoyed mild success in a few cities, indifference in most others (see TENNIS). An indoor box lacrosse league in Canada and the United States did well.

There were more leagues ahead. The National Football League (NFL) planned a six-team satellite league in Europe in 1975; an international basketball league based mainly in Europe was scheduled to start in January, 1975.

Franchise costs were high. The NFL awarded 1975 franchises to Tampa and Seattle for $16 million each. The National Basketball Association (NBA) admitted New Orleans in the 1974-1975 season for $6.15 million and voted a 1975-1976 franchise to Toronto for an undetermined, but higher, price. For $6 million each, the National Hockey League (NHL) took in Washington and Kansas City for 1974-1975. See BASKETBALL; HOCKEY.

Television was devoting 1,000 network hours a year to sports, about 11 per cent of all network time.

It was paying more than $260 million a year to show sports programs. Yet, 1973 ratings decreased in hockey, pro basketball, and pro and college football.

Racial Advances. The year saw the naming of major-league baseball's first black manager (Frank Robinson of the Cleveland Indians) and the first black head coach of the U.S. Olympic track team (Leroy Walker of North Carolina Central University).

India defaulted to South Africa in the final round of the Davis Cup tennis competition to protest South Africa's restrictive racial policies. See TENNIS.

Meanwhile, officials in November banned foreign teams from the Little League World Series, played in Williamsport, Pa. Since the series was opened to foreign teams in 1957, 20 have competed. Monterrey, Mexico, won the title in 1957 and 1958, and Taiwan won the last four series.

Among the Winners in 1974 were:

Curling. The United States won the world championship by defeating Sweden, 11-4, in the final of the 10-nation competition in March in Bern, Switzerland. Canada, world champion 12 times in the previous 15 years, was eliminated in the semifinals. The United States was represented by Superior, Wis. (Bud Somerville, skip), which had won its fourth U.S. title in seven attempts.

Fencing. Russia retained the team championship and won four of the eight titles in the world championships in June at Grenoble, France. Paul Apostol of New York City was the only American to advance beyond the second round, reaching the quarterfinals in individual saber competition. New York University captured its fourth National Collegiate overall title in five years.

Handball. Fred Lewis of Cleveland won the United States Handball Association (USHA) four-wall championship for the second time in three years. Steve Sandler of Brooklyn, N.Y., won a record seventh Amateur Athletic Union one-wall championship in June.

Rowing. An underrated eight-oared all-star crew from the United States won the world championship in September at Lucerne, Switzerland. East Germany took six of the other seven heavyweight finals. In sculling, Jim Dietz of the Bronx, N.Y., finished second to East Germany's Wolfgang Honig in the world heavyweight final; William Belden of King of Prussia, Pa., won the world lightweight title. Larry Klecatsky of New York City won five titles in the Canadian Henley Regatta and four in the U.S. championships.

Shooting. Russia won 23 titles, the United States 15, and all other nations combined 14 in the world championships in September at Thun, Switzerland. Lannie Basham of Fort Worth, Tex., was first in free rifle (prone position) and second in air rifle. Hershel Anderson of Tracy City, Tenn., won U.S. pistol titles in .22-caliber, .45-caliber, center-fire, and interservice competition.

Weight Lifting. Vassili Alexeev of Russia won his fifth straight super heavyweight world title in September in Manila. During the year, the 33-year-old Alexeev set world records of 413 pounds (187 kilograms) for the snatch, 536¾ pounds (243 kilograms) for the clean and jerk, 534 pounds (242 kilograms) for the jerk, and 937 pounds (425 kilograms) for the two lifts combined in one meet. The Russians retained the European championship, then narrowly lost their world team title to Bulgaria.

Wrestling. Russia won team honors and seven of the 10 individual titles in the world free-style champion-

Breaking the record for a midair link-up, 29 of the 32 sky divers shown
joined hands for 3 seconds during free fall from 13,500 feet (4,115 meters).

ships ending September 1 at Istanbul and six of 10 in the world Greco-Roman championships in October at Katowice, Poland. The leading American performances were fifth places by Stan Deziedzic of Lansing, Mich., in the welterweight class of free-style and Koroly Kancser of Lincoln, Nebr., in the paperweight class of Greco-Roman.

Other Champions. *Archery*, U.S. champions: men, Darrell Pace, Reading, Ohio; women, Doreen Wilber, Jefferson, Ohio. U.S. pro champions: men, Frank Gandy, Bartow, Fla.; women, Ann Butz, Corning, N.Y. *Badminton*, U.S. champions: men, Chris Kinard, Pasadena, Calif.; women, Cindy Baker, Salt Lake City, Utah. *Biathlon*, world champion: Juhani Suutarinen, Finland. *Billiards*, world pocket champion: Ray Martin, Fair Lawn, N.J. *Bobsledding*, world champions: four-man, West Germany (Wolfgang Zimmerer, driver); two-man, West Germany (Zimmerer, driver). *Canoeing*, U.S. champions: men's canoe (500 meters), Roland Muhlen, Cincinnati; men's kayak (500 meters), Steve Kelly, New York City; women's kayak (500 meters), Linda Murray, Washington, D.C. *Casting*, U.S. all-around champion: Steve Rajeff, San Francisco. *Court tennis*, world open champion: Jimmy Bostwick, New York City. *Cross-country*, A.A.U.: John Ngeno, Washington State; NCAA: Nick Rose, Western Kentucky. *Cycling*, road champions: world pro, Edd Merckx, Belgium; world amateur, Janusz Kowalski, Poland; U.S., John Allis, San Pedro, Calif. *Field hockey*, world women's champion: the Netherlands. *Gymnastics*, world all-around champions: men, Shigeru Kasamatsu, Japan; women, Ludmilla Turisheva, Russia. *Horseshoe pitching*, U.S. champion: Curt Day, Frankfort, Ind. *Judo*, A.A.U. grand champion: Irwin Cohen, Chicago. *Karate*, European open champion, J. Kallenbach, the Netherlands. *Lacrosse*, U.S. champions: NCAA, John Hopkins; club, Long Island Athletic Club. *Luge* (tobogganing), world champions: men, Josef Gendt, West Germany; women, Margit Schumann, East Germany. *Modern pentathlon*, world champion: Pavel Lednev, Russia. *Motorcycling*, U.S. grand national champion: Ken Roberts, Modesto, Calif. *Paddleball*, U.S. champion: Steve Keeley, San Diego, Calif. *Parachuting*, U.S. overall champions: men, Jack Brake, Fort Bragg, N.C.; women, Debbie Schmidt, Joliet, Ill. *Polo*, U.S. champions: open, Milwaukee. *Racquetball*, U.S. champion: Bill Schmidtke, Minneapolis. *Racquets*, U.S. open champion: William Surtees, Chicago. *Rodeo*, World all-around champion: Tom Ferguson, Miami, Okla. *Roller skating*, world champions: men, Michael Obrecht, West Germany; women, Sigrid Mullenbach, West Germany. *Softball*, U.S. fast-pitch champions: men, Santa Rosa, Calif.; women, Raybestos Brakettes, Stratford, Conn. *Squash racquets*, U.S. champions: men, Victor Neiderhoffer, New York City; women, Gretchen Spruance, Greenville, Del. *Squash tennis*, U.S. open champion: Pedro Bacallao, New York City. *Synchronized swimming*, A.A.U. outdoor champion: Gail Johnson, Santa Clara, Calif. *Table tennis*, U.S. champions: men, Kjell Johansson, Sweden; women, Yukie Ohzeki, Japan. *Team handball*, world champions: men, Romania; women, Yugoslavia. *Trampoline*, world champions: men, R. Tison, France; women, Alexandra Nicholson, Rockford, Ill. *Volleyball*, U.S. Volleyball Association champions: men, U. of California, Santa Barbara; women, Los Angeles Renegades. *Water polo*, A.A.U. champion: Fullerton, Calif. *Water skiing*, U.S. overall champions: men, Ricky McCormick, Hialeah, Fla.; women, Liz Allan Shetter, Groveland, Fla. Frank Litsky

See also OLYMPIC GAMES.

SRI LANKA

SRI LANKA is known as "the jewel of the Indian Ocean." Its soil is fertile, and its tea, rubber, and coconut-palm plantations and its forests are a deep green. Yet, few nations on the Asian continent were worse off in 1974 than Sri Lanka (formerly Ceylon). Nearly half of its imports consist of food. Its gross national product, about $1.5 billion, has not grown in years. In part, the blame rests with inefficient production and low world prices. But it also partly lies with the dogmatism of the radical politicians who rule this republic of about 13 million persons.

New Pragmatism. Sri Lanka is governed by a three-party coalition headed by Sirimavo Bandaranaike, who leads the majority Sri Lanka Freedom Party. Her unlikely allies are a pro-Russian Communist party and a Trotskyite party, the only such body that holds political power in any country. Prime Minister Bandaranaike won her last election on a leftist platform. She has carried out parts of the program, including land reform that gave nearly 600,000 acres (202,000 hectares) to landless peasants. But her extreme partners have been pressuring her to nationalize the banks and tea and coffee estates, and to arm the people "to defend socialism."

Bandaranaike decided in 1973 that a pauper state could not afford more nationalization and welfarism. The free rice ration was reduced, the free wheat-flour ration was ended, and the price of bread was raised 60 per cent. At the same time, cautious incentives were offered to foreign investors – so far, in vain.

Bandaranaike's policies added fuel to the fires of intrigue within the coalition. The climax came in November when the Trotskyites called a union rally and street demonstrations while she was visiting Russia. On the prime minister's cabled orders, the rally was banned. Seemingly, she won this showdown, but she remained dependent on the two leftist parties to keep labor from demanding higher wages.

No Peppers. The rice harvest of 79 million bushels was the best in years. But food was still in short supply, and prices kept rising. The black market provided all the essentials, from bicycle tires to hot peppers needed for the diet of curry and rice.

At one point in April, Sri Lanka reportedly had only two weeks' rice supply in stock. An emergency shipment from China averted an immediate crisis. Other nations selling food to the government were Australia, Pakistan, Russia, Canada, and the United States.

With more than 750,000 unemployed, the situation was explosive. Special courts released several thousand youths rounded up in 1971 demonstrations, when students nearly toppled the regime. But the university students remained restive and the jobless were desperate. The government doubled the size of the army and the police. It also muzzled the press by buying some newspapers, intimidating others, and closing still others. Mark Gayn

See also ASIA (Facts in Brief Table).

STAMP COLLECTING.

STAMP COLLECTING. Inflation brought sharp increases in stamp values in 1974 and attracted new collectors seeking to invest in inflation-proof commodities. The U.S. Postal Service reported that inquiries to its Philatelic Division about stamp purchases in the first third of the year had doubled over the 1973 rate and were four times the rate in 1972.

Prices obtained at the Rarities of the World stamp auction, held March 27 in New York City, exemplified the rise in stamp prices. A 5-cent, 1847 U.S. stamp in a mint pair, which was cataloged at $1,250, sold for $3,200. The total estimated catalog value of the stamps in the auction was about $666,000, but they brought $880,665. One of the famous 1918 airmail inverts sold for $41,000, which was $10,000 more than such a stamp brought in 1969. Then, at another auction in New York City on May 31, one of the airmail inverts sold for $47,000, a record price for any U.S. stamp. The unidentified seller had paid $31,000 for the stamp in 1969.

The 100th Anniversary of the Universal Postal Union, a specialized United Nations agency that makes possible the free flow of mail between nations, was the most popular subject for commemorative stamps throughout the world. On June 6, the U.S. Postal Service issued a block of 10 large five-color stamps to commemorate the Union. However, shortly after the issue was announced in April, the watchdog committee of the American Philatelic Society *black blotted* (disapproved) the issue as excessive. The society had done the same to the U.S. 10-stamp Postal People issue of 1973, which was voted the "least necessary" stamp of 1973 in a 1974 poll among stamp collectors. The same poll chose the Boston Tea Party block of four as the best issue of 1973, and the Love stamp of 1973 as the worst. Ironically, the latter was also runner-up for the best stamp of the year.

The Canadian Postal Service also incurred the displeasure of some collectors when it issued six stamps commemorating the centenary of letter-carrier service in Canada. The same collectors, however, applauded the Postal Service's announcement that it was reducing its 1974 commemoratives from a planned 45 to 33. That reduced the cost to collectors buying all the issues from $5.42 to $2.99.

New Issues. Canada's issue on March 22 of a set of 1976 Olympic Games stamps was a world first in stamp design. An engraving technique was used that provided a hidden image, the Olympic symbol, that could be seen only when the stamp was held obliquely toward a light source.

A first in United States stamp design was a set of four diamond-shaped stamps, issued June 4, to commemorate the nation's mineral heritage. Four of these stamps together also formed a diamond. A first in United States stamped envelopes was one in three colors instead of the usual one, commemorating the centenary of U.S. tennis. Theodore M. O'Leary

STATE GOVERNMENT. States closed their fiscal-year books in June, 1974, with another substantial increase in tax collections. However, they faced poor prospects in fiscal 1975, as the United States economy began to nose down in midyear.

State taxes yielded $73.9 billion for state government operations during fiscal 1974, up 9.2 per cent. General sales and gross receipts taxes accounted for the major portion of the increase, followed by corporate net income taxes, individual income taxes, and property taxes. Only 12 of the 45 states with general sales and gross receipts taxes recorded less than a 10 per cent gain in sales tax revenues. California, Indiana, Maryland, Texas, and Wyoming reported 20 per cent gains in sales tax revenues.

Tax Relief. For the second year in a row, tax relief measures far outweighed net tax increases in the states. Net tax reductions are expected to reach $685-million, while net tax increases will climb $335-million. No state had increased its income tax as of December, while at least 10 states had reduced theirs. Some form of tax relief, particularly for low-income families and the aged, was effected in at least 14 states.

Pennsylvania lowered its income tax from 2.3 to 2 per cent and established exemptions for low-income families. Nebraska reduced the personal income tax from 11 to 10 per cent of the federal income tax liability. New Mexico and New York also reduced personal income tax rates. Arizona, Vermont, and Virginia raised corporate tax rates, and Michigan and Pennsylvania lowered theirs.

Connecticut reduced its sales tax from 6.5 to 6 per cent. Increases were enacted in Arizona (3 to 4 per cent) and Tennessee (3 to 3.5 per cent). Sales tax breaks on business machinery and equipment were provided by Maine, Rhode Island, and Vermont.

Among the states providing property tax breaks for the elderly were Colorado, Georgia, Idaho, Illinois, Massachusetts, Mississippi, Oklahoma, Pennsylvania, South Dakota, and West Virginia.

State Elections saw wide Democratic gains in all branches of state government. Democrats captured 27 of the 35 governors' seats up for election; Republicans won 7; and Independent candidate James B. Longley, an insurance executive, scored an upset victory in Maine. Longley will serve with a 1975 legislature that has a Democratic-controlled House of Representatives and a Republican Senate. As a result of the elections, Democrats controlled the governor's seat in 36 of the states. Republicans won previously Democratic-held governorships in Ohio, Kansas, South Carolina, and Alaska. See ELECTIONS.

Even larger numerical gains were registered in the state legislative races. In 15 states, Democrats took control of one or both houses formerly controlled by Republicans. The Democratic Party holds the majority in both houses of 36 state legislatures. The

Republicans hold the majority in only four states, and there is divided political control of the houses in nine legislatures following the November 5 elections. Before the elections, Republicans held the majority in both houses of 16 state legislatures.

Complete turnarounds from Republican to Democratic majorities occurred in both houses of the legislatures of Connecticut, Delaware, Illinois, and Iowa. Only in the South Dakota House of Representatives did the majority change from Democratic to Republican.

At least 595 women will serve in the 1975 state legislatures compared with 470 in 1974, a 25 per cent increase. This brings the total state representation by women to 8 per cent of the total of about 7,600 state lawmakers. The new legislative season is the first in which women legislators will serve in every state lawmaking house in the nation.

Governmental Ethics became an issue in 1974 as a result of the Watergate scandal, and it showed no signs of wilting as the states prepared for their 1975 sessions. Issues such as campaign finance and disclosure laws, public disclosure of finances by state officials, and open-meetings regulations (popularly known as "sunshine" laws because of Florida's early entry into this field) were enacted in many states. New laws in 1974 require public officials and candidates to reveal their personal economic interests in

Connecticut Governor Thomas Meskill, left, and Attorney General William B. Saxbe discuss Saxbe's threat to abolish state lotteries as illegal.

Selected Statistics on State Governments

State	Resident Population(a)	Governor	Legislature(b) Senate (D.)	(R.)	House (D.)	(R.)	State tax rev. (c)	Tax rev. per cap. (d)	Public school enroll- ment 1973-74 (e)	Pub. school expenditures per pupil in aver. daily attendance 1973-74(f)
Alabama	3,577	George C. Wallace (D.)	35	0	105	0	$1,017	$284	775	$716
Alaska	337	Jay S. Hammond (R.)	13	6	30	9(g)	124	368	84	1,597
Arizona	2,153	Raul H. Castro (D.)	18	12	33	27	743	345	480	1,153
Arkansas	2,062	David Pryor (D.)	33	1(h)	97	3	605	293	457	773
California	20,907	Edmund G. Brown, Jr. (D.)	24	14(k)	55	25	7,972	381	4,457	1,170
Colorado	2,496	Richard D. Lamm (D.)	15	19(h)	39	26	798	319	569	1,075
Connecticut	3,088	Ella T. Grasso (D.)	29	7	118	33	1,092	353	658	1,283
Delaware	573	Sherman W. Tribbitt (D.)	13	8	25	16	308	537	133	1,388
Florida	8,090	Reubin O'D. Askew (D.)	27	12(g)	86	34	2,794	345	1,499	(m)
Georgia	4,882	George Busbee (D.)	51	5	157	23	1,520	311	1,079	869
Hawaii	847	George R. Ariyoshi (D.)	18	7	35	16	495	584	180	1,224
Idaho	799	Cecil D. Andrus (D.)	14	21	28	42	256	320	183	840
Illinois	11,131	Dan Walker (D.)	34	25	101	76	4,083	366	2,326	1,228
Indiana	5,330	Otis R. Bowen (R.)	23	27	55	45	1,669	313	1,209	950
Iowa	2,855	Robert D. Ray (R.)	25	24(h)	60	39(h)	987	345	640	1,113
Kansas	2,270	Robert F. Bennett (R.)	14	26	54	71	703	309	471	1,043
Kentucky	3,357	Julian Carroll (D.) (acting)	28	9(h)	80	20	1,106	329	708	727
Louisiana	3,764	Edwin W. Edwards (D.)	38	0(h)	100	4(h)	1,320	350	837	978
Maine	1,047	James B. Longley (Ind.)	14	19	91	54(g)	336	321	248	918
Maryland	4,094	Marvin Mandel (D.)	39	8	126	15	1,577	385	911	1,168
Massachusetts	5,800	Michael Dukakis (D.)	33	7	191	46(i)	2,205	380	1,191	1,136
Michigan	9,098	William G. Milliken (R.)	24	14	66	44	3,681	404	2,178	1,260
Minnesota	3,917	Wendell R. Anderson (D.)	38	28(h)	103	31	1,843	470	901	1,265
Mississippi	2,324	William L. Waller (D.)	50	2	119	2(g)	736	316	520	787
Missouri	4,777	Christopher S. Bond (R.)	23	11	113	50	1,266	265	1,020	963
Montana	735	Thomas L. Judge (D.)	30	20	67	33	220	299	179	1,186
Nebraska	1,543	J. James Exon (D.)	49(j)		(Unicameral)		406	262	326	1,040
Nevada	573	Mike O'Callaghan (D.)	17	3	31	9	251	438	131	1,032
New Hampshire	808	Meldrim Thomson, Jr. (R.)	12	12	167	233	165	204	166	900
New Jersey	7,330	Brendan T. Byrne (D.)	29	10(g)	66	14	2,044	278	1,494	1,385
New Mexico	1,122	Jerry Apodaca (D.)	27	13(k)	51	19	438	390	282	1,004
New York	18,111	Hugh L. Carey (D.)	26	34	87	63	8,516	470	3,490	1,809
North Carolina	5,363	James E. Holshouser, Jr. (R.)	49	1	111	9	1,806	336	1,150	900
North Dakota	637	Arthur A. Link (D.)	17	34(h)	40	62	219	343	140	947
Ohio	10,737	James A. Rhodes (R.)	20	12(h)	59	40	2,789	259	2,399	1,009
Oklahoma	2,709	David L. Boren (D.)	39	8	75	25(h)	778	287	601	835
Oregon	2,266	Bob Straub (D.)	22	7(g)	38	22	702	309	467	1,219
Pennsylvania	11,835	Milton J. Shapp (D.)	30	20	113	90	4,609	389	2,339	1,247
Rhode Island	937	Phillip W. Noel (D.)	46	4	83	17	334	356	188	1,295
South Carolina	2,784	James B. Edwards (R.)	43	2(h)	107	17	902	323	617	856
South Dakota	682	Richard F. Kneip (D.)	19	16	33	37	166	242	161	932
Tennessee	4,129	Ray Blanton (D.)	20	12(g)	63	34(g, h)	1,092	264	883	759
Texas	12,050	Dolph Briscoe (D.)	28	3	134	16	3,288	272	2,710	809
Utah	1,173	Calvin L. Rampton (D.)	15	14	40	35	363	309	303	816
Vermont	470	Thomas P. Salmon (D.)	12	18	74	76	180	381	104	1,109
Virginia	4,908	Mills E. Godwin, Jr. (R.)	35	5	66	19(l)	1,508	307	1,059	983
Washington	3,476	Daniel J. Evans (R.)	30	19	62	36	1,360	391	783	974
West Virginia	1,791	Arch A. Moore, Jr. (R.)	26	8	86	14	610	340	405	871
Wisconsin	4,566	Patrick J. Lucey (D.)	18	13(k)	64	35	2,032	445	986	1,200
Wyoming	359	Ed Herschler (D.)	15	15	29	32(g)	124	345	85	1,232
District of Columbia	723								138	1,523

(a) Numbers in thousands, provisional estimate as of July 1, 1974 (Bureau of the Census)
(b) As of Dec. 31, 1974
(c) 1974 preliminary figures in millions (Bureau of the Census)
(d) 1974 preliminary figures in dollars (*State Taxes 1974*)
(e) Numbers in thousands 1973-74 (U.S. Office of Education, *Digest of Educational Statistics, 1973*)
(f) Number in dollars, 1973-74 (U.S. Office of Education, *Statistics of Public Elementary and Secondary Day Schools, Fall 1973*)
(g) 1 Independent
(h) 1 vacancy
(i) 3 Independents
(j) Nonpartisan
(k) 2 vacancies
(l) 15 Independents
(m) Not available

Arizona, Florida, Indiana, Kansas, Maine, Minnesota, Oklahoma, and South Dakota. Voters approved such laws in November in California and Oregon.

Campaign finance reports were required in four more states, leaving only two states with no campaign finance reporting regulations. Individuals were limited in the amounts they may contribute to candidates by new or revised laws in 12 states. Campaign-spending lids are now in effect in 32 states, with new or revised restrictions enacted in 1974 in 15 more states.

Sex Equality. Three more states—Maine, Montana, and Ohio—ratified the Equal Rights Amendment (ERA) in early 1974, bringing the total to 33. Thirty-eight states must ratify the proposal before it becomes an amendment to the U.S. Constitution. The Tennessee and Nebraska legislatures have acted to rescind their earlier ratification.

Laws prohibiting discrimination against females continued to be placed on state lawbooks. Iowa, Kentucky, Missouri, New York, Oklahoma, and Tennessee prohibited sex or marital discrimination in extending retail credit. Other states prohibiting sex discrimination in various social areas included California, Connecticut, Idaho, and Virginia. New Mexico created a commission on the status of women, and South Dakota funded a similar commission.

Health and Welfare. Health maintenance organizations offering comprehensive health and, in some cases, dental care on a set-fee basis began to attract state government attention. Such operations were authorized by new laws in Kansas, Kentucky, New Mexico, and South Dakota. Hawaii established a comprehensive health-planning agency that includes an acupuncture board. Arizona and Rhode Island lawmakers required health insurance to cover catastrophic illnesses. Health insurance in Connecticut must now be offered to the newborn, alcoholics, and mentally disabled persons.

Abortions were regulated by 10 more states, bringing to 32 the total number of states with abortion laws since the Supreme Court of the United States ruled most state abortion laws unconstitutional in 1973. States enacting new abortion regulations or revising former laws in 1974 included California, Kentucky, Massachusetts, Minnesota, Missouri, Montana, New York, Ohio, Pennsylvania, South Carolina, Utah, and Wisconsin. However, courts ruled that some regulations in the Kentucky, Minnesota, and Utah laws were unconstitutional.

Arizona, Connecticut, Ohio, Rhode Island, and West Virginia passed new laws requiring certain minimum standards for the commitment and treatment of mental patients. Children were the specific targets of new welfare legislation in at least six states. A maternal and child health-care system designed to prevent mental retardation was established in Missouri. Child-abuse legislation was revised in Iowa and Kentucky. Maine and Wisconsin adopted laws guaranteeing rights to fathers of illegitimate children.

Crime and Law Enforcement. Death penalties were enacted in eight more states—Delaware, Kentucky, Mississippi, New Hampshire, New York, North Carolina, Pennsylvania, and South Carolina. Capital punishment laws now appear on the statute books of 28 states.

Continuing trends in law enforcement include eliminating the offense of drunkenness as a crime in six states and the addition of Minnesota to the list of a dozen states which provide aid to victims of crime. Taking action in light of the Supreme Court's ruling that obscenity regulations could be governed by local community standards, Arizona, Iowa, Kentucky, Massachusetts, New York, South Dakota, and West Virginia enacted new obscenity laws.

Drug laws were revised in at least five states. Penalties for the use of marijuana were eased in Georgia, Idaho, and South Dakota. Penalties were stiffened for illegal drug sellers in Connecticut, Georgia, and Indiana.

Energy and Environmental issues continued to dominate much legislative debate. At least 10 states enacted more emergency energy powers. Some of the legislation gives governors the authority to initiate and enforce plans to reduce gasoline use. Coal research, gasification, and removal of sulfur from coal was the subject of legislation—and state government spending—in Illinois, Iowa, and Kentucky. Trust funds for royalties from mineral revenues were authorized in Alaska, Colorado, Montana, and Wyoming. The royalty money is to help those localities most adversely affected by energy developments.

At least seven more states enacted some form of land-use legislation. About 20 states now have statewide land-use planning legislation. New laws designed to promote protection or better use of land, particularly natural or wild settings, were enacted in North Carolina, Colorado, Maryland, South Dakota, Utah, Montana, Rhode Island, Pennsylvania, and New Jersey.

Consumer Protection. Thirty states enacted some form of consumer-protection legislation in 1974. Kentucky, Mississippi, Nebraska, Ohio, and Tennessee added laws to give customers of door-to-door salesmen a period in which to cancel their purchases. Landlord-tenant laws were enacted in Alaska, Nebraska, Ohio, and Virginia.

No-fault automobile insurance legislation was enacted in Georgia, Kentucky, Minnesota, Pennsylvania, and South Carolina, bringing to 21 the number of states with no-fault auto insurance legislation.

Government Reorganization. Idaho, Kentucky, Missouri, and South Dakota acted on state government reorganization. Idaho consolidated 260 agencies into 19 cabinet-level departments. A reorganization implemented by the governor's executive orders in Kentucky was approved by the General Assembly. Missouri's government was reorganized into 14 administrative departments. Ralph Wayne Derickson

STEEL INDUSTRY. The American steel industry suffered a major setback in January, 1974, when a federal judge in Pittsburgh ruled that a European steel concern owns the patent to the basic oxygen-furnace steelmaking process used to produce the bulk of American steel. Judge Louis Rosenberg held that the Jones & Laughlin Steel Corporation owed the foreign developer an unspecified amount in royalties. He upheld a patent on the process filed 17 years ago with the United States government by an Austrian concern, VOEST. The basic oxygen-furnace method, which produces a pot of steel in less than 45 minutes, has replaced the open-hearth method as the usual process. The decision means that other U.S. steel companies using the process also may owe large amounts.

American Production through the week ending October 19 reached 117.9 million short tons (107-million metric tons) compared with the 120.2 million short tons (109 million metric tons) poured during the same period in 1973. But the November coal strike shattered chances to equal the 1973 output of 150.2 million short tons (136 million metric tons) and forced layoffs and plant closings.

Many U.S. manufacturers complained of a disturbing lack of steel during the year. Despite a sales slump in the automobile industry, a major steel market, automobile manufacturers were stockpiling steel against future price increases. Steel rods and bars were in especially short supply. With the oil shortage causing some highway traffic to be diverted to railroads, steel was also needed for more freight cars.

Meanwhile, Arnold E. Safer, an energy and minerals specialist with the Irving Trust Company in New York City, forecast that the world steel industry will have to spend over $165 billion during the 1970s to add 300 million short tons (272 million metric tons) of steelmaking capacity. Safer said in October that this would be "more than a threefold increase in investment requirement" over the 1960s, when the industry added 210 million short tons (190 million metric tons) at a cost of $50 billion.

Equal Opportunity Program. About 50,000 U.S. steelworkers will benefit from $31 million in back wages to be paid under an industrywide plan for ending racial and sex discrimination. The agreement – formalized on April 15 with the signing of two consent decrees filed in U.S. District Court in Birmingham, Ala., by officials of nine major steel firms – is believed to mark the first United States industry-wide equal employment program. The United Steelworkers Union agreed to contribute a share of the back wages.

In July, the Iranian government signed an agreement to acquire a 25 per cent equity interest in Fried. Krupp Huttenwerke, a German steel firm controlled by the Krupp interests. The deal was probably the largest single investment in Western industry yet made by a Middle Eastern country.   Mary E. Jessup

STOCKS AND BONDS. Security prices continued to fall in most of the world's financial centers throughout 1974. Stock prices in the United States slumped sharply during the first three quarters of the year, before recovering from 12-year lows. For the year, the Dow Jones industrial average fell to 616.24, down 27.6 per cent.

Foreign stock markets were equally hard hit. Prices on the London Stock Exchange plunged to 20-year lows in December. Prices also fell in Australia, Canada, France, West Germany, and other countries as the financial world reacted to tight money and fears of a worldwide recession.

U.S. Securities. The Dow Jones average of 30 blue-chip industrial stocks dropped to the year's low of 577.6 on Dec. 6, 1974, which was 45 per cent below the all-time peak of 1051.70 on Jan. 11, 1973. The bear market brought down values of railroad and public utility stocks as well as industrials. Despite the large losses, there was little panic selling. Indeed, brokers found commission profits hard to come by because of the slack volume.

The market value of the stocks listed on the New York Stock Exchange fell an estimated $400 billion during the 21 months after the market peak in 1973. This was one-third of the U.S. national income and about $50 billion more than the federal debt.

Nevertheless, the stock market had fared relatively worse during some earlier bear markets. For example, it fell 89 per cent from the 1929 peak to the 1932 trough, including a record 12.8 per cent drop on Oct. 28, 1929. No bear market since World War II had been as severe as the 1973-1974 experience.

Business Profits, however, rose to record highs in the first three quarters of 1974. Some gains were due to inventory profits gained by revaluing inventories at rising prices. Profits were a mixed blessing for U.S. companies, because inflated profits raised corporate tax liabilities. During the first half of the year, profits were running at an annual rate of $141 billion before taxes and $85 billion after taxes.

Stock Prices reflect what investors anticipate, not just current earnings. In 1974, U.S. investors observed the energy crisis that forced up prices of needed inputs and led to government controls. They observed strong anti-inflationary federal fiscal policies. They saw the tightest credit market conditions in a century, with high-grade corporate bonds yielding over 10 per cent, and the prime rate on bank loans – the interest rate charged to most-favored commercial customers – rising to 12 per cent.

As trading volume and stock prices fell during 1973, the Federal Reserve System reduced the required margin, or cash payment for buying stocks on credit, from 65 to 50 per cent, effective on Jan. 3, 1974. Despite this, loans to buy stocks on margin dropped, presumably because of high borrowing costs and lackluster prospects. High interest rates also attracted a lot of money away from the stock

Stocks Plunge in 1974

New York Stock Exchange composite averages

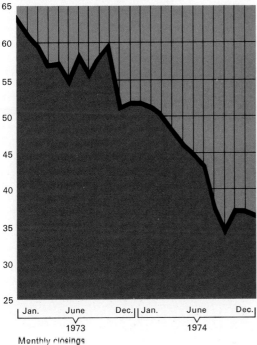

| | Jan. | June | Dec.‖Jan. | June | Dec. |
| | 1973 | | | 1974 | |

Monthly closings

SUDAN sentenced eight Palestinian guerrillas to life imprisonment on June 24, 1974, for the 1973 murder of U.S. Ambassador Cleo A. Noel, Jr., and two other diplomats in Khartoum. However, Sudanese President Sayed Gaafar Mohamed Nimeiri immediately commuted the sentences to seven years each and ordered the prisoners released to the Palestine Liberation Organization (PLO). He said that only the PLO was competent to try the men and that their return was justified by Israel's retaliatory bombings of Lebanon. He added that their crime was political, not criminal. The terrorists were flown to Beirut, Lebanon, and held under PLO supervision. The United States recalled its ambassador to Sudan.

Relations between Sudan and Libya deteriorated in May when Nimeiri accused Libya of instigating a plot against his regime and funding Sudanese insurgents. Reportedly, Libya then demanded immediate repayment of a $16.2-million loan. But Egyptian-Sudanese relations improved during the year. On February 12, the two nations set up a joint committee to foster economic and political cooperation.

On May 20, work began on a 490-mile (790-kilometer) Khartoum-Port Sudan oil pipeline and a refinery at Port Sudan. In May, the United States granted Sudan a $3-million loan to expand wheat production. Other foreign aid included loans from Denmark and the Netherlands.   William Spencer

See also AFRICA (Facts in Brief Table).

market. As stock prices declined, dividend yields rose to an average of 5.5 per cent; the ratio of earnings to stock prices rose to about 10 per cent, highest since the early post-World War II years.

Stock prices seemed so cheap after an October 4 low that investors returned to the market in sufficient volume to ignite a record one-week rally that boosted the Dow Jones average by more than 10 per cent.

Mutual Funds, which had suffered from investor pessimism, managed substantial net sales of shares in 1974 after 2½ years of net redemptions. Much of the sales gain was due to the newly formed money market funds that specialized in short-term, high-yielding securities.

Commission Changes. The Securities and Exchange Commission (SEC) continued to move toward replacing fixed brokerage fees on security transactions with negotiated commissions by May 1, 1975. Organized stock exchanges opposed the move. The SEC earlier ordered the industry to negotiate fees on transactions below $2,000 and above $300,-000. The new ruling would extend negotiated rates to all transactions. However, the House Commerce Committee cast doubt on whether the SEC would be able to meet its May 1 deadline when the committee twice refused to clear a bill on sweeping securities legislation at year-end.   William G. Dewald

See also ECONOMICS; Section One, FOCUS ON THE ECONOMY.

SUPREME COURT OF THE UNITED STATES. In a historic decision, the Supreme Court ruled 8 to 0 on July 24, 1974, that President Richard M. Nixon could not legally withhold 64 tape-recorded conversations from the special Watergate prosecutor. The decision, in *United States v. Nixon,* led directly to Nixon's resignation 16 days later. It also constituted a landmark interpretation of the division of powers among branches of the federal government.

At issue was the validity of a May 20 ruling by U.S. District Court Judge John J. Sirica ordering Nixon to comply with a subpoena issued by special prosecutor Leon Jaworski for tapes and documents for use in the fall cover-up trial of former Nixon aides. In an opinion issued by Chief Justice Warren E. Burger, a Nixon appointee, the court agreed with a key White House contention: The public interest demanded that "executive privilege" protect confidentiality of certain communications between a President and his advisers, even though that privilege was not specified in existing law. But the court rejected Nixon's claim that only the President, and not the courts, should determine when the privilege could be invoked. While one branch's interpretation of its own powers "is due great respect by the others," Burger wrote, the court must reaffirm a principle put forth in 1803 in *Marbury v. Madison:* "It is emphatically the province and duty of the judicial department to say what the law is." The President's claim of privilege "must

499

Crusader For Civil Liberties

Earl Warren, as chief justice of the United States for 16 years, presided over a Supreme Court that may have initiated more social change in the United States than any court since the time of John Marshall, who served as chief justice from 1801 to 1835. When Warren died on July 9, 1974, he left a legacy of decisions that will bolster individual liberties for years to come.

Warren was born in Los Angeles in 1891, the son of a Norwegian-born railway repairman. He earned his law degree from the University of California at Berkeley in 1914, and served as prosecuting attorney in Alameda County from 1920 to 1939. He became attorney general of California in 1939 and served in that office until he became governor in 1943.

Some say that the one blot on an otherwise outstanding record occurred early in his first term as governor, when he supported the federal order during World War II evacuating 110,000 Japanese Americans from the West Coast for fear of an imminent Japanese invasion. However, he only followed a Supreme Court decision that upheld the evacuation, but banned detention centers.

He was still serving as governor in 1953 when President Dwight D. Eisenhower named him to the Supreme Court. He took his seat on Oct. 5, 1953, and served as chief justice until he retired in 1969.

Warren, if asked, probably would have cited two leading cases as the most important ones in which he wrote the opinion of the court. In *Brown v. Board of Education* in 1954, the court held that states acted unconstitutionally when they operated dual school systems—one for whites, another for blacks. In *Reynolds v. Sims* in 1964, he put forth the "one man, one vote" principle, ruling that seats in state legislatures must be apportioned solely on the basis of population. The principle later was extended to congressional elections.

Many decisions of the "Warren Court" stirred sharp criticism. One such case was *Pennsylvania v. Nelson*. Pennsylvania was one of several states that had adopted laws making it a state crime to conspire to overthrow the federal government. Congress ear-lier had enacted legislation making such conspiracy a federal crime. Warren, writing for the court in 1956, held that Congress had pre-empted the field and struck down Pennsylvania's law. The outcry in some circles was pronounced, because the issue of subversion was a sensitive one. As a result, "Impeach Earl Warren" signs went up in some places.

A similar outcry was produced by Warren's opinion in *United States v. Robel* in 1967. Robel had been a member of the Communist Party and had worked in a defense plant for many years. His work record was impeccable; there were no signs of disloyalty or subversion in any of his activities. Yet, he had been discharged, under an act of Congress. The Warren opinion held the act, as applied to Robel, was unconstitutional.

Once a vigorous prosecutor as attorney general of California, Warren wrote numerous opinions in the area of criminal procedure. While recognizing the imperative needs of prosecutors, these opinions also made room for the demanding constitutional guarantees granted defendants. *Miranda v. Arizona* in 1966 was one of a series of cases that upheld the rights of a suspect taken into custody by the police. Under the Constitution, a suspect must be advised of his rights to keep silent and have a lawyer present. These guarantees, when honored, prevent the third degree from being used in the United States.

Warren knew of the international aspects of this and other legal problems; he was active for years in international conferences dealing with the substitution of law for force to settle disputes between nations as well as to protect the civil rights of citizens.

Warren's early career had given little indication of the role he would play on the Supreme Court. Yet, his interests in law were always humanistic, and, during his career, he became progressively more liberal. To some, the cases that the Supreme Court took to review in his day may have seemed minutiae. Yet to Warren, the measure of the law's effectiveness and rightness was in its impact on the people at the bottom, and not only on the high and mighty.   William O. Douglas

Earl Warren
(1891-1974)

yield to the demonstrated, specific need for evidence in a pending criminal trial," Burger declared. See WATERGATE; Section Two, FROM TRIUMPH TO TRAGEDY.

Race Discrimination. The court ended a 20-year pattern of decisions for plaintiffs in school desegregation cases on July 25 when it ruled that courts could not ordinarily ignore school district boundaries in combating school segregation. The 5 to 4 decision in *Milliken v. Bradley* overturned a lower court order that would have consolidated the heavily black Detroit school district with 53 mostly white suburban school districts through cross-district busing.

The court struck down the plan because the suburban districts had not been accused of unlawful segregation. "Where the schools of only one district have been affected, there is no constitutional power in the courts to decree relief balancing the racial composition of that district's schools with those of the surrounding districts," it ruled. Justice Thurgood Marshall, in a vigorous dissent, called the decision "a step backward."

Abuse of Power. In addition to the Nixon tapes case, the court dealt with several other allegations of misuse of governmental power. On April 17, the court decided that families of students wounded or killed by National Guard men at the 1970 Kent State University disturbance in Ohio should be allowed to sue state officials for civil damages. On April 29, it declared unconstitutional certain rules allowing censorship of California prisoners' mail (see PRISONS). And on May 13, the court ruled illegal a series of federal wiretaps that had been authorized by an assistant to the U.S. attorney general rather than the attorney general as specified by law. This decision forced the Justice Department to drop nearly 300 criminal prosecutions tainted by the illegal taps.

Backing away from a controversial 1973 decision, the court decided on June 24 that local juries do not have "unbridled discretion" to judge a work illegally obscene. In a 9 to 0 decision, the court held that the movie *Carnal Knowledge* did not depict sexual conduct in a "patently offensive way," and so an Albany, Ga., jury could not ban it as hard-core pornography. Although court members had predicted that guidelines issued in 1973 would allow the Supreme Court to avoid case-by-case review of allegedly obscene works, three concurring justices noted that the *Carnal Knowledge* case proved that prediction to be erroneous.

Other Decisions. In a 5 to 3 decision on June 19, in *Parker v. Levy*, the court ruled that the "general articles" of the Uniform Code of Military Justice are not unconstitutionally vague and indefinite. The decision upheld the three-year sentence given Army Captain Howard B. Levy, a doctor who was convicted of "conduct unbecoming an officer and gentleman" for publicly opposing the Vietnam War.

On June 25, in *Miami Herald v. Tornillo*, the court unanimously struck down a Florida law that allowed political candidates who had been criticized in newspaper columns the right to a printed reply in the paper. The court termed the law an abridgment of the First Amendment's free press guarantee.

In two separate opinions, the court restricted the use of the class action device, which has been used increasingly by consumer and environmental groups in bringing lawsuits. One decision forbade the grouping of claims to meet the minimum number required to bring suit in federal court. The other required the persons bringing the suit to assume the entire cost of notifying all persons in the class on whose behalf they were suing.

In *United States v. Calandra* on January 8, the court ruled 6 to 3 that the rule forbidding official use of illegally obtained evidence against a criminal suspect does not apply to grand jury proceedings. The decision legalizes use of such evidence against a suspect in seeking his indictment, but not in obtaining his conviction at trial.

In another case, *Cleveland Board v. LaFleur*, the court ruled 7 to 2 on January 21 that public-school teachers cannot be arbitrarily forced to take maternity leave after four or five months of pregnancy. The idea that teachers are unable to perform their duties after a predetermined time period violates due process of law, the majority held.   David C. Beckwith

SURGERY. See MEDICINE.

SWAZILAND. See AFRICA.

SWEDEN. The Riksdag (parliament), in which the ruling Social Democrat-Communist alliance holds exactly half the seats, resorted to a lottery to resolve a tie vote on March 27, 1974. The drawing went against the government on an Opposition bill to improve the quality of jobs in industry. Prime Minister Olof Palme accepted the lottery result to avoid confrontation and keep his government in power until the 1976 general elections.

Palme presented to parliament an $866-million package of bonus measures for taxpayers on January 30. Designed to boost the economy, the bill led to a nationwide spending spree when it took effect on April 1. The value-added tax was cut by 3.41 per cent from 17.65 per cent; parents received a tax-free bonus of about $45 for each child; and pensioner and student benefits rose. Another measure, placed before parliament on May 3, created a $238-million fund financed by companies to improve employees' working conditions and environment. Another reform, which will begin in July, 1976, lowers the pension eligibility age from 67 to 65 at an estimated cost of $71.4 million a year.

A New Constitution, formally adopted on February 27, reduced the king's role to that of a figurehead and created a single-chamber Riksdag. King Carl XVI Gustaf, who succeeded to the throne in 1973, opened the Riksdag earlier in the year for the first and last time. This and the appointment of a prime

King Carl XVI Gustaf opens Sweden's parliament for the first and last
time in January. A new Constitution adopted in February limits his powers.

minister will become the function of the speaker. The
king is no longer empowered to approve legislation
or command the armed forces, and does not have to
attend Cabinet meetings. Effective Jan. 1, 1975, the
Constitution also reduces the number of seats in the
Riksdag from 350 to 349 in the 1976 elections to
avoid "government by lottery." The voting age will
be lowered to 18.

Foreign Relations. Sweden will continue its policy
of "active neutrality," Palme pledged on August 13.
He said he feared superpower domination would
lead to social injustice for small nations. Accordingly,
the Swedish International Development Authority
proposed devoting $71.42 million, or 1 per cent of
the gross national product, for foreign aid, particularly to India, North Vietnam, and Tanzania.

The United States restored full diplomatic relations on May 22 with the arrival in Stockholm of 71-
year-old U.S. Ambassador Robert Strausz-Hupe,
former ambassador to Belgium. Relations had been
strained for two years over Palme's criticism of U.S.
policy in Vietnam.

Gasoline Rationed. On January 8, Sweden became the first West European country to ration
gasoline and heating oil following a 20 per cent cutback in oil deliveries. But so many extra coupons
were issued for "needy cases" that gasoline rationing
broke down and ended 22 days later.   Kenneth Brown

See also EUROPE (Facts in Brief Table).

SWIMMING. Tim Shaw of Long Beach, Calif., and
Jenny Turrall of Sydney, Australia, were two of the
most impressive swimmers of 1974, making frequent
appearances in the record book. In all, 14 of the 15
world records for women and 10 of the 16 for men
were broken.

Shaw, a 16-year-old high school junior, broke three
of the five world free-style records in the Amateur
Athletic Union (A.A.U.) national long-course championships in Concord, Calif., in August. He swam
200 meters in 1 minute 51.66 seconds, 400 meters in
3 minutes 54.69 seconds, and 1,500 meters in 15
minutes 31.75 seconds.

Shaw's success was unexpected, but Mark Spitz,
now retired, put it in perspective. "You can't become
an overnight star in swimming," said Spitz. "Some
kid might set his first world record, but you can bet
he worked 10 years before he set it."

Perhaps Shaw worked 10 years, but Turrall certainly did not. She turned 14 in the middle of a season
in which she lowered the women's world record for
the 1,500-meter free-style five times in 8½ months,
starting in December, 1973. By August, 1974, she
was down to 16 minutes 33.94 seconds.

Turrall stood 5 feet 2 inches (157 centimeters) and
weighed 94 pounds (43 kilograms). In most races,
she swam stroke for stroke with Sally Lockyer, also
14. They were teammates and friends, and their
parents sat together during races.

Major Meets. The year's three major meets took place in a two-week span – the European championships from August 18 to 25 in Vienna, Austria; the A.A.U. championships from August 22 to 25 in Concord; and the United States-East Germany dual meet on August 31 and September 1 in the same Concord pool. The East Germans won 17 of 29 gold medals in the European championships; their women captured 13 of 14 races. But the U.S. men's and women's combined team scored a 198-145 victory over the East Germans, mainly because the American men won all 15 races.

Shaw won three races against the East Germans. John Naber of Menlo Park, Calif., took both backstroke races, handing Roland Matthes of East Germany his first backstroke defeats in seven years, and John Hencken of Santa Clara, Calif., won both breast-stroke races in world-record time. Earlier in the year, Naber had helped Southern California lift the National Collegiate Athletic Association (NCAA) title from Indiana University by 1 point.

The East German Women continued to assault world records. Physicians at the European championships, noting their unusual bulk, body hair, and muscular development, suspected that they were taking anabolic steroids, which are male hormones.

Shirley Babashoff of Fountain Valley, Calif., and Kathy Heddy of Trenton, N.J., had record-breaking years.   Frank Litsky

SWITZERLAND. In a nationwide referendum Oct. 20, 1974, Swiss voters rejected by 2 to 1 a proposal to expel more than 500,000 foreign workers within the next three years. The government had advised voting against the proposal, which was initiated by a small right wing group. Switzerland's labor force of 3 million contains some 600,000 foreigners, the largest percentage for any European country.

The federal government began the year with attempts to reduce the 12 per cent rate of inflation. A 10 per cent limit on wage increases was adopted on February 7 for a year. On January 2, the National Bank further tightened its control of the net inflow of funds from abroad. On November 20, it imposed a 12 per cent tax on foreign-held funds to drive down the price of the Swiss franc and protect the export and tourist industries. Hotel and resort bookings fell 40 per cent as inflation hit tourism.

The Organization for Economic Cooperation and Development (OECD) reported in March that slackening consumer demand and "imported" inflation were Switzerland's main economic problems. The OECD also estimated that the oil crisis would add $750 million to the Swiss imports bill. A growing volume of exports prevented a heavy trade deficit. The 1974 federal budget showed Switzerland would face a deficit of $61.9 million, with total expenditure up 13 per cent.   Kenneth Brown

See also EUROPE (Facts in Brief Table).

SYRIA resumed diplomatic relations with the United States in June, 1974, after a seven-year break. The development came during President Richard M. Nixon's visit to Damascus, the Syrian capital. It underscored President Hafiz al-Asad's increased willingness to separate ideology from foreign policy and abandon isolationism. The resumption followed the signing on May 30 of agreements with Israel, negotiated by U.S. Secretary of State Henry A. Kissinger, that called for the disengagement of Israeli and Syrian troops on the Golan Heights, established a United Nations buffer zone between the two armies, and provided for an exchange of prisoners. It was the first formal pact between the two nations since the 1948 armistice ending Israel's war of independence.

The disengagement, completed on June 25, ended four months of artillery duels and air strikes across the Golan cease-fire line established after the October, 1973, war. Syria also received the town of Al Qunaytirah, most of which had been destroyed in the fighting. A congress of the ruling Syrian Baath Party unanimously approved the disengagement agreement in August. On August 12, Major General Hikmat al-Shehabi was named chief of staff. The fast-rising general, the former chief of Syria's military intelligence, served as Syria's military representative during the disengagement negotiations.

Economic Development. Although Russia continued to provide arms and the country remained in a state of war mobilization, the reduced border tension enabled Asad to promote economic development. Japan pledged $90 million in March for the construction of an oil refinery in Tartus; Syria's main refinery in Homs was put out of commission during the October, 1973, war. Japan also underwrote $30 million for a land reclamation project in August. The World Bank loaned Syria $73 million in March for cotton-crop expansion and the construction of 7,500 irrigated model farms averaging 70 acres (28 hectares) in the Balitch River Basin. A second World Bank loan, of $43 million and made jointly with Kuwait, would finance expansion of the national electric power grid.

Reduced Controls. The government issued a number of decrees in March aimed at reducing state control over the economy. They established duty-free zones for foreign-financed industrial plants, permitted foreign firms to transfer profits abroad in hard currencies, and granted tax exemptions for companies investing in Syria. The 1974 budget of $2.5-billion, announced March 21 by Prime Minister Mahmud al-Ayyubi, earmarked $1.2 billion for development, with $450 million for defense and $440-million for industrial and mining development.

In April, the government announced that damage to Syrian property in the October war had totaled between $200 and $250 million, all of it covered by subsidies from other Arab states.   William Spencer

See also MIDDLE EAST (Facts in Brief Table).

TAIWAN quietly weathered economic storms and maintained its isolated international position in 1974 under Prime Minister Chiang Ching-kuo. His father, President Chiang Kai-shek, remained in the ill health that forced him to give up governmental control in 1972. The president did not appear publicly, even for his 87th birthday celebration on October 31.

The Nationalist government interpreted the U.S. appointment of a senior diplomat, Leonard Unger, as ambassador to be a sure sign of continuing American support for Taiwan. There had previously been great concern because the United States also maintains relations with the People's Republic of China, which Taiwan strongly opposes. Unger arrived in Taiwan to take over the post in May.

A mutual defense treaty continued to give U.S. protection to Taiwan, subject to congressional approval of any specific action. But special presidential powers to use U.S. armed forces to defend Taiwan without specific approval ended on October 28. The U.S. military force on Taiwan was reduced in line with President Richard M. Nixon's promise to China in the Shanghai communiqué that was signed on Feb. 27, 1972.

China Reasserted on February 28 its desire to assume control of Taiwan. The date marked the anniversary of a Taiwanese uprising against Nationalist control in 1947. Peking stressed that the Taiwanese should "not miss the opportunity to contribute to the great cause of unifying the motherland" by changing sides to the Communists. No major changes occurred, but more persons of Taiwanese nationality appeared in China and as designated Chinese representatives at international events.

Because of Peking pressure, few important nations still kept diplomatic ties with Taiwan, and all references to the island were deleted from United Nations publications. But the Nationalist regime found unofficial ways to stay in contact with other countries, so this isolation had slight practical effect.

From a 1973 surplus of some $650 million on $8.3-billion worth of foreign trade, Taiwan slipped into a trade deficit beginning in March. Total 1974 foreign trade rose to more than $12 billion. This is slightly more than the estimated foreign trade of China, which has 50 times as many people but is not as oriented toward world markets as Taiwan.

Domestic Growth. Productivity, which had increased rapidly in recent years, slowed during 1974 because of the higher costs of imported fuel. But it still was over 5 per cent, better than most countries at a time of worldwide recession. Taiwan also managed to control inflation better than most other countries. Some small businesses failed, but more sophisticated industries prospered. The government continued to push projects that included new ports, a steel mill, a chemical complex, and a highway running the length of Taiwan.   Henry S. Bradsher

See also Asia (Facts in Brief Table).

TANZANIA moved in 1974 to restore relations with Great Britain, which had been strained since 1965. When the white minority in Rhodesia unilaterally declared independence from Britain in 1965, Tanzania protested that Britain should have ensured black majority rule by force if necessary. In the face of this criticism, Britain cut off aid to Tanzania.

Then in June, 1974, after weeklong talks between officials of the two governments, Britain announced it was resuming aid. Under the terms of the agreement, Britain will provide about $27.5 million in grants and loans over a three- to five-year period. In return, Tanzania will compensate British citizens for farms and businesses that were nationalized.

Chinese Aid. Tanzania was criticized during the year for allowing itself to be unduly influenced by Communist China. President Julius K. Nyerere visited China in April and secured a $77.5-million interest-free loan to develop the country's coal and iron-ore deposits. Among other development projects, China financed and helped to build the new railroad between Tanzania and Zambia.

The United Nations issued a report in June, which Tanzania protested, alleging that China had built a military base in Tanzania. Also, the white minority governments of Rhodesia and South Africa feared that China would use the new railroad to ship military supplies to black nationalist guerrillas. Tanzania stationed troops along the railway to prevent sabotage attempts by Rhodesia or South Africa.

In terms of security, Tanzania was also concerned about hostile acts by neighboring Uganda. Ugandan President Idi Amin Dada accused Nyerere of involvement in plots to assassinate him. While the tension continued, Uganda requested fighter bombers and missiles from Russia. In a show of strength, Tanzania paraded its military wares for the first time during the 20th anniversary celebrations of the ruling political party in July.

National Economy. High oil prices and the African drought adversely affected Tanzania's economy. The nation's foreign-currency reserves fell sharply, so in August, Tanzania was tentatively allocated $13.3 million from the Arab oil fund set up to help African countries.

The African drought caused widespread crop failure. Tanzania was forced to import massive amounts of food to avert starvation in some areas. This further diminished foreign-currency reserves.

Tanzania celebrated the 10th anniversary of union between the mainland (formerly Tanganyika) and the island of Zanzibar.

In May, the yearlong trial of persons accused of being involved in the 1972 assassination of Sheik Abeid A. Karume, Zanzibar's former ruler, ended. Thirty-four persons were sentenced to death and 15 were given prison sentences. Nine others were sentenced to death in 1973.   John Storm Roberts

See also Africa (Facts in Brief Table).

Parading soldiers carry pictures of Tanzanian leaders to celebrate the 10th anniversary of union between Zanzibar and mainland Tanganyika.

TAXATION. Interest in federal tax reform in the United States was kindled in 1974 by revelations about President Richard M. Nixon's nonpayment of federal income taxes. Nixon paid only $792.81 in federal taxes in 1970 on his reported income of $262,942 and $878.03 on a 1971 income of $262,385. In March, 1974, the Internal Revenue Service (IRS) said that Nixon owed $432,787 in back taxes plus interest. He agreed to pay the total without appeal. See NIXON, RICHARD M.

Nelson A. Rockefeller also found his tax payments a matter of wide public discussion and question during congressional hearings on his nomination as Vice-President. The multimillionaire paid no federal income taxes in 1970, though he paid nearly $1-million in other taxes. An IRS audit concluded that Rockefeller owed the government more than $1 million in back taxes plus interest.

Underpayment of federal income taxes is not uncommon. In 1972, for example, when the total federal tax revenue was $238 billion, the government audited only 2 per cent of the returns. It discovered 1.26 million taxpayers who had underpaid a total of $5.1 billion. Of these taxpayers, only 2,555 were charged with fraud because of willful failure to report income.

Tax Reform. The 117-measure Tax Reform Act of 1974 (which did not pass in the 93rd Congress) would have closed some of the tax loopholes through which many wealthy Americans have avoided tax payments, and would have corrected other glaring inequities in the federal tax structure. This bill would have terminated the 22 per cent depletion allowance applied to income from gas and oil wells by 1979. It also would have simplified some tax calculations and eliminated or consolidated some deductions. The standard deduction of 15 per cent of income, or $2,000, would have been raised to 17 per cent, or $2,500, to give tax relief to the working poor and to some middle-income taxpayers. The sponsors of the Tax Reform Act were reportedly planning to introduce it again in the 94th Congress.

President Gerald R. Ford endorsed the tax-reform bill in October. He also proposed that the 7 per cent investment tax credit be boosted to 10 per cent to increase the flow of money into new business facilities and equipment. He suggested a 5 per cent surtax on taxable incomes of more than $15,000 a year.

Tax Revenue. During the 1974 fiscal year (from July 1, 1973, through June 30, 1974), the federal government collected $269 billion in tax revenue. Of this, $205 billion came from individual and employment taxes; $42 billion from taxes on corporations; $5.1 billion from estate and gift taxes; and $17.1-billion from excise and other taxes.

The government had enough manpower to audit only 2.3 per cent of all tax returns in 1974. At the same time, more taxpayers were itemizing their deductions than ever before, in spite of the reinstatement of a new short form in 1972 to make the task of both taxpayer and auditor easier. The IRS estimated that almost half of all returns in 1974 were prepared by someone other than the taxpayer. One-third of all the tax returns had been prepared in this way in 1973.

Court Ruling. In October, the 10th Circuit Court of Appeals in Denver reversed a lower-court decision that had been hailed as substantially broadening a taxpayer's right to challenge the Internal Revenue Service on its rulings. The decision concerned an IRS ruling on cattle-feeding programs, which are a common tax-deferral device. Cattle-feeding tax deferrals involve the purchase of feed in one year, usually near the end of the year, and the sale of the fattened cattle the following year. The feed purchase creates a large expense deduction, without any offsetting income until the next year.

In a case involving an Oklahoma company that sponsors cattle-feeder partnerships, the lower court had ruled that taxpayers can challenge the Internal Revenue Service before filing a tax return. Normally, a taxpayer must file and then contest the tax liability in tax court, or pay the tax and sue for refund in a federal court. In dismissing the lawsuit, the appeals court said that the situation did not justify an exception to the federal Anti-Injunction Act, which generally provides that a person cannot sue to restrain the assessment or collection of any tax.

State and Local Taxes. Total state tax collections in fiscal 1974 reached $74.1 billion, an increase of 8.9 per cent over collections in fiscal 1973. Local taxes totaled about $56.2 billion, 24.2 per cent less than the state tax total.

Sales and gross receipts taxes represented the largest source of state tax revenue in fiscal 1974. All 50 states collected some form of sales and gross receipts tax, for a total of $40.5 billion. And 44 states collected a total of $17 billion in individual income taxes in the fiscal year.

Eight states accounted for more than half the total state tax revenue collected in the United States in fiscal 1974. They were (in billions of dollars): New York, $8.52; California, $7.97; Pennsylvania, $4.61; Illinois, $4.08; Michigan, $3.68; Texas, $3.29; Florida, $2.80; and Ohio, $2.79.

Tax revenues increased in 12 states by at least 15 per cent, and only seven states showed a tax revenue increase of less than 5 per cent. Connecticut was the only state showing a net decline in total tax collections in fiscal 1974, because of a reduction in its general sales tax rate and a change in the base of its individual income tax.

Seven states collected a per capita state tax revenue of $400 or more; 12 states had a per capita tax revenue of $350 to $399; 19 states, $300 to $349; 10 states, $250 to $299; and only 2 states had a per capita tax revenue of less than $250. Carol L. Thompson

TELEPHONE. The United States Department of Justice filed an antitrust suit against the American Telephone and Telegraph Company (A.T. & T.) on Nov. 20, 1974, charging A.T. & T. with illegally conspiring to monopolize communications markets. The suit seeks to force A.T. & T. to give up its manufacturing subsidiary, the Western Electric Company. It would also require that the company either get out of much of its long-distance business or else shed its 23 local telephone companies. A.T. & T. might also have to divest itself of Bell Telephone Laboratories.

The Justice Department said that winning the suit would increase competition in the telephone industry. A.T. & T. countered that it is confident that it has not violated the antitrust laws and that breaking up the nation's telephone network could lead to higher prices and a deterioration of service. The suit is not expected to reach the courts for several years and will take several more years to try.

Controversy also continued in other areas. During 1974, Microwave Communications Incorporated (MCI) and A.T. & T. disputed the right of A.T. & T. companies to restrict the interconnection of private lines, usually microwave circuits, from special carriers such as MCI into local Bell System operations. The Federal Communications Commission on November 19 refused to reconsider an earlier decision that allows such interconnection.

To ward off the loss of revenue due to such competition, the Bell System adopted a new hi-lo pricing system on private-line services. The company charges lower and more competitive rates on routes where traffic is heavy, and higher rates on routes where traffic is lower.

Directory Assistance. The Cincinnati Bell Telephone Company in March became the first company in the United States to charge for directory assistance calls. The company allows three free information calls a month and then charges for each subsequent call. Before the charge was introduced, directory assistance calls were increasing three times faster than the growth in customer service. Local information calls have dropped about 70 per cent since the charge was introduced, and the cost is being borne by those who use it. Information calls from coin phones and from handicapped persons are exempted from the charge.

New Technology. A.T. & T. in June installed 8½ miles (13.7 kilometers) of an experimental wave guide that transmits about 250,000 two-way telephone calls at one time. At that rate, the full contents of a 22-volume set of encyclopedias could be transmitted in 0.1 second.

A number of telephone companies began to offer the Bell System's Touch-a-Matic telephone to customers. The caller can dial and store up to 32 telephone numbers in a built-in integrated circuit memory by pressing a button. J. L. Peterson

See also COMMUNICATIONS.

TELEVISION entered upon its most historic 17 days in the United States on July 24, 1974, when Congress permitted live TV coverage of the six-day presidential impeachment debate by the House Judiciary Committee. The networks carried the 45-hour committee deliberations in full, on a rotation basis, at an estimated loss of $3.2 million in commercial revenue. The unprecedented national affairs drama reached its climax on August 8 with the resignation speech of President Richard M. Nixon, carried live by all three networks.

Television cameras also documented Nixon's departure from the White House the next morning, followed by the inauguration of President Gerald R. Ford. Nixon's resignation speech was witnessed by an audience estimated at from 90 million to 110 million viewers—more than double the U.S. population in 1868, the year that Andrew Johnson became the only President to be impeached.

Throughout 1974, Nixon probably garnered more network television exposure than any other U.S. President. The coverage ranged from his appearance in Houston at the National Association of Broadcasters convention in March and his trips to Russia and the Middle East to a folksy demonstration of his yoyo prowess at the opening of the new Grand Ole Opry House in Nashville, Tenn., on March 16. Also prominently covered in prime time were Nixon's

Valerie Harper, center, became one of the season's top hits when the sharp-tongued, wisecracking "Rhoda" got her own show.

Cicely Tyson aged from 19 to 110 in her moving portrayal of a former slave in *The Autobiography of Miss Jane Pittman.*

various press conferences, which usually focused on Watergate and the issue of the White House tapes.

Antitrust Suit. Notwithstanding this exposure, the battle lines were clearly drawn in 1974 between the Nixon Administration and the networks. At the beginning of the year, the networks claimed that the antitrust suit filed against them by the Department of Justice in 1972 was politically motivated.

The suit was dismissed "without prejudice" in November, clearing the way for the government to refile the case, which it did on December 10. The suit charged the networks with using their control of prime-time programming to restrain competition in the production, distribution, and sale of entertainment programs.

Series Programs. Comedy and police shows dominated major network entertainment programming in 1974. Some were spin-offs from other series and many had ethnic themes. "Kojak," starring Telly Savalas as a tough Polish-American homicide lieutenant, was big in the popularity polls in the spring.

Two ethnic comedies immediately moved into the top 10 in the fall. They were "Rhoda," a spin-off from "The Mary Tyler Moore Show," with Valerie Harper as the wisecracking, prototypical Jewish heroine; and "Chico and the Man," about a bigoted white (Jack Albertson) who owns a garage in an East Los Angeles ghetto area, and a charming Mexican-American hustler (Freddie Prinze).

Nine of the new fall entries were law-and-order series. Three starred women, one of them black—Teresa Graves in "Get Christie Love!" The other two were "Police Woman," starring Angie Dickinson, a spin-off from "Police Story"; and "Amy Prentiss," a spin-off from "Ironside," with Jessica Walters as a chief of detectives.

Consistently top-rated throughout the year were "The Waltons" and such quality-comedy series as "All in the Family," "The Mary Tyler Moore Show," "M*A*S*H," "Sanford and Son," and "Good Times," a spin-off from "Maude," itself a spin-off from "All in the Family."

Missing from 1974's weekly fall line-up were such long-time TV institutions as Lucille Ball (star of three series over the past 23 years), Dean Martin, Flip Wilson, Amanda Blake (Kitty in "Gunsmoke" since 1955), Dick Van Dyke, and Sonny and Cher.

TV Drama. Among the best dramatic programs in 1974 were *The Autobiography of Miss Jane Pittman*, a multi-Emmy winner with Cicely Tyson in the title role; *Tell Me Where It Hurts*, starring Maureen Stapleton as a painfully liberated housewife; *A Case of Rape*, with Elizabeth Montgomery; Henry Fonda's one-man tribute to Clarence Darrow; *The Execution of Private Slovik*; *The Law*, a powerful indictment of our legal system; and *QB VII*, a $2.5-million, two-part dramatization of Leon Uris' best-selling novel.

The British, as always, were richly represented. Sir Laurence Olivier was superb as *The Merchant of Venice*; and the Public Broadcasting Service (PBS) aired two engrossing English mini-series about the Edwardian era—Emmy-winner "Upstairs, Downstairs" and "The Edwardians."

The National Broadcasting Company paid a record $10 million to Paramount Picture Corporation in July for one showing (in two parts) of *The Godfather*, the biggest-grossing motion picture in history.

Networks telecast 18 daily game shows during the year, a record number. An additional 14 audience-participation programs were syndicated around the country. The most-watched game series was "Match Game," hosted by Gene Rayburn.

News and Documentaries included Walter Cronkite's one-hour interview with exiled Russian author Alexander Solzhenitsyn on June 24 and the two-hour live newscast of the shoot-out between Los Angeles police and members of the Symbionese Liberation Army on May 17.

All three networks pre-empted their entire prime-time schedules on November 5 to cover what news analysts considered to be one of the most critical off-year congressional elections in U.S. history.

President Ford's honeymoon with television soured slightly on October 15 when the networks decided that Ford's speech to the Future Farmers of America on inflation-fighting tips was not newsworthy enough to carry live. The White House then requested live coverage and got it.

An alarming trend of real-life crime imitating TV violence escalated in 1974. The networks came under pressure from the public and the government to soft-pedal sex, violence, and the general "new permissiveness" in programming. Viewers were particularly offended in September by *Born Innocent*, a film made for television that featured a vicious sexual assault on a 14-year-old girl. Congress ordered the Federal Communications Commission (FCC) to develop a plan to control such excesses.

Regulatory Progress. FCC Commissioner Richard Wiley was named chairman of the commission on March 8. Pending confirmation of new commissioners, the seven-seat FCC operated for two months with only four members. It did not reach full strength until July 10, delaying many important decisions.

However, the FCC voted in September not to renew licenses for eight Alabama stations because of a complaint filed by a local citizens' group charging discrimination against blacks. The stations were all public TV outlets owned by the Alabama Educational Television Commission. However, the decision was expected to make commercial broadcasters more sensitive to citizen complaints.

Equally vexing to broadcasters was the FCC's delay in revising its prime-time access rules. In June, the networks had to scrap six half-hour series slated for fall release after the U.S. Court of Appeals ordered the FCC to delay until at least 1975 a planned revision that would have given each network an additional 1½ hours of programming time each week.

Financial Problems. Delays in the proposed long-range funding bill for public broadcasting caused PBS to cancel a number of drama and documentary programs in favor of more shows on cooking and yoga and Japanese films. Fortunately, "Masterpiece Theatre," "Nova," and a few other fine PBS shows are underwritten by various grants and will still be carried by most public television outlets.

The financially troubled cable TV industry had hoped for some relief in 1974 in the form of pay-TV concessions from the FCC. Instead, after two years of deliberation, the FCC said in August that it needed still more data. Elaborate hearings were held in October, with testimony by more than 100 witnesses. New FCC rulings on pay TV were expected by the end of the year.

Children's Programming. The FCC issued guidelines on October 24 to upgrade children's TV fare—something Action for Children's Television had been seeking since 1970. The FCC declined to eliminate commercials entirely from children's shows, but ruled that commercials should be shorter and should be clearly separated from program material, thus excluding product plugs by a show's host. Stations were also urged to observe other recommended standards such as more weekday programming for preschoolers. June Bundy Csida

TENNESSEE. See STATE GOVERNMENT.

TENNIS. He was 22 years old, fiery, temperamental, and intimidating in his game and in his manner. She was 19, sweet, imperturbable, and, as Dave Anderson wrote in *The New York Times,* "Prim and proper in her blond ponytail and gold earrings, she resembles a poodle on parade."

He was Jimmy Connors of Belleville, Ill., the world's best male tennis player in 1974. She was Chris Evert of Fort Lauderdale, Fla., the world's best female tennis player in 1974. What's more, they were in love. She wore an 11-carat diamond they selected when they were playing tennis in South Africa. They were scheduled to be married November 8, but the marriage was later called off.

The left-handed Connors won the United States, Wimbledon, and Australian championships, routing Ken Rosewall of Australia in the United States and Wimbledon finals. Had he won the French championship, he would have achieved the grand slam, but he and others who played in the new World Team Tennis League (WTT) were barred from that tournament and several others in Europe.

Evert won the Wimbledon, French, and Italian titles. She lost to Evonne Goolagong of Australia in the Australian finals and United States semifinals. She had won 56 consecutive matches and 10 consecutive tournaments until her loss to Goolagong in the U.S. championships in Forest Hills, N.Y.

Love was more than a tennis term to Jimmy Connors and Chris Evert, but the couple finally canceled their wedding plans.

The most spectacular match of the year may have been the U.S. women's final, in which Billie Jean King of Hilton Head Island, S.C., barely defeated Goolagong, 3-6, 6-3, 7-5. The 30-year-old King spent less time playing tennis and more time with business interests. She was a spearhead of WTT as player-coach of the Philadelphia Freedoms at $100,000 a year. She had the league's best won-lost record, was Player of the Year, and was a close runner-up to Tony Roche of the Denver Racquets in voting for Coach of the Year.

The Davis Cup, long the symbol of world tennis supremacy, went to South Africa by default in 1974. With most of their leading professional players committed to playing in the WTT, the United States and Australian teams, perennial powers, were eliminated from the competition early. India beat Australia, and Colombia ousted the United States. That cleared the way to the finals for India and South Africa. But when South Africa reached the finals, the Indian team refused to play South Africa because of that nation's *apartheid* (racial segregation) policy.

"The principle of opposing apartheid is more important than a tennis championship," said R. K. Khanna, secretary of the All-India Lawn Tennis Federation. Davis Cup officials, faced with the first final-round default in the 74 years of the competition, urged India to reconsider.

This was the first time a South African team had reached the Davis Cup finals. In fact, South Africa was banned from the competition in 1970 when officials decided that a South African team's presence would disrupt the tournament. The team was reinstated in 1974 after South Africa began integrating black and white tennis players in competition. Its Davis Cup team was all white.

World Team Tennis consisted of 16 teams that played from May to August, with interruptions for the world's major tournaments. Many European nations fought WTT, because it kept leading players in America and away from lesser European tournaments. However, the International Lawn Tennis Federation gave WTT its reluctant sanction.

The league attracted such men as Connors, Tom Okker of the Netherlands, and Rosewall, John Newcombe, and Roy Emerson of Australia. The women included King, Goolagong, Rosemary Casals of San Francisco, and Maria Bueno of Brazil.

At first, a program consisted of two sets each of men's singles, women's singles, and mixed doubles, with one point for each game won. In midseason, the format was changed to one set each of men's singles, women's singles, men's doubles, women's doubles, and mixed doubles. Denver won the championship, defeating Philadelphia in the finals in August. All teams lost money and some evoked little local interest, but the league was encouraged.   Frank Litsky

TEXAS. See Dallas-Fort Worth; Houston; State Government.

Students protesting Japan's economic domination of Thailand burn effigies of Japanese TV sets during visit to Bangkok of Japan's prime minister.

THAILAND. King Phumiphon Aduldet signed a new Constitution on Oct. 7, 1974, a week before the first anniversary of student demonstrations that ended Thailand's 41 years of military rule. It was written by a 298-person assembly drawn from delegates named by the king.

Under the new Constitution, the king remains a constitutional monarch. He appoints a Cabinet whose work is based on the support of an elected Assembly. The king can veto legislation, and, in turn, can be overridden by a two-thirds vote of the Assembly. Elections for the first democratically chosen Assembly were scheduled for February, 1975. The judiciary includes a Constitutional Tribunal.

Students Object. Leaders of the 1973 student agitation failed in last-minute demonstrations in September to force four constitutional changes. These included lowering the voting age from 20 to 18 and eliminating an Assembly upper house of persons selected by the King's Privy Council. The king backed the students on the latter change, voicing strong opposition to being drawn into politics through the use of his Privy Council.

Some student leaders went to rural areas to try to educate farmers on how to participate in the new democratic system, but the response was poor. Politics remained concentrated in the capital city of Bangkok, and the traditional conservative leaders were expected to retain their influence.

Sanya Thammasak, whom the king appointed premier after military rule ended, reluctantly kept the post despite widespread criticism. He backed down before several Assembly demands, and he and Assembly Speaker M. R. Kukrit Pramoj supported demands for constitutional changes. This created a public impression of weak leadership.

U.S. Airmen Stay. The continued presence of U.S. Air Force units in Thailand, stationed there for possible use in Indochina, caused controversy. Former Foreign Minister Thanat Khoman, who had arranged the U.S. presence early in the Vietnam War, wanted it ended. The government believed, however, that the 27,500 U.S. military men and 350 planes were a valuable deterrent. It denied Thanat's assertion that North Vietnam's support for guerrillas in Thailand would end if the airmen left.

This support continued to flow across Laos, despite the Laotian cease-fire agreement's requirement that North Vietnamese forces leave Laos. Some 8,000 Communist-oriented guerrillas harassed the Thai Army in four main areas. The government accepted China's statements that it was not supporting the guerrillas, but moves to establish diplomatic relations with China made no headway.

Under new legislation, labor unions became more active, winning minimum wage laws for the first time in Thailand's long history.   Henry S. Bradsher

See also ASIA (Facts in Brief Table).

Over Here!, a musical starring Janie Sell, left, and Patty and Maxene Andrews, revived the boogie-woogie and jitterbugging of the 1940s.

THEATER. Tributary theater, the goal of stage pioneers in the 1920s, became a reality on Broadway in 1974. The richness and variety of productions were largely due to contributions from playhouses elsewhere. *Candide* came from Brooklyn; *Cat on a Hot Tin Roof* from Stratford, Conn.; and *Scapino* from London.

In an imaginative restaging of Leonard Bernstein's satiric operetta, the Chelsea Theatre Center's *Candide*, on which no Broadway producer would have gambled initially, called for tearing out all the theater seats and replacing them with stools so that the audience could be surrounded on all sides by the action. Platforms, booths, ramps, and steps became areas of a degenerate world through which the ide-

alistic innocent, Candide, moves. Although the new book by Hugh Wheeler is less than ideal for the score, the production was acclaimed. Seats at the Broadway Theatre were torn out, and *Candide* moved in for a long, prizewinning run. Another farcical romp, transported from the Brooklyn Academy of Music, was Molière's *Scapino*, staged originally by the Young Vic in England.

Cat on a Hot Tin Roof was the first modern American revival at the American Shakespeare Festival in

511

Stratford, Conn. As impressive as it was in 1955, *Cat* starred Elizabeth Ashley as Maggie, struggling for the affection of her husband, Brick, and an inheritance from her father-in-law, Big Daddy. The production effectively achieved author Tennessee Williams' aim: catching "that cloudy, flickering, evanescent – fiercely charged! – interplay of live human beings in the thundercloud of a common crisis."

Revivals of American Classics old and new thrived in 1974. Arthur Miller's 1947 success, *All My Sons*, its conflict between profit and patriotism timely again, was staged by the Roundabout Theater. Eugene O'Neill's *A Moon for the Misbegotten* was the dramatic hit of the year, with Colleen Dewhurst winning a Tony Award for her portrayal of the overweight, frustrated heroine. O'Neill's *Hughie* played in Chicago, St. Louis, and Los Angeles before its scheduled appearance in New York City, with Ben Gazzara and Peter Maloney as the talkative small-time gambler and the night clerk of a sleazy hotel. *Fashion*, an 1845 comedy by Anna Cora Mowatt, first American woman playwright, was staged off-Broadway with a new framework. Ladies of the Long Island Masque and Wig Society presented the play with a musical score reminiscent of the 1930s. The Royal Shakespeare Company of England contributed a splendid gift to the U.S. bicentennial. It brought over stylish, affectionate, and highly entertaining productions of two 19th-century works usually confined to textbooks. In *Sherlock Holmes*, John Wood played the title role of Sir Arthur Conan Doyle's hero in a thriller written in 1899 by actor William Gillette as a star vehicle for himself. *London Assurance*, a delightful comedy-melodrama, revived the reputation of Dion Boucicault, the Irish playwright who came to the United States in 1853 and whose works were prominent on the American stage until his death in 1890.

Shakespeare fans had an unusually wide choice of works. The Brooklyn Academy of Music brought from England the Royal Shakespeare Company's *Richard II*, the Actors' Company's *King Lear*, and the Young Vic's *The Taming of the Shrew*. The New York Shakespeare Festival presented *Richard III*. Off-off-Broadway, La Mama Repertory staged *Measure for Measure* and *A Midsummer Night's Dream*, the latter by a Chinese troupe in native costume.

Off-Off-Broadway is the latest economic alternative to soaring production costs off-Broadway, just as off-Broadway rose to prominence in the 1950s and 1960s as Broadway productions became increasingly expensive. On a given weekend at the height of the season, some 80 plays, entertainments, and happenings are staged in lofts, churches, warehouses, storefronts, and coffee houses. Because of the small seating areas and limited runs, producers receive concessions from the theatrical unions, and in some cases Actors Equity permits actors to work free. The productions are experimental, the plays new or classical.

The Circle Theatre Company staged James Irwin's impressive and vigorous two-character drama *The Sea Horse*. In a bar of that name on a West Coast waterfront, the tough woman owner has a brawling love affair with a seaman. Classics off-off-Broadway included *Alcestis* (New York City Repertory), Christopher Marlowe's *Edward II* (CSC Repertory), and Victor Hugo's *Hernani* (Open Eye).

New Plays were plentiful in 1974. Among them, Peter Shaffer's *Equus*, based on an actual incident, is impressive for its combination of theatricality and thoughtfulness. A young stableboy, played by Peter Firth, attacks and blinds six horses. Anthony Hopkins plays the psychiatrist who, trying to piece together the boy's motives, exposes his own shortcomings. Tom Stoppard's *Jumpers* had the dazzling verbal pyrotechnics of his earlier *Rosencrantz and Guildenstern Are Dead*, but lacked form and clarity. Real jumpers engage in acrobatics while a professor of moral philosophy lectures, his wife sings, and murders occur. Alan Ayckbourn's *Absurd Person Singular* is an adroit comic exposure of the human predicament in the face of small crises. Sandy Dennis, Geraldine Page, and Carole Shelley played the wives of an architect, a banker, and a businessman in whose homes three consecutive Christmases are celebrated. Ron Milner's *What the Wine Sellers Buy* was seen at The Mark Taper Forum in Los Angeles before its Lincoln Center debut. It is a morality play, with good and evil forces struggling for the soul of a high-school boy. A pimp tries to corrupt the boy by preaching that illegally gained money is the black man's only way to achieve status. From the Goodman Theatre Center in Chicago came Brian Friel's *The Freedom of the City*. Set in Londonderry, Northern Ireland, it depicts, within the framework of a British court of inquiry, the deaths of three civilians after an illegal civil rights march. *Short Eyes*, an exposé of prison life by a group of former prisoners, won the Critics Circle Award as the best drama.

Musicals again sought popularity through nostalgia. Best of them was *Over Here!* with the engaging Andrews sisters, Patty and Maxene, starring as wartime performers seeking a third partner. Accompanied by the boogie-woogie songs and jitterbug dances of the 1940s, the action is described by the interlocutor as "a train ride of memory cut out of America on the march." *Mack and Mabel* recalled Hollywood in the silent days, with Robert Preston as Mack Sennett and Bernadette Peters as Mabel Normand. The first musical based on magic acts, *The Magic Show*, starred 27-year-old Doug Henning delighting audiences as a master of grand illusion.

Thirty-six new plays written at U.S. colleges competed for $2,500 in cash and a production at the American College Festival in Washington, D.C., in April. The winner was *The Soft Touch* by Neil Cuthbert of Rutgers University.　　　Alice Griffin

See also AWARDS AND PRIZES (Arts Awards).

TINDEMANS, LEO (1922-   ), leader of the Flemish branch of the Christian Social Party, became premier of Belgium on April 25, 1974. This followed national elections on March 10 that gave his party only 72 of the 106 seats needed for a majority in the Chamber of Representatives. Tindemans was forced to name a minority coalition of centrists and conservatives to his Cabinet. See BELGIUM.

Tindemans was born in Antwerp on April 16, 1922. He earned a degree in political and social sciences from the University of Ghent, and then worked as a journalist in Antwerp. In 1949, he became a civil servant in the economics department of the government's Ministry of Agriculture. He also served as deputy lecturer in economics and political science at several Belgian universities.

Active in the Flemish branch of the Christian Social Party, Tindemans served as party secretary from 1958 to 1962. He was elected to the Belgian Parliament in 1961, and in 1964 became mayor of Edegem, a suburb of Antwerp.

He was named Dutch-speaking minister for community relations in the Cabinet in 1968 and played an active role in the revision of the national Constitution. He became deputy prime minister and minister of the budget in 1973.   Foster Stockwell

TOGO. See AFRICA.

TORNADOES. See DISASTERS.

TOYS. See GAMES, MODELS, AND TOYS.

TRACK AND FIELD. Sprinters spend less elapsed time in competition than any other track and field athletes, but often they gain the most attention. Such attention came to Ivory Crockett in 1974 after he ran the swiftest 100 yards in history.

On May 11, Crockett ran 100 yards in 9.0 seconds over the fast, plasticlike surface of the Tom Black Track in Knoxville, Tenn. Bob Hayes ran 100 yards in 9.1 seconds in 1963, and his record had been tied by Harry Jerome of Canada and Jim Hines, Charlie Greene, John Carlos, and Steve Williams of the United States. Even though the official watches credited Crockett with 9.0, 9.0, 8.9, and 9.1 seconds, doubters questioned the validity of the hand timing.

Crockett, a 25-year-old graduate of Southern Illinois University, had twice won Amateur Athletic Union (A.A.U.) national championships at 100 yards, but he had never run the distance faster than 9.2 seconds. And despite his record, he was far from invincible.

Williams, who earned a share of the 100-yard record in 1973, equaled the 100-meter record of 9.9 seconds in the A.A.U. championships on June 21 in Los Angeles. Delano Meriwether, the hematologist who ran in bathing trunks, ran sixth. Crockett finished seventh.

Tony Waldrop experienced a bittersweet year. The 22-year-old University of North Carolina senior had enjoyed moderate success as a half-miler and 2-

miler. Then he turned to the mile, ran it seven times indoors, and bettered 4 minutes all seven times. His fastest race was 3 minutes 55 seconds, a world indoor record, on February 17 in San Diego. Outdoors, Waldrop ran miles in 3 minutes 53.2 seconds and 3 minutes 59.8 seconds. Struck by minor injuries and illnesses, he next finished fourth in 4 minutes 5.0 seconds, ending his sub-4-minute streak at nine.

The only American men besides Crockett to break world records outdoors were Rick Wohlhuter and Jim Bolding. Wohlhuter, a Chicago insurance adjuster with a menacing mustache, set world records for 880 yards (1 minute 44.1 seconds) and 1,000 meters (2 minutes 13.9 seconds), and impressed everyone with his ability to sustain punishing paces. Bolding won consistently in the 400-meter and 440-yard hurdles in America and Europe and lowered the 440-yard hurdles record to 48.7 seconds.

Filbert Bayi of Tanzania lived up to his promise in 1974 by winning the 1,500-meter title in the Commonwealth Games on February 2 in Christchurch, New Zealand. With his usual searing pace, he led from the start and won in the world-record time of 3 minutes 32.2 seconds.

Ben Jipcho of Kenya won the Commonwealth 5,000-meter run and steeplechase and finished third in the 1,500. Those races marked the end of Jipcho's amateur career. A week later, the 31-year-old Ken-

Ivory Crockett became the world's fastest human in May, running the 100-yard dash in 9.0 seconds and breaking an 11-year-old record.

World Track and Field Records Established in 1974

Event	Holder	Country	Where made	Date	Record
Men					
100 yards	Ivory Crockett	U.S.A.	Knoxville	May 11	:09.0
100 meters	Steve Williams	U.S.A.	Los Angeles	June 21	:09.9*
880 yards	Rick Wohlhuter	U.S.A.	Eugene, Ore.	June 8	1:44.1
1,000 meters	Rick Wohlhuter	U.S.A.	Oslo	July 30	2:13.9
1,500 meters	Filbert Bayi	Tanzania	Christchurch, N.Z.	February 2	3:32.2
3,000 meters	Brendan Foster	Britain	Gateshead, England	August 3	7:35.2
440-yard hurdles	Jim Bolding	U.S.A.	Turin	July 24	:48.7
Hammer throw	Aleksei Spiridonov	U.S.S.R.	Munich	September 11	251 ft. 6 in.
Women					
200 meters	Irena Szewinska	Poland	Berlin	June 13	:22.0
400 meters	Irena Szewinska	Poland	Warsaw	June 22	:49.9
440 yards	Debra Sapenter	U.S.A.	Bakersfield, Calif.	June 29	:52.2*
3,000 meters	Ludmilla Bragina	U.S.S.R.	Durham, N.C.	July 6	8:52.74
100-meter hurdles	Annelie Ehrhardt	E. Germany	Berlin	June 12	:12.3*
400-meter hurdles	Krystyna Kacperczyk	Poland	Augsburg, W.G.	July 13	:56.51
400-meter relay	Maletzki, Stecher, Heinich, Eckert	E. Germany	Rome	September 8	:42.6
400-yard relay	Karnakova, Maslakova, Sidorova, Besfamilnaya	U.S.S.R.	Durham, N.C.	July 5	:44.15
High jump	Rosemarie Witschas	E. Germany	Rome	September 8	6 ft. 4¾ in.
Shot-put	Helena Fibingerova	Czechoslovakia	Gottwaldov, Czech.	September 21	70 ft. 9¼ in.
Discus throw	Faina Melnik	U.S.S.R.	Prague	May 28	229 ft. 4 in.
Javelin throw	Ruth Fuchs	E. Germany	Rome	September 3	220 ft. 6 in.

*Equals record

yan signed a professional contract with the International Track Association, and he became the leading money-winner and crowd favorite on the tour, often winning the mile and 2-mile the same night.

Other Americans who had successful years included Steve Prefontaine in the distance runs, Dwight Stones in the high jump, Bruce Jenner in the decathlon, and professional Steve Smith in the pole vault. The leading American women included Joni Huntley in the high jump and Francie Larrieu, Mary Decker, and Robin Campbell in the middle-distance runs.

The world's best woman athlete was 28-year-old Irena Szewinska of Poland. She broke world records for 200 and 400 meters.

International Competition. East German men and women won 10 gold medals and the Russians won nine in the 39 events of the European championships. Russia defeated the U.S. by a combined score of 192 to 184 in their annual outdoor meet. The American men won, but the Russian women beat the American women even more decisively. Kenya captured 14 of the 23 events for men in the Commonwealth Games, and Australia, Canada, and England won 12 of the 14 for women. Cuba dominated the Central American and Caribbean Games and produced two exceptional athletes in Silvio Leonard, a sprinter, and Alberto Juantorena, the year's outstanding 400-meter runner.   *Frank Litsky*

TRANSIT systems in American urban areas received a shot in the arm on Nov. 26, 1974, when President Gerald R. Ford signed into law a mass-transit aid bill that for the first time authorizes the use of federal funds to pay operating expenses. The law provides $11.8 billion in aid over six years. Many big-city mayors enthusiastically endorsed the measure as the only means of preventing further fare raises.

The measure provides $7.9 billion with which public rapid-rail and bus systems can buy new buses, subway cars, and other capital equipment. Distributed by the U.S. secretary of transportation, these funds would be 80 per cent federal and 20 per cent local. The $3.9-billion operating fund will be granted on a 50-50 matching basis, in which the city must match the federal funds.

Urban Mass Transportation Administrator Frank C. Herringer called the bill a "fundamental change in mass transit." Its provisions for operating-cost subsidies will help many transit systems that have experienced operating-cost increases of from 20 to 50 per cent since 1968. Nationally, the transit industry's total deficit has grown to about $800-million.

Total Ridership on the United States public transit systems increased for the first year since 1945. Although there were sporadic gains in some months in previous years, a continuous growth in ridership from September, 1973, to September, 1974, was reported by the American Public Transit Association. This group's figures, based on 120 cities, indicate a 7.8 per cent gain in ridership for the one-year period.

The turnaround in mass transit use was sparked by the energy crisis in late 1973 and early 1974. But many riders returned to their automobiles as gasoline supplies became plentiful again. To encourage riders to stay with public transportation, and also to promote ridership at midday, during evening hours, and on weekends, many transit systems experimented with new fare plans. These included reduced fares; cooperative fare programs in which downtown merchants pay part of the fare; "super-transfers" that provide unlimited transfer privileges all day on Sunday; annual transit passes for which the subscriber pays for 11 months and receives one month free; and family plans that provide unlimited use of transit facilities on weekends for $1.

Technology. Greater energy efficiency and economy, reduced air and noise pollution, and a more comfortable environment for riders were among the goals of mass-transit engineers in 1974. For example, two standard New York City subway cars were modified with flywheels to recoup energy of motion that is normally wasted as heat when the cars brake to a stop. Two electric buses will also be fitted with energy-saving, nonpolluting flywheels for use in San Francisco, under terms of a contract that was signed in March by the U.S. Department of Transportation (DOT).

The Urban Mass Transportation Administration began test runs of a new generation of rail cars it calls State-of-the-Art Cars. Measuring 75 feet (23 meters) in length, the plush, stainless-steel subway cars feature rapid acceleration and air suspension for a smoother ride. At its Pueblo, Colo., test facility, DOT prepared for tests of its new Advanced Concepts Train (ACT-1). The driverless vehicles are expected to provide smooth, comfortable rides while cutting maintenance costs nearly in half.

A new prototype vehicle called Transbus was also introduced. It reportedly stops with one-tenth the noise and half the odor of existing buses. Outside speakers announce passenger information. Lower floors and wider doors offer ready access.

Dial-A-Ride Systems gained in popularity during the year but remained unprofitable. The concept lets users phone a centralized computer facility that dispatches the nearest minibus to pick up the rider. For distant rides, the user transfers to a conventional bus system. In September, such a system began operating in Santa Clara County, California, the largest of some 40 systems started in 22 states during the last three years.   Kenneth E. Schaefle

President Ford discusses transit problems with 22 mayors in October. He later signed an $11.8-billion bill to aid urban transit systems.

TRANSPORTATION. Worldwide and national inflation, the energy crisis, concern for the environment, and a declining economy combined to make 1974 a year of uneasy prosperity for transportation companies in the United States. Airlines, railroads, truckers, and ocean-shipping companies generally experienced profit increases. Their profit improvement, however, stemmed primarily from higher rates and fares rather than any significant growth in freight or passenger traffic. The profits of the various transportation industries were greatly aided by more rapid approval of rate and fare increases by regulatory bodies. The agencies made an effort to be more responsive to the problems caused by soaring fuel costs and double-digit inflation.

Traffic Growth. Most transportation segments began to feel the effects of the United States economic slowdown in a major way during the last half of the year. The total U.S. transportation bill for 1974 was about $280 billion, a 6.8 per cent increase over 1973, according to preliminary estimates of the Transportation Association of America (TAA). The trade group's preliminary estimates of total U.S. mainland intercity freight volume, measured in ton-miles, showed an overall decrease of about 1 per cent, largely because of a 12 per cent drop in lakes traffic. Pipeline freight also dropped by about 1 per cent, while rails and trucks both gained 1 per cent, rivers and canals were up 2 per cent, and air freight was up 10 per cent.

The TAA's estimates for intercity passenger traffic also edged downward by about 1.7 per cent in 1974. Rail traffic was up 20 per cent, with private air travel up 8 per cent and public commercial air travel up 6 per cent. Bus travel rose about 5 per cent despite a six-day strike in November against Greyhound Bus Lines, the largest U.S. intercity bus system. Automobile traffic declined by 3 per cent.

The TAA's statistics reflect the combined impact of inflation, the declining economy, and the energy crisis upon intercity freight and passenger traffic. The slight decline in intercity freight volume was primarily the result of the slowing economy. However, the 1.7 per cent decline in intercity passenger traffic—and the shift in its composition—largely resulted from the energy crisis.

The 3 per cent decline in intercity auto traffic was the first such decline since World War II and was in contrast to an average annual growth of about 4 per cent in recent years. The upturn in intercity bus and rail passenger travel also reflected the public's shift away from automobiles and to cheaper forms of long-distance transport as the price of commercial air travel increased 14 per cent.

Inflation and a receding economy also hit the booming bicycle industry. The Bicycle Manufacturers Association of America revised its estimate of 1974 sales from 16 million to under 14 million as mounting inventories and layoffs slowed the industry.

Department of Transportation (DOT) Secretary Claude S. Brinegar announced in December his resignation effective Feb. 1, 1975. In accepting the resignation, President Gerald R. Ford expressed "deep gratitude" for Brinegar's dedicated service. On Jan. 3, 1975, President Ford signed a Transportation Safety Act that consolidates responsibility for movements of hazardous materials under DOT, makes the National Transportation Safety Board an independent agency, and directs DOT to improve its rail-safety enforcement.

Canada's Transportation Industry will be upgraded to the tune of $1.7 billion over the next five years, according to a plan proposed in June by Jean Marchand, minister of transport. It calls for total government subsidy of new passenger rail cars, 50 per cent subsidy of station improvements, and 25 per cent subsidy of Canadian-built rapid-transit cars.

Rapid intercity air travel is the goal of a two-year demonstration program that began in July with commercial flights between Montreal and Ottawa. Using planes that can take off and land on short runways located close to the downtown centers, the service is expected to carry about 100,000 passengers during the first year. Total travel time between the two city cores is about two-thirds that for bus, train, or even jet travel.   Kenneth E. Schaefle

See also AUTOMOBILE; AVIATION; RAILROAD; SHIP AND SHIPPING; TRANSIT; TRUCK AND TRUCKING.

TRAVEL. Vacation travel patterns underwent their greatest change since World War II in 1974. The postwar era of worldwide travel expansion, largely subsidized by the airlines through fare reductions and discount packages that filled seats at a loss instead of a profit, almost destroyed the international airlines and weakened many United States domestic carriers.

That era is over. The average price of a domestic airline ticket rose more than 20 per cent in 1974. Fares on many international routes increased 20 per cent, and transatlantic fares increased 30 per cent. Additionally, in June, the U.S. Civil Aeronautics Board (CAB) permitted the airlines to end cut-rate youth and family fares and drastically curtail other discount travel plans. However, air travelers were granted a measure of relief in September when the CAB approved a 25 per cent winter discount (from October 15 to March 13) for domestic midweek, 7- to 9-day round-trip flights of 1,500 miles or more. In November, the board also lowered 22- to 45-day fares by $22 between New York City and European points.

As recession fears mounted, U.S. domestic airlines suffered some of the steepest year-to-year business declines ever recorded in the industry. United Air Lines reported an 18 per cent fall in November, compared with November, 1973, figures. American Airlines had an even steeper drop of 23 per cent. Load

"Rogard him with care, you idiot.
He's an endangered species."

estimated 14 million visitors, who represented an increase of 6.9 per cent.

Some 14.3 million Americans traveled to Canada, a gain of 3 per cent over 1973. About 2.8 million Americans went to Mexico, a 10 per cent gain, and 7.6 million went overseas, an increase of 4 per cent. The United States had an estimated 8.8 million visitors from Canada who remained more than 48 hours. About 1.6 million came from Mexico and 3.5-million from overseas. Japan sent the most overseas travelers to the United States, a record 638,000.

The French Line withdrew the 66,000-ton luxury liner *France* from service in September. The ship, longest passenger liner in service – 1,035 feet (315 meters) – had been subsidized by the French government. With recent increases in fuel prices, that subsidy came to $20 million a year, a cost the government found unacceptable. The fate of the liner, which cost $75 million to build in 1961, was uncertain.

With the withdrawal of the *France*, only Cunard and Italian Line ships maintained regular service on the North Atlantic. The passenger steamship industry was engaged mainly in cruise programs.

Amtrak, the U.S. National Railroad Passenger Corporation, carried about 18 million riders during the year, an increase of about 21 per cent. Amtrak operated more than 25,000 miles (40,000 kilometers) of track, serving 450 communities. It raised fares twice in 1974, blaming increased fuel and labor costs. In April, fares were increased 5 per cent, and in November, there was an average fare boost of 10 per cent. Thirty-five new Metroliner-type coaches were ordered by the system. A total of 292 new cars were scheduled for delivery by the summer of 1976.

Hotel and Motel dollar sales were up 8 per cent. Because of soaring interest rates, however, about 36 per cent fewer U.S. hotel and motel guest rooms were built than in 1973. Intercontinental Hotels Corporation began negotiations with the Russian government for the construction of three large hotels in the Soviet Union. The hotels, to be built in Moscow, Leningrad, and Kiev, would be run by Intourist, the Soviet tourist and travel agency, under a franchise from Intercontinental Hotels.

The collapse in August of Court Line, Britain's biggest package-tour company, left 50,000 tourists stranded around the world. Another 100,000, who had paid for their vacations, were left with no place to go. Also in August, 800 British tourists were stranded in Canada and the United States by the collapse of the Tabberer Agency of England.

The U.S. Department of Commerce opposed a congressional measure granting $2.5 million to one of its agencies, the U.S. Travel Service (USTS). The grant, designed to promote domestic tourism, would have been in addition to $11.5 million that USTS spends annually persuading foreign tourists to visit the United States.   Lynn Beaumont

TRINIDAD AND TOBAGO. See West Indies.

factors (percentage of seats filled per flight) were also down on almost all major carriers. Airline officials scrambled to revise schedules, cut new equipment orders, and plan possible employee layoffs in the light of projections of continued poor business in 1975.

Air fare increases, blamed to a great extent on fuel and other operating costs and inflation abroad, pushed the cost of a two-week trip to Europe – with transportation but without frills – from about $700 in 1973 to more than $1,000 in 1974. Vacation costs in general were at least 15 per cent higher.

The U.S. Passport Office issued 2,471,461 passports during the fiscal year, a decline of 10.8 per cent. Threats of war in the Middle East; uprisings and unrest in Ethiopia, Cyprus, Greece, Northern Ireland, and Portugal; the Arab oil embargo; the devalued dollar; and rampant inflation were major factors in an overall reduction in travel.

Fewer Americans Visited Western Europe. American tourism fell 10 per cent in France, 20 per cent in Great Britain, 40 per cent in Portugal. The overall decline was estimated at from 15 to 20 per cent. The 25 million Americans who traveled abroad spent $7 billion, up 8 per cent, decreasing the travel balance-of-payments deficit by 6 per cent to $2.9-billion. Overall international tourism stayed even with 1973, with about 215 million visits across international borders. The United States welcomed an

TRUCK AND TRUCKING. The twin problems of inflation and recession had a major impact on the U.S. trucking industry in 1974. Rising costs of all items used by the industry coupled with increases in labor costs resulting from the contract agreement reached with the Teamsters Union in 1973 led to the approval of substantial rate increases by the Interstate Commerce Commission (ICC). Thus, despite a 5 per cent decline in tonnage transported, total motor-carrier revenues increased 10 per cent to $22.7 billion, according to preliminary estimates of the American Trucking Associations, Incorporated. (ATA). Net earnings were $525 million, which represented a 4 per cent increase over the $505-million earned in 1973.

Truckers' Strike. Work stoppages by independent owner-operator truckers disrupted motor-carrier operations and the industries they serve in late January and early February. The truckers were protesting higher diesel fuel costs, fuel shortages, and lower speed limits. The strike was marked by violence and the deaths of two nonstriking truckers. In many states, National Guard men were mobilized to provide safe passage for nonstriking truckers, many of whom formed caravans for protection. To end the stoppage, the ICC authorized a 6 per cent surcharge on February 7 on all motor-carrier rates to compensate for increased fuel costs.

The surcharge was reduced and incorporated into the industry's general rate structure in July, when further rate increases were approved by the ICC to offset Teamster wage increases effective July 1. However, diesel fuel prices remained approximately double those of July, 1973, through year's end.

The nationwide speed limit of 55 miles (89 kilometers) per hour, imposed in January to conserve fuel, continued in effect at year's end. To offset the decrease in productivity resulting from the limit, Congress passed legislation in December that will permit larger, heavier trucks on the nation's interstate highway system. Opposed by the National Transportation Safety Board, the provision was part of a $753-million highway-aid bill.

Declining Freight Traffic concerned many truckers. The ATA's seasonally adjusted general freight truck tonnage index began to fall below 1973 levels in April and continued to decline throughout the rest of the year. The decline was reflected in the carriers' operations in the form of layoffs and capital expenditure cutbacks that could decrease 1975 profits below those of 1974.

Minority Bias Charged. On March 21, the Department of Justice charged seven major trucking companies, 342 freight carriers, and the Teamsters Union with discriminating against black and Spanish-surnamed people. The seven companies signed consent decrees, agreeing to hire more minority members, while not acknowledging the truth of the charges. *Kenneth E. Schaefle*

TRUDEAU, PIERRE ELLIOTT (1919-   ), won his third straight election as prime minister of Canada and leader of the Liberal Party in 1974. After heading a minority government since October, 1972, Trudeau confounded his critics by leading his party to a decisive victory in the federal election on July 8. The Liberal Party gained 32 seats to emerge with a clear majority in Parliament and a margin of 46 seats over the Conservatives, the largest opposition party. See CANADA.

The election results marked an impressive personal victory for Trudeau. Crossing and recrossing the country as the constantly exposed focus of the Liberal campaign, Trudeau defended his government's record and outlined its policies for the future. His unpredictable behavior always made him news, and the presence of his attractive young wife, Margaret, helped to soften his aloof, academic image.

Without the hysterical "Trudeaumania" that swept him to power in 1968, Trudeau was forced to convince his countrymen on the basis of his record and his capacity to govern. The fact that he appealed almost as strongly in the heartland of English Canada as he did in his own province of Quebec was a measure of his achievement. After six years in a demanding office and at a time when governments in many other countries were falling because of voter disenchantment, Trudeau won a fresh personal mandate to govern Canada. *David M. L. Farr*

TUNISIA. Habib Bourguiba was named president for life of the Destourian Socialist Party in September, 1974. This made his November election as president of Tunisia for life a formality, because Bourguiba was the only candidate.

Although the government remained solidly behind Bourguiba, there was considerable dissatisfaction with single-party rule, chiefly among the young. Student unrest continued despite strict security measures. The University of Tunis was closed for three weeks in April, and 32 students received short prison sentences for subversion. Over 200 other persons, most of them students, were tried in August, and 30 received prison sentences of up to 10 years.

Bourguiba and Libyan President Muammar Muhammad al-Qadhaafi announced on January 12 that they had agreed to merge their countries into a single nation, the Islamic Arab Republic. But the Tunisian National Assembly immediately shelved the project. Algeria, which had criticized the merger, later formed a joint economic cooperation commission with Tunisia. Tunisia's development program, which included a newly completed $1.35-million phosphoric acid plant at Sfax, continued to attract foreign investment. The World Bank made three loans to Tunisia, and other loans came from Canada, France, Kuwait, Saudi Arabia, and the United Arab Emirates. *William Spencer*

See also AFRICA (Facts in Brief Table).

TURKEY. Turkish military forces invaded the island of Cyprus on July 20, 1974, after Cypriot President Archbishop Makarios III was overthrown in a Greek-supported military coup. Subsequent negotiations among Turkey, Great Britain, and Greece, the three guarantors of Cypriot independence, broke down. Turkey then acted, it said, to ensure the safety of the Turkish minority on Cyprus. By July 27, when United Nations representatives arranged a cease-fire, the 15,000-man Turkish force had seized the northern third of the island. Turkey lost 250 killed and 800 wounded in the fighting. See CYPRUS.

Strained Relations. The Cyprus adventure cracked the eastern flank of the North Atlantic Treaty Organization, to which both Greece and Turkey belong. It also increased tension between Turkey and the United States, where congressional opinion had already soured after Turkey lifted its ban on opium poppy cultivation on July 1. In October, Congress voted to cut off all military aid to Turkey after December 10, but it later postponed any cutoff until Feb. 5, 1975.

Domestic Affairs. Poppy cultivation, the Turks insisted, would be resumed under strict controls to eliminate opium smuggling. Government licensing and crop limits were imposed.

The successes on Cyprus made a national hero of Prime Minister Bülent Ecevit, who had patched together a shaky coalition of his Republican People's Party (RPP) and the right wing National Salvation Party (NSP) on January 26, following a three-month political crisis. Ecevit's government introduced legislation granting amnesty to persons jailed for "thought crimes." It also called for a voting age of 18 and for rapid industrial development. The amnesty and voting age bills were passed by the Grand National Assembly in May, though the amnesty measure aroused widespread criticism because it applied to jailed Socialists as well as to nonpolitical intellectuals.

The coalition of Ecevit's moderately leftist RPP and the NSP collapsed in September. President Fahri Koruturk asked him to form another government, but he failed. Koruturk then turned unsuccessfully first to former Premier Suleyman Demirel and once more to Ecevit. In November, Sadi Irmak, a political independent, put together a predominantly nonpolitical Cabinet. Irmak received a crushing vote of no-confidence within two weeks. Further efforts by Ziyat Baykara to form a new Cabinet failed; at year's end, the government remained in a caretaker status under Irmak.   William Spencer

See also MIDDLE EAST (Facts in Brief Table).

UNEMPLOYMENT. See ECONOMICS; LABOR.

UNION OF SOVIET SOCIALIST REPUBLICS (U.S.S.R). See RUSSIA.

Troop-laden Turkish tank lands on Cyprus in July, part of a 15,000-man invasion force that seized the northern third of that troubled island.

UNITED ARAB EMIRATES (UAE)

UNITED ARAB EMIRATES (UAE). Abu Dhabi, the main oil-producing UAE state, gained control of its oil holdings in 1974. The agreement signed on September 3 with the Abu Dhabi Petroleum Company (ADPC) gave Abu Dhabi a 60 per cent majority interest in ADPC operations. The agreement would give the group of Western oil companies owning ADPC $40 million for nationalized assets. In turn, the consortium agreed to pay Abu Dhabi $600 million for its increased share in the crude oil extracted by ADPC since January 1, 1974.

The UAE joined with Qatar, Oman, and Bahrain on May 5 in establishing a joint Arab Gulf Shipping Company, a regional shipping fleet. Also in May, the UAE loaned $75.6 million to the World Bank to finance development projects. A steel plant built in Abu Dhabi by Japan and one in Dubai built by India went into operation in June.

The emirates inaugurated their own tanker fleet, the UAE Tanker Company, in September with 49 per cent private Dutch participation. A joint Arab-British bank, ORYX (named for the rare desert antelope), opened for business in October in Dubai. It will finance Middle East development projects.

The ruler of Fujairah died in September and was succeeded by his son, Sheik Hamad bin Mohammed al-Sharqi. William Spencer

See also MIDDLE EAST (Facts in Brief Table).

UNITED ARAB REPUBLIC (U.A.R.). See EGYPT.

UNITED NATIONS (UN). The 29th UN General Assembly ended on Dec. 18, 1974, on a note of growing United States concern over a series of dramatic parliamentary triumphs by the third world. Developing countries said the trend represented the beginning of a "new international order," but Western diplomats, particularly Americans, feared the maneuvers might plunge the world organization into "rampant anarchy."

The actions that signaled a new epoch in UN history included the official appearance of Palestine Liberation Organization (PLO) chief Yasir Arafat before the 138-member forum; the unprecedented acceptance of his umbrella guerrilla group as a permanent observer – a status shared by the Vatican and Switzerland; the denial of speaking and voting rights to representatives of the white-minority government of South Africa; and the continued and increasing isolation of Israel by official condemnations and restrictions on its speaking rights.

In the closing days of the 13-week Assembly, U.S. Ambassador John A. Scali warned that "tyranny of the majority" and "one-sided, unrealistic" resolutions could erode what he said was already waning American support for the UN.

Third-World Triumphs. Buoyed by the new economic power of their oil-rich Arab colleagues, the nonwhite majority voting bloc flexed its new political muscle by convening a sixth special session of the General Assembly in April to deal with raw materials and development. A countermove to the February meeting of major oil-consuming nations in Washington, D.C., it became a spirited forum for Arab defense of high oil prices. United States Secretary of State Henry A. Kissinger cautioned on April 15 that the creation of economic "pressure blocs" would result only in "counter-pressure blocs," but his mild warning fell on deaf ears.

United Nations Secretary-General Kurt Waldheim predicted that a "new international economic order" would result from a 20-principle declaration issued by the Assembly on May 1. An accompanying action program endorsed nationalization by countries of foreign investments, regulation of multinational corporations, more equitable import-export pricing, and restitution to developing countries for past exploitation.

As if to reaffirm its new solidarity, the third-world majority brushed aside, without discussion, a U.S. proposal for a $4-billion aid program to which the United States said it would pledge a "substantial amount." Instead, the Assembly approved an "emergency operations" fund for countries "most seriously affected" by the economic crisis caused by Arab oil prices. Waldheim later declared the fund would require $4.6 billion by 1975 to meet minimum needs. By year's end, however, little more than half had been pledged, with the European Community (Common Market), a new permanent observer, promising $500 million. The United States boycotted the special fund, in a move regarded by some observers as retaliation for controversial decisions voted by a coalition of African, Arab, Asian, and Communist countries. See POVERTY.

Middle East Developments. The most dramatic evidence of third-world power was the appearance on November 13 of guerrilla leader Arafat at the UN podium, wearing a gun holster, hands clasped above his head, acknowledging cheers from a packed assembly hall. He said he had come "bearing an olive branch and a freedom fighter's gun" and warned, "Do not let the olive branch drop from my hand."

Israeli representatives, who refused to attend the session, called it a "dark day of shame" when the UN received a man who represents "nothing more than 10,000 terrorists." Outside, thousands of supporters of Israel gathered to protest the UN reception of Arafat.

The Assembly overrode U.S. and Israeli objections by recognizing the PLO as the sole representative of the Palestinians. It endorsed the Palestinians "unhindered" right to national sovereignty and to return to their homeland. It also severely curtailed Israel's right to reply to Arab speeches during the emotional debate.

Israel Condemned. By a vote of 13-0, the Security Council condemned Israel on April 24 for its strike against six Lebanese villages after an Arab terrorist

Israel's Moshe Dayan addresses New York City demonstrators protesting
United Nations recognition of the Palestine Liberation Organization.

attack on the Israeli city of Qiryat-Shemona. Israel was also condemned twice by the General Assembly – for devastating the Syrian city of Al Qunaytirah before UN troops moved into place (Israel maintained that all damage occurred during military battles before a cease-fire agreement was reached) and for strengthening economic and other ties with South Africa.

Other UN bodies joined in heaping official censure on Israel. The Human Rights Commission deplored Israel for violating human rights through annexation and settlement of occupied Arab territories. The UN Educational, Scientific, and Cultural Organization (UNESCO), by a vote of 64-27 on November 20, barred further financial aid to Israel because of its persistence in "altering the historical features" of Jerusalem during archaeological excavations.

UN Peacekeeping Actions. After the Israeli-Egyptian disengagement agreements were signed on January 18, the Security Council renewed the mandate for the second UN Emergency Force, while reducing its strength from 7,000 to 4,500 men. The Council also created a UN Disengagement Observer Force of 1,224 soldiers for the Israeli-Syrian buffer zone in the Golan Heights. Secretary-General Waldheim estimated Middle East peacekeeping costs would reach $40 million a year by April, 1975.

War in Cyprus resulted in 15 Security Council meetings in July and August, with a unanimous call for a cease-fire issued July 20, the same day Turkish troops invaded the island. The 10-year-old UN Peacekeeping Force in Cyprus was increased by 2,000 to 4,443 by August 12. On August 16, the Council issued a "formal disapproval" of continued Turkish occupation and renewed its demand for withdrawal of all foreign troops. A large-scale UN effort to help the estimated 225,000 Greek Cypriots uprooted by the conflict got underway, with Prince Sadruddin Aga Khan, the UN High Commissioner for Refugees, in charge. See CYPRUS.

In July, Khan reported the completion of a 10-month airlift, involving 27 countries and $12 million, to repatriate 250,000 persons displaced during the 1971 India-Pakistan war. About 500,000 southern Sudanese were also resettled in Sudan in 1974.

A border conflict erupted between Iran and Iraq on February 10, and the Security Council dispatched Luis Weckmann-Munoz of Mexico to the area. He arranged a troop withdrawal, adherence to a Council cease-fire demand of March 7, and the beginning of negotiations. Weckmann-Munoz was later named UN special representative in Cyprus.

African Nations. The coup in Portugal on April 25 resulted in quick independence for Guinea-Bissau, its war-ravaged former colony in West Africa. Guinea-Bissau was represented at the opening UN session on September 17, as were Grenada and Bangladesh, bringing UN membership to 138.

Portuguese President Francisco da Costa Gomes told the Assembly on October 17 that the process of decolonization was "irreversible and definitive." Independence of Portugal's other African colonies, Cape Verde Islands and Mozambique, was set for 1975, with Angola to follow soon afterward, he promised. See AFRICA; ANGOLA; GUINEA-BISSAU; MOZAMBIQUE; PORTUGAL.

United Nations committees continued to decry white-minority rule in Rhodesia and South Africa. Sean MacBride, former foreign minister of Ireland and winner of a Nobel Peace Prize in 1974, was named UN Commissioner for Namibia, formerly the territory of South West Africa. The UN revoked South Africa's mandate there in 1966, but that country continues to administer it.

South Africa, with nonwhite members in its delegation for the first time, acknowledged it was guilty of racial discrimination, "not based on any concepts of superiority or inferiority," but on historical and cultural differences, said Ambassador Roelof Botha. Nevertheless, an overwhelming majority voted to expel South Africa from the world body. Only three vetoes in the Security Council on October 30 – by the United States, Great Britain, and France – saved its permanent membership. The Assembly reacted by voting 91 to 22 to bar South Africa from voting and speaking rights for the remainder of the 29th session. Militant Algerian Abdelaziz Bouteflika, Assembly president for 1974, upheld and enforced that vote over U.S. and Western-power objections.

World Conferences. The UN Food and Agricultural Organization sponsored a World Food Conference – originally proposed to the UN by Secretary of State Kissinger – in Rome in November. The meeting produced little more than talk in the face of what the delegates called the worst food shortage in history. A related World Population Conference in Bucharest, Romania, in August, resulted in adoption of population-control guidelines. See FOOD; POPULATION, WORLD.

A third Law of the Sea Conference in Caracas, Venezuela, ended in August, taking informal steps toward global agreements on territorial limits, economic zones, and other maritime matters. See OCEAN.

International Women's Year was proclaimed for 1975, with a conference scheduled for June in Bogotá, Colombia. Helvi Sipila of Finland, the highest-ranking UN woman official, will serve as its secretary-general.

Other UN Actions. Only China voted against a General Assembly resolution asking nations to "refrain" from a military build-up in the Indian Ocean, declared a Zone of Peace in 1971. The Assembly in 1974 also recommended the Middle East, Africa, and South Asia as nuclear-free areas.

A Convention on the Limitation Period in the International Sale of Goods, giving buyers or sellers four years in which to sue in exercise of contractual rights, was adopted in June.

A revised Universal Copyright Convention went into effect July 10, protecting exclusive rights of reproduction, broadcasting, and public performance.

After 24 years, on April 12, a UN special committee completed an eight-article "definition of aggression," to help determine the legality of conflicts.

American James M. Hester, former president of New York University, was named rector of the new UN University, which is headquartered in Tokyo. Hester in November termed the university "the most ambitious ever conceived to integrate the intellectual resources of the world." It will provide a worldwide network of training, research, and data centers that will deal with such issues as peace and security, human rights and the quality of life, economic and social development, resources and environment, and application of basic science for development.

The World Court at The Hague in the Netherlands on July 25 refuted Iceland's claim to sovereign control over fishing rights within a 50-nautical-mile limit, instead of the internationally accepted 12-nautical-mile limit. The case was instituted in 1972 by Great Britain and West Germany. Iceland refused to accept the two adverse verdicts.

Finance and Organization. The 1974-1975 budget of $606 million was approved on December 18, a 12 per cent increase over the previous fiscal year. Inflation and fluctuating currencies were expected to add to the 1974 deficit of over $200 million.

Oil-rich countries gave more generously to UN programs in 1974, with Saudi Arabia alone contributing $100 million for Bangladesh UN disaster relief and $50 million to the World Food Program. The program was authorized, in another third-world show of strength, to supply food to African liberation movements.

Eighteen countries were elected to new three-year terms in the now 54-member Economic and Social Council (ECOSOC) in January. Included were Argentina, Bulgaria, Canada, China, Czechoslovakia, Denmark, Ecuador, Ethiopia, Gabon, Great Britain, Japan, Kenya, Norway, Pakistan, Peru, Russia, Yemen (Aden), and Zaire.

New Security Council members, elected October 11 to serve until 1976, include Guyana, Italy, Japan, Sweden, and Tanzania. They replace Australia, Austria, Indonesia, Kenya, and Peru. Byelorussia, Costa Rica, Iraq, Mauritania, and Cameroon will serve until the end of 1975.

Two respected UN leaders were mourned during the 29th Assembly. Paul Hoffman, an American who served as UN Development Program administrator from 1965 to 1972, died on October 8. The UN's third secretary-general, U Thant of Burma, who served from 1960 to 1971, died on November 25 at the age of 65.   Betty Flynn

See also Section One, FOCUS ON THE WORLD.

Federal Spending and Revenue Receipts

Estimated U.S. Budget for Fiscal 1975*

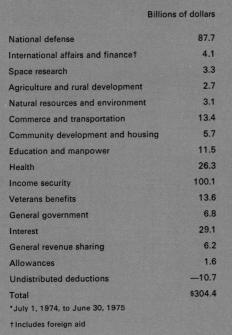

	Billions of dollars
National defense	87.7
International affairs and finance†	4.1
Space research	3.3
Agriculture and rural development	2.7
Natural resources and environment	3.1
Commerce and transportation	13.4
Community development and housing	5.7
Education and manpower	11.5
Health	26.3
Income security	100.1
Veterans benefits	13.6
General government	6.8
Interest	29.1
General revenue sharing	6.2
Allowances	1.6
Undistributed deductions	—10.7
Total	$304.4

*July 1, 1974, to June 30, 1975

†Includes foreign aid

U.S. Income and Outlays

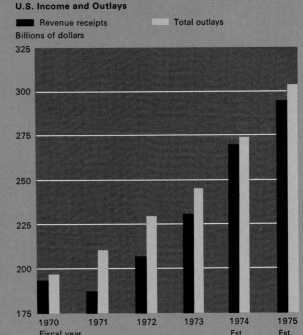

■ Revenue receipts ▢ Total outlays

Billions of dollars

Source: U.S. Office of Management and Budget

UNITED STATES, GOVERNMENT OF. The government of the United States in 1974 survived perhaps its most serious crisis since the Civil War in the 1860s. Congressional and judicial efforts to check the enormous power of the executive branch and to uncover corruption at the highest levels of the Administration of Richard M. Nixon strained the U.S. system of checks and balances and taxed the confidence of the American people.

President Nixon, under attack because of White House involvement in the Watergate affair, bowed to a July 24 ruling by the Supreme Court of the United States and surrendered incriminating tapes of conversations with his top aides. Congress, acting through various committees, persevered in its efforts to uncover executive responsibility for corruption, abuse of power, and obstruction of justice. As a result, Nixon was forced to resign on August 9, turning over the presidency to Vice-President Gerald R. Ford. The transition from one President to another was remarkably uneventful. See FORD, GERALD RUDOLPH; NIXON, RICHARD MILHOUS.

The Executive Branch. President Nixon's resignation, itself an unprecedented action, brought into play the 25th Amendment to the Constitution. For the first time in U.S. history, a man who had been appointed to the vice-presidency by the President succeeded to the presidency and in turn appointed his own Vice-President. So, for the first time, the two highest executive offices were held by men who had not been elected.

Thus, the train of events set in motion with the 1972 break-in at Democratic National Headquarters in the Watergate complex in Washington, D.C., came to an end. Nixon's first Vice-President, Spiro T. Agnew, was forced out of office in 1973; members of Nixon's staff and Cabinet confessed to crimes or were indicted on criminal charges; and Nixon himself resigned in disgrace, faced with probable impeachment and conviction. See WATERGATE; Section Two, FROM TRIUMPH TO TRAGEDY.

Yet, the world's most durable representative democracy seemed to emerge stronger than ever. Congress won new respect. The Supreme Court played its historic role with an even hand. And the growing power of the U.S. presidency was at least temporarily restrained.

President Nixon's resignation inevitably led to some changes in the Administration. President Ford named former New York Governor Nelson A. Rockefeller as Vice-President and appointed some new aides and administrative officials. But, at first, he retained Nixon appointees. However, Ford pledged to run an open Administration, and he took steps to see that his top aides did not acquire the unbridled power that Nixon's advisers had assumed.

Both Nixon and Ford emphasized foreign policy and traveled abroad in 1974. In June, President

Major Agencies and Bureaus of the U.S. Government*

Executive Office of the President
President, Gerald R. Ford
Vice-President, Nelson A. Rockefeller
White House Staff Coordinator, Donald Rumsfeld
Presidential Press Secretary, Ronald H. Nessen
Central Intelligence Agency—William E. Colby, Director
Council of Economic Advisers—Alan Greenspan, Chairman
Council on Environmental Quality — Russell W. Peterson, Chrmn.
Council on Wage and Price Stability—Albert E. Rees, Chairman
Domestic Council—Kenneth R. Cole, Jr., Executive Director
Economic Policy Board—L. William Seidman, Executive Director
Federal Energy Office—Frank G. Zarb, Administrator
Office of Consumer Affairs—Virginia H. Knauer, Director
Office of Economic Opportunity—Bert A. Gallegos, Director
Office of Management and Budget—Roy L. Ash, Director
Presidential Clemency Board—Charles E. Goodell, Chairman

State Department
Secretary of State, Henry A. Kissinger
Agency for International Development—Daniel Parker,
   Administrator
U.S. Representative to the United Nations—John A. Scali

Department of the Treasury
Secretary of the Treasury, William E. Simon
Bureau of Engraving and Printing—James A. Conlon, Director
Bureau of the Mint—Mary T. Brooks, Director
Internal Revenue Service—Donald C. Alexander, Commissioner
Treasurer of the United States—Francine Neff
U.S. Customs Service—Vernon D. Acree, Commissioner
U.S. Secret Service—H. Stuart Knight, Director

Department of Defense
Secretary of Defense, James R. Schlesinger
Joint Chiefs of Staff—General George S. Brown, Chairman
Secretary of the Air Force—John L. McLucas
Secretary of the Army—Howard H. Callaway
Secretary of the Navy—J. William Middendorf II

Department of Justice
Attorney General, William B. Saxbe
Bureau of Prisons—Norman A. Carlson, Director
Drug Enforcement Administration—John R. Bartels, Administrator
Federal Bureau of Investigation—Clarence M. Kelley, Director
Immigration and Naturalization Service—Leonard F. Chapman, Jr.,
   Commissioner
Law Enforcement Assistance Administration—Richard W. Velde,
   Administrator
Solicitor General—Robert H. Bork

Department of the Interior
Secretary of the Interior, Rogers C. B. Morton
Bureau of Indian Affairs—Morris Thompson, Commissioner
Bureau of Land Management—Curt Berklund, Director
Bureau of Mines—Thomas V. Falkie, Director
Bureau of Outdoor Recreation—James G. Watt, Director
Bureau of Reclamation—Gilbert G. Stamm, Commissioner
Geological Survey—Vincent E. McKelvey, Director
National Park Service—(vacant)
U.S. Fish and Wildlife Service—Lynn A. Greenwalt, Director

Department of Agriculture
Secretary of Agriculture, Earl L. Butz
Agricultural Economics—Don A. Paarlberg, Director
Federal Crop Insurance Corporation — Melvin R. Peterson, Mgr.
Forest Service—John R. McGuire, Chief
Soil Conservation Service—Kenneth E. Grant, Administrator

Department of Commerce
Secretary of Commerce, Frederick B. Dent
Bureau of the Census—Vincent P. Barabba, Director
National Bureau of Standards—Richard W. Roberts, Director
National Oceanic and Atmospheric Administration—Robert M.
   White, Administrator

*As of Jan. 1, 1975; **nominated but not yet confirmed

Office of Minority Business Enterprise—Alex M. Armendaris,
   Director
Patent Office—Curtis M. Dann, Commissioner

Department of Labor
Secretary of Labor, Peter J. Brennan
Bureau of Labor Statistics—Julius Shiskin, Commissioner
Labor-Management Services Administration—Paul J. Fasser, Jr.,
   Administrator
Occupational Safety and Health Administration—John H. Stender,
   Administrator

Department of Health, Education, and Welfare
Secretary of Health, Education, and Welfare, Caspar W.
   Weinberger
Alcohol, Drug Abuse, and Mental Health Administration—James
   D. Isbister,** Administrator
Food and Drug Administration—Alexander M. Schmidt,
   Commissioner
National Institutes of Health—(vacant)
Office of Education—Terrell H. Bell, Commissioner
Social Security Administration—James B. Cardwell, Commissioner

Department of Housing and Urban Development
Secretary of Housing and Urban Development, James T. Lynn
Federal Disaster Assistance Administration—Thomas P. Dunne,
   Administrator
Federal Housing Commissioner—(vacant)
Federal Insurance Administration—George K. Bernstein,
   Administrator
New Communities Administration—Otto G. Stolz, Administrator

Department of Transportation
Secretary of Transportation, Claude S. Brinegar
Federal Aviation Administration—Alexander P. Butterfield,
   Administrator
Federal Highway Administration—Norbert T. Tiemann,
   Administrator
Federal Railroad Administration—(vacant)
U.S. Coast Guard—Admiral Owen W. Siler, Commandant
Urban Mass Transportation Administration—Frank C. Herringer,
   Administrator

Independent Agencies
ACTION—Michael P. Balzano, Jr., Director
Civil Aeronautics Board—Richard J. O'Melia, Chairman
Civil Service Commission—Robert E. Hampton, Chairman
Consumer Product Safety Commission—Richard O. Simpson,
   Chairman
Energy Research and Development Administration—Robert C.
   Seamans, Jr., Administrator
Environmental Protection Agency—Russell E. Train, Administrator
Equal Employment Opportunity Commission—John H. Powell,
   Chairman
Federal Communications Commission — Richard E. Wiley, Chrmn.
Federal Deposit Insurance Corporation—Frank Wille, Chairman
Federal Maritime Commission—Helen D. Bentley, Chairman
Federal Power Commission—John N. Nassikas, Chairman
Federal Reserve System—Arthur F. Burns, Board of Governors
   Chairman
Federal Trade Commission—Lewis A. Engman, Chairman
Indian Claims Commission—Jerome K. Kuykendall, Chairman
Interstate Commerce Commission—George M. Stafford, Chairman
National Aeronautics and Space Administration—James C.
   Fletcher, Administrator
National Labor Relations Board — John H. Fanning, Acting Chrmn.
Nuclear Regulatory Commission—William A. Anders, Chairman
Securities and Exchange Commission—Ray Garrett, Jr., Chairman
Small Business Administration—Thomas S. Kleppe, Administrator
Smithsonian Institution—S. Dillon Ripley, Secretary
Tennessee Valley Authority—Aubrey J. Wagner, Chairman
U.S. Commission on Civil Rights—Arthur S. Flemming, Chairman
U.S. Postal Service—E. T. Klassen, Postmaster General
Veterans Administration—Richard L. Roudebush, Administrator

Nixon visited the Middle East and Russia. President Ford traveled to Mexico in October and to Japan, South Korea, and Russia in November. In December, he conferred with French President Valery Giscard d'Estaing on the Caribbean island of Martinique. But the Watergate scandal and the nation's economic problems caused by inflation, recession, and unemployment overshadowed foreign policy in 1974. See PRESIDENT OF THE UNITED STATES.

The Legislative Branch. The second session of the 93rd Congress braced itself for the impeachment and probable Senate trial of Nixon. The Senate Select Committee on Presidential Campaign Activities (the Watergate Committee) ended its 20-month investigation of the Watergate scandal on June 30. The House Judiciary Committee voted to recommend to the full House three articles of impeachment against the President in late July, but when Nixon resigned on August 9, the impeachment process was halted.

Despite the tumult surrounding the possibility of impeachment proceedings, Congress passed many important legislative measures. Among them were campaign-financing reform; private-pension-plan reform; new congressional procedures for dealing with the federal budget; an omnibus housing bill; a $29-billion education bill; a rise in the federal minimum wage; an $11.8-billion mass-transit bill; and legislation forbidding discrimination against women applying for mortgage and other credit. See CONGRESS OF THE UNITED STATES.

The Judicial Branch. The Supreme Court played a major role in the struggle that led to the resignation of President Nixon. On July 24, in the case of *United States v. Nixon*, the court ruled unanimously that the President did not have an absolute right to keep his records confidential. Nixon had invoked the doctrine of executive privilege in refusing to honor both congressional and court-ordered subpoenas for tapes. The High Court ruled that the interests of fairness in criminal justice outweighed the claims of executive privilege. Nixon, knowing Congress would consider defiance of the court an impeachable offense, agreed to comply.

Other important Supreme Court decisions:

• Segregation in a city's schools cannot be alleviated by combining city school districts with surrounding suburban districts unless both areas are involved in discriminatory practices. See DETROIT; EDUCATION.

• Public school systems cannot force pregnant teachers to take mandatory maternity leaves after four or five months of pregnancy.

• A Florida law requiring newspapers to print replies from political candidates attacked in their columns was unconstitutional.

• An ordinary citizen can sue a newspaper or a radio or television station for libel if it circulates false or defamatory reports. See SUPREME COURT OF THE UNITED STATES.   Carol L. Thompson

See also Section One, FOCUS ON THE NATION.

President Ford's picture replaces one of Richard Nixon in embassy in Bonn, West Germany, soon after Nixon resigned.

UNITED STATES CONSTITUTION. The U.S. Constitution underwent a severe test in 1974, culminating when President Richard M. Nixon was forced to resign on August 9 because of the scandals that had disgraced his Administration. By resigning, Nixon averted impeachment. See WATERGATE; Section Two, FROM TRIUMPH TO TRAGEDY.

The transfer of power to Vice-President Gerald R. Ford under the provisions of the 25th Amendment was accomplished with a minimum of disruption to the government. Ford then chose Nelson A. Rockefeller as Vice-President, in accord with the 25th Amendment. See ROCKEFELLER, NELSON A.

On September 8, President Ford invoked the power given to him under Article II, Section 2, of the Constitution to pardon Nixon for any crimes he committed or may have committed while in office. See NIXON, RICHARD MILHOUS; PRESIDENT OF THE UNITED STATES.

Maine, Montana, and Ohio ratified the Equal Rights Amendment in 1974, leaving the amendment five short of the 38 states needed for ratification. Nebraska and Tennessee voted to rescind their ratification, but there was a question as to whether this was legal.

Anti-abortion groups increased pressure during the year for an amendment that would outlaw abortion under almost all circumstances.   Darlene R. Stille

UPPER VOLTA. See AFRICA.

URUGUAY. President Juan María Bordaberry Arocena kept control of the government in 1974, but military leaders played a more dominant role in political and economic decisions. Under a decree signed by Bordaberry on June 27, military officers gained control of the nation's power and petroleum industries and the Central Bank. On July 12 and August 23, again acting under military pressures, Bordaberry revised his Cabinet. Among those replaced was Moises Cohen, minister of economics, whose policies had been severely criticized by the armed forces.

Bans on Political Activities, in effect since Bordaberry assumed power in March, 1972, continued. All issues of the daily newspaper *Mayoria* were confiscated on August 31, because, the government contended, it had printed "a commentary on the military situation and on the alleged pressure being applied by soldiers to obtain better-paying jobs." The government also suspended publication of *9 de Febrero*, a weekly magazine, for six weeks for "creating states of dissension between the armed forces and the executive branch." Two broadcasting stations, Radio Rural and Radio Sur, were closed briefly in August for broadcasting "statements contrary to the nation's revolutionary process."

In an effort to eliminate all alleged Marxists and left wing guerrilla sympathizers from schools, the National Education Council announced on August 11 that about 400 high-school teachers and administrators would be discharged. All had been detained or arrested at one time or another for "seditious activities." In June, the authorities drastically revised the curriculum of the University of the Republic at Montevideo and appointed "security personnel" to check on faculty members.

On June 16, Amnesty International and the International Commission of Jurists, which have consultative status with the United Nations, reported that the regime was using torture to extract confessions from political prisoners. After a seven-day fact-finding visit, they estimated that 3,500 Uruguayans had been imprisoned as security risks since July, 1972. About 1,500 were being held at the time of the visit, they said.

Financial Difficulties continued to plague the regime. On September 1, the government devalued the peso for the 30th time since Bordaberry was inaugurated. In the intervening two years, the currency had depreciated by about 400 per cent. Inflation for the first six months of the year was running at about 35 per cent. A workingman's purchasing power had fallen more than 57 per cent since January, 1968. The trade deficit for the first six months stood at $23.6 million.   Paul C. Tullier

See also LATIN AMERICA (Facts in Brief Table).
UTAH. See STATE GOVERNMENT.
UTILITIES. See COMMUNICATIONS; ENERGY; PETROLEUM AND GAS; TELEPHONE.

VENEZUELA. Carlos Andrés Pérez, leader of the Democratic Action Party, took office as president on March 12, 1974, with his followers in firm control of both houses of Congress (see PÉREZ, CARLOS ANDRÉS). Pérez began using Venezuela's soaring oil revenues – about $12 billion in 1974 – to promote a domestic program of rapid industrialization and modernization of agriculture.

Foreign Relations were dominated by Pérez' apparent ambition to play the role of spokesman for Latin American nationalism. This explained his attack on U.S. President Gerald R. Ford in September, after Ford had criticized Venezuela, along with other members of the Organization of Petroleum Exporting Countries for abusing the "oil weapon." It was also apparent in his cultivation of close relations with Cuba, Venezuela being one of the foremost champions of lifting sanctions imposed against Cuba by the Organization of American States. The leftward drift of the Pérez government, evident in its hostility toward the military regime in Chile and the restrictions placed on foreign investors, was widely attributed to the influence of Gumersindo Rodriguez, the powerful head of the state planning agency Cordiplan and a former Marxist.

The Oil Windfall, however, seemed likely to prove a transient thing for Venezuela, whose reserves will be exhausted in 12 years if production continues at the present rate of 3 million barrels a day. To effect better control, the government nationalized the oil industry effective December 31.

Nationalization plans were also mapped for the iron-ore industry, second in importance only to oil. Venezuela had long been critical of the export of iron ore by two U.S.-owned companies – U.S. Steel Corporation and Bethlehem Steel Corporation. Nationalization took effect on December 10.

The Economic Plan formulated by Cordiplan, which was given control of the budget and statistics offices as well, emphasized redistribution of wealth and rigid control of foreign investment under the terms of the Andean Pact. It also stressed the use of oil revenues to support the growth of state-run local industries and to replace food imports, which, in 1974, cost $350 million. The plan was not universally popular, however. The government became involved in a running battle with Fedecamaras, a private businessmen's association that was especially critical of price controls as well as a new law on employment security that made it almost impossible to dismiss workers. There was dissatisfaction, too, with the government's failure to curb inflation, which was running at an annual rate of 12 per cent. Finally, there was labor unrest. Despite a 25 per cent wage increase given industrial workers in April, the government had to contend in November with a major strike by iron-ore workers.   Robert Moss

See also LATIN AMERICA (Facts in Brief Table).
VERMONT. See STATE GOVERNMENT.

VETERANS, particularly those who served in the Vietnam War, got action in 1974 on complaints. They urged improvements in GI Bill benefits, an overhaul of the Veterans Administration (VA), and upgrading of VA hospitals. Under pressure from members of Congress and veterans groups, Donald E. Johnson announced in April that he would resign as administrator of veterans affairs. He was replaced in October by Richard L. Roudebush, a former Republican congressman from Indiana.

Then, on December 3, Congress overrode a veto by President Gerald R. Ford to enact a bill that increased veterans education benefits by 23 per cent, the largest increase since World War II. The new bill increased the basic monthly allowance to $270 and extended the term of eligibility for benefits to 45 months. It also provided for loans of $600 a year to student veterans. In December, Ford signed a bill raising veteran pensions by 12 per cent.

Meanwhile, many returning veterans had trouble getting jobs in 1974. The U.S. Department of Labor reported that 302,000 young veterans were unemployed in September. The unemployment rate for all Vietnam veterans from 20 to 34 years of age was 5.2 per cent, lower than the national average of 5.8 per cent. But the rate for veterans 20 to 24 was 12.4 per cent, compared with 8 per cent for nonveterans in that age group.

James Wagonseller, national commander of the American Legion, visits the White House in September to protest against amnesty program.

Delays in getting education checks added to student veterans' problems. To help unsnarl delays, the VA placed full-time representatives on those college campuses where more than 500 veterans were enrolled, and other VA representatives will visit those campuses where fewer than 500 veterans are enrolled. More than 1,300 representatives are expected to participate in the program. They will work closely with campus officials.

VA Reform. The House Veterans Affairs Committee outlined several areas where the VA needs reform. The committee encouraged revised procedures to avoid unnecessary delays in getting education checks to servicemen on time. Questioning whether the present appeals system is adequate, the committee suggested an internal ombudsman system or a more decentralized appeals board to handle complaints. They also suggested that a system be devised to get compensation checks to veterans enrolled in legitimate training programs under the GI Bill, yet prevent abuse by veterans who fraudulently claim to be enrolled in such programs.

VA Hospitals. Following criticism about the quality of care in VA hospitals and other health facilities, the VA reported to the President that it had found "significant deficiencies" in every VA hospital. The report cited a critical and immediate need for new facilities and other resources costing about $300 million. The report found the following problems:

■ Difficulty in recruiting doctors, nurses, and other staff members because the pay is lower than that offered by private hospitals or private practice.
■ Limited numbers of surgeons in VA hospitals who can provide such specialized skills as caring for paraplegics.
■ A shortage of space and adequate equipment, resulting in overcrowding and reduced care standards.
■ Complex eligibility standards that confuse veterans.

Veterans Organizations. The American Legion held its 56th national convention in Miami Beach, Fla., from August 16 to 22. Delegates elected James M. Wagonseller of Lancaster, Ohio, as national commander.

The Veterans of Foreign Wars held its 75th national convention from August 16 to 23 in Chicago. John J. Stang of La Crosse, Kans., was elected commander in chief. President Ford surprised the group with a proposal of leniency for Vietnam draft evaders and deserters and suggested that they be allowed to "work their way back" to citizenship. See NATIONAL DEFENSE.

The American Veterans Committee held its 31st convention from June 28 to 30 in South Fallsburg, N.Y. Arthur S. Freeman of Chicago was elected national chairman.   Joseph P. Anderson

VICE-PRESIDENT. See FORD, GERALD R.; ROCKEFELLER, NELSON A.

VIETNAM, NORTH. An estimated 200,000 North Vietnamese soldiers were believed to be deployed in South Vietnam during 1974. They built roads, pipelines, and other logistical support facilities. And they continued major military operations against Saigon's forces despite the Jan. 27, 1973, cease-fire agreement.

In public statements, however, North Vietnam emphasized economic development as its first priority, with secondary attention to supporting the war in the South. The Lao Dong Party, North Vietnam's Communist organization, decided on this policy at a secret meeting in late January or early February. The party's first secretary, Le Duan, said economic setbacks from the war and U.S. bombing "will take a pretty long time to eliminate."

The party's top economic expert, Deputy Premier Le Thanh Nghi, became chairman of the economic planning commission on April 2. It was hoped that he could solve the major economic problems. Premier Pham Van Dong said on September 1 that production should reach its 1965 level (before U.S. bombing began) by the end of 1974.

Russia and China increased their economic aid, largely to make up for bad harvests and food shortages, but they declined to supply much military equipment.   Henry S. Bradsher

See also ASIA (Facts in Brief Table).

A senator in South Vietnam has his head shaved to protest constitutional amendment allowing President Thieu to run for a third term.

VIETNAM, SOUTH. Economic and political pressures created by the war developed into widespread demonstrations against President Nguyen Van Thieu's regime late in 1974. Meanwhile, the war continued unchecked despite the 1973 Paris cease-fire agreement.

Two developments triggered public frustrations into the strongest challenge ever to Thieu's presidency. One was the resignation in August of President Richard M. Nixon, a strong supporter of Thieu. Nixon's fall seemed to prove to many of Thieu's opponents that the Vietnamese president might also be vulnerable. The other was U.S. congressional cuts in military aid for South Vietnam. Instead of the requested $1.45 billion for the period from July 1, 1974, to June 30, 1975, Congress voted only $700-million.

In the face of the cuts, the South Vietnamese Army had to reduce its use of planes, bombs, artillery shells, and other supplies. The resulting fears of military weakness sparked demands for new efforts to reach a political settlement with the Communists rather than accept Thieu's insistence that a political deal would be suicidal.

The two main groups agitating against Thieu were a Roman Catholic-led "People's Movement Against Corruption, for National Salvation and Peace Restoration" and "The Forces for National Reconciliation" led by the An Quang faction of Buddhists.

Thieu Moved Gradually to meet the demonstrators' complaints of corruption. He fired 377 army majors and colonels on October 25, and three generals commanding regions of Vietnam on October 30. He reshuffled his Cabinet beginning October 24. Among the ministers he dropped was his cousin and top adviser on relations with Washington, Hoang Duc Nha.

But such moves failed to satisfy the opponents. The People's Movement anticorruption leader, Tran Huu Thanh, continued to call for Thieu's resignation, as did others. Thieu denied the corruption charges and told the nation on October 1 that he would resign "if the entire people and army no longer have confidence in me."

Role of Viet Cong. The Viet Cong continued its full-scale war against the Saigon government. On October 8, it called for Thieu's overthrow, saying it would not negotiate with his regime under cease-fire agreement terms.

Declining American economic aid brought a drop in living standards. The country suffered from both recession and inflation, but the first signs of offshore oil wealth appeared. In January and February, boats of the Saigon Navy clashed with Chinese vessels over ownership of the offshore Paracel and Spratly islands. The incidents were reportedly caused by the interest in the offshore oil.   Henry S. Bradsher

See also ASIA (Facts in Brief Table).

VIRGINIA. See STATE GOVERNMENT.

VISUAL ARTS. International cooperation helped to create major old-master exhibitions in 1974. Together with the National Museums of France, the Metropolitan Museum of Art held a "Masterpieces of Tapestry" display in New York City–97 great examples of this medieval art, once again actively being made today. The exhibition was the first to result from an exchange agreement between the two museums signed in 1971. The museums pooled staff and other resources for the show, and together financed the cost of about $24 million in insurance for the loans.

The Detroit Institute of Art, in cooperation with the Pitti Palace in Florence, Italy, presented the "Twilight of the Medici: Late Baroque Art in Florence." The exhibition opened in Detroit in March, and then went on to the Pitti Palace. More than 300 examples of the extravagant baroque art style were shown, including bronze and marble sculptures, paintings, tapestries, furniture, drawings, jewelry, and many unusual decorative objects.

A great French artist of the 1700s, François Boucher, was seen in a show organized by the National Gallery of Art in Washington, D.C.

The Metropolitan Museum also signed an agreement with the Russian Ministry of Culture, which set up concurrent exhibitions in both nations in the spring of 1975. The Metropolitan Museum will lend Russia major paintings of the 1500s to 1800s and will receive in return Scythian archaeological treasures from Kiev and Leningrad.

American Exhibitions. As if in anticipation of the U.S. bicentennial in 1976, several large exhibitions at the Whitney Museum of American Art in New York City featured aspects of early U.S. art. "The Flowering of American Folk Art 1776-1876" was an attempt to document the great tradition of native art in the United States and to satisfy the current hunger for a warm, affecting art production in a time when only the craftsman and the photo-realist painter are able to do so. In the same vein was the Whitney's major exhibition of American genre painting, "The Painter's America: Rural and Urban Life 1870-1910." Finally, the tradition was brought up to date with the large "American Pop Art" show.

Among the major displays of contemporary American art held during the year was the exhibition of drawings, pastels, and bronzes of Willem de Kooning at the Walker Art Center in Minneapolis, Minn. Mark Tobey was honored with an exhibition at the National Collection of Fine Arts in Washington, D.C., and Al Held in a Whitney Museum show.

Lesser-known artists were also accorded exhibitions. The Museum of Modern Art in New York City showed the 1920s avant-gardist Gerald Murphy. The work of the important American black artist Jacob Lawrence was seen at the Whitney Museum.

European Artists. The large exhibitions of recent European art included the first retrospective of the Swiss-born constructivist sculptor Max Bill at the Albright-Knox Gallery in Buffalo, N.Y. The Alberto Giacometti exhibition at the Solomon R. Guggenheim Museum in New York City assessed that artist's vital contribution to our self-image.

The Musée de l'Orangerie in Paris exhibited the works of cubist Juan Gris in April. It was the first major Gris show since a 1958 exhibition in the Museum of Modern Art in New York City.

Three other shows all focused on the surreal. The Los Angeles County Museum of Art presented the late 19th-century French romantic Gustave Moreau. The Art Institute of Chicago hosted a traveling Max Ernst exhibition. And in New York City, the Cultural Center held "The Painter of the Mind's Eye: Belgium Symbolists and Surrealists."

Although there were at least two large exhibitions of post-object art–the "ungainly genres" as they are called–interest in such production may have waned as its sensationalism has given way to difficult searches for quality. The Walker Art Center offered "Projected Images," an exhibition by six artists who use film and video to create light environments. The Kennedy Center in Washington, D.C., presented "Art Now," the year's important gathering of conceptual and performance art.

Museum Acquisitions included two major old-master purchases. The National Gallery of Art

The Metropolitan Museum of Art in New York City sets up special lighting in February to show its 97 exhibits of medieval tapestries.

bought a rare work by the much-admired Georges de la Tour, a 17th-century French painter of simplified human forms seen against artificial light. *The Repentant Magdalen* reputedly cost $8 million. The Cleveland Museum of Art bought a *St. Catherine of Alexandria* by Matthias Grünewald, a great German artist of the 1500s. The painting formed part of an altarpiece thought lost in the 1600s.

Gifts to museums included the world's largest private collection of Rodin sculpture. Californian B. Gerald Cantor divided the collection among the Stanford University Museum, the Los Angeles County Museum, and the Museum of Modern Art in New York City.

The Asia Society, a New York City museum for Oriental art founded by John D. Rockefeller III in 1956, obtained 300 prime works from its founder. British sculptor Henry Moore presented 300 of his works to the Art Gallery of Ontario, in Toronto, Canada. Included were 18 bronzes, 41 plaster casts, and numerous drawings.

Museum Openings. The Joseph H. Hirshhorn Museum and Sculpture Garden, with 4,000 paintings and 2,000 sculptures – the largest single bequest ever made by an individual American – opened in a four-story cylindrical structure in Washington, D.C. (see Section Two, To INCREASE KNOWLEDGE AMONG MEN). The many additions to the Minneapolis Institute of Art complex, costing $26 million, were completed by Kenzo Tange, a leading Japanese architect. The Neuberger Museum at the State University of New York, Purchase, opened as the largest state university museum in the United States. In Baltimore, a new $5-million wing doubled the exhibition area at the Walters Art Gallery.

Two large photographic galleries opened in the United States. The International Center of Photography in New York City will be a print and negative archive. The Center for Photographic Arts in Chicago displays contemporary work. One of the year's important photographic exhibitions was the Metropolitan Museum's 156-print retrospective of Ansel Adams, a great landscape photographer whose work helped spread the message of conservation.

Sculpture. Chicago became home to several large-scale sculptures during the year. Most charming is *The Four Seasons*, a five-sided outdoor mosaic mural by Marc Chagall that is 50 feet (15 meters) long. It was unveiled in the First National Bank Plaza on September 27. In the nearby Federal Center Plaza, Alexander Calder's steel sculpture *Flamingo*, 55 feet (17 meters) high, was dedicated on October 25. A half-hour later, Calder's *Universe*, a large, motor-driven mobile in several sections, was dedicated in the lobby of the Sears Tower. All this coincided with the opening of a retrospective exhibition of Calder's smaller works at the Chicago Museum of Contemporary Art.

Nebraska announced that it would celebrate the bicentennial by commissioning 12 monumental sculptures that would be placed along U.S. Route 80 through the state. The program would culminate in July, 1976. Newport, R.I., presented *Monumenta*, 54 large-scale outdoor works by 40 artists that were set throughout the city.

Auction Price Records were set once again in several categories. The $444,000 paid for a Benin bronze in July was the highest price ever recorded for primitive art. A world-record price for sculpture was reached in May when Constantin Brancusi's *La Negresse Blonde II* was sold for $750,000. A record single auction total of $15 million was also reached in May in New York City's Sotheby Parke Bernet Galleries for several hundred paintings, sculptures, and drawings, with record prices for Daumier, Delacroix, and Toulouse-Lautrec. A painting by Georges Braque brought a record $552,000 in December.

Despite the record prices, there was some pessimism among dealers about continuation of the recent intense activity. During the last half of the year, some works failed to bring as much as expected. And just as Japan and Germany had offered sales potential in the past, the art world now looked to the oil-rich Arab countries, with reports that a dealer had opened an outlet in Kuwait.   Joshua B. Kind

VITAL STATISTICS. See CENSUS, UNITED STATES; POPULATION, WORLD.

WALTON, WILLIAM THEODORE (1952-   ), all-America basketball player at the University of California at Los Angeles (UCLA), won the 44th James E. Sullivan Award in 1974 as the United States outstanding amateur athlete. He signed a five-year contract to play with the Portland Trail Blazers of the National Basketball Association after graduation.

The 6-foot 11-inch (211-centimeter) star center had played in only three losing games since his junior year in high school, and he led the UCLA team to two national championships. During three seasons at UCLA, he set a rebounding record and averaged 20 points a game. He also excelled as a defensive player.

Bill Walton was born on Nov. 5, 1952, in La Mesa, near San Diego, Calif., where his father is a welfare worker. He has two brothers and a sister, all of whom stand at or over 6 feet (182 centimeters). He did not begin to play basketball seriously until his junior year in high school. He was 6 feet 7 inches (200 centimeters) tall then.

Walton, a vegetarian, practices transcendental meditation, which he says gives him a sharpened and concise thought pattern that improves his game. At UCLA, he was involved in militant political activities. He joined student demonstrators protesting when the United States mined Haiphong Harbor in North Vietnam in May, 1972.   Foster Stockwell

WASHINGTON. See STATE GOVERNMENT.

WASHINGTON, D.C. Home rule came to Washington, D.C., residents in 1974 for the first time in 104 years. On May 7, voters approved a new charter for the District of Columbia, which previously had been governed directly by the U.S. Congress.

The new governmental system calls for an elected mayor and 13-member council. The mayor has executive and appointive powers, is responsible for preparing the city budget, and has the power to reorganize city offices and agencies. The council is empowered to pass laws for the district and approve the budget. Democrat Walter E. Washington became the first elected mayor after defeating five opponents in the general election on November 5.

National Culture. A controversial new art museum, the Joseph H. Hirshhorn Museum and Sculpture Garden, opened on Washington's Mall on October 4. The $16-million facility was dubbed "the largest doughnut in the world" by one critic. It houses the Hirshhorn collection of modern art, 6,000 works from the 1800s and 1900s. The collection is considered one of the greatest of its kind. It was donated to the U.S. government by New York financier and industrialist Joseph H. Hirshhorn. See ARCHITECTURE; Section Two, TO INCREASE KNOWLEDGE AMONG MEN.

In 1974, the National Collection of Fine Arts in Washington continued reassembling works of American art produced during the 1930s and 1940s with Works Progress Administration funds. The art pieces had been scattered throughout the country.

Policewoman Dies. The first policewoman killed in the line of duty in the United States was shot on September 20 in Washington, D.C. Gail A. Cobb, 24, was killed while trying to apprehend a gunman fleeing an attempted savings and loan robbery.

On July 11, two convicts seized eight hostages and 14 other prisoners in a federal courthouse cellblock and demanded to be released. The trial of former presidential aide John D. Ehrlichman and the so-called White House "plumbers" was in session in the courthouse at the time. The convicts released 14 prisoners and one hostage, and finally surrendered after the remaining seven escaped on July 14.

According to the Federal Bureau of Investigation, serious crimes in the district rose 5 per cent during the first six months of 1974.

Economy. A survey conducted by Business International Corporation rated Washington, D.C., 17th in terms of living costs among 47 of the world's major cities. Department of Labor figures showed the city's cost of living rose 10.8 per cent between May, 1973, and May, 1974. The earnings of an average factory worker in the area rose only 8.1 per cent during the one-year period ending in July. During the same period, department store sales rose 11.2 per cent, employment increased 3 per cent, and construction activity fell by 5.9 per cent.   James M. Banovetz

See also Section Five, WASHINGTON, D.C.

Golden-plated spires top the Washington Temple, a sparkling, $15-million Mormon edifice that was completed in September near Kensington, Md.

Nixon announces on April 29 that he is releasing edited transcripts of 31 White House tapes in response to Judiciary Committee subpoena.

WATERGATE and its attendant scandals drove Richard M. Nixon from the presidency of the United States in 1974 and led to criminal trials for top officials of his Administration. On August 9, Nixon became the first U.S. President to resign his office. That historic action followed his own revelation that he was involved in the cover-up of the June, 1972, break-in, burglary, and bugging of Democratic National Committee Headquarters at the Watergate Office Building in Washington, D.C.

The revelation came on August 5, after the House Judiciary Committee had voted three articles recommending his impeachment. The belated disclosure was a deathblow to his chances of avoiding impeachment in the House and removal from office by the Senate. Vice-President Gerald R. Ford was sworn in as his successor, climaxing nearly two years of Watergate charges and denials. See Section Two, FROM TRIUMPH TO TRAGEDY.

Nixon Takes the Offensive. As 1974 began, President Nixon emerged from seclusion to try to recapture public confidence, which had been badly eroded during the closing months of 1973. His firing of Archibald Cox as special Watergate prosecutor in October, 1973, over a dispute about disclosure of taperecorded conversations had led to a public uproar and calls for his impeachment. Missing tapes and an 18½-minute gap on one White House tape added to his credibility problems. The President's

decision in December, 1973, to make public his income tax returns from 1969 to 1972 also seemed to backfire. Nixon's net worth had more than tripled from $307,141 to $988,522 while he was in the White House, yet he paid taxes of only $792.81 in 1970 and $878.03 in 1971. By January, his Gallup Poll rating had plunged to 29 per cent–a 39-point drop from the 68 per cent rating he enjoyed a year earlier.

Despite these setbacks, Nixon began 1974 by taking the offensive. He hired Boston trial lawyer James D. St. Clair on January 4 to represent him in dealings with the House Judiciary Committee and the new special Watergate prosecutor, Leon Jaworski. On January 8, Nixon issued two statements denying that his Administration had granted favors to the dairy industry or the International Telephone and Telegraph Corporation (ITT) in return for political contributions. He said he raised milk subsidies in 1971 because of congressional pressure and economic considerations, and to win the votes of dairy farmers. He rejected charges that he stopped an antitrust suit against ITT because of its $400,000 pledge to underwrite Republican convention expenses in 1972.

The President also rejected any thought of resigning. In his January 30 State of the Union message to Congress, Nixon said: "One year of Watergate is enough . . . I want you to know that I have no intention whatever of walking away from the job that the people elected me to do."

Meantime, Federal Judge John J. Sirica had appointed a panel of technical experts to determine the cause of the 18½-minute gap in the tape of a crucial conversation between Nixon and his chief of staff, H. R. Haldeman. The experts reported on January 15 that the gap was no accident. It had been caused by someone pushing the tape-recorder controls at least five separate times to erase conversation. The strong implication that White House personnel had destroyed evidence was another blow to Nixon's standing in the eyes of the public.

The Tapes Fight. The taped conversations between President Nixon and his aides regarding the Watergate cover-up became the crucial element in the Watergate case. In late 1973 and early 1974, relevant tapes were requested by the Senate Select (Watergate) Committee, the House Judiciary Committee, and special prosecutor Jaworski. But Nixon refused to turn over the tapes voluntarily, citing executive privilege. He claimed he was protecting the presidency by preserving the traditional separation of powers between the executive and legislative branches of government.

On January 4, Nixon informed Senator Sam J. Ervin, Jr. (D., N.C.), chairman of the Watergate Committee, that he would not honor the committee's subpoenas for tapes and documents. The committee then asked the courts to enforce the subpoenas. United States District Court Judge Gerhard A. Gesell dismissed the committee's suit on February 8, ruling that publicity concerning the tapes might prejudice the upcoming trials of Nixon aides charged in the Watergate affair. But Gesell rejected the President's claim of executive privilege.

On April 11, the House Judiciary Committee voted 33 to 3 to subpoena tapes and documents of 42 conversations for its impeachment inquiry. On March 18, Judge Sirica had ordered a secret Watergate grand jury report on Nixon's role in the case and copies of 19 previously released White House tapes turned over to the Judiciary Committee. These contained the heart of the case for Nixon's impeachment.

Judge Sirica issued a subpoena on April 18 for tapes of 64 conversations requested by Jaworski for use at the Watergate cover-up trial, scheduled to begin in the fall. Sirica also refused to uphold the President's claim of executive privilege.

Edited Transcripts. Confronted with these demands from Congress and the courts, the President made a dramatic gesture. In a televised address on April 29, he said he would make public the next day edited transcripts of 31 taped conversations in response to the Judiciary Committee subpoena. He asserted that they would establish his innocence and invited committee Chairman Peter W. Rodino, Jr. (D., N.J.), and the senior Republican member, Edward Hutchinson of Michigan, to listen to the actual tapes.

The 1,308 pages of transcripts provided the most intimate portrait of a President that the public had ever had. However, they caused further damage, because they showed that Nixon seriously considered paying hush money to silence Watergate burglar E. Howard Hunt about White House misconduct. A fascinated nation learned that Nixon and his advisers debated how to keep the lid on the Watergate scandal. There were countless omissions and breaks in the conversations labeled "unintelligible" or "expletive deleted."

One notable quotation was Nixon's response to an estimate by his counsel, John W. Dean III, that $1-million would be needed to seal the lips of the Watergate defendants for the next two years. "We could get that," the President replied. "On the money, if you need the money, you could get that. You could get a million dollars. You could get it in cash. I know where it could be gotten. It is not easy, but it could be done. But the question is, who the hell would handle it? Any ideas on that?"

There was immediate unfavorable congressional and public reaction. Senate Republican leader Hugh D. Scott, Jr., of Pennsylvania, who had been a key Nixon defender, said the transcripts revealed conduct that was "disgusting, shabby, and immoral." Many newspapers began calling for the President's resignation.

Instead of ending the tape controversy, Nixon's transcripts escalated the fight to new levels. His transcripts covered only 31 of the 42 tapes requested by the Judiciary Committee, and the committee voted on May 1 to inform Nixon he had not complied with the subpoena. Also, committee counsel John M. Doar announced that inaccuracies had been found in the transcripts when they were compared with other evidence. Between May 9, when the committee began its impeachment hearings, and the end of June, it issued a series of subpoenas, all of which Nixon turned down.

Meanwhile, the White House appealed the subpoena for 64 tapes requested by Jaworski for the Watergate trial. Jaworski asked the Supreme Court of the United States on May 24 to by-pass the appellate court and promptly consider Nixon's claim of executive privilege for not releasing the tapes. The High Court agreed and rendered its fateful verdict on July 24. The court ruled 8 to 0 (Associate Justice William H. Rehnquist had disqualified himself because he had served in the Justice Department under Nixon) that executive privilege does not apply to evidence for a criminal trial, and it ordered Nixon to release the 64 tapes. Reportedly, Nixon's aides and attorney persuaded him to comply with the Supreme Court order, and Sirica began receiving the tapes on July 30.

Trials and Convictions. While the Judiciary Committee pondered impeachment and the tapes disputes were raging, a series of events in federal court

At the cover-up trial of Haldeman, Ehrlichman, Mitchell, and two others in October, judge, jury, and lawyers don earphones to listen to tapes.

staggered the White House. On January 24, Egil Krogh, Jr., once head of the White House "plumbers" unit set up to stop leaks of information to the press, was sentenced to six months in prison for his role in the 1971 break-in at the office of a psychiatrist who had treated Daniel J. Ellsberg. Ellsberg had leaked the so-called Pentagon Papers to the press in 1971.

On June 3, Charles W. Colson, a former special counsel to Nixon, unexpectedly pleaded guilty to a felony charge that he had tried to deprive Ellsberg of a fair trial by waging a smear campaign against him. Colson claimed he was following Nixon's instructions. Presiding Judge Gesell sent Colson to prison for from one to three years. On July 12, former domestic affairs adviser John D. Ehrlichman was convicted of conspiracy in the Ellsberg break-in, along with three of the original Watergate burglars – G. Gordon Liddy, Bernard L. Barker, and Eugenio R. Martinez. Ehrlichman was also found guilty of perjury and sentenced to from 20 months to 5 years in prison.

Herbert W. Kalmbach, Nixon's personal lawyer and campaign fund-raiser, had pleaded guilty on February 25 to two violations of campaign fund laws, including the promise of a diplomatic post in return for a $100,000 contribution. On June 17, Judge Sirica sentenced him to from 6 to 18 months in jail. Throughout the year, executives of various corporations were tried and convicted of making illegal campaign contributions to the Nixon re-election effort.

On July 29, former Secretary of the Treasury John B. Connally, Jr., was indicted by the Watergate grand jury for accepting a $10,000 bribe from the Associated Milk Producers, Incorporated, in 1971. However, on April 28, former U.S. Attorney General John N. Mitchell and former Secretary of Commerce Maurice H. Stans were acquitted of conspiracy, perjury, and obstruction of justice charges in connection with a secret campaign contribution from financier Robert L. Vesco.

On April 5, former presidential appointments secretary Dwight L. Chapin was convicted of perjury for lying to a grand jury about White House espionage and sabotage of the 1972 Democratic presidential campaign. Richard G. Kleindienst became the first former U.S. attorney general to be convicted of a crime, for not testifying "fully and accurately" about the ITT antitrust settlement to a Senate committee looking into his nomination in April, 1972.

Jeb Stuart Magruder, deputy director of the Committee to Re-Elect the President (CRP), was sentenced to from 10 months to 4 years in prison on May 21, after pleading guilty to obstruction of justice in the Watergate burglary case. John Dean was sentenced to from one to four years in prison on August 2 for his role in the cover-up.

The Stone Wall Crumbles. On July 9, the House Judiciary Committee made public its version of the President's tape transcripts, showing that Nixon was more familiar with the cover-up than the White House version of the transcripts had indicated. The committee also disclosed a March 22, 1973, conversation in which Nixon told Mitchell: "I want you all to stonewall it, let them plead the Fifth Amendment, cover up or anything else, if it'll save it, save the plan. That's the whole point . . . . Up to this point, the whole theory has been containment, as you know, John." In mid-July, the Judiciary Committee released a massive amount of evidence alleging political manipulation of the Internal Revenue Service, illegal wiretaps on government officials and newspaper reporters, creation of a secret police unit at the White House, and other abuses of power.

The Senate Watergate Committee concluded its work on July 13. In its final report, it charged that one of Nixon's closest friends, millionaire Charles G. (Bebe) Rebozo, had spent more than $50,000 for the President's personal benefit. This included diamond earrings, given to Mrs. Nixon as a birthday gift, which – the report said – were paid for in part with $4,562.33 diverted from 1972 campaign funds.

On July 24, the Judiciary Committee opened its final, televised debate on whether to impeach Nixon. Chief counsel Doar and his Republican associate, Albert E. Jenner, Jr., both recommended impeachment, asserting the evidence showed that Nixon was involved in the cover-up almost from its inception.

St. Clair, Nixon's attorney, argued that there was no proof beyond a reasonable doubt that the President had been involved in criminal obstruction of justice. Nixon's defenders on the committee agreed, saying there was no "smoking pistol" that clearly showed his guilt.

But, when the first article of impeachment was presented on July 27, 6 Republicans joined all 21 Democrats in voting to impeach the President on a charge of blocking the Watergate investigation. Eleven Republicans voted against the article.

The second article, alleging presidential abuse of power, was approved on July 29, by 28 to 10, with one more Republican joining the majority. The third article, charging that Nixon's defiance of congressional committee subpoenas violated the Constitution, was passed on July 30 by a vote of 21 to 17. Articles accusing Nixon of exceeding his powers during the secret bombing of Cambodia and of tax fraud and improper enrichment through government-paid improvements on his property were defeated, 26 to 12.

The Smoking Pistol. On August 2, St. Clair made a shocking discovery while examining some of the 64 tapes being turned over to Jaworski. Nixon had kept secret from his own staff and attorney a taped conversation he had on June 23, 1972, with Haldeman. The tape indicated that the President was involved in the cover-up less than a week after the break-in. Reportedly, St. Clair and the new White House chief of staff, Alexander M. Haig, Jr., persuaded Nixon to make public the June 23 transcript,

in which the President directed Haldeman to tell the Federal Bureau of Investigation, "Don't go any further into this case, period."

In a statement on August 5, the President said he listened to the tape in May, 1974, before the impeachment hearings began, but did not tell anyone about it.

Once the word was out, Nixon's dwindling band of supporters in Congress almost disappeared. All his Republican defenders on the Judiciary Committee reversed themselves and voted for impeachment. "I guess we have found the smoking pistol," said Congressman Barber B. Conable, Jr. (R., N.Y.).

Battered but still battling, the President told his Cabinet on August 6 that he had no intention of resigning. The next day, however, Nixon changed his mind after Republican leaders told him that he had only a handful of supporters in the House and Senate, and that he faced certain impeachment. In a final televised presidential address on August 8, Nixon announced he would resign at noon the following day. After an emotional farewell to the White House staff on August 9, Nixon and his wife, Pat, were escorted to a waiting helicopter for the start of a journey to San Clemente that Nixon began as President and finished as a private citizen.

At noon on August 9, Ford took the oath of office and said: "My fellow Americans, our long national nightmare is over." But the specter of Watergate continued to plague the nation. On September 8, Ford astounded nearly everyone by granting Nixon a full pardon for crimes that he committed or may have committed during his years as President. The pardon, together with an agreement that gave Nixon exclusive ownership and virtual control over the White House tapes, shattered Ford's initial popularity and revived the Watergate issue in the November elections. See ELECTIONS; FORD, GERALD R.; NIXON, RICHARD M.; PRESIDENT OF THE UNITED STATES.

Cover-Up Trial. The final act of the Watergate drama took place in federal court. On October 1, former Nixon advisers Haldeman, Ehrlichman, Mitchell, Robert C. Mardian, and Kenneth W. Parkinson went on trial for conspiracy and obstruction of justice in the Watergate cover-up.

All the defendants pleaded innocent, and Ehrlichman turned against Nixon, claiming that Nixon had deliberately deceived and used him. Nixon, who had been named an unindicted co-conspirator in the March 1 indictment of the aides, was ill and unable to testify. Nevertheless, the tapes of White House conversations played at the trial provided evidence of the roles that Nixon and his aides played in the cover-up.

On Jan. 1, 1975, the jury found all the defendants except Parkinson guilty.   William J. Eaton

See also GESELL, GERHARD A.; JAWORSKI, LEON; SUPREME COURT OF THE UNITED STATES.

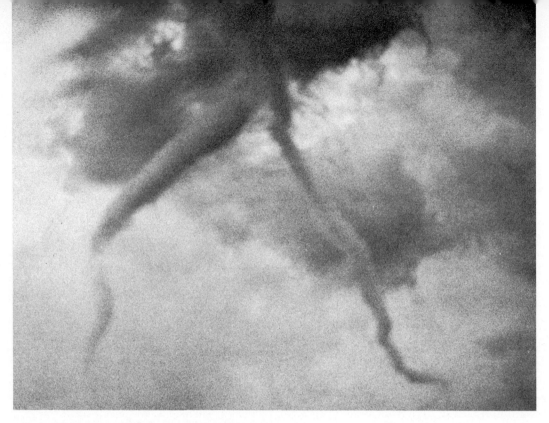

Tornado funnels struck Nashville, Tenn., on April 3, part of a series of twisters that killed over 300 along a corridor from Georgia to Ontario.

WEATHER. Scientists, ships, planes, buoys, and satellites from 72 nations joined in a 1974 study of the tropical regions that spawn hurricanes and play a crucial but poorly understood role in the world's weather. The study, from June 15 to September 23, was one of the most complex international scientific experiments ever undertaken. Called GATE – for GARP (Global Atmospheric Research Program) Atlantic Tropical Experiment – it was aimed at understanding the energy stored in tropical oceans and its influence on world weather patterns. Data were also gathered on weather conditions related to the drought that has struck Africa and Asia.

American and Russian scientists met in Leningrad in June to propose joint weather studies. The proposals ranged from surveys of air pollution to legal and administrative measures to protect the environment. The scientists also discussed the relationship of environmental change and global climate.

Aerosol Danger. Concern spread throughout the year over the increase in the amount of aerosols in the lower atmosphere. These chemical pollutants have risen sharply with increased industrialization. At the present rate, the amount of man-made aerosols in the atmosphere will equal those produced by nature by the year 2000. Some aerosols break down under the glare of ultraviolet light, releasing chlorine, which then breaks down ozone. Ozone in the lower atmosphere absorbs those wave lengths of ul-

traviolet light that would otherwise kill many plants and animals.

One of the biggest dangers, however, is the fact that aerosols in the atmosphere affect worldwide temperatures. They are known to reduce temperatures by as much as 2.3°F. (1.3°C). Recent studies of conditions at the time of the great Ice Ages show that temperature dropped only about four times as much, and the Ice Ages developed after a century or two of such temperatures. As a result, some observers believe that the present reductions may eventually cause an Ice Age. It is important to note that the snow cover and ice pack in the Northern Hemisphere in recent years have shown signs of increasing and forming earlier each year.

SMS Satellites. The Synchronous Meteorological Satellite (SMS-1) was launched on May 17 by the National Aeronautics and Space Administration (NASA). In stationary orbit over the tropical Atlantic Ocean, the satellite can photograph one portion of the earth continuously. The satellite pictures are transmitted to 500 receiving stations. A second SMS satellite was scheduled to go into orbit over the eastern Pacific. Global coverage will be attained when Japan, Russia, and the European Space Research Organization launch similar satellites.

Data from the temperature-sensing National Oceanic and Atmospheric Administration (NOAA) satellites are now being used to predict freezing temperatures. Other satellites may soon be used to determine the best crop-planting dates, and the areas where floods, blight, and fires may occur.

Weather Modification. NOAA conducted lightning-suppression research in July and August. Scientists tested the possibility of keeping the electric charge in a thunderstorm from reaching the point of explosive discharge. They dropped millions of small aluminum-coated nylon fibers into the clouds of a developing thunderstorm in the hope that the fibers would pick up and hold electric current in the clouds, relieving the storm of the excessive charges that produce lightning. Such suppression could be used to lessen the danger to spacecraft during landing and launching and reduce the danger of forest and rangeland fires.

U.S. Weather. After one of the warmest winters on record, soaking rains fell on the central United States. They continued until June in many areas, delaying crop planting. This was followed by a dry summer and an exceptionally early frost and freeze across the Midwest.

Tornadoes continued at a high rate. About 130 tornadoes occurred within an 18-hour period, beginning on April 3. The storms killed about 320 persons in an area extending from Georgia to Ontario. See Disasters.   Edward W. Pearl

WEIGHT LIFTING. See Sports.

The new weather satellite SMS-1 sent this view of the Western Hemisphere on May 28, showing five storms at the top, ranging across Canada.

WEST INDIES. The Bahamas, Jamaica, and Trinidad and Tobago sought larger shares of the revenues derived from their natural resources in 1974. Previously, foreign-owned corporations processing the islands' ore and mineral deposits kept a larger share of the profits because of their heavier investments in the enterprises.

On January 12, Prime Minister Eric E. Williams of Trinidad and Tobago announced that his government was negotiating an agreement under which it would acquire a share in the island holdings of Texaco, Incorporated. The U.S.-based company, which operates a refinery at Pointe-a-Pierre, processes about 350,000 barrels of oil per day. Simultaneously, the prime minister announced that talks were underway with an unnamed Middle East nation to establish a jointly owned refinery near Port-of-Spain.

Jamaica Took similar steps to increase its share of the profits from its bauxite deposits. In June, the Senate approved a bill increasing from $2.50 to $11.72 the levy on each short ton of bauxite exported from Jamaica. Royalties paid to the government will go up from 28 cents to 56 cents a ton. Under the bill's supplementary provisions, which included a minimum production level, the government bauxite revenues were expected to rise from the present $25-million to about $200 million a year. The companies affected included the Aluminum Company of America; the Aluminium Company of Canada; the Kaiser Aluminum and Chemical Company; the Reynolds Metals Company; and Alumina Partners, Limited, a consortium consisting of the Anaconda Company, Kaiser, and Reynolds.

In April, the Jamaican legislature unanimously passed a new gun-control law called the Suppression of Crime Act. The government acted in response to a widespread outbreak of murder and violence that was linked to drug traffic, a multimillion-dollar business that had attracted international organized crime to the island. The new law, which was enacted despite the objections of the Jamaican Bar Association and other groups concerned with civil liberties, provided for secret trials, disallowed bail, and authorized security forces to conduct searches and seize property without a warrant.

The Bahamas government planned to levy higher taxes on the earnings of the island's two principal gambling casinos. The operations have combined gross winnings of about $36 million annually. At present, the government receives 17 per cent of each casino's first $17 million in gross winnings and 10 per cent of all winnings over that. Under the proposed arrangement, the government would receive 25 per cent of the first $10 million, 20 per cent of the next $6 million, and 10 per cent of the next $4 million. Any winnings over $20 million would be subject to a 5 per cent tax.   Paul C. Tullier

See also Latin America (Facts in Brief Table).

WEST VIRGINIA. See State Government.

WHITLAM, EDWARD GOUGH (1916-), prime minister of Australia, journeyed to a number of foreign countries during 1974. He visited New Zealand and Southeast Asia in January, Indonesia in September, and the United States, Canada, and Fiji in late September and early October. During his U.S. visit, he conferred with President Gerald R. Ford. He advocated establishing a consultative body for the countries of Asia and the Pacific, collaboration among nations exporting natural resources, restraint by the United States and Russia in deploying forces in areas such as the Indian Ocean, and strengthening the nuclear nonproliferation treaty.

At home, Whitlam survived a serious challenge to his government, and his Labor Party won a special general election on May 18 (see AUSTRALIA). His leadership excited strong feelings, among both supporters and opponents. In Perth, he was punched, kicked, and pelted with rubbish at a state election rally on March 25. In Canberra, on October 30, he was derided by aboriginal demonstrators at Parliament House. Most Australians recognized, however, that he was assured of continuing as head of the Australian Labor Party. He was often described as arrogant and impetuous, but he exhibited intellectual power and creative awareness. His Cabinet colleagues acknowledged this, though sometimes quarreling with his methods.   J. D. B. Miller

WILDLIFE. See CONSERVATION.

WILSON, HAROLD (1916-   ), Labour Party leader, became prime minister of Great Britain on March 4, 1974. National elections held on February 28 failed to produce a majority in Parliament for either Labour or the ruling Conservative Party. Unable to form a coalition government, Prime Minister Edward Heath resigned and Wilson succeeded him, even though Labour had won only 301 seats in the 635-seat House of Commons. Wilson called another election on October 10, trying to gain the majority needed to pass crucial legislation. However, Labour increased its strength only to 319 seats, a scant 3-vote majority. Wilson previously served as prime minister from 1964 to 1970. See GREAT BRITAIN.

Born in Huddersfield, Yorkshire, England, Wilson graduated from Oxford University in 1937, and taught economics there for two years. During World War II, he served as a government economist. In 1945, he was elected to Parliament and named parliamentary secretary for the Ministry of Works.

In 1947, Wilson became secretary for overseas trade, and from 1947 to 1951 he was president of the Board of Trade. He scrapped many controls favored by some in his party. He became party leader in 1963. Wilson is married to the former Gladys Baldwin, and they have two sons, Giles and Robin.   Foster Stockwell

WISCONSIN. See STATE GOVERNMENT.

WRESTLING. See SPORTS.

WYOMING. See STATE GOVERNMENT.

YEMEN (ADEN). Friction with its neighbors, notably Oman, kept the Aden regime politically isolated in the Arab world in 1974. Most of the friction was caused by its militant socialism and support for such revolutionary movements as the Popular Front for the Liberation of Oman and the Arab Gulf (PFLOAG). Aden granted sanctuary to PFLOAG rebels fighting the Omani government in Dhofar Province. See OMAN.

Aden accepted the good offices of an Arab League mediation mission in May, but refused to meet with Omani representatives on the grounds that they were under the control of a "foreign power" (Iran). In October, Oman launched a major campaign to defeat the rebels, and Aden accused Iran of sending troops to occupy Arabian territory. The accusations were denied by Iran, although the Iranian government has supplied Oman with equipment and advice.

No further steps were taken toward unification of the two Yemens, though they agreed to unification in 1972. The joint committee on inter-Yemeni unity met several times, but set no firm date for unification of the two states.

Prime Minister Ali Nasir Muhammad Hasani also became minister of national education in March. Subsequently, an agreement for technical aid in building the nation's first university, in Aden, was signed with Russia on March 20.

Five-Year Plan. The Supreme People's Assembly, Aden's principal legislative body, adopted the first five-year plan in April. Its objectives were described by National Front Chairman Abdul-Fattah Ismail as "economic liberation through industrialization and exploitation of our oil and other mineral resources." Although neither plan investment figures nor the 1974-1975 budget totals were available, Aden's continued lack of significant known resources meant that economic development would have to be financed from foreign aid.

Libya loaned Aden $6.25 million on March 3. An agreement was signed with Iraq on March 15 for a $5-million interest-free loan. In May, the Kuwait Fund for Arab Economic and Social Development provided $11.97 million for irrigation in the Abyan Delta, and work started on the project. The World Bank loaned $5.4 million to Yemen in July to finance rural and vocational education centers. In July, the Organization of Arab Petroleum Exporting Countries agreed to reimburse oil-poor Aden for increased oil prices.

China Projects. The Ayn Mahfid Highway and the Zinjibar Bridge were completed on July 12. They were built by workers from the People's Republic of China under a 1970 China-Yemen cooperation agreement, and then turned over to Yemeni authorities.

The government restored diplomatic relations with West Germany in September. They had been broken off in 1969.   William Spencer

See also MIDDLE EAST (Facts in Brief Table).

YEMEN (SANA). The army seized power in a bloodless coup on June 13, 1974. It deposed the three-man Republican Council headed by President Abdul Rahman Iryani, which had governed since the civil war ended in 1967. The leader of the coup, Colonel Ibrahim Mohamed al-Hamdi, said that the armed forces acted to prevent further economic and administrative chaos. President Iryani resigned on June 18, and was exiled to Syria.

A civilian government headed by Muhsin bin Ahmad al-Ayni, who served briefly as prime minister in 1972, was formed June 21. It included former Prime Minister Hassan Makki and other holdovers from the previous Cabinet. Ayni and Interior Minister Yahya Mutawwakil, who have strong links with the ruling Baath Party of Iraq, held the most important posts. However, a provisional constitution issued June 19 vested final executive authority in a military Command Council headed by Colonel Hamdi. The constitution identified Yemen as an Arab republic under the laws of Islam. The Command Council on June 23 announced a reform of the armed forces.

The political uncertainty clouded Yemen's economic development picture. Saudi Arabia paid a fourth installment of its annual $57.6-million subsidy on March 17, and pledged an additional $34 million after the new government approved a budget of $110-million with a $31-million deficit.   William Spencer

See also MIDDLE EAST (Facts in Brief Table).

YOUNG MEN'S CHRISTIAN ASSOCIATION

(YMCA) leaders from Australia, Canada, India, Indonesia, Japan, the United States, and other countries held the first Asian-Pacific YMCA Consultation on International Cooperation in Baguio, the Philippines, in July, 1974. They discussed mutual relations and programs and differences of policy and approach. Other important international meetings were held in Asunción, Paraguay, in August, and in Accra, Ghana, in September.

YMCA's were active in such troubled parts of the world as the drought-stricken area south of the Sahara in Africa. Although hindered by the lack of facilities and personnel, the International Division of the U.S. YMCA appointed an African task force to develop programs in Senegal, Mauritania, Mali, Upper Volta, and Chad. Several important relief programs were already underway in Ethiopia, where the YMCA has traditionally been strong. They included a new orphanage at Bati and teams distributing food, clothing, and medical care.

In the United States, a major effort to find alternatives to present-day social treatment of youths in trouble with the law has greatly accelerated. Hundreds of YMCA's are participating in delinquency prevention programs. Ten residential group homes are also planned in such cities as Boston; New Haven, Conn.; and Oakland, Calif., as alternatives to putting youths in trouble in institutions.   Joseph P. Anderson

YOUNG WOMEN'S CHRISTIAN ASSOCIATION (YWCA).

In preparing for the August, 1974, World Population Conference in Bucharest, Romania, the United States YWCA and 31 other national organizations urged the United States to join in emphasizing social and economic development and respect for human rights as necessary ingredients of just and effective policy on population growth.

The YWCA also began to face a serious leadership crisis in 1974. During the next 10 years, almost 300 executive staff members will be retiring. At the same time, women and youth in developing countries need the opportunities to develop the skills that will qualify them for positions of leadership. The World Relations Unit of the YWCA accelerated its search for leadership candidates who can serve in the developing countries. Through the World YWCA, 35 program grants were made to YWCA's in 33 countries, to the Caribbean Area Committee, and to the Regional Office of YWCA.

A Consultation of Native American Women of the YWCA brought 56 women from 27 tribes to Minneapolis, Minn., in November to discuss how the YWCA can best involve American Indian women. The meeting proposed a structure to promote understanding of the concerns and issues of American Indians.

Sara-Alyce Wright was named executive director of the YWCA, effective Sept. 1, 1974. She succeeded Edith M. Lerrigo, who retired.   Joseph P. Anderson

YOUTH ORGANIZATIONS focused on sound environmental programs, saving national resources, and preventing crime and juvenile delinquency in 1974.

Boy Scouts of America (BSA). Investigation showed in June that membership rolls had been padded in 15 of the 431 local BSA councils. The national Scouting office said membership rolls had been padded in Chicago; Detroit; Evansville and Munster, Ind.; Logan, W. Va.; Birmingham, Ala.; Jackson, Ky.; Asheville, N. C.; Chattanooga, Tenn.; Columbia, Ga.; Monroe, La.; Galveston and Fort Worth, Tex.; Tulsa, Okla.; and Sacramento, Calif. After auditing records, national Scout officials censured or fired local officials responsible for falsifying membership lists.

Over 2,000 young men and women competed in 28 Olympic sports for college scholarships and medals in the Third Explorer Olympics, held in August in Fort Collins, Colo. Sanctioned by the U. S. Olympic Committee, the Explorer Olympics featured sports clinics and seminars.

The Fourth National Explorer Presidents' Congress drew 2,500 young adult delegates to Washington, D.C., in April. Mary Van Lear Wright, Auburndale, Mass., was elected national Explorer president.

Robert W. Reneker was re-elected president of the Boy Scouts of America at its 64th annual meeting in Honolulu, Hawaii, in May.

Boys' Clubs of America. "World of Work," a vocational guidance, career education, and work experience program, conducted in cooperation with the U.S. Department of Labor in test cities, produced permanent jobs for 400 participants. Working with the Department of Health, Education, and Welfare's Office of Child Development, Boys' Clubs began demonstration activities in a "Help-A-Kid" project, helping adolescent members to understand child growth and development and the responsibilities of parenthood. With the support of the Lilly Endowment, Incorporated, an Urban Fellows Training Program was implemented to help Boys' Club staff members deal more effectively with problems of urban areas.

Over 1,200 Boys' Club workers, representing nearly 1,100 clubs in 700 communities throughout the United States, attended the 68th annual conference of Boys' Clubs in New York City in May.

National Boy of the Year, George Clark, of the R.W. Brown Boys' Club in Philadelphia, was among 21 youth service organization representatives meeting with President Gerald R. Ford in August. He gave the President the results of a health survey undertaken by the Boys' Clubs, which indicated that emotional problems are the greatest single concern of young people.

Camp Fire Girls. New 1974 programs for Camp Fire members from 6 to 11 years old attempt to develop the abilities to plan and make choices, to deal with feelings and emotions, to be flexible and creative, to enjoy accomplishment and achievement, to respect oneself and others, and to learn how to learn. Camp Fire Girls from 9 to 11 years old have received a new name. They are now called Camp Fire Adventurers.

4-H Clubs. More than 5 million club members, guided by hundreds of thousands of volunteers and extension workers, were active in community projects, including health and nutrition education, recycling of natural resources, and career training. They worked with teachers, community leaders, and political leaders on a variety of projects.

Future Farmers of America (FFA). For the third consecutive year, FFA membership climbed by more than 15,000. The organization for students preparing for careers in agriculture reached a total membership of some 465,000 in 7,726 chapters.

More than 16,000 FFA members and guests attended the 47th national convention in October in Kansas City, Mo. Vernon L. Rohrscheib of Fairmount, Ill., and Ronald D. Schwerdtfeger of Capron, Okla., were named Star Farmer and Star Agribusinessman of America, which are the FFA's highest awards.

Girl Scouts of the United States of America. Leadership projects to recruit and train minority-group adults as Girl Scout leaders are now reaching thousands of girls in 26 localities across the country.

New troops now operate in Appalachia and in remote rural areas, migrant camps, inner cities, and Indian reservations. A new national Migrant Community Project will work cooperatively with thousands of Mexican-American migrant-worker families. This three-year pilot project will explore practical ways to assure continuity of Girl Scouting with migrant families.

At Rockwood National Center in Potomac, Md., Senior Scouts explored career opportunities for women in government, law, journalism, and other fields. Edith Macy National Center in Briarcliff Manor, N. Y., and Juliette Gordon Low National Center in Savannah, Ga., the birthplace of the founder of Girl Scouts of the U.S.A., hosted Cadette and Senior Scouts who studied the workings of northern and southern suburban and metropolitan communities. Nearly 5,000 girls participated in the Wyoming Trek to the National Center West, which is a 15,000-acre (6,070-hectare) wilderness site in Wyoming.

Girls Clubs of America (GCA) in 1974 introduced the "Self-Structured Way" educational approach to all its clubs. Through this process, all members, even 6- and 7-year-olds, take part in planning and deciding their own activities.

In cooperation with the *Reader's Digest*, GCA has produced a lively new 16-millimeter 13½-minute color film, *Alive and Feeling Great*, which demonstrates the Fit for Life techniques designed for and introduced to Girls Clubs in 1967 by Bonnie Prudden and Lenna Payton of the Institute for Physical Fitness in Stockbridge, Mass.

Junior Achievement (JA). The program to aid disadvantaged youths identified as potential high school dropouts, now in its fourth year, gave work experience to 1,451 students in 22 communities during the summer of 1974. Most were selected by high school counselors, others through state employment agencies.

In Job Education, local adult companies subcontract work to mini-companies made up of students who work eight-hour days and five-day workweeks during the eight-week program. Their time is divided between manufacturing the parent company's product and participating in discussions and hearing lectures on such subjects as choosing a career and how a business operates. Wages, salaries, and operating expenses are paid by the sponsoring company. The JA group makes most of the day-to-day decisions. By September, 1974, the school systems of 55 cities in the United States were offering academic credit to students involved in Junior Achievement projects.

The 31st National Junior Achievers Conference was held in August in Bloomington, Ind. Some 2,400 U.S. high school students attended, selected from over 175,000 Achievers. In addition, there were representatives from Canada, France, West Germany, Japan, and Puerto Rico.   Joseph P. Anderson

YUGOSLAVIA continued to purge liberal elements in 1974, but had second thoughts about détente with Russia. Police arrested a group of pro-Russian Communists holding a secret meeting in Bar, Montenegro, on April 6. On September 20, officials announced that 32 members of the group had been sentenced at secret trials to prison terms of up to 14 years.

Russian Relations outwardly remained correct in 1974. Russia's Deputy Premier Vladimir Novikov and Army Chief of Staff General Viktor Kulikov visited Yugoslavia in September without incident. But at the preparatory meeting for a European Communist Conference in Warsaw, Poland, in October, Yugoslavia took a strongly independent stand by opposing Russian proposals for an anti-Chinese world conference. A Yugoslav parliamentary delegation visited China in June; and, in October, a Chinese trade delegation visited Yugoslavia.

President Josip Broz Tito visited West Germany in June and Denmark in October. But he maintained a balance between East and West by visiting East Germany in November and by meeting Hungarian Party Secretary Janos Kadar in Budapest late in April. United States Secretary of State Henry A. Kissinger briefly visited Yugoslavia in early November. His visit prompted rumors of renewed sales of U.S. weapons.

Relations with Italy deteriorated in February and March when the two countries renewed an old dispute over the status of Trieste and neighboring territories. In October, Yugoslavia quarreled with Austria over the alleged unfair treatment of Austria's Croat and Slovene minorities.

On June 18, West Germany granted Yugoslavia a $300-million credit. Kuwait granted Yugoslavia a $100-million credit in June, and Libya announced that it would participate in the Adriatic Sea oil pipeline project with Yugoslavia, Czechoslovakia, and Hungary, which was officially agreed to on February 12.

Domestic Affairs. The Communist Party Congress in May tightened up party statutes, gave greater powers to the party's executive committee in Belgrade, and elected President Tito party leader for life. Under a new Constitution proclaimed on February 21, he was also elected president for life.

Unemployment rose to about 450,000 when 100,000 Yugoslavs returned from the West in the first eight months of 1974 as a result of layoffs there. Yugoslavia had a record wheat harvest, but corn, sugar beet, and other late crops suffered badly in the heavy October floods. Inflation reached 30 per cent and the balance-of-payments deficit at the end of the year was over $700 million. The dinar was devalued 7 per cent at the end of October.   Chris Cviic

See also EUROPE (Facts in Brief Table).

President Josip Broz Tito of Yugoslavia made an official state visit to Denmark in October, and he was greeted by Queen Margrethe II, left.

Zaire's 20th of May Stadium was rebuilt to host such prestige-building events as the Ali-Foreman fight and an international music festival.

ZAIRE made international headlines in 1974 by staging the on-again-off-again heavyweight championship boxing match between Muhammad Ali and George Foreman. After a month's delay, the bout finally took place at 4 A.M., October 30 (the night of October 29 in the United States), and Ali won the title. See BOXING.

In September, Zaire hosted a three-day music festival, starring black performers from Africa, the United States, and several other countries. Both the festival and the boxing match took place in the rebuilt 20th of May Stadium, which Zaire's President Mobutu Sese Seko dedicated on September 22.

The government lost an estimated $4 million on the fight, and ticket sales for the festival were low. However, Mobutu was mainly interested in bringing international prestige to this large, copper-rich African nation.

Industries Nationalized. Zaire began implementing its policy of gaining control over foreign-owned businesses and agricultural enterprises. All foreign-owned operations must eventually have Zairian citizens as owners or managing directors and board chairmen, so that foreigners will no longer control the nation's commerce.

Belgian, Lebanese, Pakistani, Portuguese, and Greek businessmen were forced to sell their companies to Zairian citizens. Reportedly, the government was also considering taking over Japanese automobile-sales outlets. The former foreign owners were invited to stay on as managers to ensure a smooth transition because of the shortage of trained businessmen among Zaire's citizenry.

Zaire began nationalizing the oil industry in January by taking over the assets of Texaco, Incorporated; the Royal Dutch-Shell Group; Mobil Oil Corporation; and Belgian and British oil interests. Oil was the only U.S. operation affected.

Yet, foreign investments continued high. Since 1970, U.S. companies have invested $110 million. General Motors Corporation opened an $8-million auto-assembly plant in November, and Gulf Oil Corporation planned to begin off-shore oil production by mid-1975.

Mobutism. The only political party, the People's Revolutionary Movement (MPR), announced in August that Mobutism would become its official doctrine. The MPR also recommended that this doctrine be incorporated into the Constitution.

In keeping with Zaire's program of African authenticity, Mobutism combines democratic practices with the tribal tradition of a strong chief, who makes all decisions. The doctrine calls for one political party and one leader to head all divisions of government. A proposed constitutional provision would exempt Mobutu from the rule that a president can serve only two five-year terms. John Storm Roberts

See also AFRICA (Facts in Brief Table).

ZOOLOGY. Amphibians get the oxygen they need to survive in various ways. Some use lungs, some use gills, and others absorb oxygen through their skin, using neither lungs nor gills. For a long time, zoologists have offered contradictory theories on how the hellbender, or giant salamander, gets its oxygen. Hellbenders have large lungs that some scientists consider important in the amphibian's absorption of oxygen. Other scientists argue that the lungs are thin sacs that cannot get enough oxygen into the blood. Adult hellbenders have no gills, so they must use either their lungs or their skin to absorb oxygen.

Salamander Study. Robert W. Guimond of Boston State College in Massachusetts and Victor H. Hutchinson of the University of Oklahoma at Norman studied the problem in 1974. They compared the oxygen consumption of hellbenders while they were out of water with that when they were in water and found that over 90 per cent of the oxygen they used was absorbed through the skin. The scientists concluded that the main function of the lungs is to provide variable buoyancy. The salamander manages to get enough oxygen because the folds in its skin have many blood vessels. Resting hellbenders rock from side to side continually to renew the layer of water that surrounds them.

Marmot Behavior. David P. Barash, zoologist at the University of Washington in Seattle, studied several different species of marmots and found that their social behavior is related to the harshness of the environmental conditions under which they live. Woodchucks, marmots that live in forests and fields where the growing season is long and life is not particularly difficult, are quarrelsome and anti-social. They socialize only during their brief breeding and weaning periods.

In contrast, Olympic marmots are much more social and gather in colonies. They live in the harsher climate of mountainous Olympic National Park in Washington, where short growing seasons and variable snow cover make life more difficult. In addition, the Olympic marmot young grow more slowly, stay with their mothers longer, and leave the colony later than do their forest cousins.

In years when the Olympic marmot population is high, the young leave their mothers earlier, but never as early as do the woodchuck young. Because the climate and food supply are more variable, Barash believes that Olympic marmot populations might easily overshoot the ability of the marginal environment to support them. The closer social integration may help them regulate the size of their population. Barash believes that the greater Olympic marmot level of interaction contributes in some unknown fashion to their earlier dispersal, thus lowering the population density. — Barbara N. Benson

In a wave that darkened the sky, 10 million birds swooped down to roost in trees at Graceham, Md., frightening residents and menacing health.

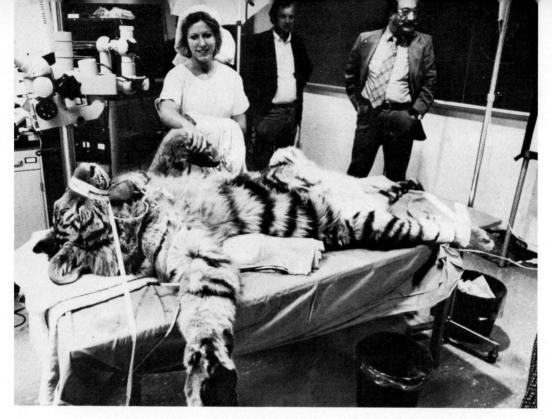

Sleeping after an anesthetic, a 10-month-old tiger from Chicago's
Lincoln Park Zoo awaits surgery to remove cataracts from its eyes.

ZOOS AND AQUARIUMS. Concern over the rapid decline in the number of wild animals throughout the world brought increasing interest in the preservation and exhibition of animal species in zoological parks. Canada saw the first visitors welcomed to the new Metropolitan Toronto Zoo. And in the United States, the Columbia Zoological Park in South Carolina and the Marine Life Aquarium in Mystic, Conn., were opened to the public.

The Philadelphia Zoological Garden, the first in the United States, celebrated its 100th year in 1974 by opening a new African Plains exhibit. But the most unusual new construction of the year was a floating pavilion for dolphins and sea lions that was added to the New England Aquarium in Boston. Elsewhere, major exhibits of tropical birds were unveiled in the zoos in Denver and Boston. Baltimore's zoo displayed a new Kodiak bear exhibit, and there was a new caribou habitat in the Vancouver, Canada, zoo.

Flight cages for birds of prey were installed in the Cheyenne Mountain Zoo in Colorado Springs, Colo., and in Jacksonville, Fla. Many other projects were under construction, from a large tide-pool exhibit in the Scripps Aquarium in La Jolla, Calif., to new grottos for lions and tigers in the National Zoo in Washington, D.C.

Conservation. The concern for conservation of animals was demonstrated by the efforts of zoo workers to breed rare species in captivity, efforts that resulted in increasing numbers of successful births of rare and endangered species. Cheetahs were born in several zoos and parks, including a second-generation litter in Whipsnade, near London, England. Golden lion marmosets and lesser pandas were also produced by captive-born parents in the National Zoological Park in Washington, D.C. In the Cincinnati Zoo and in Lincoln Park Zoo in Chicago, continued success with breeding gorillas resulted in plans for large new quarters.

Notable first births in captivity included a sea otter in Point Defiance Aquarium in Tacoma, Wash., an aardwolf in the Oklahoma City Zoo, and a hairy-nosed wombat in the Brookfield Zoo near Chicago.

The Smithsonian Institution in Washington, D.C., took over a 4,000-acre (1,618-hectare) agriculture station in Virginia as its research and conservation center. The first animals released there were a herd of Père David's deer, which are extinct in the wild. The New York and Philadelphia zoos are to join Washington's National Zoological Park in stocking the center with other rare species.

The U.S. Department of Agriculture declared a moratorium on destruction of exotic birds exposed to Newcastle disease while in quarantine. This disease of poultry is caused by a virus that attacks the bird's nervous system. The stringent quarantine was established in 1972.

George B. Rabb

World Book Supplement

In its function of keeping WORLD BOOK owners up to date, THE WORLD BOOK YEAR BOOK herewith offers significant new articles from the 1975 edition of THE WORLD BOOK ENCYCLOPEDIA. These articles should be indexed in THE WORLD BOOK ENCYCLOPEDIA by means of THE YEAR BOOK cross-reference tabs.

GERALD R. FORD

JOHNSON
36th President
1963 — 1969

NIXON
37th President
1969 — 1974

FORD, GERALD RUDOLPH (1913-   ), was the only Vice-President of the United States to become President upon the resignation of a chief executive. Richard M. Nixon resigned as President on Aug. 9, 1974, and Ford took office that same day. When Nixon left the presidency, he faced almost certain impeachment because of his role in the Watergate political scandal.

Ford had been Vice-President for only eight months when he took office as President. Nixon had appointed him to succeed Vice-President Spiro T. Agnew, who resigned while under criminal investigation for graft. Ford was the first person to be appointed to fill a vacancy in the vice-presidency. He also was the only Vice-President and President who did not win election to either office.

Ford, a Michigan Republican, had been elected to the U.S. House of Representatives 13 straight times before he replaced Agnew. He also had served as House minority leader.

The American people warmly welcomed Ford to the presidency. He had a calm, friendly manner and an unquestioned reputation for honesty. But Ford's popularity dropped sharply about a month later after he pardoned Nixon for all federal crimes that Nixon might have committed as President. Many Americans felt that Nixon should have been brought to trial in the Watergate scandal. Others believed that Nixon should not have been pardoned until he admitted his role in the scandal. Ford also caused a nationwide controversy by proposing amnesty for men who had refused to be drafted or had deserted from the armed forces during the Vietnam War.

Ford was a big, athletic man who loved sports. He often turned to the sports section of his newspaper before reading any other news. Ford starred as a football player in high school and college, and football had a major influence on his life. "Thanks to my football experience," he once said, "I know the value of team play. It is, I believe, one of the most important lessons to be learned and practiced in our lives." Ford swam regularly and also enjoyed golf and skiing.

Early Life

Family Background. Ford was born on July 14, 1913, in Omaha, Nebr. He was named for his father, Leslie Lynch King, who operated a family wool business there. Leslie's parents were divorced about two years after his birth. His mother, Dorothy Gardner King, then took him to Grand Rapids, Mich., where she had friends. In 1916, she married Gerald Rudolph Ford, the owner of a

Jerald F. terHorst, the contributor of this article, is a Columnist for The Detroit News-Universal Press Syndicate *and the author of* Gerald Ford and the Future of the Presidency.

small paint company in the city. Ford adopted the child and gave him his name. The stocky, blond youth, who became known as "Jerry," grew up with three younger half brothers, James, Richard, and Thomas.

Jerry's real father also remarried. From the King family, Jerry had a half brother, Leslie H. King; and two half sisters, Marjorie King Werner and Patricia King.

Boyhood. Jerry's parents encouraged him to develop pride in civic responsibility. His stepfather participated in programs to aid needy youths in Grand Rapids and took an active interest in local politics. His mother devoted much of her time to charity projects and other activities of the Grace Episcopal Church, where the Fords worshiped. Jerry joined the Boy Scouts and achieved the rank of Eagle Scout, the highest level in Scouting. He later proudly referred to himself as the nation's "first Eagle Scout Vice-President."

Jerry was a strong, husky boy and excelled in sports. He first gained public attention as the star center of the South High School football team. He was selected to the all-city high school football team three times and was named to the all-state team in his senior year.

At school, Jerry usually wore a suit and tie, though most boys in those days wore a sport shirt, slacks, and sweater. He studied hard and received good grades. He also won a contest sponsored by a local motion-picture theater to choose the most popular high school senior in Grand Rapids.

As a teen-ager, Jerry waited on tables and washed dishes at a small restaurant across the street from South High School. One day, his real father came in and introduced himself to the startled youth. Jerry knew about his natural father but had not seen him since his parents' divorce. King asked Jerry if he would like to live with the King family. Jerry said he considered the Fords his family. Later, in 1936, King helped Ford get a summer job as a ranger in Yellowstone National Park.

College Student. Ford entered the University of Michigan in 1931. He earned good grades and played center on the undefeated Michigan football teams of 1932 and 1933. In 1934, his teammates named him the team's most valuable player. He played center on the college team that lost to the Chicago Bears, 5 to 0, in the 1935 All-Star Football Game.

The White House

The United States flag had 50 stars when Gerald R. Ford became President.

Ford graduated from Michigan in 1935. The Detroit Lions and the Green Bay Packers offered him a contract to play professional football, but Ford had decided to study law. He accepted a job as assistant football coach and boxing coach at Yale University, hoping he could also study law there. Ford coached full time at Yale from 1935 until 1938, when he was accepted for admission by the Yale Law School.

While at Yale, Ford became a partner in a modeling agency in New York City. His partner, Harry Conover, a model, operated the agency. In March, 1940, Ford modeled sports clothes and ski apparel for an article in *Look* magazine. The agency succeeded, but Ford be-

came dissatisfied with his share of the profits and soon sold his interest.

Ford received his law degree from Yale in 1941. He ranked in the top third of his graduating class.

Grand Rapids Lawyer

In June, 1941, Ford was admitted to the Michigan bar. Shortly afterward, he and Philip W. Buchen, a former roommate at the University of Michigan, opened a law office in Grand Rapids. The United States entered World War II in December, 1941, and Ford soon volunteered for the United States Navy.

Naval Officer. Ford entered the Navy in April, 1942, and became an ensign. He taught physical training at a base in Chapel Hill, N.C., for a year. Then he became the physical-training director and assistant navigation officer of the U.S.S. *Monterrey*, an aircraft carrier. In 1943 and 1944, the *Monterrey* took part in every big naval battle in the Pacific Ocean. Ford was discharged in January, 1946, as a lieutenant commander.

Entry into Politics. Ford resumed his law career in Grand Rapids and also became active in a local Republican reform group. Leaders of the organization, called the Home Front, included U.S. Senator Arthur H. Vandenberg of Michigan, who had helped establish the United Nations, and Ford's stepfather. The two

---

IMPORTANT DATES IN FORD'S LIFE

1913 (July 14) Born in Omaha, Nebr.

1935 Graduated from the University of Michigan.

1942-1946 Served in the U.S. Navy during World War II.

1948 (Oct. 15) Married Elizabeth (Betty) Bloomer.

1948 Elected to the first of 13 successive terms in the U.S. House of Representatives.

1965 Became House minority leader.

1973 (Dec. 6) Became Vice-President of the United States.

1974 (Aug. 9) Succeeded to the presidency.

The White House

Young Jerry, shown at the age of 2½, liked to play with his dog, Spot. The youth later became active in the Boy Scouts and rose to Eagle Scout, the highest level in Scouting.

Insight, Inc.

One of Ford's Boyhood Homes was this frame house on Union Street in Grand Rapids, Mich. His family lived in the house from 1923 until 1929, when they moved to East Grand Rapids.

men urged Ford to challenge U.S. Representative Bartel J. Jonkman in the Republican primary election of 1948.

Jonkman believed that the United States should stay out of foreign affairs as much as possible. Vandenberg and Ford had supported that policy before World War II, but the war changed their views. Ford defeated Jonkman in the primary and then beat Fred Barr, his Democratic opponent in the November election. The voters of Michigan's Fifth Congressional District reelected Ford 12 straight times.

Marriage. In 1947, Ford met Elizabeth (Betty) Bloomer (April 8, 1918-   ). She was born in Chicago and moved to Grand Rapids with her family when she was 3 years old. Her father, William S. Bloomer, was a machinery salesman. Her mother, Hortense, took an active interest in Grand Rapids community affairs.

As a child, Betty became interested in dancing. She continued to study the dance and, during the 1930's, joined a New York City group directed by the noted dancer Martha Graham. Betty also worked as a fashion model. In 1942, she returned to Grand Rapids and married William Warren, a local furniture salesman. They were divorced in 1947.

When Ford met Betty, she was working as a fashion coordinator for a Grand Rapids department store. They were married on Oct. 15, 1948, just before Ford first won election to the U.S. House of Representatives. Ford campaigned on the day of his wedding and arrived late for the ceremony. The Fords had four children, Michael Gerald (1950-   ), John Gardner (1952-   ), Steven Meigs (1956-   ), and Susan Elizabeth (1957-   ).

Career in Congress

Rise to Power. Ford gained a reputation as a loyal Republican and a hard worker during his early terms in Congress. He was named to the defense subcommittee of the House Appropriations Committee in 1953 and became known as a military affairs expert. Some Republican leaders mentioned Ford as a possible candidate for the vice-presidential nomination in 1960. But the nomination went to Henry Cabot Lodge, Jr., the U.S. ambassador to the United Nations.

During the early 1960's, Ford became increasingly popular among young Republican congressmen. In 1963, they helped elect him chairman of the Republican Conference of the House. In this position, his first leadership role in the House, Ford presided at meetings of the Republican representatives.

In November, 1963, President Lyndon B. Johnson established the Warren Commission to investigate the assassination of President John F. Kennedy. Johnson appointed Ford as one of the seven members. Ford and a member of his staff, John R. Stiles, later wrote a book about Lee Harvey Oswald, *Portrait of the Assassin* (1965).

House Minority Leader. In 1965, Ford was chosen House minority leader. As minority leader, he urged Republican congressmen to do more than just criticize the proposals of Democrats, who held a majority in the House. Ford worked for Republican alternatives to Democratic programs.

Ford attracted national attention when he appeared with Senate Minority Leader Everett M. Dirksen on a series of televised Republican press conferences. The series, which reporters called the "Ev and Jerry Show," drew increased attention to Republican views.

Ford supported President Johnson's early policies in the Vietnam War. But by 1967, with no end of the war in sight, Ford began to strongly attack U.S. military strategy in Vietnam. That year, he gave a speech entitled "Why Are We Pulling Our Punches in Vietnam?" The speech encouraged Republicans to oppose

Wide World

Ford Starred at Center on the University of Michigan football team, which named him its most valuable player in 1934. He later coached football and boxing at Yale University.

The White House

The Ford Family in 1948. Seated are, *left to right,* Gerald's half brother James, Mrs. Dorothy Ford, and Gerald. Standing are half brother Thomas, Gerald R. Ford, Sr., and half brother Richard.

Johnson's war policies. In addition, Republicans and Southern Democrats joined under Ford's leadership in opposing many of Johnson's social programs. Ford considered these programs either too costly or unnecessary.

In 1968, Richard M. Nixon was elected President. The Democrats kept control of both houses of Congress, but Ford helped win approval of a number of Nixon's policies concerning the Vietnam War and inflation.

In 1970, Ford led an effort to impeach William O. Douglas, a liberal associate justice of the Supreme Court of the United States. Ford strongly criticized Douglas' vote in a case involving Ralph Ginzburg, the editor of a magazine that had paid the justice $350 for an article. Ford also objected to Douglas' encouragement of political dissent in various writings. The matter ended after a House investigating committee reported a lack of evidence to support impeachment of Douglas.

The Resignation of Agnew. In 1972, Nixon and Vice-President Spiro T. Agnew won re-election in a landslide. That same year, Ford won election to his 13th successive term in the House.

Early in 1973, federal investigators uncovered evidence that Agnew had accepted bribes. The charges covered the period that Agnew had served as Baltimore County Executive and then as governor of Maryland, and later as Vice-President. As a result of the investigation, Agnew resigned from the vice-presidency on Oct. 10, 1973. Nixon nominated Ford to replace Agnew. The nomination required the approval of both houses of Congress under procedures established in 1967 by the 25th Amendment to the United States Constitution. Previously, vacancies in the vice-presidency had remained unfilled until the next presidential election.

The Senate approved Ford's nomination by a 92 to 3 vote on November 27. The House approved it, 387 to

35, on December 6, and Ford was sworn in as the 40th Vice-President later that day. He became the first appointed Vice-President in the nation's history.

Vice-President (1973-1974)

Shortly before Ford became Vice-President, the House of Representatives started impeachment proceedings against Nixon. Some congressmen believed that Nixon was hiding evidence related to the Watergate scandal, which had begun in June, 1972. The scandal arose after Nixon's re-election committee became involved in a burglary at Democratic national headquarters in the Watergate building complex in Washington,

Wide World

As a Young Congressman, Ford gained a reputation as a hard worker and loyal Republican. He became known as a military affairs expert while serving on a defense subcommittee in Congress.

D.C. Later, evidence linked several top White House aides with the burglary or with an effort to conceal information about it.

Speaking Tour. The Watergate scandal shook public confidence in Nixon, even though he insisted he had no part in it. As Vice-President, Ford went on a nationwide speaking tour and expressed his faith in Nixon. He addressed business, civic, and youth groups in cities throughout the country. Ford also took part in many Republican fund-raising activities and campaigned for Republican candidates. By mid-1974, the Vice-President had visited about 40 states and made several hundred public appearances.

The Resignation of Nixon. In July, 1974, the House Judiciary Committee recommended that Nixon be impeached. It voted to adopt three articles of impeachment for consideration by the full House of Representatives. The first article accused the President of interfering with justice by acting to hide evidence about the Watergate burglary from federal law-enforcement officials. The other articles charged that Nixon had abused presidential powers and illegally withheld evidence from the judiciary committee.

Ford continued to defend Nixon, arguing that the President had committed no impeachable offense. Ford also predicted that the House of Representatives would not impeach Nixon.

Then, on August 5, Nixon released transcripts of taped White House conversations that clearly supported the first proposed article of impeachment. Almost all of Nixon's remaining support in Congress collapsed immediately. The Republican leaders of both the House and the Senate warned Nixon that he faced certain impeachment and removal from office.

Nixon resigned as President on the morning of August 9. At noon that day, Ford took the oath of office as the 38th President of the United States. Warren E. Burger, chief justice of the United States, administered the presidential oath of office to Ford in the East Room of the White House. Ford became the only President

Fred Ward, Black Star

Ford Accepted President Nixon's Congratulations after being sworn in as Vice-President on Dec. 6, 1973. Ford succeeded Vice-President Spiro T. Agnew, who had resigned.

in the nation's history who had not been elected to either the presidency or the vice-presidency.

Ford's Administration (1974-   )

Ford kept all of Nixon's Cabinet officers at the start of his Administration. He nominated Nelson A. Rockefeller, former governor of New York, as Vice-President. The nomination was subject to the approval of both houses of Congress under provisions of the 25th Amendment.

Early Problems. When Ford became President, he was challenged at home by soaring inflation and a loss of public confidence in the government. Inflation was causing hardship among many Americans, especially the poor and the elderly. Sharp rises in prices also threatened to cause a severe business slump.

Public faith in government had plunged to its lowest level in years, largely because of the Watergate scandal. In addition, the Nixon impeachment crisis had slowed the work of many federal agencies and created confusion about various government policies.

Fighting on the Mediterranean island of Cyprus provided the first foreign crisis for the new President. In August, 1974, Turkish troops invaded Cyprus and took control of a large part of the island. The take-over occurred after Turkish Cypriots strongly protested the formation of a new government by Greek Cypriots. Angry Greeks, Greek Cypriots, and Americans of Greek ancestry charged that the United States should have used its influence to stop the Turks.

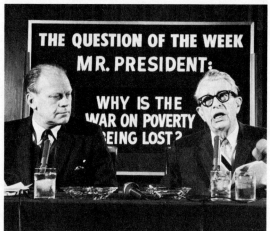

United Press Int.

House Minority Leader Ford appeared with Senate Minority Leader Everett M. Dirksen in a series of televised press conferences. Reporters nicknamed the series "The Ev and Jerry Show."

FORD'S CABINET

Secretary of State..................*Henry A. Kissinger

Secretary of the Treasury............*William E. Simon

Secretary of Defense................*James R. Schlesinger

Attorney General..................*William B. Saxbe

Secretary of the Interior............ Rogers C. B. Morton

Secretary of Agriculture.............*Earl L. Butz

Secretary of Commerce.............. Frederick B. Dent

Secretary of Labor.................. Peter J. Brennan

Secretary of Health,
    Education, and Welfare...........*Caspar Weinberger

Secretary of Housing and
    Urban Development..............*James T. Lynn

Secretary of Transportation.......... Claude S. Brinegar

---

*Has a biography in WORLD BOOK.

Sygma

Ford Took the Oath of Office As President on Aug. 9, 1974. Mrs. Betty Ford watched Warren E. Burger, chief justice of the United States, administer the oath in the East Room of the White House.

The National Scene. Ford sought to restore public faith in the government, and he promised to deal with issues openly and to cooperate with Congress. He received wide public support during his first month as President.

The Economy. Ford called inflation the nation's "public enemy Number 1." With quick congressional approval, he established the Council on Wage and Price Stability to expose any inflationary wage and price increases. Ford also proposed a one-year tax increase for corporations, families with incomes exceeding $15,000, and individuals with incomes over $7,500.

The Nixon Pardon severely hurt Ford's early popularity. On September 8, he pardoned Nixon for all federal crimes the former President might have committed as chief executive. Ford said he took the action to end divisions within the nation and to "heal the wounds that had festered too long." But the pardon angered millions of Americans. Many of them believed that the government should have brought Nixon to trial if it had enough evidence to do so. Many others felt

that Ford should not have granted the pardon until Nixon had admitted his involvement in the Watergate scandal.

The Amnesty Program was announced by Ford eight days after he pardoned Nixon. The new President offered amnesty to the approximately 28,000 draft dodgers and deserters of the Vietnam War period. The program required these men to work in a public service job for up to two years.

Foreign Affairs. Ford urged Turkey to return part of the territory it held on Cyprus to the Cypriot government. He offered United States assistance to work out a permanent peace settlement on the island. Ford also pledged to continue the policy started by Nixon to improve U.S. relations with both China and Russia.

JERALD F. terHORST

The White House

The President's Family in the White House. From left to right are sons John and Steven, Mrs. Ford, Ford, daughter Susan, and daughter-in-law Gayle and her husband, Michael.

Robert H. Glaze, Artstreet

The United States Capitol, in Washington, D.C., is the place where Congress makes the nation's laws. Tourists flock to this magnificent building to enjoy its beauty and to see Congress in action.

WASHINGTON, D.C.

WASHINGTON, D.C., is the capital and ninth largest city of the United States. It is also one of the country's most beautiful and historic cities and the site of many of its most popular tourist attractions.

As the nation's capital, Washington serves as the headquarters of the federal government. The President of the United States, the members of Congress, the Supreme Court justices, and about 375,000 other government employees work in Washington. Decisions made by government leaders in the city affect the lives of people throughout the United States and, sometimes, in other parts of the world. For example, the President suggests laws to Congress and directs U.S. relations with other countries. The members of Congress pass laws every American citizen must obey. The Supreme Court justices decide whether the government's laws and practices are constitutional.

Washington's role as the nation's capital makes it

The contributors of this article are Ronald W. Edsforth, Eunice S. Grier, and Atlee E. Shidler. All three contributors are members of the Washington Center for Metropolitan Studies in Washington, D.C.

important to the American people in another way. The city is a symbol of their country's unity, history, and democratic tradition.

Every year, millions of persons from all parts of the United States and from other countries visit Washington. They go there to see such important government buildings as the United States Capitol, where Congress meets, and the White House, where the President lives and works. They visit the Washington Monument, Lincoln Memorial, and other famous structures dedicated to American heroes of the past. They also tour the

--- FACTS IN BRIEF ---

Population: 756,510. *Metropolitan Area Population—* 2,909,316.

Area: 67 sq. mi. (174 km²). *Metropolitan Area—*2,907 sq. mi. (7,529 km²).

Altitude: 25 feet (7.6 meters) above sea level.

Climate: *Average Temperatures*—January, 37° F. (3° C); July, 78° F. (26° C). *Average Annual Precipitation* (rainfall, melted snow, and other forms of moisture)—50 in. (127 cm). For the monthly weather in Washington, D.C., see MARYLAND (Climate).

Government: Federal District under the authority of Congress. Mayor and city council, elected to four-year terms, help run the government.

Founded: Site chosen, 1791. Became capital, 1800.

city's many museums, which together house the world's largest collection of items from America's past.

Most of Washington's main government buildings, monuments, and museums stand in the west-central part of the city. This area ranks among the nation's most beautiful places. Many of its buildings and monuments are magnificent white marble structures. Scenic parks and gardens, and—in springtime—gorgeous blossoms of Japanese cherry trees, add natural beauty to the man-made splendor of the area.

Outside the west-central area, Washington is much like other big cities. It has large residential areas, including wealthy, middle-class, and poor sections. Suburbs spread out from the city in all directions. Washington faces problems common to all cities, including crime, poverty, traffic jams, and a shortage of good housing. Unlike most cities, Washington has no large industrial areas. This is so because government, rather than manufacturing, is the city's main business.

More than 70 per cent of the people who live in Washington are blacks. No other major American city has so large a percentage of black persons. In Washington's suburbs, however, whites account for more than 90 per cent of the population.

Washington lies in the southeastern United States, between Maryland and Virginia. It is the only American city or town that is not part of a state. It covers the entire area of the District of Columbia, a piece of land under the jurisdiction of the federal government.

Washington is one of the few cities in the world that was designed before it was built. President George Washington chose the city's site in 1791. He hired Pierre Charles L'Enfant, a French engineer, to draw up plans for the city. Washington replaced Philadelphia as the nation's capital in 1800. Congress named it in honor of George Washington. The *D.C.* in the city's name stands for *District of Columbia*.

WORLD BOOK map

Washington, D.C., the capital of the United States, lies between Maryland and Virginia on the east bank of the Potomac River.

Most of Washington's government buildings, famous monuments and museums, and other tourist attractions are located in the west-central part of the city. This area extends from Capitol Hill, which rises near the center of the city, westward to the Potomac River. This section describes the main features of the area. The fold-out map included in this edition of the YEAR BOOK, on pages 131, 132, and 133, provides an overview of it. The last part of the section deals with interesting sights in other parts of Washington and its suburbs. Many of Washington's points of interest also have separate articles in WORLD BOOK.

This section also tells—in general terms—about the activities of the federal government. But for much greater detail, see the article UNITED STATES, GOVERNMENT OF, and its list of *Related Articles*.

Capitol Hill

Capitol Hill rises 88 feet (26.8 meters) near the center of Washington. Several huge government buildings stand on the hill. They include the United States Capitol, congressional office buildings, the Library of Congress, the Supreme Court Building, and the conservatory of the United States Botanic Garden. The Folger Shakespeare Library and the Museum of African Art—both private institutions—are also on the hill.

United States Capitol is the place where the members of Congress meet to discuss and vote on proposed legislation. The Capitol ranks among Washington's most magnificent buildings. Many tall Corinthian columns and an enormous dome beautify its white marble exterior. A bronze Statue of Freedom 19½ feet (5.94 meters) high stands on top of the dome. The Capitol, including the statue, rises almost 300 feet (91 meters) above the ground. The Capitol has 540 rooms. Many of them contain beautiful paintings, sculptures, and wall carvings that portray events and persons important in American history. Such works of art, along with gorgeous furnishings, give the interior of the Capitol the splendor of a fine museum or a palace.

Many persons visit the Capitol just to enjoy its beauty and its reminders of the country's past. But visitors may also attend sessions of Congress. To do so, however, they must first get a pass from one of the persons who represent them in Congress.

Congressional Office Buildings. Five buildings provide office space for the members of Congress. They are the Dirksen and Russell Senate office buildings, both north of the Capitol; and the Cannon, Longworth, and Rayburn House of Representatives office buildings, south of the Capitol. The members of Congress welcome visits to their offices by people they represent.

Library of Congress is probably the world's largest library. Its collection of more than 60 million items includes books, manuscripts, films, and recordings. The collection is housed in an enormous gray sandstone main building and a white marble annex, both located east of the Capitol.

The library serves the reference needs of Congress. The public may also use its materials and tour the buildings. The library's many items of special interest to tourists include most of Mathew Brady's Civil War

Milt & Joan Mann

The Capitol's Great Rotunda, or room under its dome, contains many works of art related to American history. These works include paintings of important events and statues of famous people.

Milt & Joan Mann

The Supreme Court Building resembles a Greek temple. In a courtroom inside, the Supreme Court justices make legal decisions that may affect the lives of every American.

photographs, a Gutenberg Bible printed in the 1450's, and one of the original copies of Abraham Lincoln's Gettysburg Address.

Supreme Court Building also stands east of the Capitol. In this building, the nine justices of the Supreme Court of the United States decide on the constitutionality of laws, government practices, and decisions of lower courts.

The white marble exterior of the Supreme Court Building resembles a Greek temple. The room where the justices hear cases is decorated with long, red drapes, copper gates, and marble columns. Visitors may attend sessions of the court. But seating is limited, and is available on a first-come, first-served basis.

United States Botanic Garden is located on the southwest side of Capitol Hill. It exhibits more than 10,000 kinds of plants. The plants include many rare species.

Folger Shakespeare Library, east of the Library of Congress, houses the world's most important collection of works by and about William Shakespeare. Only scholars may use its materials. But the library displays rare books and manuscripts for public viewing.

Museum of African Art is located about 2 blocks east of the Supreme Court. It exhibits sculptures and other works of art that reflect African Negro culture. It also displays works by black American artists.

The Mall

A long, narrow, parklike area stretches westward from Capitol Hill. Called *the Mall*, it provides open space amid west-central Washington's many huge buildings.

It is also the location of some of the city's leading tourist attractions.

Several outstanding museums that are part of the Smithsonian Institution stand along the Mall a little west of Capitol Hill. Farther west are the Washington Monument and Lincoln Memorial. A long, narrow body of water called the *Reflecting Pool* lies between these two magnificent structures. Mirrorlike reflections of the monument and memorial can be seen in the pool's water. The Jefferson Memorial lies south of the Washington Monument. The memorial overlooks a lagoon called the *Tidal Basin*. Hundreds of Japanese cherry trees encircle the basin. In springtime, gorgeous pink and white cherry blossoms bloom on the trees. They create a sight of magnificent natural beauty that attracts huge crowds of visitors. The period when the trees are likely to be in bloom is set aside for a festival called the *Cherry Blossom Festival*. Other parts of Washington also have beautiful cherry trees.

Smithsonian Museums. The Smithsonian Institution is a government corporation that operates cultural, educational, and scientific facilities throughout Washington. The facilities include several museums on the Mall that house a total of more than 60 million items. Among the items in the museums are many of the world's greatest paintings, objects of importance to American history, and countless objects from the everyday life of America's past.

The original building of the Smithsonian Institution, called the *Smithsonian Building*, is one of the Mall's most impressive structures. Formerly a museum, it now houses the institution's offices. But the building remains a tourist attraction because it resembles a medieval castle. The names of the Smithsonian museums and some highlights of their collections follow.

National Air and Space Museum has exhibits that trace the history of flight. Its attractions include the airplane Orville Wright used in making man's first successful flight, and the one in which Charles Lindbergh made the first solo flight across the Atlantic Ocean. The exhibits also include spacecraft that carried American astronauts into outer space and rocks that astronauts brought back from the moon.

National Museum of History and Technology displays the flag that inspired Francis Scott Key to write the national anthem. It has large collections of historical automobiles, railroad trains, and industrial machinery. It also houses an enormous collection of everyday objects from the past, including clothing, kitchen utensils, and home furnishings.

National Museum of Natural History exhibits stuffed animals from many parts of the world and skeletons of prehistoric animals. It has lifelike exhibits that show how American Indians and Eskimos lived long ago. The museum also features an outstanding gem collection, which includes the famous Hope Diamond.

Art Museums. Three of the Smithsonian museums on the Mall are art galleries. The *National Gallery of Art* houses a world-famous collection of paintings and sculptures by Americans and Europeans. The *Hirshhorn Museum and Sculpture Garden* has an outstanding collection of modern American works of art. The *Freer Gallery*

Herbert Fristedt from Carl Östman

Visitors to the Air and Space Museum view space vehicles, above. The museum, a part of the Smithsonian Institution, also exhibits the Wright Brothers' first airplane and other early planes.

of Art features one of the world's finest collections of Oriental art.

The Smithsonian Institution also operates art museums in other parts of Washington. Its Fine Arts and Portrait Galleries Building, at 7th and F streets a few blocks north of the Mall, houses two outstanding museums. They are the *National Collection of Fine Arts*, which surveys American art from colonial days to the present; and the *National Portrait Gallery*, which includes hundreds of paintings of persons important in American history. The Smithsonian's Renwick Gallery, at 17th Street and Pennsylvania Avenue also north of the Mall, features exhibits of American crafts, design, and decorative art.

Paul S. Conklin

A Guide at the National Gallery of Art describes a famous painting to schoolchildren. One of the world's leading art museums, the gallery is part of the Smithsonian Institution.

Dean Brown from Nancy Palmer   Robert H. Glaze, Artstreet   Milt & Joan Mann

Monuments to Three American Presidents are located on the Mall. The Jefferson Memorial, *left,* stands among Japanese cherry trees at the edge of the Tidal Basin. The towering Washington Monument, *center,* ranks as the city's tallest structure. The majestic Lincoln Memorial, *right,* has a famous statue of Lincoln inside.

Washington Monument is a tall, slender, white marble *obelisk* (pillar) dedicated to the memory of George Washington. The city's tallest structure, it rises 555 feet $5\frac{1}{8}$ inches (169.29 meters). An elevator inside the monument carries visitors to the top. From there, a person can see much of the Washington area.

Lincoln Memorial is a templelike white marble monument that honors Abraham Lincoln. On the outside, 36 Doric columns—one for each state that existed when Lincoln died—support the roof. Inside the monument is a majestic marble statue of Lincoln seated in a chair. Paintings that symbolize Lincoln's accomplishments, and quotations from Lincoln's writings, appear on the interior walls.

Jefferson Memorial honors Thomas Jefferson. It is a circular white marble structure ringed by 26 Ionic columns and topped by a beautiful dome. A bronze statue of Jefferson stands inside. Quotations from Jefferson's writings appear on the walls.

North of the Mall

Many huge government buildings crowd the area north of the Mall. Most of them stand along or near Pennsylvania Avenue. This broad, tree-lined street runs northwestward from Capitol Hill. It connects the Capitol and the White House, and serves as Washington's main parade route.

The White House ranks as the most important government building in the area. Most of the other buildings house offices of the executive branch of the government. The executive branch, headed by the President, is responsible for carrying out government policies. It includes the Executive Office of the President, 11 executive departments, and many government agencies.

Several nongovernment organizations—including the American Red Cross, the Daughters of the American Revolution (DAR), the National Academy of Sciences, and the World Bank—have their headquarters near the government buildings. Also nearby are two major tourist attractions—Ford's Theatre and the John F. Kennedy Center for the Performing Arts. Watergate, a group of luxurious apartment and office buildings, stands near the Kennedy Center. It gained national fame in 1972 when campaign workers for President Richard M. Nixon, a Republican, were caught breaking into Democratic political headquarters there.

White House, at 1600 Pennsylvania Avenue, has served as the home and office of every United States President except George Washington. Some of the world's most historic decisions have been made in the building.

The White House is constructed of white sandstone and has 132 rooms. Five of the rooms are open to the public. They are the Blue Room, East Room, Green Room, Red Room, and State Dining Room. These rooms are famous for their magnificent works of art and furnishings. Visitors are not allowed in the rooms where the President lives and works. But occasionally, the President or a member of his family stops by to greet tourists in the public rooms.

The White House stands on a beautifully land-

Robert H. Glaze, Artstreet

The White House has been the home and office of every United States President with the exception of George Washington. The picture above shows the south side of the White House.

scaped plot that covers 18 acres (7.3 hectares). Lafayette Square lies north of the White House grounds and the Ellipse lies to the south. These parklike areas, together with the White House grounds, are sometimes called the *President's Square*, or *Park*. Blair House, a mansion on the west side of Lafayette Square, serves as a guesthouse for high-ranking foreign officials who come to visit the President. President Harry S. Truman lived in Blair House from 1948 to 1952, while the White House was being repaired.

Executive Branch Buildings. The main Executive Office Building stands directly west of the White House. An additional Executive Office Building is located north of the main building. Many of the President's closest advisers work in these buildings. The headquarters of the Department of the Treasury, one of the

government's executive departments, lies just east of the White House.

Several huge executive branch buildings stand close together on the south side of Pennsylvania Avenue between the White House and the Capitol. This group of buildings is called the *Federal Triangle* because it forms the shape of a triangle. It includes the headquarters of the executive departments of Commerce and Justice. It also contains the following federal government agencies: the Bureau of Customs, Federal Trade Commission, Internal Revenue Service, Interstate Commerce Commission, National Archives, and United States Postal Service.

The Department of Labor—an executive department—and the headquarters of the Federal Bureau of Investigation (FBI) lie north of Pennsylvania Avenue between the White House and the Capitol. Two other executive departments—the Department of State and the Department of the Interior—lie several blocks southwest of the White House.

Almost all the executive departments and agencies offer tours of their buildings. Especially popular are the tours of the National Archives and the FBI. The National Archives stores government documents. It displays three of the most important documents for public viewing. These are the original copies of the United States Constitution, the Bill of Rights, and the Declaration of Independence. At the FBI, bureau agents conduct tours that feature highlights of the agency's history and show how the FBI works today. The tours end with a demonstration of agents taking target practice.

Ford's Theatre, the playhouse where Abraham Lincoln was shot, stands about $1\frac{1}{2}$ blocks north of Pennsylvania Avenue, between the White House and Capitol. The theater houses a collection of items related to Lincoln's life and death. The house where Lincoln died, called *Petersen House*, is located across the street from the theater.

John F. Kennedy Center for the Performing Arts borders the Potomac River north of the Mall. Dramatic groups, ballet and opera companies, and orchestras from all parts of the world perform in the modern building. The Kennedy Center also serves as the permanent residence of the American Ballet Theatre and the National Symphony Orchestra. Performances at the center attract large crowds. Thousands of people also visit the center to honor the memory of President Kennedy, to whom it is dedicated.

South of the Mall

Originally, almost all the executive branch buildings were located near the White House. But the executive branch has grown tremendously and has spread out to other parts of Washington. Several government buildings now stand south of the Mall. They include the buildings of the three newest executive departments—Health, Education, and Welfare; Housing and Urban Development; and Transportation. The Department of Agriculture also lies south of the Mall.

The Bureau of Engraving and Printing ranks as the major tourist attraction south of the Mall. There, government workers engrave and print the country's paper

Dennis Brack, Black Star

John F. Kennedy Center for the Performing Arts features concerts, *above*, as well as ballets, operas, and plays. Its activities help make Washington a leading cultural center.

money. Large crowds of visitors flock to the bureau to see these fascinating processes.

Other Points of Interest

The Washington area has dozens of interesting sights in addition to those already described and shown on the foldout map. Some of the most famous ones appear below. Others are included under *The City* section later in this article.

National Zoological Park is a zoo about 2 miles (3 kilometers) north of the White House. The zoo contains about 3,000 animals. The animals include two pandas that the Chinese government gave to the United States in 1972.

Pentagon Building, the headquarters of the Department of Defense, ranks as the world's largest office building. It covers 29 acres (11.7 hectares) in Arlington, Va., across the Potomac from Washington.

Arlington National Cemetery, northwest of the Pentagon in Arlington, contains the graves of thousands of persons who served in the United States armed forces. It includes the Tomb of the Unknowns, where three unidentified servicemen who died in action are buried. It also includes the gravesite of President John F. Kennedy.

Marine Corps War Memorial, north of Arlington Cemetery, ranks among Washington's most famous monuments. Often called the *Iwo Jima Statue*, this dramatic bronze sculpture shows five marines and a Navy medical corpsman raising the American flag on the island of Iwo Jima during World War II.

Mount Vernon was the private estate of George Washington. It lies in Fairfax County, Virginia, about 15 miles (24 kilometers) south of the city. The first President's home and grave are there.

Other Museums. Washington has many outstanding museums in addition to the Smithsonian museums and the Museum of African Art. Two of the most famous ones are the Corcoran Gallery of Art and the Phillips

Paul S. Conklin

Arlington National Cemetery, in Arlington, Va., includes the gravesite of President John F. Kennedy, *foreground.* Thousands of men and women who served in the armed forces are buried there.

James H. Pickerell

The Marine Corps War Memorial shows servicemen raising the American flag on Iwo Jima during World War II. It stands in Arlington, Va., across the Potomac River from Washington.

Collection. The Corcoran Gallery, about 2 blocks southwest of the White House, displays masterpieces by American painters. The Phillips Collection, at 21st and Q streets about 10 blocks northwest of the White House, houses works by artists from El Greco to the present.

Architectural Styles. Many visitors to Washington enjoy the rich and varied architecture of the city's buildings and monuments. Several structures, including the Capitol, Supreme Court Building, and Lincoln Memorial are built in the classical architectural style of ancient Greece and Rome. Washington Cathedral, an Episcopal church at Massachusetts and Wisconsin avenues in northwestern Washington, features the Gothic style of medieval Europe. The National Shrine of the Immaculate Conception, near 4th Street and Michigan Avenue in northeastern Washington, has elements of two other medieval styles—Byzantine and Romanesque. The *mosque* (Moslem house of worship) of the Islamic Center is a fine example of the Islamic style of architecture. It stands along Massachusetts Avenue near Belmont Road in the northwestern part of the city.

Many buildings in Georgetown, a neighborhood northwest of the White House, provide examples of colonial American architecture. Some of the city's newest office and apartment buildings reflect modern American architecture. But a law limits the height of buildings in the city. As a result, Washington—unlike most other large cities—has no skyscrapers.

Washington, D.C., lies along the east bank of the Potomac River. The city covers 67 square miles (174 square kilometers) and has a population of 756,510. The state of Maryland borders Washington on the north, east, and south. Virginia lies across the Potomac River to the west and south.

Suburban communities of Maryland and Virginia surround Washington. The city and its suburbs form a metropolitan area that covers 2,907 square miles (7,529 square kilometers) and has a population of 2,909,316.

The United States Capitol stands near the center of Washington. Broad streets extend out from the Capitol in all directions like the spokes of a wheel. They include North Capitol Street, which runs north from the Capitol; East Capitol Street, which runs east; and South Capitol Street, which runs south. These three streets, together with the Mall that extends westward from the Capitol, divide Washington into four sections. The sections are *Northwest*, *Northeast*, *Southeast*, and *Southwest*. Each of the sections is named for its direction from the Capitol.

Each address in Washington is followed by one of four abbreviations that tells what section of the city the address is in. The abbreviations and their meanings

Paul S. Conklin

Apartment Buildings line the streets of many Washington neighborhoods. Large numbers of Washington's black residents live in neighborhoods similar to the one above.

are: *NW* (Northwest), *NE* (Northeast), *SE* (Southeast), and *SW* (Southwest).

Northwest Section includes the part of Washington between North Capitol Street and the south end of the Mall. Washington's largest section, it covers almost half the city's area and has almost half of its people. The Northwest section is also Washington's main center of cultural, economic, and government activity.

The southern part of Northwest Washington includes the White House and the many government buildings near it, the Smithsonian museums, and the Washington Monument and Lincoln Memorial. For detailed information on this part of the city, see the *Visitor's Guide* section in this article.

Washington's main shopping district lies in the Northwest section, just to the north of Pennsylvania Avenue between the White House and the Capitol. In this district, department stores and small specialty shops serve the shopping needs of residents and tourists alike.

West of the shopping district, Rock Creek Park winds through Northwest Washington in a north-south direction. The official residence of the Vice-President of the United States is located on the grounds of the Naval Observatory near the park. Dozens of embassies of countries that have diplomatic relations with the United States are also near the park.

Large residential areas lie west and east of the park. Georgetown, an area to the west, ranks among the nation's wealthiest places. It is famous for its beautiful old houses—some dating from the 1700's—and for its small shops that sell antiques and other luxury items. Other residential areas in the Northwest section of the city include high-income, middle-income, and low-income neighborhoods.

Four of the city's largest universities have their campuses in Northwest Washington. These schools are American, George Washington, Georgetown, and Howard universities.

Milt & Joan Mann

Georgetown, a wealthy neighborhood in Northwest Washington, has fine examples of early American architecture. Many of its buildings are 100 to 200 years old, but in excellent condition.

Northeast Section lies between North Capitol and East Capitol streets. It covers about a fourth of the city and has about a fourth of its people. Northeast is chiefly a residential area, and has both middle-class and low-income neighborhoods.

The Museum of African Art and other institutions dedicated to promoting black culture stand near the Capitol in the Northeast section. The campus of Catholic University of America—the national university of the Roman Catholic Church—lies about 3 miles (5 kilometers) north of the Capitol in the section.

The Anacostia River cuts through Northeast Washington east of the Capitol. The National Arboretum and the Kenilworth Aquatic Gardens lie along the river. The arboretum contains trees and shrubs from many parts of the world. The Kenilworth Gardens includes numerous ponds filled with colorful water plants.

Southeast Section is the area between East Capitol and South Capitol streets. It covers about a fourth of

the city and has about a fourth of its people. A wealthy residential neighborhood of luxury apartments and restored old houses lies close to the Capitol in the Southeast section. It also extends into the Northeast. Nearby is an old-fashioned market called the *Eastern Market*. Farmers from miles around the city come to the market to sell such products as fresh fruits and vegetables, cider, eggs, and flowers. Merchants offer bakery products, meat cut to order, and other goods.

The Anacostia River winds through the section farther south. The area south of the river, called *Anacostia*, includes many crowded and run-down sections.

Southwest Section extends from South Capitol Street to the south end of the Mall. Washington's smallest section, it covers about an eighth of the city's land and has only about 4 per cent of its people. Almost all of Southwest Washington has been rebuilt since the 1950's as part of a major urban renewal program. As a result, the section has many relatively new houses and apartment

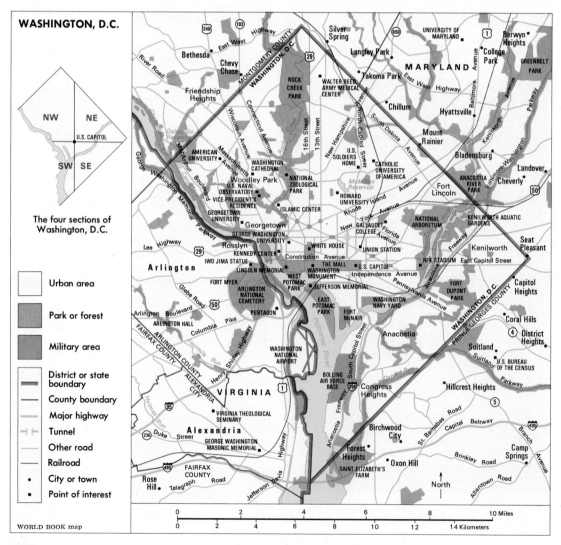

WASHINGTON, D.C.

The four sections of Washington, D.C.

Urban area

Park or forest

Military area

District or state boundary

County boundary

Major highway

Tunnel

Other road

Railroad

• City or town

▪ Point of interest

WORLD BOOK map

and office buildings. The government's three newest executive departments—Health, Education, and Welfare; Housing and Urban Development; and Transportation—are there.

Metropolitan Area. The Washington metropolitan area, as defined by the federal government, includes the city; Charles, Montgomery, and Prince Georges counties in Maryland; Arlington, Fairfax, Loudoun, and Prince William counties in Virginia; and three Virginia cities that are not part of a county—Alexandria, Fairfax, and Falls Church.

The counties of Washington's metropolitan area include both suburban cities and towns and large open areas of hills, woods, and farms. Most of the suburban cities and towns are under the jurisdiction of the counties in which they are located.

In the Washington area, as in other metropolitan areas, thousands of persons who live in the suburbs work in the city. But during the 1900's, many government agencies have moved from the city to the suburbs. Also, many private businesses have been established in the suburbs. As a result, large numbers of people—from both the city and the suburbs—work in the suburbs. For example, more than 25,000 persons work for the Department of Defense in the Pentagon in Arlington, Va. Other large government agencies in the suburbs include the National Institutes of Health and the Naval Hospital in Bethesda, Md.; the Central Intelligence Agency in McLean, Va.; and the Bureau of the Census in Suitland, Md.

James H. Pickerell

Single-Family Houses line a curving street in the Washington suburb of Bethesda, Md. Thousands of people in the Washington area live in suburbs and commute to jobs in the city.

The Washington metropolitan area includes two of the most famous *new towns* in the United States— Columbia, Md., and Reston, Va. Begun during the early 1960's, these two communities were carefully planned before they were built (see CITY PLANNING [Building New Communities]).

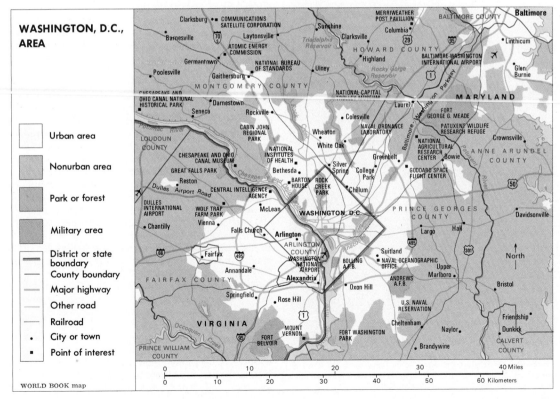

WASHINGTON, D.C., AREA

Urban area

Nonurban area

Park or forest

Military area

District or state boundary
County boundary
Major highway
Other road
Railroad
• City or town
▪ Point of interest

WORLD BOOK map

About 71 per cent of Washington's people are blacks. No other major American city has so large a percentage of black persons. Whites make up about 28 per cent of the city's population. The other 1 per cent includes small groups of American Indians and Asians—especially Chinese, Filipinos, and Japanese.

The racial makeup of Washington's suburbs contrasts sharply with that of the city. In the suburbs, about 91 per cent of the people are whites, and only about 8 per cent are blacks. American Indians, Asians, and members of other races account for the other 1 per cent of the suburban population.

About 20,000 persons who live in Washington are citizens of countries other than the United States. Many of these people work for foreign embassies or such international organizations in the city as the Organization of American States and the World Bank. The foreign population includes people from almost every country in the world, and gives the city a *cosmopolitan* (international) flavor.

Ethnic Groups. Washington differs from most big cities in that it has only one large ethnic group—blacks. More than 535,000 black persons live in the city. Blacks make up a majority of the population in each of Washington's four sections. They account for about 91 per cent of the population in Northeast Washington, 87

Robert H. Glaze, Artstreet

Black Washingtonians visit an art exhibit at Howard University, *above*. Washington has a higher percentage of black persons than any other major American city, more than 70 per cent.

per cent in Southeast, 57 per cent in Southwest, and 53 per cent in Northwest.

Thousands of Washington's blacks live in neighborhoods made up almost entirely of people of their own race. The neighborhoods range from poor, to middle-income, to upper-income ones. Many black Washingtonians also live in middle- and upper-income racially integrated areas, both in the city and the suburbs.

About 210,000 white persons live in Washington. In many cities, large numbers of whites of the same ethnic group—such as persons of Irish, Italian, or Polish ancestry—live together in the same neighborhoods. But Washington does not have such ethnic neighborhoods. Its predominantly white neighborhoods are made up of people of many ethnic backgrounds.

Housing. About half of Washington's people live in one- or two-family houses, and about half live in apartment buildings. Only about 28 per cent of Washington's families own their homes. The others rent them. The national average for the percentage of families in cities who own their homes is about 48 per cent.

Washington has some of the nation's most luxurious housing, including the Watergate apartments and the mansions and town houses of Georgetown. It also has much good middle-class housing. However, the city faces a shortage of good housing for low-income, as well as middle-income, families. This housing shortage exists in both the city and the suburbs, and ranks among the Washington area's biggest problems.

Several factors make the housing problem difficult to solve. Each year, some housing units become so run-down that people abandon them, thus reducing the number of usable low-income units. Also, such developments as urban renewal projects sometimes involve replacing housing units with higher income units, or with business or government buildings. In addition, since the 1960's, the cost of housing has risen faster in Washington than in most parts of the country. Rising costs fur-

Paul S. Conklin

Embassy Officials from many nations mix at a party at the Argentine Embassy, *above*. Washington's many embassies give the city a *cosmopolitan* (international) flavor.

ther reduce the amount of housing available to people with low and middle incomes.

Education. The Washington public school system includes about 175 schools with more than 130,000 students. An additional 25,000 students attend about 80 private schools in the city.

The District of Columbia Board of Education governs the public school system. The board consists of 11 members elected by the people to four-year terms. The board members appoint a superintendent to serve as chief administrator of the school system. About 75 per cent of the money needed to run Washington's public schools comes from local taxes, and about 25 per cent from the federal government.

Washington has 10 accredited, four-year universities and colleges. One of them, Howard University, ranks as one of the country's largest predominantly black universities. Another one, Catholic University of America, is the national university of the Roman Catholic Church in the United States.

Social Problems. Washington, like other cities, faces a variety of social problems. Among them are poverty and crime.

Overall, the people of Washington have a high standard of living. But thousands of people in both the city and suburbs do not share in the wealth. About 13 per cent of all the families in the city and about 4 per cent of the families in the suburbs have incomes that classify them as poor by federal government standards. In Washington as elsewhere, poverty affects blacks more than whites. About 15 per cent of all the black families in the metropolitan area are poor, compared to about 4 per cent of all the white families.

Paul S. Conklin

A Soccer Game on the Mall provides recreation for a group of Washington young people, *above.* The Washington Monument rises above the trees in the background.

UNIVERSITIES AND COLLEGES

Washington, D.C., has 10 universities and colleges accredited by the Middle States Association of Colleges and Secondary Schools. For enrollments and further information, see UNIVERSITIES AND COLLEGES (table).

Name	Founded
American University	1893
Catholic University of America	1887
Federal City College	1968
Gallaudet College	1864
George Washington University	1821
Georgetown University	1789
Howard University	1867
Mount Vernon College	1968
Oblate College	1958
Trinity College	1897

Most crime in the Washington area takes place in the city, especially in poor neighborhoods. But in recent years, crime rates have been rising more rapidly in the suburbs than in the city.

Washington's crime problem receives more nation-wide publicity than that of any other city with the possible exception of New York City. Whenever a government official is the victim of a crime, the news is carried throughout the country by the news media. As a result of such publicity, many persons believe Washington has the highest, or one of the highest, crime rates in the nation. This is not so, however. More than 60 metropolitan areas have a higher crime rate than the Washington area. Over a dozen metropolitan areas lead Washington in the rate of violent crimes, such as assault and murder.

Cultural Life and Recreation. The museums, government buildings, monuments, libraries, parks, and theaters described under *A Visitor's Guide* help make Washington a leading cultural and recreational center. The people of Washington as well as tourists enjoy these facilities.

Washington also has many cultural and recreational facilities used chiefly by its residents. These include a public library system with about 2 million volumes. The system includes a main library and about 20 branch libraries. The main library is the Martin Luther King Memorial Library at 9th and G streets NW. Washington has many neighborhood museums, including some that specialize in exhibits that reflect black culture. The city's main playhouses—in addition to the famous Kennedy Center—include the National Theatre at 13th and E streets NW, and the Arena Stage at 6th and M streets SW.

Washington has about 150 parks. The people use the parks for such purposes as picnics, and baseball, touch football, and soccer games. Many Washingtonians enjoy sailing on the Potomac River. Many also enjoy spectator sports. Three professional sports teams perform in the Washington area. The Washington Redskins of the National Football League play in the Robert F. Kennedy, or RFK, Stadium, about 2 miles (3 kilometers) east of the Capitol. The Washington Bullets of the National Basketball Association and the Washington Capitals of the National Hockey League play in the Capital Centre, in Largo, Md.

Washington's economy is based on the activities of the federal government. The government employs more of the Washington area's workers than does any kind of private business. It also generates much of Washington's private economic activity.

The Federal Government provides jobs for about 375,000 persons in Washington and its suburbs, or about a fourth of all the area's workers. The best-known and most important government employees include the President and his close advisers, the members of Congress, and the Supreme Court justices. But these key policy-making officials account for only a small portion of Washington's government workers. Hundreds of lower-ranking officials help carry out the day-to-day operations of the government. Thousands of office workers—including accountants, clerks, secretaries, and typists—assist them.

Private Business. The government's attractions make Washington one of the world's leading centers of tourism. Every year, about 20 million tourists visit the city to see the government in action and to enjoy its many interesting and historic sights. The money the tourists spend accounts for Washington's largest source of income other than the government's payroll. It helps support—and provides jobs in—many hotels, motels, restaurants, and other businesses.

Many other economically important businesses and private organizations are located in Washington chiefly because the government is there. They include law offices and research companies that do work for the government. They also include dozens of labor unions and professional organizations that have their headquarters in the city so they can try to influence government policies in the best interests of their members. Such businesses and organizations, as well as the city's tourist-oriented businesses, are called *service industries* because they provide service rather than produce goods. Altogether, service industries employ about 20 per cent of the Washington area's workers. The construction industry and wholesale and retail trade also provide many jobs.

Manufacturing—or the production of goods—is far less important in Washington than it is in most large cities. Only about 5 per cent of the area's labor force works in manufacturing industries. Printing and publishing firms employ most of them.

Transportation. Automobiles provide the main means of transportation within Washington and between the city and its suburbs. About 80 per cent of the people who work in the Washington area use cars to get to and from their jobs. The government has built several superhighways to handle the heavy automobile traffic. Even so, huge traffic jams often occur during morning and evening rush hours.

The Washington Metropolitan Transit Authority, a public corporation, provides public transportation in Washington. Called *Metro*, it operates a bus service throughout the city and its suburbs. In 1969, Congress passed legislation providing for a subway system to be operated by Metro. Scheduled for completion by 1980, the subway will extend throughout the city and well into the suburbs.

James H. Pickerell

Government Workers jam Pennsylvania Avenue, above, on their way to and from work. The federal government employs about a fourth of all the workers in the Washington area.

Three major airports handle Washington's commercial air traffic. Washington National Airport lies just across the Potomac River in Virginia. Dulles International Airport, also in Virginia, lies about 25 miles (40 kilometers) west of the city. Baltimore-Washington International Airport (formerly Friendship International) is in Maryland, about 30 miles (48 kilometers) northeast of Washington.

Union Station, a railroad terminal, lies north of the Capitol. It serves passenger trains that run between Washington and other parts of the country. The station also houses the National Visitor Center. Workers at the center advise visitors on what to see in Washington and how to find their way around the city.

Communication. Washington ranks as a leading communication center. Many of the world's major newspapers, magazines, and radio and television networks have permanent correspondents in the city. These newsmen provide their readers, listeners, and viewers with firsthand reports on government activities.

The government makes Washington one of the nation's chief publishing centers. Its departments and agencies produce pamphlets and books on thousands of subjects. The subjects range from census information to how to solve farm problems and where to go for medical help.

Two national magazines are published in Washington. They are *National Geographic Magazine* and *U.S. News & World Report*.

Washington has two general daily newspapers, the morning *Washington Post* and the afternoon *Washington Star-News*. Seven television stations and 18 radio stations serve the Washington area.

WASHINGTON, D.C. / Local Government

Washington has an unusual local government. As in many cities, the people elect a mayor and a city council to make laws and carry out government functions. But the federal government has final authority in all matters relating to Washington's government.

The mayor serves a four-year term. He is responsible for the administration of the government. He appoints the heads of the city's local government departments, such as the police and sanitation departments. He also prepares the city's budget and proposes local laws.

Washington's city council has 13 members. Five of the council's members—including its chairman—are elected in citywide elections. In addition, one councilman is elected from each of Washington's eight election districts. All councilmen serve four-year terms.

The city council passes local laws. But Congress also has the power to make laws for the city, including ones that overrule council decisions. The council approves the mayor's budget. But Congress and the Office of Management and Budget section of the Executive Office of the President must approve the budget.

The mayor can *veto* (reject) legislation passed by the city council. The council can *override* (set aside) a veto with a two-thirds majority vote of those voting on the question. But the President of the United States can reject council actions to override vetoes.

Washington's Flag was adopted in 1938. Its colors and design are based on George Washington's coat of arms.

The City Seal, adopted in 1871, shows Justice placing a wreath on a statue of George Washington.

Washington's city government has an annual budget of more than $1 billion. The city gets about two-thirds of its income from taxes, including property, sales, and local income taxes. The federal government provides most of the rest of the income.

Washington's present system of local government was established by an act of Congress in 1973 and approved by the people in 1974. For 100 years before that time, the people of Washington had almost no voice in their government. The President, rather than the people, chose the city's mayor and councilmen. See the *History* section of this article for details.

WASHINGTON, D.C. / History

The first people known to have lived in the Washington area were Piscataway Indians. Whites moved into the area during the late 1600's and established farms and plantations there. In 1749, settlers founded Alexandria, the area's first town, in what was then the colony of Virginia.

Washington Becomes the Capital. Several different cities served as the national capital during the early years of the United States (see UNITED STATES CAPITALS). In 1783, Congress decided that the country should have a permanent center of government. But the states could not agree on a location for it. People assumed that the new capital would become an important commercial and industrial city. As a result, each state wanted it to be located within its borders. Also, both Northerners and Southerners believed the capital should be in their part of the country.

In 1790, Secretary of the Treasury Alexander Hamilton worked out a solution. He proposed that the capital be built on land that belonged to the federal government, rather than to a state. Hamilton and others persuaded Northern political leaders to agree to locate the capital in the South. In return, Southern leaders supported certain government policies favored by the North.

Once the disagreements were settled, Congress decided to locate the capital along the Potomac River. It asked President George Washington, who had been raised in the Potomac area, to choose the exact site.

The President's choice, made in 1791, included not only the land now occupied by Washington, but also about 30 square miles (78 square kilometers) of land

west of the Potomac. The city's present territory had belonged to Maryland, and the land west of the river was part of Virginia. The two states turned over the territory to the federal government.

Early Days. George Washington hired Pierre Charles L'Enfant, a French engineer, to create a plan for the

Detail from an engraving by Andrew Ellicott (1792); Library of Congress, Geography and Map Division

Pierre L'Enfant's Plan for the city of Washington showed the location of the Capitol, White House, and Mall. President George Washington hired L'Enfant, a French engineer, to plan the city.

View of the Capitol at Washington, D.C., a hand-tinted engraving by C. J. Bentley after a painting by W. H. Bartlett; from *American Scenery*, published in 1840 by George Virtue

Pennsylvania Avenue in 1827 was a quiet dirt road. The Capitol, *background,* had a different dome and was smaller than it is today. The present Capitol design dates from the 1850's.

physical layout of the city. L'Enfant's plan dealt only with the area between the Anacostia River and Georgetown. But it established the pattern for the entire city. It made the Capitol the center of Washington. It also provided for the Mall, the broad streets that extend out from the Capitol, and many parks.

The federal government moved to Washington from its temporary capital in Philadelphia in 1800. At that time, the entire Washington area had only about 8,000 people. In 1814, during the War of 1812, British soldiers captured Washington. They burned the Capitol, the White House, and other government buildings. Reconstruction of the buildings was completed in 1819.

The Constitution of the United States gave Congress the power to govern Washington. But in 1802, Congress established a local government to help run the city. The government included a mayor and a city council. The people of Washington were given the right to elect the council members in 1802 and the mayor in 1820, but they were not allowed to vote for members of Congress or the President.

The predictions that Washington would become an important commercial and industrial center did not come true. The city could not compete economically with such long-established cities as Boston, New York, Philadelphia, Baltimore, and Charleston. Lacking economic growth, Washington remained a small city. By the 1840's, it had only about 50,000 people, and only a small part of its present area was built up. As a result,

in 1846, Congress returned to Virginia the land that the state had earlier given to the federal government.

Growth and Development. Washington's main periods of growth have been times of crisis, such as wars and depressions. During such times, the role of the federal government has been greatly expanded to help meet the crises. Large numbers of people moved to the city to handle jobs resulting from the government's growth.

The Civil War (1861-1865) was the first crisis that caused Washington to grow. During the war, the city's

The East Room, a woodcut by Benson J. Lossing, from *The Pictorial Field Book of the Civil War* (1878); Library of Congress

Union Soldiers camped in the East Room of the White House during the Civil War. They and thousands of other troops were stationed in Washington to guard it in case of Confederate attack.

Wide World

Demonstrations have long been held in Washington by people protesting government policies. These marchers are part of the Bonus Army, which demonstrated in 1932 to demand early payment of a government bonus for World War I veterans.

population soared from about 60,000 to 120,000. The Union stationed thousands of troops in Washington to protect the city from Confederate attacks. Large numbers of people flocked to the city to help direct the Union's war effort. In addition, thousands of black slaves who had been freed during the war moved to the city to find a new way of life. The enormous population growth caused by the Civil War led to a severe housing shortage in Washington. In addition, the city's streets, sewer and water systems, and other public facilities could not handle the increased population.

Congress began a major rebuilding and expansion program in Washington after the war. The program solved the city's physical problems. But it indirectly led to an end of the people's right to choose their government leaders. Congress believed that a reorganization of Washington's local government was necessary for a successful rebuilding program. At first, in 1871, it established a territorial government that included a governor appointed by the President, and an elected assembly. Then, in 1874, Congress established a local government made up of three commissioners, who were appointed by the President. As a result, Washington became the only American city in which the people did not elect its local officials.

Washington grew gradually for many years after the Civil War. But in 1917, when the United States entered World War I, another period of enormous growth began. Again, the government needed new workers to help direct a war effort. The city's population increased from about 350,000 when the United States entered the war to more than 450,000 in 1918, when the war ended. Shortages developed in housing, office space, schools, and public facilities. The automobile had replaced the horse as the main means of transportation in the city. To accommodate the cars, the Mall was turned into a parking lot. After the war, the government launched another building program. Many new houses, office buildings, and schools went up during the 1920's.

During the Great Depression of the 1930's, jobs be-

came scarce in all parts of the United States except Washington. The federal government became deeply involved in projects designed to end the depression, and thousands of new government jobs became available in the capital. The city's population grew from about 485,000 to 665,000 between 1930 and 1940.

Recent Developments. Several factors have caused the federal government to grow continuously since the depression. They include the country's participation in World War II from 1941 to 1945, and its Cold War struggle against Communism after the war. In addition, the government has taken on many responsibilities in the field of social welfare.

The government's growth has brought about steady growth of the Washington area. The city's population reached a peak of more than 800,000 by 1950. Since then, it has decreased by about 50,000, but the population of the suburbs has soared. Between 1950 and 1970, Washington's metropolitan area population grew faster than that of any other large city. It increased from about $1\frac{1}{2}$ million to almost 3 million.

Almost all the people who moved into the suburbs were whites. Blacks made up a majority of the city's population for the first time in the 1950's. The percentage of blacks in Washington has increased ever since. Blacks began moving into the suburbs in large number for the first time in the late 1960's.

In the mid-1900's, many Washingtonians began demanding the right to participate in government. In response, Congress and the states passed a constitutional amendment that allowed the people to vote in presidential elections for the first time in 1964. In 1973, Congress gave the people the right to elect local government officials for the first time in 100 years.

RONALD W. EDSFORTH, EUNICE S. GRIER, and ATLEE E. SHIDLER

Paul S. Conklin

The Watergate Complex, above, is a group of modern apartment and office buildings. Built in the 1960's, it is an example of the widespread redevelopment in Washington in recent years.

WORLD BOOK photo

Students Learn About the Metric System by Making Various Measurements with Metric Units.

METRIC SYSTEM

METRIC SYSTEM is a group of units used to make any kind of measurement, such as length, temperature, time, or weight. No other system of measurement ever used equals the metric system in simpleness. Scientists everywhere make measurements in metric units, and so do all other people in most countries.

In the mid-1970's, the United States and Canada were the only major countries not using the metric system. But there were strong efforts in both countries to convert to it. Through the years, Americans and Canadians have used the *customary*, or *English*, system for most measurements. This system was developed in England from older units, beginning in about the 1200's.

A group of French scientists created the metric system in the 1790's. The system has been revised several times. The official name of the present version is *Système International d'Unités* (International System of Units), usually known simply as *SI*. The term *metric* comes from the basic unit of length in the system, the *meter*.

Using the Metric System

The scientists who created the metric system designed it to fit their needs. They made the system logical and exact. But a nonscientist needs to know only a few metric units to make everyday measurements.

The metric system may seem difficult to someone who

Daniel V. De Simone, the contributor of this article, is Deputy Director of the Office of Technology Assessment, an agency of the United States Congress. He directed the U.S. Metric Study conducted by the government from 1968 to 1971.

has not used it. But much of this difficulty results from unfamiliarity with the units. It also comes from the need to convert measurements in the units of one system into the units of the other. After the metric system comes into widespread use in a country, the units become increasingly familiar. People no longer have to switch back and forth between two systems.

The metric system is simple to use for two reasons. First, it follows the decimal number system—that is, metric units increase or decrease in size by 10's. For example, a meter has 10 parts called *decimeters*. A decimeter has 10 parts called *centimeters*. Units in the customary system have no single number relationship between them. For example, feet and yards are related by 3's, but feet and inches are related by 12's.

Also, the metric system has only 7 basic units that make up all its measurements. The customary system has more than 20 basic units for just its common measurements. Customary units used for special purposes add many more basic units to that system.

The Decimal Arrangement. The metric system is a decimal system just as are the money systems of the United States and Canada. In a decimal system, a unit is 10 times larger than the next smaller unit. For example, a meter equals 10 decimeters just as a dollar equals 10 dimes.

Most metric units have a prefix that tells the relationship of that unit to the basic unit. These prefixes are the same no matter which base unit is used. This uniform system of names is another feature that simplifies metric measurement.

Latin prefixes are used to show the divisions of a basic unit. For example, *centi* means $\frac{1}{100}$ and *milli* means $\frac{1}{1,000}$. Greek prefixes are used to show multiples of the basic unit. For example, *hecto* means 100 times, *kilo* means 1,000 times, and *mega* means 1,000,000 times. The table on page 571 shows all the prefixes, their abbreviations, and their relationship to the basic unit.

An example will illustrate the basic simpleness of a decimal system. Suppose you want to measure the length and width of a room so you can draw a floor plan to scale. Using the customary system, you measure the room with a yardstick and get the length in units of yards, feet, and inches. To find the distance in just feet and inches, you multiply the number of yards by 3. Suppose the room measures 3 yards 1 foot 6 inches long. This measurement equals 10 feet 6 inches.

To prepare the scale drawing, you decide to let one inch of the drawing equal one foot of the room. The 10 feet in the room measurement equal 10 inches on the drawing. But the 6 inches must be divided by 12 to get the fraction of an inch needed to represent them on the drawing. Since $6 \div 12$ equals $\frac{1}{2}$, the correct scale distance for the drawing is $10\frac{1}{2}$ inches.

Using the metric system, you find the room measures 3 meters 2 decimeters long. This measurement can also be written as 3.2 meters. You let one decimeter of the drawing equal one meter of the room. Then, all you do to change the room measurement into the scale measurement is divide by 10. Moving the decimal point one place to the left divides a decimal number by 10. Therefore, the scale distance is 3.2 meters $\div$ 10, or .32 meters, which equals 3.2 decimeters.

Metric Measurement Units. Seven *base* (basic) units form the foundation of the metric system. Most everyday measurements involve only four of these units. (1) The *meter* is the base unit for length or distance. (2) The *kilogram* is the base unit for *mass*, the weight of an object when measured on the earth. (3) The *second* is the base unit for time. (4) The *kelvin* is the unit for temperature. Most people, when measuring in metric units, use *Celsius* temperatures instead of kelvin temperatures. One degree kelvin equals one degree Celsius, but the two temperature scales begin at different points. See the section *Temperature Measurements* in this article.

The three other base units have specialized uses by scientists and engineers. (5) The *ampere* is the base unit for electrical measurements. (6) The *mole* is the base unit for measuring the amount of any substance involved in a chemical or other reaction. (7) The *candela* is the base unit for measuring light.

Every base unit is defined by a *measurement standard* that gives the exact value of the unit. For information on measurement standards, see the WORLD BOOK article on MEASUREMENT.

The metric system also includes two supplementary units for measuring angles. These units are the *radian* and the *steradian* (see RADIAN).

All other units in the metric system consist of two or more base units. For example, the unit for speed, *meters per second*, combines the base units for length and time. Such combination units are called *derived units*.

Common Measurements

This section describes everyday measurements made by using the metric system. The examples give the approximate number of customary units in each metric unit. For the exact conversions between the two systems, see the WORLD BOOK article on WEIGHTS AND MEASURES. Other articles provide information on the specialized metric units used by scientists and engineers. For example, see ENERGY for the metric units related to energy.

Length and Distance Measurements. The meter is used for such measurements as the length of a rope or of a piano or other large object. It also is used to measure the height of a mountain or the altitude of an airplane. A meter is slightly longer than a yard. Short lengths are measured in centimeters, or they may be measured in *millimeters*. A centimeter equals about $\frac{2}{5}$ of an inch. Books, pencils, and other small objects may be measured in centimeters. A millimeter equals about $\frac{1}{25}$ of an inch. Photographic film, small hardware, and tiny mechanical parts are measured in millimeters.

Long distances, such as those between cities, are measured in *kilometers*. A kilometer equals about $\frac{5}{8}$ of a mile. A short distance, such as that between two buildings on the same block, is measured in meters.

Surface Measurements tell how much area something covers. For example, the amount of carpeting needed to cover a floor is measured in square units. Most areas are measured in *square meters*. A square meter equals the surface covered by a square one meter long on each side. It is slightly larger than a square yard. Smaller areas may be measured in *square centimeters* or *square millimeters*.

Land is sometimes measured in units called *hectares*. A hectare equals 10,000 square meters, or about $2\frac{1}{2}$ acres. Large land areas, such as cities and countries, are measured in *square kilometers*. One square kilometer equals about 247 acres, or about $\frac{3}{8}$ of a square mile.

Volume and Capacity Measurements tell how much space something occupies or encloses. A volume measurement tells the size of a box, and a capacity measurement tells how much the box can hold. Volume and capacity are both measured in cubic units, such as *cubic meters* or *cubic decimeters*. The volume of a box with each side 1 meter long equals 1 cubic meter. A cubic meter contains 1,000 cubic decimeters and equals about $1\frac{1}{3}$ cubic yards.

Most capacity measurements for liquids are made in units called *liters*. A liter equals a cubic decimeter and is slightly larger than a liquid quart. Smaller units include the *deciliter* ($\frac{1}{10}$ of a liter) and the *milliliter* ($\frac{1}{1,000}$ of a liter). A milliliter equals a *cubic centimeter*.

Weight and Mass Measurements. The mass of an object is not really the same as its weight because its weight changes with altitude. However, the two measurements are equal at sea level on the earth. The kilogram is a unit of mass. But most people who use the metric system think of the kilogram as a unit of weight.

A kilogram equals about $2\frac{1}{5}$ avoirdupois pounds. The *gram* is used for small weight measurements. A gram equals $\frac{1}{1,000}$ of a kilogram. Manufacturers and shippers weigh bulk goods in *metric tons*. A metric ton equals 1,000 kilograms, or about $1\frac{1}{10}$ short tons in the customary system.

Time Measurements. The metric system measures time exactly as the customary system does for measurements longer than a second. For such measurements, the

THE METRIC SYSTEM AT A GLANCE

Length and Distance

Length and distance measurements in the metric system are based on the meter. All units for length and distance are decimal fractions or multiples of the meter. Commonly used units for such measurements include the millimeter, centimeter, meter, and kilometer.

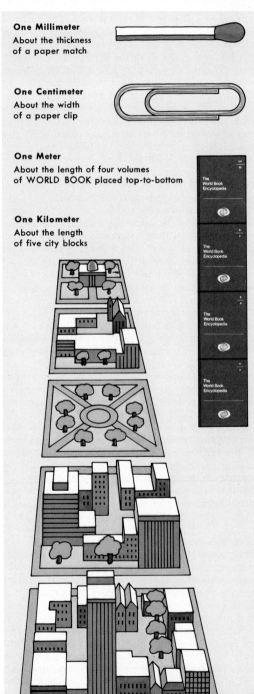

One Millimeter
About the thickness of a paper match

One Centimeter
About the width of a paper clip

One Meter
About the length of four volumes of WORLD BOOK placed top-to-bottom

One Kilometer
About the length of five city blocks

Surface or Area

Surface or area measurements in the metric system are also based on the meter. But area is measured in square units. Common units for these measurements include the square centimeter, square meter, hectare (10,000 square meters), and square kilometer.

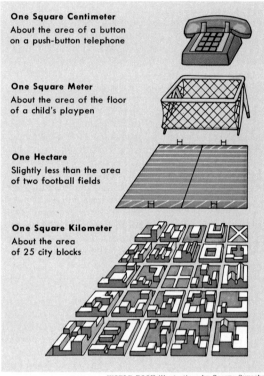

One Square Centimeter
About the area of a button on a push-button telephone

One Square Meter
About the area of the floor of a child's playpen

One Hectare
Slightly less than the area of two football fields

One Square Kilometer
About the area of 25 city blocks

WORLD BOOK illustrations by George Suyeoka

Volume and Capacity

Volume and capacity measurements in the metric system are based on the meter, but these measurements are made in cubic units. Common volume and capacity units include the cubic centimeter, liter (1,000 cubic centimeters), and cubic meter.

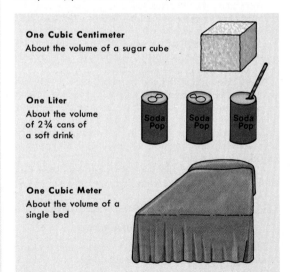

One Cubic Centimeter
About the volume of a sugar cube

One Liter
About the volume of 2¾ cans of a soft drink

One Cubic Meter
About the volume of a single bed

The illustrations on these pages will help show the size of the most common metric units. The metric conversion table will aid in the quick conversion of measurements into or out of the metric system.

Weight and Mass

Weight measurement in the metric system is based on mass, the amount of matter an object contains. The metric unit for mass—and thus weight—is the gram. Commonly used weight units include the gram, kilogram, and metric ton (1,000 kilograms).

One Gram
About the weight of two paper clips

One Kilogram
About the weight of the U-V volume of WORLD BOOK

One Metric Ton
About the weight of a small automobile

Metric Conversion Table

This table can help you change common measurements into or out of metric units. To use it, look up the unit you know in the left-hand column and multiply it by the number given. Your answer will be approximately the number of units in the right-hand column.

WHEN YOU KNOW:	MULTIPLY BY:	TO FIND:
Length and Distance		
inches	25	millimeters
feet	30	centimeters
yards	0.9	meters
miles	1.6	kilometers
millimeters	0.04	inches
centimeters	0.4	inches
meters	1.1	yards
kilometers	0.6	miles
Surface or Area		
square inches	6.5	square centimeters
square feet	0.09	square meters
square yards	0.8	square meters
square miles	2.6	square kilometers
acres	0.4	hectares
square centimeters	0.16	square inches
square meters	1.2	square yards
square kilometers	0.4	square miles
hectares	2.5	acres
Volume and Capacity		
ounces (fluid)	30	milliliters
pints	0.47	liters
quarts	0.95	liters
gallons	3.8	liters
milliliters	0.034	ounces (fluid)
liters	2.1	pints
liters	1.06	quarts
liters	0.26	gallons
Weight and Mass		
ounces	28	grams
pounds	0.45	kilograms
short tons	0.9	metric tons
grams	0.035	ounces
kilograms	2.2	pounds
metric tons	1.1	short tons
Temperature		
degrees Fahrenheit	5/9 (after subtracting 32)	degrees Celsius
degrees Celsius	9/5 (then add 32)	degrees Fahrenheit

Source: *A Metric America*, National Bureau of Standards, 1971

Temperature

Everyday temperature measurements in the metric system are made on the Celsius scale. This scale was once called the centigrade scale. Water freezes at 0°C and boils at 100°C.

Water at 0°C (ice)   Water at 100°C (steam)

Metric Prefixes

These prefixes can be added to any metric unit to increase or decrease its size. For example, a kilometer equals 1,000 meters. Centi, kilo, and milli are the most commonly used prefixes.

Prefix	Abbreviation	Increase or decrease in unit
tera (*TEHR uh*)	T	1,000,000,000,000 (One trillion)
giga (*JIHG uh*)	G	1,000,000,000 (One billion)
mega (*MEHG uh*)	M	1,000,000 (One million)
kilo (*KIHL uh*)	k	1,000 (One thousand)
hecto (*HEHK tuh*)	h	100 (One hundred)
deka (*DEHK uh*)	da	10 (Ten)
deci (*DEHS uh*)	d	0.1 (One-tenth)
centi (*SEHN tuh*)	c	0.01 (One-hundredth)
milli (*MIHL uh*)	m	0.001 (One-thousandth)
micro (*MY kroh*)	μ	0.000001 (One-millionth)
nano (*NAY nuh*)	n	0.000000001 (One-billionth)
pico (*PY koh*)	p	0.000000000001 (One-trillionth)
femto (*FEHM toh*)	f	0.000000000000001 (One-quadrillionth)
atto (*AT toh*)	a	0.000000000000000001 (One-quintillionth)

metric system does not follow the decimal system. For example, 60—not 100—seconds equal a minute, and 60 minutes equal an hour. Time measurements in both systems use a decimal arrangement for units longer than a year. Ten years equal a *decade*, 10 decades are a *century*, and 10 centuries are a *millennium*. For more information about time measurement, see TIME.

The metric system follows a decimal arrangement for time measurements shorter than a second. Scientists and others who work with electronic equipment, including computers and radar, use such measurements. For example, some electronic computers perform mathematical operations in *microseconds* and *nanoseconds*. A microsecond is $\frac{1}{1,000,000}$ of a second, and a nanosecond is $\frac{1}{1,000,000,000}$ of a second.

Temperature Measurements. Most people who use the metric system have thermometers marked in degrees Celsius (° C). Water freezes at 0° C and boils at 100° C. The normal body temperature of human beings is 37° C.

Celsius has been the official name of the metric scale for temperature since 1948. But many people still call this scale by its old name of *centigrade scale*. The word *centigrade* means *divided into 100 parts*. The Celsius scale has 100 degrees between the freezing and boiling temperatures of water.

Scientists do not know of any limit on how high a temperature may be. The temperature at the center of the sun is about 15,000,000° C, for example, but other stars may have an even higher temperature. On the other hand, nothing can have a temperature lower than −273.15° C. This temperature is called *absolute zero*. It forms the basis of the *kelvin scale* used by some scientists. One degree Celsius equals one degree on the kelvin scale. Because the kelvin scale begins at absolute zero,

0 K equals −273.15° C, and 273.15 K equals 0° C. See ABSOLUTE ZERO.

History

Before the development of the metric system, every nation used measurement units that had grown from local customs. For example, the English once used "three barleycorns, round and dry" as their standard for an inch. Grains of barley varied in size, of course—and so did the inch. As a result, no one could be sure that their measurements of the same thing would be equal.

During the 1600's, some people recognized the need for a single, accurate, worldwide measurement system. In 1670, Gabriel Mouton, the vicar of St. Paul's Church in Lyons, France, proposed a decimal measurement system. He based his unit of length on the length of one minute ($\frac{1}{21,600}$) of the earth's circumference. In 1671, Jean Picard, a French astronomer, proposed the length of a pendulum that swung once per second as the standard unit of length. Such a standard would have been more accurate than barleycorns because it was based on the physical laws of motion. In addition, a pendulum could have been duplicated easily to provide uniform measurement standards for everyone. Through the years, other people suggested various systems and standards of measurement.

The Creation of the Metric System. In 1790, the National Assembly of France asked the French Academy of Sciences to create a standard system of weights and measures. A commission appointed by the academy proposed a system that was both simple and scientific. This system became known as the metric system, and France officially adopted it in 1795. But the government did not require the French people to use the new units of measurement until 1840.

IMPORTANT DATES IN THE DEVELOPMENT OF THE METRIC SYSTEM

1670 Gabriel Mouton, a French clergyman, proposed a decimal system of measurement based on a fraction of the earth's circumference.

1671 Jean Picard, a French astronomer, proposed using the length of a pendulum swinging once each second as a standard unit of length.

1790 The National Assembly of France requested the French Academy of Sciences to develop a standard system of weights and measures. The system the academy developed became known as the metric system. Also in 1790, Thomas Jefferson, then U.S. secretary of state, recommended that the United States use a decimal system of measurement. Congress rejected the idea.

1795 France adopted the metric system but allowed people to continue using other measurement units.

1821 John Quincy Adams, then U.S. secretary of state, proposed conversion to the metric system. Congress again rejected the proposal.

1837 France passed a law that required all Frenchmen to begin using the metric system on Jan. 1, 1840.

1866 Congress legalized the use of the metric system in the United States but did not require that it be used.

1870-1875 An international conference on the metric system met to update the system and adopt new measurement standards for the kilogram and meter. Seventeen nations, including the United States, took part in the conference.

1875 The Treaty of the Meter was signed at the close of the 1870-1875 international conference. The treaty set up a permanent organization, the International Bureau of Weights and Measures, to change the metric system as necessary.

1889 New meter and kilogram standards based on those adopted by the 1870-1875 conference were made and sent to all countries that signed the Treaty of the Meter.

1893 The United States began defining all its measurement units as fractions of the standard meter and kilogram.

1890's Attempts were made in Congress to change U.S. measurements to metric, but none were successful. Many people, especially those in industry, opposed any change in the nation's measurement system.

1957 The U.S. Army and Marine Corps adopted the metric system as the basis for its weapons and equipment.

1960 A General Conference of Weights and Measures held by countries using the metric system adopted the present version of the system.

1965 Great Britain began a 10-year changeover to the metric system.

1968-1971 A congressional study explored the costs and benefits to the United States of converting to the metric system. The study recommended that the country make a planned conversion.

1970 Canada and Australia set up a commission to plan conversion to the metric system.

1974 The U.S. House of Representatives defeated a bill calling for a conversion to the metric system.

In the original metric system, the unit of length equaled a fraction of the earth's circumference. This fraction was $\frac{1}{10,000,000}$ of the distance from the North Pole to the equator along the line of longitude near Dunkerque, France; and Barcelona, Spain. The French scientists named this unit of length the *metre*, from the Greek word *metron*, meaning *a measure.*

The units for capacity and mass came from the meter. The commission chose the cubic decimeter as the unit of fluid capacity and named it the liter. The scientists defined the metric unit for mass, the gram, as the mass of a cubic centimeter of water at the temperature where it weighs the most. That temperature is about 4° C (39° F.).

The original measurement standards of the metric units have been replaced by more accurate ones, and other units have been added to the system. Whenever necessary, an international group of scientists holds a General Conference of Weights and Measures to revise the system. The General Conference of 1960 named the system Système International d'Unités.

International Acceptance. Other nations began to convert to the metric system after 1840, when the French people were first required to use it. By 1850, Greece, The Netherlands, Spain, and parts of Italy had adopted the new units of measurement.

An international metric convention, held from 1870 to 1875, created measurement standards of greater accuracy for length and mass. Seventeen nations, including the United States, participated in this convention. In 1875, they signed the Treaty of the Meter, which established a permanent organization to change the metric system as necessary. This organization, called the International Bureau of Weights and Measures, has its headquarters near Paris.

By 1900, 35 nations had adopted the metric system. They included the major countries of continental Europe and South America. By the mid-1970's, almost every country in the world had either converted to the system or planned to do so. The United States and Canada were the only major countries not using the metric system. In 1970, Canada and Australia each established a commission to plan for conversion.

The United States and the Metric System. In 1790, Secretary of State Thomas Jefferson recommended that the United States use a decimal measurement system. That same year, work leading to the metric system began in France. Congress rejected Jefferson's recommendation. In 1821, Secretary of State John Quincy Adams also proposed conversion to the metric system. But Congress again turned down such action. At that time, the United States traded mostly with England and Canada, neither of which was considering any change in its measurements. A conversion of U.S. measurements would have interfered with this trade.

The United States showed little interest in the metric system for more than 40 years following Adams' proposal. Meanwhile, the nation's industries developed machines and products based on customary units. Until the mid-1900's, many industries opposed conversion to metric measurements. They believed such a step would require costly changes in their machines and manufacturing methods. In 1866, Congress made the metric system legal in the United States. But it took no action toward requiring the use of metric measurements.

In 1893, the United States based the yard and the pound on fractions of the international metric standards for the meter and the kilogram. But during the next 70 years, only a few metric measurements began to come into daily use. In the 1950's, for example, pharmacists started to use metric units to fill prescriptions. In 1957, the U.S. Army and the Marine Corps began to measure in metric units. During the 1960's, because of the increasing number of foreign cars, many mechanics had to use tools based on the metric system. Also in the 1960's, the National Aeronautics and Space Administration (NASA) began to use metric units.

In 1965, Great Britain began a 10-year changeover to the metric system. Other members of the Commonwealth of Nations later decided to convert. The action of the Commonwealth governments created new interest in the metric system in the United States. More and more people began to realize that, in time, the United States would be the only major country that used customary measurements.

In 1968, Congress authorized a three-year study of metric conversion. This study recommended a step-by-step conversion to the metric system during a period of 10 years. Such a planned conversion would help reduce the cost and problems of changing the nation's measurement system. However, in 1974, the House of Representatives defeated a bill calling for a conversion. But some industries and other groups continued with their own plans for conversion.   DANIEL V. DE SIMONE

Related Articles. See MEASUREMENT with its list of *Related Articles.* See also the following articles:

Absolute Zero	International Bureau	Mole
Ampere	of Weights and	National Bureau
Candela	Measures	of Standards
Celsius Scale	Kilogram	Time
Centimeter	Kilometer	Ton
Gram	Liter	Weights and
	Meter	Measures

Outline

I. **Using the Metric System**
   A. The Decimal Arrangement
   B. Metric Measurement Units
II. **Common Measurements**
   A. Length and Distance Measurements
   B. Surface Measurements
   C. Volume and Capacity Measurements
   D. Weight and Mass Measurements
   E. Time Measurements
   F. Temperature Measurements
III. **History**

Questions

Why is a decimal system of measurement easier to work with than a nondecimal system?

What are the seven basic metric units?

What do the letters *SI* stand for?

What is a *derived unit?*

What prefix is used to increase a unit by 1,000?

Where was the metric system developed? When?

Why did U.S. industry oppose the metric system?

Where does the term *metric* come from?

What was Gabriel Mouton's proposal for a decimal unit of length?

What did the Treaty of the Meter accomplish?

METROLINER. See ELECTRIC RAILROAD (History).

George Mars Cassidy, Van Cleve Photography

Baseball is often called the *national pastime of the United States.* Millions of Americans enjoy playing and watching this exciting "bat and ball" game.

BASEBALL

BASEBALL is a sport that is so popular in the United States that it is often called the *national pastime.* Every spring and summer, millions of people throughout the country play this exciting "bat and ball" game. Millions also watch baseball games and closely follow the progress of their favorite teams and players.

There are organized baseball teams for every age group from 8-year-olds to adults. The teams that at-

Joseph L. Reichler, the contributor of this article, is the Special Assistant to the Commissioner of Professional Baseball, and the author of many books about baseball. The illustrations throughout the article were prepared for WORLD BOOK *by Charles Slack unless otherwise credited.*

tract the most interest are those of the two major leagues: the American League and the National League. These teams are made up of men who rank as the world's best players. Every year, about 30 million persons flock to ballparks to watch major league baseball games. Many more millions watch games on television, listen to them on radio, read about them in newspapers, and discuss them with their friends.

Baseball began in the eastern United States in the mid-1800's. By the late 1800's, people throughout the country were playing the game. The National League was founded in 1876, and the American League in 1900. Through the years, baseball spread from the United States to other parts of the world. Today, it ranks as a major sport in such countries as Canada, Italy, Japan, Taiwan, The Netherlands, South Africa, and many Latin-American nations.

BASEBALL TERMS*

Balk is an illegal act by a pitcher with one or more runners on base. Runners advance one base on a balk. There are 13 ways to balk. For an example, a pitcher balks when, with his foot on the pitcher's plate, he feints a throw to a base but does not throw.

Batting Average shows the percentage of times that a player gets a base hit. To find a player's batting average, divide his number of hits by the number of official times he batted. Carry the answer to three decimal places.

Diamond is a nickname for the infield, used because the infield is shaped somewhat like a diamond. Sometimes, the term is used to mean the entire field.

Double Play is a play on which the fielders put out two opponents. Most double plays result from ground balls hit in force situations.

Earned-Run Average is the average number of *earned runs* scored against a pitcher every nine innings. An earned run is one that is scored without the aid of an error. To find a pitcher's earned-run average, divide the number of innings he pitched by 9. Then, divide that

total into the number of earned runs the pitcher allowed. Carry the answer to two decimal places.

Hit-and-Run Play occurs when a runner on first base runs toward second when the pitcher releases the ball. This forces the second baseman or shortstop to cover second base. The batter tries to hit the ball through the "hole" left open by the fielder.

Official Scorer is an official of a baseball game who keeps a record of every play. He also makes such decisions as whether a batter reached base as the result of a base hit or by a hit on error. Usually, a newspaper reporter serves as the official scorer.

Runs Batted In are runs scored as a result of a batter's base hits, outs (except double plays), sacrifices and sacrifice flies, walks, or when he is hit by a pitch.

Sacrifice occurs when a batter bunts a ball on which he is put out, but which allows a base runner to advance. When a batter flies out and a runner advances after the catch, it is a *sacrifice fly.*

Squeeze Play calls for a batter to bunt the ball so that a runner can score from third base.

*This table includes terms that do not appear in the text.

A baseball game is played on a large field between two teams of 9 or 10 players each. The teams take turns *at bat* (on offense) and *in the field* (on defense). A player of the team in the field, called the *pitcher*, throws a baseball toward a player of the team at bat, called the *batter*. The batter tries to hit the ball with a bat and drive it out of the reach of the players in the field. By hitting the ball, and in other ways, players can advance around the four bases that lie on the field. A player who does so scores a *run* for his team. The team that scores the most runs wins the game.

The information in this section is based on the rules of major league baseball. Most other leagues follow much the same rules. The section on *Baseball Leagues* later in this article lists some exceptions. For information on softball, a popular game based on baseball, see SOFTBALL.

Players and Equipment

Players. National League baseball teams include nine players: a *pitcher, catcher, first baseman, second baseman, shortstop, third baseman, left fielder, center fielder,* and *right fielder.* Each player plays a defensive position when his team is in the field and takes a turn as the batter when his team is at bat.

American League teams include the same players, but they may—and almost always do—use a tenth player. This player, called the *designated hitter (dh)*, bats in place of the pitcher. He does not play a defensive position. All other players except the dh and the pitcher both bat and play in the field. The American League adopted the designated hitter rule in 1973.

Baseball teams also have substitute players. A substitute may replace any player except the pitcher at any time. A pitcher must face at least one batter before leaving the game. A player who leaves a game for a substitute may not return to the game.

Other members of a baseball team include a *manager* and several *coaches*. The manager decides which players will play in the game and directs the team's strategy. The coaches assist the manager.

Equipment. A *baseball* is a small, hard, round ball. It measures from 9 to $9\frac{1}{4}$ inches (23 to 23.5 centimeters) in circumference and weighs between 5 and $5\frac{1}{4}$ ounces (142 and 148.8 grams). A tiny cork ball forms the center of the ball. Tightly wrapped layers of rubber and yarn surround the cork. Two strips of white cowhide sewn together with thick red thread cover the ball. Until 1974, the cover was made of horsehide, rather than cowhide. For this reason, baseballs are sometimes called *horsehides*.

A *baseball bat* is a long, rounded piece of wood. Most bats are made of ash wood, but some are made of hackberry or hickory. A major league bat may not be more than 42 inches (107 centimeters) long or $2\frac{3}{4}$ inches (7 centimeters) in diameter at its thickest point.

Each defensive player wears a padded leather *glove*, and uses it to catch the ball. There are three kinds of gloves: the *catcher's mitt*, worn by the catcher; the *first baseman's glove*, worn by the first baseman; and the *fielder's glove*, worn by all other players.

All players wear shoes with spikes on the soles so they can stop and start quickly. Most players wear shoes with metal spikes. But some wear shoes with synthetic rubber spikes when they play on fields covered by artificial turf. Players also wear uniforms, which include socks, knickers, a jersey, and a cap. The batter wears a special plastic cap called a *batting helmet*. The helmets are designed to avoid injuries to batters who are hit in the head with a ball.

A catcher wears special equipment for protection. A metal *mask* protects his face. A *chest protector* of padded

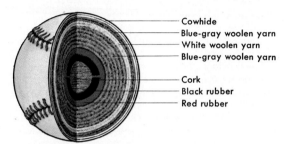

The Inside of a Baseball has a cork center and layers of rubber and yarn. Strips of cowhide sewn together cover the ball.

Labels on illustration:
- Cowhide
- Blue-gray woolen yarn
- White woolen yarn
- Blue-gray woolen yarn
- Cork
- Black rubber
- Red rubber

The Three Kinds of Baseball Gloves are, *left to right*, the catcher's mitt, first baseman's glove, and fielder's glove.

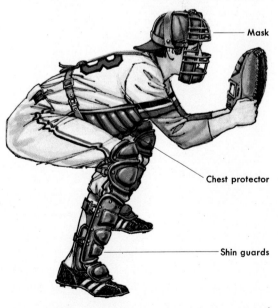

Labels on illustration:
- Mask
- Chest protector
- Shin guards

The Catcher wears special protective equipment—a metal mask, a padded chest protector, and plastic shin guards.

cloth covers his chest and stomach. Plastic *shin guards* protect his legs.

The Field

A baseball field includes three sections: (1) an infield, (2) an outfield, and (3) foul territory. The infield and outfield make up *fair territory*. Walls or fences surround the field. The size and shape of the outfield and foul territory vary from ballpark to ballpark. But the infield has the same size and shape in every ballpark.

A baseball field is covered partly by grass, or artificial turf, and partly by dirt. The illustration of the field in this article shows a typical field. But some of the newest fields have artificial turf, rather than dirt, between the bases.

The Infield is a square area with a base at each corner. The bases are—in counterclockwise order—*home plate*, *first base*, *second base*, and *third base*. Each base lies 90 feet (27.4 meters) from the next one.

Home plate is a slab of white rubber sunk into the ground so that its top is level with the ground. The front of the plate—the part that faces the rest of the infield—is 17 inches (43 centimeters) wide. The plate tapers off to a point in the back. First base, second base, and third base are white canvas bags filled with *kapok* or some other soft material. Each bag is 15 inches (38 centimeters) square and from 3 to 5 inches (8 to 13 centimeters) thick. Spikes anchor the bags to the ground.

White lines made by chalk, lime, or some other material mark the boundaries of a *batter's box* on the left and right sides of home plate. Each box is 6 feet (1.8 meters) long and 4 feet (1.2 meters) wide. A *catcher's box* 5 feet (1.5 meters) long and 3 feet 7 inches (1.1 meters) wide lies behind the plate. Technically, the catcher's box lies in foul territory. But it is usually considered part of the infield.

A straight white line called a *foul line* extends out from each side of home plate. These lines run past first and third base to the walls or fences at the end of the outfield. Each foul line is 3 inches (8 centimeters) wide.

A *pitcher's mound* rises near the center of the infield. The mound measures 18 feet (5.5 meters) in diameter and reaches a height of 10 inches (25 centimeters) at its center. A slab of white rubber called the *pitcher's plate*, or *the rubber*, is sunk into the ground at the center of the mound. The plate measures 24 inches (61 centimeters) by 6 inches (15 centimeters). It lies 60 feet 6 inches (18.4 meters) from home plate.

The Outfield lies between the infield and the walls or fences farthest from home plate. Technically, the outfield begins directly behind first, second, and third base. But people usually think of the area just behind the bases as part of the infield. They consider the *grass line* the dividing point between the infield and the outfield.

DIAGRAM OF A BASEBALL FIELD

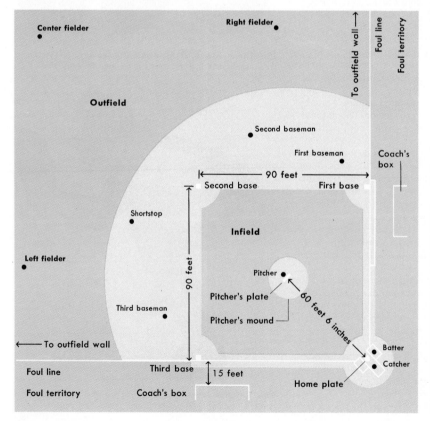

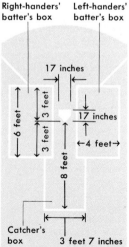

The diagram at the left shows a baseball field and the usual positions of the players. The outfield and foul territory extend beyond the area shown to the outer fences or walls. A detailed drawing of the home plate area appears below.

WORLD BOOK diagram

The grass line is the part of the field where the dirt beyond the bases ends and grass or artificial turf begins. In fields that have an artificial turf infield, a white line marks the location of the grass line.

The size of the outfield varies from field to field. But a major league rule sets minimum sizes. The rule requires that in ballparks opened before June 1, 1958, the outfield must be big enough so that the distance from home plate to the left and right field walls or fences at the foul lines is at least 250 feet (76.2 meters). The distance for ballparks opened after that date must be at least 325 feet (99.1 meters) down each foul line and at least 400 feet (121.9 meters) in center field.

Foul Territory is the part of the field behind home plate and across the foul lines from the infield and the outfield. There is no standard size for foul territory. But the major league rule book recommends that the distance between home plate and the wall behind it be at least 60 feet (18.3 meters).

Two *dugouts*—one for each team—are built into the wall in foul territory. One lies behind first base, and the other behind third. Usually, the managers and other team members not required to be on the field sit in the dugouts.

White lines outline two *coach's boxes* in foul territory—one near first and one near third. The boxes measure 10 feet by 20 feet (3 by 6.1 meters).

An *on-deck circle* 5 feet (1.5 meters) in diameter lies between each dugout and home plate. The batter who follows the one at bat awaits his turn in the circle nearest his dugout.

A field also includes a *bull pen* for each team. These areas have space where substitutes can *warm up* (practice) before entering the game. In some ballparks, the bull pens lie in foul territory across the foul lines from the outfield. In other parks, they are located beyond the outfield walls or fences.

Player Positions. The pitcher of the team in the field stands on the pitcher's mound. He must have one foot in contact with the pitcher's plate when he throws the ball. The catcher crouches behind home plate, within the boundaries of the catcher's box. He makes hand signals that tell the pitcher what kind of pitches to throw and catches balls that pass the batter. The pitcher and catcher are called the team's *battery*.

The first baseman and second baseman play between first and second base, and the shortstop and third baseman between second and third. These players, called *infielders*, try to catch balls hit short distances by batters.

The left fielder, center fielder, and right fielder spread out across the outfield. Called *outfielders*, these players try to catch balls hit past and over the heads of the infielders.

The batter of the team at bat stands in a batter's box. Left-handed batters stand in the box to the right of home plate. Right-handers stand in the box to the left of the plate.

A coach of the team at bat stands in each coach's box. The coaches receive hand signals regarding strategy from the manager. They relay the signals to batters and base runners.

Umpires serve as the officials of baseball games. In most major league games, there are four umpires. One umpire stands near each base.

Baseball Skills

Basically, baseball matches the skills of the pitcher against those of the batter. But fielders and base runners also play key roles in the game.

Pitching. A good pitcher can throw a variety of pitches. The most common pitches are the *fast ball*, the *curve ball*, and the *slider*. A fast ball thrown by a major league pitcher may travel at a speed close to 100 miles (160 kilometers) per hour. A curve ball thrown by a right-handed pitcher breaks sharply to the left and downward as it reaches the batter. A left-hander's curve breaks to the right and downward. A slider resembles a curve ball. But it seems to "slide" rather than break sharply, and it does not move downward. Other pitches include the *screwball*, which breaks just like—but in the

Pitching Deliveries, or the ways pitchers throw the ball, vary widely. The series of pictures above shows a typical delivery of a right-handed pitcher. With his right foot on the pitcher's plate, the pitcher (1) raises his hands above his head, (2) lifts his left leg, (3) pushes forward using the plate for leverage, (4) releases the ball, and (5) follows through.

WORLD BOOK photo

A Batter should grip the bat, stand in the batter's box, and swing in ways that make him feel comfortable. But a good batter follows certain basic batting "rules," as shown above. He takes a level, or fairly level, swing, keeps his head from jerking so he can follow the flight of the ball, and follows through with his swing.

WORLD BOOK photo

A Batter Bunts by tapping the ball a short distance into the infield. To bunt, a batter slides his upper hand up to about the middle of the bat, *above*, and moves his feet so he faces the pitcher, *right*. He then lets the ball hit the bat.

opposite direction from—the curve ball; the *sinker*, which drops sharply as it reaches the batter; and the *knuckle ball*, which may break to the left or right, or downward.

Batting. Many experts believe that a batter's job of hitting a ball thrown by a major league pitcher is the hardest thing to do in any sport. The ball reaches the batter in a fraction of a second. It may move in any of the ways described above as it reaches home plate. Even so, batters are able to follow the flight of the ball, whip the bat around quickly, and drive the ball sharply into the field. A batter may take a full swing and try to hit the ball as far and hard as he can. Or, he may take less than a full swing and try to poke the ball between fielders. This batting strategy is called *place hitting*.

Fielding. Good fielders can catch almost any ball hit near them and race far after balls and catch them. They can also throw the ball with great speed and accuracy to put out runners. A single outstanding play by a fielder can win a game for a team.

Base Running. Good base runners can steal bases, and take an *extra base* (one more base than usual) on

batted balls. They can quickly judge when to try to advance and when to stay near the base. A runner, like a fielder, can win a game with one outstanding play.

The Game

Before a baseball game begins, each manager makes a list that shows his team's *lineup* and *batting order*. A lineup tells which player will play each defensive position. A batting order shows the order in which the players will take their turns at bat.

The team on whose field the game is played is called the *home team*. The other team is the *visiting team*. The visiting team takes the first turn at bat and the home team players go to their positions in the field. The team's turn at bat lasts until its players make three *outs*. Every time a player advances around the bases during the turn at bat, the team is credited with a *run*. When the visiting team's turn at bat is over, the home team comes to bat and the visitors take the field.

One turn at bat by each team is called an *inning*. A regulation baseball game lasts nine innings. The team with the most runs at the end of the game wins. If the two teams have the same number of runs after nine innings, they play *extra innings* until one of them scores more runs than the other in an inning.

Each player who comes to bat during a baseball game tries to reach base and advance around the bases. The pitcher of the team in the field and his teammates try to put each batter out. There are many ways to make outs, reach base, and advance around the bases.

Outs by Batters. Most batters make outs in one of three ways—by strikeouts, ground outs, or fly outs.

Strikeouts. A batter strikes out when he makes three strikes during his turn at bat. There are four kinds of strikes—*swinging strikes*, *called strikes*, *foul strikes*, and *foul tips*.

A batter makes a swinging strike when he swings at a pitch and misses it. A called strike occurs when a batter *takes* (does not swing at) a pitch and the home plate umpire rules that the pitch was within the *strike zone*. A pitch within the strike zone is one that passes over any part of home plate between the batter's armpits and the top of his knees.

A batter makes a foul strike if he hits a *foul ball* when he has fewer than two strikes against him. Foul balls include all batted balls that: (1) settle in foul territory between home plate and first base or home plate and third base, (2) bounce or roll past first or third in foul territory, or (3) land in foul territory beyond first or third. Usually, a foul ball hit after two strikes does not count as a strike. But if the batter *bunts* (taps the ball) foul after two strikes, it does count as a strike.

A foul tip occurs when a batter hits a ball directly back to the catcher and the catcher catches the ball on the fly. All foul tips count as strikes, no matter how many strikes the batter has against him.

Ground Outs. A batter grounds out if he hits a *fair ball* that touches the ground and fails to reach first base before a fielder holding the ball touches the base or tags the batter with the ball. Fair balls include all batted balls that: (1) settle in fair territory between home plate and first base or home plate and third base, (2) bounce or roll past first or third in fair territory or hit either base, (3) land in fair territory beyond first or third, or (4) pass over an outfield wall or fence in fair territory. Almost all ground outs result from balls hit to infielders or the pitcher.

Fly Outs. A batter flies out if he hits a fair ball or foul ball and a fielder catches the ball on the fly. The foul tip, described earlier, is an exception to the fly out rule. Foul tips count as strikes, rather than outs.

Fly outs hit short distances and high into the air are often called *pop outs*. Those hit hard and on a fairly straight line are *line outs*.

Other Outs. There are several less common ways in which batters can make outs. For example, a batter is out if he hits a fair ball and runs into the ball, or if he bats out of turn and the opposing manager points out this violation to the home plate umpire.

Reaching Base. Most batters reach base through *base hits*. A batter makes a base hit when he (1) hits a fair ball that is not caught on the fly, and (2) reaches first base before a fielder holding the ball touches the base or tags the batter with the ball. A batter who makes a base hit may continue to run around the bases. But if a fielder tags the batter with the ball while he is off base, the batter is out.

A base hit that enables a batter to reach first base is

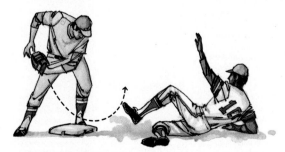

An Infielder Tags a Base Runner with a quick, sweeping motion. The runner slides to try to avoid the tag.

called a *single*. One on which a batter reaches second base is a *double*, third base a *triple*, and home plate a *home run*. Most singles result from balls hit into the infield or past the infielders but in front of the outfielders. Most doubles and triples are made on hits that get past outfielders. Almost all home runs result from batted balls hit over an outfield wall or fence. A batter who makes such a hit can simply trot around the bases, and cannot be tagged out.

A batter who hits a ball and reaches base because of a fielder's mistake is credited with a *hit on error*, rather than a base hit. One who reaches base because the fielders tried to put a base runner out is credited with a *fielder's choice*.

Batters can also reach base without hitting the ball. The most common way is to receive a *walk*, or *base on balls*. A batter walks if the pitcher throws four *balls* (pitches outside the strike zone) during his turn at bat. A batter who walks goes to first base. A batter also goes to first base if the pitcher hits him with the ball. In addition, he goes to first on *catcher interference*. Catcher interference occurs when the catcher touches the bat when a batter is swinging.

Base Runners—Advancing and Outs. A batter who reaches base becomes a base runner. Base runners try to advance around the bases and score runs for their team. The defensive players try to put them out.

Base runners may try to advance at any time. But they usually wait until the batter hits the ball, and then decide whether or not to try to advance. If there are no outs or one out and a batter hits a ball that is likely to be caught on the fly, base runners stay near their bases. They do so because they must *tag up* (touch their bases) after a fly out. If a runner fails to tag up before a fielder holding the ball touches the runner's base or tags the runner with the ball, the runner is out. After a runner tags up, he can try to advance to the next base. He must reach the base before a fielder tags him with the ball, or else he is out.

When there are two outs, runners usually try to advance as soon as a fly ball is hit. They do so because their team's turn at bat ends as soon as a fielder catches the ball.

Base runners do not have to tag up if a batter hits a ball that touches the ground. But depending on the situation, runners may stay near their bases or run toward the next base on a ground ball. They stay near their bases if they judge that they will not be able to reach the next base before being tagged with the ball by a fielder. This situation usually occurs on ground balls hit sharply to infielders. If a runner believes he can get to the next base before being tagged, he runs toward the base. He is out if he fails, and safe if he succeeds.

In some situations—called *force situations*—base runners must try to advance to the next base. A force situation exists when a batter hits a ground ball and a runner occupies a base another player is entitled to. A batter who hits a ground ball is always entitled to first base. As a result, a runner on first is always forced to advance on a ground ball. If a team has runners on first and second base—or on first, second, and third base—all the runners are forced to advance on ground balls. In such

A BASEBALL BOX SCORE

Robins	ab	r	h	bi		Blue Sox	ab	r	h	bi
Thomson, rf	5	0	1	0		Bruner, 2b	4	0	2	0
Peters, cf	4	1	0	0		Jones, ss	4	1	2	1
Smith, 1b	4	0	1	1		Osgood, lf	4	1	1	1
Baker, 3b	4	0	0	0		Simon, 1b	4	0	0	0
Rogers, lf	4	2	3	1		Adams, 3b	4	0	1	1
Cain, 2b	3	1	1	1		Hood, c	4	0	0	0
Ruiz, ss	4	0	2	1		Walker, rf	3	0	0	0
Meyer, c	3	0	0	0		Tobin, cf	4	0	0	0
Irwin, p	4	0	0	0		Hayden, p	3	1	1	0
Totals	35	4	8	4		Totals	34	3	7	3

Robins . . . . 010 002 100—4
Blue Sox . . . . 100 100 010—3

E—Bruner, Thomson. DP—Blue Sox 1. LOB—
Robins 7, Blue Sox 5. 2B—Rogers. 3B—
Jones. HR—Rogers. SB—Peters.

Pitching Summary

	IP	H	R	ER	BB	SO
Irwin (W, 8-7)	9	7	3	3	1	5
Hayden (L, 4-5)	9	8	4	4	3	4

T—2:31. A—21,112.

A Box Score is a statistical summary of a baseball game. Box scores appear in newspapers. The listing at the right explains the meaning of many abbreviations used in box scores.

ABBREVIATIONS

ab—times at bat
r—runs scored
h—base hits
bi—runs batted in

Runs per inning and total

E—errors
DP—double plays
LOB—runners left on base
2B—doubles
3B—triples
HR—home runs
SB—stolen bases

IP—innings pitched
H—base hits allowed
R—runs allowed
ER—earned runs allowed
BB—bases on balls
SO—strikeouts
W—winning pitcher and won-lost record
L—losing pitcher and won-lost record
T—time of game
A—paid attendance

cases, each runner forces the runner in front of him.

A runner in a force situation makes an out if he fails to reach the next base before a fielder holding the ball touches the base. The fielder does not have to tag the runner. Such an out is called a *force out*.

Sometimes, base runners *run with the pitch*. That is, they race toward the next base as soon as the pitcher throws the ball. This strategy has both advantages and disadvantages. If the batter takes the pitch, and the runner gets to the next base before a fielder tags him with the ball, the runner is safe at the base. This play is called a *stolen base*. But if the runner fails to reach the base before being tagged, he is out. A runner who runs with the pitch can often advance farther on a hit than he can if he waits until the batter hits the ball. However, the runner risks being put out on a fly ball. He may end up so far from his base that he cannot get back to tag up before a fielder holding the ball touches the base.

Base runners can make outs and advance in other ways than those already described. For example, a runner is out if a batted ball hits him while he is in fair territory and not on a base. A runner on first base advances to second if the batter walks or is hit by a pitch. If the team also has a runner on second—or runners on second or third—those runners also move to the next base.

Umpires. Most major league games have four umpires. They are the *home plate umpire, first base umpire, second base umpire,* and *third base umpire.* The home plate umpire has the most important job. Every time a batter takes a pitch, he must decide whether the pitch was a ball or a strike. The home plate umpire also decides whether runners attempting to reach home plate were safe or out. The first base umpire rules on plays at first base, the second base umpire on plays at second, and the third base umpire on plays at third. The first base and third base umpires also decide whether batted balls hit down the foul lines were fair or foul.

Many people play baseball on an informal basis. They get together with their friends, *choose up sides* (divide into two teams), and play a ball game. But millions of people also play baseball on a formal, organized basis. They join teams that belong to a league. The teams play regularly scheduled games against other teams in their league. The team that has the best record at the end of the schedule, or that wins a play-off, becomes the champion.

Baseball leagues range from those for players as young as 8 years old to leagues for adults. The adult leagues include the major leagues and the minor leagues. These leagues are professional leagues. Almost all other leagues are amateur leagues.

Major league and minor league teams consist entirely of men. Almost all players on most amateur teams are boys or men. But in the 1970's, many girls began demanding the right to play on boys' teams. Some teams now allow girls to join their teams.

Major Leagues

There are two major leagues, the American League and the National League. Each league has 12 teams and consists of two 6-team divisions—an Eastern Division and a Western Division. Of the 24 major league teams, 23 represent United States cities, and 1—the Montreal Expos—represents a Canadian city. See the table in this section for a list of the teams.

Regular Season. Every major league team plays 162 games during the regular season. The season starts in early April and ends in late September or early October. A team plays 18 games against each of the other 5 teams in its division. It plays 12 games against each of the 6 teams in the other division in its league. Each team plays half of its games *at home* (on its own field) and half *on the road,* or *away* (on the fields of opponents). The teams that finish the season with the best record in each division win the division championships.

Play-Offs. The two division champions in each league meet in a play-off after the regular season. The first team to win three games in each play-off wins the *pennant* (becomes the champion of its league).

World Series. The American and National League pennant winners meet in the World Series. The first

MAJOR LEAGUE BASEBALL TEAMS

AMERICAN LEAGUE

Eastern Division	Western Division
Baltimore Orioles	California Angels
Boston Red Sox	Chicago White Sox
Cleveland Indians	Kansas City Royals
Detroit Tigers	Minnesota Twins
Milwaukee Brewers	Oakland Athletics
New York Yankees	Texas Rangers

NATIONAL LEAGUE

Eastern Division	Western Division
Chicago Cubs	Atlanta Braves
Montreal Expos	Cincinnati Reds
New York Mets	Houston Astros
Philadelphia Phillies	Los Angeles Dodgers
Pittsburgh Pirates	San Diego Padres
St. Louis Cardinals	San Francisco Giants

team to win four series games wins the *world champion-ship*. The World Series ranks among the world's major sports events. Played every year since 1903—except in 1904—it captures the interest of millions of people. Many people who have only a small interest in baseball follow the series. Television and radio stations send play-by-play coverage of the games throughout the United States and to many other countries.

All-Star Game is a special game played during the regular season. It matches outstanding American League players against stars of the National League. Baseball fans choose the starting lineups—except the pitchers—for the two teams. The team managers select the starting pitchers and all substitutes. An All-Star Game has been played every year since 1933, except in 1945. From 1959 through 1962, there were two games each year.

Minor Leagues

Minor leagues serve chiefly as training grounds for major league players. Most minor league teams are either owned by, or have a *working agreement* with, a major league team. Under a working agreement, the major league team helps support the minor league team. The minor league team trains players for the major league team.

There are 18 minor leagues with a total of more than 140 teams. Most minor league teams play in small cities or towns in the United States. Some play in Mexico, and a few in southern Canada. The minor leagues are divided into four classifications. The classifications—from the highest to the lowest—are Class AAA, Class

AA, Class A, and Rookie Leagues. Most players start their professional careers in a Rookie or Class A league. If they improve enough, they move up to Class AA or Class AAA, and then to a major league.

Amateur Leagues

Three national organizations administer amateur baseball programs for young players. They are the American Amateur Baseball Congress; Boys Baseball, Inc.; and Little League Baseball, Inc. A player can join a league in one of these programs when he is 8 years old, and advance to other leagues in the program until his late teens. Local organizations, such as park districts, have similar programs for young players.

Teen-agers also play amateur baseball in American Legion leagues and Babe Ruth leagues. Most high schools and colleges have baseball teams that belong to a league. The National Baseball Congress sponsors amateur leagues for adults.

Most amateur baseball leagues follow the same rules as the major leagues. But some leagues have special rules to accommodate their players. For example, the teams of leagues for young players play on fields that are smaller than those of the major leagues. Often, games involving young players are scheduled for fewer than nine innings. Some leagues allow players to use aluminum bats to hold down the cost of equipment. Wooden bats sometimes break when a batter hits the ball, but aluminum bats do not. High school leagues allow starting players to leave and return to the game once. This rule enables more players to participate in a game.

THE WORLD SERIES

Year	Winner	Loser	Games Won-Lost	Year	Winner	Loser	Games Won-Lost
1903	Boston (AL)*	Pittsburgh (NL)†	5-3	1940	Cincinnati (NL)	Detroit (AL)	4-3
1905	New York (NL)	Philadelphia (AL)	4-1	1941	New York (AL)	Brooklyn (NL)	4-1
1906	Chicago (AL)	Chicago (NL)	4-2	1942	St. Louis (NL)	New York (AL)	4-1
1907	**Chicago (NL)	Detroit (AL)	4-0	1943	New York (AL)	St. Louis (NL)	4-1
1908	Chicago (NL)	Detroit (AL)	4-1	1944	St. Louis (NL)	St. Louis (AL)	4-2
1909	Pittsburgh (NL)	Detroit (AL)	4-3	1945	Detroit (AL)	Chicago (NL)	4-3
1910	Philadelphia (AL)	Chicago (NL)	4-1	1946	St. Louis (NL)	Boston (AL)	4-3
1911	Philadelphia (AL)	New York (NL)	4-2	1947	New York (AL)	Brooklyn (NL)	4-3
1912	**Boston (AL)	New York (NL)	4-3	1948	Cleveland (AL)	Boston (NL)	4-2
1913	Philadelphia (AL)	New York (NL)	4-1	1949	New York (AL)	Brooklyn (NL)	4-1
1914	Boston (NL)	Philadelphia (AL)	4-0	1950	New York (AL)	Philadelphia (NL)	4-0
1915	Boston (AL)	Philadelphia (NL)	4-1	1951	New York (AL)	New York (NL)	4-2
1916	Boston (AL)	Brooklyn (NL)	4-1	1952	New York (AL)	Brooklyn (NL)	4-3
1917	Chicago (AL)	New York (NL)	4-2	1953	New York (AL)	Brooklyn (NL)	4-2
1918	Boston (AL)	Chicago (NL)	4-2	1954	New York (NL)	Cleveland (AL)	4-0
1919	Cincinnati (NL)	Chicago (AL)	5-3	1955	Brooklyn (NL)	New York (AL)	4-3
1920	Cleveland (AL)	Brooklyn (NL)	5-2	1956	New York (AL)	Brooklyn (NL)	4-3
1921	New York (NL)	New York (AL)	5-3	1957	Milwaukee (NL)	New York (AL)	4-3
1922	**New York (NL)	New York (AL)	4-0	1958	New York (AL)	Milwaukee (NL)	4-3
1923	New York (AL)	New York (NL)	4-2	1959	Los Angeles (NL)	Chicago (AL)	4-2
1924	Washington (AL)	New York (NL)	4-3	1960	Pittsburgh (NL)	New York (AL)	4-3
1925	Pittsburgh (NL)	Washington (AL)	4-3	1961	New York (AL)	Cincinnati (NL)	4-1
1926	St. Louis (NL)	New York (AL)	4-3	1962	New York (AL)	San Francisco (NL)	4-3
1927	New York (AL)	Pittsburgh (NL)	4-0	1963	Los Angeles (NL)	New York (AL)	4-0
1928	New York (AL)	St. Louis (NL)	4-0	1964	St. Louis (NL)	New York (AL)	4-3
1929	Philadelphia (AL)	Chicago (NL)	4-1	1965	Los Angeles (NL)	Minnesota (AL)	4-3
1930	Philadelphia (AL)	St. Louis (NL)	4-2	1966	Baltimore (AL)	Los Angeles (NL)	4-0
1931	St. Louis (NL)	Philadelphia (AL)	4-3	1967	St. Louis (NL)	Boston (AL)	4-3
1932	New York (AL)	Chicago (NL)	4-0	1968	Detroit (AL)	St. Louis (NL)	4-3
1933	New York (NL)	Washington (AL)	4-1	1969	New York (NL)	Baltimore (AL)	4-1
1934	St. Louis (NL)	Detroit (AL)	4-3	1970	Baltimore (AL)	Cincinnati (NL)	4-1
1935	Detroit (AL)	Chicago (NL)	4-2	1971	Pittsburgh (NL)	Baltimore (AL)	4-3
1936	New York (AL)	New York (NL)	4-2	1972	Oakland (AL)	Cincinnati (NL)	4-3
1937	New York (AL)	New York (NL)	4-1	1973	Oakland (AL)	New York (NL)	4-3
1938	New York (AL)	Chicago (NL)	4-0	1974	Oakland (AL)	Los Angeles (NL)	4-1
1939	New York (AL)	Cincinnati (NL)	4-0				

*(AL) American League.   †(NL) National League.   **Series included a tie game called off because of darkness.

The American National Game of Baseball (1846), a color lithograph by Currier & Ives;
(WORLD BOOK photo of a lithographic reproduction published by Shorewood Publishers, Inc.)

The First Baseball Game between two organized teams took place on the Elysian Fields in Hoboken, N.J., on June 19, 1846. It matched the Knickerbocker Base Ball Club of New York and the New York Nine. The New York Nine won the game, 23 to 1.

Baseball began in the United States in the mid-1800's. Historical evidence indicates that Americans developed the game from an old English sport called *rounders*. But in spite of this evidence, many people believe that Abner Doubleday of the United States invented baseball.

Early Development

Rounders. People in England played rounders as early as the 1600's. Rounders, like baseball, involved hitting a ball with a bat and advancing around bases. Although rounders resembled baseball, there were many differences between the two games. Perhaps the main difference was the way in which fielders put out base runners. Fielders threw the ball at runners. If the ball hit a runner who was off base, the runner was out. This practice was called *soaking* or *plugging* runners.

From Rounders to Baseball. American colonists in New England played rounders as early as the 1700's. They called the game by several names, including *town ball*, the *Massachusetts game*, and—sometimes—*base ball*. Rules for the game appeared in books from time to time. Even so, people generally played the game according to their local customs. The number of players on a side, the number of bases and distance between them, and other rules varied from place to place.

Americans gradually changed the game into baseball. One of the key points in this development took place when players replaced the practice of soaking runners with the present practice of tagging them. Historians believe players in New York City probably made the change in the 1830's or 1840's.

The Abner Doubleday Theory. In spite of evidence showing that baseball developed from rounders, many people believe that Abner Doubleday invented baseball in Cooperstown, N.Y., in 1839. Doubleday later became a United States Army general and died in 1893.

The Doubleday Theory arose from a dispute over the origin of baseball in the early 1900's. In 1906, major league officials appointed a commission to investigate the question of the game's origin. Many people told the commission that baseball developed from rounders. But the commission reported that Doubleday invented the game. It based its conclusion on a letter from Abner Graves, who had been a boyhood friend of Doubleday's. Graves said he had been present when Doubleday invented baseball in Cooperstown in 1839.

Historians now believe that Doubleday had little, if anything, to do with baseball. They also point out that the game described by Graves included the practice of soaking runners. Thus, it was not essentially different from rounders.

Alexander Cartwright, a New York City sportsman, is called the *father of organized baseball*. In 1845, he started a club whose only purpose was playing baseball. Called the *Knickerbocker Base Ball Club of New York*, it was the first organization of its kind. Cartwright wrote a set of baseball rules when he organized the club. These rules, together with rules added in 1848 and 1854, did much to make baseball the game it is today.

The 1845 rules set the distance between the bases at 90 feet (27.4 meters), and provided for nine players on a side. They contain the first known mention of the need to tag runners rather than soaking them. The 1848 addition included the present-day rule of tagging first base to put a batter out on a ground ball. The force out rule was added in 1854.

On June 19, 1846, the Knickerbocker Club met the New York Nine in the first baseball game between two organized teams. The game took place on the Elysian Fields in Hoboken, N.J. The New York Nine won the game, 23 to 1.

Rule Changes. Although Cartwright's rules and today's rules are alike in many ways, there are also many differences between the two. Following are some of the original rules and the dates when they were changed.

Length of Game. Cartwright provided that the first team to have 21 or more runs at the end of an inning won the game. The present rule in which the team with the most runs after nine innings wins was adopted in 1857.

Pitching. At first, the pitcher stood 45 feet (13.7 meters) from home plate and had to throw the ball underhanded. The pitching distance was increased to 50 feet (15.2 meters) in 1881 and to the present 60 feet 6 inches (18.4 meters) in 1893. The rule that allows the pitcher to throw overhanded was adopted in 1884.

Fly Outs. Originally, a batter was out if a fielder caught the ball either on the fly or on the first bounce. An 1864 rule change provided that fair balls caught on the bounce were not outs. A change adopted in 1883 provided that foul balls caught on the bounce were not outs.

Strikes and Balls. In early baseball, as in today's game, three strikes counted as a strikeout. But batters only made strikes by swinging and missing. Called strikes became part of the game in 1868. The National League adopted the foul strike rule in 1901, and the American League in 1903. There was no such thing as a walk in early baseball. An 1879 rule change provided that a batter walked after nine balls. The present four ball rule was introduced in 1889, after several changes.

The Spread of the Game

Groups throughout the eastern United States formed baseball clubs shortly after the Knickerbocker Club began. The Civil War (1861-1865) helped spread baseball to all parts of the country. Union soldiers who knew about the game often played it for recreation. Other Union troops and Confederate prisoners watched them. In this way, people from many parts of the nation learned baseball. They taught it to others when they returned home after the war. Soon, people in cities and towns and on farms in all parts of the country began playing baseball.

Professional Baseball. All early baseball players were amateurs. But many teams soon began attracting top players by offering them jobs or money. In 1869, the

Cincinnati Red Stockings decided to pay all its players. The Red Stockings thus became the first professional baseball team. Many other teams then turned professional. In 1876, eight professional teams formed the National League, the first major league. Eight teams formed the American League in 1900. The American League became the second major league in 1901.

At first, the cities represented by major league teams changed often. By 1900, the National League had teams in Boston, Brooklyn, Chicago, Cincinnati, New York City, Philadelphia, Pittsburgh, and St. Louis. By 1903, the American League teams represented Boston, Chicago, Cleveland, Detroit, New York City, Philadelphia, St. Louis, and Washington, D.C. The same 16 teams were to make up the major leagues and play in the same cities for 50 years.

Early Strategy and Stars. Early major league baseball is sometimes called the *dead ball era*. Baseballs used from the start of the game until about 1920 were "dead"; that is, less lively than those used today. Most batters were place hitters rather than long ball hitters. Wee Willie Keeler, a leading batter of baseball's early days, stated the batting philosophy of the era. His famous motto was: "I hit 'em where they ain't."

Bunting and base stealing were more common in the early days than they are today. King Kelly probably ranked as the most popular player of the late 1800's. His fame came from his ability to run the bases. Fans urged Kelly on with the chant, "Slide, Kelly, Slide."

Other stars of the 1800's included Cap Anson and Charlie (Old Hoss) Radbourn. Anson became the first player to make more than 3,000 base hits during a career. Radbourn pitched 73 complete games in 1884, and won 60 of them.

The 1900's

Interest in baseball soared after 1900. The game soon played such an important part in American life that it became known as the *national pastime*. Many boys spent almost all their leisure time during warm weather playing baseball. People in all walks of life eagerly followed the major league pennant races and the World Series. Star players became local, or even national, heroes. Many people could name every major league player, and knew the batting averages and other accomplishments of players. Jacques Barzun, a famous philosopher and educator, perhaps best summed up the importance of baseball in American life. Barzun wrote: "Whoever wants to know the heart and mind of America had better learn baseball."

The Early 1900's. The year 1900 marks the beginning of the *modern era* of major league baseball. By that time, the two major leagues had been formed and most baseball rules were the same as today. Records established by players and teams are divided into two categories: *modern* (since 1900) and *premodern* (before 1900). Records made by players who played during both periods are counted as modern records. For example, Cy Young holds the modern record for most games won by a pitcher (511). But Young won about half of these games before, and half after, 1900.

Ty Cobb, a Detroit Tiger outfielder of the early

1900's, became one of the greatest and most exciting players of all time. His many records include most base hits (4,191), highest career batting average (.367), and most career stolen bases (892). Honus Wagner of the Pittsburgh Pirates was another great star of the era. A bowlegged shortstop, Wagner led the National League in batting eight times and ranked among the best fielders and base runners. Outstanding early pitchers included Christy Mathewson of the New York Giants, Grover Cleveland Alexander of the Philadelphia Phillies and other teams, and Walter Johnson of the Washington Senators. Mathewson and Alexander hold the record for most games won by a pitcher in the National League (373). Johnson's blazing fast ball helped him become baseball's "strikeout king." He struck out more batters than any other pitcher in history (3,508). He won 416 games, more than any pitcher except Cy Young.

The Black Sox Scandal. In 1919, the Cincinnati Reds defeated the Chicago White Sox in the World Series. The next year, eight White Sox players were accused of *throwing* (trying to lose) the series in return for money from gamblers. Baseball Commissioner Kenesaw Moun-

tain Landis banned the players from baseball. This scandal, called the *Black Sox Scandal*, shocked baseball fans and hurt the game's reputation.

Landis had been appointed commissioner in 1920 especially to investigate the scandal. A federal judge with a reputation for honesty, he helped restore public confidence in baseball.

The Babe Ruth Era. Also in 1920, Babe Ruth joined the New York Yankees. At about the same time, teams began using livelier baseballs than before. Ruth, an outfielder, began hitting more and longer home runs than anyone thought possible. During the 1920's, he hit more than 50 homers in four different seasons, including a record 60 in 1927. Before Ruth, no player had hit more than 24 homers in a season. Ruth had hit a record 714 home runs when he retired in 1935.

Ruth's fame became so great that the 1920's in baseball is often called the *Babe Ruth Era*. Wherever the Yankees played, fans flocked to ballparks to see Ruth. Large numbers of people who knew nothing about baseball began following Ruth's career, and became interested in the game. Ruth's success also helped change

United Press Int.

Ty Cobb, *sliding,* became one of baseball's greatest all-around players. He stole more bases, made more base hits, and had a higher lifetime batting average than any player in history.

Brown Bros.

Christy Mathewson, *left,* pitched a record three shutouts for the New York Giants in the 1905 World Series. John McGraw, *center,* was his manager. Joe McGinnity, *right,* was a pitcher.

United Press Int.

Babe Ruth ranks as the most famous player in baseball history. He thrilled fans with his long and frequent home runs. Ruth hit 714 homers, including more than 50 in four different seasons.

Players may be elected to the Hall of Fame by (1) the 10-year members of the Baseball Writers Association, (2) the Hall of Fame Committee on Baseball Veterans, or (3) the Negro Leagues Selection Committee. Candidates must be retired and have played at least 10 years in the major leagues or Negro leagues.

Name	Position	Elected	Life Dates
Alexander, Grover	Pitcher	1938	1887-1950
Anson, Cap	First baseman	1939	1852-1922
Appling, Luke	Shortstop	1964	1907-
Baker, Home Run	Third baseman	1955	1886-1963
Bancroft, Dave	Shortstop; manager	1971	1891-1972
Barrow, Edward G.	Executive	1953	1868-1953
Beckley, Jake	First baseman	1971	1867-1918
Bell, Cool Papa	Outfielder	1974	1903-
Bender, Chief	Pitcher	1953	1883-1954
Berra, Yogi	Catcher	1972	1925-
Bottomley, Jim	First baseman	1974	1900-1959
Boudreau, Lou	Shortstop; manager	1970	1917-
Bresnahan, Roger	Catcher	1945	1879-1944
Brouthers, Dan	First baseman	1945	1858-1932
Brown, Mordecai	Pitcher	1949	1876-1948
Bulkeley, Morgan G.	First President, National League	1937	1837-1922
Burkett, Jesse	Outfielder	1946	1868-1953
Campanella, Roy	Catcher	1969	1921-
Carey, Max	Outfielder	1961	1890-
Cartwright, Alexander	"Father of Organized Baseball"	1938	1820-1892
Chadwick, Henry	Writer; author of first rule book	1938	1824-1908
Chance, Frank	First baseman	1946	1877-1924
Chesbro, Jack	Pitcher	1946	1874-1931
Clarke, Fred	Outfielder	1945	1872-1960
Clarkson, John	Pitcher	1963	1861-1909
Clemente, Roberto	Outfielder	1973	1934-1972
Cobb, Ty	Outfielder	1936	1886-1961
Cochrane, Mickey	Catcher	1947	1903-1962
Collins, Eddie	Second baseman	1939	1887-1951
Collins, Jimmy	Third baseman	1945	1870-1943
Combs, Earle	Outfielder	1970	1899-
Comiskey, Charles A.	First baseman; owner	1939	1859-1931
Conlan, Jocko	Umpire	1974	1899-
Connolly, Tom	Umpire	1953	1870-1961
Coveleski, Stan	Pitcher	1969	1889-
Crawford, Sam	Outfielder	1957	1880-1968
Cronin, Joe	Shortstop	1956	1906-
Cummings, Candy	Pitcher	1939	1848-1924
Cuyler, Kiki	Outfielder	1968	1899-1950
Dean, Dizzy	Pitcher	1953	1911-1974
Delahanty, Ed	Outfielder	1945	1867-1903
Dickey, Bill	Catcher	1954	1907-
DiMaggio, Joe	Outfielder	1955	1914-
Duffy, Hugh	Outfielder	1945	1866-1954
Evans, Billy	Umpire	1973	1884-1956
Evers, Johnny	Second baseman	1946	1881-1947
Ewing, Buck	Catcher	1939	1859-1906
Faber, Red	Pitcher	1964	1888-
Feller, Bob	Pitcher	1962	1918-
Flick, Elmer	Outfielder	1963	1876-1971
Ford, Whitey	Pitcher	1974	1928-
Foxx, Jimmy	First baseman	1951	1907-1967
Frick, Ford	Commissioner	1970	1894-
Frisch, Frankie	Second baseman	1947	1898-1973
Galvin, Pud	Pitcher	1965	1855-1902
Gehrig, Lou	First baseman	1939	1903-1941
Gehringer, Charley	Second baseman	1949	1903-
Gibson, Josh	Catcher	1972	1911-1947
Gomez, Lefty	Pitcher	1972	1908-
Goslin, Goose	Outfielder	1968	1900-1971
Greenberg, Hank	First baseman	1956	1911-
Griffith, Clark	Pitcher; owner	1946	1869-1955
Grimes, Burleigh	Pitcher	1964	1893-
Grove, Lefty	Pitcher	1947	1900-
Hafey, Chick	Outfielder	1971	1903-1973
Haines, Jesse	Pitcher	1970	1893-
Hamilton, Billy	Outfielder	1961	1866-1940
Harridge, Will	President, American League	1972	1881-1971
Hartnett, Gabby	Catcher	1955	1900-1972
Heilmann, Harry	Outfielder	1952	1894-1951
Hooper, Harry	Outfielder	1971	1887-
Hornsby, Rogers	Second baseman	1942	1896-1963
Hoyt, Waite	Pitcher	1969	1899-
Hubbell, Carl	Pitcher	1947	1903-
Huggins, Miller	Second baseman; manager	1964	1879-1929
Irvin, Monte	Outfielder	1973	1919-
Jennings, Hugh	Shortstop	1945	1869-1928
Johnson, Ban	Organizer	1937	1864-1931
Johnson, Walter	Pitcher	1936	1887-1946
Keefe, Tim	Pitcher	1964	1856-1933
Keeler, Wee Willie	Outfielder	1939	1872-1923
Kelley, Joe	Outfielder	1971	1871-1943
Kelly, George	First baseman	1973	1895-
Kelly, King	Catcher; outfielder	1945	1857-1894
Klem, Bill	Umpire	1953	1874-1951
Koufax, Sandy	Pitcher	1972	1935-
Lajoie, Napoleon	Second baseman	1937	1875-1959
Landis, Kenesaw Mountain	First commissioner	1944	1866-1944
Leonard, Buck	First baseman	1972	1907-
Lyons, Ted	Pitcher	1955	1900-
Mack, Connie	Catcher; owner	1937	1862-1956
Mantle, Mickey	Outfielder	1974	1931-
Manush, Heinie	Outfielder	1964	1901-1971
Maranville, Rabbit	Shortstop	1954	1891-1954
Marquard, Rube	Pitcher	1971	1889-
Mathewson, Christy	Pitcher	1936	1880-1925
McCarthy, Joe	Manager	1957	1887-
McCarthy, Tommy	Outfielder	1946	1864-1922
McGinnity, Joe	Pitcher	1946	1871-1929
McGraw, John	Third baseman; manager	1937	1873-1934
McKechnie, Bill	Manager	1962	1886-1965
Medwick, Ducky	Outfielder	1968	1911-
Musial, Stan	Outfielder; first baseman	1969	1920-
Nichols, Kid	Pitcher	1949	1869-1953
O'Rourke, Jim	Outfielder; catcher	1945	1852-1919
Ott, Mel	Outfielder	1951	1909-1958
Paige, Satchel	Pitcher	1971	1906-
Pennock, Herb	Pitcher	1948	1894-1948
Plank, Ed	Pitcher	1946	1875-1926
Radbourn, Charlie	Pitcher	1939	1854-1897
Rice, Sam	Outfielder	1963	1890-
Rickey, Branch	Catcher; executive	1967	1881-1965
Rixey, Eppa	Pitcher	1963	1891-1963
Robinson, Jackie	Second baseman	1962	1919-1972
Robinson, Wilbert	Catcher; manager	1945	1863-1934
Roush, Edd	Outfielder	1962	1893-
Ruffing, Red	Pitcher	1967	1904-
Ruth, Babe	Outfielder; pitcher	1936	1895-1948
Schalk, Ray	Catcher	1955	1892-1970
Simmons, Al	Outfielder	1953	1902-1956
Sisler, George	First baseman	1939	1893-1973
Spahn, Warren	Pitcher	1973	1921-
Spalding, Albert G.	Pitcher	1939	1850-1915
Speaker, Tris	Outfielder	1937	1888-1958
Stengel, Casey	Outfielder; manager	1966	1890?-
Terry, Bill	First baseman	1954	1898-
Thompson, Sam	Outfielder	1974	1860-1922
Tinker, Joe	Shortstop	1946	1880-1948
Traynor, Pie	Third baseman	1948	1899-1972
Vance, Dazzy	Pitcher	1955	1891-1961
Waddell, Rube	Pitcher	1946	1876-1914
Wagner, Honus	Shortstop	1936	1874-1955
Wallace, Bobby	Shortstop; pitcher	1953	1873-1960
Walsh, Ed	Pitcher	1946	1881-1959
Waner, Lloyd	Outfielder	1967	1906-
Waner, Paul	Outfielder	1952	1903-1965
Ward, John M.	Infielder; outfielder; pitcher	1964	1860-1925
Weiss, George	Executive	1971	1894-1972
Welch, Mickey	Pitcher	1973	1859-1941
Wheat, Zack	Outfielder	1959	1888-1972
Williams, Ted	Outfielder	1966	1918-
Wright, George	Shortstop	1937	1847-1937
Wright, Harry	Manager	1953	1835-1895
Wynn, Early	Pitcher	1972	1920-
Young, Cy	Pitcher	1937	1867-1955
Youngs, Ross	Outfielder	1972	1897-1927

BASEBALL

United Press Int.

Joe DiMaggio helped lead the New York Yankees to 9 world championships during his 13-year career. In 1941, he established a record by making one or more base hits in 56 consecutive games.

Wide World

Ted Williams ranks among the top 10 modern players in both lifetime batting average and home runs. In 1941, he batted .406, marking the last time any player hit over .400 in a season.

MODERN MAJOR LEAGUE RECORDS

Record	Total	Player	Year(s)
Home Runs:			
Season (154 games)	60	Babe Ruth	1927
Season (162 games)	61	Roger Maris	1961
Career	733	Henry Aaron	1954- *
Batting Average:			
Season	.424	Rogers Hornsby	1924
Career	.367	Ty Cobb	1905-1928
Runs Batted In:			
Season	190	Hack Wilson	1930
Career	2,209	Babe Ruth	1914-1935
Runs Scored:			
Season	177	Babe Ruth	1921
Career	2,244	Ty Cobb	1905-1928
Base Hits:			
Season	257	George Sisler	1920
Career	4,191	Ty Cobb	1905-1928
Consecutive Game Hitting Streak:			
	56	Joe DiMaggio	1941
Stolen Bases:			
Season	118	Lou Brock	1974
Career	892	Ty Cobb	1905-1928
Wins (Pitching):			
Season	41	Jack Chesbro	1904
Career	511	Cy Young	1890-1911
Strikeouts (Pitching):			
Season	383	Nolan Ryan	1973
Career	3,508	Walter Johnson	1907-1927
Shutouts:			
Season	16	Grover Alexander	1916
Career	113	Walter Johnson	1907-1927
Consecutive	6	Don Drysdale	1968
Consecutive Scoreless Innings:			
	58⅔	Don Drysdale	1968
Consecutive Games Played:			
	2,130	Lou Gehrig	1925-1939

*As of the end of the 1974 season

United Press Int.

Jackie Robinson became the first black player in modern major league baseball. He joined the Brooklyn Dodgers in 1947.

Culver

Satchel Paige was a star pitcher for Negro teams for about 30 years. He entered the major leagues in 1948 at the age of 42.

Jack Zehrt

Wide World

United Press Int.

Sandy Koufax became the only player to pitch four no-hit games. He pitched one each year from 1962 through 1965.

Willie Mays won fame for his sensational catches, as well as for his outstanding hitting and base running.

Henry Aaron hit more home runs than any other player, 733 through the 1974 season. His 715th homer, above, broke Babe Ruth's record.

baseball strategy. More and more batters became full swingers rather than place hitters, and home runs became one of the most important parts of the game.

Baseball's many other stars of the Babe Ruth Era included first baseman Lou Gehrig, who batted right after Ruth in the Yankee batting order. Gehrig became the first modern player to hit four home runs in a game. He also set the record for most consecutive games played (2,130). Rogers Hornsby, a second baseman, reached his peak during the era. In 1924, he batted .424 for the St. Louis Cardinals, a modern record.

Many radio stations began broadcasting baseball games during the 1920's. As a result, play-by-play accounts of games reached millions of people.

Depression and War. Major league baseball, like other businesses, faced economic hardship during the Great Depression of the 1930's. Money received from radio stations in return for the right to broadcast games helped teams financially. Also, some team owners installed lights in ballparks so that teams could play at night and attract fans who worked during the day. The first night game took place in Crosley Field, Cincinnati, between the Cincinnati Reds and Philadelphia Phillies on May 24, 1935. The first All-Star Game was played in Comiskey (now White Sox) Park in Chicago on July 6, 1933. Baseball officials opened the Baseball Hall of Fame in Cooperstown in 1939.

The United States entered World War II in 1941. Many major league players served in the armed forces. From 1942 through 1945, teams used many players who were too old, too young, or physically unable to serve in

the armed forces. The war ended in 1945, and most of the players returned to baseball for the 1946 season.

The many stars who played both before and after the war included Joe DiMaggio, Ted Williams, Stan Musial, and Bob Feller. DiMaggio, a Yankee outfielder, became one of the game's greatest all-around players. He set a record when he made one or more base hits in 56 consecutive games in 1941. Williams, a Boston Red Sox outfielder, ranks among baseball's all-time great hitters. His lifetime batting average of .344 is one of the highest in history. In 1941, Williams batted .406, marking the last time anyone hit over .400. Musial starred as a first baseman and outfielder for the Cardinals. He won seven National League batting titles. He also made 3,630 base hits, more than any player except Ty Cobb. Feller, a pitcher for the Cleveland Indians, won fame for his blazing fast ball and strikeout ability.

Postwar Baseball. Attendance at baseball games soared after World War II. In the late 1940's and early 1950's, many teams began televising some games.

Until the mid-1940's, black players were not allowed to play in the major leagues. Instead, they played in leagues made up entirely of blacks. These *Negro leagues* received little publicity, but they had many outstanding players. Negro league stars included Cool Papa Bell, an outfielder; Josh Gibson, a catcher; and Satchel Paige, a pitcher.

Jackie Robinson became the first black player in modern major league baseball, when he joined the Brooklyn Dodgers in 1947. Many other black players entered the major leagues after Robinson.

The Yankees had become baseball's strongest team during the Babe Ruth Era. From then until the 1960's, they dominated the game more than any other team before or since. From 1949 through 1953, they established a record by winning five straight pennants and World Series. Casey Stengel was their manager.

Franchise Shifts and Expansion brought about important changes in the major leagues. In 1953, the Boston Braves moved to Milwaukee, marking the first time a National League *franchise* (team) had moved since 1900. In 1954, the St. Louis Browns moved to Baltimore in the first American League shift since 1903. Several other teams later moved to other cities. Also, during the 1960's, the American and National leagues expanded. Each league added four new teams. In 1969, each split into two 6-team divisions.

Before the franchise shifts and expansion, all major league teams played in the Eastern and Midwestern United States. The changes resulted in the establishment of teams on the West Coast, in the South and Southwest, and one in Canada.

Recent Developments. In 1961, the American League increased the number of games played by each team yearly from 154 to 162. Roger Maris, a Yankee outfielder, hit a record 61 home runs that year. But he passed Babe Ruth's record of 60 homers after his team had played 154 games. As a result, the achievements of both Maris and Ruth are listed as records.

The National League increased the number of games from 154 to 162 in 1962. At that time, Ty Cobb held the single-season record for stolen bases (96). Maury Wills, a Los Angeles Dodger shortstop, stole 104 bases in 1962. But like Maris, he passed the old record after his team had played 154 games. Therefore, the marks of both Wills and Cobb were listed as records. Later, Lou Brock, a Cardinal outfielder, broke both records. In 1974, he stole 118 bases, breaking Wills's record. He also broke Cobb's record because he had stolen 97 bases before his team had played 154 games.

Sandy Koufax, a Dodger star of the 1960's, became one of baseball's greatest pitchers. He was the only person ever to pitch four no-hit games.

Baseball's many other great stars of recent years include Willie Mays and Henry Aaron, both outfielders. Mays played for the New York (later San Francisco) Giants in the 1950's, 1960's, and early 1970's. He became one of the game's greatest all-around players, starring as a hitter, fielder, and base runner.

Aaron joined the Milwaukee (now Atlanta) Braves in 1954. Several players received more publicity than Aaron. But year after year, Aaron ranked among the game's leading hitters. He established many batting records. Finally, he broke what was probably baseball's most glamorous record—Babe Ruth's career home run total. On April 8, 1974, Aaron hit his 715th career home run in Atlanta Stadium as thousands of spectators and millions of television viewers looked on. By the end of the 1974 season, Aaron had hit 733 home runs.

Frank Robinson, another outstanding player, became the first black manager in major league history. The Cleveland Indians hired him as their manager at the end of the 1974 season.　　　　Joseph L. Reichler

---

FRANCHISE SHIFTS AND EXPANSION

1953 The Boston Braves moved to Milwaukee.

1954 The St. Louis Browns moved to Baltimore and became the Baltimore Orioles.

1955 The Philadelphia Athletics moved to Kansas City, Mo.

1958 The Brooklyn Dodgers moved to Los Angeles. The New York Giants moved to San Francisco.

1961 The Washington Senators moved to Minneapolis-St. Paul and became the Minnesota Twins. The American League expanded to 10 teams, adding the Los Angeles Angels and a new Washington Senators team.

1962 The National League expanded to 10 teams, adding the Houston Astros and the New York Mets. (The Astros were nicknamed the Colt .45's until 1965.)

1966 The Los Angeles Angels moved to Anaheim and became the California Angels. The Milwaukee Braves moved to Atlanta.

1968 The Kansas City Athletics moved to Oakland.

1969 Both leagues expanded to 12 teams. The American League added the Kansas City Royals and Seattle Pilots. The National League added the Montreal Expos and San Diego Padres. Both leagues split into two 6-team divisions.

1970 The Seattle Pilots moved to Milwaukee and became the Milwaukee Brewers.

1972 The Washington Senators expansion team moved to Dallas-Fort Worth and became the Texas Rangers.

BASEBALL/*Study Aids*

Related Articles in WORLD BOOK include:

Outline

I. **How the Game Is Played**

    A. Players and Equipment   C. Baseball Skills

    B. The Field   D. The Game

II. **Baseball Leagues**

    A. Major Leagues   C. Amateur Leagues

    B. Minor Leagues

III. **History**

Questions

What is a force play?

How are players chosen for the All-Star Game?

Who holds the career record for most base hits?

Who was Alexander Cartwright?

When does a base runner have to tag up?

What are some of the main baseball pitches?

What were some of Babe Ruth's accomplishments?

What is a working agreement?

What is the Abner Doubleday Theory?

How did World War II affect baseball?

Section Six

Dictionary Supplement

This section lists important words to be included in the 1975 edition of THE WORLD BOOK DICTIONARY. This dictionary, first published by Field Enterprises Educational Corporation in 1963, keeps abreast of our living language with a program of continuous editorial revision. The following supplement has been prepared under the direction of the editors of THE WORLD BOOK ENCYCLOPEDIA and Clarence L. Barnhart, editor in chief of THE WORLD BOOK DICTIONARY. It is presented as a service to owners of the dictionary and as an informative feature to subscribers of THE WORLD BOOK YEAR BOOK.

A

animal park, a zoo where animals live in open surroundings similar to their natural habitats instead of being displayed in cages: *In the new animal parks now opening all over the United States ... animals have the space in which to interact with their own and other species in a natural way* (Barbara Ford).

B

Ban·gla·de·shi (bäng′glə desh′ē, -dā′shē), *n., pl.* **-shis** or **-shi,** *adj.* —*n.* a native or inhabitant of Bangladesh (the former province of East Pakistan): *The Bangladeshis [are] still five-sixths agricultural* (London Times). —*adj.* of or having to do with Bangladesh or its people.

barefoot doctor, an agricultural worker in China who has been trained to serve as a part-time medical auxiliary: *The barefoot doctors, estimated at more than 1 million, represent a major addition to China's stock of medical manpower* (Eli Ginzberg).

bi·o·rhe·ol·o·gy (bī′ō rē ol′ə jē), *n.* the study of the flow and deformation of blood, mucus, and other fluids in plants and animals: *Of the many facets of biorheology, ... significant rheological changes are observed in several blood diseases* (Henry L. Gabelnick).

book bank, a place where used books are collected and usually sold to raise funds for a charitable cause: *Groups of young people of high school age ... served their schools and communities through creation of book banks and libraries* (Joseph P. Anderson).

book·tel·ler (book′tel′ər), *n.* a person who records the text of a book on tape or record, which is then reproduced and sold as a talking book: *The actors he hires as booktellers are, he says, "highly skilled pros, who are not superstars"* (New York Post).

butt·leg·ger (but′leg′ər), *n. U.S.* a person who engages in buttlegging: *New York State gathers in $325-million a year in cigaret taxes, despite the losses to the buttleggers* (Yonkers, N.Y., Herald-Statesman).

butt·leg·ging (but′leg′ing), *n. U.S.* the illegal transportation and sale of cigarettes on which a very low or no cigarette sales tax has been paid. [American English < *butt* cigarette + (*boot*) *legging*]

C

ca·ble·cast·ing (kā′bəl kas′ting, -käs′-), *n.* broadcasting by cable TV: *Cablecasting is emerging as a kind of television not dependent on advertising ... and with strong local roots* (Ralph Lee Smith).

co·ter·mi·nal·i·ty (kō′tėr mə nal′ə tē), *n. U.S.* the establishment by city departments, such as the police and sanitation, of coinciding geographical boundaries or districts, in order to coordinate their services to the public: *Achieving coterminality would not necessarily require a new city charter ...: it could be implemented by a mayor* (New York Post).

culture shock, the disorientation a person experiences when thrust into a foreign culture or a new way of life: *Able boys were repelled by the belief that they could only be "cogs" in industry, and they were also repelled by the "culture shock" they experienced on entering it* (New Scientist).

cy·cle·way (sī′kəl wā′), *n. British.* a road reserved for cyclists; bikeway: *There are 14 miles of cycleway separate from the roads, and they have been designed to be a joy to use* (London Times).

D

dan² (dän, dan), *n.* any one of several grades or ranks of proficiency in the martial arts: *Mr. Burns [is] a judo black belt and fourth dan* (London Times). [< Japanese *dan*]

den·tur·ist (den′chər′ist), *n.* (in Canada) a person who sells and fits false teeth, and is legally authorized to do so in some provinces, although not a dentist. [< *denture* + *-ist*; patterned after *optometrist*]

de·pro·gram (dē prō′gram, -grəm), *v.i., v.t.,* **-grammed, -gram·ming** or **-gramed, -gram·ing.** to try to dissuade (a person) from a set of wayward ideas or beliefs, often by forceful means: *Other accounts of deprogramming indicate that the process, which can last from two days to two weeks, is something between a brainwashing and an inquisition* (Time). —**de·pro′gram·mer,** *n.*

DH (no periods), designated hitter: *One manager ... was thinking of using Don Buford as a leadoff DH* (National Review).

dialogue of the deaf, a discussion or negotiation in which each side completely ignores the needs or arguments of the other: *Better communication is no panacea for every industrial dispute ... But English reserve does seem to lead, all too often, to a muted dialogue of the deaf* (London Times). [translation of French *dialogue des sourds*]

E

ek·pwe·le (ek′pwə lā′), *n.* the unit of money of Equatorial Guinea, introduced in 1973, replacing the peseta. [< a native word in western Africa]

F

fi·brin·bi·o·plast (fī′brən bī′ō-plast), *n.* a synthetic fibrous tissue used to replace missing human tissue in surgical operations: *The Hungarian biochemical invention "fibrinbioplast" ... also stimulates regeneration of the body's own tissue* (Richard A. Pierce). [< *fibrin* + *bioplast*]

fly·off (flī′ôf′, -of′), *n.* a contest in flying between two or more aircraft: *A flyoff ... between the two prototypes is tentatively scheduled for 1976; the winner will become the army's new attack helicopter* (William K. West).

H

hang glider, 1. a device like a large kite or wing, beneath which a person hangs prone in a harness, used for gliding or soaring as a sport; Rogallo: *The most common type of hang glider is an A-shaped kite about 20 feet wide and weighing about 40 pounds* (New York Sunday News). **2.** a person who rides such a device; Rogallist.

hyp·no·dra·ma (hip′nə drä′mə, -dram′ə), *n.* a form of psychodrama in which a situation experienced under hypnosis is acted out: *We were to be hypnotized, and were to ... regress to forgotten states; once these states were recalled, hypnodrama could be used to act them out, enabling us finally to gratify the unsatisfied nurture needs of infancy* (Leo Litwak).

I

in·com·mu·ta·tion (in′kom yə-tā′shən), *n. U.S.* commutation from the city to work in the suburbs: *The report explained the growth of incommutation as a result of the movement of major companies and industries into the suburbs, combined with the decision of employes to remain in the central cities* (Yonkers, N.Y., Herald-Statesman).

in·dex (in′deks), *n., pl.* **-dex·es** or **-di·ces,**-*v.* —*v.t.* to adjust (income, rates of interest, and the like) to price changes in goods and services as reflected by the cost-of-living index: *Brazil has sharply lowered its rate of inflation by "indexing" its economy* (Newsweek).

K

kick·box·ing (kik′bok′sing), *n.* an Oriental method of fighting in which the feet are used to deliver blows like those given in boxing.

Kir·li·an (kir′lē ən), *adj.* having to do with or designating a method of photography in which unexposed film is placed between an electrode and the object to be photographed, so that the finished photograph exhibits a bright glow of different colors that seems to emanate from the photographed object: *Kirlian imagery, the Kirlian process. Soviet parapsychologists believe ... that all living structures are encompassed by a "bioplasm," or energy field, and that the Kirlian photograph records the surrounding field* (New York Times Magazine). [< Semyon and Valentina *Kirlian,* Russian researchers, who developed this method]

Kwan·za (kwän′zə), *n.* an annual Afro-American cultural festival celebrated during the seven-day period from December 26 to January 1: *Although Africans themselves do not celebrate Kwanza, it has been growing in popularity in black communities ... Kwanza is actually an*

American compendium of African festivals, especially the one that marks the end of the harvest and the beginning of the new planting season (Stephen Gayle). [< Swahili *kwanza*, infinitive of *anza* to begin]

L

liv·ing will, a formal document expressing a person's wishes as to how he should be treated medically if he were to become permanently brain-damaged, comatose, or the like: *"Living wills" prepared in advance of illness . . . typically state the conditions under which the future patient would like life-prolonging treatment to be omitted and death-hastening treatments (narcotics) to be used* (Diana Crane).

lump·ec·to·my (lum pek′tə mē), *n., pl.* **-mies.** the surgical removal of a cancerous lump in the breast: *For certain of her patients in cases in which early diagnosis has been made, she favors "lumpectomy," the removal of the cancer alone rather than the entire breast* (Time). [< *lump*[1] + (mast)*ectomy*]

M

mail·gram (māl′gram), *n. U.S.* a letter transmitted electronically from a telegraph office to a local post office for delivery to the addressee.

main·stream (mān′strēm′), —*v.t., v.i. U.S.* to integrate (handicapped children) with other schoolchildren by transferring them from special classes to regular classrooms, usually on a gradual or part-time basis: *That children will be mainstreamed without backup services is always a danger in times of financial stress* (Myron Brenton).

martial art, any of the Oriental arts of fighting or self-defense, such as karate and aikido: *Mike first entered the martial arts at the age of thirteen when he began studying judo* (Eric Lee).

memory television, a device that can record and play back televised pictures, either attached to or incorporated in a standard television set: *Memory television . . . has a refreshable memory capable of storing one or more frames of a television signal* (Kimio Ito).

mi·cro·map (mī′krə map′), *v.t.,* **-mapped, -map·ping.** to map microscopic parts or details of: *This effect makes it possible to locate—or micromap—the distribution of uranium and thorium in different samples* (Robert M. Walker).

Min·a·ma·ta disease (min′ə mä′tə), poisoning by ingestion of mercury from contaminated fish and shellfish. [< *Minamata* Bay, in western Kyushu, Japan, where it was first identified]

mus·ca·lure (mus′kə lúr′), *n.* a synthetic form of the sex attractant of houseflies: *The potential useful-*

ness of muscalure in reducing the need for insecticides was greatly enhanced by its ability to attract both males and females (Marcella M. Memolo). [< Latin *musca* fly + English *lure*]

muscle car, a medium-sized automobile with a powerful engine, designed for high speed and acceleration: *Muscle cars—equipped with huge engines, high rear-axle ratios, heavy duty suspensions, and oversized tires . . .* (Jim Dunne). *The Cortina body is known generically as a British-look, high-style muscle car* (Listener).

N

neu·ter·cane (nü′tər kān, nyü′-), *n.* a storm that draws its force from both tropical and cold-front disturbances in the atmosphere: *Weather satellites have been providing pictures of the progress and development of neutercanes* (Allan Yale Brooks). [< *neuter* + (hurri)-*cane*]

nun·cha·ku (nún′chə kə), *n., pl.* **-kus.** a weapon of defense against frontal assault, used especially in karate, consisting of two wooden sticks connected by a rawhide or nylon cord: *Nunchakus are a dangerous, deadly weapon and . . . not everyone is psychologically prepared to learn how to use them* (Andrew Lunick). [< Japanese *nunchaku*]

O

open dating, the practice of stamping on packaged food the date when it was packaged or the limit of its shelf life: *Consumer groups campaigned for legislation demanding . . . "open dating" practices at other stores* (Norman Thompson).

ou·gui·ya (wä gē′yə), *n.* the unit of money of Mauritania, introduced in 1973 and replacing the franc. [< French *ouguiya* < Arabic *wagīya*]

P

pa·ro·chi·aid (pə rō′kē ād′), *n. U.S.* governmental aid to parochial schools: *Both presidential candidates came out for one form or another of "parochiaid," . . . and it was an issue in many state legislatures* (Martin E. Marty). [< *parochi*(al) *aid*]

patrimonial waters, the waters off the coastline of a state, usually extending up to 200 miles out to sea, within which the state may exercise jurisdiction over natural resources but may not restrict the freedom of navigation of other states: *"Patrimonial" waters is the term they use, as opposed to "territorial" waters, where full sovereignty is exercised* (Peter Tonge).

patz·er (pats′ər, pots′-), *n. Slang.* an amateur chess player, especially one who plays the game without

skill or style: *He played as though Petrosian were a patzer, and nobody can take that kind of liberty with so great a player* (Harold C. Schonberg). [probably < German (dialectal) *Patzer* spoiler < *patzen* to spoil, botch]

plea bargaining, an informal practice in which the prosecuting attorney in a criminal action agrees to allow a defendant to plead guilty to a lesser charge, in order to avoid a lengthy trial, assure a conviction, or gain the defendant's cooperation as a witness in a criminal action against another: *Plea bargaining in criminal cases was condemned . . . by Lord Parker of Waddington, Lord Chief Justice* (London Times). *U.S. District Judge William J. Campbell . . . believes "plea bargaining should be acknowledged, legitimized, and encouraged"* (Jack Star).

po·si·tion (pə zish′ən), —*v.t.* **3.** to market or advertise (a product) by appealing to a particular type of consumer or specific segment of the public: *The main difficulty manufacturers have in positioning a new product is [that] they want everybody to love their product* (Jack Springer).

pro·hor·mone (prō hôr′mōn), *n.* the inactive forerunner of a hormone; substance from which a hormone is built: *In the body, the molecule is first synthesized in the parathyroid gland as a prohormone, a long chain of 106 amino acids that are chemically linked together* (Earl A. Evans).

psy·cho·his·to·ry (sī′kō his′tər ē, -trē), *n., pl.* **-ries. 1.** a historical account written from a psychological point of view. **2.** the writing of such a history or histories: *There has been a bit of a history of psychohistory. Beginning with Freud, there have been a number of attempts . . . to apply psychological methods to historical events* (Robert Jay Lifton).

R

reg·gae (reg′ā, rā′gā), *n.* a simple, lively, rhythmic form of rock'n'roll music of West Indian origin: *Reggae is characterized by a loping beat and sparing use of instrumental effects* (Ed Ward). [< a native name in the British West Indies]

Ro·gal·list (rō gal′ist), *n.* a person who engages in hang gliding: *One of the most spectacular take-off points for Rogallists is . . . 1300 feet above Lake Elsinore, Calif.* (Wolfgang Langewiesche).

rolf·ing (rol′fing), *n.* a method of correcting bodily deformities by manipulating the fascial tissue of the muscles in order to reorganize the body's natural orientation to the force of gravity: *Rolfing is a system of deep massage that stretches and rearranges the tissues surrounding the muscles* (New Yorker). [< Ida *Rolf*, an American biochemist and physiotherapist, who developed the method]

PRONUNCIATION KEY: hat, āge, cãre, fär; let, ēqual, tėrm; it, īce; hot, ōpen, ôrder; oil, out; cup, pút, rüle, ūse; child; long; thin; ŦHen; zh, measure; ə represents a in about, e in taken, i in pencil, o in lemon, u in circus.

591

S

shield law, *U.S.* a law that permits a member of the press to protect his confidential sources: *Under "shield laws" in twelve States, newsmen can refuse to reveal their sources* (Time).

sin tax, *U.S. Informal.* a tax on alcoholic liquor, cigarettes, sweepstakes tickets, and the like: *The state's antiquated tax structure ... relies heavily on revenue from so-called "sin taxes" on alcoholic beverages, tobacco, and racing* (Joseph P. Ford).

sissy bar, *U.S.* a curved metal piece attached to the back of a bicycle seat to support or protect the rider's back: *Sissy bars will be lower this year* (Esquire).

ski flying, the sport of jumping on skis to cover as much ground as possible: *In ski flying, only distance counts, with no marks for form* (James O. Dunaway).

slow virus, a virus that may remain present in the body of an infected person for most or all of his life, believed to be the cause of many chronic diseases: *Evidence recently came to light that implicated slow viruses in such neurological disorders of humans as multiple sclerosis ... as well as in rheumatoid arthritis* (Robert G. Eagon).

Sri Lan·kan (srē' läng'kən), **1.** a native or inhabitant of the Republic of Sri Lanka (formerly Ceylon); Ceylonese; Singhalese: *Thousands of Sri Lankans applauded May Day speakers* (New York Times). **2.** of or having to do with the Republic of Sri Lanka or its people. [< *Sri Lanka*, the Singhalese name of Ceylon + English *-an*]

stop-out (stop'out'), *n. U.S.* a college student who interrupts his education to pursue some other activity for a year: *Many stop-outs do better academically than their less seasoned classmates, if only because they are a year older* (Time). [patterned on *drop-out*]

streak·ing (strē'king), *n.* the practice of running or riding naked through a public area, especially as a fad: *Motives for streaking appear to vary. In some instances it has become a form of political protest. Some people go naked for a bet* (London Times).

stun gun, a long-barreled gun that shoots a compressed bag filled with sand, bird shot, or the like, used especially in riot control: *The stun gun is ... fired from a 40-mm. shell* (Newsweek).

sub·op·ti·mize (sub op'tə mīz), *v.t., v.i., -mized, -miz·ing.* to fail to make the most of (a system, process, plan, or the like): *It is more difficult for them to sense needs beyond those institutions ... In the language of the systems analyst, they have a strong tendency to suboptimize* (Atlantic).

su·per·fec·ta (sü'pər fek'tə), *n. U.S.* a form of betting on a horse race in which the better must pick in their exact order the first four horses to finish the race: *The superfecta is a betting gimmick popular at the trots* (New Yorker). [American

English, blend of *super-* and *perfecta*]

swerp·ing (swėr'ping), *n. U.S.* a sound distortion on a magnetic tape, supposedly produced by an automatic tape recorder as it accelerates to full recording speed after being actuated by a sound: *Swerping ... normally obscures the first few syllables spoken after the interruption of speech* (J. Fred Buzhardt). [imitative]

Sym·bi·o·nese (sim'bī ə nēz', -nēs'), *adj.* of or belonging to a secret paramilitary group of terrorists, formed in 1974: *the Symbionese Liberation Army.* [< Greek *symbiôn* living together (see SYMBIONT) + English *-ese*]

T

tae kwon do (tī' kwon dō), the Korean form of karate: *Huey Daniels, a tae kwon do stylist from Canton, Ohio, took third place and Ron Shaw from Kent State won 4th* (Mary Townsley). [< Korean *tae kwon do*]

t'ai chi chu'an (tī' jē chwän'), a Chinese system of physical exercises similar to shadowboxing. [< Chinese (Peking) *t'ai chi chu'an*]

ta·ka (tä'kə), *n., pl. -ka.* the unit of money of Bangladesh, worth 100 paise, established in 1972. [< Bengali *taka*]

technology assessment, 1. the attempt to make advance assessments on the impact or effect of a new technological process or system on society: *Technology assessment aims to look beyond the cost-effectiveness of new technology, in an attempt to recognize as many potential side effects as possible* (New Scientist). **2.** a study or analysis of such a potential impact or effect: *The board would award contracts to industrial, non-profit, or academic groups for specific technology assessments as they are needed by Congressional committees* (Science News).

theme park, an amusement park in which all the attractions have to do with a single, or several, themes, such as wildlife, marine life, fantasyland, or African and Asian culture: *The number of Americans who visit the theme parks which now dot the U.S. landscape from coast to coast has soared ... to more than 54 million* (Sylvia Porter).

transcendental meditation, a Hindu system of meditation designed to produce a relaxed state of consciousness intermediate between wakefulness and sleep: *The practice of transcendental meditation leads to greatly reduced physiological activity, indicative of an "inner calm"* (Gary E. Schwartz). *Transcendental meditation ... is advocacy of the egoless state* (Science News).

transfer factor, a substance in cells, smaller than an antibody, that is believed to cause immunity against foreign substances even when transferred from one person to another: *Transfer factor ... can apparently, when given to people suffering from immune deficiency

diseases, transfer to them the immunological status of the donor* (New Scientist and Science Journal).

tri·fec·ta (trī fek'tə), *n. U.S.* a form of betting on a horse race in which the better picks the winners of the first, second, and third place in their order of finish. [American English < *tri-* three + (per)*fecta*]

U

ul·tra·mi·cro·fiche (ul'trə mī'krə fēsh'), *n., pl. -fich·es, -fiche* (-fēsh'). ultrafiche: *Ultramicrofiche achieves a reduction ratio of more than 200 and puts up to 8,000 pages on a single film* (Lawrence Lessing).

up·val·ue (up'val'yü), *v.t., v.i., -ued, -u·ing.* to fix a higher legal value on (currency that has depreciated) in relation to gold: *If the franc were devalued and the Deutsche mark upvalued, French food prices in francs would rise proportionately overnight and German food prices in marks would fall proportionately* (Listener).

V

ver·ti·port (vėr'tə pôrt', -pōrt'), *n.* a small airport for aircraft that can take off and land vertically. [< *verti-* (cal take-off and landing) + (air)*port*]

W

Wa·ter·gate (wôt'ər gāt', wot'-), *n.* **1.** a major political scandal involving illegal activities directed against political opponents of President Richard Nixon and subsequent attempts to cover up these activities: *... the disclosures of misconduct in high places loosely defined as "Watergate"* (James A. Wechsler). **2.** any widespread public scandal: *If there is a British Watergate who will expose it and track it down?* (New Statesman). *The incident ... is being referred to in the scientific community as "a medical Watergate"* (New York Times). [< the *Watergate*, an apartment-house and office-building complex in Washington, D.C., where men connected with the Republican Committee for the Reelection of the President were arrested burglarizing Democratic National Committee headquarters]

white death, *Informal.* heroin: *U.S. narcotics agents around the world ... are engaged in an escalating war against the "white death"* (Newsweek). [so called from the color of most types of heroin]

white hole, a hypothetical hole in outer space from which energy and stars and other heavenly matter emerge or explode, as distinguished from a black hole: *White holes are more than simply mirror images of black holes. They are sources of matter that could literally come out of this world* (Time). *At present, nobody knows how white holes express themselves in the vast regions of distant space* (Mort LaBrecque).

Index

How to Use the Index

This index covers the contents of the 1973, 1974, and 1975 editions of
THE WORLD BOOK YEAR BOOK.

Each index entry is followed by the edition year (in *italics*) and the page
numbers, as:
    ADVERTISING, *75*–184, *74*–178, *73*–194

This means that information about Advertising begins on the pages
indicated for each of the editions.

An index entry that is the title of an article appearing in THE YEAR BOOK is
printed in capital letters, as: **AUTOMOBILE.** An entry that is not an article
title, but a subject discussed in an article of some other title, is printed: **Pollution.**

The various "See" and "See also" cross references in the index list are to
other entries within the index. Clue words or phrases are used when two or
more references to the same subject appear in the same edition of THE YEAR
BOOK. These make it easy to locate the material on the page, since they refer to
an article title or article subsection in which the reference appears, as:
    Endangered species: conservation, *74*–271; whales, *Special Report*, *75*–97;
        zoos, *74*–542

The indication *"il."* means that the reference is to an illustration only. An index
entry in capital letters followed by *"WBE"* refers to a new or revised WORLD BOOK
ENCYCLOPEDIA article that is printed in the supplement section, as:
    METRIC SYSTEM, *WBE*, *75*–568

Acknowledgments

The publishers acknowledge the following sources for illustrations. Credits read from left to right, top to bottom, on their respective pages. An asterisk (*) denotes illustrations created exclusively for THE YEAR BOOK. All maps, charts, and diagrams were prepared by THE YEAR BOOK staff unless otherwise noted.

3	WORLD BOOK photo; WORLD BOOK diagram
8-10	Wide World
11	Photo Trends; Wide World
12	Wide World; Wide World; Camera Pix from Keystone
13	Keystone; Wide World; NBC Television
14	Wide World
16	Francoise Nicolas Fried*
17	Boris Spremo*
18-19	Wide World
20	Keystone
21	United Nations
22	Francoise Nicolas Fried*
23	Robert Isear*
24	Fred Ward, Black Star
25-26	Wide World
28	Francoise Nicolas Fried*
29	Robert Isear*
31	Wide World
32	United Press Int.
33	Wide World
34	Francoise Nicolas Fried*
35	Joseph Erhardt*
36	U.S. Department of Defense
37	Arnold Ryan Chalfant & Associates
38	National Academy of Sciences
40	Francoise Nicolas Fried*
41	Dan Budnik*
42	United Press Int.
43-44	Wide World
45	Harris & Ewing
46	Francoise Nicolas Fried*
47	Dan Budnik*
48	Field Enterprises, Inc.
49	Daniel J. Edelman, Inc.
50	United Press Int.
51	Masterpiece Theatre
52	Francoise Nicolas Fried*
53	J. R. Eyeman*
54	United Press Int.
55	Atlanta Braves
56	Wide World
59	Don Carl Steffen
61-62	Dennis Brack, Black Star
63	Wally McNamee, *Newsweek*; Allen Green from Nancy Palmer
64-65	Wally McNamee, *Newsweek*
66	Wally McNamee, *Newsweek*; Fred Ward, Black Star; Fred Ward, Black Star
67	Larry McIntosh, *Newsweek*; Dennis Brack, Black Star; Fred Ward, Black Star
68	Dennis Brack, Black Star
69	United Press Int.
70-73	Dennis Brack, Black Star
74	Wally McNamee, *Newsweek*
75	J. P. Laffont, Sygma
76	Dennis Brack, Black Star
77	J. P. Laffont, Sygma; *Newsweek*
78-79	Alex Webb, Magnum
81-94	Frank Rakoncey*
96-97	John Dominis, Time/Life Picture Agency
98-99	Bettmann Archive
100-101	Gordon Williamson, Bruce Coleman, Inc.; Wedigo Ferchland, Bruce Coleman, Inc.
102	Ramon Goas
103	Gordon Williamson, Bruce Coleman, Inc.
104	John Wittbold, Clipper Exxpress; Joanne Kalish, Sea Library
107-108	Sea World
110-121	Patrick Maloney*
124-126	Dennis Brack, Black Star*
128-130	Robert Lautman*
131-133	George Suyeoka
135-136	Dennis Brack, Black Star*
139	Sven Simon from Katherine Young
140	Reg Hunt
142-143	Audrey Topping, Rapho Guillumette; Harrison Forman
145	Ralph Herrmanns from Carl Östman
146	Jerry Cooke
148-149	V. Rastelli, Woodfin Camp, Inc.
151	Joel Morwood from Katherine Young
153	Paolo Koch, Rapho Guillumette
156-170	Paul S. Conklin*
172	Wide World
174	Library of Congress
175	Historical Pictures Service
177	Culver Pictures
178	Bettmann Archive; Brown Brothers; Brown Brothers
181-182	Bettmann Archive
184	© 1974 The American Heart Association, Inc.
185	National Safety Council
186	Wide World
187	Keystone
191	Carl Davaz, *Topeka Capital-Journal*
194	Richard Melloul, Sygma
196	University of California
197	Pictorial Parade
199	United Press Int.
200	American Institute of Architects
201	Photo Trends
202-203	Daniel Mularoni, Sygma
206	Wide World
207	NASA
209	Wide World
210	John Fairfax and Sons, Ltd.
211	Wide World
213	United Press Int.
214	J. P. Laffont, Sygma
215-216	Wide World
217	Pictorial Parade
219	Keystone
220	Pete Schmick, *Washington Star-News*
222	Wide World
224	Tony Rollo, *Newsweek*
225	Morrie Brickman, Washington Star Syndicate, Inc.
227	Wide World
228	William E. Sauro, *The New York Times*
231	William E. Sauro, *The New York Times*
233	Eleanor E. Storrs, Gulf South Research Institute, New Iberia, Louisiana
237-238	Wide World
240	United Press Int.
242	Wide World
244	Blaine, *The Spectator*, Canada
247	*The New York Times*
250	*The New York Times*
251-253	Keystone
255	Keystone; Chicago Police Department
257-260	Wide World
261	Andrew Sacks, *The New York Times*
263-264	*The New York Times*
265	Santa Fe Railway
267	Wide World
268	Sarita Kendall, *The New York Times*
269	NASA
270-271	Wide World
275	Pictorial Parade
276	United Press Int.
277	William Mauldin, © 1974 *Chicago Sun-Times*
278	*U.S. News & World Report*
280	Wide World
281	Don Bierman, *Chicago Daily News*
282	Wide World
283	Keystone
284	Pictorial Parade
287	Martha Swope
288	Costas; Louis Péres
289	Planned Parenthood-World Population; Wide World; Pictorial Parade; Wide World

290	NBC Television; Wide World; Wide World; Pictorial Parade
291-292	Wide World
293	Wide World; Wide World; Wide World; United Press Int.
294	Wide World; Wide World; Wide World; United Nations
295	Wide World
297	Keystone
299	Wide World
300	James Andanson, Sygma
301	Wide World
303	Howard D. Simmons, *Chicago Sun-Times*
304	Jacques Pavlovsky, Sygma
305	*The Sankei Shimbun;* Pictorial Parade
311	Arthur Grace, *The New York Times*
312	*U.S. News & World Report*
314	Wide World
317	Pictorial Parade
319	Wide World
320	From *Krokodil*, Moscow, reprinted in *Atlas World Press Review*, June, 1974
321	Keystone
322	Canadian Press Photo
323	Pictorial Parade
326	Expo '74
328	Joseph Erhardt*/Shirt courtesy of JBT Chroma, Inc.; Joseph Erhardt*/Shirt courtesy of JBT Chroma, Inc.; Joseph Erhardt*
330	Wide World
331	Gene Maggio, *The New York Times*
334	Wide World
336	White House
337	Wide World
338-339	Alain Nogues, Sygma
340	Pictorial Parade
341	Talis Bergmanis, *The New York Times*
342	Woods Hole Oceanographic Institution
344	Henri Bureau, Sygma
346	Wide World
347	Pictorial Parade
348	Keystone
349	The Press Association Limited
350	Keystone
356	Wide World
358	Jim Hedrich, Hedrich-Blessing
359	Wide World
360	Gene Basset, Scripps-Howard
361	Nik Wheeler, Sygma
363	Wide World
364	Gary Settle, *The New York Times*
366	Sovfoto
367	Reprinted by permission of Chicago Tribune-New York News Syndicate, Inc., © 1974. All rights reserved.
368	Wide World
370	Wide World; Keystone
372	*The Sankei Shimbun*
373	Pictorial Parade
375-377	Wide World
378	James Mayo, *Chicago Tribune*
379	Wide World
380-382	United Press Int.
387	Edward Hausner, *The New York Times*
388	United Press Int.
389	Auth, *The Philadelphia Inquirer*, © 1974, Chicago Tribune-New York News Syndicate, Inc.
391	Pictorial Parade
392	Jill Krementz
394	Reprinted with the permission of Farrar, Straus & Giroux, Inc. from *Duffy and the Devil* by Harve Zemach, illustrated by Margot Zemach, Copyright © 1973 by Farrar, Straus & Giroux, Inc.
399	Lee Baker Johnson, *Business Week*
400	Bruce Roberts, Rapho Guillumette
401	Hahnemann Medical College and Hospital, Philadelphia
404-405	Neal Boenzi, *The New York Times*
410	Wide World
411	Cinema 5 Ltd.
412	Wide World
413	Keystone
414	Henry Grossman
416	Photo Trends
417-418	Wide World
419	J. P. Laffont, Sygma
420	Wide World
423	Dick De Marsico
424	New Zealand Embassy
425	Wide World; World News Corporation
427	United Press Int.
428	Wide World
429	Photo Trends
431	Drawing by Stan Hunt, © 1974 The New Yorker Magazine, Inc.
432	Map data courtesy of Ian W. D. Dalziel, Lamont-Doherty Geological Observatory of Columbia University
433	Wide World
434	United Press Int.
437-438	Wide World
439	Wide World; Daniel J. Edelman, Inc.
441	United Press Int.
442	Larry Morris, *The New York Times*
443	Edward Hausner, *The New York Times*
444	Wide World
446	NASA
449	Wide World
450	Le Lieu Browne, *The New York Times*
451	Wide World
452	Gary Settle, *The New York Times*
454	Wide World
455	J. P. Laffont, Sygma
456-457	White House
458	Orion Press from Katherine Young
460	Åke G. Lundberg, The Billy Graham Evangelistic Association
463	Wide World
465	CBS Radio
466	*Topeka Capital-Journal*
467	ABC Television; Pictorial Parade
469	Wide World
470-473	United Press Int.
476-478	Sovfoto
479-488	Wide World
491	NASA
493	*National Enquirer;* United Press Int.
495	Wide World
500	Wide World
502	United Press Int.
505	Keystone
507	CBS Television
509-510	Wide World
511	Betty Lee Hunt Associates
513	United Press Int.
515	Wide World
517	William Mauldin, © 1974 *Chicago Sun-Times*
519	Cuneyt Arcayurek/Sipa from Liaison Agency
521-528	Wide World
529	Paul Hosefros, *The New York Times*
531	*U.S. News & World Report*
532	Wide World
534	Betty Wells, NBC News
537-542	Wide World
543	Andrew Keen, Jr., *Baltimore News-American*
544	Jerry Tomaselli, *Chicago Sun-Times*

A Preview of 1975

January

S	M	T	W	T	F	S
			1	2	3	4
5	6	7	8	9	10	11
12	13	14	15	16	17	18
19	20	21	22	23	24	25
26	27	28	29	30	31	

1 **New Year's Day.**

6 **Epiphany,** 12th day of Christmas, celebrates visit of the Three Wise Men.

14 **94th Congress** convenes for first session.

19 **Jaycee Week,** through January 25, marks founding of Jaycees.
World Religion Day, emphasizes need for world religious unity.

February

S	M	T	W	T	F	S
						1
2	3	4	5	6	7	8
9	10	11	12	13	14	15
16	17	18	19	20	21	22
23	24	25	26	27	28	

1 **National Freedom Day.**
American Heart Month through February 28.
Boy Scouts of America Anniversary Celebration through February 28.

2 **Ground-Hog Day.** Legend says six weeks of winter weather will follow if ground hog sees its shadow.

11 **Mardi Gras,** last celebration before Lent, observed in New Orleans, La., and many Roman Catholic countries.
Chinese New Year, begins year 4673 of the ancient Chinese calendar, the Year of the Hare.

12 **Abraham Lincoln's Birthday,** observed in 26 states.
Ash Wednesday, first day of Lent, the penitential period that precedes Easter.
Holiday of the Three Hierarchs. Eastern Orthodox holy day, commemorating Saints Basil, Gregory, and John Chrysostom.

14 **Saint Valentine's Day,** festival of romance and affection.

15 **National FFA Week,** through February 22, publicizing the role of Future Farmers of America in U.S. agriculture.
Susan B. Anthony Day, commemorates the birth of the suffragist leader.

16 **Brotherhood Week** to February 23.

17 **George Washington's Birthday,** according to law, is now legally celebrated by federal employees, the District of Columbia, and 42 states on the third Monday in February, not on the actual anniversary, the 22nd.

24 **Easter Seal Campaign** through March 30.

25 **Purim,** commemorates the saving of Jews through the death of the ancient Persian despot Haman.

March

S	M	T	W	T	F	S
						1
2	3	4	5	6	7	8
9	10	11	12	13	14	15
16	17	18	19	20	21	22
23	24	25	26	27	28	29
30	31					

1 **Red Cross Month** through March 31.

2 **Save Your Vision Week** through March 8.

7 **World Day of Prayer.**

9 **Girl Scout Week,** through March 15, marks the 63rd birthday of U.S. Girl Scouts.

16 **Camp Fire Girls Birthday Week,** to March 22, marks 65th birthday of the organization.
National Boys' Club Week through March 22.

17 **St. Patrick's Day,** honoring the patron saint of Ireland.

21 **First Day of Spring,** 12.57 A.M. E.S.T.
Earth Day, opens yearlong program to replenish the earth.

23 **Palm Sunday,** marks Jesus' final entry into Jerusalem along streets festively covered with palm branches.
Holy Week, through March 29, commemorates the Crucifixion and Resurrection of Jesus Christ.

27 **Maundy Thursday,** celebrates Christ's injunction to love each other.
Passover, or Pesah, first day, starting the 15th day of the Hebrew month of Nisan. The eight-day festival celebrates the deliverance of the ancient Jews from bondage in Egypt.

28 **Good Friday,** marks the death of Jesus on the cross. It is observed as a public holiday in 17 states.

30 **Easter Sunday,** commemorating the Resurrection of Jesus Christ.

April

S	M	T	W	T	F	S
		1	2	3	4	5
6	7	8	9	10	11	12
13	14	15	16	17	18	19
20	21	22	23	24	25	26
27	28	29	30			

1 **April Fools' Day.**
Cancer Control Month through April 30.

13 **National Library Week** through April 19.
Pan American Week through April 19.

30 **Walpurgis Night,** according to legend, the night of the witches' Sabbath gathering in Germany's Harz Mountains.

May

S	M	T	W	T	F	S
				1	2	3
4	5	6	7	8	9	10
11	12	13	14	15	16	17
18	19	20	21	22	23	24
25	26	27	28	29	30	31

1 **May Day,** observed as a festival of spring in many countries.
Law Day, U.S.A.
Mental Health Month through May 31.

4 **National Music Week** through May 11.

8 **Ascension Day,** 40 days after Easter Sunday, commemorating the ascent of Jesus into heaven.

11 **Mother's Day.**

12 **Salvation Army Week** through May 18.

16 **Shabuot,** Jewish Feast of Weeks, marks the revealing of the Ten Commandments to Moses on Mt. Sinai.

17 **Armed Forces Day.**

18 **Whitsunday,** or Pentecost, the seventh Sunday after Easter, commemorating the descent of the Holy Spirit upon Jesus' 12 apostles.

22 **National Maritime Day.**

25 **Indianapolis 500-Mile Race** in Indianapolis, Ind.

26 **Memorial Day,** according to law, is the last Monday in May.

June

S	M	T	W	T	F	S
1	2	3	4	5	6	7
8	9	10	11	12	13	14
15	16	17	18	19	20	21
22	23	24	25	26	27	28
29	30					

6 **D-Day,** commemorates the day the Allies landed to assault the German-held continent of Europe in 1944.

8 **National Flag Week** through June 14.

9 **Stratford Festival,** drama and music, Ontario, Canada, through October 11.

14 **Flag Day,** commemorates the adoption of the Stars and Stripes in 1777 as the official U.S. flag.
Queen's Official Birthday, marked by trooping of the colors in London.

15 **Father's Day.**

21 **First Day of Summer,** 7:27 P.M. E.S.T.

27 **Freedom Week** through July 4.

A Preview of 1975

July

S	M	T	W	T	F	S
		1	2	3	4	5
6	7	8	9	10	11	12
13	14	15	16	17	18	19
20	21	22	23	24	25	26
27	28	29	30	31		

1 Dominion Day (Canada), celebrates the confederation of the provinces in 1867.
4 Independence Day, marks Continental Congress's adoption of Declaration of Independence in 1776.
13 Captive Nations Week through July 19.
14 Bastille Day (France), commemorates popular uprising against Louis XVI in 1789 and seizure of the Bastille, the infamous French prison.
15 Saint Swithin's Day. According to legend, if it rains on this day, it will rain for 40 days.
17 Tishah B'ab, Jewish fast day, on ninth day of Hebrew month of Ab, marking Babylonians' destruction of the First Temple in Jerusalem in 587 B.C.; Roman destruction of the Second Temple in A.D. 70; and Roman suppression of Jewish revolt in A.D. 135.
20 Moon Day, the anniversary of man's first landing on the moon in 1969.
26 Salzburg International Music and Drama Festival, Salzburg, Austria, through August 30.

August

S	M	T	W	T	F	S
					1	2
3	4	5	6	7	8	9
10	11	12	13	14	15	16
17	18	19	20	21	22	23
24	25	26	27	28	29	30
31						

14 V-J Day (original), marks Allied victory over Japan in 1945.
15 Feast of the Assumption, Roman Catholic and Eastern Orthodox holy day, celebrates the ascent of the Virgin Mary into heaven.
19 National Aviation Day.
24 Edinburgh International Festival, music, drama, and film, through September 13.
26 Women's Equality Day, commemorating the ratification of the 19th Amendment, giving women the vote.

September

S	M	T	W	T	F	S
	1	2	3	4	5	6
7	8	9	10	11	12	13
14	15	16	17	18	19	20
21	22	23	24	25	26	27
28	29	30				

1 Labor Day in the United States and Canada.
6 Rosh Hashanah, or Jewish New Year, the year 5736 beginning at sunset. It falls on the first day of the Hebrew month of Tishri and lasts for two days.
8 Ramadan, the ninth month of the Moslem calendar begins, observed by fasting.
15 Yom Kippur, or Day of Atonement, most solemn day in the Jewish calendar, marking the end of the period of penitence.
17 Citizenship Day.
Constitution Week, through September 23, commemorates the signing of the U.S. Constitution in Philadelphia, on Sept. 17, 1787.
20 Sukkot, or Feast of Tabernacles, begins the nine-day Jewish observance, which originally celebrated the end of harvest season.
Harvest Moon, the full moon nearest the autumnal equinox of the sun, shines with special brilliance for several days and helps farmers in the Northern Hemisphere to get more field work done after sunset.
23 First Day of Autumn, 10:55 A.M. E.S.T.
27 American Indian Day, honoring native Americans.

October

S	M	T	W	T	F	S
			1	2	3	4
5	6	7	8	9	10	11
12	13	14	15	16	17	18
19	20	21	22	23	24	25
26	27	28	29	30	31	

1 Anniversary of the 1949 Chinese Communist Revolution, China's national holiday.
5 National Employ the Physically Handicapped Week through October 11.
National 4-H Week through October 11.
Fire Prevention Week through October 11.
9 Leif Ericson Day, honoring early Norse explorer of North America.
12 National Y-Teen Week through October 18.
13 Thanksgiving Day, Canada.
Columbus Day, commemorates Columbus' discovery of America in 1492. Previously celebrated on October 12.
19 National Cleaner Air Week through October 25.
26 American Education Week through November 1.
27 Veterans Day, observed on the fourth Monday in October.
31 Halloween, or All Hallows' Eve.
Reformation Day, celebrated by Protestants, marks the day in 1517 when Martin Luther nailed his Ninety-Five Theses of protest to the door of a church in Wittenberg, Germany.
United Nations Children's Fund (UNICEF) Day.

November

S	M	T	W	T	F	S
						1
2	3	4	5	6	7	8
9	10	11	12	13	14	15
16	17	18	19	20	21	22
23	24	25	26	27	28	29
30						

1 All Saints' Day, observed by the Roman Catholic Church.
Christmas Seal Campaign through December 31.
4 Election Day, United States.
5 Guy Fawkes Day (Great Britain), marks the failure of a plot to blow up King James I and Parliament in 1605 with ceremonial burning of Guy Fawkes in effigy.
7 Anniversary of 1917 Bolshevik Revolution, Russia's national holiday, through November 8.
17 National Children's Book Week through November 23.
27 Thanksgiving Day, United States.
29 Hanukkah, or Feast of Lights, eight-day Jewish holiday beginning on the 25th day of the Hebrew month of Kislev that celebrates the Jewish defeat of the Syrian tyrant Antiochus IV in 165 B.C. and the rededication of The Temple in Jerusalem.
30 Advent, first of the four Sundays in the season preceding Christmas.

December

S	M	T	W	T	F	S
	1	2	3	4	5	6
7	8	9	10	11	12	13
14	15	16	17	18	19	20
21	22	23	24	25	26	27
28	29	30	31			

2 Pan American Health Day.
6 Saint Nicholas Day, when children in parts of Europe receive gifts.
10 Human Rights Week through December 17.
Nobel Peace Prize Presentation, in Oslo, Norway.
15 Bill of Rights Day, marks the ratification of that document in 1791.
22 First Day of Winter, 6:46 A.M. E.S.T.
25 Christmas.
31 New Year's Eve.